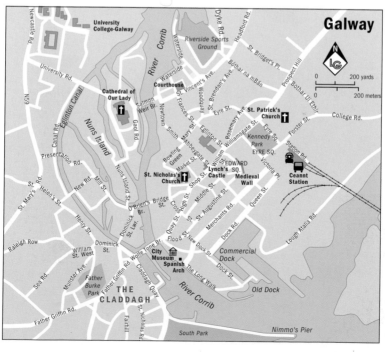

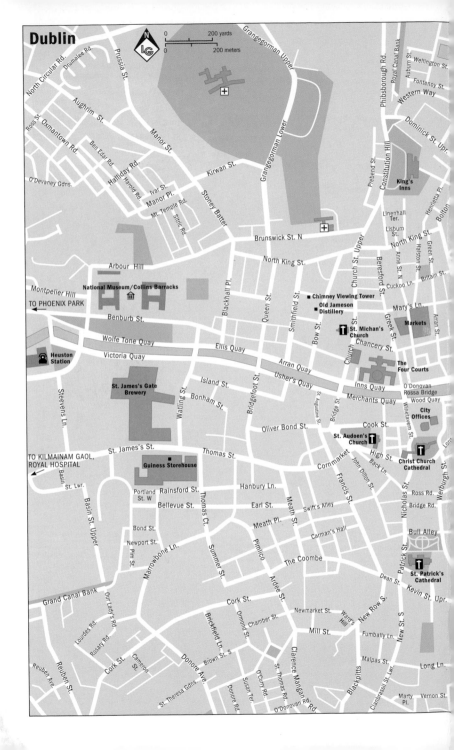

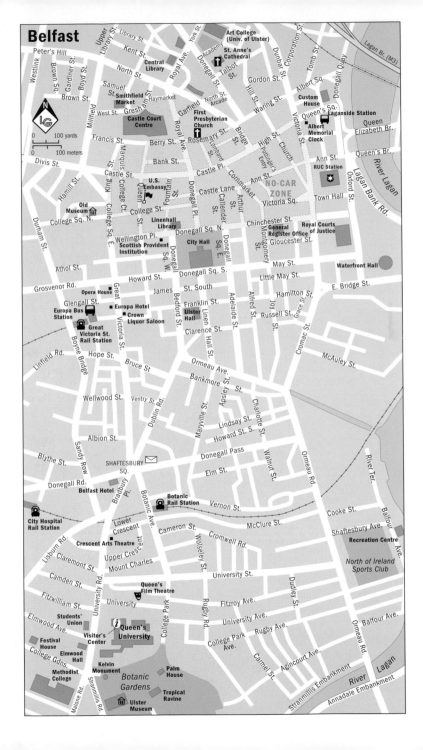

LET'S GO

■ PAGES PACKED WITH ESSENTIAL INFORMATION

"Value-packed, unbeatable, accurate, and comprehensive."

—The Los Angeles Times

"The guides are aimed not only at young budget travelers but at the independent traveler; a sort of streetwise cookbook for traveling alone."

—The New York Times

"Unbeatable; good sight-seeing advice; up-to-date info on restaurants, hotels, and inns; a commitment to money-saving travel; and a wry style that brightens nearly every page."

—The Washington Post

■ THE BEST TRAVEL BARGAINS IN YOUR BUDGET

"All the dirt, dirt cheap."

—People

"Let's Go follows the creed that you don't have to toss your life's savings to the wind to travel—unless you want to."

—The Salt Lake Tribune

■ REAL ADVICE FOR REAL EXPERIENCES

"The writers seem to have experienced every rooster-packed bus and lunar-surfaced mattress about which they write."

—The New York Times

"[Let's Go's] devoted updaters really walk the walk (and thumb the ride, and trek the trail). Learn how to fish, haggle, find work—anywhere."

—Food & Wine

"A world-wise traveling companion—always ready with friendly advice and helpful hints, all sprinkled with a bit of wit."

—The Philadelphia Inquirer

■ A GUIDE WITH A SPIRIT AND A SOCIAL CONSCIENCE

"Lighthearted and sophisticated, informative and fun to read. [Let's Go] helps the novice traveler navigate like a knowledgeable old hand."

—Atlanta Journal-Constitution

"The serious mission at the book's core reveals itself in exhortations to respect the culture and the environment—and, if possible, to visit as a volunteer, a student, or a teacher rather than a tourist."

—San Francisco Chronicle

LET'S GO PUBLICATIONS

TRAVEL GUIDES

Australia 9th edition
Austria & Switzerland 12th edition
Brazil 1st edition
Britain 2008
California 10th edition
Central America 9th edition
Chile 2nd edition
China 5th edition
Costa Rica 3rd edition
Eastern Europe 13th edition
Ecuador 1st edition
Egypt 2nd edition
Europe 2008
France 2008
Germany 13th edition
Greece 9th edition
Hawaii 4th edition
India & Nepal 8th edition
Ireland 13th edition
Israel 4th edition
Italy 2008
Japan 1st edition
Mexico 22nd edition
New Zealand 8th edition
Peru 1st edition
Puerto Rico 3rd edition
Southeast Asia 9th edition
Spain & Portugal 2008
Thailand 3rd edition
USA 24th edition
Vietnam 2nd edition
Western Europe 2008

ROADTRIP GUIDE

Roadtripping USA 2nd edition

ADVENTURE GUIDES

Alaska 1st edition
Pacific Northwest 1st edition
Southwest USA 3rd edition

CITY GUIDES

Amsterdam 5th edition
Barcelona 3rd edition
Boston 4th edition
London 16th edition
New York City 16th edition
Paris 14th edition
Rome 12th edition
San Francisco 4th edition
Washington, D.C. 13th edition

POCKET CITY GUIDES

Amsterdam
Berlin
Boston
Chicago
London
New York City
Paris
San Francisco
Venice
Washington, D.C.

LET'S GO

IRELAND

EDITORS
MATTHEW R. CONROY
MOLLY DONOVAN

RESEARCHER-WRITERS
KYLE DALTON
ALEX ELLIS
ANNIE LEVENSON
J.P. SHARP

JOY DING MAP EDITOR
SILVIA GONZALEZ KILLINGSWORTH MANAGING EDITOR

ST. MARTIN'S PRESS ✦ NEW YORK

Maps by David Lindroth copyright © 2008 by St. Martin's Press.

Distributed outside the USA and Canada by Macmillan.

Let's Go: Ireland Copyright © 2008 by Let's Go, Inc. All rights reserved. Printed in the United States of America. No part of this book may be used or reproduced in any manner whatsoever without written permission except in the case of brief quotations embodied in critical articles or reviews. Let's Go is available for purchase in bulk by institutions and authorized resellers. For information, address St. Martin's Press, 175 Fifth Avenue, New York, NY 10010, USA.

ISBN-13: 978-0-312-37456-3
ISBN-10: 0-312-37456-9
Thirteenth edition
10 9 8 7 6 5 4 3 2 1

Let's Go: Ireland is written by Let's Go Publications, 67 Mount Auburn St., Cambridge, MA 02138, USA.

Let's Go® and the LG logo are trademarks of Let's Go, Inc.

CONTENTS

HOW TO USE THIS BOOK

Bienvenidos. Oh wait, you're headed to Ireland, where the locals, for the most part, speak English. Well, that takes away half the trouble. This book will help you with any other difficulties you may have. Read on to find out how to use the invaluable chapters of this guide:

DISCOVER. Discover Ireland (see p. 1) holds **suggested itineraries** and Let's Go's picks. If you can't decide what your favorite part of Ireland is, use this chapter as a cheat-sheet to answer your relatives' nosy questions.

ESSENTIALS. This section outlines the practical information you need for traveling in Ireland, including logistical details, packing tips, and comprehensive safety and health information. (see p. 8).

LIFE AND TIMES. After reading our extensive coverage of Irish history, politics, and culture (see p. 49), you could probably fool people into thinking that you were already an expert on the Emerald Isle.

BEYOND TOURISM. To find out how where to volunteer, study, or work abroad in the short- or long-term, check out **Beyond Tourism** (see p. 79).

TRANSPORTATION INFO. Before coasting on to the next leg of your journey, check the transportation section at the beginning of each town to find out trip durations, departure frequencies, and prices. Fares, unless otherwise noted, are one-way. "Return" indicates round-trip fares.

COVERAGE. The chapters circle the island clockwise, beginning with **County Dublin,** devoted to the city and its suburbs. Next is **Eastern Ireland,** then **Southeast Ireland** and its hub, Kilkenny. From there, the spiral continues to **Southwest Ireland** and Cork, **Western Ireland** and Galway, and **Northwest Ireland** with Donegal Town. The final chapter completes the cycle, crossing over into **Northern Ireland,** starring Belfast and Derry/Londonderry.

FEATURES. This guide holds many juicy sidebar articles exploring topics from matchmaking festivals to the King of Tory Island. Also keep your eyes peeled for in-depth essays on the walls of Belfast and volunteering in Ireland. Our book also includes tipboxes, advising you where to snag free hamburgers or how to enjoy a large city on a budget, and the "Real Deal" on how to avoid tourist traps.

PRICE DIVERSITY. All of our food and accommodations listings are followed by a price diversity icon (see p. XI) to let you know at a glance how much you can expect to spend. Our researchers rank listings starting with the best and give their absolute favorites the *Let's Go* thumbs-up (◪).

A NOTE TO OUR READERS. The information for this book was gathered by *Let's Go* researchers from May through August of 2007. Each listing is based on one researcher's opinion, formed during his or her visit at a particular time. Those traveling at other times may have different experiences since prices, dates, hours, and conditions are always subject to change. You are urged to check the facts presented in this book beforehand to avoid inconvenience and surprises.

RESEARCHER-WRITERS

Kyle Dalton *Dublin, Cork, Southern Coast*

This former team captain who appeared in the 2007 NCAA Women's Basketball tournament took her game from the hardwood to the streets of Dublin and Cork. Kyle canvassed the comedy scene in Dublin, the scuba sites of Baltimore, and everything in between. Though challenged by flat tires and the demands of researching two world-class cities, she found her groove along the coast, producing witty prose along the way and netting nothing but great copy.

Alex Ellis *Northern Ireland, Northwest Ireland*

Before beginning a graduate program in England, Alex thought he might do a little traveling. His interest in country-hopping through Europe was quickly put to the test with a diverse and challenging route in the North. While pubbing in Belfast, this mathematical genius received a tutorial in the city's rich social and political history. While practicing the popular sport of coasteering in Antrim, this former rugby player took on a new athletic challenge. Travelers in the North will owe a lot to this dogged researcher.

Annie Levenson *Galway, Eastern and Western Ireland*

This former roadtripper let the road rise up to meet her as she trekked all over Ireland. A travel-holic, Annie was the perfect choice for researching the meandering route that took her from daytripping in Dublin's suburbs to wandering the Wicklow Way to pubcrawling in Galway. Though a vegetarian in the land of meat and potatoes and our only researcher without a car, Annie thrived wherever she went, bringing sunshine to even the rainiest days.

J.P. Sharp *Western Ireland, Southwest Ireland*

This gregarious graduate set off for Ireland in search of a little relaxation and a lot of *craic*. He ultimately found breathtaking scenery, effervescent locals, and countless fond memories. During his travels, J.P. lived like the Irish: he rambled over their land, drank their Guinness (last count: 50½ pints!), and flirted with their women. But have no fear—all this revelry never detracted from the consistently outstanding quality of his coverage of the Island's islands and the Western coast.

CONTRIBUTING WRITERS

Emily Simon is a former *Let's Go: France* researcher who volunteered at the Birr Castle Demesne, Co. Offaly.

Brenna Powell works for the Stanford Center on Conflict and Negotiation with grassroots organizations in Northern Ireland.

ACKNOWLEDGMENTS

LET'S GO

TEAM IRELAND THANKS: ⚑Alex, Annie, Kyle, and J.P. for your tireless effort and dedication and your bravery in facing difficult routes, horrible weather, and the occasional flat tire. ⚑Silvia for being our *craic*-baby and ensuring the quality of our book. Our map editor ⚑Joy for guaranteeing that none of our readers get lost. Our mad scientist and best friend, ⚑Noga, for making every single day as enjoyable as possible and ensuring that we always had a comfy chair for a siesta. ⚑Vicki and Jansen for always handling all of our problems. ⚑Anne for making sure that at least some work was done each day. We would also like to thank everyone else at LG for a wonderful year. Special thanks to our friends and family. Last but not least, we thank Michaela for assisting our weary RWs on the road.

MATT THANKS: Molls, for being an amazing partner on this book. I can't possibly say how much I enjoyed spending time with you this summer. Here's to living in Boston! Silvia, for deftly guiding us through a million things that went into this book. Joy, for your attention to detail. The 6ex family and everyone at LG. Mom, Dad, and friends for four great years.

MOLLY THANKS: Matt, for answering all my questions, for not judging, for the surprises, and for everything else; it's good to have you on my team. Silvia, I think we now understand each other. Yay. Joy, for all your help. The fourth floor, for putting up with the snorts. Mom, Dad, Cait, and tKat for everything.

JOY THANKS: Matt and Molly for being punctual perfectionists, and so much fun! Alex for witticisms, Annie for gusto, JP for keenness, Kyle for resilience—all the RWs for making maps a priority. BW and AB for entertaining me at work. Mom and Dad for putting up with an MIA daughter all summer. And LG love.

Editors
Matthew R. Conroy
Molly Donovan
Managing Editor
Silvia Gonzalez Killingsworth
Map Editor
Joy Ding
Typesetter
Alexandra Hoffer

Publishing Director
Jennifer Q. Wong
Editor-in-Chief
Silvia Gonzalez Killingsworth
Production Manager
Victoria Esquivel-Korsiak
Cartography Manager
Thomas MacDonald Barron
Editorial Managers
Anne Bensson, Calina Ciobanu, Rachel Nolan
Financial Manager
Sara Culver
Business and Marketing Manager
Julie Vodhanel
Personnel Manager
Victoria Norelid
Production Associate
Jansen A. S. Thurmer
Director of E-Commerce & IT
Patrick Carroll
Website Manager
Kathryne A. Bevilacqua
Office Coordinators
Juan L. Peña, Bradley J. Jones

Director of Advertising Sales
Hunter McDonald
Senior Advertising Associate
Daniel Lee

President
William Hauser
General Managers
Bob Rombauer, Jim McKellar

IX

ABOUT LET'S GO

NOT YOUR PARENTS' TRAVEL GUIDE

At Let's Go, we see every trip as the chance of a lifetime. If your dream is to grab a machete and forge through the jungles of Costa Rica, we can take you there. If you'd rather bask in the Riviera sun at a beachside cafe, we'll set you a table. We write for readers who know that there's more to travel than sharing double deckers with tourists and who believe that travel can change both themselves and the world—whether they plan to spend six days in Mexico City or six months in Europe. We'll show you just how far your money can go, and prove that the greatest limitation on your adventures is not your wallet, but your imagination.

BEYOND THE TOURIST EXPERIENCE

To help you gain a deeper connection with the places you travel, our fearless researchers scour the globe to give you the heads-up on both world-renowned and off-the-beaten-track attractions, sights, and destinations. They engage with the local culture only to emerge with the freshest insights on everything from local festivals to regional cuisine. We've also opened our pages to respected writers and scholars to hear their takes on the countries and regions we cover, and asked travelers who have worked, studied, or volunteered abroad to contribute first-person accounts of their experiences. In addition, we increased our coverage of responsible travel and expanded each guide's Beyond Tourism chapter to share more ideas about how to give back while on the road.

FORTY-EIGHT YEARS OF WISDOM

Let's Go got its start in 1960, when a group of creative and well-traveled students compiled their experience and advice into a 20-page mimeographed pamphlet, which they gave to travelers on charter flights to Europe. Four and a half decades later, we've expanded to cover six continents and all kinds of travel—while retaining our founders' adventurous attitude toward the world. Laced with witty prose and total candor, our guides are still researched and written entirely by students on shoestring budgets, experienced travelers who know that train strikes, stolen luggage, food poisoning, and marriage proposals are all part of a day's work.

THE LET'S GO COMMUNITY

More than just a travel guide company, Let's Go is a community. Our small staff comes together because of our shared passion for travel and our desire to help other travelers see the world the way it was meant to be seen. We love it when our readers become part of the Let's Go community as well—when you travel, drop us a postcard (67 Mt. Auburn St., Cambridge, MA 02138, USA), send us an e-mail (feedback@letsgo.com), or post on our forum (http://www.letsgo.com/connect/forum) to tell us about your adventures and discoveries.

For more information, visit us online: www.letsgo.com.

2 PRICE RANGES 3 4
IRELAND 5
1 5

Our researchers list establishments in order of value from best to worst; our favorites are denoted by the Let's Go thumbs-up (🔼). However, because the best value is not always the cheapest price, we have also incorporated a system of price ranges, based on a rough expectation of what you'll spend. For **accommodations,** we base our range on the cheapest price for which a single traveler can stay for one night. For **restaurants** and other dining establishments, we estimate the average amount a traveler will spend. The table tells you what you'll *typically* find in Ireland at the corresponding price range; keep in mind that no system can allow for every individual establishment's quirks, and you'll typically get more for your money in larger cities. In other words: expect anything.

ACCOMMODATIONS	RANGE	WHAT YOU'RE *LIKELY* TO FIND
❶	under €20	Campgrounds, dorm rooms, or dorm-style rooms. Expect bunk beds and a communal bath; you may have to provide or rent towels and sheets.
❷	€21-35	Upper-end hostels or lower-end B&Bs. You may have a private bathroom, or there may be a sink in your room and a communal shower in the hall.
❸	€36-45	A small room with a private bath, probably in a great hostel or B&B. Should have decent amenities, such as phone and TV. Breakfast may be included in the price of the room.
❹	€46-60	Similar to 3, but may have more amenities or be in a more highly-touristed or conveniently-located area.
❺	above €60	Fancy hotels or upscale B&Bs. If it's a 5 and it doesn't have the perks you want, you've paid too much.

FOOD	RANGE	WHAT YOU'RE *LIKELY* TO FIND
❶	under €10	Probably a fast-food stand, chipper, university cafeteria, or bakery. Rarely ever a sit-down meal.
❷	€11-20	Some sandwich shops, pubs, pizzerias, and take-out options, but also quite a few ethnic restaurants. May be take-out or sit-down.
❸	€21-30	Entrées are more expensive, but chances are you're paying for decor and ambience. Here's a chance to escape the pub culture for a meal.
❹	€31-40	As in 3, higher prices are probably related to better service, but in these restaurants, the food will tend to be fancier or more elaborate, or the location will be especially convenient.
❺	above €40	Your meal might cost more than your room, but there's a reason—it's fabulous or famous, and you'll probably need to wear something other than sandals and a t-shirt; but don't worry—you'll need that kind of garb for the classy club later.

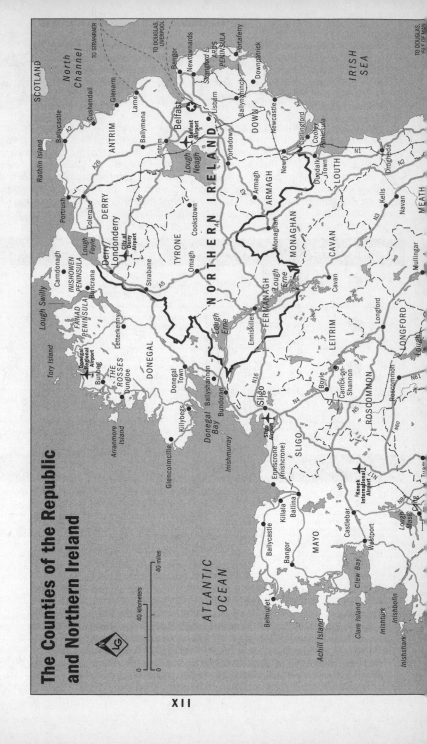

The Counties of the Republic and Northern Ireland

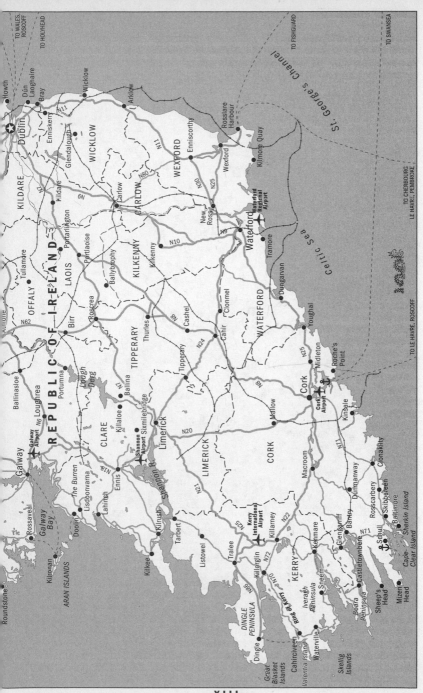

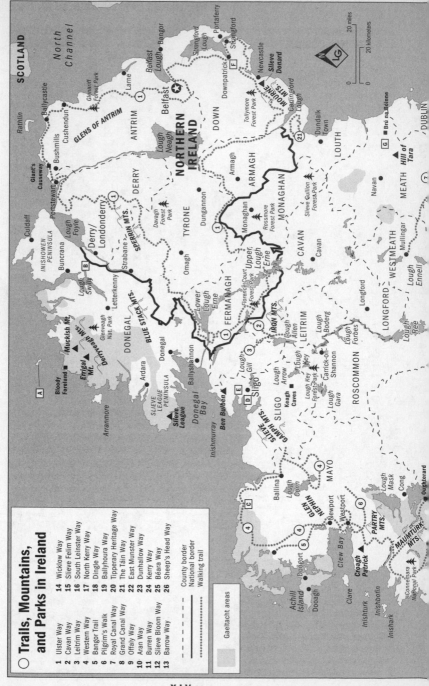

○ Trails, Mountains, and Parks in Ireland

1 Ulster Way	14 Wicklow Way
2 Cavan Way	15 Slieve Felim Way
3 Leitrim Way	16 South Leinster Way
4 Western Way	17 North Kerry Way
5 Bangor Trail	18 Dingle Way
6 Pilgrim's Walk	19 Ballyhoura Way
7 Royal Canal Way	20 Tipperary Heritage Way
8 Grand Canal Way	21 The Táin Way
9 Offaly Way	22 East Munster Way
10 Aran Way	23 Dunhallow Way
11 Burren Way	24 Kerry Way
12 Slieve Bloom Way	25 Béara Way
13 Barrow Way	26 Sheep's Head Way

County border
National border
Walking trail

Gaeltacht areas

XIV

Historical Sights in Ireland

A	Tory Island	J	Glendalough
B	Grianán Ailigh	K	Bunratty Castle
C	Ceide Fields	L	Kilkenny Castle
D	Carrowmore	M	Jerpoint Abbey
E	Drumcliffe Churchyard	N	Rock of Cashel
F	Grave of St. Patrick	O	Dunquin (Dún Chaoin)
G	Newgrange	P	Muckross House
H	James Joyce Tower	Q	Blarney Castle
I	Dún Aengus (Dún Aonghasa)	R	Staigue Fort

IRISH SEA

St. George's Channel

CELTIC SEA

ATLANTIC OCEAN

REPUBLIC OF IRELAND

Dublin

Dún Laoghaire

Wicklow

Arklow

Rosslare Harbour

Wexford

Waterford

Dungarvan

Kinsale

Cork

Fermoy

Clonmel

Cashel

Tipperary

Limerick

Ennis

Galway

Athlone

Tullamore

Portlaoise

Kilkenny

Clonegal

WICKLOW

KILDARE

LAOIS

OFFALY

CARLOW

WEXFORD

KILKENNY

TIPPERARY

WATERFORD

CORK

LIMERICK

CLARE

GALWAY

KERRY

WICKLOW MTS.

BLACKSTAIRS MTS.

SLIEVEARDAGH HILLS

SLIEVE BLOOM MTS.

COMERAGH MTS.

KNOCKMEALDOWN MTS.

GALTY MTS.

SLIEVE AUGHTY MTS.

THE BURREN

Cliffs of Moher

BOGGERAGH MTS.

MULLAGHEREIGH MTS.

SHEHY MTS.

DERRYNASAGGART MTS.

GLANARUDDERY MTS.

SLIEVE MISH MTS.

MACGILLICUDDY'S REEKS

CAHA MTS.

Reservoir

Lough Derg

Lough Corrib

Galway Bay

Lough Leane

Bantry Bay

Dingle Bay

Killarney

Killarney Nat. Park

Tralee

Dingle

Bantry

Skibbereen

Great Blasket Islands

ARAN ISLANDS

Thoor Ballylee

Coole Park

Burren National Park

XV

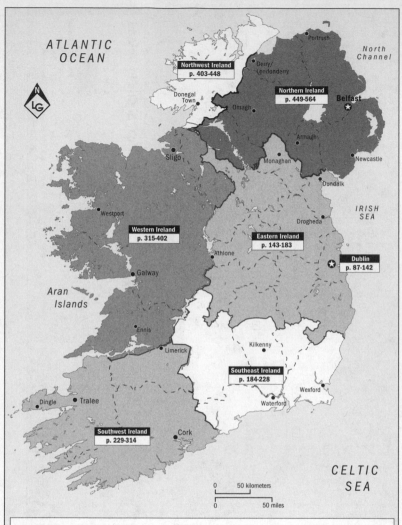

ATLANTIC
OCEAN

North
Channel

Portrush

Northwest Ireland
p. 403-448

Derry/
Londonderry

Northern Ireland
p. 449-564

Belfast ★

Donegal
Town

Omagh

Armagh

Newcastle

Sligo

Monaghan

Dundalk

IRISH
SEA

Westport

Drogheda

Western Ireland
p. 315-402

Eastern Ireland
p. 143-183

Athlone

Dublin
p. 87-142
★

Galway

Aran
Islands

Ennis

Limerick

Kilkenny

Southeast Ireland
p. 184-228

Wexford

Dingle ● Tralee

Waterford

Southwest Ireland
p. 229-314

Cork

CELTIC
SEA

0   50 kilometers

0   50 miles

Chapter Divisions

County Dublin
County Dublin

Eastern Ireland
Counties: Monaghan, Cavan, Louth,
Meath, Longford, Westmeath, Offaly,
Laois, Kildare, and Wicklow

Southeast Ireland
Counties: Tipperary, Kilkenny, Carlow,
Wexford, and Waterford

Southwest Ireland
Counties: Cork, Kerry, and Limerick

Western Ireland
Counties: Clare, Galway, Mayo,
Roscommon, Leitrim, and Sligo

Northwest Ireland
County Donegal

Northern Ireland
Counties: Derry, Antrim, Tyrone,
Fermanagh, Armagh, and Down

DISCOVER
IRELAND

Welcome to Ireland, the land of congeniality, camaraderie, and *craic*. Visitors come to Ireland for its rustic charm: its emerald hills, heathered crags, and misty seacliffs. They also come to see its up-and-coming cities with their festivals and exhibits, musical performances, and rollicking nightlife, but they stay for the hospitality and friendliness that flow from the very pores of the Irish people. Whether you choose to relax in the countryside or absorb as much culture and history as possible during your stay, your travel opportunities are endless. Learn all there is to know about Yeats in County Sligo, stagger through a pub crawl in Dublin, meander through a seaside village, or sway to traditional music in a local pub as you swill a pint of Guinness with your new Irish friends.

WHEN TO GO

Travelers in the low season (mid-Sept. to May) score cheaper airfares and accommodations and dodge the tourist hordes. But budget travelers beware: many sights, hostels, B&Bs, and tourist offices close in the winter, and in some rural areas, local transportation is either severely limited or may shut down completely. Most of Ireland's best festivals also occur in the summer. Irish weather is relatively constant; rain, like Guinness and *craic*, abounds in Ireland. (See **Temperature and Climate,** p. 594.) The southeastern coast is relatively dry and sunny, while western Ireland is considerably wetter and cloudier. July and August are the warmest months, but May and June are the sunniest. December and January are very rainy and cold. Year-round, take heart—cloudy mornings often clear by noon.

THINGS TO DO

COMMUNE WITH THE COLOR GREEN

The tranquil, gorgeous **Beara Peninsula** (p. 276) and its 200km of **Beara Way** offer an opportunity for lone travelers to brood as they enjoy beautiful scenery. **Killarney National Park** (p. 291) is a hiking-biking-climbing paradise that makes a good gateway to the understandably heavily touristed **Ring of Kerry** (p. 295). Trekkers along the **Kerry Way** (p. 295) traverse the same countryside without quite so much company. Several developed paths allow hikers to spend any number of days exploring Ireland's mountain chains—the **Wicklow Way** passes through the **Wicklow Mountains** (p. 152) in Dublin's backyard, while the new **Sperrin Way** treks through the **Sperrin Mountains** (p. 582). South of Tipperary Town, follow the river **Aherlow** (p. 207) as it cuts through the **Galty Mountains** (p. 207). In remote Co. Donegal, the **Slieve League Mountains** (p. 441) reach their dramatic end at the highest sea cliffs in Europe. The west coast is densely strewn with strange and beautiful geologic curiosities, including the limestone moonscape of **The Burren** (p. 352) and towering **Cliffs of Moher** (p. 352), which soar 700 ft. above the sea. The bizarre honeycomb columns of **Giant's Causeway** (p. 567) spill out from the **Antrim Coast**, a long strip of rocky crags and white beaches. Donegal's **Glenveagh National Park** (p. 453) contains salt-and-peppered **Mount Errigal.** Near Enniskillen, a series of underground caves carved the limestone earth into haunting **Marble Arch Caves** (p. 592). And just northwest of Galway lies **Connemara** (p. 387), studded with two mountain ranges (the **Twelve Bens** and the **Maamturks**), the **Western Way**

1

TOP 10 FESTIVALS

The Irish, with their relaxed attitude and effervescent love of *craic*, know how to celebrate. Festivals abound throughout the year and throughout the island; *Let's Go* has compiled a list of the country's top ten festivals for your enjoyment.

1. Get your Joyce on at the **Bloomsday Festival** in Dublin on June 16 (p. 136).

2. Place your bets at the **Galway Races** in July, and order a pint ordered from the longest bar in Europe (p. 375)

3. If you're in search of love, head to Lisdoonvarna for the annual **Lisdoonvarna Matchmaking Festival** in September (p. 354).

4. Sit back and relax at the **Dublin Film Festival** (p. 137).

5. Walk the way during the **Wicklow Mountains Spring Walking Festival** in May.

6. Celebrate the arts with the students at Belfast's Queen's University during the **Festival at Queen's** in November (p. 516).

7. Show your pride at the **Dublin Gay and Lesbian Film Festival** in June (p. 137).

8. Get spooky at the **Banks of the Foyle Halloween Carnival** in Derry (p. 581).

9. Don't miss the **Galway Arts Festival** in mid-July, Ireland's largest arts festival in its most up-and-coming cultural city (p. 375).

10. Be sure to check out the **Cork Midsummer Festival,** replete with two weeks of artistic performances in mid-June (p. 249).

(p. 386) footpath that twists through the Maamturks, and **Connemara National Park** (p. 396).

WAX POETIC

Natural beauty and urban grime have inspired centuries of superb literature, and the Irish are fiercely proud of the literary luminaries they have produced. Dublin (p. 91) has promoted (and suffered) the caustic wit of **Jonathan Swift, Oscar Wilde, George Bernard Shaw, James Joyce, Sean O'Casey, Samuel Beckett, Brendan Behan, Flann O'Brien, Eavan Boland,** and **Roddy Doyle,** to name but a few. **W.B. Yeats** expressed poetry all over the island, but chose Co. Sligo for his grave (p. 422). **John Millington Synge** found literary greatness depicting the domestic trials of Aran Islanders (p. 377). **Seamus Heaney** compared the bogland's fossilized remains of pre-Christian sacrifices to the Troubles. In Belfast (p. 491), **Brian Moore, Bernard MacLaverty,** and **Paul Muldoon** capture ordinary lives in a city known only for its extraordinary events. **Brian Friel's** plays bring to life the wilds of Co. Donegal (p. 427). Limerick (p. 326) has had a successful face-lift since the poverty-stricken childhood of **Frank McCourt.** Farther south, the dwindling *gaeltacht* of Co. Kerry is preserved through the autobiography of Blasket-Islander **Peig Sayers** and the poetry of **Nuala Ni Dhomhnaill.** Ancient **mythology** is the most pervasive of Ireland's literary forms—nearly every landmark is attributable to fairies, giants, or heroes.

DRINK UP

The Irish claim that stout is blessed and that whiskey is the "water of life." It follows that the island's breweries and distilleries are its holy wells. The **Guinness Storehouse** (p. 126) guards the secret of its black magic, but doles out plenty of samples at tours end as consolation. **Smithwicks** (p. 196), the oldest brewery in Ireland, stores a blonder brew in a former monastery in Kilkenny. Back in Dublin, the **Old Jameson Distillery** (p. 130) makes a slightly sweeter whiskey than the hard stuff stored at **Bushmills Distillery** (p. 568) in Co. Antrim, but the folks at Bushmills provide more "fulfilling" tours.

BE A GOOD SPORT

With its expansive fields, sandy beaches, and mild climate, Ireland is the perfect place for athletics. If oceanside during the summer, sail in one of Ireland's many **regattas,** at locales such as **Bantry** (p. 273) in early May, **Bangor** (p. 518) in early July, or **Wicklow** (p. 146) in late July or early August. Try surfing off the duned beaches of the **Strandhill Peninsula** (p. 419) in County Sligo. For more firmly-grounded fun, visit **Croke Park** in Dublin to see the **All-Ireland Hurling Finals** (p. 74) in early September and the **All-Ireland Gaelic Football Finals** (p. 74) in late September. Go road-bowling with the like of pros like Mike Barry in **County Cork,** or watch the **horse races** in **Killarney** (p. 285), **Galway** (p. 359), or **Dingle** (p. 311).

ROCK OUT

Though Ireland's national instrument is the harp, you'll be able to find a much wider variety of music throughout the island. For traditional culture, jam during **trad sessions** at pubs in almost any city or town; counties Kerry, Galway, Sligo, and Donegal all have good reputations. Head over to **Buncrana** (p. 469) in late July for the **Buncrana Music Festival**, and then to **Glencolmcille** (p. 441) for the **Folk Festival** in early August. Enjoy the November **Trad Festival** in **Ennis** (p. 335) and the **Jazz Festival** in **Dungarvan** (p. 231) in mid-February. Check listings of **Riverdance** tours and other musical performances throughout the country.

VISIT THE ISLAND'S ISLANDS

The people of the **Aran Islands** (see p. 377) live much like the rest of the country did around 1900—speaking Irish, eking out their living fishing in *curraghs* at the mercy of the sea. Off the Dingle Peninsula, the now deserted **Blasket Islands** (p. 317) were once home to several impoverished memoirists. Now they hold only pensive walks through haunting village ruins. Electricity and tap water are recent introductions to Donegal's **Inishbofin Island** (p. 393), but serenity and camaraderie are longstanding. **Sherkin Island** (p. 269) beckons visitors to its sandy, cliff-enclosed beaches, over-abundance of cows, and under-abundance of people. Nearby **Cape Clear Island** (p. 267) trades cows for goats, to produce the best homemade goat's milk ice cream in all of Ireland.

PLAY EXPLORER

In Co. Meath, the 5000-year-old passage tombs of the **Boyne Valley** (p. 164), including sights at **Newgrange, Knowth, and Dowth,** are architectural feats that stump modern engineers. Nearby **Hill of Tara** (p. 166) has been the symbolic Irish throne from Celtic chieftains to St. Patrick to 19th-century Nationalists. On the west coast, **Poulnebrane Dolmen** marks a group gravesite with a 25-ton capstone atop two standing rocks. Bend over backwards and kiss the **Blarney Stone** (p. 251) to gain the distinctly Irish gift of the gab. On the magnificent limestone **Rock of Cashel** (p. 204), a mishmash of early Christian structures defines the skyline. **Glendalough** (p. 152) is the picturesque home of St. Kevin's 6th-century monastery, a 100 ft. round tower, and the saint's small stone kitchen. In Donegal, near Derry, **Grianán Ailigh** (p. 467) was first a Druidic temple, then the burial place for Aedh (divine king of the Túatha De Dannan), and finally a seat of power for the northern branch of the Uí Néill (O'Neill) Clan. The monastic ruins of **Clonmacnois** (p. 184), south of Athlone, keep watch over the River Shannon's boglands. St. Ciaran founded his monastery here in AD 548, and the gorgeous remains lure many a traveler to the otherwise untouristed midlands. The otherworldly **Skellig Rocks** (p. 305) astound visitors to the Iveragh Peninsula. The **Rock of Dunamaise** (p. 187) rises in Portlaoise, a scar left by Cromwell.

FROLIC

Guinness runs freely during the island-wide frenzy of **St. Patrick's Day** (March 17th). Mid-May brings **Armagh's Apple Blossom Festival** (p. 549). James Joyce enthusiasts ramble for 18 hours through Dublin every June 16, **Bloomsday** (p. 136). In mid-July, the **Galway Arts Festival** (p. 375) hosts theater, trad, rock, and film for two weeks of revelry. Early August brings all types of musicians, artists, and merrymakers to Waterford's **Spraoi festival** (p. 237). He-goats compete for the title of alpha male in **Killorglin's Puck Fair** (p. 295) in mid-August. In late August, Cape Clear Island welcomes tale-spinners to the **International Storytelling Festival** (p. 268), while everyone in Ireland tunes in to the nationally televised **Rose of Tralee Festival and Pageant** (p. 325). Many return happy from the **Lisdoonvarna Matchmaking Festival** (p. 354) in early September. Fat ladies sing at the **Wexford Opera** (p. 220) in late October, and ghouls and goblins mob **Derry** for its carnival-like **Halloween** celebration (p. 581). Ireland's largest arts celebration, the **Belfast Festival** (p. 516) at Queen's College, is a three-week winter potluck of cultural events.

DISCOVER

BEST CLUB FOR YOU AND YOUR POSSE: Zanzibar (p. 116) in Dublin reserves swanky private rooms for free. The Liffey Room overlooks the river, the Star Room has huge stars deep-cut in the wooden ceiling.

BEST HOME MAKEOVER: The citizens of Baltimore can thank the new owners of **Dún na Sead** (p. 267) for pimping their castle. It took the couple six years to turn a nondescript pile of rubble into an artfully decorated dreamhouse.

BEST BIPOLAR ARCHITECTURE: An antagonistic marriage is responsible for the battling styles of the **Castle Ward House** (p. 529) near Mountstewart. One wing is classical, the other gothic.

BEST PLACE TO TALK TO DEAD ANIMALS: Dublin's **Natural History Museum** (p. 122) crams a dodo skeleton and a lemur frozen in maniacal frenzy, among other expired monstrosities, into three floors of gallery space.

BEST PLACE TO TALK TO PERSONIFIED ANIMALS: The Dodo Terrace in the botanical gardens of **Mount Stewart House** (p. 526) contains a menagerie of animal statues intended to represent various upper-crust characters, including Winston Churchill.

BEST PLACE TO GET TO KNOW YOUR VACUUM CLEANER: The owner of **Fox's Lane Folk Museum** (p. 255) in Youghal will give you the lowdown on every household implement since the 70s.

BEST PLACE TO TRAIN FOR THE OLYMPICS (OR LEARN TO KAYAK): Schull's **Fastnet Marine Outdoor Education Centre** (p. 271) trains Olympic athletes and teaches novices the basics of kayaking, sailing, and windsurfing.

BEST ROOM TO SHACK UP WITH PRINCESS BARBIE: Each room in the **Bridge House B&B** in Skibbereen (p. 264) has its own motif. The Pink Room, is, unsurprisingly, pink, with pink curtains, a gazillion pink pillows, and a mannequin dressed in formal wear.

BEST PLACE TO TREASURE HUNT: The **raised beaches** around Malin Head (p. 474) are studded with semi-precious stones; sifting through the sands may reveal jasper, quartz, small opals, and amethysts beneath more prosaic stones.

BEST PLACE TO SOB OVER SCENERY: The only thing missing from the beautiful Howth **cliff walk** (p. 140) is a box of kleenex.

BEST PLACE TO ABANDON YOUR CHILD: Malahide's **Museum of Childhood** (p. 137) plays host to the world's oldest known dollhouse and a model mansion that fills an entire room.

BEST PUB FOR RUGBY (AND A RUGBURN): Fealty's bar (p. 521) in Bantry is renowned for spreading turf on its floor for rugby season.

BEST MONARCH: Patsy Dan (p. 455), the current King (Rí) of Tory Island, maintains a unique monarchical style with an earring, a motorcycle, a penchant for impressionistic painting, and a bartending gig on the side.

BEST MODERN ART: Sligo's **Model Arts and Niland Gallery** (p. 418) holds one of the country's finest collections of Irish art, including a number of works by Jack Yeats, WB's brother.

BEST CAB RIDE: Black Cab Tours (p. 507) highlight the murals and sights on both sides of Belfast's Peace Line.

BEST PUB TO GET A NOSEBLEED: Extremely motivated beer lovers and thirsty Wicklow Way hikers climb to **Johnnie Fox's** (p. 158), 400m above sea level.

BEST ABBA IMITATION: The bartenders at the **Old Oak** (p. 246), one of the finest traditional pubs in Ireland, flaunt hairstyles and wigs reminiscent of the übersuccessful Swedish pop group.

BEST PUBLIC PARK (WORST PLACE TO FIND A TOOTHBRUSH): Cork's **Public Museum** (p. 249), attached to the botanically blessed Fiztgerald Park, holds a collection of 18th-century toothbrushes.

SUGGESTED INTINERARIES

TOURISTY FOR A REASON (4 WEEKS)

Malin Head (1 day)
Semi-precious stones are hidden under the sand on these raised beaches at Ireland's northernmost point (p. 474).

Giant's Causeway (1 day)
A strange formation of octagonal rock pillars and the earth's eighth natural wonder, this geological oddity is the North's must-see (p. 567).

Slieve League (1 day)
Hike around Europe's tallest sea cliffs (p. 438).

Donegal Town (2 days)
Catch some rest at one of Ireland's best hostels, and soak in the untamed scenery (p. 430).

Sligo (2 days)
The beautiful and isolated Burren was once the beloved home of W.B. Yeats (p. 414).

END

Belfast (2 days)
Experience this city's complex history, illustrated in the murals decorating its sectarian neighborhoods (p. 491).

Galway (2 days)
Ireland's third largest city is a lively student center that draws many of the best musicians on the island (p. 359).

Howth (1 day)
This affluent suburb contains Howth Castle and Salman Rushdie's lighthouse hideout (p. 138).

Dublin (4 days)
Dublin is hopping with people from all over the world, here for the history, the pub crawls, and the Gaelic football matches at Croke Park (p. 93). START

Aran Islands (3 days)
Ferry to these desolate islands to purchase the namesake sweater, or just relax (p. 377).

Cliffs of Moher (1 day)
Marvel at the sheer 200m drop as wind gusts try to blow tourists over the edge (p. 352).

Doolin (1 day)
Swill Guinness with locals in this small town (p. 350).

Kilkenny (2 days)
This classic Irish city houses a former monastery which is now Ireland's oldest brewery (p. 189).

Cork (2 days)
Up-and-coming Cork has one of the best rock music and nightclub scenes in the country (p. 238).

Ring of Kerry (2 days)
Take a bus or bike ride around the Ring of Kerry a peninsula captured on Irish postcards worldwide (p. 295).

Blarney (1 day)
Kiss the Blarney Stone to gain the Irish "gift of the gab" (p. 251).

DISCOVER

I ONLY HAVE A WEEK (1 WEEK)

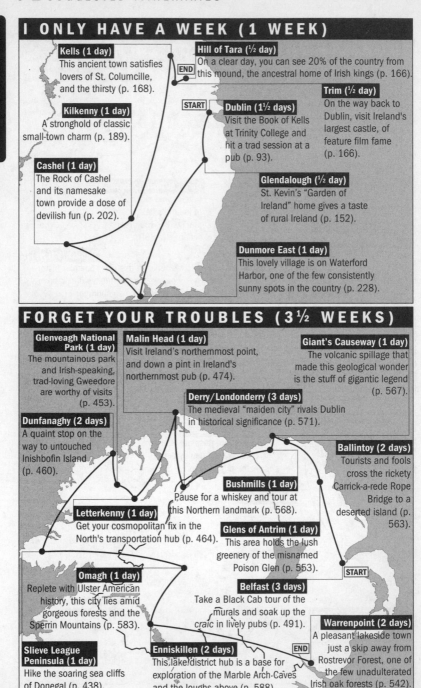

Kells (1 day)
This ancient town satisfies lovers of St. Columcille, and the thirsty (p. 168).

Hill of Tara (½ day)
On a clear day, you can see 20% of the country from this mound, the ancestral home of Irish kings (p. 166).

END

START

Kilkenny (1 day)
A stronghold of classic small-town charm (p. 189).

Dublin (1½ days)
Visit the Book of Kells at Trinity College and hit a trad session at a pub (p. 93).

Trim (½ day)
On the way back to Dublin, visit Ireland's largest castle, of feature film fame (p. 166).

Cashel (1 day)
The Rock of Cashel and its namesake town provide a dose of devilish fun (p. 202).

Glendalough (½ day)
St. Kevin's "Garden of Ireland" home gives a taste of rural Ireland (p. 152).

Dunmore East (1 day)
This lovely village is on Waterford Harbor, one of the few consistently sunny spots in the country (p. 228).

FORGET YOUR TROUBLES (3½ WEEKS)

Glenveagh National Park (1 day)
The mountainous park and Irish-speaking, trad-loving Gweedore are worthy of visits (p. 453).

Malin Head (1 day)
Visit Ireland's northernmost point, and down a pint in Ireland's northernmost pub (p. 474).

Giant's Causeway (1 day)
The volcanic spillage that made this geological wonder is the stuff of gigantic legend (p. 567).

Derry/Londonderry (3 days)
The medieval "maiden city" rivals Dublin in historical significance (p. 571).

Dunfanaghy (2 days)
A quaint stop on the way to untouched Inishbofin Island (p. 460).

Ballintoy (2 days)
Tourists and fools cross the rickety Carrick-a-rede Rope Bridge to a deserted island (p. 563).

Bushmills (1 day)
Pause for a whiskey and tour at this Northern landmark (p. 568).

Letterkenny (1 day)
Get your cosmopolitan fix in the North's transportation hub (p. 464).

Glens of Antrim (1 day)
This area holds the lush greenery of the misnamed Poison Glen (p. 553).

START

Omagh (1 day)
Replete with Ulster American history, this city lies amid gorgeous forests and the Sperrin Mountains (p. 583).

Belfast (3 days)
Take a Black Cab tour of the murals and soak up the craic in lively pubs (p. 491).

Warrenpoint (2 days)
A pleasant lakeside town just a skip away from Rostrevor Forest, one of the few unadulterated Irish oak forests (p. 542).

Slieve League Peninsula (1 day)
Hike the soaring sea cliffs of Donegal (p. 438).

Enniskillen (2 days)
This lake district hub is a base for exploration of the Marble Arch Caves and the loughs above (p. 588).

END

CULTURE 'N' OLD STUFF (2 WEEKS)

Inishmurray Island (1 day)
This uninhabited island harbors early monastic structures built on ancient Druidic sites (p. 422).

END

Sligo (2 days)
Visit Yeats's grave and the scenery that inspired his poetry (p. 414).

Newgrange (1 day)
This Neolithic burial site is older than the Egyptian pyramids (p. 164).

Athlone (1 day)
Take a rest from the tourism machine at everyone's favorite transportation hub, home to the monastic Clonmacnoise (p. 181).

Galway (2 days)
Ireland's leading musical city is home to thousands of students and one of Ireland's liveliest art scenes (p. 359).

START

The Hill of Tara (1 day)
Feel the power at what was the seat of Irish kings from pre-Christian times until just 400 years ago (p. 166).

Aran Islands (2 days)
Cycle past ancient ring forts and contented seals sunning themselves on the rocky shore(p. 377).

Doolin (2 days)
Trad-seeking pilgrims find this song-filled village snuggled into the rocky landscape of the Burren (p. 350).

Dublin (3 days)
Study up for free on Irish history at the National Museums by day, and spend the evening on a literary pub crawl or at the Irish Film Institute (p. 93).

TREE-HUGGING IN THE WEST (3 WEEKS)

Dingle Peninsula (3 days)
Mountains, beaches, and Irish-speakers abound in this scenic destination (p. 311).

START

Sixmilebridge (1 day)
Land at Shannon Airport and overnight in this sleepy town (p. 342).

Blasket Islands (1 day)
Don't leave before hitting the isolated *gaeltacht* off Ireland's west coast (p. 317).

Tarbert (2 days)
This peaceful seaside spot is home to a restored 17th-century home and a convenient ferry to Kerry (p. 326).

Ring of Kerry (3 days)
Move clockwise to avoid tour buses on this deservedly popular destination, and spend time in magnificent Killarney National Park (p. 295).

Valentia Island (2 days)
This often bypassed island has winding paths perfect for biking (p. 299).

END

Skellig Rocks (1 day)
Get chills from the ancient Christian ruins and gorgeous scenery on the Skellig Islands (p. 305).

Beara Peninsula (7 days)
Don't miss the third and least visited finger of land—hike the Beara Way over Healy Pass (p. 276).

ESSENTIALS

PLANNING YOUR TRIP

ENTRANCE REQUIREMENTS.
Passport (p. 10). Required of all foreign nationals except UK citizens traveling direct from the UK and nationals of Belgium, France, Germany, Luxembourg, and the Netherlands holding a valid national photo ID card. Advisable to bring passport regardless.
Visa (p. 11). Required of citizens of Afghanistan, Albania, Cuba, Democratic Republic of the Congo, Eritrea, Ethiopia, Ghana, Iran, Iraq, Lebanon, Moldova, Montenegro, Nigeria, Serbia, Somalia, Sri Lanka, Zimbabwe.
Work Permit (p. 11). Required for all non-EEA (European Economic Area) citizens planning to work in Ireland.

EMBASSIES AND CONSULATES

IRISH CONSULAR SERVICES ABROAD

For other Irish embassies, check the embassies and consulates search engines at www.embassyworld.com and www.irelandemb.org.

Australia: Irish Embassy, 20 Arkana St., Yarralumla, Canberra ACT 2600 (☎06 273 3022).

Canada: Irish Embassy, Ste. 1105, 130 Albert St., Ottawa, ON K1P 5G4 (☎613-233-6281; embassyofireland@rogers.com).

New Zealand: Consulate-General, 6th fl., 18 Shortland St., Auckland, NZ (☎0064 9 977 2255; www.ireland.co.nz).

UK: Irish Embassy, 17 Grosvenor Pl., London SW1X 7HR (☎020 7235 2171). **Passport and Visa Office:** Montpelier House, 106 Brompton Rd., London SW31LJ (☎00 44 20 7225 7700; passportlondon@dfa.ie/0906 661 0917; visamail@justice.ie). **Consulates:** 16 Randolph Crescent., Edinburgh EH3 7TT, Scotland (☎00 44 131 226 7711); Brunel House, 2 Fitzalan Rd., Cardiff CF24 0EB (☎00 44 29 20662 000).

US: Irish Embassy, 2234 Massachusetts Ave. N.W. Washington, D.C. 20008-2849 (☎202-462-3939). **Consulates:** 345 Park Ave., 17th fl., New York, NY 10154-0037 (☎212-319-2555); 400 N. Michigan Ave., Ste. 911 Chicago, IL 60611 (☎312-337-1868); 535 Boylston St., Boston, MA 02116 (☎617-267-9330); 100 Pine St., 33rd fl., San Francisco, CA 94111 (☎415-392-4214).

UK CONSULAR SERVICES ABROAD

For addresses of British embassies in countries not listed here, consult the **Foreign and Commonwealth Office** (☎020 7008 1500; www.fco.gov.uk). Some cities have a local British consulate that can handle most of the same functions as an embassy.

Australia: British High Commission, Commonwealth Ave., Yarralumla, ACT 2600 (☎02 6270 6666; http://bhc.britaus.net). **Consulates:** The Gateway, Level UK (16), 1 Macquarie Place, Sydney, NSW 2000; also in Adelaide, Brisbane, Darwin, Hobart, Melbourne, and Perth.

Canada: British High Commission, 80 Elgin St., Ottawa, ON K1P 5K7 (☎613-237-1530; www.britishhighcommission.gov.uk). **Consulates:** 777 Bay St., Ste. 2800, Toronto, ON M5G 2G2 (☎416-593-1290); also in Calgary, Dartmouth, Montreal, Quebec City, St. John's, Vancouver, and Winnipeg.

Ireland: British Embassy, 29 Merrion Rd., Ballsbridge, Dublin 4 (☎01 205 3700; www.britishembassy.ie).

New Zealand: British High Commission, 44 Hill St., Thorndon, Wellington 6011, P.O. Box 1812, Wellington 6140 (☎04 924 2888; www.britain.org.nz); mail to P.O. Box 1812, Wellington. **Consulate:** Level 17, IAG House, 151 Queen St., Auckland (☎09 303 2973); mail Private Bag 92014, Auckland.

US: British Embassy, 3100 Massachusetts Ave. N.W. Washington, D.C. 20008 (☎202-588-6500; www.britainusa.com). **Consulate:** 845 Third Ave., New York, NY 10022 (☎212-745-0200); also in Atlanta, Boston, Chicago, Houston, Los Angeles, and San Francisco.

CONSULAR SERVICES IN IRELAND

Australia: The Republic, 7th fl., Fitzwilton House, Wilton Terr., Dublin 2 (☎664 5300).

Canada: The Republic, 65 St. Stephen's Green, 4th fl., Dublin 2 (☎353 01 417 4100). **Northern Ireland,** Consulate of Canada, Unit 3, Ormeau Business Park, 8, Cromac Ave., Belfast, Northern Ireland, BT7 2JA (☎+44 2891 272060). Mailing address: P.O. Box 405, Belfast, BT3 5BL.

New Zealand: The Republic, 37 Leeson Park, Dublin 6 (☎01 660 4233). **UK,** New Zealand Consulate, New Zealand House, 80 the Haymarket, London SW1Y 4TQ (☎020 7930 8422).

UK: See **UK Consular Services Abroad,** p. 8.

US: The Republic, 42 Elgin Rd., Ballsbridge, Dublin 4 (☎01 668 8777). **Northern Ireland,** Consulate General, Danesfort House, 223 Stranmillis Rd., Belfast BT9 5GR (☎028 9038 6100).

TOURIST OFFICES

Almost every town in Ireland has a tourist office, with services ranging from useful (free local maps and pamphlets, transportation schedules, and accommodations booking services) to partial (e.g., a list of only those accommodations that have paid them a fee). All national tourist boards offer information on hikes, parks, and trails. Below are the main offices of the national tourist boards; for countries not listed here, check www.ireland.ie and www.discovernorthernireland.com.

Irish Tourist Board (Bord Fáilte): Main office at Suffolk St., Dublin 2 (☎353 1 605 7799; www.ireland.ie). **Tourism Ireland:** Bishops Sq., Redmonds Hill, Dublin 2 (☎01 476 3400; www.tourismireland.com). **Northern Ireland:** 47 Donegall Pl., Belfast BJ1 5AD (☎028 9024 6609). **Australia:** 5th Level, 36 Carrington St., Sydney NSW 2000 (☎02 9299 6177). **Canada:** 2 Bloor St. West, Ste. 3403, Toronto, ON M4W 3E2 (☎800-223-6470). **New Zealand:** Dingwall Building, 2nd fl., 87 Queen St., Auckland 1 (☎09 379 8720). **UK:** Nations House, 103 Wigmore St., London W1U 1QS (☎0800 039 7000). **US:** 345 Park Ave., New York, NY 10154 (☎800-223-6470; www.tourismireland.com).

Northern Ireland Tourist Board: Main Office at 59 North St., Belfast, BT1 1NB, Northern Ireland (☎028 9089 5512; www.discovernorthernireland.com). **The Republic:** 16 Nassau St., Dublin 2 (☎01 679 1977; infodublin@nitb.com). **UK:** Nations House, 103 Wigmore St., London W1U 1QS (☎0800 039 7000; info.gb@toursismireland.com). **Australia:** 36 Carrington St., 5th Level, Sydney NSW 2000 (☎02 9299 6177; info@tourismireland.com.au). **Canada:** 2 Bloor St. West, Ste. 1501, Toronto, ON M4W

3E2 (☎800-223-6470; info@shamrock.org). **New Zealand:** 6th fl., 18 Shortland St., Private Bag 92136, Auckland 1 (☎09 379 8720). **UK:** Nations House, 103 Wigmore St., London W1U 1QS (☎020 75180800). **US:** 345 Park Ave., New York, NY 10154 (☎800-223-6470; info@shamrock.org). From elsewhere, contact any British Tourist Office. Tourist boards have free brochures and sell lists of all B&Bs and campgrounds.

DOCUMENTS AND FORMALITIES

PASSPORTS

REQUIREMENTS
Citizens of Australia, Canada, New Zealand, the UK, and the US need valid passports to enter Ireland and to re-enter their home countries. Ireland does not allow entrance if the holder's passport expires in under six months; returning home with an expired passport is illegal and may result in a fine.

NEW PASSPORTS
Citizens of Australia, Canada, Ireland, New Zealand, the UK, and the US can apply for a passport at any post office, passport office, or court of law. Any new passport or renewal applications must be filed well in advance of the departure date, though most passport offices offer rush services for a very steep fee.

> **ONE EUROPE.** European unity has come a long way since 1958, when the European Economic Community (EEC) was created to promote cooperation. Since then, the EEC has become the European Union (EU), a mighty political, legal, and economic institution. On May 1, 2004, ten South, Central, and Eastern European countries—Cyprus, the Czech Republic, Estonia, Hungary, Latvia, Lithuania, Malta, Poland, the Slovak Republic, and Slovenia—joined the 15 member states: Austria, Belgium, Denmark, Finland, France, Germany, Greece, Ireland, Italy, Luxembourg, the Netherlands, Portugal, Spain, Sweden, and the UK. Bulgaria and Romania joined on January 1, 2007.
>
> What does this have to do with the average non-EU tourist? The EU's policy of **freedom of movement** means that border controls between the first fifteen member states (minus Ireland and the UK, but plus Norway and Iceland) have been abolished, and visa policies have become harmonized. While you're still required to carry a passport (or government-issued ID card for EU citizens) when crossing an internal border, once you've been admitted into one country, you're free to travel to other participating states. Britain and Ireland have also formed a **common travel area,** abolishing passport controls between the UK and the Republic of Ireland.
>
> For more important consequences of the EU for travelers, see **The Euro** (p. 13) and **Customs in the EU** (p. 12).

PASSPORT MAINTENANCE
Photocopy your passport, as well as your visas, traveler's check serial numbers, and other important documents. Carry one set of copies in a safe place, apart from the originals, and leave another set at home. You can also carry an expired passport or an official copy of your birth certificate separate from other documents.

If you lose your passport, notify the local police and your country's nearest embassy or consulate. To expedite its replacement, you will need to know all information previously recorded and show ID and proof of citizenship. In some cases, a replacement may take weeks to process, and it may be valid only for a limited time. Any visas stamped in your old passport will be lost. In an emergency, ask for temporary traveling papers to re-enter your home country.

VISAS

Citizens of most countries, including Australia, Canada, the EU, New Zealand, the UK, and the US, do not need visas for visits of less than 90 days. For longer stays, non-citizens of the EU must register for free with the **Garda National Immigration Bureau**, 13-14 Burgh Quay, Dublin 2 (☎01 666 9100) or in the local police station. If in doubt, or if your home country is not one of these, check with your embassy.

Double-check entrance requirements at the nearest embassy or consulate of Ireland (see p. 8) for up-to-date info before departure. US citizens can also consult www.pueblo.gsa.gov/cic_text/travel/foreign/foreignentryreqs.html.

WORK PERMITS

Admission as a visitor does not include the right to work, which is only authorized by a work permit. Students studying in Ireland may enter without a visa but must apply to the **Aliens Office** (Harcourt Sq., Dublin 2; ☎01 475 5555) upon entering the country (not necessary for UK residents). Contact your embassy for information, and see **Beyond Tourism**, p. 79.

IDENTIFICATION

When you travel, always have at least two forms of identification on you, including at least one photo ID; a passport and a driver's license or birth certificate is usually adequate. **Never carry all of your IDs together;** split them up in case of theft or loss, and keep photocopies of all of them in your luggage and at home.

STUDENT, TEACHER, AND YOUTH IDENTIFICATION

The **International Student Identity Card (ISIC)**, the most widely accepted form of student ID, provides discounts on some sights, accommodations, food, and transport; access to a free 24hr. multilingual emergency helpline; and insurance benefits for US cardholders (see **Insurance**, p. 21). Applicants must be full-time secondary or post-secondary school students at least 12 years of age. Because of the proliferation of fake ISICs, some services (particularly airlines) require additional proof of student identity.

The **International Teacher Identity Card (ITIC)** offers full-time teachers the same insurance coverage as the ISIC and similar but much more limited discounts. For travelers who are 25 years old or under but are not students, the **International Youth Travel Card (IYTC)** offers many of the same benefits as the ISIC.

Each of these identity cards costs US$22-25 or equivalent. ISICs and ITICs are valid for a maximum of 16 months; IYTCs are valid for one year. Many student travel agencies (see p. 24) issue the cards; for a list of agencies or more information, see the **International Student Travel Confederation** website (www.istc.org).

The **International Student Exchange Card (ISE)** is a similar identification card available to students, faculty, and youth aged 12 to 26. The card (US$25) provides discounts, medical benefits, and access to a 24hr. emergency helpline. Call US ☎800-255-8000 or international 480-951-1177 for more info, or visit www.isecard.com.

CUSTOMS

Upon entering Ireland, you must declare certain items from abroad and pay a duty on their value if they exceed the allowance established by Ireland's customs service. Goods and gifts purchased at **duty-free** shops abroad are not exempt from duty or sales tax; "duty-free" merely means that you need not pay a tax in the country of purchase. Duty-free allowances were abolished for travel between EU member states but still exist for those arriving from outside the EU. Upon returning

ESSENTIALS

home, you must likewise declare all articles acquired abroad and pay a duty on the value of articles in excess of your home country's allowance. In order to expedite your return, make a list of any valuables brought from home and register them with customs before traveling abroad, and keep receipts for all goods acquired abroad.

If you're leaving for a non-EU country, you can reclaim any **Value Added Tax (VAT)** you paid on goods purchased in Ireland. See p. 16.

> **CUSTOMS IN THE EU.** As well as freedom of movement of people within the EU (see p. 10), travelers in the 15 original EU member countries (Austria, Belgium, Denmark, Finland, France, Germany, Greece, Ireland, Italy, Luxembourg, the Netherlands, Portugal, Spain, Sweden, and the UK) can also take advantage of the freedom of movement of goods. This means that there are no customs controls at internal EU borders (you can take the blue customs channel at the airport), and travelers are free to transport whatever legal substances they like as long as it is for their own personal (non-commercial) use—up to 800 cigarettes, 10L of spirits, 45L of wine, and 55L of beer. Duty-free allowances were abolished on June 30, 1999 for travel between EU member states; however, travelers between the EU and the rest of the world still get a duty-free allowance when passing through customs.

MONEY

CURRENCY AND EXCHANGE

The Republic of Ireland uses the euro and Northern Ireland still uses the pound sterling. The currency chart below is based on August 2007 exchange rates between local currency and Australian dollars (AUS$), Canadian dollars (CDN$), European Union euro (EUR€), New Zealand dollars (NZ$), British pounds (UK£), and US dollars (US$). Check the currency converter on websites like www.xe.com or www.bloomberg.com, or a large newspaper for the latest exchange rates.

EURO (€)		
AUS$1 = €0.63		€1 = AUS$1.59
CDN$1 = €0.70		€1 = CDN$1.44
NZ$1 = €0.57		€1 = NZ$1.76
UK£1 = €1.48		€1 = UK£0.67
US$1 = €0.74		€1 = US$1.34

POUND (£)		
AUS$1 = £0.424		£1 = AUS$2.36
CDN$1 = £0.470		£1 = CDN$2.13
EUR€1 = £0.672		£1 = EUR€1.49
NZ$1 = £0.381		£1 = NZ$2.62
US$1 = £0.501		£1 = US$1.99

As a general rule, it's cheaper to convert money in Ireland than at home. While currency exchange will probably be available in your arrival airport, it's wise to bring enough foreign currency to last for the first 24 to 72 hours of your trip.

When changing money abroad, try to go only to banks or bureaux de change that have at most a 5% margin between their buy and sell prices. Since you lose money with every transaction, **convert large sums** (unless the currency is depreciating rapidly), but **no more than you'll need.**

If you use traveler's checks or bills, carry some in small denominations (the equivalent of US$50 or less) for times when you are forced to exchange money at disadvantageous rates, but bring a range of denominations since charges may be levied per check cashed. Store your money in a variety of forms; ideally, at any given time you will be carrying some cash, some traveler's checks, and an ATM and/or credit card. All travelers should also consider carrying some US dollars (about US$50 worth), which are often preferred by local tellers.

THE EURO. The official currency of 13 members of the European Union— Austria, Belgium, Finland, France, Germany, Greece, Ireland, Italy, Luxembourg, the Netherlands, Portugal, Slovenia, and Spain—is now the euro.

The currency has some important—and positive—consequences for travelers hitting more than one euro-zone country. For one thing, money-changers across the euro-zone are obliged to exchange money at the official, fixed rate (see above), and at no commission (though they may still charge a small service fee). Second, euro-denominated traveler's checks allow you to pay for goods and services across the euro-zone, again at the official rate and commission-free.

TRAVELER'S CHECKS

Traveler's checks are one of the safest and least troublesome means of carrying funds. American Express and Visa are the most recognized brands. Many banks and agencies sell them for a small commission. Check issuers provide refunds if the checks are lost or stolen, and many provide additional services, such as toll-free refund hotlines abroad, emergency message services, and assistance with lost and stolen credit cards or passports. Traveler's checks are readily accepted in most cities and large towns. Ireland also accepts Thomas Cook checks (☎1800 411 021; www.travelex.co.uk). Ask about toll-free refund hotlines and the location of refund centers when purchasing checks, and always carry emergency cash.

American Express: Checks available with commission at select banks, at all AmEx offices, and online (www.americanexpress.com; US residents only). American Express cardholders can also purchase checks by phone (☎800-528-4800). Checks available in Australian, British, Canadian, European, Japanese, and US currencies, among others. American Express also offers the Travelers Cheque Card, a prepaid reloadable card. Cheques for Two can be signed by either of two people traveling together. For purchase locations or more information, contact AmEx's service centers: in Australia ☎+61 29 271 8666, in New Zealand +649 367 4567, in the UK +441 273 696 933, in the US and Canada 800-221-7282; elsewhere, call the US collect 336-393-1111.

Travelex: Visa TravelMoney prepaid cash card and Visa traveler's checks available. For information about Thomas Cook MasterCard in Canada and the US call ☎800-223-7373, in the UK 0800 622 101; elsewhere call the UK collect +44 1733 318 950. For information about Interpayment Visa in the US and Canada call ☎800-732-1322, in the UK 0800 515 884; elsewhere call the UK collect +44 1733 318 949. For more information, visit www.travelex.com.

Visa: Checks available (generally with commission) at banks worldwide. For the location of the nearest office, call the Visa Travelers Cheque Global Refund and Assistance Center: in the UK ☎0800 895 078, in the US 800-227-6811; elsewhere, call the UK collect +44 2079 378 091. Checks available in British, Canadian, European, Japanese, and US currencies, among others. Visa also offers TravelMoney, a prepaid debit card that can be reloaded online or by phone. For more information on Visa travel services, see http:/ /usa.visa.com/personal/using_visa/travel_with_visa.html.

CREDIT, DEBIT, AND ATM CARDS

Where they are accepted, credit cards often offer superior exchange rates—up to 5% better than the retail rate used by banks and other currency exchange establishments. Credit cards may also offer services such as insurance or emergency

ESSENTIALS

help, and are sometimes required to reserve hotel rooms or rental cars. **MasterCard** (a.k.a. EuroCard in Europe) and **Visa** (e.g., Carte Bleue) are the most frequently accepted; **American Express** cards work at some ATMs and at AmEx offices and major airports, but are almost never accepted elsewhere.

The use of ATM cards is widespread in Ireland. Depending on the system that your home bank uses, you can most likely access your personal bank account from abroad. ATMs get the same wholesale exchange rate as credit cards, but there is often a limit on the amount of money you can withdraw per day (usually around US$500). There is typically also a surcharge of US$1-5 per withdrawal.

Debit cards are as convenient as credit cards but withdraw money directly from the holder's checking account. A debit card can be used wherever its associated credit card company (usually MasterCard or Visa) is accepted. Debit cards often also function as ATM cards and can be used to withdraw cash from associated banks and ATMs throughout Ireland. The two major international money networks are **MasterCard/Maestro/Cirrus** (emergency services US ☎800-622-7747, Ireland 1-800 557 378; from Northern Ireland 0800 964 767; www.mastercard.com) and **Visa/PLUS** (for assistance US ☎800-847-2911, Ireland 800-55-8002; www.visa.com). Most ATMs charge a transaction fee that is paid to the bank that owns the ATM.

PINS AND ATMS. To use a cash or credit card to withdraw money from a cash machine (ATM) in Europe, you must have a four-digit **Personal Identification Number (PIN).** If your PIN is longer than four digits, ask your bank whether you can just use the first four, or whether you'll need a new one. **Credit cards** don't usually come with PINs, so if you intend to hit up ATMs in Europe with a credit card to get cash advances, call your credit card company before leaving to request one.

Travelers with alphabetic, rather than numerical, PINs may also be thrown off by the lack of letters on European cash machines. The following are the corresponding numbers to use: 1=QZ; 2=ABC; 3=DEF; 4=GHI; 5=JKL; 6=MNO; 7=PRS; 8=TUV; and 9=WXY. Note that if you mistakenly punch the wrong code into the machine three times, it will swallow your card for good.

GETTING MONEY FROM HOME

If you run out of money while traveling, the easiest and cheapest solution is to have someone back home make a deposit to your bank account. Failing that, consider one of the following options.

WIRING MONEY

It is possible to arrange a **bank money transfer,** which means asking a bank back home to wire money to a bank in Ireland. This is the cheapest way to transfer cash, but it's also the slowest, usually taking several days or more. Note that some banks may only release your funds in local currency, potentially sticking you with a poor exchange rate; inquire about this in advance. Money transfer services like **Western Union** are faster and more convenient than bank transfers—but also much pricier. Western Union has many locations worldwide. To find one, visit www.westernunion.com, or call in Australia ☎1800 173 833, in Canada and the US ☎800-325-6000, in the UK ☎0800 833 833, or in Ireland ☎1800 395 395. To wire money using a credit card (Discover, MasterCard, Visa), call in Canada and the US 800-CALL-CASH, in the UK ☎0800 833 833. Money transfer services are also available to **American Express** cardholders and at selected **Thomas Cook** offices.

US STATE DEPARTMENT (US CITIZENS ONLY)

In serious emergencies only, the US State Department will forward money within hours to the nearest consular office, which will then disburse it according to instructions for a US$30 fee. If you wish to use this service, you must contact the Overseas Citizens Service division of the US State Department (☎202-647-5225, toll-free 888-407-4747).

COSTS

The cost of your trip will vary considerably, depending on where you go, how you travel, and where you stay. The most significant expenses will probably be your round-trip (return) **airfare** to Ireland (see **Getting to Ireland: By Plane**, p. 24) and a **railpass** or **bus pass**. Before you go, spend some time calculating a reasonable daily **budget**.

STAYING ON A BUDGET

To give you a general idea, a bare-bones day in Ireland (camping or sleeping in hostels/guesthouses, buying food at supermarkets) would cost about US$47 (€35); a slightly more comfortable day (sleeping in hostels/guesthouses and the occasional budget hotel, eating one meal per day at a restaurant, going out at night) would cost US$94 (€70) and for a luxurious day, the sky's the limit. Don't forget to factor in emergency reserve funds (at least US$200) when planning how much money you'll need.

TIPS FOR SAVING MONEY

Some simpler ways include searching out opportunities for free entertainment, splitting accommodation and food costs with trustworthy fellow travelers, and buying food in supermarkets rather than eating out. Bring a **sleepsack** (p. 17) to save on sheet charges in European hostels, and do your **laundry** in the sink (unless you're explicitly prohibited from doing so). Museums often have certain days once a month or once a week when admission is free; plan accordingly. If you are eligible, consider getting an ISIC or an IYTC (p. 21); many sights and museums offer reduced admission to students and youths. For getting around quickly, bikes are the most economical option. Renting a bike is cheaper than renting a moped or scooter. Don't forget about walking, though; you can learn a lot about a city by seeing it on foot. Drinking at bars and clubs quickly becomes expensive. It's cheaper to buy alcohol at a supermarket and imbibe before going out. That said, don't go overboard. Though staying within your budget is important, don't do so at the expense of your health or a great travel experience.

TOP TEN LIST

TOP 10 WAYS TO SAVE IN IRELAND

As long as the dollar cowers before the almighty euro, here are some tips to guard your cash:

1. Buy food at markets and grocery stores, like the St. George's Market (p. 500) in Belfast, instead of restaurants.

2. Get the Heritage Card (p. 94) for discounts to over 85 sights, and be on the lookout for days when you can get into sights or museums for free.

3. Rather than spend €8 on laundry, buy cheaper new clothing at Penneys, a national clothing chain.

4. Find accommodations that let you stay for free if you work part-time.

5. Abuse free Internet access in libraries and tourist offices; use your hostel's address to gain membership at certain libraries.

6. If you're focusing on a specific region for a while, look into holiday homes, which can be cheaper in the long run. You don't need to find a new home every time you explore a new town.

7. Buy beer and liquor at markets instead of bars.

8. Build more outdoors experiences into your itinerary—many Irish National Parks have entrance fees, but no one collecting.

9. Take public transportation or walk instead of renting a car.

10. Forget the hostels or the fancy B&Bs. To live on the cheap, grab a tent and camp for the night amid the starry skies.

ESSENTIALS

TIPPING AND BARGAINING

Some restaurants in Ireland figure a service charge into the bill; some even calculate it into the cost of the dishes themselves. The menu often indicates whether or not service is included. If gratuity is not included, consider leaving 10-15%, depending upon the quality of the service. Tipping is very uncommon for other services, such as taxis and hairdressers, especially in rural areas. In most cases, people are usually happy if you simply round up the bill to the nearest euro. **Never tip in pubs**—it's considered condescending (see p. 65). In general, do not tip bartenders, though some bartenders at hip urban bars may expect a tip; watch and learn from other customers.

VALUE ADDED TAX

Both the Republic and Northern Ireland charge a **value added tax (VAT),** a national sales tax on most goods and some services. In Ireland, the 21% VAT does not apply to food, health services, agricultural fertilizers, insurance and banking services, and children's clothing. The VAT is almost always included in listed prices. The British rate, applicable to Northern Ireland, is 17.5% on many services (such as car rental, hairdressers, hotels, and restaurants) and on all goods (except books, food, and medicine). Refunds are available only to non-EU citizens and only for goods taken out of the country. In Ireland, **VAT refunds** are available on goods from stores displaying a "Cashback" sticker (ask if you don't see one). Request a voucher with your purchase, which you must present at the Cashback service desk in Dublin or Shannon airport. Purchases greater than €250 must be approved at the customs desk. Your money can also be refunded by mail.

Visitors to Northern Ireland can get a **VAT refund** on goods taken out of the country within three months of purchase through the **Retail Export Scheme.** Look for signs like "Tax Free Shopping" or "Tax Free for Tourists" and ask the shopkeeper about minimum purchases (usually €65-130) and get a form. Keep purchases in carry-on luggage so a customs officer can inspect the goods and validate refund forms. Some places give on-the-spot refunds, but most require that you mail the stamped forms back to the store in the envelope provided.

PACKING

Pack lightly: Lay out only what you absolutely need, then take half the clothes and twice the money. The Travelite FAQ (www.travelite.org) is a good resource for tips on traveling light. The online **Universal Packing List** (http://upl.codeq.info) will generate a customized list of suggested items based on your trip length, the expected climate, your planned activities, and other factors. If you plan to do a lot of hiking, also consult **The Great Outdoors,** p. 41. Some frequent travelers keep a bag packed with all the essentials: passport, money belt, hat, socks, etc. Then, when they decide to leave, they know they haven't forgotten anything.

Luggage: If you plan to cover most of your itinerary by foot, a sturdy **frame backpack** is unbeatable. (For the basics on buying a pack, see p. 42.) Toting a **suitcase** or **trunk** is fine if you plan to live in one or two cities and explore from there, but not a great idea if you plan to move around frequently. In addition to your main piece of luggage, a **daypack** (a small backpack or courier bag) is useful.

Clothing: No matter when you're traveling, it's a good idea to bring a warm jacket or wool sweater, a rain jacket (Gore-Tex® is both waterproof and breathable), sturdy shoes or hiking boots, and thick socks. Flip-flops or waterproof sandals are must-haves for grubby hostel showers, and extra socks are always a good idea. You may also want one outfit for going out, and maybe a nicer pair of shoes. If you plan to visit religious or cultural sites, remember that you will need modest and respectful dress. Some religious or cultural sites require modest dress and sometimes covered shoulders.

Sleepsack: Some hostels require that you either provide your own linen or rent sheets from them. Save cash by making your own sleepsack: fold a full-size sheet in half the long way, then sew it closed along the long side and one of the short sides.

Converters and Adapters: In Ireland, electricity is 230 volts AC, enough to fry any 120V North American appliance. 220/240V electrical appliances won't work with a 120V current, either. Americans and Canadians should buy an adapter (which changes the shape of the plug; US$5) and a converter (which changes the voltage; US$10-30). Don't make the mistake of using only an adapter (unless appliance instructions explicitly state otherwise). [Australians and New Zealanders (who use 230V at home) won't need a converter, but will need a set of adapters to use anything electrical.] For more on all things adaptable, check out http://kropla.com/electric.htm.

Toiletries: Toothbrushes, towels, cold-water soap, condoms, razors, tampons, and deodorant are often available, but it may be difficult to find your preferred brand; bring extras. **Contact lenses** are likely to be expensive and difficult to find, so bring enough extra pairs and solution for your entire trip. Also bring your glasses and a copy of your prescription in case you need emergency replacements. If you use heat-disinfection, either switch temporarily to a chemical disinfection system (check first to make sure it's safe with your brand of lenses), or buy a converter to 220/240V.

First-Aid Kit: For a basic first-aid kit, pack bandages, a pain reliever, antibiotic cream, a thermometer, a multifunction pocketknife, tweezers, moleskin, decongestant, motion-sickness remedy, diarrhea or upset-stomach medication (Pepto Bismol® or Imodium®), an antihistamine, sunscreen, insect repellent, burn ointment, and a syringe for emergencies (get an explanatory letter from your doctor).

Film: Film and developing in Ireland are expensive, so consider bringing along enough film for your entire trip and developing it at home. If you don't want to bother with film, consider using a digital camera. Although it requires a steep initial investment, a digital camera means you never have to buy film again. Just be sure to bring along a large enough memory card and extra (or rechargeable) batteries.

Other Useful Items: For safety purposes, you should bring a **money belt** and a small **padlock.** Basic **outdoors equipment** (plastic water bottle, compass, waterproof matches, pocketknife, sunglasses, sunscreen, hat) may also prove useful. **Quick repairs** of torn garments can be done on the road with a needle and thread; also consider bringing electrical tape for patching tears. If you want to do laundry by hand, bring detergent, a small rubber ball to stop up the sink, and string for a makeshift clothes line. Other things you're liable to forget include: an umbrella, sealable **plastic bags** (for damp clothes, soap, food, shampoo, and other spillables), an **alarm clock,** safety pins, rubber bands, a flashlight, earplugs, garbage bags, and a small calculator. A **cell phone** can be a lifesaver (literally) on the road; see p. 37 for information on acquiring one that will work in Ireland.

Important Documents: Don't forget your passport, traveler's checks, ATM and/or credit cards, adequate ID, and photocopies of all of the aforementioned in case these documents are lost or stolen. Also check that you have any of the following that might apply to you: a hosteling membership card (p. 39); driver's license (p. 11); travel insurance forms (p. 21); ISIC (p. 11), and/or rail or bus pass (p. 29).

SAFETY AND HEALTH

GENERAL ADVICE

In any type of crisis situation, the most important thing to do is **stay calm.** Your country's embassy abroad (p. 9) is usually your best resource when things go wrong; registering with that embassy upon arrival in the country is often a good idea. The government offices listed in the **Travel Advisories** box (p. 19) can provide information on the services they offer their citizens in case of emergencies abroad.

LOCAL LAWS AND POLICE

Ireland's police force, or *Garda Síochána*, is committed to guarding the peace on the island. Though an unarmed force, the *Garda* does enforce the law. If you're traveling throughout the country by car, there's no need to worry about security checkpoints; there are no longer border checkpoints throughout the Republic and Northern Ireland.

DRUGS AND ALCOHOL

The Republic and the UK both regulate the possession of recreational drugs, with penalties ranging from a warning to lengthy prison sentences. Possession of marijuana results in a fine, though repeated offenses can result in prosecution. Harder substances are treated with severity. If you carry **prescription drugs** with you, have a copy of the prescription and a note from a doctor readily accessible at country borders. The drinking age, 18 in both Ireland and Northern Ireland, is more strictly enforced in urban areas.

SPECIFIC CONCERNS

DEMONSTRATIONS AND POLITICAL GATHERINGS

Although sectarian violence is dramatically less common than in the height of the **Troubles** (see p. 483), some neighborhoods and towns still experience unrest during sensitive political times. It's best to remain alert and cautious while traveling in Northern Ireland, especially during **Marching Season**, which reaches its height around July 12. August 12, when the **Apprentice Boys** march in Derry/Londonderry, is also a testy period when urban areas should be traversed with caution. The most common form of violence is property damage, and tourists are unlikely targets (though their cars may be if they bear Republic license plates). In general, if you are traveling in Northern Ireland during Marching Season, prepare for transport delays and for some B&Bs, shops, and services to be closed. Vacation areas like the Glens and the Causeway Coast are less affected. In general, use common sense in conversation and be respectful of religious and political perspectives.

Border checkpoints have been removed, and armed soldiers and vehicles are less visible in Belfast and Derry/Londonderry. Do not take **photographs** of soldiers, military installations, or vehicles; the film will be confiscated and you may be detained for questioning. Taking pictures of political murals is not a crime, although many people feel uncomfortable doing so in residential neighborhoods. Unattended luggage is always considered suspicious and worthy of confiscation.

TERRORISM

Terrorism has become a serious international concern, but it is enormously difficult to predict where or when attacks will occur. Northern Ireland has its own domestic terrorist organizations. Most of these terrorist organizations set out to cause maximum monetary damage but minimum casualties. Travelers are almost never targeted, and, since the Good Friday Agreement in 1998, terrorism has ceased to be a major concern for most Irish, even in the North, though Troubles-related violence still occurs especially during the summer Marching Season.

Travelers should gather as much information as possible before and during their trips. The US Department of State website (www.travel.state.gov) is a good place to research the current situation anywhere you may be planning to travel. The **UK Civil Contingencies Secretariat** website at www.ukresilience.gov.uk features updates and warnings for citizens of and travelers to the UK. Depending on the circumstances, you may want to register with your home embassy or consulate when you arrive. The box (see below) lists contacts and webpages with updated government travel advisories.

 TRAVEL ADVISORIES. The following government offices provide travel information and advisories by telephone, by fax, or via the web:

Australian Department of Foreign Affairs and Trade: ☎612 6261 1111; www.dfat.gov.au.

Canadian Department of Foreign Affairs and International Trade (DFAIT): Call ☎800-267-8376; www.dfait-maeci.gc.ca. Call for their free booklet, *Bon Voyage...But.*

New Zealand Ministry of Foreign Affairs: ☎044 398 000; www.mfat.govt.nz.

United Kingdom Foreign and Commonwealth Office: ☎020 7008 1500; www.fco.gov.uk.

US Department of State: ☎888-407-4747; http://travel.state.gov. Visit the website for the booklet *A Safe Trip Abroad.*

ESSENTIALS

PERSONAL SAFETY

EXPLORING AND TRAVELING

To avoid unwanted attention, try to blend in as much as possible. Respecting local customs (in many cases, dressing more conservatively than you would at home) may placate would-be hecklers. Familiarize yourself with your surroundings before setting out and carry yourself with confidence. Check maps in shops and restaurants rather than on the street. If you are traveling alone, be sure someone at home knows your itinerary, and never admit that you're by yourself. When walking at night, stick to busy, well-lit streets and avoid dark alleyways. If you ever feel uncomfortable, leave the area as quickly as you can.

There is no sure-fire way to avoid all the threatening situations you might encounter while traveling, but a good **self-defense course** will give you concrete ways to react to unwanted advances. **Impact, Prepare,** and **Model Mugging** can refer you to local self-defense courses in Australia, Canada, Switzerland and the US. Visit the website at www.modelmugging.org for a list of nearby chapters.

If you are using a **car,** learn local driving signals and wear a seatbelt. The main concern for most drivers visiting the Republic or Northern Ireland is adjusting to **driving on the left-hand side of the road** (especially dealing with right turns).

 WHEN RIGHT IS WRONG. For drivers hailing from the US, Canada, and other countries where cars drive on the right side of the road, adjusting to driving on the left can be confusing. Remember to take your time—especially when turning right—to always be aware of your surroundings, and to avoid driving on narrow roads until you become more comfortable.

Rotaries (roundabouts) flow right to left and are a major site of tourist crashes; they often lie directly outside airports. Children under 40 lb. should ride only in specially designed carseats, available for a small fee from most car-rental agencies. Study route maps before you hit the road, and if you plan on spending a lot of time driving, consider bringing spare parts. If your car breaks down, wait for the police to assist you. For long drives in rural areas, invest in a cellular phone and a **roadside assistance program** (see **By Car,** p. 30). Park your vehicle in a garage or well-traveled area, and use a steering wheel locking device in larger cities. **Sleeping in your car** is one of the most dangerous (and often illegal) ways to get your rest. For info on the perils of **hitchhiking,** see p. 34.

POSSESSIONS AND VALUABLES

Never leave your belongings unattended; crime occurs in even the most demure-looking hostel or hotel. Bring your own **padlock** for hostel lockers, and don't ever store valuables in any locker. Be particularly careful on **buses** and **trains**. Carry your backpack in front of you where you can see it. When traveling with others, sleep in shifts. When alone, use good judgment in selecting a train compartment: never stay in an empty one, and use a lock to secure your pack to the luggage rack. Try to sleep on top bunks with your luggage stored above you (if not in bed with you), and keep important documents and valuables on your person.

To minimize the financial risk associated with traveling, bring as little with you as possible, buy a few combination **padlocks** to secure your belongings either in your pack or in a hostel or train station locker, and **carry as little cash as possible.** Keep your traveler's checks and ATM/credit cards in a **money belt**—not a "fanny pack"—along with your passport and ID cards. **Keep a small cash reserve separate from your primary stash.** This should be about US$50 (euro are best) sewn into or stored in the depths of your pack, along with your traveler's check numbers.

In large cities **con artists** often work in groups and may involve children in their routines. Beware of certain classics: sob stories that require money, rolls of bills "found" on the street, mustard spilled (or saliva spit) onto your shoulder to distract you while they snatch your bag. **Never let your passport and your bags out of your sight.** Beware of **pickpockets** in city crowds, especially on public transportation. Also, be alert in public telephone booths: If you must say your calling card number, do so quietly; if you punch it in, make sure no one looks over your shoulder.

If you will be traveling with electronic devices, such as a laptop computer or a PDA, check whether your homeowner's insurance covers loss, theft, or damage when you travel. If not, you might consider purchasing a low-cost separate insurance policy. **Safeware** (☎ US 800-800-1492; www.safeware.com) specializes in covering computers and charges $90 for 90-day comprehensive international travel coverage up to $4000.

PRE-DEPARTURE HEALTH

In your **passport,** write the names of any people you wish to be contacted in case of a medical emergency, and list any allergies or medical conditions. Matching a prescription to a foreign equivalent is not always easy, safe, or possible, so if you take prescription drugs, consider carrying up-to-date prescriptions or a statement from your doctor stating the medication's trade name, manufacturer, chemical name, and dosage. While traveling, be sure to keep all medication with you in your carry-on luggage. For tips on packing a **first-aid kit** and other health essentials, see p. 17.

Some common drugs may have different names in Ireland than in your home country. For example, what is referred to as acetaminophen (brand name: Tylenol) in the US is known as paracetamol in Europe. A common brand name for this drug in Ireland is Panadol. Pseudoephedrine, a decongestant, is commonly known as Sudafed. Ibuprofen (known as Advil®, Motrin®, etc. in the US) is commonly referred to as Nurofen® in Ireland.

IMMUNIZATIONS AND PRECAUTIONS

Travelers over two years old should make sure that the following vaccines are up to date: MMR (for measles, mumps, and rubella); DTaP or Td (for diphtheria, tetanus, and pertussis); IPV (for polio); Hib (for *haemophilus influenzae* B); and HepB (for Hepatitis B). For recommendations on immunizations and prophylaxis, consult the Centers for Disease Control and Prevention (CDC; see below) in the US or the equivalent in your home country, and check with a doctor for guidance.

INSURANCE

Travel insurance covers four basic areas: medical/health problems, property loss, trip cancellation/interruption, and emergency evacuation. Though regular insurance policies may well extend to travel-related accidents, you may consider purchasing separate travel insurance if the cost of potential trip cancellation, interruption, or emergency medical evacuation is greater than you can absorb. Prices for travel insurance purchased separately generally run about US$50 per week for full coverage, while trip cancellation/interruption may be purchased separately at a rate of US$3-5 per day depending on length of stay.

Medical insurance (especially university policies) often covers costs incurred abroad; check with your provider. **US Medicare** does not cover foreign travel. **Canadian** provincial health insurance plans increasingly do not cover foreign travel; check with the provincial Ministry of Health or Health Plan Headquarters for details. **Australians** traveling in Northern Ireland are entitled to many of the services they would receive at home as part of the Reciprocal Health Care Agreement. **Homeowners' insurance** (or your family's coverage) often covers theft during travel and loss of documents (passport, plane ticket, railpass, etc.) up to US$500.

ISIC and **ITIC** (p. 11) provide basic insurance benefits to US cardholders, including US$100 per day of in-hospital sickness for up to 100 days and US$10,000 of accident-related medical reimbursement (see www.isicus.com for details). Cardholders have access to a toll-free 24hr. helpline for medical, legal, and financial emergencies overseas. **American Express** (☎ 800-338-1670) grants most cardholders automatic collision and theft insurance on rentals made with the card.

USEFUL ORGANIZATIONS AND PUBLICATIONS

The American **Centers for Disease Control and Prevention** (**CDC;** ☎ 877-FYI-TRIP; www.cdc.gov/travel) maintains an international travelers' hotline and an informative website. Consult the appropriate government agency of your home country for consular information sheets on health, entry requirements, and other issues for various countries (see the listings in the box on **Travel Advisories,** p. 19). For quick information on health and other travel warnings, call the **Overseas Citizens Services** (M-F 8am-8pm from US ☎ 888-407-4747, from overseas 202-501-4444), or contact a passport agency, embassy, or consulate abroad. For information on medical evacuation services and travel insurance firms, see the US government's website at http://travel.state.gov/travel/abroad_health.html or the **British Foreign and Commonwealth Office** (www.fco.gov.uk). For general health information, contact the **American Red Cross** (☎ 202-303-4498; www.redcross.org).

STAYING HEALTHY

Common sense is the simplest prescription for good health while you travel. Drink lots of fluids to prevent dehydration and constipation, and wear sturdy, broken-in shoes and clean socks. Use talcum powder to keep your feet dry in the Irish rain, and always remember to drink responsibly: don't drink and drive.

ONCE IN IRELAND

ENVIRONMENTAL HAZARDS

Heat exhaustion and dehydration: Heat exhaustion leads to nausea, excessive thirst, headaches, and dizziness. Avoid it by drinking plenty of fluids, eating salty foods (e.g., crackers), abstaining from dehydrating beverages (e.g., alcohol and caffeinated beverages), and wearing sunscreen. Continuous heat stress can eventually lead to heatstroke, characterized by a rising temperature, severe headache, delirium and cessation of sweating. Victims should be cooled off with wet towels and taken to a doctor.

INSECT-BORNE DISEASES

Many diseases are transmitted by insects—mainly mosquitoes, fleas, ticks, and lice. Be aware of insects in wet or forested areas, especially while hiking and camping; wear long pants and long sleeves, tuck your pants into your socks, and use a mosquito net. Use insect repellents such as DEET and soak or spray your gear with permethrin (licensed in the US only for use on clothing). **Ticks**— which can carry Lyme and other diseases—can be particularly dangerous in rural and forested regions.

Lyme disease: A bacterial infection carried by ticks and marked by a circular bull's-eye rash of 2 in. or more. Later symptoms include fever, headache, fatigue, and aches and pains. Antibiotics are effective if administered early. Left untreated, Lyme can cause problems in joints, the heart, and the nervous system. If you find a tick attached to your skin, grasp the head with tweezers as close to your skin as possible and apply slow, steady traction. Removing a tick within 24hr. greatly reduces the risk of infection. Do not try to remove ticks with petroleum jelly, nail polish remover, or a hot match. Ticks usually inhabit moist, shaded environments and heavily wooded areas. If you are going to be hiking in these areas, wear long clothes and DEET.

Other insect-borne diseases: Lymphatic filariasis is a roundworm infestation transmitted by mosquitoes. Infection causes enlargement of extremities and has no vaccine. **Leishmaniasis,** a parasite transmitted by sand flies, can occur in Europe. Common symptoms are fever, weakness, and swelling of the spleen, as well as skin sores. There is a treatment, but no vaccine.

FOOD- AND WATER-BORNE DISEASES

Prevention is the best cure: be sure that your food is properly cooked and the water you drink is clean. If the region's tap water is known to be unsanitary, peel fruits and vegetables before eating them and avoid tap water (including ice cubes and anything washed in tap water, like salad). Watch out for food from markets or street vendors that may have been cooked in unhygienic conditions. Other culprits are raw shellfish, unpasteurized milk, and sauces containing raw eggs. Buy bottled water, or purify your own water by bringing it to a rolling boil or treating it with **iodine tablets;** note, however, that some parasites such as *giardia* have exteriors that resist iodine treatment, so boiling is more reliable. Always wash your hands before eating or bring a quick-drying purifying liquid hand cleaner.

Giardiasis: Transmitted through parasites and acquired by drinking untreated water from streams or lakes. Symptoms include diarrhea, cramps, bloating, fatigue, weight loss, and nausea. If untreated, it can lead to severe dehydration. Giardiasis occurs worldwide.

Leptospirosis: A bacterial disease caused by exposure to fresh water or soil contaminated by the urine of infected animals. Able to enter the human body through cut skin, mucus membranes, and through ingestion, it is most common in tropical climates. Symptoms include a high fever, chills, nausea, and vomiting. If not treated it can lead to liver failure and meningitis. There is no vaccine; consult a doctor for treatment.

OTHER INFECTIOUS DISEASES

The following diseases exist in every part of the world. Travelers should know how to recognize them and what to do if they suspect they have been infected.

Rabies: Transmitted through the saliva of infected animals; fatal if untreated. By the time symptoms (thirst and muscle spasms) appear, the disease is in its terminal stage. If you are bitten, wash the wound, seek immediate medical care, and try to have the animal located. A rabies vaccine, which consists of 3 shots given over a 21-day period, is available and recommended for developing world travel, but is only semi-effective.

Hepatitis B: A viral infection of the liver transmitted via blood or other bodily fluids. Symptoms, which may not surface until years after infection, include jaundice, appetite loss, fever, and joint pain. It is transmitted through unprotected sex and unclean needles. A 3-shot vaccination sequence is recommended for sexually-active travelers and anyone planning to seek medical treatment abroad; it must begin 6 months before traveling.

Hepatitis C: Like Hepatitis B, but the mode of transmission differs. IV drug users, those with occupational exposure to blood, hemodialysis patients, and recipients of blood transfusions are at the highest risk, but the disease can also be spread through sexual contact or sharing items like razors and toothbrushes that may have traces of blood on them. No symptoms are usually exhibited. If untreated, Hep C can lead to liver failure.

AIDS and HIV: For detailed information on Acquired Immune Deficiency Syndrome (AIDS) in Ireland, call the 24hr. National AIDS Hotline at ☎800-342-2437.

Sexually transmitted infections (STIs): Gonorrhea, chlamydia, genital warts, syphilis, herpes, HPV, and other STIs are easier to catch than HIV and can be just as serious. Though condoms may protect you from some STIs, oral or even tactile contact can lead to transmission. If you think you may have contracted an STI, see a doctor immediately.

OTHER HEALTH CONCERNS

MEDICAL CARE ON THE ROAD

In the event of sudden illness or an accident, dial ☎**999,** the general **emergency** number for the Republic and Northern Ireland. It's a free call from any pay phone to an operator who will connect you to the local police, hospital, or fire brigade. EU citizens receive health care; others must have medical insurance or be prepared to pay, though emergency care is provided free of charge. Hospitals are plentiful and listed in the **Practical Information** sections. Note that though emergency care is free in Ireland, there are often long waiting lists that may prevent patients from acquiring the immediate attention they require.

If you are concerned about obtaining medical assistance while traveling, you may wish to employ special support services. The *MedPass* from **GlobalCare, Inc.,** 6875 Shiloh Rd. East, Alpharetta, GA 30005, USA (☎800-860-1111; www.global-care.net), provides 24hr. international medical assistance, support, and medical evacuation resources. The **International Association for Medical Assistance to Travelers** (**IAMAT;** US ☎716-754-4883, Canada 519-836-0102; www.iamat.org) has free membership, lists English-speaking doctors worldwide, and offers detailed info on immunization requirements and sanitation. If your regular **insurance** policy does not cover travel abroad, you may wish to purchase additional coverage (see p. 21).

Those with medical conditions (such as diabetes, allergies to antibiotics, epilepsy, or heart conditions) may want to obtain a **MedicAlert** membership (US$40 per year), which includes among other things a stainless steel ID tag and a 24hr. collect-call number. Contact the MedicAlert Foundation International, 2323 Colorado Ave., Turlock, CA 95382, USA (☎888-633-4298, outside US ☎209-668-3333; www.medicalert.org).

WOMEN'S HEALTH

Women traveling in unsanitary conditions are vulnerable to **urinary tract (including bladder and kidney) infections.** Over-the-counter medicines can sometimes alleviate symptoms, but if they persist, see a doctor. **Vaginal yeast infections** may flare up in hot and humid climates. Wearing loosely fitting trousers or a skirt and cotton underwear will help, as will over-the-counter remedies like Monistat or Gynelotrimin. Bring supplies from home if you are prone to infection, as they may be difficult to find on the road. And, since **tampons, pads,** and reliable **contraceptive devices** are sometimes hard to find when traveling (especially in rural areas), bring supplies with you. **Abortion** is not legal in Ireland; for questions or help regarding an unplanned pregnancy, contact the **National Pregnancy Helpline** ☎01 850

495 051 or the **Irish Family Planning Association (IFPA)** ☎01 850 425 262. Visit www.positiveoptions.ie for a full list of regional telephone helplines.

GETTING TO IRELAND

BY PLANE

When it comes to airfare, a little effort can save you a bundle. Courier fares are the cheapest for those whose plans are flexible enough to deal with the restrictions. Tickets sold by consolidators and standby seating are also good deals, but last-minute specials, airfare wars, and charter flights often beat these fares. The key is to hunt around, be flexible, and ask about discounts. Students, seniors, and those under 26 should never pay full price for a ticket.

AIRFARES

Airfares to Ireland peak between early June and late August; holidays are also expensive. The cheapest times to travel are October and February. Midweek (M-Th morning) round-trip flights run US$40-50 cheaper than weekend flights, but they are generally more crowded and less likely to permit frequent-flier upgrades. Not fixing a return date ("open return") or arriving in and departing from different cities ("open-jaw") can be pricier than round-trip flights. Patching one-way flights together is the most expensive way to travel. Flights between Ireland's capitals or regional hubs—Dublin, Cork, Galway, and Belfast—will tend to be cheaper.

If Ireland is only one stop on a more extensive globe-hop, consider a round-the-world (RTW) ticket. Tickets usually include at least five stops and are valid for about a year; prices range US$1200-5000. Try **Northwest Airlines/KLM** (☎800-225-2525; www.nwa.com) or **Star Alliance,** a consortium of 16 airlines including United Airlines (www.staralliance.com).

Fares for round-trip flights to Dublin from the US or Canadian east coast average US$900, US$500 in the low season (Oct.-Apr.); from the US or Canadian west coast US$1000/600; from the UK, UK£100/75; from Australia AUS$3500/2400; from New Zealand NZ$4000/2600.

BUDGET AND STUDENT TRAVEL AGENCIES

While knowledgeable agents specializing in flights to Ireland can make your life easy and help you save, they may not spend the time to find you the lowest possible fare—they get paid on commission. Travelers holding **ISICs** and **IYTCs** (see p. 11) qualify for big discounts from student travel agencies. Most flights from budget agencies are on major airlines, but in peak season some may sell seats on less reliable chartered aircraft.

CTS Travel, 30 Rathbone Pl., London W1T 1GQ, UK (☎020 7447 5000; www.ctstravel.co.uk). A British student travel agent with offices in 39 countries including the US, Empire State Building, 350 Fifth Ave., Ste. 7813, New York, NY 10118 (☎877-287-6665; www.ctstravelusa.com).

STA Travel, 5900 Wilshire Blvd., Ste. 900, Los Angeles, CA 90036, USA (24hr. reservations and info ☎800-781-4040; www.statravel.com). A student and youth travel organization with over 150 offices worldwide (check their website for a listing of all their offices), including US offices in Boston, Chicago, Los Angeles, New York, Seattle, San Francisco, and Washington, D.C. Ticket booking, travel insurance, railpasses, and more.

Walk-in offices are located throughout Australia (☎03 9207 5900), New Zealand (☎09 309 9723), and the UK (☎08701 630 026).

Travel CUTS (Canadian Universities Travel Services Limited), 187 College St., Toronto, ON M5T 1P7, Canada (☎888-592-2887; www.travelcuts.com). Offices across Canada and the US including Los Angeles, New York, Seattle, and San Francisco.

USIT, 19-21 Aston Quay, Dublin 2, Ireland (☎01 602 1904; www.usit.ie), Ireland's leading student/budget travel agency has 20 offices throughout Northern Ireland and the Republic of Ireland. Offers programs to work, study, and volunteer worldwide.

Wasteels, Skoubogade 6, 1158 Copenhagen K., Denmark (☎3314 4633; www.wasteels.com). A huge chain with 180 locations across Europe. Sells Wasteels BIJ tickets discounted 30-45% off regular fare, 2nd-class international point-to-point train tickets with unlimited stopovers for those under 26 (sold only in Europe).

ESSENTIALS

 FLIGHT PLANNING ON THE INTERNET. The Internet may be the budget traveler's dream when it comes to finding and booking bargain fares, but the array of options can be overwhelming. Many airline sites offer special last-minute deals on the Web.

STA (www.statravel.com) and **StudentUniverse** (www.studentuniverse.com) provide quotes on student tickets, while **Orbitz** (www.orbitz.com), **Expedia** (www.expedia.com), and **Travelocity** (www.travelocity.com) offer full travel services. **Priceline** (www.priceline.com) lets you specify a price, and obligates you to buy any ticket that meets or beats it; **Hotwire** (www.hotwire.com) offers bargain fares, but won't reveal the airline or flight times until you buy. Other sites that compile deals include www.bestfares.com, www.flights.com, www.lowestfare.com, www.onetravel.com, and www.travelzoo.com.

SideStep (www.sidestep.com) and **Booking Buddy** (www.bookingbuddy.com) are online tools that can help sift through multiple offers; these two let you enter your trip information once and search multiple sites.

Air Traveler's Handbook (www.faqs.org/faqs/travel/air/handbook) is an indispensable resource on the Internet; it has a comprehensive listing of links to everything you need to know before you board a plane.

COMMERCIAL AIRLINES

The commercial airlines' lowest regular offer is the **APEX** (Advance Purchase Excursion) fare, which provides confirmed reservations and allows "open-jaw" tickets. Generally, reservations must be made seven to 21 days ahead of departure, with seven- to 14-day minimum-stay and up to 90-day maximum-stay restrictions. These fares carry hefty cancellation and change penalties (fees rise in summer). Book peak-season APEX fares early. Use **Expedia** (www.expedia.com) or **Travelocity** (www.travelocity.com) to get an idea of the lowest published fares, then use the resources outlined here to try to beat those fares. Low-season fares should be appreciably cheaper than the **high-season** (early June-Aug.) ones listed here.

TRAVELING FROM NORTH AMERICA

Basic round-trip fares to Ireland range from roughly US$200-900. Standard commercial carriers like **American** (☎800-433-7300; www.aa.com), **United** (☎800-538-2929; www.ual.com), and **Northwest** (☎800-447-4747; www.nwa.com) will probably offer the most convenient flights, but they may not be the cheapest. Check **Lufthansa** (☎800-399-5838; www.lufthansa.com), **British Airways** (☎800-247-9297; www.britishairways.com), **Air France** (☎800-237-2747; www.airfrance.us), and **Ali-**

talia (☎800-223-5730; www.alitaliausa.com) for cheap tickets from destinations throughout the US to all over Europe.

TRAVELING FROM THE UK

Because of the great number of carriers flying from the British Isles to the continent, we only include discount airlines or those with cheap specials here. The **Air Travel Advisory Bureau** in London (☎870 737 0021; www.atab.co.uk) provides referrals to travel agencies and consolidators that offer discounted airfares out of the UK. **Cheapflights** (www.cheapflights.co.uk) publishes airfare bargains.

Aer Lingus: Ireland ☎0818 365 000; www.aerlingus.ie. Return tickets from Dublin, Cork, Galway, Kerry, and Shannon to Amsterdam, Brussels, Düsseldorf, Frankfurt, Helsinki, Madrid, Milan, Munich, Paris, Rennes, Rome, Stockholm, and Zürich (EUR€102-244).

bmibaby: UK ☎08702 642 229; www.bmibaby.com. Departures from throughout the UK. London to Cork (UK£60).

easyJet: UK ☎08712 442 366; www.easyjet.com. London to Belfast (UK£46).

KLM: UK ☎08705 074 074; www.klmuk.com. Cheap return tickets from London and elsewhere to Dublin and Cork.

Ryanair: Ireland ☎0818 303 030, UK 08712 460 000; www.ryanair.com. From Dublin, Glasgow, Liverpool, London, and Shannon to destinations throughout Western Europe. Low price guarantee.

TRAVELING FROM AUSTRALIA AND NEW ZEALAND

Air New Zealand: New Zealand ☎0800 73 70 00; www.airnz.co.nz. Auckland to London.

Qantas Air: Australia ☎13 13 13, New Zealand ☎0800 808 767; www.qantas.com.au. Flights from Australia and New Zealand to London for around AUS$2000.

Singapore Air: Australia ☎13 10 11, New Zealand ☎0800 808 909; www.singaporeair.com. Flies from Auckland, Christchurch, Melbourne, Perth, and Sydney to London.

Thai Airways: Australia ☎1300 65 19 60, New Zealand ☎09 377 38 86; www.thaiair.com. Auckland, Melbourne, Perth, and Sydney to London.

AIR COURIER FLIGHTS

FROM NORTH AMERICA

Round-trip courier fares from the US to Ireland run about US$200-500. Most flights leave from New York, Los Angeles, San Francisco, or Miami in the US; and from Montreal, Toronto, or Vancouver in Canada. The organizations below provide members with lists of opportunities and courier brokers for an annual fee. Prices quoted below are round-trip.

Air Courier Association, 1767 A Denver West Blvd., Golden, CO 80401 (☎800-211-5119; www.aircourier.org). 10 departure cities throughout the US and Canada to London, Madrid, Paris, Rome, and throughout Western Europe (high-season US$130-640). 1-year membership US$49.

International Association of Air Travel Couriers (IAATC; www.courier.org). From 7 North American cities to Western European cities, including London, Madrid, Paris, and Rome. 1-year membership US$45.

Courier Travel (www.couriertravel.org). Searchable online database. Multiple departure points in the US to various European destinations.

FROM THE UK, AUSTRALIA, AND NEW ZEALAND

The minimum age for couriers from the **UK** is usually 18. The **International Association of Air Travel Couriers** (www.courier.org) often offers courier flights from London to Tokyo, Sydney, and Bangkok and from Auckland to Frankfurt and London. **Courier Travel** also offers flights from London and Sydney.

STANDBY FLIGHTS

Traveling standby requires considerable flexibility in arrival and departure dates. Companies dealing in standby flights sell vouchers rather than tickets, along with the promise to get you to your destination (or near your destination) within a certain window of time (typically 1-5 days). You call in before your specific window of time to hear your flight options and the probability that you will be able to board each flight. You can then decide which flights you want to try to catch, show up at the appropriate airport at the appropriate time, present your voucher, and board if space is available. Vouchers can usually be bought for both one-way and round-trip travel. You may receive a monetary refund only if every available flight within your date range is full; if you opt not to take an available (but perhaps less convenient) flight, you can only get credit toward future travel. Read agreements with any company offering standby flights with care, as tricky fine print can leave you in the lurch. To check on a company's service record in the US, contact the Better Business Bureau (☎703-276-0100; www.bbb.org). It is difficult to receive refunds, and clients' vouchers won't be honored when an airline fails to receive payment in time.

TICKET CONSOLIDATORS

Ticket consolidators, or **"bucket shops,"** buy unsold tickets in bulk from commercial airlines and sell them at discounted rates. The best place to look is in the Sunday travel section of any major newspaper (such as *The New York Times*), where many bucket shops place tiny ads. Call quickly, as availability is extremely limited. Not all bucket shops are reliable, so insist on a receipt that gives full details of restrictions, refunds, and tickets, and pay by credit card (in spite of the 2-5% fee) so you can stop payment if you never receive your tickets. For more info, see www.travel-library.com/air-travel/consolidators.html.

TRAVELING FROM CANADA AND THE US

Some consolidators worth trying are **Rebel** (☎800-732-3588; www.rebeltours.com), **Cheap Tickets** (www.cheaptickets.com), **Flights.com** (www.flights.com), and **TravelHUB** (www.travelhub.com). Let's Go does not endorse any of these agencies. As always, be cautious, and research companies thoroughly before you hand over your credit card number.

CHARTER FLIGHTS

Tour operators contract charter flights with airlines in order to fly extra loads of passengers during peak season. These flights are far from hassle free. They occur less frequently than major airlines, make refunds particularly difficult, and are almost always fully booked. Their scheduled times may change and they may be cancelled at the last moment (as late as 48hr. before the trip, and without a full refund). And check-in, boarding, and baggage claim for them are often much slower. They can be, however, much cheaper.

Discount clubs and fare brokers offer members savings on last-minute charter and tour deals. Study contracts closely; you don't want to end up with an unwanted overnight layover. **Travelers Advantage** (☎800-835-8747; www.travelersadvantage.com; US$90 annual fee includes discounts and cheap flight directories) specializes in European travel and tour packages.

BY BOAT

Ferries are popular and easy on the wallet, but time-pressed travelers and world-roving secret agents will have to settle for air travel; cruising across northern seas, a ferry from France takes 14 hours to reach the Emerald Isle. Almost all sailings in June, July, and August are "controlled sailings," which means that you must book the crossing ahead of time (a few days in advance is usually sufficient).

Fares vary significantly depending on time of year, time of day, and type of boat. Traveling mid-week, at night, in spring, fall, or winter promises the cheapest fares. Adult single tickets usually run €28-60, but there are discount rates available. Some people tag along with car drivers who are allowed four free passengers. Bikes can usually be brought on for no extra charge. Students, seniors, families, and youth traveling alone typically receive discounts; **ISIC cardholders** typically receive a 25-50% discount.

Bus and train tickets that include ferry connections between Britain and Ireland are also available as package deals through ferry companies, travel agents, and USIT offices. Contact Bus Éireann for information (see **By Bus**, p. 28).

The fares below are **one-way** for **adult foot passengers** unless otherwise noted. Though standard return fares are usually double the one-way fare, **fixed-period returns** (usually within five days) are almost invariably cheaper. Ferries run **year-round** unless otherwise noted. **Bike storage** is usually free, although you may have to pay up to €15 in high season. For a **camper/trailer** supplement, you will have to add €30-210 to the "with car" fare. A directory of ferries to and from Ireland can be found at www.seaview.co.uk/ferries.html.

Brittany Ferries: France ☎08 25 82 88 28, Ireland ☎021 427 7801, Spain ☎942 360 611; www.brittany-ferries.com. **Roscoff** to **Cork** (12-14hr., late Mar. to early Nov. F inbound, Sa outbound; €52-99).

Irish Ferries: France ☎01 56 93 43 40, Ireland ☎0818 300 400, UK ☎0870 517 1717; www.irishferries.com. **Cherbourg** and **Roscoff** to **Rosslare** (19hr., Apr.-Aug. 1-9 per week, €56-69). **Pembroke, UK** to **Rosslare** (3¾hr.; £20). **Holyhead, UK** to **Dublin** (2-3hr.; £20, 50% student discount).

Stena Line: UK ☎08705 707 070; www.stenaline.co.uk. **Fishguard** to **Rosslare** (2hr., from £63 for motorists). **Holyhead** to **Dublin** or **Dún Laoghaire** (1¾hr., from £68 for motorists). **Stranraer** to **Belfast** (3¼hr., from £48 for motorists).

Steam Packet Company: UK ☎871 222 1333; www.steam-packet.com. **Isle of Man** to **Belfast** (2¾hr., €33). **Isle of Man** to **Dublin** (4hr., €15).

BY BUS

Bus Éireann (the Irish national bus company) reaches Britain and even the continent by working in conjunction with ferry services and the bus company **Eurolines** (Republic ☎01 836 6111, UK ☎08705 143 219; www.eurolines.com). Most buses leave from Victoria Station in London. They go to **Belfast** (15hr.) and **Dublin** (16hr.), and other major cities, including Birmingham, Bristol, Cardiff, Glasgow, and Liverpool. Services run to Cork, Derry/Londonderry, Galway, Limerick, Tralee, and Waterford, among others. Prices given are for adult fares during the summer— cheaper fares are available in the low season, as well as for those under 13, under 26, and over 60. Tickets can be booked through USIT, Bus Éireann, Irish Ferries, Stena Line, Eurolines, or a **National Express** office in Britain.

GETTING AROUND IRELAND

In most of Ireland, public transportation is regular and extensive. Most travelers go by bus, as trains can only effectively be used to travel between urban centers. Travel in Counties Clare, Kerry, and Donegal can be difficult without a car.

Fares on all modes of transportation are either **single** (one-way) or **return** (round-trip). **"Period returns"** require you to return within a specific number of days; **"day**

return" means you must return on the same day. Unless stated otherwise, *Let's Go* lists single fares. Return fares are generally 30% above the one-way fare.

Roads between Irish cities and towns have official letters and numbers ("N" and "R" in the Republic; "M," "A," and "B" in the North), but most locals refer to them by destination ("the Kerry road"). Signs and printed directions sometimes give only the numbered and lettered designations, sometimes only the destination. Most signs are in English and Irish; destination signs in outlying *gaeltacht* are most often only in Irish. In the Republic, all black-and-white signs giving distance in miles were removed in 2006 and replaced with green-and-white signs that use kilometers. Speed limit signs are in miles per hour in Northern Ireland and kilometers per hour in the Republic.

BY BUS

Buses in the Republic reach many more destinations and are cheaper than trains. Bus drivers are often very accommodating in where they will pick up and drop off. The national bus company, **Bus Éireann** (Dublin general helpline ☎01 836 6111; www.buseireann.ie), operates both long-distance Expressway buses, which link larger cities, and local buses, which serve the countryside and smaller towns. The invaluable bus timetable book is difficult to obtain; check at the Busáras Central Station in Dublin. In Donegal, **private bus providers** take the place of Bus Éireann's nearly-nonexistent local service. *Let's Go* lists these providers where applicable.

Bus Éireann's **Irish Rover Bus** ticket offers unlimited bus travel within Ireland for three of eight consecutive days (€73, under 16 €42), eight of 15 consecutive days (€165/90), or 15 of 30 consecutive days (€245/133), but is generally less cost-effective than buying individual tickets. A combined **Irish Explorer Bus & Rail** ticket allows unlimited travel on trains and buses for eight of 15 consecutive days (€210/105). Tickets can be purchased at any urban Bus Éireann terminal or online, www.buseireann.ie.

Ulsterbus, (☎028 9066 6630; www.ulsterbus.co.uk), the North's version of Bus Éireann, runs extensive, reliable routes throughout Northern Ireland, where there is no private bus service. Coverage expands in summer, with several coastal routes and full- and half-day tours leaving from Belfast for key tourist spots. Pick up a free regional timetable at any station. There are discounts for families and students; inquire by phone for details of various programs.

The **Emerald Card** offers unlimited travel on: Ulsterbus; Northern Ireland Railways; Bus Éireann Expressway, Local, and City services in Cork, Dublin, Galway, Limerick, and Waterford; and intercity DART and suburban rail Iarnród Éireann services. The card works for eight out of 15 consecutive days (€236, under 16 €118) or 15 out of 30 (€406/202).

BUS TOURS. In exchange for some of your independence, bus tours can free you from agonizing over minutia and connect you with a knowledgeable tour leader. Tours cost around €50 per day, with longer tours costing less per day. **Paddywagon Tours** (☎01 823 0822; www.paddywagontours.com) has one-, three-, four-, six- and 10-day packages, including breakfast, hostels, and sights. **Contiki Travel** (US ☎866-266-8454; www.contiki.com) runs comprehensive bus tours starting at around $1149. Tours include accommodations, transportation and some meals.

BY TRAIN

Iarnród Éireann (Irish Rail), is useful only for travel to urban areas—you'll need to find another form of transportation to reach villages and wilderness. Trains from Dublin's Heuston Station chug toward Cork, Ennis, Galway, Limerick, Tralee, Waterford, and Westport; others leave from Dublin's Connolly Station to head for Belfast (express), Rosslare (express), Sligo, and Wexford. For schedule information, pick up an *InterCity Rail Travelers Guide* (€1.20), available at most train stations. An **ISIC** allows you to purchase a **National Student Travel Card** (€12), which cuts fares by 30-50% on national rail. A **Faircard** (€10-15) can get anyone age 16 to 26 a significant discount on the price of any InterCity trip. Those over 26 can get the less potent **Weekender card** (€7). Both are valid through the end of the year. For combined bus-and-train travel passes, see **By Bus**, p. 28. Information is available from the Irish Rail information office (☎ 01 85036 6222; www.irishrail.ie). Unlike bus tickets, train tickets sometimes allow travelers to break a journey in stages yet still pay the price of a single-phase trip. Bikes may be carried on some trains; check at the station for specific restrictions.

While the **Eurailpass** is not accepted in Northern Ireland, it is accepted on trains in the Republic. It will be tough to make your railpass pay for itself, since train fares are reasonable, distances short, or buses preferable. If, however, the total cost of your trips nears the price of the pass, the convenience of avoiding ticket lines may be worth the difference. Youth and family passes are also available but are worth it only if you plan to travel to the Continent as well. The BritRail pass does not cover travel in Northern Ireland, but the month-long **BritRail+Ireland** works in both the North and the Republic with rail options and return ferry service between Britain and Ireland (5 days US$462, 10 days US$733). Travelers under 26 should look into a youth pass. You'll find it easiest to buy a Eurailpass before you arrive in Europe; contact STA, Travel CUTS, or another travel agent. **Rail Europe Group** (US ☎ 877-257-2887; www.raileurope.com) also sells point-to-point tickets.

Northern Ireland Railways (☎ 028 9066 6630; www.nirailways.co.uk) is not extensive but covers the northeastern coastal region well. The major line connects Dublin to Belfast. When it reaches Belfast, this line splits, with one branch ending at Bangor and another at Larne. There is also rail service from Belfast and Lisburn west to Derry/Londonderry and Portrush, stopping at three towns between Antrim and the coast. British Rail passes are not valid here, but Northern Ireland Railways offers its own discounts. A valid **Translink Student Discount Card** (£7) will get you up to 33% off all trains and 15% discounts on many bus fares within Northern Ireland. The **Freedom of Northern Ireland** ticket allows unlimited travel by train and Ulsterbus and can be purchased for seven consecutive days (£50), three out of eight days (£34), or a single day (£14).

BY CAR

Traveling by car offers speed, freedom, and easy access to the countryside. Disadvantages include high gas (petrol) prices (about €1 per liter), unfamiliar automobile laws, and **driving on the left side of the road**. Be particularly cautious at roundabouts (rotary interchanges): remember to **give way to traffic from the right.** Speed limits in the Republic are given in kilometers per hour, not miles per hour.

RENTING

Renting (hiring) an automobile is the cheapest option if you plan to drive for a month or less, but the initial cost of renting a car and the price of gas in Ireland will astound you. Cheaper cars tend to be less reliable and harder to handle on difficult terrain. Less expensive 4WD vehicles in particular tend to be top heavy and more dangerous when navigating particularly bumpy roads.

RENTAL AGENCIES

You can rent a car from a US-based firm (Alamo, Avis, Budget, or Hertz) with European offices, from a European-based company (Europcar) with local representatives, or from a tour operator (Auto Europe, Europe By Car, and Kemwel Holiday Autos) that will arrange a rental for you from a local company at its own rates. It is always significantly less expensive to reserve a car from the US than from Europe. You can generally make reservations before you leave by calling major international offices in your home country. However, occasionally the price and availability information they give doesn't jive with what the local offices in your country will tell you. Try checking with both numbers to make sure you get the best price and accurate information. Local desk numbers are included in town listings in this book; for home-country numbers, call your toll-free directory. Ask airlines about special fly-and-drive packages; you may get up to a week of free or discounted rental. Expect to pay US$90-200 per week, plus VAT, for a tiny car. Reserve ahead and pay in advance if at all possible. Always check if prices quoted include tax and collision insurance; some credit card companies provide insurance, allowing their customers to decline the collision damage waiver. Ask about discounts and check the terms of insurance, particularly the size of the deductible. For insurance reasons, most companies require renters to be over 21 or 23 and under 70. **Dan Dooley** (☎ 800-331-9301; www.dandooley.com), **Easy Car** (www.easy-car.com), and **Enterprise** (within Ireland ☎ 890-227-999, UK 0870 350 3000, US 800-261-7331; www.enterprise.com) are the only major companies in Ireland that will rent to drivers between 21 and 24, though such drivers incur an added daily surcharge. At most agencies, all that's needed to rent a car is a license from home and proof that you've had it for at least a year.

Major rental agencies convenient to major airports are **Enterprise** (Dublin and Shannon Airports), **Budget Rent-A-Car** (Central Office ☎ 090 662 7711, Dublin Airport 01 844 5150, Shannon Airport 061 471 361; www.budgetcarrental.ie), and **Thrifty** (☎ 800 515 800, Dublin Airport 01 844 1950, Shannon Airport 361 471 770; www.thrifty.ie). It is always significantly less expensive to reserve a car from the US than from Europe. Major rental agencies easily reached from home include:

Auto Europe (US and Canada ☎ 888-223-5555 or 207-842-2000; www.autoeurope.com).

Avis (Australia ☎ 136 333; New Zealand 0800 65 51 11; UK 8445 81 81 81; Canada and the US 800-331-1212; www.avis.com).

Budget (Canada ☎ 800-268-8900; UK 8701 565 656; US 800-527-0700; www.budgetrentacar.com).

Europe by Car (US ☎ 800-223-1516 or 212-581-3040; www.europebycar.com).

Europcar International (UK ☎ 870 607 5000; US 877-940-6900; www.europcar.com).

Hertz (Australia ☎ 9698 2555; UK 0870 844 8844; US and Canada 800-654-3001; www.hertz.com).

Kemwel (US ☎ 877-820-0668; www.kemwel.com).

COSTS AND INSURANCE

Prices range €90-200 (plus VAT) per week with insurance and unlimited mileage. Expect to pay more for larger cars and for 4WD. Cars with **automatic transmission** cost 40% more than standard manuals (stick shift), and in some places automatic transmission is hard to find in the first place. It is virtually impossible, no matter where you are, to find an automatic 4WD.

Return the car with a full tank of petrol to avoid high fuel charges at the end. Be sure to ask whether the price includes **insurance** against theft and collision. Remember that if you are driving a conventional vehicle on an **unpaved road** in a rental car, you are almost never covered by insurance; ask before leaving the rental agency. Beware that cars rented on an **American Express** or **Visa/Mastercard Gold or Platinum** credit cards in Ireland might not carry the automatic insurance that they would in some other countries; check with your credit card company. Insurance plans almost always come with an **excess** (or deductible) of around $500 for conventional vehicles. This means you pay for all damages up to that sum, unless they are the fault of another vehicle. The excess you will be quoted applies to collisions with other vehicles; collisions with non-vehicles, such as trees, ("single-vehicle collisions") will cost you even more. The excess can often be reduced or waived entirely if you pay an exorbitant additional daily charge.

National chains often allow one-way rentals, picking up in one city and dropping off in another; yet, this often will not apply in picking up in the Republic and dropping off in Northern Ireland (and vice versa). There is usually a minimum hire period and sometimes an extra drop-off charge of several hundred dollars.

DRIVING PERMITS AND CAR INSURANCE

INTERNATIONAL DRIVING PERMIT (IDP)

If you plan to drive a car while in Ireland for longer than a three-month period, you must have an International Driving Permit (IDP). If you intend to drive for longer than one year, you'll need to get an Irish driver's permit.

Your IDP, valid for one year, must be issued in your home country before you depart. The application for an IDP usually requires one or two photos, a current local license, an additional form of identification, and a fee. To apply, contact the national or local branch of your home country's automobile association. Be careful when purchasing an IDP online or anywhere other than your home automobile association. Many vendors sell permits of questionable legitimacy at higher prices.

CAR INSURANCE

Most credit cards cover standard insurance. If you rent, lease, or borrow a car, you will need a **Green Card,** or **International Insurance Certificate,** to certify that you have liability insurance and that it applies abroad. Green cards can be obtained at car rental agencies, car dealers (for those leasing cars), some travel agents, and some border crossings. Rental agencies may require you to purchase theft insurance in countries that they consider to have a high risk of auto theft.

DRIVING PRECAUTIONS. When traveling in the summer, bring substantial amounts of water (a suggested 5 liters of water per person per day) for drinking and for the radiator. For long drives to unpopulated areas, register with police before beginning the trek and again upon arrival at the destination. Check with the local automobile club for details. When traveling for long distances, make sure tires are in good repair and have enough air, and get good maps. A compass and a car manual can also be very useful. You should always carry a spare tire and jack, jumper cables, extra oil, flares, a flashlight, and heavy blankets (in case your car breaks down at night or in the winter). If you don't know how to change a tire, learn before heading out, especially if you are planning on traveling in deserted areas. Blowouts on dirt roads are very common. If your car breaks down, stay in your vehicle; if you wander off, there's less likelihood trackers will find you.

ON THE ROAD

On a two-way street, driving travelers should remember to use the **left side of the road.** At roundabouts (rotary inter-changes), **yield to traffic from the right.** The **Association for Safe International Road Travel (ASIRT),** 11769 Gainsborough Rd., Potomac, MD 20854 (US ☎301-983-5542; www.asirt.org), can provide specific information on road conditions.

Roads are identified by letters and numbers ("N" and "R" in the Republic; "M," "A," and "B" in the North), but most locals refer to them by destination ("the Kerry road"). Signs and printed directions sometimes give only the numbered and lettered designations, sometimes only the destination. Most signs are in English and Irish; destination signs in outlying *gaeltacht* are most often only in Irish. The green-and-white signs posted along the roadways post speed limits in kilometers per hour. A typical speed limit outside of town is 80 km/hr.; in town, the speed limit is 50 km/hr. National roads (green signs) have a set 100 km/hr. speed limit and motorways (blue signs) have a 120 km/hr. speed limit. For an informal primer on European road signs and conventions, check out www.travlang.com/signs. For more details on Irish speed limits, visit www.citizensinformation.ie.

DANGERS
Take care when straying from national roads and motorways; Ireland's windy backroads are often narrow and uneven. Farm animals, such as horses and cattle, may cross some rural roads. Cell phone use while driving is illegal in Ireland. So is drinking and driving; police *(Garda)* officers enforce a strict blood-alcohol limit of 80 milligrams of alcohol per 100 milliliters of blood. Seat belts are required to be worn at all times. The emergency roadside number is ☎999.

BY BICYCLE

Many insist that cycling is *the* way to see Ireland and Northern Ireland. Much of the island's countryside is well suited for pedaling by daylight, as many roads are not heavily traveled. Single-digit "N" roads in the Republic and "M" roads in the North are more busily trafficked; try to avoid these. Begin your trip in the south or west to take advantage of prevailing winds.

Many **airlines** will count your bike as your second free piece of luggage, but some charge extra (around US$80 one-way). Check with the individual company for any special packaging procedures. Most ferries let you take your bike for free or for a small fee. You can bring your bike on some **trains,** but the cost varies; inquire at the information desk. You'll have better luck getting your bike on a **bus** if you depart from a terminal, not a wayside stop. Bikes are allowed on Bus Éireann at the driver's discretion for a fee of €10 (not always enforced).

Riding a bike with a frame pack strapped on it or on your back is extremely dangerous; **panniers** (US$10-40) are essential. The first thing to buy, however, is a suitable **bike helmet** (US$15-50). U-shaped **locks** are expensive (from US$25), but most companies insure their locks against theft.

Raleigh Rent-A-Bike (☎01 465 9659; www.raleigh.ie) has rental shops across Ireland. You can hire a bike for usually as little as €20 per day, €80 per week, plus deposit (€80). The shops will equip you with locks, patch kits, pumps, and, for longer journeys, pannier bags (€20 per week). **Celtic Cycling** (☎059 977 5282; www.celticcycling.com) serves the Southeast, including Carlow, Kilkenny, Waterford, and Wexford. They also offer cycling tour packages of varying length (€595 for 7 days), that include accommodations and pickup at the train station.

Many small local dealers and hostels also rent bikes. Rates are about €8-18 per day and €40-80 per week. Tourist offices can direct you to bike rental establishments and distribute leaflets on local biking routes, and provide the extensive *Cycle Touring Ireland*. Adequate **maps** are a necessity; *Ordnance Survey* maps (€7) or Bartholomew maps are available in most bookstores. For more information on biking through Ireland, find a copy of *Ireland by Bike*, by Robin Krause (Mountaineers Books ☎206-233-6303; www.mountaineersbooks.org).

Those who are nervous about striking out on their own should consult **Trek Travel,** 4617 Dovetail Dr., Ste. 3, Madison, WI 53704, USA (☎866-464-8735; www.trektravel.com), which offers full-package luxury cycling excursions (US$3795, based on double occupancy). Contact Trek Travel for more information on a variety of tour options.

BY THUMB

 Let's Go never recommends hitchhiking as a safe means of transportation, and none of the information presented here is intended to do so.

Let's Go strongly urges you to consider the risks before you choose to hitchhike. Hitching means entrusting your life to a random person, risking theft, assault, sexual harassment, and unsafe driving. Locals do not recommend hitchhiking in Northern Ireland or in County Dublin; many also caution against it in the Midlands. Hitching is more common on the west coast than the east.

For women traveling alone, hitching is just too dangerous. A man and a woman are a less dangerous combination, two men will have a harder time, and three will go nowhere. In all cases, **safety** should be the first concern. Safety-minded hitchers avoid getting in the back of a two-door car (or any car they wouldn't be able to get out of in a hurry) and never let go of their backpacks. If they ever feel threatened, they insist on being let off immediately. Acting as if they are going to open the car door or vomit will usually get a driver to stop.

In the **Practical Information** section of many cities, *Let's Go* lists the tram or bus lines that take travelers to strategic hitching points. Placement is crucial—experienced hitchers stand where drivers can stop, have time to look over potential passengers, and return to the road without causing an accident. Hitching on hills or curves is hazardous and usually fruitless; roundabouts and access roads to highways are better. You can get a sense of the amount of traffic a road sees by its letter and number: in the Republic, single-digit N-roads (A-roads in the North) are as close as Ireland gets to highways, double-digit N-roads see some intercity traffic, R-roads (B-roads in the North) generally only carry local traffic but are easy hitches, and non-lettered roads are a hitcher's purgatory. Hitching (or even standing) on motorways (M-roads) is illegal. Entrance ramps in front of the blue-and-white superhighway pictograph (a bridge over a road) would be a better choice.

KEEPING IN TOUCH

BY EMAIL AND INTERNET

The Irish postal service is both reliable and speedy. Though Internet is readily available in cities, it can often be hard to find in rural Donegal and Kerry. **Email** is an easy way to stay in touch, though slow connections in Ireland may make the experience more trying than you're accustomed to. Connecting to your home server will probably be considerably slower than connecting to **web-based email providers** (like www.hotmail.com, www.yahoo.com and, in Ireland, ireland.com). In Irish cities, Internet access is available in cafes, hostels, and usually in libraries. One hour of webtime costs about €3-6 (an ISIC may win you a discount). Look into a county library membership in the Republic (€2.50-3), which will give you unlimited access to participating libraries and their Internet connections. Such membership is particularly useful in counties where Internet cafes are sparse, like Donegal, Kerry, and Mayo.

Increasingly, travelers find that taking their **laptop computers** on the road with them can be a convenient option for staying connected. Laptop users can call an Internet service provider via a modem using long-distance phone cards specifically intended for such calls. They may also find Internet cafes that allow them to connect their laptops to the Internet. And most excitingly, travelers with wireless-enabled computers may be able to take advantage of an increasing number of Internet "hot spots" to get online for free or for a small fee. Newer computers can detect these hotspots automatically; otherwise, websites like www.jiwire.com and www.locfinder.net can help you find them. For information on insuring your laptop while traveling, see p. 21.

WARY WI-FI. Wireless hot spots make Internet access possible in public and remote places. Unfortunately, they also pose security risks. Hot spots are public, open networks that use unencrypted, unsecured connections. They are susceptible to hacks and "packet sniffing"—ways of stealing passwords and other private information. To prevent problems, disable ad hoc mode, turn off file sharing, turn off network discovery, encrypt your e-mail, turn on your firewall, beware of phony networks, and watch for over-the-shoulder creeps. Ask the establishment whose wireless you're using for the name of the network so you know you're on the right one. If you are in the vicinity and do not plan to access the Internet, turn off your wireless adapter completely.

BY TELEPHONE

CALLING HOME FROM IRELAND

You can usually make **direct international calls** from pay phones. A **calling card** is probably your cheapest bet. Calls are billed collect or to your account. You can frequently call collect without even possessing a company's calling card just by calling their access number and following the instructions. Each one comes with a Personal Identification Number (PIN) and a toll-free access number. You call the access number and then follow the directions for dialing your PIN. To purchase prepaid phone cards, check online for the best rates; www.calling-cards.com is a good place to start. Online providers generally send your access number and PIN via email, with no actual "card" involved. You can also call home with prepaid phone cards purchased in Ireland (see **Calling Within Ireland,** p. 36). **Swiftcall** phone cards or other prepaid Irish phone cards (available at post offices and newsagents) can score you great rates after 9pm, Irish time—often as low as €0.15-0.20 per minute. **To obtain a calling card** from your national tele-communications service before leaving home, contact the appropriate company listed below (using the numbers in the first column). To **call home with a calling card,** contact the operator for your service provider in Ireland by dialing the appropriate toll-free access number (listed below in the second column).

COMPANY	TO OBTAIN A CARD, DIAL:	TO CALL ABROAD, DIAL:
AT&T (US)	800-364-9292 or www.att.com	800 550 000 (Republic) 0800 89 0011 (Northern Ireland)
Canada Direct	800-561-8868 or www.infocanada-direct.com	800 555 001 (Republic) 0800 89 0016 (Northern Ireland)
MCI (US)	800-777-5000 or con-sumer.mci.com	800 55 1001 (Republic and North-ern Ireland)
Telstra Australia	13 22 00 or www.telstra.com	800 55 00 61 (Republic) 0800 8566161 (Northern Ireland)

You can also usually make **direct international calls** from pay phones, but if you aren't using a calling card, you may need to drop your coins as quickly as your words. Prepaid phone cards and occasionally major credit cards can be used for direct international calls, but they are generally less cost-efficient. Placing a **collect call** through an international operator is even more expensive, but may be necessary in case of emergency. You can place collect calls through the service providers listed above even if you don't have one of their phone cards.

PLACING INTERNATIONAL CALLS. To call Ireland from home or to call home from Ireland, dial:

1. The **international dialing prefix.** To call from **Australia,** dial 0011; **Canada** or the **US,** 011; **Ireland, New Zealand,** or the **UK (including Northern Ireland),** 00.
2. The **country code** of the country you're calling. For **Australia,** dial 61; **Canada** or the **US,** 1; **Ireland,** 353; **New Zealand,** 64; the **UK (including Northern Ireland),** 44. To reach **Northern Ireland from the Republic,** dial 048.
3. The **city/area code.** *Let's Go* lists the city/area codes for cities and towns in the Republic opposite the city or town name; **the city code for all towns in the North is 028.** If the first digit is a zero (e.g., 020 for London), omit the zero when calling from abroad (e.g., dial 20 from Canada to reach London).
4. The **local number.**

CALLING WITHIN IRELAND

Using Irish pay phones can be tricky. Public phones come in two varieties: **coin** and **card.** Public coin phones will give you back unused coins (not fractions of coins; don't insert a €1 coin for a 20-euro cent call), but private pay phones (called "one-armed bandits") in hostels and restaurants do not—once you plunk in your change, kiss it good-bye. In any pay phone, do not insert money until asked to, or until the call goes through. The pip-pip noise the phone makes as you wait for it to start ringing is normal and can last up to 10 seconds. Local calls cost 40 euro cents for 4min. on public phones; "one-armed bandits" charge more.

CALLING FROM THE REPUBLIC OF IRELAND
Operator: ☎ 10 (not available from card phones).
Directory inquiries: ☎ 11 850 or 11 811 (for the Republic and the North).
International access code: ☎ 00.
International operator: ☎ 114.
International directory inquiries: ☎ 11 818.

CALLING FROM NORTHERN IRELAND AND LONDON
Operator: ☎ 100.
Directory inquiries: ☎ 192.
International access code: ☎ 00.
International operator: ☎ 155.
International directory assistance: ☎ 153.

The smart option for long-distance calls is buying a **prepaid phone card,** which carries a certain amount of phone time depending on the card's denomination. The time is measured in minutes or talk units (e.g., one unit or one minute), and the card usually has a toll-free access telephone number and a personal identification number (PIN). News agents sell phone cards in denominations of €5, €10, €20, or €30. Card phones have a digital display that ticks off your units' perilous plunge. When the unit number starts flashing, you may push the eject button on the card phone; you can then pull out your expired calling card and replace it with a fresh one. If you wait until your card's units fall to zero, you'll be disconnected. Eject your card early and use the remaining unit or two for a local call. Phone rates tend to be highest in the morning, lower in the evening, and lowest on Sunday or late at

ESSENTIALS

night. Before settling on a calling card plan, be sure to research your options in order to pick the one that best fits both your needs and your destination.

Pay phones in Northern Ireland initially charge €0.10 for local calls; most calls cost €0.20. A series of harsh beeps warns you to insert more money when your time is up. The digital display ticks off your credit in 1p increments so you can watch your pence in suspense. Only unused coins are returned. You may use all remaining credit on a second call by pressing the "follow on call" button (often marked "FC"). Phones don't accept 1p, 2p, or 5p coins. The dial tone is a continuous purring sound; a repeated double-purr means the line is ringing. Northern **British Telecom Phonecards,** in denominations of UK£2, £5, £10, and £20, are sold at post offices and newsstands, and are accepted at most public phones.

CELLULAR PHONES

The international standard for cell phones is **Global System for Mobile Communication (GSM).** To make and receive calls in Ireland you will need a **GSM-compatible phone** and a **SIM (Subscriber Identity Module) card,** a country-specific, thumbnail-sized chip that gives you a local phone number and plugs you into the local network. Companies like **Cellular Abroad** (www.cellularabroad.com) rent cell phones that work in a variety of destinations around the world, providing a simpler option than picking up a phone in-country.

GSM PHONES. Just having a GSM phone doesn't mean you're necessarily good to go when you travel abroad. The majority of GSM phones sold in the United States operate on a different **frequency** (1900) than international phones (900/1800) and will not work abroad. Tri-band phones work on all three frequencies (900/1800/1900) and will operate through most of the world. Additionally, some GSM phones are **SIM-locked** and will only accept SIM cards from a single carrier. You'll need a **SIM-unlocked** phone to use a SIM card from a local carrier when you travel.

TIME DIFFERENCES

Britain and Ireland are on **Greenwich Mean Time (GMT).** GMT is 5hr. ahead of New York, 8hr. ahead of Vancouver and San Francisco, 10hr. behind Sydney, and 12hr. behind Auckland, although the actual time differences depend on daylight savings time. Both Britain and Ireland observe **daylight saving time** between the last Sunday of March and the last Sunday of October.

The following table applies from late October to early April.

4AM	5AM	6AM	7AM	8AM	NOON	10PM
Vancouver Seattle San Francisco Los Angeles	Denver	Chicago	New York Toronto	New Brunswick	London **DUBLIN**	Sydney Canberra Melbourne

This table is applicable from early April to late October.

4AM	5AM	6AM	7AM	8AM	NOON	9PM
Vancouver Seattle San Francisco Los Angeles	Denver	Chicago	New York Toronto	New Brunswick	London **DUBLIN**	Sydney Canberra Melbourne

BY MAIL

SENDING MAIL HOME FROM IRELAND

Airmail is the best way to send mail home from Ireland; just write "airmail" on the front. **Surface mail** is by far the cheapest and slowest way to send mail. It takes one to two months to cross the Atlantic and one to three to cross the Pacific—good for heavy items you won't need for a while, such as souvenirs that you've acquired along the way. These are standard rates for mail from Ireland to:

Australia: Allow 5-7 days for regular airmail home. Postcards/letters cost €0.78; packages up to 0.5kg €21, up to 2kg €35.

Canada: Allow 5-7 days for regular airmail home. Postcards/letters cost €0.78; packages up to 0.5kg €21, up to 2kg €35.

New Zealand: Allow 5-7 days for regular airmail home. Postcards/letters cost €0.78; packages up to 0.5kg €21, up to 2kg €35.

UK: Allow 2-3 days for regular airmail home. Postcards/letters cost €0.78; packages up to 0.5kg €17.50, up to 2kg €24.

US: Allow 5-7 days for regular airmail home. Postcards/letters cost €0.78; packages up to 0.5kg €21, up to 2kg €35.

SENDING MAIL TO IRELAND

An Post is Ireland's national postal service (☎01 705 7600; customer.services@anpost.ie, www.anpost.ie). Dublin is the only place in the Republic with postal codes. Even-numbered codes are for areas south of the Liffey, odd-numbered for Northern Ireland. Northern Ireland has number and letter postal codes like the UK.

To ensure timely delivery, mark envelopes "airmail". In addition to the standard postage system whose rates are listed above, **Federal Express** (Australia ☎ 13 26 10, Canada and the US 800-463-3339, Ireland 1800 535 800, New Zealand 0800 733 339, the UK 08456 070 809; www.fedex.com) handles express mail services from most countries to Ireland. Sending a postcard within Ireland costs €0.55, while sending packages up to 0.5g domestically requires €6.25; up to 2kg costs €7.25.

There are several ways to arrange pick up of letters sent to you while you are abroad. Mail can be sent via **Poste Restante** (General Delivery) to almost any city or town in Ireland with a post office and it is fairly reliable. Address *Poste Restante* letters like so:

Bono

Poste Restante

City, Ireland

The mail will go to a special desk in the central post office, unless you specify a post office by street address or postal code. It's best to use the largest post office, since mail may be sent there regardless. It is usually safer and quicker, though more expensive, to send mail express or registered. Bring your passport (or other photo ID) for pick up; there is no fee. If the clerks insist that there is nothing for you, ask them to check under your first name as well. *Let's Go* lists post offices in the **Practical Information** section for each city and most towns.

American Express travel offices throughout the world offer a free **Client Letter Service** (mail held up to 30 days and forwarded upon request) for cardholders who contact them in advance. *Let's Go* lists AmEx office locations for most large cities in **Practical Information** sections; for a complete list, call ☎800-528-4800 or visit www.americanexpress.com/travel.

ACCOMMODATIONS

HOSTELS

Hostels are usually laid out dorm-style, often with large rooms and bunk beds, although private rooms that sleep two to four are becoming more common. They sometimes have kitchens and utensils, bike or moped rentals, storage areas, transportation to airports, breakfast and other meals, laundry facilities, and Internet access (which is often extremely slow). There can be drawbacks: some hostels close during daytime "lockout" hours, have a curfew, don't accept reservations, impose a maximum stay, and a few require that you do chores. In Ireland, a dorm bed in a hostel will average around €16-24 and a private room around €25-40.

In Ireland more than anywhere else, senior travelers and families are invariably welcome. Some hostels are strikingly beautiful (a few are even housed in castles), but others are little more than run-down barracks. You can expect every Irish hostel to provide blankets, although you may have to pay extra for sheets (see **Packing**, p. 16). In recent years, a number of Irish hostels have been turned into refugee houses and have closed their doors—it is always a good idea to call ahead to hostels to ensure that they are open for business.

A HOSTELER'S BILL OF RIGHTS. There are certain standard features that we do not include in our hostel listings. Unless we state otherwise, you can expect that every hostel has no lockout, no curfew, free hot showers, some system of secure luggage storage, and no key deposit.

HOSTELLING INTERNATIONAL

Joining the youth hostel association in your own country (listed below) automatically grants you membership privileges in **Hostelling International (HI),** a federation of national hosteling associations. Non-HI members are welcome in all Irish HI hostels, though there are occasional member discounts. Many HI hostels accept reservations via the **International Booking Network** (www.hostelbooking.com). HI's umbrella organization's website (www.hihostels.com) lists the web addresses and phone numbers of all national associations. Other comprehensive hosteling websites include www.hostels.com and www.hostelplanet.com.

In Ireland, **An Óige** (an-OYJ), 61 Mountjoy St., Dublin 7, the HI affiliate, operates 26 hostels countrywide. (☎01 830 4555; www.anoige.ie. One-year membership €20, under 18 €10). Many An Óige hostels are in remote areas or small villages and were designed primarily to serve those seeking nature, not noise. The North's HI affiliate, **HINI** (Hostelling International Northern Ireland; formerly known as **YHANI**), 22-32 Donegal Rd., Belfast BT12 5JN, operates eight hostels. (☎028 9032 4733; www.hini.org.uk. One-year membership £15, under 25, £10.)

Most HI hostels also honor **guest memberships**—you'll get a blank card with space for six validation stamps. Each night you'll pay a nonmember supplement (one-sixth the membership fee) and earn one guest stamp; get six stamps, and you're a member. A new membership benefit is the **FreeNites** program, which allows hostelers to gain points toward free rooms. Most student travel agencies (see p. 24) sell HI cards, as do all of the national hosteling organizations below. All prices listed below are valid for **one-year memberships** unless otherwise noted.

Australian Youth Hostels Association (AYHA), 422 Kent St., Sydney, NSW 200 (☎02 9261 1111; www.yha.com.au). AUS$52, under 18 AUS$19.

Hostelling International-Canada (HI-C), 205 Catherine St. Ste. 400, Ottawa, ON K2P 1C3 (☎613-237-7884; www.hihostels.ca). CDN$35, under 18 free.

An Óige (Irish Youth Hostel Association), 61 Mountjoy St., Dublin 7 (☎830 4555; www.irelandyha.org). EUR€20, under 18 EUR€10.

Hostelling International Northern Ireland (HINI), 22-32 Donegall Rd., Belfast BT12 5JN (☎02890 32 47 33; www.hini.org.uk). UK£15, under 25 UK£10.

Youth Hostels Association of New Zealand Inc. (YHANZ), Level 1, 166 Moorhouse Ave., P.O. Box 436, Christchurch (☎0800 278 299 (NZ only) or 03 379 9970; www.yha.org.nz). NZ$40, under 18 free.

Scottish Youth Hostels Association (SYHA), 7 Glebe Crescent, Stirling FK8 2JA (☎01786 89 14 00; www.syha.org.uk). UK£8, under 18 £4.

Youth Hostels Association (England and Wales), Trevelyan House, Dimple Rd., Matlock, Derbyshire DE4 3YH (☎08707 708 868; www.yha.org.uk). UK£16, under 26 UK£10.

Hostelling International-USA, 8401 Colesville Rd., Ste. 600, Silver Spring, MD 20910 (☎301-495-1240; www.hiayh.org). US$28, under 18 free.

BOOKING HOSTELS ONLINE. One of the easiest ways to ensure you've got a bed for the night is by reserving online. Click to the **Hostelworld** booking engine through **www.letsgo.com,** and you'll have access to bargain accommodations from Argentina to Zimbabwe with no added commission.

INDEPENDENT HOLIDAY HOSTELS

In Ireland a number of hostels belong to the Independent Holiday Hostels (IHH). Most of the 140 IHH hostels have no lockout or curfew, accept guests of all ages, require no membership card, and have a comfortable atmosphere that generally feels less institutional than at An Óige hostels; all are Bord Fáilte-approved. Grab a free booklet with complete descriptions of each at any IHH hostel. Contact IHH at 57 Lower Gardiner St., Dublin 1 (☎01 836 4700; www.hostels-ireland.com).

OTHER TYPES OF ACCOMMODATIONS

B&BS

For a cozy alternative to impersonal hostel dorms, B&Bs (private homes with rooms available to travelers) range from the tolerable to the sublime. Hosts will sometimes go out of their way to be welcoming, often accepting travelers with pets or giving local tours. "Full Irish breakfasts" (eggs, bacon, bread, sometimes black or white pudding, fried vegetables, cereal, orange juice, and coffee or tea) fill stomachs until dinner. Singles run about €30-40, doubles €45-65. Many B&Bs do not provide phones, TVs, or private baths. Irish B&Bs tend to be cozy and are usually staffed by knowledgeable and friendly locals. B&Bs displaying a shamrock are officially approved by Bord Fáilte. For accommodations in Northern Ireland, check the Northern Ireland Tourist Board's *Where to Stay in Northern Ireland,* available at most tourist offices. For more information, check out **InnSite** (www.innsite.com) or **BedandBreakfast.com** (www.bedandbreakfast.com).

UNIVERSITY DORMS

Many **colleges and universities** open their residence halls to travelers when school is out; some do so even during term-time. These dorms are often close to student areas—typically chock-full of things to do and people to meet—and are usually very clean. Getting a room may take a couple of phone calls and some planning, but rates tend to be low, and many residence halls offer free local calls. For appropriate cities, including **Belfast, Dublin,** and **Galway.** *Let's Go* lists colleges which rent dorm rooms in the **Accommodations** sections of towns and cities. **Cork** and **Limerick** are also big university towns with student housing available in summer.

HOME EXCHANGES AND HOSPITALITY CLUBS

Home exchange offers the traveler various types of homes (houses, apartments, condominiums, villas, even castles in some cases), plus the opportunity to live like a native and to cut down on accommodation fees. For more information, contact HomeExchange.com Inc., P.O. Box 787, Hermosa Beach, CA 90254, USA (☎310 798 3864 or toll free 800-877-8723; www.homeexchange.com), or Intervac International Home Exchange in Ireland (☎041 98 30930; www.intervac.org/ireland).

Hospitality clubs link their members with individuals or families abroad who are willing to host travelers for free or for a small fee to promote cultural exchange and general good karma. In exchange, members usually must be willing to host travelers in their own homes; a small membership fee may also be required. **The Hospitality Club** (www.hospitalityclub.org) is a good place to start. **Servas** (www.servas.org) is an established, more formal, peace-based organization, and requires a fee and an interview to join. An Internet search will find many similar organizations, some of which cater to special interests (e.g., women, GLBT travelers, or members of certain professions). As always, use common sense when planning to stay with or host someone you do not know.

GOING GREEN

ECEAT International (the European Centre for Ecological and Agricultural Tourism) publishes a *Green Holiday Guide to Great Britain and Ireland* (€15), which lists places to stay on organic farms or otherwise environmentally friendly establishments. All ECEAT-listed accommodations are in lovely, wild areas. Contact ECEAT International at Radnicni 14, 66601 Tisnov, Czech Republic (☎420 541 235 080; www.eceat.org). For more about Irish organic farms see **Beyond Tourism**, p. 79.

THE GREAT OUTDOORS

Camping brings you closest to the land, the water, the insects, and continued financial solvency. Hostels often have camping facilities, but many campsites are designed for people with caravans (RVs), not tents. Sites cost €5-15, depending on the level of luxury. It is legal to cross private land by **public rights of way;** any other use of private land without permission is considered trespassing. Whenever camping, remember that **bogs catch fire** extremely easily.

Camping in State Forests and National Parks is not allowed, nor is camping on public land if an official campsite is in the area. It is also illegal to start campfires within 3km of these forests and parks. Caravan and camping parks provide all the accoutrements of bourgeois civilization: toilets, showers, and sometimes kitchens, laundry facilities, and game rooms. At many sites, caravans are available for hire. Northern Ireland treats its campers well; there are equipped campsites throughout the country, and spectacular parks often house equally desirable sites.

The **Great Outdoor Recreation Pages** (www.gorp.com) provides excellent general information for travelers planning on camping or spending time in the outdoors.

USEFUL RESOURCES

A variety of publishing companies offer hiking guidebooks to meet the educational needs of novice or expert. For information about camping, hiking, and biking, write or call the publishers listed below to receive a free catalog. Campers heading to Europe should consider buying an **International Camping Carnet.** Similar to a hostel membership card, it's required at a few campgrounds and sometimes provides

LEAVE NO TRACE. Let's Go encourages travelers to embrace the "Leave No Trace" ethic, minimizing their impact on natural environments and protecting them for future generations. Trekkers and wilderness enthusiasts should set up camp on durable surfaces, use cookstoves instead of campfires, bury human waste away from water supplies, bag trash and carry it out with them, and respect wildlife and natural objects. For more detailed information, contact the **Leave No Trace Center for Outdoor Ethics,** P.O. Box 997, Boulder, CO 80306 (☎800-332-4100 or 303-442-8222; www.lnt.org).

discounts. It is available in North America from the **Family Campers and RVers Association** and in the UK from **The Caravan Club** (see below).

Automobile Association, Contact Centre, Lambert House, Stockport Rd., Cheadle SK8 2DY, UK (☎08706 000 371; www.theAA.com). Publishes *Caravan and Camping Europe* and *Britain & Ireland* (UK£10) as well as road atlases for Europe, Britain, France, Germany, Ireland, Italy, Spain, and the US.

The Caravan Club, East Grinstead House, East Grinstead, West Sussex, RH19 1UA, UK (☎01342 326 944; www.caravanclub.co.uk). For UK£34, members receive access to sites, insurance services, equipment discounts, maps, and a monthly magazine.

Mountaineering Council of Ireland (☎01 625 1115; www.mountaineering.ie), safety tips and local resources for hillwalking and climbing.

WILDERNESS SAFETY

Staying **warm, dry,** and **well hydrated** is key to a happy and safe wilderness experience. For any hike, prepare yourself for an emergency by packing a first-aid kit, a reflector, a whistle, high-energy food, extra water, raingear, a hat, mittens, and extra socks. For warmth, wear wool or insulating synthetic materials designed for the outdoors. Cotton is a bad choice as it dries painfully slowly.

Check **weather forecasts** often and pay attention to the skies when hiking, as weather patterns can change suddenly. Always let someone—a friend, your hostel, a park ranger, or a local hiking organization—know when and where you are going. Know your physical limits and do not attempt a hike beyond your ability. See **Safety and Health,** p. 17, for information on outdoor medical concerns.

CAMPING AND HIKING EQUIPMENT

WHAT TO BUY

Good camping equipment is both sturdy and light. North American suppliers tend to offer the most competitive prices.

Sleeping Bags: Most sleeping bags are rated by season; "summer" means 30-40°F (around 0°C) at night; "four-season" or "winter" often means below 0°F (-17°C). Bags are made of **down** (warm and light, but expensive, and miserable when wet) or of **synthetic** material (heavy, durable, and warm when wet). Prices range US$50-250 for a summer synthetic to US$200-300 for a good down winter bag. **Sleeping bag pads** include foam pads (US$10-30), air mattresses (US$15-50), and self-inflating mats (US$30-120). Bring a **stuff sack** to store your bag and keep it dry.

Tents: The best tents are free-standing (with their own frames and suspension systems), set up quickly, and only require staking in high winds. Low-profile dome tents are the best all-around. Worthy 2-person tents start at US$100, 4-person tents start at US$160. Make sure your tent has a rain fly and seal its seams with waterproofer. Other useful accessories include a **battery-operated lantern,** a plastic **groundcloth,** and a nylon **tarp.**

Backpacks: Internal-frame packs mold well to your back, keep a lower center of gravity, and flex adequately to allow you to hike difficult trails, while **external-frame packs** are more comfortable for long hikes over even terrain, as they carry weight higher and distribute it more evenly. Make sure your pack has a strong, padded hip-belt to transfer weight to your legs. There are models designed specifically for women. Any serious backpacking requires a pack of at least 4000 cu. in. (16,000cc), plus 500 cu. in. for sleeping bags in internal-frame packs. Sturdy backpacks cost US$125-420—your pack is an area where it doesn't pay to economize. On your hunt for the perfect pack, fill up prospective models with something heavy, strap it on correctly, and walk around the store to get a sense of how the model distributes weight. Either buy a **rain cover** (US$10-20) or store all of your belongings in plastic bags inside your pack.

Boots: Be sure to wear hiking boots with good **ankle support.** They should fit snugly and comfortably over 1-2 pairs of **wool socks** and a pair of thin **liner socks.** Break in boots over several weeks before you go to spare yourself blisters.

Other Necessities: Synthetic layers, like those made of polypropylene or polyester, and a pile jacket will keep you warm even when wet. A **space blanket** (US$5-15) will help you to retain body heat and doubles as a groundcloth. Plastic **water bottles** are vital; look for shatter- and leak-resistant models. Carry **water-purification tablets** for when you can't boil water. Although most campgrounds provide campfire sites, you may want to bring a small **metal grate** or **grill.** For those places that forbid fires or the gathering of firewood, you'll need a **camp stove** (the classic Coleman starts at US$50) and a propane-filled **fuel bottle** to operate it. Also bring a **first-aid kit, pocketknife, insect repellent,** and **waterproof matches** or a **lighter.**

WHERE TO BUY IT

The online and mail-order companies listed below offer lower prices than many retail stores. A visit to a local camping or outdoors store will give you a good sense of the look and weight of certain items before you buy.

Campmor, 400 Corporate Dr., PO Box 680, Mahwah, NJ 07430, USA (☎800-525-4784; www.campmor.com).

Cotswold Outdoor, Unit 11 Kemble Business Park, Crudwell, Malmesbury Wiltshire, SN16 9SH, UK (☎08704 427 755; www.cotswoldoutdoor.com).

Discount Camping, 833 Main North Rd., Pooraka, South Australia 5095, Australia (☎618 8262 3399; www.discountcamping.com.au).

Eastern Mountain Sports (EMS), 1 Vose Farm Rd., Peterborough, 03458 NH, USA (☎888-463-6367; www.ems.com).

Gear-Zone, 8 Burnet Rd., Sweetbriar Rd. Industrial Estate, Norwich, NR3 2BS, UK (☎1603 410 108; www.gear-zone.co.uk).

L.L. Bean, Freeport, ME 04033, USA (US and Canada ☎800-441-5713; UK 0800 891 297; www.llbean.com).

Mountain Designs, 443a Nudgee Rd., Hendra, Queensland 4011, Australia (☎+617 3114 4300; www.mountaindesigns.com).

Recreational Equipment, Inc. (REI), Sumner, WA 98352, USA (US and Canada ☎800-426-4840, elsewhere 253-891-2500; www.rei.com).

CAMPERS AND RVS

Renting an RV costs more than tenting or hosteling but less than staying in hotels while renting a car (see **Rental Cars,** p. 30). The convenience of bringing along your own bedroom, bathroom, and kitchen makes RVing an attractive option, especially for older travelers and families with children.

Rates vary by region, season (summer is most expensive), and type of RV. Rental prices for a standard RV are around €850 per week. **Motorhome Ireland,**

Ratoath Rd., Kilbride, Dublin 15; and, 17 Valley Rd., Banbridge, Co. Down Northern Ireland, BT32 4HP (☎01 869 8000, 028 4062 1800; www.motorhome-irl.co.uk) rents a range of motorhome models starting at €175 per day (7-day minimum) during the summer; prices significantly cheaper in the low season.

ORGANIZED ADVENTURE TRIPS

Organized adventure tours include hiking, biking, skiing, canoeing, kayaking, rafting, climbing, photo safaris, and archaeological digs. Tourism bureaus often can suggest parks, trails, and outfitters. Stores like REI and EMS (see above) that specialize in camping and outdoor equipment also are good sources for info. Below are several additional resources in organized travel:

Specialty Travel Index (US ☎888-624-4030, elsewhere 415-455-1643; www.specialtytravel.com) leads Emerald Isle excursions.

GORP Travel (www.gorptravel.com) lists organized trips in Ireland on its website.

Green Earth Travel (☎888-246-8343; www.greenearthtravel.com) arranges environmentally-friendly travel packages to Ireland.

SPECIFIC CONCERNS

SUSTAINABLE TRAVEL

As the number of travelers on the road continues to rise, the detrimental effect they can have on natural environments becomes an increasing concern. With this in mind, Let's Go promotes the philosophy of **sustainable travel.** Through a sensitivity to issues of ecology and sustainability, today's travelers can be a powerful force in preserving as well as restoring the places they visit.

Ecotourism, a rising trend in sustainable travel, focuses on the conservation of natural habitats and how to use them to build up the economy without exploitation or overdevelopment. Travelers can make a difference by doing research in advance and by supporting organizations and establishments that pay attention to their impact on their natural surroundings and that strive to be environmentally friendly. For more information, see **Beyond Tourism,** p. 79.

ECOTOURISM RESOURCES. For more information on environmentally responsible tourism, contact one of the organizations below:

Earthwatch, 3 Clock Tower Place, Ste. 100, Box 75, Maynard, MA 01754, USA (☎800-776-0188 or 978-461-0081; www.earthwatch.org).

The Green Box (☎071 985 6898; www.greenbox.ie) has developed an "ecotourism plan" for Ireland.

The International Ecotourism Society, 1333 H St. NW, Ste. 300E, Washington, D.C. 20005, USA (☎202-347-9203; www.ecotourism.org).

Sustainable Ireland (☎01 674 5773; www.sustainable.ie) focuses its efforts on sustainable living projects in Ireland.

RESPONSIBLE TRAVEL

The impact of tourist expenditures on the destinations you visit should not be underestimated. The choices you make during your trip can have powerful effects on local communities—for better or for worse. Travelers who care about the destinations and environments they explore should make themselves aware of the social, cultural, and political implications of the choices they make when they travel. Simple decisions such as buying local products instead of globally available ones, paying fair prices for products or services, and attempting to say a few words in the local language can have a strong, positive effect on the community.

Community-based tourism aims to channel tourist funds into the local economy by emphasizing tours and cultural programs that are run by members of the host community and that often benefit disadvantaged groups. This type of tourism also benefits the tourists themselves, as it often takes them beyond the traditional tours of the region. The *Ethical Travel Guide* (UK£13), a project of **Tourism Concern** (☎+44 020 7133 3330; www.tourismconcern.org.uk), is an excellent resource for information on community-based travel with a directory of 300 establishments in 60 countries.

TRAVELING ALONE

There are benefits to traveling alone, including independence and greater interaction with locals. On the other hand, any solo traveler is a more vulnerable target for harassment and street theft. As a lone traveler, try not to stand out as a tourist, look confident, be especially careful in deserted or very crowded areas, and never admit that you are alone. For more tips, pick up *Traveling Solo*, by Eleanor Berman (Globe Pequot Press, US$14), visit www.travelaloneandloveit.com, or subscribe to **Connecting: Solo Travel Network**, 689 Park Rd., Unit 6, Gibsons, BC V0N 1V7, Canada (☎800-557-1757; www.cstn.org; membership US$30-50).

WOMEN TRAVELERS

Women exploring on their own inevitably face some additional safety concerns, but it's easy to be adventurous without taking undue risks. If you are concerned, consider staying in hostels which offer single rooms that lock from the inside or in religious organizations with rooms for women only. Stick to centrally located accommodations and avoid solitary late-night treks or metro rides.

Always carry extra money for a phone call, bus, or taxi. **Hitchhiking** is never safe for lone women, or even for two women traveling together. Look as if you know where you're going and approach older women or couples for directions if you're lost or uncomfortable. Wearing a conspicuous **wedding band** sometimes helps to prevent unwanted overtures. Your best answer to verbal harassment is no answer at all; feigning deafness, sitting motionless, and staring straight ahead at nothing in particular will do a world of good that reactions usually don't achieve. The extremely persistent can sometimes be dissuaded by a firm, loud, and very public "Go away!" Don't hesitate to seek out a police officer or a passerby if you are being harassed. Memorize the emergency numbers in places you visit, and consider carrying a whistle on your keychain. A self-defense course will both prepare you for a potential attack and raise your level of awareness of your surroundings. Also be aware of the health concerns (see p. 23) that women face when traveling.

GLBT TRAVELERS

Homosexual acts were decriminalized in the Republic in 1993, but the countryside remains largely suspicious of homosexuals. Dublin now supports a small gay community, with growing student societies at Trinity and UCD and an expanding array of pubs and clubs. Belfast and, to a lesser degree, Cork and Galway, also have small gay communities. *Gay Community News* covers Irish gay-related news, and its listings page covers gay locales in all of Ireland. Listed below are contact organizations, mail-order bookstores, and publishers that offer materials addressing some specific concerns. **PlanetOut** (www.planetout.com) offers a bi-weekly newsletter and a comprehensive site addressing gay travel concerns. **Gay Ireland**

ESSENTIALS

(www.gay-ireland.com) provides information on gay locales and events in Ireland and offers personal and chat services.

Gay and Lesbian Youth in Northern Ireland (GYLNI), Cathedral Buildings, 64 Donegall St., Belfast, BT1 2GT (☎077 0721 6921; www.glyni.org.uk). Offers a forum for meeting gay men and lesbians (ages 16-25) and info on gay locales in the North.

Ireland's Pink Pages (www.pink-pages.org). Ireland's web-based bisexual, gay, and lesbian directory. Extensive urban and regional info for both the Republic and the North.

International Lesbian and Gay Association (ILGA), 17 Rue de la Charité, 1210 Brussels, Belgium (☎32 2502 2471; www.ilga.org). Provides political information, such as homosexuality laws of individual countries.

ADDITIONAL RESOURCES: GLBT.
Spartacus 2005-2006: International Gay Guide. Bruno Gmunder Verlag (US$33).
Damron Men's Travel Guide, Damron Road Atlas, Damron Accommodations Guide, Damron City Guide, and *Damron Women's Traveller.* Damron Travel Guides (US$18-24). For info, call ☎800-462-6654 or visit www.damron.com.
The Gay Vacation Guide: The Best Trips and How to Plan Them, Mark Chesnut. Kensington Books (US$15).

TRAVELERS WITH DISABILITIES

Ireland is not wheelchair-friendly. Ramps, wide doors, and accessible bathrooms are less common than in the US, even in cities like Dublin. *Let's Go* lists **wheelchair-accessible facilities** wherever possible. **Guide dogs** are always conveyed free, but both the UK and Ireland impose a six-month quarantine on all animals entering the country and require that the owner obtain an import license. For more information, call the Department for Environment, Food, and Rural Affairs helpline at ☎084 5933 5577 (www.defra.gov.uk). For general information and free guides on disability access, write to the British Tourist Authority or Bord Fáilte. **Rail** is (probably) the most convenient form of travel for disabled travelers in Ireland: many stations have ramps, and some trains have wheelchair lifts, special seating areas, and specially equipped bathrooms.

USEFUL ORGANIZATIONS

Access Abroad, www.umabroad.umn.edu/access. A website devoted to making study abroad available to students with disabilities. The site is maintained by Disability Services and the Learning Abroad Center, University of Minnesota, 230 Heller Hall, 271 19th Ave. South, Minneapolis, MN 55455, USA (☎612-626-9000).

Accessible Journeys, 35 West Sellers Ave., Ridley Park, PA 19078, USA (☎800-846-4537; www.disabilitytravel.com). Designs tours for wheelchair users and slow walkers. The site has tips and forums for all travelers.

The Guided Tour Inc., 7900 Old York Rd., Ste. 114B, Elkins Park, PA 19027, USA (☎800-783-5841; www.guidedtour.com). Organizes travel programs for persons with developmental and physical challenges in Ireland.

MINORITY TRAVELERS

The cosmopolitan cities of Dublin and Cork are surprisingly diverse. Rural areas, however, remain prevalently white and Christian (largely Catholic in the Republic, mixed Catholic and Protestant in the North). Darker-skinned travelers are common subjects of attention, especially in rural areas. Most comments and stares are motivated by curiosity rather than ill will, but in rare cases minority travelers face derogatory comments or a refusal of service in pubs, B&Bs, and shops. For community resources, consult The Northern Ireland Council for Ehnic Minorities at www.nicem.org.uk.

DIETARY CONCERNS

Outside city centers, you're not likely to find much pub grub without meat, but in almost every town at least one restaurant will have something for vegetarians; *Let's Go* lists these locations accordingly. Vegans may need to cook for themselves. The travel section of the Vegetarian Resource Group's website (www.vrg.org/travel) has a list of organizations that are geared toward helping vegetarians and vegans traveling abroad. Visit the website of the Vegetarian Society of Ireland at www.vegetarian.ie to learn more about vegetarian restaurants and health food shops in Ireland. **Green Lodge,** Bantry, Co. Cork (☎027 66146; greenlodge@eircom.net), offers accommodations for vegan and vegetarian travelers. Travelers who keep kosher should contact synagogues in larger cities for information on kosher restaurants. **Kosher Ireland** (☎086 2788326; www.kosherireland.com) will deliver kosher meals anywhere in the Republic. Kosher is not a common term or practice in Ireland; if you are strict in your observance, you may have to prepare your own food. A good resource is the *Jewish Travel Guide*, edited by Michael Zaidner (Vallentine Mitchell; US$19). Travelers looking for halal restaurants may find www.zabihah.com a useful resource.

OTHER RESOURCES

Let's Go tries to cover all aspects of budget travel, but we can't put *everything* in our guides. Listed below are books and websites that can serve as jumping-off points for your own research.

WORLD WIDE WEB

Almost every aspect of budget travel is accessible via the web. In 10 min. at the keyboard, you can make a hostel reservation, get advice on travel hotspots from other travelers, or find out how much a train from Dublin to Galway costs.

Listed here are some regional and travel-related sites to start off your surfing; other relevant websites are listed throughout the book. Because website turnover is high, use search engines (such as www.google.com) to strike out on your own.

 WWW.LETSGO.COM. Let's Go's website features a wealth of information. It offers excerpts from all our guides as well as monthly features on new hot spots in the most popular destinations. In addition to our online bookstore, we have great deals on everything from airfares to cell phones. Our resources section is full of information you'll need before you hit the road, and our forums are buzzing with advice from other travelers. Check back often to see constant updates, exciting new tips, and prize giveaways.

THE ART OF TRAVEL

Backpacker's Ultimate Guide: www.bugeurope.com. Tips on packing, transportation, and where to go. Also tons of country-specific travel information.

BootsnAll.com: www.bootsnall.com. Numerous resources for independent travelers, from planning your trip to reporting on it when you get back.

How to See the World: www.artoftravel.com. A compendium of great travel tips, from cheap flights to self defense to interacting with local culture.

Travel Intelligence: www.travelintelligence.net. A large collection of travel writing by distinguished travel writers.

Travel Library: www.travel-library.com. A fantastic set of links for general information and personal travelogues.

World Hum: www.worldhum.com. An independently produced collection of "travel dispatches from a shrinking planet."

INFORMATION ON IRELAND

The BBC Northern Ireland: www.bbc.co.uk/northernireland. The best source of news for the North.

CIA World Factbook: www.odci.gov/cia/publications/factbook/index.html. Tons of vital statistics on Ireland's geography, government, economy, and people.

Geographia: www.geographia.com. Highlights, culture, and people of Ireland.

Ireland: Information on the Irish State: www.irlgov.ie. A comprehensive website about the government of the Republic.

Tourism Ireland: www.tourismireland.com. Information-packed site aimed at helping travelers get to and around the country.

LIFE AND TIMES

Travelers expecting Ireland to consist of thatched cottages, rolling hills, and vistas of jagged cliffs will not be disappointed, but those seeking a warm, traditional Irish welcome may be surprised. Irish friendliness and hospitality are not entirely relics of the past, but since Ireland joined the European Union in 1973, the joke that it has abandoned the rainbow for the pot of gold has become common. With its booming economy in the 1990s earning it the nickname the "Celtic Tiger," Ireland's prosperity has brought mixed blessings. Urban gourmands rejoice at the arrival of the "gastropub," while others lament the decline of the slow-paced Irish way of life. In the countryside, however, the traditional lifestyle is still visible in tight-knit communities centered around sports, music, the church, and the pub.

Northern Ireland (see p. 478), officially a territory of the UK, comprises six of Ulster's nine counties. "Ulster" is a term used exclusively by Protestants in the North. Under the 1998 Northern Ireland Peace Agreement, residents of Northern Ireland may choose whether to identify themselves individually as Irish or British, but word choice can still be tricky, as some identify with neither. People refer to "Northern Ireland" or "the North" and "the Republic" or "the South"; the term "Southern Ireland" is never used.

HISTORY

ANCIENT IRELAND (UP TO AD 350)

Archaeologists and historians have pieced together a fragmented understanding of ancient Irish culture from the scant remains of its stone structures and metalwork. These clues indicate that Ireland's first settlers quickly founded an agrarian civilization upon arriving from Britain around 7000 BC. These people created many structures that still loom large in the Irish landscape. Among them are **dolmens,** tombs and shrines for the dead made of huge stones in table-like forms, some of which were etched with geometric designs. **Passage tombs** are less common; these underground stone hallways and chambers often contained corpses and cinerary urns (see **Newgrange,** p. 164). **Stone circles** are rings of gravestones that likely marked spots of religious significance.

Bronze poured into Ireland circa 2000 BC, and the agrarian society was retooled into a warrior aristocracy. Starting in 900 BC, the **Irish Golden Age** brought grander structures: **ring forts** (see **Dún Aengus,** p. 381), protective walls that circled encampments and villages; **souterrains,** underground hideouts for storing loot and escaping from various marauders; and **clochans,** mortarless beehive-shaped huts.

Although a few groups of **Celts** (KELTS) may have arrived as early as 2000 BC, extensive migration didn't begin until 600 BC. They were first referred to by the Greeks as the *Keltoi*, translated as "hidden people" or "barbarians" depending on the source—the former referring to their vast but unwritten scholarship and knowledge. The Celts quickly settled down to their

circa 7000 BC
Ireland's first settlers arrive from Britain. Ireland is one of the last areas in Europe to be colonized.

circa 3000 BC
Mound-builders do their thing. The Hill of Tara is established.

2000 BC
Bronze becomes the latest craze.

900 BC-700 BC
Irish Golden Age brings prosperity.

600 BC-AD 1
The Celts migrate from central Europe.

new western outpost. Known for their ferocity, the Celts were famous for cutting off their enemies' heads and nailing them over the doors of their huts. They were free to wreak havoc, as the Romans were too busy conquering Germanic tribes to set their greedy sights on Ireland.

The Celts prospered on the peaceful isle, speaking a hybrid of Celtic and indigenous languages (collectively called Old Irish) and living in small farming communities. Regional chieftains ruled territories called *tuath*, while provincial kings controlled several *tuatha*. The **Uliad of Ulster,** a northern kingdom of chariot warriors, dominated the La Tène culture from their capital near Armagh (see **Navan Fort,** p. 549). These kings organized raids on Britain and established settlements in Scotland and Wales; their valor and success inspired tales of mythic heroism recounted in the *Táin Bó Cuailnge* and other epics (p. 68).

CHRISTIANS AND VIKINGS AND PIRATES, OH MY! (350-1200)

Starting in the late 4th century AD, a series of missionaries showed Ireland the light, Christian-style. The most important and successful of these was **Saint Patrick**—for more about his life and miracles see p. 59.

The missionaries and monks who followed St. Patrick recorded observations of the unfamiliar Celtic culture, describing, among other things, the system of writing found on **ogham stones.** These large obelisks, which recorded lineages in a script of dots and slashes, are still present in the **Burren** (p. 352), at the **Hill of Tara** (p. 166), and at **Brú na Bóinne** in Co. Meath (p. 164). Missionaries introduced the Viking-inspired **round tower** to the architectural lexicon. These structures were built as bell towers to call monks in to prayer but also served as fortifications against invaders. As Christianity spread through Ireland and mixed with indigenous Celtic beliefs, **high crosses,** or Celtic crosses, sprung up throughout the landscape. These large stone crucifixes, which combine the Christian cross with the Celtic circle, sometimes feature elaborate carvings of Biblical stories or saintly legends. Like stained-glass windows, these often served the purpose of educating illiterate Christians.

In monastic cities **Glendalough** (p. 152) and **Clonmacnois** (p. 184), refugee Catholic monks recorded the old epics and composed long religious poems in both Latin and Old Irish. The monks also created some of Europe's most beautiful **illuminated manuscripts,** handwritten books illustrated with paintings and gold leaf. The 7th-century **Book of Durrow** is the earliest surviving manuscript of this type; it is now exhibited at Trinity College (p. 121) with the early 9th-century **Book of Kells.**

The Golden Age of Irish Scholasticism (not to be confused with the Irish Golden Age from 900 BC-700 BC) was interrupted by **Viking** invasions in the 9th and 10th centuries. Their raids were most frequent along the southern coast, where they founded permanent settlements at Limerick, Waterford, and Dublin. The horned ones built Ireland's first castles, allied themselves with fierce chieftains, and littered the southeast with Norse-derived place names like Smerwick and Fota.

AD 200
High Kings set up shop in Tara.

432
St. Patrick arrives in Ireland (by our best estimate).

500-700
Huge monastic cities flourish.

circa 600
Monks create the Book of Durrow.

795
Full-scale Viking invasions begin.

early 800s
Monks ignore Vikings and instead spend time illuminating the Book of Kells.

914-919
Vikings found Waterford, Dublin, and Limerick.

999
King Brian Ború defeats Vikings.

LIFE AND TIMES

The epic **Battle of Clontarf,** where the Vikings were trounced near Dublin in 1014, signaled the decline of their control. The island was then divided between chieftains **Rory O'Connor** and **Dermot MacMurrough,** who continued to duke it out for the crown. Dermot ill-advisedly sought the assistance of English Norman nobles, and Richard de Clare (a.k.a. **Strongbow**) was all too willing to help. Strongbow and his Anglo-Normans arrived in 1169 and cut a bloody swath through South Leinster. Strongbow married Dermot's daughter Aoife after Dermot's death in 1171 and for a time seemed ready to proclaim an independent Norman kingdom in Ireland. Instead, he affirmed his loyalty to King Henry II and with characteristic generosity offered to govern Leinster on England's behalf.

FEUDALISM AND ITS DISCONTENTS (1200-1607)

Throughout the next few centuries, the English came to Ireland and settled down for a nice, long occupation. The Norman strongholds in Leinster had more towns—including the **Pale,** a fortified domain around Dublin—and more trade, while Gaelic Connacht and Ulster were agrarian. The two sides displayed a surprisingly unified culture: English and Irish lords built similar castles, ate similar foods, enjoyed the same poets, and hired the same mercenaries. The Crown fretted over this cultural cross-pollination and sponsored the notoriously unsuccessful **Statutes of Kilkenny** in 1366. These decrees banned English colonists from speaking Gaelic and intermarrying with the Irish, and it forbade the Irish from entering walled cities like Derry.

The English Crown successfully wrested more control. In 1495, **Poynings' Law** declared that the Irish Parliament could convene only with English consent and could not pass laws that did not meet with the Crown's approval. When Henry VIII created the Church of England, the Dublin Parliament passed the 1537 **Irish Supremacy Act,** declaring Henry head of the Protestant **Church of Ireland** and effectively making the island property of the Crown. The Church of Ireland held a privileged position over Irish Catholicism, even though the English neither articulated any difference between the two religious outlooks nor attempted to convert the Irish people. The lords of Ireland wished to remain loyal both to Catholicism and to the Crown—a daunting proposition even by 16th-century standards. Bold **Thomas FitzGerald** sent a missive to Henry VIII stating this position. In response, Henry revoked his aristocratic title. FitzGerald, not easily silenced, sponsored an uprising in Munster in 1579, an early hint to the English that a loyal Ireland could only be achieved under direct Protestant control.

Not to be outdone by FitzGerald, the equally defiant Ulster Earl **Hugh O'Neill** led a rebellion in the late 1590s. The King of Spain promised naval assistance and his Armada arrived in Kinsale Harbour in 1601 but did little to stop the English army from demolishing Irish forces. Relieved of their power, O'Neill and the rest of the major Gaelic lords bolted from Ireland in 1607 in what came to be known as the **Flight of the Earls.** Despite their grandiose plans to reappear with assistance from the Catholic rulers on the mainland continent, few ever returned to Ireland.

1014
Battle of Clontarf: Vikings get trounced once and for all.

1171
Strongbow grovels before English crown.

1172
Pope decrees that Henry II of England is feudal lord of Ireland.

1361
Irish pure-bloods banned from positions of power.

1366
Statutes of Kilkenny are passed.

1470-1534
Anglo-Irish Earls of Kildare bring relative stability to Irish politics.

1494
The Fretful Crown attempts to limit the Earls' power through Poynings' Law.

1537
Henry VIII claims Ireland for his own. Yoink!

1579
Catholic-minded FitzGerald stages an uprising against the English.

1595-1601
Another uprising: Hugh O'Neill vs. English Crown.

LIFE AND TIMES

While the world looked on in feigned astonishment, the English took control of Irish land and parceled it out to Protestants.

CROMWELL (1607-1688)

The English project of dispossessing Catholics of their land and replacing them with Protestants was most successful in Ulster, partially because the Earls had left a power vacuum. In a move known as the **Ulster Plantation,** Scottish tenants and laborers, themselves displaced by the English, joined the rag-tag mix of adventurers, ne'er-do-wells, and ex-soldiers bent on resettling the North. In 1641, a loose-knit group of Gaelic-Irish chiefs led the now landless Irish in an unsuccessful revolt in Ulster.

After his victory in the English Civil War, **Oliver Cromwell** turned his army to Ireland in 1649. Following standard Cromwellian procedure, the Lord Protector destroyed anything he did not occupy and then some. Catholics were massacred and whole towns razed. Over 25% of Irish land was confiscated and awarded to soldiers and Protestant vagabonds. Native Irish landowners were presented with the option of going **"to Hell or to Connacht"**—both desolate and infertile, one with a slightly warmer climate. By 1660, the tenant system was in full swing; the vast majority of Irish land was owned, maintained, and policed by Protestant immigrants. After Cromwell's death in 1658, Restored English King Charles II passed the 1665 **Act of Explanation.** The poorly enforced Act required Protestants to relinquish one-third of their land to the "innocent papists." Unsurprisingly, this never happened.

MORE BRITISH PROBLEMS (1688-1801)

More than thirty years after the English Civil War, political disruption again resulted in Irish bloodshed. In 1688, Catholic **James II,** driven from England by the Glorious Revolution led by Protestant William of Orange, came to Ireland to gather military support and reclaim his throne. Irish Jacobites and Williamites engaged in civil war. James tried to take Derry in 1689, but a rascally band of Protestant **Apprentice Boys** closed the gates on him and started the 105-day **Siege of Derry** (p. 571). William ended the war and sent his rival into exile on July 12, 1690 at the **Battle of the Boyne.** Northern Protestants still celebrate the victory on July 12 (called **Orange Day** in honor of King Billy; for more on **"the Marching Season,"** see **Northern Ireland,** p. 494). Five years later, the British enacted a set of **Penal Laws** for the purposes of further oppression, banning (among other things) the practice of Catholicism.

In Dublin and the Pale, the bourgeois Anglo-Irish tried to create a second London. This group defined the **"Ascendancy,"** a social elite whose elitism depended upon Anglicanism. **Trinity College,** chartered in 1592, was the quintessential institution of Ascended Protestants. Cultural ties notwithstanding, many aristocrats felt little political allegiance to England. **Jonathan Swift** pamphleteered on behalf of the Protestant Church and the Irish masses. Meanwhile, displaced peasants filled Dublin's poor areas, creating the horrific slums that led to Swift's "Modest Proposal" (see **Wit and Resistance,** p. 68).

Early 18th-century Catholics practiced their religion furtively, using large, flat rocks (dubbed **Mass rocks**) when they couldn't get their hands on an altar.

REBELLION AND UNION (1775-1848)

The Irish were not immune to the bold notions of independence that emerged from the American and French Revolutions. The *liberté*-fever was particularly strong among the **United Irishmen**, a group that had begun as a Protestant Ulster debating society with the nerve to challenge English rule. Outlawed in 1794, the United Irishmen reorganized as a more radical secret society. Their leader, a Kildare Protestant named **Theobald Wolfe Tone**, hoped that a general rebellion would create an independent, non-sectarian Ireland. To this end, he admitted nationalist Catholics among the ranks of the United Irishmen. The bloody **Rebellion of 1798** erupted with a furious band of peasants led by priests and ended with their last stand at **Vinegar Hill,** near Enniscorthy in Co. Wexford (p. 213). Always looking for an excuse to tussle with the Brits, French troops arrived and managed to hold their ground for about a month before being utterly destroyed. Wolfe Tone committed suicide in captivity, and other United Irishmen escaped to France.

With the 1800 **Act of Union,** the Crown abolished Irish self-government altogether. The Dublin Parliament died and "The United Kingdom of Great Britain and Ireland" was born. The Church of Ireland entered into an unequal marriage, changing its name to the "United Church of England and Ireland."

As the Napoleonic Wars raged in Europe, many feared that Bonaparte would notice the little green island in the Atlantic. Paranoid generals constructed squatty structures along the coast called **Martello towers** (see **Dún Laoghaire,** p. 140) which were never tested by French armies.

Under the terms of Union, Irish representatives held seats in the British Parliament, and thanks to a long awaited set of electoral reforms, Catholic farmers found that they too could go to the polls. With their newfound suffrage they elected Catholic **Daniel O'Connell** in 1829, forcing Westminster to repeal the remaining anti-Catholic laws that would have barred him from taking his seat. "The Liberator" promptly forced Parliament to allot money for improving Irish living conditions, healthcare, and trade. When unsympathetic Tories took power, O'Connell convened huge rallies in Ireland, showing popular support for repealing the Act of Union.

THE FAMINE AND ITS AFTERMATH (1845-1870)

During the first half of the 19th century, the potato was the wondercrop of the rapidly growing Irish population. Overreliance on potatoes had devastating effects when these tubers fell victim to a fungal disease. During the years of the **Great Famine** (1847-49), an estimated two to three million people died and another million emigrated to Liverpool, London, Australia, and the US on overcrowded boats called **coffin ships** because of their low survival rates (see **New Ross,** p. 224). British authori-

1695
Penal Laws make life miserable for Catholics.

1713
Jonathan "Baby-eater" Swift becomes Dean of St. Patrick's Cathedral in Dublin.

1775-1789
The American and French Revolutions foment Irish unrest.

1798
The bloody, unsuccessful, but heroic Rebellion of 1798.

1800
The Act of Union: British dissolve the Irish Parliament and create "the United Kingdom of Great Britain and Ireland."

1829
Daniel "The Liberator" O'Connell is elected; Catholics finally allowed to sit in Parliament.

1841
Population of Ireland surpasses 8 million.

1845-1847
Potato and other crops fall victim to a fungal disease.

1847-1851
The Great Famine: 2 to 3 million people die, another million emigrate.

1849-1899
The British begin to remove the Irish landlords from their properties.

1858
Irish Republican Brotherhood (IRB), a.k.a the Fenians, founded.

1870
Isaac Butt founds the Irish Home Rule Party and seeks to disrupt parliamentary procedure. Gladstone and Parnell's Home Rule Bill is defeated.

1884
The Gaelic Athletic Association is founded.

1890
Parnell scandal divides the Home Rule contingent.

1893
Gaelic League founded to reinvigorate the Irish language.

1905
Arthur Griffith forms Sinn Féin.

1911
Women's Suffrage movement.

1910-1913
Northern Protestants rally to protest Home Rule.

LIFE AND TIMES

ties often forcibly traded inedible grain for the few potatoes peasants could find and the Irish, whose diet was supplemented by delicacies like grass, had little choice but to accept. Hungry Catholics converted to Protestantism in exchange for British soup, earning for themselves the disdainful title "soupers." Ulster, which had a more diversified economy, was not hit nearly as hard by the Famine as the rest of Ireland.

After the Famine, the social structure of the Irish peasantry was completely reorganized. The bottom layer of truly penniless farmers had been eliminated. Eldest sons inherited family farms, while unskilled younger sons often had little choice but to leave the Emerald Isle. Depopulation continued, and **emigration** became an Irish way of life. Fifty years of land legislation converted Ireland, with the exception of Dublin and industrial northeast Ulster, into a nation of conservative, culturally uniform smallholders.

English injustice fueled the formation of more pugnacious young Nationalist groups. In 1858, crusaders for a violent removal of their oppressors founded the Irish Republican Brotherhood (IRB), a secret society known as the **Fenians.** Encouraged by a purportedly sympathetic Parliament, agrarian thinkers and republican Fenians created the **Land League** of the 1870s and pushed for further reforms.

PARNELL AND IRISH NATIONALISM (1870-1914)
In 1870, Member of Parliament **Isaac Butt** founded the **Irish Home Rule Party.** Its several dozen members adopted obstructionist tactics—they made long speeches and introduced amendments in the hopes of keeping the opposing MPs so angry, bored, and impotent that they would have little choice but to grant Ireland autonomy. **Charles Stewart Parnell** was a charismatic Protestant aristocrat with a hatred for everything English whose major accomplishment was to mobilize the Catholic church in support of Home Rule. Backed by Parnell's invigorated Irish party, British Prime Minister **William Gladstone** introduced an ill-fated **Home Rule Bill.** Though Parnell survived implication in the **Phoenix Park murders** (see p. 130), allegations were confirmed in 1890 that he was having an extramarital affair and his influence declined.

While politicians, engrossed by the scandal, let their ideals fall by the wayside, civil society waxed ambitious. Following their British and American sisters, the fairer sex established the **Irish Women's Suffrage Federation** in 1911. Marxist **James Connolly** led strikes in Belfast, and English-born Dubliner **Jim Larkin** spearheaded a general strike in 1913. Conservatives, attempting to "kill Home Rule by kindness," pushed for social reform.

Meanwhile, various groups tried to revive an essential "Gaelic" culture, unpolluted by foreign influence. The **Gaelic Athletic Association** (see p. 74) attempted to replace English with hurling, camogie, and Gaelic football. The **Gaelic League** spread the use of the Irish language (see **The Revival,** p. 69). Culture was not only trendy, but also was a politically viable weapon—the Fenians seized the opportunity to disseminate their ideas and became the movers and shakers in Gaelic organizations. Arthur Griffith began a tiny movement and a little-read newspaper advocating Irish abstention from British politics, both of which went by the name **Sinn Féin** (SHIN FAYN, "Ourselves Alone"). Reacting to the threat of Home Rule, Northern Protestants joined mass rallies, signed a covenant, and organized the paramilitary **Ulster Volunteer Force (UVF)** in 1913. The same year, nationalists led by **Eoin MacNeill** in Dublin responded by forming the **Irish Volunteers;** the two paramilitary groups were only kept from civil war by the onset of WWI.

THE EASTER RISING (1914-1918)

At the outbreak of WWI in 1914, British Prime Minister Henry Asquith passed a Home Rule Bill in return for Irish bodies to fill trenches. A Suspensory Act followed, delaying home rule until peacetime, and putting off the Ulster Unionist issue for another six years in exchange for Ulster's participation in the war effort. In all, 670,000 Irishmen enlisted to fight the Kaiser.

An 11,000-member armed guard, the remnants of the Irish Volunteers, stayed behind to defend Ireland. They were nominally led by Eoin MacNeill, who knew nothing of the revolt that the Fenians were brewing. If an architect could be ascribed to the ensuing mayhem, it would be poet and schoolteacher **Padraig Pearse**, who won his co-conspirators over to an ideology of "bloody sacrifice"—the notion that if a few men died martyrs' deaths, the entire population would eventually join the struggle for independence.

The Volunteers conducted a series of unarmed parades in an effort to convince the Dublin government of their harmlessness. Meanwhile, Fenian leaders were plotting to receive a shipment of German arms for use in a nationwide revolt on **Easter Sunday 1916,** with the notion that "England's emergency was Ireland's opportunity." The delivery of weapons was unsuccessful, but unsuspecting Fenian leaders continued planning their rebellion. They attempted to coerce MacNeill, who gave orders for Volunteer mobilization on Easter Sunday. The day before the insurrection, he learned that he had been manipulated by a weaponless bunch of brigands. Putting his trust in mass media, he inserted a plea into the Sunday papers asking all Volunteers to forgo the rebellion and stay home.

Although MacNeill and most Fenian leaders had been working toward military success, Pearse's followers wanted martyrdom. On Sunday, the group met and rescheduled their uprising for the following Monday, April 24. Pearse, James Connolly, and 1600 volunteers seized the **General Post Office** on O'Connell St. (see p. 128), read aloud the *Poblacht Na H Éireann* ("Proclamation of the Republic of Ireland"), and hunkered down for five days of brawling in the streets of Dublin. As their only tangible accomplishment was massive property damage, the rebels were seen initially as criminals by most Dubliners and were pelted with tomatoes by disapproving women.

The Crown retaliated with swift, vindictive punishments—in May, 15 "ringleaders" received the death sentence. Among the executed were Padraig Pearse, William Pearse (whose primary

1913
Dublin general strike. Nationalist Irish Volunteers founded. Unionist Ulster Volunteers founded.

1914
Home Rule Bill passes with an amendment excluding Ulster.

1916
Easter Rising begins a day late in Dublin. The insurrection fails and its leaders are executed straight into martyrdom.

1917
Sinn Féin is reorganized under Éamon de Valera as a national movement fighting for Irish independence. The Irish Volunteers reorganize under Fenian Michael Collins.

1919
Ireland fights for its Independence.

LIFE AND TIMES

crime was that he was Padraig Pearse's brother), and James Connolly, who was shot while tied to a chair because his wounds prevented him from standing. **Éamon de Valera** was spared when the Crown discovered he was American.

The British, with their hasty martial law, proved Pearse a true prophet—the public grew increasingly anti-British and sympathetic to the rebels. Dublin's **Kilmainham Gaol** (see p. 126), the site of the executions, became a shrine of martyrdom. The Volunteers reorganized under master spy and Fenian bigwig **Michael Collins**, and the Sinn Féin party became the political voice of military nationalism. Collins orchestrated the collusion between the Volunteers and Sinn Féin, and Éamon de Valera became the party president. The last straw came when the British tried to introduce a military draft in Ireland in 1918.

INDEPENDENCE AND CIVIL WAR (1919-1922)

Under the guidance of de Valera, Sinn Féin declared independence and formed a parliament named the **Dáil** (DOY-il). Extremist Irish Volunteers became Sinn Féin's military wing and started calling themselves the **Irish Republican Army (IRA).** Thus, the British saw another, though not their last, **War for Independence.** The Crown reinforced its police with the infamously brutal **Black and Tans**—ex-soldiers nicknamed after their patched-together uniforms. In 1920, after the six-year grace period was up, British Prime Minister **David Lloyd George** passed the **Government of Ireland Act,** which divided the island into Northern Ireland and Southern Ireland, two partially self-governing areas within the United Kingdom. Pressed by a newly elected Parliament, George conducted hurried negotiations with Collins and produced the **Anglo-Irish Treaty,** creating a 26-county Irish Free State but recognizing British rule over the northern counties. (For a more in-depth history of Northern Ireland, see **A Divided Island,** p. 479.) The treaty imposed on Irish officials an oath of allegiance to the Crown but not to the British government. Resourceful Lloyd George pushed the treaty through with the threat of war on Ireland.

The IRA, Sinn Féin, and the population split on whether to accept the treaty. Collins said yes; de Valera said no. Parliament said yes, and de Valera resigned the presidency. Arthur Griffith said he'd assume the position. The capable Collins government began the business of setting up a nation. A portion of the IRA, led by **General Rory O'Connor,** opposed the treaty; these nay-sayers occupied the Four Courts in Dublin, took a pro-treaty general hostage, and were attacked by the forces of Collins's government. Two years of **civil war** followed; the pro-treaty government won, Griffith died of a heart attack, Collins was assassinated (see **Clonakilty,** p. 260), and the dwindling minority of anti-treaty IRA officers went into hiding. Sinn Féin denied the legitimacy of the Free State government and voiced their disapproval by referring to the Republic as "the 26-county state" or "the Dublin Government," rather than the official "Éire."

1920
The first Black and Tans are recruited. Government of Ireland Act passes, separating Northern Ireland from the rest of the island.

1921
The Anglo-Irish Treaty produces the 26-county Free State of Ireland. The British retain control of the six Northern counties.

1922-1923
The Irish Civil War.

Dec. 1922
A first constitution is framed for the Irish Free State.

THE ERA OF DE VALERA (1922-1960)

Éire emerged from its civil war having lost its prominent leaders and looking quite a bit worse for the wear. The Anglo-Irish Treaty required a constitution by December 6, 1922. With time running out, **W.T. Cosgrave** was elected prime minister and passed a hasty preliminary constitution. Under the guidance of **Éamon de Valera,** the government ended armed resistance by Republican insurgents, executed 77 of them, and imprisoned several more. Cosgrave and his party, **Cumann na nGaedheal,** (today's **Fine Gael**) headed the first stable Free State administration. Then, in 1927, de Valera broke with Sinn Féin and the IRA and founded his own political party, **Fianna Fáil** ("Soldiers of Destiny"), to oppose the treaty non-violently and participate in government. Fianna Fáil won the 1932 election, and de Valera held power through the next two decades. Fianna Fáil broke up the remaining large landholdings and imposed high tariffs, instigating a trade war with Britain that battered the Irish economy until 1938. Although they were outlawed in 1936, IRA hardliners continued to trickle out of jails and resumed violence.

In 1937, de Valera proposed and voters approved the permanent Irish Constitution. It declared the state's name to be Éire and established the country's bicameral legislature. The more powerful **Dáil** (DOY-il), or lower house, is composed of 166 seats directly elected in proportional representation. The upper house, or **Seanad** (SHA-nud), has 60 members chosen by electoral colleges and partially functions to protect minority opinions. The Prime Minister, called the **Taoiseach** (TEE-shuch), and his deputy the **Tánaiste** (tah-NESH-tuh) lead a Cabinet. The **President** is the ceremonial head of state, with a seven-year term.

Ireland stayed neutral during WWII (known as **The Emergency**), though many Irish citizens identified with the Allies and about 50,000 served in the British army. Éire's brand of neutrality didn't exactly hinder the Allies; downed American or British airmen were shipped north to non-neutral Belfast while German pilots were detained in P.O.W. camps.

In 1948, a Fine Gael government under **John Costello** had the honor of officially proclaiming "the Republic of Ireland" free. The Republic left the British Commonwealth altogether in 1949, finally severing all ties with Britain, who recognized the Republic a year later. The Republic declared that the UK would maintain control over Ulster until the Parliament of Northern Ireland consented to join the Republic.

The last de Valera government (1951-59), and its successor, led by **Sean Lemass,** boosted the Irish economy by ditching protective tariffs in favor of attracting foreign investment. Instead of the verbal and military skirmishes over constitutional issues that dominated the 1920s, Irish politics became a contest between the ideologically similar Fianna Fáil and Fine Gael.

THE REPUBLIC TODAY

Ireland's post-war boom, ushered in with the efforts of Lemass, didn't arrive until the early 1960s. Economic mismanagement

1923
de Valera's government squelches Republican insurgents and ends armed resistance to the Irish State.

1923-1932
Cosgrave rules, granting women's suffrage and bringing electricity to the West.

1927
de Valera splits with Sinn Féin and establishes Fianna Fáil.

1936
The IRA is outlawed.

1948
The Republic of Ireland is officially free from British rule

1983
A public referendum reaffirms the Republic's ban on abortion.

1985
The Republic gains an official place in Northern Ireland negotiations.

1990
Mary Robinson is elected President.

1994
Peace-minded President Reynolds is forced to step down over Church scandals.

LIFE AND TIMES

LIFE AND TIMES

1995
Divorce is legalized in Ireland.

1997
Bertie Ahern becomes the youngest Prime Minister ever.

1998
The Good Friday Peace begins in the North.

2002
The Euro is introduced to Ireland and the punt is phased out.

2004
Bertie Ahern becomes President of the European Council.

2005
Cork is named the European Capital of Culture.

2006
On October 18th, the Republic of Ireland is overtaken by Northern Ireland in the FIFA world rankings for the first time in history.

2007
Bertie Ahern is reelected as Prime Minister of the Republic of Ireland for a third term.

and poor governmental policies kept the boom short. By the early 1970s, Ireland was on its way back down again. In an effort to revitalize the nation, Ireland entered the European Economic Community, now the **European Union** (EU), in 1973. EU membership and an increased number of international visitors spurred by the creation of Bord Fáilte helped introduce the slow, painful process of secularization. Garret FitzGerald revamped Fine Gael under a secular banner and alternated Prime Ministership with Fianna Fáil's Charlie Haughey throughout the late 70s and early 80s. EU funds proved crucial to helping Ireland out of a severe mid-80s recession and reducing its dependence on the UK. In 1985, FitzGerald signed the Anglo-Irish agreement, which allowed Éire to stick an official nose into Northern negotiations.

The Irish broke social and political ground in 1990 by choosing **Mary Robinson** as their president. Formerly a progressive barrister who had championed the rights of single mothers and gays, Robinson fought vigorously to overcome the international (and local) perception of the Irish as conservative cronies. In 1995, a national referendum narrowly made divorce legal in the Republic. When Mary was appointed the United Nation's High Commissioner for Human Rights in 1997, she was replaced by **Mary McAleese,** a native of Belfast.

Robinson's small, leftist **Labour Party** enjoyed unexpected success, paving the way for further social reform. In 1993, Taoiseach **Albert Reynolds** made ending violence in Northern Ireland his top priority. A year later he announced a cease-fire agreement between Unionists and the IRA. Despite his miracle-working in the North, Reynolds was forced to resign following a scandal involving his appointee for President of the High Court. After Reynolds's resignation, the Labour Party formed a coalition with Fine Gael, led by John Bruton as Taoiseach.

In June 1997, Fianna Fáil won the general election, making **Bertie Ahern,** at 45, the youngest Taoiseach in Irish history. Ahern joined the peace talks that produced the **Good Friday Agreement** (see p. 488) in April of 1998. On May 22, 1998, in the first island-wide election since 1918, an overwhelming 94% of voters in the Republic voted for the enactment of the Agreement, which ended their territorial designs on the North. (For the recent status of the Good Friday Agreement, see p. 490.)

In the summer of 2001, the Irish populace trickled out to the polls and defeated the **Nice Treaty.** The Treaty was the first step in the addition of 12 eastern European nations to the European Union. The result of the referendum shocked Ireland's pro-Treaty government and caused quite a stir on the continent. The government began a campaign to clarify the details of the treaty, as opinion polls found the Irish public pro-expansion but wary of union collapse. The treaty was eventually passed, admitting Poland and 11 other eastern European countries. On May 11, 2004, Bertie Ahern welcomed the new countries into the union as President of the European Council.

With money coming to Ireland from the European Union, increased foreign investment, and a thriving tourism industry, the Irish economy is booming as never before. Ireland now leads Europe in the percentage of university-educated adults.

This educated, flexible work force has invited foreign investment, further boosting the economy to the tune of over 5% growth in real GDP based on an estimate from 2006. In 2006, Ireland boasted the lowest unemployment rate in the EU at 4.2%. Recently, in June 2007, the leader of Fianna Fáil, Bertie Ahern, was re-elected to a third term as the Republic's Prime Minister.

SAINTS AND HEROES

SAINT PATRICK

In a country where over ninety percent of the population practices Catholicism, it's no surprise that the man who introduced the religion to Ireland is considered a pretty big deal. Indeed, Saint Patrick (AD 387-493) is the best known and most loved of the Irish saints. Captured by pirates and sent to tend the sheep of a druid warlord in **Country Antrim** (p. 551) at age 16, Patrick's only solace in life was constant, fervent prayer. Though he loathed his master and his mindless labor, Patrick's acquired familiarity with the Celtic language and traditional druidic practices aided him in his later quest to "liberate the Irish" from the bonds of druidism. After six years in captivity, Patrick fled his master and journeyed to the Continent, where he entered the priesthood. In 433, he returned to Ireland under the instruction of **Pope Celestine** and his mentor **Saint Germain** as a missionary.

Throughout his journeys, Patrick was able to connect with the Irish people by preaching the "glad tidings of redemption" in their native tongue. He gained many devoted followers, including Dichu, a chieftain who once threatened to behead the wandering saint. When Dichu went to smite Patrick with a fatal blow, he turned as rigid as stone and, amazed, became one of Patrick's most loyal disciples. Dichu donated a large barn named **Saul** (after *sabhal*, meaning barn) to serve as a chapel for Patrick, and this building became the first church in Ireland.

Patrick gained eternal fame for his actions on Easter Sunday of 433. On that day, druid **High King Laoghaire** (LEE-ree) had assembled the druid chieftains at the **Hill of Tara** (p. 166) for a feast. The King decreed that no one in the country would light a fire until the signal blaze in the castle had been lit. Patrick, celebrating Easter Eve with his followers across the way at the **Hill of Slane** (p. 175), ignited the Paschal Flame, both in defiance of the king's proclamation and in propagation of his own religion. Despite attempts by the druids to extinguish the flame, it burned on, and Patrick, dressed in vestments and clutching the gospel before the fire, struck an imposing figure. In the series of magical duels that ensued between Patrick and the druids, the saint was victorious. Patrick then produced a **shamrock** to explain the Holy Trinity: on one stem grow three leaves, just as Father, Son, and Holy Spirit are three divine persons in one God.

Patrick continued to use the shamrock as a visual aid in his teachings as he traveled throughout Ireland, preaching and converting people as he journeyed. Patrick built his cathedral in **Armagh,** Ulster (p. 544), and he baptized the King of Munster at the **Rock of Cashel** (p. 204). One of Patrick's favorite spots—and a place that remains a place of penance for modern pilgrims—was **Station Island,** a tiny island on Lough Derg. Patrick died in 493, and his body now rests in the Cathedral at **Downpatrick** (p. 530).

SAINT COLUMCILLE

Saint Columcille (a.k.a Columba, Columbcille, or Colmkille), the father of Celtic monasticism, was a renowned saint whose nose was always stuck in a book. He was born into wealth, to the lords of the O'Donnell clan in **Donegal** in AD 521. He went to school at Clonard in County Meath and studied under an ancient bard, an Irish poet who recited history in poetic form. Under his instruction, Columcille became an able poet as well. The bookish saint felt a calling to the church, and over the course of 15 years he founded monasteries throughout Durrow and **Kells** (p. 168). He led by example, and his monasteries promoted the values of asceticism, austerity, and scholarship by which he lived. Columcille transcribed over 300 books, and he composed the **Book of Durrow,** a later copy of which rests in the library of Trinity College in Dublin (p. 121).

According to legend, Columcille instigated war in 561 between the O'Neills of Ulster and King Diarmait after the king murdered one of the O'Neills. Another tale has it slightly differently: Columcille secretly copied the psalter of Saint Finnian—a big no-no that prompted Finnian to tattle to Diarmait. When Columcille refused the king's order to return the book, war ensued. Columcille chose to pray for the O'Neill clan, while Finnian prayed for the king's army. Columcille's prayers proved stronger, for Diarmait lost 3,000 men at the Battle of Cooldrevny. Filled with remorse, Columcille exiled himself from Ireland and vowed to convert 3,000 men to Christianity as penance. It is said that he spent his last night in Ireland on the **Bed of Loneliness** in Gartan Parish (p. 452) as he stared at the stars—the last time he would behold them over his native Ireland.

He subsequently sailed **Iona,** an island off the Scottish coast, where he established a monastery and continued to found churches and abbeys throughout the Great Glen. He had one more adventure in his life: confronting the Scottish **Loch Ness Monster** when Nessie tried to make off with one of his monks.

SAINT BRIGID

Saint Brigid (AD 451-525), the **Patroness of Ireland,** was a no-nonsense, religious beauty who knew exactly what she wanted. Born the daughter of a Leinster Prince in **Faughart,** five kilometers north of **Dundalk** (p. 176), Brigid refused several good offers of marriage, praying that God would relieve her of the bonds of her beauty so she could become a nun. Legend has it God answered her prayers, and Brigid took the veil from St. Macaille, soon rising to the rank of abbess under St. Mel.

According to legend, Brigid, seeking land on which her community of followers could thrive, asked the King of Leinster to grant her only the land over which her cloak would spread. Miraculously, her cloak covered all of Curragh. Brigid erected the Convent of *Cill-Dara* (Kildare), or "the church of the oak." She settled there with seven other nuns, and she soon established a neighboring monastery and a school of art. In conjunction with the convent, these additions made Kildare a bustling city of art and scholarship, featuring famous illuminated manuscripts, including the **Book of Kells** (p. 168).

After a life of traveling throughout Ireland, converting and healing people, Brigid died in Kildare in 525. She was originally laid to rest in the Kildare Cathedral, but in 879, due to Viking invasions, her body was moved to **Downpatrick** and placed alongside **St. Patrick** and **St. Columcille.** Devotees still visit Kildare, Downpatrick, and Faughart to worship her.

CÚCHULAINN

Cúchulainn, also known as the "Hound of Culann," or the "Hound of Ulster," is one of Ireland's best known semi-mythical heroes. Born to the mortal Diechtine and either Sualtam, her husband, or the god Lugh, Cúchulainn possessed semi-divine strength and became a great warrior. Known in childhood as Setanta, Cúchulainn gained his name by slaying (in alleged self-defense) the fierce watchdog of Culann the smith. According to legend, Cúchulainn took up arms at age 7 when he heard the druid prophesy that anyone who armed himself that day would be famous, though short-lived. This prophesy was fulfilled throughout Cúchulainn's life.

Cúchulainn fell in love with Emer, the daughter of Forgall the Wily. Forgall took being a protective father to a whole new level when he insisted that Cúchulainn train with warrior-woman Scathach, secretly hoping that Cúchulainn would be killed. Instead, the young hero learned much from Scathach, and he became a skilled warrior. At age 17, he single-handedly defended Ulster from the army of Connact in the Cattle Raid of Cooley. His demise came after he killed Cu Roi of Munster. Cu Roi's son, Lugaid, vowed to avenge his father's death by murdering Cúchulainn. Cúchulainn, as was customary of Celtic heroes, had taken a vow, or *gaesa*, both to always accept any meat offered to him and to never eat dog meat. Armed with this information, Lugaid was able to concoct a brilliant plan that caused Cúchulainn to break his *gaesa*—he offered him dog meat. Cúchulainn entered the impending fight with Lugaid spiritually weakened, and he was mortally wounded by Lugaid's spear. He tied himself to a pillar so he could remain standing, and his enemies only approached his corpse after a raven had landed on his shoulder. Lugaid beheaded Cúchulainn, but as he did so, Cúchulainn's sword fell, severing Lugaid's hand. Even in death, the hero remained an effective fighter.

FINN MCCOOL

Raised by a druidess and a warrior-woman, Liath Luachra, Finn McCool is one of Ireland's best-loved legendary heroes. Finn allegedly lived a life of hunting, fighting, sorcery, passion, and love. His greatest accomplishment was the creation of the **Giant's Causeway** (p. 567) near Portrush. According to legend, Finn single-handedly created this formation of volcanic rock after a Scottish giant mocked his fighting ability. Outraged, Finn threw a rock that included a challenge inside it all the way to Scotland. The cowardly giant refused the challenge, saying that he couldn't swim to far-away Ireland. Ever the gentleman, Finn took volcanic pillars and formed a causeway so that the giant could reach him and accept his challenge. Whether or not the causeway was the work of Finn McCool, it remains a remarkable attraction and is considered one of Great Britain's natural wonders.

FANTASTICAL FIGURES

LEPRECHAUNS

These mischievous little men are Ireland's best-known imaginary creation. Leprechauns are shoemakers by trade, but that's just their day job: their main responsibility is to guard the ancient treasure of the Danes. Leprechauns try their best to avoid greedy humans—they can vanish instantly if humans take their eyes off them—but if caught, they will offer either a pot of gold or three wishes for their freedom. Be careful, though; if you get a leprechaun to make this offer, it doesn't necessarily mean you've won. Leprechauns are notoriously crafty and foil many humans with their clever tricks. Though leprechauns consider themselves superior to the foolish, miserly Irishmen, they are undoubtedly Irish through and through: the little men like to maintain a slight buzz from home-brewed *poitín*.

BANSHEES

Banshees, ghost-like women who wail to signal someone's imminent death, are tragically misunderstood figures who get a bad rap just for being creepy. These women protect five ancient Irish families: the O'Neills, the O'Briens, the O'Connors, the O'Gradys, and the Kavanaghs. Banshees, complete with long, fair hair and blood-red eyes from incessant crying, adorn themselves in seriously eerie garb: either a long gray hooded cloak or a death shroud. It's understandable that the Banshee's appearance, coupled with her woeful wailing, creates a combination that can really freak people out. But the Banshee's cry is intended to be a helpful warning that gives the members of the family time to prepare themselves for death. If you've heard the cry of the Banshee, count your blessings: a dying person never hears her strident wail—no matter how hard he listens.

MERROWS

Merrows are the beautiful and clever mermaids who swim off the Irish coasts. Renowned for their grace and beauty, these creatures have the torsos of human women and the tails of fish. In counties Kerry, Cork, and Wexford, they wear small red feather caps that enable them to move swiftly through the water. In the north, they wear sealskins and adopt the appearance of seals while in the water. Whether she wears a cap or sealskin, if a merrow removes her clothes and abandons them, she cannot return to the sea until she retrieves them. Many lovesick Irishmen have stolen the discarded clothing of the beautiful merrows, luring them into marriage. Without her clothes, the merrow will be an obedient and docile wife, but as soon as she finds these clothes, remnants of her nautical past, the merrow will inevitably abandon her family and resume her life as a mermaid.

THE IRISH

DEMOGRAPHICS

Recent estimates put the Republic of Ireland's population at around 4.1 million—with approximately 40% living within 100km of Dublin—and Northern Ireland's at approximately 1.7 million. According to the most recent census, over 21% of Ireland's population is under 15. Ireland's birthrate is the highest in the EU, with an average 14.40 children per 1,000 people. However, rates are expected to drop slightly with increased use of contraception and as Irish couples begin to wait longer before having children.

The demographic composition of Ireland is usually described as mono-racial, but recent economic growth has inspired unprecedented immigration. This influx, a happy reverse of the historic emigration of the Irish people, includes the return of Irish citizens and people of Irish heritage, foreigners (including many Eastern Europeans) in search of jobs, and refugees seeking asylum. Racial diversity is still rare, especially in rural areas.

Though Britain itself boasts a multi-racial population, the demographic make-up of Northern Ireland resembles that of the Republic. Pervading cultural distinctions and disagreements in the Republic, and especially in Northern Ireland, continue to exist between people of different creeds (Protestants and Catholics, Republicans and Loyalists), not color.

RELIGION

The Republic of Ireland's population is almost 90% Catholic, making it one of the most Christian countries in the world. But the emergence of Catholicism didn't begin until St. Patrick's arrival some 1500 years ago. Before then, the island belonged to the Celts, a pagan people who worshipped a number of nature gods. When Christian missionaries arrived in the 5th century, they incorporated many Celtic traditions into Christian practice, easing Ireland's transformation into a devoutly Catholic land.

Since the days of St. Patrick, Catholicism has strongly influenced daily life and politics. The Church controls many state-funded hospitals, social services, and public schools that have mandatory religion classes. Sunday mass is a family event (often followed by a pint in the pub) and extreme respect is garnered by the local parish priests (who often share a round with parishioners after services). However, recent declines in church attendance reveal a society in the often paradoxical process of secularization. Though divorce has been legalized, the Republic officially restricts abortions to cases of danger to the mother (although it is common for Irish women seeking abortions to travel to England). Contraception was legalized in 1979, the same year that one third of the Irish population turned out to see the Pope speak in Phoenix Park. Homosexual acts were decriminalized in 1993. Christianity is nearly the only religion on the island, but tiny Jewish and Buddhist populations can be found in the cities.

The overlapping of religion, politics, and culture is more obvious in the North. Northern Ireland's primary religions are Protestantism and Catholicism (a minority at 40%). Though Protestants currently have a larger population, it is predicted that due to the higher birth rates of Catholics in the country, Catholics will outnumber Protestants within a couple of decades.

Though the Troubles in the North are often attributed to religious disagreement (which is certainly part of the problem), nationalism is the main cause of strife. Protestants, descended from Englishmen who were imported to Ireland, more often than not claim loyalty to England (Loyalists), while Catholics, more likely to be descended from the Irish masses abused by the English over the years, support the Republic (Republicans). Fighting usually erupts over a person's loyalty to country. For a complete history of the **Troubles,** see p. 483.

LANGUAGE

The English language came to Ireland with the Normans in the 12th century and eventually became the primary tongue. Like many things British, the Irish have molded the language to make it their own. The Irish accent, or "lilt," differs from county to county. In the southern and western counties, bring a notebook for communication, as the accent is often so thick and guttural that visitors may find it hard to understand conversations. In Dublin and in the North, expect clearer pronunciation and a sing-song style of conversing. Northerners' speech bears the mark of Scottish settlement.

Many people outside of Ireland do not realize that "Irish" is not just an accent. Because English is so commonly spoken in Ireland, the strong linguistic history of the **Irish language (Gaelic)** is often invisible to the average traveler. Though the constitution declares Irish the national language of the Republic, there are only 85,000 individuals living in exclusively Irish-speaking communities, or **gaeltacht** (GAYL-tacht). The *gaeltacht* is composed of small settlements scattered about the most remote regions of the island; those who wish to move there must be fluent. The most prominent of these are located in Connemara (see p. 387), in patches of Co. Donegal (p. 427), on the Dingle Peninsula (p. 311), on Cape Clear Island (p. 267), and in the Aran Islands (p. 377). These geographically disparate communities are further divided by four dialects: Ulster, Connacht, Munster, and An Caighdeán, the last of which is a combination of elements from each of the first three.

The Irish government continues efforts to preserve and promote modern Irish; Irish citizens are required to take *Gaelige* throughout their educational experience. Just over 40% of Irish are able to speak Gaelic, but only 1% are native speakers. A Connemara-based Irish radio station and an Irish-language television station, *Telifís na Gaelige* (T na G to locals), expand language opportunities for those interested in Irish. Peruse the **Glossary,** p. 595, for useful words and phrases.

IRISH CULTURE

MEAT AND POTATOES

Irish gastronomy has tended to center itself unequivocally on the staple of a truly Irish diet: the potato. Other ingredients may vary, but since its introduction to Ireland in the sixteenth century, the potato has been a constant feature in Irish meals. For just about 400 years, the Irish stuck to the potato and what they knew: bland, no-nonsense, traditional dishes that had been prepared for generations. In recent decades, a movement to westernize Irish food has diversified options throughout the country. New innovations and ideas have enabled the Irish to blend their traditional cuisine with the western passion for fresh produce, light cooking, and an array of flavorful sauces and accents. Though quality international restaurants can now be found throughout the island, don't worry—if you're craving a truly Irish concoction, you'll be able to find it.

Unsurprisingly, most Irish dishes feature potatoes. Traditional specialties include **colcannon** (potato with garlic and cabbage), **champ** (mashed potatoes with green onions and butter), and **boxty** (fried potato pancakes). **Irish stew,** a thick, hearty dish of lamb or mutton, potatoes, onions, parsley, and often Guinness, remains a popular choice, as does the traditional **Irish Breakfast** of bacon, eggs, sausage, fried tomatoes, and fried potatoes.

Many subsist on **pub grub,** cheap and tasty food served in local eateries. Typical pub grub includes Irish stew, meat pies, burgers, soup, and sandwiches. If you're in the mood for something quick, check out a **chipper** (fish and chips shop) or **takeaway** (takeout restaurant). Chippers feature fried whitefish and chips (french fries) served with salt and vinegar; ketchup sometimes costs extra.

Irish bards still sing the praises of the Clonakilty man who first concocted **black pudding.** This delicacy makes the most of the bits of the pig not usually eaten (some for good reason). Black pudding is, as one local butcher put it, "some pork, a good deal of blood, and grains and things—all wrapped up in a tube." Luckily, fewer and fewer pubs entice visitors with tubes of pork and blood, as eater-friendly **gastropubs** have become increasingly popular, especially in cities.

In addition to their meat and potatoes, the Irish love their bread. Be sure to try thick, fluffy loaves of **soda bread,** a heavy white bread made with soda instead of yeast, often prepared with raisins or spices. **Wheaten bread** is exactly the same as soda bread, except made with whole wheat rather than white flour. Other popular breads include **blaa,** a doughy white bun native to Waterford, **brown bread,** which is thick and grainy, and **batch loaves,** square-shaped bread used for sandwiches.

Recently, seafood—particularly shellfish—has become increasingly popular. Some cities hold oyster festivals; mussels and oysters can be found in the small fishing villages peppered across the Irish coast.

CUSTOMS AND ETIQUETTE

JUMPING THE QUEUE

In Ireland, when the occasion calls, people usually form orderly lines, or "queues." When people line up to get on a bus or enter a theater, the "queue" that forms is considered quite sacred. To "jump the queue"—to ignore the order of the line and push your way to the front—will earn you disapproving stares, and often, verbal confrontations or "flipped birds."

FLIPPING THE BIRD(S)

Another easy way to anger the locals is to flip someone the fingers. While in other countries people usually flip only their middle finger when someone lights their lawn on fire or steals their bike, the Irish flip both their middle finger and their index finger, forming a V shape. Flipping the birds is only insulting when you position your hand so that the palm is facing inward and move it upwards; if the palm is facing outward, you've just said "peace," you damned hippie.

BEING A PEOPLE-PERSON

The Irish are notoriously friendly and welcoming, and they stress the importance of being gregarious. Make sure to give everyone you meet a firm handshake—complete with eye contact—and to strike up conversation, even if you're in a taxi cab.

HOLDING YOUR TONGUE

There are certain topics that should never be brought up in casual conversation in Ireland, because the feelings that they instill in Irishfolk are anything but casual. Unless you're very familiar with your companions, avoid discussing the Troubles in Northern Ireland. Steer clear from conversations about religion as well. And remember that what may be funny in one culture can be terribly annoying in another. Unless you want to participate in a pub brawl, don't reference leprechauns, Lucky Charms, pots of gold, or the wee people. And of course, remember to reign in any proclivity for loud, obnoxious, or arrogant behavior. These traits will not earn you any friends at the local pub.

WATCH THE PDA

The Irish are incredibly reserved people, so try not to be too touchy-feely with them or in their presence. While a handshake is encouraged, a bear-hug is overwhelming. Irish conservatism extends to wardrobe as well: dress modestly and mind your manners.

THE PUB

The pub is the living room of the Irish household. Locals of all ages from every social milieu head to the public house for conversation, food, singing, and *craic* (KRACK), an Irish word meaning "a good time." Before hitting the pub, you should learn the ground rules.

GROUND RULES

Pub hours in the Republic are generally Monday through Saturday from 10:30am to 11:30pm (11pm in winter) and Sunday from 12:30 to 2pm and 4 to 11pm. **Late licenses,** increasingly common in Dublin, allow some pubs to stay open until midnight or 2am. Other pubs, especially ones catering to fishermen, have been granted special "early" licenses, requiring an act of Parliament to revoke, which allow them to open at 7:30am. Pubs almost never charge a cover or have a drink minimum. Pubs in the North tend to be open Monday through Saturday 11:30am to 11pm, until 1 or 2am on weekends, and Sunday from 12:30 to 2:30pm and 7 to 10pm. Some rural pubs close for a few hours on weekday afternoons. Pub **lunches** are usually served Monday through Saturday from 12:30 to 2:30pm, while soup, soda bread, and sandwiches are served all day. **Children** are often not allowed in pubs after 7pm. The legal drinking age in Ireland and Northern Ireland is 18.

DRINKS

Cocktails are a rarity found mainly in American-style bars and discos. In Ireland, expect **beer, whiskey,** and not much else.

BEER

Beer comes in two basic varieties: **lagers** (blond, fizzy brews served cold, a bit weaker than ales or stouts) and **ales** (slightly darker, more bitter, and sometimes served warmer than lagers). **Stout,** a type of ale, is thick, black in color, and made

WHISKEY BUSINESS

While Guinness is synonymous with Ireland the world over, Irish whiskey comes a close second as the unofficial national drink of the Emerald Isle. Indeed, seasoned Irish drinkers often chase a pint of Guinness ("a big one") with a glass of whiskey ("a small one"). Whiskey in Ireland was created by Medieval monks, who used the fiery tipple as an antidote to cold winters. In later years it was distilled at dangerous strengths in Irish homes, where the phrase "blind drunk" was sometimes quite literal. At the end of the 16th century, the English government cited spirits as the source of Irish unrest and declared martial law against all moonshiners, leading to the emergence of illegal establishments called *shabeens* selling extra-potent *poitín.*

Poitín is a 140-proof kick in the face. Culled from potatoes steeped in a mixture of apples, berries, and barley, then thrice-distilled in a gigantic copper worm, it is a clear liquid with a bouquet reminiscent of paint thinner. Because of its high alcohol content and risky mode of preparation, *poitín* is illegal. It is not served in pubs or brought out in polite company.

Most whiskey drinkers take their spirits neat, over ice, or with a bit of water. Other popular whiskey-based drinks are "hot Irish" (whiskey, lemon, cloves, brown sugar, and boiling water) and Irish coffee (black coffee, sugar, and whiskey, topped with cream).

from roasted barley, imparting a meaty flavor. **Guinness** stout is a rich, dark brew with a head thick enough for a match—or an incredibly small human—to stand on. For a sweeter taste, try it with black currant, cider, or other flavors. **Murphy's,** brewed in Cork, is a similar, slightly creamier stout. Cork also produces **Beamish,** a tasty "economy" stout (read: cheap date drink). Stout takes a while to pour properly (usually 3-4min.); it should be enjoyed in slow measure as well, and never before it settles. **Smithwicks** and **Kilkenny** are hoppy, English-style red ales. **Harp** is a popular domestic lager. Many young people swig imported American lagers, even though the worst Irish beer is far better than Budweiser. Beer is served in pint glasses (20 oz.) or half-pints (called a "glass"). Ordering a beer by name will bring you a full pint, so be loud and clear if you only want a half. A pint of Guinness costs about €4-6 in the Republic and about ₤3 in the North.

WHISKEY

Anyone who drinks this aggressive liquor as it's meant to be drunk—"neat," or straight—can tell you that there's a huge difference between Scotch whiskys (without an "e"), American whiskeys, and Irish whiskeys. Travelers to the island earn brownie points for preferring the local variety—but what actually makes an Irish whiskey Irish? The basic ingredients in whiskey—water, barley (which becomes malt once processed), and heat from a fuel source—are always the same. It's the quality of these ingredients, the way in which they're combined, and the means by which they're stored that gives each product its flavor. Irish whiskey is triple distilled in closed kilns, so it lacks the smoky flavor of Scotch and is much smoother. Apart from single malts, which are made from a single batch of malted barley and aged in casks, most Irish whiskey is blended from whiskeys made of malted and unmalted grain spirits.

Walk into a bar anywhere in the world, and you'll be able to find **Jameson,** the quintessential export of the Irish whiskey industry. Jameson, however, is only the tip of the iceberg. Ireland's two largest distilleries, **Bushmills** in Co. Antrim in the North (p. 568), and **Midleton** in Co. Cork (p. 250), produce the vast majority of Irish whiskey. Here are some of our picks, arranged by distillery:

BUSHMILLS. Bushmills distillery is the oldest licensed whiskey distillery in the world, having received its first grant to produce liquor in 1608.

■ **Black Bush:** More complex than Jameson, aged in Oloroso sherry casks, with a rewarding kick at the end.

Bushmills 16-year Single Malt: A high-end whiskey that's smooth as silk, aged successively in three casks made from three different kinds of wood. Goes down easy with pleasant aftertastes.

Bushmills 10-year Single Malt: Only connoisseurs can tell you what makes this different from the 16-year. The aging process yields a smooth finish with hints of vanilla.

MIDLETON. Midleton is the largest distillery in Ireland, home to Jameson and dozens of other brands. Use the cash you've been saving to splurge on **Midleton Very Rare,** Ireland's most fashionable whiskey. It's produced in limited quantities, with each bottle numbered and signed by the head distiller. At €120 a bottle, expect the best. If you haven't got hundreds of euro to spare, try these:

▨ **Powers:** One of the most popular Irish whiskeys, and one of the few available outside Ireland. Powers has a smooth, straightforward flavor with no frills.

Redbreast: A higher price pure pot still whiskey that's smoky, mysterious and altogether satisfying.

Crested 10: A first-rate blend of aged whiskeys put out by Jameson, with a light color and refreshingly crisp flavor.

Jameson: Originally distilled in Dublin, this hard-hitting whiskey is famous the world over as the benchmark of Irish whiskey. Has some tooth to it.

Paddy: A mostly unremarkable but drinkable whiskey that's popular for its lower price; a good choice for Irish coffee.

COOLEY. Ireland's only independent distillery (Bushmills and Midleton are both owned by Irish Distillers, a subsidiary of the French Pernod Ricard company), is the **Cooley distillery** in Co. Louth. It produces a number of fine whiskeys including **Locke's, Tyrconnell,** and **Connemara.** They're almost impossible to find, even in Ireland, but they're well worth the search (www.cooleywhiskey.com).

OTHER DRINKS. Urban pubs usually have a fully stocked bar and can make you whatever you desire, but outside of Dublin and Belfast your choices are often limited to whiskey or beer. It might take a little work to get a cocktail of any sort; if you do choose to humble yourself and try, expect to pay high prices, upwards of €9 for a basic cocktail in some pubs.

Irish coffee is sweetened with brown sugar and whipped cream and laced with whiskey. It's been more popular among tourists than natives ever since its alleged invention at Shannon Airport by a desperate bartender looking to appease cranky travelers on a layover. **Hot whiskey** (spiced up with lemon, cloves, and brown sugar) provides a cozy buzz. In the west, you may hear some locals praise **mountain dew,** code for **poitín** (pah-CHEEN), an illegal distillation sometimes given to cows in labor that ranges in strength from 115 to 140 proof. *Poitín* makes after-hours appearances in pubs throughout Ireland, but be warned that *poitín* is highly toxic: while most alcoholic drinks are based on ethanol, *poitín* uses lethal methanol.

HOW TO GET YOUR DRINK

Pubs have no waitstaff. Try to catch the barman's eye and wait your turn. If you're in a group, don't order individual drinks: have one person buy the whole round. Once these drinks are finished, someone else buys the next round. This continues until everyone has bought a round. Order at the bar, pay the bartender, and carry your drink anywhere in the pub. Most pubs reward exploration with outlandishly cozy nooks and galleries or outdoor tables. A bell will ring to announce last call.

Never tip in a pub. Doing so implies that the bartender is inferior rather than an equal. If you want to thank him or her (e.g., if you're ordering a large number of drinks), you can end your order with "And one for yourself?" The bartender may accept your offer and add the price of his drink onto your order, though he or she might not pour for themselves right away. This is a courtesy and is never expected.

FOOD

WHAT TO EXPECT

Pub lunches are usually served Monday to Saturday from 12:30 to 2:30pm, while soup, soda bread, and sandwiches are served all day. Standard pub grub consists of sandwiches and soup in the afternoon and Irish classics in the evening: sausages, meat pies, and jacket (baked) potatoes. The **gastropub**, a new type of pub proliferating in urban areas, serves modern, trendy food in a traditional atmosphere, usually with delicious results but higher prices.

HOW TO GET YOUR FOOD

Choose from the chalkboard menu, then order at the bar. Bring your drink to your table; the bartender will bring you your meal when it's ready. **Never tip.**

IRISH LITERARY TRADITIONS

THE IRISH LANGUAGE

The Irish language is called *Gaeilge* (GALE-ga) by its speakers; the English translation "Gaelic" (GAY-lik) can also refer to Scottish Gaelic, another Celtic language. In 1600, the Irish language matched the popularity of English worldwide. The Anglophones, however, had more money and better armies; over the next 250 years, Irish became the language of the disenfranchised (see **Language,** p. 63).

Irish re-entered the lives of the privileged classes with the Gaelic Revival. In 1893, **Douglas Hyde** (Éire's first President) founded the **Gaelic League** to spread the everyday use of Irish as part of a larger project of de-Anglicization.

LEGENDS AND FOLKTALES

In early Irish society, a bard's (from the Irish *baird*) songs of battles, valor, and lineage served as a chieftain's sole news source for state affairs. Poetry and politics were so intertwined that the *fili*, trained poets, and *breitheamh* (BREH-huv), judges of the Brehon Laws, were often the same people. The poet-patron relationship was as symbiotic in Ireland as anywhere else—the poet earned his lord's favor (and food and shelter) by dishing out praise and mystical support.

In later years, legendary tales were written down for posterity. The famous **Book of Invasions** (*Leabhar Gabhála;* LOWR GA-vah-lah) is a long-winded record of the pre-Christian cultures and armies that have invaded Ireland. The **Ulster Cycle,** a collection of old Irish folktales, includes the adventures of King Conchobar (Conor) of Ulster and his clan, the **Ulaid.** The central tale of the *Ulster Cycle* is the **Táin Bó Cuailnge** (Cattle Raid of Cooley), in which Queen Medbh—Conchobar's archenemy and, incidentally, his ex-wife—decides first to steal the most famous bull in the country, the Donn of Cooley. For more on Cú Chulainn, see **Saints and Heroes,** p. 59.

WIT AND RESISTANCE

After the English dispossessed the Irish chieftains at the **Battle of Kinsale** (see p. 52), most Irish writers foresaw the imminent collapse of Irish language and culture. As the bards of the Irish courts lost their high status, they carried on their work among the peasant classes. Thus began Ireland's vernacular literary culture. Most of the authors writing in Irish at this time lamented their home as a land under cultural attack; a common metaphor treated Ireland as a captive woman, like the dark and beautiful *Roisin Dubh* ("black rose").

By the 17th century, wit and satire began to characterize the emerging modern Irish literature. In Dublin, **Jonathan Swift** (1667-1745), Dean of St. Patrick's Cathedral, addressed the state of the Irish peasant with sophisticated and misanthropic wit. Swift's razor-sharp satiric pamphlets and essays took pot-shots at cruel English lords but still managed to defend the Protestant Church of Ireland. Most notable is his "A Modest Proposal," in which he facetiously argues that the way to cure overpopulation and poverty in one stroke is for the wealthy lords to eat the babies of the poor.

In the mid-19th century, the Famine hit, and folk culture fell by the wayside in the face of destitution. Cosmopolitan Dublin managed to breed talent, but gifted young writers traded the Liffey for the Thames in order to make their names. **Oscar Wilde** (1856-1900) moved to, or perhaps created, the high aesthetic culture of London. More witty than insightful, and more vicious than profound, his best-known play is ▨*The Importance of Being Earnest* (1895). Prolific playwright **George Bernard Shaw** (1856-1950) was also born in Dublin but moved to London in 1876, where he became an active socialist. His work *John Bull's Other Island* (1904) depicts the increasing hardships of the Irish peasant laborer.

THE REVIVAL

Toward the end of the 19th century, the crop of young Irish writers no longer turned to London to cultivate their talent. Rather, a vigorous and enduring effort known today as the **Irish Literary Revival** took over the scene. Members of this movement turned to Irish culture, from its ancient mythology to contemporary folktales, for inspiration. At the forefront of the movement was **Lady Augusta Gregory** (1852-1932), who brought Irish culture to the masses by translating forgotten texts and collecting the folktales and legends of Galway's poor residents.

Gregory joined poet **William Butler Yeats** (1865-1939), the first Irishman to win the Nobel Prize, in founding the **Abbey Theatre** in Dublin to bolster a school of Irish dramatic literature (see p. 132). But conflict almost immediately arose among various contributors. Was this new body of drama to be written in verse or prose, in the tradition of the realistic or the fantastic and heroic? In theory, the plays would be written in Irish, but in practice they needed to be written in English. A sort of compromise was found in the work of **John Millington Synge** (1871-1909), whose English plays were perfectly Irish in essence. His experiences with locals in bucolic Ireland gave him the subject matter for his black comedy *The Playboy of the Western World* (1907), which destroys the pastoral myth of Irish peasantry. His masterpiece, ▨*Riders to the Sea*, imbues the struggles of a family on the Aran Islands with sublime and mythic gravity. **Sean O'Casey** (1880-1964) caused riots at the Abbey with the 1926 premiere of *The Plough and Star*, which depicted the Easter Rebellion without mythologizing its leaders.

MODERNISM: JOYCE AND BECKETT

Many authors still found Ireland too insular an island to suit their literary aspirations. **James Joyce** (1882-1941) headlines the cast of inky Irish expatriates. Joyce was born and educated in Dublin, but he left forever in 1904, saying: "How sick, sick, sick, I am of Dublin! It is the city of failure, of rancour and of unhappiness. I long to be out of it." Joyce's writing, however, always clung to Ireland—describing exclusively the lives of the denizens of Dublin. Joyce's most accessible work is a collection of short stories titled *Dubliners* (1914). His first novel, *A Portrait of the Artist as a Young Man* (1914), recounts Joyce's own youth and his decision to abandon his country, religion, and family. The structure of *Ulysses* (1922), Joyce's ground-breaking Modernist (mock) epic loosely resembles Homer's *Odyssey*—hence the title—but rather than tackling 10 years and half the known world, Joyce deals with a single day in 1904 Dublin. This epic day is marked each June 16 by "Bloomsday" festivities of the literary and inebriate kind (see p. 136). While the Republic forked over big bucks to host a six-month retrospective of *Ulysses* in

2004, culminating in the centenary Bloomsday festival, Joyce's home has not always been so kind to him; his works faced a de facto ban until the 1960s.

Samuel Beckett (1906-89), a postmodern writer before the term existed, concerned himself with the pain, loneliness, and minutiae that many of his characters mistook for living. During expat reunions in Paris, Joyce dictated parts of *Finnegan's Wake* to Beckett. Beckett's poems, novels, and plays, including the absurdist masterpiece *Waiting for Godot*, earned him a place in the canon alongside his mentor Joyce. Unlike Joyce, Beckett sought to rid his prose of Irishness. By writing much of his work in French before translating it into English, he eliminated the colloquialisms that might have worked against his universal subject matter.

POEMS, PLAYS, AND PLOTS

After the 1940s, Irish poetry once again commanded widespread appreciation. Living in the backwash of the Revival and the Civil War, this generation of Irish poets questioned their cultural inheritance, finding a new version of Ireland to complicate the old one. **Patrick Kavanaugh** (1906-67) debunked a mythical Ireland in poems such as *The Great Hunger* (1945), which was banned for its obscenities and prompted the Irish police to visit Kavanaugh's house and seize the manuscript. The works of **Thomas Kinsella** and **John Montague** display an awareness of the history of Irish poetry with a sensitivity to mid-19th-century civil strife. Although some poets are political to the point of propaganda, much contemporary Irish poetry is intensely private. Poets like **Eavan Boland** treat political issues only indirectly. Perhaps the most famous contemporary Irish poet is **Seamus Heaney** ("Famous Seamus"), winner of the 1995 Nobel Prize in Literature. Born in rural County Derry, Heaney became a controversial figure after leaving the North for the Republic. For more on Heaney, see **Literary Voices,** p. 490.

The dirt of Dublin continues to provide fodder for generations of writers. Notorious wit, playwright, poet, and terrorist **Brendan Behan** strung together semi-autobiographical works about delinquent life, such as his play *The Quare Fellow* (1954). Mild-mannered schoolteacher **Roddy Doyle** wrote the well-known Barrytown trilogy about the Rabbitte family in Dublin (see **Film,** p. 77), as well as the acclaimed *The Woman Who Walked Into Doors* (1996). Doyle won the Booker Prize in 1994 for *Paddy Clarke Ha Ha Ha.*

Frank McGuinness and **Brian Friel** top the list of contemporary Irish playwrights. Friel's *Dancing at Lughnasa* (1990) became a Broadway hit and a Meryl Streep-blessed movie, and McGuinness's war drama *Observe the Sons of Ulster Marching Towards the Somme* has enjoyed international success. **Martin McDonagh's** *The Beauty Queen of Leenane* (1996) has gained fame and four Tony awards. **Conor McPherson's** *The Weir* won the 1998 Olivier Award for "Best New Play" and captivated sold-out Broadway audiences with comic and poignant tales told in a rural Irish pub. Important critics and essayists include **Conor Cruise O'Brien,** a former diplomat who writes about everything—history, literature, politics; **Denis Donoghue** and his vigorous, skeptical *We Irish;* and the provocative **Declan Kiberd,** whose Ireland is a postcolonial society more like India than England.

A pair of Limerick-born brothers immigrated to New York and caught the next train to best-sellerdom. **Frank McCourt** won the Pulitzer Prize for his 1996 memoir about his poverty-stricken childhood, *Angela's Ashes* (1996), and followed up with the sequel *'Tis* (2000). His most recent work, *Teacher Man* (2006), chronicles his experiences as both a high school teacher and college professor. Not to be outdone, **Malachy** "the brother of Frank" **McCourt** published his own memoir *A Monk Swimming* (1999), and has since authored a number of other books, including *Danny Boy: The Legend of the Beloved Irish Ballad* (2002) and *A History of Ireland* (2004).

MUSIC

TRADITIONAL FOLK MUSIC AND DANCE

Despite Queen Elizabeth I's best efforts to extinguish it, Irish traditional music has continued rollicking through the centuries. **Trad** is the array of dance rhythms, repeated melodies, and embellishments that has been passed down through countless generations of musicians. A typical pub session will sample from a variety of types, including reels, jigs, hornpipes, and slow airs. These tunes can be written down, but a traditional musician's training consists largely of listening to and reproducing others' tunes. As a result of this inexact way of teaching and training, the same tune may sound different each time it's played.

Trad may be heard in two ways: studio-canned and pub-impromptu. Best-selling recording artists include **Altan, De Danann,** and the **Chieftains.** Equally excellent groups are the **Bothy Band** and **Planxty** of the 1970s, and, more recently, **Nomos, Solas, Dervish,** and **Deanta.** These bands have brought Irish music into international prominence, starting with the early recordings of the Chieftains and their mentor **Sean O'Riada,** who fostered the resurrection of trad from near-extinction to a national art form. While recording bands perform regularly at concerts, most traditional musicians play before more intimate audiences at their local pubs. A **session** occurs when musicians gather at the pub to play together; they are the best way to witness authentic musical performances. Though anyone can join in the music, trad sessions are not just casual jams. Musicians are expected to know the melodies. *Let's Go* lists many pubs with regular trad, but you'll find the best sessions by asking local enthusiasts. Pubs in Counties Kerry, Galway, Sligo, and Donegal have deservedly good reputations. For the best trad in quantity and quality, find a **fleadh** (FLAH), a musical festival at which musicians' scheduled sessions spill over into nearby pubs. **Comhaltas Ceoltóirí Éireann,** the national Trad music association, organizes *fleadhs.* (☎01 280 0295; www.comhaltas.com.)

Purists get in heated arguments about what constitutes "traditional" singing. A style of unaccompanied vocals called *sean-nós* ("old-time") is the oldest form on the island, though perhaps not the easiest on the ears. This style of nasal singing descends from keening, an ancient practice of wailing lamentation. Vocalists sing each verse of a song differently, peppering the song with syllabic embellishments and tonal variations. A popular young practitioner of this style is **Iarla O'Lionaird** of Cork. More common than *sean-nós* is folk singing, usually guitar- or mandolin-accompanied ballads. Harps, though the national symbol, are tough to drag through a pub door; you're more likely to find an assortment of fiddles, accordions, tin whistles, and guitars as well as the more traditional *uilleann* pipes (a more sophisticated version of the bagpipe) and *bodhrán* (a hand-held drum struck with a double-ended mallet). Sessions in pubs typically alternate between fast-paced traditional instrumental music and folk songs. Ireland's favorite traditional songsters include **Dominick Behan, The Dubliners, Christy Moore,** and **Sean Tyrell.**

Hard-shoe dancing involves creating a percussion accompaniment by pounding the floor with foot-loose fury. Individual **step-dancing** and group **set-dancing** are centuries-old practices, but the spontaneous and innovative streak in each is fading fast. Today, traditional dancing follows the regimentation of formal competitions, where rigid-torsoed dancers compete according to rote standards of perfection. *Céilís* (KAY-lees), at which attendants participate in traditional Irish set-dancing, still take place in most towns. The televised, pyrotechnic-accompanied spectacles *Riverdance* and *Lord of the Dance* offer loose, stylized interpretations—don't expect any of that Michael Flatley nonsense at the local pub.

IRISH ROCK, PUNK, AND POP

Just as they adapted and exported trad, the Irish also have become adept at transforming outside forms of music to fit their native style. Starting in the 1970s, Irish music fused with British and American Rock and Roll, ultimately crating a uniquely Irish sound. **Van Morrison** was particularly skilled at drawing inspiration from American rhythm and blues, which he combined with Celtic "soul." **Horslips** became hugely popular in the 70s by trying to merge trad and rock forms but wound up shuffling uneasily between the two. **The Pogues** succeeded where Horslips failed, fusing angry, drunken post-punk with whirling trad and Shane MacGowan's slurred, poetic lyrics. **Enya** used Irish lyricism and electronics to create a bland New Age sound. More recently, **Afro-Celt Sound System** achieved popular and critical success through its fusion of traditional Celtic and African sounds with manic rhythms of drum and bass. Irish-American fiddler **Eileen Ivers** is known as the "Jimi Hendrix of the violin."

Irish musicians have dabbled in practically every genre of purebred rock. In the 70s, **Thin Lizzy** produced early heavy metal. Dublin nurtured a thriving post-punk scene in the late 70s and 80s. In Belfast, **Stiff Little Fingers** spat forth three years' worth of excellent anthems. **Ash** heralded a 90s revival of the Belfast punk aesthetic; their album *1977* (1996) reached number one on the UK charts. **My Bloody Valentine** formed in Ireland in 1984 before moving to London; music critics commonly call their 1991 album **Loveless** the best rock album ever recorded.

Ireland's musicians have also set their sights on mainstream superstardom— exemplified by ▨**U2**, Ireland's biggest rock export. From the adrenaline-soaked promise of 1980's *Boy*, the band ascended into the stratosphere, culminating in world-wide fame with *The Joshua Tree* (1987) and the sublime *Achtung, Baby* (1991). The acclaimed *How to Dismantle an Atomic Bomb* (2005) reiterated the overwhelming success of the group, which has won 22 Grammys—a record number tied with Stevie Wonder for contemporary artists. **Sinéad O'Connor** became a phenomenon in the 1990s, not only for her breathy lyrics but also for her vocal support of the IRA. The lowercase **cranberries** and the sibling-based **Corrs** cornered the international soft rock market in the 1990s. The boy-group **Boyzone** conquered the UK charts and the hearts of millions of pre-adolescent girls; similar black magic was practiced on the opposite sex by the girl-group **B*witched.**

New bands continue to draw inspiration from the Irish, incorporating pub-style music into their songs. Irish-American bands **Flogging Molly, the Dropkick Murphys,** and **the LeperKhanz** all share this style.

FILM

Since the 1950s, when John Wayne's 1952 film *The Quiet Man* gave an international audience of millions their first view of the island, Ireland's lush landscape and low labor costs have lured mainstream directors to the Emerald Isle. Alfred Hitchcock filmed Sean O'Casey's *Juno and the Paycock* with the Abbey Theatre Players in 1930. Robert Flaherty's classic documentary about coastal fishermen, *Man of Aran* (1934) has become a favorite. American director John Huston, who eventually made Ireland his home, shot many films there; his last work, *The Dead* (1987), is the film version of the masterpiece from Joyce's *Dubliners*.

In the last few decades, the Irish film industry has grown, thanks to the Irish Film Board (*Bord Scannan na hEireann*). Recently, the industry has become increasingly focused on creating uniquely Irish films. In the past, many films were censored or banned due to the involvement of the Catholic Church, but such censorship has decreased significantly in recent years. A new desire to portray the real Ireland has resulted in a less idealistic but equally tender vision of the country. **Jim Sheridan** helped kick off the Irish cinematic renaissance with his universally acclaimed adaptation of Christy Brown's autobiography, *My Left Foot* (1991). More recently, Sheridan has worked again with actor Daniel Day-Lewis in two films that take a humanistic approach to the lives of Catholics and Protestants during the Troubles with *In the Name of the Father* (1993) and *The Boxer* (1997). Another Dublin saga, *The General* (1998), by the English director John Boorman, remembers the rise and fall of one of the most notorious criminals in recent Irish history, Martin Cahill. *Roddy Doyle* (see **Irish Literary Traditions,** p. 68) saw the first slice of his Barrytown trilogy, ◪*The Commitments*, hit the silver screen in 1991. Dublin native **Neil Jordan** has become a much sought-after director thanks to the success of *Michael Collins* (1996), *The Good Thief* (2002), and *Breakfast on Pluto* (2005). Fairytale Ireland is captured in *The Secret of Roan Inish* (1995) and *Into the West* (1993). *An Everlasting Piece* (2000), about a wig salesman in Belfast, found international success for its comedic portrayal of the everyday interactions of Protestants and Catholics. The tradition of creating films that depict political and religious troubles in Ireland lives on in *The Wind that Shakes the Barley* (2006), the story of two brothers who are torn apart by anti-British sentiment, and the winner of the Palme d'Or at the Cannes Film Festival, 2006. The Irish are also exploring new genres of film, including musicals: *Once* (2006) is an acclaimed modern-day musical love story.

The **Galway Film Fleadh,** held in July, is Ireland's version of Cannes, appropriately reduced in scale but still featuring a week's worth of quality films. If you're interested in attending a festival that focuses on creativity and filmmakers who work with new technology, check out the early summer's **Darklight Film Festival** in Dublin. The **Dublin Film Festival** runs for a week in the early spring. Dublin also hosts the **Junior Dublin Film Festival** in late November, showing the world's best children's films. In Northern Ireland, the **Foyle Film Festival** takes place in Derry in November. The **Belfast Film Festival** in Belfast runs for a week in early spring.

NEWSPAPERS AND OTHER MEDIA

The Irish media style is more similar to that of Great Britain than other countries in Europe given the prominence of national daily newspapers over local newspapers. Traditionally, Irish people are fond of their newspapers—91% of Irish adults read newspapers regularly. Together, the Republic and Northern Ireland support eight national **dailies,** the most popular in the Republic being the *Irish Independent* (www.independent.ie) and the *Irish Time* (www.ireland.com). Other papers in the Republic include the *Irish Examiner*, *Irish Daily Star*, and *Evening Herald*. The best-selling paper in the North is the *Belfast Telegraph* (www.belfasttelegraph.co.uk). Other Northern papers include the *Irish News*, a pro-democratic labor party paper, the *Belfast Newsletter*, a socialist party publication, and the evening *Belfast Telegraph.* Many towns also have weekly local newspapers, and some larger cities have two. Dublin remains one of the only cities that does not have its own paper. The country also has several Republic of Ireland editions of British Newspapers, especially **tabloids,** such as the *Irish Sun*, *Irish Mirror*, and *Irish Star*.

Radio came to Ireland when the BBC started broadcasting in Belfast in 1924. Two years later, the Irish Free State started the radio station 2RN in Dublin. Television invaded the country in 1953 with the BBC's first broadcast in Northern Ireland, quickly followed by Ulster TV (UTV) in 1959. In 1961, the Republic's national radio service made its first television broadcast under the name **Radio Telefís Eireann (RTE).** In 1994, **TG4** came out with the Irish Language Service, and commercial broadcasts started in 1998 with **TV3.**

SPORTS AND RECREATION

The Irish take enormous pride in their two native sports: **Gaelic football** and **hurling.** Any Irish sporting event can end in hysteria, when hordes of fans bedecked in their county colors bring bedlam to Irish city streets. Attending a pub the day of its county's game will leave you deaf, drunk, and counting down to the next round.

Most traditional Irish sports are modern versions of contests fought between whole clans across expanses of countryside. In 1884, the **Gaelic Athletic Association**

(GAA) was founded to establish official rules and regulations for hurling, Gaelic football, and other ancient Irish recreational activities (www.gaa.ie). A secondary function of their efforts was to promote a truly Irish identity, free of Anglo intrusion. The organization's first patron was Archbishop Croke of Cashel and Emly; his name later came to adorn Croke Park in Dublin, Ireland's biggest Gaelic-games stadium. The GAA divided the island on a club-county-province level, in which the club teams are organized mostly according to parish lines. Ultimately arranged into the four provinces, Connacht, Munster, Leinster, and Ulster, all 32 counties of the island compete in the knockout rounds of the two "All Ireland" Championships, but only two make it to the finals in September. Despite the nationalism of its beginnings, the GAA has always included teams from Northern Ireland in these leagues. At the moment, the GAA identity is undergoing a major transition. In April 2005, it voted to lift its longstanding ban on foreign sports, opening Croke Park to soccer and rugby. Up until 1971, the GAA did not permit its members to attend, let alone to host, soccer or rugby matches. The 2005 vote was deeply symbolic; many remember Croke Park as the site where British paramilitaries opened fire at a Gaelic football match in 1920, killing 13.

GAELIC FOOTBALL

Although it may seem like the love-child of American football and British rugby, Gaelic football is older than both. Players may run holding the leather ball for no more than four paces, after which they must bounce, kick, or punch it. One point is scored for putting the ball over the crossbar between the posts, three for netting it. The game is played by both men and women in teams of 15 for two 30-minute periods. The finals of the inter-county competition, known as the All-Ireland Final, are held at the end of September in Croke Park. The winning team receives the Sam Maguire Cup.

HURLING

As fans like to say, if football is a game, then hurling is an art. This fast and dangerous-looking sport named after the stick with which it is played—the *caman* or "hurley"—started in the 13th century. The hurley—like a hockey stick with a shorter and wider blade—is used to hit the ball along the ground or as far as 80m overhead. Players also kick the ball or hit it with the flat of their hands. The *sliothar* (ball) is leather-covered and can be either caught for hitting or carried along on the stick. Teams of 15 players each try to score a point by hitting the ball over the eight-foot-high crossbar of the goalposts. By hitting the ball under the crossbar past the goalkeeper players can score a "goal" (or *cúl*) worth three points. The female version of hurling is called **camogie,** and requires considerably more protective wear. Athletes have the opportunity to compete in the All-Ireland Senior Hurling Championship for the Liam McCarthy Cup. The finals are held in early September at Croke Park.

ROAD BOWLING

Imagine a game of golf. Make the fairway a nice winding stretch of Irish asphalt, about 4km long, lined with screaming fans who place bets on the action. Replace that cute little white dimpled ball with 28 oz. of solid iron. Now you've got something like road bowling. Oh, and clubs are for wimps. Just wind up and fling that sucker—check for cars first. The player who reaches the pre-determined destination with the fewest strokes wins. The sport enjoys its most enthusiastic following in the North, particularly in County Armagh, but can also be found on the twisty roads of County Cork. Ireland's most famous road bowler is County Cork's own Mike Barry. He won an unprecedented eight All-Ireland titles from 1965 to 1975.

FOOTBALL AND OTHERS

Imported to Ireland in 1878, **football** (or soccer) inspires an equally fanatical, if less patriotic, following as do hurling and Gaelic football. The Irish are also fiercely devoted to the football clubs of England, with Liverpool and Manchester United as the local favorites. Much to the dismay of football fans in Ireland, the Republic failed to qualify for the recent World Cup in Germany in 2006. The disappointing result led to the retirement of popular footballer Roy Keane. **Rugby** has a strong fan base in both the Republic and Northern Ireland; when Ireland's not playing, expect people to cheer for the English team. One of the most popular teams is the British and Irish Lions, which consists of the top players from England, Ireland, Scotland, and Wales. The Lions typically go on tour to play Australia, New Zealand, and South Africa. **Horse racing** maintains a devoted following in the Republic, thanks to Co. Kildare's championship breeding grounds. The **Galway Races** festival, held during the last week of July, draws thoroughbred racing fans from throughout the country. Water like **surfing** and **sailing** are popular hobbies, particularly along the Western and Northwestern coasts. The lawns of world-class **golf courses** line the Irish countryside.

HOLIDAYS AND FESTIVALS

For more information, contact the appropriate regional tourist office, or the national tourist boards for the Republic and Northern Ireland. **Starred dates** are national holidays—expect businesses to be closed or operating on Sunday hours.

DATE 2008	DATE 2009	CITY OR REGION	FESTIVAL
WINTER			
*December 25	*December 25	Republic and UK	Christmas Day
*December 26	*December 26	Republic and UK	Boxing Day/St. Stephen's Day
*January 1	*January 1	Republic and UK	New Year's Day
Mid-February	Mid-February	Dungarvan	Dungarvan Jazz Festival
Feb.-Mar.	Feb.-Mar.	Dublin	Dublin Film Festival
*March 17	*March 17	Republic and Northern Ireland	St. Patrick's Day
March	March	Achill Island	Achill Island Walking Festival
SPRING			
*March 21	*April 10	Republic and UK	Good Friday
*March 23	*April 12	Republic and UK	Easter Sunday
*March 24	*April 13	Republic and UK	Easter Monday
Late April	Late April	Galway	Cúirt International Literary Festival
*May 5	*May 4	Republic and UK	May Day Bank Holiday
Early May	Early May	Wicklow	Wicklow Mountains Spring Walking Festival
Early May	Early May	Bantry	Bantry Regatta
*June 2	*June 1	Republic and UK	Bank Holiday
Mid-June	Mid-June	Dublin	Bloomsday Festivities
SUMMER			
Mid-Late June	Mid-Late June	Cork	Cork Midsummer Festival
Mid-Late June	Mid-Late June	Dublin	Dublin Gay Pride Festival
Late June	Late June	The Curragh, Co. Kildare	Irish Derby
Early July	Early July	Kells	Kells Heritage Festival
Early July	Early July	Bangor	Bangor Regatta
Early July	Early July	Bray	Bray Seaside Festival
Early July	Early July	Galway	Galway Film Fleadh
July	July	Tipperary	Pride of Tipperary Festival
*July 12	*July 12	Northern Ireland	Orange Day
July 14	July 13	Northern Ireland	Battle of the Boyne (Orangemen's Day)

Mid-July	Mid-July	Drogheda	Samba Festival
Mid-July	Mid-July	Killarney	Killarney Races
Mid-July	Mid-July	Ballina	Ballina Street Festival
Mid-Late July	Mid-Late July	Galway	Galway Arts Festival
Late July-Early August	Late July-Early August	Belfast	Belfast Gay Pride Festival
Late July	Late July	Buncrana, Co. Donegal	Buncrana Music Festival
Late July	Late July	Galway	Galway Races
Late July-Early August	Late July-Early August	Dungloe	Mary from Dungloe International Festival
Late July-Early August	Late July-Early August	Wicklow	Regatta Festival
Early August	Early August	Waterford Harbor	Spraoi Festival
*August 4	*August 3	Republic of Ireland	Bank Holiday
Early August	Early August	Kinsale	Regatta and Welcome Home Festival
Early August	Early August	Glencolmcille	Folk Festival
Early August	Early August	Dingle	Dingle Races
August	August	Warrenpoint	Maiden of Mournes Festival
Mid-August	Mid-August	Cobh	Cobh People's Regatta
Mid-August	Mid-August	Cushendall	Heart of the Glens Festival
August 18	Mid-August	Clifden	Connemara Pony Show
August 21	August 21	Knock	Feast of Our Lady of Knock
Mid-Late August	Mid-Late August	Kilkenny	Arts Week
Late August	Late August	Derry/Londonderry	Feile An Chreagain
Late August	Late August	Armagh	All-Ireland Road Bowl Finals
Late August	Late August	Tralee	Rose of Tralee International Festival
Late August	Late August	Republic of Ireland	Fleadh Cheoil na hÉireann
August and September	August and September	Lisdoonvarna	Lisdoonvarna Matchmaking Festival
Early September	Early September	Cape Clear Island	International Storytelling Festival
Early September	Early September	Cork	Folk Festival
September	September	Dublin	All-Ireland Hurling and Football Finals
September	September	Dublin	Dublin Fringe Festival
September	September	Glenties	Fiddlers' Weekend
AUTUMN			
Late September	Late September	Galway	Galway International Oyster Festival
Late September	Late September	Westport	Arts Festival
Late September	Late September	Clifden	Community Arts Festival
Early to Mid-October	Early to Mid-October	Cork	Murphy's Film Festival
October	October	Kinsale	Kinsale Fringe Jazz Festival
Mid-October	Mid-October	Belfast	Festival at Queen's
October	October	Ennis	October Arts Festival
October	October	Kinsale	Kinsale International Festival of Food and Wine
*October 27	*October 26	Republic and UK	Halloween
October 31	October 31	Derry/Londonderry	Banks of the Foyle Carnival
Late October	Late October	Dublin	Samhain Halloween Parade
Late October	Late October	Cork	Guinness Jazz Festival
November	November	Ennis	November Trad Festival

ADDITIONAL RESOURCES

GENERAL HISTORY

A History of Ireland, by Mike Cronin. St. Martin's Press, 2001.

Eyewitness to Irish History, by Peter Berresford Ellis. Wiley Publishing, 2007.

Hope Against History: The Course of Conflict in Northern Ireland, by Jack Holland. Henry Holt, 1999.

In Search of Ireland Heroes: The Story of the Irish from the English Invasion to the Present Day, by Carmel McCaffrey. Ivan R. Dee Publishing, 2006.

The IRA, by Tim Pat Coogan. St. Martin's Press, 2001.

The Irish Famine, by Gray and Burns. Abrams, Harry N Inc., 1995.

Malachy McCourt's History of Ireland, by Malachy McCourt. Running Press, 2004.

The Oxford History of Ireland, by R.F. Foster. Oxford University Press, 2001.

Reinventing Ireland: Culture and the Celtic Tiger, by Cronin, Kirby, and Gibbons. Pluto Press, 2002.

FICTION AND NON-FICTION

The Cambridge Companion to Modern Irish Culture, by Cleary and Connolly. Cambridge University Press, 2005.

The Cambridge Companion to Twentieth-Century Irish Drama, by Shaun Richards. Cambridge University Press, 2004.

The Contemporary Irish Novel, by Linden Peach. Palgrave MacMillan, 2004.

How the Irish Saved Civilization: The Untold Story of Ireland's Heroic Role from the Fall of Rome to the Rise of Medieval Europe, by Thomas Cahill. Doubleday, 1995.

The Irish Martyr, by Russell Working. University of Notre Dame Press, 2006.

Ireland: A Novel, by Frank Delaney. HarperCollins, 2005.

Killing Rage, by Eamon Collins. Granta Books, 1999.

Pint-Sized Ireland: In Search of the Perfect Guinness, by Evan McHugh. Thomas Dunne Books, 2007.

Round Ireland With a Fridge, by Tony Hawks. St. Martin's Press, 2000.

FILM

For Irish films, search the websites www.irishfilmboard.ie, www.irishfilm.net and www.irishfilm.ie, or peruse the following books.

Contemporary Irish Cinema: From the Quiet Man to Dancing at Lughnasa, by James MacKillop. Syracuse University Press, 1999.

Irish Film: The Emergence of a Contemporary Cinema, by Martin McLoone. University of California Press, 2001.

National Cinema and Beyond: Studies in Irish Film, by Rockett and Hill. Four Courts Press, 2004.

TRAVEL BOOKS

Bed and Breakfast Ireland: A Trusted Guide to Over 400 of Ireland's Best Bed and Breakfasts, by Dillard and Causin. Chronicle Books, 2005.

Daytrips Ireland: 55 One-Day Adventures by Car, Rail, or Bus, by Patricia Tunison Preston. Hastings House Daytrips, 2000.

Ireland by Bike: 21 Tours Geared for Discovery (by bike), by Robin Krause. Mountaineers Books, 1999.

The Most Beautiful Villages of Ireland, Fitz-Simon and Palmer. Thames & Hudson, 2000.

Spectacular Ireland, by Harbison. Beaux Arts Editions, 2001.

Teach Yourself Irish, by Diarmuid O Se and Joseph Sheils. McGraw Hill, 2004.

The Wicklow Way, by Fewer Micheal. Ordnance Survey, 1999.

BEYOND TOURISM

A PHILOSOPHY FOR TRAVELERS

BEYOND TOURISM HIGHLIGHTS

CREATE artwork in the otherwordly surroundings of **the Burren** (p. 352).

SPEAK Gaelic like a pro after studying in isolated **gaeltachts** (p. 84).

STUDY conflict resolution and peace in **Belfast** (p. 491).

TEACH people with learning disabilities in **Kilkenny** (p. 189).

As a tourist, you are always a foreigner. While hostel-hopping and sightseeing can be great fun, you may want to consider going *beyond* tourism. Experiencing a foreign place through studying, volunteering, or working can help reduce that touristy stranger-in-a-strange-land feeling. Furthermore, travelers can make a positive impact on the natural and cultural environments they visit. With this Beyond Tourism chapter, *Let's Go* hopes to promote a better understanding of Ireland and to provide suggestions for those who want to get more than a photo album out of their travels. The "Giving Back" sidebar feature (p. 165, p. 254) also highlights regional Beyond Tourism opportunities.

There are several options for those who seek to participate in Beyond Tourism activities. Opportunities for **volunteering** abound, with both local and international organizations. **Studying** in a new environment can be enlightening, whether through direct enrollment in a local university or in an independent research project. **Working** is a way to immerse yourself in local culture while financing your travels.

As a **volunteer** in Ireland, you can participate in projects ranging from organic farming to advocacy for the homeless, either on a short-term basis or as the main component of your trip. Later in this chapter, we recommend organizations that can help you find the opportunities that best suit your interests, whether you're looking to get involved for a day or for a year.

Studying at a college or in a language program is another option; more and more students are visiting Ireland to learn Gaelic. Many travelers structure their trips by the **work** available to them along the way, ranging from odd jobs on the go to full-time, long-term stints in cities.

VOLUNTEERING

Volunteering can be a powerful and fulfilling experience, especially when combined with the thrill of traveling in a new place. In Ireland, opportunities abound for community development, peace efforts, and ecological preservation.

One great way to find opportunities that match up with your interests and schedule is to check with national volunteer agencies, such as **Volunteering Ireland** (www.volunteeringireland.com) or the **Northern Ireland Volunteer Development Agency** (www.volunteering-ni.org). Sometimes, contacting individual sites and workcamps directly helps to avoid high application fees. Northern Ireland's **FREE PHONE** (☎0800 052 2212) connects callers to local volunteer bureaus. Worldwide service databases **Idealist** (www.idealist.org) and **ServeNet** (www.servenet.org) have plenty of listings in the Republic and Northern Ireland.

Those looking for longer, more intensive volunteer opportunities usually choose to go through a parent organization that takes care of logistical details and often

WHY PAY MONEY TO VOLUNTEER? Many volunteers are surprised to learn that some organizations require large fees or "donations." While this may seem ridiculous at first glance, such fees often keep the organization afloat, in addition to covering airfare, room, board, and administrative expenses for the volunteers. (Other organizations rely on private donations and government subsidies.) If you're concerned about how a program spends its fees, request an annual report or finance account. A reputable organization won't refuse to inform you of how volunteer money is spent.

Pay-to-volunteer programs might be a good idea for young travelers who are looking for more support and structure (such as pre-arranged transportation and housing), or anyone who would rather not deal with the uncertainty implicit in designing a volunteer experience from scratch.

provides a group environment and support system—for a fee. There are two main types of organizations (religious and non-sectarian), although there are rarely restrictions on participating for either.

URBAN ISSUES

Though Ireland is a fully modernized nation, community and urban development will always be needed. With over 10,000 homeless people living in Ireland, those who volunteer to do anything from building homes to helping with childcare will be welcomed with open arms. If hands-on volunteering is unappealing, many organizations need volunteers for fundraising efforts.

Christian Aid, The Republic: 17 Clanwilliam Terr., Grand Canal Dock, Dublin 2, Ireland (☎01 611 0801; www.christianaidconnect.org). Northern Ireland: 30 Wellington Park, Belfast, BT9 6DL (☎028 9038 1204; www.christian-aid.org.uk). Volunteers work to strengthen communities and alleviate poverty. Small stipends may be available.

Focus Ireland, 9-12 High St., Dublin 8, Ireland (☎01 881 5900; www.focusireland.ie). Volunteers get involved in advocacy and fundraising for the homeless in Dublin, Limerick, or Waterford.

Habitat for Humanity International, 121 Habitat St., Americus, GA 31709, USA (☎229-924-6935; www.habitat.org). Volunteers build houses in Northern Ireland and the Republic on trips of 2 weeks to 1 yr. Costs start at US$1300. 18+; under 18 must be accompanied by a guardian.

Merchant's Quay Ireland, 4 Merchant's Quay, Dublin 8, Ireland (☎01 679 0044; email info@mqi.ie, www.mqi.ie/Home.shtml). Works for justice and increased opportunities for the homeless.

Service Civil International Voluntary Service (SCI-IVS), 5030 Walnut Level Rd., Crozet, VA 22932, USA (☎206 350 6585; www.sci-ivs.org). Arranges short-term placement in several types of volunteer camps to work on grassroots issues in Dublin and Northern Ireland. 18+. Registration typically $80-195.

Simon Communities of Ireland, St. Andrew's House, 28-30 Exchequer St., Dublin 2, Ireland (☎01 671 1606; www.simoncommunity.com). Full- or part-time volunteers assist homeless and at-risk individuals.

Voluntary Service Bureau, 34 Shaftesbury Sq., Belfast, BT2 7DB, Ireland (☎028 9020 0850; www.vsb.org.uk). Umbrella organization for charitable works in the greater Belfast area. Fifteen other locations throughout Northern Ireland.

Volunteering Ireland, Coleraine House, Coleraine St., Dublin 7, Ireland (☎01 872 2622; www.volunteeringireland.com). Opportunities for individuals or groups in various volunteering and advocacy settings. Options listed online. Free placement service.

COMMUNITY ISSUES

Ireland offers opportunities to work with communities troubled by issues such as poverty, substance abuse, and mental health problems. Many programs demand a long-term commitment, and some involve volunteers in projects of reconciliation and ecological conservation. Several prominent programs are listed below.

▓ **L'Arche Ireland,** "Seolta," Warrenhouse Rd., Baldoyle, Dublin 13, Ireland (☎01 839 4356; www.larche.ie). Assistants become part of a residential community in Dublin, Belfast, Cork, or Kilkenny, to live with, work with, and teach people with learning or mental health disabilities. Room, board, and a small stipend provided. Commitment of 1-2 years expected.

Camphill Communities of Ireland, Gorey, Co. Wexford, Ireland (☎053 942 5911; www.camphill.ie). Volunteers live and work with disabled children and adults in one of 12 communities in the Republic and 5 in Northern Ireland. Focus is on communal work and education. Room and board provided. Volunteers commonly stay between 6 months and 2 years.

Foróige, Block 12D, Joyce Way, Park West, Dublin 12, Ireland (☎01 630 1560; www.foroige.ie), is the Irish branch of Big Brothers Big Sisters International, a mentoring program for young kids in need of long-term guidance. Serves Counties Galway, Mayo, Roscommon, and Sligo.

Mental Health Ireland, Mensana House, 6 Adelaide St., Dun Laoghaire, County Dublin, Ireland (☎01 284 1166; www.mentalhealthireland.ie). Volunteer activities include fundraising, housing, "befriending," and promoting mental health in various regions of Ireland. Opportunities listed in their online newsletter, *Mensana News*.

Rainbow Project N.I., 33 Church Ln., Belfast BT1 2JF, and 37 Clarendon St., Derry/Londonderry, BT48 7ER (☎028 9031 9030; Derry 028 7128 3060; www.rainbow-project.org). Volunteers act as peer educators and health promoters in gay venues. Short- and long-term opportunities available.

PEACE PROCESS

The deep-rooted conflict in Northern Ireland has plagued Britain and Ireland for centuries, resulting in uprisings of violence from both sides. Over the past 30 years, the peace process has grown international in scope. In 1998, Catholic John Hume and Protestant David Trimble were awarded the Nobel Peace Prize for their work on the Good Friday Peace Agreement earlier that year. However, violence is still very much a concern, and the peace process remains a high priority. Volunteering for these organizations is a particularly good opportunity for foreigners whose primary objective is peace, not the promotion of one side over the other.

▓ **Kilcranny House,** 21 Cranagh Rd., Coleraine BT51 3NN, Northern Ireland (☎028 7032 1816; www.kilcrannyhouse.org). A residential educational center provides a safe space for both sides to interact and explore issues of non-violence, prejudice awareness, and conflict resolution. Volunteer opportunities range from 6 months to 2 years. Room and board (vegetarians accommodated) provided.

Corrymeela Community, Corrymeela House 8, Upper Crescent, Belfast BT7 1NT, Northern Ireland (☎028 9050 8080; www.corrymeela.org). A residential community committed to bringing Protestants and Catholics together to work toward peace. Volunteer opportunities range from 1week to 1 year. Ages 18-30 preferred for long-term positions.

Global Volunteers, 375 East Little Canada Rd., St. Paul, MN 55117, USA (☎800 487 1074; www.globalvolunteers.org). Opportunities at Glencree Centre for Reconciliation in the Wicklow Mountains. 1week US$2095, 2weeks US$2295; discounts available.

Harmony Community Trust, Glebe House, Bishops Court Rd., Strangford BT30 7NZ, Northern Ireland (☎028 4488 1374). Encourages cross-community interaction through social and educational programs for all ages. Volunteer opportunities range from 1 week to 2 years. Short-term volunteers 18+, long-term volunteers 21+.

NICHS, 547 Antrim Rd., Belfast BT15 3BU, Northern Ireland (☎028 9037 0373; www.nichs.org). Volunteers work with young people in Belfast to promote reconciliation and mutual understanding. Day, evening, and residential weekend opportunities are available. 18+. Room, board, and travel costs provided.

Northern Ireland Volunteer Development Agency, 58 Howard St., 4th fl., Belfast BT1 6PG, Northern Ireland (☎028 9023 6100; www.volunteering-ni.org). Helps arrange individual and group volunteer efforts in Northern Ireland. Membership fees £15 per year, groups £30-40 per year.

Quaker Service Committee, 541 Lisburn Rd., Belfast BT9 7GQ, Northern Ireland (☎028 9020 1444; www.ulsterquakerservice.com), runs programs for Protestant and Catholic children from inner-city Belfast. Accommodations and a small stipend for food provided. Short-term volunteers (summer) 18+, long-term volunteers (up to 2yr.) 21+.

Volunteers for Peace, 1034 Tiffany Rd., Belmont., VT 05730, USA (☎802-259-2759; www.vfp.org). Runs work camps in Ireland. Space is limited. Membership (US $30) required for registration. Programs average US$250 for 2-3weeks.

FARMING AND CONSERVATION

Volunteers who choose to work for a conservation project or an environmentally conscious farm can forge new connections with the countryside of the Emerald Isle. For those enthralled by Ireland's rich ancient and medieval past, archaeological conservation may be the better fit.

Archaeological Institute of America, Boston University, 656 Beacon St., Boston, MA 02215, USA (☎617-353-9361; www.archaeological.org). *Archaeological Fieldwork Opportunities Bulletin,* on their website, lists field sites in Ireland.

Conservation Volunteers Northern Ireland, Beech House, 159 Ravenhill Rd., Belfast BT6 0BP, Northern Ireland (☎028 9064 5169; www.cvni.org). Involves volunteers in short-term practical conservation work, from tree-planting to trail-building. The Belfast office also welcomes long-term volunteers (min. 6 mo. commitment). 18+.

The Donegal Organic Farm, Doorian, Glenties, Co. Donegal, Ireland (☎074 94 95 51286; www.donegalorganic.ie). Offers opportunities for farming, forestry, habitat maintenance, and wildlife inventory.

i-to-i, 32 Grattan Sq., Dungarvan, Co. Waterford (☎58 40050). Provides volunteering and internship opportunities in conservation, media, and marketing. 1-12 weeks. Accommodations provided. 18+.

Worldwide Opportunities on Organic Farms (WWOOF), P.O. Box 2675, Lewes BN7 1RB, England, UK (www.wwoof.org). Provides room and board at a variety of organic farms in Ireland in exchange for help on the farm. Membership UK£15.

STUDYING

Study-abroad programs range from basic language and culture courses to college-level classes, often for credit. In order to choose a program that best fits your needs, research as much as you can before making your decision; determine costs and duration, as well as what kind of students participate in the program and what sort of accommodations are provided.

For accommodations, dorm life provides a better opportunity to mingle with fellow students, but there is less of a chance to experience the local scene. If you live with a

VISA INFORMATION. Citizens of the EU and most Western countries need only a passport to enter Ireland. To stay longer than 90 days, visitors must obtain permission from the Alien's Registration Office in Dublin, or register with the local police *(Garda)* station (both free). To **study in Ireland,** students need to submit a copy of their acceptance letter from an educational institution in Ireland, verifying the duration and nature of the course and that requisite fees have been paid, to the Department of Foreign Affairs Visa Office at 69/71 St. Stephen's Green, Dublin.

family, there is a potential to build lifelong friendships with natives and to experience day-to-day life in more depth, but conditions can vary greatly from family to family

UNIVERSITIES

In this section, we list both American organizations and local Irish programs that enable students to study at Irish universities. You can search **www.studyabroad.com** for various semester-abroad programs that meet your criteria, including your desired location and focus of study.

AMERICAN PROGRAMS

Academic Programs International, 107 E. Hopkins, San Marcos, TX 78666, USA (☎800-844-4124 or 512-392-8520; www.academicintl.com). Arranges placement in Galway, Limerick and Cork. Fees range US$4550 (summer) to US$30,910 (full-year).

American Institute for Foreign Study, College Division, River Plaza, 9 West Broad St., Stamford, CT 06902, USA (☎800-727-2437, ext. 5163; www.aifsabroad.com). Organizes programs at the University of Limerick. All-inclusive costs range US$6300 (summer), to US$15,455 (semester), to US$26,690 (full year). Scholarships available.

Arcadia University, Center for Education Abroad, 450 S. Easton Rd., Glenside, PA 19038, USA (☎866-927-2234; www.arcadia.edu/cea). Operates programs throughout the island. Costs range US$13,990 (semester) to US$34,400 (full year).

College Consortium for International Studies, 2000 P Street. NW, Ste. 503, Washington, D.C. 20036, USA (☎800-453-6956; www.ccisabroad.org). Summer and term-time programs. Contact sponsor for cost information.

Council on International Educational Exchange (CIEE), 7 Custom House St., 3rd fl., Portland, ME 04101, USA (☎800-407-8839; www.ciee.org/study). Sponsors semester or full-year study abroad in Dublin and places college students in local internships.

Institute for the International Education of Students (IES), 33 N. LaSalle St., 15th fl., Chicago, IL 60602, USA (☎800-995-2300 or 312-944-1750; www.iesabroad.org). Offers year-long (US$29,480), semester (US$18,180), and summer programs (US$5700) for college study in Dublin. Scholarships available.

Institute for Study Abroad, Butler University, 1100 W. 42nd St., Ste. 305, Indianapolis, IN 46208, USA (☎800 858 0229 or 317-940-9336; www.ifsa-butler.org). Arranges study abroad at a variety of universities in the Republic and the North in several fields. Fees range from US$20,000-30,000; check website for details.

University Studies Abroad Consortium, University of Nevada, Reno, NV 89557, USA (☎866-404-8722; 775-784-6569; www.usac.unr.edu). Offers a full curriculum of study in Cork from US$3980 (summer) to US$7980 (semester) to US$15,960 (full year).

IRISH PROGRAMS

Most American undergraduates enroll in programs sponsored by US universities. Local universities in Ireland can be much cheaper, though it may be more difficult to receive academic credit. Some schools that offer study-abroad programs to international students are listed below.

Irish Studies Summer School, USIT NOW, 19-21 Aston Quay, Dublin 2, Ireland (☎01 602 1904; www.usitnow.ie). Seven-week program (€6340) offering courses in Irish history and contemporary culture. USIT also administrates the summer program **Ireland in Europe,** a 2-week course focusing on Irish civilization (€1600-1865).

National University of Ireland, Galway, University Rd., Co. Galway, Ireland (☎091 524 411; www.nuigalway.ie). Offers half- or full-year opportunities for junior-year students who meet the college's entry requirements. Summer school courses include Irish Studies, Gaelic Language, and Creative Writing. Fees vary by field.

Queen's University Belfast, International Office, Belfast BT7 1NN, Northern Ireland (☎028 9097 5088; www.qub.ac.uk/ilo). Study in Belfast for a summer (UK£1125), a semester (UK£3850), or a full year (UK£7700).

Trinity College Dublin, Office of International Student Affairs, East Theatre, Trinity College, Dublin 2, Ireland (☎01 896 3150; www.tcd.ie/isa). Offers year-long programs of undergraduate courses for visiting students. Tuition fees €13,566-17,775.

University College Cork, International Education Office, "Roseleigh," Western Rd., University College, Cork, Co. Cork, Ireland (☎021 490 4730; www.ucc.ie/international). Students can choose from a wide array of subjects and classes. Fees vary by course.

University College Dublin, International Summer School, Newman House, 86 St. Stephen's Green, Dublin 2, Ireland (☎01 716 1565; www.ucd.ie/summerschool). A 2½-week international summer course examining Irish culture and tradition. Contact for more information, including fees.

University of Ulster, Shore Rd., Newtownabbey, Co. Antrim BT37 0QB, Northern Ireland (☎28 70 324138; www.ulst.ac.uk/international). Offers semester- or year-long programs for visiting international students. Fees UK£3070-8290. See website for details.

LANGUAGE SCHOOLS

While some nationals do not look back fondly on their days of required Gaelic study, many travelers are eager to learn the Irish tongue. Language programs, often lodged in *gaeltacht* districts, deliver introductory Irish courses that vary in intensity, inside and outside the classroom. The academically challenging programs will ask you to restrict your conversations to Gaelic. The physically challenging send their visitors on hiking trips and adventure outings. Others offer the peace and quiet of a resort setting with a less-than-rigorous workload that many diligent Irish schoolchildren would die for. Notable programs include:

Gaelachas Teo, Gleann Maghair, Co Corchai, Ireland (☎021 482 1116; www.gaelachas.com/chiarain.htm). 3-week Irish language school for ages 11 to 18 years. In addition, students are taught Irish dancing, drama, and singing, and participate in canoeing and snorkeling trips led by Cape Clear Adventure Centre. €750.

Daltaí na Gaeilge (☎732-571-1890; www.daltai.com). Irish for "Students of the Irish Language." This non-profit corporation runs language-immersion programs throughout North America. Website also lists teachers in Ireland.

Ionad Foghlama Chléire, Cape Clear Island, Skibbereen, Co. Cork, Ireland (☎028 39190; www.cleire.com). Week-long course in Irish language and culture. Includes visits to historical and archaeological sites. Tuition €225. Room €110.

Oideas Gael, Glencolmcille, Co. Donegal, Ireland (☎074 97 30248; www.oideasgael.com). Week-long and weekend courses (€190/€95) attended by natives and travelers alike. €150.

Oidhreacht Chorca Dhuibhne, Ballyferriter, Co. Kerry, Ireland (☎066 915 6100; www.corca-dhuibhne.com). "Irish for Beginners" course designed specifically for non-nationals, €390.

BEYOND TOURISM

Taisce Árainn Teoranta, Árainn Mhór Island, Co. Donegal, Ireland (☎074 95 21593). On secluded Árainn Mhór Island in the Donegal *Gaeltacht,* Taisce offers week-long language courses and a range of outdoor activities.

OTHER STUDY ABROAD

Say farewell to tradition and pursue your passion: opportunities abound in Ireland to participate in specialized and highly focused study programs. A few examples in archaeology, art, classics, and cooking are listed below.

Achill Archaeological Field School, Achill Archaeology Centre, Dooagh, Achill Island, Co. Mayo, Ireland (☎098 43564; www.achill-fieldschool.com). 4-, 6-, or 8-week summer courses (€2750/€3650/€4250) surveying and excavating the deserted village of Slievemore. 3-day archaeology "taster"(€250), introduction to archaeology (€795).

Ballymaloe Cookery School, Shanagarry, Midleton, Co. Cork, Ireland (☎021 464 6785; www.cookingisfun.ie). Courses run the gamut, from the half-day "Sushi Made Simple" (€105), to a 12-week certificate course (€9395). Accommodations available from €28 per night for short courses, €95 per week for the 12-week programs.

Burren College of Art, Newtown Castle, Ballyvaughan, Co. Clare, Ireland (☎065 707 7200; www.burrencollege.ie). Offers 1-week summer courses (approx. US$400) and a 2-yr. Master of Fine Arts (approx. US$25,000 per yr.). Subjects include photography, drawing, painting, and sculpture. Beginner and advanced courses in summer.

Dunbrody Cookery School, Dunbrody Country House Hotel and Restaurant, Arthurstown, New Ross, Co. Wexford, Ireland (☎051 389 600; www.dunbrodyhouse.com/html-files/school.htm). Offers cooking courses in various cuisines and styles, always based on the simple use of the best Irish ingredients. Costs are €150 or €295 for 1- or 2-day courses; participants get a discount at the adjoining Dunbrody Country House Hotel.

Latin and Greek Summer School, Department of Ancient Classics, University College Cork, Ireland (☎021 490 3618; www.ucc.ie/acad/classics/summ_sch.html). Offers intensive 8-week courses during July and August in either Latin (both classical and medieval) or Greek. €1400, with housing and textbooks €2300.

Summer Art Program in Ireland, Office of International Programs, SUNY Cortland, B-15 Old Main, P.O. Box 2000, Cortland, NY 13045, USA(☎607-753-2209; www.cortlandabroad.com). Intense 5-week summer program in landscape-drawing and painting amidst the beautiful cliffs and beaches of the Dingle Peninsula in Dingle Town. Fees vary by institution.

Yeats International Summer School, Yeats Society Sligo, Hyde Bridge, Sligo, Ireland (☎353 071 91 42693). Offers Yeats-related lectures and seminars to students of all ages during the first 2 weeks of August. Applications available on website. €350 for 1 week, €575 for 2 weeks. Scholarships available.

WORKING

Ireland's low unemployment rates make it easy for travelers to find work. Securing a job legally is another story. A strict work permit policy that favors nationals and members of the EU complicates visitors' dreams of paying their way around the island. The Department of Enterprise recently announced it will not grant any work permits to hotel clerks, barstaff, and bus drivers. Expedited work visas, however, are available to skilled employees in certain sectors of the medical, technical, and construction fields. Professionals in these fields report receiving their work visas in a matter of days. For more information, direct questions to the **Department of Enterprise, Trade, and Employment** (www.entemp.ie).

Since April of 2007, students with primary, masters, or doctorate degrees from an Irish third-level educational institution have qualified to apply for the **Third Level**

Graduate Scheme, which allows foreigners and non-EU members to continue living in Ireland while they apply for a green card or work permit.

> **VISA INFORMATION.** Citizens of the EU and most Western countries need only a passport to enter Ireland. To remain for longer than 90 days, visitors must obtain permission from the Alien's Registration Office in Dublin (☎01 660 9100), or the local police (*Garda*) station (see p. 11). Though EU nationals may work in Ireland without a permit, non-EU visitors must have potential employers submit a work permit application to the Department of Enterprise, Trade and Employment (☎01 631 3333; www.entemp.ie). Only if the worker has technical skills will employers agree to pay the large renewable fees attached to the application. Employers must list the position for at least one month on the National Training and Employment Authority website (www.fas.ie) and prove that there is not a more qualified national or EU-member candidate before the work permit will be issued. The permit takes seven to nine weeks to process, is valid for between one month and one year, and can be renewed upon expiration. If your 90-day visit period has expired by then, you will have to reenter the island with your new work permit visa. It's the sort of struggle that would have inspired an Upton Sinclair tome. For this reason, it is advisable that visitors seeking employment begin their job search before making their way to the Emerald Island. Those with Australian, Canadian, and New Zealand visas will have an easier time. A Working Holiday Authorization permits you to work in Ireland for twelve months; contact your Irish Embassy for details.

For full-time students, there is a costly but effective loophole in the bureaucratic madness. **BUNAC, USA** offers students the ability to work anywhere in the Republic of Ireland for up to four months. The company also offers an "Ireland/Britain Combo Package," which includes a four-month work permit in Ireland and a six-month work permit in the United Kingdom and Northern Ireland. (☎203-264-0901; www.bunac.org. Ireland permit US$400. Combo package US$690.)

Those whose parents were born in an EU country may be able to claim dual citizenship in Ireland, or at least the right to a work permit. Commonwealth residents with a parent or grandparent born in the UK do not need a work permit to work in Northern Ireland. Contact your British Consulate or High Commission (see p. 8) for details before departure and the Department of Enterprise upon arrival.

LONG-TERM WORK

If you're planning on spending a substantial amount of time (more than three months) working in Ireland, search for a job well in advance. The Maryland-based **Association for International Practical Training** helps obtain visas and work permits lasting 12-18 months for travelers who have found their own jobs or internships, primarily in the technical fields. (☎410-997-2200; www.aipt.org.) Job-seeking travelers report having the best luck in the touristed urban areas of Dublin, Belfast, and Cork. Students in the **Work Abroad Program** typically find work at cafes, pubs, hotels, banks, and libraries.

Teachers (see below) should check job listings in Irish newspapers. **Internships,** usually for college students, are a good way to transition into working abroad, though they are often unpaid or poorly paid.

International placement agencies can be the easiest way to find employment. Be wary of companies that claim the ability to get you a job abroad for a fee—often the same job listings are available online or in newspapers or are out-of-date. **Ask**

Ireland (www.askireland.com/work.asp) offers a listing of available jobs, as well as helpful information about working in Ireland. In the South, the **Job Options Bureau,** Tourist House, 40-41 Grand Parade, Cork, Ireland (☎21 427 5369; www.joboption-bureau.com) offers internship placement for three-month to year-long programs.

TEACHING

Teaching jobs abroad are rarely well paid, though some private American schools in Ireland pay relatively competitive salaries. American schools overseas require American teaching certification. In most cases, you must have a bachelors degree to work as a full-time teacher. Irish primary schools sometimes require teachers to demonstrate a level of competency in all areas of the curriculum, including Gaelic. College undergraduates can often get summer positions teaching or tutoring.

The International Educator (☎508-362-1414; www.tieonline.com) lists overseas teaching vacancies and offers job search and resume posting online (fees vary based on ad size). **Search Associates** recruits for both teaching internships and administrative positions abroad. **Teach Abroad** (www.teachabroad.com) lists options for oversees teaching. A popular option is to volunteer as a teacher. While most fund their own way, some volunteers get free accommodations; others manage to obtain a daily stipend from their college. Those interested are encouraged to inquire at colleges and secondary schools for school-specific information.

AU PAIR WORK

Au pairs are typically women, aged 18-27, who work as live-in nannies in exchange for room, board, and a small spending allowance or stipend (usually €60-70 per week in Ireland). American au pairs may have a difficult time finding employment in Ireland, as English training is considered a major benefit of the au pair experience. Those lucky enough to connect with a host family often speak favorably of their experience, despite the long hours and mediocre pay; on days off au pairs have the chance to explore Ireland on the cheap. You may find the most success finding a host family by word of mouth, but there are a number of agencies willing to serve you—some at no cost. Several starting points are listed below.

Douglas Au Pair Agency Ltd., 28 Frankfield, Douglas, Co. Cork, Ireland (☎21 489 1489; www.aupairhere.com). No placement fee.

Dublin Childcare Recruitment Agency, Newcourt House, Strandville Ave., Clontarf, Dublin 3, Ireland (☎01 833 2281; www.childcare-recruitment.com). Applicants must hold an EU passport. Additional positions available for nurses and nannies.

Shamrock Au Pair Agency, Magheree, Kilmoroney, Athy, Co. Kildare, Ireland (☎059 862 5533; www.aupairireland.com). No placement fee. Actively seeks non-English speakers.

SHORT-TERM WORK

Work and live in the same place at **The Ark** hostel (p. 431) in Belfast or the **Dublin International Youth Hostel** (see p. 106). From waitressing and bartending, to childcare and farmwork, temporary workers find their way to enter the workforce. Most often, these short-term jobs are found by word of mouth, or simply by talking to the owner of a hostel or restaurant. Due to the high turnover in the tourism industry, many places are eager for help, even if it is only temporary. *Let's Go* lists temporary jobs whenever possible; check under the practical information sections of towns and cities for work opportunity listings.

BEYOND TOURISM

FOR FURTHER READING ON WORK ABROAD.

Au Pair in Ireland, by Richard Marsh, 2004 (richardmarsh@legendarytours.com).

How to Get a Job in Europe, by Sanborn and Matherly. Surrey Books, 1999 (US$22).

How to Live Your Dream of Volunteering Overseas, by Collins, DeZerega, and Heckscher. Penguin Books, 2002 (US$17).

International Directory of Voluntary Work, by Whetter and Pybus. Peterson's Guides and Vacation Work, 2000 (US$16).

International Jobs, by Kocher and Segal. Perseus Books, 1999 (US$18).

Live and Work in Ireland, by Dan Boothby, 2004 (US$20).

Overseas Summer Jobs 2002, by Collier and Woodworth. Peterson's Guides and Vacation Work, 2002 (US$18).

Work Abroad: The Complete Guide to Finding a Job Overseas, by Hubbs, Griffith, and Nolting. Transitions Abroad Publishing, 2000 ($16).

Work Your Way Around the World, by Susan Griffith. Worldview Publishing Services, 2001 (US$18).

Invest Yourself: The Catalogue of Volunteer Opportunities, published by the Commission on Voluntary Service and Action (☎718-638-8487).

BEYOND TOURISM

it's easy being green

It's no great secret—even to the first-time traveler—that Ireland is green. But most people aren't aware that Ireland is also home to some of the world's finest horticultural estates. I volunteered at Birr Castle, Demesne, in Birr, Co. Offaly, and found that the heart of Ireland offers an incredible collection of flora that puts your average shamrock to shame.

The Birr program was established 20 years ago by the 7th Earl of Rosse, who lives in the castle with his family. After years of volunteer work for the United Nations in the Middle East, Lord Rosse decided to set something up closer to home. He is a down-to-earth, but nevertheless royal, presence at Birr who often joins the volunteers for planting, or leads daytrips to the peat bogs.

Coming from as far as Nepal, and as close as Dublin, most volunteers are between the ages of 20 and 25, and tend to stay at Birr for two or three months. The program can accommodate up to six at a time in rustic cottages just outside the castle wall. While many volunteers have worked in botanic gardens before and are looking to further their knowledge for educational or career purposes, novices are also welcome.

I arrived at Birr in mid-June, just in time for the "low season" (most of the major seed propagation takes place during the fall or spring). With two volunteers from Northern Ireland, I tended the greenhouse, planted shrubs, looked after the rose beds, and pulled weeds from just about everywhere. We worked from 8am to 5pm daily, with breaks for tea and lunch, under the supervision of the full-time staff.

Birr Castle Demesne is located in the Midlands, a quiet, unspoiled region of Ireland that most travelers miss as they hurry to reach the coast. Those savvy enough to stop in Birr find a Georgian heritage town flanked by a stunning 17th-century castle and 50 hectares of dramatic gardens. The Demesne is the largest of its kind in Ireland, with waterfalls, fountains, two rivers, formal gardens, a fernery, a five-hectare lake, and—according to the *Guinness Book of World Records*—the tallest box hedges in the world. Birr also contains exotic plants and trees collected from more than 40 countries. Gardens of this size take a lot of work to maintain, but a team of year-round interns (or "stagaires," as they are called here) helps to keep the grounds looking glorious.

Some of the my most remarkable discoveries, however, came after work and on the weekends, as I adjusted to Irish small-town life. My fellow volunteers and I soon relied on each other for everything, and shared rounds at our favorite pub, the Chestnut. Because Birr is in the center of Ireland, it was easy to travel just about anywhere. One weekend took us to the International Sheep Dog Competition in Tullamore, where we tromped through hectares of mud in our Wellies to toast a crowd of Tipperary farmers with Tullamore Dew Whiskey.

Lord Rosse likes to say that his exotic plants are as "happy as are our visitors." It must be something in the water, because after a week here I was already staring at the real-estate window in town and contemplating life as a full-time gardener. I couldn't help but

"Lord Rosse likes to say that his exotic plants are as 'happy as are our visitors.'"

envision Birr in spring, with magnolias, roses, and tree peonies in full bloom.

If you are interested in volunteering at Birr, send a formal application (complete with cover letter, and recommendation) to:

The Earl of Rosse

Birr Castle

Birr, Co. Offaly, IRELAND

Lord Rosse requests that applications be sent at least two months in advance of the desired start date.

Emily Simon worked at a Birr Castle, Demesne during the summer of 2005. She studies History and Literature at Harvard University, and was a Researcher-Writer for Let's Go France *2005.*

A DIFFERENT PATH

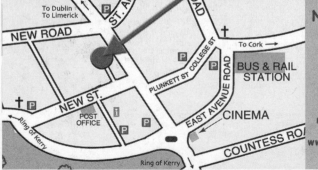

COUNTY DUBLIN

Dublin and its suburbs spill into the surrounding counties, but they form a single economic and commercial region linked by a web of mass transit. Dubliners reap the success of the Celtic Tiger and take it out to play, cultivating a culture so magnetic that weekending suburbanites and international hipsters come body-slamming into hotel mattresses. While Dublin's suburbs offer a less polluted alternative, the housing developments staked around their peripheries dissolve any notions of romantic Irish villages. However, beautiful beaches, literary landmarks, and well-preserved castles enveloping the area around the big city still give Dublin's environs an air of much-missed country calm.

COUNTY DUBLIN HIGHLIGHTS

GO WILD for hurling or Gaelic football at legendary **Croke Park** (p. 131).

MEASURE Ireland's tallest permanent waterfall on **Powerscourt Island** (p. 145).

TOUCH the hand of an 800-year-old mummy at **St. Michan's Church** (p. 129).

VIEW cutting-edge drama at Dublin's famous **Abbey Theatre** (p. 132).

◧ TRANSPORTATION

Rail lines, bus routes, and the national highway system all radiate from the capital. Transport between the country's major cities is so Dublin-centric that visitors often find it more convenient to arrange travel to other parts of Ireland from the city, taking daytrips into the countryside while retaining a base in Dublin. For more information on transportation, see **Essentials**, p. 8.

BY BUS

Dublin Buses (☎ 873 4222; www.dublinbus.ie) service the entire county. The buses, which come in a variety of shapes, sizes, and colors (all sporting "db" logos), run 6am-11:30pm and cover the city and its suburbs comprehensively: north to **Howth, Donabate,** and **Malahide;** west to **Rathcoole, Maynooth,** and **Celbridge;** and south to **Blessington, Enniskerry, Dún Laoghaire,** and **Bray.** Buses are cheap (€1-4; prices rise according to distance, which is measured in "stages") and run generally 8am-6pm every 8-20min. and 6am-8am and 6pm-midnight every 30-45min. Inner-city buses run about every 15min., while suburban routes are often staggered every hour.

 BUS-TED. Dublin buses have a few eccentricities besides their funky double-deckered appearance. To save you from angry stares and embarrassment, note that they only accept coins and do not provide change, so have the exact amount ready. Also, buses in Dublin must be hailed like a cab to let them know you want on; otherwise, they may not stop even if their route says they should. If you're planning to use public transportation frequently, a bus timetable book will soon become your bible. Ask for a copy at the Dublin Busáras, and keep it close to your heart. (Free.)

Most bus routes terminate in the city center, at stops located near Christ Church, the Trinity College facade, St. Stephen's Green, O'Connell St., and Parnell St. Bus stands along the quays post timetables of routes around the city center. Various pamphlets, like the *Quick Guide to Cash Fares* and *Dublin Visitor Map & Guide* (both free), and the *Dublin Bus Timetables* (€2) allow the traveler to plan an organized tour or solo trips. The latter two are available from some newsagents; all can be picked up from the **Dublin Bus Office,** 59 Upper O'Connell St. (☎873 4222. Open M 8:30am-5:30pm, Tu-F 9am-5:30pm, Sa 9am-2pm, Su 9:30am-2pm.) The Trinity College Student Union and Busáras in the Central Bus Station have handy Travel Information sheets with fares and timetables for many routes.

Dublin Bus runs the **NiteLink** service to the suburbs. (M-Th 12:30am and 2am, F-Sa every 20min. 12:30-4:30am, or 12:30, 2, and 3:30am, depending on destination. €4; Celbridge/Maynooth €6. Most passes not valid.) Tickets for the NiteLink are sold at the Dublin Bus Office, by Nitelink bus drivers, and from "ticket buses" on the corner of Westmoreland and Fleet St. or on D'Olier St. next to Trinity College. NiteLink leaves for the northern suburbs from D'Olier St., the southern suburbs from College St., and the western suburbs from Westmoreland St. The **Airlink** service (#747 and 748; €6, children €3) connects **Dublin Airport** to Busáras and Heuston Station, stopping on O'Connell St. and the quays along the way. (Every 10-15min. 5:45am-11:30pm.) **Wheelchair-accessible buses** are ever more prevalent, with around 60% of Dublin Buses now accessible and a commitment by Dublin Bus to purchase only accessible buses in the future. Check with the Bus Office or visit (www.dublinbus.ie) to find fully accessible routes.

Travel passes, called "Ramblers," are designed for those planning to use the bus system frequently in a short amount of time; passes are sold for one-, three-, five-, or seven-day periods. **Rambler** and **Travel Wide** passes offer unlimited rides (1-day €6, 3-day €11, 5-day €17.30, 7-day €21). Other tickets allow for both bus and suburban rail/DART travel (1 day **short hop** €8.80; weekly €28; monthly €98). While the seven-day pass can be used for a seven-day increment starting on any day, Dublin Bus months are calendar months. Discount tickets are available at the bus office and from city newsagents. Only Irish students with student Travelcards are eligible for student prices.

BY TRAIN

Electric **DART** (Dublin Area Rapid Transit) trains run up and down the coast, connecting the city and its suburbs. The DART puts buses to shame in terms of cost and speed, but reaches a more limited number of destinations. From **Connolly, Pearse,** and **Tara Street Stations** in the city center, trains shoot south past **Bray** and north to **Howth, Malahide,** and **Belfast.** Tickets are sold in the station and must be presented at the end of the trip (every 10-15min. 6am-10:30pm; €1.30-2). The orange trains of the **suburban rail** network continue north to **Malahide, Donabate,** and **Drogheda;** south to **Wicklow** and **Arklow;** and west to **Maynooth** and **Mullingar.** These trains all leave from Connolly Station. The north- and southbound lines stop at Tara St. and Pearse Stations as well. Suburban trains to **Kildare** leave from **Heuston Station.** Trains leave frequently (M-Sa 30 per day, Su 13 per day). Timetables are available at the stations and online. **Bicycles** are only allowed in DART passenger cars if they are folded and packed. Special rail and bus/rail tickets are cost-effective only for travelers addicted to mass transit.

The **Luas** (☎461 4910 or Customer Care Freefone 1800 300 604; www.luas.ie; free phone line open M-F 7am-7pm, Sa 10am-2pm), Dublin's Light Rail Transit System, is the city's newest form of mass transit. With just two lines, it's still in its early stages of development. However, it's growing quickly; the Luas went from carrying 22 million passengers in 2005 to 26 million in 2006. The more central **red line** is 14km long and runs from **Connolly Station** to **Tallaght** with a total of 23 stops, including **Heuston Station.** The **green line** is just 9km long, running south from **St.**

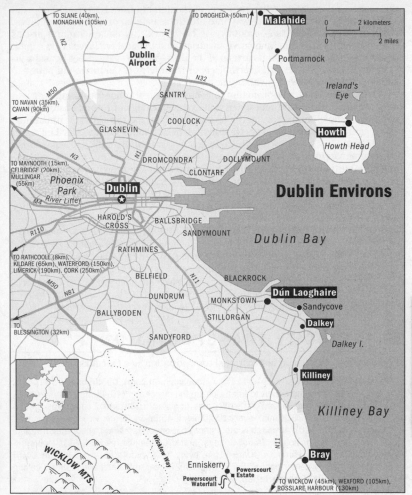

Stephen's Green to **Sandyford** with 13 total stops. Prices for single Luas tickets range €1.40-2.20, depending on how many "zones" you go through. It may be wise (and eco-friendly) to purchase a Luas **SmartCard** (€10; €3 for card, €7 credit) if you plan to use the Luas frequently. It offers discount rates and works by deducting the maximum fare when you "TAG ON" (climb aboard) and refunding whatever you didn't use when you "TAG OFF" (part ways). The Luas does not welcome **bikes.**

DUBLIN (BAILE ÁTHA CLIATH) ☎01

The spirit of Dublin mirrors the spirit of Ireland; small but lively, the city is now experiencing something of a renaissance. Modern Dublin is home to nearly half of the country's population. With an influx of immigrants from Eastern Europe and Africa, Dublin has muscled its way into an exclusive club of international cities. Not quite as cosmopolitan or as large as New York City or London, but just as eclectic, Dublin supports innovative theatrical and musical enclaves. This capital on the rise refuses to forget its artists of the past—nearly every street boasts a literary landmark, be it a statue, birthplace, or favorite pub. Centuries-old pubs rub shoulders, and share walls, with hip newcomers.

The local watering holes remain the center of neighborhood communities and also play host to a world-renowned music scene. Gangs of tourists fought their way into Temple Bar and claimed it as their own, but the nightlife hub remains as lively and entertaining as ever. New late-night hot spots glimmer farther south along Great Georges St., while the area around Grafton St. continues to flourish under a monarchy of designer fashion.

While the Irish worry that Dublin has contracted the growl of big-city crime, poverty, and apathy, its cultural and pub-happy attractions retain that famous Irish charm. At the same time, Dublin exudes an air of urban sophistication, making it an exhilarating and deservedly popular destination.

 ACT LIKE YOU OWN THE PLACE. The Heritage Card, a VIP pass for anyone, provides admission year-round to 80 historical sites around the Republic. With individual admission costing up to €10, this card (€21, students €8) is well worth the investment, even if you only get to visit 2 or 3 sites. Cards can be purchased at most of the 80 sites, all of which are managed by the Office for Public Works or the Department of the Environment, Heritage and Local Government. For more info, call ☎0164 76597, or visit www.heritageireland.ie.

◪ INTERCITY TRANSPORTATION

For more on national and international transportation, see **Essentials**, p. 8.

Airport: Dublin Airport (☎814 1111; www.dublinairport.com). **Dublin buses** #41, 41B, and 41C run from the airport to Eden Quay in the city center (40-45min., every 20min., €1.75). **Airlink shuttle** (☎703 3092) runs non-stop to Busáras Central Bus Station and O'Connell St. (20-25min., every 10-20min. 5:45am-11:30pm, €6), and to Heuston Station (50min., €6). **Aircoach** is more pricey but operates 24hr., transporting travelers to and from major hotels, Trinity College, and O'Connell St. (☎844 7118; www.aircoach.com. Every 15min. 4:30am-11pm, every hr. 11pm-4:30am; €6, return €10.) **Taxis** to the city center cost €20-25. Wheelchair-accessible cabs available by calling ahead; see **Local Transportation**, p. 100.

Trains: Tickets can be purchased at Dublin's 3 major stations (purchase at least 20min. ahead to beat crowds, especially during rush hour), but they can also be bought in advance at the **Irish Rail Travel Centre**, 35 Lower Abbey St. (Information ☎836 6222; www.irishrail.ie. Open M-F 9am-5pm.) The center has **Iarnród Éireann** (EER-ann-road AIR-ann), **British** and **European Rail** agents as well as pamphlets and a phone that directly connects you to an agent who can help with DART, suburban rail, international train tickets, and cross-channel ferries (only in conjunction with train purchases, known as "sail and rail" packages). Booking also available by credit card over the phone (☎703 4070 for Iarnród; ☎703 1885 for European and British rail). Bus #90 runs from Connolly, Tara St., and Heuston Stations. The Luas also runs from Connolly to Heuston (see **By Train**, p. 29). Connolly and Pearse are also **DART** stations serving the north and south coasts; see **Local Transportation**, p. 100.

Connolly Station, Amiens St. (☎703 2358), north of the Liffey, close to Busáras. Ticketing open M-Sa 7am-10:20pm, Su 8am-9:30pm. Bus #20b heads south of the river and #130 goes to the city center, while the DART runs to Tara Station on the south quay. Trains to: **Belfast** (2hr.; M-Sa 8 per day, Su 5 per day; €50 monthly return, €36.50 day return); **Sligo** (3hr.; 3-4 per day; €33.50 monthly return, €25.50 day return); **Wexford** and **Rosslare** (3hr.; 2 per day; €25 monthly return, €19.50 day return).

Heuston Station (☎703 3299), south of Victoria Quay and west of the city center, a 25min. walk from Trinity College. Ticketing open M-Sa 6:30am-9pm, Su 7:30am-9:30pm. Buses #78, and 79 run from Heuston to the city center. Trains to: **Cork** (3hr.; 6 per day; €67 monthly return, €61 day return); **Galway** (2¾hr.; 7 per day; €42 monthly return, €30 day return); **Kilkenny** (2hr.; M-Th and Sa 5 per day, F 1 per day, Su 4 per day; €27.50 monthly return, €22 day return); **Limerick** (2½hr.; 9 per day; €55 monthly return, €50 day return); **Tralee** (4hr.; 3-4 per day; €70 monthly return, €62 day return); **Waterford** (2½hr.; 4-5 per day; €30 monthly return, €23.50 day return).

Pearse Station (☎828 6000), east of Trinity College at the intersection of Pearse St. and Westland Row. Ticketing open M-Sa 7:30am-11:50pm, Su 9am-9:50pm. Receives southbound trains from Connolly Station.

Buses: Intercity buses to Dublin arrive at **Busáras Central Bus Station,** Store St. (☎836 6111; www.buseireann.ie; Schedules and general information M-Sa 8:30am-7pm, Su 9am-7pm), directly behind the Customs House and next to Connolly Station. **Bus Éireann** runs buses to: **Belfast** (3hr., 6-7 per day, €20); **Cork** (4½hr., 6 per day, €18); **Derry/Londonderry** (4¼hr., 4-5 per day, €27.50); **Donegal** (4¼hr., 4-5 per day, €12.50); **Galway** (3½hr., 15 per day, €8.50); **Kilkenny** (2hr., 6-7 per day, €6.25); **Killarney** (6hr., 5 per day, €17); **Limerick** (3½hr., 13 per day, €20.50); **Rosslare** (3hr., 13 per day, €20.50); **Shannon Airport** (4½hr., 13 per day, €12.50); **Sligo** (4hr., 4-6 per day, €26.50); **Tralee** (6hr., 6 per day, €33.60); **Waterford** (3hr., 10 per day, €10); **Westport** (5hr., 2-3 per day, €26.50); **Wexford** (2¾hr.; M-Sa 13 per day, Su 10 per day; €11.50). All prices are adult return. **PAMBO** (Private Association of Motor Bus Owners), 32 Lower Abbey St. (☎878 8422), provides names and numbers of private operators presently in service. Open M-F; call ahead. For more info on all types of buses, see **By Bus,** p. 28.

Ferries: Book ferries through the ferry company or through the Irish Rail office if in conjunction with train tickets (see **Trains,** p. 92). **Irish Ferries,** 2-4 Merrion Row, off St. Stephen's Green. (☎661 0511; www.irishferries.com. Open M-F 9am-5pm, Sa 9am-1pm.) **Stena Line** ferries arrive from Holyhead at the **Dún Laoghaire** ferry terminal (☎204 7777; www.stenaline.com); from there, the **DART** shuttles passengers into central Dublin (€2). **Buses** #7, 7a and 46a run from Georges St. in Dún Laoghaire to O'Connell St., but the DART is easier. Irish Ferries arrive from Holyhead at the **Dublin Port** (☎607 5665). From there, bus #53 runs to the city center (1 per hr., €1.40); **Dublin Bus** also runs buses tailored to ferry schedules (M-Sa 6:45, 7:30am, 1:15, 8pm, Su 7:30am, 1:15, 8pm; €2.50). **Norfolkline Ferries** (☎819 2999; www.norfolkline-ferries.co.uk) docks at Dublin Port and goes to **Liverpool** (7hr.; daily 10pm; Tu-Sa 10am; foot passengers €30-45, with car €150-240). **Isle of Man Steam Packet Company** (☎800 805 055; www.steam-packet.com) docks at Dublin Port and sends 1 boat per day to the small island; rates depend on dates and term of stay (from about €50, only about €20 if you're on foot).

⚡ ORIENTATION

A compact city, Dublin would be relatively easy to navigate if its street names didn't change so frequently. Street names are posted on the side of buildings at (most) intersections and hardly ever on street-level signs. Buying a map with a street index is a good idea. The tourist office has enough maps to fill a treasure chest, including the detailed *Ordnance City Centre Tourist Map* (€4) and *City Centre Street Atlas* (small €5.50, large €12). The smallest one, *The Berlitz Pocket Map: Dublin* (€2), is about as inconspicuous as a pop-up map can be.

The **River Liffey** forms a natural boundary between Dublin's North and South Sides. Most of the notable sights, shops, and restaurants are on the **South Side**. The rival **North Side** claims most of the hostels, Busáras, Connolly Station, and a whole lot of heart. It also contains a convenient 393 ft. tall orienting device for tourists: the Dublin spire (or as locals lovingly refer to it: "the stiletto in the

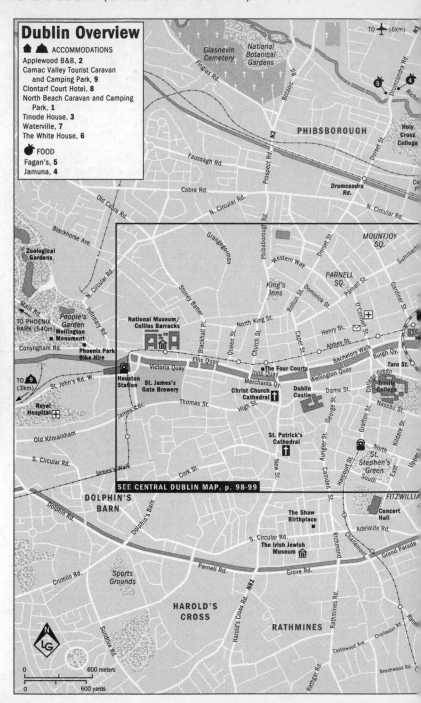

Dublin Overview

🏠 🏠 ACCOMMODATIONS

Applewood B&B, **2**
Camac Valley Tourist Caravan
 and Camping Park, **9**
Clontarf Court Hotel, **8**
North Beach Caravan and Camping
 Park, **1**
Tinode House, **3**
Waterville, **7**
The White House, **6**

🍎 FOOD
Fagan's, **5**
Jamuna, **4**

SEE CENTRAL DUBLIN MAP, p. 98-99

COUNTY DUBLIN

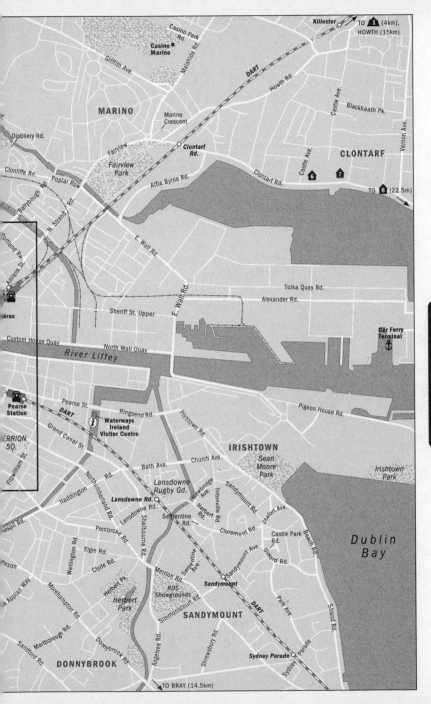

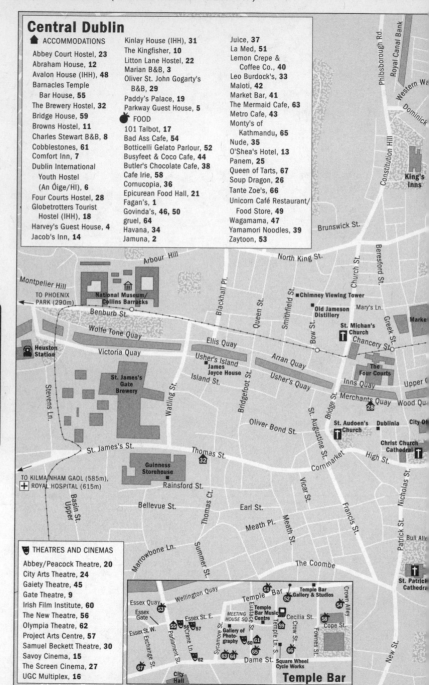

Central Dublin

ACCOMMODATIONS

Abbey Court Hostel, **23**
Abraham House, **12**
Avalon House (IHH), **48**
Barnacles Temple
  Bar House, **55**
The Brewery Hostel, **32**
Bridge House, **59**
Browns Hostel, **11**
Charles Stewart B&B, **8**
Cobblestones, **61**
Comfort Inn, **7**
Dublin International
  Youth Hostel
  (An Óige/HI), **6**
Four Courts Hostel, **28**
Globetrotters Tourist
  Hostel (IHH), **18**
Harvey's Guest House, **4**
Jacob's Inn, **14**

Kinlay House (IHH), **31**
The Kingfisher, **10**
Litton Lane Hostel, **22**
Marian B&B, **3**
Oliver St. John Gogarty's
  B&B, **29**
Paddy's Palace, **19**
Parkway Guest House, **5**

FOOD

101 Talbot, **17**
Bad Ass Cafe, **54**
Botticelli Gelato Parlour, **52**
Busyfeet & Coco Cafe, **44**
Butler's Chocolate Cafe, **38**
Cafe Irie, **58**
Cornucopia, **36**
Epicurean Food Hall, **21**
Fagan's, **1**
Govinda's, **46, 50**
gruel, **64**
Havana, **34**
Jamuna, **2**

Juice, **37**
La Med, **51**
Lemon Crepe &
  Coffee Co., **40**
Leo Burdock's, **33**
Maloti, **42**
Market Bar, **41**
The Mermaid Cafe, **63**
Metro Cafe, **43**
Monty's of
  Kathmandu, **65**
Nude, **35**
O'Shea's Hotel, **13**
Panem, **25**
Queen of Tarts, **67**
Soup Dragon, **26**
Tante Zoe's, **66**
Unicorn Café Restaurant/
  Food Store, **49**
Wagamama, **47**
Yamamori Noodles, **39**
Zaytoon, **53**

THEATRES AND CINEMAS

Abbey/Peacock Theatre, **20**
City Arts Theatre, **24**
Gaiety Theatre, **45**
Gate Theatre, **9**
Irish Film Institute, **60**
The New Theatre, **56**
Olympia Theatre, **62**
Project Arts Centre, **57**
Samuel Beckett Theatre, **30**
Savoy Cinema, **15**
The Screen Cinema, **27**
UGC Multiplex, **16**

COUNTY DUBLIN

Phibsborough Rd.
Royal Canal Bank
Western Wa
Dominick
Constitution Hill
King's Inns
Brunswick St.
Beresford St.
Church St.
North King St.
Arbour Hill
Montpelier Hill
TO PHOENIX
PARK (290m)
National Museum/
Collins Barracks
Benburb St.
Chimney Viewing Tower
Old Jameson
Distillery
Mary's Ln.
Smithfield St.
Queen St.
Blackhall Pl.
Bow St.
St. Michan's
Church
Chancery St.
Greek St.
Marke
Wolfe Tone Quay
Ellis Quay
Arran Quay
Inns Quay
The
Four Courts
Upper C
Heuston
Station
Victoria Quay
Usher's Island
James
Joyce House
Island St.
Usher's Quay
Merchants Quay
Wood Qu.
St. James's
Gate Brewery
Watling St.
Bridgefoot St.
Bridge St.
St. Augustine St.
St. Audoen's
Church
Dublinia
City Of
Christ Church
Cathedral
Stevens Ln.
Oliver Bond St.
High St.
St. James's St.
Thomas St.
Cornmarket
Vicar St.
Guinness
Storehouse
Rainsford St.
Nicholas St.
TO KILMAINHAM GAOL (585m),
ROYAL HOSPITAL (615m)
Bellevue St.
Earl St.
Meath Pl.
Meath St.
Francis St.
Patrick St.
Bull Alle
Basin St.
Upper
Marrowbone Ln.
Summer St.
The Coombe
St. Patrick's
Cathedra
Wellington Quay
Temple Bar
Temple Bar
Gallery & Studios
Crow Alley
Essex Quay
Essex
Gate
Essex St. E.
Temple
Bar Music
Centre
Cecilia St.
Crow St.
Fownes St.
Cope St.
New St.
Essex St. W.
Parliament St.
Exchange St.
Crane Ln.
Sycamore St.
MEETING
HOUSE SQ.
Eustace St.
Gallery of
Photo-
graphy
Temple Ln. S.
Dame St.
Square Wheel
Cycle Works
City
Hall
Temple Bar

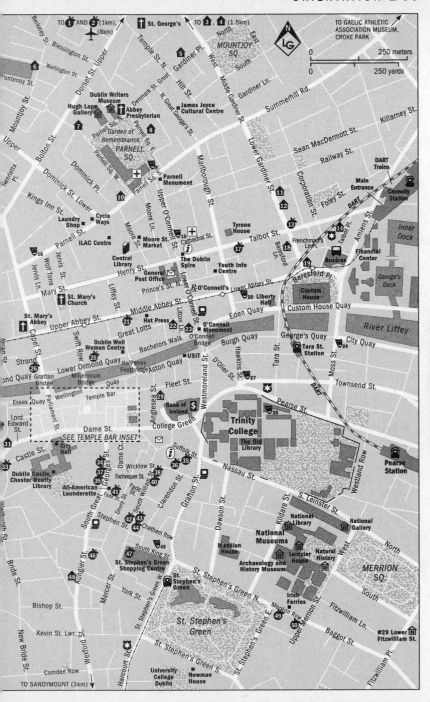

TO ❶ AND ❷ (1km),
(8km)

St. George's

TO ❸ ❹ (1.5km)

TO GAELIC ATHLETIC
ASSOCIATION MUSEUM,
CROKE PARK

N
LG

0   250 meters
0   250 yards

Berkeley St.
Blessington St.
Wellington St.

MOUNTJOY
SQ.
North
West
East
South

Temple St. Upper

Gardiner Pl.

❺

Dorset St. Upper

Hill St.

Gardiner Ln.

Summerhill Rd.

Killarney St.

Fontenoy St.
❻
Mountjoy
Upper
Henrietta
Pl.

Wellington St.

Dublin Writers
Museum
Hugh Lane
Gallery
❼

Denmark St. Great
N. Great George's St.

Abbey
Presbyterian

James Joyce
Cultural Centre

❽

Lower Gardiner St.

Sean MacDermott St.

Railway St.

DART
Trains

Bolton St.
Dominick St. Lower

Parnell Sq. W.
Parnell Sq. N.
Parnell Sq. E.
Garden of
Remembrance

PARNELL
SQ.

Marlborough St.

Corporation St.

Foley St.

Main
Entrance

DART

Connolly
Station

Kings Inn St.

Dominick St. Lower
Parnell St.
Parnell Sq. W.

❿
❾
Parnell
Monument

Upper O'Connell St.

Lower Gardiner St.

❶❶
❶❷

Amiens St.

Busáras
❶❹

Financial
Center

Inner
Dock

Laundry
Shop
Cycle
Ways

Moore Ln.
Moore St.

Tyrone
House

Talbot St.

❶❸
Frenchman's
Ln.

Talbot Pl.

George's
Dock

ILAC Centre

Central
Library

Moore St.
Market

Cathedral St.

❶❼

Belfast Ln.

❶❽

Parnell St.
Jervis St.
Wolf Tone St.
❶❻

Henry St.

General
Post Office

The Dublin
Spire

Youth Info
Centre

❶❾

Beresford Pl.

Custom
House

Financial
Center

St. Mary's
Church
Mary St.

Liffey St.
Middle Abbey St.
Upper Abbey St.

Prince's St. N.
O'Connell's

Lower Abbey St.

❷⓿ Liberty
Hall

Custom House Quay

River Liffey

St. Mary's
Abbey

Capel St.
Swift's Row
Great Lotts

Hot Press
❷❶
❷❷ ❷❸

O'Connell
Monument
O'Connell
Bridge

George's Quay

Tara St.
Station

City Quay
❷❹

Strand St.
Ormond Quay
❷❻

Dublin Well
Woman Centre

Bachelors Walk

Ha'penny
Footbridge

Millennium
Bridge

Lower Ormond Quay

Aston Quay
USIT

Burgh Quay

Hawkins St.
D'Olier St.

❷❼

Moss St.

Townsend St.

DART

Essex
Quay
Grattan
Bridge

Wellington

Temple Bar

Fleet St.

Anglesea St.
❷❾

Westmoreland St.

Pearse St.

❸⓿

Lord
Edward
St.
❸❶

Parliament St.
Dame St.

SEE TEMPLE BAR INSET

Bank of
Ireland
$

College Green

Trinity
College

Westland Row

Pearse
Station

Castle St.
❸❸
Dublin Castle
Chester Beatty
Library

City
Hall

❸❹
❸❼
❸❾
All-American
Launderette

South Great Georges St.
Dame Ct.

Wicklow St.
Exchequer St.
❸❽
❹⓿
Fade St.

Suffolk St.
❸❻ ❹❺
The Old
Library

Nassau St.

S. Leinster St.

Wigtown St.
❹❶
Drury St.
South William St.
Clarendon St.

Grafton St.

Dawson St.

Kildare St.

National
Library

National
Gallery

❹❷ ❹❸
❹❹ Chatham Row

National
Museums

Natural
History

MERRION
SQ.

Aungier St.
❹❻

South King St.
❹❺

Mansion
House

Leinster
House

North
West
South

❹❽

Mercer St.
York St.

St. Stephen's Green
Shopping Centre

❺

St. Stephen's Green W.
St. Stephen's Green N.

St.
Stephen's
Green

Archaeology and
History Museum

Irish
Ferries
❹❾
❺⓿

Merrion Row
Upper Merrion St.

Fitzwilliam Ln.
Fitzwilliam Pl.

#29 Lower
Fitzwilliam St.

Bishop St.

St. Stephen's
Green

St. Stephen's Green S.

Baggot St.

Kevin St. Lwr.

New Bride St.
Bride St.
Wexford St.

Camden Row

TO SANDYMOUNT (3km)

Harcourt St.

University
College
Dublin

Newman
House

ghetto"). The core of Dublin is ringed by **North** and **South Circular Roads,** each with its own creative assortment of pseudonyms and name changes. Most of the city's major sights are located within this area; the walk from one end to the other takes about one hour. **O'Connell Street,** three blocks west of Busáras, is the primary link between north and south Dublin. The streets running alongside the Liffey are called **quays** (KEEZ); the name of the quay changes with every block. Dubliners are more likely to direct by quays, rather than by street name or address. If a street is split into "Upper" and "Lower" (which occurs on both sides of the river) the "Lower" is the section closer to the Liffey.

South of the Liffey, O'Connell St. becomes **Westmoreland Street,** passes **Fleet Street,** curves around the western side of Trinity College, and then becomes **Grafton Street. Fleet Street** becomes **Temple Bar.** Temple Bar is also the term for the area bordered by the Liffey, Dame St., Westmoreland St., and Parliament St., which is invaded nightly by battalions of pub-seeking students and tourists, armed with proper identification. By day, Temple Bar's funky restaurants, art museums, and workshops attract well-heeled locals. The southern edge, **Dame Street,** which runs parallel to Temple Bar and terminates at Trinity College, is a major artery full of restaurants and cafes that are easier on the wallet. **Trinity College** is the nexus of Dublin's cultural activity, pulling many bookshops and student-oriented pubs into its orbit. The college touches the northern end of **Grafton Street,** where street entertainers brush elbows with big-league shoppers. Grafton's southern end opens onto **St. Stephen's Green,** the famous public park and a site of pilgrimage for Dubliners when they're blessed with a few minutes of sun.

Merchants on the North Side unload goods for better prices than those in the more touristed South. **Henry Street** and **Mary Street** comprise a pedestrian shopping zone that intersects with O'Connell St. just after the **General Post Office,** two blocks from the Liffey. The North Side has a reputation for being a rougher area, especially after dark. This reputation may not be wholly deserved, but tourists should avoid walking in unfamiliar areas on either side of the Liffey at night. As in any big city, the best advice is to not walk alone and to avoid parks at night.

⌐ LOCAL TRANSPORTATION

Buses: Dublin Bus, 59 O'Connell St. (☎873 4222; www.dublinbus.ie). Open M-F 8:30am-5:30pm, Sa 9am-2pm, Su 9:30am-2pm. See **By Bus,** p. 28.)

Taxis: Blue Cabs (☎802 2222), **ABC** (☎285 5444), and **City Metro Cabs** (☎872 7272) have wheelchair-accessible cabs (call ahead). **Taxi stands** are located outside Trinity College, behind the Bank of Ireland, on Lower Abbey St. at the bus station (Busáras), on the north side of St. Stephen's Green, and on Parnell St. All available 24hr. Taxis are notoriously expensive in Dublin; ask how much a route is expected to cost before getting in. Typical charges start at €2 with a rolling rate of €0.30-0.45 per min. A cheaper, environmentally-safer, albeit slightly slower alternative is the newly-debuted fleet of **Ecocabs** (www.ecocabs.ie). Ecocabs are passenger bikes run on the muscles of operators and self-charging battery power. The very fit drivers will take up to 2 passengers anywhere in the city center completely free of charge, though tips (anywhere between €0.50 and €5) are appreciated. The bikes cluster around the spire, Trinity college area, and Grafton, and run daily 10am-8pm.

Car Rental: Alamo, Dublin Airport (☎844 4162; www.alamo.com). Economy €47 per day, €160-200 per wk. Ages 24-74. **Argus,** Woodlawn Industrial Estate (☎4999 600; www.argusrentals.com), also in the airport. Economy €28 per day, from €120 per wk. Ages 25-70. **Avis,** Dublin airport and 35-39 Old Kilmainham, city center (☎605 7500; www.avis.ie). Economy €65 per day, €162 per wk. Long-term rentals available. Minimum age 21; €15 per day under-25 surcharge. **Budget,** 151 Lower Drumcondra Rd. (☎837 9611; www.budget.ie) and at the airport. Economy from €49 per day, €160 per wk. Ages 23-75. **Enterprise,** Russell St. (☎836 6577; www.enterprise.com) and at the airport, rents from €30 per day to 21+. Rates vary; a bit of online research usually pays off. Be warned that Dublin traffic is heavy, and parking spaces are scarce.

Bike Rental: Cycle Ways, 185-6 Parnell St. (☎873 4748). Rents quality hybrid or mountain bikes. €20 per day, €80 per wk. with €200 deposit. Open M-W and F-Sa 9:30am-6pm, Th 9:30am-8pm, Su 11am-5pm. **Neill's Wheels,** 9 Capel St. (085 153 0648), rents bikes at the same rates, helmets for €5, and has the added service of delivery and daily 2hr. tours, starting at 6:30pm on Essex bridge. **Square Wheel Cylcle Works,** 21 Temple Lane S. (☎086 081 4417; squarewheel_dublin@yahoo.com), in Temple Bar. Owner lets customers buy any used bike with the agreement to buy it back. Call ahead as bikes are subject to availability.

Hitchhiking: Since Dublin is well served by bus and rail, there is no good reason to thumb it. **Hitchhiking in Co. Dublin and its vicinity is extremely unsafe,** especially for women, who have met tragic fates hitching in the area in the past. *Let's Go* never recommends hitchhiking.

☑ PRACTICAL INFORMATION

TOURIST AND FINANCIAL SERVICES

Tourist Information: Main Office, Suffolk St. (☎6697 92083; international ☎0800 039 7000; www.visitdublin.com). From Connolly Station, walk left down Amiens St., take a right onto Lower Abbey St., pass Busáras, and continue until O'Connell St. Turn left, cross the bridge, and walk past Trinity College; the office is on the right, down Suffolk St., in a converted church. Books accommodations for €4, contracting with the **Gulliver Ireland** travel agency for credit card bookings by phone (☎6697 92082). **Fexco** provides **currency exchange** and money transfers. (☎605 7709. Open M-Sa 9am-5:30pm, Su 10:30am-3pm.) **Bus Éireann** provides info and tickets. **Dollar** and **Thrifty** car rentals have desks here. (M-F 9am-5pm, Sa 9am-1pm.) **Fáilte Ireland** provides a list of car rental agencies and also books tours, concerts, plays, and most anything else in Dublin that requires a ticket (through **Ticketmaster**); booking fee €2 for Ticketmaster. Main Office open M-Sa 9am-5:30pm, Su 10:30am-3pm; July-Aug. hours extended M-Sa 9am-7pm. Reservation desks close 30min. early. Tourist info within Ireland also available at ☎850 230 330.

Tourist Office Branches: Dublin Airport. Open daily 8am-10pm. **Dún Laoghaire Harbour,** Ferry Terminal Building. Open M-Sa 10am-1pm and 2-6pm. **Baggot St.** Open M-F 9:30am-noon and 12:30-5pm. **13 Upper O'Connell St.** Open M-Sa 9am-5pm. The latter 3 branches are well stocked and less crowded than the airport and main branches. All telephone inquiries handled by the central office (☎850 230 330).

Northern Ireland Tourist Board: 16 Nassau St. (☎679 1977 or 850 230 230). Books accommodations in the North. Open M-F 9:15am-5:30pm, Sa 10am-5pm.

THE REAL DEAL. Similar in concept to the Heritage Card (p. 94), the Dublin Pass really makes its carriers feel important as it allows those who purchase it (€31) to skip the queues. However, you'll need a lot more time-savers and a pure love of touristy attractions to get your money's worth; the card is only valid for one day. Additional durations are offered (up to 6 days) but are similarly steep (€89). If you think you're up for the challenge, cards can be purchased at Dublin tourist offices or online, www.dublinpass.ie.

Budget Travel: USIT, 19-21 Aston Quay (☎602 1600), near O'Connell Bridge. The place for Irish travel discounts. ISIC, HI, Student Travelcard and EYC cards. Photo booths €6. Student Travelcard most widely accepted for Irish public transportation. Also books flights. Open M-F 9:30am-7pm, Sa 10am-5pm. The Student Union in Trinity College also sells Student Travelcards for €12 (☎896 1268).

Hosteling Organization: An Óige Head Office (Irish Youth Hostel Association/HI), 61 Mountjoy St. (☎830 4555; www.irelandyha.org), at Wellington St. Follow O'Connell St. north, ignoring its name changes. Mountjoy St. is on the left, 20min. from O'Connell Bridge. Book and pay for HI hostels here. Also sells bike and rail package tours. The An Óige Handbook lists all HI hostels in Ireland and Northern Ireland. Hugely beneficial membership card valid for the calendar year €20, under 18 €10. Open M-F 9:30am-5:30pm. (Also see **Hostels,** p. 39.)

Embassies: For an extensive list of embassies and consulates, see **Essentials,** p. 8.

Banks: Bank of Ireland, AIB, and **TSB** branches with **bureaux de change** and 24hr. **ATMs** cluster on Lower O'Connell St., Grafton St., and near Suffolk and Dame St. Bureaux de change also in the General Post Office and in the tourist office main branch, and scattered about the city. At lunch hour (typically 1-2pm) and on F evenings, long lines form outside the ATMs, which aren't replenished over the weekends. Most banks open M-W and F 10am-4pm, Th 10am-5pm.

LOCAL SERVICES

Luggage Storage: Connolly Station. Small lockers €4, large lockers €6. Open daily 7am-10pm. **Busáras.** Lockers €5/7/10. Open 24hr. The **Global Internet Cafe** (see **Internet,** p. 103), in the city center, stores luggage for €4 1st day, €2 per extra day.

Library: Dublin Corporation Central Library, Henry and Moore St. (☎873 4333), upstairs in the ILAC Centre. Video and CD sampling facilities, EU telephone directories, and free **Internet** access (book ahead). Checking out books requires proof of residence in Dublin. Tourists may apply for a reference ticket, which allows use of library facilities, minus check-out privileges. Open M-Th 10am-8pm, F-Sa 10am-5pm.

Women's Resources: Women's Aid Helpline (☎800 341 900; www.womensaid.ie) offers support groups and info on legal matters (10am-10pm). **Dublin Rape Crisis Centre,** 70 Lower Leeson St. (☎661 4911; 24hr. hotline ☎800 778 888). Office open M-F 8am-7pm, Sa 9am-4pm; call for an appointment. **Dublin Well Woman Centre,** 35 Lower Liffey St. (☎872 8051; www.wellwomancentre.ie), is a private health center for women. It also runs a clinic (☎660 9860), 67 Pembroke Rd. Offers student discount on services to USIT cardholders.

Ticket Agencies: Try the Ticketmaster ticket desk at the Suffolk St. tourist office or www.ticketmaster.ie.

Laundry: All-American Launderette, 40 South Great Georges St. (☎677 2779). Self-service €6.50; full-service €9.50. Detergent €2 extra. Open M-Sa 8:30am-7pm, Su 10am-6pm. **Laundry Shop,** 191 Parnell St. (☎872 3541). Self-service €8.80; full-service €10. Detergent €1.10 extra. Open M-F 9am-7pm, Sa 9am-6pm.

EMERGENCY AND COMMUNICATIONS

Emergency: ☎999 or 112; no coins required.

Police *(Garda):* Dublin Metro Headquarters, Harcourt Terr. (☎666 9500); Store St. Station (☎666 8000); Fitzgibbon St. Station (☎666 8400); Pearse St. Station (☎666 9000). **Police Confidential Report Line:** ☎800 666 111.

Counseling and Support: Irish Tourist Assistance Service, Harcourt Sq. (☎478 5295; www.itas.ie). Helps robbery victims find accommodations and contact embassies or families. A loss or crime report must first be filed with the police. Also offers telephones, email, assistance with language difficulties, emergency meals and shelter, and help with re-issuing travel tickets and canceling credit cards. Open M-Sa 10am-6pm, Su noon-6pm. **Samaritans,** 112 Marlborough St. (office ☎872 7700; 24hr. helpline ☎850 609 090), offers general counseling. **Dublin Rape Crisis Centre,** 70 Lower Leeson St. (☎661 4911; 24hr. hotline ☎800 778 888). Office open M-F 8am-7pm, Sa 9am-4pm; call for an appointment. **Cura,** 30 South Anne St. (☎850 622 626; Dublin office ☎671 0598), is a Catholic support organization for women with unplanned pregnancies. Open M-W 10:30am-6:30pm, Th-F 10:30am-2:30pm, Sa 1-4pm. **AIDS Helpline** (☎800 459 459). Open daily 10am-5pm.

Pharmacy: O'Connell's, 56 Lower O'Connell St. (☎873 0427). Convenient to city bus routes. Open M-F 7:30am-10pm, Sa 8am-10pm, Su 10am-10pm. Other branches scattered about the city, including locations on Grafton St. and Westmoreland St. **Dowling's,** 6 Baggot St. (☎678 5612), near the Shelbourne Hotel and St. Stephen's Green. Open M-W and F 8am-7pm, Th 8am-8pm, Sa 9am-7pm.

Hospital: St. James's Hospital, James St. (☎410 3000). Bus #123. **Mater Misericordiae Hospital,** Eccles St. (☎803 2000), off Lower Dorset St. Buses #3, 10, 11, 16, 22. **Beaumont Hospital,** Beaumont Rd. (☎809 3000). Buses #103, 104, 27b, 42a, 51a. **The Adelaide and Meath Hospital** (☎414 2000), farther south, is served by buses #49, 49A, 50, 54A, 65, 65B, 75, 76, 77, 77A, 201, 202.

Phones: Telecom Éireann (inquiries ☎1901). Public pay phones are on almost every corner. Privatization of Ireland's phone industry has led other companies to put up their own pay phones; pay careful attention to varying rates for local calls, which start at about €0.50 per 2min. and rise with distance. (Also see **Telephones,** p. 35.)

Directory Inquiries: ☎11811 (free) or 11850 (€0.65 first min., €0.10 each additional min.); international ☎11866 (€1.20 first min., €0.60 each additional min.).

Internet: Free Internet access is available at the **Central Library** (see **Local Services,** p. 102), but slots fill up quickly. Chains abound; the best are **Global Internet Cafe,** 8 Lower O'Connell St. (☎878 0295; www.globalcafe.ie) and its partner **Central Cyber Cafe,** 6 Grafton St. (☎677 8298; www.centralcafe.ie), though Global tends to be cheaper and has longer hours. Central's 2nd fl. (without cafe) is also cheaper. They offer a wide array of services, plus excellent coffee. €3-4.50 per hr., students €2.65-4, members €2.25-3. Membership €5 weekly; €10 monthly. Wi-Fi €2 per hr. or €10 per 8hr. over a 7-day period. Global open M-F 8am-11pm, Sa 9am-11pm, Su 10am-11pm. Central open M-F 9am-10pm, Sa-Su 10am-9pm. **The Internet Exchange,** with branches at Cecilia St. (☎670 3000) and Fownes St. in Temple Bar (☎635 1680). €3 per hr. Cecilia location open M-F 8am-2am, Sa-Su 10am-2am; Fownes location open M-Th and Su 9am-12:30am, F-Sa 10am-1am. **Wired,** 15 Aungier St. (☎405 4814), with other locations around the city, charges €16 per 10hr. in addition to its normal rates of €1 per 20 min. and €2 per hr. Open daily 9am-midnight. **The Planet Cyber Cafe,** 13 St. Andrews St. (☎670 5182) has a sci-fi theme and tasty food. €0.05 per min. before noon, €0.10 per min. after noon. Open M-F 10am-8pm.

Post Office: General Post Office (GPO), O'Connell St. (☎705 7000). *Poste Restante* pickup at the **Poste Restante** window (see **Mail,** p. 38). Open M-Sa 8am-8pm. Smaller post offices, including one on Suffolk St. across from the tourist office, are typically open M-Tu and Th-F 9am-6pm, W 9:30am-6pm.

Postal Code: Dublin is the only place in the Republic that uses postal codes. The city is organized into regions numbered 1-18, 20, 22, and 24; even-numbered codes are for areas south of the Liffey, while odd-numbered ones are for the north. The numbers radiate out from the city center: North City Centre is 1, South City Centre is 2.

⌐ ACCOMMODATIONS

Because Dublin is an incredibly popular destination, it is necessary to book accommodations at least one week in advance, particularly around Easter weekend, bank holiday weekends, sporting weekends, St. Patrick's Day, New Year's, and June through August. The tourist office books local accommodations for a fee of €4, but they only deal in Fáilte Ireland-approved B&Bs and hostels. Approved accommodations aren't necessarily better than unapproved ones, though they do tend to be a bit cleaner. Phoenix Park may tempt the desperate, but camping there is a terrible idea, not to mention illegal—if the *Garda* or park rangers don't deter you, the threat of thieves should. If the following accommodations are full, consult Dublin Tourism's annual *Sleep! Guide* (€2.50), or ask hostel staff for referrals.

Accommodations with a nifty green shamrock sign out front are registered, occasionally checked, and approved by Fáilte Ireland. Hostels and B&Bs without the shamrock haven't been inspected but may be cheaper and better located—some owners with a streak of individualism often find that Fáilte Ireland's advertising is unnecessary. Rooms range from €15 at the very lowest to upwards of €50 per person. On the North Side, B&Bs cluster along **Upper** and **Lower Gardiner Street,** on **Sheriff Street,** and near **Parnell Square.** Exercise caution when walking home through the inner-city area at night. **Clonliffe Road, Sandymount,** and **Clontarf** are no more than a 15min. bus ride from Eden Quay. If you don't have a reservation, chances of finding an available room in a decent B&B are better farther out.

INSIDE THE CITY CENTER

TEMPLE BAR AND THE QUAYS

Chic cafes and ethnic restaurants crowd the cobblestone streets of Temple Bar. Unfortunately, so do throngs of tourists and drunken revelers. Located close to all the major sights and pubs, Temple Bar accommodations are convenient and relatively safe, but often quite loud, especially on weekends.

Barnacles Temple Bar House, 19 Temple Ln. (☎671 6277). Patrons can nearly jump into bed from Temple Bar pubs, including the actual Temple Bar, next door. Spacious, sky-lit lounge with open fire and TV, and a colorfully tiled and well-kept kitchen. All rooms with bath. Continental breakfast included. Free luggage storage. Laundry €6.50, dry only €3.50. Internet access €1 per 15min. 11-bed dorms €15.50-18.50; 6-bed €21-25.50; quads €25.50-28.50; doubles €68-82. ❶

Oliver St. John Gogarty's Temple Bar B&B, 18-21 Anglesea St. (☎671 1822; www.gogartys.ie). Bright, clean dorms in an old, well-maintained building above a popular pub of the same name. Great location for Temple Bar enthusiasts. Elevator access. Laundry €5. 8- to 10-bed dorms €18-25; 4 to 6-bed €20-35; doubles €30-45. Self-catering quad €200-250; 6-person €210-300. ❷

Bridge House (☎672 5811; www.thebridgehouse.net), corner of Parliament and Essex St. Comfortable ensuite rooms in an elegant Georgian townhouse. Continental breakfast included. Singles €69-85; doubles €85-130; triples €105-185. ❹

Litton Lane Hostel, 2-4 Litton Ln. (☎872 8389; www.littonlane.hostel.com), off Bachelor's Walk. Coolest history and staff. Former studio for U2, Van Morrison, and Sinéad O'Connor is full of personality (murals and silkscreens) and personableness (staff is likely to remember your name). Not the cleanest or the most modern, but a laid-back atmosphere ensures a comfortable stay. Free Wi-Fi. Free luggage storage. Key deposit €1. Dorms €20-22; doubles €80. ❷

Cobblestones, 29 Eustace St. (☎677 8154 or 677 5422), in the middle of Temple Bar. Snug rooms with large windows, nice showers, and a fantastic location. Book before Feb. and watch the St. Patrick's Day parade from the patio roof. Continental breakfast included. Free Wi-Fi. Dorms €19-22; doubles €55-60. Discounts available mid-week, for stays 1 wk. or longer, and for groups. ❷

GARDINER STREET AND CUSTOMS HOUSE

The area near the train and bus station holds some of Dublin's best hostels in one of its less desirable neighborhoods. These are fine places to stay for late arrivals or early departures, or for those who don't mind a walk to good food and nightlife. **Gardiner Street** runs north from the **Custom House** and parallel to **O'Connell Street. Parnell Square** sits at the top of **Upper Gardiner Street.** Both Lower and Upper Gardiner St. are within walking distance of **Busáras** and **Connolly Station;** buses #41, 41B, and 41C from Eden Quay travel to the end of the road.

■ **Globetrotters Tourist Hostel (IHH),** 46-47 Lower Gardiner St. (☎878 8808; www.globe-trottersdublin.com or www.townhouseofdublin.com). Dose of luxury at a budget price. Trendy pop art, tropical fish, a lush courtyard, well-dressed staff, and all-you-can-eat Irish breakfast make this Georgian mansion more like a posh B&B than a hostel. Private rooms with TV in adjacent **townhouse.** Free Internet access. Free luggage storage. Towels €1 with €6 deposit. Dorms €24-29; singles €70; triples €132; quads €140. ❷

Browns Hostel, 89-90 Lower Gardiner St. (☎855 0034; www.brownshostelireland.com). Long-term residents cook and play pool in the cavernous wine-cellar-turned-kitchen and lounge of this friendly hostel. Closets and A/C in every room, TVs in most. Locker-room-like showers in the basement. Skylights in the Shannon room. Breakfast included. Next door cafe (same owners) serves €5 pizza meal to hostelers. Internet €5 per hr. Lockers €1. Blankets €2. Towels €1-1.50. 20-bed dorms €15; 10- to 14-bed €20; 4- to 6-bed €25. Long-term stays €100 per wk. ❶

Abraham House, 82-3 Lower Gardiner St. (☎855 0600). Dependable staff and large dorms with ensuite baths. Comfortable private bedrooms sleep up to 4 and have TVs and kettles. Bureau de change. Free Wi-Fi. Light breakfast included. Free luggage storage. Security box €5 deposit and €1 per day. 20- and 10-bed dorms €10-29; 8- and 6-bed €18-25; 4-bed €23-33. Private rooms €80. ❷

Jacob's Inn, 21-28 Talbot Pl. (☎855 5660; www.isaacs.ie). 2 blocks north of the Custom House. Elevator, cleanliness and all ensuite rooms all say hotel more than hostel; unfortunately, so does its lack of character and community. Bike storage. Wheelchair-accessible. Light breakfast included. Lockers €1.50 per night. Towels €2. Lockout 11am-3pm. Dorms €15-26; doubles €80-130; triples €81-120. ❷

Paddy's Palace ❷, 5 Beresford Place (☎823 0822; www.paddywagontours.com), off Lower Gardiner St. Bright Irish colors and painted leprechaun logo are gimmicky, but kind staff, enormous tapestry curtains, and modern facilities add substance. Internet access €1 per 30min. Free Wi-Fi. Safe €2. Breakfast included. 6- to 10-bed dorms €17-21; 4-bed €20-23; doubles €54-66.

WEST OF TEMPLE BAR

Though the area west of Temple Bar is more industrial than the city center and farther from anything resembling nightlife, it has several excellent accommodations and is close to some of the city's main sights, including the Guinness Brewery and so many churches you can't help but feel blessed.

■ **Four Courts Hostel,** 15-17 Merchants Quay (☎672 5862). On the south bank of the river. Bus #748 from the airport stops next door. Friendly, helpful staff runs this 250-bed hostel, which has pristine, well-lit rooms and hardwood floors. Quiet lounge and a combination TV/game room provide plenty of space to wind down. Car park. Continental breakfast included. In-room lockers. Laundry €7. 8- to 16-bed dorms €15-20; 4- to 6-bed €24-27; doubles €62-70; triples €90. ❷

Kinlay House (IHH), 2-12 Lord Edward St. (☎679 6644). Great location a few blocks from Temple Bar. If you don't a get a room with a view of the Christ Church Cathedral, at least you can watch the plasma TV. Free Internet access. Continental breakfast included. Lockers €1 with €5 deposit. Laundry €8. 16- to 24-bed dorms €17-20; 4- to 6-bed €24-29; singles €44-56; doubles €29-33; triples €27-33. ❷

Avalon House (IHH), 55 Aungier St. (☎475 0001; www.avalon-house.ie). Performers from salsa dancers to musicians get free accommodation if they spend one hour teaching other guests. Foosball, ping-pong, air hockey and video games also save hostelers from boredom and emptying their wallets in the city. Wheelchair-accessible with elevator. Free Internet access. Light continental breakfast included. Lockers and smaller lockboxes €1 each. Laundry €5. Large dorms €14-20; 4- to 6-bed dorms €24-27; singles €30-39; doubles €66-74. ❷

The Brewery Hostel, 22-23 Thomas St. (☎453 8600). Follow Dame St. past Christ Church through its name changes, or take bus #123. So close to the Guinness Brewery that it smells of hops. 15-20min. walk from Temple Bar. Accommodating staff. Picnic area with grill. Free car park. All rooms with bath. Continental breakfast included. Free luggage storage. Free Internet access. 8- and 10-bed dorms €18-25; doubles €70. ❷

NORTH OF O'CONNELL STREET

Since the area north of O'Connell St., around Parnell Sq. and beyond, is generally less ritzy and touristed than Temple Bar and its environs, it's also much quieter. While the more eclectic and avant-garde artistic tastes lie south of the Liffey, there are still plenty of attractions here; elegant architecture and sights like the Dublin Writers Museum and the Gate Theatre sparkle with their own charm.

■ **Parkway Guest House,** 5 Gardiner Pl. (☎874 0469; www.parkway-guesthouse.com). Sports fans bond with the proprietor, a former hurling star, while those less athletically inclined still appreciate his great eye for interior design, consistent delivery of great advice, and all-star breakfasts. Car park available for 4 cars. Singles €40; doubles €60-70, €65-80 with bath.❸

■ **Abbey Court Hostel,** 29 Bachelor's Walk (☎878 0700; www.abbey-court.com). Corner of O'Connell St. and Bachelor's Walk near bridge. Hostel boasts clean yet narrow rooms overlooking the Liffey, a greenhouse-like common room, and a newly refurbished kitchen. Hidden apartments each have lounge, TV, and lush courtyard. Internet access €1 per 15min., €2 per 40min. Continental breakfast included at NYStyle cafe next door. Free luggage storage; security box €1. Full-service laundry €8. 12-bed dorms €19-22; 6-bed €24-27; 4-bed €27-30; doubles €78-88. Long-term rate €119 per wk. includes breakfast. Apartments from €30 per person per night. ❷

Harvey's Guest House, 11 Upper Gardiner St. (☎874 8384; www.harveysguesthouse.com). 2 adjoining Georgian houses offer wooden sleigh beds, TVs, and well-appointed bathrooms. Full breakfast included in a charming converted cellar. Car park in back. €55-65 per person. ❹

Charles Stewart B&B, 5-6 Parnell Sq. E. (☎878 0350; www.charlesstewart.com). Birthplace of the infamous author Oliver St. John Gogarty, this home has a great location in the oasis of Parnell Sq. Its proximity to the Dublin Writer's Museum only adds to the literary feel. Irish breakfast included. Singles €57-63; doubles €69-99; triples €120. ❺

Dublin International Youth Hostel (An Óige/HI), 61 Mountjoy St. (☎830 4555; www.irelandyha.org). Huge, rambling hostel housed in a converted convent and 18th-century school. Complimentary breakfast served in the former chapel with arched wooden ceilings. Wheelchair-accessible. Bureau de change. Car park and buses to Temple Bar. In-room storage; luggage storage at reception €1.25 per day. Towels €1. Laundry €5. Internet access €1 for 15min., €2 for 40min. HI €2 discount per person per night. Dorms €19-22; doubles €48-52; triples €72-78; quads €86-100. Ask at the desk about **work opportunities.** ❷

The Kingfisher, 166 Parnell St. (☎872 8732; www.kingfisherdublin.com). Inn, restaurant, and cafe in one. Bathrooms clean enough to sleep in, but the rooms are more comfortable. Irish breakfast included. Restaurant offers cheap takeaway. Free Wi-Fi in cafe. Sleek TV/VCR in each room; kitchenettes in some. €35-45 per person; with 4-course dinner from €65 per person. Discounts for stays longer than 5 days. ❹

Marian B&B, 21 Upper Gardiner St. (☎874 4129; marianbb@gofree.indigo.ie). Fine rooms near Mountjoy St. Irish breakfast included. Singles €40; doubles €70. ❸

OUTSIDE THE CITY CENTER

DORSET TO DRUMCONDRA

This is an ideal place to stay if you're planning on paying a visit to **Croke Park** or **The National Botanic Gardens.** Not having to constantly bob and weave through packs of people is a plus. Additionally, most spots are a straight shot to the airport; those flying out of Dublin will appreciate not having to deal with city center traffic. To make the 20min. walk from the city center, go up O'Connell St., turn right on Dorset St., head across the Royal Canal, then turn right onto Clonliffe Rd. Buses #3 and 11 run to the city center; #41A/B/C, 746, and 747 run to and from the airport.

Applewood B&B, 144 Upper Drumcondra Rd. (☎837 8328; www.applewood.ie). Proprietress can tell you exactly how to get anywhere you want to go, but you'll probably be content to stay in her simple, comfy beds. Singles €40-50; doubles €65-75. ❸

Tinode House, 170 Upper Drumcondra Rd. (☎837 2277; www.tinodehouse.com). Big beds, cozy conservatory, and smoked salmon on the menu at this Edwardian home. Singles €55-70; doubles €35-45 per person. ❹

Comfort Inn, Granby Row/Parnell Sq. (☎0818 333 444; www.comfortinns.ie), off Dorset St. Don't be deterred by the chain name—this brand new model's got a little flair; funky modern decor and techno-savvy suites heat up former wax museum location. Flatscreen TVs. Free broadband in rooms, Wi-Fi in lobby and bar. Doubles from €89. ❸

CLONTARF

Clontarf Rd. runs north along Dublin Bay. Bus #130 takes 15min. to go from Lower Abbey St. to Clontarf Rd.

Waterville, 154 Clontarf Rd. (☎833 0238), past Oulton Rd. Wooden floors, a modern space, and a dining room overlooking the bay. All rooms with bath, TV, and phone. Internet access available. Doubles €70. ❹

The White House, 125 Clontarf Rd. (☎833 3196). Sink into bed and gaze out at the spacious backyard. Irish breakfast included. Singles €45; doubles €70. ❸

Clontarf Court Hotel, 225 Clontarf Rd. (☎833 2680). Family-owned hotel overlooks a sailboat harbor and the heavy machinery behind it. Room 104 has the best views. Irish breakfast included. Singles €65; doubles €95; family room €130. ❺

CAMPING

Most campsites are far from the city center, but plenty of camping equipment is available in the heart of the city. **The Great Outdoors,** on Chatham St. off Grafton St., has an excellent selection of tents, packs, and cookware. (☎679 4293; www.greatoutdoors.ie. An Óige members 10% discount. Open M-W and F-Sa 9:30am-6pm, Th 9:30am-8pm, Su 12:30-5:30pm.) On the north side, the **Outdoor Adventure Store,** Upper Liffey St., has enthusiastic owners and an extensive selection. (☎872 5177; www.outdooradventurestore.ie. Open M-W and F-Sa 9am-6pm, Th 9am-7pm, Su noon-5pm.) It is illegal and unsafe to camp in Phoenix Park.

North Beach Caravan and Camping Park (☎843 7131; www.northbeach.ie), in Rush. Accessible by bus #33 from Lower Abbey St. (45 min., 25 per day) and suburban rail. Quiet, beachside location outside the urban jumble. Kitchen for washing dishes. Showers €2. Electricity €3. Open Apr.-Sept. €9 per adult, €5 per child. ❶

Camac Valley Tourist Caravan and Camping Park, Naas Rd. (☎464 0644; www.camacvalley.com), in Clondalkin near Corkagh Park. Take bus #69 (45 min. from city center) and ask to be let off at Camac. Wheelchair-accessible. Dogs welcome. Showers €1. Laundry €4.50. €9-10 per person; €22 per 2 people with car or camper; €24 per caravan. ❶

LONG-TERM STAYS

Visitors expecting to spend several weeks in Dublin may want to consider a bedsit or a sublet, since longer stays are often most economical when sharing the cost of rent. Many hostels offer special rates for long-termers, especially in the winter; ask at individual hostels for details. Rooms in locations outside the city center, like Marino and Rathmines, go for about €70-110 per week (ask whether electricity, phone, and water are included). Some B&Bs also offer reduced rates for long-term stays but are generally reluctant to do so in the summer.

There are a number of sources for finding roommates and sublets. Dublin's countless university students often seek roommates, usually in the summer. The most up-to-date and comprehensive postings of vacancies are at **USIT,** 19-21 Aston Quay (see **Tourist and Financial Services,** p. 101). Supermarket notice boards are another source. **Trinity College** has a jam-packed board inside the main gate. Also check out the tourist office's *Sleep!* accommodation guide (€2.50) or classified ads in the *Irish Independent, the Irish Times,* and particularly the *Evening Herald.* Find plenty of apartment postings at **www.daft.ie.**

Another reasonable option is **university housing,** although it does cost more than hostels and is only available during the summer holiday—roughly mid-June to mid-September. **Trinity College** is in a perfectly central location and offers single and shared rooms, some with bath. (☎608 1177; www.tcd.ie/accommodations. Singles €58-70; doubles €75-140.) The **Mercer Court Campus,** lower Mercer St., near Grafton St. and St. Stephen's Green, has single and double rooms, all with bath and TV. (☎474 4120; www.mercercourt.ie. Singles €52; doubles €82.) **Dublin City University,** Glasnevin, can be reached by bus #747 (the Airlink shuttle), 16A, 41, 41A, 41B, 41C, 46X, 58X, or 746 from the city center. (☎700 5000. Breakfast included. Singles with bath €47-60; doubles with bath €84-88.) Other options are available through **USIT,** which operates **University College Dublin** dorms in Belfield. (☎269 7111 during summer. Take bus #3. Single private room in 4-bed apartment €25-30.)

◪ FOOD

Dublin's many **open-air markets** sell fresh food at relatively cheap prices. Vendors deal fruit, fresh strawberries, flowers, and fish from their pushcarts. The later in the week, the livelier the market. Bustling **Moore Street Market** is a great place to get fresh veggies. (Between Henry St. and Parnell St. Open M-Sa 10am-5pm.) The **Thomas Street Market,** along the continuation of Dame St., is a calmer alternative for fruit and veggie shopping. (Generally open Th-Sa 11am-5pm, although some stalls are open during the week; drop by to check.) Produce can be found every day along **Wexford St.** The best value for **supermarkets** around Dublin is in the **Dunnes Stores** chain, with full branches at St. Stephen's Green (☎478 0188; open M and F 8:30am-8pm, Tu-W and Sa 8:30am-7pm, Th 8:30am-9pm, Su 10am-7pm), the ILAC Centre off Henry St., and N. Earl St. off O'Connell; a small convenience version is on Georges St. The dueling German discount stores **Lidl** and **Aldi** continue their invasion of the Irish grocery market; their most central locations are also near the ILAC Centre, with entrances off Parnell St. (Lidl open M-Sa 8am-10pm, Su 12:30pm-7pm. Aldi open M-W 9am-8pm, Th-F 9am-9pm, Sa 9am-7pm, Su 11am-

7pm.) **Down to Earth,** 73 S. Great Georges St., stocks health foods, herbal medicines, and a dozen different options for granola fanatics. (☎671 9702. Open M-Sa 8:30am-6:30pm.) Health food is also available around the city at various branches of **Nature's Way;** the biggest is at the St. Stephen's Green Shopping Centre. (☎478 0165. Open M-W and F-Sa 9am-6pm, Th 9am-8pm, Su noon-6pm.)

FOOD BY TYPE

JAPANESE

Wagamama (111)	GGS ❸
Yamamori Noodles (111)	GGS ❸

CAFES

Butler's Chocolate Cafe (111)	GGS ❶
Lemon Crepe & Coffee Co. (111)	GGS ❶
Metro Cafe (111)	GGS ❶
🖾Queen of Tarts (109)	TB ❶

CONTINENTAL

Bad Ass Cafe (110)	TB ❸
Botticelli Gelato Parlour (110)	TB ❶
Busyfeet & Coco Cafe (111)	GGS ❶
Fagan's (112)	NL ❸
Havana (111)	GGS ❷
🖾Market Bar (110)	GGS ❶
The Mermaid Cafe (109)	TB ❺
O'Shea's Hotel (112)	NL ❷
Panem (112)	NL ❶
Tante Zoe's (109)	TB ❹

FISH AND CHIPS

Leo Burdock's (110)	GGS ❶

MEDITERRANEAN

🖾101 Talbot (112)	NL ❹
La Med (110)	TB ❸
🖾Unicorn Café Restaurant (110)	GGS ❷

ORGANIC/VEGETARIAN

Cafe Irie (110)	TB ❶
🖾Cornucopia (110)	GGS ❷
gruel (110)	TB ❷
Juice (111)	GGS ❷
Nude (110)	GGS ❶
Soup Dragon (112)	NL ❷

SOUTH ASIAN/MIDDLE EASTERN

Govinda's (111)	GGS ❷
Jamuna (112)	NL ❸
Maloti (111)	GGS ❶
Monty's of Kathmandu (110)	TB ❹
Zaytoon (110)	TB ❷

TB Temple Bar **GGS** Grafton and South Great Georges St. **NL** North of Liffey

TEMPLE BAR

Creative restaurants with local and ethnic fare cater to every budget in this food-happy corner of the city center. Outstanding coffee shops keep the hangovers at bay before the pubs reopen.

🖾 **Queen of Tarts,** Dame St. (☎670 7499), across from City Hall. Addictive pastries, light meals, and coffee. Scones (raspberry, raisin, chocolate, or plain), flaky and baked to perfection; €3. Breakfast €3-8. Inventive sandwich varieties €7. Open M-F 7:30am-7pm, Sa-Su 9am-7pm. ❶

Tante Zoe's, 1 Crow St. (☎679 4407), across from the back entrance of the Foggy Dew pub. Cajun-Creole food in a casual setting. Mellow instrumental music may whisper "elevator," but the food shouts "delicious." Gumbos €7; entrees €18-28. 2-course lunch €15. Open M-Sa noon-4pm and 5:30pm-midnight, Su 1-10pm. ❹

The Mermaid Cafe, 69-70 Dame St. (☎670 8236; www.mermaid.ie), near S. Great Georges St. Chunky wooden tables and beads hanging in the door frame. Unusual entrees like aubergine schnitzel (€23-28). Outstanding Su brunch. Menu changes frequently. Open M-Sa 12:30-2:30pm and 6-11pm, Su 12:30-3:30pm and 6-9pm. ❺

Zaytoon, 14-15 Parliament St. (☎677 3595). Don't let the fast-food-style counter fool you; this corner restaurant serves top-notch Persian food late into the night. Choose a cheap lunch or one of the healthier ways to satisfy the raging post-pub munchies. Excellent mixed döner meal (lamb and chicken; €9). Open daily noon-4am. ❷

Monty's of Kathmandu, 28 Eustace St. (☎670 4911; www.montys.ie), on the left just before Dame St. Native landscape murals set the scene for Nepalese cuisine. Spicy Begum Bahar, chicken covered with fried minced lamb (€15.50), pleases meat-lovers while regional specialty vegetable Jyogi Bhat (€14.50) makes vegetarians feel at home. Early-bird menu served daily 6-7pm (2-course €20, 3-course €24). Entrees €14-23. Open M-Sa noon-2:30pm and 6-11:30pm, Su 6-11:30pm. AmEx/MC/V. ❹

Cafe Irie, 11 Fownes St. (☎672 5090). Above clothing store Sé Sí Progressive. Just about every guide has sung this favorite lunch spot's praises, and *Let's Go* can't help but join the chorus. Artsy cafe with assortment of delicious sandwiches (€6-7), including great vegetarian and vegan options. Smoothies €3.80. Open daily 9am-9pm. ❶

Botticelli Gelato Parlour, 1-3 Temple Bar. (☎672 7289; www.botticelli.ie). Tourists soaking up Irish trad drool over the Italian ice cream beckoning from the window. Scooper will translate Italian flavors, but the one to remember is "nocciola," for their sublime hazelnut. 1 scoop €2.50. Open daily 12:30pm-midnight. ❶

La Med, 22 East Essex St. (☎670 7358; www.lamed.ie). Mediterranean seafood, which, thankfully, comes from waters cleaner than the nearby Liffey. Start a meal with mussels *Provençale* or *mariniere* (€9) and then try one of the richer meat dishes. Early-bird special (€19) of appetizer and entree served 4-7pm. Entrees €11-19. Open M-Tu and Su 4pm-11pm, W-F noon-11pm, Sa 10am-11pm. AmEx/MC/V. ❸

Bad Ass Cafe, 9-11 Crown Alley (☎671 2596; www.badasscafe.com). Locals and tourists chow down in a big pizza parlor. Huge windows overlooking Temple Bar. Large pizza €13-14. Other entrees €8-16. Lunch special, choice of pizza, burger, or pasta; €9. Open daily 11:30am-late. ❸

gruel, 68a Dame St. (☎670 7119). Ambience is actively ugly while the dishes are undeniably beautiful. Offers meat and organic vegetarian options, including Irish stew or unique summer vegetable stew with goat cheese. Entrees €6-12. Brownies (€2.50) are heavenly. Open M-Sa 9am-8pm, Su 11:30am-8pm. ❷

GRAFTON AND SOUTH GREAT GEORGES STREETS

▨ **Market Bar,** Fade St. (☎613 9094; www.tapas.ie). Right off S. Great Georges after Lower Stephen St. Huge old sausage factory given classy makeover; now serves tasty tapas in heaping portions. High-ceilinged house usually packed to gills for fish pie. Small tapas €7.50; large tapas €11. Kitchen open M-W noon-9:30pm, Th noon-10pm, F-Sa noon-10:30pm, Su 3-9:30pm. ❶

▨ **Unicorn Café Restaurant,** 12B Merrion Court (☎676 2182; www.unicornrestaurant.com). Left off Merrion Row, behind Unicorn Food Store and Café. Legendary Italian restaurant serves classic dishes with panache. Lunch €16-30; dinner €19-32. Open M-Th 12:30-3:30pm and 6-11pm, F-Sa 12:30-3:30pm and 6-11:30pm. **Unicorn Food Store and Café ❷,** Merrion Row (☎678 8588), offers food from the same kitchen, at a fraction of the price, for sit-down or takeaway. St. Stephen's Green, down the block, is perfect for a picnic. *Panini* €7.50; pasta €7.50-9. Open daily 8am-7pm. ❹

▨ **Cornucopia,** 19 Wicklow St. (☎677 7583). If there's space, sit down in this cozy and very popular spot for a delicious and filling meal (€11-12) or a cheaper but equally tasty salad smorgasbord (€3-8 for choice of 2, 4, or 6 salads). Open M-W and F-Sa 8:30am-8pm, Th 8:30am-9pm, Su noon-7pm. ❷

Leo Burdock's, 2 Werburgh St. (☎454 0306), behind The Lord Edward pub across from Christ Church Cathedral. Additional location on Lower Liffey St. Lip-smacking fish 'n' chips served the right way, in brown paper. A nightly pilgrimage for many Dubliners. Takeaway only. Fish €4-6.75; chips €2.65. Open daily noon-midnight. ❶

Nude, 21 Suffolk St. (☎677 4804). Organic, free-range/free-trade food served in a modern space on hefty communal tables. Grab-N-Go selection for those in a hurry. Choose from a selection of fresh-squeezed juices and smoothies (€4.10), salads (€4), hot *panini* (€5.10), and wraps (€5.75). Also on Grafton St. above BT2. Open M-Sa 7:30am-10pm, Su 10am-8pm. ❶

Butler's Chocolate Cafe, 24 Wicklow St. (☎671 0591; www.butlerschocolates.com). Decadence never felt so good. Luxury chocolate shop also offers a tempting selection of hot and cold coffee drinks, with branches throughout the city. Chocolates can be shipped worldwide from the website. Cookie hot chocolate €3.50. Open M-Sa 7:30am-8pm, Su 10am-7pm. ❶

Juice, 73-83 S. Great Georges St. (☎475 7856; www.juicerestaurant.ie). Meat-lovers stay away, vegetarians rule the day. Makes the most of mother nature's bounty in bright setting. Open daily 11am-11pm. ❷

Maloti, 34-35 S. William St. (☎671 0428). Authentic Indian food with artistic style and presentation. Great lunch specials. 1-course €6, 2-course €8.45. Open M-Th noon-2:30pm and 5:30-11:30pm, F-Sa noon-2:30pm and 5:30-midnight, Su 1-11pm. ❶

Havana, S. Great Georges St., second location at Camden Market (☎400 5990/476 0046; havana.ie). Share tapas in fun, busy setting. Tapas €9-15. "MTW deal": M-W any 2 tapas €13. Open M-W 11:30am-10:30pm, Th-F 11:30am-11:30pm, Sa 1-11:30pm, Su 5-10:30pm. ❷

Lemon Crepe & Coffee Co., 66 S. William St. (☎672 9044). Squeeze into this tiny, trendy joint for crepes made on the spot. Chill at one of the streetside tables, or get takeaway. Savory and sweet crepes big enough to share; €5-8. Gluten-free buckwheat crepes available. Vegetarian-friendly. Open M-W 8am-7:30pm, Th 8am-9pm, F-Sa 9am-7:30pm, Su 10am-6:30pm. ❶

Govinda's, 4 Aungier St. (☎475 0309; www.govindas.ie) and 83 Middle Abbey St. Fabulous Indian food in a colorful oasis with soothing music and a karma-conscious menu. Offers classes in vegetarian *bhakti* cuisine with local chef. Dinner special €9. Open M-Sa noon-9pm. ❷

Yamamori Noodles, 71-72 S. Great Georges St. (☎475 5001). Delicious Japanese cuisine served in an elegant dining room with white paper lanterns. Free Wi-Fi. Maki roll €7-8; lunch €10; entrees €14.50-18.50. Open M-W and Su 12:30-11pm, Th-Sa 12:30-11:30pm. ❸

Busyfeet & Coco Cafe, 41-2 S. William St. (☎671 9514). Some may feel slightly out of place at this health and socially conscious cafe; menu includes organic breads and Fair Trade coffee. Gourmet burger menu (€7.25-12) served from 4pm. Sandwiches €6-8. Outdoor seating. Open M-Tu 10am-9pm, W-Sa 10am-10pm, Su 11am-8pm. ❶

Wagamama, S. King St. (☎478 2152; www.wagamama.com). Pre-theater and post-shopping crowds sate their noodle lust at this London-based chain. Service is efficient at long, communal tables. Vegetarian- and vegan-friendly. Ramen €11-16. Open M-Sa noon-11pm, Su noon-10pm. ❸

Metro Cafe, 43 S. William St. (☎679 4515). Satisfying Parisian-style cafe with fresh coffee, homemade breads, and outdoor seating. Daily sandwich special board (€5-6) actually changes daily (a rarity in a country where toasted ham is king). Open M-Tu and F-Sa 8am-8pm, W 8am-9pm, Th 8am-10pm, Su 10:15am-7pm. ❶

NORTH OF THE LIFFEY

Eateries here tend to be less interesting than their South Side rivals. **O'Connell Street** sports blocks of neon-signed fast-food chains and tourist traps, but a few notable exceptions brighten the north city center's gastronomic landscape. Several of the best and cheapest options cluster in the **Epicurean Food Hall,** accessible from Lower Liffey St. and Middle Abbey St. Under the glass roof is a mix of aromas from nearly every corner of the globe. From Mediterranean and kebabs (€8.50-9.50) at **Istanbul** to Italian coffee and *panini* (€4-7) at **La Corte,** plus the inevitable chipper in the superior **Leo Burdock's** (see **Grafton St.** and **South St. Georges**), there's something to placate every ethnic foodcrush. (Most shops open M-W 9am-8pm, Th 9am-9pm, F-Su 9am-7pm. Leo Burdock's street window open until midnight.)

COUNTY DUBLIN

■ **101 Talbot,** 101 Talbot St. (☎874 5011), between Marlborough and Gardiner St., 1 flight up through the red doors. Excellent Italian-Mediterranean food catered to Abbey Theatre-goers. Large windows look onto busy Talbot St. below. Menu changes frequently but always has vegetarian specialties. Book ahead. Entrees €14-20. Early-bird 5-8pm €21. Open Tu-Sa 5-11pm. ❹

Fagan's, Lower Drumcondra Rd. (☎836 9491), just before Botanic Ave. Relaxed atmosphere in attractive indoor and outdoor setting combines with gorgeous food to produce a friendly pub. Worthy of a trek from the city and a must-stop for anyone staying in the north. Carvery €11; entrees €10-15. Kitchen open daily 12:30-3pm and 4-9pm. ❸

Panem, 21 Lower Ormond Quay (☎872 8510). Tight squeeze but packed for a reason. Mastered the art of the sandwich (€4.50) in a sort of croissant-foccacia combination whose main ingredient is delicious with a side of cheap. Open M-Sa 9am-5:30pm. ❶

Soup Dragon, 168 Capel St. (☎872 3277). Bigger location around corner on Ormand Quay. Fierce name, mean stews (€4.50-8.50). Homemade concoctions vary by day. Healthy fruits, juices, and breads round out the vegetarian-friendly menu. Open M-F 8am-4:30pm. Ormand Quay location also open Sa 11am-5pm. ❷

Jamuna, 157 Lower Drumcondra Rd. (☎857 3000). Ordinary decor belies exceptional Indian cuisine. 2-course "business lunch" (€9) is favorite of young professionals while single course (€5) suits most. Naan (Indian bread) included. Several vegetarian options. Entrees €12-15. Open daily noon-9pm. ❸

O'Shea's Hotel, 19 Talbot St. (☎836 5665), at the corner of Lower Gardiner St. Generous portions of tasty bar food. Cozy brick space with large windows perfect for people-watching behind the bar of the same name. Convenient to north city center hostelers. Entrees €10-19; "bar bites" (bigger than they sound) €7-12. Open daily 8am-10pm. ❷

▇ PUBLIN

James Joyce proposed that a "good puzzle would be to cross Dublin without passing a pub." When a local radio station once offered £100 to the first person to solve the puzzle, the winner explained that any route worked—you'd just have to stop in each one along the way. Dublin's pubs come in all shapes, sizes, and specialties. This is the place to hear trad, Irish rock, and country western in abundance. Ask around or check the publications *In Dublin, Hot Press,* or *Event Guide* for music listings. Normal **pub hours** in Ireland end at 11:30pm Sunday through Wednesday and 12:30am Thursday through Saturday. The laws that dictate these hours are changing—patrons often get about a half-hour after "closing" to finish off their drinks. An increasing number of pubs have **late permits** that allow them to remain open until at least 2am; drink prices tend to rise around midnight to cover the permit's cost (or so they claim). Bars that post their closing time as "late" mean after midnight and, sometimes, after what is legally mandated. **ID-checking** almost always happens at the door rather than at the bar and is more often enforced in Dublin than in other parts of Ireland. Note that a growing number of bars are blurring the distinction between pub and club by hosting live music and staying open late into the night on weekdays. So pay attention and hit two birds with one pint.

The *Let's Go* **Dublin Pub Crawl** (p. 111) will aid in discovering the city while researching the perfect pint. If you're looking for Guinness, try **Mulligan's, The Stag's Head,** and **Brogan's Bar;** each claims to pour the best pint, though some say the title belongs to the **Gravity Bar** at the top of the **Guinness Storehouse.** To judge for yourself, try them all, and be sure to congratulate the winner.

GRAFTON STREET AND TRINITY COLLEGE AREA

McDaid's, 3 Harry St. (☎679 4395), across from Anne St. Once the center of the Irish literary scene in the 50s. Today the gregarious crowd spills out onto the street in nice weather. Open M-W 10:30am-11:30pm, Th-Sa 10:30am-12:30am, Su 12:30-11pm.

COUNTY DUBLIN

Dublin Pub Crawl

4 Dame Lane, 17
Bailey, 22
The Bleeding Horse, 36
The Brazen Head, 11
Brogan's Bar, 14
Bruxelles, 27
Café en Seine, 31
The Capitol Lounge, 29
The Celt, 6
Davy Byrne's, 25
Dawson Lounge, 28
The Foggy Dew, 15
The Globe, 20
Hairy Lemon, 26
Hogan's, 23
The International Bar, 21
Life, 5
The Long Stone, 9
M. Hughes, 1
McGruders, 19
M.J. O'Neill's, 16
McDaid's, 30
Messrs. Maguire, 4
Mulligan's, 7
The Odeon, 35
Oliver St. John Gogarty, 10
The Palace, 8
The Porterhouse, 12
Pravda, 2
Sinnott's, 32
Solas, 33
Southwilliam, 24
The Stag's Head, 18
Temple Bar Pub, 13
Whelan's, 34
Zanzibar, 3

The International Bar, 23 Wicklow St. (☎677 9250), on the corner of S. William St. Great place to meet kindred wandering spirits. Downstairs lounge hosts excellent M improv comedy; Tu jazz; W-Su stand-up; Su house music. Arrive early to comedy nights for a seat. W-F cover €10, students €8. Open M-W 10:30am-11:30pm, Th-Sa 10:30am-12:30am, Su 12:30-11pm.

Café en Seine, 40 Dawson St. (☎677 4567; www.capitalbars.com). Glittery mosaic ceiling, massive potted plants, and 3-story atrium belong in an Egyptian palace but are resigned to this yuppie bar. Free Wi-Fi. M live jazz 10pm-midnight, Su 3-5pm. F-Sa DJ. Coffee bar daily 11am-7pm. Kitchen open daily noon-3pm and 4-10pm. Open M-W 11am-1:30am, Th-Sa 11am-2:30am, Su 11am-1:30am.

Bailey, Duke St. (☎670 4939). Trendy cocktail spot a step away from Grafton St. for the post-shopping set. Mod white leather bar stools, technicolor lighting, and tons of outdoor seating. Open M-Th noon-11:30pm, F-Sa noon-12:30am, Su 12:30-11pm.

Bruxelles, Harry St. (☎677 5362), across from McDaid's. Classy bar with glass chandeliers and a constant crowd of young trendsetters. M-Tu and Su blues/soul draws crowds. Open M-W 10:30am-1:30am, Th-Sa 10:30am-2:30am, Su 10:30am-1am.

Sinnott's, S. King St. (☎478 4698). Cave-like basement pub devoid of Cro-Magnons but full of twentysomethings. 3 massive projection screens show sports. Dance floor packed until 2am. Open M-W 10:30am-11:30pm, Th-Sa 10:30am-2:30am, F-Sa 11am-2:45am, Su noon-11pm.

Davy Byrne's, 21 Duke St. (☎677 5217; www.davybyrnespub.com), off Grafton St. Lively, middle-aged crowd fills the pub where Joyce set *Ulysses'* Cyclops chapter; come on Bloomsday for a taste of Joycean Dublin. Plenty of stylish seating curves around the long art-deco bar. Gourmet pub food served all day. Open M-W 9am-11:30pm, Th-Sa 9am-12:30am, Su 12:30-11pm.

Dawson Lounge, 25 Dawson St. (☎671 0311), downstairs. Smallest pub in Dublin (only 23 sq. meters, including restrooms and storage) is classy, wood-paneled, and, needless to say, intimate. Open M-Sa 12:30-11:30pm.

M.J. O'Neill's, Suffolk St. (☎679 3656), across from the tourist office. Enormous maze of rooms is fairly quiet by day, but by night a fun, young crowd keeps it pulsing. A central wraparound bar leaves space to find a drink. M and Su 9pm trad. Open M-Th 12:30-11:30pm, F-Sa 10:30am-12:30am, Su 12:30-11pm.

HARCOURT, CAMDEN, AND WEXFORD STREETS

■ **Whelan's,** 25 Wexford St. (☎478 0766; www.whelanslive.com). Pub hosts big-name trad, rock, and everything in between in attached music venue. Live music nightly starting at 8:30pm (doors open at 8pm). Th DJs' Fear and Loathing night. Cover €7-15. Open for lunch (€8-12) 12:30-2pm. Open M-W until 2am and Th-Sa until 3am.

The Bleeding Horse, 24 Upper Camden St. (☎475 2705). Labyrinth of cozy nooks for private affairs surround a sprawling central bar. F-Sa late bar with DJ. Open M-Th and Su until midnight, F-Sa until 2am.

The Odeon, Old Harcourt Train Station (☎478 2088). Has a young, well-heeled clientele who come to be seen. Th-Sa DJ; other nights lounge and dance. Cover €10. Open M-W until 11pm, Th until 12:30am, F-Sa until 2:30am.

Solas, 31 Wexford St. (☎478 0583). Sidle into one of the huge velvet booths and check out the circular fish tank on the stairs in this plush red- and green-themed lounge. Popular with students. DJ every night spins urban and soul, starting around 9pm. Open M-W noon-11:30pm, Th-Sa noon-12:30am, Su 4-11pm.

AROUND SOUTH GREAT GEORGES STREET

■ **The Stag's Head,** 1 Dame Ct. (☎679 3701). Atmospheric Victorian pub with stained glass, round marble-topped tables, and evidence of deer decapitation front and center above the bar. Student crowd dons everything from T-shirts to tuxes and spills into the alleys (especially now that they can't smoke indoors). Excellent pub grub. Entrees €7.50-11. Kitchen open M-F noon-3:30pm and 5-7pm, Sa noon-2:30pm. Bar open M-Th 10:30am-11:30pm, F-Sa 10:30am-12:30am.

The Capitol Lounge, 18-19 Lower Stephen St. (☎475 7166). Special deal includes delicious cocktails (€5) from extensive list until midnight. Bump with DJ nightly downstairs or head upstairs for more intimate setting. Open daily 3pm-2:30am.

Southwilliam, 52 S. William St. (☎672 5946; www.southwilliam.ie). Urbanites gather day and night for pies and pints. Savory pastries (€9) are the only items on the menu, but with the likes of duck *confit,* it more than satisfies. Th-F and Su live music. Sa DJ. Open M-W noon-midnight, Th and Su noon-1am, F-Sa noon-2:30am.

The Globe, 11 S. Great Georges St. (☎671 1220). Frequented by a laid-back, hip crowd with a Guinness or a frothy cappuccino in hand. Frequent DJs. Open M-Sa noon-3am, Su 4pm-1am.

4 Dame Lane, 4 Dame Ln. (☎679 2901). Look for the 2 flaming torches. A crowd gets down to 2 DJs on 2 floors, playing mostly house in this high-ceilinged, votive-lit space. Live DJ nearly every night. 23+. Open daily 5pm-3am.

Hairy Lemon (☎678 7724), corner of Drury and Lower Stephen St. Spacious, comfortable neighborhood announces itself loudly with its bright green-and-yellow exterior, but inside a casual and welcoming ambience awaits. Heated beer garden popular with smokers. F-Sa bar open late. Open daily noon-11:30pm.

Hogan's, 35 S. Great Georges St. (☎677 5904). Attractive crowd but the ambience is lacking. F-Sa basement DJ spins pop, funk, or soul; Th hip-hop upstairs. Open M-W 12:30-11:30pm, Th 12:30pm-1am, F-Sa 12:30pm-2:30am, Su 4-11:30pm.

TEMPLE BAR

▨**The Porterhouse,** 16-18 Parliament St. (☎671 5715). Way, way more than 99 bottles of beer on the wall, including 10 self-brewed porters, stouts, and ales. Tough choices, but the Porterhouse Red is a must. 3½ spacious floors fill nightly with great crowd for trad, blues, and rock. Open M-W 11:30am-11:30pm, Th 11:30am-2am, F-Sa 11:30am-2:30am, Su 11:30am-1:30am.

Temple Bar Pub, Temple Ln. S. (☎672 5286). Pre-packaged entertainment but still great space, especially for smokers, with garden right in the middle. Wheelchair-accessible. 2hr. trad sessions M-Th 4:30 and 8:30pm, F-Sa 4:30pm. Open M-Th 11am-12:30am, F-Sa 11am-1:30am, Su noon-12:30am.

Brogan's Bar, 75 Dame St. (☎671 1844). Unassuming little spot ignored by tourists despite its location. Somewhat fatherly crowd. Enjoy a pint of the "black magic" as you examine the extensive collection of Guinness paraphernalia that adorns the walls. Open M-W 4-11:30pm, Th 4pm-12:30am, F-Sa 1pm-12:30am, Su 1-11:30pm.

Messrs. Maguire, Burgh Quay (☎670 5777). Explore this classy watering hole under the spell of homemade brews. M trad 9:30-11:30pm, Su ballads 9-11pm. W-Sa late bar with DJ. Kitchen open all day. Open M-Tu 10:30am-12:30am, W 11am-1:30am, Th 10:30am-2am, F-Sa 11am-2:30am, Su noon-12:30am.

The Foggy Dew, Fownes St. (☎677 9328). Friendly pub with less flash than other Temple Bar joints, but its rock vibe gives it an edge. F-Sa DJ. Open M-W 11am-11:30pm, Th 11am-12:30am, F-Sa 11am-1:30am, Su 12:30-11pm.

The Palace, 21 Fleet St. (☎677 9290), on the corner near Westmoreland St. Neighborly pub has an old-fashioned, saloon-like feel. Comfy seats in the stained-glass, sky-lit back room. Open M-Th 10:30am-11:30pm, F-Sa 10:30am-12:30am, Su 12:30-11pm.

Oliver St. John Gogarty (☎671 1822), corner of Fleet St. and Anglesea St. Convivial atmosphere in a traditional but touristed pub. Named for the surgeon and poet who was Joyce's roommate/nemesis and appeared in *Ulysses* as Buck Mulligan. Much-sought-after trad daily 2:30pm-2:30am, with a break from 7-8pm. Open M-Sa 10:30am-2:30am, Su 10:30am-1am.

THE BEST OF THE REST

Zanzibar (☎878 7212), at the Ha'penny Bridge. Dances between club and pub with explosive results. Unique private rooms on the balcony, one overlooking the Liffey. M-Th and Su €5 mixed drinks before midnight. Tu-Su DJ plays R&B, blues, and chart-toppers. Cover after 11pm F €5, Sa €7. Kitchen open until 10pm. Open M-Th 5pm-2:30am, F 4pm-2:30am, Sa 2pm-2:30am, Su 2pm-1:30am.

The Long Stone, 10-11 Townsend St. (☎671 8102). Scurry through this multi-level maze of comfortable booths and rooms. Frequent live bands. W and Sa 8-10pm live music. Kitchen open M-F 5-8pm, Sa 4-8pm. Open M-Th noon-11:30pm, F-Sa noon-12:30am, Su 4pm-12:30am.

Pravda, 35 Lower Liffey St. (☎874 0090), on the north side of the Ha'penny Bridge. There's nothing Russian about the place, other than the Cyrillic on the wall murals and the stores of vodka inside. Trendy, gay-friendly, and crowded. DJ W-Sa. Bar menu daily noon-9pm. Th-Sa late bar until 2:30am.

The Celt, 81-82 Talbot St. (☎878 8665). Packed with locals of all ages who stay for the nightly trad sessions featuring some of the best up and comers. Some of the cheapest pints in the city center (€3.80). Open M-Th 10:30am-11:30pm, F-Sa 10:30am-12:30am, Su 12:30-11pm.

Mulligan's, 8 Poolbeg St. (☎677 5582), behind Burgh Quay, off Tara St. Upholds its reputation as one of the best pint-pourers in Dublin. A taste of the typical Irish pub: low-key and "strictly drink," with no touristy trad to be found. Open M-Th 10:30am-11:30pm, F-Sa 10:30am-12:30am, Su noon-11pm.

The Brazen Head, 20 North Bridge St. (☎679 5186), off Merchant's Quay. Established in 1198, Dublin's oldest pub was once the location of the United Irishmen's secret meetings. Cobbled courtyard with beer barrel tables. Nightly trad. Carvery and pub grub menu served 12:30-9pm. Open M-W 10:30am-11:30pm, Th-Sa 10:30am-12:30am, Su 12:30pm-midnight.

Life, Lower Abbey St. (☎878 1032), left of the Irish Life Centre. The young, the beautiful, and the hangers-on trickle in after work, so things don't heat up until later in this live music venue. Pink-tinted skylights on the upper level and quite possibly the best bar aquarium in Dublin. Lunch €8-12. F-Sa DJ and late bar until 2:30am.

M. Hughes, 19 Chancery St. (☎872 6540), behind Four Courts. Felons beware: this comfy venue for nightly trad attracts the prosecution and the defense and is loaded with *Garda* at lunch. M and W-Th set dancing around 9:30pm. If you're aching to be the first in the city to down a Guinness, come M-Sa when the pub opens promptly at 7am. Open M-Th 7am-11:30pm, F-Sa 7am-12:30am, Su noon-11pm.

McGruders, Thomas St. (☎453 9022), next to the Brewery hostel. After a visit to gravity bar, meet the storehouse workers for a pint of their own. Same owners as Brewery Hostel so low-key backpacker fun abounds. M live trad 9-11pm, F blues 6-9pm. Soup and sandwich €8. Kitchen open daily noon-9pm.

▓ CLUBLIN

As a rule, clubs open at 10 or 10:30pm but don't heat up until the pubs empty around 12:30am. Clubbing is an expensive end to the evening, since covers run €5-20 and pints can surpass €5. To save some money, find a club with an expensive cover but cheap drink prices and stay all night. **Concessions** provide discounts with varying restrictions. The Stag's Head (see **Publin,** p. 114) offers them around 11pm, but any nightclub attached to a pub distributes them in its home bar. A handful of smaller clubs on **Harcourt** and **Camden Streets** are basic but fun. Most clubs close between 1:30 and 3am, but a few have been known to stay open until daybreak. To get home after 11:30pm, when Dublin Bus stops running, take the **NiteLink bus** (M-W 12:30am and 2am, Th-Sa every 20min. from 12:30am to 4:30am; €4), which runs designated routes from the corner of Westmoreland and College St. to Dublin's suburbs. **Taxi** stands are sprinkled throughout the city, the most central being in front of Trinity, at the top of Grafton St. by St. Stephen's Green, at Upper O'Connell St., and on Lower Abbey St. Be prepared to wait 30-45min. on weekend nights. For the most up-to-date information on clubs, check the *Event Guide*.

▓ **The PoD,** 35 Harcourt St. (☎478 0225; www.pod.ie), corner of Hatch St., in an old train station. Stylishly futuristic, orange interior. Serious about its music. Upstairs is **The Red Box** (☎478 0225), a huge, separate club with brain-crushing music and a crowd at the bar so deep it seems designed to winnow out the weak. Mellow train-station-turned-bar **Crawdaddy** hosts musical gigs, including some world stars. Cover €10-20; Th students €5; can rise fast when big-name DJs perform. Open until 3am on weekends.

▓ **Spirit,** 57 Middle Abbey St. (☎877 9999). Huge, popular club with a daunting queue on weekends. Each of the 4 floors has its own name and musical vibe. "Mind" (basement level): the rock room, with music to match. "Soul" (ground floor): main bar, with R&B, blindingly colorful lights and a medium-sized dance floor. "Body" (first floor): huge dance floor, and a giant egg-shaped fortress in the middle for the DJs to hatch pounding house music. The top floor, "Virtue," may be the coolest of all, but it's only for VIPs and clubbers with invisibility cloaks. Cover €10-20. Su gay night. Th €5 for students. Open Th-Su 10:30pm-3:30am. Occasional club nights during the week; call for details.

The Village, 26 Wexford St. (☎475 8555). Ground-floor bar is swanky or posh, depending on your vocabulary. Occasional live music sits below a popular upstairs weekend club. Th-Sa bands play from 7-10:30pm (about €20), then DJs come in for chill-out, jungle, and house downstairs. Tickets for live bands available next door. Club F €7, Sa €9. Bar open until 1:30am; club open Th-Sa until 3am.

Gaiety, S. King St. (☎679 5622; www.gaietytheatre.com), off Grafton St. 3 bar areas and the best of all musical worlds with salsa, jazz, swing, latin, and soul. F-Sa Elegant theater shows late-night wild side. Cover F €12, Sa €15. Open F-Sa midnight-4am.

Traffic, 54 Middle Abbey St. (☎873 4038; www.traffic54.net). Nightly DJ spins hip-hop, house, or techno for a young crowd from his throne at the end of the long bar. Flanking TVs flash images to accompany the music. M-Th and Su 2 cocktails for the price of 1; F-Sa they may seem like 1 for the price of 2. Rush-hour traffic jam awaits anyone venturing into the dark downstairs on weekends. 21+. Cover after 11pm Th €6, F-Sa €8-10. Open M-W 3-11:30pm, Th-Sa 3pm-2:30am, Su 3pm-midnight.

Club M, Blooms Hotel (☎671 5622), on Cope St. in Temple Bar. One of Dublin's largest clubs attracts a mixed crowd with multiple levels and bars. 18+ pushes the conversation closer to gym class than career moves. Cover M-Th €5; F-Sa €12-15. Free tickets often distributed in Temple Bar. Open M-Th 11pm-2:30am, F-Sa 10pm-2:30am.

The Mezz (The Hub), 21-25 Eustace St. (☎670 7655). Live bands rock nightly right inside the entrance of this low-ceilinged, atmospheric club—try not to knock over a drumset as you make your way toward the bar. Quiet pub by day transforms into a loud live-music cauldron at night. No cover. It shares the building with **The Hub,** which, as one of the only 18+ clubs in Temple Bar, attracts the younger crowd. Cover at The Hub €5-10. Open daily until 2:30am.

The Turk's Head, Parliament St. (☎679 2606). Atmospheric bar with a richly exotic interior, complete with huge potted plants. 70s and 80s classics. No cover. Open M-Tu until 12:30am, W-Sa until 2:30am, Su until 1am.

Fibber Magee's, 80-82 Parnell St. (☎872 2575). No charts here. Mostly alt, rock, and industrial, with bands on weekends. Cover Th €3, F-Su free unless a band comes to play (€2-3). Open Th-Sa until 2:30am, Su until 1:30am.

DISTANCE: 3.5km
DURATION: 8hr.
WHEN TO GO: Begin the tour at 8am

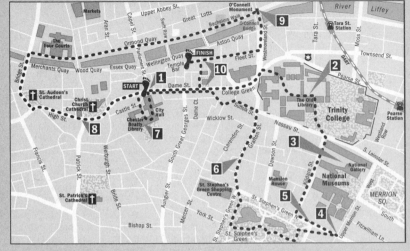

DUBLIN WALKING TOUR

1. QUEEN OF TARTS CAFE. Begin the day with a delicious scone. (See p. 109.)

2. TRINITY COLLEGE. The Old Library, one of the many stately edifices of Dublin's most famous university, holds the **Book of Kells.** (See p. 121.)

3. NATIONAL GALLERY. This gallery has a major collection of international works, from paintings by Picasso and Goya to a wing dedicated to the Yeats family. (See p. 122.)

4. NATURAL HISTORY MUSEUM. A marvel of taxidermy and preservation; everything from beetles to bears are jam-packed into three floors of flora and fauna. (See p. 122.)

5. UNICORN FOOD STORE. This Italian bistro is a great place to grab some lunch. Bring some pasta or a sandwich with you to St. Stephen's Green. (See p.110.)

6. ST. STEPHEN'S GREEN. Linger over a picnic and enjoy the streams, trees, and flowers in Dublin's answer to Central Park. (See p. 123.)

7. GRAFTON STREET. Try to catch some of the street performers or window-shop on Dublin's trendiest shopping avenue. (See p.121.)

8. CHESTER BEATTY LIBRARY. Walk through the grounds of Dublin Castle to reach this library of treasures, and gawk over the ancient illuminated texts. (See p. 124.)

9. CHRIST CHURCH CATHEDRAL. Dublin's oldest structure is also, supposedly, the burial place of Strongbow. (See p. 125.)

10. O'CONNELL STREET. Stop to admire the O'Connell Monument. (See p. 127)

11. PUB STOP. Because no day in Dublin is complete without a pub experience, seek out Temple Bar Pub's daily trad session at 4:50pm. (See p. 115.) Alternatively, drink with the locals at Brogan's Bar, Dame St. (See p. 115.)

GAY AND LESBIAN NIGHTLIFE

Gay and lesbian nightlife centers around several options mentioned below; also keep a lookout for clubs that have running gay nights.

■ **The Dragon,** S. Great Georges St. (☎478 1590), a few doors down from The George. Opened in May 2005 as Dublin's newest gay club, although everyone is welcome. It's packed to its trendy rafters on weekend nights. Quieter lounge area in front gives way to a DJ spinning house by the dance floor in back. Massive sculpture of Hercules wrestling a snake floats above the pulsing crowd. 18+. Open M 5pm-2:30am, Tu-W 5-11:30pm, Th-Sa 5pm-2:30am, Su 5-11pm.

The Front Lounge, Parliament St. (☎670 4112). Red velvet seats in this more subdued gay bar are filled nightly by a young, trendy crowd. Open M and W noon-11:30pm, Tu noon-12:30am, Th noon-1:30am, F-Sa noon-2am, Su 4-11:30pm.

The George, 89 S. Great Georges St. (☎478 2983; www.capitalbars.com). Deep purple facade loudly proclaims itself as Dublin's oldest and most prominent gay bar. Theoretically mixed in age and gender but seems to draw a decidedly older male crowd. Attached nightclub open W-Su until 2:30am. Frequent theme nights and cabaret. Cover after 10pm €8-10. Open M-Tu 12:30-11:30pm, W-Su 12:30pm-2:30am.

Company, 27 Upper Ormond Quay (☎872 2480). Formerly named Out on the Liffey. Quiet location along the quays ensures a local crowd most nights. Tu game show, Sa men's night, Su karaoke 4-7pm. F-Sa DJ. No cover. Open M-Tu noon-11:30pm, W-Th 10:30am-12:30am, F-Sa 10:30am-2:30am, Su noon-11:30pm.

🔍 TOURS

SELF-GUIDED WALKING TOURS

Dublin is definitely a walking city, as most major sights lie within 1km of O'Connell Bridge. The tourist office's website (www.visitdublin.com) caters directly to our iPod-loving generation with **free downloadable iWalks.** The 9-40MB MP3 files are guided audio tours by author and historian Pat Liddy including trails for the Guinness Storehouse, Temple Bar, and the Historic Northside, among others. The offices also sells *Must-Do's!* (€2.50), which detail directions to the main attractions. The first three walking tours listed below are mapped out in the *Dublin Walkabout City Map and Guide.* Trail pamphlets can be purchased for the Ulysses Trail. All guides are available at the tourist office (€1-4). *Let's Go* also features its own **Dublin Walking Tour** (p. 116).

THE CULTURAL EXPERIENCE. This tour covers all of the important Northside sights: the shopping meccas of Henry St. and the Fruit Market, the Custom House and King's Inns, the Municipal Gallery, and the Dublin Writers Museum.

THE HERITAGE EXPERIENCE. The walk begins on College Green and weaves its way past theaters, churches, and markets, and ends in Grafton St.

THE GEORGIAN EXPERIENCE. No visitor to Dublin should be denied the aesthetic pleasure of the best-preserved Georgian streets, terraces, and public buildings south of the Liffey; this tour includes such landmarks as Merrion Square, the National Gallery, and Newman House.

ULYSSES MAP OF DUBLIN. Chart Poldy's haunts and retrace his heroic actions, beginning with kidneys for breakfast. The walk takes a full 18hr. (including drinking), but it's faster than reading *Ulysses* yourself. Walking while reading is not recommended. Guide €1.

GUIDED WALKING TOURS

For those who enjoy big groups and don't mind a tour guide prodding them along, there are several tours to try. Most are about 2hr. long, but entertaining anecdotes and continuous movement often make them more fun than going it alone.

HISTORICAL WALKING TOUR. Trinity College history graduates provide a crash course in the city and country's history, stopping at a variety of Dublin sights. Guides seamlessly transition from one era to another and from one street to the next, protecting their listeners from ignorance and Dublin's maniacal drivers. *(Meet at Trinity's front gate. ☎087 688 9412. May-Sept. daily 11am and 3pm, Apr.-Oct. 11am; Nov.-Mar. F-Su 11am. Special tours available for groups; call for more info. €12, students €10.)*

TRINITY COLLEGE WALKING TOUR. Moderately irreverent and sufficiently stuck-up, this student-led tour concentrates on University lore. All that pretension does propel tourists to the front of the line at the *Book of Kells* exhibit. *(30min. tours May-Oct. 10:15am-3:40pm leave every 40min. from the info booth inside the front gate; Oct.-Jan. weekends only. Wheelchair-accessible. Tour €5, with admission to the Old Library and the Book of Kells €10. Under 12 free.)*

1916 REBELLION WALKING TOUR. The creation of the Republic was precipitated by the 1916 Rebellion, which took place solely in Dublin. See the scars it left and the state it created. *(Meet inside the International Bar, 23 Wicklow St. ☎086 858 3847; www.1916rising.com. 2hr. tour Mar. 1-Oct. 31 M-Sa 11:30am, Su 1pm. €12.)*

GUIDED PUB CRAWLS

THE DUBLIN LITERARY PUB CRAWL. Trained actors lead participants on a trek spliced with reenactments of comical anecdotes of the city's literary history. Jokes get funnier as the tour progresses through four stops. *(Meet at The Duke, 9 Duke St. ☎670 5602; www.dublinpubcrawl.com. Apr.-Nov. M-Sa 7:30pm, Su noon and 7:30pm; Dec.-Mar. Th-Sa 7:30pm, Su noon and 7:30pm. €12, students €10. Reserve at Suffolk St. tourist office.)*

MUSICAL PUB CRAWL. An enjoyable jaunt led by two musicians (and their instruments), who teach aspiring trad-heads how to differentiate between one session and another. *(Arrive a little early upstairs at Oliver St. John Gogarty's, on the corner of Fleet and Anglesea St. ☎475 3313; www.discoverdublin.ie. Apr.-Oct. daily 7:30pm; Nov.-Mar. Th-Sa 7:30pm. €12, students and seniors €10.)*

BUS TOURS

Dublin Bus runs a number of tours around the city, including the Ghostbus tour below. Check out www.dublinbus.ie for more information. Buses depart from the Dublin Bus office at 59 O'Connell St. *(☎873 4222. Open M-Sa 9am-7pm.)*

HOP-ON HOP-OFF TOUR OF DUBLIN. This tour allows an in-depth exploration of Dublin's major sights, including the National Gallery, Dublin Castle, and the Guinness Brewery, with special discounts. *(Tour begins at Cathal Brugha St. Pass valid 24hr., bus portion 90min. Departs May-Sept. 30 per day every 10min.; Oct. every 15min. Operates daily May-Sept. 9:30am-6:30pm, Oct. 9:30am-4pm. €14, seniors €12.50, children €6.)*

THE GHOSTBUS TOUR. The "world's only Ghostbus" shows you Dublin in all of its undead glory. *(Tours begin and end at Dublin Bus, 59 Upper O'Connell St. ☎873 4222. 2hr. M-F 8pm and Sa-Su 7 and 9:30pm. €25.)*

VIKING SPLASH TOURS. Cruise on land and water in converted WWII amphibious vehicles. Rattle other tours and let everyone in Dublin know you're a tourist with the "Viking Roar." You'll hear diverse tales of Dublin history from the surprisingly amiable Norsemen at the helm. *(Tours depart from Bull Alley St. behind St. Patrick's Cathedral and St. Stephen's Green North. ☎707 6000; www.vikingsplash.ie. 1½hr. Mar.-Oct. 10+ tours daily, Feb. W-Su, Nov. Tu-Su. Call for times and to book ahead. June weekends and July-Aug. €20, children €10; Sept.-May and June weekdays €15.50, children €8.50.)*

◉ 🏛 SIGHTS AND MUSEUMS

SOUTH OF THE LIFFEY
TRINITY COLLEGE AND NEARBY

With 12,000 students and 1200 staff, Trinity College is like a self-contained city within a city. To get there from North of the Liffey, follow O'Connell St. across the river and bear right onto Westmoreland St.

TRINITY COLLEGE. Behind ancient walls sprawls Trinity's expanse of stone build-ings, cobblestone walks, and grassy-green grounds. The British built Trinity in 1592 as a Protestant seminary that would "civilize the Irish and cure them of Pop-ery." The college became part of the path on which members of the Anglo-Irish elite trod on their way to high positions and has educated such luminaries as Jonathan Swift, Robert Emmett, Thomas Moore, Oscar Wilde, and Samuel Beck-ett. The Catholic Jacobites who briefly held Dublin in 1689 used the campus as a barracks and a prison (see **More British Problems,** p. 52). Bullet holes from the 1916 Easter Rebellion still mar the stone entrance. Until the 1960s, the Catholic Church deemed it a cardinal sin to attend Trinity; when the Church lifted the ban, the size of the student body tripled. Today, it's a celebrated center of learning, located steps away from the teeming center of a cosmopolitan capital, and an unmissable stop on the tourist trail. *(Between Westmoreland and Grafton St., South Dublin. Main entrance fronts the traffic circle now called College Green. Pearse St. runs along the north edge of the college, Nassau St. the south. ☎608 1724; www.tcd.ie. Grounds always open. Free.)*

THE OLD LIBRARY. This 1712 chamber holds an invaluable collection of ancient manuscripts, including the renowned **Book of Kells** (p. 50). Around AD 800, four Irish monks squeezed multicolored ink from bugs and plants to illustrate a four-volume edition of the Gospels. Each page holds intricate Celtic designs, interwo-ven with images of animals and Latin text. In 1007, the books were unearthed at Kells (p. 168), where thieves had buried them. For preservation purposes, the dis-play is limited to two volumes and only one page is turned per month. Two of the library's four other most celebrated books, the *Books of Dimma, Durrow, Armagh,* and *Mulling,* are on rotating display. A new exhibit, "Turning Darkness Into Light," highlights the details of their production and significance. Upstairs, the library's **Long Room** contains Ireland's oldest harp—the **Brian Ború Harp,** used as the design model for Irish coins—and one of the few remaining copies of the orig-inal **1916 proclamation** of the Republic of Ireland (p. 55). The room oozes with scholarship, although the catalogue system (smallest books on the top shelf, larg-est on the bottom) seems to be for reasons more practical than academic. *(From the main gate, the library is to the right, on the south side of Library Sq. ☎608 2320; www.tcd.ie/Library. Open May-Sept. M-Sa 9:30am-5pm, Su 9:30-4:30pm; Oct.-Apr. M-Sa 9:30am-5pm, Su noon-4:30pm. €8, students and seniors €7.)*

BANK OF IRELAND. Staring down Trinity from across College Green is the mono-lithic Bank of Ireland. Built in 1729, the building originally housed the **Irish Parliament,** a body that represented only the Anglo-Irish landowner class. After the Act of Union (see **Rebellion and Union,** p. 53), the Brits sold the building to the bank on the condition that it destroy all material evidence of Parliament's previous existence. But some rem-nants have persisted. Tourists can still visit the former chamber of the **House of Lords,** a small, elegant stateroom with impressive tapestries and an eye-catching 1780s chande-lier. *(☎671 2261. Corner of Westmoreland and College Green. Open M-Tu and F 10am-4pm, W 10:30am-4pm, Th 10am-5pm. 45min. guided talks Tu 10:30, 11:30am, 1:45pm. Free.)*

GRAFTON STREET. The few blocks south of College Green are off-limits to cars. The area's nucleus, Grafton St., meanders southward and connects with St. Stephen's Green. Its shops showcase everything from fast-food to haute couture, while its wide variety of **buskers** (street performers) entertain the crowds.

KILDARE STREET

The block bordered by Kildare St., Nassau St., Upper Merrion St., and Merrion Row is loaded with impressive buildings and many of the city's major museums.

▧ THE NATURAL HISTORY MUSEUM. Closed in 2007 for lengthy renovations, but sure to regain its beloved status when it finally reopens, the museum showcases Victorian taxidermy at its strangest and best, with exotic stuffed animals from all over the globe. Three giant Irish deer skeletons and more examples of classic taxidermy stare out from old Victorian cabinets. The dodo skeleton fights Irish parasitic worms for prime face-time, and mysterious red tarps, when lifted, reveal the tiny but complex world of preserved insects. *(Upper Merrion St.* ☎ *677 7444. Plans to re-open by summer 2009.)*

THE NATIONAL GALLERY. This collection of over 2500 canvases, only 800 of which are on active display, contains a comprehensive mix of internationally and locally renowned artists. Paintings by Brueghel, Goya, Carravaggio, Vermeer, and Rembrandt can be seen in the European exhibits, while a major part of the collection is dedicated to the Irish tradition. The works of **Jack Yeats,** brother of poet W.B., and Ireland's most celebrated artist of the 20th century, are of particular interest. Portraits of Lady Gregory, James Joyce, and George Bernard Shaw complete the display. The new **Millennium Wing** houses a 20th-Century Irish Art exhibit, a Yeats archive which celebrates the combined talents of father John B. and his four children, and computer stations that give "virtual tours" of the museum. Summertime brings concerts, lectures, and art classes; inquire at the front desk for schedules. *(Merrion Sq. W.* ☎ *661 5133; www.nationalgallery.ie. Open M-W and F-Sa 9:30am-5:30pm, Th 9:30am-8:30pm, Su noon-5:30pm. Free guided tours Sa 3pm, Su 2, 3, 4pm; July also daily 3pm. Admission free. Temporary exhibits €10, students and seniors €6.)*

LEINSTER HOUSE. The Duke of Leinster made his home on Kildare St. back in 1745, when most of the urban upper-crust lived north of the Liffey. By building his house so far south, where land was cheaper, he could afford an enormous front lawn. Today, Leinster House provides chambers for the **Irish Parliament,** or **Tithe An Oireachtais** (on tir-OCH-tas). It holds both the **Dáil** (DOIL), which does most of the governmental work, and the **Seanad** (SHAN-ad), the less powerful upper house (p. 57). The Dáil meets, somewhat sporadically, from October to Easter, Tuesday beginning at 2:30pm and Wednesday and Thursday beginning at 10:30am. When the Dáil is in session, visitors can view the proceedings by contacting their embassy to get security clearance. **Tours** of the galleries are given on Saturday and Sunday (between 10am and 4pm on the hour) and are conducted by the Captain of the Guard. *(☎ 678 9911. Passport required. Tours leave from the front entrance of Leinster House, which is between the National Library and the Archaeology and History Museum.)*

THE NATIONAL MUSEUM OF ARCHAEOLOGY AND HISTORY. Dublin's largest museum has incredible artifacts spanning the last two millennia. One room gleams with the **Tara Brooch,** the **Ardagh Hoard,** and other Celtic goldwork. Another section is devoted to the Republic's founding years and flaunts the bloody vest of nationalist hero **James Connolly.** *(Kildare St., next to Leinster House.* ☎ *677 7444; www.museum.ie. Open Tu-Sa 10am-5pm and Su 2-5pm. Guided tours €2; call for times. Museum free.)*

THE NATIONAL LIBRARY. The end of 2008 will unveil the finishing touches on the Library's state-of-the art W.B. Yeats exhibition. The **Yeats Collection** comprises over 2000 items from the celebrated poet's life, many of which are perusable via cool, techno-savvy touchscreens. Aside from the impressive futuristic displays, the interactive collection also lets visitors depart with a deeper appreciation of one of Ireland's most fascinating literary figures. Before entering the WBY area, be sure not to miss the library's chronicles of Irish history and literary goodies in its entrance room. Further in, a genealogical research room helps visitors trace even the thinnest twigs of their Irish family trees. Don't miss the reading room and its soaring domed ceiling shaded with beautiful green hues. *(Kildare St., adjacent to Lein-ster House. ☎603 0200. Open M-W 9:30am-9pm, Th-F 9:30am-5pm, Sa 9:30am-1pm. Guided tours of Yeats collection M-F 3:30pm, Sa 11am. Free. Academic reason required to obtain a library card and entrance to the reading room.)*

ST. STEPHEN'S GREEN AND MERRION SQUARE

Home to Ireland's trendiest shops and priciest homes, Merrion Sq. draws shoppers and gawkers, while the grass of Dublin's finest park beckons weary travelers.

ST. STEPHEN'S GREEN. This nine-hectare park was a private estate until the Guinness clan bequeathed it to the city. Today, the grounds are teeming with public life. Artificial lakes and hills, carefully manicured gardens, and couples nuzzling in gazebos all make you feel like you've died and gone to Wicklow. After the bustle of Grafton St. and the rowdiness of pub life, St. Stephen's Green is a welcome return to the elements. *(Kildare, Dawson, and Grafton St. all lead to the park. ☎475 7826. Open M-Sa 8am-dusk, Su 10am-dusk.)*

MERRION SQUARE. The Georgian buildings and elaborate doorways of Merrion Sq. and adjacent Fitzwilliam St. satisfy any longings for classic European architecture. After leaving 18 Fitzwilliam St., **W.B. Yeats** took up residence at 82 Merrion Sq. Farther south on Harcourt St., playwright **George Bernard Shaw** and Dracula's creator, **Bram Stoker,** were neighbors at #61 and 16, respectively. In the 1960s, the Electricity Supply Board tore down a row of the townhouses and built a monstrous new office. Irate Dubliners had a row of a different sort, and to compensate, the ESB now funds **#29 Lower Fitzwilliam St.,** also known as the **Georgian House Museum,** a restored townhouse-turned-museum that demonstrates the lifestyle of the 18th-century Anglo-Irish elite. The friendly curators are extremely knowledgeable about the life and times of Dublin back in the day. *(☎702 6165; www.esb.ie/numbertwentynine. Open Tu-Sa 10am-5pm, Su 1-5pm. A short audio-visual show leads to a 40min. tour of the house. €5, students and seniors €2.50, children free.)* The prim Georgians continue up Dawson St., which connects St. Stephen's Green to Trinity College one block south of Grafton St. Dawson St. has the honor of bestowing an address on the Mansion House, home to the Lord Mayors of Dublin since 1715. The Irish state declared its independence here in 1919, and the Anglo-Irish truce was signed in the mansion two years later. *(Closed to the public. Feel free to gawk outside.)*

NEWMAN HOUSE. This fully restored building was once the seat of **University College Dublin,** the Catholic answer to Trinity. *A Portrait of the Artist as a Young Man* chronicles Joyce's time here. The poet Gerard Manley Hopkins spent the last years of his life teaching classics at the college. The cursory tour is geared to the architecturally and literary-minded. *(86 St. Stephen's Green S. ☎716 7422. Admission by guided tour. Open to individuals June-Aug. Tu-F at 2, 3, 4pm; groups admitted throughout the year with 2 wk. advance booking. €5, concessions €4.)*

THE SHAW BIRTHPLACE. This house offers a glimpse into G.B. Shaw's childhood. Mrs. Shaw held recitals here, sparking little George's interest in music. Her lovely Victorian garden also inspired his fascination with landscape painting. *(33 Synge St. Stroll south on Camden St., make a right on Harrington St., and turn left onto Synge St. Conveniently close to buses #19, 19a, or 122 from O'Connell St. ☎872 2077. Open May-Sept. M-Tu and Th-Sa 10am-1pm and 2-5pm, Sa-Su 2-5pm. Open for groups outside hours by request. €7, concessions €6, children €4.40.)* Nearby is the **Grand Canal,** where a statue of poet **Patrick Kavanagh** sits on his favorite bench by the water.

THE IRISH JEWISH MUSEUM. This museum is in a restored former synagogue and houses a large collection of artifacts, documents, and photographs chronicling the history of the tiny Jewish community in Ireland from 1079, when five Jews arrived and were sent packing, through later and more successful European migrations. *(3-4 Walworth Rd., off Victoria St. South Circular Rd. runs to Victoria*

COUNTY DUBLIN

St.; from there the museum is signposted. ☎453 1797. Open May-Sept. Tu, Th, Su 11am-3:30pm; Oct.-Apr. Su 10:30am-2:30pm. Free, donations accepted.)

TEMPLE BAR

West of Trinity, between Dame St. and the Liffey, the Temple Bar neighborhood hums with activity. Narrow cobblestone streets link quirky cafes and upscale eateries, hole-in-the-wall theaters, rock venues, and used-clothing and record stores. In the early 1980s, the Irish transport authority intended to replace the neighborhood with a three-hectare transportation center. In 1985, the artists who lived in the area circulated petitions and ultimately saved their homes and businesses from the corporate cash cow. Ironically, Temple Bar quickly grew into one of Europe's hottest nightlife spots, forcing the artists out anyway. To steer the growth toward more cultural ends, the government-sponsored Temple Bar Properties has spent over €40 million to build a flock of arts-related tourist attractions, with independent coattail-riders springing up as well. Even so, weekend nights tend to be wild. Dublin is referred to by some as "The Las Vegas of Europe" with its plethora of costume-clad **stag and hen** (bachelor and bachelorette) parties pub-hopping with the throngs of tourists.

■**THE IRISH FILM INSTITUTE.** The Institute is a modern complex of two theaters, a trendy and popular **restaurant and bar,** a bookshop, and an archive that are all situated around a light-filled courtyard. Its theaters screen a continual series of new releases, focusing on independent and foreign cinema, and also hold festivals and special retrospectives ranging from Mexican Film Week to the Lesbian and Gay Film Festival. The institute's inner sanctum, the **Irish Film Archive,** is dedicated specifically to Irish film. It holds its own screenings and also contains an archive that can be viewed upon request. *(6 Eustace St. ☎679 5744, box office 679 3477; www.irishfilm.ie. Open M-F 10am-6pm. IFI Restaurant and bar open daily 10am-11pm. Entrees €7.50-9.50. See **Cinema**, p. 133.)*

TEMPLE BAR MUSIC CENTRE. After renovations in 2007, the center promises to bring back its terrific musical events virtually every night of the week. It also houses its own pub and cafe. *(Curved St. ☎670 9202; www.tbmc.ie. Music nightly 7:30pm, club 11pm. Cover varies according to act; check with box office for details.)*

GALLERY OF PHOTOGRAPHY. Above a photography bookstore is Ireland's largest photo studio. The walls of this four-story gallery are lined with contemporary photographs by mostly Irish and some international photographers. The gallery also runs workshops and an advanced photography course, and has black-and-white and color darkrooms available for rent. New digital photography resources also available. *(Meeting House Sq. ☎671 4654; www.galleryofphotography.ie. Open Tu-Sa 11am-6pm, Su 1-6pm. Offers several photography courses from €175-245. 3hr. darkroom rental €15.)*

TEMPLE BAR GALLERY AND STUDIOS. One of Europe's largest studio complexes, the gallery draws mostly contemporary artists from all over Ireland and the world. Though the studio has several dozen live-in artists, the gallery is free and open to the public. *(5-9 Temple Bar. ☎671 0073; www.templebargallery.com. Open Tu-W and F-Sa 11am-6pm, Th 11am-7pm.)*

DAME STREET AND THE CATHEDRALS

Those in search of medieval castles, religious ruins, and tales of Vikings and past Irish warriors need look no further than Dame St. and its environs, host to some of Dublin's oldest religious and state buildings.

■**CHESTER BEATTY LIBRARY.** Honorary Irish citizen Alfred Chester Beatty was an American mining magnate who amassed a beautiful collection of Asian and Middle Eastern art, sacred scriptures, and illustrated texts. He donated this collection to Ireland upon his death, and a new library behind Dublin Castle houses his abundance of cultural artifacts. It's no wonder that the library won

the title of European Museum of the Year in 2002. This collection of truly fascinating objects, from intricate Chinese snuff bottles to some of the earliest fragments of the Biblical Gospels, are arranged on the first floor by region of the
world. The second floor contains Beatty's extensive collection of texts from
nearly every major world religion. On the roof, a specially designed garden
incorporates surfaces of plant life and stones to create a serene space suspended above the urban landscape. *(Behind Dublin Castle. ☎ 407 0750; www.cbl.ie.
45min. tours W 1pm, Su 3 and 4pm. Open May-Sept. M-F 10am-5pm, Sa 11am-5pm, Su
1-5pm; Oct.-Apr. Tu-F 10am-5pm, Sa 11am-5pm, Su 1-5pm. Closed Jan. 1, Good Friday,
Dec. 24-26, and M bank holidays. Free.)*

DUBLINIA. This three-story interactive exhibition, which culls its name from one
of the ancient Latin terms for the city, is housed on the site of the medieval parish
of St. Michael the Archangel. The setting reflects the subject; figures come to life
as visitors are ushered through Dublin's medieval history from AD 1170 to 1540. A
highlight is the re-creation of a 13th-century Dublin Fair, where you can don
period clothes, play games, and catch a glimpse into the archaic world of medieval
medicine. The top floor contains a brand-new exhibit of the history of the Vikings
and their legacy in Dublin. *(Across from Christ Church Cathedral. ☎ 679 4611;
www.dublinia.ie. Open Apr.-Sept. daily 10am-5pm; Oct.-Mar. M-F 11am-4pm, Sa-Su 10am-4pm.
Last admission 45min. before closing. €6.25, students and seniors €5.25, children €3.75. Combined admission with Christ Church Cathedral €9.50.)*

DUBLIN CASTLE. Norman King John built the castle in 1204 on top of the Viking
settlement *Dubh Linn* ("black pool"); more recently, a series of structures from
the 18th and 19th centuries has covered the site, culminating in an uninspired
20th-century office complex. But for the 700 years after its construction, Dublin
Castle was the seat of British rule in Ireland, and its state apartments, which are
open to the public for tours, are still used for state functions, and since 1938, every
Irish president has been inaugurated here. For the best view of the castle—and a
nice picnic—head to the Irish-knot lawn in the back of the complex, next to the
Chester Beatty Library. Next door, the intricate inner dome of Dublin City Hall
(designed as the Royal Exchange in 1779) shelters statues of national heroes like
Daniel O'Connell. *(Dame St., at the intersection of Parliament and Castle St. ☎ 677 7129;
www.dublincastle.ie. State Apartments open M-F 10am-4:45pm, Sa-Su and holidays 2-4:45pm;
closed during official functions. €4.50, students and seniors €3.50, children €2. Grounds free.)*

CHRIST CHURCH CATHEDRAL. Built in the name of the universal Church, Irish
cathedrals were forced to convert to the Church of Ireland in the 16th century.
Sitric Silkenbeard, King of the Dublin Norsemen, built a wooden church on this
site around 1038, and the Anglo-Norman Strongbow rebuilt it in stone in 1169. Further additions were made in the following century and again in the 1870s. Stained
glass sparkles above the raised crypts, one of which supposedly belongs to Strongbow. In merrier times the cavernous crypt held shops and drinking houses, but
nowadays cobwebs hang from the ceiling, fragments of ancient pillars lie about
like bleached bones, and in every corner a looming stone memorial serves as an
eerie reminder of the human history captured within its walls. The entrance fee
includes admission to the "Treasure of Christ Church," a rotating exhibit that displays the church's hoard of medieval manuscripts, gleaming gold vessels, and
funereal busts. *(At the end of Dame St., uphill and across from the Castle. A 10min. walk from
O'Connell Bride, or take bus #50 from Eden Quay or 78A from Aston Quay. ☎ 677 8099. Open
daily 9:45am-5pm except during services. €5, students and seniors €2.50.)*

ST. PATRICK'S CATHEDRAL. This church dates back to the 12th century,
although Sir Benjamin Guinness remodeled much of the building in 1864. At 100m
long, it's Ireland's largest cathedral. Richard Boyle, father of scientist Robert, has
a memorial here, and the writer Jonathan Swift spent his last years as Dean of St.
Patrick's; his grave is marked on the floor of the south nave. *(From Christ Church,*

Nicholas St. runs south and downhill, eventually becoming Patrick St. Take bus #49, 49A, 50, 54A, 56A, 65, 65B, 77, or 77A from Eden Quay. ☎ 475 4817; www.stpatrickscathe-dral.ie. Open Mar.-Oct. daily 9am-6pm; Nov.-Feb. Sa 9am-5pm, Su 10am-3pm. Church closed to tours Su for 2hr. services beginning at 10:30am and 2:30pm, although visitors are welcome to attend. €5, students and seniors €4.) **Marsh's Library,** beside the cathedral, is Ireland's oldest public library. A peek inside reveals elegant wire alcoves, a collection of early maps, and exhibits of its holdings. *(☎ 454 3511. Open M and W-F 10am-1pm and 2-5pm, Sa 10:30am-1pm. €2.50, students and seniors €1.50.)*

ST. AUDOEN'S CHURCH. Founded by the Normans, this parish church is Dublin's oldest. It now contains an exhibit detailing the importance of this only remaining medieval parish that is still in use within the city of Dublin. *(High St. ☎ 677 0088. Open June-Sept. daily 9:30am-4:45pm, except during Su services. €2.10, students and seniors €1.30.)* **St. Audoen's Arch,** built in 1215 and now obscured by a narrow alley, is the only surviving gate from Dublin's medieval **city walls.** During the 16th century, the walls ran from Parliament St. to the castle, then to Little Ship St., along Francis St. to Bridge St., and then along the Liffey.

GUINNESS BREWERY AND KILMAINHAM GAOL

If you're within walking distance of central Dublin, it's best to take a bus west along the quays or to hop on a train to nearby Heuston Station to get to the *gaol* and Guinness Storehouse.

GUINNESS STOREHOUSE. The abundance of stout-stamped paper bags hanging from the arms of tourists are a good indication of Ireland's number one tourist attraction. Most can't resist the chance to discover the ins and outs of the famed black magic. Forward-looking Arthur Guinness ensured that his original 1759 brewery would become the success that it is today by signing a 9000-year lease, which is dramatically set into the floor of the massive reception hall. The building itself is an architectural wonder; seven floors of glass and suspended metal catwalks coax you through the production and legacy of Ireland's most famous brew. The self-guided tour ends with a complimentary pint in the top floor's Gravity Bar, a modern, light-filled space that commands a stunning panoramic view of the city. A massive empty pint glass that could hold the equivalent of 14.3 million pints forms the central column of the complex, rising from reception up to the bar's floor. Even if the Guinness phenomenon doesn't float your boat, you'll revel at the pyrotechnics that are marketing at its best. *(St. James's Gate. From Christ Church Cathedral, follow High St. west through its name changes—Cornmarket, Thomas, and James. Or, take bus #51B or 78A from Aston Quay or #123 from O'Connell St. ☎ 408 4800; www.guinness-store-house.com. Open daily July-Aug. 9:30am-8pm, Sept.-June 9am-5pm. €14, students over 18 and seniors €9.50, students under 18 €7.50, ages 6-12 €5, under 6—start them young!—free.)*

 THE REAL DEAL. Self-guided tours like the one at the Guinness Store-house are usually what you make of them. If you're are too eager for the prize at the top, you might miss some of the treasures in the middle, like the tasting lab, personal kiosks to view vintage Guinness ads, and the history of famous Guinness symbols like the Book of Records and Tookie the Toucan. About that pint in the sky, though...For a more jovial but crowded atmosphere, go in the evening; for a relaxed, comfortable setting, early is best. -*Kyle Dalton, RW '08*

KILMAINHAM GAOL. Almost all the rebels who fought in Ireland's struggle for independence between 1792 and 1921 spent time here, and the jail's last occupant was **Éamon de Valera,** the former leader of Éire. Built on raised land outside of the city, its open-barred windows left prisoners exposed to the elements with the belief that the air would dispel disease. The prison's dark history echoes through its frigid, eerie passages. The ghastly but compelling stories of the prisoners are dealt out in two doses, first in the comprehensive museum that sets the *gaol* in the context of its socio-political history, and then in a 1hr. tour of the dank chambers that ends in the haunting wasteland of an execution yard. *(Inchicore Rd. Take bus #51b, 51c, 78a, or 79 from Aston Quay. ☎ 453 5984. Open Apr.-Sept. daily 9:30am-5pm, Oct.-Mar. M-F 9:30am-4pm, Su 10am-5pm. Tours every 30min. €5.30, seniors €3.50, students €2.10. Small museum, separate from tour, is free of charge.)*

OTHER SIGHTS

THE ROYAL HOSPITAL KILMAINHAM. Now home to the Irish Museum of Modern Art (IMMA), this grandiose estate was built in 1679 as a hospice for retired and disabled soldiers. Its facade mimics that of the famed Les Invalides in Paris, and the grounds contain highlights like an interior courtyard ringed by stone walkways and a spectacular Baroque chapel. Inside, a series of rotating modern art exhibitions are on display, some of them in conjunction with major museums worldwide. IMMA also hosts resident artists whose works can be seen in their own exhibit hall. *(Military Rd. 5 min. walk from Heuston Station—bus #51 or 70 from Aston Quay. ☎ 612 9900; www.imma.ie. Open Tu-Sa 10am-5:30pm, Su noon-5:30pm. Guided tours W and F 2:30pm, Su 12:15pm. Free. Call ahead for special events.)*

THE COLLINS BARRACKS. Housed in former military barracks, the **National Museum of Decorative Arts and History** has an extensive collection of objects, ranging from Irish silver to scientific instruments to period clothing from Ireland's past. The central courtyard is enclosed by four wings which hold a variety of interesting exhibits. Don't miss the first gallery, Curator's Choice, which showcases 25 objects chosen by the museum's curators for their power to tell a story. *(Benburb St., off Wolfe Tone Quay. Take buses #25, 66, or 67 from Middle Abbey St. or #79, 90, or 91 from Aston Quay, which goes to Heuston Station and stops across the street from the museum. The Luas red line also stops directly in front of the museum. ☎ 677 7444; www.museum.ie. Open Tu-Sa 10am-5pm, Su 2-5pm. Public guided tours usually daily 3pm; €2. Museum free.)*

NORTH OF THE LIFFEY

O'CONNELL STREET AND PARNELL SQUARE

While tourists tend to stick to the south and the central drag of O'Connell St., the north retains a local feel. Less trendy than its southern counterpart, the area north of the Liffey is flooded with cheap stores and construction vehicles. The elusive real Dublin lies just a step off onto one of the many side streets, where fresh fruit and fish markets abound.

O'CONNELL STREET. This shopping thoroughfare starts at the Liffey and leads to **Parnell Square.** At 45m, it was once the widest street in Europe. In its pre-Joycean heyday, it was known as Sackville St., but its name was changed in honor of "The Liberator" Joseph Parnell. The central traffic islands contain monuments to Irish leaders such as James Larkin—who organized the heroic Dublin general strike of 1913—O'Connell, and Parnell (see **Infidelity on O'Connell Street,** p. 130). **O'Connell's statue** faces the Liffey and O'Connell Bridge; the winged women aren't angels but Winged Victories, although one has a bullet hole from 1916 in a rather inglorious place. At the other end of the street, **Parnell's statue** points toward nearby Parnell Mooney's pub, while the engraved words at his feet proclaim: "Thus far and no further." In front of the General Post Office stands the recently erected 120m **Dublin Spire.** Originally planned as a Millennium Spire, it wasn't actually completed until early 2003. The spire and the recently planted trees lining the lower part of the street are the first steps to restoring it to its former glory. One of the street's monuments that visitors won't see is **Nelson's Pillar,** a freestanding column that recalled Trafalgar and stood outside the General Post Office for 150 years; in 1966 the IRA com-

INFIDELITY ON O'CONNELL STREET

This main drag was once called the Street of the Three Adulterers.

1 **O'Connell Monument:** Daniel O'Connell led the 19th-century Catholic Emancipation movement, but he also sparked controversy with his purported infidelity.

2 **Dublin Spire:** Dublin's Millennium Spire, unceremoniously nicknamed "Stiffy by the Liffey," was once the site of a pillar erected in honor of Horatio Nelson, a British Admiral whose extramarital affair produced his only child. The pillar was blown up by former IRA members in 1966.

3 **Parnell Monument:** Charles Stewart Parnell was the leader of the Home Rule Party whose infamous, long-term affair with Kitty O'Shea led to his political downfall. Parnell's statue points in the direction of the Rotunda Hospital, which was formerly Dublin's primary maternity ward.

memorated the 50th anniversary of the Easter Rising by blowing the Admiral out of the water.

THE GENERAL POST OFFICE. Today, it may be just a place to send a postcard, but in 1916 the GPO was likely the most important building in Dublin. Its imposing edifice was the eye of the 1916 Easter Rising (p. 55), and Padraig Pearse read the Proclamation of Irish Independence from its steps. Stop on your way along O'Connell St. to examine the bullet nicks that still pit the front of the exterior and the series of paintings recounting the struggle for independence that hang in the main hall. (*O'Connell St. ☎705 7000. Open M-Sa 8am-8pm.*)

DUBLIN CITY GALLERY: THE HUGH LANE. An impressive collection of Irish and international art, including works by Renoir, Manet, and Degas, are on display in the Georgian **Charlemont House.** When American painter Hugh Lane offered to donate his collection of French Impressionist paintings to the city, he did so on the condition that the people of Dublin contribute to this gallery's construction. But the artist's death aboard the *Lusitania* in 1915 raised decades of disputes over his will that were eventually resolved in an agreement to divide parts of the collection between this site and London's Tate Gallery. (*Parnell Sq. North Buses #10, 10a, 11, 11a, 11b, 13, 13a, 39x, and 70x all stop at Parnell Sq. East just around the corner, while 46a and City Tour bus stop directly in front. ☎874 1903; www.hughlane.ie. Open Tu-Th 9:30am-6pm, F-Sa 9:30am-5pm, Su 11am-5pm. €7, students and seniors €3.50, under 18 free.*)

THE DUBLIN WRITERS MUSEUM. Sure to delight wordsmiths, this enthralling museum documents Dublin's rich literary heritage and the famous figures who played a part. Manuscripts, rare editions, and memorabilia of giants like Swift, Shaw, Wilde, Yeats, Beckett, Behan, Kavanagh, and O'Casey share space with caricatures and paintings. Don't miss the Gallery of Writers upstairs, an ornate, bust-lined room that harbors one of the most personal items of the collection: James Joyce's piano. Also worth checking out is the one-man performance titled "The Writers Entertain," about some of Ireland's most famous literary figures. (*18 Parnell Sq. N. ☎872 2077; www.visitdublin.com. Open June-Aug. M-F 10am-6pm, Sa 10am-5pm, Su 11am-5pm; Sept.-May M-Sa 10am-5pm, Su 11am-5pm. €6.50, students and seniors €5.50. Combined ticket with the Shaw birthplace €11, students and seniors €9. Performance daily 1:10-2pm; €11-13 includes tour.*) The **Irish Writers Centre** adjacent to the museum is the hub of Ireland's living community of writers, providing today's aspiring writers with frequent fiction and poetry readings. It is not a museum but it does provide information about Dublin's literary happenings. (*19 Parnell Sq. N. ☎872 1302; www.writers-centre.ie. Open M-F 10am-5:30pm.*)

JAMES JOYCE CULTURAL CENTRE. Mock-ups reveal reams of insight into Joyce's life, love, and labor, while intriguing items like the original door to his home at 7 Eccles St., a map tracing Stephen Daedalus's and Leopold Bloom's relative movements, and a 1921 *Ulysses* schema pique literary interest. If in town on June 16th, don't miss the center's Bloomsday festivities, when the halls come alive with reenactments and guided tours. *(35 N. Great Georges St., up Marlborough St. and past Parnell Sq. ☎878 8547; www.jamesjoyce.ie. Open Sept.-June M-Sa 9:30am-5pm, Su 12:30-5pm; July-Aug. M-Sa 9:30am-5pm, Su 11am-5pm. Guided tour daily 2pm; €10, students and seniors €9. Admission to the center €5, students and seniors €4.)*

OTHER SIGHTS. Along the northern edge of Parnell Sq., the **Garden of Remembrance** eulogizes the martyrs who seized the General Post Office and were subsequently executed (see **The Easter Rising,** p. 55). The cross-shaped, mosaic-floored pool is anchored at one end by an arresting statue that represents the mythical Children of Lir, who turned into swans. The Irish proclamation of their faith is inscribed in the wall behind them, while a smaller plaque translates it into English: "In the winter of bondage we saw a vision. We melted the snows of lethargy and the river of resurrection flowed from it." Legend has it that when Ireland is wholly united, the swans will turn back into children and fly away. *(Open until dusk.)* On Cathedral St. lies the inconspicuous **Dublin Pro-Cathedral,** the city's center of Catholic worship. Tens of thousands gathered here for Daniel O'Connell's memorial service. "Pro" means "provisional"—many Dublin Catholics want Christ Church Cathedral returned. The **National Wax Museum,** which is relocating to Smithfield Village, near the Guinness storehouse at the end of 2007, features life-size replicas of Hitler, the Teletubbies, the Pope with his Popemobile, and others. *(☎872 6340. Open M-Sa 10am-5:30pm, Su noon-5:30pm. €7, students €6, children €5.)*

ALONG THE QUAYS

With neither the grace of the Seine nor the grandeur of the Thames, the Liffey, in all its mucky glory, is still Dublin's major artery. On a (rare) sunny day, a walk along the river can be pleasant enough, especially when broken up by quick visits to the following sights, listed from east to west.

THE CUSTOM HOUSE. Dublin's greatest architectural triumph, the Custom House was designed and built in the 1780s by London-born **James Gandon,** who gave up the chance to be Russia's state architect so that he could settle in Dublin. The Roman and Venetian columns and domes give the cityscape a taste of what the city's 18th-century Anglo-Irish brahmins wanted Dublin to become. There's a small exhibit of the building's design and creation on display inside, but its facade is by far more interesting. Carved heads along the frieze represent the rivers of Ireland; the sole woman is the Liffey. *(East of O'Connell St. at Custom House Quay, where Gardiner St. meets the river. ☎888 2538. Visitors Centre open mid-Mar. to Nov. M-F 10am-12:30pm, Sa-Su 2-5pm; Nov. to mid-Mar. W-F 10am-12:30pm, Su 2-5pm. €1, students free.)*

FOUR COURTS. This Gandon masterpiece was built to consolidate Dublin's scattered legal courts in one place. It now houses the Supreme Court and the High Court, the two most important in the land. There's not much to see, but don't miss a peek into the grand central rotunda, where lawyers and judges hurry back and forth on their way to court. Yet another Dublin building affected by the War of Independence, Four Courts was burned and largely destroyed in 1921, only to be rebuilt and altered later that decade. *(Inn's Quay, several quays west of O'Connell Bridge. ☎888 6000. Open M-F 9am-4:30pm. No scheduled tours. Free.)*

ST. MICHAN'S CHURCH. This modest church, dating back to 1095, is noteworthy for its ancient and creepy limestone vaults, which may have inspired Bram Stoker's *Dracula*. Everything in here is real, from the mummified corpses dating back as many as 800 years to the grisly execution order of two 1798 rebels. Touch the hand of the Cavalier, the oldest mummy on display, and you're rumored to be blessed with good luck—not to mention centuries-old dust and a big case of the willies. *(Church St. ☎872 4154. Open Mar. 18-Oct. M-F 10am-12:45pm and 2-4:30pm, Sa 10am-12:45pm; Nov.-Mar. 16 M-F 12:30-3:30pm, Sa 10am-12:45pm. Crypt tours €3.50, students and seniors €3, under 16 €2.50. Church of Ireland services Su 10am.)*

JAMES JOYCE HOUSE. This address, at the foot of the four-year-old **James Joyce Bridge,** played a major part in Joyce's real and fictional pursuits; the house of his aunts, it was also the setting of his renowned short story "The Dead." The owner now remarkably blends fiction and reality for Joyce enthusiasts who want to re-create the dinner party exactly how it was told by the story's narrator. The "Dead Dinners" include the precise menu of the story (including goose, ham, spiced beef, floury potatoes, and pyramids of apples and oranges), period music, and the utmost in hospitality. *(15 Usher's Island Quay. ☎086 157 9546; www.jamesjoyce-house.com. House free and open to the public but call ahead. Dinners €45-80 per person.)*

SMITHFIELD

With the government pouring thousands of euro into local development, this area may be on its way to becoming the next Temple Bar. Don't rush here yet, though, the area still has a ways to go before it's complete. In the meantime, drink up.

OLD JAMESON DISTILLERY. Learn how science, grain, and tradition come together to form liquid gold—whiskey, that is. The tour walks visitors through the creation of the drink, although the stuff is really distilled in Co. Clare. Not to disappoint those hankering for a taste after all that talking, the tour ends at the bar with a free drink (soft drinks for the uninitiated). Volunteer in the beginning to get the chance to taste-test a tray of six different whiskeys from around the world. *(Bow St. From O'Connell St., turn onto Henry St. and continue straight as the street dwindles to Mary St., then Mary Ln.; the warehouse is on a cobblestone street on the left. Buses #68, 69, and 79 run from city center to Merchant's Quay. ☎807 2355. Tours daily 9:30am-5:30pm, typically every 45min. €9.75, students and seniors €8, children €6.)*

THE CHIMNEY VIEWING TOWER. Smithfield's answer to the Guinness Gravity Bar, the Old Jameson Distillery Chimney rises 60m above the ground; an elevator takes you up to a glass viewing platform that offers a 360° urban panorama. *(Follow the "Ceol" sign outside of the Old Jameson Distillery; the tower is outside of a hotel and shop. ☎817 3838, ask for the Ceol Shop. Tours M-Sa 10-5pm, Su 11am-5pm. €5; students, seniors, and children €3.50.)*

DISTANT SIGHTS

Far removed from the flurry of Dublin's main center, the outskirts of the city offer several major attractions to tempt visitors.

PHOENIX PARK AND DUBLIN ZOO. Europe's largest enclosed public park is most famous for the "Phoenix Park murders" of 1882, when The Invincibles, a Republican splinter group, stabbed Lord Cavendish, Chief Secretary of Ireland, and his trusty Under Secretary a mere 180 meters from the **Phoenix Column.** Complications ensued when a Unionist journalist forged a series of letters linking Parnell to the murderers (see **Parnell,** p. 54). The Phoenix Column itself, which is capped with a phoenix rising from flames, is something of an inside joke—the park's name actually comes from the Irish *Fionn Uisce,* meaning "clean water." The 714 hectares also harbor the **President's Residence** *(Áras an Uachtaraín),* the US Ambassador's residence, cricket pitches, polo grounds, and lots of red deer. The deer are quite tame and beautiful to watch; they often graze in the thickets near Castleknock Gate. To view all the sights without all the hikes, see the friendly owners of **Phoenix Park Bike Hire,** located at the Conyngham Rd. entrance *(☎086 265 6258. Bikes €5 per hr., €15 per ½ day, €20 per day; tandem €10/25/40.)* Even though the park is also home to one of the *Garda's* largest headquarters, the park is still not safe to travel in at night, especially alone, as it is poorly lit. *(Take bus #10 from O'Connell St. or #25 or 26 from Middle Abbey St. west along the river.)* The most notable attraction within its grounds is **Dublin Zoo,** one of the world's oldest and Europe's largest. It contains 700 critters and the world's biggest egg. For an urban zoo, the habitats are large and the animals tend to move around—the elephants even swim, something visitors rarely see elsewhere. *(Bus #10 from O'Connell St.; #25 or 26 from Wellington Quay. ☎474 8900. Open M-Sa 9:30am-6pm, Su 10:30am-6pm. Last admission 5pm. Zoo closes at dusk in winter. €14, students and seniors €11.50, children €9.50.)*

CASINO MARINO. An architectural gem and house of tricks, this 16-room country house was built for the Earl of Charlemont in 1758 as a seaside villa. Funeral urns on the roof are actually chimneys, and hollow columns serve as drains. Other highlights include secret tunnels, trick doors, and stone lions standing guard. *(Off Malahide Rd. Bus #123 from O'Connell St.; #27 or 42 from the quays. ☎833 1618. Open June-Sept. daily 10am-6pm; Feb.-Mar. and Nov.-Dec. M-F 10am-5pm, Sa-Su noon-4pm; Apr. M-F 10am-5pm, Sa-Su noon-5pm; May and Oct. daily 10am-5pm. Admission by tour only. €3, students and children €1.30, seniors €2.10.)*

GAELIC ATHLETIC ASSOCIATION MUSEUM AND CROKE PARK. Those intrigued or mystified by the world of Irish sports—hurling, camogie, Gaelic football, and handball—should follow the path forged by thousands of maniacal fans every Sunday in the summer to the historic **Croke Park Stadium** and its museum. An extensive exhibit spells out the rules and history of each Gaelic sport with the help of high-tech touchscreens and audio-visual displays. A 1hr. tour of the massive 82,500-seat stadium puts visitors in the shoes of both players and spectators, bringing them out onto the field for a taste of glory and into premium and corporate seating for a taste of exclusivity. Multi-million euro plans are currently in place to refurbish the museum in stages; it will continue to be open and improve its exhibits. *(Take bus #3, 11, 11a, 16, 16a or 123 from O'Connell St. and ask for directions, or bus #51a from Lower Abbey St. to Clonliffe. ☎819 2323. Museum open M-Sa 9:30am-5pm, Su noon-5pm. Game days open to Cusack Stand ticketholders only. Last admission 4:30pm. Museum €5.50, students and seniors €4, children €3.50; museum and stadium tour €9.50/7/6. For more info, see **Sports,** p. 73.)*

 KNOW YOUR SPORTS. The GAA Museum is a great way to get initiated into the world of Irish sport. If there's anything the Irish are more passionate about than beer, it's their games. (The two also complement each other quite well.) Still, no visit to Ireland seems complete without a working knowledge of these incredibly fast-paced and fun-to-watch battles, and the earlier you catch on, the better. The incredibly friendly staff at the museum are ready and willing to answer all your questions about their sports and share their passion for the games.

THE NATIONAL BOTANIC GARDENS. A beautiful blend of royalty and research, the National Botanic Gardens was founded in 1795 by the Royal Dublin Society but is now primarily used for educational research on plant diversity and sustainability. Its glasshouses, the kingly version of greenhouses, rise ornately above the 19.5 hectares of various gardens like plant-friendly castles. Inside, over 17,000 plant species find a steamy home while the rose garden and other temporary attractions (such as the sunflower maze) prefer the open air and nearby ponds and creeks. *(Take bus #13, 13a, 19, and 19a from O'Connell. The gardens are in Glasnevin off Botanic Ave. ☎804 0300. Open summer M-Sa 9am-6pm, Su 10am-6pm; winter M-Su 9am-4:30pm. Grounds free. Guided tours Su 12:30 and 2:30pm; €2.)*

WATERWAYS IRELAND VISITOR CENTRE. Known as the "box on the docks" in Dublinese, this floating museum educates those ignorant of the significance of the inland waterway. Often overlooked among Dublin's parade of sites, the 200-year-old system of waterways gets the spotlight here. *(Take buses #2 or 3 south to the Grand Canal. ☎677 7510. Open June-Sept. daily 9:30am-5:30pm; Oct.-May W-Su 12:30-5pm. €2.50, students and children €1.20, seniors €2, families €6.35.)*

COUNTY DUBLIN

♫ ARTS AND ENTERTAINMENT

Whether you seek poetry, punk, or something in between, Dublin is ready to entertain. The free *Event Guide* is available at music stores and hotels throughout the city. It comes out every other Friday and has decent listings. The glossier *In Dublin* (free at Tower Records) comes out every two weeks with feature articles and listings for music, theater, art exhibitions, comedy shows, clubs, museums, and movie theaters. *Events of the Week*—a much smaller free booklet—is jammed with ads but also has some good info. Hostel staffers are often reliable, if biased, sources of information. Go to www.visitdublin.com for the latest hot spots.

MUSIC

Dublin's music scene attracts performers worldwide. Pubs, which provide musicians with a free beer and a venue, see a lot of musical action. There is often a cover charge (€5-15) for better-known acts. *Hot Press* (€3.50) has the most up-to-date listings, particularly for rock. Its commentaries on the musical scene are insightful, and its left-leaning editorials give you an idea of what the Dublin artistic community is thinking. **Tower Records,** on Wicklow St., carries *Hot Press* and posts reams of leaflets and bills across the city that broadcast upcoming events. Scheduled concerts tend to start at 8pm or later; impromptu ones tend to start later.

Traditional music (trad) is an important element of Dublin's heritage and continues to thrive today. Some pubs in the city center have trad sessions every night: **Oliver St. John Gogarty, The Porter House, The Long Stone, The Celt,** and **Temple Bar Pub** are all good choices for sessions (see **Publin,** p. 112). The city's best pub for trad is ▧**Cobblestones,** King St. N. (☎872 1799), in Smithfield. There's no rock here, but live shows keep things lively, and basement sessions add an air of spontaneity. (Open M-Th 5-11:30pm, F-Sa 4pm-12:30am, Su 1-11pm. Sessions begin M-W 9:30pm, Th-Sa 7:30pm, Su 2pm.) Another intimate venue for live music is ▧**Whelan's,** 25 Wexford St, which also frequently hosts noted international acts. (p. 114.) Big-deal bands frequent the **Baggot Inn,** 143 Baggot St. (☎676 1430).

The Temple Bar Music Centre, Curved St. (☎670 9202), hosts events and concerts every night. The **National Concert Hall,** Earlsfort Terr., provides a venue for classical concerts and performances. They have nightly shows in July and August and a summer lunchtime series on occasional Tuesdays and Fridays. (☎417 0077. Tickets €8-16, students €4-8; summer lunchtime tickets Tu €8, F €16.) Programs for the **National Symphony** and smaller local groups are available at classical music stores and the tourist office. **Isaac Butt** on Store St. and the **Life** bar (see **Publin,** p. 112) have periodic jazz. Big acts play **Olympia Theatre,** 72 Dame St. (☎677 7744), and **Vicar St.,** 99 Vicar St. (☎7755 800; www.vicarstreet.com), off Thomas St. The stars also perform for huge crowds at the **Tivoli Theatre,** 135-138 Francis St. (☎454 4472); **Croke Park,** Clonliffe Rd.; and the **Royal Dublin Society (RDS),** in Ballsbridge. Tickets for major shows are available at **Ticketmaster** venues throughout the city, usually in music stores, and also online.

THEATER

Dublin has one of the world's premier national theaters and a long history of theatrical experimentation. Check the *Event Guide* and look for flyers about the shows in any given week, available in many restaurants and hostels throughout the city. There is no true theater district, but smaller theater companies thrive on Dame St. and Temple Bar. Box office hours are usually for phone reservations, while box offices stay open until curtain on performance nights. Showtime is generally 8pm.

▧ **Abbey Theatre,** 26 Lower Abbey St. (☎878 7222; www.abbeytheatre.ie). Founded by Yeats and his collaborator Lady Gregory in 1904 to promote the Irish cultural revival and modernist theater, a combination that didn't go over well with audiences. The Abbey's 1907 premiere of J. M. Synge's *Playboy of the Western World* led to storms of protest (see **The Revival,** p. 69). Today, the Abbey (like Synge) has gained respectability: it is now Ireland's National Theatre and on the cutting edge of international drama. Tickets €15-30; Sa 2:30pm matinee €18, students and seniors with ID €14. Box office open M-Sa 10:30am-7pm.

Peacock Theatre, 26 Lower Abbey St. (☎878 7222). The Abbey's experimental downstairs studio theater. Evening shows, plus occasional lunchtime plays, concerts, and poetry. Doors open M-Sa at 7:30pm. Tickets €10-17; Sa 2:45pm matinees €12.50. Available at Abbey box office.

Gate Theatre, 1 Cavendish Row (☎874 4045; www.gate-theatre.ie). Contemporary Irish and classic international dramas in intimate yet elegant setting. Wheelchair-accessible. Box office open M-Sa 10am-7:30pm. Tickets €16-30; M-Th student ticket at curtain €16 with ID, subject to availability.

Project Arts Centre, 39 E. Essex St. (☎881 9613; www.project.ie). Showcase every imaginable type of artistic production, from modern art exhibitions to plays to the Dublin Writers Festival, with an eye for the avant-garde. Box office open M-Sa 10am-6pm. Tickets under €20; student discounts available. The **gallery** hosts rotating visual arts exhibits. Open same time as box office. Free.

The New Theatre, 43 E. Essex St. (☎670 3361; www.thenewtheatre.com), in Temple Bar. Opposite the Clarence Hotel, inside Connolly Books. Brand new avant-garde plays focused on social issues of modern Irish society. Small and intimate. Box office open M-Sa 11am-7:30pm. Tickets €20, students €15.

Gaiety, South King St. (☎677 1717; www.gaietytheatre.ie), just off Grafton St. Provides space for modern drama, ballet, music, and the Opera Ireland Society. Box office open M-Sa 10am-8pm. Tickets €15-70. Also see **Clublin,** p. 117.

City Arts Centre, 23-25 Moss St. (☎677 0643), parallel to Tara St. off Georges Quay. Avant-garde exploration of significant contemporary issues. Box office open daily 9:15am-5pm. Tickets €8, students €5.

Samuel Beckett Theatre, Trinity College (☎608 2461, phone bookings 896 2242 or 960 3138), inside the campus. Hosts anything it happens upon, including scores of student shows. Tickets €18, students €14. Previews and matinees €12.

Olympia Theatre, 72 Dame St. (☎679 3323, phone bookings 081 871 9330). Specializes in commercial musical theater, plus midnight revues and tributes to the likes of ABBA and other pivotal Northern European pop bands. Box office open M-Sa 10:30am-6:30pm on days with no show, M-Sa 10:30am-9pm on show days. Tickets €17-45.

COMEDY

If the weather's got you down, Dublin's vibrant comedy scene should pick you right back up. The Irish are renowned for their wit, and they've learned to channel it into standard forms of improv and stand-up. Comedy nights and clubs are popping up around every corner, all promising *craic* and crack-ups. More festivals are making their way onto the calendar as well, including July 2007's inaugural **Bud Light Revue,** a 3-day laughfest in the Iveagh Gardens, and the very successful **Bulmers International Comedy Festival,** which spans the month of September. It's hard to go wrong in any of the clubs, but check out any of Dublin's free event guides (see **Arts and Entertainment,** p. 132) for weekly listings.

The Capital Comedy Club, Wellington Quay (☎677 0616; www.capitalcomedyclub.com). Upstairs from Ha'penny Bridge Inn. Intimate and engaging setting with comics sure to give you an ab workout. MC is an up-and-coming stand-up and keeps the laughter rolling between gigs by local comedians. Doors open W and Su 9pm; show starts 9:30pm. Cover €7, students €5.

The International Comedy Club, 23 Wicklow St. (☎677 9250; www.theinternationalcomedyclub.com). Popular club packs a punch...line. Claim to fame: Eddie Izzard stopped by and spontaneously performed. M Improv. Arrive early. Doors open Th-Sa 8:45pm; shows 9:15pm. Cover €10, students €8.

The Bankers Comedy Club, Trinity St. (☎679 3697), off Dame St. Showcases improv and stand-up 2 nights per week to get you guffawing. W and F improv; Th and Sa stand-up. Doors open 9pm. Cover €10, students €8.

The Laughter Lounge, Eden Quay (☎ 1800 266 339; www.laughterlounge.com). Self-described as "the most fantabulous comedy experience in the whole wide world." Bigger venue gets the giggles going early. Th-Sa stand-up. Doors open 7pm; show starts 8:30pm. Tickets €20-30.

CINEMA

Ireland's well-subsidized film industry reeled with the arrival of the **Irish Film Institute,** 6 Eustace St., in Temple Bar. The Institute is home to the Irish-focused Irish Film Archive, but it also hosts tributes and festivals that pay homage to films from all over the world, including French and Spanish celebrations and Bloomsday screenings. It also shows a variety of classic and European arthouse films throughout the year. (☎ 679 3477; www.irishfilm.ie. Membership required to buy most tickets. Weekly membership €1; yearly membership €20, students €15. Memberships allow 3 guests and must be purchased at least 15min. before show. M-F matinees €6-7.50; after 5pm all shows €7.50-8.) **The Screen,** D'Olier St. (☎ 672 5500), also rolls artsy reels. First-run movie houses cluster on O'Connell St., the quays, and Middle Abbey St. The **Savoy,** O'Connell St. (☎ 874 6000), and **UGC Multiplex,** Parnell St. (☎ 872 8444), screen major releases for about €7.50, and UGC offers an unlimited monthly pass for €17.50.

GALLERIES

Kerlin Gallery, Anne's Ln. (☎ 670 9093; www.kerlin.ie), across from Hillsboro Fine Art. Open, experimental space, full of national and international contemporary art. Open M-F 10am-5:45pm, Sa 11am-4:30pm.

Solomon Gallery, Powerscourt Townhouse Centre (☎ 679 2437; www.solomongallery.com), on South William St. Inside the beautiful ballroom of an old Palladian Mansion. Exhibits modern and contemporary prints, paintings, and sculptures. Open M-Sa 10am-5:30pm.

Graphic Studio Gallery (☎ 679 8021; www.graphicstudiodublin.com), off Cope St., through the arch. First gallery in Dublin to focus exclusively on contemporary prints. Open M-F 10am-5:30pm, Sa 11am-5pm.

Hillsboro Fine Art, 3 Anne's Ln. (☎ 677 7905; www.hillsborofineart.com), paintings by young talent in a cozy, 2-level space. Open M-F 10:30am-6pm, Sa 10:30am-4pm.

SPORTS AND RECREATION

Games are serious business in the big city, especially since most tournament finals take place here. The season for **Gaelic football** and **hurling** (see **Sports,** p. 73) runs from mid-February to November. Provincial finals take place in July, national semifinals on Sundays in August (hurling the first week, football the second and third), and **All-Ireland Finals** in either late August or early September. Games are played on **Phibsborough Road** and in **Croke Park.** (Clonliffe Rd., a 15min. walk from Connolly station. Bus routes #3, 11, 11A, 16, 16A, 51A, 123. ☎ 836 3222; www.gaa.ie. Tickets €20-60.) Tickets are theoretically available at the turnstiles, but they tend to sell out quickly; All-Ireland Finals sell out immediately. Home games of the Irish **rugby** team are typically played in **Lansdowne Road Stadium** but may also be played at Croke Park during Lansdowne's redevelopment; the peak season runs from February to early April. **Camogie** (women's hurling) finals are in September. For more sports information, check the Friday papers or contact the **Gaelic Athletic Association** (☎ 836 3222; www.gaa.ie). **Greyhounds** race all year. (☎ 668 3502, 497 1081. W-Th and Sa 8pm at Shelbourne Park. M-Tu and F 8pm at Harold's Cross.) **Horse racing** and its attendant gambling run rampant at Leopardstown Racetrack (☎ 289 2888), in Foxrock. At the beginning of August, the **Royal Dublin Horse Show** comes to the RDS in Ballsbridge (see **Music,** p. 132). For the weekend warrior, St. Stephens Park is always ready for a game of footies.

⬛ SHOPPING

Dublin hardly rivals the European shopping meccas of London and Paris, but it has some hot spots of its own. Tiny shops pop up everywhere along the streets both north and south of the Liffey, but Dublin's most serious shopping is on **Grafton** and **O'Connell Streets.** On pedestrian Grafton St., well-dressed consumers crowd clothing stores to become even better dressed while street performers ("buskers") keep things lively outside. Most of the street's stores are international chains, but the side streets between Grafton and **South Great Georges Street** are full of more unique boutiques. Teens and barely-twenties buy used clothes and punk discs in **Temple Bar** and newer versions of the same in the **St. Stephens Green Shopping Centre,** an undistinguished mall on the northwest corner of its namesake, at the end of Grafton St. Across the river, **Mary** and **Henry Streets** have still more chains for those on a tighter budget. Stores are generally open Monday through Saturday from 9am to 6pm, with later hours on Thursdays (until 7-8pm). On **Moore Street,** vendors sell fresh produce at low prices. (Open M-Sa 10am-5pm.) **Clery's,** Upper O'Connell St., is Dublin's principal department store. (☎878 6000. Open M-W and Sa 9am-7pm, Th 9am-9pm, F 9am-8pm.)

At the top of Grafton St. is the aforementioned **St. Stephen's Green Shopping Centre.** Lord Powerscourt's 200-year-old townhouse on Clarendon St. has been converted into the **Powerscourt Townhouse Centre,** a string of chic boutiques selling antiques and Irish crafts. Gen-Xers and hippie-holdouts head to **Georges St. Market Arcade,** on South Great Georges St. near Dame St., home to a fortune-teller and many vintage clothing and used-record stalls. (Shops generally open M-W and F-Sa 10am-6pm, Th 10am-7pm; some shops open Su noon-6pm.)

DUBLIN'S LITERARY SHOPPING

Dawson St. and **Middle Abbey St.** house many of Dublin's bookstores. On Saturdays, **Temple Bar's** used-book sellers take over Meeting House Sq.

Chapters, Ivy Exchange, Parnell St. (☎879 2700 or 872 3297; www.chapters.ie), beside rotunda Hospital at the end of Moore St. Vast collection of new and used books, with a top floor selling new and used CDs, DVDs, and VHS tapes. Come here to jettison those finished paperbacks—they'll buy or trade almost any used book. Open M-W and F-Sa 9:30am-6:30pm, Th 9:30am-8pm, Su noon-6:30pm.

International Books, 18 South Frederick St. (☎679 9385; www.internationalbooks.ie), around the corner from Nassau St. Stocks excellent collections of non-English fiction, DVDs, and dictionaries. Multi-lingual muggles can purchase *Harry Potter* here in 10 languages. Open M-Sa 9am-5:30pm.

Eason, in 5 locations throughout the city, the largest of which is on 40 Lower O'Connell St. (☎858 3800). Lots of serious tomes and an extensive "Irish interest" section. Wide selection of local and foreign magazines and newspapers. Open M-W and Sa 8:30am-6:45pm, Th 8:30am-8:45pm, F 8:30am-7:45pm, Su noon-5:45pm.

RECORDS, TAPES, AND CDS

Freebird Records, 5 Cope St. (☎675 9856), off Anglesea St. in Temple Bar. Dublin's best selection of indie rock, vinyl, and used CDs. Knowledgeable staff can recommend local bands. Another location on Wicklow St. with the same hours (☎707 9955). Open M-W and F-Su 11am-6:30pm, Th 11am-7:30pm.

Claddagh Records, 2 Cecilia St. (☎677 0262; www.claddaghrecords.com), in Temple Bar between Temple Ln. and Crow St. Good selection of trad and a variety of international music. Open summer M-F 10:30am-8pm, Sa-Su noon-8pm; winter M-F 10:30am-5:30pm, Sa noon-5:30pm.

City Disks, Temple Ln. (☎633 0066). Good selection of new and used indie rock, hip-hop, and blues, on disc or vinyl. Also sells concert tickets for just about any venue, whether through Ticketmaster or independently. Open M-W and F 11am-7pm, Th 11am-8pm, Sa 10am-6pm, Su noon-6pm.

Celtic Note, 14-15 Nassau St. (☎670 4157). Specializes in traditional Irish music. Also a Ticketmaster outlet. Open M-W and F-Sa 9am-7pm, Th 9am-8pm, Su 11am-6pm.

CLOTHING

While Merrion Sq. and St. Stephen's Green may tempt the traveler in search of haute couture, stores offering alternative styles, lower prices, or vintage relics can be found all over the city. Temple Bar is the place to go for vintage clothing, with stores offering a standard assortment of clothes from the 1960s to today at prices higher than you'd expect—don't be surprised to find a faded t-shirt for €15.

■ **The Eager Beaver,** 17 Crown Alley (☎677 3342). Treasure trove of T-shirts, track suits, and more. 2 fl. of tightly packed clothes in a building that takes up half a block—shopping here can be daunting, but the intrepid rummager finds the occasional sweet leather jacket. Open M-W 9:30am-6pm, Th 9am-7:30pm, F 9am-7pm, Sa 9:30am-6pm, Su noon-6pm. Students, seniors, and unemployed 10% discount.

Jenny Vander, 2 Drury St. (☎677 0406), behind S. Great Georges St. Market Arcade. Redefines vintage: their oldest dresses date back to the 1870s. Women come here for embroidered corsets, antique kimonos, or the perfect Bloomsday outfit. Not for the casual shopper—prices reflect the rarity of their collection—but the knowledgeable staff can point out hidden deals. Open M-Sa 9:30am-5:45pm.

Wild Child, 8 Crow St. (☎633 7748), off Dame St. Psychedelic 60s-70s garb, funky music, and a shelf of gag gifts and practical jokes. Extensive men's and women's selection. Sister shop on S. Great Georges St. sells furniture originals (☎475 5099). Open M-W and F-Sa 10am-6pm, Th 10am-7pm, Su 1-6pm.

Costelloe and Costelloe, 14A Chatham St. (☎671 4209; www.costelloeandcostelloe.com), at the corner of Clarendon. Tiny shop full of glittering handbags (from €35), beaded jewelry (from €12.50), and silk scarves (from €24.50). Open M-W and F 10am-6:30pm, Th 10am-8pm, F 10am-6:30pm, Sa 10am-7pm, Su 1:30-5pm.

❀ FESTIVALS

Failte Ireland's annual *Calendar of Events* (€1.30) offers info on events throughout Ireland, including Dublin's many festivals, antique and craft fairs, flower marts, horse shows, and the like. The biweekly *Events Guide* or *weekly indublin* (free in stores) are also good sources.

BLOOMSDAY. James Joyce's Dublin comes alive each year on June 16, the date of protagonist Leopold Bloom's 18hr. journey in the famed *Ulysses.* Festivities are held all week leading up to the big day and culminate on the 16th with a slate of events ranging from reenactments to concerts to guided tours of many of the Dublin spots mentioned in the book. The James Joyce Cultural Centre (p. 129) sponsors a reenactment of the funeral and wake, a lunch at Davy Byrne's, and a Guinness breakfast, among other activities. *(Call ☎ 280 9265 for info.)*

STREET PERFORMANCE WORLD CHAMPIONSHIP. Three days of free entertainment. Buskers battle it out on the street for the world title while onlookers search their pockets for spare coins. (Mid-June. ☎639 4850; www.spwc.ie.)

MUSIC FESTIVALS. The **Festival of Music in Great Irish Houses,** held in mid-June, organizes concerts of period music in 18th-century homes across the country, including some in the city. *(☎278 1528.)* **Feis Ceoil** in mid-March is the longest-running classical music festival in Europe and attracts groups from dozens of countries to its prized competitions. *(☎676 7365.)* The **Dublin International Organ and Choral Festival,** or **Pipeworks,** features both international ensembles and the three cathedral choirs of Dublin and also holds an organ-playing competition and master classes. It is set to take place June 20-28 in 2008. *(☎633 7392; www.pipeworksfestival.com.)* The **Guinness Blues Festival,** a three-day extravaganza in late July, showcases blues performances, films, workshops, a blues trail pub crawl of live music, and a free outdoor concert on College Green. (☎ 497 0381.) Ask at the tourist office about *fleadhs* (FLAHS), day-long trad festivals that pop up periodically.

ST. PATRICK'S DAY. The week encompassing March 17 occasions a city-wide carnival of concerts, fireworks, street theater, and intoxicated madness. Many pubs offer special promotions, contests, and extended hours. (☎ 676 3205; also contact the tourist center for more information.)

THE DUBLIN THEATRE FESTIVAL. This premier cultural event, held from late September to early October, showcases works from Ireland and around the world at major theaters like the Abbey, the Gate, the Olympia, and the Gaeity. Tickets may be purchased all year at participating theaters, and, as the festival draws near, at the Festival Booking Office. (44 East Essex St. ☎ 677 8439, box office 677 8899; www.dublintheatrefestival.com. Tickets €13-20, student discounts vary by venue.)

THE DUBLIN FILM FESTIVAL. Nearly two weeks of Irish and international movies are screened at all of the major cinematic venues throughout the city, including UGC, the Savoy, and the Screen, with a panoply of seminars in tow. (Early to mid-Mar. ☎ 661 6216; www.dubliniff.com.)

GAZE: THE DUBLIN INTERNATIONAL LESBIAN AND GAY FILM FESTIVAL. Over 15 years celebrating GLBT on the big screen, the festival hosts a weeks worth of screenings at the IFI, which showcases the best in gay and lesbian film. (First week in August. www.gaze.ie. Tickets €8-20.)

◪ GLBT DUBLIN

PRIDE (www.dublinpride.org), is a week-long celebration complete with a parade, club nights, panels, theatricals, and even a sports day in Phoenix Park. To find out what's going on, check out the **Gay Community News (GCN),** Unit 2 Scarlet Row, W. Essex St. (☎ 671 9076; www.gcn.ie), a free monthly guide with information on gay life and nightlife in Dublin and beyond. **Gay Switchboard Dublin** sponsors a hotline. (☎ 872 1055. Available M-F and Su 8-10pm, Sa 3:30-6pm). **OUThouse,** 105 Capel St., is a community resource center, offering a library, cafe, support groups, information sessions, and social events listings. (☎ 873 4932. Drop-in hours M-F noon-6pm.)

◪ DAYTRIP FROM DUBLIN: MALAHIDE

DART serves Malahide station (20 min., daily 2 per hr, roundtrip €3.40). From the DART station, turn right on Main St. and over the bridge (15min.) to get to the castle entrance gate. **Malahide Garda Station,** Main St., ☎ 666 4600. Castle ☎ 846 2184; www.malahidecastle.com. Park open dawn until dusk. Castle open Jan.-Dec. M-Sa 10am-12:45pm and 2-5pm, Apr.-Sept. Su and bank holidays 10am-12:45pm and 2-6pm, Oct.-Mar. Su and bank holidays 11am-12:45pm and 2-5pm. Admission only by 35min. tour. €7, students and seniors €6, children €4.40. Museum open M-Sa 10am-1pm and 2-5pm, Su 2-6pm. €2. Gardens open May-Sept. 2-5pm. €4.

Malahide Castle is more than an 800-year-old blend of architectural styles surrounded by hectares of perfectly manicured parklands. It is also an impressive cultural complex, housing several museums. The castle includes rooms full of 14th-through 19th-century furnishings and portraits; the paneled oak room and the great hall are magnificent. The audio tour is incredibly (sometimes overly) detailed. A live peacock welcomes those who discover the castle's best secret: the ◪**Museum of Childhood,** a veritable Antiques Roadshow of 18th-century dollhouses and toys. This charity trust can't afford to advertise, so few are aware of the world's oldest known dollhouse, finished in 1700. Upstairs sits the spectacular **Tara's Palace,** a huge model mansion that fills an entire room. Beyond the main drag of clothing and craft boutiques, you'll find the gorgeous Malahide beach, as well as a beach-side walking path. Closer to neighboring Portmarnock (2km) is the even softer, more luxurious 2 mi. stretch of beach known as the **Velvet Strand.**

Malahidean restaurants tend to cater to heavy purses, but budget travelers can certainly find a smattering of affordable spots. **Coffee Scene ❷,** on Main St. and Old St., has more than just your daily fix of caffeine. Patrons enjoy hot soup (€4) and jacket potatoes (€7) with their newspapers in or just outside the cozy shop. (☎845 7175. Open daily 8am-5:30pm. MC/V.) Inside Malahide Castle, dine like royalty at **The Restaurant ❶,** a casual cafe offering ham, turkey, and cheese sandwiches (€3.65, on fresh bread €5.75), as well as scones (€1.65), to complement afternoon tea. (☎846 3027. Open M-Sa 10am-5pm, Su 11am-6pm. MC/V, min €10.) **Mario's Pizza ❷,** off Main St. at 1 New St., serves up hot pies for a little cold cash. Aside from ordinary cheese pizza (10 in. €7.80), Mario's offers BBQ chicken pizza (€11.80) and—why not—fish and chips (€6) to suit all tastes. (☎845 0989. Open daily 12:30pm-midnight. MC/V.) Grab supplies for beachside picnics at **SuperValu,** in the shopping center on Main St. and Townyard Ln. (☎845 0233. Open M-W 8am-8pm, Th-Sa 8am-9pm, Su 9:30am-6:30pm.)

DUBLIN'S SUBURBS

Strung along the Irish Sea from Donabate in the north to Bray in the south, Dublin's suburbs offer harried travelers an accessible, calm alternative to the voracious human tide swarming about the Liffey. Old ruins and new shopping centers intermix, both clamoring for a view of the rocky shore. Natural beauty combined with small village streets help two regions stand out from the sprawl: tranquil Howth Peninsula to the north and the cluster of suburbs around Dún Laoghaire to the south. The two regions are surprisingly close: you can see right across the bay from one to the other. Howth offers splendid views of the water and Dublin city. Bragging rights for Dublin's best beach go to the Velvet Strand, a plush stretch of rock and water between Malahide and Portmarnock. Dublin's southern suburbs are tidy and fairly well-off—the coastal yuppie towns form a chain of snazzy houses and bright surf. The suburban rail and local buses service the area, but the fastest and most convenient way to travel is by the DART, which connects all the coastal towns, making them easily accessible for afternoon or day outings.

HOWTH (BINN ÉADAIR) ☎01

Favored by Ireland's literary lasses, Howth (rhymes with "both") was the childhood home of Maud Gonne, Yeats's wife, and the location of Molly Bloom's reminiscences in Joyce's *Ulysses*. Only 14.5km from Dublin, Howth peninsula is an extremely popular evening and weekend destination for Dubliners looking to escape the stress of city life. If the weekend sun is shining, expect crowds. And who could blame them? Howth is an inexpensive wonderland, with hiking trails ringing a cliff, a hill of flowers, and a towering castle. At the end of the day, after the salty air and steep trails have whetted your appetite, there's plenty of seafood to enjoy from right out of the harbor.

🖪🔃 TRANSPORTATION AND PRACTICAL INFORMATION. The easiest way to reach Howth is by **DART.** Take a northbound train to the Howth end of the line (30min., 4 per hr., €3.60). **Buses** leave from Dublin's Lower Abbey St. Bus #31 runs every hour from the center of Howth, near the DART station; #31 adds a loop that climbs to the Howth Summit. To get into town, turn left out of the DART station and walk toward the harbor on Harbour Rd. A general map of the peninsula is posted at the harbor entrance.

Services include: an **ATM,** inside of SPAR off Main St. just before the church; the **police** *(Garda)* station, at Howth Terr. and Church Rd. (☎666 4900; open 24hr.); **McDermott's Pharmacy,** 5 Main St. (☎832 2069; open M-Sa 9am-6pm, Su 9am-1pm);

free **Internet** access at the **library**, on Main St. across from the pharmacy (☎ 832 2130; open M and W 2-8:30pm, Tu and Th 10am-1pm and 2-5:15pm, F and Sa 10am-1pm and 2-5pm; call ahead to reserve a time); the **post office**, Abbey St. (☎ 832 0899; open M-F 9am-1pm and 2:15-5:30pm, Sa 9am-1pm).

⛩ ACCOMMODATIONS. The B&Bs in Howth provide guests with full Irish breakfasts and ensuite bathrooms. Many are a long climb or a short bus ride up Thormanby Rd., but most proprietors will pick visitors up at the DART stop. Bus #31 makes regular stops running up Thormanby Rd. You'll findn delightful hosts at at ▒Gleann na Smól ❸ ("The Valley of the Thrush"), a left off Thormanby Rd., at the end of Nashville Rd. on the left. An affordable option close to the harbor, it has five rooms with TVs and a generous supply of reading material. The owners exemplify Irish hospitality: Kitty makes fresh brown and Irish soda breads daily, and her son, Sean, is happy to share his wealth of knowledge about Howth's history and attractions. (☎ 832 2936. Singles €50, doubles €64. Cash only.) ▒**High Field ❸**, farther up Thormanby Rd., is on the left, up a winding driveway. A lovely harbor view from the dining room and front bedrooms complements the old Victorian house. Couples may enjoy swinging in the loveseat in the front yard, and the young (or young at heart) are welcome to jump on the trampoline. (☎ 832 3936. Doubles €72. Cash only.) With a great location right by the light house, **Ann's Guest Accommodations ❸** is a brand new B&B situated where East Pier meets Harbour Rd. Don't be confused by the shop selling ice cream and postcards downstairs—there are rooms up there! (☎ 832 3197; www.annsofhowth.com. Singles €60, doubles €85. MC/V.) Sounds of the owner strumming his guitar greet patrons of **Hazelwood ❸**, 1.6km up Thormanby Rd., in the Thormanby Woods estate, at the end of the first cul-de-sac on the left. You'll feel like royalty when you eat breakfast in the dining room, richly decorated with dark wood and elaborate goblets. (☎ 839 1391; www.hazelwood.net. Singles €50; doubles €72. Cash only.) On the side of a hill lies **Inisradharc ❸**, with brilliant views of Ireland's Eye from its sunny conservatory. The view atop the steep hill is great, but prepare for the long trek up it. From Abbey Rd., bear right at the church and follow Balkill Rd. up the hillside; the hotel is on the right. (☎ 832 2306. Doubles €80, with children 25% discount. AmEx/MC/V.)

▨▨ FOOD AND PUBS. Fried seafood, especially local cod, haddock, or Dublin Bay prawns, is the thing to eat in Howth. **Caffé Caira ❷**, on the corner of Harbour Rd. and Abbey St., fries up classic fishy fare. The takeaway window serves the same food at a breakneck pace for a fraction of the price. (☎ 832 2600. Cod fish and chips at restaurant €9.50; takeaway €7.70; burger €6.60/2.20. Open daily noon-9:30pm; takeaway noon-1am. Cash only.) **The Country Kitchen ❶**, 15 Main St., to the right of the church, packs fresh baguette sandwiches (€3.40) for hungry hikers. Attached is a market with drinks, fruits, and veggies to round out the meal. (☎ 832 2033. Open M-Sa 8am-7pm, Su 8am-5pm. MC/V.) **Maud's ❷**, Harbour Rd., is a casual cafe with sandwiches (veggie *panini* €6.45) and award-winning ice cream (most €1-4.50; signature "Pooh Bear Delight" €5.50) to sweeten anyone's day. (☎ 839 5450. Open daily 9am-6pm. Cash only.) Near Country Kitchen on Main St., **Kruger's ❸**, offers bar bites and Irish entrees (€8-11) to go with a pint (€4), and occasionally offers live trad. (☎ 832 2229. Kitchen open daily 12:30-9:45pm. MC/V.) **The Oar House ❹**, 8 West Pier, serves up chowder (€5) and Howth crab cakes (tapas €10, main course €20) just feet from the water. The decor is an eclectic mix of shabby and chic: the table settings are beautifully fancy, but nautical buoys line the walls. (☎ 839 4568; www.theoarhouse.ie. Open daily 12:30-10:30pm. Reservations recommended for dinner. MC/V.) Top off your cliff walk with a pint and an incredible view of North Howth at **The Summit**, located at the top of Thormanby Rd. (☎ 832 4615. Bar open M-Th and Su 11:30am-11:30pm, F-Sa 11:30am-12:30am. MC/V.) The ceiling aquarium and later hours attract locals to **bá mizu** (which means "water bar" in Japanese) on Main St, despite the slightly pricier drinks (beer €4-5, cocktails €9-11). Japanese cartoons play on TVs by the bar. (☎832 2691. Open M-W and Su 4pm-11:30pm, Th-Sa 12:30pm-2:30am. MC/V.)

◙ ⚑ SIGHTS AND OUTDOOR ACTIVITIES. The well-trod but narrow ▨**cliff walk** (4hr.) ringing the Howth peninsula is a breathtaking sea-side adventure. Visitors have a variety of routes to choose from, including a lovely jaunt along the lower cliff. The walk starts near the town center and wanders through heather-covered hills and stone ruins, all bordered by 30-60m of cliffs and open sea. Hikers will see **Puck's Rock** at the harbor's end, marking the spot where the devil allegedly fell when St. Nessan shook a Bible at him. The nearby **lighthouse,** surrounded by tremendous cliffs, housed Salman Rushdie for a night during the height of the *fatwa* against him. To get to the trailhead from town, turn left at the DART and bus station and follow Harbour Rd. for about 20min. past East Pier. To avoid the long trek back over the cliff walk, climb the path from the lighthouse to the Summit Carpark and either hop the #31B back down to the heart of town or walk down Thormanby Rd. The parking lot offers a magnificent view: on a clear day, Wales and the Mourne Mountains in Northern Ireland are visible. **Ireland's Eye,** a small island just offshore, once provided sanctuary for monks, whose legacy is memorialized in the ruins of **St. Nessan's Church.** The monks abandoned their island refuge when they tired of marauding pirates. The island's long beach is now primarily a bird haven, with 177 species calling it home. Visitors can also spot Lambay, an island beyond Ireland's Eye, home to a large seal colony. Hungry seals flock to **Nicky's Plaice** on West Pier (☎ 832 3557; www.nickysplaice.ie), lured by a bell that announces feeding times at noon and 3pm.

Several sights are clustered in the middle of the peninsula; head right as you exit the DART station and then left after 400m, on the same road as the entrance to the Deer Park Hotel. Up this road lies the private Howth Castle, a charmingly awkward patchwork of materials, styles, and degrees of upkeep. Unfortunately, the castle's denizens prefer to keep to themselves and don't open their house to the public. Commoners can instead ramble in the ▨**Rhododendron Gardens,** the site of Molly Bloom's musings at the end of Joyce's *Ulysses.* Follow the signs up the road and past the golf course to the flowerbeds, where you can get a scented view of the harbor and Ireland's Eye. (Gardens always open. Rhododendrons in bloom Apr.-June. Free.) For a day of golf, play one of the glorious courses at Deer Park Golf Club, just past the castle. (☎832 2624. M-F €18.50 per 18-hole round, Sa-Su €27. Club rental €16.50 full set, €7.50 half set. Open M-F 8am-dusk, Sa-Su 6:30am-dusk.) Get a military outlook at one of the coast's many Martello towers (see Rebellion, p. 53) on Abbey St., which now houses ▨**Ye Old Hurdy-Gurdy Museum of Vintage Radio,** the result of one man's 40-year love affair with radios. (☎086 815 4189. Open daily May-Oct. from 11am-4pm, Nov.-Apr. weekends 11am-4pm. €5.) Little boys and not-so-little train and car enthusiasts may be interested in the National Transport Museum, an old tin warehouse packed with restored trains, trams, tanks, and ambulances from the 1880s to the 1970s. Sadly, climbing aboard the old firetrucks is forbidden. (☎848 0831; www.nationaltransportmuseum.org. Open June-Aug. M-F 10am-5pm and every Sa-Su and bank holiday 2-5pm. €3; students, children, and seniors €1.50.)

DÚN LAOGHAIRE ☎01

As one of Co. Dublin's major ferryports, with boats coming over from Holly Head in Wales, Dún Laoghaire (dun-LEER-ee) is many tourists' first peek at Ireland. It's a good place to begin your rambles along the coast, and it's easy to see why it has been immortalized in Joyce's and Shaw's writings—the seaviews are spectacular. The surrounding towns, from north to south, are Blackrock, Monkstown, Dalkey, and Killiney. Getting from one town to the next is quick and simple for those staying within a few blocks of the sea, because all have stops on the DART. For those who have time, it's also lovely to walk along the shore from one town to the next—

benches line the way, so you're never too far from a spot to rest. On summer evenings, couples stroll down the Dún Laoghaire waterfront, and the whole town turns out for weekly sailboat races.

ORIENTATION AND PRACTICAL INFORMATION. Dún Laoghaire is easily reached on the **DART** from Dublin (€2) or southbound **buses** #7, 7A, 8, or (a longer, inland route) 46A from Eden Quay. For those who want to party downtown by night, the #7N **nightbus** departs for Dún Laoghaire from College St. in Dublin. (M-Th 12:30 and 2am, F-Sa every 30min. 12:30-4:30am. €4.) From the ferryport, **Marine Road** climbs up to the center of town. **George's Street,** at the top of Marine Rd., holds most of Dún Laoghaire's shops; many lie at the intersection in the 70s-inspired **Dún Laoghaire Shopping Centre.** The section of the street to the right of Marine Rd. is Lower George's St. To the left is Upper George's St. At the end of this street you'll find Peoples Park, a lovely place to take relax and survey the scenery.To reach **Bloomfield Shopping Centre,** head up Marine Rd. from the harbor, take a right on George's St., and then take the third left. **Patrick Street,** the continuation of Marine Rd., has some good, cheap eateries.

The **tourist office** at the ferry terminal is constantly humming as it outfits visitors with maps and pamphlets. Ask for the series of six walks on the Dún Laoghaire Way. The pamphlets cover easy-to-miss sights and provide the maps needed to find them. (Open M-Sa 10am-1pm and 2-6pm.) Banks, 24hr. **ATMs** and **bureaux de change** cluster around the intersection of Marine Rd. and George's St. **Ulster Bank,** on Upper George's St., has a 24hr. **ATM.** (☎280 8596. Open M-W and F 10am-4pm, Th 10am-5pm.) The **post office** is beyond the bank on Upper George's St. (☎230 0140. Open M and W-F 9am-6pm, Tu 9:30am-6pm, Sa 9am-1pm.) **St. Michael's Hospital** is on Lower George's St. (☎280 6901). Just off Upper George's St., on Corrig Ave., is the **Police** *(Garda)* **Station.** (☎666 5000. Open 24hr.) **Star Laundry,** 47A Upper George's St., will wash your duds. (☎280 5074. Open M-Sa 8:30am-6pm. 3kg €7.50.) On the corner of Marine Rd. and George's St. is **O'Mahoney & Ennis Pharmacy.** (☎280 1163. Open M-Sa 9am-6pm.) **Dún Laoghaire Youth Info Centre,** in the church on Marine Rd., helps travelers find **work opportunities.** (☎280 9363; www.youthquest.ie. Open M-F 9:30am-5pm, Sa 10am-4pm.) Free **Internet** access is available at the Youth Info Centre and at the **Carnegie Library,** toward the end of Lower George's St. (☎280 1147. Open M and Sa 10am-1pm and 2-5pm, Tu and Th 1:15-8pm, W and F 10am-5pm.)

ACCOMMODATIONS. **Belgrave Hall ❷,** 34 Belgrave Sq., is a 20min. walk from the town center and accessible from the Seapoint DART station. Head left down the coast, right on Belgrave Rd., left on Eaton Pl., right across from the blue and yellow doors, and left again across from Belgrave House. Hostelers live in style in this splendid, well-maintained old mansion. A richly decorated dining/sitting room with a marble fireplace and an ornately patterned ceiling contribute to the decor, and one-of-a-kind antique furniture pieces in each room make you feel like royalty. (☎284 2106. Continental breakfast included. Laundry €7. Free parking. 10-bed dorm €25. Cash only.) Closer to town, **Marina House ❷,** 7 Old Dunleary Rd., is a clean, well-run hostel just next to West Pier. The kitchen's wall is painted to look like the nearby harbor. (☎284 1524. Continental breakfast included. 10-bed dorm €19; 4-bed ensuite dorm €22.50. Wash €2, dry €2. MC/V.) Hop off the DART into bed at **Marleen's B&B ❸,** 9 Marine Rd. Its convenient location attracts those catching an early-morning ferry. (☎280 2456. TV and tea facilities. Singles €35; doubles €64. Cash only.)

FOOD AND PUBS. **Tesco** sells groceries downstairs in the Dún Laoghaire Shopping Centre. (☎280 0668. Open M-W and Sa 8:30am-7pm, Th-F 8:30am-9pm.) Fast-food restaurants and inexpensive coffee shops line George's St. The menu is in both English and Polish at **Harry's Cafe Bar ❷,** 21 Upper George's St. Pierogi (€4.50) and meatballs (€10.50) are delicious—no matter what language you use to order them. (☎280 8337. Open M-F 8am-6pm, Sa-Su 9am-6pm. MC/V.) The best family res-

COUNTY DUBLIN

taurant in town is **Bits and Pizzas ❸**, 15 Patrick St. Go early or be prepared to wait. (☎284 2411. Pizza and pasta €9-14; homemade ice cream €2.15. Open M-W noon-10:30pm, Th-Su noon-11pm. MC/V.) For home-baked vegetarian fare, travel to bohemian **World Cafe ❷**, 56 Lower George's St., where paintings of vegetables adorn the walls. (☎284 1024. Avocado sandwich €7. Open M-F 9am-5pm, Sa 10am-5pm. MC/V.) For vegetarian-friendly Asian-influenced cuisine, pick up sushi (€5) or sandwiches (€4.50-5) at **The Art of Eating ❷**, 47 Upper George's St. If the wholesome food doesn't cure what ails you, you can visit the Chinese medical center behind the restaurant. (☎663 9049. Open M-F 10:30am-6:30pm, Sa 10:30am-5:30pm. MC/V.) At **Weir's ❸**, 88 Lower George's St., mahogany, brass, and a wrought-iron spiral staircase add upscale style to the classic pub meal. (☎230 4654; www.weirs.ie. Carvery lunch noon-2:30pm; €8-11. Kitchen open daily 9am-9pm. MC/V.) Stylish 🖩**Purty Kitchen Seafood Bar**, Old Dunleary Rd., transforms its loft into a nightclub with trad Tuesdays and rock Fridays and Sundays. Pricey dinners and a fabulous wine list are also available. (☎284 3576. Open M-Th and Su 10am-11:30pm, F-Sa 10am-1:30am. No cover. MC/V.) **Scott's Bar**, 17 Upper George's St., has music six nights per week, with everything from karaoke to 70s. (☎280 2657. F karaoke, Sa local rock bands. No cover. Open M-W and Su 10:30am-11:30pm, Th-Sa 10:30am-1:30am.)

⑤ SIGHTS. To get to **James Joyce Tower** from the Sandycove DART station, turn left onto Islington Ave., go down to the coast, turn right, and continue to the Martello tower in Sandycove; or take bus #8 from Burgh Quay in Dublin to Sandycove Ave. From Dún Laoghaire center, it's about a 20min. walk. In September 1904, James Joyce stayed here for six tense days as a guest of Oliver St. John Gogarty, the witty surgeon, man-about-town, and first civilian tenant of the tower. Joyce later infamized Gogarty in the first chapter of *Ulysses*. The novel's opening is set in and around the tower, with Buck Mulligan portraying Gogarty. The tower's museum is a motherload of Joycenalia: his death mask, love letters to Nora Barnacle, library card, and many editions of *Ulysses* abound. The **Round Room** upstairs, described by Joyce as the "gloomy domed living room," is a reconstruction of the author's bedroom, while the gun platform looks out over the ocean. If you're lucky enough to be in the area on Bloomsday, you'll find a parade of Joyce-lovin' galore. (☎280 9265. Open Mar.-Oct. M-Sa 10am-1pm and 2-5pm, Su 2-6pm; Nov.-Feb. by appointment. €7, students €6.) At the base of the tower lies another Joyce-blessed spot, the 40 ft. **bathing place**, formerly open only to men. Now, a wholesome co-ed crowd and a bevy of toddlers splash in the shallow pool facing the road. But be warned: male skinny-dippers still frequent the water on the rocks adjacent to the tower.

🖩🎵 ENTERTAINMENT AND OUTDOOR ACTIVITIES. Dún Laoghaire harbor, full of boat tours, car ferries, fishermen, and yachts cruising around the **new marina**, is a friendly oceanside metropolis. Frequent summer **boat races**, usually on Saturday mornings, draw large crowds. Head to the piers—the setting for Samuel Beckett's *Krapp's Last Tape*—to soak up the sun or brood over the meaning of life. A number of outdoor and water activities are available in town. The **Irish National Sailing School & Club**, at the base of West Pier, offers beginner weekend and week-long sailing courses. (☎284 4195; www.inss.ie. €268 per course.) Dún Laoghaire's best *craic* is at 🖩**Comhaltas Ceoltoiri Éireann** (COLE-tus KEE-ole-to-ri AIR-run), 32 Belgrave Sq., next door to Belgrave Hall hostel. This is the national headquarters of a huge international organization for Irish traditional music; it hosts *seisiúns* (sessions), performances of traditional song, dance, and storytelling, and *céilí* dancing on Friday nights year-round. *Céilí* dancing is not a spectator sport, so bring your dancing shoes. Of course, pints are also available. (☎280 0295; www.comhaltas.com. *Seisiúns* July to mid-Aug. M-Th at 9pm; €10. *Céilí* €10. Free trad sessions Tu-W; F-Sa €3.)

▶ DAYTRIPS FROM DÚN LAOGHAIRE: DALKEY AND KILLINEY. A medieval heritage town with its own castle, island, and restaurants, **Dalkey** toes the

COUNTY DUBLIN

line between ritzy and quaint. The town features both fancy and budget-style restaurants. Most shops and restaurants are on or around Castle St. At the far end of Castle St. (from the DART station) is **Dalkey Castle** (a.k.a. **Goat Castle,** for a local medieval family's coat-of-arms) and its **Heritage Centre.** Actors dressed as medieval maids and guards lead visitors through the castle and puzzle over modern dress and speech. The center also runs guided walks of Dalkey. (☎ 285 8366; www.dalkey-castle.com. Open M-F 9:30am-5pm, Sa-Su 11am-5pm. €6, students and seniors €5. Tours every 30 min. Walks May-Aug. M and F 11am, W 2pm from the Heritage Centre.)

On Castle St., **Eurospar** is the place to stock up on groceries. *(☎ 285 9477. Open daily 8am-10pm.)* **Mugs Cafe Bar ❷,** 61 Castle St., offers creative *panini*, like the cranberry and brie (€7), as well as various forms of caffeine. *(☎ 284 0419. Open daily 8am-6pm. Cash only.)* Just off Castle St., The **Idlewilde Cafe ❷,** 20 St. Patrick's Rd., has sandwiches galore, plus burgers (€9) and readings later in the evening. *(☎ 235 4501. Open daily 8am-6pm, W-Sa also 7pm-late. MC/V.)* **Benito's ❸,** 47 Castle St., serves classic Italian favorites across from the Heritage Centre. (☎ 285 1010. Pizza and pasta €12-14. Open M-F 5:30-11pm, Sa noon-11pm, Su 3-11pm. MC/V.) For a change of scenery and pace, enjoy a boat trip to **Dalkey Island** from Coliemore Harbor. Dalkey Island, or Thorn Island (so named for the wooden spars that protruded from its shores when it served as a Viking stronghold), is thought to have been a haven for 14th-century Dublin city-dwellers attempting to escape the Black Death. The island's **Martello Tower Number Nine** was one of the many towers built in anticipation of Napoleon's ultimately unfulfilled invasion of the coast.

To the south of Dún Laoghaire, **Killiney** (kill-EYE-nee), Dublin's poshest suburb, may have the most dazzling beach around. Head to the Dún Laoghaire tourist office to pick up the heritage map of Dún Laoghaire or the **Killiney Walk** pamphlet of the Dún Laoghaire Way series for details on seven Killiney-area walks. From the top of **Killiney Hill Park,** the breathtaking views extend as far as the eye can see—that dark smudge on the horizon is Wales. (To reach the park from Castle St., turn left on Dalkey Ave. and climb Dalkey Hill, then take Burmah Rd. into the park.) Before entering the park, slip down to Torca Rd., where **Shaw's Cottage,** up the road on the left, once housed young George Bernard. This is a private home; Shaw enthusiasts will have to make do with visiting his birthplace on 33 Synge St. in Dublin (see **Merrion Square,** p. 123). As Shaw wrote, "I lived on a hill top with the most beautiful views in the world." Visitors can content themselves with seeing what the artist himself saw. Among Killiney's scattered B&Bs, the best views, both inside and outside the house, are found at **Druid Lodge ❺,** on Killiney Rd. Follow the road to Dalkey and look for white boulders on the right; the lodge is on the left. (☎ 285 1632. Singles €60-70; doubles €90.)

BRAY (BRÍ CHUALAIN)   ☎ 01

Although officially located in Co. Wicklow, Bray functions as a suburb of Dublin: the DART and Dublin Bus trundle through the town regularly, bringing flocks of city-folk to its beach. Well-tended gardens set against a commercialized, cotton candy and arcade-laden seafront exemplify Bray's compromise between beach town and Victorian haven. Whether you're into ice cream cones or Palladian architecture, you'll find a quaint beauty in the stunning seafront.

🖪🔢 TRANSPORTATION AND PRACTICAL INFORMATION. Bray is a 40min. **DART** ride from Dublin's Connolly Station (€4.10 return). **Buses** #45 and 84 arrive from Eden Quay. Bray has reliable travel options to **Enniskerry** in Co. Wicklow: from the Bray DART station, bus #185 runs to Enniskerry (€1.90; 1 per hr. on: 45). **St. Kevin's Bus Service** (☎ 281 8119) shuttles passengers from the town hall on Main St. to Glendalough. (1hr., 2 per day, €15 return.)

Maps are posted in the DART station and are available at the tourist office, which is the first stop south of Dublin for those in search of info on Wicklow. The

COUNTY DUBLIN

office, which shares a building with the **Heritage Centre,** is downhill on Main St. (☎286 7128. Open July-Aug. M-F 9am-1pm and 2-5pm, Sa 10am-3pm; Sept.-June M-F 9:30am-1pm and 2-4:30pm, Sa 10am-3pm. Heritage Centre admission €3.) To reach **Main Street** from the DART station, take **Quinsborough Road** or **Florence Road,** both of which run uphill and perpendicular to the tracks. Quinsborough Rd. has shops and restaurants. **The Strand,** which has cotton candy stands and nicer restaurants, runs parallel to **Meath Road** along the beach. **Bray Cycle Centre,** in the Boulevard Centre on Quinsborough Rd., rents **bikes** and does quick repairs. (☎286 3357. Open M-Sa 9:30am-6pm. €35 per day, €100 per week.) **AIB** on Main St., near Quinsborough Rd., has a 24hr. **ATM** and **bureau de change.** (☎286 7771. Open M-Tu and F 10am-4pm, W 10:30am-4pm, Th 10am-5pm.) There are also ATMs at the DART station and at several banks on Quinsborough and Main St. Call ahead to snag a seat at one of the popular, free computers with **Internet** access in the **library,** located on the corner of Florence Rd. and Eglinton Rd., off Quinsborough Rd. (☎286 2600. Open M, W, F-Sa 10am-5pm, Tu and Th 10am-8:30pm.) The **Youth Information Center,** 1 Brennan's Pde., on Albert Ave. (off the Strand) also has free **Internet** access and provides information on area **work** and **volunteer opportunities.** (☎276 2818. Open M-F 10am-1pm and 2-5pm.) The **Police** *(Garda)* station is on Convent Ave., off The Strand. (☎666 5300. Open 24hr.) The **post office** is at 18 Quinsborough Rd. (☎286 2012. Open M and W-F 9am-5:30pm, Tu 9:30am-5:30pm, Sa 9am-1pm.) A few doors down is **Lawlor's Pharmacy,** 16 Quinsborough Rd. (☎286 2048. Open M-Sa 9am-6pm.) Get dirty duds clean at the **Bray Launderette,** 9 Quinsborough Rd. (☎282 8298. Open M-F 8am-6:30pm, Sa 9am-6pm. Wash and dry up to 7lb.; €9.30.)

⌘ ACCOMMODATIONS. B&Bs line the Strand; the cheaper ones are on Meath Rd., away from the water and flocks of people. **Bayview ❸,** is a small B&B on Meath Rd. The rooms are tiny in terms of floorspace, but they compensate with soaring ceilings. The owner, a master craftsman, has installed beautiful wood floors in the dining room. (☎286 0887. Singles €35; doubles €70. Cash only.) Anne and Pat Duffy welcome guests to **Moytura ❸,** 2 Herbert Park. Take Herbert Rd., the continuation of Quinsborough Rd. after Main St. The B&B is on the right before the fork with King Edward Rd. The Duffys provide homemade bread, freshly squeezed orange juice, and chats on Irish history and literature. (☎282 9827. All rooms with bath. Singles €45; doubles €70.) **Ulysses ❹,** a green building in the middle of the Strand, is a 200-year-old house once operated as a B&B by Joyce's niece. Its prime location offers a great lookout over the beach and promenade. (☎286 3860. Free parking. Singles €47; doubles €86. Cash only.)

◧▦ FOOD AND PUBS. SuperQuinn, across the bridge from the tourist office on Castle St. (the continuation of Main St.) sells groceries (☎286 7779. Open M-F 8:30am-11pm, Sa 8am-9pm, Su 9am-8pm), as does **Dunnes** on 7 Quinsborough Rd. (☎286 7611. Open M-W and Sa 8:30am-7pm, Th-F 8:30am-8pm, Su 11am-6pm). **Campo de' Fiori ❸,** 1 Albert Ave., at the intersection with the Strand, has garlic hanging from the walls, and they're not afraid to use it. (☎276 4257; www.campodefiori.ie. Pasta €8-16; entrees €15-23. Open M and W-Th 5-10:30pm, F-Sa 5-11pm, Su 2-9pm. MC/V.) **Molloy's ❷,** 14 Quinsborough Rd., serves up classic Irish fare, such as the full breakfast (€8), as well as eclectic favorites including chicken tikka masala (€7.50). A bicycle hangs over a selection of baked goodies. (☎286 2196. Open M-Sa 7am-6pm, Su 8am-6pm. Cash only.) Pick up a sandwich (from €2.60) and some chocolate mousse (€0.80) for a picnic by the water at **The Larder ❶,** 19 Main St., which has no seating. (☎286 5093. Open M-Sa 9am-5:30pm. Cash only.)

For a night out, try **Clancy's,** 5 Quinsborough Rd. It's a dark, old-time pub with wooden plank tables and trad on Tuesdays and Thursdays around 10pm. (☎286 2362. Open M-Th 10:30am-11:30pm, F-Sa 10:30am-12:30am, Su 12:30-11pm. MC/V.) Pubs abound, like **The Porterhouse,** which gathers a young crowd in its outdoor beer garden in summer, and inside year-round. Attached is a nightclub, which plays mainly chart-toppers until late. (☎286 0668. Pint and slice of pizza €5. Kitchen open M-W until 10pm. Pub open M-Tu noon-midnight, W-Sa noon-2am, Su 12:30pm-1:30am. Club open Th-Su 8:30pm-3am. F-Sa cover €8 after 10pm. MC/V.)

◪ SIGHTS. For gorgeous views of the Wicklow Mountains and Bray Bay, hike to the summit of **Bray Head**, high above the south end of the Strand and away from the neon lights. The trail starts after the short paved pedestrian walkway begins to curve up the hill. On the right, past the picnic area, a set of steps signals the start of one of several winding trails to the top. The 30min. hike is very steep and requires some climbing over rocks, but a breathtaking panorama at the top is worth the effort. Ramblers can also follow the 2-2½hr. cliff walk, which heads from Bray Harbour to Greystones. Along the way you may come face to face with kittiwakes, seals, and goats. Ask for a pamphlet detailing the route at the Tourist Office. Just outside of town, **Killruddery House and Gardens** has plots as beautiful as those of the not-too-distant Powerscourt Estate. Its Elizabethan-Revival house has a domed roof and a six-meter pendulum clock. **Finnegan's Bus** (€1.30) departs for the house every 20min. from the DART station. (☎286 3405. Gardens open daily Apr.-Sept. 1-5pm. House open daily May-June and Sept. 1-5pm. Call for tour times. House and gardens €10, students and seniors €8, children €3.)

◪ DAYTRIPS FROM BRAY. Lordly **Powerscourt Estate** sits near **Enniskerry** in Co. Wicklow, 8km east of Bray. Built in the 1730s, the house has become an architectural landmark. Powerscourt was gutted by flames in 1974, but the owner has recently begun to repair the lost interior, and it now houses shops and a cafe. Outside, the brightly colored and immaculately maintained terraced gardens—displaying a fusion of Italian opulence and Japanese elegance—justify the high admission price. **Sugar Loaf Mountain** looms in the distance, and four-legged companions rest in peace under the headstones of the pet cemetery behind the estate. Make time for the "long walk," which takes roughly 1hr. but can last considerably longer for the thorough botanical aficionado. *(From Bray, take bus #185 to Enniskerry; #44 runs direct from Dublin (1hr.; 2 per hr.; €1.90). Facing the town clock, take the left fork; the house and gardens are a few hundred meters beyond the gatehouse. ☎ 204 6000; www.powerscourt.ie. Open daily 9:30am-5:30pm. Gardens €7.50, students and seniors €6.50. Exhibition detailing history of home and gardens €2.50/2.20.)*

THE REAL DEAL. Three Palladian homes are situated within an easy day's trek from Dublin: Powerscourt Estate, Castletown House, and Russborough House. As grand as each of these old houses may be, you'll probably only have time to see one of them. If you just want your Palladian grandeur, thank you very much, head to Castletown House. If stamens and pistols pull your trigger, check out Powerscourt Estate. And if you're only in it for the artwork, it's got to be Russborough House.

The 120m plunge makes of the **Powerscourt Waterfall** makes it Ireland's tallest permanent waterfall. The waters above the falls were dammed to ensure a spectacular flow and a viewing platform was constructed in preparation for King George IV's 1821 visit to Powerscourt. Luckily, the King never made it to the falls—when the dam was released, the entire platform was swept away. Although they're worth a visit during any season, the falls are most impressive in late spring and after heavy rains. A 40min. nature walk begins at the base and winds through quiet, untended woods. *(The falls are located 5.6km outside Enniskerry. Take a bus to Enniskerry and follow the somewhat cryptic signs from town. There is no public transportation to the falls. Waterfall open Jan.-Feb. and Nov.-Dec. daily 10:30am-4pm, Mar.-Apr. and Sept.-Oct. 10:30am-5:30pm, May-Aug. 9:30am-7pm; €5, students €4.50.)*

EASTERN IRELAND

Those unfortunate souls who see eastern Ireland only through the windows of a westbound bus out of Dublin don't know what they're missing—Counties Wicklow, Kildare, Meath, and Louth deserve a closer look than daytrips from the city allow. The monastic town at Clonmacnoise and the passage tombs in Meath continue to fascinate archaeologists. The Wicklow Mountains offer spectacular views, and those too tired to continue hiking can head downhill to relax on the beautiful beaches. Not too far north, the tiny lakeside towns of Monaghan (see **Northern Ireland**, p. 478) harbor the warmest waters in the northern half of the island. Most of the tourist industry is still in its adolescent stages, but the committed guardians of their respective local treasures help the homesteads and ruins come alive.

EASTERN IRELAND HIGHLIGHTS

HOSTEL HOP across the spectacular **Wicklow Way** (p. 155).

IMPROVE YOUR POSTURE among the world's tallest hedges at Birr Castle (p. 187).

SIZE UP Ireland's studliest horses in **Kildare** (p. 162).

SOLVE the mystery of the **Newgrange** passage tomb (p. 164).

COUNTY WICKLOW

Despite being exhausted of its gold during the Bronze Age, sacked by Vikings in the 9th century, and then crushed under the English thumb after the conflicts of 1798 (see **Rebellion and Union**, p. 53), Co. Wicklow has always been an attractive piece of real estate. The mountainous county offers outdoor enthusiasts deserted back roads and seesawing ridges for cycling. Wicklow is right in the capital's backyard; its major sights are accessible by bus from downtown Dublin, though bikes or cars are best for moving about within the county. Visitors flock to Wicklow's historic *gaol*, the monastic ruins at Glendalough, and the birthplace of political leader Charles Parnell near Rathdrum. The Wicklow Way, the first of Ireland's waymarked trails, invites travelers to rough it for a week, and Brittas Bay's golden beaches provide the ideal setting to perfect the art of lounging in the sun.

WICKLOW COAST

The sparsely populated towns of the Wicklow coast seem a world away from jet-setting Dublin, although the allure of the capital draws commuters from as far away as Wicklow Town. The area lacks the heavy-hitting historical hot spots of the inland route through Glendalough and Kilkenny but provides kilometers of untouristed, sheep-filled fields that wind over cliffs and dunes to the sparkling sea. Hikers and cyclists can find plenty of fantastic routes to enjoy.

WICKLOW TOWN (CILL MHANTÁIN) ☎0404

Touted both for its seaside vistas and as a base camp for aspiring Wicklow mountaineers, Wicklow Town has a wide selection of restaurants and plenty of accom-

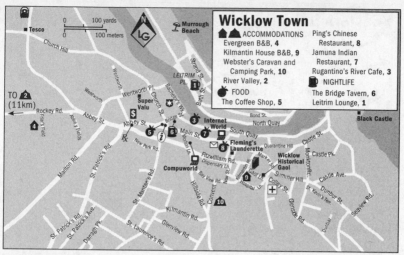

Wicklow Town

▲■ ACCOMMODATIONS
Evergreen B&B, **4**
Kilmantin House B&B, **9**
Webster's Caravan and
  Camping Park, **10**
River Valley, **2**
● FOOD
The Coffee Shop, **5**

Ping's Chinese
  Restaurant, **8**
Jamuna Indian
  Restaurant, **7**
Rugantino's River Cafe, **3**
● NIGHTLIFE
The Bridge Tavern, **6**
Leitrim Lounge, **1**

modations within walking distance of its pubs. An eager traveler can exhaust the sightseeing potential of the town fairly quickly, but many days' worth of hiking and cycling excursions lie within the hills.

TRANSPORTATION. Trains run to **Dublin's** Connolly Station (1¼hr.; M-Sa 5 per day, Su 3 per day; €13.40 return) and to **Rosslare Harbour** via **Wexford** (2hr., 4 per day, €19 return). The station is 15min. east of town on N11; walk along Main St. until it becomes Abbey St., pass the Grand Hotel and bear right, then follow signs. **Bus Éireann** (www.buseireann.ie) leaves for **Dublin** near the *gaol* at the other end of Main St. and the Grand Hotel (1½hr.; M-Sa 13 per day, Su 7 per day; €10.50 return). **Bus tours** navigate the Wicklow Mountains, including **Bus Éireann's** tour (☎ 836 6111. Departs Dublin Mar.-Oct. daily 10:30am. €30, students €28.) and **Wild Wicklow Tour.** (☎ 280 1899. Departs St. Stephen's Green in Dublin daily 8:50am. €28, students/children €25.)

ORIENTATION AND PRACTICAL INFORMATION. Coming from Dublin or the train station, the N11 becomes **Abbey Street** and snakes past the Grand Hotel to the grassy triangle of **Fitzwilliam Square.** It continues as **Main Street** becomes **The Mall** and ends in **Market Square.** Across the street from the Grand Hotel, Wentworth Pl. heads down the hill to the **Leitrim River.** The historic **gaol** sits up the hill from Market Sq. The **tourist office** is in Fitzwilliam Sq. (☎ 69117. Open M-Sa 9:30am-5:15pm.) **AIB,** on Abbey St., has a 24hr. **ATM.** (☎ 67311. Open M 10am-5pm, W 10:30am-4pm, Tu and Th-F 10am-4pm.) Nearby on Abbey St. is the **Abbey Pharmacy** (☎ 67459. Open M-Sa 9am-6pm.) Free **Internet** access is available at the **Wicklow Library,** next to the *gaol.* (☎ 67025. Open M-Sa 10am-1pm and 2-5pm, W-Th also 6-8:30pm.) **Internet** access is also available for a fee at **Internet World,** 9 Lower Mall (☎ 62609. Open M-Sa 11am-10pm, Su noon-8pm; €5 per hr., students €4) and at **Compuworld,** on Morton's Ln. off Main St. (☎ 62773. Open M-F 9:30am-6pm, Sa 10am-6pm; €5 per hr.) On New St., **Fleming's Launderette** will get your clothes clean. (☎ 95329. Open M-Sa 9am-1pm and 2-6pm. Wash and dry €8.) From the town center, walk down Main St. toward Market Sq.; the **post office** is on the right. (☎ 674 71. Open M and W-F 9am-5:30pm, Tu 9:30am-5:30pm, Sa 9:30am-1pm.) The Police *(Garda)* Station is on Bachelor's Walk, off Bridge St. (☎ 60140. 24hr.)

Eastern Ireland

EASTERN IRELAND

NORTHERN IRELAND

Belfast

Cookstown
Omagh
Castlereagh
Lough Neagh
Lisburn
CO. TYRONE
Dungannon
Lurgan
Ballynahinch
Portadown
Banbridge
Armagh
CO. DOWN
Lower Lough Erne
A47
A46
A35
A32
A45
A4
M1
A27
A50
A25
Newcastle
CO. FERMANAGH
Enniskillen
A41
A3
A29
CO. ARMAGH
A28
A1
N16
A4
A32
Monaghan
N54
A25
Newry
Marble Arch Caves
Florence Court
Upper Lough Erne
A509
A34
Clones
CO. MONAGHAN
Warrenpoint
Rostrevor
Kilkeel
Lough Allen
Ballyconnell
Belturbet
Castleblaney
Carlingford
Carlingford Lough
Drumshanbo
Killashandra
Dundalk Town
Cavan
Carrickmacross
N52
Castlebellingham
Dundalk Bay
Carrick-on-Shannon
N3
CO. CAVAN
N2
CO. LOUTH
Irish Sea
CO. LEITRIM
N4
Granard
Finnea
Lough Sheelin
N52
Monasterboice
Mellifont
N5
CO. LONGFORD
Kells
N3
Slane
Boyne Valley
Drogheda
Longford
N63
Coole
Fore
Navan
N51
Newgrange
Balbriggan
Lough Derravaragh
N55
N51
Rush
Lambay I.
Lough Owel
N52
Trim
Hill of Tara
Donabate
Malahide
Mullingar
N4
CO. MEATH
Howth Head
CO. WESTMEATH
Lough Ennel
Dunboyne
N3
N2
CO. DUBLIN
Howth
Athlone
N6
Kilbeggan
Kilcock
Maynooth
N4
Leiplix
Dublin
Moate
N80
N52
Edenderry
Celbridge
Dún Laoghaire
Dublin Bay
Clonmacnoise
CO. OFFALY
CO. KILDARE
N81
Banagher
Tullamore
Newbridge
Naas
Powerscourt Estate
Bray
Kilcormac
N52
N80
Blessington
Greystones
Birr
Mountmellick
Kildare
The Curragh
Blessington Lake
CO. WICKLOW
Ashford
SLIEVE BLOOM MTS.
Portlaoise
N7
N78
N81
Glendalough
Laragh
Roscrea
Dunamaise Castle
N80
Athy
N9
WICKLOW MTS.
Wicklow
CO. LAOIS
Baltinglass
Rathdrum
Wicklow Head
Templemore
N7
N8
N78
Avoca
R747
CO. TIPPERARY
CO. KILKENNY
Carlow
N81
N80
Arklow
CO. CARLOW
Arklow Head
Kilkenny
N10
Bagenalstown
Bunclody
N11
Ferns
N76
N10
N9
N9
Enniscorthy
CO. WEXFORD
N79
N11
Irish National Heritage Park

0   15 kilometers
0   15 miles

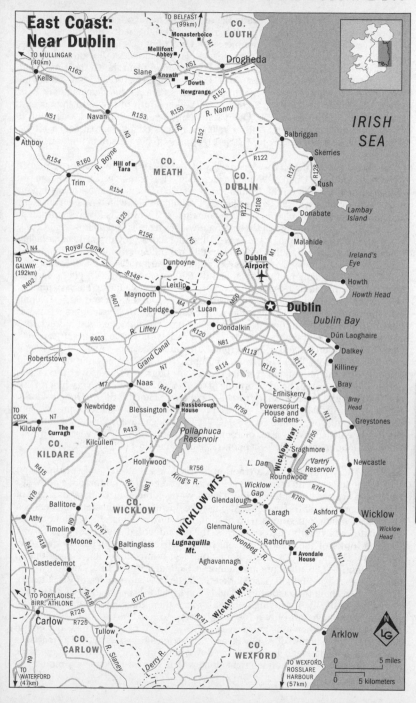

East Coast: Near Dublin

TO BELFAST (99km)

CO. LOUTH

Monasterboice

Mellifont Abbey

Drogheda

TO MULLINGAR (40km)

R163

Kells

Slane

Knowth

Dowth

Newgrange

R152

R51

N51

M1

Navan

R153

R150

N2

R152

R. Nanny

Balbriggan

IRISH SEA

Athboy

R154

R160

R. Boyne

Hill of Tara

Trim

CO. MEATH

Skerries

R127

R128

Rush

R122

CO. DUBLIN

R154

R125

R156

N3

R121

R122

R108

Donabate

Lambay Island

Royal Canal

N4

TO GALWAY (192km)

R402

Dunboyne

Leixlip

Maynooth

Celbridge

M4

Lucan

Malahide

Ireland's Eye

Dublin Airport

N2

M1

Howth

Howth Head

R407

R. Liffey

R120

Clondalkin

⊛ Dublin

Dublin Bay

R403

Grand Canal

N7

N81

R113

R114

R116

R117

Dún Laoghaire

Dalkey

Killiney

Robertstown

M7

Naas

R410

Enniskerry

Bray

Bray Head

TO CORK

N7

Newbridge

Blessington

Russborough House

R759

Powerscourt House and Gardens

Greystones

Kildare

The Curragh

CO. KILDARE

Kilcullen

R413

Pollaphuca Reservoir

Wicklow Way

Sraghmore

R55

L. Dan

Vartry Reservoir

Newcastle

R415

Hollywood

R756

R412

N81

King's R.

Roundwood

R764

R763

Ballitore

CO. WICKLOW

WICKLOW MTS.

Wicklow Gap

Glendalough

Laragh

Ashford

Wicklow

N78

Athy

Timolin

Moone

R747

Baltinglass

Lugnaquilla Mt.

Glenmalure

Avonbeg R.

R755

Rathdrum

R752

Wicklow Head

Castledermot

R418

Aghavannagh

Avondale House

N11

TO PORTLAOISE, BIRR, ATHLONE

R417

R416

R727

Wicklow Way

R747

Carlow

R726

R725

Tullow

CO. CARLOW

R. Slaney

Derry R.

CO. WEXFORD

Arklow

TO WEXFORD, ROSSLARE HARBOUR (57km)

N9

TO WATERFORD (47km)

CO. DUBLIN

N

0   5 miles

0   5 kilometers

⌐ ACCOMMODATIONS. Kilmantin House B&B ❸, next to the *gaol*, is decidedly un-prisonlike with its sunny breakfast room and bright bedrooms, all with bath and TV. (☎67373. Singles €55; doubles €80. Cash only.) **Evergreen B&B ❸**, Friarsfield Rd., is a lovely home with parking and tasty breakfasts. All rooms equipped with private bath. Turn onto Friar's Hill Rd., downhill from the Grand Hotel, and then right onto Friarsfield Rd. (☎68347. Doubles €80. Cash only.) Several campgrounds are scattered around the area. **Webster's Caravan and Camping Park ❶** is located on Silver Strand (see **Sights**, p. 150), 4km south of town on the coastal road. (☎67615. Showers €1.50. Open June-Sept. 2-person tent €18. Cash only.) Twelve kilometers down N11, **River Valley ❶** boasts cushy campsites. (☎41647. Showers €0.50. Open Mar.-Sept. €12 per tent plus €6 per person in tent. MC/V.)

◨▥ FOOD AND PUBS. Buy groceries at **SuperValu,** on Wentworth Pl. off Church St. (☎61888. Open M-W and Sa 8am-8pm, Th-F 8am-9pm, Su 10am-7pm) or the superior **Tesco,** out on the Dublin road. (☎69250. Open 24hr.) All of the baked goods and hot dishes at **The Coffee Shop ❷**, Fitzwilliam Sq., which range from soup and sandwiches to shepherds pie, are homemade. The cafe is always charming, even when its menu changes. (☎68194. Sandwiches from €4; daily hot meal €9.50. Open M-Sa 9:15am-5:30pm. Cash only.) Dine like exotic royalty at **Jamuna Indian Restaurant ❸**, 1 Lower Mall, which has traditional Indian cuisine, white linen, and sparkling glasses. (☎64628. Entrees €8.50-12, vegetarian dishes €5-6. Lunch special €8.50. Open daily noon-2:30pm and 6-11:30pm. AmEx/MC/V.) **Ping's Chinese Restaurant ❸**, on Main St. by the post office, serves great Chinese food; try prawns (€13) in Szechuan sauce. (☎62763. Entrees €10-13. Open M-Th and Su 5-11:30pm, F-Sa 5pm-midnight. MC/V.) **Rugantino's River Cafe ❺**, South Quay, offers a tranquil view of the water from their deck. The early bird special gives you a crack at 3 courses for €22; later diners pay €18-22 for a variety of seafood entrees. (☎61900. Open M-Th and Su 6-10pm, F-Sa 6-11pm. Early bird special 6-7:30pm. MC/V.)

A bus runs from Wicklow Town to Dublin (F-Sa; €10), leaving at 1:45 and 4:45pm from the Monument. **Leitrim Lounge,** on Leitrim Pl. just over the bridge across the river, serves hearty portions of traditional bar food (carvery lunch €10) and features live music F-Su. (☎67443. Local cover bands F-Sa 10:30pm, rock Su. Kitchen open 12:30-9pm. Pub open M-Th 10:30am-11:30pm, F-Sa 10:30am-12:30am, Su noon-11pm. Cover some Sa €5. MC/V.) The **Bridge Tavern**, Bridge St., attracts the locals with acoustic, jazz, or rock music every night of the week. (☎67718. Open M-Th noon-midnight, F-Sa noon-12:30am, Su noon-11:30pm. MC/V.)

◎ SIGHTS. Wicklow's top attraction is **Wicklow's Historic Gaol** (pronounced "jail"). The museum fills nearly 40 cells with audio clips and interactive activities relating to every detail of the facility's history—even the controversial business of shipping convicts off to Australia. At times the downtrodden plaster prisoners can seem a bit much, but guides who describe the horrendous conditions of early prison life keep visitors engrossed. Even the most devoted exercise fanatics won't like the looks of the treadwheel out back. (☎61599; www.wicklowshistoric-gaol.com. Open Mar.-Oct. daily 10am-6pm; last admission 5pm. Tours 40min., every 10min. €7.30, students and seniors €5.50, children €4.25. Limited wheelchair access.) The first left past Market Sq. leads to what remains of **Black Castle.** The Normans built the castle in 1178 and local Irish lords began attacking it almost immediately, finally destroying it in 1301. Since then, many assaults and changes in ownership have left only a few wind-worn stones, but the site offers a seasprayed view of green hills and waves. (Always open. Free.) At the other end of Main St., at the juncture of Abbey St. and St. Patrick's Rd., the ruins of a **Franciscan friary** hide behind a small gate and a run-down hut. The friary was built at the same time as the Black Castle and fell right along with it. It was subsequently rebuilt and became a place of retirement for both Normans and native Irish who considered it neutral ground. Now wildflowers grow in its arches. (Always open. Free.)

A somewhat precarious cliff trail (5km return) over spongy turf provides smashing views of the coast en route to ▓St. Bride's Head (Wicklow Head), where St. Patrick landed on Travilahawk Strand in AD 432. Legend has it that the townspeople greeted him by knocking out the teeth of his sidekick, Mantan ("the toothless one" or "gubby"), who was later assigned to convert the same local hooligans. Facing Black Castle, pick up the trail to your right and continue for over an hour to get to the head and its pristine rock beach nestled into the cliffs. Another 10min. up the unimproved road brings you to the **lighthouse** at Wicklow Head. At Market Sq., Main St. becomes Summer Hill and then Dunbur Rd., the coastal road, from which beaches extend south to **Arklow**. Locals head over the bridge and left to pebbly Murrough Beach, which is popular with dog walkers. From Wicklow, the closest strips of sun and sand are **Silver Strand** and **Jack's Hole**, though most people head to the larger ▓**Brittas Bay**, which is located halfway to Arklow.

▓ **FESTIVALS.** Every August, Wicklow hosts its annual five-day **Regatta Festival**, the oldest such celebration in Ireland. The two-week festivities feature hard-core skiff racing and a parade of whimsical homemade barges; join the spectators on the bridge and let loose with eggs and tomatoes. At night, amicable pub rivalries foster serious singing competitions and barmen's races with pints in hand. The **Wicklow Arts Festival** livens up May with plays, poetry readings, trad, and concerts. Most activities, including lunchtime concerts, are free. (www.wicklowarts.ie. Tickets €5-10.) Contact the tourist office for more information.

AVONDALE HOUSE AND RATHDRUM   ☎ 0404

The birthplace and residence of Charles Stewart Parnell, political champion of tenant rights and home rule, **Avondale House** is now a museum devoted to the ill-fated hero and a relic of Ireland's early 19th-century upper-class lifestyle. More interesting than the house itself is the 20min. video that provides a cinematic glimpse into Parnell's life and his role in the fight for Irish independence (see **Parnell and Irish Nationalism**, p. 54). The house has a small **cafe** downstairs and holds week-long **summer school** opportunities for all ages. (☎46111; www.coillte.ie. Cafe sandwiches €3.50-4.25, lasagne €8.75. House open mid-Mar. to Oct. daily 11am-6pm, last admission 5pm. Mar.-Apr. and Sept.-Oct. closed M. Open by arrangement during the offseason. Guided tours for groups of any size upon request. €6, students and seniors €5.50. Parking €5. MC/V.) Floraphiles and hikers explore the 500 acres of **Avondale Forest Park** that surrounds the house and spreads along the west bank of **Avonmore River**. Avondale House sells guides (€2.50) that detail the grounds, complete with **maps** and extensive information on three walks of varying length. The 5.6km **Centenary Walk** is especially nice. The trail is not on the map but is well signposted with informational blurbs and takes walkers through the arboretum. If you haven't had enough walking, stop by the tourist office for the *Rambles Round Rathdrum* guide, which has 14 more routes through the countryside.

Also in town, **Old Presbytery Hostel (IHH) ❶** has fine beds and bathrooms. Continue past the tourist office, turn left after the grocery store and then right at the top of the hill; look for the pink building. (☎46930. Laundry €6. Dorms €18; singles €22-25. AmEx/MC/V.) You'll feel at home at **Stirabout Lane B&B ❸**, located in the center of town on Main St. This B&B has large, doll-filled rooms and a lovely back garden. The comfortable sitting room has piles of books and DVDs. (☎43142; www.stiraboutlane.com. Off-street parking available. Singles €40; doubles €60-70. MC/V.) Just past Avondale House, 1.6km from town, **An Loudubh ❸** offers 500 acres of walks starting only steps from the sitting room. The owner is happy to help visitors find the perfect trails. (☎46202. Singles €40; doubles €70. Cash only.)

Hidden Valley Holiday Park ❶ campground has tent and trailer sites, as well as cabins, overlooking the river. Campers can boat, fish, or swim in the rushing water. Turn right out of the train station and go down the hill; turn left just before the stone bridge; the campground is about 375m down the path. (☎46080; www.irelandholidaypark.com. Kayaks €5 per hr., rowboats €2 per hr, daily fishing license €5. Open May-Sept. Tents €10 per person, children €5. Electricity €3. MC/V.) **Centra,** located on Main St., sells groceries. (☎43161. Open M-F 7am-9pm, Sa 7am-8pm, Su 8am-6pm.) Locals pack into **Jacob's Well ❸**, Main St., at mealtimes for home-cooked portions of traditional fish, meats and stews (€11-13) complemented by brown bread, potatoes, and vegetables. Jacob's is the local place for eating, drinking and socializing at all hours of the day. (☎46282. Open M-Th 9am-11pm, F-Sa 9am-12:30am, Su 10:30am-11pm. Kitchen closes at 9. MC/V.) **The Coffin Shed ❷**, Main St., has subdued white plaster walls, but the delicious sandwiches (€4-5) and risotto (€10) keep the place lively. (☎43486. Open M-Sa 9am-4:30pm, Su 12:30-8:30pm. MC/V.) For nightly refreshment, check out **The Cornerhouse**, just beyond the square. Live trad and rock music on Sa and Su nights. (☎46654. Pint €3.65. Open M-Th 10:30am-11:30pm, F-Sa 10:30am-12:30am, Su 12:30pm-11pm. Cash only.) **Cartoon Inn,** Main St., is a pub with a lively, mixed clientele and wacky walls decorated by artists from a now-defunct cartoon festival. (☎46774. Open M-Th 10:30am-11:30pm, F-Sa 10:30am-12:30am, Su noon-11pm. Cash only.)

Avondale House is on the road from Wicklow Town to **Avoca,** 1.5km after **Rathdrum** and before the **Meeting of the Waters.** From Rathdrum, take Main St. toward Avoca (downhill) and follow the signs. **Bus** #133 arrives in Rathdrum from **Dublin** (2¾hr.; €9.70; M-Sa depart Dublin 9am and 5:30pm, Su 2pm), as do **trains** (1¼hr.; M-Sa 5 per day, Su 3 per day; €13.40). Rathdrum is not easily visible from the train station; after exiting the station's driveway, turn left at the Police *(Garda)* station and stroll 200m uphill to a path on the right through the stone gate—the path cuts through the Parnell National Memorial Park and up to Main St. Avondale House is to the left; the town center is to the right. The **tourist office,** in the square, offers pamphlets on hikes and area attractions. (☎46262. Open M-F 9:30am-1pm and 2-5pm.) The **Bank of Ireland,** with its 24hr. **ATM** and **bureau de change** (☎46162; open M-Tu, Th-F 10am-12:30pm and 1:30-4pm, W 10:30am-12:30pm and 1:30-4pm), the pharmacy (☎46157; open M-F 9am-1pm and 2-6pm, Sa 9am-1pm and 2-5:30pm), and the **post office** (☎46211; open M-F 9am-1pm and 2-5:30pm, Sa 9am-1pm) are in the square. The **library** has free **Internet** access. (☎43232. Open Tu, Th, Sa 2-4pm; W 11am-1pm, 2-4pm, and 6:30-7:30pm.) **T. McGrath,** Main St., rents bicycles. (☎46172. Open M-Tu and Th-F 9am-6pm, W 9am-1pm, Sa 9am-4:30pm. €10 per day.) The **Police** *(Garda)* is by the train station. (☎46127.)

WICKLOW MOUNTAINS

Carpeted in heather and rushing with water, the 600m high Wicklow summits are home to scattered villages and grazing sheep. Glendalough, a valley renowned as a medieval monastic village, draws a steady stream of coach tours from Dublin. Drivers should be careful as they maneuver around hikers, bikers, tour buses, and flocks of sheep. All but the most weathered hikers find portions of the Wicklow Way challenging, but the effort is rewarded with the best-maintained trailpath in the country and its charming hostels and B&Bs. Stop by the tourist offices in Glendalough, Bray, Wicklow Town, Arklow, and Rathdrum for maps and advice.

GLENDALOUGH (GLEANN DÁ LOCH)   ☎ 0404

In the 6th century, a vision inspired St. Kevin to give up his life of ascetic isolation and establish a monastery. He offset the austerity of monastic life by choosing one of Ireland's most spectacular valleys in which to found Glendalough ("glen of two lakes"; pronounced glen-DA-lock), and had no trouble finding followers to join him. The valley has remained busy to this day, though swarms of nature-loving tourists have replaced St. Kevin's disciples. Glendalough, no longer a true town, consists of St. Kevin's habitat, composed of a hostel, a hotel, and a smattering of roads barely wide enough for the convoy of tour buses that service the valley. Though gaggles of visitors frequent the main road, a brief walk on any trail leads to the proverbial road less traveled. One kilometer up the road, the village of **Laragh** has food options and plenty of B&Bs.

🖪🔁 TRANSPORTATION AND PRACTICAL INFORMATION. If they're not arriving on one of the countless charter bus tours, pilgrims come by **car** on R756, on **foot** along the Wicklow Way, or in **buses** run by St. Kevin's Bus Service. (☎0128 18119; www.glendaloughbus.com. Buses leave from St. Stephen's Green in **Dublin** M-Sa 11:30am and 6pm, Su 11:30am and 7pm; return €18.) Buses also leave from **Bray,** past the Town Hall on the right. (M-Sa 12:10 and 6:40pm, Su 12:10 and 7:30pm; return €15.) Bus Éireann (☎0183 66111; www.buseireann.ie) also runs **day tours** from Dublin's Busáras Station through the mountains and to **Glendalough.** (Tours Apr.-Oct. daily 10:30am, return 5:45pm. €30, students and seniors €28, children €19.50.) Hitching to Glendalough, though never recommended by *Let's Go,* is fairly easy from Co. Wicklow towns, but most Glendalough-bound traffic from Dublin is via bus. Hitchers at the beginning of N11 in southwest Dublin report receiving rides via the juncture of N11 with Glendalough's R755 with relative ease.

Just off R756, little Glendalough sits on a tributary where **Glenealo River** pools into its **Upper and Lower Lakes.** The **Glendalough Visitors Centre** (see **Sights,** p. 154) provides a wealth of both information and parking spaces. The **National Park Information Office,** between the lakes, is the best source in the region for hiking advice. (☎45425. Open May-Aug. daily 10am-1pm and 2-6pm, Sept.-Apr. Sa-Su 10am-dusk.) When the park office is closed, call the **ranger office** (☎45800), located in nearby Trooperstown Wood. **Laragh IT,** located in the **Brockagh Resource Center,** a right turn off the road from Laragh, has **Internet** access. (☎45600. Open M-F. €3 per hr.) The Glendalough and Laragh **post office** is next to the **Wicklow Heather restaurant** (☎45669. Open M-F 9am-1pm and 2-5:30pm, Sa 9am-1pm.)

🛏 ACCOMMODATIONS. The Glendaloch Hostel (An Óige/HI) ❷ lies 5min. up the road on the left past the Glendalough Visitor Centre. Though pretty standard, good beds, excellent security, and an in-house cafe make it by far the best option in the area. As with all accommodations in the area, book in advance during the summer. (☎45342. All rooms single-sex with bath. Wheelchair-accessible. Picnic lunch €5.50, order the day before; Irish or continental breakfast €6.50/4.50; dinner €11. Laundry €5. Dorms €23, €2 YHA discount. MC/V.)

On the road from Laragh to the Visitors Centre lie three B&Bs with similar prices and accommodations. The front door of **The Arch ❷** stands beyond an enormous, leafy archway. Oddly, this B&B offers no breakfast, but it's got TVs and tea sets in every room. (☎45384. Singles €25; doubles €50. Cash only.) Tucked into the forest on the way to St. Kevin's Church, **Pinewood Lodge ❹** offers immaculate rooms furnished with its namesake. (☎45437. All rooms with bath. Wheelchair-accessible. Singles €55; doubles €80. Apartments €250-400 per wk. MC/V.) Tired hikers rest their weary feet at **Dunroamin House ❸** in large, well-decorated rooms. (☎45487. Doubles €70. Cash only.)

🍴🔳 FOOD AND PUBS. The walls of **Ann's Coffee Shop ❶** are decorated with maps and paintings of local flora and fauna. Aside from coffee, there are sandwiches (€3.40-4.20) and fauna-free soup (€4) for vegetarians. (☎45454. Open daily 10am-5pm. MC/V.) **Lynham's ❸** piles plates high with hearty fare: the Guinness beef stew (€13) is tasty and filling. There's also a carvery lunch (€12) daily from 12:30-3pm. The attached **Lynham's Pub** lures travelers with easy-listening music and bands on Thursdays and Saturdays. (☎45345. Entrees €18-23. Open daily 11am-midnight. MC/V.) **Wicklow Heather** ❸ is family- and vegetarian-friendly and has a dark wood floor, ceiling, and bar. (☎45157. Breakfast €5-10; entrees €13-21. Open daily 8:30am-9:30pm. MC/V.) **McCoy's** has gas, groceries, and snacks for the trail. (☎45475. Open daily 8am-8:30pm.)

◖ SIGHTS. The attractions are divided into two categories: first, the ruins, and second, the valley and its trails. Each section has its own parking lot and information center. The educationally-minded traveler should head to the first lot on the road from Laragh to visit the **Glendalough Visitors Centre,** which offers ample information on the valley's intriguing past. The admission fee covers an exhibit and a 17min. audio-visual show on the history of Irish monasteries—St. Kevin's in particular—followed by a tour of the ruins. Visitors learn, among other interesting tidbits, that St. Kevin used to stand in one of the frigid lakes long enough for birds to make nests in his outstretched hands—before, of course, returning home to pray. (☎45325 or 45352. Open daily mid-Mar. to mid-Oct. 9:30am-6pm; mid-Oct. to mid-Mar. 9:30am-5pm; last admission 45min. before closing. 30min. tours follow the audio-visual presentation and run every 30min. in the summer. Admission €3, students €1.30. Free parking available.)

Glendalough's well-preserved ruins are free and always open for exploration. A 1m base supports the 30m **Round Tower** of Glendalough, one of the best-preserved in all of Ireland (see **Christians and Vikings,** p. 50), complete with its conical cap. It was built in the 10th century, to be used primarily as a belltower, but it also served as a watchtower and retreat in tumultuous times. The entrance is 3.5m above the ground; when Vikings threatened, the monks would climb the inside of the tower floor by floor and draw up the ladders behind them. The **cathedral,** constructed using a combination of Romanesque architectural styles, was once the largest in the country. In its shadow stands **St. Kevin's Cross,** an unadorned high cross that was carved before the monks had tools to cut holes through stone. The 11th-century **St. Kevin's Church,** whose stone roof remains intact, acquired the misnomer "St. Kevin's Kitchen" because of its chimney-like tower. After 500 years, it has remained in disrepair except for a brief revival in the 19th century. To peek inside, join one of the visitor center's tours.

The **Upper and Lower Lakes** and their surrounding walks are Glendalough's true attraction. Head straight toward the second parking lot (parking €4; the lot closes at 10pm) located off the road from Laragh at Upper Lake and the National Park Information Office. Or, walking from the ruins, cross the bridge at the far side of the monastery and head right on the paved path for about 20min. until it hits the magnificent Upper Lake and park, which has plenty of outdoor options to suit every age and ability. The park has fields for lounging and areas for barbecuing and picnicking; in the summer months children splash around in both lakes. On the shore of Upper Lake is **St. Kevin's Bed,** the cave in which he prayed. Legend has it that when St. Kevin went there, his words ascended in a vortex of light and flames that burned over the Upper Lake's dark waters with such intensity that no one but the most righteous monks could witness it without going blind. A network of nine well-marked walking trails lead from the Information Office, ranging from short, wheelchair-friendly strolls to 4hr. hillwalks over boggy, mountainous terrain. Two walks in particular come highly recommended. Marked by the brown arrows, St. Kevin's Cell path (moderate; about 45min.) is a quick jaunt up near the Poulanass waterfall, stopping on the way down at **St. Kevin's Cell** and **Reefert Church,** where local chieftains found their eternal resting places. For a longer route (3½hr.), the Spinc and Glenealo Valley path is marked by white arrows. The trail ascends to a glorious lookout over Upper Lake, circles the valley where goats and deer wander on the mountainside, and passes old mining ruins before looping back. This walk has several steep inclines and descents in addition to rocky terrain, so hikers should wear good boots and be mindful of variations in terrain.

Prominently displayed maps point out these as well as other trails. Visitors can also obtain their own copies (for further walking inspiration) in the form of a pamphlet entitled *The Walking Trails of Glendalough* (€0.50), available at the Visitors Centre or the National Park Information Office.

Experienced hikers may also want to check out the nearby peaks of **Camaderry Mountain,** which afford beautiful views of the nearby lakes. However, the land is boggy and featureless, and trails aren't marked; it's easy to get lost without a **compass** and **elevation map.** Rangers say the average hiker shouldn't attempt it, but experienced mountain walkers with good boots and a good eye for maps may enjoy hiking off the beaten path in the Wicklow Mountains.

THE WICKLOW WAY

Ireland's oldest marked hiking trail (est. 1981) is also its most spectacular. Stretching from **Marlay Park** at the border of Dublin to **Clonegal** in Co. Carlow, the 122km Wicklow Way meanders north to south through Ireland's largest highland expanse. As hikers weave over heathered summits and through steep glacial valleys, yellow arrows and signs mark the Way's various footpaths, dirt tracks, and paved roads. Civilization is rarely more than 3km away, but appropriate wilderness precautions should still be taken: bring warm, windproof layers and raingear for the exposed hills. Though the terrain never gets frighteningly rugged, sturdy footwear is a must (see **Wilderness Safety,** p. 42). Cell phones often don't work along the Way, so don't rely on them—bring a GPS device if you have one. Water is best taken (with permission) from farmhouses, not streams. Open fires should be carefully monitored and are illegal within a kilometer of the forest. Hikers of all ages and walks of life have completed the entire Way, but many people find that they can still get a delightful taste of the mountains with only a little hiking.

⌐ TRANSPORTATION

Dublin Bus (☎0187 34222) runs frequently to **Marlay Park** in **Rathfarnham** (#16 from O'Connell St.) and **Enniskerry** (#44 or 185 from Bray), and less frequently to **Glencullen** (#44B; M-Sa 1-2 per day). **Bus Éireann** (☎0183 66111) comes somewhat near the Way farther south, with infrequent service from Busáras in Dublin to **Tinahely** and **Shillelagh** (1hr. 45min., 1-2 per day). From the south, Bus Éireann runs from **Bunclody** (5km from Clonegal) and **Kildavin** (3.2km from Clonegal) back to Dublin (2hr., 1-2 per day). **St. Kevin's** runs shuttles from Dublin to **Bray, Roundwood, Laraugh,** and **Glendalough.** (☎0128 18119; www.glendaloughbus.com. Buses depart Dublin M-Sa 11:30am and 6pm, Su 11:30am and 7pm, and depart Glendalough M-F 7:15, 9:45am, 4:30pm; Sa-Su 9:45am and 5:40pm. €18 return.) **Bikes** are allowed on forest tracks and paved sections. For a particularly scenic route, take R759 to **Sally Gap,** west of the trail near Lough Tay, then head south on R115 past **Glenmacnass Waterfall** (roughly 25km).

 TIP | **WICKLOW WAYWARD.** Public transportation along the Wicklow Way is spotty at best. If you don't have a car, be sure to plan a realistic route: if you get tired, you may even have trouble finding a cab to take you to a major town served by Bus Éireann.

⊹ ? ORIENTATION AND PRACTICAL INFORMATION

An excellent resource for information on the Way is **www.wicklowway.com,** a comprehensive website that gives detailed directions and day-to-day suggestions for hiking all or part of the trail. It also offers maps and accommodations listings, including basic amenities and their distances from the trail. Another useful

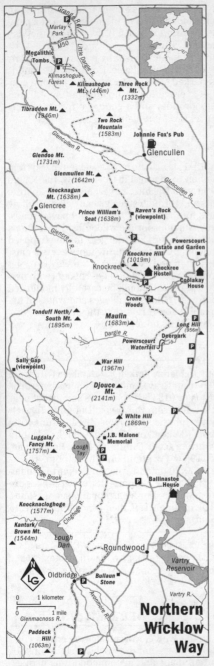

Northern Wicklow Way

resource is **www.walkireland.ie,** which details and rates each section of the route. Most tourist offices in the county sell the **Wicklow Way Map Guide** (€9), a good source of information on the trail and its sights. Don't let the unconventional compass confuse you. (The map is oriented with North pointing down.) Hiking 7-8hr. each day for six days leads backpackers from one end to the other. There are plenty of attractive abbreviated routes; numerous side trails make excellent day hikes—**Wicklow Way Walks** (€7.60) outlines several short ones. **Dirty Boots Treks** leads both day- and week-long treks. (☎01623 6785. Dayhike with guide, food, and transport to and from Dublin €45, students €39.) The northern 71km of the Way (from Dublin to Aghavannagh) is the older section and, with the best scenery and hostels, it attracts the most visitors. A long but rewarding hike extends from Enniskerry to Roundwood. From there, a lovely and manageable 12km route runs from Roundwood to Glendalough (see **Accommodations,** p. 156). One more 18km day brings you to Glenmalure, where Stirabout Lane B&B (see **Rathdrum,** p. 151) picks up from the trailhead. An Óige publishes a pamphlet detailing 4-5hr. hostel-to-hostel walks that often include sections of the Way (available at An Óige hostels in Co. Wicklow and Dublin). To see the true highlights of the Way, hike the 32km from Powerscourt Waterfall near Enniskerry to Glendalough, passing stupendous **Lough Dan** and gorgeous **Lough Tay.** For more information, contact the **National Park Information Office** (☎45425), between Glendalough's lakes (p. 154). Forestry lands are governed by **Coillte** (KWEEL-chuh; ☎01201 1111), but much of the Way is simply on a right-of-way arrangement through private lands.

⌂ ACCOMMODATIONS

The splendor of the Wicklow Way isn't exactly a well-kept secret—many accommodations take advantage of the endless stream of hikers who plan to tackle the route. **Camping** is feasible along the Way; several B&Bs even have camping facilities. Many local farmhouses allow tents on their land, but planning ahead is difficult. Hikers who ask permission to camp when they come to a stopping point often find landowners accommodating. National Park lands are fine for low-impact camping, but pitching a tent in state plantations is prohibited.

HOSTELS

Hostels include self-catering facilities, but only Glendaloch sells meals and boxed lunches; bring food or expect to walk several kilometers to reach a grocery store. Except for the Glendaloch Hostel, **An Óige Head Office** (☎0183 04555; www.irelandyha.org) handles bookings. Hostels run north to south in the following order:

Knockree (An Óige/HI), Lacken House, Enniskerry (☎0128 64036), on the Way. Farmhouse 6km from the village and 3km from Powerscourt Waterfall. From Enniskerry, take the right fork in the road leading uphill from the village green and follow the signs to the hostel. Lockout 10am-5pm. Dorms €12-16. **Closed** until March 2008. ❶

🏠 **Glendaloch (An Óige/HI),** a stone's throw from the Way (☎0404 45342), by the monastic ruins. Well worth a 2- to 3-day break from hiking. Dorms €23-25. MC/V. See **Glendalough,** p. 152. ❷

🏠 **Glenmalure (An Óige/HI),** Glenmalure. At the end of a dead-end road 12km along the Way south from Glendalough. By car, head from Glendalough to Laragh and take each major right turn. Back-to-nature lodging: no telephone, running water, or electricity (but it does have beds). Showers available at the nearby Glenmalure Lodge for a small fee. Open June-Oct. daily; Nov.-May weekends only. Dorms €11-15. ❶

Old Presbytery Hostel (IHH), Rathdrum (☎0404 46930). From town, make a left at the Centra and head uphill; it's a pink house on the right. Dorms €18 (See Rathdrum, p. 151). AmEx/MC/V. ❷

EASTERN IRELAND

BED AND BREAKFASTS

Approved accommodations can be booked with a credit card through the **All-Ireland Room Reservation** service (☎1850 230 330; www.ireland.travel.ie). A number of B&Bs offer **camping** and pickup if booked ahead; the **Wicklow Way Map Guide** comes with a sheet that lists about 20 B&Bs. Those listed below have nice hiker perks.

Coolakay House (☎0128 62423), 4km outside Enniskerry, next to the Powerscourt Waterfall. Does pickups from Cronewood trailhead (4.5km away) and shuttles to Enniskerry. Lovely sunroom for tired hikers and luxurious rooms with TVs and hair dryers. Packed lunch €8-10. Singles €60; doubles €90. Cash only. ❹

Ballinastoe House, Roundwood (☎01281 8940; www.ballinastoe.com). Claims to be the highest B&B in Ireland. Great views. Guest collection from the trail. Luggage transfer on request. Dinner €20. Open Mar.-Oct. Singles €45; doubles €75. Cash only. ❸

Ashfield House, Curravanish, Tinahely (☎0402 38146; www.tinahelyashfield-house.com). 2km from town, just off the Way. Pickup from trailhead and shuttles to town. Vegetarian dinner options (€20). Singles €45; doubles €66-70. MC/V. ❸

Rosbane Farmhouse, Rosbane (☎0402 38100). 7min. walk from the Way, near the summit of Garryhoe. Trail pickups on request. Private B&B with plenty of space to relax. Lunch about €4. Singles €40; doubles €70. Camping €85 per tent. Cash only. ❸

Ballinavortha House, Clonegal (☎05991 55848; www.ballinavorthahouse.com). 4km from Clonegal, 1.2km from the trail. Trail pickups on request. Luggage transfer to next accommodation. Dinner €15. Singles €30; doubles €60. Cash only.

🄲🄼 FOOD AND PUBS

All hikers should carry enough food to last through the length of the journey (5-6 days), as restaurants and groceries are only found in towns located off the Way (Glendalough and Laragh excepted). **Water** can be found at hostels and B&Bs along the Way; it is vital that hikers drink plenty of water during the strenuous trek to avoid dehydration. Hikers who reach Glencullen or Enniskerry and are in need of alcoholic rehydration should make an extra effort to climb to **Johnnie Fox's ❸**, Ireland's highest pub. Established in 1798, Johnnie's is 365m above sea level. Here, Wicklow Way walkers drink and dine while enjoying the pub's excellent *craic*. The nightly trad sessions and delicious food (entrees €16.50-25) make the journey worthwhile. Locals usually crowd into the back. (☎0129 55647; www.jfp.ie. Open M-Sa 10:30am-11:30pm, Su noon-11pm. Kitchen open daily 12:30-9:30pm. MC/V.)

WESTERN WICKLOW

Squatter, lumpier, and less traveled than the rest of the county, western Wicklow is green, friendly, and free from crowds of tourists. It's possible to hike between western Wicklow and the Wicklow Way, but turn around at red flags; the Irish Army maintains a few shooting ranges in the region. Hiking is relatively safe in unflagged areas. Lungnaquilla Mountain, the highest peak in Co. Wicklow, has stunning views and challenging hiking trails.

BLESSINGTON (BAILE COIMÍN)   ☎045

Blessington lies beside Blessington Lake close to the intersection of N81 from Dublin (1hr. by car) and R410 from Naas. (20min.) Wilderness lovers explore the waters—created by damming the River Liffey in the 1930s and 40s—and the rugged, sheep-spotted hills. Cultured types make the daytrip from Dublin for the world-class art inside the exceptionally well-maintained Palladian **Russborough House,** which sprawls amid its vast parkland 3.2km south of Blessington on N81 toward Baltinglass. Richard Cassells, who also designed Dublin's Leinster House and much of Trinity College, built the house in 1741 for Joseph Leeson, an Anglo-Irish man-about-Parliament who later became Lord Milltown. Russborough now houses the impressive Beit Collection of predominantly 17th- and 18th-century European paintings and furniture, as well as many intricate plaster ceiling pieces. The museum has been robbed four times, most notably in 1986, when the Dublin mobster "The General" orchestrated the theft of the 17 most valuable paintings, including works by Goya, Vermeer, and Velasquez. Fortunately, all have since been recovered. The best pieces are now in the National Gallery in Dublin (p. 122), but a few excellent ones remain here in Wicklow. Unfortunately, the paintings were removed in 2004 during efforts to conserve the ornate Rococo-style plaster ceiling work, but they are expected to have returned by summer 2007. For the time being, tours visit upstairs bedrooms to make up for the missing paintings. In the summertime, explorers get lost in the garden's **hedge maze.** Entrance to the maze is found through the equestrian school in the second parking lot. (☎865 239; russborough@eircom.net. Open May-Sept. daily 10am-5pm; Apr. and Oct. Su 10am-5pm. Hourly admission by 1hr. tours. €6, students and seniors €4.50, children €3. Maze open June-Aug. 12:30-5pm. €2.)

Hayland's House B&B ❸, a convenient 10min. walk out of town on the N81 to Dublin, across the road from the #65 bus stop, offers warm hospitality and pristine accommodations, despite the fact that the decor looks like it hasn't changed since the 70s. (☎865 183. Singles €35-40; doubles €65-70. Cash only.) On the other side of town, 1.6km out on the road to Naas, the friendly owners of **Fairhill B&B ❸,** 5 Pipers Stones, provide excellent rooms and a well-manicured lawn. (☎865 692. Ensuite singles €40; doubles €70. Cash only.) The **West Wicklow House ❸,** Main St., serves tasty pub grub all day, such as the joint-of-the-day (€12) or the more exotic vegetarian-friendly curry (€12). In the evening, have a pint and listen to live trad on Wednesday nights. (☎865 214. F-Sa DJs. Su cover bands. Restaurant open M-F noon-8:30pm, Sa noon-7:30pm, Su noon-7pm. Pub open M-Th 10:30am-11:30pm, F-Sa 10:30am-12:30am, Su 12:30-11pm. MC/V.) You can smell **Macari's ❶** all the way down Main St.—it's the place to go for greasy delights. It might not be light on the stomach, but it's light on the wallet. (☎891 906. ¼-pounder €3.40, chips €2.30. Cash only. Open M and W-F noon-midnight, Sa-Su 2-11pm.) For groceries, there's **Dunnes,** behind the tourist office off of Main St. (☎857 732. Open M-F 8:30am-8pm, Sa 8:30am-8pm, Su 9am-8pm. MC/V.)

The easiest way for non-drivers to reach Blessington is by the #65 **bus** (M-Sa 14 per day, Sa 14 per day, Su 17 per day; €3.20) from Eden Quay in Dublin. Some buses continue to Ballymore and will stop at the entrance to Russborough House on request. However, getting picked up again is not quite so simple. The **tourist office,** next to Ulster Bank, gives advice on outdoor activities. (☎865 850. Open M-F 9:30am-5pm.) You'll find the **Police** *(Garda)* **Station** on Main St. (☎884 300. Open M-Sa 10am-1pm and 7-10pm, Su 11am-1pm and 7-9pm.) **Unicare Pharmacy** is in the shopping center behind the tourist office. (☎857 582. Open M-W and Sa 9am-6pm, Th-F 9am-9pm, Su noon-5pm.) **Ulster Bank,** on Main St., has a 24hr. **ATM.** (☎865 125. Open M-W and F 10am-4pm, Th 10am-5pm.)

COUNTY KILDARE

The towns immediately west of Dublin in Co. Kildare are still well within the city's orbit. The best sights—Kildare's horses and Castletown House—can be visited as easy daytrips from the capital. From the 13th to the 16th century, the Fitzgerald Earls of Kildare controlled all of eastern Ireland. Today, mansions and the big-money Irish Derby evoke Kildare's former prominence. The Irish National Stud rears horses that win the world's greatest derbies, at the Curragh Racecourse.

MAYNOOTH (MAIGH NUAD) ☎01

Maynooth (ma-NOOTH) is an active town of the erudite and religious. In 1795, St. Patrick's College, the first Catholic seminary in Ireland, opened with George III's encouragement—the monarch was concerned that priests educated in Revolutionary France would acquire dangerous notions of independence. Priests are still ordained here, but the 120 clerical students are now outnumbered by their 6000 peers at what is now the National University of Ireland at Maynooth. The serene campus includes **College Chapel, Bicentenary Garden,** and A.W. Pugin's Gothic **St. Mary's Square.** The **St. Patrick's National Science Museum** displays scientific and clerical artifacts. (☎708 3780. Open May-Sept. Tu and Th 2pm-4pm, Su 2-6pm. Free.) **Maynooth Conference & Accommodations,** under the arch of the large building directly in front of the Main St. entrance, provides campus maps and housing information (see housing information at St. Patrick's College, below). (☎708 6200. Open M-F 8:30am-7:30pm and 8-11pm, Sa-Su 8:30am-12:30pm, 1:30-7:30pm, and 8-11pm.) Tours of the college campus for groups of five or more can be arranged by calling Mary O'Malley (☎087 668 5009; €60 per group). The Fitzgerald family controlled its vast domain from 12th-century **Maynooth Castle,** located near the college. The castle's exhibition room is lined with comic-book-style panels explaining the history of the castle and the Fitzgerald family. Excellent guided tours pass through the remnants of the fortress and grounds. (☎628 6744. Open June-Sept. daily 10am-6pm; Oct. Su and bank holidays 10am-5pm. Free.)

⬛**St. Patrick's College** ❸ rents student apartments and rooms during the summer and a small number of rooms during the year. The cost includes access to computer terminals (with free Internet access), the college swimming pool, weight room, tennis courts, and playing fields. (☎708 6400; www.maynoothcampus.com. Rooms available early June to mid-Sept.; limited number Oct.-May. Singles €28-57, with breakfast €35.40-64.40; doubles €46-70. MC/V.) Enjoy light fare and delicious baked goods on a student budget (€1-4) at **Elite Confectionery** ❶ on Main St. (☎628 5521. Open M-Sa 8:30am-6pm. Cash only.) **Centra,** Main St., has groceries. (☎628 5247. Open M-Sa 6:30am-9pm, Su 7am-9pm. MC/V.)

Maynooth is 24km west of Dublin on the M4. The **suburban rail** runs from Connolly Station in Dublin every 30min. (€5.10 return); **bus** #66 goes directly to Maynooth, and #67A runs via Celbridge (€2.10), with both departing from Pearse St. If you take the #67A, walk down the hill with the Glenroyal Hotel on your right until you hit town. The **Citizens Information Centre,** on Dublin Rd., around the corner from Main St. farthest from St. Patrick's, mainly serves locals, but has tourist maps to spare. (☎628 5477. Open M-F 9:30am-5pm.) Several banks line Main St., including **Ulster Bank** and **Bank of Ireland,** which both have 24hr. **ATMs.** Also on Main St. is **McCormack's Pharmacy.** (☎628 6274. Open M-F 9am-6pm, Sa 9:30am-6pm.) The **police** *(Garda)* **Station** is located at the corner of Main St. and Canal Pl. (☎629 1444. Open M-Sa 10am-1pm, 2-6pm, and 7-9pm, Su noon-2pm). **Internet** access is available at **Maynooth Netcafe & Callshop** on Leinster St., off Main St. one block from St. Patrick's. (☎629 1817. Open daily 9am-11pm.)

CELBRIDGE ☎01

Little Celbridge (SELL-bridge) lies 8km south of Maynooth on Celbridge Rd. At the end of a long, tree-lined lane is **Castletown House**—magnificent home of William Connolly, the Speaker of the Irish House of Commons—built to showcase Ireland's treasures. The richest man in 1720s Ireland, Connolly built this grandiose mansion (the largest of its kind in the country) and sparked a nationwide penchant for Palladian architecture. Detailed tours cover the history of the house and its inhabitants and locally made furnishings. The saccharine pink-and-blue glass chandeliers in the Long Gallery are a sight to behold. From the window, a memorial obelisk known as **Connolly's Folly** is visible 3.2km behind the estate. Connolly's "philanthropic" widow (who turned the upstairs into a casino after his death) had the monument built to employ famine-starved locals in 1740. An on-site **coffee shop** ❶ offers drinks and pastries for €1-3. (☎ 628 8252. Open Apr.-Sept. M-F 10am-6pm, Sa-Su 1-6pm; Oct. M-F 10am-5pm, Su 1-5pm; Nov. Su 1-5pm. Admission by guided tour only. €3.70, students and children €1.30, seniors €2.60, family €8.70.) Castletown House's beautifully groomed front lawn and tree-lined fields, which include a path along the Liffey River, are a great place to picnic or spend a relaxing afternoon. If the weather holds up, put together the ingredients for your picnic at **Centra**, on Main St. (☎ 628 8337. Open daily 6am-11pm. MC/V.) Across the street, **Ulster Bank** has a 24hr. **ATM.** (☎ 627 0657. Open M-W and F 10am-4pm, Th 10am-5pm.) Also on Main St. is **Blake's Pharmacy.** (☎ 627 1141. Open daily 9am-9pm.) Follow the road out of town to Maynooth to find the **Police** *(Garda)* **Station.** (☎ 627 1181. Open M-Sa 10am-1pm, 2-6pm, and 7-9pm, Su noon-2pm.) **Buses** #67 and 67A run to Celbridge town center from Dublin. (€3.80 return.) The less convenient **suburban rail** (€2, 9 per day) leaves from Heuston Station and arrives roughly every hour at the Hazelhatch and Celbridge stops. A complimentary shuttle outside the station gate leaves after every train and runs the 4km to the town center.

KILDARE (CILL DARA)   ☎ 045

While Ireland is full of ancient monuments and sacred Christian sights, Kildare is the holy land for the country's other religion: horse racing. Carefully bred, raised, and raced here, thoroughbreds are the lifeblood of the town, and bookies almost outnumber pubs. The town grew around a church founded in AD 480 by St. Brigid, who chose a site next to an oak tree she saw in a vision, hence the town's Irish name, which means "Church of the Oak." Just west of Kildare, horses gallop through the greenery of the Curragh Plains, which stretch majestically across the gentle landscape. Back in the town center, the triangular plaza hosts some pleasant restaurants and pubs in the shadows of St. Brigid's, but the quiet of the cathedral is often upset by traffic from N7.

█🚹 TRANSPORTATION AND PRACTICAL INFORMATION. Kildare straddles busy N7 (Dublin-Limerick) and connects to Heuston Station by **suburban rail.** (40min., M-Sa every hr. 6am-10:30pm.) **Bus Éireann** goes to **Dublin** en route from **Limerick** and **Cork.** (1½hr.; M-F 28 per day, Sa 27 per day, Su 20 per day; €9.70/6.40.) **J.J. Kavanagh/Rapid Express Coaches** offers cheaper service between Dublin's Middle Abbey St. and Kildare. (☎ 883 1106. M-Sa 5 per day, Su 4 per day; €9.) The **tourist office,** in the Market House in the square, books accommodations for a €4 fee and distributes free copies of a Kildare Town guided walking tour. (☎ 530 672. Open May-Sept. M-Sa 9:30am-1pm and 2-5pm; Oct.-Apr. 10am-1pm and 2-5pm.) The same building houses the **Heritage Centre** upstairs, which shows a short video, narrated by the ghost of a local monk. (☎ 530 672. Open same hours as tourist office. Free.) The **Bank of Ireland,** the Square, has a 24hr. **ATM** and a **bureau de change.** (☎ 521 276. Open M 10am-5pm, Tu and Th-F 10am-4pm, W 10:30am-4pm.) Free **Internet** access is available at the **library** in the square. (☎ 520 235. Open Tu 2:30-5pm and 6-8pm, W 10am-1pm and 2-5pm, F 2:30-5pm, Sa 11am-1pm and 3-5pm.) The **post office** is in a brick building on Dublin St., past the Silken Thomas pub and across the road. (☎ 521 349. Open M and W-F 9am-5:30pm, Tu 9:30am-5:30pm, Sa 10am-1pm.) For **taxis,** call **Taxi-Express** (☎ 520 038).

🏠 ACCOMMODATIONS. Lord Edward Guest House ❷, behind the Silken Thomas pub and under the same ownership, has spacious, spotless, sometimes elegant rooms with coffee, tea, TV, and bath. (☎ 522 389 or 521 695. Wheelchair-accessible. Singles €30; doubles €65. MC/V.) **Singleton's ❸,** 1 Dara Park, is in town and has three rooms with TV and bath. From the Heritage Centre, follow Station Rd. to the right; it's on the right before the Esso station. (☎ 521 964. Laundry €5 per load. Open Mar.-Sept. Singles €40; doubles €60.) Seven kilometers from town, situated on a poultry farm, is the peaceful **Eagle Hill B&B** ❸. Call for pickup or take Tully Rd. 9km out of town, following the signs, to reach top-notch rooms. (☎526 097. Free bike rental. Laundry and Internet access available on request. All rooms with bath. Singles €35-40; doubles €60.) Five well-signposted kilometers from town toward Monasterevin, the cows at comfortable **Castleview Farm and B&B** ❸ produce milk for Bailey's Irish Cream in the shadows of a crumbling church. A self-catering thatched-roofed cottage is available for longer stays. (☎521 816; www.kildare-bandb.com. Singles €40-50; doubles €68-76. Cottage €300-500 per wk.)

◻◻ FOOD AND PUBS. Food and entertainment in Kildare center around the massive Flanagan family complex that manages to maintain a unique character in spite of its monopoly. The sprawling **Silken Thomas Restaurant and Lounge** ❷, the Square (☎522 232), stands out from the rest of the pubs, offering locally renowned sandwiches (€4-6) and meals (entrees €17-24); try the Chinese-inspired "from the wok" options. The pub's name refers to "Silken Thomas" FitzGerald, who raised Dublin in revolt against the British in 1534. **Flanagan's Lounge,** behind Silken Thomas, does a good job of faking authenticity with low ceilings, muraled wood-beams, open peat fires, and an impressive matchbox collection hanging above the bar. The other pub on the premise is the **Public Bar** (a.k.a. **Squires**), an attractive re-creation of an antique Dublin watering hole that shows GAA matches on a projector screen. (☎521 389.) **Lil's,** at the back of Silken Thomas, is the new upscale lounge. Between Lord Edward's and the Silken Thomas lies the friendly Flanagan family's most recent success, the chic **◻Tigerlily** nightclub. An attached outdoor beer garden comforts those whom the smoking ban has forced outside, while lamps and heaters repel the cold. (☎521 389. Cover F €10, Sa €12, Su €8. Open F-Su 11:30am-3pm.) Next to the cathedral in the unlabeled brick building with the black awning, **Top Nolan's,** the Square, is a low-key joint with a pool table in the back. Trad sessions have replaced the hammers and handsaws in this former hardware store. (☎521 528. Tu and Su trad. Open M-Th 4-11:30pm, F 4pm-12:30am, Sa 11am-12:30am, Su 11am-11pm.) For a quiet pint, join the well-heeled crowd at the refined **J.J. Mahon and Son,** Claregate St. at the corner of Market Sq. The "snug" off to the side is a comfy drawing room where patrons are free to chat and channel surf amid some old photographs. (☎521 316. 21+. Open M-Th 10:30am-11:30pm, F-Sa 10:30am-12:30am, Su 12:30-11pm.) Great Chinese food is conveniently located on Market Sq. in the overly floral **Kingsland** ❷. (☎521 052 or 531 688. Entrees €8-14. Open M-Th 5:30pm-12:30am, Sa 5:30pm-1am, Su 12:30-3pm and 5:30-11pm.) Just off the square toward the railway station on Station Rd., **Agape Gourmet Sandwich Bar** ❶ has tasty *panini*, wraps, and bagel sandwiches (€5-6), including a good selection of vegetarian options. (☎533 711. Open M-F 8am-6pm, Sa 10am-6pm.) **La Pizza Ristorante** ❸, the Square, next to Top Nolan's, is an average Italian eatery with pizza and pasta for €10-15. (☎533 507. Open Tu-W 6-9:30pm, Th 6-10pm, F 5-11pm, Sa 6-11pm, Su noon-4pm and 5-9pm.) Also on Station Rd., **Mizzoni Pizza Co.** offers personal pizzas (€5) as well as the larger and more imaginative kebab pizza (€10). Bring some friends and tackle the "wagon wheel," a 20 in. monster of a pie (€18.50). Grab food extra late on Friday and Saturday nights. (☎535 100. Open M-Th and Su 4:30pm-1am, F-Sa 4:30pm-3am.)

◻ SIGHTS. The **◻Irish National Stud and Japanese Gardens,** 1km from the square on Tully Rd., were founded by the eccentric Colonel William Hall-Walker in 1900. The son of a Scottish brewer, the colonel studied each foal's horoscope at its birth—if the stars weren't lined up favorably, the foal would be sold, regardless of its lineage. These days, the Irish National Stud is in the big-money business of rearing the world's best thoroughbred racehorses. Mating season kicks off, naturally, on Valentine's Day, and the current top stud and high-class "whorsetitute," Indian Ridge, is insured for €30 million and charges €75,000 per romantic rendezvous. Other options include Celtic Swing and Desert Prince. The Stud's small **Irish Horse**

Museum tells the history of the horse with a few informative displays. A looped video about the legendary champion is complemented by a horse's skeleton. **Guided tours** educate the ignorant about the bizarre and incredibly lucrative world of stud farms and horse racing. Along with the gorgeous, sinewy thoroughbreds, visitors can see the world's smallest breed of horse and Tommy "the teaser," a pony whose job is to make sure the mares are "ready" for the stud. The **Japanese Gardens** allegorize the "life of man" through a beautiful, semi-narrative trail. From the cave of birth to the hill of mourning, visitors experience learning, disappointment, and marriage as they wander through the maze of caves, bridges, and bonsai trees. If you choose to follow the "rugged path" after the Gate of Oblivion, the path of life may be unexpectedly more difficult. The Japanese Gardens seem tiny in comparison with the enormous 1.5-hectare **St. Fiachra's Garden,** opened for the new millennium. Peaceful St. Fiachra's evokes "monastic spirituality" with quiet, swan-filled lakes, waterfalls, and monastic cells, with a subterranean garden partially crafted of Waterford crystal. (☎521 617; www.irish-national-stud.ie. Open mid-Feb. to mid-Nov. daily 9:30am-6pm; last admission 5pm. 35min. tours of the National Stud begin at noon, 2:30, and 4pm. €10, students and seniors €8, children €5, under 5 free, families €25.)

Right off the square in town, recently restored **St. Brigid's,** a Church of Ireland cathedral that lay derelict for over 200 years, stands in the shadow of the tower. The cathedral dates from the 12th century and sits on the site of a church founded by St. Brigid in AD 480. The site seems to attract untraditional bishops; a *sheela-na-gig* (erotic female figure carving) spreads her legs under the lid of Bishop Wellesley's tomb. The staff gives out a free guide of the other, less erotic, monuments and statues that surround the cathedral. (Open May-Sept. M-Sa 10am-1pm and 2-5pm, Su 2-5pm. Services Su at 11:30am. Suggested donation €1.50.) Next to the church is **St. Brigid's Fire Temple,** a pagan ritual site that St. Brigid repossessed for Christianity. Only female virgins were allowed to tend the fire, which burned continuously for 1000 years. Archbishop George Browne of Dublin ended this tradition in the 16th century—by extinguishing the flames, not the virginity. (Free.) Behind the church, the 10th-century **round tower** is one of two in Ireland that visitors can enter and climb (the other is in Kilkenny); most others lack floors. The climb up the steep ladders is harrowing. (Open May-Sept. M-Sa 10am-1pm and 2-5pm, Su 2-5pm. €4; children are often waved in for free.)

▶ **DAYTRIP FROM KILDARE: THE CURRAGH.** Between Newbridge and Kildare on N7 lie the Curragh Plains, 5000 acres of perhaps the greenest fields in Ireland. Thoroughbred horses, hoping to one day earn fame and fortune at the **Curragh Racecourse,** host of the annual **Irish Derby,** graze and train here. The Derby is Ireland's premier sporting and social event and one of the world's most prestigious races. Hit the Curragh as early as 7:30am and watch scores of horses take their daily training run on one of the five gallops, each 2-3km long. (☎441 205; www.curragh.ie. Bus Éireann serves the Curragh on race days, leaving from Busáras in Dublin and from the square in Kildare. Races every other weekend late Mar.-Oct. Sa-Su 2:15 or 2:30pm. Tickets usually start at €15, €50 for the Derby; limited access Derby tickets from €25.) One kilometer toward Allenwood, the family-oriented **Lullymore Heritage and Discovery Park** uses re-created villages set amid woodland walks to explore life in the boglands from the Mesolithic era to the Famine. Visitors can ride a train to a farm, explore themed gardens, play mini golf, and visit the peat bog. Little ones run amuck in the new Funky Forest indoor playground. (From Kildare, take R401 to Rathangan and then R414 toward Allenwood. ☎870 238. Tours available upon request. Open Easter-Oct. M-Sa 10am-6pm, Su 11am-6pm; Nov.-Easter and bank holidays Sa-Su 11am-6pm; other times by appointment. €9, seniors €7, families €22.) Also in Lullymore, signposted from town, is the **Bog of Allen Nature Centre,** where visitors can learn about the history of the surrounding bogs and see the **Flytraps Greenhouse,** which features insect-eating plants from all over the world. The **Yin and Yang Garden** juxtaposes wet and dry environments. *(☎045 860 133; bogs@ipcc.ie. Open every M-F and the last Su of May, July, and Nov. 10am-4pm. €5.)*

COUNTY MEATH

Meath's farmlands and meadows hide a wealth of history both above and below ground. The Hill of Tara was Ireland's political and spiritual center in prehistoric times, and the marks it has left on the landscape retain an air of solemn mystery for today's visitors. The countryside, with its winding roads, rolling hills, and castle-filled towns, provides the perfect backdrop for a Sunday bike ride or drive.

BOYNE VALLEY

The thinly populated Boyne Valley hides Ireland's greatest archaeological treasures, and farmers, plowing around an impressive archaeological cache, still appreciate the rich soil that has made the Boyne Valley a farmland since the Stone Age. Massive passage tombs create subtle bumps in the landscape that belie their cavernous underground chambers, which are older than the Egyptian pyramids and at least as puzzling. Celtic High Kings once ruled from atop the **Hill of Tara,** leaving a wealth of mysterious folklore in their wake. The Hill's enduring significance and incredible views attract visitors aplenty, as do the well-preserved Norman fortifications in Trim. According to legend, St. Patrick lit a flame that helped bring Christianity to Ireland atop the **Hill of Slane.** (see **St. Patrick,** p. 59). Every so often, farmers uncover artifacts from the 1690 Battle of the Boyne, resurfacing powerful memories for Irish Protestants (see **More British Problems,** p. 52).

NEWGRANGE, KNOWTH AND DOWTH ☎041

Along the River Boyne, between Slane and Centre, sprawls Brú na Bóinne (BREW-nah BOY-nya; "homestead of the Boyne"). The Boyne Valley boasts three main passage tombs at Newgrange, Knowth and Dowth, which share the title of World Heritage Sites with other impressive world landmarks, including their younger sisters, Stonehenge and the Pyramids of Giza. Though these large tombs were probably reserved for the remains of the ancient rich and famous, some 37 other satellite tombs, comparable to modern day family plots, can be found in this 2500-acre region, all with more than five millennia of history behind them. Neolithic engineers constructed Newgrange, Dowth, and Knowth within walking distance of each other, possibly with the weary travelers of the future in mind.

Archaeologists suspect the 5000-year-old mounds had some sort of religious or magical significance. Long before the wheel was invented, they moved 1-ton kerbstones from 15km away, probably using a log-rolling mechanism. The work was sluggish (it took as many as 80 men four days to move one kerbstone to the site), and the larger mounds took a half-century to build—twice the length of the average Neolithic man's life span. Some of the stones are decorated with Neolithic art which either have religious or linguistic significance, depending on whom you ask.

■**Newgrange** offers the best glimpse of the structure and interior of a passage tomb. After 1000 years of existence, the front of this circular mound collapsed and fell into disrepair. It remained hidden for 4000 years and was only rediscovered in 1699; many of the stones bear 200-year-old graffiti. During the reconstruction in 1963, archaeologists discovered a roof box over the passage entrance that channels sunlight down the 20m passageway. The sunlight illuminates the burial chamber for 17 gilded minutes during the winter equinox. The tour provides a brilliant simulation of this experience, leaving visitors in awe. Those wishing to see the real event must sign up for a lottery, held every October. Unfortunately, the temperamental Irish weather sometimes clouds those 17 minutes of sun.

The most impressive of the three main sights, for archaeologists if not for visitors, is **Knowth** (rhymes with "mouth"). Hunter-gatherers settled here in 4000 BC, followed by Stone Age folks who built the mound visible today, Iron Age Celts who left behind some of their dead and the earliest writing found in Ireland, and—as late as the 12th century—Christians who dug a network of underground tunnels into the mounds and the surrounding area for speedy escape from Viking raids. The enormous passage tomb houses two back-to-back burial chambers with separate east and west entrances, possibly an allusion to the sun's movement across the horizon. The tomb is surrounded by an incredible 127 of the kerbstones, many of which are decorated, as well as a cluster of the smaller satellite tombs. Knowth's carvings are relatively well-preserved, with unexplained spirals and etchings adorning the outside of the mound.

The mound at **Dowth** (also rhymes with "mouth") was damaged during excavations in the 1840s. While the public isn't allowed inside, people are welcome to explore the outside; it's probably only worth your time if you haven't toured Newgrange or Knowth. To see Dowth, cars and bikers can explore the roads off N51 between Slane and Drogheda; by foot, it's about 15-20min. up the road.

Access to Knowth and Newgrange requires admission to ⬛**Brú na Bóinne Visitors Centre,** located near Donore on the south side of the River Boyne, across from the tombs themselves. Allow 3-4hr. for the center and the tours of both tombs. Especially on Sundays, arrive before lunch for the best chance of seeing the tombs, as only 500 visitors are admitted each day. August is the busiest month; arrive at 9am to ensure a spot. While awaiting a tour, check out the center's excellent exhibit on the lives of the gifted and talented Stone Agers or grab a quick bite at the downstairs **tea room,** where drinks and pastries are €2-5. (☎988 0300. Open June to mid-Sept. 9am-7pm; May and mid to late Sept. 9am-6:30pm; Mar.-Apr. and Oct. 9:30am-5:30pm; Nov.-Feb. 9:30am-5pm. Admission to the Visitors Centre €3, students/children €1.60, seniors €2; center and Newgrange tour €6/3/4.50; center, Newgrange, and Knowth €10.30/4.50/7.40. Last tour 45min. before closing. Last admission to center 45min. before closing.) Downstairs, a **tourist office** distributes area maps and information (☎988 0305. Open daily 9am-7pm). To reach the Visitors

GIVING BACK

PAY IT FORWARD

Once your international ramblings are over, your clothes finally washed, and your backpack stowed away, you may start to feel grateful to all the kind people who aided you on your journeys. The old man who bought you a pint when you were drenched by an Irish rainstorm. The little freckled kid who waved at you as the bus you were meant to catch pulled away. Everyone who ever smilingly said "no bother" when you apologized for yet another cultural gaffe.

Servas is an organization that allows travelers to fulfill their traveling karma once they've returned home. It was founded in 1948 by a group of pacifists who wanted to encourage international peace, love, and understanding (Servas means "you serve" in Esperanto). Individuals sign up to host travelers for two nights, taking them into their homes without pay.

The idea is that it's a cultural exchange: travelers benefit from free lodging and a real look at life in an average family, while hosts broaden their horizons by striking up friendships with foreigners. The organization screens both hosts and travelers to protect the safety of everyone involved. So once you're back home, think about pulling out the futon for a couple of fellow travelers. If nothing else, they'll be a good audience for your 500-picture slideshow.

For more info, visit www.servas.org; or write to helpdesk@servas.org.

Centre from Drogheda by bike, turn left by the bus station and head straight on the uphill road for 8km. **Bus Éireann** (☎ 836 6111) sends shuttles to the Visitors Centre from **Drogheda** (10min., every hr., €5.25 return). Several **bus tours** from Dublin include admission to the sights, including Bus Éireann's. (Oct.-Apr. Th and Sa, May-Sept. M-Th and Sa-Su. €30, student €28.)

HILL OF TARA ☎ 046

Tara, marked by a long, enigmatic history, serenely awaits its many visitors. From prehistoric times until the 10th century, **Tara** was the social, political, and cultural heart of Ireland. Standing atop the hill, it's not hard to see why; on a good day, it's said that you can see 20% of the country. A sacred site for ancient Irish religion and home to 142 former Irish kings and the largest collection of Celtic monuments in the world, Tara hides its many secrets beneath its 40 hectares of oddly shaped grassy mounds. Secret-seeking is allowed, but don't bring a shovel—in the early 20th century, a misguided cult on a hunt for the Arc of the Covenant used one to damage the Mound of the Synods. Though they failed to find the arc, they did manage to unearth a few ancient Roman coins. Located at Tara is the sacred *Lia Fail* ("Stone of Destiny"), an ancient rock once used as a coronation stone. The rock was said to roar when the rightful king of Tara placed his hands upon it. The **Mound of Hostages,** Tara's resident burial mound, dates back to 2500 BC. Finally, like any ancient Irish sight, Tara has its own St. Patrick tale—according to legend, it was here that St. Paddy used a shamrock to explain the Holy Trinity to a high king, and from this tale the shamrock emerged as Ireland's national symbol (p. 59).

The grounds are free and open to the public. The enormous site is about 7km east of Navan on N3. Take any **local bus** from Dublin to **Navan** (1hr.; M-Sa 37 per day, Su 15 per day; €9.70, children €6.40) and ask to stop at the signposted turn-off on the left; then it's 2km of uphill legwork. The actual buildings—largely ringforts of wattle, wood, and earth—have long been buried or destroyed; what remains are concentric rings of grassy dunes. While 360° views and the allure of ancient history should excite the imagination, the remains are not visually overwhelming and it is worth stopping by the **Visitors Centre** in the old church to see aerial photos and an excellent **audio-visual show** (20min.) on Tara's history. After the show, take a **guided tour** (35min., times vary but always available if you show up at least an 1hr. before closing). The tour covers only the sights at the top of the hill, though Tara actually encompasses a larger number of smaller mounds and ring forts. (☎ 046 902 5903. Access to hill free. Center open mid-May to mid-Sept. daily 10am-6pm. Last admission 5:15pm. €2.10, students €1.10, seniors and children €1.30, under 5 free.)

TRIM (BAILE ATHÁ TROIM) ☎ 04694

Jaded travelers looking for a break from Dublin should treat themselves to a visit to Trim, a tidy heritage town located just an hour outside the capital. Ireland's largest Anglo-Norman castle (and occasional Hollywood backdrop) oversees the proceedings, while the gentle currents of the River Boyne run through town and maintain its tranquil mood.

◪◪ TRANSPORTATION AND PRACTICAL INFORMATION. Bus Éireann stops in front of Trim Castle on its way to and from **Dublin** (1hr.; M-F 14 per day, Sa 8 per day, Su 4 per day; €7). **Castle Street** intersects central **Market Street,** which has most of the town's shops, then crosses the **River Boyne** under the alias of **Bridge Street.** The first left after crossing the bridge is **Mill Street.** Bridge St. curves uphill on the far side, turning into **High Street** before splitting. The left fork becomes **Haggard Street,** and the right becomes **Navan Gate Street,** the road to the nearby Newtown ruins. The **Visitors Centre** and **tourist office** is on Castle St., below the castle and next to the bus stop. It distributes a useful map of Trim's sights, sells souvenirs, and presents an audio-visual tour of the town's history. (☎37227; www.meathtourism.ie. Open M-Sa 9:30am-5:30pm, bank holidays and Su noon-5:30pm.) **Bank of Ireland**, with a 24hr. **ATM**, is on Market St. (☎31230. Open M 10am-5pm, Tu-F 10am-4pm.) The **library**, on High St., has free **Internet** access. (Open Tu and Th 10am-8:30pm, W and F-Sa 10am-1pm and 2-5pm.) **Emmy Cyber Cafe,** Market St., at the roundabout by Emmet St., also provides Internet access. (☎83498. Open M-F 10am-8pm, Sa noon-8pm, Su 2-8pm. €1 per 20min.) In a purple building on Market St. is **Trim Pharmacy, Ltd.** (☎31279. Open M-Sa 9am-6pm). The **post office** is at the intersection of Market and Emmet St., inside Spar. (☎31268. Open M-F 9am-1pm and 2-5:30pm, Sa 9am-1pm.)

⌖ ACCOMMODATIONS. The family-run ⬛**Highfield House B&B ❸** on Maudlins Rd., a spectacular stone building with views of the Yellow Steeple and the river, used to be a maternity hospital but now offers a fine maternal welcome and the most luxurious stay in town. From the bus stop, walk away from the bridge and center of town; it's on the right (5min.) past the *Garda* station. (☎36386. Free Internet access. Singles €55; doubles €84; triples €108. MC/V.) The **Bridge House Tourist Hostel ❷,** tucked away down a driveway from High St. and the Mill St. bridge, is in a 600-year-old building nestled up against the gentle waters of the Boyne. The largest dorms have four beds and all rooms are ensuite. The intimate TV lounge is a converted medieval wine cellar. Call ahead in summer when the 15 beds fill quickly. (☎31848. Check-in 6-7pm or by phone arrangement. Kitchen and free Internet access. 4-bed dorms €20; private rooms €25 per person. MC/V with surcharge.) **Brogan's ❹,** a 3min. walk up High St., has brightly painted rooms with TVs, showers, coffee- and tea-making facilities, and telephones. A mellow in-house pub and beer garden offer good eats and frequent live music. Behind the pub is a lounge which hosts live music most weekend nights. (☎31237. Breakfast included. Oct.-Feb. ensuite singles €45; doubles €90; Mar.-Sept. €55/99. MC/V.)

◪🔄 FOOD AND PUBS. Grab groceries at **Spar,** Market St., which is also home to the post office. (☎38870. Open daily 8am-9pm.) **Watson's Elementary Café ❷,** Market St., serves an adequate, inexpensive breakfast with sizes that fit all appetites, and is the only eatery open early Sundays. An a la carte lunch menu (W-Sa) offers entrees for €8.50-9.50. They also sell delicious homemade breads. (☎38575. Filled baguette €6-7; Irish breakfast €5.50-9.50. Open daily 7:30am-7pm.) For quality sandwiches (€5.25-6.26) and cappuccino head to **Ego's ❶,** Emmet St., across from the Emmet Tavern. The excellent blackboard bagel and sandwich specials run €6-6.50. (☎86731. Open M-Sa 8am-6pm. MC/V.) The **An Troman Food Hall** ("tra-MANN") ❶ on Market St. sells baked goods, wines, and fine foods. They also sell interesting sandwiches for €5-6.50, such as the tuna and corn with lemongrass dressing. (☎83703. Open M-Sa 8:30am-6pm.) Cheerful **Bennini's ❷,** in the car park next to Trim Castle, is known for its creative salads and a number of healthy options which help those trying to stay trim. (☎31002. Sandwiches €5; lunch specials €11. Open M-F 9:30am-6pm, Sa-Su 10am-6pm. MC/V.) Next door, under the same ownership and with a bright-red color scheme, **Franzini O'Brien's ❸** boasts Trim's most eclectic menu, blending Italian, Asian, and Mexican culinary influences. (☎31002. Entrees €15-22. Open M-Sa 6:30-10pm, Su 5-9pm. AmEx/MC/V.) Overlooking the River Boyne on Bridge St., **Sally Rogers** matches its classy interior and impressive collection of single-malt whiskeys (only for show) with a peaceful waterside deck that puts most beer gardens to shame. (☎38926. Th-Sa band or DJ, Su karaoke. Open M-F 5-11:30pm, Sa-Su 1-11:30pm.) **Emmet Tavern,** Emmet St., to the left when facing the post office, has boisterous local customers and a popular pub lunch. (☎31378. W trad or ballads; F-Su DJ or a live band. Open M-Th 10:30am-11:30pm, F-Sa 10:30am-12:30am, Su 12:30-11pm.)

EASTERN IRELAND

◉ 🄰 **SIGHTS AND OUTDOOR ACTIVITIES.** ◪**Trim Castle,** built by Norman invader Hugh de Lacy in 1172 and now open to the public after a regal £3 million face-lift, presides over Trim. After the original wooden structure burned down, de Lacy built the towering stone keep seen today to which various defense elements have since been added. Tours of the castle detail these defenses and describe the area's role as a social hub during the Middle Ages, when the powerful and populous town supported seven monasteries. When Norman power collapsed, the castle lost nearly all its strategic importance and thus survived the centuries relatively untouched. It costs a little extra to see the keep, but the renovations inside are extraordinarily well done, and the views from the top are fabulous: the Hill of Tara is visible on a clear day. If the household doesn't inspire you, try to recognize the gate from the siege of York from *Braveheart*, which was filmed along the barbican gate, the only one of its kind in Ireland. (☎38619. Open Easter-Sept. daily 10am-6pm; Oct. daily 10am-5:30pm; Nov.-Easter Sa-Su 10am-5pm. First tour 10:30am, last tour 1hr. before closing. Admission to keep with 35-45min. guided tour only; tours generally leave on the hr. or on the ½hr., when enough people show up. Tour and grounds €3.70, students and children €1.30, seniors €2.60, families €8.70; grounds only €1.60/1.10/4.50.)

Across the river stand the remains of the 12th-century **Yellow Steeple,** a belltower named for its twilight gleam. The gleam, however, left with the lichen that were removed during restoration. Nonetheless, the crumbling tower is a stunning landmark that can be seen from almost anywhere in town. In its shadow, **Talbot's Castle,** adapted from the steeple's original abbey, was home to Jonathan Swift and later became a school attended by the undefeated Duke of Wellington. Though a private residence, it is funded by the government and open to the public during certain times of the year, and the owner will provide tours to groups on requests from June to July and September. (☎31213.) Walking from the Castle car park or making the first right before the bridge brings wanderers to the **Millennium Bridge,** which leads across the Boyne to the Yellow Steeple and **Sheep Gate,** the only surviving piece of the town's medieval walls. Ten minutes out on the Dublin road in the direction opposite the castle, shout your name at the reverberating ruins of St. Peter and St. Paul's Cathedral, across the river from Echo Gate and the ruined Hospital of St. John the Baptist. The cathedral grounds contain a tomb with two figures mistakenly called the Jealous Man and Woman. The sword between them conventionally signified chastity, not resentment.

BEYOND THE VALLEY OF THE BOYNE

KELLS (CEANANNAS MÓR)   ☎046

Kells, hailed by Columban monks as "The Splendor of Ireland," is best known for its religious significance but has lost the asceticism of monastic times—you'll find pubs on almost every street. In AD 559, St. Columcille (p. 59) founded a monastery here before continuing to Iona. At Iona, the monks began the famous **Book of Kells,** an elaborately decorated copy of the Gospels. It came to Kells when the Columbans fled Iona to escape the Vikings in 804. In 1007, the book was stolen, its gold cover ripped off and its pages buried in a bog. The book was rescued two months later and remained in Kells until 1661, when it was carted off to Trinity College where it now dwells.

🄲 🄿 **TRANSPORTATION AND PRACTICAL INFORMATION. Bus Éireann** runs from **Dublin** (1hr.; M-Sa 2-4 per hr., Su 15 per day; €10) and stops in front of Headfort Arms Hotel. Services include: 24hr. **ATMs** on John St. at **AIB** (☎924 0610; open M 10am-12:30pm and 1:30-5pm, Tu-F 10am-12:30pm and 1:30-4pm) and by Headfort at **Bank of Ireland** (☎924 0032; open M 10am-5pm, Tu and Th-F 10am-4pm, W 10:30am-4pm); free **Internet** access at the **library,** on Maudlin St. (☎924 1592; open Tu and Th 1:30-5pm and 6-8:30pm, W and F-Sa 10am-1pm   and   2-

5pm); **gas** at **Murphy's Service Station,** across from Headfort (☎924 0695; open M-F 6:30am-10pm, Sa 7am-9pm, Su 8am-9pm); the **post office,** on Farrel St. (☎924 0598; open M-F 9am-5:30pm, Sa 9am-1pm); the **police** *(Garda)* **station,** on Circular Rd. (☎924 0999; open 24hr.); up Carrick St., on Circular Rd., is **Grimes Pharmacy** (☎924 0950; open M-F 9am-6:30pm, Sa 9:30am-6pm); there's also a **Laundrette** on Farrel St. (☎087 957 6918. Open M-Sa 9am-6pm; €12-15.)

F ACCOMMODATIONS. Kells Hostel ❶, Carrick St., sports a renovated kitchen, back patio, blueprints of the area on the wall, and basic, spotless facilities. From the center of town, head uphill, bearing right, on Carrick St. When SuperValu is on your left, look right (beside Carrick House) for the big blue letters. (☎924 9995; www.kellshostel.com. Laundry €6. Reception 5-8pm. Access code needed afterhours. 6- to 8-bed dorms €15; private 2- to 4-bed rooms with baths €20 per person. Camping €8. MC/V.) B&Bs are closer to town but more expensive. Partway down a cul-de-sac across from the tourist office is **Avalon B&B ❸,** 5 Headfort Park, which offers homestyle luxury, including TVs and a lovely front yard. (☎924 1536. Singles €45; doubles €70. Cash only.) Directly across from the Heritage Center, the **Janetta B&B ❸,** 2 Headfort Rd., welcomes guests into a spacious, centrally located suburban home with ornate decorations. The six rooms all have TV, bath, and tea and coffee. (☎924 9678. Singles €45; doubles €70. Cash only.)

🖸 FOOD. SuperValu grocery store is on Circular Rd. across from the hostel. (☎924 0983. Open M-W and Sa 8am-7:30pm, Th-F 8am-9pm, Su 9am-6:30pm. MC/V.) **Pebbles ❶,** Newmarket St., is a popular coffee shop that serves inexpensive full Irish breakfasts (€6) and sandwiches (€3-4) on red checkered tablecloths. (☎924 9229. Open M-F 8am-5:30pm, Sa 8am-5pm. Cash only.) Order before taking a seat at **Owen's Deli and Cafe ❶,** Carrick St. Try the fantastically flavorful pesto and mozzarella *panini* (€5, €3.60 takeaway), or load up on bread, scones, and jams. (☎929 3458. Open M 9am-2pm, T-Th and Sa 9am-6pm, F 9am-8pm. Cash only.) Though an ocean away from Cuba, **Café Havana ❶,** on Kenli's Pl., serves a tasty Havana special wrap (€5.70), with ham, pineapple, and mozzarella. They've also got shepherd's pie (€5.45) for those whose taste buds don't want to stray so far from home. (☎924 7716. Open M-Sa 9am-5pm. Cash only.) With vegetarian-friendly delights, carnivorous fare, and sweet 70s funk, **The Ground Floor ❹,** Bective Sq., serves burgers (€14.50) and bangers and mash (€15) and is still endorsed by the Irish Heart Association. (☎924 9688. Entrees €15-22. Open M-Sa 5:30pm-late, Su 4pm-late. MC/V.) **Tower Grille ❶,** Farrell St., is the hot spot for takeaway grease: fried chicken, kebabs, burgers, and spring rolls run €3-6. Vegetarians can spend €2.60 to clog their arteries with a veggie burger. (☎469 2403. Open daily noon-1am.)

🅼🅺 PUBS AND CLUBS. Arches, Farrell St., on the left, is a classy, clean, well-lit pub with an art-deco fireplace. It hosts live alternative bands without a cover on Fridays. Just below it is the newest, slickest nightclub in town, **Kaktus,** owned by the same people who run Arches. (☎929 3866. Th ladies night with raffle. Bar open M-F and Su noon-11:30pm, Sa noon-12:30am. Club open F-Su 11:30pm-2:30am. Cover €8. MC/V.) Join the crowd at **The Chaser,** Cross St., where students play pool and dance to chart-toppers in an adjoining room. (Open M and Th afternoon-11:30pm, F-Sa 2pm-12:30am. Cash only.) **The Blackwater Inn,** Farrell St., has a dark interior with church-like stained-glass windows. It's anything but clerical when a one-man band plays trad on Wednesday. Enjoy a refreshing pint (€4) after a game of pool. (☎924 0386. Open M-Th noon-11:30pm, F-Sa noon-12:30am, Su noon-11pm. Cash only.) Weekend partygoers start at **The Kelltic Bar,** where DJs spin Th-Sa then move to the adjoining nightclub, the small and modern **Vibe,** where the music is a mix of pop and techno. Live rock bands call the place home on Sunday. (☎924

8300. F 80s night. Bar open M-W 4-11:30pm, Th-F 4pm-2am; club open F-Sa 12:30pm-2:30am, Su 12:30pm-2am. Cover €3. MC/V.)

⬛ SIGHTS. Kells is best known for being a center of Christian learning from the 9th to the 12th century. With Headfort behind, the outstanding **Heritage Center** is to the left, in the former courthouse between the fork in the road. A 15min. video details Kells' history, including numerous Viking raids, and visitors can examine a replica *Book of Kells*, with enlarged copies of selected pages. (☎924 7840. Open May-Sept. M-Sa 10am-5:30pm, Su and bank holidays 2-6pm; Oct.-Apr. M-Sa 10am-5pm. Last admission 45min. before closing. €4, students and seniors €3. Town walking tours €10 per person, minimum of 2 people.)

Most points of interest lie up the street from the Heritage Center. The grounds of **St. Columba's Church** on Church St. and Market St. host four **high crosses** covered with Biblical scenes. The western cross is little more than a stump, but the southern cross, with its instructional depictions of crucifix-making, remains intact. Go upstairs inside the church for detailed explanations of each drawing and for more information and photos. A 12th-century wall encircled the church until 1997, when the County Council decided to build a path alongside it that undermined its foundations and caused the walls to come tumbling down. The nearby 30m **round tower's** door is located halfway up the wall and was supposed to protect people and treasures from Viking raids, but it didn't succeed; its monks were torched, its books and saintly relics stolen, and would-be High King Murchadh Mac Flainn was murdered here in 1076. (☎929 3626. Church grounds open dawn to dusk. Church open M-F 10am-1pm and 2-5pm, Sa 10am-1pm, Su for services only at 11:30am.)

Time has been kinder to **St. Columcille's House,** across Church Ln., an awe-inspiring oratory where the *Book of Kells* may have been completed. Pick up the key from amiable retiree Mrs. Carpenter, who often escorts visitors up the hill (groups preferred). Visit her house, adorned with roses on the door and four green pillars in the front, to the right of the church at 10 Church View, or ask the Heritage Center to phone her, then head up 200m to the oratory. The place looks almost exactly as it would have in St. Columcille's day; the only difference is the current doorway, which now leads to the basement. Originally, the basement connected to the church by a secret tunnel. The daring can climb the extremely steep staircase and walk around the tiny attic (those over four feet tall must crouch).

Three kilometers down Oldcastle Rd., within People's Park, is the **Spire of Loyd,** a 50m mock lighthouse erected by the old Headfort landlords at the end of the 18th century. (☎924 7840. Tour through Heritage Center €10. Group bookings available for up to 10.) The first week of July is a popular time to visit for the **Kells Summer Festival,** which offers open tours of the Spire, along with food and dance.

COUNTY LOUTH

On its way between the lively capitals of Dublin and Belfast, N1 winds through Louth, a county filled with small towns, crumbling ruins, and soaring mountains. History buffs appreciate Drogheda, which lies 5km east of where William and James battled on the Boyne, and 8km south of Monasterboice and Mellifont Abbey. Dundalk is a convenient place to cross into the North and is also home to the Harp lager brewery. The hills and seacoasts of the Cooley Peninsula command the affections of hikers, bikers, and—in ancient times—bards.

TO ✚ (2km), MELLIFONT ABBEY (6.5km),
MONASTERBOICE (8km), BELFAST (96km).

Bothar Brugha

North Rd.

Hardman's Gdns.

Drogheda

🏠 ACCOMMODATIONS
Abbey Lodge B&B, **2**
Green Door Hostel, **17**
Green Door Lodge, **16**
Harpur Lodge, **4**
Roseville Lodge B&B, **1**

🍴 FOOD
Garam Masala, **13**
La Pizzeria, **9**
The Mariner, **14**

Monk's, **15**
Moorland Cafe, **10**

🍺⭐ PUBS AND CLUBS
c. ni carbre, **7**
Earth, **11**
Fusion, **3**
McHugh's, **5**
Peter Matthews, **8**
Sarsfield's, **6**
Storm, **12**

Patrick St.

Magdalen Tower

Upper Magdalene St.

Rope Walk

BOLTON SQ.   Green Lanes

Market

TO OLDBRIDGE (5km)

Trinity St.

Narrow West St.

Fair St.

St. Peter's R.C. Church

Permanent TSB Bank

Tesco

West St.

Droichead Arts Centre

Stockwell Ln.

Hickey's Pharmacy

Dunnes Stores

Wellington Quay

Dyer St.

Rathmullen Rd.

AIB Bank

St. Mary's Bridge

South Quay

James St.

John St.

Donore Rd.

Barrack St.

Millmount Museum

Mount St. Oliver

Derek St.

Mary St.

St. Mary's Church of Ireland

Georges St.

Dominick St.

Mill Ln.

St. Peter's Church of Ireland

William St.

King St.

Francis St.

Palace St.

St. Peter's St.

TAXI

St. Laurence St.

Bachelors Ln.

Shop St.

Quay Cycles

North Quay

St. Lawrence's Gate

Constitution Hill

Cord Rd.

North Strand

Merchants Quay

River Boyne

The Mall

Dublin Rd.

Marsh Rd.

TO 🚂 (1.6km)

0   200 meters
0   200 yards

DROGHEDA (DROICHEAD ÁTHA)   ☎ 041

An up-and-coming tourist hot spot, this growing town is still small enough to be
easily navigable by foot. Drogheda (DRAW-head-ah) is a convenient starting point
from which to visit Newgrange, Dowth, and Knowth, as well as Monasterboice,
Mellifont, and Slane. Authentic Irish pubs and an active art and nightclub scene
mix with religious and historic landmarks.

▮ TRANSPORTATION

Trains: Station (☎983 8749) on the Dublin road east of town. Follow John St. south of
the river. To: **Belfast** (2hr.; M-Sa 7 per day every 2hr., Su 4 per day; €41) and **Dublin**
(1hr., express 30min.; M-Sa 16 per day, Su 14 per day, every hr; €13).

Buses: ☎983 5023. Station on John St. at Donore Rd. Inquiries desk open daily 7am-6pm. To:
Athlone (2½hr.; 1 per day, 11:13am; €16.50); **Belfast** (1½hr.; 9 per day, every 2-3hr.; €14,
students €12.50); **Dublin** (1¼hr.; daily every hr.; €5); **Galway** (4½hr.; 11:13; €19, students
€15.50.); **Mullingar** (1½hr.; 2 per day, Su 1 per day; €14, students €11.30).

Bike Rental: Quay Cycles, 11 North Quay (☎983 4526). €14 per 24hr.; ID deposit
required. Open M-Sa 9am-6pm, Su 2-6pm. AmEx/MC/V.

⚡ PRACTICAL INFORMATION

Tourist Office: Located on Mayorally St., the brand-new office is a great starting point for exploring the sights of Drogheda and the surrounding areas. A walking tour leaves from Millmount Museum daily at 2pm. Complete the walk solo with the guidance of the "Drogheda Heritage Route" pamphlet, free at the tourist office. The office also offers hop-on/hop-off bus tours of Drogheda, Mellifont Abbey, Monasterboice, and Newgrange. (☎983 7070; www.drogheda.ie. Open M-F 9:30am-1pm and 2-5pm. Bus tours leave from tourist center daily at 9am and noon; €15, students €12. Walking tours by appointment only; ☎983 3097. €5, students €4, children and seniors €3.)

Banks: Cross St. Mary's Bridge and take the 2nd left to find numerous banks lining West St., including **Permanent TSB** (☎983 8703; open M-F 10am-5pm, W opens 10:30am.) Both **TSB** and **AIB** on Dyer St., parallel to West. St. toward the river (☎983 6523; open M 10am-5pm, Tu and Th-F 10am-4pm, W 10:30am-4pm) have 24hr. **ATMs.**

Emergency: ☎999; no coins required. **Police** *(Garda)*: West Gate (☎987 4200. Open 24hr.).

Pharmacy: Hickey's, West St. (☎983 8650). Open M-F 9am-9pm, Su 10:30am-6:30pm.

Hospital: Our Lady of Lourdes, Cross Lanes (☎983 7601).

Internet: On Stockwell Ln. find free Internet access at the **library** (☎983 6649; open Tu and Th 10am-5pm and 6-8pm, W and F-Sa 10am-5pm). For cheaper rates, try **Zenith Systems** on 34 James St., by the Green Door Hostel. (☎987 4439; open daily 10am-10pm; €1 per hr.)

Post Office: West St. (☎983 8157). Open M-F 9am-5:30pm, Sa 9am-1pm.

⌂ ACCOMMODATIONS

■ **Green Door Hostel,** 13 Dublin Rd. (☎983 4422; www.greendoorireland.com). Sunny, comfortable, and clean dorms with spotless baths more than compensate for the small kitchen and common area. Young, friendly staff with lots of nightlife knowledge and a love for American movies. Laundry wash €3.00, dry €3.50. Breakfast included. Reception 9am-9pm. 10-bed dorms €18. MC/V. ❷

Harpur Lodge (IHO), Platin Rd. (☎983 2736; www.harpurlodge.ie). Take Shop St. from the bridge uphill, head up Peter St. and turn right onto William St.; the B&B is the last house on right. Drogheda's older—though equally comfortable—B&B. Small kitchen. Full Irish breakfast €5. 3-bed dorms €20; private rooms ensuite €30. Cash only. ❷

Green Door Lodge, 47 John St. (☎983 4422), owned by the same folks as the Hostel. Reception at 13 Dublin Rd. Clean, colorful rooms with bath (some with tubs) and TV. Singles €40-45; doubles €56-64. MC/V. ❹

Abbey Lodge B&B, 72 Georges St. (☎086 854 7657). A friendly B&B not far from the center of town. All rooms ensuite with TV. Singles €35, €45 with breakfast. Doubles €60/75. Cash only. ❸

Roseville Lodge B&B, Georges St. (☎983 4046). Seven luxurious rooms, all ensuite; some include bathtubs. Singles €50, doubles €70. Cash only. ❹

◖ FOOD

An **open-air market** selling produce and meats has been held in Bolton Sq. every Saturday since 1317, while the newer **Dunnes Stores** (☎983 7063. Open M-Tu and Sa 8:30am-7:30pm, W-F 8:30am-9pm, Su 10am-7:30pm) and **Tesco** (☎983 7209. Open M-Sa 8am-10pm, Su 10am-6pm), West St., sell groceries all week.

■ **Monk's,** 1 North Quay (☎984 5630). Couches line the walls of Monk's, where cuddling couples snuggle over brunch and the rest of us order another coffee. Try a veggie wrap (€4) or one of the many breakfast options, such as the heavenly french toast (€4). The delicious monk's power breakfast (€6.50) is so good it's almost holy. Open daily 8:30am-6:15pm. MC/V. ❶

La Pizzeria, 38 Peter St. (☎983 4208). Garlic hangs from the ceilings of this romantic yet bustling Italian restaurant. Very popular with locals; call after 4pm to make reservations. Pasta and pizza €9-10. Open M-Tu and Th-Su 6-11pm. MC/V. ❷

Moorland Cafe, 96/97 West St. (☎983 3951). It looks a bit like a cafeteria, but don't be dismayed—the food, like the brie, ham, and relish wrap (€6.30) and daily home-made soups (€4), is anything but ordinary. Sandwiches on fresh bread with any three fillings €4. Open M-Sa 9am-6pm. Cash only. ❶

The Mariner, 6 North Quay (☎983 7401). Primarily a pub, The Mariner serves cheap seafood from the banks of the river. Try it fried, poached, grilled, or any other way imaginable. Cod €8, salads €6.50-7. Kitchen open daily 9:30am-4:30pm. MC/V. ❷

Garam Masala, 10 Stockwell St. (☎980 3862). If you're tired of pub grub, spice up your palate with some tasty Indian food—try tandoori tikka masala (€9.45) or aloo gobii (€5). Prices slightly higher during dinner. Open M-Sa noon-3pm and 5-11:30pm, Su 1-4pm and 5-11pm. AmEx/MC/V. ❷

▼ PUBS

As the largest town in the area, Drogheda has an active, expansive nightlife scene. Venues stay open slightly longer on Friday and Saturday nights and in the summer, but in general, assume that pubs close by midnight; expect to be kicked out by 12:30am.

▨ Peter Matthews, 9 Laurence St. (☎983 7371). Head to the back of the pub for a summer beer garden or check out one of the many nooks and crannies indoors. Very popular with locals. Live alternative/indie music M and Th-Su; cover €3. Pint €4. Open daily 2pm-2am. Cash only.

c. ni carbre's, 11 North Strand. The 2 sisters who run this pub open and close it when they feel like it. Open daily around 8:30pm. Cash only. Don't try to call—they can't be bothered by a phone. Small, dark interior whose ceilings and walls are still plastered with original posters from the 50s. Great trad sessions Tu and acoustic blues/bluegrass some Su. Pint €4.

McHugh's, 1-2 Cord Rd. (☎983 5995). Stationed at the edge of Cord Rd. Home to many of Drogheda's musicians, McHugh's offers live rock, pop, and jazz Th-Su. To keep visitors on their toes, they also have an 80s club night. Cover €4-15. Open M-Th and Su noon-11:30pm, F-Sa noon-12:30am. MC/V.

Sarsfield's, Lawrence Gate (☎983 8032). Across the street from McHugh's. TVs and Louth county flags adorn the dark wood walls of this manly man's pub. Beer garden out back. Su trad. Open M-Sa 10:30am-12:30am, Su 12:30-11pm. MC/V.

◖ CLUBS

After the pubs close around midnight, Drogheda's clubs start rocking.

Earth, Stockwell Ln. (☎984 7070), in back of Westcourt Hotel. Plays a mix of hip-hop, chart-toppers, and dance music to a 20s-30s crowd. Dress code strictly enforced—leave your sneakers at home. Beers €5, cocktails €9. Cover Th-F €10, Sa €12, Su €9. 21+. Open Th-Su 11:30pm-3am.

Storm, 4 Stockwell Ln. (☎987 5170), across from Earth. Futuristic neon lighting helps clubbers see one another in a new light. Plays Top 40 hits to a 20s crowd. Cover M, Th, Su €6; F €10; Sa €12. Beer €4. 21+. Open M and Th-Su 11:30pm-2:30am. Cash only.

Fusion, 12 Georges St. (☎983 0088). Funky alternative/indie music and decor with attached beer garden. Draws the pub crowd after midnight. Cover Th €5, F €8, Sa-Su €10. Vodka and Red Bull €7.40. Open Th-Su 11:30pm-3am. Cash only.

EASTERN IRELAND

👁 SIGHTS

ST. PETER'S CHURCHES. Drogheda has two St. Peter's Churches, and both have an undeniably morbid feel. The imposing, neo-Gothic **St. Peter's Church on West Street,** built in the 1880s, safeguards what's left of the sainted martyr Oliver Plunkett. Visitors can come face-to-face with his blackened, shriveled head. A handful of his bones is on display, as is the door of his London prison cell. *(Open daily 8:30am-8:30pm. Free.)* The other **St. Peter's Church (Church of Ireland)** conjures bad luck at the top of Peter St. The tower of the original timber structure was destroyed in a 1548 storm. Another wooden structure was built to replace it, only to be torched (with refugees inside) by Cromwell. The present church was built in 1751 and is being renovated after falling victim to another, more recent, fire. Mounted on the wall of the cemetery's far left corner are cadaver tombs, with brutally realistic carvings of the half-decayed bodies of a man and woman. *(Free.)*

DROICHEAD ARTS CENTRE. With artwork lining the stairway, the Arts Centre on Stockwell St. offers an alternative to ancient ruins and religious artifacts. The gallery has monthly art exhibits, and the theater puts on amateur and professional music, dance, and drama presentations. *(Shows €15-20, workshops €8.) The center also hosts creative classes year-round and a town-wide Samba festival in late June. (☎983 3946; www.droicheadartscentre.com. Open daily 10am-5pm. Free.)*

MILLMOUNT MUSEUM. Reputed to be the burial place of the old Celtic poet Amergin, Millmount was guarded by the Normans, defended against Cromwell and the free state army, used by the British for a Martello lookout tower (see Martello Tower, p. 53), and captured by the IRA during the Civil War. Visitors can now take advantage of its height to obtain a great view of the town and surrounding hills from the tower. In the nearby Millmount Museum, check out the only three Norman guild banners left in Ireland, as well as local artifacts, including surprisingly well-preserved 230-year-old butter. *(☎983 3097. Open M-Sa 10:30am-5pm, Su 2:30-6pm. Admission to museum and tower by 1hr. tour; €5.50, students €4, children/seniors €3.)*

BATTLE OF THE BOYNE. The Battle of the Boyne raged at **Oldbridge,** 5km west of Drogheda on Slane Rd. In 1690, Protestant William of Orange's victory over James II secured the English Crown and far more than the half of Ireland (see **The Ascendancy,** p. 52). For the slightly more ambitious traveler, a brisk 45min. walk brings you to the **Obelisk Centre** (located in a small trailer), which offers visitors a view of the battle site. *(Head 2.5km down Slane Rd. to the Obelisk Bridge; the Centre is on the right. ☎988 4343. Open June-late Aug., daily 9:30am-5:30pm. Free.)* The **Battle of the Boyne Oldbridge Estate Center** offers an informative 30min. tour recreating the battle on the old battlefield. On Sundays from June-Sept. it hosts a living history program, complete with cannons and live cavalry. *(3.2km north of Donore Village, on the right. ☎980 9950; www.battleoftheboyne.ie. Open daily 10am-6pm. Free.)*

OTHER SIGHTS. At the end of West St. are the four-story towers of 13th-century **St. Laurence's Gate.** At the top of the hill, on Peter St., the 14th-century **Magdalen Tower** is all that remains of the Dominican Friary that once stood on the spot. The tower was damaged in Cromwell's attack in 1649. The largest remaining segment of the Norman wall which used to enclose the entire village can be found in front of St. Mary's Church of Ireland on Mary's St. behind the Martello tower. Cheery **Harry Hall** offers daytrip tours to neighboring towns accessible from Drogheda in his **hackney** service (☎0866 71608; www.harryhall.org. 3 hr tour €12.).

📑 DAYTRIPS FROM DROGHEDA

MONASTERBOICE AND MELLIFONT ABBEY

Both ruins are signposted off the Drogheda-Collon Rd. (R168). Motorists and cyclists head 8km north on N1 until the Dunleer exit. At the bottom of the ramp, turn left and fol-

low the Monasterboice signs. From Monasterboice, continue following the road until turning right where it connects with main Drogheda-Collon Rd. Take the 2nd street on the right to Mellifont Abbey. About 5km separate the two sites. By taxi—settle the price at the start—the trip should cost no more than €20. To reach Mellifont Abbey by bus, take #182 (€1.75), which leaves 5 times a day, to Ardee; it's a 1m walk from the station to the abbey. To reach Monasterboice, take bus #100 (€2.25) 10min. up the road. Monasterboice Information Office is open July-Aug. M-Sa 10am-6pm; the site is always open. Mellifont Abbey Information Office (☎ 982 6459. Open May-Sept. daily 10am-5:15pm) offers tours on demand for €2.10, students €1.10, seniors €1.30. The site is free after hours.

What were once two of the most important monasteries in Ireland now stand crumbling 8km north of Drogheda. The grounds of **Monasterboice** (MON-uh-ster-boyce) include a round tower and some of the most detailed high crosses in existence. The crosses, which date from the 10th century, are widely believed to have acted as durable visual storybooks to spell out Biblical history for the illiterate masses. **Muireadach's Cross,** the first visible ruin upon entering the grounds, is considered one of the most typical examples of its kind in the country. It's certainly jam-packed with biblical highlights, spotlighting the Crucifixion and the Last Judgment while cramming in an all-star cast including Adam, Eve, Cain, Abel, Satan, and the Savior himself, all on a mere (yet still impressive) 5.5m of stone. On one end, Satan pulls down his side of the Judgment scales and herds 14 souls to Hell. At a height of nearly 6m, the **West Cross** is the tallest cross in Ireland, covered from head to toe with wonderfully intricate work. The **North Cross** is relatively undecorated compared to its showy brethren, but it includes an ancient sundial. Not very much is known about the original abbey, since the round tower which purportedly served as treasury and belfry caught fire in 1097 with all the abbey books and annals inside. Still, an **information office** is on site, from which volunteers offer impromptu tours and information on the crosses in the summer months.

Monasterboice stayed active until 1142, when the Cistercians planted their first foothold in Ireland a few kilometers away. **Mellifont Abbey** quickly grew to be a wealthy and powerful organization—by the time it was dissolved in 1539, it was the second most valuable Cistercian house in the country. What's left of the Abbey is mostly fragments, and it takes a good deal of creativity to envision what the original structure must have looked like. The ornate Romanesque **lavabo** (wash basin) and the decorated **chapter house** were the two places that allowed luxurious architecture in the otherwise simple Abbey. The vow of silence is not imposed upon visitors, who are welcome to chat as they explore the site on their own or with the help of a guide. The **Visitors Centre** houses a small exhibition of mostly building fragments, provides a hand-drawn map of the surrounding area, and leads excellent tours that help visitors visualize life in the abbey.

THE HILL OF SLANE AND SLANE CASTLE

To get to Slane, take bus #188 from Drogheda (€3.60, M-Sa 6 per day), or bus #32 or 33 to Letterkenny from Dublin (1 every 2hr.). Entrance to Hill of Slane is free. Admission to Slane Castle (☎ 988 4400; www.slanecastle.ie) by 30min. tour only. Open May-Aug. M-Th and Su noon-5pm. €7, students and seniors €5, families €20. For info and tickets to Slane Concert, visit www.ticketmaster.ie. Concert takes place on the last Sa in Aug. Tickets average €80.

In the year 433, the famed St. Patrick lit the first paschal fire on the **Hill of Slane,** defying the druid king Laoghaire. Luckily, some intense prayer got St. Patrick off the hook (see **St. Patrick,** p. 59) and out of trouble. Though Laoghaire remained a pagan, he allowed his subjects to convert to Christianity. The rest is history. Buses drive into town, unless the driver agrees to stop next to the hill. Take a left at the town intersection and walk up the road until the hill and tower are visible on the left. Explorers can ramble among the ancient stone spiral staircases in the ruins but should watch out for the errant cow. Less than 16km away is **Newgrange,** whose white-rimmed, grass-covered mound can be seen in front of the left edge of the distant Wicklow mountains.

EASTERN IRELAND

Coming from the hill, you'll see the four nearly identical **Georgian houses** on each corner of the central intersection, which at one time housed all the major figures in the town: the priest, the police, the doctor, and the judge. Head left on N51 for about 10 min. to find the tiny four-room cottage that was once the home of poet Francis Ledwidge and his eight siblings. A small exhibit and a quiet, shady back garden comprise the **Francis Ledwidge Museum.** (☎982 4544; ledwidgemuseum@eircom.net. Open daily 10am-1pm and 2-5:30pm. €2.50, students and seniors €1.50.)

One kilometer outside of town on N51 is **Slane Castle,** reopened to the public in 2001 after renovations following a tragic fire ten years earlier (in an uncanny coincidence, U2 recorded "Unforgettable Fire" in the castle's dining room years before the blaze). Completed in 1785, the castle is a spectacular example of Gothic Revival architecture. However, the site has seen better days: though it's been refurbished since the fire, most of the antiques and paintings were destroyed. Now it's mainly used for corporate gatherings and weddings. Each August, the castle opens its doors to the likes of U2, Madonna, and the Rolling Stones for the annual **Slane Concert.** The concert is one of Ireland's most popular, drawing crowds of over 80,000 fans. Tickets usually go on sale in March or April and sell out at the beginning of summer. Only wedding parties and corporate events can book space and accommodations in the castle. At ■ **Slane Farm Hostel ❷,** Paddy Macken welcomes music lovers and others into spacious, comfortable dorm rooms, as well as a modern kitchen and game room with darts, a DVD player, and beanbag chairs. Guests wake up to the sound of sheep bleating in the back field. The hostel is on R163, the road directly across from the entrance to Slane Castle on the right. (☎982 4390; www.slanefarmhostel.ie. Laundry €8. Dorms €18; singles €35, doubles €50; **camping** €8. Free wireless. Reservations recommended. AmEx/MC/V.) A sweet-smelling rose garden complements a cheery blue and yellow interior at **The Fáilte B&B ❸,** 6 Castle Hill Rd., halfway between the Castle and the town center of N51. All rooms are private with ensuite bathrooms and TV. (☎086 398 4260. Singles or doubles €35. Cash only.) There's no postage necessary at **The Old Post Office ❷,** Main St., which serves beef and Guinness stew (€9.50), vegetarian wraps (€5), and chicken and goat cheese sandwiches (€7.75), a special favorite. (☎982 3090. Open daily 9am-5pm, Tu-Sa also 6:30-9:30pm. MC/V.) For fresh-baked bread and mouth-watering cakes, head to **George's Patisserie & Delicatessen ❶,** on Chapel St. Try the ham sandwich (€4.50) and soup (€4), or pick up cheese, olives, and delicious soda bread from the deli to put together your own feast. (☎982 4493. Open Tu-Sa 9am-6pm. Cash only.) The **police** *(Garda)* is on N51 on the way out of town (☎982 4202; always open). Internet access is free at the public **library** on Castle St. off N51 (☎046 982 4955; open T and Th 2-5:30pm and 6:30-8:30pm, W and F-Sa 10:30am-1:30pm). The **post office** is inside Mimnagh's on Main St. (☎982 4218; open M-F 9am-1pm and 2-5:30pm, Sa 9am-1pm.)

DUNDALK TOWN (DÚN DEALGAN)   ☎042

Dundalk, home of the Harp Brewery and Celtic folk group, The Corrs, sits at the mouth of Dundalk Bay, halfway between Dublin and Belfast. Though it tries to associate itself with mythic Cooley Peninsula, the congested criss-crossing streets may disappoint visitors expecting a rustic escape from the congestion of other east-coast cities. Unfortunately, the brewery is closed to the public, but Harp flows freely every night at Dundalk's 141 pubs. Dundalk has long been a republican stronghold; one neighborhood is even nicknamed "Little Belfast." Pedestrians should be cautious walking after dark, as Dundalk's streets are unsafe at night. Dundalk is also becoming a major destination for greyhound-racing fans; Ireland's first all-weather race track has opened just north of town (see **Sights,** p. 178).

🚍 **TRANSPORTATION.** N1 zips south to **Dublin** and north to **Belfast,** turning into A1 at the border. The **train station** (☎933 5521; open daily 5:15am-5:45pm) is on Carrickmacross Rd. From Clanbrassil St., turn right on Park St., then right again on Anne St., which becomes Carrickmacross across the roundabout. Service to: **Belfast** (1hr.; M-F 8 per day, Sa 7 per day, Su 4 per day; €17.50, children €8.50), **Dublin** (1¼hr.; M-Sa 7 per day, Su 4 per day; €18.50/9); and **Newry** (20min.; M-F 8 per day, Sa 7 per day, Su 4 per day; €8/4). **Buses** stop at the **Bus Éireann station** (☎933 4075; open daily 8:30am-12:30pm and 1-6:10pm), on Long Walk, and go to: **Belfast** (1¼hr.; 10 per day; €12, children €7.50) via **Newry** (20 min., 10 per day, €4.30/2.80) and **Dublin** (1½hr.; 9 per day; €7, 6am-6pm €5). **A1 Cabs,** 9 Crowe St. (☎932 6666), runs cabs day and night. There is a taxi stand on Crowe St.

🗺📠 **ORIENTATION AND PRACTICAL INFORMATION.** Dundalk's main street is **Clanbrassil Street; Park Street** is its busiest. The street names change often. Clanbrassil enters **Market Square** as it moves south past the post office and courthouse and becomes **Earl Street** before intersecting **Park Street,** which becomes Dublin St. to the right. Left of this intersection, Park turns into **Francis Street,** then **Roden Place,** then **Jocelyn Street** as it moves east toward the waterfront. Grab free maps and brochures detailing the city's sights from the **tourist office;** they also book accommodations for €4 plus a 10% deposit. From the bus stop, walk down Long Walk, turn right onto Crowe St., passing the main square on the left. Continue until the road becomes Jocelyn St.; the office is on the right past the cathedral. (☎933 5484; www.ecoast-midlands.travel.ie. Open June-Aug. M and W-F 9am-6pm, Tu and Sa 9:30am-1pm and 2-5:15pm; Sept.-May M-F 9:30am-1pm and 2-5:30pm.) **Ulster Bank, AIB,** and **Bank of Ireland,** all on Clanbrassil St., have 24hr. **ATMs.** (All open M 10am-5pm and Tu-F 10am-4pm; AIB and Bank of Ireland open W 10:30am.) Prescriptions can be filled at **Smyth's Pharmacy,** 86 Clanbrassil St., at the corner with Bachelor's Walk. (☎27766. Open M-Sa 9am-6pm.) **Tommy the Bike's Outdoor World,** 11 Earl St., past the courthouse, sells **camping equipment.** (☎933 3399. Open M-Sa 9am-6pm.) **Datastore,** 58 Dublin St., provides **Internet** access, a scanner, a printer, and a **fax** machine. (☎31579. Internet access €1 per 5min., €2 per 11-59min., €3 per hr. Fax €1.50 for the first page and €0.50 per page thereafter to Ireland and Northern Ireland; €2.50/1 to the rest of Europe. Open M-Sa 9:30am-7pm.) The **post office** is located at 2 Clanbrassil St. (☎933 4444. Open M and W-F 9am-5:30pm, Tu 9:30am-5:30pm; Sa 9am-1pm; first Tu of the month open 9am.) The **police** station is across the street from the train station, at The Crescent.

🏠 **ACCOMMODATIONS.** Dundalk's B&B options are extensive, but most are outside the town center. If not traveling by car, ask carefully about locations. **Glengat House ❸,** 18-19 The Crescent, a left off Anne St. before the train station, has comfy rooms and an oddball collection of antiques and curiosities in the foyer. (☎933 7938; www.glengathouse.com. 1st fl. wheelchair-accessible bathrooms. Internet access. All rooms with bath. Singles €50; doubles €80. MC/V.) In town, **Oriel House ❷,** 63 Dublin St., is convenient and inexpensive, and provides basic rooms. (☎933 1347. Singles €30; doubles €50; triples €75.) For those with cars, **Krakow ❸,** 190 Ard Easmuinn, signposted from the train station, is a good but distant option, complete with TVs, hair dryers, and tidy rooms in a modern bungalow. A pedestrian shortcut goes to the city center, but taking it after dark can be dangerous. (☎933 7535. Singles €45; doubles €65.) Across from the shopping center on Dublin St., make a right to get to **Lismar B&B ❹,** 8 Stapleton Pl., which has a large number of motel-style rooms; the free Internet access is an extra perk. (☎57246; lismar@aol.ie. Singles €50; doubles €40.)

▣ ▨ FOOD AND PUBS. Groceries can be bought at the large **Tesco** in the Long Walk Shopping Centre next to the bus station. (☎27277. Open M-Tu 8:30am-7pm, W 8:30am-8pm, Th-F 8:30am-10pm, Sa 8:30am-7pm, Su 10am-6pm.) At the museum on Saturday mornings, the **Farmers' Market** sells fresh local produce. Restaurants and late-night fast-food joints clutter the main streets of town. **La Cantina ❷,** 1 River Ln., a left off Park St. at the Imperial Hotel heading away from the water, is a local favorite for affordable Italian. (☎932 7970. Pizza and pasta €10-15. Open Tu-Sa 6-10:30pm, Su 6-10pm.) **Deli Lites ❶,** with its two locations at 20 Clanbrassil St. and on Park St. across from the parking lot, is a colorful cafe with a wide range of sandwiches, wraps, and melts (€3.30-4.50) to satisfy the lunchtime crowds. The menu will please travelers who don't fear an impending coronary with a full fry breakfast for €6. (Clanbrassil St. ☎932 9555, Park St. ☎54385. Clanbrassil St. open M-Sa 8:30am-6pm; Park St. open M-Sa 8:30am-4pm.) The refined **Windsor Bar ❹,** 36-37 Dublin St., across the street and one block out from Oriel House, serves a reasonably priced bar menu by day (specials €9.50) and a more expensive a la carte seafood menu by night. (☎933 8146; windsorbar@eircom.ie. Sandwiches €5.50; dinner from €13. Bar menu daily 10:30am-6pm; kitchen open 6-10pm. Bar open M-Th 10:30am-11:30pm, F-Sa 10:30am-midnight, Su 10:30am-11pm.) The flavorful dishes (€10-12.50) at **Punjab Curry House ❸,** 79 Dublin St., across from the Ford dealership, are not necessarily cheap, but the €32.50 set menu for two is a solid deal. (☎938 6711. Takeaway available. Open daily 5-11pm.)

With 141 pubs lining the streets, Dundalk has a ready pint at every turn. The interior of **Courtney's,** 49 Park St., resembles a Gothic church, though the prevailing theme is more death by football. Locals pile in for Sunday evening live rock and blues performances. (☎932 6652. Open M-Th 3-11:30pm, F 3pm-12:30am, Sa noon-12:30am, Su noon-11:30pm.) **The Spirit Store,** located at Georges Quay on the waterfront, is worth the €8 cab ride down Jocelyn St. There is frequently live music upstairs (cover €5-45; the more expensive ones are ticketed events, so call ahead or visit the website), hosting trad and alternative rock. International beers from local Harp to Belgian cherry beer to Zimbabwe's finest brew draw crowds from ages 18 to 80. Sunday brings weekly trad sessions and the **Spot on Comedy Club** is hosted about once per month. (☎29649; www.spiritstore.ie. Comedy club cover €12-15; visit website for schedule.)

◪ SIGHTS. Grab the tourist office's free brochure on the Dundalk Heritage Trail, a pictorial map detailing the town's historical sights. Gothic **St. Patrick's Cathedral,** Francis St., was modeled after King's College Chapel in Cambridge and rescaled to Dundalk's more modest skyline. (☎933 4648. Open daily 7:30am-6pm.) Next to the tourist office, the award-winning **County Museum,** Jocelyn St., is a cut above average, which is probably why you have to pay for it. The multimedia exhibits tell the story of County Louth from the Bronze Age. Even those short on time and money can wander into the foyer to see the museum's best exhibit: the **Heinkel Bubble Car.** This was the only car manufactured in the Republic by the German Heinkel company, famous for building many planes for the Luftwaffe during WWII. The car looks like a cockpit on wheels. (☎932 7056. Open Tu-Sa 10:30am-5:30pm, Su 2-6pm. €3.80, students and seniors €2.50, children €1.20, families €10.15.) Past the far northwest corner of town, about 5km out on Castletown Rd. (N51), and a left after St. Louis Secondary School, the 12th-century **Cúchulainn's Castle** is said to stand on the birthplace of the Ulster Cycle's famous hero. The seven-story **Seatown Windmill,** on Seatown Pl., was once the largest in Ireland, but it lost its clout when it was removed in 1890. (Castle and Windmill always open and free, as are many of the Heritage Trail sights. Contact the tourist office for more information.) On sunny days, nice beaches and restaurants beckon from

Blackrock, 5km south on R172. Just finished in the summer of 2007, the **Dundalk Stadium** is home to Ireland's only all-weather greyhound track. Take N1 toward Newry; the stadium is signposted (and quite visible) from the road just past the roundabout. Without a car, you'll need to call a cab. (☎34438; www.igb.ie.)

COOLEY PENINSULA

The numerous trails in the mountains surrounding the Cooley Peninsula are a hiker's paradise: the Táin Trail traverses the mountains with ideal paths for bikers, and Carlingford Lough has the warmest waters in the northern half of Ireland, though some locals still claim they are cursed. Several ancient Irish myths are set in this dramatic landscape, including the epic *Táin Bó Cuailnge*, "The Cattle Raid of Cooley," one of the oldest stories in any European language. Remarkably well-preserved remnants of medieval settlements are scattered across the peninsula.

CARLINGFORD (CARLINN)   ☎042

The earthy scent of the mountains mingles with the salty breeze rising off the lough in the quiet village of Carlingford. Overlooking the water in the shadow of Slieve Foy, the nearest and highest of the Cooley Mountains, the attractive town incorporates medieval ruins and cobbled streets to stunning effect. Many rewarding hikes begin in Carlingford, but many visitors seem content to wander the charming streets, relax in quiet cafes and B&Bs, and enjoy the stunning views across the water to the Mourne Mountains.

🖪🚹 **TRANSPORTATION AND PRACTICAL INFORMATION. Buses** (☎933 4075) stop at the waterfront en route to **Dundalk** (40min., M-Sa 5 per day) and **Newry** (20-30min., M-Sa 4 per day). For **taxis,** call **Gally Cabs** (☎937 3777). The **tourist office** is by the bus stop and books accommodations for €2. They also have copies of the *Heritage Town Trail*, which points out historical sights in town. (☎937 3033; www.carlingford.ie. Open Mar.-Oct. daily 10am-5pm; Nov.-Feb. M and W-Su 10am-5pm.) While there is no bank branch in town, **AIB** has a 24hr. **ATM** on Newry St., next to O'Hare's. Those with outdoors experience may find **work opportunities** at the **Carlingford Adventure Centre.** A minimum two-month stay is requested; call ☎937 3100 for more info. There is a **police** station on Newry St., next door to Belvedere House. **Murphy's Laundry** (☎83891; open M-Sa 9am-6pm; €14 per load) is next to the **post office,** in Trinity Gifts on Dundalk St. (☎937 3171. Open M-F 9am-1pm and 2-5:30pm, Sa 9am-1pm.)

🛏 **ACCOMMODATIONS.** The **Foy Centre ❷,** just off Dundalk St., is a community center that also has 32 hostel-style beds. (☎83624; info@carlingfordbeds.com. Dorms €23; ensuite private doubles €50.) On Tholsel St., one block inland toward the ruins of King John's Castle and left into town, **Carlingford Adventure Centre and Hostel (IHH) ❷** provides small dorms on the first floor, nicer rooms with bath on the second, and private rooms detached from the busy adventure center. The adventure center offers over 20 land- and water-based activities (from €49 per ½-day, children from €44), and the hostel is often filled with school groups, so book ahead. (☎937 3100; www.carlingfordadventure.com. Internet access €1 per 15min. Open Feb.-Nov., year-round for groups. Dorms €26; singles €35, with bath €40; ensuite doubles €60. AmEx/MC/V.) Carlingford has many posh and pricey B&Bs; most outside the village center advertise lake views. By far the best value is the welcoming **Shalom B&B ❸,** Ghan Rd., a short drive or reasonable walk from the waterfront. Tasteful decorations, free chocolate in every room, a 2nd fl. dining room with great views, and free Internet access make this an unbeatable option. (☎937 3151; www.jackiewoods.com. All rooms with bath. Singles €45; doubles €70; 4-person apartments €110.) In the center of town, **Belvedere House ❹** on Newry St., a right at the ruins of King John's Castle, has themed rooms all related to the legend of Cúchulainn. Rejoice in ensuite double-powered showers. The reception is next door in the owner's restaurant, Bay Tree. (☎937 3731; www.belvederehouse.ie. Free Internet access. Singles M-Th and Su €40, F-Sa €50; doubles €60/70. AmEx/MC/V.) Around the bend from Shalom on Ghan Rd., **Beaufort House ❹** is Carlingford's award-winning guesthouse with large, elegant rooms. (☎937 3879; www.beauforthouse.net. Rooms €45-60 per person. MC/V.) Above **Saints & Sinners** pub on Newry St., the owners offer accommodations, though the sinners at the town's hottest spot may keep you from using your paid-for bed. (☎087 256 3025. Rooms €35 per person, with breakfast €40.)

◪▨ FOOD AND PUBS. For groceries, head to **Londis** on Dundalk St. (☎76602. Open daily 7am-10pm.) Carlingford offers a few pubs; its most popular is **PJ O'Hare's,** otherwise known as **The Anchor Bar.** Upon entering town, turn left at King John's Castle. The bar was once only slightly bigger than a breadbox, but popularity forced a makeover that more than doubled the space, which includes another extension that will house a full restaurant. (☎937 3106. ½-dozen oysters €9.50, 1 dozen €18. Entrees €17-26. Tu, Th, F and Su live bands, Th trad, Sa disco, and Su afternoon jazz. Open M-Th and Su 11am-11:30pm, F-Sa 11am-12:30am.) The Italian chef at **Captain Corelli's Mandolin ❹**, connected to Belvedere House, prepares seafood, meat dishes (€16-22), and pasta dishes (€11-13) fit for a king. (☎938 3848. Open M-Th 6-9:30pm, F 6-10pm, Sa 6-10:30pm, Su 5-9pm. AmEx/MC/V.) The serious foodie owner of **Bay Tree ❸**, Newry St., makes every single thing from scratch and obtains all produce locally—and by locally, we mean often in his own backyard. (Entrees €17-24. Open W-Su 6-10pm.) For daytime fare, follow the signs up the hill to **Georgina's Bakehouse ❶**, a homey bakery and teahouse specializing in light lunches and delectable desserts; try any of the sandwiches, and you won't be disappointed. (☎937 3346. Soups, salads, and sandwiches €3-7; desserts €2.50-4.40. Open daily 10am-6pm.)

◪ SIGHTS. The **Holy Trinity Heritage Centre** is housed in a renovated medieval church squeezed among several more recent buildings. The center's staff and a small exhibition educates visitors on the history and local lore of Carlingford from the 9th century to the present. (☎937 3454. Open M-F 10am-12:30pm and 2-4:30pm. €3, children often free if you ask.) The nearby ruins of the **Dominican Friary** have retained some of their high walls and dramatic arches and are open for exploration. Carlingford's three other surviving pre-Renaissance buildings create interesting scenery, but their interiors are closed to visitors. **King John's Castle,** by the waterfront, is the most impressive of Carlingford's medieval remains. It was built in the 1190s and named for King John, who visited briefly in 1210. **Taaffe's Castle,** along the quay, was built during the 16th century as a merchant house and contains classic Norman defensive features. In a tiny alley off Market Sq., the turreted 16th-century **Mint,** which never actually produced any coins, is notable for its ornate limestone windows displaying Celtic designs. At the end of the street, one of the old 15th-century town gates, the **Tholsel** (TAH-sehl), frames a scenic pedestrian entrance to the town's old thoroughfare. Visitors can join **Carlingford Walks** for an informative guided walking tour of the medieval village. (☎086 352 2732; cfdwtours@yahoo.ie. 1hr. tours Mar.-Oct. M and W-Sa 2pm. Call ahead. €6 per person, min. 4 people.) Carlingford also lies along the 585km **Táin Trail,** a route that alternates between surfaced roads and forested tracks as it retraces the footsteps of Queen Maeve and Cúchulainn in the *Tain Bo Cauilgne;* a 40km loop cover the

Cooley Peninsula through the Cooley Mountains. Maps are available at the tourist offices in Carlingford or Dundalk. Although Carlingford is normally known for its serenity, a weekend-long **Oyster Festival** in late-August draws musicians, and of course, seafood, from all over the island. In August, Carlingford folk head to the hills for the **Poc Fada,** an event based on an ancient Celtic sport in which hurlers hit a ball across the mountains to see who can finish with the fewest strokes. (For information on both festivals, contact the Carlingford tourist office.)

THE MIDLANDS

The Irish Midlands comprise six counties that are often passageways rather than destinations: Cavan, Monaghan, Laois, Offaly, Longford, and Westmeath. Counties Monaghan and Cavan's friendly villages beckon travelers seeking rest on their way to the Northwest. The 19 lakes of Co. Westmeath have earned it the nickname "Land of Lakes and Legends," while Athlone overcomes its crossroads status with its bohemian left bank and beautiful setting on the Shannon. Soggy Co. Offaly is dotted with small towns and home to the impressive ruins of Clonmacnoise. The underappreciated Slieve Bloom Mountains straddle the border between Offaly and Laois,while Co. Longford is calm and collected but not very exciting.

ATHLONE (BAILE ÁTHA LUAIN)   ☎09064

Settled in the flatlands on the border of Counties Roscommon and Westmeath, Athlone sits in the center of everything and in the middle of nowhere. Located at the intersection of the Shannon River and the Dublin-Galway road, it is the transportation hub of Ireland, but visitors will be relieved to find that it has far more to offer than its bus connections and heavy traffic. A 13th-century Norman castle attests to the city's former strategic importance. The scenic Shannon River offers enough fishing and boating to fulfill any water-baby's dream, and the monastic ruins of nearby Clonmacnoise are reachable by road or boat. Sitting in the shadow of the castle, the left bank has developed into an enclave of Athlone hipsters, filling its colorful facades with ethnic eateries, trendy boutiques, and lively bars.

◾ TRANSPORTATION. Athlone's **train** and **bus depots** are on Southern Station Rd., which runs parallel to Church St. (☎73322. Tickets M-Th and Sa 8:15am-12:45pm and 1:45-4:15pm, F 8:15am-12:45pm and 1:45-8:30pm, Su 9:15-11am and 2:30-9pm.) **Trains** to: **Dublin** (2hr.; M-Sa 11 per day, Su 10 per day; M-Th and Sa €19, F and Su €27; children €9.50/13.50) and **Galway** (1hr.; M-Sa 8 per day, Su 5 per day; €15/25, children €7.50/12.50). This is the center of **Bus Éireann** services; on their map, all roads lead to Athlone. At least one bus per day departs to almost all major cities, including **Belfast, Cork** (4½hr.; M-Sa 2 per day, Su 1 per day; €21, children €13.90), **Derry, Waterford, Tralee,** and **Killarney.** The main route from Dublin to Galway trundles through frequently. (17-21 per day; Dublin and Galway each €11, children €8.) There is also service to Birr. (50min.; M-Sa 4 per day, Su 2 per day; €8.40/5.35.)

◾◪ ORIENTATION AND PRACTICAL INFORMATION. The River Shannon splits Athlone into the **left bank** and **right bank.** The former is more exciting and claims the castle, but the latter holds most of the shops and services. **Church Street** cuts through the right bank, while most of the action on the left bank goes down between **High Street** and the castle. Church Street becomes **Custume Place** as it approaches the bridge. The besieged **tourist office,** in the castle, provides the *Athlone and District Visitors Guide* and books accommodations for a €4 fee. (☎94630. Open Apr. or May through Sept. or Oct. M-F 9:30am-5:30pm, Sa 10am-5:30pm). **Bank of Ireland** (☎92747), Church St., **National Irish Bank** (☎1890 882 557), and **AIB** (☎75101), Custume Pl., all have 24hr. **ATMs.** (All three open M 10am-5pm, Tu-F 10am-4pm; W 10:30am-4pm.) **Internet** access is available at **Aidan Heavey Public Library,** off Church St., in the modern white building behind the church. (☎42158. Open M 10am-5:30pm, Tu and Th 10am-8pm, W 11am-5:30pm, F 10am-5pm, Sa 10am-1:30pm. €1.50 per 50min., students €1 per 50min.) There are also Internet cafes on Irishtown Rd. and Dublin Rd. The **police** station is one block up from the castle on Barrack St. The **post office** is by the castle on Barrack St. (☎83544. Open M-F 9am-5:30pm, Tu opens 9:30am, Sa 9am-1pm.)

⌖⌗ ACCOMMODATIONS AND FOOD. Right at the epicenter of the Shannon's lively left bank, ▪**The Bastion ❸**, 2 Bastion St., is a funky B&B with an mix of art and tapestries that give it a mellow vibe. The decor will soothe your soul while the breakfast buffet of fresh fruit, yogurt, and other non-fried goodies will take care of your heart. Next door, the **Bastion Gallery** sells everything from natural remedies to quirky crafts. (☎94954. Superior continental breakfast included. Free Internet access. Singles €35-50; doubles €45-80. MC/V.) **Higgins' ❸**, 2 Pearse St., on the left bank, has decent rooms above a friendly pub. (☎92509. Singles €35; doubles €65, €5 extra per person with breakfast included. MC/V.) Across the street from the Bastion is **Marie's B&B ❹**, 8 High St. The owners use their keen eye for design to conjure up a beautiful home. (☎92494. Free Internet access. Singles €40; doubles €70.) **Lough Ree East Caravan and Camping Park ❶** stakes tents 5km northeast on N55 (the Longford road) by a pleasant inlet on the lake; follow signs for the lough. (☎78561 or 74414. Showers €0.20 per min. Laundry wash €6, dry €2. Electricity €3. Open Apr.-Sept. Tents and caravan sites from €10; €4 per adult, €4 per child.)

Dunnes, Irishtown Rd., sells groceries. (☎75212. Open M-W and Sa 9am-7pm, Th-F 9am-9pm, Su noon-6pm), but Athlone has a lively restaurant scene that's worth the splurge. The bright yellow **Kin Khao Thai ❸**, tucked away off High St., a left before Food for Thought, is hailed by critics as the best Thai restaurant in Ireland, and serves nostril-clearing curries in a lively orange room. Food-lovers on a budget should capitalize on the two-course express lunch (W-Su 12:30-2:20pm; €10) or early-bird dinner (M-Th and Su 5:30-7:30pm, F-Sa 5:30-7pm), which offers an appetizer, entree, and coffee or tea for €18. (☎98806. Entrees €14-19. Open M-Tu and Sa 5:30-10:30pm, W-F and Su 1:30-10:30pm. MC/V.) **The Left Bank Bistro ❹**, Fry Pl. at the bottom of the Bastion St. hill, was named one of the 100 best restaurants in Ireland in 2005. The lunches are affordable and filling; try the various open-face sandwiches for €8.50. (☎94446; info@leftbankbistro.com. Dinner entrees €21-29. Early-bird set menu Tu-F 5:30-7:30pm; €25. Open Tu-Sa 10:30am-9:30pm. MC/V.) **Pizza Mama ❷**, 4 Pearse St., is quickly becoming a left bank favorite for its pizza and pasta (€10.50-15), as well as lunchtime *panini* for €8.50. (☎44009. BYOB; corkage €2. Open M-F noon-3pm and 5-11pm, Sa-Su 1-11pm.) **Bonne Bouche ❷**, 21 Church St., upstairs in Rick's Bar, feels a bit like a hotel lobby but serves better-than-average entrees. (☎72112. Lunch specials €8-9. Open M-Sa 9:30am-6pm.)

▮▮ PUBS AND CLUBS. The weekend *Westmeath Independent* has entertainment listings, as does the biweekly *B-Scene* magazine, which is sold in local cafes. The ever-busy ▪**Sean's Bar,** 13 Main St., is recognized by the *Guinness Book of World Records* as Ireland's oldest inn, dating back to AD 900. Sawdust-covered floors around the bar and a piece of the original wood-and-wattle wall attest to its age, but the Shannon-side beer garden with a retractable roof is state of the art. (☎92358. Music every night, mostly trad and ballads. Open M-Th noon-11pm, F-Sa noon-12:30am, Su noon-11pm.) **Gertie Brown's,** 9 Custume Pl., formerly The Hooker, pleases regulars with perfect pints, low ceilings, and paintings and artifacts of a bygone era. Don't mind the stern portrait of Gertie above the fire-

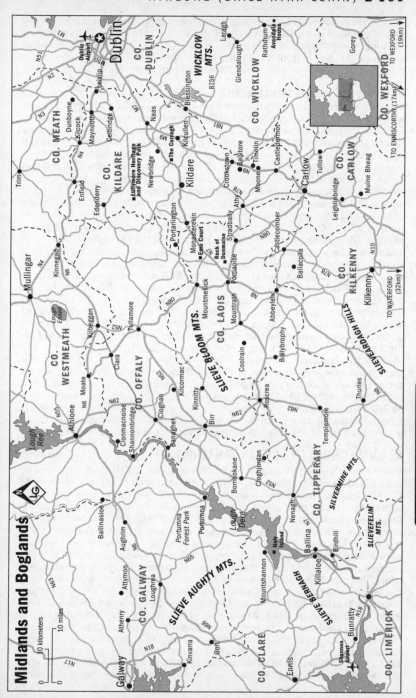

Midlands and Boglands

place—you're probably not doing anything she hasn't done. And if you are, you should probably stop immediately. (☎74848. W trad.) **The Palace,** Market Sq., is a disco bar that plays pop in a red-lit bar. (☎92229. Open Th-Sa 10pm-2am.) **BoZo's,** on Church St. across from the library, brings out the clubbers for DJs spinning chart-topping music. (☎74376. Open Th-Sa 11:30pm-2:30am. Cover €8-11.)

◐ ※ **SIGHTS AND FESTIVALS.** Athlone's historical fame can be traced to a single crushing defeat. Orange Williamite forces besieged **Athlone Castle** in 1691 and, with the help of 12,000 cannonballs, easily crossed the river and conquered their foes. The defending Jacobites, unskilled soldiers at best, suffered countless casualties; the attackers lost fewer than 100 of their 25,000 (see **Rebellion and Union,** p. 53). The castle is free for all to wander, and provides some grand Shannon views. (Open daily May-Sept. 9:30am-5:30pm.) Inside, the **Visitors Centre** tells a 45min. audio-visual tale of the battle and marches on through Athlone history to relate the stories of home-grown tenor **John McCormack** and the river Shannon. There was once a dull **museum** inside the Visitors Centre which featured gramophones and uniforms from the Irish Civil War; it is currently closed but may re-open in the future. (☎92912. Open daily May-Sept. 10am-4:30pm. €4, seniors and students €2, children €1.20.) **Viking Tours,** 7 St. Mary's Terr., on the right bank, supplies helmets and swords for a light-hearted "authentic" Viking experience on a replica Viking ship that sails up the Shannon to Lough Ree and, depending on demand, to Clonmacnoise. The Clonmacnoise ride includes a guided tour of the monastic ruins. (☎73383 or 086 262 1136; www.vikingtoursireland.com. 1½hr. Lough Ree and 4hr. Clonmacnoise voyages depart from the Strand across the river from the castle. Generally 2 per day, but call ahead as frequency and times will vary with demand. Lough Ree €12, children €10, families €40; Clonmacnoise €20/15/60.) If you want to drop a line while near the lake, **fishing permits** are available from Strand Fishing Tackle, next to Viking Tours on The Strand (☎79277).

Athlonians becomes athletes for July's **Tri-Athlone,** a triathlon competition. But jocks are not the only ones who flock to visit the local festivals: April brings the **Drama Festival,** which features Irish plays and actors. The end of September ushers in the **Literary Festival,** which consists mostly of readings. Contact the tourist office (☎94630) or the Athlone Chamber of Commerce (☎73173) for details on the Tri-Athlone or the Literary Festival. For the Drama Festival, contact the Mullingar tourist office (☎044 934 8761), as the Athlone branch is closed that time of year.

CLONMACNOISE (CLUAIN MHIC NÓIS)   ☎09096

Twenty-three sparsely populated kilometers southwest of Athlone, the monastic ruins of Clonmacnoise (clon-muk-NOYS) keep watch over Shannon's boglands. St. Ciaran (KEER-on) founded his monastery here in AD 548; the settlement grew into an important center for worship and scholarship. Monks wrote the **Book of the Dun Cow** here around 1100, on vellum from St. Ciaran's cow. The holy heifer traveled everywhere with the saint and miraculously produced enough milk for the whole monastery. The cows munching their way across the landscape today have ordinary udders, but the grandness of the sight still excites the imagination. The ruin's **cathedral** has seen its share of attacks over the course of its thousand years, both from Vikings and English garrisons at Athlone. One of its doorways is known as the **whispering arch;** faint sounds travel up one side over to the other. **O'Connor's Church,** built in the 12th century, has Church of Ireland services from June through August on Sundays at 4pm. The extensive ruins also include a **round tower,** the remains of a **castle,** and many early **grave slabs.** Peaceful **Nun's Church** lies beyond the modern graveyard behind the main site, about 500m down the path. Its finely detailed doorways are some of Ireland's most impressive examples of Romanesque architecture. The **Visitors Centre** provides access to the monastery and screens a 23min. film. (☎74195. The center, unlike the sites, is wheelchair-accessible.

Open daily June to early Sept. 9am-7pm; mid-Sept. to Oct. and mid-March to May 10am-6pm; Nov. to mid-March 10am-5pm. €5.30, students and children €2.10, seniors €3.70, families €11.50.) The **Clonmacnoise and West Offaly Railway** runs 9km through a peat bog and allows passengers to try their hand at turf cutting. (☎74450; www.bnm.ie. Open June-Aug. daily 10am-5pm; Apr.-May and Sept. M-F 10am-5pm. Trains run on the hr. €6.50, children €4.80, families €22.)

One outstanding B&B is 🖪**Kajon House ❸**, on Shannonbridge Rd. near the ruins. The owners make fabulous dinners (€20-22), soups, and desserts (€8), and greet guests with delicious homemade scones and a good sense of humor. If the cooking and hospitality somehow fail to warm you, the electric blankets will. (☎74191; www.kajonhouse.cjb.net. Call ahead for pickup. Singles €45; doubles €67. Discount 10% for 3+ night stays.) The **Ely Lodge B&B ❸**, Cloghan Rd. (R357), is between Kajon and the West Offaly Railroad. Its spacious rooms with wood finish all have bathrooms and TV and are completely child-proof. (☎74205 or 086 264 7719. Singles €37; doubles €70.) The **Glebe Touring Caravan and Camping Park ❶** is 5km to the east. (☎09064 30277. Open Easter-Oct. Laundry wash €2, dry €2. 2-person caravans €14; 2-person tents €12, extra person €6.)

To reach Clonmacnoise from Athlone or Birr by car, take N62 to **Ballynahown** and follow the signs from there. Cycling to town involves a 22.5km gauntlet of hilly terrain. The **tourist office**, at the Clonmacnoise car park, sells guides to the ruins for €5. (☎74134. Open Mar.-Nov. daily 10am-5:30pm.)

THE SLIEVE BLOOM MOUNTAINS ☎05791

Though lower than 610m at their highest point, the Slieve Bloom Mountains create a gentle break from the plains between **Birr, Roscrea, Portlaoise**, and **Tullamore**. Hiking trails abound in the forests and energy-rich bogland. The 70km circular **Slieve Bloom Way** is accessible at dozens of points along its path for those who prefer shorter hikes. The 4.5km return hike from **Monicknew Bridge,** heading counter-clockwise toward the Ridge of Capard, offers an excellent sampling of the region's terrain. From the gatepost, walk up the road beneath the stately evergreens. Mossy undergrowth and trickles of bogwater increase with the altitude, forming small glens barely visible from the trail. At the acute right turn at the top of the first road, feast on the sweeping westerly view of the valleys below. A similar but more expansive eastward vista awaits around a few bends and over the ridge. Turn back at any point once you've reached the bog plateau. For other information on walks, trailheads, and directions, pick up the *Slieve Bloom Way Walking Guide* (€5) from the tourist offices at Birr or Portlaoise. The mountains' greatest asset is their lack of tourist-oriented activity—there's nothing to do but relax. The towns around the mountains are bastions of Ireland's rural lifestyle.

For an oddly Lilliputian experience, visit the **Old Time Village** a few kilometers from the Glebe Caravan Park. In his backyard, the owner has built an entire miniature famine-era village and manor estate; placards are liberally sprinkled throughout, containing both explanatory information and a few prayers. Finding the village can be a challenge, so the most reliable way to find it is to ask the locals. (15min. from Birr. €3, children free.)

The friendly owners of the family-run **Traditional Farm Hostel ❶** give guests lifts from **Ballacolla**, a town reached twice a day by bus from Portlaoise. Follow signs if you're traveling there on your own. Though a bit off the beaten path, the hostel is worth the trip for its country welcome, comfy rooms, and funky sculptures made from scraps of farmyard junk. (☎057 873 4032; info@farmhostel.com. Wheelchair-accessible. Continental breakfast €5. Laundry €5-7. All rooms with bath. Private 2- to 5-person rooms €20. **Camping** €10.) **Roundwood House ❺**, a gorgeous 16th-century Georgian house with a resident peacock, is in a world of its own just 5km on R440 from Mountrath. Guests enjoy free Internet access, as well as a 20% discount for stays of at least three nights. (☎057 873 2120. Dinner €50. Singles €100-110;

doubles €150-170. Three self-catering cottages of various sizes are available for €280-500 per wk. Under 12 50% discount. AmEx/MC/V.)

The *craic* can be mighty in Slieve Bloom villages, but it's all about the timing. On Thursday nights, the thatch-roofed **Village Inn** (☎35277) in **Coolrain,** about 8km from Mountrath, gets the locals together for some infectiously fun set-dancing. The **Irish Music and Set Dancing Festival** jigs into Coolrain on the first weekend in May. Contact Micheál Lalor (☎086 260 7658) for info on either festival.

Transportation can be tricky. Two of the best towns for entry to the mountains are **Kinnitty** to the northwest, and **Mountrath** to the south; between them runs a winding road. Travelers reliant on public transportation, however, are considerably inconvenienced. The **Portlaoise** tourist office (☎057 862 1178) provides a handy list of Co. Laois residents who have been trained as tour guides.

BIRR (BIORRA) ☎05791

William Petty named Birr "the belly button of Ireland," though the town's none-too-central location leads some to suspect that old Will may have been speaking from behind a pint glass. Nonetheless, Birr's castle alone has plenty of scientific and natural wonders to warrant a visit, and the tourist office packs visitors off to the Slieve Bloom Mountains, a 14km bike ride east to Kinnitty.

⊟⚡ TRANSPORTATION AND PRACTICAL INFORMATION. Buses stop at the post office in Emmet Sq. **Bus Éireann** runs to: **Athlone** (50min.; M-Sa 4 per day, Su 2 per day; €6); **Cahir** (2hr.; M-Sa 3 per day, Su 1 per day); **Dublin** (2½hr.; M-Sa 4 per day, Su 2 per day); **Limerick** (1½hr.; M-F 5 per day, Su 2 per day). **Kearns Coaches** (☎0509 20124; www.kearnstransport.com) has better fares to **Dublin** (M-F and Su 3 per day, Sa 2 per day; €10, children €5); get info at Square News in Emmet Sq.

The umbilicus of Birr is **Emmet Square.** Most shops and pubs are either in the square or south down **O'Connell Street,** which becomes **Main Street** after one block. Residential areas lie to the north and west, down **Emmet** and **Green Street.** East from Emmet Sq. is **Johns Mall.** The **tourist office** is on Brendan St., the continuation of Castle St. after it crosses Main St. (☎20110. Open mid-May to mid-Sept. daily 9:30am-1pm and 2-5:30pm.) It has a free heritage map of town, sells the *Slieve Bloom Way Walking Guide* (€5), and connects travelers with the Slieve Bloom Rural Development Society. The office may soon be moving to the Civic Buildings next to the Catholic Church on Wilmer Rd., which is off Johns Mall. (☎37299. Accommodations bookings €4 plus a 10% deposit.) The **Bank of Ireland,** Emmet Sq. (☎20092; open M 10am-5pm, Tu and Th-F 10am-4pm, W 10:30am-4pm), has an **ATM,** as does **AIB,** on Johns Mall (☎20069; open M 10am-5pm and Tu-F 10am-4pm). **Internet** access is generally €2 per hr. at the **library,** in the former Chapel of the Mercy Sisters on Wilmer Rd., but 10min. checking email is free. (☎24950. Open Tu and Th-F 9:30am-1pm and 2-5:30pm, W 1:30-5:30pm and 6-9pm.) The **police station** is at 4 Emmet Sq. (☎20016). The **post office** is in Emmet Sq. (☎20397. Open M-F 9am-5:30pm and Sa 10am-1pm; Tu open 9:30am except 1st Tu of the month.)

⌂ ACCOMMODATIONS. Birr's B&Bs are expensive, but they're often worth the price. **Spinner's Town House ❹,** Castle St., epitomizes country elegance with its crisp decor and spacious rooms. A charming **bistro ❹** downstairs serves scrambled eggs with smoked salmon for breakfast; dinner (most entrees €16-22.50) costs a bit more. (☎21673. Free Internet access. Singles from €55; doubles from €80; "Gothic wing" suites €100, but the castle view and pointed arches aren't worth the markup. Standby rooms from €30 are a steal. AmEx/MC/V.) If Spinner's is full, head across the road to **Maltings Guest House ❹,** Castle St., part of a large complex with impersonal but comfortable rooms, many overlooking the river. (☎21345. Singles Oct.-Mar. €50, Apr.-Sept. €55; doubles €80. MC/V.) The attached **restau-**

rant ❷, one of the few in town, serves vegetarian-friendly meals. (Entrees €13-24. Open daily 7:30am-9pm; Oct.-May M-Th and Su closes 3pm.)

🖸🖥 **FOOD AND PUBS. SuperValu** sells groceries at 25 Main St. and has an **ATM** inside. (☎20015. Open M-W and Sa 8am-7:30pm, Th-F 8am-9pm, Su 9am-6pm.) **Londis,** in the other direction from Emmet Sq., stays open daily until 9pm. (☎21250.) Locals point to the pink storefront of **Kong Lam ❷**, Main St., for cheap Chinese takeaway. (☎21253. Entrees €8-11. Open M-Th and Su 5pm-12:30am, F-Sa 5pm-1:30am.) Spend a bit more on lunch and eat *al fresco* in the beer garden at the **Coachhouse Lounge ❸**, in Dooly's Hotel in the square. The **cafeteria ❶** serves sandwiches and fresh smoothies for €4. (☎20032. *Panini* €6; lunches and daily specials €9-11. Dinner €9-13. MC/V.) **Melba's** is Dooly's nightclub. (Cover before midnight €5, after midnight €7. Open F-Sa 11:30pm-1:30am, Su 11:30pm-1am. Bar open M-Th 10am-11:30pm, F-Sa 10am-12:30am, Su noon-11pm.) **Whelehan's,** Connaught St., off Main St., owned by members of the Offaly hurling team, is the liveliest place in town. (☎21349. Open M-Th and Su noon-midnight, F-Sa noon-12:30am.)

🖸 **SIGHTS.** Visitors are welcome (for a fee) to tread on the Earl of Rosse's turf at 🖪**Birr Castle,** which remains his private home. The 48-hectare estate has babbling brooks, the tallest box hedges in the world, and paths perfect for aimless wandering. The most recent botanical feat is the formal **Millennium Gardens.** The inhabitants of the castle have left a legacy of scientific discovery around the grounds and it is said that Birr had electricity before Edison patented it. The **Historic Science Centre,** inside the Visitors Centre, showcases the noteworthy strides in astronomy and photography that were made in the castle in the 19th century. The Third Earl of Rosse discovered the Whirlpool Nebula with the **Leviathan,** an immense telescope whose 2m mirror was the world's largest for 72 years. To build the telescope he had to invent metal alloys strong and shiny enough to give his mirrors a clear surface. The starry-eyed can still observe the Leviathan (outside in a stone enclosure) in action today, but only on clear days. The mammoth device is hard to miss on the grounds, but the **suspension bridge** in the southeast corner, the first of its kind on the British Isles, is more easily overlooked. (☎20336; www.birrcastle.com. Castle open daily Mar.-Oct. 9am-6pm; Nov.-Feb. 10am-4pm. Wheelchair-accessible. Leviathan tours during the summer daily 12:30 and 3pm. Castle and science center €9, students and seniors €7.50, children €5, under 5 free.)

PORTLAOISE (PORT LAOISE)   ☎05791

Travelers who ask at the tourist office what there is to do in Portlaoise (port-LEESH) are likely to be directed outside of town, though not for a lack of local hospitality. The **Rock of Dunamaise** is close by. It was the model of impregnability until Cromwell cannonballed onto the scene 400 years ago. The crumbling ruins cling to a limestone outcropping that offers spectacular views of the Slieve Bloom Mountains in the distance. Six kilometers outside of town on N7 toward Dublin, **Emo Court** offers more panoramic views. James Gandon, famous for the Four Courts and Custom House in Dublin, designed the house in the 1780s for the first Earl of Portarlington. Gandon's obsessive attention to detail (the court was constructed over a period of 84 years) is apparent throughout the house. In the foyer, two of the four stately doors are merely decorative. The manicured gardens and 10-hectare man-made lake make for a pleasant stroll, and the grand avenue leading to the house is lined with sequoias. (☎26573. Open mid-June to mid-Sept. daily 10am-6pm; tours every hr. 10am-5pm. Gardens open during daylight hours for free. €3, seniors €2.10, students and children €1.30, families €7.40.)

The stark white facade of **Oakville ❸**, Mountrath Rd., a 5min. walk from Main St., on the left after the train tracks, contrasts its cozy rooms and friendly proprietors.

EASTERN IRELAND

Morris, a trained tour guide, briefs guests on local history over tea in the conservatory. (☎61970; oakvillebandb@eircom.net. Free Internet access. All rooms with bath and TV. Singles €40; shared rooms €35 per person.) **Donoghue's B&B ❸,** 1 Kellyville Park, on the roundabout at the end of Lawlor Ave., offers convenience and ensuite rooms. (☎21353. Singles €50; doubles €75.) For groceries, try **Tesco,** located inside the mall on Lawlor Ave., opposite Main St. (☎21730. Open M-Tu and Sa 9am-7pm, W-F 9am-9pm, Su noon-6pm.) Local favorite **The Kitchen and Foodhall** (a.k.a. **Jim's Kitchen**) ❷, in Hynds Sq. off Main St., serves the best lunches in town. The entrees (€11.50), which vary daily, are served with a great selection of salads. The gourmet grocer in front sells cheese and other goodies. (☎62061. Sandwiches €4-5. Open M-Sa 9am-6pm.) As the evening wears on, try **The Kingfisher ❹,** in the old brick AIB building on Main St., an upscale Indian restaurant that specializes in baltis and raitas. The takeaway menu is cheaper, with entrees from €8.50-10.50. (☎62500; www.kingfisherrestaurant.com. Entrees €13.50-19.50. Open M-Tu and Sa 5:30-11:30pm, W-F 12:30-2:30pm and 5:30-11:30pm. MC/V.) Another local favorite is **Egan's Hostelry ❶,** Lower Main St., with sandwiches (€5.50-6), a carvery lunch (daily 9am-4pm; entrees €8-11) by day, and a solid bar menu at night. (☎21106 or 21101. Dinner €15-25. Open daily 9am-9:30pm. MC/V.) The sandwiches next door in **Egan's New Cafe ❶** are cheaper than the hostelry's meals (€5.50-6) and are served on funky parchment-like wooden placemats. (☎21106. Open daily 9am-6pm.) **Dunamaise Arts Centre,** the large orange building on the corner just up Church St. from Main St., on the right. The arts center holds a 250-seat theater and has a varied program of music, theater, and international film. On the second floor, a free **gallery** displays work by local artists. (Cafe Latte ☎63515. Internet access €2.50 per hr. Entrees €5-8. Cafe open M-Sa 8:30am-5:30pm. Arts center ☎63355; www.dunmaise.ie. Tickets €12-30. Films €8; children, seniors, and students €6. Box office open M-Sa 10am-5:30pm; also performance nights 7-8:30pm.)

Pubs in Portlaoise are centered around Market Sq. The largest is **Bar Mondays,** 15 Market Sq., which features a menu of 40 shooters (€4, F €3) designed by the bar staff (10-15 on the menu at a time) with erotic names like "Peter's Chocolate Monkey," which is made with banana Bols and Baileys. (☎057 862 2416; www.barmondays.com. M trad, Th karaoke, F-Sa DJ, Su live band. Open M-Th 5-11:30pm, F 5pm-12:30am, Sa noon-12:30am, Su noon-11pm.)

In late August or early September, the **Electric Picnic** weekend rock & pop festival in Stradbally draws music fans from all over Ireland to the Portlaoise area. To get to Stradbally, take N80 east toward Carlow and Waterford. (☎081 871 9300; www.electricpicnic.ie. Buy tickets online or visit Tracks in the Portlaoise shopping center.) Also in Stradbally, the **Stradbally Steam Rally** hosts a display of steam engines. (Contact the tourist office for more info.)

James Fintan Lawlor Avenue runs parallel to **Main Street.** Lawlor Ave. is a four-lane highway that opens onto Portlaoise's shopping centers, the most prominent of which is **Lyster Square.** The **train station** (☎21303; open daily 6am-11pm) is at the curve on **Railway Street,** which follows **Church Street** from Main St. **Trains** run to **Dublin** (1hr.; M-Sa 13 per day, Su 6 per day; €18.50, children €9.25) and **Kildare** (25min.; M-Sa 8 per day, Su 6 per day; €8.20/4.10). **Bus Éireann** stops on Lawlor Ave. on its way to **Dublin** (1½hr., 18-20 per day, €10.30/7.20). **J.J. Kavanagh/Rapid Express** (☎883 1106) also serves **Carlow** (2 per day; €6.50, under 3 free) and **Dublin** (M-Sa 5 per day, Su 4 per day; €10, under 3 free) from Lawlor Ave. The **tourist office** is in Lyster Sq., on Lawlor Ave. (☎21178. Open M-Sa 9:30am-1pm and 2-5:30pm; Oct.-June closed Sa.) **AIB,** Lawlor Ave. (☎21349), has an **ATM,** as does the **Bank of Ireland.** (☎21414. Both open M 10am-5pm, Tu and Th-F 10am-4pm, W 10:30am-4pm.) The **library,** across from the tourist office, has **Internet** access. (☎22333. €2.50 per 30min. Open Tu and F 10am-5pm, W-Th 10am-7pm, Sa 10am-1pm.) The regional **post office** is inside the shopping center on Lawlor Ave. (☎74220. Open M and W-F 9am-5:30pm, Tu 9:30am-5:30pm; open 9am first Tu of each month.)

SOUTHEAST IRELAND

Southeast Ireland has all the coast can offer, from the incredibly fresh fish and quaint thatched-roofed cottages in tiny Kilmore Quay to the sandy beaches and sunshine in Ardmore, Duncannon, Dunmore East, and Wexford. The region is famous for its strawberries and oysters, whose aphrodisiacal powers may account for the gaggles of children who play on its shores. Round towers litter the countryside, most notably St. Canice's in Kilkenny and the Rock of Cashel's tower in Cashel. Inland, mesmerizing green fields and stunning mountain views provide an exciting contrast to the trad and rock that pump through the pubs of Carlow, Kilkenny, Waterford, and Wexford. The region is most easily seen by automobile and best experienced by bicycle, although buses and trains serve most cities and towns.

SOUTHEAST IRELAND HIGHLIGHTS

DESCEND into the subterranean chambers of the **Mitchelstown Caves** (p. 207).

HONK at a white-fronted goose at the **Wexford Wildfowl Reserve** (p. 220).

GET YOUR TRAD ON at the **Brú Ború Heritage Centre** (p. 204).

MASTER the waves after a surf lesson in **Tramore** (p. 229).

COUNTIES KILKENNY AND CARLOW

Northwest of Co. Wexford and Waterford and southwest of Dublin, Counties Kilkenny and Carlow largely consist of lightly populated hills, small farming villages, and scattered ruins. The medieval city of Kilkenny, a popular destination for international tourists and Irish youth, is the bustling exception. The town of Carlow, though much smaller, still produces an after-hours buzz of its own.

KILKENNY CITY   ☎05677

Kilkenny (pop. 30,000) is a perfect destination for travelers in search of the classic Irish city. In proud Irish fashion, it has a renowned medieval namesake castle, bright storefronts with excellent shopping, a tremendous selection of pubs, and its own brewery. While Dublin is becoming increasingly international, Kilkenny staunchly clings to its roots; it's much easier to find a traditional pub filled with the sounds of an *uillean* pipe than a trendy gastropub.

The city cemented itself in the history books in 1172 when Strongbow built Kilkenny Castle to command the crossing of the River Nore (p. 50). His son-in-law later replaced

Southeast Ireland

the original structure with sturdier stone and incorporated the town in 1204. The town wall, part of which still stands today, once designated the border between "English Town," inside the gates and governed by the Normans, and "Irish Town," governed by the local bishop. The two governments were apt to quarrel, and Kilkenny's nickname, "the fighting cats," stems from their behavior (see **Entertainment**, p. 185). Their sportsmen haven't lost their pugnacious tendencies, and they now field one of Ireland's best hurling teams. Today, a casual walk down its handsome streets reveals Kilkenny's attempt to recreate its 15th-century charm. The city's buildings and sidewalks glint with indigenous polished black limestone which Kilkennians fondly refer to as "black marble," and storefronts have eliminated tacky neon—even fast-food joints have hand-painted facades. These efforts are reaping their touristic reward: the city has twice earned the coveted title of Tidy Town, and its population doubles during high season.

KILKENNY FOR POCKET CHANGE. Begin the day at **SuperQuinn** (see p. 193), where free food samples abound in the morning and early afternoon. Next, the Smithwick's **Brewery Tour** (see p. 196) is worth sitting through for the free all-you-can-drink hour in the brewery's basement pub. Finally, relax in the gorgeous **Kilkenny Castle** grounds (see p. 196). For €5, take a guided tour inside and check out the spectacular Long and Butler art galleries.

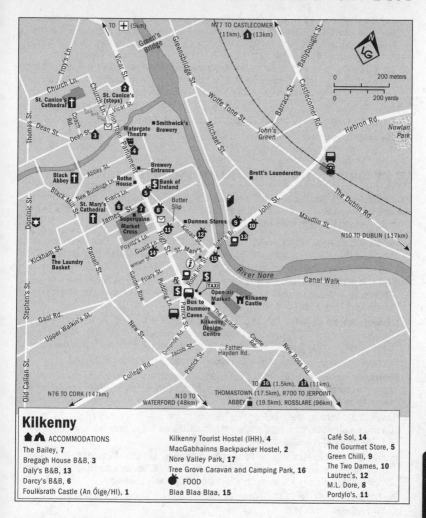

Kilkenny

🏠🏕 **ACCOMMODATIONS**
The Bailey, **7**
Bregagh House B&B, **3**
Daly's B&B, **13**
Darcy's B&B, **6**
Foulksrath Castle (An Óige/HI), **1**

Kilkenny Tourist Hostel (IHH), **4**
MacGabhainns Backpacker Hostel, **2**
Nore Valley Park, **17**
Tree Grove Caravan and Camping Park, **16**
🍎 **FOOD**
Blaa Blaa Blaa, **15**

Café Sol, **14**
The Gourmet Store, **5**
Green Chilli, **9**
The Two Dames, **10**
Lautrec's, **12**
M.L. Dore, **8**
Pordylo's, **11**

🔲 TRANSPORTATION

Trains: Kilkenny MacDonagh Station, the Dublin road (☎22024). Open M-Sa 7:45am-7:20pm, Su 9:45am-7:45pm. Kilkenny is on the main **Dublin-Waterford** rail route (4-6 per day in each direction). To: **Dublin** (2hr., €22-27.50); **Thomastown** (15min., €9.20 return); **Waterford.** (45min., €9.80-12.50) Connections to the west can be made at **Kildare Station,** 1¼hr. north on the Dublin-Waterford line.

Buses: Kilkenny Station, the Dublin road (☎051 317 864). Buses also depart from the city center at **Cafe Net,** Patrick St. Tickets also available at the tourist office. To: **Clonmel** (1¼hr., 6 per day, €7.50); **Cork** (3hr.; M-Sa 3 per day, Su 2 per day; €16.50); **Dublin** (2hr., 5-6 per day, €10.80); **Galway** via **Athlone** or **Clonmel** (5hr.; M-Sa 6 per day, Su 3 per day; €21); **Limerick** via **Clonmel** (2½hr.; M-Sa 4 per day, Su 2 per day; €16.50); **Rosslare Harbour** via **Waterford** (2hr.; M-Sa 2 per day, Su 3 per day; €16.50); **Waterford** (1½hr., M-Sa 2 per day, €9). **Buggy's Coaches** (☎41264) run from **Kilkenny** to **Ballyragget** (30min., M-Sa 3 per day) and **Castlecomer** (15min., M-Sa 3 per day, €4) with stops at the **An Óige hostel** (15min.) and **Dunmore Cave** (20min.). Buggy's also runs **bus tours** of the area. **J.J. Kavanagh's Rapid Express** (☎31106) runs to **Dublin** (M-Sa 5 per day, Su 2 per day; €8).

Taxis: €3.80-4.10 min. charge, plus €1.25 per km and €1 per additional passenger. **Bridge Cabs** (☎086 177 1626); **Kilkenny Cabs** (☎52000); **Chris Vaughan** (☎25215).

Bike Rental: Treegrove Campground (☎70302). €15 per day. Pass the castle and take the 1st right after the roundabout (a 20min. walk). ID required. Closed Nov.-Jan.

▣ 🛈 ORIENTATION AND PRACTICAL INFORMATION

From **MacDonagh Station**, turn left onto **John Street** and downhill across the bridge toward the intersection with **High Street** and **the Parade**. Most activity occurs in the triangle formed by **High, Rose Inn**, and **Kieran Streets**.

Tourist Office: Rose Inn St. (☎51500), in a 1582 pauper house. Free maps and bus info; bus tickets can also be purchased here. Open July-Aug. M-F 9am-6:30pm, Sa 10am-6pm, Su 11am-5pm; Sept.-June M-F 9:30am-5:30pm, Sa 10am-6pm.

Banks: Bank of Ireland, Parliament St. (☎21155), has a 24hr. **ATM;** the High St. and Parade St. intersection has several more. Banks open M 10am-5pm, Tu-Th and F 10am-4pm, W 10:30am-4pm.

Laundry: Brett's Launderette, Michael St. (☎63200). Wash and dry €16. Open M-Sa 8:30am-8pm; last wash 6:30pm. **The Laundry Basket** (☎70355), at the top of James St. Full-service wash and dry €1 per lb. Dry-cleaning facilities. Open M-F 8:30am-7pm, Sa 9am-5pm.

Emergency: ☎999; no coins required. **Police** (Garda): Dominic St. (☎22222).

Pharmacy: Several on High St. All open M-Sa 9am-6pm (some closed for lunch, 1-2pm); Su rotation system. **White's Pharmacy,** 5 High St. (☎21328), specializes in cameras and film developing.

Hospital: St. Luke's, Freshford Rd. (☎85000). Continue down Parliament St. to St. Canice's Cathedral, turn right and veer left onto Vicars St., then left onto Freshford Rd. The hospital is on the right.

Internet: The cheapest option is **Powers Newsagency,** John St. €2 per hr. Open 8am-10pm. There are several Internet cafes on Rose Inn St. **Kilkenny e.centre,** 26 Rose Inn St. (☎60093). €6 per hr., students €5 per hr. Open daily 9am-9pm.

Post Office: High St. (☎62327). Open M and W-F 9am-5:30pm, Tu 9:30am-5:30pm, Sa 9am-1pm and 2-5:30pm.

▮ ACCOMMODATIONS AND CAMPING

The average Kilkenny B&B costs around €35 per person, but some places hike prices up to €40 on weekends. B&Bs tend to be slightly impersonal; hostels are more homey. Call ahead in the summer, during festivals, or on weekends. The Waterford road and more remote Castlecomer Rd. have the most guesthouses.

▨ **Kilkenny Tourist Hostel (IHH),** 35 Parliament St. (☎63541). Near the popular pubs and next to Smithwick's Brewery. Guests bustle about in the kitchen and dining room, living room, and front steps. Town info posted in the front hall. Great place to meet pub-crawling companions, but evening common-space lockout can be annoying. Non-smoking. Kitchen and living room open 7am-11pm. Laundry €5. Free Wi-Fi. Check-out 10am. 6-to 8-bed dorms €17; 4-bed €19; doubles €21. Jan.-Mar. €1 less. Cash only. ❶

MacGabhainns Backpacker Hostel, 24 Vicar St. (☎70970). Small hostel. 16 beds, freshly painted rooms, free breakfast, and great location make this a good bet. Laundry €6.50. Towels €1. Dorms M-Th and Su €16, F-Sa €17. MC/V. ❶

Foulksrath Castle (An Óige/HI), Jenkinstown (☎67674). On N77 (Durrow Rd.), 13km north of town. Turn right at signs for Connahy; the hostel is 400m down on the left. Buggy's Buses (€4) run from the Parade M-Sa from Kilkenny 5:30pm, from Jenkinstown 8:05am and 11:50am. A royal accommodation, Foulksrath is housed in a 15th-century castle, but infrequent buses sometimes make getting there an arduous journey. Lock-out 10am-5pm. Check-in after 5pm, curfew midnight. Dorms €15. Cash only. ❶

Bregagh House B&B, Dean St. (☎22315; www.bregaghhouse.com), the 1st B&B on the left turning off High St. Clean rooms, handsome wooden furniture, and firm beds. Lovely back garden and sunny conservatory. Singles €50; doubles €74. Cash only. ❸

Daly's B&B, 82 John's St. (☎62866). Ferns and other hanging plants greet guests in the sky-lit entrance hall, along with an aquarium full of cheerful fish; they're not for breakfast. Immaculate, spacious rooms and a large breakfast area lie beyond. Check-out 11:30am. Singles €45; doubles €68. Cash only. ❸

Darcy's B&B, 26 James St. (☎21954). A little old house by the SuperQuinn market, off High St. Delightful proprietors rent out simple, clean rooms with TVs. Free parking. Singles €55; doubles with bath M-Th and Su €70, F-Sa €100. Cash only. ❸

Nore Valley Park (☎27229). 11.3km south of Kilkenny between Bennetsbridge and Stonyford, marked from town. Take the New Ross road (R700) to Bennetsbridge, and the signposted right before the bridge. Hot showers, TV room, and children's play area (€3). Mini-golf (€2.50), go-carts (€1.50), tractor rides (€1), picnic and barbecue areas. Wheelchair-accessible. Open Mar.-Oct. Laundry €5.70. Backpackers €6.50. €3 per person, €8 per tent. MC/V. ❶

Tree Grove Caravan and Camping Park (☎70302). 1.6km past the castle on the New Ross road (R700). €8 per person, caravans €20. Free showers. Cash only. ❶

🦞 FOOD

Dunnes Stores, Kieran St., sells housewares and food. (☎61655. Open 24hr.) **SuperQuinn,** in the Market Cross shopping center off High St., has an equally huge selection and free samples. (☎52444. Open M-Tu 8am-8pm, W-F 8am-9pm, Sa 8am-7pm, Su 10am-7pm.) You can pick up fresh, local grub at the **market** by Kilkenny Castle every Th 9am-2:30pm. Everything about Kilkenny's restaurants is great except the prices, which hover somewhere in the lower stratosphere. Below are some of the best or most reasonable options; otherwise, your best bet is a pub.

🦞 **Café Sol,** William St. (☎64987; www.cafesofkilkenny.com). Delicious, award-winning bistro fare with reasonably priced, creative lunch menu (salads, stir fries €8-11) served noon-6pm. Entrees €21-29. Open M-Sa 11:30am-10pm, Su noon-9pm. MC/V. ❸

🦞 **Pordylo's,** Butter Slip (☎70660), between Kieran and High St. Zesty global dinners (€20-25). Plentiful vegetarian options. Early-bird menu until 7pm (2 courses €22; 3 courses €27). Reservations recommended. Open daily 5-11pm. AmEx/MC/V. ❹

The Two Dames, 80 John St. No phone. Small cafe with food that tastes as good as it smells. Creative sandwiches, like the Two Dames special (cranberry sauce, brie, grapes, stuffing; €5.50) give it an edge over similar restaurants. Takeaway €1.50 less. Open M-F 8:30am-5pm, Sa 10am-4:30pm. Cash only. ❶

The Gourmet Store, 56 High St. (☎71727). Huge gourmet sandwiches, like the goat cheese, sun-dried tomato, and pesto (€3.50). The attached grocery is the best place to pick up all the fancy foods your heart desires. Open M-Sa 9am-6pm. MC/V. ❶

Lautrec's, 9 Kieran St. (☎62720; www.lautrecs.com). Glorious French and Italian bistro food in a jazzy, rustic wine cellar. Pizza and pasta €8.50-14. Entrees €19-25. Open M-Th 5-10pm, F 5-11pm, Sa-Su 2-11pm. MC/V. ❸

Green Chilli, 8 John St. (☎86990 or 86988). Exquisite Indian food served in a dimly lit, tastefully decorated eatery. Vegetarian dishes €8.50. Meat entrees €13-15. Takeaway €2 less. Open M-Sa 5pm-midnight, Su 5-11pm. MC/V. ❸

Blaa Blaa Blaa, Canal Square. (☎52212). Just before the John Bridge. A hole-in-the-wall takeaway sandwich shop with the queue always out the door. Try the Wake-Up Call (€3.20) with sausage and chili jam. Open 8:30am-4pm. Cash only. ❶

M.L. Dore, High St. (☎63374). Entrance on High and Kieran St. Large, fresh deli case lures passersby into this nostalgic cafe, with old beer posters and wooden statues for sale. Sandwiches €4-7. Light entrees €7-15. Open daily 8am-10pm. Cash only. ❷

 PUBS

Kilkenny, "The Marble City," is also known as the "Oasis of Ireland"—its watering holes host live music most nights, especially in summer. On weekends, partygoers swarm off trains and buses onto John St. and often don't make it past the bridge; hen and stag parties abound at modern pubs and clubs. Several more subdued, traditional pubs line Parliament St. *Let's Go* has picked 14 of the best for a ▨**Kilkenny Pub Crawl** (p. 197). Pubbers who want to wind the night down slowly begin the crawl at the top of John St., while those who want to keep tossing back the Smithwick's well into the night should begin at the end of Parliament St. Alternatively, start at 3pm in the **Smithwick's Brewery** and begin the buzz on the house (tickets required, see **Sights,** p. 196). All pubs close at regulation hours (M-Th 11:30pm, F-Sa 12:30am, Su 11pm) unless otherwise noted. Music is almost always free.

▨ **The Pump House,** 26 Parliament St. (☎63924). A favorite among locals and hostelers. Loud, convenient, and complete with a vintage water pump. There's a fire burning in the grate, in case the scene's not hot enough. M-W great trad. F-Su bands upstairs, Sa DJ. Sandwiches (€4.25-4.75) served M-Sa noon-6pm. Opens daily at noon. Cash only.

▨ **Tynan's Bridge House Bar,** Johns Bridge (☎21291), on the river. Clocks in at 304 years, and it's had the same interior for much of its life span. Small, with terrific atmosphere, local art, and old spice drawers behind the bar. Lack of music keeps it subdued; locals fill the beer garden to chat every night of the week. Cash only.

▨ **Ryan's,** Friary St. off High St. No frills and no phone—just a good crowd and a beer garden. The ceiling's covered in photos of very happy patrons. Tu swing or jazz, W-Th trad; Sa mongrel mix of rock, blues, and soul. Opens M-F 4pm, Sa-Su 2pm. Cash only.

Cleere's, 28 Parliament St. (☎62573). Thespians from the Watergate Theatre across the street converge here during intermission. Black-box theater in back hosts vivacious musical and theatrical acts (tickets €5-25); periodic poetry readings. The same musicians have been playing every M for 18 years, making Cleere's home to the oldest-running session in Kilkenny. Open M-F 4pm, Sa-Su noon. MC/V.

Anna Conda, 1 Watergate St. (☎71657), near Cleere's. Great beer garden overlooks the ducks on the Suir. DJ on F-Sa night spins 60s-90s hits. Mixed crowd. Late bar F-Sa until 1:30am, July-Aug. also Th. MC/V.

Kyteler's Inn, Kieran St. (☎21064). The 1324 house of Kilkenny's witch, whose husbands (all 4) had a knack for poisoning themselves on their 1st anniversaries. The food and drink have since become safer. Watch out for the wax beauty in the basement. Trad nightly 9:30pm, Su 6pm. The attached nightclub **Nero's,** burns down the house F-Sa. Cover €7-10. Th-Su open until 1:30am. AmEx/MC/V.

Bollards, 31-32 St. Kiernan St. (☎21353). Pub fills on Tu and Th nights for excellent trad sessions. Serves pub grub like filling beef and Guinness stew (€10) and sandwiches (€6). Kitchen open daily noon-9:30pm. Open M-Sa 10:30am, Su 2pm. MC/V.

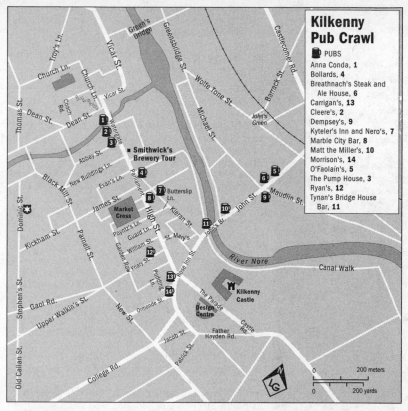

Kilkenny Pub Crawl

🍺 PUBS

Anna Conda, **1**
Bollards, **4**
Breathnach's Steak and
  Ale House, **6**
Carrigan's, **13**
Cleere's, **2**
Dempsey's, **9**
Kyteler's Inn and Nero's, **7**
Marble City Bar, **8**
Matt the Miller's, **10**
Morrison's, **14**
O'Faoláin's, **5**
The Pump House, **3**
Ryan's, **12**
Tynan's Bridge House
  Bar, **11**

Morrison's, 1 Ormond St. (☎71888). Kilkenny's newest late bar. Latin music grooves downstairs F-Su, while upstairs is a more traditional pub. Late bar until 1am. MC/V.

O'Faoláin's, John St. (☎61018). Throbbing new 3-fl. bar with a stunning restored Welsh church crafted into the walls. Tu trad. Late bar (nightly until 2am) and dance club (F-Sa; cover €10) make for a great place to end the night. MC/V.

Marble City Bar, 66 High St. (☎61143). Hip, modern pub tucked between High and Kieran St. Glowing marble countertop and occasional live music. Huge platters of pub grub (€12-16) served 9:30am-10pm. Tearoom (entrance on Kieran St.) with outdoor seating is a great place to relax and people-watch. MC/V.

Matt the Miller's, 1 John St. (☎61696), at the bridge. Huge, thronged, and alluring. Monday nights are mayhem. Pub fare €5-11 served M-F noon-4pm, Sa-Su noon-6:30pm. M rock music; Sa-Su DJ; M-F live bands, mainly covers. M, Th, Su late bar until 1:30am. Cover €5 after 10:30pm M and Sa. MC/V.

Dempsey's, 61 John St. (☎21543). Examine the musty tomes in the big bookcase. As traditional as it gets, with a charming back beer garden. Great €8-10 carvery lunches served daily noon-3:30pm and MC/V.

Breathnach's Steak and Ale House, 23-24 John St. (☎56737). Sports bar through and through—even the artwork features horses and footballers. Best place to watch if the Kilkenny Cats are on. W trad. Sa DJ. Cash only.

Carrigans, 2 High St. (☎02763). Ultra-hip, with marble walls and a tiled ceiling. The fresh new face of Kilkenny's drinking scene. Check out the old-fashioned grand luxury

The Chronicle

IN RECENT NEWS

KISS YOUR BUTTS GOODBYE

Step into an Irish pub, and you'll find it different from its international counterparts. Why? It's not the Guinness posters or the music—it's the air.

In March 2004, Ireland implemented a nationwide ban on smoking in workplaces, including restaurants and pubs. Though similar measures have been passed in parts of the United States and New South Wales, Ireland was the first country in the world to instate a ban of this kind. Though some feared that the ban would diminish pubs' business, concerns for the health of restaurant workers prevailed.

Three years later, studies have shown that the law has had its intended effect. The British Medical Journal published a study demonstrating that the number of non-smoking bar workers with respiratory problems has fallen 17% since the ban was first implemented. The law is also correlated with a drop in smoking: a study by the national Quitline service shows that 7000 people have stopped smoking since 2004, and half of those report that the ban influenced their decision.

It also turns out that businessmen had nothing to fear—according to the Central Statistics Office of Ireland, the ban has not decreased pub and restaurant business. So while you're out on your pub crawl, bring your ibuprofen, but leave those cigarettes at home.

bathrooms. Pizza, *panini*, and meals €8-11 served until 8:30pm. M Trad. W and Su late bar until 1:30am. Gay night every 2nd F. MC/V.

◉ SIGHTS

KILKENNY CASTLE. ▨**Kilkenny Castle,** the Parade, is the city's crown jewel. The castle housed the Earls of Ormonde from the 1300s through 1935, and many rooms have been restored to their former opulence. **Long Galley,** reminiscent of a Viking ship, is chock-full of portraits of English bigwigs and giant tapestries. The vaulted ceiling is especially impressive—it took the artist over two years to decorate with Celtic revival painting, which was fashionable in the 1850s. The basement houses **Butler Gallery** and its excellent modern art exhibits, which rotate every 6 weeks. (☎21450. *Castle and gallery open daily June-Aug. 9:30am-7pm; Sept. 10am-6:30pm; Oct.-Mar. 10:30am-12:45pm and 2-5pm; Apr.-May 10:30am-5pm. Castle access by 1hr. guided tour only. €5.30, students €2.10. Free every F in March. 1st fl. of castle and 10min. audio-visual presentation are wheelchair-accessible. MC/V.*) The 21-hectare **park** adjoining the castle provides excellent scenery for an afternoon jaunt. (*Open daily 8am-8:30pm; earlier closing hours in the low season. Free.*) Across the street, the internationally known **Kilkenny Design Centre** fills the castle's former stables with expensive Irish crafts. Past the gallery and workshops, the Butler House **gardens** are much quieter than the castle grounds and are a lovely place to sit or stroll. (☎22118; *www.kilkennydesign.com. Open Apr.-Dec. M-Sa 9am-6pm, Su 10am-6pm; Jan.-Mar. M-Sa 9am-6pm.*)

SMITHWICK'S BREWERY. Ireland's oldest brewery, Smithwick's has 50 years on its darker cousin, although Guinness had the last laugh when it purchased the brewery several years ago (to add insult to injury, it now brews Budweiser on-site). Head to the security station, on the right after Watergate Theatre, early in the morning (9-10am) to collect one of 50 free tickets. Show up at 3pm outside the green doors on Parliament St. to the left of the courthouse for a tedious 15min. virtual tour and ▨**free pints** in the private pub below the factory. A history of accidents keeps visitors out of the actual factory. (☎21014. *Tours July-Aug. M-F.*)

ST. CANICE'S CATHEDRAL. "Kilkenny" is derived from the Gaelic *Cill Chainnigh,* meaning "Church of St. Canice." With an impressive wooden ceiling and expertly carved tombs, the Romanesque gothic cathedral holds plenty of eye candy, including its original 12th-century baptismal font. The 30m **round tower** next to the cathedral is 1200 years old, but it's none the worse for the wear. With €3 and a bit of faith, the brave can climb the six steep ladders to a gorgeous panoramic view of the town and its surroundings. *(☎64971. On a hill off Dean St. Open June-Aug. M-Sa 9am-6pm, Su 2-6pm; Apr.-May and Sept. M-Sa 10am-1pm and 2-5pm, Su 2-5pm; Oct.-Mar. M-Sa 10am-1pm and 2-4pm, Su 2-4pm. Tower open at 10am. Cathedral entrance €4, students €3; round tower €3/2.50; combined ticket €6. Guided tours available but must be pre-booked.)*

THE BLACK ABBEY. Off Abbey St., Black Abbey was founded in 1225 by Dominican friars. A row of coffins that used to contain bodies struck by the Plague lie outside. Inside, An awe-inspiring, wall-size stained-glass window depicts the 15 mysteries of the rosary, while a 600-year-old statue saved from Cromwell's cronies stands guard nearby. *(☎21279. Free.)*

ROTHE HOUSE. Rothe House, Parliament St., was a Tudor merchant house when it was built in 1594. Now it's a small museum of local archaeological finds and Kilkennian curiosities, including 1830-1990 period costumes. The self-guided tour is mildly stimulating at best, though the displays of vintage clothing, including a section devoted to undergarments, are a sight. Some bypass the museum altogether and access the quiet, original stone courtyards through the welcome office. *(☎22893. Open Apr.-Oct. M-Sa 10:30am-5pm, Su 3-5pm; Nov.-Mar. M-Sa 1-5pm, Su 3-5pm. Last admission 4:15pm. Guided tours available on request, min. 10 people. €4, students €3.)*

WALKING TOUR. The weekday **Tynan Walking Tours,** adequate but not stellar, are the only way to take a peek inside a cell in the **old city gaol.** Save your euros and explore the town yourself with a free map from the tourist office. Tours depart from the tourist office on Rose Inn St. *(☎63955; www.tynantours.com. 1hr. tours mid-Mar.-Oct. M-Sa 10:30am, 12:15, 3, 4:30pm, Su 11:15am and 12:30pm; call for winter hours. €6, students and seniors €5.50.)*

🎵 ENTERTAINMENT

The Kilkenny People (€1.30) is a good resource for art and music listings. **The Watergate Theatre,** Parliament St., stages drama, dance, and opera year-round. (☎61674; www.watergatekilkenny.com. Box office open M-F 10am-7pm, Sa 2-6pm, Su 1hr. before curtain. Tickets €15-25, student tickets usually €12.) In mid-August, Kilkenny holds its **Arts Festival,** a daily program of theater, concerts, dance, and readings by famous European and Irish artists. (☎52175; www.kilkennyarts.ie. Some event tickets are free, others €15-25; student/senior discounts vary by venue. Sold at the box office in the Parade in the old Bank of Ireland, by phone, or online. Box office open M-F 10am-6pm.) The city's population increases by more than 10,000 when the **Cat Laughs;** this **comedy festival** features international the first weekend in June. (www.smithwickscatlaughs.ie. Some events free, others €20-30; book in advance.) The **Rhythm and Roots Festival,** a celebration of country music, comes a-knockin' on the bank holiday in May (www.kilkennyroots.com).

🏞 OUTDOOR ACTIVITIES

Many options await the outdoor enthusiast in and around Kilkenny. **Noreside Outdoors** (☎93966) sets up **fishing** on the Nore and sells permits to make it legal. To **canoe** on the river Barrow, call **Go with the Flow River Adventures** (☎08725 29700. Rental €25 per day). Those with equestrian aspirations choose **Kilkenny Top Flight Equestrian Centre** (☎22682) to ride along the banks of the Nore, or the pricier **Mount**

Juliet (☎73000) for trail rides on a country estate; pre-booking is essential. The **Kilkenny Golf Club** (☎65400), out Castlecomer Rd., is an 18-hole championship course open to non-members. To watch rather than participate, see the "Fighting Cats" in a **hurling match** in Nowlan Park, near the train station. (kilkenny.gaa.ie.) **Horseracing** thrills fans in **Gowran Park** (☎26225; www.gowranpark.ie), on N9.

▶ DAYTRIPS FROM KILKENNY

THOMASTOWN AND JERPOINT ABBEY. **Thomastown,** a tiny community on the Nore River south of Kilkenny, is the gateway to the stately ▩**Jerpoint Abbey,** located only 2.4km away. The strict order of Cistercian monks who founded Jerpoint in 1180 stressed simplicity, but at some point they loosened up and decorated their home with beautiful stone carvings of their favorite saints. The trend caught on, and soon almost every stone surface displayed beautiful carvings; virtually every pillar and wall is now decorated with a figure. Much of the original structure fell apart and had to be reconstructed, but some original plaster with still-decipherable paintings remains in the sacristy. Tours (45min.) upon request discuss the lives of medieval monks and offer insight into the meanings of the stonework and paintings. At one end of Market St. lie the 13th-century remnants of **Thomastown Church,** which is currently being restored. A trilogy of curious objects remains among the church's gravestones: an ancient ogham stone, a Celtic cross, and a weathered 13th-century effigy. (*Bus Éireann stops at Jerpoint Inn in Thomastown on its way from Waterford to Kilkenny, 2 per day. The folks at the Inn have a schedule for Rapid Express ☎31106, a private bus running between Dublin and Tramore; 9 per day. Trains run from Waterford to Dublin through Thomastown and Kilkenny 4-5 per day 9am-9pm; €12.30 return. The train station is a 10min. walk out on Marshes Rd. From the station, turn left and head downhill to get to town. Jerpoint Abbey ☎24623. Open daily June-Sept. 9:30am-6pm; Oct. and Mar.-May 10am-5pm; Nov. 10am-4pm. €3, students €1.30.*)

DUNMORE CAVE. On the road to **Castlecomer,** 10km north of Kilkenny, eerie **Dunmore Cave** lies underfoot. The only Irish cave documented in ancient annals, it's known as one of the three darkest places in Ireland (the others being Newgrange and Knowth). Recently unearthed human bones dating from AD 928, mostly belonging to women and children and some showing signs of brutality, are remnants of a tragic Viking massacre of over 100 local people that year. A few years back, a tour guide who strayed outside the marked boundaries of the cave discovered a valuable Viking stash of silver thread, coins, and other spoils that still confound archaeologists. The 40min. tours repeat the information given in the 10min. audio-visual presentation, but they're the only way to gain admission to the caves; guides point out the important stalactites and stalagmites and accompany visitors up and down the over 700 steps. The limestone caverns, which remain a constant 50°F year-round, make a perfect habitat for bats but can be chilly for humans. (*Buggy's Coaches, ☎41264, stops at the cave between Kilkenny and Castlecomer. 20min., M-Sa 1 per day, 12:45pm with 4pm return. From drop-off point, the 10min. walk is well signposted. By car, take N78, the Dublin-Castlecomer road, from Kilkenny; turn right after the split with N77, the Durrow road. Cave ☎67726. Open Mar.-Nov. daily 9:30am-5:30pm; Nov.-Mar. F-Su 9:30am-5:30pm. Last admission 1hr. before closing. €3, students €1.30.*)

CARLOW TOWN (CEATHARLACH) ☎05991

The unassuming but vibrant town of Carlow lies along the eastern side of River Barrow, between Dublin and Waterford on the N9. Its picturesque river scenery and towering cathedral spire, combined with winding, pub-filled streets, mark it as more than a nondescript pit stop. Today, Carlow's rather bellicose history has been relegated to the county museum, where visitors can steal a look at what remains of the gallows from which insurgents of the **1798 Rebellion** (p. 53) were hanged. Still, Carlow is determined not to live in the past. The busy town has found ways to please its growing population of young people and travelers with a variety of activities and festivals, as well as wireless Internet hotspots and lively pubs and cafes.

⌷ TRANSPORTATION. Trains (☎31633) run through Carlow from Dublin's Heuston Station on their way to **Waterford** (1¼hr.; M-Sa 5 per day, Su 3 per day; €15.20 from Carlow). **Bus Éireann** (☎051 879 000; www.buseireann.ie) leaves from the corner of Barrack and Kennedy, in a little bus park, for **Athlone** (2¼hr., M-Sa 11:20am, €15), **Dublin** (1¾hr.; M-Sa 10 per day, Su 6 per day; €9.50), and **Waterford** (1¼hr.; M-Sa 10 per day, Su 6 per day; €9.50). **Rapid Express Travel,** Barrack St. (☎43081 or 016 791 549 for Dublin office), run a Tramore-Waterford-Carlow-Thomastown-Dublin route daily (10 per day to Waterford or Tramore 8:30am-midnight, 8 per day to Dublin 9:45am-9:45pm; €8 to Tramore and Waterford, €9 to Dublin); call or visit www.jjkavanagh.ie to book ahead or see Midland destinations. For a **taxi,** call **Carlow Cab** (☎914 0000), or head to the taxi stand at Potato Market, off Tullow St.

⌷⌷ ORIENTATION AND PRACTICAL INFORMATION. From the train station, it's a 10min. walk to the town center; head down **Railway Road,** turn left onto the **Old Dublin Road,** and make another left at the Court House onto **College Street.** The **tourist office** is on College St., off Tullow St. behind the library. (☎31554; www.carlowtourism.ie. Open M-F 9:30am-1pm and 2-5:30pm; June-Aug. also Sa 10am-1pm and 2-5:30pm.) Services include: a **bureau de change** and a 24hr. **ATM** at the **AIB,** Tullow St. (☎32315; open M 10am-5pm, Tu and Th-F 10am-4pm, W 10:30am-4pm); another 24hr. **ATM** at the **TSB** across from the SuperValu on Tullow St., and another at **Bank of Ireland** underneath the Dinn Rí complex entrance also on Tullow St.; **Internet** access at a few locations but **Enter and Escape,** 91 Tullow St., is central and relatively cheap (☎30345. €1 per 15min.; open M-F 10am-10pm, Sa 10am-6pm, Su noon-6pm); the **post office,** on the corner of Kennedy Ave. and Burrin St. (☎31783. Open M-F 9am-5:30pm, Sa 9am-1pm.)

⌷⌷ ACCOMMODATIONS AND FOOD. The local B&Bs are a traveler's best bet for safe, affordable accommodation as Carlow Town is still in need of an accredited hostel. The **Redsetter Guesthouse ❸,** 14 Dublin St., is in the center of town, but it somehow manages to feel like a quiet, country home. (☎41848. Parking available. €40 per person.) Similarly, the **Carlow Guesthouse ❸** casts off its ordinary hotel-like outer appearance in order to give its guests a personal experience with loads of amenities. Take the Green Ln. toward the Dublin N9 route and look for the yellow house with the horse statue on the right. (☎36033; www.carlowguesthouse.com. €40-45 per person ensuite.) Speaking of cozy, the **Westlow B&B ❸,** just before the Carlow Guesthouse, offers small rooms with a warm welcome and the right price. Your wallet will thank you. (☎43964. €35 per person ensuite.) In contrast, the **Dinn Rí Hotel ❹** prides itself less in its more ordinary yet pricier rooms, and more in its association with some of the town's best food and entertainment hot spots. (☎33111; www.dinnri.com. Singles €50-65, not available Sa; doubles €100-150; triples €125-195.)

Supermarkets **Aldi,** on Hanover Rd. off N9 toward Kilkenny (open M-W 9am-8pm, Th-F 9am-9pm, Sa 9am-7pm, Su 11am-7pm) and **Lidl,** on Tullow St. two blocks past the Fairgreen Shopping Centre (open M-Sa 8am-9pm, Su 12:30pm-7pm) compete on the outskirts of town for local shoppers. An even fresher stock of local ingredients can be purchased at the town's **Farmers' Market,** set up on Saturday mornings in the Potato Market behind Haddens Car Park (9am-2pm). For a stylish meal at a surprisingly reasonable price, visit the town's entertainment mecca at Dinn Rí and turn right to find **Brooks Cafe Bar ❸.** The menu offers specialty teas and coffees alongside tempting sandwiches, while the evening menu, served when the restaurant becomes considerably more bar than cafe, is better known for its inventive burgers. Aside from the hip food and atmosphere, Brooks attracts customers with its designation as a Wi-Fi hot spot. (☎33111. Sandwiches €6; burgers €13; dinner €16-27. Open 8:30am-11pm, cafe bar menu 8:30am-5:30pm, evening menu 5:30-9:45pm.) **Lennon's ❷**, 121 Tullow St., is also a crowd-pleaser among the locals for its long list of home-made favorites such as soups and brown bread sandwiches. (☎31575. Sandwiches and wraps €7-8; entrees €11-12. Open for breakfast M-Sa 10am-11am; lunch M-F noon-3pm, Sa noon-4pm; dinner Th-F 5:30-9pm.)

🖼🎵 PUBS AND CLUBS. Unsurprisingly, the Dinn Rí pub and entertainment complex, which spans the entire block between Tullow St. and Kennedy Ave., dominates Carlow nightlife. The pub has plenty of seats to go around for the Sunday trad sessions. Its two nightclubs unite on Saturday nights, admitting a crowd larger than the populations of most Irish towns. Of the two, **The Foundry** is rumored to be cooler, but **The Towers Live!** does live up to its namesake by host-ing live music. (☎33111. Nightclub open F-Su from 11pm. Cover €5-10; check club or www.dinnri.com for upcoming performances.) Other venues still get their due, especially ▨**Scragg's Alley**, 12 Tullow St., where local hipsters schmooze around the stylish bar (☎42233.) Renowned **Teach Dolmain** (CHOCK DOL-men), 76 Tullow St., also hosts trad music on Thursday nights. (☎30911. Bar kitchen open daily noon-9pm.)

◧🎭 SIGHTS AND FESTIVALS. In the middle of a field 4km from Carlow lies the **Brownshill Dolmen.** Marking a 6000-year-old burial site, the 150-ton granite capstone is the largest of its kind in Europe. No one knows how those Neolithic lads managed to schlep it up there. Follow Tullow St. through the traffic light and keep going straight until the roundabout pointing to Dublin. Turn left, then right at the next roundabout and follow the signs. Near the Barrow Bridge, **Carlow Castle** hangs on by a fingernail behind the storefronts on Castle St. The building's decrepit condition can be blamed on one Dr. Middleton, who used dynamite to remodel the castle. The doctor, incidentally, was trying to turn the castle into an insane asylum; now it's in disrepair, but visitors can still walk around its base and peer at the rubble.

In June, Carlow hosts **Éigse** (AIG-sha, "gathering"), a 10-day arts festival. Fantas-tic Irish talent gathers to present visual, musical, and theatrical works. The festival office is on College St. (☎40491; www.eigsecarlow.ie.)

Carlow also boasts of its great walking and cycling cites nearby, not the least of which include the serene **Oak Park Forest Park.** Located on N9 en route to Castled-ermot, this diverse, 120-acre woodland provides a variety of walking loops. For more information on outdoor activities, consult the tourist office.

COUNTY TIPPERARY

In southern Tipperary, the towns of Clonmel, Cahir, and Cashel rest among a sprawling idyllic countryside and medieval ruins. Farmers outnumber tourists in this fertile region—even during the summer months you might find yourself the only occupant of your hostel. The Rock of Cashel looms over the countryside, topped only by the Comeragh, Galty, and Knockmealdown Mountains to the south of the Cahir-Cashel-Tipperary triangle. Lismore, though located in Co. Waterford, is covered here in Co. Tipperary with the Knockmealdowns. Those traveling by public transportation must head to Cahir to connect to the surrounding towns.

TIPPERARY TOWN (THIOBRAID ARANN)   ☎ 062

"It's a long way to Tipperary," as the Judge and Williams song goes, but once you get there there's not much to see. Affectionately known as "Tipp Town," Tipperary is a market center for the Golden Vale farming region. Compared with the surrounding hills and the **Glen of Aherlow** to the south, Tipp doesn't have a particularly star-studded collection of sights; in fact, there are no sights, museums, or tourist attractions within walking distance. However, this doesn't stop happy Tippers from singing its praises from July through the first week in August during the **Pride of Tipperary Festival,** which names one local lass the "Pride of Tipperary." Buses leave from Abbey St.; a block up the hill on Bridge St. brings you to Main St. To the left is Church St. and to the right are Davis and Mitchell St.

The aptly named **Central House B&B ❸,** 45 Main St., has a welcoming owner, comfortable beds and a great location. (☎51117. Rooms €30 per person, €35 with breakfast. MC/V.) Other B&Bs are on **Emly Road,** about 800m west of town off Main St.; in addition, several pubs offer accommodation upstairs. **Emmett House ❹,** above T. C. Ryan's, has rooms from €45-90 that make the stumble home that much easier. **SuperValu** sells groceries on Kickham Pl., at the foot of Abbey St. (☎52930. Open M-F 8am-9pm, Sa 8am-7pm, Su 8:30am-6pm.) Depending on your point of view, the interior of **Kiely's Bar ❷,** 22 Main St., could be described as "minimalist and modern" or "bare and gloomy." But, as pub grub goes, it has the cheapest, tastiest food around. (☎51239. Lunch €8-10; dinner €13-17. Kitchen open 10:30am-9pm. MC/V.) The walls outside **Mary Hanna's ❷,** 51 Main St., are emblazoned with mottos like "in vino, veritas." It's clear that those eating inside have taken that slogan to heart. (☎80503. Lunch €6-11. Dinner from €20. Open M-W 9:30am-5:30pm, Th-F 9:30am-5:30pm and 9-10pm, Sa 10am-5:30pm and 7-10pm. MC/V.) For a taste of the sea in the middle of the island, try the **The Brown Trout ❷** on Abbey St., one block from Main St., where there is a framed fish tank on the wall. (☎51912. Lunch €10-11; dinner €12-17. Open daily 12:30-2:30pm and W-Su 6-9:30pm. MC/V.) For those seeking simple cafe fare, the bright, colorful **Shamrog's Bistro ❸,** 1 Davis St., dishes out everything from sandwiches (€3.50-4) to steaks. (☎82847. Lunch €8-13, dinner €9-15. Open M-Th 9am-6pm, F-Su 9am-8pm. Cash only.) A pub with old-time charm, **Kickham House,** 50 Main St., draws a wide range of ages and has the most frequent live music. (☎51716. Open daily from 10:30am. Tu and Sa 9:45pm trad. Cash only.) Sit back as you watch Ireland's best battle it out on the big screen or enjoy the fabulous soups of the day at **Tony Lowry's,** 46 Main St., next to Central House B&B. (☎52774. Th live music. Lunch 10:30am-3pm. Cash only.) Across the street, **T.C. Ryan's,** 34 Main St., has pool and darts for those who want to get in the game. (☎51465. Kitchen open from 10:30am. Cash only.)

Buses go from Tipp's **Abbey Street** to Limerick (40min.; M-F 8 per day, Sa 7 per day, Su 6 per day 10:30am-10:15pm; €5); Rosslare Harbor (4½hr.; M-Sa 3 per day, Su 2 per day 8:25am-4:15pm); and Waterford (2½hr.; M-Sa 7 per day, Su 6 per day 8:25am-8:40pm). The **tourist office,** on Mitchell St. in the Excel Centre—a large orange building that also houses the **Family Historical Research Centre** and a cineplex—is a useful resource for preparing trips into the glen and mountains. Glen of Aherlow trail maps are free. Ask the Galtee Walking Club (☎56331) about group hill walks. (☎80520; www.tipperary-excel.com. Internet €1 per 15min. Cineplex films €8, M-Th students €7. Open M-Sa 9:30am-5:30pm and 7-10pm, Su 2-5:30pm and 7-10pm.) **AIB** (☎51139) is on Main St., along with **Bank of Ireland** (☎50160). Each has a 24hr. **ATM.** (Both open M 10am-5pm, Tu-F 10am-4pm; AIB Th open 10:30am-4pm.) The **library** on Davis St. provides **Internet** access—call in advance to get on the waiting list. (☎51761. 1hr. per day €2. Open Tu and F-Sa 10am-1pm and 2-5:30pm, W 1-5:15pm and 6:30-8:30pm, Th 10am-1pm and 2-6:30pm.) The **post**

office is on Davis St. (☎51216. Open M and W-F 9am-5:30pm, Tu 9:30am-5:30pm, Sa 9:30am-1pm.), while the **police** *(Garda)* is just around the corner on St. Michael St. (☎51212. Open 24hr.) **Castigan's,** 52 Main St., is one of the many pharmacies on the main drag. (☎51132. Open M-Sa 9:30am-6pm.)

CASHEL (CAISEAL MUMHAN)   ☎062

The town of Cashel sits among green fields, tucked between a series of mountain ranges on N8, 19km east of Tipperary Town. Visitors stream out of tour buses for a peek at the Rock, a remarkably well-preserved collection of medieval buildings. There's little else in Cashel, but no one seems to mind; two fine hostels and a street full of pubs keep backpackers happy.

◪◨ TRANSPORTATION AND PRACTICAL INFORMATION. Bus Éireann (☎0613 3333; www.buseireann.ie) runs to **Dublin** (3hr., 6 per day 9:35am-7:35pm, €10) and **Cork** (30min., 6 per day 10:50am-8:50pm, €10.50) via **Cahir** (15min., €4.20) Buses depart from Main St. near the tourist office. Pick up schedules at the tourist office and purchase tickets across the street at SPAR. Traveling to most nearby towns requires a connection in Cahir. **Main Street** has everything you want to see—except the Rock, which is up a hill and very well signposted from Main St. At the top of Main St., Lady's Well St. is to the left and Friar St. is to the right. Cashel's **tourist office** splits rent with the **Heritage Centre** in the City Hall on Main St. and leads **walking tours** every Tu-Th at 7pm. (☎62511; e-mail jhugheso@eircom.net to confirm. Tours €7.50, students €5. Open daily 9:30am-5:30pm.) **Bank of Ireland** (☎61200; open M 10am-5pm, Tu and Th-F 10am-4pm, W 10:30am-4pm) and **AIB** (☎61144; open M 10am-5pm, Tu 10:30am-4pm, W-F 10am-4pm) are neighbors on Main St.; the AIB has a 24hr. **ATM. McInerney's,** three doors down from the SuperValu, **rents bikes.** (☎61225. €10 per day, €60 per week. Open Th-Tu 9:30am-1pm and 2-6pm, W 9:30am-1pm.) The **library,** located under the arch on Friar St., about a minute from Main St., provides **Internet** access. (☎63825. €2 per hr. Open M and W 10am-5pm, Tu and Th 10am-5pm and 6-8:30pm, F-Sa 10am-1pm and 2-5pm.) The **post office** is on Main St. (☎61418. Open M and W-F 9am-5:30pm, Tu 9:30am-5:30pm, Sa 9am-1pm.) The **police** *(Garda)* station is on Hogan Sq., near the bottom of Main St. (☎75840. Open daily 9am-5pm.) **O'Dwyer's Pharmacy,** Main St., fulfills all your medicinal and beauty needs. (☎61318. Open M-Sa 9am-6pm.) **Tivoli Cleaners,** Friar St., does laundry for €1 per lb., which usually works out to €8-10 per load. (☎62517. Open M-Sa 9:30am-6:30pm.)

◪◪ ACCOMMODATIONS AND CAMPING. It's almost a shame that Cashel has two fine hostels, because the B&Bs are reasonably priced treats. A 10min. walk from central Cashel on Dundrum Rd., which intersects Main St. toward the bottom of the hill, lies the incredible ◪**O'Brien's Farm House Hostel ❷.** O'Brien's has an incredible view of the Rock, cheerful, spacious rooms, and a common room with armchairs around a fire. (☎61003. Full-service laundry €12. Dorms €17.50; doubles €65. **Camping** €9 per person, with separate bathroom facilities and kitchen. MC/V.) **Cashel Holiday Hostel (IHH) ❶,** on John St. just off Main St., is the more social of the two hostels, though with slightly less comfy digs. Avoid the cramped bunk rooms by sticking to the spacious kitchen, which is illuminated by the huge skylight. Next door, the owners also operate the **Cashel Town B&B ❸,** featuring themed rooms based on a popular mystery series. (☎62330; www.cashelhostel.com; www.cashelbandb.com. Laundry €10. Dorms €15; 4-bed dorms with bath €18. Discount for long-term stays. B&B singles €40, ensuite €45; doubles €60/70. €5 less without breakfast. MC/V.) Several B&Bs rest in the quiet residential neighborhood of Dominic St. en route to the Rock and castle. Just steps from the Rock, the sunny, comfortable and immaculate rooms of **Rockville House ❸**, Dominic St., are a great bargain. Check out the stuffed bird in the hallway. (☎61760. All rooms with bath. Singles €40; doubles €60. Cash only.) **Thornbrook House ❸** is about 2.5km up Dualla Rd. From Main St., turn onto Friar St. and then left onto Dualla. The house shimmers with elegant chandeliers and sparkling bathrooms. For 25 years, caring hostess Mary Kennedy has been brewing warm tea for her guests. All rooms have TV, coffee, and tea. (☎62388. Singles €55; doubles €75. MC/V.)

▯▣ FOOD AND PUBS. SuperValu, Main St., sells groceries. (☎61555. Open M-F 8am-10pm, Sa-Su 8am-9pm.) **Spearman's ❶,** near the Friary St. end of Main St., serves hot sandwiches and *panini* (€3.50-6) on freshly baked bread. (☎61143. Open M-F 9am-5:45pm, Sa 9am-5pm. MC/V.) Head to **Café Hans ❸,** off Lady's Well St. on the road to the Rock, for first-rate salads and grilled salmon. (☎63660. Entrees €9-15. Open Tu-Sa noon-5:30pm. Cash only.) At the bottom of Main St., **Indo Spice ❷** serves steaming plates of samosas and pakoras. Entrees €9-10, take-out €1-2 less. (☎63801. Open M-Th and Su 5-11:30pm, F-Sa 5pm-midnight, Sa-Su also noon-3pm. Cash only.) Enjoy decadent sweets at **The Bake House ❶,** across from the tourist office. Coffee and light meals are served upstairs, but you're better off sticking to the sticky buns. (☎61680. Entrees €4-7. Open M-Sa 8:30am-5:30pm, Su 10am-5:30pm. Cash only.)

Cashel's pub crawl is a straight shot down Main St. All of the following close at standard pub hours (M-Th 11:30pm, F-Sa 12:30am, Su 11pm). Start the night next door to the tourist office at **Feehan's,** where the decor is timeless and the chips are hot and crispy. (☎61929. Kitchen open M-F noon-6pm, Sa noon-3pm.) Head left out the back door to get to **Moor Lane Tavern** for darts, snooker, or dancing. (☎62093. Tu and Th country, F-Sa rock, Su trad 8-10pm.) If the stars are out, move next door to the gorgeous multi-level beer garden at wheelchair-accessible **Mikey Ryan's** (☎61431). Cross over Main St. for some singing, joke-telling *craic* on the green couches at **Davern's** (☎61121; M and W live music after 9pm), before heading down the street to **Pat and Fox,** a younger scene with a trendy, lively vibe, run by a 1992 All-Star Hurler. (☎62428. Daily poker games. Th solo singer.) End the night at **Brian Ború,** where there's live music—everything from rock and alternative to

TOP 10 FOODS TO TRY ON THE ROAD

1. Brown bread: Whole meal goodness. Best from the corner bakery.

2. Muller Rice: Sweet dairy rice with a layer of fruit on the bottom. Find it in the dairy section with the yogurt.

3. Garlic Chips: A real heartstopper. French fries smothered in garlic mayonnaise (known as "salad cream"). Find them at the local greasy spoon.

4. Rashers: Thick, juicy strips of fried pork with a piece of fat dangling off the end. A key component of the full Irish breakfast.

5. Black pudding: Sausages held together by blood, which gives it its signature black color. Served at breakfast.

6. Chocolate muffins: Chunks of chocolate in every bite. Try Cadbury's version, which has a creamy filling and a bar of milk chocolate poured over the top.

7. Guinness and beef stew: Traditional favorite combines the two with vegetables and potatoes.

8. Döner Kebab: A Persian dish popular on the island. Shaved lamb smothered in a tangy sauce and wrapped up in a pita with all the fixings.

9. Sponge Toffee: Crunchy yellow candy looks like honeycomb and tastes like burnt sugar.

10. Muesli: The Irish version of granola, loaded with oats, dried fruit, seeds, and nuts.

trad—five nights per week and a DJ on weekends. (☎ 63381. Music M and Th-Su. M trad. F-Sa DJ. Open daily at 10:30am. Kitchen open noon-8pm.)

▶ THE ROCK OF CASHEL. It looms majestically on the horizon—a huge limestone outcropping topped with medieval buildings. Welcome to the Rock. Also known as Cashel of the Kings, or St. Patrick's Rock, the **▧Rock of Cashel** is associated with a number of legends, some historically substantiated, others more dubious. St. Patrick almost certainly baptized the King of Munster here around AD 450; whether he accidentally stabbed the king's feet in the process is debatable. Guided tours (every hr. on the ½hr.) are informative, if a bit dry. Mounted plaques point out the important parts, so exploring at your own pace is a viable and perhaps more attractive option. Avoid showing up near noon to steer clear of tour buses dropping off throngs of visitors. The bi-steepled **Cormac's Chapel,** consecrated in 1134, holds semi-restored Romanesque paintings, disintegrating stone arches, and an ornately carved sarcophagus used as a "flesh-eater" to prepare bodies for burial. Visitors wander beneath the vaulted Gothic arches of the **Cashel Cathedral,** which was nearly lost in 1495 when the Earl of Kildare lit it on fire. Kildare defended himself to Henry VII by saying, "I thought the Archbishop was in it." The King promoted him to Lord Deputy. Next to the cathedral, a 27m **round tower,** built circa 1101, is the oldest and best-preserved part of the Rock. The old Vicar's choir building now houses a **museum,** at the entrance to the castle complex, which contains the 12th-century **St. Patrick's Cross.** It is said that anyone who can wrap their arms around the cross will never get a toothache again—possibly because they'll lose their teeth in the attempt. Upstairs, the choir's **dining room** has been beautifully reconstructed. A disappointing film on medieval religious structures is shown every hour or so. As impressive as the Rock is during the day, it's truly inspiring by night, when it's flooded with light. The best view is from the cow path leading down from the Rock toward Hore Abbey. (☎ 61437. Rock open daily June to mid-Sept. 9am-7pm; mid-Mar. to mid-June 9am-5:30pm; mid-Sept. to mid-Oct. 9am-5:30pm; mid-Oct. to mid-Mar. 9am-4:30pm. Last admission 45min. before closing. €5.30, students €2.10, seniors €3.70.) Visitors may want to head to the **Heritage Centre,** in the same building as the tourist office on Main St., to brush up on their history before making the trek to the rock, but most of the information is covered in the tour. The Centre features temporary exhibits and permanent installations such as "The Rock: From the 4th-11th Century" and its much-anticipated sequel, "The Rock: 12th-18th Century." (☎ 62511. Open daily 9:30am-5:30pm. Free.)

◎ OTHER SIGHTS. It's a shame that **Hore Abbey,** the last Cistercian monastery built in Ireland, lies in the shadow of The Rock, because it's often overlooked by travelers on the hill. The intact ceiling is majestic, and there are few tourists to elbow out of the way. A quick jog down the hill near The Rock is the fastest route to the abbey. (Always open. Free.) **Brú Ború Heritage Centre** (pronounced "brew-brew"), at the base of The Rock, hosts wonderful, if stagey, traditional music and dance sessions. Afterward, musicians invite the audience to the bar for a round of informal trad. The Centre also houses the **Sounds of History** audio-visual museum; visit for a crash course in Irish song and dance. (☎ 61122; www.comhaltas.com. Performances mid-June to mid-Sept. Tu-Sa 9pm. €18, students €10; with pre-show dinner €48/24. Centre open mid-June to mid-Sept. Tu-Sa 9am-11:30pm; mid-Sept. to mid-June M 9am-5pm, Tu-Sa 9am-11:30pm. Sounds of History display €5, students €3.) The **GPA-Bolton Library,** John St., displays a musty collection of books and silver that once belonged to Theophilus Bolton, an Anglican archbishop of Cashel. The tiny library harbors ecclesiastical texts and rare manuscripts, including the first English translation of *Don Quixote* and an English Bible that is (locally) reputed to be the **smallest book in the world.** (☎ 61944. Open M-Th 10am-2:30pm. €2.) **St. John the Baptist Church,** Friar St., has a magnificent mosaic on its front facade and eerily realistic sculptures inside. (Open daily 9am-7pm. Free.)

The quiet **St. Dominick's Abbey,** on Dominic St., built in 1243 by Dominican friars, houses a graveyard in its ruins. Get a key to the gate from Mrs. McDonnell, 19 Dominic St., the first house on the right, 45m after the abbey. (Free.) In the town of **Golden,** 8km west of Cashel on the Tipperary Rd., stand the ruins of lovely **Althassel Abbey,** a 12th-century Augustinian priory founded by the Red Earl of Dunster. The Tipperary Heritage Way Walk, which is signposted from Cashel, follows the banks of the River Suir for 11km to Golden.

FETHARD (FIODH ARD)

Within cycling distance from Cashel (15km) and a short bus ride away from Clonmel (14km), the medieval town of Fethard (FEH-TARD) is protected by an impressive intact stone wall dating as far back as the 13th century. From Cashel, follow Friary Rd. (R692) to the roundabout, then follow signs to town. Behind the wall, the medieval **Holy Trinity Church** (not to be confused with the modern Holy Trinity Church at the opposite end of Main St.) looms over the surrounding graveyard. For a peek into the church itself, talk to someone in the **Community Office** on Barrack St. and pick up general **tourist information** and a guide to the town's sights, which are particularly well-signposted. (☎31000; www.fethardonline.com. Open M-F 9am-5pm.) Next to the churchyard's entrance is the **Town Hall** building, which dates back to the 17th century and is one of the oldest urban buildings of its type in Ireland. Fethard also hosts two **sheela-na-gig,** bizarre 15th-century stone carvings of nude women performing lewd acts. The more scandalous of the two is adjacent to the Watergate Bridge; the other is through the yard and next to the **Augustine Friary,** which is on Burke St. past the gate on the far end of town. The Friary also has an ornate, recently restored stained-glass window. Just outside town, toward Cashel, the **Fethard Folk Museum** holds thousands of items from the 19th and early 20th centuries, including farm tools, bicycles, and a horse-drawn carriage. On Sundays, hundreds of people flock to the grounds for the biggest **car boot sale** (flea market) in Ireland. (☎31516. Museum and boot sale Su 11am-4pm and noon-5pm. €1.50, children €1.) About 3km up the Killenaule Rd. from Fethard lie the well groomed and strictly secured grounds of **Coolmore** (☎31298; www.coolmore.com), the world's leading **stud farm.** Breeders from all over the world shell out upwards of €45,000 for these stellar stallions to "cover" their mares. The grounds are not open to the public—even horses deserve some privacy.

Travelers flock to the **Gateway B&B ❸,** Rocklow Rd., for its sunny breakfast room, soft beds, and accommodating owner. (☎31701; www.gatewaybandb.com. €25-28 per person. Singles €35; doubles €55. Cash only.) For a pint, head down Burke St. around the corner from Main Square to **The Well,** the town's resident provider of Guinness and good cheer. (☎31053. Open daily from 8pm.) **McCarthy's,** 2 Main St., has everything you need from cradle to grave: food, drink, and a casket. (**McCarthy's Restaurant ❷** ☎31176. **G&T's Restaurant ❶** ☎32050. Pub ☎31149. McCarthy's entrees €15-20. G&T's entrees €2-6. McCarthy's open daily 6-10pm. MC/V. G&T's open M-Sa 9am-6pm. Cash only. Pub opens daily at noon; F trad sessions.) **Emily's Delicatessen ❶,** Burke St., has hearty breakfasts and inexpensive sandwiches, as well as a fully stocked specialty foods shop. (☎32728. Food €2-5. Open M-F 8:30am-6:30pm, Sa 8:30am-5pm. Cash only.)

Shamrock Coaches runs a bus from Clonmel, in front of Eason's, on Mary St. (☎050 422 266. Departs Clonmel 11:30am, 3:15, 6pm. €3.40.) **Centra,** on the continuation of Main St., sells groceries and sandwiches and has the only **ATM** in town. (☎31383. Open daily 7am-9pm.) Also on Main St. are the **pharmacy** (☎32111; open M-W 9am-6:45pm, Th-Sa 9am-6pm) and **post office** (☎31217; open M-F 9am-12:30pm and 1:30-5:30pm, Sa 9am-12:30pm).

CAHIR (AN CATHAIR)   ☎052

The small town of Cahir (CARE) sits on the edge of the Galty Mountains. Its plethora of walking trails for hikers and pubs for social butterflies compensate for its limited number of restaurants and accommodations. At the crossroads of the Waterford-Limerick and Dublin-Cork roads, it's a good base for the bus-reliant, although smaller attractions and hostels can be difficult to reach. A lovely afternoon might include a riverside stroll to the well-preserved medieval Cahir Castle and the secluded, thatched-roofed Swiss Cottage.

⬛🄬 TRANSPORTATION AND PRACTICAL INFORMATION. Buses stop on Castle Rd., near its namesake, Cahir Castle. Up the hill, Church St. runs through the square. Bus Éireann is the cheapest and most convenient way to travel to and from Cahir. Buses go from the tourist office to: **Cashel** (15min., 6-7 per day, €4.20); **Cork** (1½hr., 7 per day, €9.50); **Dublin** (3hr., 6-7 per day, €9.50); **Limerick** via **Tipperary** (1hr., 5-7 per day, €6.30); **Waterford** (1¼hr., 6-7 per day, €6.30). The train station is 5min. out of town on Cashel Rd.; from Castle Rd., take a left at the square and bear right. Trains go to **Dublin** via **Limerick** (3hr.; M-Sa 7, 11am, 3:30pm; €34) and **Waterford** (4hr., M-Sa 9:30am and 1:20pm). *Let's Go* does not recommend hitchhiking, but hitchers to Dublin or Cork reportedly position themselves on N8, a 20min. hike from the center of town. Those hitching to Limerick or Waterford wait outside town on N24, which passes through the town square. The **tourist office,** Castle St., offers many goodies: the free *Southeast Guide*, which includes a map; *Ordnance Survey #74* and *75*, which cover hill walks in the area (€8.25), and one of Ireland's best postcard selections. (☎41453. Open Apr.-Oct. M-Sa 9:30am-1pm and 2-6pm.) **AIB,** up the street from the tourist office (☎41277; open M-F 9:45am-5:15pm), has a 24hr. **ATM.** In the square across from Cahir House Hotel is **Bank of Ireland.** (☎41299. Open M 10am-5pm, Tu and Th-F 10am-4pm, W 10:30am-4pm; closed 12:30-1:30pm.) The **post office** is on Church St. (☎41275; open M-F 9:30am-1pm and 2-5:30pm, Sa 9:30am-1pm.) **Internet** access is available at the **Enterprise Centre,** set back from the square under the arch. (☎43224. Open M-F 9am-6pm. €4 per hr.) Several pharmacies are in the square; **Morrison's Pharmacy** is the best-stocked. (☎41241. Open M-Sa 9am-6pm.)

🄶 ACCOMMODATIONS. On the town square, the modest exterior of **Tinsley House B&B ❸** gives way to splendid, spacious rooms, all with TV and bath and named after local historical figures. The elegant sitting room has tea, coffee, and cookies, as well as plenty of notable folks on the walls. (☎41947; www.tinsley-house.com. Singles €40; doubles €65. Cash only.) Located on the square above a barber, the rooms at **Arch House ❸** all have TV and tea and coffee facilities. (☎41922. Singles €40; doubles €60. Cash only.) There are two hostels relatively close to Cahir. **Lisakyle Hostel (IHH) ❶,** 2.5km south on Ardfinnan Rd., is the more accessible. From the bus station, walk up the hill, make a right at Cahir House Hotel, and keep walking for 800m after the turn-off to the Swiss Cottage. The quiet country location, ivy-covered walls, and wooden bunks with wool blankets make it feel like you're visiting grandma's summer cottage; cobwebs under the beds add authenticity to the rusticity. The entire hostel shares two single bathrooms, but there are usually too few guests for it to matter. The gregarious owner does pick-up service from the bus or train station. Stop into the office in town on Main St., across from the post office, to find out when he's heading over. (☎41963. Dorms €15. Private family room €18 per person. **Camping** €8. Cash only.)

🄲🄼 FOOD AND PUBS. For groceries, try **SuperValu,** on Bridge St., across the bridge from the castle. (☎41515. Open M-Th and Sa 8am-8pm, F 8am-9pm, Su 9am-6pm.) On Saturdays, there's a **farmers' market** at the end of Main St. (9am-1pm.) ◪**Lazy Bean Cafe ❷** offers fresh sandwiches (€7), soups and salads, greasy-spoon breakfasts, and ice cream in a bright, modern interior. (☎42038. Open M-Sa 9am-6pm, Su 10am-6pm. MC/V.) Overlooking the River Suir on Castle St., **River House ❷** has vegetarian-friendly quiche (€8), drool-worthy desserts, and free Wi-Fi. (☎41951; www.riverhouse.ie. Open daily 9am-5pm. MC/V.) Enjoy pizza, pasta, and coffee in the small **Galileo's Cafe ❷**, 4 Gladstone St., which shares the building with the Craft Granary. (☎45689. Salads €5-6; pizza and pasta €9-11. Open M-Sa noon-10pm, Su 1-9pm. MC/V.) **Galtee Inn ❸**, the Square, is a local favorite. Lunches are small and cheap (€9-11), but dinners swell in size and price, up to €23. (☎41247. Kitchen open M-Sa 9:30am-10pm, Su 12:30-9:30pm. MC/V.) **Irwin's**, Church St., an old fashioned pint-puller, has a sunny beer garden and a good daytime crowd. (No phone. Music some weekends, sometimes €5 cover. Open M-Th 10:30am-11:30pm, F-Sa 10:30am-12:30am, Su 12:30-11pm. Cash only.) **Castle Arms ❷**, Castle St., has an old set of spice drawers behind the bar. (☎42506. Pub grub around €8. Kitchen open daily 11am-3pm. Cash only.)

◨ SIGHTS. Cahir's most famous landmark is 13th-century **◪Cahir Castle.** This typical medieval castle later became home to the well-known Butler family. Unfortunately, the castle's defenses couldn't hold out after the invention of gunpowder, and in 1599 the Earl of Essex successfully bombarded the castle by lobbing a few cannonballs, one of which is still stuck in the wall of the square tower. Some rooms are furnished, while others illustrate castle life in medieval Ireland with sleek panels. Don't miss the 11,000-year-old Irish deer antlers, which have been preserved in the peat bogs since the last ice age. The 15min. video presentation, which provides an overview of castles in the area, is a good prequel to the optional guided tours. (☎41011. Open daily mid-June to mid-Sept. 9am-7pm; mid-Sept. to mid-Oct. and Apr. to mid-June 9:30am-5:30pm; mid-Oct. to Mar. 9:30am-4:30pm. Last admission 45min. before closing. 30min. tours every hr. €3, students €1.30, seniors €2.10.)

The broad **River Suir** that rushes into Waterford Harbour is but a wee stream in Cahir. A forested **river walk** starts at the tourist office and winds past the 19th-century **Swiss Cottage,** located 1.5km from town. Built with nature-inspired curvilinear forms inside and out, the ornamental cottage was a place for the Butler family to entertain guests and pretend to be peasants when they tired of life in the castle. The cottage is nicely restored, with an undulating thatched roof, but it's the scenic walk there that makes it worthwhile. (☎41144. Open mid-Apr. to mid-Oct. daily 10am-6pm; mid-Mar. to mid-Apr. Tu-Su 10am-1pm and 2-6pm; mid-Oct. to mid-Nov. Tu-Su 10am-1pm and 2-4:30pm. Last admission 45min. before closing. Grounds are free; admission to the cottage is by 20min. guided tour only. €3, students and children €1.30, seniors €2.10.) **Fly Fishing** opportunities line the river walk past the Swiss Cottage. Fishing licenses (€20 per day) can be obtained at the Heritage Cornerstone on Church St., right on the town square. (☎42730. Open daily 7am-11pm.)

The refreshingly uncommercialized **Mitchelstown Caves** are 13km off the Cork road, halfway between Cahir and Mitchelstown in the hamlet of **Burncourt.** Ask the Cork bus driver to stop at the caves; it's a 3.2km walk from N8. As you descend into the deep subterranean chambers, which were discovered just 170 years ago by a local farmer, you will feel like you're entering an alternate universe. With a bit of imagination, you can make out numerous whimsically named mineral formations like Streaky Bacon or the Towel of Babel. Unfortunately, the 30min. mandatory tour covers just a quarter of the caves' length and ends far too soon. (☎67246; www.mitchelstowncave.com. Open daily 10am-6pm. Last tour 5:30pm. €6.)

GALTY MOUNTAINS AND GLEN OF AHERLOW

South of Tipperary Town, the river **Aherlow** cuts through a richly scenic valley called the Glen of Aherlow. West of Cahir, the **Galty Mountains** rise abruptly along the southern edge of the Glen. The purple-tinted, lake-studded range boasts **Galtymore Mountain** (920m), Ireland's third-highest peak. The glen and mountains are ideal settings for both picnicking and full-fledged trekking. Serious hikers should invest in *Ordnance Survey #66* and *74* (€6.60), available at tourist offices and bookstores in Tipperary and Cahir. The Tipp Town tourist office sells Gill and

MacMillan's helpful *Best Irish Walks* (€11.50), which details several day hikes in the area as well as others around the country. **Glenbarra** is also a popular base camp. To get there, drive west from Cahir toward Mitchelstown. The **Glen of Aherlow Fáilte Society** releases a series of pamphlets (€1) detailing walks, including an 11km walk around Lake Muskry and a 12km route to Lake Curra. They also put on a walking festival during the bank holiday weekend in June. Call the **Glen of Aherlow Info Point** (☎0625 6331; www.aherlow.com) for information on the area.

There are no marked trails in the Galtees, but a popular 14.5km, 6hr. loop summits Galtymore Mountain. *Ordnance Survey #74* and a good pair of boots are a must for this lovely hike. It departs from **Mountain Lodge (An Óige/HI)** ❶, in Burncourt, a gas-lit Georgian hunting lodge with a gorgeous round sitting room. No electricity is a reminder that the wilderness is literally at your doorstep. From Cahir, follow the Mitchelstown road (N8) for 13km, turn right at the sign, and continue another 3km on the unpaved path. Alternatively, take the Cork bus (#8) to the Glengarra Woods stop; the entrance to the woods and the 3.2km walk to the hostel are about 275m to the left. (☎0526 7277. Open daily Apr.-Sept.; closed 10am-5pm. €15, under 18 €12, An Óige members €13/10. Cash only.) For a shorter route to the summit (2½hr.), follow N8 for about a mile toward Mitchelstown before heading into the woods. The staff of the **Ballinacourty House** ❶, an excellent campsite in the Aherlow valley, provide detailed information on the Glen. (☎0625 6230. Meals and cooking facilities available. Open Easter-Sept. €18-20 for 2 adults in a tent. MC/V.) They also operate a pricey **restaurant** ❸ and a pleasant **B&B** ❸. (Dinner for guests €18. Singles €45; doubles with bath €68.) To reach Ballinacourty House, take R663 off the Cahir-Tipperary road (N24) in **Bansha** and follow it for 13km to the signposted turn-off. Newly opened **Glen of Aherlow Caravan and Camping Park** ❶, on R663 between Bansha and Lisvernane, offers the weary traveler a place to shower and pitch a tent. (☎0625 6555; www.tipperarycamping.com. Electricity €2. Free showers and kitchens. 2 adults with tent €20. Cash only.)

CLONMEL (CLUAIN MEALA)   ☎052

As Co. Tipperary's economic hub, Clonmel (pop. 20,000) offers visitors returning from a day in the Comeragh Mountains all the comforts of modern life. While it makes for a good base for hikers with a car, Clonmel doesn't have much in the way of tourist attractions or budget-friendly accommodations. While in town, drink up: Clonmel produces the apples that are crushed into Bulmer's Cider.

■ **TRANSPORTATION.** Clonmel's train station is on Prior Park Rd. (☎21982), less than 2km north of the town center. Trains go to: **Limerick** (1hr., M-Sa 3 per day 6:45am-3:15pm, €11); **Waterford** (10:46am; 12:22, 7:20pm; €5); and **Rosslare Harbour** (1¼hr., M-Sa 12:40pm, €11). **Bus** info is available at the tourist office and train station. Coaches run from the front of the train station to: **Cork** (2hr.; M-Sa 4 per day 8am-5pm, Su 2:30 and 8:15pm; €15); **Dublin** (3¼hr.; M-Sa 6-7 per day 6:45am-5:30pm, Su 9am-8:30pm; €13); **Galway** (3¾hr., 7 per day 9:45am-6:25pm, €19); **Kilkenny** (1hr., 8 per day 6:45am-8:25pm, €7.50) via **Carrick-on-Suir** (20min.); **Limerick** (1½hr., 8-9 per day 9:45am-9:25pm, €8) via **Tipperary** (1hr.); **Rosslare** (3½hr., 2-3 per day 9:50am-5:40pm, €6); **Waterford** (1hr., 10 per day 7:30am-10:05pm, €6).

■▐ **ORIENTATION AND PRACTICAL INFORMATION.** Clonmel's central street runs parallel to the **Suir River.** From the station, take a right and then the first left and follow **Prior Park Road** straight into town. Prior Park Rd. becomes commercial **Gladstone Street,** which intersects the main drag, known successively as **Irishtown, O'Connell,** pedestrian-only **Mitchell,** and **Parnell Street. Mary Street** runs parallel to Gladstone St. **Sarsfield Street** is the continuation of Gladstone St., and **Abbey Street** runs off Parnell toward the riverside quays. The **tourist office** is located in the basement of St. Mary's Church, off Mary St. (☎22960. Open M-Th 9:30am-

4:30pm, F 9:30am-3:45pm; closed 1-2pm.) The **AIB** (☎22500) and **Bank of Ireland** (☎21011) are neighbors on Parnell St. and both have **ATMs**. (Both open M 10am-5pm, Tu and Th-F 10am-4pm, W 10:30am-4pm.) Visit **Citizens Information**, 2-3 Emmet St., to check for **work opportunities**. (☎22267. Open M-F 10am-4pm, W-Th 10am-4pm and 7-9pm.) The **police** *(Garda)* station is on Emmet St. (☎77640). **Mulligan's**, Market Pl. and O'Connell St., is the local **pharmacy**. (☎29202. Open M-W and Sa 9am-6pm, Th 9am-7pm, F 9am-9pm.) Do laundry at **Cleanwell**, 48 O'Connell St. (☎21969. Wash and dry €5-10. Open M-Sa 9am-6pm.) **St. Joseph's and St. Michael's Hospital** is on Western Rd. (☎77000). The snooker club **Circles**, 16 Market St., doubles as an **Internet** cafe. (☎23115. €0.10 per min., €5.70 per hr. Open daily 11am-11pm.) The **library**, Emmet St., also provides Internet access. (☎24545. €2 per 50min. Open M-Tu 10am-5:30pm, W-Th 10am-8:30pm, F-Sa 10am-1pm and 2-5pm.) The **post office** is also on Emmet St., by the library. (☎21742. Open M and W-F 9am-5:30pm, Tu 9:30am-5:30pm, Sa 9:30am-1pm.)

▐▌▐▌ ACCOMMODATIONS AND CAMPING.

Clonmel, full of hotels and B&Bs, is not the most backpacker-friendly town. The area along the Cahir road past Irishtown is patched with B&Bs. You'll sit in the lap of luxury at **Brighton House ❸**, 1 Brighton Pl. The elegant 200-year-old Georgian guest house has beautiful, spacious rooms with their own sitting areas and a working well in the garden. From the train and bus station, walk toward town; it's on the left at the first set of lights. (☎23665; www.tipp.ie/brighton.htm. Singles €45-50; doubles €90. MC/V.) Close to downtown at the **Riverside House ❸**, New Quay, guests watch swans swim by from the windows of the expansive rooms. This stately house has been overlooking the Suir for more than a century. (☎25781. Singles €30; doubles €60, ensuite €65. Cash only.) Budget options increase a kilometer from town. Halfway between Clonmel and Cahir on N24 is **The Apple Farm ❶**, a grove turned campsite. (☎41459; www.theapplefarm.com. Open May-Sept. Electricity €2.50. Showers free. €6 per person, children €4. MC/V.) Well outside town—but well worth the trip—is **Powers-the-Pot Camping & Caravan Park ❶**, Harney's Cross. Follow Parnell St. east from town, turn right at the first traffic light (not N24), cross the Suir, and continue for 9km over a mountain road to the signposted turn-off. Gracious owners Niall and Jo provide maps and guides for the Munster Way and answer all outdoors-related questions. (☎23085; www.powersthepot.net. Open May-Sept. Free kitchen and showers. 2-person tent €12.50; each additional adult €4, child €1.50. MC/V.)

▐▌▐▌ FOOD AND PUBS.

SuperQuinn dominates Market Pl. (☎27222. Open M-F 8:30am-10pm, Sa 8am-7pm, Su 10am-7pm.) Find health food at **The Honey Pot**, 14 Abbey St. (☎21457. Open M-Sa 9:30am-6pm.) ▧ **O Tuama's Cafe ❷**, 5-6 Market Pl., serves healthy, filling meals for under €9 in an upbeat environment. Top off your meal with a smoothie (€4) from the juice bar. (☎27170. Open M-Sa 8:30am-5:30pm, F 8:30am-6pm, Sa 9am-5:30pm. MC/V.) **Niamh's ❷** (NEEVS), at the corner of Mitchell St. at Gladstone St., offers specialty coffees, hot lunches, sandwiches (€7), and all-day breakfast (€4.50-8) in a deli-style restaurant. The same sandwiches are €3 less for takeaway. (☎25698. Open M-F 9am-5:45pm, Sa 9am-5pm. MC/V.) **Home Bakery ❶**, 26 Mitchell St., has inexpensive filled sandwiches (€4) and all the artery-clogging fare your heart can handle. (☎22375. Open M-Sa 9am-6pm. Cash only.) Locally acclaimed **Catalpa ❹**, on Sarsfield St., hosts Italian feasts in a former bank vault. (☎26821. Pizza and pasta €10-14. Meat dishes €15-22. Open Tu-Su 6-9:30pm, W-F also 12:30-2pm. AmEx/MC/V.) **Tom Skinny's Pizza Parlor ❷**, Market St., specializes in deep dish pizza—made fresh before your eyes—and ice cream. Glorious aromas, a shiny jukebox, and a portrait of Marilyn Monroe complement the delightful decor. (☎26006. Pizza €6-14. Ice cream €1.50-2.50. Open M-F noon-midnight, Sa-Su noon-1am. MC/V.)

At enormous **Mulcahy's**, 47 Gladstone St., pubbers compete on a plateau of shiny snooker tables or head upstairs to Danno's for dancing. (☎22825; www.mulcahys.ie. Carvery lunch noon-5:30pm, à la carte 8am-9:30pm. Entrees €8-11. W trad. Sa hosts **Danno's,** an 18+ disco. Cover €10. MC/V until 9:30pm.) Four-time winner of the Munster Pub of the Year, **Tierney's,** 13 O'Connell St., is full of odd knickknacks, from a shelf of musty books to a life-sized Guinness toucan. If it all gets to be too much, head out back to the heated beer garden. (☎24467. Open from 10:30am. Kitchen open 12:30-9:30pm. Entrees €13-18. MC/V.) **O'Keefe's,** 33 Parnell St., next to Hearns Hotel, is Clonmel's newest nightspot, with leather-covered barstools, a half-dozen widescreen TVs showing football and rugby, and a back room reserved for dancing. Every weekend two DJs light up the floor. Leave your sweatpants at home—"neat dress" is required. (☎21611. Comedy club every 3rd Su; trad W 9pm, Th-Su late bar until 2am. €15. MC/V only M-W.)

◑ ❀ **SIGHTS AND FESTIVALS.** The Heritage Trail map points pedestrians to some great spots in Clonmel. Stops along the way include the **West Gate,** at the western end of O'Connell St., an 1831 reproduction of the medieval gate that once separated Irishtown from the more prosperous Anglo-Norman area. The 25m octagonal tower of **Old St. Mary's Church,** Mary St., stands near the remnants of the town wall that fell to Cromwell's advances in 1650. Just inside the door of the **Franciscan Friary** on Abbey St. are the 15th-century tomb effigies of a knight and lady of the Butler family. The **South Tipperary County Museum,** Mick Delahunty Sq., off Emmet St. across from the library, tells of the county's history since the Stone Age and hosts small traveling exhibitions. The beautifully lit permanent gallery displays retro and modern art, as well as schoolchildren's work. (☎34550; www.southtippcoco.ie. Open Tu-Sa 10am-5pm. Last admission 45min. before closing. Free.) **South Tipperary Arts Centre,** Nelson St., hosts monthly visual art exhibitions. (☎27877; www.southtippparts.com. Open M-F 10am-5:30pm, Sa noon-5pm. Free.) Clonmel's history as a transport hub is celebrated at the **Museum of Transport,** 2km outside town on Gortafleur Rd. To check out the collection of antique cars, head past the train station, make a right onto the Waterford Rd., and then a left onto Gortafleur Rd., past the racecourse. Every July, Clonmel comes alive with nine days of music, theatre, and dance for the **Clonmel Junction Festival.** Past performances have included everything from Afro-Cuban music to Polish DJs. (☎28521; www.junctionfestival.com. Tickets €8-30.)

🞮 **OUTDOOR ACTIVITIES.** The tourist office's books and leaflets describe several **walks** in the area and nearby **Nire Valley.** The **East Munster Way** begins as a gentle footpath through the lowland hills of **Carrick-on-Suir, Kilsheelan,** and **Clonmel,** extends to a perch on the **Comeragh Mountains,** and then runs full-force into the **Knockmealdowns** before ending 70km later in **Clogheen.** Along the way hikers pass the **Kilsheelan Woods,** the glistening Suir River, and the magnificent vistas in the Comeragh Mountains. In Clogheen, ambitious hikers can follow the **Druhallow Way,** which connects with the **Kerry Way** (p. 295), or take **Blackwater Way** into isolated Araglin Valley. The best maps to use are *Ordnance Survey #74* and *75* (available at the Clonmel tourist office; €8.25). For specific information on the East Munster Way, consult guides such as the *East Munster Way Map Guide,* available at **Parson's Green,** a garden, campsite, and activity center all rolled into one outside of the Clogheen town center. (☎65290; www.clogheen.com. Open M-F 9am-6pm.) **Powers-the-Pot Campground** (p. 209) is also a sure bet for information on hikes in the Comeragh and Knockmealdown Mountains.

The **Comeragh Mountains** are wave-shaped, which means that trails vary greatly in difficulty depending on the direction of approach. The terrain ranges from the soft and wet lowlands to the rocky and challenging *coums* (Irish for "mountain hollows"), which often house lakes. The Comeragh terrain includes marshy plateaus that are manageable even for city folk in sneakers. The excellent *Nire Valley Walks* maps #1-12 (available at Powers-the-Pot; €1) illustrate two- to four-hour day hikes from Clonmel. More challenging treks can also be found in this region. One such option begins from Powers-the-Pot, a half-mile off the Munster Way. With *Ordnance Survey #75* in hand, head east from the campsite and follow the ridges south. It is relatively hard to get lost in good weather, but be sure someone knows you're out there. Guided hikes are also available; ask Niall at Powers-the-Pot.

The **Knockmealdown Mountains** are a dramatic collection of roughly contoured summits straddling the Tipperary-Waterford border 19.3km south of Cahir. Many hikes begin in either **Clogheen** or, for a less challenging route, **Newcastle**, the location of the tiny but locally renowned **Nugent's Pub.** One sight of particular interest is the spectacular **Vee Road,** which runs south from Clogheen to the **Knockmealdown Gap** and erupts with purple rhododendrons in May and June. If you're not in the mood for hiking, driving the Vee Rd. between Lismore and Clogheen gives you an exhilarating look at the Gap, the Knockmealdowns, and the beautiful **Bay Loch,** a supposedly bottomless lake whose mystique lies in a local legend about a woman who haunts its waters. Two-thirds of the way up the Gap, as pines give way to heather and bracken, a parking lot marks the path up **Sugarloaf Hill.** From there you can continue to **Knockmealdown Peak** (795m), the highest in the range. The beautiful trail over the western half of the Knockmealdowns begins along the Vee at the same place and heads west, up the lower peaks of Knockshanahullion and Farbreaga, ending at the Kilcaroon Bridge on R665 between Ballyporeen and Clogheen. The unofficial **tourist office** in Clogheen, across from the turn-off for Vee Rd., serves generous portions of maps with a side of local lore, but sometimes observes irregular hours. (☎65258. Usually open M-F 10am-5pm.)

LISMORE (LIOS MÓR)   ☎058

Lismore's grand castle and cathedral remind visitors that this charming little town was once a thriving monastic center. Seated at the banks of the Blackwater River, the stunning Lismore Castle supports a booming tourist business; the town is also worth a visit for its beautiful walks and proximity to the hiking trails of Co. Tipperary's Knockmealdown Mountains. All this history and beauty makes Lismore a great travel destination, so it's no wonder the **Immrama Festival of Travel Writing** is held here in early June. As a distinguished travel guide reader (considering the object currently in your hands), it is definitely worth checking out (contact the **Heritage Center** for details).

█🛈 TRANSPORTATION AND PRACTICAL INFORMATION. Bus Éireann stops across from the tourist office and runs to **Cork** (1¼hr.; M, Th, Sa 9:35am, F 9:50am, Su 6:20pm except July and Aug.; €9.30), **Dublin** (M-Sa 6:55am, 3:09pm, also Th 3:24pm, F 5:40pm, Su 3:45pm) and **Waterford** via **Dungarvan** (1¼hr.; M-Sa 6:55am, also Th 3:24 and 6:25pm, F 5:40pm, Sa 6:25pm; €10.20). The Vee road represents a spectacular scenic route to reach Lismore from Clogheen; its many roadside "viewpoints" are popular for a reason. Hitchers wishing to get to Cork ride east to Fermoy, then south on N8. Hitching to Dungarvan is also common, but not recommended by *Let's Go*. The well-staffed and extremely helpful **Heritage Centre** occupies the old courthouse. (☎54975. Open year-round M-F 9:30am-5:30pm; May-Oct. also Sa 10am-5:30pm, Su noon-5:30pm.) Free **Internet** access is available at the **library** on Main St. (Open M, W, F 11:30am-1pm and 2-6pm; Tu and Th 1-4:30pm and 5:30-8pm.) The **post office** is on E. Main St. (☎54220. Open M-F 9am-1pm and 2-5:30pm, Sa 9am-1pm.)

🏠 ACCOMMODATIONS. Accommodations in Lismore are sparse and can dent the budget traveler's wallet, but inviting B&Bs can be found on either side of the town. From the tourist office, take a right at the statue and head up Main St. out of town to reach **Beechcroft ❸,** whose impeccably manicured front lawn, hardwood floors, and luxurious bedding feel simply indulgent. (☎54273. Singles €40; doubles €60. Family rooms available.) Right in the heart of town, **The Castle Lodge ❸** offers bright, large rooms above its eponymous pub and restaurant. (☎53077. Rooms €35 per person.) On

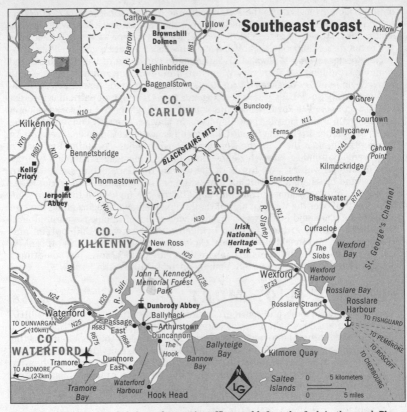

the other side of town, left from the tourist office and left at the fork in the road, **Pine Tree House** ❸ has an expansive front yard and comfortable rooms. (☎53282; www.pinetreehouselismore.com. €35 per person. Discount for longer-term stays.)

FOOD AND PUBS. Lismore's **Farmer's Market**, Lismore Castle Ave., is quite popular. (Su 11am-3pm.) **Centra**, E. Main St., sells groceries. (☎54122. Open M-F 8:30am-8pm, Sa 8:30am-8:30pm, Su 10am-6pm.) **Eamonn's Place** ❸, E. Main St., is a pub with a lot to be proud of: a gorgeous waterfall in its beer garden, tasty homemade, seasonal meals featuring fish snagged straight from the Blackwater, and fantastic desserts. With so much going for it, its no wonder its great *craic* is what people talk about most. (☎54025. Lunch from €7; served M-F 12:30-2:30pm. Dinner €10-17; served M-Sa 6-9pm during the summer.) **Il Castello** ❶, across from the Castle Lodge, has satisfying staple takeaway items, such as burgers (€2-4), chicken (€4), and cheap kebabs. (Open daily 5:15-11pm.) Tiny **Movenpick** ❶, off Main St., obliges the sweet tooth with ice cream flavors like tiramisu. (1 scoop €1.75. Open daily noon-5pm.)

SIGHTS. Gorgeous **Lismore Castle** looms over the Blackwater River, swathed in foliage and aristocratic grandeur. The building has served as a medieval fort, Sir Walter Raleigh's residence, and the birthplace of the 17th-century father of modern chemistry, Robert Boyle (of PV=nRT fame). Remodeled with great imagination in the 19th century, the castle is now privately owned by the English Duke of

Devonshire, whose apartment can be leased by the ambitious—and very rich—for €25,000 per week (yeah, that's a ➎). The fabled Lismore Crozier and the *Book of Lismore*, two priceless artifacts thought to have been lost forever, were found hidden in the castle walls in 1814; the crozier can be seen at Dublin's National Museum. Visitors can tour the lush **gardens,** walking in the legendary footsteps of *The Faerie Queen* poet Edmund Spenser. (☎54424; www.lismorecastle.com. Open mid-Apr. to Sept. daily 1:45-4:45pm. Garden tours €7, under 16 €3.50.) The castle's bridge is also the starting point for the peaceful, tree-lined **Lady Louisa's Walk,** which clings to the banks of the Blackwater.

The castle was once connected by an underground passage, long since closed off, to **St. Carthagh's Cathedral,** on Deanery Hill. A number of tombs in the cathedral's ancient graveyard are sealed with heavy stone slabs, relics of Lismore's past as a hot spot for body-snatching. The cathedral did a better job of retaining historical markers—a collection of 9th- and 10th-century engraved commemorative stones are set into one of its walls. The **Heritage Centre,** in the town square, has a 30min. video presentation of Lismore's past and a cursory exhibit highlighting the 1000-year-old *Book of Lismore*, with a replica of the original, which is privately owned and not accessible to the public. A new science room is dedicated to the life and works of Robert Boyle. (€4.50, seniors and students €4.) The center also runs **guided tours** of town during the summer (June-Aug.; €3) and sells self-guided tour booklets (€3). A few kilometers from Lismore is a car park for the locally beloved **Towerswalk,** a casual amble through the woods and greenery of the countryside. From the castle, cross the bridge and turn left; after 4.8km, Towerswalk is on the right. A local landlord named Keily-Ussher, reviled for his cruelty to starving tenant farmers during the Great Irish Famine of the 1840s, began constructing the tower and entrance gate to what was to be a castle; today, all that remains at the end of the woodsy 1hr. walk are ruins known as "The Grand Folly."

Lismore is also conveniently close to the myriad hiking trails of the Knockmeal-down Mountains and the East Munster Way (see **Outdoor Activities,** p. 210).

COUNTIES WEXFORD AND WATERFORD

Wexford and Waterford may be a little too welcoming for their own good—Ireland's invaders, from Celts to Vikings and Norsemen to hordes of modern backpackers, have all begun their island-conquering here. Metropolitan Waterford (famous for its crystal), the picturesque Comeragh Mountains, the salty pubs and crowded streets of Wexford Town, and the waves of Tramore's beaches present a veritable feast of temptations. New Ross, with its fine hostels, is a good base for exploring the southeast. The best way to experience the region's beauty is along Slí Charman (SHLEE KAR-man), usually referred to as "An Slí," a pathway that runs 217km along Co. Wexford's coast from the Co. Wicklow border to Waterford Harbour.

ENNISCORTHY (INIS COIRTHAIDTH) ☎05392

Back in the day, the people of Enniscorthy certainly had spunk. During the failed revolution of 1798, a local priest led an uprising at nearby Vinegar Hill and held the British at bay for 12 days (p. 53). The 1798 Visitors Centre, dedicated to chronicling the event, highlights with relish the fact that 20,000 residents of county Wexford died during the skirmish. Later, hot-headed residents of Enniscorthy joined others from Dublin and surrounding towns in the 1916 Easter Rising; Enniscorthy was the last to surrender (p. 55). Modern Enniscorthians channel their rebellious natures into musical pursuits, filling pubs with raucous music during their two largest festivals: the Strawberry Festival and the Blues Festival. Still, it's probably not a good idea to make locals angry.

⧉ TRANSPORTATION. N11 passes through Enniscorthy, heading south to **Wexford** and north to **Arklow, Wicklow,** and **Dublin. Trains** run to: **Dublin** (2½hr., 3 per day, €19.50) and **Rosslare** (50min., 3 per day, €6.70). **Buses** stop outside the Bus Stop Shop on Shannon Quay, between the two bridges and across the river from the squares, on their way north to **Dublin** via Ferns (2½hr., 5-7 per day, €13.10), and south to **Waterford** (1hr., 8-10 per day, €13.10) and **Wexford** (30min., 9-12 per day, €6.40 return). For **taxis,** call ☎36333, 33975, or 36666.

◢◪ ORIENTATION AND PRACTICAL INFORMATION. From the railway station, turn right onto Templeshannon then cross the Enniscorthy Bridge over the River Slaney into the center of town; turn left into **Abbey Square,** one of the main shopping areas, or continue uphill to **Market Square.** From there, Main St., Rafter St., and Weafer St. fan out, leading the way to plenty of shops and restaurants. Tourist information is available at the **1798 Visitors Centre** (p. 215), signposted after a 10min. walk from Abbey Sq. down Mill Park Rd. For further Enniscorthian lore and a free monthly events guide, see Maura Flannery in **Castle Hill Crafts,** 4 Castle Hill (☎36800), across from the Castle and up the hill from Abbey Sq. Several banks, including **AIB,** Slaney Pl. (☎33163; open M 10am-5pm, Tu and Th-F 10am-4pm, W 10:30am-4pm) and **Permanent TSB,** Market Sq. (☎35700; open M-Tu and Th-F 10am-5pm, W 10:30am-5pm) have 24hr. **ATMs.** The **Police** *(Garda)* station, on Lymington Rd., one street over from the visitor center, is open 24hr. (☎42580). Next door, The **library** has free **Internet** access. (☎36055. Open M 2:30-5:30pm, Tu-W and F 10:30am-1pm and 2:30-5:30pm, Th 10:30am-1pm, 2:30-4:30pm, and 6-8pm.) **Softech Communications,** on Church St., offers Internet access for €2 per hr. (30833. Open M-F 10am-10pm, Sa-Su noon-10pm.) Next to the Abbey Sq. shopping center is **Enniscorthy Cleaners.** (☎36466. Open M-Sa 8am-6pm. Wash and dry €12-16.) The **post office** is by the Abbey Sq. roundabout. (☎33226; open M and W-F 9am-5:30pm, Tu 9:30am-5:30pm, Sa 9am-1pm.)

⌂ ACCOMMODATIONS. Right in town, between Market Sq. and the cathedral is **Murphy's B&B ❸,** 9 Main St. Simple, stylish art hangs on the walls, and the guest sitting room is full of plump cushions. (☎37837. All rooms ensuite. Singles €35-40; doubles €70-80. Cash only.) The **Old Bridge House ❸** is next to the Old Bridge on Slaney Pl. Large rooms, friendly proprietors, and a river view compensate for occasionally noisy traffic. (☎34222. Singles €40; doubles €70. MC/V.) At **Adelmar ❷,** Summerhill, Mrs. Agnes Barry offers her hospitality. Follow N11 toward Dublin, take a left at the Shell station, and follow the signs up the hill. (☎33668; www.adelmar.com. Open June-Oct. Singles €30; doubles €56. Cash only.) **Vale View Farmhouse ❸,** St. Johns Rd., off N30, is a modern farm bungalow 2.5km outside of town. Tea, coffee, homemade treats, and dinner entrees (€25-30) await guests. (☎35262. Singles €50; doubles €65-75. Cash only.)

▣▨ FOOD AND PUBS. Dunnes Stores, on the right off Main St. in the Mill Centre, has groceries (☎30222. Open M-Sa 8:30am-midnight, Su 9am-10pm). There's a smaller selection at **Caulfield's SuperValu,** located in the shopping center on Mill Park Rd. at the Abbey Sq. roundabout. (☎34541. Open M-W 8am-9pm, Th-F 8am-10pm, Sa 8am-8pm, Su 10am-6pm.) **The Baked Potato ❶,** 18 Rafter St., serves delicious homemade open-face sandwiches (€4-4.50), quiches (€5.50), and stuffed baked potatoes (€3-5), as its name implies. (☎34085. Open M-Sa 8am-6pm. MC/V.) **Zorba Restaurant ❷,** 11 Rafter St., serves up hearty Lebanese and Mediterranean dishes, such as kofka (€9.50) or vegetarian mosaka (€8.50). Tempting pastries linger just by the register. (☎35901. Open daily 9am-9pm. MC/V.) **Galo Char Grill ❸**, 19 Main St., serves exquisitely grilled Portuguese dishes, like the chicken roti (€9.10), as well as several vegetarian options. Galo's is incredibly popular, so call ahead. (☎38077. Open M-Sa noon-3pm and 5:30-10pm, Su noon-9pm. MC/V.) **Shenanigans ❸** serves quality pub grub for €8-10 in Market Sq. Be sure to check out the mosaics. (☎36272. Kitchen open daily 10am-6pm. MC/V.) Follow the yellow-brick road to the **Golden City ❷**, 9 Market Sq., for traditional Chinese dishes such as hot and sour soup (€3.30), hot pot (€8.70), and other delicious delicacies. (☎38521. Open M-Sa 12:30-2:30pm and 4-11:30pm, Su 12:30-11:30pm. MC/V.)

The Bailey, on Barrick St. by the river, is a swanky new pub/nightclub with free live music on Fridays. Attached is **Vertigo,** a club with high standards: there are hair straighteners for hire in the bathrooms, so guests have no excuse not to look good. (☎30353. Su 80s-90s music. Pub open M-Th 10:30am-11:30pm, F-Sa 10:30am-12:30am, Su 12:30-11pm. Club open Th-Su 11:30pm-2am. Cover Th €10 with €3 drinks all night, F €8, Sa €10, Su €5. MC/V.) **Rackard's,** 23 Rafter St., is among the hippest spots in town. (☎33747. Open M-Th 10:30am-11:30pm, F-Sa 10:30am-12:30am, Su 12:30-11pm. W Trad sessions. MC/V.) **The Antique Tavern,** 14 Slaney Pl., lives up to its name, with Enniscorthy artifacts and other antiques from around the world plastered to the walls. (☎33428. Free Wi-Fi. Open M-Th 10:30am-11:30pm, F-Sa 10:30am-12:30am, Su 12:30-11pm. MC/V.)

🎞🌸 **SIGHTS AND FESTIVALS.** The **National 1798 Visitors Centre,** a 5min. walk from town on Mill Park Rd., is an impressive multimedia experience examining the failed Rebellion of 1798 and the Battle of Vinegar Hill. In general, the museum's exhibits are excellent, though occasionally all the audio-visual gizmos and gadgets—like the life-size chess pieces—obscure the history. The 14min. film projects blood and guts onto four screens. (☎37596; www.1798centre.com. Open May-Sept. M-F 9:30am-5:30pm, Sa-Su noon-4pm; Oct.-Apr. M-F 9:30am-4pm. Last admission 5pm. €6, students and seniors €3.50.) An uphill 4km walk from town, across the river, the actual **Vinegar Hill** battle site offers a fantastic battle's-eye view of the town below. For a more intimate perspective, enthusiastic Maura Flannery's **Walking Tour of Enniscorthy** is unbeatable. The 1hr. trek reveals the dirty little secrets of the town's past. Find out about the time in 1649 when Enniscorthy women got Cromwell's soldiers drunk and killed them or learn why, after flagrantly kissing up to Queen Elizabeth with *The Faerie Queene,* poet Edmund Spenser refused her gift of the local castle. (☎36800. Tours daily 12:45pm or by arrangement for groups of 5 or more. Tours at 6pm on request. €5, students, seniors, and children €3.)

St. Aidan's Cathedral, on Cathedral St. uphill from Murphy's Hotel, has been completely restored. The stencil work on the arches and the plethora of stained-glass windows are incredibly impressive. Original construction began in 1843 under the close supervision of architect Augustus Pugin. An architectural genius, Pugin designed over 40 churches with soaring ceilings that make the spaces light and airy. A €1 brochure is a good touring companion. (Open daily 10am-6pm. Free.) In Market Sq., a statue commemorates **Father Murphy,** who fanned the flames of rebellion in 1798. The priest was a Loyalist sympathizer before an angry mob threatened to burn down his church. He installed himself at the head of the United Irishmen (see **Rebellion and Union,** p. 53) and led the pikemen of Enniscorthy into battle.

The **Wexford County Museum** fills the bulk of the **Norman Castle** on Castle Hill, chronicling Wexford's history and exhibiting an eclectic collection of castaway oddities from all over the world. The rooms display the original letters and belongings of principal players in the rebellions of 1798 and 1916. Since the museum's days as a single 13-object display back in 1960, the curators have stuffed it from dungeon to eaves with odd bits like ship figureheads and a collection of international police patches; spiders now call a lot of the nooks and crannies home. The model boats and ships in the third floor maritime room, and the graffiti made by an inmate in the musty dungeon, are worth a quick look. (☎35926. Closed for renovations until summer 2008. Open Feb.-Nov. M-Sa 10am-6pm, Su 2-5:30pm; Dec.-Jan. Su 2-5pm. €4.50, students and seniors €3.50, children €1.) If the walking tour wasn't enough exercise, sweat it out on the new machines or jump in the pool at the **Waterford Pool and Leisure Centre,** on the left past the train station. (☎34443. Open M-F 7am-10pm, Sa-Su 9am-8pm. Pool and gym €5.50-6 per hr.)

The first weekend in July ushers in the annual **Strawberry Fair's** long weekend of festivities and fructose. Market Square fills to the brim with outdoor entertainment and vendors selling strawberries and cream. Free music from trad to bluegrass plays nightly in various pubs. Local businesses sponsor Strawberry Princesses; for the culmination of the festivities the town votes on which prom-gown-clad teen should become the Strawberry Queen. (www.strawberryfestival.ie has exact dates and info on music and entertainment events.) The mid-September **Blues Festival** brings three days of entertainment by renowned musicians. Book accommodations well in advance for dates around both festivals.

WEXFORD (LOCH GARMAN)   ☎05391

Wexford's narrow, winding streets are so small that cars along Main St. must yield to baby carriages. The town's quality pubs and restaurants line stone passageways that were built in the 12th century when the Normans conquered the Viking settlement of Waesfjord. Today, fishing trawlers line the harbor, and a newly constructed promenade encourages leisurely strolling by the waterside. Though Wexford has plenty of great shops, restaurants, and (of course) pubs, its compact size helps retain a small-town feel.

▐ TRANSPORTATION

Drivers from Dublin arrive via N11; N25 heads along the Southern coast to Cork.

Trains: O'Hanranhan (North) Station, Redmond Sq. (☎22522). Facing away from the water at Crescent Quay, turn right and walk for about 5min. If office is closed, buy tickets onboard. Services Connolly Station in **Dublin** (2¾hr., 3 per day, return €23) and **Rosslare** (15min., 3 per day, €4).

Buses: Buses stop at the train station. **Mace** (☎24056), across the street, has info and sells tickets. Buses run to **Dublin** (2¾hr., 8-10 per day, €14.40) and **Rosslare** (20min., 9-12 per day, €5.20). Buses to and from **Limerick** (3½hr.; M-Sa 6 per day, Su beginning after noon 2 per day; €23) connect with **Irish Ferries** and **Stena-Sealink** ships.

Taxis: Noel Ryan (☎24056); **Wexford Taxis** (☎46666). There's also a taxi stand at Redmond Sq.

◈ ▮ ORIENTATION AND PRACTICAL INFORMATION

Most of the town's action takes place one block inland along twisting, turning **Main Street.** A plaza called the **Bullring** is near the center of town, a few blocks from where North Main St. changes to South. Another plaza, **Redmond Square,** sits at the northern end of the quays near the train station. Two steeples and a number of towers—including the hilltop Franciscan Friary—define the town's skyline.

Tourist Office: Crescent Quay. (☎23111). Pick up *Discover Wexford* (€2), *Front Door to Ireland* (free), or *Welcome to Wexford* (free). Open M-F 9:30am-6pm, Sa 10am-6pm.

Banks: 24hr. **ATMs** are available at: **Permanent TSB,** the Bullring. (☎24355; open M-Tu and Th-F 10am-5pm, W 10:30am-5pm); **AIB,** S. Main St. (☎22444; open M 10am-

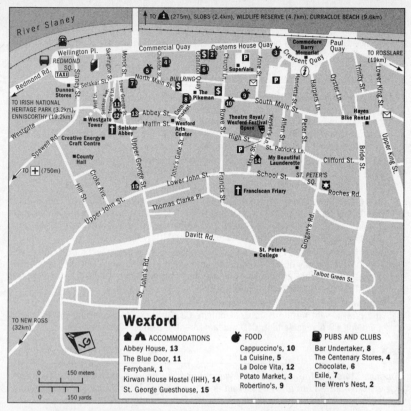

Wexford

🏠🏡 **ACCOMMODATIONS**
Abbey House, **13**
The Blue Door, **11**
Ferrybank, **1**
Kirwan House Hostel (IHH), **14**
St. George Guesthouse, **15**

🍎 **FOOD**
Cappuccino's, **10**
La Cuisine, **5**
La Dolce Vita, **12**
Potato Market, **3**
Robertino's, **9**

🍺 **PUBS AND CLUBS**
Bar Undertaker, **8**
The Centenary Stores, **4**
Chocolate, **6**
Exile, **7**
The Wren's Nest, **2**

5pm, Tu and Th-F 10am-4pm, W 10:30am-4pm); and **Bank of Ireland,** Commercial Quay (☎23022; open M 10am-5pm, Tu and Th-F 10am-4pm, W 10:30am-4pm).

Laundry: My Beautiful Launderette (☎24317), St. Peter's Sq. Open M-F 9:30am-1pm and 2-5pm, Sa 9:30am-1pm. Self service €10; wash and dry €17.

Emergency: ☎999; no coins required. **Police** (*Garda*): Roches Rd. (☎22333).

Pharmacy: Pharmacies along Main St. rotate Su, late, and lunchtime hours. Most are open M-Sa 9am-6pm.

Hospital: Wexford General Hospital, Newtown Rd. (☎42233), on N25/N11.

Internet: Wexford Library (☎21637), Redmond Sq. In a parking lot—enter through the drugstore on Slaney Pl. or lot entrance on Wellinton Pl. Call to reserve a 1hr. slot. Open Tu 1-5:30pm, W 10am-5:30pm and 6-8pm, Th-F 10am-5:30pm, Sa 10am-1pm. Free.

Post Office: Anne St. (☎22587). Open M and W-F 9am-5:30pm, Tu 9:30am-5:30pm, Sa 9am-1pm. Smaller offices on S. Main St. and in Mace at Redmond Sq.

Bike Rentals: Hayes (☎22462), 108 South Main St. Rents bikes for €20 per 24hr., €15 for less than 24hr. Open M-Sa 9am-6pm.

Work Opportunities: Farm Solutions Ltd. hires farm workers. (☎0539 236 222; www.farmsolutions.ie.)

ACCOMMODATIONS

If the hostels and B&Bs below are full, ask the proprietors for recommendations or look along N25 (the Rosslare road or New Town Rd.). If you plan to be in town during the opera festival (see **Entertainment,** p. 220), book as far in advance as possible; rooms are often reserved up to a year ahead of time.

Kirwan House Hostel (IHH), 3 Mary St. (☎21208; www.wexfordhostel.com). A refurbished 200-year-old Georgian house in the heart of town. Brightly painted, clean but smallish quarters don't cramp; they just make fellow bunkers feel like family. Young, friendly staff lead impromptu area excursions and lively pub crawls. Dorms €18-24; private rooms for 3-5 €72-110. Cash only. ❶

The Blue Door, 18 Lower Georges St. (☎21047). Well-kept building with, of course, a blue front door as well as blue carpets. Views of the castle from immaculate ensuite rooms with biscuits, coffee, and tea. Singles €40; doubles €70. MC/V. ❸

St. George Guesthouse, Georges St. (☎43474; www.stgeorgeguesthouse.com). 4min. uphill from North Main St. in a sprawling yellow and white house. More like a hotel than a B&B, with bright, well-kept rooms and plants on the stairs. TVs, tea/coffee, and phones in rooms. Free parking. Doubles €70-80. MC/V. ❸

Abbey House, 34 Abbey St. (☎24408; www.abbeyhouse.ie). Family-run B&B with a central location, comfy quarters with large baths, and a dining room with an electric fireplace; the pleasant exterior has friendly flower boxes. Singles €35-40; doubles with bath €56-80. MC/V 2% charge. ❸

Ferrybank, (☎66926; ferrybank@wexfordboroughcouncil.ie). Just across the bridge from the quays, right on the Harbor. Electricity €3. Shower €1. Wash and dry €4 each. Camping €9 per single tent, €19 per family tent or camper. Cash only. ❶

FOOD

Dunnes Store, Redmond Sq., has everything from groceries to clothes. (☎45688. Open daily 8am-midnight.) **SuperValu** is in the parking lot off Custom House Quay. (☎22290. Open M-W and Sa 8:30am-7pm, Th-F 8:30am-9pm, Su noon-6pm.)

La Dolce Vita, 6-7 Trimmer's Ln. (☎70806). Small but bustling cafe is lined with wine bottles. Creative *panini,* like the pesto, mozzarella, and sun-dried tomato, are €7.50, or €5 takeaway. Pasta €9-10. Open daily 9am-5:30pm. MC/V. ❷

Cappuccino's, 25 North Main St. (☎23669). Great coffees and sandwiches in an energetic atmosphere. Lunch €8. ❷

Robertino's, 19 S. Main St. (☎23334). Excellent pizza at this classic and popular Italian restaurant. Renaissance statues adorn the walls. Pizza and pastas €10-15. Open daily 10am-10:30pm. AmEx/MC/V. ❸

La Cuisine, 80 N. Main St. (☎24986). Homey bakery with snug seating area behind the busy takeaway counter. Good sandwiches (€3-5) and amazing desserts (€2-4). The apple sponge-cake is addictive. Open M-Sa 9am-5:30pm. MC/V. ❶

Potato Market, Crescent Quay. (☎41131). Mythical figures with swords battle it out on the windows of this quayside cafe. With delicious soups (€4) and sandwiches and pastas galore (€9-11), we're the victors. Open daily 7:30am-9pm. MC/V. ❸

PUBS AND CLUBS

The Centenary Stores, Charlotte St. (☎24424), off Commercial Quay. A classy crowd flocks to this stylish pub/cafe situated in a former warehouse. Patio for those sunny-afternoon pints. Excellent trad Su mornings. Attached club, **The Back Door,** has bands M and Th, DJs Th-Su. No cover Th-F and Su before 11:30pm, afterwards €8. Open M-Tu and Th-Sa 10:30am-2am, W 10:30am-11:30pm, Su noon-2am. AmEx/MC/V.

 BETTER THAN A BREAD LINE. On Monday nights, Centenary Stores on Charlotte St. serves free BBQ with all the fixings after 11pm until they run out. No one knows why they do it, but patrons theorize that the hearty food pads the stomach so you're ready to go for another round of drinks. Line up early or expect to wait. See **Centenary Stores,** above, for more information.

Exile, 87 N. Main St. (☎74222). Live rock and trad bands most F-Su nights, otherwise DJs spinning everything from chart-toppers to techno. Open F-Su 10:30pm-3am, depending on the live acts. Free before 11:30pm, afterwards €10. MC/V.

Chocolate, on Common Quay. (☎21131). Hip drinks include an extensive coffee menu and frozen vodkas in the club (Cocktails €6-7.50). Slick interior and sophisticated patrons. W Live trad, Sa rock. Cover for nightclub F and Su €8 after 11pm, Sa €10 after 11pm. Open M, W, F-Sa 9am-2am, Tu and Th 9am-11:30pm, Su noon-11pm. MC/V.

Bar Undertaker/Cape Bar, in the Bullring (☎22949), next to the Pikeman. So named because its owners also have a small undertaking business on the other side of town. Th and Sa-Su live acoustic guitar. Open M-Th 10:30am-11:30pm, F-Sa 10:30am-12:30am, Su 5-11pm. Cash only.

The Wren's Nest, on Customs House Quay (☎22359). Earned a James Joyce award for Authentic Irish Pubs. Charmingly antiquated interior and dart board. Open M-Th 10:30am-11:30pm, F-Sa 10:30am-12:30am, Su 4-11pm. Cash only.

👁 🔺 SIGHTS AND OUTDOOR ACTIVITIES

WESTGATE TOWER. The remains of the Norman **city walls** run the length of High St. **Westgate Tower** is the only one of the wall's original six gates still standing. The tower gate now holds the **Westgate Heritage Centre,** where an excellent 30min. audio-visual show recounts the town's history. *(☎46506; www.wexfordtourism.com. Near the intersection of Abbey and Slaney Pl. Center open M-Sa 10am-5:30pm, occasionally Su during summer. Audio-visual show €3.)*

SELSKAR ABBEY. The serene ruins of Selskar Abbey mark the site of Henry II's penance for his role in St. Thomas Beckett's murder. At the Creative Energy Craft Gallery, behind the Selskar Abbey, you can observe or participate in various craft demonstrations, watch a movie about Wexford, or visit the fair trade coffee shop. *(Enter through the gate by the heritage center. Abbey open daily. Gallery ☎46506; selskardesign@eircom.net. Gallery open M-Sa 10am-6pm, Su noon-6pm.)*

THE BULLRING. In 1621, the town's butcher guild inaugurated bull baiting as a promotional device—the mayor got the hide and the poor got the meat. In the ring stands a statue of a stalwart peasant fearlessly brandishing his homemade weaponry. Known as **The Pikeman,** the edifice commemorates the 1798 uprising (see **Rebellion and Union,** p. 53) and is the main attraction of today's less lively Bullring. Nearby, another statue presides over Crescent Quay. It displays the dashing Commodore John Barry, native son and founder of the U.S. Navy, facing the sea. *(The Bullring is marked by an open area between North and South Main St.)*

FRIARY CHURCH. Franciscan monks have called Wexford home since 1230. The Friary Church houses the "Little Saint" in the back corner of the nave. The wax effigy of young, half-lidded St. Adjutor shows the gash inflicted by the martyr's Roman father. *(☎22758; located in the Franciscan Friary on School St. Open daily. Free.)*

HORSEBACK RIDING. Wexford's countryside and beaches make for great riding. Shelmalier Riding Stables has horses waiting for interested visitors. *(Stables 6km away off R733 at Forth Mountain on the way to the Wildfowl Reserve. ☎39251; book ahead.)*

♫ ENTERTAINMENT

For detailed information on events throughout the county, pick up *The Wexford People* (€1.50) from any local newsstand or pub. The funky **Wexford Arts Centre,** in Cornmarket, presents free art exhibitions. Evening performances of music, dance, and drama occur here throughout the year. (☎23764; www.wexfordartscentre.ie. Center open M-W 10am-6pm, Th-Sa 10am-9pm. Tickets generally €10-15.) The **Theatre Royal,** High St., produces shows throughout the year, culminating in the internationally acclaimed **Wexford Opera Festival,** held for three weeks starting at the end of October. The festival uncovers three obscure but deserving operas from the artistic attic and performs them in an intimate setting. (☎22400, box office 22144; www.wexfordopera.com. Box office open M-F 9am-5pm. Tickets €12-100.) Enniscorthy's Strawberry Festival leads into Wexford's **Hooves and Grooves Festival,** complete with horse racing and plenty of free music in June and July (www.wexlive.com/grooves).

🗺 DAYTRIPS FROM WEXFORD

THE SLOBS AND CURRACLOE BEACH

The Wildfowl Reserve is on the North Slob, 3.2km north of Wexford. Take Castlebridge/Gorey Rd. to well-signposted Ardcavan Ln. (€10 cab ride), or hike through the Ferrybank caravan park and along the increasingly sandy, picturesque beach for 40min. Bus Éireann departs Wexford for Curracloe M 10:15am, Sa 8:15am and 4:30pm; departs Curracloe M 4:36pm, Sa 1:11 and 5:43pm. Reserve Centre ☎23129. Open daily 9am-5pm. Free. Guided tours on request.

In the late 1840s the Slobs, which were originally boglands, were filled to create more land for agriculture. Actually two meters below sea level, they are constantly pumped out to keep the spongy land from being immersed in water. Though they're still used for growing grasses and cereals, the Slobs are better known for attracting spectacular wildlife. **The Wexford Wildfowl Reserve,** a research center and haven for rare birds from around the world, covers 420 acres. Ten thousand of Greenland's white-fronted geese (half of the entire species population) descend on the Sloblands between October and April, cohabiting with other birds from as far as Siberia and Iceland. You can spy on them, as well as on the resident Irish birds who are mating along the channels, from one of the many hides. The **Reserve Centre** has a new wing that details the creation of the Slobs, highlights the wildlife, and displays a water-based cannon formerly used to kill dozens of birds at one time. The observation tower affords a great lookout over the Reserve, and the Centre lends binoculars for better glimpses of the fowl.

Ten more kilometers down the coast lies broad **Curracloe Beach,** and beyond it **Ballinesker Beach,** where Spielberg filmed the D-Day landings in *Saving Private Ryan.* It doesn't look all that much like Normandy, but it sure is beautiful. Untainted by buildings or other civilization markers, the beach is peaceful and the sand is soft; the exceptionally clean water looks almost tropical but is a good deal colder. Curracloe makes a fabulous cycling daytrip; the beach is lined with dune bluffs whose stature rivals the steeples on the far side of the Slaney. To get there by bike, follow Castlebridge/Gorey Rd. beyond the turnoff for the Slobs to a signposted right turn for Curracloe Town. Cycle past fields of sheep and turn right in Curracloe Town at the post office (35min. from the bridge, 10min. by car).

THE IRISH NATIONAL HERITAGE PARK

The park is 5km outside Wexford on N11. Taxis cost about €8. ☎20733; www.inhp.com. Open daily 9:30am-6:30pm, last admission 5pm, subject to seasonal change. Hourly guided tours included in the price of admission. Wheelchair-accessible. €7.50, students €6.

The Irish National Heritage Park packs 9000 years of history into a park barely 20 years old. Visitors stroll through reconstructions of a Stone Age campsite, an early Norman tower, and old Irish homesteads, tombs, and fortifications. Since the real sites are in various states of disrepair and are scattered across the country, the park attempts to show the sites as they would have looked in their heydays. It's a good idea in theory, but the costumed guides, fake food and bones, and recorded noises make the whole thing seem a little artificial. A fake round tower just isn't the same. If you get hungry afterward, hop over to the park's restaurant, **Fulacht Faidh ❷**, which serves carvery food and excellent chips. (Entrees €9-10. Open daily 12:30-5:30pm.)

ROSSLARE HARBOUR (ROS LÁIR) ☎05391

Rosslare Harbour, best viewed when waving from the deck of a departing ship, is a decidedly dull seaside village whose primary function is welcoming voyagers and bidding them *bon voyage* as they depart for France or Wales. Unlike the seaports of popular imagination, Rosslare doesn't conjure international intrigue; it doesn't even have many good pubs or restaurants. Plan on shipping out as soon as your bags are off the ferry.

▐ TRANSPORTATION. Trains run from the ferry port to: **Dublin** (3hr., 3 per day, €19.50); **Limerick** (2½hr., 1-2 per day, €17) via **Waterford** (1¼hr., 1 per day, €10); and **Wexford** (15min., 3 per day, €4). The rail office (☎57930) is open daily 6:15am-9:15pm. The same office houses the bus station (☎57930). Most **buses** stop at the ferry terminal, by the Kilrane Church and the Catholic church, and go to: **Dublin** (3hr., 14 per day, €16); **Galway** via **Waterford** (6½hr., 4 per day, €25.50); **Killarney** (6hr., M-Sa 4 per day, Su 3 per day; €24.50) via **Cork** (3½ hr., €21) and **Waterford** (1½hr., €14.40); **Limerick** (4hr., M-Sa 5 per day, Su 3 per day; €21); **Tralee** (M-Sa 4 per day, Su 2 per day; €25.50); **Wexford** (20min., 13-17 per day, €4.30). **Stena Line** (☎61560) and **Irish Ferries** (☎0818 300 400) serve the port. **Ferries** shove off for: **Wales** (summer 5-6 per day, winter 2 per day); **Britain** (2 per day); and **France** (1 every other day). For more info see **By Boat**, p. 27. For a **taxi** out of town, check for phone numbers at the blue information board to the left of the bureau de change, or try Meg Browne (☎08729 47883), Jimmy Ferguson (☎08723 24618), or Harbour Cabs (☎08727 37466). An office in the ferry terminal offers **Europcar** (☎33634), **Hertz** (☎33238), and **Budget** (☎33318) **car rentals**. Prices hover around €80-90 for one to two days and €200-235 per week.

▐▌ ORIENTATION AND PRACTICAL INFORMATION. To get from the ferry port into town, climb the ramp or walk the steps up the cliff; the path goes to N25 which cuts through town. Contact the Wexford **tourist office** (see p. 216) with travel questions, or head to the **port authority desk** for ferry information (☎33114). **Exchange currency** at the **Bank of Ireland**, on St. Martin Rd. (☎33304. 24hr. **ATM.** Open M-F 10:30am-12:30pm and 1:30-4pm.) The **post office** in the SuperValu shopping center has a **bureau de change.** (☎33201. Open M-F 9am-1pm and 2-5:30pm, Sa 9am-1pm.) **Gouldson's Pharmacy** is next door. (☎33551. Open M-F 9am-1pm and 2-6pm, Sa 9am-1pm and 2-5:30pm.)

▐▌ ACCOMMODATIONS AND FOOD. B&Bs swamp N25 just outside Rosslare. **▧Mrs. O'Leary's Farmhouse ❷**, off N25 in Kilrane, a 15min. drive from town, towers above the rest. Open since 1955 and set on a glorious 40-hectare seaside farm, Mrs. O'Leary's is a holiday in and of itself. On fine days, stroll down to the quiet beach. If the weather threatens, stay inside by the fireplace with tea and scones. Breakfasts are varied and tasty, with vegan and vegetarian options plus homemade bread and jam. Pickup from town when available. (☎33134. Singles €40-45; doubles €70. Cash only.) Four-poster beds in some rooms add a touch of old-fashioned grandeur to **St. Martin's B&B** ❹, on St. Martin's Rd., near the bank. Rooms include minifridges and hair dryers. (☎33133; www.saintmartinsross-lare.com. Singles €50; doubles €70. Free Wi-Fi. MC/V in summer.)

The few restaurants in town tend to be expensive and uninspiring—cooking is the best bet. The **SuperValu,** on N25, has groceries. (☎33107. Open M-W and Sa 8am-7pm, Th 8am-8pm, F 8am-9pm, Su 9am-5pm.) For chipper lovers, there is no better place than Rosslare, land of fried fish. The best pub is **Culleton's,** on N25 about 1.5km out of town. The *craic* here is as good as it gets, so it's worth the walk. (☎33590. Open M-Th 10:30am-11:30pm, F-Sa 10:30am-12:30am, Su 12:30-11pm. Sa live rock, Su trad. MC/V.) The **Kilrane Inn,** on N25 in Kilrane, across from Culleton's, has a large eating area where pub food (sandwiches €5-6; roasts and fish €10-13) is served from 12:30-3pm and 5-9pm. (☎33661. Open M-Th 10:30am-11:30pm, F-Sa 10:30am-12:30am, Su 12:30-11pm. Trad sessions F-Sa. MC/V.)

KILMORE QUAY AND THE SALTEE ISLANDS ☎05391

Twenty kilometers southwest of Rosslare Harbour on Forlorn Point, whitewashed seaside cottages line the main road of Kilmore Quay. The small fishing village (pop. 400) isn't even large enough to have a bank, but its harbor—shared by fishermen, seals, and visitors venturing to and around the uninhabited Saltee Islands—is quite active. The quiet village, with few sounds beside the whispering wind and the crashing waves, is the perfect setting for a lovely and relaxing afternoon.

■⊞ **ORIENTATION AND PRACTICAL INFORMATION.** To reach Kilmore Quay from Rosslare Harbour, take the Wexford road to Tagoat and turn left; from Wexford, take the Rosslare road, turn right on R739 near Piercetown, and continue for 6.5km. **Viking Buses** (☎21053) runs from **Wexford** to Kilmore Quay—look for "Shuttle Bus" signs in Redmond Sq. and Kilmore Quay roundabout. (30min. Departs Wexford M-Tu and Th-F 7:30, 10am, 1:30, 5:45pm; W and Sa 7:30am, 1:30, 5:45pm. Departs Kilmore Quay M-Sa 8:10, 10:30am, 2:15, 6:30pm; return €8.) **Bus Éireann** runs between **Wexford** and Kilmore Quay (30min.; departs Wexford W 10am and 3:30pm, Sa 11am and 4:20pm; departs Kilmore Quay W 10:35am and 4:10pm, Sa 11:35am and 5pm; €4). In town, two streets diverge from the harbor: **Wexford road** and **back road.** A small beach lies to the left of the harbor, and the 11km **Ballyteige Beach** to the right of the harbor. **Tourist information** is available at **Stella Maris Community Centre** on Wexford road, which also has individual public and private showers (€3 per hr.) and **Internet** access for €4 per hr. (☎29922. Open M-F 9am-5pm, Sa 9am-12:30pm, Su 9am-1pm. Showers open June-Sept. daily 5-8pm.) There are **no banks** or **ATMs** in town but you can use a bank card to withdraw money at the **post office,** which is on the Wexford road, just beyond the church. (☎29641. Open M-F 9am-12:30pm and 1:30-5:30pm.)

⛨ **ACCOMMODATIONS.** May Bates's **Harbour Lights B&B** ❸, New Ross Rd., has a good view of the Saltee Islands, free parking, and insider advice on the restaurants in town. It's in the middle of town across from the Silver Fox restaurant. (☎29881. Singles €45; doubles €70. MC/V.) The **Quay House** ❹, just beyond the post office on the Wexford road, is more like a hotel than a B&B. The breakfast options are colorfully displayed on a chalkboard. (☎29988. Doubles €90. MC/V.)

🌃🖼 **FOOD AND PUBS.** The closest thing to a grocery store in town is **Cullens,** by the roundabout. (☎48971. Open daily 8am-9pm.) Reel in the best meal around at the ⚑**Silver Fox ❹,** across from the Maritime Museum. The fresh seafood is served up just down the street from the harbor. (☎29888. Call ahead. Entrees €15-30; vegetarian entrees €14-15. 3-course early-bird menu €25, 5-7pm. Open June-Sept. daily 12:30-9:30pm, Oct.-May M-Sa 5-9:30pm, Su 12:30-9:30pm. MC/V.) **Bird Rock ❷,** a coffee shop housed in the Stella Maris Community Centre (see above), is the place for affordable food. It serves huge dishes (€4-6), including breakfast all day. (☎29922. Open Tu-F 9am-2pm, Sa 9:30am-12:30pm, Su 9am-noon. Cash only.) **James Kehoe's Pub ❸,** on the Wexford road directly across from St. Peter's Church, is an eatery, watering hole, and museum all in one with a steering wheel, menu from the *Lusitania,* and binnacle on display. Try the superb seafood chowder (€6) and check out the handy pamphlets (€4, but free to look) on Kilmore Quay lore. (☎29830. Entrees €15-18, sandwiches €4.25-7. Sa live trad. Kitchen open noon-10pm. MC/V.) There's a bit more variety than a typical pub usually offers at **The Wooden House ❸,** with greek salad and stuffed baked potatoes in addition to typical roasts. (☎48879. Sandwiches €8-9, entrees €12-19. Kitchen open noon-8pm. F-Su live music. MC/V.)

🌄🌿 **SIGHTS AND FESTIVALS.** Kilmore Quay runs daily boat trips to the **Saltee Islands,** formerly a pagan pilgrimage site and now Ireland's largest **bird sanctuary.** The winged population numbers nearly 50,000 and sings loudly on the rocks and in every crevice of the cliff banks. There's little more than salt and feathers on this refuge for puffins, razorbills, and gray seals, but it's an ideal place for a long picnic. Prominent granite monuments and a throne in the middle of one of the islands are reminders that the Saltees belonged to the late self-proclaimed Prince Michael Neale. For more royal family history, check www.salteeislands.info. A narrow ridge of rock is thought to have connected the smaller island to the mainland in ancient times. This land bridge, called **St. Patrick's Causeway,** was used for driving cattle to pasture on the islands. The beginning of the Causeway is visible from town at low tide. To get there, take the road to Kilmore town and turn right at the signpost, roughly 1.6km from town, or scramble over rocks on the beach, turn left, and walk 20min. from the harbor. **Boats** leave the mainland each morning, weather permitting. **Declan Bates** offers a 1½hr. cruise around the islands. (☎29684. €18, children €9. Phone for sailing times.) **Eamonn Hayes** brings visitors aboard for **deep-sea angling, reef-fishing,** and scenic trips around the islands. Call ahead to arrange a time or to rent equipment. (☎29723 or 087 213 5308; www.kilmoreangling.com. Full-day boat rental €360; evening rental 4:30-8pm €285. Rods €10.)

The village floats its **Maritime Museum** in the lightship *Guillemot,* once anchored near the harbor and now cemented into it. Climb into the hold and view Irish naval artifacts and marine accessories, then read the tragic stories of local shipwrecks, recorded on somewhat decrepit and waterlogged posterboards. Unfortunately, the museum is closed for renovations until mid-summer 2008. (☎29655. Open June-Aug. daily noon-6pm. €4; students/children/seniors €2.) Through town and just around the corner, the **Millennium Memorial Hiking Trail** winds a short route to Forlorn Point, adjacent to the main jetty. Handouts detailing flora, fauna, and history of this walk and two others in the area are available at the Stella Maris Centre. A giant whalebone that washed ashore in 2000 and a stone ship overlooking the majestic ocean pay tribute to local sailors lost at sea in the Memorial Park. The **Kilmore Seafood Festival** hauls in seafood, music, and games for four raucous days in July. Call the Stella Maris Centre (☎29922) for information.

SOUTHEAST IRELAND

NEW ROSS (ROS MHIC TREOIN)   ☎051

New Ross makes for a great place to rest after a tour of Ireland's southeast corner, as Waterford, the Hook, Wexford, and Kilkenny lie within easy reach of this tiny yet bustling town. Home to the beloved Kennedy family, this ancient maritime port has a tidy little list of sights, most of which involve its favorite great-grandson John F. Kennedy and the Irish exodus. *Dunbrody*, a coffin ship replica from the Famine era, is an awe-inspiring must-see.

■■ **ORIENTATION AND PRACTICAL INFORMATION.** Most events in New Ross occur on a strip of waterfront known as **the Quay.** Other major thoroughfares are **Mary Street,** which extends uphill from the bridge, and **South Street,** which runs parallel to the Quay one block inland between Mary St. and Cross St. New Ross is on N25 (to Wexford and Waterford) and N30 (to Enniscorthy): though *Let's Go* does not recommend hitchhiking, hitchers report finding plenty of rides on either, especially in the morning and late afternoon.

Bus Éireann (☎051 879 000; www.buseireann.ie) runs from the Riverview Hotel on the Quay to **Dublin** (3hr.; M-Sa 7:10, 11am, 1:25, 4:28pm, Su 11am, 1:25, 5:45pm; €10.50); **Rosslare Harbour** (1hr.; M-Sa 7:10, 11:50am, 1:35, 7:50pm, Su 7:10am, 1:35, 7:50pm; €11); and **Waterford** (25min.; M-Sa 10 per day 7:50am-8:55pm, Su 6 per day 8am-9pm; €5.50). **Donovan's Taxi** (☎425 100) will drive you to your hostel after an exhausting day. The New Ross **tourist office,** in **Dunbrody Centre** next to the famine ship, provides useful town information as well as an Internet cafe (€2 per 30min.) and tickets for the Dunbrody ship tour. (☎421 857; www.newrosschamber.ie. Open Oct.-Mar. daily 9am-5pm; Apr.-Sept. daily 9am-6pm.) Banks with 24hr. **ATMs** abound: **Bank of Ireland,** on Quay St. (☎421 267; open M 10am-5pm, Tu-F 10am-4pm); **AIB** (☎421 319; open M 10am-5pm, Tu-F 10am-4pm) and **TSB** (☎422 060; open M-F 10:30am-5pm) are across from each other on South St. The **post office** is on Charles St., off the Quay. (☎421 261. Open M-F 9am-5:30pm, Sa 9am-1pm.) New Ross is also newly wired up with two Internet cafe options across the street from each other on the Quay: **Internet Cafe** (€1.50 per 15min., €4 per 30-60min.) and the cafe in the Dunbrody Centre (2€ per 20min.).

▐▐ **ACCOMMODATIONS AND FOOD.** ▨**Mac Murrough Farm Hostel ❶** provides a family-friendly respite in a converted farmhouse. From the bridge, follow Quay St. up one block, then turn left onto North St. and follow N30 toward Enniscorthy. Take a right onto Bosheen Rd., then turn left immediately after the Statoil station and continue straight until you see the "hostel" sign; the remaining mile is signposted. The owners will pick you up if you call ahead. Check out is at 10:30am, but don't worry about sleeping in—the roosters will give you a real wake-up call (☎421 383; www.macmurrough.com. Dorms €16-18; ensuite twin €20.) For a bed in town and a bigger dent in the wallet, try **Riversdale House B&B ❸,** William St. Follow South St. to William St. and turn left up the hill. The owners take pride in their snazzy rooms with great views of town. (☎422 515. Ensuite rooms €35 per person.) **Glendower House B&B ❸,** on Ring Road near N25, has a more modern feel with TVs in every one of its pristine rooms. (☎421 989. Singles €40; doubles €40.)

SuperValu grocery store is on the Quay. (☎421 392. Open M-Th 8am-9pm, F 8am-10pm, Sa 8am-7:30pm, Su 9am-6pm.) **Café Nutshell ❶,** 8 South St., tucked away in the back of the health-food shop "In a Nutshell Emporium," serves breakfast, sandwiches, and excellent coffee in a skylighted seating area. (☎422 777. Breakfast €3-6; sandwiches €3.50-7. Open M-Sa 9am-5pm.) For those in the mood for something greasier, **Kaan Kebab ❶,** 2 John St., offers a variety of kebabs, burgers, and chips (kebabs €5-6; burgers €3-4; chips €3). For a unique dining experience, board **The Galley Cruising Restaurant ❹** (☎421 723), which travels from New Ross into either

Waterford Harbour or up the River Nore, depending on the tide. An Irish culinary stronghold, their yeast malt brown bread is considered their signature. It is served with all of their fresh, seasonal meals: lunch (2hr.; 12:30pm; €25, cruise only €12), tea (2hr., 3pm, €12/10), or dinner (2-3hr., 6 or 7pm, €40/15).

◙ **SIGHTS.** During the **Great Famine,** thousands of emigrants made the torturous 50-day journey to America in the dank and dreary holds of wooden ships. Many left from New Ross in the *Dunbrody,* which sank off the coast of Canada after her days as a famine ship were over. Today, a brand-new 54m oak replica sits at the docks, inviting visitors to observe the conditions both first-class and steerage passengers had to endure. Tours start with a 10min. video highlighting the making of the new ▧**Dunbrody,** then move into the ship, where actors relive the ordeal. A computerized database of coffin ship passengers is free to explore. (☎425 239; www.dunbrody.com. Open Apr.-Oct. daily 9am-6pm; Nov.-Mar. daily 9am-5pm; last admission 1hr. before closing. €7, seniors €5, students and children €4.) After learning about your Irish roots, get a load of the natural ones at the **John F. Kennedy Arboretum,** which lies 11.3km south of New Ross on Ballyhack Rd. (R733). Stroll around 623 gorgeous acres of nearly 6000 different species dedicated to Ireland's favorite U.S. President. The small **cafe** doubles as a gift shop but many visitors bring their own lunch to this perfect picnicking place. (☎388 171. Open May-Aug. daily 10am-8pm; Apr. and Sept. 10am-6:30pm; Oct.-Mar. 10am-5pm. Last admission 45min. before closing. €2.20, seniors €2, children €1.20.) Nearby, at the **Kennedy Homestead** in Dunganstown, Kennedy fans can visit the home and working farm of JFK's great-grandfather and see an archival video of the 35th President's visit to Ireland in 1963. (☎388 264; www.kennedyhomestead.com. Open July-Aug. daily 10am-5pm; May-June and Sept. M-F 11:30am-4:30pm. €5, seniors €4.30.)

THE HOOK PENINSULA

South of New Ross and west of Waterford, the Hook is a peaceful peninsula renowned for its historic abbeys, forts, and lighthouses. Sun-drenched coastlines draw deep-sea anglers to Waterford Harbour and Tramore Bay, while the pubs on the oceanfront keep the midnight oil burning long past midnight. Unfortunately, public transportation does not reach this burgeoning vacation region, so itinerant travelers must depend on cars or bikes. The peninsula is accessed by heading south along R733 from New Ross, or by crossing Waterford Harbour on the Ballyhack-Passage East ferry (every 10min.; cars €8, €12 round-trip). *Let's Go* doesn't endorse hitchhiking, though hitchers find rides fairly easily. Those who make it around the Ring of Hook are rewarded with stunning coastal views. Plan ahead at www.thehook-wexford.com.

BALLYHACK AND ARTHURSTOWN   ☎051

Sixteen kilometers south of New Ross, **Ballyhack** threatens its cross-channel neighbor, Passage East, with 15th-century **Ballyhack Castle.** Although the Castle fails to strike fear into the hearts of invading tourists, it was built around 1450 by William Marshall (Strongbow's heir; see **Feudalism,** p. 51) to protect his precious port at New Ross. To make sure the job was done right, Marshall hired the Crusading Order of the Knights Hospitallers, known for battlefield valor. Tours lead visitors up the castle tower and take delight in displaying the ghastly methods of self-defense employed by the knights. (☎389 468. Open mid-June to mid-Sept. daily 10am-6pm; last tour 45min. before closing. Free.)

Three kilometers north of Ballyhack on the New Ross Rd. lies **Dunbrody Abbey,** a magnificent 12th-century Cistercian monastery. Visitors can take a guided tour through the massive monastery and then head across the road to lose themselves in the breathtaking **hedge-row maze,** located just beyond the Abbey's **Visitors Centre.** If you emerge, reward yourself with one of Greta's homemade scones or brown bread open-faced sandwiches in the nearby **tea room.** Once refueled, visitors can also enjoy a lovely **pitch and putt course** near the maze. (☎388 603. Call ahead. Center and tea room open June-Aug. daily 11am-5pm. Abbey €2. Castle and maze €5.)

If history and religion weren't inspiring enough, perhaps some of nature's best work will do the trick in the form of the majestic **Kilmokea Gardens.** To visit this seven-acre horticulturist's dream, complete with over 130 plant species manicured to embrace its far eastern influence, continue up R733 toward New Ross; brown signs guide visitors the rest of the way. Also a country manor, Kilmokea has become a popular wedding location. Visitors not intending to get hitched can still enjoy the **craft shop** and a respite in the **Pink Teacup Cafe** in addition to a stroll through the flora and fauna paradise (☎388 109; www.kilmokea.com. Gardens and craft shop open June-Aug. daily 11am-5pm. Cafe serves lunch noon-3pm. €6, children €3.)

The Ballyhack-bound find lodgings in **Arthurstown.** Take a right from the Ballyhack ferryport's landing area and follow the **Slí Charman** (SHLEE KAR-man) coastal path; the village lies half a mile up the trail. **Glendine Country House B&B ❹,** is a step up from the typical cozy B&B experience but still offers a personal touch. This ivy-covered Georgian manor, located on the left just through town (look for the shetland cows on the lawn), has thoughtfully decorated and spacious rooms. Breakfasts feature homemade breads and organic produce. Freshly made light meals are also available. (☎389 258; www.glendinehouse.com. Singles €60; doubles €120; family rooms €45 per person.) The new **Willow Lodge B&B ❸** offers clean and comfortable rooms close to town without burning a hole in your wallet. From Ballyhack, follow the main road up the hill and take the first road on your left. (☎389686. €35 per person ensuite.) Even closer to Ballyhack, the **Marsh Mere Lodge ❹** will be one of the first houses on the left. In this elegant B&B, the deck overlooks the ocean and the sitting room has an antique grand piano. (☎389 186 or 08722 27303; www.marshmerelodge.com. Singles €50; doubles €100.) Modest and modern **Arthur's Rest B&B ❸,** on the left up the hill on Duncannon Rd., has immaculate rooms and a cozy living room with a flat-screen TV. (☎389 192. Singles €40; ensuite doubles €35 per person.) Arthurstown has a pub and views of the water, but nary a bite to eat; cook for yourself or head to Duncannon, a few kilometers away. The closest large grocery stores are in Wexford, New Ross, and Waterford. Back in Ballyhack, the only edibles are found at **Byrne's ❷,** by the ferry port. The pub serves sandwiches (€2.50-4.50), and the store has a limited grocery selection. (☎389 107. Open M-Th 10:30am-11:30pm, F-Sa 10:30am-12:15am, Su noon-11pm; lunch served M-Sa 11am-7pm.)

DUNCANNON
☎051

The warmth of its people and its rich history make this quaint town that clings to the eastern coast of Waterford Harbour worth a visit. A beautiful beach below town also makes Duncannon a popular spot for Irish vacation homes. The **Duncannon Fort Visitor Centre** is located inside **Duncannon Fort,** an array of stone structures looming over the harbor. Built in 1586 by the ruling English to protect themselves from the threat of the Spanish armada, its location on the extremely exposed harbor has made it strategically important for centuries. The complex also houses an excellent **Maritime Museum,** a cafe and craft shop, and the **Cockleshell Art Centre,** which showcases the work of both locally and nationally prominent artists. Increasingly popular **military reenactments,** staging battles from World War I and other major conflicts go down the first weekend in June. (☎389 454. Center open June to mid-Sept. daily 10am-5:30pm; low-season tours available by appointment. Admission includes guided tour. €5, children and seniors €3.)

Seashells B&B ❸, on the beach, has sleek rooms with tall windows and great views of the water. (☎389 195. Ensuite rooms €35 per person, under 14 €20. Continental breakfast only.) **Mona Lisa B&B ❸,** on the right heading up the hill toward Duncannon Fort, has bright rooms with white linens. (☎389 335. Singles €45; doubles €75.) Up the hill past Mona Lisa's, after the only right turn, is **The Moorings B&B ❸,** with pretty, spacious rooms. (☎389 242. Breakfast included. €35-40 per person ensuite.)

Given Duncannon's size, there aren't many culinary options, but two pubs in the main intersection of town offer good grub. Historic **Strand Tavern ❷** has been recognized in the short list of "Irish Pubs of Distinction" (www.ipodltd.com) due in part to its authentic wooden decor taken directly from a ship washed ashore in 1888, its signature seafood chowder, and its very friendly staff. (☎389 109. *Panini* €6; entrees €10-24. Breakfast available daily 10-11:30am, bar food noon-9pm.) Across the street to the right, **Roche's Traditional Bar ❷** serves classic Irish fare from 12:30-6pm and shares a kitchen with **Squigl ❷,** which opens from 7-9pm for a fine dining experience. Roche's also hosts trad sessions every Friday night (☎389 188. Entrees €7-11.)

Duncannon has a **post office** in the center of town. (Open M-F 9am-5:30pm.) **New Ross Bus Service** (☎389 418) runs one mid-morning bus per day to and from their respective destinations; see the schedule posted outside of the post office or call for more details.

HOOK HEAD ☎051

Hook Head's 13th-century **Hook Lighthouse** is the oldest operating beacon in the British Isles. Tours run up its 115 steps in search of panoramic views of the peninsula. Visitors are treated to a hearty dose of history and lighthouse lore. The Visitors Centre has a small gift shop and a cafe serving soup and sandwiches. (☎397 055. Open Mar.-Oct. daily 9:30am-5:30pm. Guided tours every 30min. €5.50, students and seniors €3.50.) On the eastern side of the peninsula at the bottom of a valley is Ireland's own gloriously secluded **Tintern Abbey,** founded in the 13th century. (☎562 650.

WAR GAMES

For most of the year, the seaside town of Duncannon is sleepy and content, whiling away the off-season months until the heat of summer entices throngs of vacationers back to its beaches. Every year at the end of May, its lords play proud host to a series of military reenactments at their own major historical landmark, Duncannon Fort, which looms on the cliff overlooking Waterford Harbour.

Staged battles range from the fight for Irish independence—when rebel prisoners, captured by the ruling English, were held in cells at the same site—to the American Civil War. Spectators and participants the world over come to watch famous historical battles erupt on the grounds of the fort. Accuracy is of the utmost concern; the World War II scenes, for example, feature vintage military vehicles of both the Allies and Axis Powers. After the appropriate country surrenders, the audience has a chance to interview the veteran soldiers, who answer in character. The festivities conclude with a parade of soldiers from the Middle Ages to the present, marching in one long line.

*For more information, contact the **Visitor Centre** at ☎0513 89454. The festival generally runs the last weekend in May or the first weekend in June.*

Open May-Nov. daily 10am-6pm. Wander freely or take a tour: €2, students €1.10, seniors €1.30.) The abbey is 4.8km from the Ballycullane stop on the Waterford-Rosslare rail line.

WATERFORD HARBOUR

Beautiful Waterford Harbour straddles the Waterford-Wexford county line east of Waterford City. Its orientation and proximity to England once made it a prime target for invasion, which led to the construction of Duncannon Fort under the supervision of Queen Elizabeth. It also inspired Oliver Cromwell's catchy phrase "by hook or by crook"; he schemed to capture Waterford City via either Hook Head or its cross-harbor neighbor Crooke Village. The **Passage East Car Ferry** (☎382 480) provides a fast and convenient alternative to circumnavigating the harbor—it zips you across the water between Ballyhack and Passage East in under ten minutes (€8 one-way, €12 return). While the trip is a swell ride by car, the roads outside of Waterford are hilly and windy, and the long journey tests the stamina of even the staunchest cyclists.

DUNMORE EAST (DÚN MÓR) ☎051

Vacationing Irish families have made Dunmore East their summertime mecca. Watch your step: in good weather, droves of children swarm the beaches. When not people-watching, look out to sea—the harbor, cliffs, and distant Hook make for spectacular views. Dunmore's beaches are great for swimming, especially at several points where trails descend into isolated coves. Central Dunmore Beach is the most popular. Kittiwakes (small gulls) throng the coastline, building their nests in cliff faces unusually close to human habitation—hundreds of nests clutter the cliffs of Badger's Cove. Big waves crash onto the rocks at the few fowl-free rock faces, which are accessible via the dirt road past Dock Rd. For off-shore thrills, the friendly folks at **Dunmore East Adventure Centre,** on the docks, teach windsurfing, kayaking, canoeing, sailing, and rock climbing, and provide the equipment. The Centre also offers excellent day-camps for children and 2-, 3-, or 5-day sailing courses. (☎383 783; www.dunmoreadventure.com. Book ahead. 2hr. sessions: adults €40-45, children €23-30.) Music buffs will especially appreciate the **Guinness Bluegrass Festival,** entering its second decade, which dominates the social life of the village every August.

Dunmore East's two main streets run the length of the beach: **the Strand** comprises the lower part of town and **Dock Road** leads uphill and to the docks. **Creaden View B&B ❸**, next to the post office on Dock Rd., has a neat garden, rooms overlooking the bay, and a diverse and delicious breakfast menu. (☎383 339. Singles €45-50; doubles €70.) ▓**Church Villa ❸**, across from the church between Dock Rd. and the Strand, has bright rooms, a conservatory dining room, and a sunny owner to match. (☎383 390. Singles €45; doubles €70.) **Springfield B&B ❸**, the second left from the beginning of the Strand, leading up and away from Dock Rd., has pristine, modern rooms and a well-lit breakfast room. (☎383 448. Open Mar.-Nov. Singles €45-60; doubles €60-70.)

Buy groceries at **Londis Supermarket,** Dock Rd., on the right after passing the Ocean Hotel. (☎383 471. Open June-Sept. M-Th 8:30am-8pm, F-Su 8:30am-9pm; Oct.-May M-F 8:30am-7pm, Sa-Su 8:30am-8pm.) The best sandwiches in town are served up at the **Bay Cafe ❷**, on Dock Rd. (☎383 900. Sandwiches €3-6. Open summer daily 9am-6pm; low-season 9am-4:30pm.) Cheap yet satisfying grub can also be found at **The Pirate ❶**, a small chipper and kebab stand at the east entrance to town. (Fish €5; kebab and chips €7.) For a sit-down meal, a lively bunch gather nightly at the **Spinnaker Bar ❷**, also on the Strand. On Saturday nights, this popular

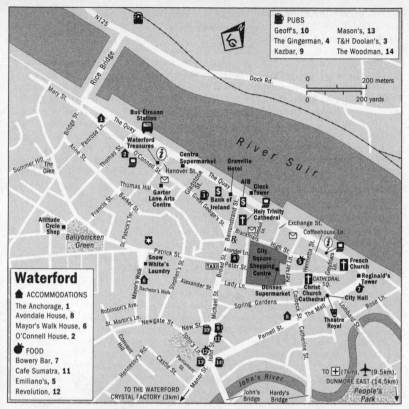

PUBS

Geoff's, **10**		Mason's, **13**	
The Gingerman, **4**		T&H Doolan's, **3**	
Kazbar, **9**		The Woodman, **14**	

0   200 meters

0   200 yards

Waterford

🏠 ACCOMMODATIONS

The Anchorage, **1**
Avondale House, **8**
Mayor's Walk House, **6**
O'Connell House, **2**

🍴 FOOD

Bowery Bar, **7**
Cafe Sumatra, **11**
Emiliano's, **5**
Revolution, **12**

hangout offers live music, as well as plenty of beer and pizza, proving that life doesn't get much better than on the beach. (Pizza €7 small, €9 large. Open daily M-Th 2pm-midnight, F-Su 2pm-2am.) Alternatively, **Power's Bar,** on Dock Rd. across from the post office, is a proudly traditional pub and the favorite of local fishermen. (☎383 318. Open trad sessions Tu night begin at 9:30pm.)

Suirway Coaches (☎382 209; www.suirway.com. 24hr. timetable ☎382 422) runs the 15.3km between **Waterford** and **Dunmore East** (30min., M-Sa 7:50, 10:30am, noon, 2:30, 3:30, 5pm; Sa first bus 8:30am, otherwise same as weekday times; €3). Wait outside Dingley's shop on Dock Rd. or flag it down anywhere on its route. Ulster Bank has a 24hr. **ATM** outside the Londis Supermarket on Dock Rd.

TRAMORE (TRÁ MHÓR)   ☎051

Despite the pastel amusement parks that dot the shore, Tramore manages to avoid seeming tacky or honky-tonk. When you get beyond the strip, it's still a regular old Irish town, with friendly, unflappable locals and gorgeous views. Don't miss the cliffs rising above the beach—the views of the coast are fantastic, and you might spot a newbie surfer wiping out in the sea.

🚍🚶 TRANSPORTATION AND PRACTICAL INFORMATION. Buses connect Tramore to **Waterford. Bus Éireann** runs every half hour (40min., 6:20am-11pm,

€2.50). **Rapid Express Coaches** (☎872 149) sends buses from the station to Waterford every 2hr. (9 per day, €2.50), and to **Dublin** (M-Sa 9 per day 5:15am-8pm, Su 8 per day 6:15am-8pm). Call **Coast Cabs** (☎330989) or **Atlantic Cabs** (☎386 177) for a **taxi.**

Tramore can be difficult to navigate; few streets keep their names for long and not even the tourist office has a good map. The town is small, though, so you won't stay lost for long. The bus station is on the **Waterford road** (technically **Turkey Road**), a block from the intersection of **Strand Street** (which becomes **Main Street,** then **Summer Hill**) and **Gallwey's Hill** (which joins **Church Road** up the cliff). The **tourist office** is next to the bus station. (☎381 250. Open June-Aug. Tu-Sa 10am-1pm and 2-5:30pm.) **AIB** (☎381 216) is on Strand St., and the **Bank of Ireland** is on Summer Hill (☎386 611. Both open M 10am-5pm, Tu and Th-F 10am-4pm, W 10:30am-4pm); both have **bureaux de change** and 24hr. **ATMs.** Inquire at the **library,** Market St., about free **Internet** access. (☎381 479. Open M-Tu 11am-1pm and 2-6pm, W-F 11am-1pm and 2-8pm.) Also on Market St. is the **Police** (*Garda*) station. (☎391 620. Open 24hr.) The **post office** is on Main St. (☎390 196. Open M-F 9am-1pm and 2-5:30pm, Sa 9am-1pm), as is **Hogan's Pharmacy.** (☎395 000; open M-Sa 9am-6pm.)

⚑ ACCOMMODATIONS. There's no shortage of B&Bs in Tramore—this beach town is a popular summer destination for families. The first weekend in June, Tramore hosts TraFest, with free live music in every pub in town. Book well in advance, as accommodations fill up with music-lovers. The only budget option near Tramore is the ▣**Beach Haven Hostel ❶,** but it's a gem: a refitted 160-year-old building with comfy beds, a laid-back surfer vibe, and a friendly, knowledgeable staff. From the bus station, turn right and walk about two blocks; it's on the right. For more pampering, head next door, where owners Niamh and Avery also operate the **Beach Haven House ❷.** Hostelers can get a full Irish breakfast in the B&B for €7. (☎390 208; www.beachhavenhouse.com. Dorms Sept.-June €15, July-Aug. €20; private rooms €20/25. B&B singles €35/45; doubles €70/80. Coin laundry €4 wash/dry. Hot water 7-11am and 5-8pm. MC/V.) Among the many B&Bs, the most competitive rates are at **The Cliff ❸,** Church St., a first-rate YWCA guesthouse. The views of the beach from the spacious garden are grand. (☎381 363; www.thecliff.org. Per person June-Sept. €26-32, Oct.-May €24-28. Check-in 2-6pm, check-out 10:30am. Only groups of 4 or more in winter. MC/V.) **Cloneen B&B ❸,** on Love Ln., lives up to its address with romantic rooms with flatscreen TVs and a fantastic garden; one room has a private patio. Take Church St. and bear left as it becomes Newton Rd.; Love Ln. is immediately on the left. (☎38126; www.cloneen.net. Open Mar.-Oct. Doubles €70. MC/V.) In the center of town, The **Cuckoo's Nest ❸,** Main St., has bright, simple rooms at good prices. (☎391 477. €30 per person. Cash only.) Two and a half kilometers out Dungarvan Coast Rd., between the golf course and the Metal Man monument, the family-style **Newtown Caravan and Camping Park ❶** is the best of several nearby campsites. (☎381 979. Showers €1. July-Aug. 2 people in tent or caravan €23, each additional adult €5, €2 children. Low season €5 less. Open Easter-Sept. MC/V.)

◩▦ FOOD AND PUBS. Up Main St., **Quish's SuperValu** sells groceries. (☎386 036. Open daily 8am-10pm.) Schools of frying fish are as ubiquitous in Tramore as in any other Irish sea town. **Indulge Bakery ❶,** 7 Main St., packs delicious sandwiches on freshly baked bread (€2.50-3.50). You'll also find cheeses, olives, and desserts. (☎815 6182. Open summer M-Sa 9am-5pm, Su 9am-3pm. Cash only.) Dinner at the **Vic Cafe ❷,** 1 Lower Main St., is pricey, but lunch is a bargain, with inventive sandwiches and liver pate (€7-8). Take a cushioned seat under the art and feel like you're really splurging. (☎386 144. Open M-W 9am-8pm, Th and Su 9am-9pm, F 9am-9:30pm, Sa 9am-10pm. Entrees €18-21. MC/V.) **Apple Brown Betty ❶,** in a tiny beach hut, directly across from the lifeguard station, has filling crepes (€4.80-6.80) designed to satisfy beachgoers' appetites. Open Apr.-Sept. daily 10am-8pm. Cash only.) Trot over to **The Sea Horse ❷**, Strand St., for pub chow, coffee, and a friendly atmosphere. (☎386 091. Snacks €5.50, entrees €12-13. Kitchen open 12:30-9pm. MC/V.) For drinks and dance, the three floors of **The Victoria House ("The Vic")**, Queens St., get younger, louder, and more crowded as you descend. The spacious beer garden is a huge selling point. (☎390 338. Open summer M-Th 2-11:30pm, F-Sa 12:30pm-12:30am, Su 12:30-11pm, winter open M-Th 4pm. Live music most Sa, usually local indie bands. Cash only.) On Saturdays, music lovers join the regulars at **Murph's**, Strand St., to bang their heads to live rock. (☎386 440. Open M-Th noon-11:30pm, F-Sa noon-12:30am, Su 12:30-11pm. Cash only.) A young set also fills **The Cellar**, at the intersection of Gallwey's Hill and Strand St., before heading upstairs to the nightclub, **Charlie Strings**. (☎386 396. Open M-Th 10:30am-11:30pm, F-Su 10:30am-2am. Cover €5 after 11pm. Su live cover bands. MC/V.)

🏃 OUTDOOR ACTIVITIES. The **cliffs** outside town are truly spectacular. The tourist office provides a list of historic and scenic walks along them. The best is **Doneraile Walk**, a path that stems off Church Rd. Follow the little red markers away from Tramore and into a land of cliff, ocean, and cloud. About 1.5km out, you can jump off the diving board and into the clear water of ⚑**Guillamene Cove**. Ignore the "Men Only" sign—a smaller one underneath explains that it's been "retained merely as a relic of the past." Cliff-diving is dangerous, illegal, and not recommended by *Let's Go*. A shorter version of the walk is 5.6km and takes about 1½hr. to complete; turn right after passing the cove and picnic area. Turn left for the extended loop (about 2hr.), which passes the three pillars and the **Metal Man**, who points to sea and warns sailors that they're straying close to land. Another beautiful route, the 6km **Strand Walk**, heads down Tramore Beach to sand dunes surrounded by salt marsh. **T-Bay Surf Centre** rents surfboards, bodyboards, wetsuits, and other surfing accessories. The only surfing school in the area approved by the Irish Surfing Association, T-Bay offers fantastic individual and group lessons and weekend packages to help make you an Irish Big Kahuna. Call ahead to check the variable surf: generally, the summer months are good for beginners, while winter brings bigger waves. (☎391 297; www.surftbay.com. Open daily 10am-5pm; call ahead to book. Complete surf rental package and 2hr. group lessons €65, large groups €45.) **Seapaddling.com** (☎358 995) offers scenic guided paddles around the area. The waterfront promenade offers all sorts of entertainment, including **Splashworld** indoor waterpark, an assortment of rides, pools, and screaming children, as well as an attached gym and health center. (☎390 176. Open daily 10am-7pm, gym open 7am-10pm. €10, students €7.50. Gym day pass €9.) The **Tramore Amusement Park**, by the shore, has plenty of ways to make you toss your cookies, while arcades are nearby. (☎086 838 1586. Open Mar.-June and Sept. M-F 2-8pm, Sa-Su 1-10pm; July-Aug. daily 1-11pm. Rides €2-4.)

DUNGARVAN (DUN GARBHÁN)   ☎058

Filled with fishermen, bustling markets, ocean breezes, and rollicking pubs, Dungarvan is endearing and lively. Pub-goers on Davitt's Quay watch harbor boats ground themselves as the water ebbs. There are plenty of opportunities to shop and eat in the town's central square and its surrounding streets, and those hankering for another castle tour delight in **King John's Dungarvan Castle**. Presiding over Davitt's Quay, the castle fell into disrepair in the early 14th century, after being periodically under siege for 100 years. It was further damaged when the Provisional IRA set it on fire in 1922. The *Garda* later took control of the building and used it as barracks until 1987, when it was finally vacated for renovations. A short video and tour take visitors through the castle's turbulent history and its various reconstructions. (☎48144. Guided tours 10:30am and 2pm. Free.) The deep-sea fishing in Dungarvan is excellent, though nearby waters do have a reputation for harboring sharks. For more info on fishing licenses, see the Southern Regional Fisheries Board website at www.srfb.ie. Capt. John Tynan also leads expeditions on the *Avoca*. (☎41327. €60 per day or €25 for an evening excursion.) **Baumann's Jewelers,** 6 St. Mary Street (☎41395), has tackle and a wealth of free information. After catching loads of fish, tired sportsmen can catch the newest release at SGC Cinemas off Davitts Quay, next to the town's shopping center. **Dungarvan's Féile na nDéise** (FAY-la nah ne-DAY-sha, "local area festival") packs the square with free concerts and historical reenactments the first weekend in May (called the May Bank Holiday weekend). Those missing the May festivities can still find a taste of Dungarvan culture at its weekly **Farmer's Market** and smaller **Country Market** (Farmer's Market in the town's central Grattan Sq., Th 9am-2pm; Country Market at the Causeway Tennis Club, Abbeyside on Strand Side North, F 11am-1pm.)

There are surprisingly few B&Bs in Dungarvan, perhaps because the few that are there set such a high standard. If you're psyched for incredible ocean views, head 8km up the N25 west toward Cork to the aptly named **Seaview Guesthouse ❷**, featuring bright dining and sitting rooms with a view that will prompt guests to ignore the added ensuite TV bonus. (☎41583; www.seaviewdungarvan.com. Wheelchair-accessible. €30 per person.) Closer to town, the passionate proprietor of the historic **Caibre House ❹** ensures that your stay will be worth every penny. Situated on the banks of River Colligan, the beautiful 1819 home lets guests enjoy their evening wine or freshly prepared breakfast featuring cage-free eggs and local salmon in a tropical garden out back (where owner Brian Wickham also grows his own herbs). To find this multi-award-winning B&B (which has been in business since 1912), cross the Shandon Bridge on N25 toward Waterford and take an immediate left on Strand Side North. The house will be on the left after 200m (☎42338; www.cairbrehouse.com. Wheelchair-accessible. €40-50 per person ensuite.) **Mountain View House ❹**, off O'Connell St., also caters to its guests with modern amenities, a gorgeous dining room and a deer head in the entryway. (☎42588; www.mountainviewhse.com. Singles €45; doubles €85.)

Grocery shoppers find the lowest prices and widest selection at **Dunnes Stores** in the town's shopping center off Bridge St. (☎24766. Open M-W and Sa 9am-10pm, Th-F 9am-midnight, Su 10am-8pm.) Food-lovers flock from far and wide to sample celebrity chef Paul Flynn's gourmet take on Irish cuisine served at **The Tannery ❸**, behind the Arts Centre on Quay St. Gastronomically minded travelers make room in their stomach and budget for the three-course early-bird special (☎45420; www.tannery.ie. Lunch entrees €15-17.50. Dinner entrees €23-29. Early-bird €28. Open for lunch Tu-F and Su 12:30-2:30pm; dinner Tu-F 6:30-9:30pm, Su 6:30-9pm (July-Aug. only); early-bird Tu-F 6:30-7:30pm.) **Davitt's Pub ❸,** Davitt's Quay, is fabulous and frequently packed. A crowd of 18- to 80-year-olds enjoys everything from intimate booths and tables overlooking the river by day to a large dance floor that forms around the circular bar as the night wears on. An interesting mix of Asian, Irish, and Mexican food is served daily 10:30am-11:30pm weekdays and until 2am on weekends. (☎44900. Lunch €7-8; dinner €12-24. Club open Th-Su 11pm-2:30am, often with live music. Cover charge may apply.) In true seaside form, Dungarvan has its own **Anchor Bar** (☎41249), on Davitt's Quay. The small and colorful Anchor hosts rock and trad most weekends. **The Shamrock Restaurant ❶**, 4 O'Connell St., stretches a Euro and your stomach by serving heaping portions of simple, homemade Irish food in a soothing peach-walled diner. (☎42242. Sandwiches €3-4. Dinner €7.50-13. Open M-Sa 9am-9pm.) Good, cheap eats can also be found at **Jumbos ❷**, which offers Chinese takeaway on the Abbeyside of the Causeway. (☎41677. Delivery 6-11pm; €1.20, min. €5 order. Entrees €7-9. Open daily 5-11:30pm.)

Buses (☎05187 9000; www.buseireann.com) leave from Davitt's Quay. They run east to **Waterford** (1hr.; M-Sa 7 per day 7:30am-6pm, Su 5 per day 8:30am-6:05pm; €8.80, students €7), west to **Cork** (M-Sa 13 per day 8:50am-7:50pm, Su 13 per day; €13, students €10.70), and south to **Ardmore** (M-F 8:50 and 9:30am, F also 2:55pm; Sa 8:50am and 2:55pm; €15), **Dublin** (M-Sa 5 per day, Su 6 per day; €13.10, students €11.30), and **Lismore** (F and Su 9:20am and 5:50pm; €13, students €10.70). **Main Street,** which becomes **O'Connell Street** at the traffic light, runs through the town's central square. The **tourist office,** outside the square in the Courthouse building, has free maps and music listings for area pubs. (☎41741. Open M-Sa 9am-5:30pm, until 5pm during low season.) **Bank of Ireland,** the Square, and **AIB,** Meagher St., both have 24hr. **ATMs.** (Both open M 10am-5pm, Tu and Th-F 10am-4pm, W 10:30am-4pm.) **Internet** access is available at the **library** on Davitt's Quay (☎41231. Open Tu-Sa 10am-5pm and W-Th 6-8pm. Free with a membership, which is free for students, €7.60 otherwise, and available at the reference desk.) For the less academically inclined, there's also the **Sip 'N' Surf cafe** next to Davitt's pub. (☎48658. €1.50 per 15min., €5 per hr. Open M-F 8:30am-8pm, Sa 10:30am-8pm, Su 2-6pm.) The **post office** is on Bridge St. past the square. (☎41176. Open M and W-F 9am-5:30pm, Tu 9:30am-5:30pm, Sa 9am-1pm.)

ARDMORE (AIRD MHÓR) ☎024

St. Declan christianized Ardmore in the 4th century, and the ruins support the town's claim that it is the island's oldest Christian settlement. Ardmore's five beaches draw the locals every summer, but the town empties drastically during the low season. The **cliff walk,** a 4.8km path blessed with great ocean views, stops at all of the sights associated with the St. Declan legend. Maps can be found in the tourist offices of nearby cities and most local accommodations. At one end of the walk is Ardmore's **cathedral,** built piecemeal on the site of St. Declan's monastery between 800 and 1400. St. Declan himself is said to be buried here, and the faithful swear that soil from the saint's grave cures diseases. In addition to its own collection of carvings, the cathedral houses two **ogham stones** (p. 50). Nearby stands a 97-foot **round tower** (p. 50). **St. Declan's Stone** is perched at the water's edge, on the right from Main St. along the shore. This intrepid stone purportedly floated from Wales after the holy man visited there. Another highlight along the way is **St. Declan's Well,** which contains water rumored to cure all afflictions. Hikers trek on the 90km **St. Declan's Way,** which starts in town and runs up to Cahir in Co. Tipperary. The "gorges" view of the ocean from the cliffs makes many visitors want to dive right in; for that, **Ardmore Diving** is most helpful. It offers courses, boat trips, and equipment for hire to satisfy all your scuba needs (☎058 46577; www.ardmorediving.com. Basic courses €50, children €35.)

Accommodations in Ardmore tend to be rather unstable so it may be a good idea to check the Dungarvan tourist office ahead of time (☎058 41741). **Duncrone B&B** ❸ rewards those who make the 20min. uphill journey afoot with incredible views of the round tower and ocean from spacious and colorful rooms. From Main St., turn right at the round tower and walk about 8km; the driveway is signposted on the right. (☎94860. Singles €38-45; doubles €65; triples €90.) If staying with a group for a week or more, **Ardmore Holiday Homes** ❷ has three- and four-bed houses with kitchens just a short stroll from sandy shores. (☎058 44310; www.ardmoreholidayhomes.com. 3-bed houses €450-735 per wk., 4-bed houses €450-750 per wk. Weekend rates also available.) Those with a car might also consider commuting out of town in order to get the best value; **Seaview Guesthouse** ❷ (p. 231) and nearby **Maple Leaf B&B** ❸, the first right after Seaview, are good options at comparable rates. (Maple Leaf ☎058 41921. €34 per person ensuite.)

Quinn's Foodstore, at the top of Main St., has groceries. (☎94250. Open M-Tu and Th-F 8am-7pm, W 8am-8pm, Sa 8am-7:15pm, Su 9am-6pm.) **Whitehorses** ❹ serves fresh fish and outstanding desserts. Call for reservations. (☎94040. Lunch €13-22; dinner €22-33. Open Tu-Sa 11am-11pm, Su noon-11pm.) If the sun is shining, search for coveted outdoor seating at **The Old Forge Restaurant ❸**, which serves fresh traditional Irish food all day long. (Sandwiches €6-9; entrees €10-18. Open daily 8:30am-9pm.) **An Tobar,** Main St. (☎94166), has pub grub noon-3:30pm and 6-8:30pm and a variety of weekend music; local trad starts up F-Sa 10pm and Su 6pm. **Keever's Bar,** Main St. (☎94141), is a favorite of the older Ardmore crowd. **An Seanachai ❸** (SHAWN-ah-KEY), one of the most heralded of all heritage pubs, is just a 10min. drive east of Ardmore. (☎058 46755. Entrees €10-14. Open for lunch 12:30-2:30pm, bar menu 3-9:30pm, dinner 6:30-9:30pm, Su carvery 12:30-4pm.)

Buses leave from the stop across from Whitehorses and run to **Cork** via **Youghal** (M-Sa 9:45am, 3:40, 7:20pm, Su 7:35pm; €12) and **Waterford** via **Dungarvan** (2hr., M-Sa 10:17am and 3:44pm, €12.80). **Ardmore** is a 4.8km detour south off the Cork-Waterford road (N25). Hitching, which is never recommended by *Let's Go*, can be slow from the junction. The **post office** is on Main St. (☎94191. Open M-F 9am-1pm and 2-5:30pm, Sa 9am-1pm.)

WATERFORD (PORT LÁIRGE)   ☎051

Past the glistening waters of the harbor gleams Waterford, Ireland's oldest city, which was settled by the Vikings in the late 10th century. Nowadays, the crystal factory is the town's biggest sell, and you'll even find crystal chandeliers in the local churches. Beyond the factory, the town's got plenty of sparkle, with excellent museums and well-preserved remnants of its Viking past. Unlike that of most of southeast Ireland, Waterford's nightlife is best during the winter, when college students pack John St. bars.

▐ TRANSPORTATION

Let's Go does not recommend hitchhiking. Waterford's few hitchers stick to main routes away from the city center. To reach N24 (Cahir, Limerick), N10 (Kilkenny, Dublin), or N25 (New Ross, Wexford, Rosslare), they head over the bridge toward the train station. For N25 to Cork, hitchers continue down Parnell St.

Flights: ☎875 589. **Waterford Airport.** Follow the Quay, turn right at Reginald's Tower, then left at the sign 20min. from town.

Trains: Plunkett Station (☎873 401. M-Sa 6:35am-7:05pm, Su 8:30am-6:45pm), across the bridge from the Quay. To: **Dublin** (2½hr., M-Sa 5-6 per day, Su 4 per day; €23.50); **Kilkenny** (40min., 3-5 per day, €9.80); **Limerick** (2¼hr., M-Sa 2 per day, €29.50); **Rosslare Harbour** (1hr., M-Sa 1 per day, €9.80).

Buses: The station is on the Quay, across from the tourist office (☎317 815). Office open M-Sa 8:15am-6pm. To: **Cork** (2½hr., 10-13 per day, €16.50); **Dublin** (2¾hr., M-Sa 14 per day, Su 9 per day; €11.50); **Galway** (5hr., 5-6 per day, €21); **Kilkenny** (1hr., 2 per day, €9); **Limerick** (2½hr., M-Th and Su 7 per day, F 8 per day; €10); **Rosslare Harbour** (1¼hr., 3-5 per day, €14.40). **City buses** leave from the Clock Tower on the Quay (M-Sa, €1.35). **Night bus** runs to Tramore on Saturdays (Departs Waterford 12:30, 1:30, 2:30am; departs Tramore 1, 2, 3am. €5.)

Taxis: Easy to find, 24hr. Either go to the **cab stand** on Broad St. or try: **Rapid Cabs** (☎858 585); **Deise Cabs** (☎820 500).

✳ ▐ ORIENTATION AND PRACTICAL INFORMATION

Waterford's founders must have had a knack for urban planning, because the area between **the Quay, Parnell Street (the Mall),** and **Barronstrand Street (Michael and**

Broad Street) still lies at the heart of the action. Pedestrian-only Hanover and Barronstrand St. branch off the Quay and its wide waterside promenade.

Tourist Office: ☎875 823, on the Quay, across from the bus station. From the train station, cross Rice Bridge and turn left. Attached to the Waterford Treasures Museum. Hours vary, but generally open summer M-Sa 9am-6pm, Su 10am-5pm, winter M-F 9:15am-5pm, Sa 10am-6pm.

Banks: 24hr. **ATMs** line the streets. On the Quay, they're at **AIB** (☎873 494), by the clock tower, and **Bank of Ireland** (☎872 074). Both open M 10am-5pm, Tu and Th-F 10am-4pm, W 10:30am-4pm.

Emergency: Dial ☎999 or 112; no coins. **Police** (Garda): Patrick St. (☎305 300).

Pharmacy: Gallagher Pharmacy, 29 Barronstrand St. (☎878 103). Open M-Th and Sa 9am-6pm, F 9am-9pm. MC/V.

Hospital: Waterford Regional Hospital (☎848 000). Follow the Quay east to the Tower Hotel and follow the signs. Turn left on Lombard St., which becomes Newtown Rd. (R683) and leads to the hospital. Then follow signs straight ahead to the hospital.

Internet: Waterford e-Centre, 10 O'Connell St. (☎878 448). €4.50 per hr.; 10% student discount. Open M-Th 9:30am-9pm, F-Sa 9:30am-8pm, Su 11am-6pm. **Voyager Internet Cafe,** 85 the Quay (☎843 843). €4 per hr. Open M-Sa 10am-9pm, Su 2-6pm.

Bike Rentals: Altitude Cycle and Outdoor Centre, 22 Ballybricken (☎870 356; www.altitude.ie). Open M-Sa 9:30am-5:30pm. Rentals May-Aug. €15 per day.

Laundry: Snow Whites, 61 Mayor's Walk (☎858 905). Wash and dry €15. Open M-Sa 9:15am-6pm.

Post Office: The Quay (☎317 321). The largest of several. Open M-F 9am-5:30pm, Sa 9am-1pm. Smaller offices located on O'Connell St. and corner of Exchange and High St.

Work Opportunities: The **Youth Information Centre,** 130 the Quay (☎877 328), helps with finding short-term work. Open M-F 9:30am-5:30pm. **Internet** access €4 per hr.

▐ ACCOMMODATIONS

Most B&Bs in the city center are nothing to write home about; those outside town on the Cork Rd. are better. Waterford has no hostels, but just a 40min. bus ride gets you to Tramore, where you'll find the ▧**Beach Haven Hostel** (p. 229).

Mayor's Walk House, 12 Mayor's Walk (☎855 427; www.mayorswalk.com). A short walk from the quay, off Patrick St. Conveniently close to many pubs. Quiet, simple rooms—no frills, but great prices and friendly management. All rooms with shared bathrooms. Open Feb.-Nov. Singles €28; doubles €50. Cash only. ❷

O'Connell House, 3 O'Connell St. (☎874175). Centrally located, with cheerful rooms. The house's little dog is cute, but his barking might get old after a while. Some rooms with shared bath, others ensuite; all €35 per person. Cash only. ❸

Avondale House, 2 Parnell St. (☎852 267; www.staywithus.net). Old Georgian mansion with plenty of modern luxuries, including TVs, phones, and hair dryers. Just a short walk from the pubs of John St. No breakfast. Singles €45; doubles €60. MC/V. ❸

The Anchorage, 9 the Quay (☎854 302; www.theanchorage.net). For those with early buses or trains, location is unbeatable at this B&B, but frayed carpets inside show its age. TV, phone, and tea- and coffee-making facilities. Singles €45; doubles €70. ❹

▐ FOOD

Buy groceries at **Dunnes Stores** in the square's shopping center. (☎853 100. Open M-W and Sa 9am-7pm, Th-F 9am-9pm, Su noon-6pm.) or **Centra,** on the

SOUTHEAST IRELAND

Quay next to the Granville Hotel. (☎841 626. Open M-F 6:30am-11pm, Sa-Su 7am-11pm.) For cheap fast food, head to John St.

Revolution, 19 John St. (☎844 444; www.revolutionwaterford.com). Revolution's leather seating pods are just as conducive to eating as they are to entertainment; laugh while you eat as you enjoy the comedy club on Th weekly in winter, monthly in summer, and DJs F-Su. Salads, wraps, and sambos (€4-10) in addition to typical pub food. Kitchen open daily noon-midnight. Comedy club €10, F-Su no cover. AmEx/MC/V. ❷

Cafe Sumatra, 53 John St. (☎876 404). With colorful, funky couches and a budget-friendly menu, it's a good choice for travelers who want a little funk for less. Lots of vegetarian options, including the Mediterranean wrap (€7), as well as meatier *panini* (€6-7). Open M-Th 8:30am-7pm, F-Sa 8:30am-11pm, Su 11am-9pm. MC/V. ❷

Emiliano's, 21 High St. (☎820 333). Candlelit tables and a well-dressed crowd set a romantic atmosphere for authentic Italian cuisine. Call ahead for reservations or you'll get no *amore*. Pizza €11-14. Pasta €13-15. Entrees €16-24. Open Tu-Su 5-10pm. AmEx/MC/V. ❹

The Bowery Bar, 5-6 the Mall (☎855 087; www.bowery-bar.com), behind Reginald's Tower. Classy bar/restaurant/nightclub with leather walls, a fish tank and tealights. Kitchen open daily noon-9pm. Burgers €9-10, pasta and vegetarian options €8.50-9.50. Th-Sa rock/jazz, Su trad. Nightclub open 11pm-2:30am. Sa cover €10. MC/V. ❸

🍸🎵 PUBS AND CLUBS

The Quays are flooded with old-fashioned pubs, but the corner of John and Parnell St. is where local youngsters get their drink on in the newer, flashier late bars. When pubs close at 12:30am, late bars and weekend discos kick it into high gear.

Geoff's, 8 John St. (☎874 787). Locals of all ages drop into this deceptively spacious wood-paneled pub for pints and laughs. Beer garden. Italian-style sandwiches (€5) and pasta (€9.50) served M-Sa noon-9pm. Battle of the Bands every February. Open M-Th 11am-11:30pm, F-Sa 11am-12:30am, Su 12:30-11pm. MC/V.

T&H Doolan's, George's St. (☎841 504). Serving for 300 years; its building, part of the medieval city walls, has been standing for 800. Sinéad O'Connor once crooned here. Crowd is split between natives and imports. Plenty of dollars stuck to the rafters, but you won't see many euro coins with pins through them. Live trad every night at 9:30pm. Open M-Th 10:30am-11:30pm, F-Sa 10:30am-12:30am, Su 12:30-11pm. MC/V.

The Woodman, 42 John St. (☎858 130). Small, traditional pub. Shuts down at 12:30am on weekends, so click those heels and head to the adjoining **Ruby Lounge,** which rocks Th-Su until 2am. MC/V.

The Gingerman, 6-7 Arundel Ln. (☎879 522). Looks like a dark French bistro, but pints, not merlot, are *à la mode* at this popular pub. Elegant and dramatic dark-wood-and-mirrors back room. F live music. Open M-Th 10am-11:30pm, F-Sa 10am-12:30pm, Su 12:30-11pm. Kitchen open M-Sa 10am-6pm, Su 12:30-4pm. Entrees €6-10. MC/V.

Kazbar, 57 John St. (☎843 730). Posh urbanites flock to the outdoor tables of this Middle-Eastern-themed bar/cafe to pretend they're somewhere truly exotic. Heated roof garden. F-Sa live music. Sandwiches €4.50-8. Kitchen open 10:30am-8pm. MC/V.

Mason's, 97 Manor St. (☎875 881), at Parnell and John St. Slick, clubby pub with flatscreen TVs and a dress code. M rat pack, Su pop and classic rock. Open M-F 7pm-11:30pm, Sa 1pm-2am, Su 1-11pm. MC/V.

👁 SIGHTS

To cover all of Waterford's sights in a day requires the swiftness of a Viking raider.

THE WATERFORD CRYSTAL FACTORY. What links fancy dinner sets, the Times Square Millennium Ball, and all major glass sporting trophies? The spectacular

Waterford Crystal Factory, where they were all handcrafted. The factory is located 3.2km from the city center on N25 (the Cork road), and it's worth sitting through a couple of glorified commercials to see workers up close. Watch master craftsmen transform molten goo into sparkling crystal or admire the finished products and tremble at their sky-high prices. *(Catch the City bus outside Dunnes on Michael St. and ask to stop at the factory. M-Sa. 10-15min., every 15-20min. €1.35. Or take city bus #3, which leaves across from the Clock Tower every 15min M-Sa. The 20min. walk is a straight shot down Manor St. Factory ☎332 500; www.waterfordvisitorcentre.com. Gallery open daily Mar.-Oct. 8:30am-6pm; Nov.-Feb. 9am-5pm. Tours Mar.-Oct. daily 8:30am-4pm, Nov.-Feb. M-F 9am-3:15pm. 1hr. tours every 15min. during high season. Gallery free; tours €9.50, students €6.50.)*

▧**WATERFORD TREASURES.** To catch up on the 1000-year history of Waterford, head to Waterford Treasures at the restored Granary, connected to the tourist office. The multimedia barrage of kinetic, visual, and aural displays appeals to all learning styles; perhaps that's why the €4.5 million museum was named the 1999-2000 Ireland Museum of the Year. The actual artifacts, including plenty of Viking goods and the only extant item of Henry VIII's clothing (a velvet hat) make quite an impressive show. *(☎304 500. Open Apr.-Sept. M-Sa 9:30am-6pm, Su 11am-6pm; Oct.-Mar. M-Sa 10am-5pm, Su 11am-6pm. €7, students and seniors €5.)*

REGINALD'S TOWER. From its perch at the end of the Quay, Reginald's tower has guarded the city entrance since the 12th century. Its virtually impenetrable 10-foot-thick walls have housed a prison, a mint, and generations of cannon-toting town defenders; 1004 years make it the oldest continuously operating building in Ireland. Tiny models illustrate the contributions of Vikings, Normans, and English kings to Waterford's growth, while an audio-visual presentation on the top floor explains the history of the city's walls. Try it in Irish. *(☎304 220. Open Apr.-Oct. daily 10am-5:30pm; Nov.-Mar. W-Su 10am-5pm; last admission 45min. before closing. Tours by request. €2.10, students €1.10, seniors €1.30.)*

OTHER SIGHTS. Stellar guide Jack Burtchaell helps sort out the city's mongrel lineage, keeping visitors involved and enthralled on ▧**The Walking Tour of Historic Waterford.** Well worth the €7, the tour's a great way to get a feel for Waterford and for Ireland itself. *(☎873 711. 1hr. tours depart from the Waterford Treasures Museum and 15min. later from the Granville Hotel on the Quay. Tours mid-Mar. to mid-Oct. daily 11:45am and 1:45pm. €7.)* Many of the more recent buildings were the brainchildren of 18th-century architect John Roberts. The Theatre Royal and City Hall, both on the Mall, are his masterpieces. He's also responsible for Catholic Holy Trinity Cathedral, Barronstrand St., and the Church of Ireland's Christ Church Cathedral, Cathedral Sq. (up Henrietta St. from the Quay), making Waterford the only city in Europe where Catholics and Protestants worship in buildings designed by the same architect.

🎵 🌺 ENTERTAINMENT AND FESTIVALS

The tourist office provides an annual list of major events in town, and any local newspaper, including the free *Waterford Today*, should have more specific entertainment listings. Watch for posters as well. The **Garter Lane Arts Centre,** 22a O'Connell St., supports different forms of art inside its old Georgian brick. Visual exhibits adorn the walls and are usually free. Concerts cost around €15-20, and dance and theater productions grace its stage year-round. *(☎855 038. Center and box office open Tu-Sa 11am-6pm; performance nights later. Excellent films shown Su at 7pm; €8, students and seniors €6.)* Waterford's largest festival is the **Spraoi** ("spree"), held during the August bank holiday weekend. A celebration of life with a carnival atmosphere that inundates the streets of the city, the *Spraoi* attracts street theater troupes and bands from around the globe, and culminates in a sizable parade, fireworks, and an original production. *(☎841 808; www.spraoi.com.)* Greyhound racing takes place year-round, twice weekly at Kilcohan Park. *(☎874 531. Races F-Sa 8:02pm. €10, students €5.e)*

SOUTHWEST IRELAND

With the inspiration of a dramatic landscape ranging from lush lakes and mountains to stark, ocean-battered cliffs, Southwest Ireland is a place where artists and storytellers thrive. Its position as a backdoor to the isle also gives it a darker, more storied past; outlaws and rebels once struggled for power in hidden coves and glens, and the abundance of ancient forts and castles in the area is a testament to their legacy. Today, the urban activity of Cork City and the area's frantic pace of growth balance the calm of neighboring rural villages. The Iveragh Peninsula's Killarney and Ring of Kerry draw huge numbers of visitors every year, as they flock to some of the most stunning scenery in the world. The southern peninsulas of Mizen Head, Sheep's Head, and the Beara, are equally beautiful, though not as busy. Not surprisingly, those who visit often decide to stay—real estate in western Cork is readily snapped up by foreigners who have fallen in love with its way of life.

SOUTHWEST IRELAND HIGHLIGHTS

BREATHE IN the fresh air of **Killarney National Park** (p. 291).

FERRY over to the rugged **Skellig Rocks** for a taste of monastic life (p. 305).

KISS the **Blarney Stone** and earn the traditionally Irish gift of the gab (p. 251).

WORK behind the scenes at the **Cork International Film Festival** (p. 249).

EASTERN COUNTY CORK

One of Ireland's most celebrated and visited areas, Eastern County Cork was historically a place of prosperity, with its natural harbors sustaining a thriving trade center. Its distance from Dublin and the English Pale saved the area from complete English domination during the 1600s and afforded locals freedom from the ruling British; as a result, Co. Cork seethed with patriotic activity during the 19th and 20th centuries. It was the headquarters of the "Munster Republic" and the birthplace of patriot Michael Collins. Modern Cork City is a hotbed of industry and culture, while the seaside towns of Kinsale and Cobh entertain tall ships and stooped backpackers, and Blarney Castle still draws droves of visitors to kiss its famous stone.

CORK CITY (AN CORCAIGH)   ☎ 021

Heralded as Europe's 2005 "Capital of Culture," Cork (pop. 150,000) hosts most of the athletic, musical, and artistic activities of the southwest. The river quays and pub-lined streets display architecture both grand and grimy, evidence of "Rebel

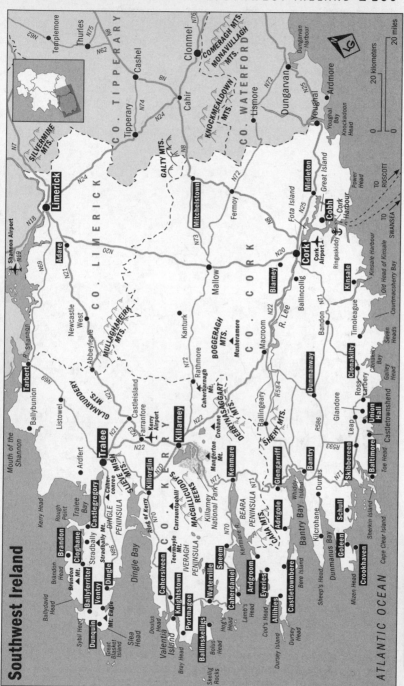

Southwest Ireland

Orrery Rd.

Cathedral Rd.

Mount Nebo Ave.

Gurranbraher Ave.

St. Ann's Rd.

Mary Aikenhead Pl.

Gurranbraher Rd.

Boyce's St.

Glen Ryan Rd.

Blarney St.

Blarney St.

TO CORK CITY
GAOL (90m)

Convent Ave.

Sunday's Well Rd.

Sunday's Well Rd.

North Mall

Bachelor's Quay

Grenville Pl.

Grattan St.

Henry St.

River Lee (North Channel)

Sheares' St.

Liberty

**Fitzgerald
Park**

Cork Public
Museum

Mardyke Walk

Dyke Parade

Granary
Theatre

8

Washington St.

Hanover S

7

Western Rd.

Lancaster Quay

TO MARDYKE CENTRE
(135m)

Wandesford
Quay

R. Lee (South Channel)

Sharman
Crawford

Glucksman
Gallery

Donovan's Rd.

**University
College**

Connaught Ave.

Gill Abbey St.

Bishop St.

**St. Finbarr's
Cathedral**

Proby's Qua

Gaol Walk

College Rd.

Dean St.

**Elizabeth
Fort**

Barrack St.

13

Cork Center

Corn Market St.

St. Paul's Ave.

Merchant's Quay

**Opera
House**

14

Emmet Pl.

Grattan St.

N. Main St.

**Coal Quay
Market**

15

16

**Crawford
Art Gallery**

Sheares St.

Liberty St.

Castle St.

Paul St.

17

French Church St.

Academy

Faulkner

Bowling

William

19

**Queens Old
Castle**

**Bank of
Ireland**

Carey's Lane

Washington St.

18

Grand Parade

Cinema

20

**Ulster
Bank**

St. Patrick's St.

Cook St.

Robert St.

Morgan St.

Winthrop

Maylor St.

Hanover St.

**Triskel
Arts Centre**

SAYIT

**Cork City
Library**

Princes St.

Web Workhouse

21

**Christ
Church**

**Bishop
Lucy
Park**

**English
Market**

Marlborough St.

Pembroke

Oliver Plunkett St.

Wandesford
Quay

South Main St.

Tuckey St.

22

USIT

Princes St.

Cook St.

**Beamish &
Crawford
Brewery**

i

South Mall

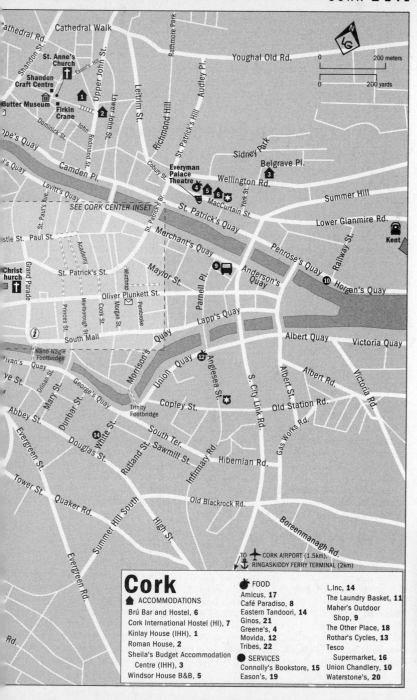

Cork

▲ ACCOMMODATIONS

Brú Bar and Hostel, **6**
Cork International Hostel (HI), **7**
Kinlay House (IHH), **1**
Roman House, **2**
Sheila's Budget Accommodation
  Centre (IHH), **3**
Windsor House B&B, **5**

🍴 FOOD

Amicus, **17**
Café Paradiso, **8**
Eastern Tandoori, **14**
Ginos, **21**
Greene's, **4**
Movida, **12**
Tribes, **22**

● SERVICES

Connolly's Bookstore, **15**
Eason's, **19**

L.Inc, **14**
The Laundry Basket, **11**
Maher's Outdoor
  Shop, **9**
The Other Place, **18**
Rothar's Cycles, **13**
Tesco
  Supermarket, **16**
Union Chandlery, **10**
Waterstone's, **20**

Cork's" history of resistance, ruin, and rebuilding. What few pre-industrial charms smokestacks didn't blacken, the English blighted. Cork burned down in 1622, Cromwell expelled half its citizens in the 1640s, and the city flamed up again in 1920 during the Irish War for Independence. In true Darwinian form, Cork's trying past has only caused it to evolve, becoming stronger, prouder, and increasingly diversified. Its economy is booming, trad music fills the streets on a nightly basis, and it has a palpable international flavor. Ireland's third-largest city, Cork continues to win over the hearts of its visitors with its charm.

✈ INTERCITY TRANSPORTATION

Flights: Cork Airport (☎431 3131; www.corkairport.com), 8km south of Cork on the Kinsale Rd. (N27). 9 airlines operate out of Cork, including **Aer Lingus** (☎818 365 000), **Ryanair** (☎818 30 30 30), and several others offering low fares to European cities. Taxis (€15-18) or buses (M-F 36-40 per day 7:50am-11:12pm, Sa 25 per day 7:50am-8:45pm, Su 22 per day 7:50am-11:10pm; €4) run from the airport to the bus station on Parnell Pl.

Trains: Kent Station, Lower Glanmire Rd. (☎450 6766; www.irishrail.ie), in the northeast part of town across the river from the city center. Open M-Sa 6am-8pm, Su 8am-8:50pm. Trains to: **Dublin** via **Limerick** (3hr.; M-Sa 15 per day 5:15am-8:30pm, Su 10 per day 8:30am-7:30pm; €55); **Cobh** (30min.; M-Sa 22 per day 5:20am-10:30pm, Su 9 per day 8:45am-9:50pm; €3.55); **Mallow** (which has connections to **Killarney** and **Tralee**; M-Sa 27 per day 5:15am-7:30pm, Su 16 per day 8am-8:50pm; €8.20).

Buses: Parnell Pl. (☎450 8188), 2 blocks east of Patrick's Bridge on Merchant's Quay. Inquiries desk open daily 9am-5:30pm. **Bus Éireann** runs to all major cities: **Bantry** (2hr.; M-Sa 8-9 per day 9:15am-7pm, Su 5 per day 10:30am-7:30pm; €13.50, students €11.20); **Dublin** (4½hr.; M-Sa 6 per day 8am-6pm; €9.50/€8.60); **Galway** (4hr.; 12 per day 7:25am-6:25pm; €14.40/€12.60); **Killarney** (2hr.; M-Sa 14 per day 8:30am-8:30pm, Su 11 per day 8:30am-8:30pm; €13.50/€11.20); **Limerick** (2hr.; 14 per day 7:25am-10:40pm; €10.80/€9); **Rosslare Harbour** (4hr.; M-Sa 8:40, 10:40am, 4:40pm, Su 10:40am and 4:40pm; €19/€15.30); **Sligo** (7hr.; 8:25, 10:25am, 12:15pm; €23/€18); **Tralee** (2½hr., same times as Killarney; €14.40/€11.70); **Waterford** (2¼hr., same times as Rosslare Harbour; €15/€12.10). Return fares offer better deals.

Ferries: Ringaskiddy Terminal (☎437 8036), 13km south of the city, is the closest port. **Brittany Ferries** (☎427 7801; www.brittanyferries.ie) sends boats to **Roscoff, France** (12hr., Sa only; single from €108) and has an office on the Grand Parade by the tourist office. Open M-F 9am-5:30pm, Sa 9am-1pm. **Swansea-Cork Ferries** (☎483 6000; www.swanseacorkferries.com) suspended its service in 2007 but typically sends daily ferries to **Swansea, Wales** (10hr., from €39). Both companies take online bookings. **Bus Éireann** (☎450 8188) makes the 45min. trip from the Cork bus station to the ferry. Buses leave 1¼hr. prior to ferry departure.

✴ ORIENTATION

Cork's compact city center wasn't always a single island. Before it was diverted to create the modern moat, the River Lee's north and south channels ran straight through the city. **St. Patrick Street** was laid directly over the water's course, hence its unconventional U-shape. St. Patrick St. ends its horseshoe and becomes **Grand Parade** to the west; to the north it crosses **Merchant's Quay,** home of the bus station. North across St. Patrick's bridge, **MacCurtain Street** runs east to **Lower Glanmire Road** and the train station before becoming the **N8** to Dublin, Waterford, and Cobh. Generally parallel **Paul, St. Patrick,** and **Oliver Plunkett Street** are the heart of downtown, with shop-lined and largely pedestrian avenues connecting them from north to south. Heading west from Grand Parade, **Washington Street** eventually becomes **Western Road** before reaching **University College Cork** and the **N22** to Killarney.

⊏ LOCAL TRANSPORTATION

Let's Go does not recommend hitchhiking, but hitchers headed for West Cork and Co. Kerry walk down Western Rd. past the An Óige hostel and the dog track to the Crow's Nest Pub, or they take bus #8. Those hoping to get to Dublin or Waterford tend to stand on the hill next to the train station on Lower Glanmire Rd.

Bus: The main bus station (☎ 450 8188), at Parnell Pl., offers free timetables for the **city buses.** From downtown, catch the buses (and their schedules) at the bus station on Merchant's Quay, across from the Father Matthew statue. Bus #8 runs down Western Rd. toward UCC and the An Óige hostel. Downtown buses run M-Sa every 10-30min. 7:30am-11:15pm, with reduced service Su 10am-11:15pm. Fares from €1.

Car Rental: Several companies offer competitive rates at the Cork Airport, including **Avis** (☎ 432 7460; www.avis.ie), **Irish Car Rentals** (from USA: 1877 347 3227, from Ireland: 1850 206 088; www.irishcarrentals.com), and **Auto Europe** (1800 923 154; www.autoeurope.ie.). Within the city, **Great Island Car Rentals** is on 47 MacCurtain St. (☎ 811 609). €80 per day, €250-340 per wk. 23+. Open M-Sa 9am-5:30pm.

Bike Rental: In Shandon, **AA Bike Shop,** self-proclaimed "Munster's oldest cycle shop" off the North Gate Bridge rents bikes returnable at 6 other locations across Ireland for no extra fee. (☎ 087 945 1635; www.irishcyclehire.com. €12 per day, €70 per wk. Open daily 9am-6pm. **Rothar Cycles,** 55 Barrack St. (☎ 431 3133), has more expensive rates but is the only shop that also rents mountain bikes. €25 per day, €80 per wk.; €30 one-way fee. €100 deposit or credit card. Open M-Sa 10am-6pm.

⊉ PRACTICAL INFORMATION

TOURIST AND FINANCIAL SERVICES

Tourist Office: Tourist House, Grand Parade (☎ 425 5100), near the corner of South Mall, across from the National Monument along the river's south channel. Offers accommodation booking (€4, 10% deposit) and a **free city guide and map.** Open June-Aug. M-F 9am-7pm, Sa 9am-5pm, July-Aug. also Su 10am-5pm; Sept.-May M-Sa 9:15am-5:15pm. **The Cork City Tour** is a 1hr. bus ride that leaves from the tourist office and stops at locations all over town; you can join at any of its stops. (July-Aug. tours every 30min., Apr. and Oct. every 45min.; €13, students and seniors €11, children €5.) Mike Collins also begins his thorough **Historic Walking Tours** (☎ 085 100 7300), loaded with insider's tidbits, at the tourist office. Tours M-F 10am, noon, 2, 4pm.

Budget Travel: SAYIT, 76 Grand Parade (☎ 427 9188), sells Interrail tickets among other services. Open M-W and F 9am-5:30pm, Th 10am-5:30pm, Sa 10am-4pm. **USIT,** Oliver Plunkett St. (☎ 427 0900), around the corner from the tourist office, has similar offerings. Open M-F 9:30am-5:30pm, Sa 10am-5pm. Oliver Plunkett St. has several budget travel businesses, so shop around for the best deals.

Banks: Most larger banks can be found on the South Mall. Others include: **Ulster Bank Ltd.,** 88 St. Patrick St. (☎ 427 0618). Open M 10am-5pm, Tu-F 10am-4pm. **Bank of Ireland,** 70 St. Patrick St. (☎ 427 7177). Open M 10am-5pm, Tu-F 10am-4pm. Most banks in Cork have 24hr. **ATMs.**

LOCAL SERVICES

Luggage Storage: At the **bus station** (€2.70 per item 1st day; €2.50 each additional day). Open M-F 7:45am-7pm, Sa 9am-6pm; June-Aug. also open Su 9am-6pm.

GLBT Information: The Other Place, 8 South Main St. (☎427 8470; www.gayproject-cork.com), is a resource center for gay and bisexual men in Cork; it has tourist information, a resource library, and a cafe. Cafe/drop-in hours M-F 11am-10pm, Sa-Su noon-6:30pm. Also hosts a gay bar 1st Sa of every month (see **Clubs,** p. 247). **Gay Information Cork** (☎427 1087) has a helpline M-Th 7-9pm. **Lesbians In Cork (L.Inc.),** White St. (☎480 8600), has information on local events, support, and social groups. Open M-F 11am-3pm. Drop-in service Tu noon-3pm, Th 8-10pm, Sa 2-4pm. Helpline (☎431 8318) available Th 8pm-10pm). Consult the *Gay Community News* (GCN, available at The Other Place) for more info on events.

Laundry: The Laundry Basket, 2 Barrack St. (☎469 1234), does drop-off wash and fold service by the lb. as well as dry cleaning. Wash/dry/fold up to 2lb. €4, each additional lb. €1. Dry cleaning: shirt €4.50, blouse €6.50. Open M-Sa 9am-6pm.

EMERGENCY AND COMMUNICATIONS

Emergency: ☎999; no coins required. **Police** *(Garda):* Anglesea St. (☎452 2000).

Crisis and Support: Sexual Violence Centre, 5 Camden Pl. (☎1800 496 496 or 450 5577). Open M-F 9am-5pm. **AIDS Helpline** (☎427 6676). Open M-F 10am-5pm, Tu 7-9pm. **Samaritans,** Coach St., offers confidential emotional support. (Office ☎427 1323; 24hr. support line ☎1850 609 090.)

Pharmacies: Regional Late Night Pharmacy, Wilton Rd. (☎434 4575), opposite the Regional Hospital on bus #8. Open M-F 9am-10pm, Sa-Su 10am-10pm. **Late Night,** 9 Patrick St. (☎427 2511). Open M-F 8:30am-10pm, Sa 9am-10pm, Su 10am-10pm.

Hospital: Mercy Hospital, Grenville Pl. (☎427 1971). €60 fee for emergency room access. **Cork University Hospital,** Wilton St. (☎454 6400), on the #8 bus route.

Internet: North of River Lee: **Wired To The World Internet Cafe,** 6 Thompson House, MacCurtain St. (www.wiredtotheworld.ie). Gaming, phone booths, and Wi-Fi. Internet €1 per hr. Open M-Sa 9am-midnight, Su 10am-midnight. City Centre: ⬛**Web Workhouse,** Winthrop St. (☎427 3090), near the post office between St. Patrick's and Oliver Plunkett St., has over 30 high-speed computers, tea, coffee, and snacks. M-Sa 8am-5pm €3 per hr., 5pm-3am €2.50, 3-8am €1.50; Su €2.50 per hr. all day. Open 24hr. Old city: **Surf City,** 11 Barrack St., has a €10 no-limit day pass. Open M-Su 10am-11pm. **Cork City Library** (☎492 4908), on Grand Parade also provides Internet access. Open M-Sa 10am-5:10pm. €1 per 30min.

Post Office: Main office: Oliver Plunkett St. (☎485 1049). Open M-Sa 9am-5:30pm. For other locations, see map.

⌐ ACCOMMODATIONS

Cork's fine array of hostels should put a smile on any budget traveler's face, but not if you can't get a room, so call ahead. For full Irish breakfasts, more privacy, and more cash, **Western Road,** near the University, is the veritable land of B&Bs.

⬛ **Sheila's Budget Accommodation Centre (IHH),** 4 Belgrave Pl. (☎450 5562; www.sheilashostel.ie), at the intersection of Wellington Rd. and York Street Hill. A perennial *Let's Go* favorite. Its friendly and trustworthy staff are the biggest reason for its glowing reputation; they take great pride in ensuring their guests feel safe and have fun too. 24hr. reception desk doubles as general store. Free luggage storage. Free Internet access. Breakfast €3. Sauna €2 per 4min. Laundry €6.50. Check-out 10:30am. Dorms €15-20; doubles €48-50. Ensuite rooms available. ❷

Brú Bar and Hostel, 57 MacCurtain St. (☎455 9667; www.bruhostel.com). High-class appearance and low-class price. Atmosphere is controlled and friendly. Free

Internet access and continental breakfast. Bar open 4pm-4am. Towels €2. Laundry €5. Check-in 1pm. Check-out 10:30am. 6-bed dorms €17; 4-bed dorms €21-23; doubles €50; private rooms €60. MC/V. ❷

Kinlay House (IHH), Bob and Joan's Walk (☎450 8966; www.kinlayhouse.ie), down the alley to the right of St. Anne's Church. Bright colors and warm atmosphere; some rooms have great views of the city. Plush lounge with TV and sunny Internet room. Internet access €1 per 15min. Continental breakfast included. Laundry €8. Free parking. 8- to 15-bed dorms €15-18; doubles €46-54. Ensuite rooms available. AmEx/MC/V. ❷

Roman House, 3 St. John's Terr., Upper John St. (☎450 3606; www.interglobal.ie/romanhouse), in a muted red building with a black door, across from Quality Hotel. Near the city center. Caters specifically to gay and lesbian visitors. Breakfast room is adorned with the friendly proprietor's artwork. Rooms ensuite with TV and tea/coffee. Singles €55; doubles €75. ❹

Cork International Hostel (An Óige/HI), 1-2 Redclyffe, Western Rd. (☎454 3289), a 15min. walk from Grand Parade. Bus #8 stops across the street; turn left and walk about 2 blocks. Clean, spacious rooms with high ceilings and a nice lawn. All rooms ensuite. Continental breakfast €4, full Irish €6.50. Internet access €1 per 15min., €2 per 40min. Check-in 8am-midnight. Dorms €18; 4-bed €20; doubles €40. ❶

Windsor House B&B, 54/55 MacCurtain St. (☎455 2615). Owned by 2 young brothers who aim to fully refurbish the old house. They intend to add a personal touch without a big hike in price. Check up on their progress and any new additions to the funky dining room. Rooms €30-35 per person. ❸

☐ FOOD

Cork is blessed with delicious restaurants and cafes, especially on the lanes connecting Patrick, Paul, and Oliver Plunkett St. The **English Market,** accessible from Grand Parade, Patrick, and Oliver Plunkett St., displays meats, fish, cheeses, and fresh fruit from the farms and fisheries of West Cork. Be especially sure to locate the ◪**Sandwich Stall;** the sandwich was invented in England and is now perfected in Cork's English Market (M-Sa 9:30am-6pm). **Tesco,** on Paul St. inside the Paul St. Shopping Centre, is the biggest supermarket around. (☎427 0791. Open M-Sa 8am-10pm, Su 10am-8pm.) In the wee hours after the pubs and clubs close, nothing satisfies like **Hillbillies** chicken, with two central locations: Grand Parade near Tuckey St. and MacCurtain St. (☎425 1059. Entrees €7-8. Open daily noon-3:30am.)

◪ **Eastern Tandoori,** 1-2 Emmett Pl. (☎427 2232), across from Opera House. Cork is renowned for its international flavor; this East Asian gem proves it. Elegant dining room overlooks the water. Early-bird 3-course menu is a steal. Entrees €12-19. Early-bird €15: M-Th 5-7pm, F-Sa 5-6pm, Su 5-6:30pm. Open daily 5-11:30pm. ❷

Ginos, 7 Winthrop St. (☎427 4485). Though the pizza is good, the gelato brings the crowds during summer. Heavenly flavors like honeycomb and hazelnut in heaping scoops. Small pizza €5; ice cream €1.35 per scoop. Open daily noon-10pm. ❶

Tribes, 8 Tuckey St. (☎427 4446). Late-night, low-light java shop with south-islander theme. Serves sandwiches and other meals and coffee (more than 11 kinds from all over the globe) and tea into the wee hours. Sandwiches €5; entrees €8-10. Open Tu-Th 10:30am-midnight, F-Sa 10:30am-4am, Su noon-11pm. ❷

Amicus, Paul St. (☎427 6455), across from Tesco. Artistically presented dishes that taste as good as they look. Modern yet down-to-earth; vegetarian Sicilian curry balances "Massive Beef Burger." Lunch €7-10; entrees €10-23. Open daily 8am-late. ❸

Greene's, 48 MacCurtain St. (☎455 2279). Walk through the stone arch past Isaac's Hotel. Warm colors, a waterfall, and grand skylights complement an exquisite menu.

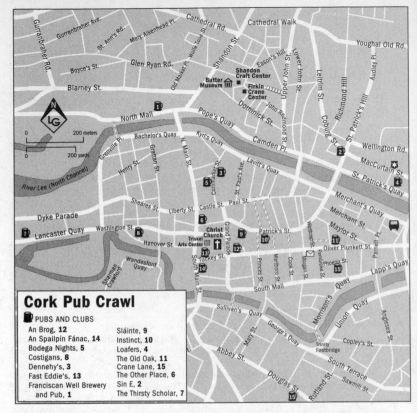

Cork Pub Crawl

PUBS AND CLUBS

An Brog, **12**	Sláinte, **9**
An Spailpín Fánac, **14**	Instinct, **10**
Bodega Nights, **5**	Loafers, **4**
Costigans, **8**	The Old Oak, **11**
Dennehy's, **3**	Crane Lane, **15**
Fast Eddie's, **13**	The Other Place, **6**
Franciscan Well Brewery	Sin E, **2**
and Pub, **1**	The Thirsty Scholar, **7**

Entrees €18-27. Open M-Th noon-10pm, F-Sa noon-10:30pm, Su noon-9:30pm. Early-bird 3-course menu €25; served daily 6-7pm. ❹

Café Paradiso, 16 Lancaster Quay (☎427 7939). Award-winning vegetarian meals make the most of what mother nature has to offer. Lunch €6-15; dinner €8-22. Open Tu-Sa noon-3pm and 6:30-10:30pm. ❸

Movida, 1 Union Quay (☎879 976 433). Inexpensive tapas menu mixes it up Spanish style. Tapas €3-11. Dinner M-Th and Su 5-10pm, F-Sa 5pm-12:30am. ❶

⌖ PUBS

Cork's pub scene has the variety of music and atmosphere expected of the Republic's second-largest city. Pubs crowd along Union Quay, Oliver Plunkett, and South Main St. To guide you on your tipsy quest, *Let's Go* offers our very own **Cork City Pub Crawl** (see **map**, p. 242). The city is especially proud of native Murphy's, a thick, creamy stout that some say rivals Guinness. A cheaper stout, Beamish, is also brewed here and is unique to Cork. Nearly all pubs stop serving at 11:30pm on weekdays, 12:30am on Fridays and Saturdays.

▧ **The Old Oak,** Oliver Plunkett St. (☎427 6165), across from the General Post Office. Year after year it wins a "Best Traditional Pub in Ireland" award. Kitchen open M-Sa noon-3pm. Bar closes F-Sa 2am, Su 1am.

☒ **An Spailpín Fánac** (on spal-PEEN FAW-nuhk), 28 South Main St. (☎427 7949), across from Beamish Brewery. One of Cork's oldest (est. 1779) and favorite pubs. Live trad every night. Storytelling last Tu of every month. Su Singers Club.

Sláinte, Market Ln. (☎427 4793), off Patrick St. Newer pub with a name far less sketchy than that of its comedy club, **The Craichouse,** is quickly becoming known for hosting some of the area's best upcoming comedians. W trad; F jazz/rock or funk; Su comedy. Club €7, students €5.

An Brog (☎427 0074), at the corner of Oliver Plunkett St. and Grand Parade. Ideal scene for those who crave good alternative rock and are working up the courage to sport eyebrow rings. Crowd weighted toward the student and 20s set. **Qube** club next door open until 2am. Cover varies.

Sin E, 8 Coburg St. (☎450 2266), just left off MacCurtain St. after crossing St. Patrick's Bridge. Candlelit interior. Some of Cork's best live music Tu-F and Su.

Franciscan Well Brewery and Pub, 14b North Mall (☎439 3434), along the North Quay, just east of Sundays Well Rd. Home-brewed Purgatory Pale Ale and Rebel Red. During summer, beer garden fills up fast for popular barbecue 5:30-11pm.

Loafers, 26 Douglas St. (☎431 1612). Ireland's oldest gay and lesbian pub fills every night with all age groups. Weekend DJ. Summer barbecue. No cover.

The Thirsty Scholar, Lancaster Quay (☎427 6209), next to Café Paradiso. An intimate, student-filled pub an easy stumble from campus. Th live rock.

Dennehy's (☎427 2343), across from Bodega Nights on Cornmarket St., close to the river. Small, packed, nothing fancy; just good craic.

▨ CLUBS

Cork nurtures aspiring young bands, but the turnover rate is high. To keep on top of the scene, check out *WhazOn? Cork,* a free bi-weekly performance schedule available at local stores. The Thursday "Downtown" Section in the *Evening Echo* newspaper also lists potential hotspots. Cork is also full of nightclubs that await the sloshed and swaying student population once the pubs have closed. Before forking over the €5-10 cover, remember that clubs close at 2am.

Crane Lane, 1 Phoenix St. (☎427 8487). From Oliver Plunkett St., walk toward Parnell Pl., turn right onto Smith St., and right again onto Phoenix St. Live rock, trad, and folk music 5-6 nights per week attracts locals and those lucky enough to find it.

Bodega Nights, 46-49 Cornmarket St. (☎427 2878), north of Grand Parade, newly reinvented itself into a DJ-friendly club with occasional live gigs. Large enough to house 5 bars including "world's first organic bar" for the seriously yuppie.

Instinct, Sullivan's Quay (☎496 6726), near Quay Co-op. Self-termed "lifestyle bar" regularly hosts DJs. Th-Su late bar helps it get jumping on the weekends. Sa cover €5.

Fast Eddie's (☎425 1438), off S. Main St. A young, thumping club popular with the student and 20s set. Strictly 18+. Cover €3-12, depending on the night.

The Other Place (☎427 8470), in a lane off South Main St. by the resource center. Gay and lesbian disco 1st Sa of every month. Cover €5. 18+.

◉ SIGHTS

Cork's sights are in three areas: the Old City, in the center of town; the Shandon neighborhood north of the river; and around University College Cork in the west.

THE OLD CITY

TRISKEL ARTS CENTRE. The small but dynamic Centre maintains two small galleries with rotating exhibits, and organizes music, film, literature, theater, and visual arts events. *(Tobin St. ☎ 427 2022; www.triskelart.com. Open M-F 9:30am-5:30pm, Sa noon-4pm. Cafe open 9:30am-5pm. Gallery free; consult desk for event prices.)*

ST. FIN BARRE'S CATHEDRAL. Looming over Proby's Quay, St. Fin's is a testament to the Victorian obsession with the Neo-Gothic. The cathedral, built between 1865 and 1879, houses contemporary art exhibits during the summer. *(Bishop St. ☎ 496 3387. Open M-Sa Oct.-Mar. 10am-5pm; Apr.-Sept. 10am-5:30pm. €3, students €1.50.)*

CHRIST CHURCH. Bishop Lucy Park, around the steeple-less Christ Church, provides a quiet spot to rest in a city center otherwise lacking green space. The site, scattered with eclectic statues, suffered Protestant torching three times between its consecration in 1270 and the construction of the final version in 1729. It is now used as an archive. *(Off Grand Parade, north of Bishop Lucy Park. Walk down Christ Church Ln., with the park on your left, until you emerge on S. Main St.; the church is on your right. Free.)*

SHANDON AND EMMET PLACE

ST. ANNE'S CHURCH. Commonly called Shandon Church, St. Anne's houses the famous Bells of Shandon, which visitors can ring before climbing the stone stairs for a great view of the city. The clocks on the church tower have always been notoriously out of sync—the eastern and western minute hands tick ahead of their northern and southern neighbors—and have earned the church its nickname, "the four-faced liar." The church is now small and intimate, with a collection of rare books along the left wall and an organ in the rear choir loft. *(Walk up John Redmond St. and take a right in front of the Shandon Craft Centre; St. Anne's is on your right. ☎ 450 5906. Usually open June-Sept. M-Sa 10am-5:30pm. Tower €6, students and seniors €5, families €12. Church free. Group rates available.)*

OTHER SIGHTS. The brick-and-glass **Opera House,** home to operas, ballets, and musicals, was erected two decades ago after its more elegant predecessor went up in flames. *(Emmet Pl. Over the hill from Shandon Church and across the north fork of the Lee. ☎ 427 0022.)* You can smell the hops from the **Beamish and Crawford Brewery** on South Main St. where visitors can enjoy a pint (or two) of stout while watching a DVD presentation about it in the hospitality room. *(☎ 491 1100. Open to visitors Oct.-Mar. Tu and Th 10:30am, noon. €5, students and seniors €4.)* The **Cork Vision Centre** is located in the heart of Cork's historic district as it is one of the best places to learn about the city's past. Its incredible scale model is also worth a gander. *(North Main St. ☎ 427 9925. Open Tu-Sa 10am-5pm. Free.)* The **Cork Butter Museum** unfortunately isn't made of butter...but it does make Cork's history as a major center of dairy commerce surprisingly interesting. *(Church St. ☎ 430 0600. Open Mar.-Oct. daily 9am-6pm. €3.50, students and seniors €2.50.)* The **Crawford Art Gallery** runs a program highlighting temporary Irish and international exhibitions. The striking main gallery room is filled with classical sculptures. *(Emmet Pl., off Paul St. ☎ 490 7855. Open M-Sa 10am-5pm. Guided tours Sa 2:30pm. Free.)* At the **Shandon Craft Centre,** potters and crystal-blowers display and sell their wares. *(O'Connell Sq., across from St. Anne's Church. Open M-F.)*

WESTERN CORK CITY

■ **UNIVERSITY COLLEGE CORK (UCC).** UCC's campus is a collection of brooding Gothic buildings, manicured lawns, and sculpture-studded grounds. Be sure not to miss the collection of Ogham stones, ancient gravestones marked with coded lines—an early example of the Irish language—in the appropriately classic Stone Corridor. The campus is also now home to the acclaimed and architecturally-striking **Lewis Glucksman Gallery** *(☎ 490 1844). (Main gate on Western Rd. ☎ 490 3000; www.ucc.ie. Gallery open Tu-Sa 10am-5pm, late night Th until 8pm, Su noon-5pm)*

▓ **FITZGERALD PARK.** This charming park boasts rose gardens, playgrounds, and a pond; it's a common canoodling spot for young lovers. It also contains the befuddling, esoteric exhibitions of the **Cork Public Museum,** which features such goodies as 18th-century toothbrushes and the clothes of James Dwyer, Sheriff of Cork. Next door is the Riverview **cafe,** with meals and refreshments available to enjoy outside. *(From the front gate of UCC, follow the signposted walkway across the street.* ☎ *427 0679. Museum usually open M-F 11am-1pm and 2:15-5pm, Su 3-5pm. Free.)*

CORK CITY GAOL. This not-to-be-missed museum is a reconstruction of the jail as it appeared in the 1800s, complete with eerily lifelike wax figures. An account of Cork's social history accompanies stories of miserable punishments, such as the "human treadmill" that was used to grind grain. The building also used to house the headquarters of the Radio Broadcasting Studio, which exists today in the form of an intriguing radio museum. *(From Fitzgerald Park, cross the white footbridge at the western end of the park, turn right onto Sunday's Well Rd. and follow the signs.* ☎ *430 5022. Open daily Mar.-Oct. 9:30am-6pm; Nov.-Feb. 10am-4pm. Last admission 1hr. before closing. €7, students and seniors €6. Admission includes audio tour.)*

🎭 🌿 ENTERTAINMENT AND FESTIVALS

In the lively streets of Cork, amusement is easy to find. Those who tire of the pubs can take advantage of the music venues, dance clubs, theaters, and sports arenas.

THEATER. Everyman Palace, MacCurtain St., hosts big-name musicals, plays, operas, and concerts. (☎450 1673. Box office open M-Sa 10am-6pm, Su 2-7:30pm, until 7:30pm on show nights. Tickets €10-23.) The **Opera House,** Emmet Pl., next to the river, presents dance and performance art. (See **Other Sights,** p. 248.) **The Granary,** Mardyke (☎490 4275), stages performances by local and visiting theater companies. **Triskel Arts Centre,** Tobin St., simmers with avant-garde theater and regular concert and film series. (☎427 2022.) **Firkin Crane,** Shandon Court, houses two theaters dedicated to developing local dance talent. Performance dates vary throughout the year. (☎450 7487. Call for details.)

SPORTS. Cork is mad for sports. Its Gaelic football, hurling, and soccer teams are perennial contenders for national titles (see **Sports and Recreation,** p. 73). From June through September, **hurling** and **Gaelic football** take place every Sunday afternoon at 2 and 4pm. For additional details, consult the Gaelic Athletic Association (www.gaa.ie) or the *Cork Examiner.* Be cautious in the streets on football game days, especially during championships—jubilant fans have been known to mow tourists down. Tickets to big games (€17-20) are scarce, but Wednesday, Saturday, and Sunday evening matches are cheap (€1.50-5) or free. To buy tickets to these local games, visit **Pairc Uí Chaoimh** (park EE KWEEV), the GAA stadium. Take the #2 bus to Blackrock and ask the driver to stop at the stadium. The newly opened **Mardyke Arena** at University College Cork provides a break from the Irish rain. The massive complex holds three training gyms, a lap pool, basketball courts, and climbing walls. (☎490 4751. Open M-F 7am-10:30pm, Sa 9am-7pm, Su 10am-7pm. Day passes available in the summer. €10, families €20. Call ahead.*)*

MUSIC. Big-name musicians play for free in local pubs and hotels during the three-day **Guinness Cork Jazz Festival** (www.guinnessjazzfestival.com) in late October. Book rooms well ahead of time if you're visiting that weekend. The weeklong **Corona Cork Film Festival** (☎427 5945; www.corkfilmfest.org), in early October at the Opera House and the Triskel Arts Centre, is another popular event. The **Cork Midsummer Festival** (☎421 5131; www.corkfestival.com) promises to enchant in mid-June with two weeks of visual arts, theater, music, and dance

BEHIND THE BIG SCREEN. During the 1st week of October, Cork hosts one of its most celebrated events—the International Film Festival, a showcase of big-budget and independent films, documentaries, and Irish-directed works. The organizers need 150 volunteers to help make the festival a smashing success. Committing to a minimum of 20 hours of work, volunteers assist in ticket sales, production, and guest and press reception. In return, volunteers are given free admission to festival films. For contact info, see below.

performances. At the end of April, the **Cork International Choral Festival** (☎421 5125) fills City Hall, churches, and outdoor venues with voices from across the globe. The smaller **Shandon Street Festival** kicked off during the Midsummer Festival 2007 and hopes to offer more food and fun in the coming years. (Contact festival director Linda O'Halloran ☎439 6082.) **Corkpride**, a week-long series of events celebrating Cork's gay and lesbian community, begins at the end of May. (Contact The Other Place and L.Inc for details, see Local Services.)

NEAR CORK CITY: MIDLETON   ☎021

Sixteen kilometers from Cork, Midleton *(Mainstir na Corann)* is home to historic—and popular—**Jameson Heritage Centre** and **Old Midleton Distillery,** where visitors learn why Queen Elizabeth I called Irish whiskey her one true Irish friend. A 1hr. **tour** engages visitors on the history and craft of whiskey production at the site and includes a free glass at the end; three lucky volunteers get to sample six different kinds of whiskey as their fellow tourists look on. (☎461 3594. Wheelchair-accessible. Open Mar.-Oct. daily 10am-6pm; tours every 30-45min., last tour 5pm; Nov.-Feb. by tour only 11:30am, 2:30, 4pm. €9.75, students and seniors €8.)

Though Midleton is better known as a pit stop rather than a tourist destination, the town's only hostel, **An Stór (IHH) ❶,** translated as "the treasure," is reason enough to stay. With cozy beds, nice showers, a spacious kitchen and lounge, and a wealth of information from its incredibly friendly and helpful owners, it's not a hostel, it's a "homestel." There aren't even numbers on the rooms, which are instead each named after a species of bird in Ireland. To see exactly how this hostel continually lives up to its name, turn onto Connolly St. from Main St. and take the first left onto Drury's Ave. (☎463 3106. Internet access available. Laundry €5. All rooms ensuite. Dorms €18; private rooms €24.)

Those not too distracted by the distillery will notice that Midleton has developed a reputation for something else: its food. Its **farmers' market** is extremely popular, and deservedly so. On the roundabout on the northern end of Main St., follow Park St. (after Fermoy Rd.) and take a right past the Tesco (www.midletonfarmersmarket.com; open Sa 9am-1pm). During the first weekend in September, the two-day binge known as the **Midleton Food and Drink Festival** lines the streets with live music and enticing edibles. When those options aren't available, **Tesco,** at the end of Main St. past the roundabout, sells groceries around the clock. (☎463 6151. Open 24hr.) The **Fire and Ice Cafe ❷,** the Courtyard, 8 Main St., is home to Midleton's own up-and-coming chef, Gary Masterson. He is so set in his ways that all his dishes, such as the grilled portobello mushroom on sourdough toast, wilted spinach, and gorgonzola cheese, must be made from scratch. Find Gary and his wife, Winnie, hard at work in the courtyard, off 8 Main St.; don't forget to try one their five types of lemonade such as passion fruit or ginger. (☎463 9682; www.fireandicecafe.ie. Lunch €10-12. Open M-F 9am-5pm, Sa 9am-11:30pm.) Significantly less gourmet and proud of it, **Ua Ceochain ❶,** 40 Main St., is the town's favorite chipper. Their minimalist menu shows they know what they do best. Rumors are even the town's millionaire can't resist. (Fish €3; chips €1.50-2.50. Open M 9pm-midnight, Tu-W 12:15-1:45pm and 9pm-midnight, F 12:15-1:45pm, 5:15-6:50pm, and 9pm-midnight, Sa 5:15pm-6:50pm and 9pm-midnight.) Another spot for delicious baked goods and meals, including sweet-and-sour chicken with veggies and the classic shepherd's pie, is Eleanor O'Sullivan's **The Granary Foodstore ❷**, in Coachhorse Ln. off Main St. (☎461 3366. Entrees €4-10. Open M-F 9am-6pm, Sa 9am-5:30pm.) Italian eatery **La Trattoria ❸** serves a variety of fun *panini*, pizza, and entrees. (☎463 1341. *Panini* €9. Pizza €10-13. Entrees €11-16. Breakfast 8:30am-noon, lunch noon-5pm, dinner 3-10pm.)

At night, **Wallis's**, 74 Main St., has become the place for music in town. Dig the modern sound system among the cavernous stone pillars and flagstones. (☎463 3185. Tu and Th live trad, Su live rock.) Head to **The Meeting Place** and the adjoining **Rory Gallagher's Bar**, Connolly St., for pints in the beer garden, which stays open rain or shine thanks to the retractable awning. (☎463 1928.) **McDaid's**, toward the end of Main St., has turned a historic hostel into a fun and lively pub attracting a mixed crowd to its regular live gigs upstairs. (☎463 1559. Th live trad, F live rock.)

To get to Midleton, a **bus** from **Cork** (20min.; M-F 32 per day 6:10am-11pm, Sa 23 per day 7:55am-11pm, Su 14 per day 7:50am-11pm; €5), or drive from Cork or Cobh on the Cork-Waterford highway (N25). The town's **tourist office** is located on Distillery road and has free maps of the town (☎461 3702. Open Easter-Sept. 9:30am-1pm and 2-5:15pm.) **Internet** access is free for members of the **library,** whose staff is also a reliable source for information about the area. Located on Main St. in the old 1789 Market House building. (Membership €2.50. Open M-Sa 9:30am-5:30pm.) Right alongside the library is the **post office.** (☎463 3621. Open M-F 9am-1pm and 2-5:30pm, Sa 9:15am-12:30pm.) Next to the post office is a **Permanent TSB** 24hr. **ATM; Bank of Ireland** and **Ulster** also have 24hr. **ATMs** on Main St. **Owenacurra Pharmacy** on Main St. is open late and also has an **ATM** inside. (☎463 1632. Open M-Sa 8:30am-10pm.)

◙ DAYTRIP FROM CORK: BLARNEY

Bus Éireann runs buses from Cork to Blarney M-F 15 per day, Sa 16 per day, Su 10 per day; €4.80 return. Blarney Castle ☎438 5252. Open June-Aug. M-Sa 9am-7pm, Su 9:30am-5:30pm; Sept. M-Sa 9am-6:30pm, Su 9:30am-dusk; Oct.-Apr. M-Sa 9am-6pm, Su 9:30am-5pm; May M-Sa 9am-6:30pm, Su 9:30am-5:30pm. Last admission 30min. before closing. Castle and grounds €8, students and seniors €6, children €2.50.

Blarney Castle, home of the legendary **Blarney Stone,** sits in a lush park 8km from Cork City. The original castle at the site, dating back to the 10th century, was made of wood, and was later replaced with stone by King Dermot McCarthy of Munster in 1446. Visitors can explore the many rooms of the castle, retracing the steps of medieval royalty and the men who defended the family. At the top of the castle is the famous stone, which must be kissed in dramatic fashion: by lying face-up partially suspended over a precipice. Legend has it that Queen Elizabeth I coined the name during her long and tiring negotiations for control of the castle. The owner, Cormac McCarthy, Earl of Blarney, followed the rules of 16th-century diplomacy, writing grandiose letters in praise of the Queen, but never gave up the land. Her royal feathers sufficiently ruffled, Her Majesty exclaimed: "This is all blarney—he never says what he means!" The stone allegedly imparts this gift of gab to whomever kisses it. When you've had your smooch, visit the dreamlike **rock close,** a rock garden built on an ancient druidic site. South American plants and groves of tall trees cradle eerie rock formations like the **wishing steps, witches' kitchen,** and **dolmen.** While the famous stone may bestow eloquence, these mystical grounds tend to leave its visitors speechless.

SOUTHWEST IRELAND

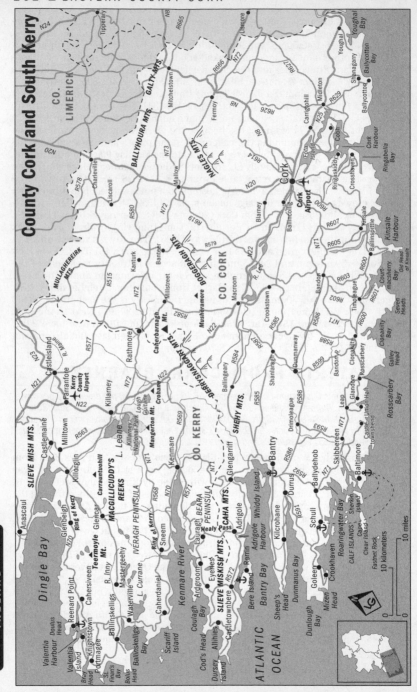

County Cork and South Kerry

COBH (AN CÓBH)   ☎021

Now a quiet harbor across from bustling of Cork, Cobh (KOVE) was Ireland's main transatlantic port until the 1960s. The town's steep hillside, lined with multicolored houses, was the final glimpse of Ireland for many of the emigrants who left between 1848 and 1950. Present-day Cobh offers visitors numerous occasions for more measured ocean adventure, and lies just a short train ride away from both the excitement of Cork City and the exoticism of the best wildlife park in Ireland.

☲🗗 TRANSPORTATION AND PRACTICAL INFORMATION. Cobh is an easy train ride from **Cork** (25min.; M-Sa 22 per day 5:20am-10:30pm, Su 9 per day 8:45-9:50pm; €4.40 return). Drivers take N25, then R624. The **tourist office,** along the water next to the train station, is in the restored Royal Cork Yacht Club, founded in 1854. It gives out free **maps.** (☎481 3301; www.cobhharbourchamber.ie. Open M-F 9:30am-5:30pm, during the summer additionally Sa-Su 1-5pm.) The **Cobh Internet Cafe & Call Shop,** on Main St., has Internet access. (☎485 5353. Open M-Sa 10am-10pm, Su 2-10pm. €2 per 35min., €3 per hr., €5 per 2hr. Min. €2.) The **library,** underneath the bridge after the second left from the tourist office, has free **Internet** access in 50min. slots (limit 1 per day) for members. (☎481 1130. Membership €2.50. Internet available Tu-Sa 11am-5pm.) Two 24hr. **ATMs** are located on W. Beach; an **AIB** at 4 W. Beach and a **Permanent TSB** across from the Centra.

🗂 ACCOMMODATIONS. Beds in this oceanfront town don't come cheap. Kevin Murphy, the owner of the **Bella Vista Hotel and Self-Catering Suites ❹** and **Harley's B&B ❸** doesn't quite have a monopoly on the accommodations in Cobh, but he does offer a range of appropriately priced options. The hotel, on Bishop's Rd., which also contains the **China Sea Restaurant and Takeaway** and rustic **bar,** has diverse rooms (ask for the one with the globe and telescope). Next door are snazzy, modern suites with two double rooms. (☎481 2215; www.bellavistahotel.ie. Hotel singles €45-60; doubles and triples €33-48 per person. Breakfast included. Self-catering €120 per night. Breakfast €6.50.) His B&B, located above **Harleys Coffee Shop** on 24 Harbour Row, also has rooms with personality, and runs a bit cheaper. (☎481 4290; www.harleysbnb.com. Singles €35-40; doubles €30-33 per person. Self-catering rooms available. Inquire about fishing packages.) Murphy's competition is stiff in the large yet very welcoming **Amberleigh House ❸,** which boasts a scenic view of its green garden and the sea. (☎481 4069. Singles €55; doubles €43 per person.) **Ardeen B&B ❸** also offers spacious rooms overlooking the harbor at lower rates. (☎481 1803. Singles €45; doubles €36 per person.)

☷🗹 FOOD AND PUBS. For the largest selection of groceries, a massive **Super-Valu** greets those on the way into town from Midleton Rd. (☎490 8340. Open M-F 8:30am-9pm, Sa 8:30am-8pm, Su 9:30am-8pm.) **The Lazy Bean Cafe ❷** defies its name with the obvious effort put into its stylish and health-conscious cuisine. The toffee nut delight latte (€3) is as tasty as it looks. (☎481 1999. Breakfast €6-7; sandwiches €4-7; salads €8-9.) Rival cafe **The River Room ❷,** on West Beach, has more local flavor; their large and tasty ciabatta sandwiches (€6) and lunchtime quiche are very popular. (☎481 5650. Open M-Sa 9am-5pm.) **The Quays Bar and Restaurant ❷,** 17 Westbourne Pl., attracts tourists with its expansive outdoor waterfront seating and surprisingly reasonable prices. (☎481 3539. Entrees €13-17. Open M-Th 10:30am-11:30pm, F-Sa 10:30am-12:30pm, Su 12:30-11pm.) For takeaway, **Indian Kitchen ❷** serves satisfying, spicy meals. (☎481 6494. Entrees €9-14. Delivery available. Open M-Th and Su 5-11pm, F-Sa 5-11:30pm.)

◪ SIGHTS. In 1912, Cobh was the *Titanic's* last port of call before the "unsinkable" ship went down. Just four years later, when the Germans torpedoed the

DO IT FOTA ANIMALS

You've marvelled at the bison lumbering along, the baby cheetahs at play, and the peacocks preening on the path in front of you—now, how would you like to adopt one?

Of course you shouldn't flee Fota Wildlife Park with one of their beloved animals wrapped around your neck like a summer sweater, but you can do something to help. The non-profit park runs an "Adopt an Animal at Fota" program, which allows visitors to sponsor an animal. Almost all—92.5%—of the proceeds go toward care for that particular species within the park, while the rest helps to sponsor conservation projects in the animal's native homeland.

Saving the world one animal at a time isn't cheap, but neither is taking care of these animals, many of which are endangered. If you visit the park with friends, chipping in to sponsor one together isn't unmanageable. Plus, in recognition of your generosity, you get a certificate of adoption, a glamor shot of the animal, and your name displayed at the park—not to mention the novel chance to sponsor a cheetah or a penguin in the Emerald Isle.

Information about the animals and an adoption brochure are available at the **Fota Wildlife Park** *on Fota Island. Call* ☎*02148 12678 or visit www.fotawildlife.ie for more details.*

Lusitania during WWI, most survivors and some of the dead were taken back to Cobh in lifeboats. The town commemorates its eminent but tragic history with respect and dramatic flair at ◙**The Queenstown Story**, a heritage center next to the railway station. The museum's flashy multimedia exhibit traces the port's past, with sections devoted to emigration, the *Titanic*, the *Lusitania*, and the peak of transatlantic travel. Informational panels help to resolve confusion over the town's three names—the original Cove, Victoria-inspired Queenstown, and finally Cobh, from Gaelic. The glass-roofed building has a marketplace feel and houses a large souvenir shop selling anything Irish. (☎481 3591; www.cobhheritage.com. Open daily 9:30am-6pm; last admission 5pm. €6, students €5.50.) **St. Colman's Cathedral** dominates the skyline on the hill high above town with its Gothic spire; the view of the harbor is well worth the hike up to its entrance. Completed in 1915, the cathedral boasts the largest carillon in Ireland, consisting of 47 bells weighing over 4600kg. (☎481 3222. Open daily 7am-8pm. Guided tours available by arrangement. Free.) The **Sirius Arts Centre** has been home to some serious artistic talent, including the live acoustics of Damien Rice. Located in the same building as the tourist office, the center is dedicated to the display of art as well as the restoration of the historic Old Yacht Club in which it resides.

Marine Transport Services, at the harbor across from the *Titanic* monument, launches 1hr. **Harbour Cruises.** (☎481 1485. June-Sept. tours leave daily at noon, 2, 3, and 4pm. €6.50, children €4.) For landlocked history, guided walking tours or bus rides on the **Titanic trail** stop at sites in town that are directly connected with the famed ship and offer related anecdotes. (☎481 5211; www.titanic.ie. 1-1¼hr. walking tour leaves from the Commodore Hotel Cobh daily at 11am throughout the year; June-Aug. additional tour at 2pm. €9.50, including a Guinness at the end of the tour. Contact Michael Martin ☎481 5211 for minibus tours.)

▶ **DAYTRIP FROM COBH: FOTA ISLAND.** Ten minutes from Cobh lies Fota Island, where more than 90 species of animals from all over the world—including bison, zebras, and giraffes—roam in the ◙**Fota Wildlife Park.** Opened in 1983 by the President of Ireland, the non-profit wildlife park is dedicated to conservation and education. Its 78 acres recreate the natural habitats of animals while also allowing many of them to roam freely, making it as close to a safari experience as you can get north of the equator. A **snack bar** at the far end of the park, where the

Cork-Cobh train stops, serves lunches (€3-6) to eat at the picnic areas available outside the park. The **Fota Arboretum,** next to the park, 1.6km from the station, cares for greenery as exotic as the beasts next door. *(Fota is an intermediate stop on the train from Cork to Cobh. Get off at Fota and re-board afterward for about €4.* ☎ *481 2678. Open daily except Dec. 25-26; Mar. 17-Nov. 4 M-Sa 10am-5pm, Su 11am-5pm; Nov. 5-Mar. 16 M-Sa 10am-3:30pm, Su 11am-3:30pm. €12.50, students and seniors €8. Parking €3.)*

YOUGHAL (EOCHAILL)   ☎ 024

Fifty kilometers east of Cork on N25, sun-kissed Youghal (YAWL) was immortalized in the 1954 version of *Moby Dick* starring Gregory Peck. A popular beach and a wealth of remarkable history have kept Youghal interesting even after its 15 minutes of fame elapsed. The huge **Clockgate,** which was built in 1777 and served as a prison and makeshift gallows, straddles crowded Main St. On Church St., the beautiful **St. Mary's Church** and **Myrtle Grove** estate stand side-by-side. The former features parts from the original Danish structure of 1020; behind the building, visitors can walk along the old **city walls,** built between the 13th and 17th centuries. Inside the church rests the elaborate grave of Robert Boyle, first Earl of Cork. Myrtle Grove was the residence of Sir Walter Raleigh, who served as mayor of Youghal from 1588-89. The house is privately owned, but literary buffs can glimpse the window where Raleigh's buddy Edmund Spenser is said to have finished *The Faerie Queen.* For a condensed history of Youghal since the 9th century, drop by the tourist office's **heritage center.** (☎20170. Same hours as tourist office.) Across the street and up an alley from the center, 🖾**Fox's Lane Folk Museum** is a surprisingly fascinating collection of household implements from razor blades and sewing machines to vacuum cleaners. (☎91145. Wheelchair-accessible. Open July 1-Sept. 30 Tu-Sa 10am-1pm and 2-6pm or by appointment. Last admission 5:30pm; €4.) Youghal's rich history and beautiful landscape likely influenced the opening of the new **White Gables Art and Photography Studio,** 11 Strand St., which specializes in local and Irish national art.

For a change of pace, crowds pack the **Greyhound Stadium,** located on N25 toward Cork, on Tuesday and Friday nights. (☎92305. First race 8pm. Admission €7, students €4.) Throughout July and August, get your trad on at the annual **Dancing Thru the Ages** show featuring Irish music and dance every Wednesday and Thursday night in the Mall Arts Centre. (☎92571; www.dancingthrutheages.com. W-Th 8:30pm; €20, students and seniors €18.50.) Those inspired by the town's association with Moby Dick can go on a quest of their own with **A Whale of a Time** dolphin- and whale- watching trips. (☎086 328 3256; www.whaleofatime.ie. Book ahead.) If that sounds like a ship-load of money, you can try getting closer on your own by renting a canoe or kayak from Mick, whose store is located on Main St. just past the clock tower. (☎087 629 4930. Open daily 5:30pm-12:30am.) Or just try to catch a glimpse of the dolphins for free while walking the beautiful promenade.

Youghal has only one hostel in town, but it's a great one. 🖾**Evergreen House Accommodation ❶,** on the Strand, has the appearance and comfort of home for an unbeatable price. Either walk the 20min. from town along N25 and just past the Tides restaurant, or ask the bus to let you off out front. (☎92877. Dorms €19; private rooms €23.) **Roseville ❸,** on New Catherine St. behind Brooke's SuperValu, may be worth the extra dough; if not for its homemade bread at breakfast, then at least for the inside scoop you'll get on the town's *Dancing thru the Ages* shows. (☎92571; www.rosevillebb.com. €33-35 per person. Student discount available.) If you'd rather look at the Atlantic from bed, then head up the Front Strand away from town until you reach **Bayview House B&B ❸.** (☎92824; www.bayviewhouse.net. Ensuite rooms €30 per person.) Elegant **Avonmore**

House ❸, South Abbey, has stylish rooms and a diverse breakfast menu. (☎92617; www.avonmoreyoughal.com. Ensuite rooms €35-45 per person.)

Plenty of food options cater to any budget. **Brooke's SuperValu** sells groceries on N. Main St. (☎92279. Open M-F 8am-9pm, Sa 8am-8pm, Su 9am-7pm.) For scrumptious scones, a full dinner menu, and great ambience, try ❧**The Red Store Pub & Restaurant ❸,** 150-151 N. Main St. (☎90144. Scone and coffee €3. *Panini* €8. Entrees €10-15. Scones and drinks daily 10:30am-12:30pm; carvery lunch until 2:30pm; dinner 5:30-9pm.) On weekends, music fills the popular **Treacy's Nook Pub,** Church St. The Treacy family celebrated the pub's 100th year under their ownership in 2001 and has also added a hip coffee bar in front. (☎92225. *Panini* €8. Coffee bar M-F 12:30-5pm.) The younger set heads to **The Gate,** S. Main St., where dark recesses echo with rock music. (☎93052. Th-F and Su live music. Occasional cover €2.) The rafters of roomy **Moby Dick's,** Market Sq., are decked out in nautical regalia. (☎92756. Sa ballads.) After hitting the streets, snack on some good eats at one of these late-night options: **Doyle a Meal,** 13 S. Main St. (☎93069. Chips €2-4; chicken €3-7; pizza €7-8; delivery €2.50); or **Roma Grill,** 50 N. Main St. (☎92142. Pizza €6-8; burgers €5; grilled entrees €4-14. Open M and W-Su takeaway noon-midnight, sit-down noon-10am.)

Buses stop on Main St. in front of the public restrooms, across from Dempsey's Bar. They travel to Cork (50min.; M-Sa 19 per day 7:30am-10:25pm, Su 17 per day 9:25am-10:25pm; €8.80, students €7) and Waterford via Dungarvan (1½-2hr.; M-Sa 10 per day 7:20am-10:25pm, Su 8 per day 9:25am-10:25pm; €13, students €10.70). **Youghal Cabs** (☎91818) also runs 24hr. service. The **tourist office,** Market Sq., on the waterfront behind the clocktower, distributes a free "tourist trail" booklet, which lays out a walk covering Youghal's historical sites. (☎20170. Open May-Sept. M-F 9am-5:30pm, Sa-Su 9:30am-5pm; Oct.-Apr. M-F 9am-5:30pm.) Souvenirs can be sent via the **Post Office** on Main St. (☎92161. Open M-F 9am-5:30pm, Sa 9:30am-1pm.) **TSB** and **Bank of Ireland** can both be found with **ATMs** on N. Main St. The **Aura Leisure Centre** satisfies those looking to for a way to burn off those full Irish breakfasts with its large gym and pool. (☎91614. Open M, W, F 7:30am-10pm, Tu and Th 9am-10pm, Sa-Su 10am-7pm. Pool per hr.: €6.75, students €5; gym per hr.: €8.50, students €5.50.) Of course, a swim in the big blue ocean or a jog on the promenade works well, too (and it's free). Afterwards, the **Laundrette** near the clock tower gate on Main St. will take care of your sweaty clothes with its wash, dry, and press services. (Open M-Sa 9:30am-1pm and 2-6pm.) The **library,** on Church St., off Main St., provides free **Internet** access with membership to Cork County libraries. (☎93459. Membership €2.50. Open Tu-Sa 9:30am-1pm and 2-5pm.) If the library is full, try **Cyberoom Internet Cafe,** on N. Main St. (☎90555. Open M-F 10:30am-8pm, Su 2-6pm. €1.50 per 15min., €8 per 2hr.; student discount 25%.)

WESTERN COUNTY CORK

Western Cork, the southwestern third of the vast county, was once the "badlands" of Ireland; its ruggedness and isolation rendered it lawless and largely uninhabitable. Wave-whipped Mizen Head and the stoic, rock-streaked heights of Sheep's Head mark the southwestern bounds of the Emerald Isle. From Cork City, there are two choices for westward bus routes: inland or coastal. The **coastal bus** runs from Cork to Skibbereen, stopping in Bandon, Clonakilty, and Rosscarbery (M-Sa 7-8 per day 9:45am-8:15pm, Su 6-7 per day; €11.30), while the **inland bus** travels from Cork to Bantry, via Bandon and Dunmanway (M-Sa 7 per day 9:15am-7pm, Su 3-5 per day 10:30am-7:30pm). Travelers who venture away from the bus routes at any point along the trip (via car, bicycle, or foot) will invariably be rewarded with a more memorable trip. Hitchers report having little trouble finding a ride in these parts, though *Let's Go* never recommends hitchhiking.

THE INLAND ROUTE

Those looking to avoid the tourist crowds should consider one of the winding scenic inland routes that run westward from Cork. These roads aren't meant to save time but to highlight the scenery. Many travelers head northwest to stop in Macroom and Killarney; west toward Macroom, Ballingeary, Bantry, and Glengarriff; and southwest toward Dunmanway, Bantry, and Skibbereen. The rocky faces of the Shehy Mountains, between Dunmanway and Ballingeary, have some of Ireland's best-preserved wilderness areas, and are best explored by bike or on foot.

DUNMANWAY (DÚN MÁNMHAI)   ☎023

Located in relative isolation at the intersection of R586, R587, and R599, **Dunmanway** ("Fort of the Middle Plains") is a quiet town with authentic Irish charm. There's not much in the way of attractions in the town itself, but its proximity to other sights of interest makes it a convenient place to stop. To the northwest and over the mountains lies **Ballingeary** (*Béal Athán Ghaorthaidh*), the heart of one of West Cork's declining *gaeltachts* and the entry point to **Gougane Barra Forest.** The forest has a hotel and national park and is also the site of **St. Finbarr's monastery,** the original location of which is now marked by a church. (For more information about the hotel and park, check out www.gouganebarra.com.) Past the Shiplake Hostel turn-off, 10km out of Dunmanway, lies **Lakes Cullenagh and Coolkellure,** both of which are lovely walking and picnicking areas. Specific information on scenic walks can be found at the **library** (An Leabharlann), in Market Sq., which lends out **West Cork Walks** to members as well as a free brochure on garden trails in west Cork. (☎55411. Membership €2.50. Open Tu 1-8pm, W-Sa 10am-5:30pm.) If it's local history you're interested in, try and catch the friendly staff at the **Dunmanway Heritage Centre,** on Main St. (☎086 177 7483. Open M noon-5pm, F 9am-1:30pm.)

Hostelers' little hearts will break to learn the future of popular **Shiplake Mountain Hostel ❶** is uncertain, as it was up for sale in the summer of 2007. If you're lucky, the new owners will have kept the charming farmhouse and its colorful gypsy caravans, 5km from town on Castle St., as a place for shallow-pocketed visitors to stay. If not, alternative lodgings can be found in the more modern **Galvins on the Greene B&B ❸,** next to the Southern Bar on East Greene. (☎45625. Private car park. TV. Singles €40; doubles €70.) The **Parkway Hotel ❹,** farther down East Greene, is great: its guests can enjoy its four lively bars and restaurant serving food from 8am-9pm, including free breakfast and daily carvery lunch (not free). Its friendly owners also belie the typical hotel experience. (☎45236; www.parkwayhotel.ie. Free bike storage, TV, phone. Singles €55; doubles €90.)

EuroSpar on Main St. stocks food and drink, has an **ATM** (☎45457; open M-W 8am-8pm, Th-Sa 8am-9pm, Su 8am-6pm), and contains a **post office** (open M-F 9am-5:30pm, Sa 9am-1pm). **An Chistin ❶,** near the end of Main St., starts your day off right or keeps it going with fresh breakfast served all day. (☎56943. Breakfast €6-10. *Panini* €5-8. Open daily 9am-4pm.) **Mirabelle's ❶** in the Market Sq. has a more modern setting and menu, including fresh smoothies. (☎087 994 3872. Takeaway available. Smoothies €4. Sandwiches and wraps €7-8. Open daily 10am-6pm.)

🍺**The Shamrock,** Market Sq., is owned and operated by a fifth-generation O'Donovan who lives up to his good name by passionately overseeing that people of all ages and types find what they're looking for; from the restaurant's homemade favorites to the beer garden's burrito stand, from trad music to disco DJs, Shamrock's got you covered. (☎45142. Pub hosts F trad. Nightclub F-Su DJ. Bar

SOUTHWEST IRELAND

food €9-19.) In stark opposition, **Wrynn's Bar** wouldn't even try and advertise its quiet, cozy atmosphere, whose warmth comes from both its fireplace and old-time charm. The locals, however, couldn't keep their mouths shut about it. If that's too full and your stomach's on empty, the **Southern Bar** on East Greene serves great bar food on weekends in its spacious pub. (☎45625. Kitchen open Th-Su 4pm-8pm.)

Bus Éireann runs from **Cork** to **Dunmanway** (M-Sa 6-7 per day 9:15am-7pm, Su 4-5 per day 10:30am-7:30pm; €11.60); buses depart in front of James MacCarthy's in **Market Square.** A **police** *(garda)* station is located at the end of Main St. (☎45202). 24hr. **ATMs** are located at the **AIB** on East Greene and the **Bank of Ireland** at the end of Main St. The **Dunmanway Laundrette,** also on Main St., offers wash/dry, dry cleaning, and shoe repair services. (☎56943. Open M-Sa 9:30am-1pm and 2-6pm.) **Internet** access is available in the library to members. To reach Ballingeary from Dunmanway, take R587 northeast until you get to R584, then head westbound; it's on the Macroom to Bantry/Glengariff road. In this *gaeltacht*, signs are posted in traditional script, including Ballingeary's Irish name, *Béal athán Ghaorthaídh.*

SOUTHERN COAST

West of Cork City, N71 threads through Clonakilty and Skibbereen before the land branches into the smaller and more remote fingers of Sheep's Head, Mizen Head, and the Beara Peninsula. Along the way, rolling green hills and lush pastures are slowly replaced by craggy hilltops, dramatic cliffs, and towering mountain peaks as Ireland's southern coast begins to look more like its western one. This stunning backdrop is mere window-dressing for a populace that may be small, but has the warmth and hospitality that fulfill the stereotype of the friendly local. With tourism here relatively less rampant than in the neighboring superstars of the Ring of Kerry and Cork City, people are better left to shape their distinct regional culture to their own tastes.

KINSALE (CIONN TSÁILE)   ☎021

Every summer the population of small, upscale Kinsale quintuples with a flood of tourists. Gastrophiles flock to Kinsale's 11 famed "Good Food Circle" restaurants, and locals claim it is the only town in Ireland with more restaurants than pubs. Culture vultures and aquatic daredevils can get their fixes too in the town's beach, castle, forts, galleries, and coastal walks. But the postcard-inspiring beauty of today hides its grim past: the victory of Elizabethan England at the 1601 Battle of Kinsale cleared the way for several centuries of colonialism. Deposed Catholic King James II came here 80 years later for a final failed attempt to reclaim his throne, and in 1915, the *Lusitania* was sunk just off Kinsale's Old Head. These days, boats from Britain bring vacationers eager to fill the town's coffers.

■ 🗺 **ORIENTATION AND PRACTICAL INFORMATION.** Kinsale lies at the base of a U-shaped inlet, a 40min. drive southwest of Cork on R600. Facing the water, **Charles Fort** and the **Scilly Walk** (SILL-ee) are to the left; the piers, **Compass Hill,** and **James Fort** are to the right. **Buses** to **Cork** stop at the Esso station on the Pier. (40min.; M-Sa 11-14 per day 7:30am-10:40pm, Su 5 per day 10:30am-7pm; €9.50. return.)

Services include: **bike rental** and **fishing supplies** at **Mylie Murphy's,** one of the first storefronts on the right coming into town (☎477 2703; open M-Sa 9am-6pm, call ahead Su in summer; bike or fishing pole rental €10 per day, €60 per wk.; deposit or credit card required); the **tourist office,** Emmet Pl., in the black-and-red building on the waterfront (☎477 2234; open June daily 9:15am-6pm, July-Aug. 9am-7pm, Sept.-Apr. 9:15am-5pm. Free maps and brochures); 24hr. **ATMs** at **Bank of Ireland,** at the corner of Main St. and Emmet Pl. (☎477 2521; open M 10am-5pm, Tu-F 10am-4pm) and **AIB** on Pearse St. (☎477 2765; open M 10am-5pm, Tu and Th-F 10am-4pm, W 10:30am-4pm); **Internet** access at **Elasnik Web Cafe**, 6A Exchange Bldg., Market Sq. (☎477 7356; www.elasnikcomputers.com. €5 per hr., students €4 per hr.; open daily 10am-10pm. Snacks/coffee; free coffee with every hr.); **Bookstór**, an independent, family-run, yet modern **bookstore** with a wide selection of Irish interests and other unique genres (☎477 4966; www.bookstor.ie; open M-W and Sa 9:30am-6pm, Th-F 9:30am-7pm, Su 11:30am-6pm).

⊠⊠ ACCOMMODATIONS AND CAMPING. As a tourist-crazy town, Kinsale's center and environs are bursting with B&Bs. Most of them cater to an affluent crowd, so the budget-oriented beds fill up quickly. If budget is a bit less of a concern and the company of a jazz recording artist among a fine array of art sounds like your tune, head up the Glen Rd. past Toddies Restaurant and look for the purple and yellow **Gallery Guesthouse ❹**. Guests who don't join jam sessions with proprietor Tom O'Hare on his vibraphone can easily entertain themselves with in-room satellite TV and DVD players. The delightful quirkiness only continues in the morning with items like "a colorful creation of ice cream with summer fruits" contrasted with the bacon and leek quiche on the menu. (☎477 4558. Rooms €45-55 per person.) Be especially sure to call ahead or book online for the **Kinsale Arms Guesthouse ❸**, 55 Main St., whose young owners are eager to please their guests. With their tastefully decorated rooms in the heart of town at unbeatable rates, they usually succeed. (☎477 2233; www.kinsalearms.com. Rooms €35 per person.) **Dempsey's Hostel ❶**, on Eastern Rd. on the way out of town, appears rather bare, but its range of affordable accommodations and low-cost services will at least not empty your wallet. Guests also enjoy use of the herb garden and spacious TV room. (☎477 4111. Parking available. Laundry €5. Dorms €15; private doubles €36. Camping €7.) Those bringing their own roof can camp at the **Garrettstown House Holiday Park ❷**, 9.7km west of Kinsale outside Ballinspittle on the R600. The facilities include tennis courts, minigolf, and game room. (☎477 8156; www.garrettstownhouse.com. Open May to late Sept. 1 adult with tent €12.50-14.50.)

☐⊠ FOOD AND PUBS. Tourists 'round the globe have long had Kinsale on their map as a gourmet destination. Those not ambitious or deep-pocketed enough to try all 11 in the formal "Good Food Circle" (Chairperson: Carole Norman ☎477 2847) should at least consider a bite in one of our chosen few. In spite of this rich tradition of cuisine, **SuperValu**, Pearse St., sells groceries. (☎477 2843. Open M-Sa 8:30am-9pm, Su 10am-9pm.) If you're going to try one of the elite 11, make it Georgina Campbell's "2007 Seafood Restaurant of the Year" award-winning **Fishy Fishy Cafe ❸**, in one of its two locations. The older one, on Guardwell St., is a combination seafood restaurant and gourmet store that serves lunch to a packed crowd. (☎477 4453. Lunch €12.50-19. Shop open Tu-Sa 9am-5:30pm; cafe Tu-Sa noon-3pm.) Its newer spot ups the scale but retains the charm and offers four items on its appealing menu in "taste" portions for just €10. (☎470 0415; www.fishyfishy.ie. Entrees €14-23. Open daily noon-4:30pm; summer also Tu-F noon-8pm.) When Miss Campbell's awards fail to impress (they're a dime a dozen in this town), perhaps a stopover at 3 Market St.'s **Daltons Bar ❷**, will suffice. (☎477 7957. Lunch €10-15. Open daily noon-4pm.) Seeking noteworthy cafe fare, locals pack behind the wraparound corner window at **Patsy's Corner ❶**, Market Sq., for sandwiches and salads (€3.50-7.30) and homemade cakes. (☎086 865 8143. Open Sept.-July M-Sa 9am-5:30pm; Aug. daily 9am-5:30pm.) On Main St., **Muddy Maher's ❶** supplies dependable pub grub and music four to five nights per week during the summer. (☎477 4602. Entrees €6-11. Kitchen open daily until 9:30pm.)

Those who make the hike to the vicinity of Charles Fort should enjoy a pint at the unparalleled **Bulman Bar** (☎477 2131), the 2004 Black and White Pub of the Year. Locals spill outside on sunny days to enjoy the view over the bay; rainy days crowd them inside by one of two cozy fireplaces. A proper pub crawl will take you beyond Kinsale's small maze of streets. **The Spaniard,** atop the hill out of town along the Scilly Walk, is well worth the trip. Two bars and a restaurant, with thick stone walls, low-beamed ceilings, and dark wood paneling, lure fishermen and other locals to foot-tapping trad sessions several nights per week. To reach the pub, follow the signs to Charles Fort along the water's edge and around the bend. (☎477 2436. W trad sessions, other nights impromptu. Pub entrees €6-17; restaurant entrees €19-24. Pub food daily 12:30-3pm; restaurant open daily 6:30-10pm.) The owners have improved the beloved **An Seanachaí,** 6 Market St. Among the changes, the one constant is the ample supply of *craic.* (☎477 7077.)

◙ **SIGHTS.** A 30min. trek up and around **Compass Hill,** south of Main St., affords wide views of the town and its seascapes. Even more impressive is the vista from the star-shaped **Charles Fort,** which served as a British naval base from the 17th century until 1921. The battlements overlook the water and a stunning spread of town, harbor, and coastline. (☎477 2263. daily Open mid-Mar. to Oct. 10am-6pm; Nov. to mid-Mar. 10am-5pm. €3.50, seniors €2.50, students and children €1.25.) To reach Charles Fort, follow the 2km **Scilly Walk** (30min.), a path along the coast starting at the end of Pearse St. that boasts some scenery of its own. Across the harbor from Charles Fort, the much less extensive but nonetheless remarkable ruins of ▨**James Fort** tempt explorers with secret passageways and panoramic views of Kinsale. Follow the pier away from town, turn left after crossing the Duggan bridge and park at the end of the road. From there, follow the signs.

Back in town, **Desmond Castle,** Cork St., broods with a gloomy history. The 15th-century customs house served as an arsenal during the 100-day Spanish occupation of 1601 and as a naval prison in the 17th century. Inside, the **International Museum of Wine** chronicles both Kinsale's history as a wine port and its legions of emigrants who established themselves as vintners in continental Europe. (☎477 4855. Open mid-Apr. to Oct. daily 10am-6pm. Last admission 45min. before closing. €3, seniors €2.10, students and children €1.30.) More history comes to life in the **Kinsale Courthouse,** Market Sq., site of the hearings for the case of the famous British ocean liner *Lusitania,* which was sunk in 1915 by a German torpedo off the coast of Kinsale. This hodgepodge of brick and slate now contains the **Kinsale Regional Museum.** (Open W-Sa 10:30am-5:30pm, Su 2-4:15pm. €2.50, students €1.50.) Up the hill from Market Sq. is the restored west tower of the 12th-century **Church of St. Multose,** the patron saint of Kinsale, and an ancient graveyard worth a peek. (☎477 2220. Church open daily 10am-5pm. Graveyard always open. Free.) For current artistic attractions, the **Kinsale Arts Week** kicks off in early July with a range of events throughout town. (☎477 2348; www.kinsaleartsweek.com.)

CLONAKILTY (CLOCH NA COILLTE)   ☎023

Once a linen-making town with a workforce of over 10,000, Clonakilty ("Clon" for short), which lies between Bandon and Skibbereen on the N71, is now a calm town of 3500. Henry Ford was born nearby, but the favorite native is military leader, spy, organizational genius, and Irish hero Michael Collins. The wily Collins came home during the Civil War, thinking "they surely won't kill me in my own country." So much for nationalist bravado—he was murdered 40km from town. Most visitors, looking for relaxation rather than revolution, head to nearby Inchydoney Beach. The sound of crashing waves mixes with riffs reverberating during early September's **Guitar Festival,** featuring music on the town's sandy shores.

🔊 🄵 ORIENTATION AND PRACTICAL INFORMATION. Clonakilty's main drag begins at the tourist office on **Ashe Street** and becomes **Pearse Street** (known as Main St.) and then **Western Road** in quick succession. A stone tribute to axe-wielding rebel Tadgh an Astna serves as a central point. To the statue's left, **Rossa Street** runs into **Connelly Street** near the Wheel of Fortune water pump. **Astna Street** angles off the statue toward the harbor and **Inchydoney Beach** (bear right). **Buses** from **Cork** (M-Sa 9-10 per day 9am-11pm, €12.50) arrive on the corner of Clarke St., by Spar, and routes from **Skibbereen** (M-Sa 5-6 per day 7am-midnight, Su 4 per day 11am-6pm; €9.40) stop in front of Lehane's Supermarket on Pearse St. Walk the 4.8km to Inchydoney or **rent bikes** at **MTM Cycles**, 33 Ashe St. (☎ 33584. €2.50 per hr., €10 per day, €45 per wk.) The **tourist office**, 25 Ashe St., hands out maps and plenty of friendly advice. (☎ 33226. Open July-Aug. daily 9am-6pm; Sept.-June M-Sa 9:15am-6pm.) **AIB** and **Bank of Ireland** are on Pearse St. and have 24hr. **ATMs,** while **Permanent TSB** has one in its Rossa St. location. (Opening times for each approx. M 10am-5pm, Tu-F 10am-4pm.) For **Internet** access, a membership (€2.50) to the library in the Old Mill on Kent St. grants free access (☎ 34275; open Tu-Sa 10am-6pm), while **fast.net,** Pearse St., also has fax and photocopy services (☎ 34515; €1 per 10min., €3 per 30min., €5 per hr.; open M-F 9am-6pm, Sa 10am-5pm).

🄵 ACCOMMODATIONS. Clonakilty joins the growing group of towns in need of more budget accommodations. Of course, the cozy and elegant B&B **Nordav ❸**, just off Western Rd. behind the museum, may be an exception to the rule. Removed from the road by a well-groomed lawn and splendid rose gardens, it features sweet suites. (☎ 33655. €40-50 per person.) Bubblegum pink **Aisling Heights ❸**, off the bypass to Clogheen Meadows, also offers spacious ensuite rooms with TV. (☎ 33491. Singles €40-45; doubles €64-70.) **Desert House Camping Park ❶** is connected to a dairy farm, 800m southeast of town. It provides spots on a wide, sloping lawn. (☎ 33331. Showers €1.30; electricity €3.50. 1-person tent €8.50; 2-person tent €17.50; 4-person tent €21.50.)

🄲🄼 FOOD AND PUBS. Clonakilty's culinary fame derives from its unique type of **black pudding**, a sausage-like concoction of beef, blood, and grains. Those eager to try it or its pasty **white pudding** sister (substitute pork and milk for blood), should head to the award-winning butcher at **Twomey's.** (☎ 33365. Open M-Sa 9am-6pm.) But fear not—Clon has many other options for sustenance. **Betty Brosnans ❶**, 58 Pearse St. (☎ 33685), offers a feast for the eyes and the stomach; visitors enjoy her photo gallery of local scenes as they nosh on her "shopper's special" including a mug of soup, a mug of coffee or tea, and a toasted ham and cheese sandwich for just €8.50. Those late-night Chinese food cravings can be curbed at **Sea Palace ❶**, on McCurtain Hill. (☎ 36694. Entrees €8-11. Open M-Th and Su 5pm-midnight, F-Sa 5pm-12:30pm.) For dessert, pick up a box of Belgian bites of heaven at tiny **Choc Box** on 9 Ashe St. (☎ 21605. Open M-Sa 10am-5:30pm, Su 10am-4pm.) Or, for sheer sinful indulgence, check out the **Ice Cream Parlour** on Pearse St. They carry 14 homemade flavors, but their milkshakes take the cake. (☎ 33699. 1 scoop €1.50. Open M-Sa 10am-6pm, Su 1pm-6pm.) Buy groceries at **Londis Supermarket,** Pearse St. (☎ 33685. Open M-Sa 7am-10pm, Su 8am-10pm.)

Clonakilty is justifiably famous for its great music scene. It was also home to world-famous Noah Redding, the bass player for Jimi Hendrix but locally known for being the Friday-night regular at **De Barra's,** Pearse St., for 25 years. This pub, which boasts a superb sound system and ample space, has also drawn names like Damien Rice and Roy Harper. The way people rave about the *craic* found nightly at De Barra's, you'd think it actually was a drug. (☎ 33381. M trad night. Cover W-Th and Su €6-10. Open M-Th 10:30am-11:30pm, F-Sa 10:30am-12:30am, Su

10:30am-11pm.) Through the arched Recorders' Alley off Pearse St., behind O'Donovan's Hotel, **An Teach Beag** (☎33250) is Clonakilty's center for a communal type of storytelling called **scríoch**, where one storyteller oversees while others take turns. It's also a huge center for trad, ballads, folk, and other music; there are performances every night of the summer and a few nights per week in winter. Around the corner, **Shanley's**, 11 Connolly St. (☎33790), is equally reputable for its frequent music showcases and reliable doses of *craic*.

◨ **SIGHTS.** To fill the hours before the pubs pick up, join the locals at ▨**Inchydoney,** one of the prettiest beaches this side of Malibu, California. The water might be a bit less temperate than the tropics, but water-adverse individuals can still enjoy views of the big blue among surrounding cliffs and rolling hills. And for the adventurous, the **West Cork Surf School** offers 2hr. beginner lessons daily at 10am and 2pm. (☎086 869 5396; www.westcorksurfing.com. Book ahead.) The Inchydoney Rd. passes the **West Cork Model Railway Village,** where the Kinsale, Bandon, and Clonakilty of 1940 are reborn in miniature. Kids will enjoy the mini-railroad rides through town. (☎33224. Open Feb.-Oct. daily 11am-5pm. €10.) Back in town, the **West Cork Regional Museum,** Western Rd., displays an early 20th-century beer-pouring machine and the christening shawl of patriot O'Donovan Rossa and even lets visitors play dress-up with an antique silk cloak. (Open May-Oct. Tu and Th-Sa 10:30am-5pm, Su 2-5pm. €3, students €1.50, children free.) While in Clonakilty, don't miss the opportunity to learn about the heroic Michael Collins. Seven different **tours** of sights relating to his life and death can be arranged through the tourist office or Timothy Crowley (☎46107). The Crowleys also operate the **Michael Collins Centre,** a hilltop cottage with a wealth of information on both the man and the area's traditions and folklore. (☎46107; www.reachireland.com. Open mid-June to mid-Sept. M-Sa 10:30am-5pm, Su by appointment. Guided walking tours of surrounding countryside also available. "Michael Collins Experience" slide show M-Th 7:45pm; €5.) Just over 3km east lies the **Lios na gCon Ring Fort,** which was "fully restored" based on excavators' estimates of its 10th-century form; it's the only ring fort in Ireland reconstructed on its original site.

UNION HALL (BREANTRA)   ☎028

En route to the larger centers of Clonakilty and Skibbereen, tiny **Union Hall** sits serenely across the water from equally small **Glandore.** Set amid rolling green pastures and forested land too rocky for farming, this fishing village was once a hangout of **Jonathan Swift.** Those looking for shade in what used to be the **Rineen Forest** will have to wait until it grows back; the trees were recently cut down (and replanted) for timber. In the meantime, the area still has picnic tables and lovely walking paths. Those looking for an even more intimate experience with nature and have the means to camp should head to beautiful **Meadow Camping Park ❶,** just past Glandore on the N71 toward Rosscarbery. (☎33280. Showers €1; electricity €3. 1-person tent €8; 2-person tent €17; 4-person family tent €24.) **Knockdrum Fort,** also to the west, represents the remnants of an Iron Age Celtic fort.

Five kilometers out of town, an unorthodox but singular experience awaits at the ▨**Ceim Hill Museum.** The term unique doesn't begin to describe the gregarious proprietress, who displays an eclectic collection of pterodactyl teeth, dinosaur droppings, stone-age calendars, and Easter Rising rifles in her rambling farmhouse high on a hill above town. Visitors to Miss O'Mahony's "museum" depart with a deeper appreciation for what may appear to be just piles of "stuff" than ever thought imaginable. From Union Hall, continue past the closed down Maria's Holiday Hostel on the road to Reen Pier and take the steep right turn before descending down to the pier. The museum is signposted at the top of the hill on the left.

(☎36280. Open daily 10am-7pm. €4, children €2. Large groups call ahead.) For **dolphin and whale watching expeditions,** you have your choice of joining captain Nic Slocum aboard his *Voyager* or Colin Barnes on the *Holly Jo*. Both depart from nearby Reen Pier daily at 10am during the summer and both captains are well qualified to help you in your quest to spot the spectacular species. From the bridge into town, pass through the village and follow the sign near the church for Reen Pier. (Captain Slocum: ☎08612 00027 or 0283 3357; www.whalewatchwestcork.com. 4hr. tour. Additional afternoon tour when busy. Book ahead. Captain Barnes: ☎36832. Additional tour Mar.-Oct. 3pm. €40, students and seniors €30.)

The immaculate and well-located ■**Seascape B&B ❸** has beautiful, airy rooms with hardwood floors and a gorgeous view of the bay below. (☎33920. €35 per person.) **Casey's Bar ❸** also offers comfortable rooms in a prime location overlooking the bay. The proximity to the bar's kitchen is also a perk, as it serves delicious, generously portioned dishes featuring fresh local seafood. (☎33590. Sandwiches €4-10. Entrees €14-22. Kitchen open daily noon-8:30pm. Suites €40 per person.) **Dinty's Bar ❸** serves steak and seafood. (☎33373. Entrees €13-22. Kitchen open daily 12:30-2:30pm and 5-9pm.) Enjoy freshly baked bread at **Marinero's ❶,** which makes its cafe fare with mostly local or organic products following time-tested family recipes. (☎34708. Lunch €7-8. Open daily during summer 9:30am-6pm; winter 10am-4pm.) **Centra** stocks groceries (☎34955. Open summer M-Sa 8am-9pm, Su 8am-5pm; in winter M-Sa 8am-9pm, Su 8am-2pm.) The jovial atmosphere and billiard tables at **Maloney's** (☎33610) draw a crowd, while **Nolan's Bar** (☎33758) keeps it simple with no food or music but plenty of patronage.

SKIBBEREEN (AN SCIOBAIRIN) ☎028

The biggest town in Western Cork, Skibbereen (or "Skib" as it is sometimes affectionately called) is a convenient stop for travelers roaming the coastal wilds of the peninsula or on their way to points east or west. Skib was established in 1631 by refugees fleeing Algerian pirates and was one of the hardest-hit areas in the country during the Great Famine. Skib has transcended its darker past; brighter times are reflected in its colorful houses and the cheerful Irish music which plays over load speakers in the streets on Sundays. All of Skib turns out for the bustling weekend markets for local farmers. (**Country market:** F 12:30-2:30pm, church hall off Bridge St. **Farmers' market:** Sa 10am-1pm, church parking lot.) Skib is also a good base for daytrips to seaside towns like Baltimore and Castletownshend.

■◪ **ORIENTATION AND PRACTICAL INFORMATION.** Skibbereen's major roads are laid out in an L-shape, with **North Street** running perpendicular to **Main Street** and **Bridge Street** (the name-change occurs at the small bridge). The clock tower, post office, and stately Maid of Erin statue surround the intersection that forms the elbow. **Buses** stop at Cahalane's Pub on Bridge St. and run to Baltimore (M-F 5 per day 8am-5pm, Sa 4 per day 9:30am-5pm; €2.80); Cork (M-Sa 4 per day 1:15-6:30pm, Su 5 per day 11:15am-6:30pm; €11.30) via Clonakilty (€5.65) and Killarney (10:50am; €14). **Roycroft Cycles,** on Ilen St. off Bridge St., **rents bikes** and can provide an **airport pickup service;** call for details. (☎21235. €12-17 per day, including helmet. Credit card deposit. Open M-W and F-Sa 9:15am-6pm.) Hitchers typically stay on N71 to go east or west but switch to R595 to go south; *Let's Go* doesn't recommend hitchhiking. The **tourist office** is next to the Town Hall on North St. (☎21766. Open July-Aug. M-Sa 9am-7pm, Su 10am-5pm; June M-Sa 9am-6pm; Sept.-May M-F 9am-5pm.) **AIB** has an **ATM,** on Bridge St., as does **Bank of Ireland,** on Market St., in front of the SuperValu on Main St.; **Permanent TSB** on Main St. also has one. (☎21388, 21700, and 21524, respectively.) AIB and Bank of Ireland open M 10am-5pm, Tu and Th-F 10am-4pm, W 10:30am-4pm; **Permanent TSB** open

M-Tu and Th-F 10am-5pm, W 10:30am-5pm.) **West Cork Dry Cleaners** is across from the bus stop on Bridge St. (☎21627. €1 per lb., min. €8. Open M-F 10am-5:30pm, Sa 10am-5pm.) **Cleary's Pharmacy** and **O'Byrne's Pharmacy** are affiliated and sit directly across from each other on Main St. (☎21543 and 21491, respectively; Cleary's after-hours emergencies ☎086 193 6668. Both open M-Sa 9am-6pm.) **Internet** access is free to members in 45min. increments at the **library,** across from the Arts Centre on North St. A one-time membership fee of €2.50 (under 16 free) is required but also provides access to all County Cork libraries. (☎22400. Open M-Sa 10am-5:30pm; Internet access 10am-4:45pm. Slots tend to fill up the day before, so book ahead.) The **Flexible Learning IT Center** has an Internet station filled with computers across the street on the third floor of the Arts Centre building. (☎40297. €0.09 per min. Open M-F 9:30am-1pm and 2-5pm.) The **post office** is on Market St. (☎21144. Open M-F 9am-5:30pm, Sa 9am-1pm.)

⊠⊠ ACCOMMODATIONS AND CAMPING. ⊠**Russagh Mill Hostel and Adventure Centre (IHH) ❷** is brimming with character; hostelers can't help but fall in love with it. From the climbing wall to the tire swings, the generous owners to the enormous amount of hangout space, a stay at the Russagh Mill is a taste of the way life on the road should be. (☎22451; www.russaghmillhostel.com. Wi-Fi available. Check-out 11am. Open Feb.-Nov. Dorms €15; singles €25; doubles €20; family rooms €40.) The sign outside of ⊠**Bridge House ❸,** in the middle of town on Bridge St., proclaims its status as Ireland's most unusual B&B. The friendly proprietress is also an artist, and her trade is evident in quirky bedrooms with unique color schemes and character. She also serves a lavish breakfast. (☎21273. €35 per person.) The **Hideaway Campground ❶,** before the hostel on Castletownshend road, provides space for campers and caravaners and also has a game room, self-service kitchen, and playground. (☎22254. Laundry wash €3; dry €1 per 20min. Showers €1. 2-person tent €17, with car €20; extra adult €6.)

⊠⊠ FOOD AND PUBS. For groceries, **J.J. Field & Co.'s SuperValu,** Main St., has a nice selection as well as a small street cafe that serves a variety of sandwiches for €3. (☎21400. Open M-Tu 8am-7pm, W-F 8am-9pm, Sa 8am-6:30pm, Su 9:30am-6pm.) The pubs don't open until the afternoon, but fear not. **Tipsy Muffin ❶** gets its name from the owner's special baked goods that include a healthy dose of "medicine." Look for the window with the painting of the inebriated pastry on 26 North St. to try a treat touched by Bailey's or Tia Maria. If they've sold out (and they do) or you're abstaining, her chocolate muffins are equally delicious if less mind-altering. (Hot breakfast €6-7. Open daily 9:15am-5:30pm.) **Annie May's ❷,** 11 Bridge St., is Skib's best spot for stew and other Irish staples. (☎22930. Open daily summer 9am-10pm; winter 9am-7pm. Occasional live trad.) When not craving cuisine from the Emerald Isle, get your Greek on at **Yassou ❶,** on the corner of Bridge St. (☎21157. Lunch €7-12; dinner €10-24. Open daily noon-9:30pm.)

The Paragon, Main St., is a spacious, popular pub that hosts nightly music of all types, including trad and live bands, and a weekend disco nightclub. (M live guitarist, Tu trad, Th live band, F-Su disco. Disco cover €10, band cover €15.) **Corner Bar,** on the corner of Bridge and Ilen St., draws a local crowd with trad on Mondays and Saturdays; it also showcases a **singers' club,** which performs traditional Irish vocals on the first Friday of every month. More local flavor can be found at **Kearney's Well,** past the tourist office on North St. Nearby **An Goban Saor** attracts the older locals but in accordance with its name ("Saor" roughly translates to mean "freedom"); it welcomes all types and treats them to music on weekends.

⊠⊠ SIGHTS AND OUTDOOR ACTIVITIES. In the old gasworks building on Upper Bridge St., the **Skibbereen Heritage Centre** introduces visitors to the town's

legacy of want and plenty: the history and devastating effects of the Great Famine are presented in a detailed interactive exhibit. Visitors also get a first taste of
the natural beauty and biological wealth of nearby **Lough Ine** (also spelled Hyne;
see **Baltimore,** p. 265) through a short video and photographic display. (☎40900;
www.skibbheritage.com. Open mid-May to mid-Sept. daily 10am-6pm; mid-Mar.
to mid-May and mid-Sept. to Oct. Tu-Sa 10am-6pm. Last admission 5:15pm. €6,
students and seniors €4.50, children €3, families €14.) **Skibbereen Historical
Walks** offers guided tours through the town with a well-informed dose of history.
(☎087 930 5735. 1½hr. tours leave from Skibbereen Heritage Centre Tu and Sa
6:30pm. €4.50, under 15 €2.) The **West Cork Arts Centre,** North St., rotates exhibits of modern Irish art. (☎22090. Gallery open M-Sa 10am-6pm. Free.) Get wired
into the local arts scene with *Art Beat*, free at the arts center. For a self-guided
tour of the town's major sights, pick up a copy of *The Skibbereen Trail* map
(€1.75) at the tourist office. Included on this tour is the **Abbeystrewery Cemetery,**
where between 8000 and 10,000 Famine victims are buried. **Liss Ard Estate Gardens,** just out of town on the Castletownshend road, comprise nine hectares of
diverse flora created with the intent of promoting creative methods of natural
conservation. (☎086 820 2241. Open Apr.-Oct. M-F 10am-4:30pm; gates close
promptly at 5pm. Free.) Based just 13km from Skib, Jim Kennedy at **❦Atlantic
Sea Kayaking** offers a huge range of kayaking excursions in the region, from
nighttime paddles to half-, full-, and multiple-day jaunts. Consult the website for
a full list of trips—there are even international expeditions. (☎21058 or 086 606
5973; www.atlanticseakayaking.com. Night paddle €45; ½ day paddle €40.)

BALTIMORE (BAILE TAIGH MÓR)   ☎028

The tiny fishing village of Baltimore (pop. 200) has traded its pirates for tourists
and is now also a popular center for aquatic sports and the major point of departure for Sherkin and Cape Clear Island. The recently restored castle *Dún na Sead*
(The Fort of the Jewels), one of nine regional 16th-century castles belonging to the
prolific O'Driscoll clan, overlooks the harbor from the (admittedly small) center of
town. O'Driscolls from near and far congregate here for a weekend every June to
elect a chieftain and stage a family gathering, complete with live music, jammed
pubs, and convivial inebriation. When ancient lineages aren't being toasted, Baltimore keeps itself busy with local artists and vacationers—not to mention the ubiquitous tourists—flocking to enjoy its bright, dramatic seascapes.

🚌 TRANSPORTATION AND PRACTICAL INFORMATION. The main road
from Skibbereen passes along the water before running 2.5km out of town to the
milk bottle-shaped **Beacon,** a clifftop lighthouse that once guided ships between
the mainland and Sherkin Island. Buses run to **Skibbereen** regularly. (M-F 3-5 per
day 8:10am-5:30pm, Sa 4 per day during summer 10am-5:25pm; €3.) **Ferries** to **Cape
Clear** (☎086 346 5110; M-F 8:15, 10:45am, 2pm; W also 4:45pm, F also 8pm; Sa
10:45am and 8pm; Su 11:45am, 2, 5:30pm; €14) and **Sherkin Island** (☎087 244 7828;
5-7 per day; €7, return €10), leave from the pier. The small **Islands Craft Office,** in a
small building along the pier, is run by an artists' collective from Sherkin and Cape
Clear Island and also serves as a **tourist office** with general information about the
area. (☎20441. Summer hours vary depending on the ferry schedule but are
roughly M and W-Su 11am-6pm.) Cotter's Gala, above the pier, sells **stamps.**

🏠 ACCOMMODATIONS. With popular Rolf's Hostel completely converted to
pricier holiday cottages, budget travelers can head up the main road from the
pier to **Top of the Hill Hostel ❶,** for clean, affordable rooms. The general lack of
decor yields to the wide range of channels available on the common room satel-

DEEP SEA POCKETS

If you liked the view of Ireland's spellbinding southern coast from above, wait until you see it from below. With its wealth of aquatic life, proximity to the unique salt-water lake, Lough Ine, and plethora of wrecked ships to turn others' misfortune of long ago into your own viewing pleasure, southern Ireland may be the place to learn how to scuba dive. And there may be no one better to help you in that quest than the exuberant professionals at Aquaventures, Baltimore, Co. Cork.

Aquaventures offers a variety of fun programs for all skill and experience levels, including the 4-5 day Open Water Diver course (€575). That may sound like a lot of quid...but you'll make up for it in squid...and other underwater species you'll see in the process. Afterward, you'll receive an internationally recognized PADI (Professional Association of Diving Instructors) certification, allowing you to use your newly acquired scuba skills anywhere in the world.

However, there's more than enough to explore in Ireland's waters before you move on. Beginners can start out with some light shore dives, eventually working their way up to the challenging but rewarding underwater tour of the famous Fastnet Rock and Lighthouse.

Aquaventures Dive Centre, Baltimore (☎20511; www.aquaventures.ie; info@aquaventures.ie). Call ahead for certification program. completed before visit.

lite TV. Other perks include an outside picnic area, a modern kitchen, and a fireplace. (☎20094; www.topofthehillhostel.ie. Dorms €15.) For the full package (and then some), **The Stone House B&B ❹** is run by the enthusiastic owners of Aquaventures (see **Sights and Outdoor Activities**, p. 267, and **The Big Splurge**, left sidebar). You may think your hostess, Rianne, has had one too many Lucozades, but her energy is both genuine and contagious, and will likely inspire you to take a bite out of life after you've finished her renowned breakfast. (☎20511. Singles €45-60; doubles €70-80.) **Fastnet B&B ❹**, just around the corner from the waterfront, provides spacious rooms with shale stone walls. (☎20515. Singles €45; doubles €60-80. Discounts for children.) **The Old Posthouse B&B ❸**, just across from Fastnet B&B and next door to Algiers Inn, provides ensuite rooms and a large, stone-floored dining room in a building dating back to the 1880s. (☎20155. Singles €40; doubles €66.)

🛋🍽 **FOOD AND PUBS.** Buy provisions for extended island stays at **Cotter's Gala**, on the main road past the circle of pubs facing the harbor. (☎20106. Open June-Aug. daily 8:30am-9pm; Sept.-May daily 9am-7:30pm.) Rolf may have upped the prices of his accommodation, but there is good reason to follow the signs from the top of the main road to his Holiday Cottages. His classy **Cafe Art and Restaurant ❷** still serves his famous (and affordable) salads. Dine in one of the elegant rooms with a plate of fresh greens and a selection from the wine bar on the patio. (☎20289. Open Apr.-Sept. daily 8am-9pm; Oct.-Mar. W-Su 8am-9pm. Sandwiches €4-5; entrees €12-20. Occasional live music.) **La Jolie Brise ❸**, right on the town square overlooking the pier, dishes out tasty pizzas and a good selection of seafood. Even with the generous portions don't skip on their famous chips (€3). The owners put a lot of money and effort into renovating **Jacob's Bar** and **The Waterfront**, which is sure to make the establishments even more popular. (☎20600; www.youenjacob.com. Bar Th-F and Su live music. Pizza and seafood €7-16.50. Kid-friendly. Open daily 8:30am-11pm.) Just around the corner in a little alleyway, **Mews Restaurant ❺** serves a sophisticated but short menu away from the hubbub. (☎20390. Steak €26. Entrees €20-26. Open June-Sept. M-Sa 6-10pm. Cash only.) Join in on the mariners' merriment at **Bushe's Bar** (☎20125; open M-Sa 5-10pm), and cushioned **Algiers Inn** (☎20145; F disco May-June), just around the corner.

◙ ⚐ SIGHTS AND OUTDOOR ACTIVITIES. In the center of town, **◙Dún na Sead** is an intimate and intriguing look into a distinctly modern castle. Now privately owned by a couple who have put six years of labor into restoring its once-derelict stones, the castle abode now displays a small exhibit of O'Driscoll history. The balcony has incredible views of the town and waterfront, and the building itself is a marvel of hardwood floors and soaring beamed ceilings. (☎087 290 3236. Open June-Sept. daily 11am-6pm. €3; under 12 free.) Most of Baltimore's best sights are underwater. Wrecked U-boats, galleons, and other sub-aquatic curiosities await amphibious visitors. To arrange dives or equipment rentals, contact the passionate experts at **Aquaventures,** located next to their Stone House B&B. (Follow signs from main road. ☎20511. ½ day snorkel tour €40, children €30; scuba dives €40 without equipment, full rental €80. See **The Big Splurge,** p. 266 and inquire about other packages and courses.) The views from above water aren't bad either. **Atlantic Boating Service,** in a shack at the bottom of the hill leading to the pier, rents small orkney boats. (☎22145; www.atlanticboat.ie. **Boat rental** €60 per day; life jacket rental €3; wetsuit rental €5.) Or contact **Baltimore Sea Safari** to reserve a spot on one of the many sightseeing trips they offer around the surrounding waters. (☎20753. 1½hr. Sea Safari trip daily 11am and 2pm; €25. 15min. Harbour Thrill Trips €10. 40min. evening adventure trips daily 7pm; €15.) Explorers with wheels can head east to circular **Lough Ine** (sometimes spelled Hyne), Northern Europe's only saltwater lake, where rapids change direction with the tide. The lough, which originally contained fresh water, was transformed by rising sea levels following the last Ice Age. These days Ine is a stomping ground for marine biologists searching for its myriad sub-tropical species. **Walking trails** wind through the woods around the lake and up the slopes. The lake is clearly signposted on the road between Skibbereen and Baltimore, as is the privately owned **Glebe Gardens and Cafe,** which houses 1.8 hectares of plant and flower gardens. After a leisurely amble, visitors can snack on delicious sandwiches (€4.75) and light meals in the outdoor cafe. It also offers romantic evening meals (Th-Sa) and sells a small selection of plants. (☎20232; www.glebegardens.com. Open Easter-Sept. daily 10am-6pm. €4, under 16 free.)

CAPE CLEAR ISLAND ☎028

If you find the dramatic landscape of steep, rugged hills ending in cliffs and laced with stone walls and fences arresting from the water; it only gets better upon closer exploration. Cape Clear may be tiny (pop. 129), but its beautiful scenery keeps the visitors coming back, while a unique history as a seat of the local O'Driscoll clan makes it a place of ancestral affection. Indeed, Cleire (the island's *gaeltacht* and primary name) holds strongly to its Irish roots, relegating English to the seat of the second language and offering opportunities for visiting youngsters to learn the native tongue in the summer (visit www.gaelachas.com for details).

▣ 🛈 TRANSPORTATION AND PRACTICAL INFORMATION. Ferries run to and from **Baltimore.** (☎086 346 5110; www.islandtripper.com. 45min.; departs Cape Clear M-F 9:15, 11:45am, 5:30pm, W also 4pm, Sa 9:15am, 6:15pm, Su 10:30am, 12:30, 4:40, 6:15pm; return €14.) *The Karycraft* takes passengers directly to **Schull.** (☎28138. 45min.; June-Aug. 11:30am, 3:30, 5:30pm; Sept. 5:30pm; €11.50 return.) Life here is leisurely and hours are approximate—don't be surprised if something is not open during its posted hours. For current opening hours and general island information as well as a free map and several brochures, consult the

information office in the Pottery Shop, on the left at the end of the pier. (☎39100. Open daily June-Aug. 11am-1pm and 3-6pm; Sept. 3-5pm.) There are **no banks or ATMs** on the island, but the shop and local pubs do offer a cash back service. The green box trailer on the far side of the pier houses a temporary **library,** including Irish language instruction tapes and books as well as **Internet** access for members. (Open W and F-Sa 2-5pm, Th 2-5pm and 7-9pm. Membership €2.)

⌐ ACCOMMODATIONS. An Óige/HI ❶ is a 10min. walk from the pier; follow the main road to the right outside of pottery shop and the hostel is on your right on the far side of the south harbor. The secluded and refurbished stone building has a kitchen with hot plates, a small, cozy common room, and basic bunks. (☎41968; www.mamut.com/anoigecapeclear. Occasionally closed in winter. Dorms €16.) Up the stairs and opposite Ciarán Danny Mike's (p. 268), the **Cluain Mara B&B ❷** has sunny rooms with harbor views. (☎39153. Singles €40; doubles €60. Self-catering 8-person apartment €550 per wk.) The steep road on the left after the hostel leads to charming **Ard Na Gaoithe ❸**, which houses spacious doubles and family rooms. (☎39160. Rooms €30 per person.) Eco-friendly **Cuas an Uisce Camp-site ❶** is a sloping field right on the secluded south harbor, directly across the water from the hostel. Bear right before colorful Ciarán Danny Mike's; the site is 400m up on the left. (☎39119. Open June-Sept. Showers €1. Limited tent rental €6. Camping €6 per person, under 16 €3.)

⌐⌐ FOOD AND PUBS. The versatile **An Siopa Beag,** on the pier, stocks basic groceries and has a small **coffee dock** that dispenses breakfast, fresh scones and cakes, crepes, sandwiches, and homemade soups and is a Wi-Fi hot spot. Diners can also enjoy "healthy, fresh" full meals outdoors on nice summer days. (☎39099. Internet €3.50 per hr. Entrees €10-16. Open June-Aug. daily 10am-8:30pm; Sept.-May M-Th 11am-6pm.) **Ciarán Danny Mike's ❸** is Ireland's southernmost pub and restaurant. Sunny couple Ciarán and Mary serve delectable soups (€3) and entrees (€10-15) in a homey pub filled with memorabilia from the local O'Driscoll clan. (☎39172.) The same owners spice it up a bit at **Cotter's Cape Clear Bar ❶**, located closer to the pier, with a surprisingly sophisticated menu featuring a variety of tapas. (☎39102. Tapas €3-6. Open daily 11am-9pm.) What Cape Clear's pub scene lacks in quantity it makes up for in stamina; without a resident island *Garda* to regulate after-hours drinking, the fun can roll on as long as people stay—sometimes as late as 3am. **Club Cleire,** just above An Siopa Beag, takes best advantage of this arrangement, filling the isle with music every summer's eve, including live trad on Friday and Saturday nights. (☎39119. Open June-Sept. daily 8pm-late.)

⌐⌐ SIGHTS AND OUTDOOR ACTIVITIES. A steep 25min. hike up the narrow hill to the left past the harbor reaches the Cape Clear **Heritage Centre,** packed with everything from a family tree of the O'Driscolls to a history of local saint *Naomh Ciarán* to a deck chair from the *Lusitania*. (Open June-Aug. M-Sa noon-5pm, Su 2-5pm. Librarian has the key in winter. €3, students and seniors €2, children free.) Just before the center, **Cléire Goats** (☎39126) is home to some of the best-bred furry beasts in Ireland. The small shop sells a long list of goat products including goat burgers, goat sausage, goat's milk garlic cottage cheese, and the popular, creamy **goat's milk ice cream** (€2.50). To see them in action, daily milkings are advertised at 10am and noon. To get even closer, the owners are involved with the WWOOF program which places individuals seeking **work opportunities** on organic farms (see **Beyond Tourism,** p. 79). For exhilarating views of the hills and valleys of the craggy island and of the surrounding oceanscape, the road to the heritage center and the **old lighthouse** at the southeastern corner of Cape Clear make the best vantage points. Though not officially operated as a tourist site, the lighthouse's grounds are open to visitors. Throughout the centuries, the **marriage stones,** on the northeast corner of the island, were visited throughout the centuries by intrepid lovebirds hoping to gain greater fertility. The **bird observatory,** a white farmhouse to the right of the pier, organizes bird watches, primarily for die-hard ornithologists. (☎39181. €14 per night.) Five kilometers off the east shore is **Fastnet Rock Lighthouse,** namesake of the famous Fastnet boat race. Capt. Ciarán O'Driscoll runs "Spirit of the Isles," a boat ride around the lighthouse and back that doubles as a **whale, dolphin, and bird-watching** excursion. (☎39153; or inquire in person at Ciarán Danny Mike's. Summer sailings daily 4pm, returning at 5:30pm. €15; €20 if leaving from Baltimore, where pickup is at 11:30am. Times subject to change, so call ahead.) Swallow a hefty dose of island lore in early September at Cape Clear's annual **International Storytelling Festival** (☎087 971 1223) near the end of August, which features puppet workshops, music sessions, and a weekend of memorable tales by storytellers from Ireland, the British Isles, and the United States.

SHERKIN ISLAND (INIS ARCAIN)   ☎028

Just 10min. across the water from Baltimore, Sherkin Island (pop. 100) lures visitors with its sandy, cliff-enclosed beaches, windswept heaths, overabundance of cows, and lack of people. Today, the island's tiny population swells during the summer with tourists and vacationing locals from the mainland who seek its beautiful beaches. Overland navigation of the island is simple; from the ferry dock the main road passes **Kinnish Harbour** and the **Sherkin Art Exhibition Community Hall,** which hosts summer exhibits. (☎20336. Open July-Aug.; call for specific hours.) To reach Sherkin's best beaches, continue down the main road to the east side of the island and the glorious **Silver Strand.** Nearby lie secluded **Cow Strand** and **Trabawn,** which are smaller and great for swimming. For views from the island's east side, turn left at the signs for **Horseshoe Harbour** and its defunct **lighthouse.** Sherkin is liveliest on the last Sunday of July during the **Sherkin Family Regatta.**

Frequent **Ferries** depart for Baltimore. (☎087 911 7377. 10min.; 10 per day in summer, 5-8 per day in winter; €10 return.) Ferry schedules are posted outside the **Islands Craft Office** in Baltimore (p. 265) and on the back of the Sherkin brochure, which can be found in, among other places, the Islands Craft Office and the Clonakilty tourist office. Ferries also depart less frequently from **Cunnamore,** off the N71. (☎086 888 7799. 1hr., June-Sept. 3-4 per day, €11.50 return.) Fresh air, fresh produce, and perhaps a fresh outlook on life (or at least great views of the harbor) await at **The Horseshoe Cottage ❸.** The passionate owners offer posh massages (€40) and sailing trips, but also cater to the thriftier crowd by allowing camping and discounts for helping out on the farm. (☎20598. Breakfast included. Camping €28. Singles €40; doubles €70-76. Inquire about sailing packages and work opportunities.) **The Islander's Rest ❹,** across the street from the Jolly Roger pub, overlooks Baltimore and has warm-toned bedrooms. It is also home to one of the island's two bars, which serves food daily starting at noon. (☎20116; www.islandersrest.ie. Showers €5. Towels €1. Rooms €45-60 per person.) However, most island-dwellers will head to the legendary **Jolly Roger ❸.** Many an Irishman gets misty-eyed with nostalgia when thinking about the good times they've had in this pub, which serves food daily from noon to 8pm and *craic* until dawn. (☎20379. Lunch €3.50-6.50; entrees €9-20. Impromptu live music.) For **stamps,** ice cream, and the latest news on the island, see the kind Mays O'Reilly in her informally christened **"An Tigin"** (or "little shop") on the main road past the pier and the school. Since the island's one store closed, the craftswoman has stepped in to fill the people's postal needs. She also offers coffee, tea, and pastries for takeaway (☎20009).

SCHULL (AN SCOIL) ☎028

Schull's name, when pronounced correctly ("skull"), may make it sound a little spooky, buts the town's true character better fits its Gaelic translation to "school" as it is a lesson in charm and beauty. An ideal base for forays onto Mizen Head and ferry trips to the nearby Sherkin Islands and Cape Clear, the seaside town of Schull is situated 6.5km west of **Ballydehob**, on R592, off of N71. Schull is a hub of outdoor activities on both land and sea, but its tranquil surroundings are also cause for pause. Be warned that many other travelers are wise to Schull's charms; it's a popular summer mecca, and its flashy new hotel, holiday cottages, and B&Bs draw droves of travelers.

🖃 🖾 TRANSPORTATION AND PRACTICAL INFORMATION. Buses to **Cork** via **Skibbereen** (M-Sa 8:05am, 1:40, 5:50pm, Su 1:55 and 5:50pm; €12.10) and **Goleen** (M-Sa 8:30pm, Su noon and 1:35pm; €3.50) stop next to the AIB on Main St. (☎021 450 8188; www.buseireann.com.) **Ferries** regularly go to **Cape Clear Island** (June-Aug. daily 10:30am, 2:30, 4:30pm; €13 return) and occasionally to other destinations; ask at the pier or in any local business for further details. Pick up the detailed *Visitor's Guide* (€2 suggested donation), complete with suggestions for good walking and cycling tours in the area, at the **library** or in many of the stores along Main St. The library also has **Internet** access in 30min. slots for members but keeps odd hours. (☎28290. Membership €2.50. Open Tu and Th-F 3-6pm, W 10am-noon, Su 11:30am-1:30pm.) **@ Your Leisure,** on Main St., has Internet access and **Newman's West** (see **Food and Pubs,** p. 253) on Main St. is a Wi-Fi hot spot. (☎28600. €2 per 15min., €3 per 30min. Open June-Aug. daily 10am-10pm; Sept.-May M-F 3-8pm, Sa-Su noon-9pm.) **AIB,** at the top of Main St., has a 24hr. **ATM.** (☎28132. Bank open M-F 10am-12:30pm and 1:30-4pm.) There's a **pharmacy** on Main St. (☎28108. Open M-Sa 9:30am-1:15pm and 2:15-6pm.) The **post office** is located on Main St. (☎28110. Open M-F 9am-1pm and 2-5:30pm, Sa 9:30am-1pm and 2-5:30pm.)

🗔 ACCOMMODATIONS. Schull is yet another example of how the true budget accommodation is a dying breed in Ireland, with the Backpacker's Lodge and campsites going the way of the buffalo. Travelers' best source of consolation may be a homecooked meal served up at one of these choice B&Bs. The hardest part about staying at the **Hillside B&B ❸,** up Cooryderrigan from Main St. is deciding if you want sea or mountain views in one of its color-themed rooms (☎28248. Singles €40; ensuite doubles €64-68.) At **Sea View B&B ❸,** just before Hillside, the choice is made for you; every room has a sea view (hence the name). You will have to choose from one of its many scrumptious breakfast menu options, which early risers enjoy in its high-ceilinged breakfast conservatory. (☎28373. Singles €50; doubles €70-80. Discounts in winter.) **Rookery Cottage ❸,** on Air Hill off the left end of Main St., may not have the postcard-worthy views, but it boasts a genuinely kind proprietress, her two adorable dogs, and a fantastic garden. (☎28660. Rooms €35 per person.) For some pure indulgence, take the short walk up Main St. to Culla Rd. and stay at the historic **Grove House ❹.** Now a B&B, this vine-covered manor was once a hotel that catered to the likes of George Bernard Shaw and Jack B. Yeats. You don't have to be famous to enjoy its spacious outdoor patio, elegant rooms, or its (optional) multi-course dinner using only the finest, freshest ingredients—but you do need a bit more cash. (☎28067; www.grovehouseschull.com. Entrees from €30. Suites €50 per person.)

🖸 🖾 FOOD AND PUBS. From the simple fish 'n' chips to the exotic handmade chocolates, Schull's eateries have one thing in common: quality. If you're in a rush, groceries can be purchased at **Eurospar,** which also has an AIB **ATM** inside.

(☎28236. Open July-Sept. M-Sa 8am-9pm, Su 8am-7pm; Oct.-June M-F 8am-7:30pm, Sa 8am-9pm, Su 8am-7pm.) Or, try smaller **Hegarty's Centra,** complete with a Bank of Ireland ATM (☎28520; open daily 7am-10pm), across from Eurospar on Main St. The freshest produce can be found on Sundays at the **Country Market** located on the East End tennis courts. (Open daily 10am-2pm.) Leaving Ireland without sampling the fried deliciousness at the simply named **Fish Shop** ❶ on the pier is a serious error. (☎28599. Glass of wine €2. Fish 'n' chips €8. Open daily during summer noon-10pm.) However, be sure to try the sensational pub grub served in several of Schull's bars. The exemplary **Hackett's Bar** ❶, Main St., recently had the distinction of being named one of the best gastropubs in the UK and Ireland by *The Guardian.* It offers a range of affordable lunches, from a hummus and salad plate (€8) to smoked salmon with gubbeen cheese on brown bread (€8). As the weekend evening hours draw near, it also features live rock bands on Fridays and occasional live music throughout the week. It also boasts a French farmhouse-style restaurant upstairs. (☎28625. Kitchen open daily noon-3pm; dinner F-Sa 7-9pm.) Not to be outdone, the **Bunratty Inn** ❷, at the top of Main St., also serves award-winning pub food all day and has a scenic patio out front. (☎28341.) Perhaps outshined by the two big boys on the block, **The Black Sheep** ❷ is appropriately named but shouldn't be overlooked, with jolly atmosphere and generously portioned classic Irish fare and seafood. July and August bring nightly live music, while the low season still has trad Friday through Sunday night. (☎28022. Catch of the day with mashed potatoes and veggies €12.50.) For an alternative scene, **Newman's West** ❷ features a lengthy cocktail menu and wine list to complement its inventive menu items served late into the night (☎27776. Sandwiches €5. cocktails €8. Open M-Th and Su 10am-11:30pm, F-Sa 10am-12:30am.) If you think you've had enough, don't walk near **Jagoe's** ❶ on Main St. The aroma of her freshly baked chocolate cake is simply irresistible. (☎28028. Breakfast €2-5. Lunch €6-12. Open daily 9:30am-5:30pm.) Or perhaps it's ◙**Gwen's chocolates** next door you smell. Artisans in the truest sense of the word, these chocolatiers let sweet-toothed shoppers watch as they hand-make their little drops of cocoa-heaven. Equally drool-inducing is their ice cream. (☎27853. Open during summer daily 8am-6pm; winter F-Su 10am-5pm.)

◙ ⚑ SIGHTS AND OUTDOOR ACTIVITIES. ◙**Fastnet Marine Outdoor Education Centre,** on Colla Rd. past the pier along the water, is a nationally recognized kayaking, sailing, and windsurfing center; everyone from novices to Olympic athletes train with its instructors. It offers year-round courses in all three activities, but you can only take advantage if you're planning on staying for a few days; classes start at five days in length. It's also extremely busy, so be sure to book far in advance—months ahead for July and August. (☎28515; www.schullsailing.ie. 5-day sailing course €275 per person.) Another option for aquatic fun is **Watersports Centre Ltd.,** on the pier, which rents and sells wetsuits and fishing gear, and offers **kayak** and **sailing courses.** (☎28554. Open June-Oct. M-Sa 9:30am-1pm and 2-5:30pm. Sailing dinghies and motorboats €80 per ½ day. 2½hr. kayak trip €30. 2½hr. sailing course €30.) The **Planetarium,** Colla Rd., delights crowds with summer star shows. (☎28552; www.schullcommunitycollege.com. 45min. shows June-Aug. M and Th 8pm; July-Aug. also W and Sa 4pm. Schedule may vary. €5, seniors and children €3.50.) For **walking trails,** consult the *Visitor's Guide* for a thorough walking map. Or let the horse do most of the work by calling **Ballycummisk Riding School** for a pony-trekking lesson (☎37246.) And in mid-summer, Schull makes its own contribution to the busy West Cork art scene with the annual **Art in Schull** festival, a week of literary workshops, musical performances, and art exhibitions, including a display in nearly every shop on Main St.

MIZEN HEAD AND SHEEP'S HEAD

The serene southwestern tip of Ireland is composed of two narrow peninsulas. Mountainous Sheep's Head, to the north, is the smaller of the two, extending out into the ocean along Bantry Bay. Across Dunmanus Bay to the south, Mizen Head stretches out to the southwest before ending in spectacular craggy cliffs. Both make for excellent day-long cycling trips, but the isolated coves and wild beaches along the coast merit more careful exploration.

GOLEEN, CROOKHAVEN, AND MIZEN HEAD   ☎ 028

The Mizen becomes more scenic and less populated west of Schull, but it's mobbed during July and August when sun-loving vacationers pack the sandy beaches. The most reliable transit is **Betty Johnson's Bus Hire,** which gives tours of the Mizen via the scenic northern coast road. The tour includes bits of local history and runs to the **Mizen Vision** (p. 273). Call Betty for her schedule; she will make a run any day when there are at least eight people interested. (☎28410. About 3hr. €10.) **Bus Éireann** only goes as far as Goleen (2 per day on the Cork-West Cork line; inquire in Schull or Ballydehob for a schedule). **Bantry Rural Transport** offers limited service from Bantry to Goleen and Schull. (☎ 027 52727. Arrives in Goleen Tu and F 10am.) The **night bus** (better known as the "booze bus") leaves Bantry at 7pm and does a four westward loops, servicing Dunbeacon, Lowertown, Toormore, Goleen, Crookhaven, and Barleycove every Thursday through Saturday, making the pub-crawling crowd all the merrier. (Call Michael Collins ☎086 317 4606. €5) **Hitching,** though not recommended by *Let's Go,* is possible in the summer, when hitchers often perch at the crossroads on the Goleen Rd. just outside town. Die-hard **cyclists** can daytrip to Mizen Head from Schull (58km round-trip). Schull currently has no bike rental options; the nearest shops are in Skibbereen or Bantry.

The block-long village of **Goleen** *(Goilín)* is a convenient place to stop for lunch if you're on your way to places in the southwest. **Richie's Take Away ❶** may be short on ambience, but it serves surprisingly delicious burgers, fries, and Indian staples (any Indian or Pakistani dish on request) late into the night for some of the cheapest prices around. Try the vegetable *pakoras* (€4) with mango chutney. (☎35829. Burgers €2.50-4; Kebabs €6-7. Open daily noon-3am.) **The Fastnet ❶** is a roomy pub that serves simple sandwiches (€3) by day and has live music on summer weekends. (☎35877. Kitchen open daily noon-6pm.) If you're staying in Goleen, you might as well do it in style at ⊠**Heron's Cove B&B ❸,** down the hill from Goleen on the water. (☎35225; www.heroncove.ie. All rooms with bath and TV. Single €50-70; double €80.) The elegant **restaurant ❹** downstairs serves delicious seafood, meat, and pasta in a dining room overlooking the small cove. (☎35225. Reservations required Oct.-Apr. Entrees €19-30. Open daily at 7pm. MC/V.)

Tiny **Crookhaven** *(An Cruachan;* pop. 37), about 8km southwest off the Mizen coastal road, is perched at the end of its own peninsula. Once people glimpse Crookhaven's beautiful beaches they naturally want to stay longer; for that, Maureen at **The Galley Cove House ❹,** located a few kilometers before town on the Goleen Rd., is more than happy to oblige. The nautical theme that abounds in the ship on the mantle, the Titanic bell, and the wooden floors and ceilings may be predictable, but the homey touches like fresh flowers in the entryway and an especially friendly welcome are a delightful surprise. (☎35137; www.galleycovehouse.com. Rooms ensuite with TV. Single €45-55; doubles €37-45 per person.) Of course, the seafood chowder (€6) at the **Crookhaven Inn ❷** may be reason enough to stay alone, while its oriental lamb burger (€10) isn't a bad excuse either. (☎35309. Sandwiches €4-12; entrees €10-20. Tu and Th live music. Kitchen open Easter-Oct. daily noon-8pm.) Join half the population at **O'Sullivan's ❷,** which serves sandwiches, soups, and cold pints by the water's edge, and hosts live music up to five times per week from June through August. (☎35319. Kitchen open daily noon-9pm.) The coastal road west from Goleen is a marvel of stone-streaked hills and valleys interrupted by the expanse of **Barley Cove Beach,** a magnet for vacationers whether the sun is out or not. Five kilometers past the beach, Ireland comes to an abrupt end at **Mizen Head,** where cliffs rise 213m above the waves. **Mizen Head Lighthouse,** built in 1909, was recently automated and electrified, and the nearby buildings turned into a museum, the **Mizen Vision,** accessible by a narrow bridge between jagged cliffs. The museum illuminates the solitary lives of lighthouse keepers and their homes and has a windy viewing platform that is the most southwesterly point in Ireland. Although overcast skies may evoke less than positive reactions, they actually create ideal visiting conditions: you can revel in the sight of the tossing sea dissolving into a cloud-wreathed horizon. Return via the Head's 99 steps (or take the ramp) to the new **Visitors Centre,** where you can peruse more exhibits or have a light meal. (☎35115. Open June-Sept. daily 10am-6pm; mid-Mar. to May and Oct. daily 10:30am-5pm; Nov. to mid-Mar. Sa-Su 11am-4pm. €6, students €5, under 12 €3.50, under 5 free.)

BANTRY (BEANNTRAI) ☎027

According to the big *Book of Invasions*, Ireland's first human inhabitants landed just 1.6km from Bantry (p. 68). Later, 17th-century English settlers arrived in the bay and drove the Irish out; in 1796, Wolfe Tone and a band of Irish patriots made an ill-fated attempt to return the favor with the help of the French Armada. These days, the St. Brendan's statue greets all new arrivals with open metallic arms, and charming Bantry makes visitors feel far more welcome than it historically has. Stately Bantry House and its gardens wow visitors, while the authentic pubs scattered throughout its main streets invite them in for a pint. For daytrips out onto the Sheep's Head peninsula or to Whiddy Island, this is the best place to drop anchor for the night.

█ TRANSPORTATION. Buses stop outside Julie's Diner in Wolfe Tone Sq. Bus Éireann heads to **Cork** via **Bandon** (M-Sa 12 per day 7am-6:30pm, Su 4 per day 10:30am-6:30pm; €13.50) and to **Glengarriff** (M-Sa 5 per day, Su 3 per day 11:20am-8:40pm; €3.30). From June to September, buses go to **Killarney** (1 per day, €13). Berehaven Bus Service (☎70007) also stops here on the way to and from **Cork** on Thursdays while Harrington's stops on nearby Ballylicky bridge everyday except Thursday (☎74003, call ahead). **Glengariff Tours** offers half- and full-day guided tours of the Beara Peninsula, the Ring of Kerry, and the Mizen Peninsula, or any other customized tour of Ireland with daily pickup in Bantry and Glengarriff. Call or email for bookings. It also operates a 24hr. cab service, with additional pickup available at Shannon, Cork, and Kerry airports. (☎63060 or 087 973 0741; www.glengarifftours.ie, glengarriffcabs@hotmail.com. From €14 per person.) **Rent bikes** from Nigel's Bicycle Shop on the Glengarriff Rd. (☎52657. €15 per day, discount for 2 or more days; helmet included. ID or credit card deposit. Open June-Aug. M-Sa 10am-6pm; Sept.-May Tu-Sa 10am-5pm.)

█▐ ORIENTATION AND PRACTICAL INFORMATION. Bantry lies at the eastern end of **Bantry Bay,** which forms the western side of the town's epicenter, **Wolfe Tone Square.** At the northeast corner of the square, **Marino Street** extends eastward and then splits into **Old Barrack Road** and **Glengarriff Road.** At the southeast corner, **New Street** also runs east, then becomes **Bridge Street** (which runs up to the library). **Main Street** begins to stretch north where the name change occurs. Sheep's Head lies just southwest of town; the Beara Peninsula is to the northwest. Cars, cyclists, and hitchers stay on N71 to get into or out of Bantry. The **tourist office,** on the east side of Wolfe Tone Sq., has maps of Bantry and Sheep's Head, and a helpful, patient staff. (☎50229. Open July-Aug. daily 9am-6pm; Apr.-June and Sept.-Oct. M-Sa 9:15am-6pm.) **AIB** and **Bank of Ireland,** both of which are on the south side of the square, have 24hr. **ATMs.** (☎50008 and 50377. Both open M 10am-12:30pm and 1:30-5pm, Tu-F 10am-12:30pm and 1:30-4pm.) **Coen's Pharmacy** is one of several in the square. (☎50531. Open M-Sa 9am-6pm.) The **police** *(Garda)* are also on the square (☎50045). **Bantry Laundrette & Dry Cleaning** on Warners Ln., with access from Marino or Barrack St., will keep you smelling fresh (☎55904. €1 per lb., min. €8. Open M-Sa 9am-5pm.) **St. Joseph's Bantry Hospital,** Dromleigh Rd. (☎50133), is 400m past the library. There are several places in town for **Internet** access: on Bridge St., **fast.net Business Services** has a room full of computers in addition to printing and fax services (☎51624; €1 per 10min., €5 per hr.; open M-F 9am-6pm, Sa 10am-5pm); **Organico,** on Glengarriff Rd., is a cafe as well (☎55905; €1 per 15min., €4 per 1hr.; open M-Sa 10am-6pm); while the **library,** at the top of Bridge St., provides free access to its members (€2.50) in 1hr. increments (☎50460; open Tu-W and F-Sa 10am-1pm and 2:30-6pm, Th 10am-6pm). For snail mail, the **post office** is at 2 William St., which branches off the Square's southeast corner next to New St. (☎50041. Open M and W-F 9am-5:30pm, Tu 9:30am-5:30pm, Sa 9am-1pm.)

◪◪ ACCOMMODATIONS AND CAMPING. Coming into town on N71 to the north, be sure not to pass ◪**The Mill B&B ❸** to your right. Its immense lawn, fountain, and gorgeous glass breakfast room are hard to miss. However, these amenities are trumped by the spunky Dutch proprietress, her cooking, and her spotless, spacious rooms adorned with her equally friendly husband's colorful artwork. (☎50278; www.the-mill.net. Ensuite rooms with TV. Car park. Laundry service available. €35 per person.) Closer to town, **The Harbour View Guest House and Hostel ❶,** across the bay from the N71 into town on the road to the beach, offers dirt-cheap rates and attractive bay views. The hostel includes a TV lounge and kitchen facilities while the guest house rate includes breakfast. (☎51140. Car park nearby. 8- to 10-bed dorms €12.50; private €15 per night, €70 per wk.; B&B rooms €30 per person.) The formal, high-ceilinged rooms at **Atlanta Guest House B&B ❸,** Main St., are larger than those of most B&Bs. If you book early enough to stay during the Chamber Music Festival, you may hear the strains of professional performers rehearsing in their rooms or getting together for mini-sessions. (☎50237; www.atlantaguesthouse.com. Singles €40-50; shared rooms €30-35 per person.) For upscale rooms on the square, check out the posh **Bantry Bay Hotel ❹.** With frequent live music during the summer in the ground-floor bar and big, hangover-curing breakfasts the next morning, guests are all taken care of. (☎50062. Singles €45-65; doubles €90-100.) Five kilometers from town, off the Glengarriff Rd. past Ballylickey, family-friendly **Eagle Point Camping and Caravan Park ❶** has a beautiful private beach, tennis courts, several TV rooms, a lounge, and free showers. (☎50630. Open May-Sept. Laundry €6. €10 per person; 2-person tent €23-24.)

◪◪ FOOD AND PUBS. SuperValu, New St., sells groceries. (☎50001. Open M-Th and Sa 8am-8pm, F 8am-9pm, Su 9am-6pm.) Bantry has a wealth of wonderful cafes and fresh food stores. It's difficult to go wrong, but popular ◪**Organico Cafe ❶,** Glengarriff Rd., distinguishes itself with a creative menu, 95% of which is organic and vegetarian, served in an airy loft. The downstairs **shop** sells everything from homemade organic bread (€2.50-5) to organic shampoo. (Cafe ☎55905; shop ☎51391. Soup €6; entrees €8.50. Cafe open M-Sa 10am-6pm; hot food available 11:30pm-3:30pm. Shop open M-Sa 9:30am-6pm. MC/V.) Less hippie, more homey **Floury Hands Cafe and Bakery ❶,** on Main St., delights with delicious toasted sandwiches (€3-5) and dangerously decadent desserts. (☎52590. Specials €5-8. Open M-Sa 8am-5:30pm.) **The Attic ❶**, Bantry's youth cafe located upstairs on 9 Marino St., operates on a "no adult policy," giving teens exclusive access to its air hockey, pool table, and healthy refreshments. (☎56856. Smoothies €2. Ages 14-19. Open Tu-Th 3-6:30pm, F 3-11pm, Sa 6-11pm.) A few pubs happily serve traditional Irish faves alongside your pint. **The Quays ❷** in the square has prices that will leave enough room in your wallet for another round, or their enticing pear and almond flan for €4.50. (☎50900. Lunch €4-10. Dinner €12-22. Kitchen open daily 12:30pm-late.) For yummy in your tummy without much money, follow your nose to **The Brick Oven ❷** in the square. (☎52500. Pizzas €10-18. Open daily noon-9pm.)

Like its food, the entertainment at The Quays is mostly old-fashioned but occasionally hip; their big, lofty bar often holds live music sets on weekends, alternating between trad and pop. **Anchor Bar,** New St. (☎50012), brings in da noise and da occasional funk band on Thursday and every other Saturday. It also kicks off your Sunday morning on the right note with more live music. **The Schooner,** Barrack St. (☎52115), draws a younger crowd with live DJs on Saturdays and Sundays and a more mixed one with live music on Fridays. In the square, **J.J. Crowley's** (☎50029) attracts the ballad-lovers to its popular Wednesday trad, only to be outdone by its Friday *craic*. After the pubs shut down, night owls head to the disco (open June-Aug. F-Su 11:30pm-2:30am; cover €10) in the **Bantry Bay Hotel** (p. 274).

◙ ♫ SIGHTS AND ENTERTAINMENT. Bantry's main tourist attraction lies a 10min. walk from town up a long, shady driveway off the coastal Cork road. **▓Bantry House and Gardens,** a Georgian manor with grounds overlooking the bay, is a visual feast that shouldn't be missed. The house was the former seat of the Earls of Bantry but was later converted into a hospital during Ireland's Civil War and again during the Emergency (neutral Éire's term for WWII). Full admission allows visitors to explore the interior of the elegant house and the manicured rear gardens, which include a fountain ringed by trees and a challenging ascent up the "Stairway to the Sky" that rewards visitors with a view of the bay and manor.

The Earls had to flee when Irish rebel **Theobald Wolfe Tone** harnessed some of France's anti-English sentiment for a nationalist insurrection (p. 53). Learn about Wolfe Tone's naval assault and the 1980s discovery of a French Armada ship in the harbor at the **1796 Bantry French Armada Exhibition Centre,** which occupies the house's former stables. Ironically, Bantry House was the former residence of Richard White, the man who mobilized British resistance to Wolfe Tone's invasion. Enjoy refreshments in a **tea room** in the house. (☎50047; www.bantryhouse.com. House and exhibit open mid-Mar. to Oct. daily 10am-6pm. Garden and exhibit €5. House, exhibit, and gardens €10; students and seniors €8; children free.)

As if a stately mansion wasn't sophisticated enough, Bantry further gussies itself up in mid-summer with back-to-back prestigious arts festivals. Beginning with the renowned **West Cork Chamber Music Festival** during the last week of June, musicians from around the world, including the **RTE Vanburgh String Quartet,** perform in the sanctuary of St. Brendan's Church and the rooms of Bantry House. (☎52788; www.westcorkmusic.ie. Tickets €11-39; daily passes €32-55, full-wk. €225-440; master classes €5.) Immediately following is the equally distinguished **West Cork Literary Festival,** which draws bigger names every year and holds readings and workshops at venues including the Bantry Library. The festival also frequently hosts post-event gatherings at the Organico cafe. (☎61157; www.westcorkliterary-festival.ie. Afternoon sessions €10-30; workshops €150 per 5 days; some readings and discussions free.) Those who prefer rod and reel to pen or piano will be happy to know Bantry is also well known as an excellent **fishing** port. Nearby Lough Boffin is a popular spot and **McCarthy Sports,** in the round tower on Main St., supplies fishing equipment, permit and tackle needs as well as **camping** gear. (☎51133. Permits €12 per day, children €6; €30 per 3wk.; €60 for season.)

SHEEP'S HEAD (MUINTIR BHAIRE) ☎027

Though largely ignored by tourists passing through Skibbereen and Bantry en route to the better publicized peninsulas of Mizen and Beara, Sheep's Head is a spectacular, tour-bus-free alternative. **Walkers** and **cyclists** take advantage of peaceful roads and the well-plotted **Sheep's Head Way**—one of Ireland's most recently marked walking trails. The coastal roads running along the northern and southern edges are markedly different but have their own advantages; the best way of experiencing the peninsula's stark, rugged beauty is to set out west from Bantry and take the northern road, locally called Goat's Path, as it climbs to the highest heights of the jagged hills with an incredible ocean vista to your right. From there, the road into the tiny village of **Kilcrohane** curves sharply down the descent but has an unbroken panorama of the breathtaking valley below. The road back along the southern coast is less scenic, but wider, flatter, and faster.

Sheep's Head is a daytrip by bike from Bantry for the extremely fit (65km), but those who prefer a more leisurely pace will find peaceful lodging at any of the B&Bs speckling the peninsula or at the tiny **Carbery's View Hostel ❶** in Kilcrohane. The hostel is signposted from the western end of town and is situated over the bay. (☎67035. Dorms €14.) Head to **Fitzpatrick's ❶** (☎67057) for a pint, a sandwich (€3), and warm company. If you're staying in Kilcrohane, visit the **post office** and pick up supplies, coffee, or a sandwich at **O'Mahoney's Shop,** on the main road. (☎67001. Open M-Sa 9am-9pm, Su 10:30am-1pm and 7-9pm.)

BEARA PENINSULA

Beara Peninsula's desolate landscape offers haunting treks for the lonely explorer. The tourist mobs circling the nearby Ring of Kerry usually skip the Beara altogether, and therefore miss some of the best views of the Iveragh from across the bay. This is a place for unspoiled scenery and solitude; travelers seeking pubs, people, and other signs of civilization might be happier on Iveragh or Dingle. The spectacular **Caha** and **Slieve Miskish Mountains** march down the center of the peninsula, separating the Beara's rocky south from its lush northern shore. West Beara remains remote—travelers wander treacherous single-track roads along the stark Atlantic coastline, picking their way though mountains, rocky outcrops, and the occasional herd of sheep. The dearth of cars west of Glengarriff makes **cycling** the 200km of the **Beara Way** a joy, but makes hitchhiking almost impossible.

GLENGARRIFF (AN GLEANN GARBH) ☎027

Glengarriff may only be one street long, but its role as the gateway to the Beara Peninsula and its prominence in the wool industry draw hordes of summer touristsr. Most visitors do their shopping and get back on their buses, but anyone with a hint of a green thumb will not want to miss this village's three main attractions.

◪◪ TRANSPORTATION AND PRACTICAL INFORMATION. Bus Éireann stops in front of Casey's Hotel on Main St. Buses run to **Bantry** (25min.; M-Sa 3-4 per day 8am-6pm, Su 3 per day 11:30am-8:15pm; €3.30), **Castletownbere** (45min.; June-Aug. 1-2 per day 11:50am, F 8:40pm; €3.10) via **Adrigole** (30min.), and **Cork** (2½hr.; M-Sa 8am, 2:15, 6pm, Su 1:55 and 6pm; €13.50). From June to mid-September, a bus departs at 11:55am to: Kenmare (45min.), Killarney (1¾hr.), and Tralee (3hr.).

Berehaven Bus Service (☎70007) also serves **Bantry** (M 2 per day, Tu and F-Sa 1 per day; €8), **Castletownbere** (Th-F 1 per day, €6), and **Cork** (2hr., Th 1 per day, €15.)

Glengarriff is graced with two **tourist offices.** A large, **privately run office,** next to Murphy's Village Hostel on the main road just down from the bus stop, has an extremely helpful staff and a good selection of area maps and brochures. (☎63000. Open May-Sept. daily 9:30am-6pm.) The smaller **Bord Fáilte** office is at the end of the main road on the way to Bantry. (☎63084. Open June-Sept. M-Tu and Th-Sa 9:15am-1pm and 2-5pm.) There are several **bureaux de change** (in tourist offices and B&Bs) but **no bank** or **ATM** in Glengarriff, so stock up on cash before visiting. The **post office** is inside O'Shea's Market on Main St. (☎63001. Open M-F 9am-1pm and 2-5:30pm, Sa 9am-1pm.)

⌂ ⛺ ACCOMMODATIONS AND CAMPING. Triumphing over its mere village status, Glengariff offers fantastic accommodations to cater to any budget. Several mid-range B&Bs are scattered throughout but cheaper, comfortable, clean rooms and a spacious 24hr. kitchen with patio deck await at cozy **Murphy's Village Hostel ❶**, in the middle of town above the Village Kitchen. (☎63555. Laundry €8. Dorms €15; doubles €40.) Just across the street, but at the other end of the price spectrum, the newly re-vamped and re-christened **Glengariff Park Hotel ❺** has a nice, central location, while the satellite TV, room service and a luxurious spa let guests feel worlds away. (☎63000; www.glengarriffpark.com. July-Aug. €69-79 per person; June-Apr. €49-59 per person.) Two excellent **campsites** are neighbors on the Castletownbere road 2.5km from town and offer very different experiences. Those lookin' for *craic* before closing the flap should head a little farther down for the turn-off to **Dowling's ❶** to get their fix; their huge on-site bar and lounge welcomes all to their regular trad sessions, occasionally featuring campers as performers. (☎63154. Open Apr.-Oct. €8 per person, €20-23 per unit for 2 adults). In contrast, quiet **O'Shea's ❶**, to the right, boasts lush, well-manicured lawns with high hedgerows for privacy. (☎63140. Open mid-Mar. to Oct.; €7 per person.)

◨ ⛾ FOOD AND PUBS. O'Shea's Market sells groceries on Main St. (☎63346. Open M-Sa 8am-9pm, Su 9am-7pm.) Glengarriff doesn't have many affordable dining options, but several cafes and pubs provide a decent bite to eat. Across from the Queen Harbour Ferry dock on the Bantry road isn't just any old cafe. The owners of **The Old Church Cafe ❷** live on-site and have transformed the tiny chapel into a unique eatery. Parents enjoy the popular goat cheese salad with rhubarb compote (€11.50) with a glass of wine (€4) on outdoor picnic tables while watching their kids attempt kayaking in the bay below (☎63663. Entrees €11-15. Open Mar.-Oct. daily noon-5pm.) **The Village Kitchen ❷**, attached to Murphy's Hostel, serves all-day breakfasts, pancakes, pastries, and hot and cold sandwiches. Their banana and chocolate muffins (€3) are a crowd fave. (☎63555. *Panini* and quiche €5.50. Open Apr.-Oct. 9am-6pm.) **The Hawthorn Bar ❷**, on the Kenmare-Castletownbere end of the main road, serves fresh and delicious daily specials at especially low prices (€11) and showcases live music during summer every night except Tuesday. (☎63625. Entrees €9-16. Kitchen open daily 11am-9:30pm.) **The Blue Pool Bistro and Bar ❷**, connected to the Glengariff Park Hotel, has a more modern feel and menu, but keeps its music traditional every Tuesday through Saturday. (☎63000. Entrees €11-28. Open M-Sa 10:30am-1am, Su carvery 12:30-5pm.) The **Blue Loo Lounge,** at the end of the main road near the Kenmare and Castletownbere turn-offs, is the place to go for a pint and lively company. It too has frequent live music, with a mix of everything Sunday nights. Two connected pubs next door, **Harrington's** and **The Maple Leaf** (☎63021), host live music virtually every night of the week; Harrington's is more trad-oriented, while the Maple Leaf often has DJs on weekends who put the rock in the rocky waterfall in the pub's beer garden.

🖻 🗻 SIGHTS AND OUTDOOR ACTIVITIES. Lush, calm **Glengarriff National Nature Reserve and Ancient Oak Forest** has a number of light walks that make for a beautiful morning or afternoon excursion. The short but steep hike up to **Lady Bantry's Lookout** is a popular walk with a stunning panoramic view of Glengarriff Harbor to the south and the woodland glens bordered by the Caha Mountains to the north. (1km; 30min. return from the park's entrance.) Other pleasant walks include the largely flat **Big Meadow Walk** (3km; 1½hr.), which takes you around a grassland of anthills, oaks, and wildflowers, and the shorter, self-explanatory **Waterfall Walk** (500m; 15min.). *Walking Trails in Glengarriff Woods Nature Reserve* (€0.40), available at the tourist office and in the leaflet box in the reserve's main car park, outlines all of the walks in the park. For those with a good pair of boots and a yearning for hilly thrills, there are more detailed *Ordnance Survey* maps (€8) available at both tourist offices. The **Magannagan Way,** the local segment of the peninsula-long Beara Way, travels through woodlands and bogs to the foot of 574m **Sugarloaf Mountain.** Named for its resemblance to old-fashioned conical sugar lumps, the Sugarloaf is one of three peaks, including Hungry Hill and Slieve Miskish, that form the skeleton of the craggy Caha Mountain range. Although there are no official paths up the mountain and the area around its base is privately owned, hikers climb to the summit to relish its breathtaking views of the Caha Mountains, more distant peaks of the Iveragh peninsula, and islands floating in Bantry Bay. For more information about Magannagan Way and Sugarloaf Mountain, inquire at the tourist office or the nature reserve.

Glengariff is well known as a picnicker's paradise. Perhaps the best spot is **Garinish Island** (known locally as *Ilnacullin*, or "island of holly"), a 15-hectare islet oasis in Glengarriff Harbour. When English financier Annan Bryce acquired the island from the War Office in 1900, it was just a rocky outcrop inhabited by a thriving community of gorse bushes. But a million hours of labor and countless boatloads of topsoil later, Bryce saw his dreams of a fairyland for his family come true in the form of an elaborately designed exotic garden (plans for a mansion were never realized). Bryce's diplomat son bequeathed their blooming island to the Irish people in 1953, and it has been considered a national treasure ever since. Areas named "Happy Valley" and "The Jungle" further furnish fantastical notions, but the garden's lush and diverse flora are only the icing on the cake; sites such as an **Italian Garden** and **walled garden** are augmented by a **Grecian temple** and the 1805 **Martello tower.** (☎63040. Open July-Aug. M-Sa 9:30am-6:30pm; June M-Sa 10am-6:30pm, Su 11am-6:30pm; May and Sept. M-Sa 10am-6:30pm, Su noon-6:30pm; Apr. M-Sa 10am-6:30pm, Su 1-6:30pm; Mar. and Oct. M-Sa 10am-4:30pm, Su 1-5pm. Last admission 30min. before closing. Guidebook €2. €3.70, students and children €1.30, seniors €2.60, families €8.70.) Three separate boat services run to the island. **Blue Pool Ferry** leaves from the pier in town, next to the Village Kitchen and Murphy's Village Hostel. (☎63333 or 63555; €10 return; boats depart every 20min. daily 10am-6pm), while **Harbour Queen Ferry** leaves from the pier across from the Eccles Hotel (☎63116; every 20min. daily 9:30am-6pm; €12 return, students €10) and smaller **Ellen's Rock Boat Trips** depart from near the campsites (☎63110. €10). The sunbathing **seals** are easy to spot, looking far less dignified than gorgeous actress Maureen O'Hara's white chimney-house in the distance.

Next, enjoy an Asian-inspired picnic by the sea or under the gazebo at the **Glengariff Bamboo Park.** The French Thibault family was eager to give the famous Bambouseraie in France a little sister here in Ireland. Head to Bantry from Glengariff on the N71 and watch for signs and bamboo fences. Visitors wander through 13 acres of thoroughly un-Irish vegetation, trying to spot the 30 different species of bamboo and 12 distinct varieties of palm trees. (☎63570 or 63975; www.bamboo-park.com. Open daily 9am-7pm; Dec.-Feb. closes at dusk. Hours contingent upon weather. €5, seniors €4, students €3, disabled €1, children free.)

Capping off the Lewis Carrollesque picnicking tour is **The Ewe Gallery and Sculpture Garden.** This interactive and extremely unique garden is the open home of artist Sheena Wood and her writer husband, Kurt Lyndorff. Giant snails and ill-proportioned pink men beckon visitors into this playground for the imagination. The colorful invitation is hard to resist. (☎ 63840; www.theewe.com. Open daily 10am-6pm, closed during winter. €3.50.)

Even with all its hoopla about gorgeous landscapes, Glengariff has much to offer the watersportsmen as well. The many lakes and inlets around Glengarriff provide wonderful spots to fish. Nearby, **Barley Lake** and **Glasslough Lake** are unstocked and can be fished without a permit. **Upper and Lower Lough Avaul** are well stocked with trout, but require a permit. (Permits available at the Cottage Bar and the Maple Leaf Pub. One-day permit €12, children €6; 3-week permit €30; seasonal permit June-Aug. €60.) For more specific info about good spots to cast your line, pick up the pamphlet *Fishing in Glengarriff* (€0.10) at the privately owned tourist office. You can also ask about locations at the piers or call the regional Fisheries Board (☎ 0264 1221). Additionally, **Glengarriff Harbour** is a prime location for kayaking trips. For half-day (€45) or full-day (€80) excursions, contact **Sea Kayaking West Cork** (☎ 70962; www.seakayakingwestcork.com).

THE HEALY PASS

Former Governor General of Ireland and Co. Cork native Tim Healy advocated for the completion of the road from Adrigole to Lauragh that had been started, but never finished, as a Famine-relief project in 1847. After his death in 1931, the government christened it in his name. R574 winds up between some of the highest peaks in the **Caha Mountains,** connecting the two tiny towns of Adrigole and Lauragh over the border between counties Cork and Kerry. Since the roads are narrow, steep, long, and winding, the pass is best explored by car. To enjoy the full effect of the breathtaking views, travel from south to north: the road loops through a rocky, gently sloping meadow populated by sheep, and then becomes increasingly steep as it ascends the valley wall. At the top, **Don's Mountain Cabin** perches on the Cork/Kerry border. The owners stock a great selection of local-interest books in addition to sweaters, knickknacks, and the essentials, like ice cream, candy, and drinks. (Open daily 10am-6pm, depending on the weather.) Forty-five meters beyond, the rocky mountain curtain opens onto the green sweep of Co. Kerry, nearby Glenmore Lake, and the distant mountains of the Iveragh Peninsula. This is also the last parking and viewing spot before the ride down to Lauragh, which is steeper and more harrowing than the County Cork side of the Pass; go slowly and watch the road instead of the arresting scenery. The challenge of **biking** the pass intimidates all but the most experienced cyclists. Some hitchers, on the other hand, judge the panoramic payoff to be worth the long wait for a lift. *Let's Go* does not recommend hitchhiking.

ADRIGOLE (EADARGOIL)   ☎ 027

Before taking the pass north to Lauragh, many travelers spend a night in Adrigole. The tiny village doesn't have a downtown; instead, restaurants and accommodations are scattered along the Glengarriff-Castletownbere road. **Peg's Shop,** just before the Healy Pass turn-off coming from Castletownbere, has groceries and supplies including **stamps.** (☎ 60007. Open M-F and Su 8:30am-8pm, Sa 9am-9:30pm. AmEx/MC/V.) The spacious dorms and extensive facilities at the **Hungry Hill Lodge ❶,** along the Castletownbere road beyond the Healy Pass turn-off, make Adrigole a good base for outdoor expeditions. After your adventure, relax in the attached **coffee shop ❶** and **pub.** (☎ 60228; www.hungryhilllodge.com. Diving compressor available. Laundry €4. Dorms €17 for the 1st night, each additional night

€15. Doubles €35; family rooms €50. **Camping** €8 for 1 person, €15 for 2.) Thrill seekers can attempt to tackle 685m **Hungry Hill**, where a mountaintop lake overflows on rainy days to create Ireland's tallest **waterfall**. After conquering the mountain, take on the sea; the **West Cork Sailing Centre** rents kayaks and offers weeklong sailing courses. (☎60132; www.westcorksailing.com. Open year-round. Kayak rental €10 per hr. 1-wk. sailing course €410.)

CASTLETOWNBERE (BAILE CHAISLEAIN BHEARRA) ☎027

As one of Ireland's largest fishing ports and the biggest town on the Beara Peninsula, Castletownbere attracts both commercial rigs from as far as Spain and cyclists en route to points west and north. With energetic, authentic pubs and phenomenal seafood restaurants sure to revitalize trekkers, the town serves as a good base for daytrips out to its cross-harbor neighbor, Bere Island.

⊑ TRANSPORTATION. Bus Éireann offers year-round service to **Cork** via **Glengarriff** (3hr.; M, W, F June-Aug. daily; €15.50) and a summer route between **Castletownbere** and **Killarney** (M-Sa 11am and 5:40pm, €14.10) via **Kenmare,** where it's necessary to change buses. Two **minibuses** operate between **Cork** and **Castletownbere** via **Bantry** and **Glengarriff;** they will take interested groups on tours of the **Beara.** For reservations, call **Harrington's** (☎74003; departs outside SuperValu M-W and F-Sa 8am, Su 5pm; departs Cork from the bus station M-W and F-Sa 6pm, Su 7:30pm), or **O'Donoghue's Berehaven** (☎70007; departs from the square Th 7:30am, departs Cork from the bus station Th 6pm). **SuperValu,** on Main St. across from the pier, **rents bikes.** Reservations recommended. (☎74898; denvercal@oceanfree.net. €12.50 per day. Open for rentals daily 9am-9pm.)

⊒⊓ ORIENTATION AND PRACTICAL INFORMATION. Castletownbere centers on **Main Street** and the small square halfway down its length. The molehill-size **tourist office** sits just inside the Church grounds past the square on the Allihies road. (☎70054. Open June-Sept. M-Sa 9am-5pm.) **SuperValu** and the **AIB** across the square have the only **ATMs** on the peninsula. (AIB ☎70015. Open M 10am-5pm, Tu and Th-F 10am-4pm, W 10:30am-4pm.) For **laundry,** head to **O'Shea's Launderette** on Main St. near SuperValu. (☎70994. €8 per load. Open M-F 9am-6pm, Sa 9:30am-6pm.) The **police** *(Garda),* toward the end of Main St., can be reached at ☎70002. Neighboring **Beara Computers** (☎71040; open M-Sa 10am-9pm) and **Beara Action** (☎70880; open M-F 9:30am-5:30pm), across from Main St. on the square, both provide Internet access at the rate of €1 per 15min. The **library,** on Main St. next to the Collins butcher shop, offers free Internet access for members but has limited hours. (☎70233. Membership €2.50. Open Tu 6-8pm, W 2-6pm, Th 11am-1:30pm, F 10:30am-1pm and 3-6pm, Sa 10am-1pm.) The **post office** is on Main St. (☎70001. Open M-F 9am-2pm and 3-5:30pm, Sa 9am-1pm.)

⋔ ACCOMMODATIONS. The views at the **Garranes Farmhouse Hostel (IHH) ❶,** perched on a cliff 10km (€12-15 cab ride) west of town on the Allihies road, might literally be breathtaking. Not to worry, the equally tranquil Buddhist Centre located conveniently next door (see **Sights,** p. 281) teaches techniques to get it back. The hostel also has **volunteer opportunities** available: 6hr. per day in exchange for room and board. Call ahead as vacancies may be hard to come by, especially during the center's monthly retreats. (☎73032. Laundry €5. Dorms €15; family rooms €40. Cottages available for weekly rental.) In town, **Ocean View Lodge ❶,** in the pink building on the far corner of the square, is a quiet hostel with excellent kitchen facilities, a common room with TV, and spacious rooms. (☎71693; info@bearahostel.com. Wheelchair-accessible. Dorms €20; singles €25; doubles and family rooms €20 per person. Discounts for longer stays.) **Harbour Lodge Hostel ❶**, located behind the church in a former convent (up the church's front steps and through the gate to the right), provides decent if spare rooms and a self-catering kitchen. (☎71043. Wheelchair-accessible. Laundry €7. Rooms €18 per person.)

🛒🍴 **FOOD AND PUBS. SuperValu,** on the Adrigole end of Main St. across from the harbor, is the biggest grocery store in town. (☎70020. Open M-Sa 8am-9pm, Su 9am-9pm.) A smaller **Spar,** on Main St. at the square, sells groceries as well. (☎70057. Open M-F 7:30am-1pm, Sa 8am-10pm, Su 9am-10pm.) 🍴**Breen's Lobster Bar ❸**, the Square, is equally friendly and serves filling meals and great soups. (☎70031. Main menu only served June-Aug. noon-6:30pm.) A friendly German cooking French pancakes in a small Irish town proves to be a unique but success-ful combo; so are his Nutella and Bailey's (€3.20) and Irish coffee (€3.30) crepes. If the popular cook hasn't moved on, find his **Creperie ❶** stand in the square for weekend evening meals or snacks. (Sweet and savory crepes €2-4. Open F 4pm-1:30am, Sa 1pm-3:30am, Su 4pm-midnight.) A few doors down, **The Copper Kettle ❶**, also on the square, is a charming cafe offering a superior selection of sand-wiches, salads, and far too tempting treats. (☎71792. Sandwiches from €3.40; sal-ads €5-9. Open M-Sa 10am-5pm.) **Jack Patrick's ❷** serves standard Irish fare and gets its meat fresh from the butcher next door. (☎70319. Lunches €7-11; entrees from €9. Open M-Sa 10am-9pm; June-Sept. also Su 1-9pm.) The less epicurean **Cronin's Hideaway ❷** serves fish, chips, and burgers in its takeaway joint and class-ier Irish food in its restaurant next door. (☎70386. Takeaway €2-7. Restaurant entrees €7-11. Takeaway open M-Th and Su 5:30pm-midnight, F-Sa 5:30am-1am. Restaurant open M-Sa 5:30pm-9pm, Su 4pm-9pm. Closed W in winter.) When the boats are in, fishermen and landlubbers alike head to the pubs. The front of **McCarthy's,** on the corner of the square, might look familiar; it was featured on the cover of a popular Pete McCarthy novel. The pub offers everything from a light lunch to groceries, along with great *craic*. (☎70014. *Panini* and wraps €3-7. Kitchen open 11am-5pm. Trad and ballads June-Sept. 4-5 nights per wk., Oct.-May. weekends.) **O'Donoghue's** (☎70007), the square, lures a mixed crowd of tourists and locals with sunny (or starry) outdoor tables and live bands on occasional summer Fridays. Live music on Fridays and Saturdays keeps feet tapping at **Twomey's Ivy Bar** (☎70114), Main St., past the square on the way to Allihies.

📷📷 **SIGHTS AND OUTDOOR ACTIVITIES.** Three kilometers southwest of Castletownbere on the Allihies road rest the ruins of **Dunboy Castle,** which has the distinction of being the inspiration for not one, but two, novels (Froude's *The Two Chiefs of Dunboy* and du Maurier's *Hungry Hill*). After extensive renovations, the castle has become the latest five-star hotel, taking "the royal treatment" to a quite literal level (www.dunboycastle.com). Four hundred meters down the road past the mansion, the 14th-century fortress, **O'Sullivan Bere,** is in worse shape. The original owner accidentally blew up the fort in 1594 and English armies finished the job eight years later. Today, only two sides of the castle and its low outer wall remain, but their grassy tops and panoramic view of the bay evoke a haunting beauty. A small detour off the Allihies Rd., bearing right at the fork on the way out of town, leads to a cluster of ancient structures representative of ones common to the area. The first is a **stone circle,** at Derrintaggart West, where 12 of the original 15 stones still stand. At Teernahillane, about 1.5km farther along, lies a raised **ring fort** 27m in diameter and 1.8m high. A 800m hike up the hill leads to a **wedge tomb.**

Castletownbere's seat at the foot of **Hungry Hill** (685m) makes it a fine base for daytrips up the mountain. (Ask at the tourist office; see **Adrigole,** p. 280.) For those who prefer to while away in the harbor, Frank Conroy at **Sea Kayaking West Cork** has a base here and in Glengariff (see **Glengariff,** p. 276.) 10km west of town, adjoining the Garranes Farm Hostel, perches the **Dzogchen Beara Tibetan Buddhist Retreat Centre** (☎73032; www.dzogchenbeara.org). As the international center of the Rigpa (Tibetan for "intelligence" or "awareness") tradition, Dzogchen Beara welcomes students for retreats lasting anywhere from two weeks to one year and also offers a daily program with meditation and compassion exercises. The view from the meditation room is inspiring. (Meditation class daily 9:45-10:30am, Loving kindness class M-F 3-4pm. Fees by donation. Call ahead to confirm.)

▶ DAYTRIPS FROM CASTLETOWNBERE. A 15min. ferry ride across the harbor to tranquil and picturesque **Bere Island** (pop. 222) makes for a lovely daytrip. In addition to its beautiful scenery, the island has more quirky sights, from the Irish reserve army barracks lining the northeastern coast (explaining that camo-clad company on the ferry over) to the rusty, abandoned vehicles on the roadsides. (Until recently there was no junk-metal service to transport old autos to the mainland.) Across the harbor from Rerrin, the masts of a fishing ship jut from the sea; the ship burned in 1982 under mysterious circumstances after her owner ran out of money to pay the crew. The abandonment issues apparently don't too run deep, however; the British government wouldn't hand the island back until 1938, 17 years after Ireland gained its independence. The best option for a long-term stay is located almost directly off the Murphy Ferry at the sparkling ▣**Lawrence Cove Lodge ❶,** where a cozy living room with a hearth and TV, bright ensuite rooms, and enthusiastic, friendly owners will make you feel right at home. (☎75988; www.bereislandlodge.com. Wheelchair-accessible. Breakfast €7. Laundry €9. Apr.-Sept. dorms €20; private rooms €22-30; large family rooms €90; group rate €18 per person.) **Martello View B&B ❸,** a 10 min. walk from the village following the signs to the left, is a superb choice for a short stay. Its spacious, pristine rooms contrast the awesome ancient towers they overlook. (☎75052 or 086 198 1541. Singles €40-45; doubles €35-40 per person.) The island also offers a variety of great accommodations for larger groups and longer stays. In addition to their B&B, Martello View rents a smaller cottage with kitchen and TV room where up to five people can comfortably crash. (€350-400 per wk.) **Barry Hanley's Bere Island Holiday Homes ❶** hooks you and eight lucky friends up in style with amenities such as a widescreen TV with DVD player, a modern kitchen, and outdoor barbecue. (☎086 884 5709 or 021 437 2531; www.bereislandholidayhomes.com. €300-700 per wk.; €180-200 per weekend; €200-300 midweek 3 nights.) Finally, **The Admiral's House ❷** has transformed itself from a hostel into a deluxe self-catering complex big enough to fit 18 people, accommodating even the largest Irish families. (☎75213; www.visitbereisland.com. Sept.-June €600-900 per wk.; July-Aug. €1500 per wk.)

There is a small **shop** across from the hostel which stocks groceries and also houses a post office. (Shop ☎75004, post office ☎75001. Shop open June-Aug. M-Sa 9am-9:30pm, Su noon-9:30pm; Sept.-May M-Sa 9am-6pm, Su noon-3pm. Post office open M-F 9am-1:30pm and 2:30-5:30pm, Sa 9am-1pm.) Meet the locals next door at **Desmond O'Sullivan's** (☎027 75192) over a pint. Nearby Kitty Murphy's Cafe is shutting her doors but another restaurant will likely open them again. In the meantime, proper meals, a plasma TV, and a pool table attract those to the western side of the island, near the Bere Island Ferry pier, to **The Lookout Cafe ❶.** (☎75999. Entrees €5-18. Takeaway available. Open daily 9:30am-9pm.) Outside the village, a number of attractions make short or long jaunts around the island tempting, including an ancient wedge tomb just outside of Rerrin, a standing stone that marks the central axis of the island, and four Martello towers dotting the coastline.

Beach bums and vacationers make their sunny-weather pilgrimages to Cloughland Beach, directly south of the village. Connecting many of the major sites of Bere Island is the Beara Way; many hikers find it convenient to take one of the ferries to either the eastern or western end of the island, then take the other one back. Be sure to plan ahead, however, as the 6 mi. trek takes time; those wishing to see the whole island more quickly should consider the well-marked cycling route. *(Murphy's Ferry Service leaves from the dock 5km east of Castletownbere off the Glengarriff road and lands in the island's "center" at Rerrin. ☎75014 or 087 238 6095; www.murphysferry.com. 20min.; June-Aug. 8 per day 7:30am-8:30pm, Sept.-May 4 per day 7:30am-8:30pm; return €6, children free; car and 2 passengers return €20; each additional passenger €5. Bere Island Ferry leaves from the center of Castletownbere and lands on the western end of the island, near the walking paths, many of the ruins, and the cafe. ☎027 75009; www.bereislandferries.com. June-Sept. M-Sa 7 per day 8:30am-8:30pm, Su 5 per day noon-8pm; call for winter schedule; return €7, return with car €25. Phone ahead during low season.)*

DURSEY ISLAND. A copy of the 91st Psalm adorns the wall of the cable car out to Dursey Island—passengers may want to be reassured that "You have made the Lord your defender, the most High your protector" as they dangle above the Atlantic. While peering down to the ocean as the snug wooden compartment whistles in the wind may be the most thrilling aspect of the trip, the land brings rewards of its own—its roads and trails are part of the Beara Way. The English army laid waste to Dursey Fort in 1602, but only after raiding the unarmed garrison and tossing soldiers over the cliffs to their doom. Today, the western tip has exhilarating views over sea cliffs and a chance to observe the island's flocks of migrant birds, who have the edge in numbers over Dursey's seven human residents. **Windy Point House ❷**, near the base of the cable car on the mainland, treats guests to luxurious ensuite rooms, evening meals, and stunning views of Dursey Sound. (☎73017. Singles €50; doubles €35 per person.) Camping is permitted on the island. *(Just off the tip of the Beara, accessible by Ireland's only cable car. The cables begin 8km out from Allihies, off the Castletownbere road. Due to the weight limit, capacity is limited to 6 persons; islanders, animals, and cargo get priority over tourists. 10min.; M-Sa 9-10:30am, 2:30-4:30pm, 7-7:30pm; Su 9-10am, 1-1:30pm, 4-4:30pm, 7-7:30pm. €4, children €1.)*

NORTHERN BEARA PENINSULA

Past Castletownbere, the Beara Peninsula stretches out into the Atlantic, while the landscape becomes rocky and rugged, but sojourners find fulfillment in the lonely beauty of the cliff-lined coast and distant villages. Despite steep hills and strong winds, **biking** is a beautiful, if occasionally terrifying, way to tour the area; the road hugs the coastline for most of its route. The adventurer can take to the hills along the **Beara Way.** The barren beauty of the Beara cannot be fully experienced from behind a windshield, but motoring around the peninsula does have its benefits.

ALLIHIES (NA HAILICNI) ☎027

Set between the Slieve Miskish Mountains and the sea, Allihies's abandoned cottages nearly outnumber its inhabitants. Fenced-off mine shafts, empty buildings, and a carved-up hillside testify that this was once a booming copper-mining town. The vibrantly colored facades form a charming cluster of civilization resting between the towering crags of the neighboring Slieve Miskish Mountains and the rolling waves of the Atlantic. Allihies's economy now stems from a different source: its arresting scenery has been the setting for several films, and its location along the Beara Way makes it a popular tourist stop. It's also home to two pristine beaches, **Ballydonegan Strand** and **Garinish Strand,** which lie a few kilometers down the road toward Dursey; follow the signs to the right at the fork. At the turn-off to Dursey, look for the largest **wedge tomb** on the Beara peninsula—it consists of two sidestones and a single capstone. The road to the Dursey cable car, off the Castletownbere road, passes the crumbling but still impressive **Lehanmore Ring Fort.**

The newly renovated ⊠**Village Hostel (IHH)** ❶, next to O'Neill's pub on the main street, pleasantly blends the simple life (no TV) with modern style in its roomy common areas and outdoor barbecue. (☎73107; www.allihieshostel.net. Laundry available. Open May-Oct. Dorms €16-18; doubles €45-50; family rooms €55-65.) If you're in search of a place with a few more amenities and an even better location, **The Sea View House** ❸ is true to its name. (☎73004; www.seaviewallihies.com. Singles €40; doubles €75.) Allihies's three pubs cater mostly to locals, but they guarantee a good time for all. **O'Neill's** ❷ hosts trad and ballads on Wednesdays and weekends; it's also the best bet for a meal, even for vegetarians. (☎73008. Sandwiches €3-10; entrees from €9. Bar menu served noon-9pm, restaurant menu Th-Sa 6pm-9pm, Su lunch noon-3:30pm.) Just next door, **The Lighthouse** (☎73937) has folk on Saturdays during the summer. **Jimmy's,** a.k.a. The Oak Bar (☎73110), is a few doors down and holds occasional music sessions.

EYERIES AND ARDGROOM ☎027

The road north from Allihies climbs through stone-streaked hills adorned with tufts of green and culminates in the even tinier village of **Eyeries** *(Na Haorai)*. In the uppermost reaches of the pass, where sheep wander freely, look for the **Mass Rock,** which was once used as a secret altar by persecuted Catholics. The stretch between Eyeries and Ardgroom is home to several notable sights; at **Ballycrovane,** the tallest ogham stone in Europe rises majestically on a hill above the coastline. It lies on a well-signposted route off of the main road beyond the northern end of town; it's also on private property, and the owners charge a €2 toll (children free). According to legend, the **Hag of Beara,** a natural rock formation in nearby Kilcatherine, is actually the petrified remains of an ancient woman. In the 18th-century ruins nearby, an unusual stone carving of a cat's head adorns the entrance.

In summer, Bus Éireann runs **buses** between **Castletownbere** and **Kenmare,** stopping in Eyeries and Ardgroom twice daily in each direction. The **Urhan Hostel** ❶ lies 5km before Eyeries on the main road from Allihies and possibly has the lowest rates for a private room on the island. Its adjoining **post office** and **general store** are added bonuses. (☎74005. Store open M-Sa 9am-6pm. Dorms €12; private rooms €15. **Camping** allowed.) The **Urhan Inn Pub** (☎74288), just down the road, provides pints and pool tables. Within the village itself, food options are limited. **O'Sullivan's** has groceries on the main street. (☎74016. Open daily 8:30am-9pm.) **Causkey's** (☎74161) hosts year-round trad on Sundays and more spontaneously other nights. The huge picture window in the back, unusual decor for a pub, offers an amazing view of the ocean. **O'Shea's** (☎74025) entertains locals with occasional trad.

For a divine meal and lively *craic,* head down the road to the village of **Ardgroom** *(Dha Dhrom)*. Friendly owners and ensuite rooms greet you at **O'Brien's B&B** ❷. (☎74019. Open May-Sept. Singles €25; doubles €50.) ⊠**The Village Inn Bar and Restaurant** ❷, next door, will be busy; its fresh seafood and meat dishes are delicious and cheap. (☎74067. Lunch €3-8; dinner from €10-24. Kitchen open daily noon-4:30pm and Tu-Su 6-8pm.) Down the street at the gas station, **Harrington's General Store** stocks provisions and serves tea, coffee, and sandwiches. (☎74003. Open M-Sa 7:30am-9:30pm, Su 9am-9:30pm.) **The Holly Bar** (☎74433), a few doors down from The Village Inn, buzzes with locals and often hosts ballads and trad on weekends.

COUNTIES LIMERICK AND KERRY

The romanticized Ireland of charming seaside villages, enchanted green mountains, and jagged coastal cliffs finds its inspiration in Co. Kerry. Arguably the most beautiful region on the island, it is indisputably the most touristed. Each summer, tiny towns open their doors to an influx of visitors from around the globe. The Iveragh Peninsula, home to the Ring of Kerry, is anchored at its base by the lake-smattered Killarney National Park and extends west to tranquil Valentia Island and the ancient monastic settlement of Skellig Michael, 13km off its western shore. The Dingle Peninsula's popularity is growing rapidly, but skinny roads help preserve the ancient sights and traditional feel of Slea Head, the West Dingle *gaeltacht*, and the haunting Blasket Islands. Farther North, ancient castle ruins pepper the rich green pastures in Co. Limerick. Historically noted for its monasteries, the area is now known for its dairy cattle, the sloping Galtee Mountains, and the metropolitan center of Limerick City. In summer, buses run to most areas in these counties, but public transportation evaporates during the low season.

IVERAGH PENINSULA

As the Southwest's most celebrated peninsula, the Iveragh's picturesque villages, ancient forts, and romantic scenery justifiably serve as the backbone of the Irish postcard industry. Its appeal is traditionally advertised in the form of the breathtaking but limiting "Ring of Kerry," a series of highways manhandled by tour buses that shadow the coastline. While glimpses of the ocean and mountains through the window of a moving vehicle are beautiful, the mountainous landscape has a lot more in store off the beaten track. The Kerry Way, a long-distance walking path that roughly mimics the shape of the Ring, sweeps hikers above the asphalt and lays the best views at their feet. The smaller Skellig Ring, a remote roadway which swings through Ballinskelligs and Portmagee along the westernmost tip of the peninsula, deserves a trip to its ruined abbey for beautiful, unspoiled scenery.

KILLARNEY (CILL AIRNE)   ☎ 064

As the largest town on the Iveragh Peninsula and the starting point for the fabled Ring of Kerry, Killarney's cafes, restaurants, and hopping, music-filled pubs keep the more urban-oriented happy. Those who tire of its heavily touristed streets are usually rejuvenated by the natural beauty that awaits in the nearby national park.

▉ TRANSPORTATION

Flights: Kerry Airport, Farranfore (☎ 066 976 4644), halfway between Killarney and Tralee just off N22. 20min. from Killarney. Cabs and buses serve town. **Ryanair** (☎ 01813 03030; www.ryanair.com) flies to **London Stansted** (2 per day) and **Frankfurt-Hahn** (1 per day). **Aer Arann** (☎ 08182 10210; www.aerarann.com) flies to **Dublin** (2-4 per day), **Manchester** (4 per wk.), and **Lorient** (1 per wk.).

Trains: Killarney Station (☎ 31067, recorded info 890 778 899, inquiries 850 366 222). Off E. Avenue Rd., near the intersection with Park Rd. Open M-Sa 6am-1pm and 2-7pm, Su 30min. before departures. Killarney is on the Dublin-Tralee Intercity route with connections available to **Cork** (2hr., €20); **Dublin** (3½hr., €59), and **Limerick** (3hr., €22). Book ahead online for the best rates and special deals.

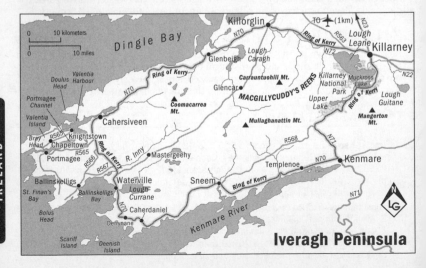

County Kerry

ATLANTIC OCEAN

0   10 kilometers
0   10 miles

Loop Head
Kilbaha
Kilkee
R487
CO. CLARE
Kilrush
Mouth of the Shannon
Bunnaclugga Bay
R551
Tarbert
Kerry Head
Ballybunion
TO LIMERICK (95km)
N69
Listowel
R556
R557
N69
Smerwick Harbour
Inishtooskert
Ballydavid
Brandon
Brandon Bay
Ballyheige Bay
R551
Ballyferriter
Mt. Brandon
Cloghane
Castlegregory
CO. KERRY
Inishnabró
DINGLE PENINSULA
Stradbally
Great Blasket I.
Dunquin
Conor Pass
Slea Head
Ventry
Beenoskee Mt.
Tralee Bay
Dingle
Camp
N86
Inishvickillane
Ventry Harbour
Anascaul
Tralee
N21
N21
Dingle Harbour
R561
SLIEVE MISH MTS.
Castlemaine
Castleisland
Dingle Bay
R. Maine
R23
Doulus Head
Glenbeigh
Killorglin
Milltown
Farranfore
R577
Valentia I.
Cahersiveen
Ring of Kerry
N70
Kerry County Airport
Bray Head
Knightstown
Coomacarrea Mt.
Carrauntuohill Mt.
R563
N22
Portmagee
Skellig Ring
Glencar
MACGILLYCUDDY'S REEKS
Killarney
St. Finan's Bay
Ballinskelligs
R. Inny
Mastergeehy
L. Leane
Bolus Head
Waterville
IVERAGH PENINSULA
Killarney National Park
Rathmore
Ballinskelligs Bay
L. Currane
N71
Caherbarnagh Mt.
Caherdaniel
Sneem
R568
Ring of Kerry
Mangerton Mt.
DERRYNASAGGART MTS.
Scariff I.
N70
Kenmare River
R571
Kenmare
R569
Cod's Head
Coulagh Bay
Ardgroom
BEARA PENNISULA
SHEHY MTS.
Dursey I.
Eyeries
Lauragh
CAHA MTS.
N71
CO. CORK
Allihies
SLIEVE MISKISH MTS.
Healy Pass
TO CORK (65km)
R572
Castletownbere
Adrigole
Glengarriff
N22
Bere I.
Rerrin
R584

Dingle Bay

Killorglin
TO ✈ (1km)
N23
Lough Leane
Killarney
N70
Ring of Kerry
R563
N72
N22
Glenbeigh
Lough Caragh
Doulus Head
Valentia Harbour
Ring of Kerry
Carrauntuohill Mt.
Killarney National Park
Muckross Lake
Portmagee Channel
N70
Glencar
MACGILLYCUDDY'S REEKS
Lough Guitane
Valentia Island
Upper Lake
Bray Head
R565
Knightstown
Chapeltown
Cahersiveen
Ring of Kerry
Mangerton Mt.
Portmagee
R565
R566
Mullaghanattin Mt.
Ballinskelligs
R567
R. Inny
Mastergeehy
R568
N70
Kenmare
St. Finan's Bay
Waterville
Sneem
Ring of Kerry
Templenoe
N71
Bolus Head
Ballinskelligs Bay
Lough Currane
N70
Caherdaniel
Derrynane
Kenmare River
N71
Scariff Island
Deenish Island

Iveragh Peninsula

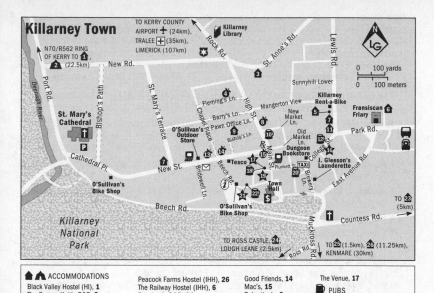

Killarney Town

TO KERRY COUNTY AIRPORT ✈ (24km), TRALEE ✚ (35km), LIMERICK (107km)

Killarney Library

N70/R562 RING OF KERRY TO ❶ (22.5km)

New Rd.

St. Anne's Rd.

Lewis Rd.

Rock Rd.

Port Rd.

Deenagh River

Bishop's Path

St. Mary's Terrace

St. Mary's Cathedral

Cathedral Pl.

O'Sullivan's Bike Shop

Killarney National Park

Fleming's Ln.

Chapel Place

Barry's Ln.

O'Sullivan's Outdoor Store

Pawn Office Ln.

Bishop's Ln.

High St.

New St.

Bridewell Ln.

Beech Rd.

Beech Rd.

New Market Ln.

Sunnyhill Lower

Mangerton View

Old Market Ln.

Dungeon Bookstore

Main St.

Tesco

Plunkett St.

TAXI

Town Hall

O'Sullivan's Bike Shop

Killarney Rent-a-Bike

Franiscan Friary

Park Rd.

College St.

Brewery Ln.

East Avenue Rd.

J. Gleeson's Launderette

Muckross Rd.

Countess Rd.

Ross Rd.

TO ROSS CASTLE, ❷⁴ LOUGH LEANE (2.5km)

TO ❷⁵ (1.5km), ❷⁶ (11.25km), KENMARE (30km)

TO ❷³ (5km)

0   100 yards
0   100 meters

N

ACCOMMODATIONS
Black Valley Hostel (HI), **1**
The Copper Kettle B&B, **5**
The Fairview Guest House, **11**
Killarney Hostel (HI), **23**
Kiltrasna Farmhouse B&B, **25**
Neptune's (IHH), **9**
Orchard House B&B, **3**
Paddy's Palace Hostel (IHH), **7**

Peacock Farms Hostel (IHH), **26**
The Railway Hostel (IHH), **6**
Rosslands B&B, **24**
The Súgán (IHH), **7**
White Bridge Caravan and
Camping Park, **2**

FOOD
Cathleen's Country Kitchen, **13**

Good Friends, **14**
Mac's, **15**
Robertino's, **8**
The Stonechat, **4**

★ **NIGHTLIFE**
The Grand, **19**
G2 Bar and Club, **21**
McSorley's, **16**

The Venue, **17**

PUBS
Courtney's Bar, **20**
The Granary, **22**
Mustang Sally's, **18**
O'Connor's Traditional Pub, **10**
Scott's Bar, **12**

Buses: Park Rd. (☎30011), connected to the outlet mall. Open mid-Sept. to June M-Sa 8:30am-5pm; July to mid-Sept. M-Sa 8:30am-6pm, Su 8:30am-4pm. Buses to: **Belfast** (9hr.; daily 9, 10am, noon, plus M 6:15am; €32.50); **Cork** (2hr., 11-14 per day 6:55am-7:30pm, €15); **Dingle** (2hr.; 7-8 per day 8am-5:05pm, plus F 7:20pm; €12.30); **Dublin** (6hr.; 5-6 per day 9am-4pm, plus M 6:15am; €22.50); **Farranfore/Kerry Airport** (15min.; 7-8 per day 9am-6pm, plus M 6:15am; €4); **Galway** (4½hr.; 7-8 per day 9am-6pm, plus M 6:15am; €21-24); **Kenmare** (1hr., 3-5 per day 7:40am-5pm, €8.40); **Kilkenny** (5hr., 3-4 per day 6:55am-3:30pm, €21); **Limerick** (2hr.; 6-7 per day 9am-6pm, plus M 6:15am; €15.40); **Shannon Airport** (2½hr.; 6-7 per day 9am-6pm, plus M 6:15am; €17); **Skibbereen** (4hr., 1:45pm, €15.40); **Tralee** (40min., 11-17 per day 8am-10:20pm, €7.50); **Waterford** (5hr., 9-12 per day 6:55am-6:30pm, €21). Additionally, hostels can book buses for discounted rates to the **Ring of Kerry Circuit** (€16.50), **Dingle** (€23), and **Gap of Dunloe** (€23). **Bus Éireann** runs a no-frills Ring of Kerry loop in the summer (M-Sa 1:15 and 3pm, Su 1:15pm; see **Ring of Kerry,** p. 295).

Taxis: Taxi Cab Rank, College Sq. (☎31331).

Bike Rental: O'Sullivans, Beech Rd. (☎31282), across from the tourist office (☎22389), and on lower New St., near Cathedral. Free panniers, locks, repair kits, and maps. €15 per day, €85 per wk. Lodgers at Neptune's pay €12.50 per day. Open daily 9am-6pm. **Killarney Rent-a-Bike** (☎087 236 3044), with locations at The Súgán hostel and the Flesk Campsite out on Muckross Rd. €12 per day, €60 per wk.

✈ ? ORIENTATION AND PRACTICAL INFORMATION

Most of Killarney is packed into three crowded streets. **Main Street,** in the center of town, begins at the **Town Hall** and generally runs north, becoming **High Street** where

New Street intersects it from the west. **Plunkett Street** runs east from Main St. just south of the New St. intersection; it curves into **College Road,** which continues east, toward the bus and train stations, as **Park Road. East Avenue Road** wraps to the southwest from Park Road and connects the train station back to town hall at **Kenmare Place.** From Kenmare Place, **Southlink Road** heads west in the direction of Killorglin, and **Muckross Road** runs south to the Muckross Estate and Kenmare.

Tourist Office: Beech Rd. (☎31633). Open July-Aug. M-Sa 9am-8pm, Su 10am-5:45pm; June and Sept. M-Sa 9am-6pm, Su 10am-5:45pm; Oct.-May M-Sa 9:15am-5pm.

Banks: AIB, Main St. (☎31047), next to the town hall; **Ulster,** New St. (☎36166), after Beech St.; and **Permanent TSB,** 23-24 New St. (☎33666), have 24hr. ATMs. All open M-Tu and Th-F 10am-4pm, W 10am-5:30pm. Other banks scattered throughout town.

Luggage Storage: Bus Station, Park Rd. (☎30011), see Buses. €2 per bag per day. Open daily 7am-6pm.

Laundry: J. Gleeson's Launderette, Brewery Ln. (☎33877), off College St. Self-service €9; full-service €10. Open M-Sa 9am-6pm.

Emergency: ☎999; no coins required. **Police** (Garda): New Rd. (☎31222).

Pharmacy: McSweeney, The Courtyard, Fairhill (☎35931), near College St. Large store with friendly service. Open M-Sa 8:30am-8pm, Su 11am-6pm.

Hospital: Nearest emergency facilities are in Tralee (☎06671 84000). Killarney's emergency hotline, **Southdoc,** with offices on Park Rd. (☎850 335 999), is in operation after 6pm on weekdays (when doctors' offices close) and all day on weekends.

Internet Access: Killarney Library (☎32655), on Rock Rd., at the top of High St. Free. Call ahead to reserve a time. ID required. Open M-Sa 10am-5pm, Tu and Th until 8pm. **Ri-Ra** (☎38729), on Plunkett St. €3 per hr.; 10hr. pre-paid account €20. Open June-Sept. M-Sa 9:15am-11pm, Su noon-9pm; Oct.-May daily 10am-10pm.

Post Office: New St. (☎31051). Open M and W-F 9am-5:30pm, Tu 9:30am-5:30pm, Sa 9am-1pm.

ACCOMMODATIONS

Cushy B&Bs and four-star hotels line the roads coming into town, but Killarney has quality hostels and more central B&Bs downtown. Camping is not allowed in the National Park, but there are several excellent campgrounds nearby.

IN TOWN

■ **Neptune's (IHH),** Bishop's Ln. (☎35255), 1st walkway off New St. on right. Immense and immaculate. Wheelchair-accessible. Breakfast €2.50. Free Internet access. Free luggage storage. Locker deposit €10. Laundry €7. 8-bed dorms €12.50-16; 4- to 6-bed dorms €13-16; doubles €36-42. Student discount 10% 1st night. ❶

■ **The Fairview Guest House** ❹, College St. (☎34164; www.fairviewkillarney.com). Ultra-luxurious B&B just minutes from the bus station. (€40-65 per person with €5-15 room discount for Let's Go readers and 10% off at its restaurant, **The Fifth Season** ❸; entrees €22-27). Ridiculously nice owners also run its two less expensive annexes.

The Copper Kettle ❸, just up the street from Fairview. Wooden and warm. €32-50 per person.

Rosslands ❸, near the Park. Colorful and quaint. €30-45 per person.

The Súgán (IHH), Lewis Rd. (☎33104), 2min. from the bus or train station. Go left onto College St.; Lewis Rd. is the 1st right. Funky and fun inside and out. Exuberant staff, impromptu storytelling, and music in the common room and neighboring pub keep hostelers happy. Towels €1. "Chillout time is midnight." Bike rental discount €2 per day at Killarney Rent-a-Bike. Dorms €15; doubles €40. ❶

The Railway Hostel (IHH), Park Rd. (☎35299). 1st right as you head to town from the bus station. Modern building with large beds and access to public transportation. Laundry €5. Internet access €1 per 15min. Dorms €16-19; doubles €50; triples €66. ❶

Orchard House B&B, St. Anne's Rd. (☎31879), off High St. Fancy rooms and a bay-windowed breakfast nook in a quiet, convenient new location with private parking. Cheerful proprietors readily give advice about activities in the area. Individually tailored breakfasts. Rooms €35 per person. ❸

Paddy's Palace Hostel (IHH), 31 New St. (☎35382), 1 block past the post office. Low price but not big on space or atmosphere. Part of Paddywagon Tours based in Dublin (www.paddywagontours.com). 4- to 6-bed dorms €15; doubles €40; triples €45. ❶

OUTSIDE TOWN

■ **Peacock Farms Hostel (IHH),** Gortdromakiery (☎33557), 11.25km from town. Take the Muckross Rd. out of town, turn left at the signpost before the Muckross post office, and go 3.2km, following signs up a steep hill. Cheap, clean, cheerful digs boast an unsurpassed view of Lough Guitane. Worth the cab fare for a Killarney experience free of tourist kitsch. Wheelchair-accessible. Open Apr.-Oct. Dorms €12; private rooms €18. ❶

Killarney Hostel (An Óige/HI), Aghadoe (☎31240), 5km west of town off the Killorglin road; turn right before the Golden Nugget and take the 4th left on a concealed drive. Free bus runs June-Aug. 5 times per day; from Oct.-May take the Killorglin bus and ask to stop at the Golden Nugget. Kitchen, TV room, and occasional barbecue in a stone mansion. Arranges various park tours. Parking available. Bike rental €13 per day; deposit €10. Internet €1 per 15min., €2 per 40min. Breakfast €5-7; packed lunch €6; dinner €13. Laundry €5. Reception 7:30am-midnight. Dorms €15-19, under 18 and members €14-16. Doubles €40-46; quads €68-88. ❶

Black Valley Hostel (An Óige/HI), Black Valley (☎34712). 22.5km from town on the Gap of Dunloe Rd., a few km from Lord Brandon's Cottage. Street signs are scarce, so call ahead for directions. Buses stop 10km away in Beaufort Bridge. Spotless hostel. Friendly owners have a small shop that sells groceries. Sheets €2. Midnight curfew. Lockout 10am-5pm. Open Mar.-Oct. Dorms €16, with membership €14. Shop open 9:30am-9pm. ❶

Kiltrasna Farmhouse B&B, Loughguittane Rd. (☎31643), off Muckross Rd. 2nd road on the left after Gleneagle Hotel, about 800m uphill from the main road. 6 bedrooms, 5 with bath and 1 wheelchair-accessible, tastefully decorated with colorful bedspreads. In the guestbook, previous guests laud the peace and tranquility. Open Mar. to mid-Oct. Singles €40; doubles €60; inquire about group rates. ❸

White Bridge Caravan and Camping Park, the Ballycasheen road (☎31590; www.killarneycamping.com). 2nd site in Glenbeigh (☎976 8451), near the beach. Well-groomed, award-winning park offers laundry, TV lounge, game room, a shop for essentials, and modern shower facilities. Enticing grassy stretches inspire impromptu football matches. €9 per person with tent; 2-person tent with car €23, each additional person €7. ❶

Hillcrest Farmhouse, Black Valley (☎34702; www.hillcrestfarmhouse.com). Signposted at Moll's Gap. Follow Gap of Dunloe Rd. turning right at sign before Black Valley Hostel. TV, ensuite rooms, dinner option, and gorgeous views make a great home for tired trekkers. Breakfast included. Tea and scones served throughout day. Dinner €27. Boats to Killarney (☎37430) leave nearby starting 10:30am, €14-15. Bikes permitted. Singles €49; doubles €35 per person. ❹

◨ FOOD

Food in Killarney is affordable at lunch, but prices rise as the sun sets. On **Plunkett Street** and **New Street,** a number of fast-food joints and **takeaways** stay open until 3 or 4am, and cheap, quality food is available around the clock. **Tesco,** in an arcade accessible by New St. or Beech Rd. (also on Cork Rd., beyond MacDonald's), sells groceries. (☎32866. Open M-W and Sa 8:30am-7pm, Th-F 8:30am-9pm, Su 10am-6pm.) For organic foods, try **Horan's,** in Innisfallen Centre near the tourist office car park. (☎35399. Open M-W and Sa 9am-6:30pm, Th 9am-7pm, F 9am-8pm.)

■ **The Stonechat,** Fleming's Ln. (☎34295). Down to earth despite its soaring reputation. Hanging plants nicely complement the stone and tomato-colored walls of this cottage. Serves excellent chicken, fish, and vegetarian dishes. 4-course early-bird menu (€22) available daily from 6-7:30pm. Lunch €7-9; dinner €13-18. Open M 6:30-10pm, Tu-Sa 12:30-3pm and 6:30-10pm. ❷

Mac's, 6 Main St. (☎35213). Newly renovated family-friendly restaurant whose best feature is still the homemade ice cream (1 scoop €2) that made it famous. Excellent desserts. Vegetarian options. Desserts €2-6.50. Entrees €13-19. Open M and W-Su noon-9:30pm, Tu 6-9:30pm. ❷

Cathleen's Country Kitchen, 17 New St. (☎33778). Busy takeaway and sit-down restaurant serves baked goods, sandwiches, dinners, and delicious desserts. Meals €3-10. Open June-Aug. M-F 9am-8pm, Sa 9am-6pm; Sept.-June M-Sa 9am-6pm. ❶

Robertino's, High St. (☎34966). Candlelit date spot with Italian serenades, frescoes and savory pastas (€14-16), pizza (€13.50-19), and meat dishes (€20-26). Open during summer daily noon-4pm and 5-10:30pm; winter daily 4-10:30pm. ❹

Good Friends, 13 New St. (☎38225). Chinese takeaway keeps prices low (meat entrees €8) and style high in elegant restaurant area. Amicable service stays true to name. Open for lunch Th-F 12:30-2:30pm, Su 1-4pm; dinner daily 5pm-midnight. ❶

🔛 PUBS AND CLUBS

Live music is a staple in Killarney's pubs on summer nights, so herds of tourists seeking the next great jig make for a crowded, noisy drinking experience. Several nightclubs simmer from 10:30pm until 2:30am; most charge €6-8 cover but offer discounts before 11pm or midnight.

■ **McSorley's,** College St. (☎39770). Trendy 20s crowd gets down to a huge variety of live music on the dance floor or simply listens from the dark haven of lounge-like seating. Nightly trad 8-10pm, live band 11pm-1am, and a late DJ. Cover: F €7, Sa €10.

■ **The Grand,** Main St. (☎31159). Popular club for locals and tourists of all ages. Night begins with live trad (9-11pm), then switches to rock (11:30pm-1:30am) as the bar fills up. Disco in back 11pm-3am. Arrive before 11pm and dodge the €5-8 cover.

Scott's Bar, College St. (☎31060), part of Scott's Gardens Hotel. Relaxed, yet classy. Modern, yet full of character. Tourists and locals rub elbows to hear nightly trad in summer, or F-Su in winter. Kitchen open daily noon-9pm.

Courtney's Bar, Plunkett St. (☎32689). 2 bars on 2 dark floors serve a local, hip crowd. W-F and Su live music/open-mic session. Sa DJ. Occasional cover for live band €5.

O'Connor's Traditional Pub, 7 High St. (☎31115). Foreign and domestic patrons mingle in spacious, casual atmosphere. Traditional Irish food (try the Irish stew or the chowder) served daily 5-10pm. M-Sa 9:30-11:30pm and Su 8-10pm trad; winter F-Su only.

Mustang Sally's, Main St. (☎35790). Blues lovers are drawn in by the name and stay for the atmosphere. Massive pub pleases with plasma TVs and 2 dance floors until its nightclub, **The Venue,** opens up. Kitchen open noon-8pm (most dishes €9.50-12.50). Nightclub cover F-Sa after midnight €8. F-Su 9pm-late DJ in the pub, later in the disco.

The Granary, Beech Rd. (☎20075; www.granarykillarney.com), across from the tourist office. Live music (from rock to country) caters to the young and trendy every night in this stylish, cavernous pub. F-Sa after midnight cover €5. Visit website or call for event schedule. Low-key, trendy **G2 Bar and Club** upstairs open F-Sa 11:30pm-2:30am.

👁 🏃 SIGHTS AND OUTDOOR ACTIVITIES

Congested with bureaux de change, souvenir shops, and disoriented foreigners, Killarney plays second fiddle to the massive National Park just across the road, but has some attractions of its own and is the place to find information and transportation for visits to the park. The soaring, Neo-Gothic **St. Mary's Cathedral,** at the western end of New St., was built during the Great Famine and can seat 1400 within its limestone walls. (Open 24hr. Free.) The area has excellent salmon and trout **fishing,** especially in early fall. Unrestricted fishing is allowed in nearly all of Killarney's lakes, but it requires a permit (€12 per day) in rivers and Barfinnihy Lake. **O'Neill's Fishing Shop,** Plunkett St. (☎31970), rents rods (€10 per day).

Steeds are available from the **Killarney Riding Stables** (☎31686; €30 per hr., €50 per 2hr.) and **Muckross Stables** (☎32238; €30 per hr.; no children under 8).

Killarney's **festivals** are big events on the local social calendar. During the first two weeks of July, the town goes all out for **Killarney Summerfest,** when musicians, artists, and entertainers fill the streets and big-name bands draw crowds to evening concerts. With Pink headlining in 2007, organizers knew they had better "get this party started" right; a colorful kick-off parade and ferris wheel did the trick. (☎71560; www.killarneysummerfest.com.) In mid-May and mid-July, horses gallop in the **Killarney Races** at the race course on Ross Rd. (Tickets available at gate; €10-15.) The **Killarney Regatta,** the oldest in Ireland, draws rowers and spectators to Lough Leane the first Sunday in July.

KILLARNEY NATIONAL PARK

Thousands of years ago, Ice Age glaciers sliced up the Killarney region, scooping out a series of lakes and glens and scattering boulders across the terrain. Today, visitors reap the visual bounty of nature's cycle of change; Killarney National Park is a paradise of tree-carpeted mountain peaks and blue waters, making for unparalleled hiking, biking, and climbing. The park, stretched across 96 square kilometers of prime Kerry real estate, bordered by Killarney to the northeast and Kenmare to the southwest, encompasses a string of forested mountains and the famous **Lakes of Killarney:** huge **Lough Leane (Lower Lake),** medium-sized **Muckross (Middle) Lake,** and the small **Upper Lake,** connected to the others by a channel 3.2km to the southwest. **Japanese Sika Deer,** introduced to Killarney in 1865, can be spotted in the glens surrounding the lakes, but you may have to hike a bit farther up the mountains (primarily Torc and Mangerton) to see Ireland's only remaining indigenous herd of **Red Deer** who returned after the last Ice Age. Also along the lakes's shores are the majority of the park's **historical sights. The Kenmare road** curves along the southeastern shores of the lakes, providing awe-inspiring vistas for motorists, but the park's diversity of landscape and wildlife can only be truly experienced by bike, horse-drawn carriage, or on foot. With so many tourists driving the roads in and around the park, hitching can be difficult as well as risky. Given the park's size, the best place to start is at the Killarney tourist office, which provides a number of detailed maps and information about guided tours.

The park's popular heritage destinations include **Ross Castle** on **Lough Leane** and **Muckross House** on **Middle Lake,** while the **Gap of Dunloe**—running from north to south, where it is bordered by the **Macgillycuddy's Reeks**—is a major pilgrimage site for hikers (see **Sights and Outdoor Activities,** p. 297). Visits to most of these sights can be managed in several hours or stretched over a full day, depending on the mode of transport. Hikers and bikers should be wary of cars and buses on narrow roads, especially the Kenmare Rd., which climbs into a steep and winding maze.

Hiking and biking trails for all levels of experience litter the park's environs. Three leisurely self-guided rambles stay within its borders: the **Old Boat House Nature Trail** (less than 1km) around the tiny Muckross Peninsula and Gardens; the **Blue Pool Nature Trail** (2km), highlighted by a small lake that includes a pool; and **Arthur Young's Walk** (4km), through woods filled with the Japanese Sika deer. For a more difficult and scenic trek, the 8km (about 4hr.) hike up **Torc Mountain,** just south of Muckross Lake, rewards the intrepid with panoramic views of the three lakes below. Farther to the southeast, a trek through the passes of **Mangerton Mountain,** a little more taxing, descends along the **Devil's Punch Bowl.** Stunning sights await those with wheels high in the mountains along the Kenmare Rd. (N71) at **Ladies' View** and **Moll's Gap.** Navigating the traffic jam of private cars and tour buses at the car parks can be a minor hassle, but the array of mountains, water, and sky that await are more than worth it.

Killarney is also a perfect starting point for adventurers who aspire to walk the 208km **Kerry Way** (p. 295). It begins down the Muckross Road leading out of town; immediately after the Flesk Bridge, the clearly signposted trail slopes down to the right. It's also possible to get a shorter taste of the Way via the **Old Kenmare Road.** This first (or last) leg of the route passes through the spectacular Torc and Mangerton Mountains and can be managed in a day. From Killarney, follow the Kenmare road for 6.5km and turn left just beyond the main entrance to Muckross House—the Way leaves from the car park on the side road. The Killarney tourist office sells a Kerry Way guide with topographic maps. *Ordnance Survey #78* and *83* (€8 each) include roads, trails, and archaeological points of interest.

🛡 ROSS CASTLE AND LOUGH LEANE

Several major attractions perch along the banks of Lough Leane. The closest to town is **Knockreer Estate,** which lies a short walk down New St. past the cathedral. The original mansion housed the Catholic Earls of Kenmare and, later, the Grosvenor family of National Geographic fame. The current building, which was built in the 1950s, is unimpressive and closed to the public, but nearby **Deenagh Lodge Tearooms** is quite quaint and welcomes visitors for scrumptious sandwiches (€5) and homemade desserts. (☎087 949 8183. Open Easter-Oct. daily 10:30am-5pm.) The **nature trails** accessible from the estate afford views of the mountains and roaming deer. Visitors can drive or walk out to the older and more famous **Ross Castle** (from the Muckross road turn right on Ross Rd. 3km from Killarney), but the numerous footpaths from Knockreer (15min.) are more scenic. The castle, built by the O'Donoghue chieftains in the 14th century, was the last in Munster to fall to Cromwell's army. Its complete refurbishment in the 1960s dispelled the mystique that inspired centuries of poets and artists, but enabled it to be opened to the public. Today, tours detail the typical life of a 16th-century chieftain. (☎35851. Guided tour only. 40min. tours every 30-40min. Open mid-Mar. to May daily 9:30am-5:30pm, June-Aug. daily 9am-6:30pm; Sept. to mid-Oct. daily 9:30am-5:30pm; mid-Oct. to mid-Nov. Tu-Su 9:30am-5:30pm. Last admission 45min. before closing. €5.30, students €2.10, seniors €3.70, families €11.50.) Paths continue to the secluded **Ross Island,** which is actually a lobster-claw-shaped peninsula stretching into Lough Leane. Its greenish pools testify to the area's copper mining past.

The best way to see Lough Leane is from the water. The pier by Ross Castle offers several options: **Lily of Killarney Watercoach** cruises around the giant lake, covering local history and folklore (☎31068; departs during summer noon, 1:45, 3:15, 4:30pm; €8), while a **motorboat trip** (☎087 675 7791 or 087 689 9241) travels to Innisfallen Island (€7), the Meeting of the Waters via Lough Leane and Muckross

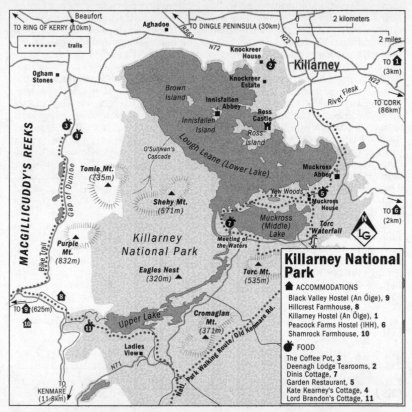

Lake (€10), or the Gap of Dunloe via Lough Leane, Muckross Lake, and Upper Lake (€15, return €25). Or, rent your own **rowboat**. (☎32252. €10 per boat.)

On Innisfallen Island, the husk of **Innisfallen Abbey** remains stoic and graceful, despite its age. The Abbey was founded circa AD 600 by St. Finian the Leper; in the Middle Ages it became a university and opened its doors to students. The Annals of Innisfallen, now housed at Oxford, were written here by 39 monastic scribes around 1326. They recount the Abbey's take on Irish and world history in both Irish and Latin. At the Abbey's center is a yew tree; yew and oak groves were sacred to the druids, and resolutely non-druidic abbeys were often built among and around them. The separate **Augustinian Abbey** is so derelict that it might be a challenge to identify, but it's still worth a visit.

🔲 MUCKROSS AND THE MEETING OF THE WATERS

The roofless crumblings of **Muckross Abbey,** built in 1448, lie 5km south of Killarney on the Kenmare road. The abbey's grounds, which contain the ruins of the abbey itself and a modern graveyard, are haunting and serene. (Always open. Free.) From the abbey, signs point the 1.5km way to **Muckross House,** a Victorian manor impressive to all but Queen Victoria herself. Unfortunately for the owners, the mansion's elaborate furnishings, walled garden, and magnificently manicured lawns apparently failed to woo Her Majesty into giving the man of the house his coveted royal title. She stayed a mere two days in 1861, leaving the owners titleless and bankrupt. Visitors today can access the estate on guided tours and peep through each one of its 365 windows themselves (an even more astonishing number considering the steep glass tax in those days that led to the expression "daylight robbery"). Within the grounds also lie the **Muckross Traditional Farms,** a living history museum designed to depict rural life in 1930s Kerry. Help costumed demonstrators whip up traditional cuisine and crafts, or try to catch one of its special events such as storytelling or traditional dance. Buffet-style fare (sandwiches and salads €4-10; entrees €10) can be enjoyed among tourist throngs at the spacious **Garden Restaurant ❶**, next to the **craft shop**, which is often very busy selling its products made on the estate. (☎31440; www.muckross-house.ie. House open daily July-Aug. 9am-7pm; Sept.-Oct. and mid-Mar. to June 9am-6pm; Nov. to mid-Mar. 9am-5:30pm. Farms open June-Sept. daily 10am-6pm, May daily 1-6pm; Oct. Sa-Su 1-6pm. Call ahead for the summer schedule. House or farms each €5.75, students €2.35, families €14.50. Joint admission to house and farms €8.50/4/25. Last admission 1hr. before closing. Restaurant credit card min. €20.)

Muckross House is also the access point to several sights in the area. A 2km path follows the water to the 18m drop of **Torc Waterfall** and a 5km stroll in the opposite direction leads to the **Meeting of the Waters,** where channels from the Upper Lough introduce themselves to the Middle. The paved path is pretty, but the dirt trail through the **Yew Woods** is more secluded and not accessible to bikes. Nearby, **Dinis Cottage ❶** refuels hikers and bikers with sandwiches (€4) and sweets (€3.50). It also offers **boat service** to Muckross House. (☎31954. Open mid-May to Sept. daily 10:30am-6pm. Boats €7, €10 return) Park explorers should note that there's no direct route from the Muckross sights to Ross Castle; those wishing to conquer both in one day must return to Killarney, making for a total trip of 16km.

🗝 GAP OF DUNLOE

Expect both misty mountain vistas and a generous dose of physical exertion on a Gap of Dunloe hike. **Organized treks** to the Gap can be booked at area hostels or at the Killarney tourist office. (☎31633. €27, with hostel discount €23.) Such treks, which include a boat trip across Muckross Lake, shuttle visitors to the foot of the Gap, eliminating the 11.2km hike from town. After hiking the Gap, trekkers meet the boat that takes them across the lake to Ross Castle, where a bus picks them up and drops them back in Killarney. Attempting the Gap on foot using this route, however, requires a trek up the long side of the mountain. It is far easier, and potentially less expensive, to attack by bike from the opposite direction; the same motorboat service that travels over to Ross Castle from the end of the Gap can also bring hikers and bikers in the opposite direction. (1½hr. €15 per person; bikes free of charge. Book ahead at the Killarney tourist office or local hostels.) To get to the Gap from Lord Brandon's Cottage, the pickup and drop-off point across the lake, turn left over the stone bridge and continue for 3km to the hostel and church. Hang a right onto a hairpin-turn-laden road that winds up to the top of the Gap (2.5km). What follows is a well-deserved 11km downhill coast through the park's most magical scenery.

Opportunities for nourishment conveniently sandwich the trail. At the foot of the Gap is **Kate Kearney's Cottage ❸**, named for a mountain-dwelling woman famous for brewing and serving a near-poisonous *poitín*. Her former home is now a pub and restaurant that sucks in droves of tourists with its nightly Irish music extravaganzas. (☎44146. Summer W trad. Sandwiches €3-7; bar food specials €12. Kitchen open 12:30-9pm. Irish Night daily €35-40, including 4-course meal, live music, and dancing. Book ahead.) A nearby cafe, **The Coffee Pot ❷**, fuels visitors with the full Irish breakfast (€7.50) and cliff-conquering caffeine. (☎087 236 0602. Lunch €8-10. Open daily 9am-6pm.) At the other end of the gap, a light snack of tea and freshly baked scones is served at **The Hillcrest Farmhouse** (see **Killarney accommodations,** p. 288), while **Lord Brandon's Cottage ❶** greets masters of the mountain with more substantial fare and a celebratory cold pint. (☎34730. Sandwiches from €3. Open daily July-Aug. 10am-5pm; May-June and Sept.-Oct. 10am-4pm. Public restrooms available.) Those who ended the tour at Kate Kearney's Cottage can return to Killarney by continuing on the road to Fossa, then turning right on the Killorglin Rd. The 11.2km ride back to Killarney passes the ruins of Dunloe Castle, an Anglo-Norman stronghold demolished by Cromwell's army, and a set of ogham stones, circa AD 300. The nearby golf course also hosts the **Gap of Dunloe Farmer's Market** (1-5pm), which combines a good deal of mother nature's greatest gifts.

RING OF KERRY AND THE KERRY WAY

The term **"Ring of Kerry"** is generally used to describe the entire Iveragh Peninsula, but it actually refers to a particular set of roads: N71 from Kenmare to Killarney, N72 from Killarney to Killorglin, and the long loop of N70 west to Cahersiveen, south to Caherdaniel, and finally east back to Kenmare. If the captivity of a prepackaged private bus tour out of Killarney isn't appealing, **Bus Éireann** offers a regular summer circuit through the major towns on the Ring. (☎30011. Departs Killarney mid-June to Aug. M-Sa 1:15, 3pm, Su 1:15pm; entire ring in 1 day €21.70.) Buses travel counterclockwise, from Killarney to Killorglin, along Dingle Bay, east by the Kenmare River, and north from Sneem back to Killarney. Another bus runs year-round in the mornings, traveling clockwise from Waterville back to Killarney (M-Sa 1 per day, 7:30am). **Bikers** may find themselves jammed between buses and cliffs on the narrow, bumpy roads, though traffic can often be avoided by doing the Ring clockwise, the direction that faces the scenery. Fortunately for cyclists, signposts lead to a new bike route that avoids most main roads and has better views. Drivers must choose between lurching behind large tour buses and meeting them face-to-face on narrow roads.

Those who wish to avoid the impossibly narrow tour-bus superhighway of the Ring of Kerry road need not write off the Iveragh Peninsula entirely. A step away from N70, solitude and superior scenery reward walkers along The Kerry Way. This well-signposted route (look for the yellow walking man) traverses a wide variety of terrain, from rugged inland expanses to soaring coastal cliffs. Described as an "inner" ring of Kerry, the Way brings walkers above the road, to higher ground and more scenic vistas. Its 217km route follows an array of paths, including pastures, old "butter roads" (constructed for horses lugging butter), and ancient thoroughfares between early Christian settlements. The Way also crosses the main road often enough to make daytrips convenient from almost anywhere on the Ring. Some noteworthy outings include a boat trip to the haunting Skellig Rocks and a day spent biking or hiking along the byways of Valentia Island. Both lie just off the northwestern coast of the peninsula and are most easily accessed from the village of Portmagee. For the best of the Way itself, traverse the dramatic stretch from Kenmare through Killarney and northwest to Glenbeigh and the inspiring passage between Waterville and Caherdaniel.

KILLORGLIN (CILL ORGLAN) ☎066

Killorglin lounges along the banks of the River Larne, 21km west of Killarney in the shadow of Iveragh's mountainous spine. Tourists tend to pass through fast on their way west to the peninsula's more touristy spots, but what the town lacks in sights it more than makes up for with its annual festival dedicated to goats.

⊟⬛ TRANSPORTATION AND PRACTICAL INFORMATION. Several **buses** travel during summer from **Killarney** to the Killorglin stop outside the Catholic Church on Mill Rd., including the Ring of Kerry bus leaving Killarney at 1:15pm daily (others leave Killarney June-Sept. daily 12:45, 4, 4:45, 6:45pm; M-Sa also 9:50am and 3pm; €4.40). The 9:50am, 1:15, and 3pm continue to **Cahersiveen** (50min., €7.50), the 1:15 and 3pm to **Waterville** (1¼hr., €7.50), and the 1:15pm to **Sneem** (3hr., €9.50). Also during summer, the bus from **Waterville** to Killarney departs M-Sa at 7:30am, stopping in **Killorglin** at 8:55am. Additionally, a bus travels to **Tralee** (June-Sept. M-Sa 9:15am, 1:15, 4:30, 5:15pm, 6:40pm, Su 1:15pm and 3:30pm, also M-F 8am). During the winter, the bus to Killarney stops in town once per day (Killarney bus station ☎064 34777). For a **taxi**, call Mid-Kerry Cabs (☎087 258 2040). Killorglin's **Main Street** runs from the river and widens into the **square**, then continues up the hill, where it intersects with **Iveragh Road;** the **tourist office** is across the street at the intersection. The tourist office's friendly staff has plenty of info about the area. (☎976 1451. Open May-Oct. M-F 9am-1pm and 2-7:30pm, Sa 10:30am-5:30pm; Nov.-Apr. M-F 9am-1pm.) **AIB,** on Main St., has an **ATM.** (☎976 1134. Open M 10am-5pm, Tu-F 10am-4pm.) Other **ATMs** are located inside the **Bank of Ireland** on Market St. (☎976 1147; open M 10am-12:30pm and 1:30-5pm, Tu-F 10am-12:30pm and 1:30-4pm) and the **Eurospar** (see **Food and Pubs,** p. 296). **Laune Dry Cleaners and Launderette** is on Iveragh Rd. (€9 per load. Open M-Sa 9am-6pm; Oct.-June closes W 1pm.) **Mulvihill Pharmacy** is halfway up Main St. (☎976 1115, after-hours 976 1387. Open M-Tu and Th-F 9am-6:30pm, W and Sa 9am-6pm.) Get 50min. of fast, free **Internet** access by signing up at the **library,** set back from Iveragh Rd. near the tourist office. (☎976 1272. Open Tu-Sa 10am-1:30pm and 2:30-5pm.) The **post office** is a bit farther down on Iveragh Rd. (☎976 1101. Open M-Tu and Th-F 9am-1pm and 2-5:30pm, W 9am-1pm and 2-5pm, Sa 9am-1pm.)

⬛⬛ ACCOMMODATIONS AND CAMPING. Killorglin's great overnight options defy its "pitstop" status. Even without charging practically the lowest rates for B&B and self-catering in all of Kerry, the **Hill Top View ❸,** located 1km from town on the Glenbeigh Rd., would be a smart choice for its clean ensuite rooms equipped with TVs and Wi-Fi, and its large dining room filled with the fragrance of freshly baked goods. (☎976 1932. Kitchen and laundry available. Evening 4-course meal €15. B&B rooms €25 per person. Self-catering €450 per wk., fits up to 10 people.) **⬛Orglan House B&B ❸,** a 5min. walk from town over the bridge on Killarney Rd., has more standard rates but far above-average hospitality and simply unbeatable views of the goat-crazy town. (☎976 1540. Rooms €30-35 per person.) Bright, bountiful **Laune Valley Farm Hostel (IHH) ❶,** 1.6km from town off the Tralee Rd., houses guests in the hostel and cows, chickens, dogs, and ducks on the farm. Farm-fresh milk and eggs for sale make whipping up scrambled eggs irresistible. The deck with mountain views is a dining spot. (☎976 1488. Wheelchair-accessible. Free showers. Dorms €16-17; doubles €40-50. **Camping** €8 per person.) **Laune Bridge House B&B ❸** is a few doors closer to town than Orglan and offers beautiful, spacious bedrooms. (☎976 1161. Singles €45; doubles €70.) Tent up at **West's Caravan and Camping Park ❶,** 2km east of town on the Killarney road in the shadow of **Carrantoohill,** Ireland's tallest peak. Fishing, table tennis, and a tennis court are available. (☎976 1240. Open Easter to mid-Oct. Showers €2. Laundry from €5. 1-person tent €7.50; car, tent, and 2 adults €18. Mobile home rental from €250-570 per wk.)

◧⬛ FOOD AND PUBS. Eurospar, in the square, stocks groceries and serves deli sandwiches. (☎976 1117. Open M-F 9am-9pm, Sa 9am-9:30pm, Su 9:30am-6pm.) Killorglin's newest culinary adventure is a testament to how far Irish cuisine has come. Forget pub grub; **Sol y Sombra ❶** is an inventive, inexpensive Spanish tapas and wine bar housed within a beautiful old church off Lower Bridge St. (☎976 2347; www.solysombra.ie. Tapas €6-11. Open M and W-F 5-11:30pm, Sa 5pm-12:30am, Su 5-11pm.) For more familiar cafe fare, tiny **Benz Cafe ❷**, in the square, which dishes out sandwiches, burgers, and salads (€4.25-12), as well as an excellent Irish breakfast. (☎976 2653. Open M-W 9am-6pm, Th-Sa 9am-9pm.) **Dev's 'n the square ❷**, the square, satisfies seafood lovers and vegetarians with its diverse menu. (☎979 0812. Lunch €4-10; dinner €18-26. Open daily 9am-3pm and 6-10pm. MC/V.) **Bunker's ❷**, across from the tourist office, is also crowded as it doubles as a restaurant and a coffee shop with a pub next door. (☎976 1381. Entrees €8-13. Open daily 9:30am-10:30pm. AmEx/MC/V.) At night, relaxed fun, a friendly atmosphere, and fine food can be found at legendary **Nick's Seafood Restaurant and Piano Bar ❷** on Lower Bridge St. (☎976 1219. Lunch €6-12; dinner €15-30. Open daily 12:30-11:30pm.) Locals quench their thirst at **Old Forge**, Main St., a lively stone pub with big screen TVs. (☎976 1231. F-Su disco. F-Sa cover €5.) An older crowd fills **Laune Bar**, Lower Main St., on the water.

◙ ♫ SIGHTS AND OUTDOOR ACTIVITIES. Every year from August 10 through 12, thousands of goat lovers journey from around the globe to Killorglin for the ancient **Puck Fair.** On August 10th, a **goat** from the Kerry mountainside is crowned king in the town square by a local girl dressed in period garb, and three days of revelry ensue. But it's all in good fun; at the end of the festival, the newest addition to the Killorglin royal line is released back into nature and the town regains some semblance of everyday life. If you're visiting Killorglin when goat's not on the social menu, catch up on spectacles past at **The Basement Museum**, housed in a private home past the church down Mill Rd. The owner recounts stories in a room overflowing with festival memorabilia, as well as an archive of old photos and a collection of circus posters from around the world. (☎976 1353. €2. Call ahead.) Eight kilometers from town off the Killarney Rd., **Ballymalis Castle** rests on its 16th-century laurels, dozing on the banks of the Laune in view of Macgillycuddy's Reeks. Head west off N70 to hit two beaches suitable for swimming: pebbled **Cromane Beach** and the less rocky **Rossbeigh Beach** (10km and 16km away, respectively). **Cappanalea Outdoor Education Centre,** 12km to the southwest off the Ring of Kerry Rd., offers canoeing, rock climbing, windsurfing, sailing, and hill-walking in a green, hilly region of pristine beauty. (☎976 9244; www.oec.ie/cappanalea. Open daily 10am-5pm. Day course with any 2 activities €55, children €35; any 1 activity €30/18. Individual booking July-Aug. only; group booking year-round, min. of 6.)

CAHERSIVEEN (CATHAIR SAIDBHIN)   ☎066

Best known in Ireland as the birthplace of patriot Daniel O'Connell (p. 53), Cahersiveen (CAH-her-sah-veen) serves as a base for exploring nearby archaeological sites and for short trips to Valentia Island and the Skelligs. But its pub charm and nightlife, popular restaurants, outstanding campground, and cozy hostel are more than enough reason to spend a night here on your way around the Ring.

⊟ ⁊ TRANSPORTATION AND PRACTICAL INFORMATION. Buses from **Killorglin** stop in front of Banks Store on Main St. (mid-June to Aug. M-Sa 4 per day, Su 2 per day. See **Killorglin transportation,** p. 296) and continues to **Killarney** (2½hr., €11.50) via **Waterville** (25min., €4), **Caherdaniel** (1hr., €4.25), and **Sneem** (1½hr., €8). Another bus heads east to **Killarney** (M-Sa 8am and 12:15pm). The town centers around one street, N70 **Ring of Kerry Road,** which is called **New Market Street, Church Street, Main Street, New Street,** and finally **Valentia Road** as it travels from east to west through town. **Casey Cycles,** Main St., **rents bikes.** (☎947 2474. €14 per day, €70 per wk. Helmet and lock included. Open July-Aug. M-Sa 9am-6pm, Su

10:30am-noon; Sept.-June M-Sa 9am-6pm and by appointment.) Cahersiveen's **tourist office** is across from the bus stop. (☎947 2589. Open June to mid-Sept. M-Tu, Th, Sa 9:15am-5pm; W and F 9:15am-12:45pm.) Find a **map** and walking guide to the Heritage Trail at Quirk's newsagent (see **Sights**, p. 298). An **AIB** with **ATM** is on Main St. The **Bank of Ireland** near the church also has a 24hr. **ATM**. (☎947 2022. Open M 10am-5pm, Tu-F 10am-4pm.) **O'Connor's Pharmacy** is near the church. (☎222 0798. Open M-W and F-Sa 9am-6pm, Th 9am-1:30pm.) At the **library** on Main St., two 50min. **Internet** sessions per week are free for those over 18. (☎947 2287. Open Tu-W and F-Sa 10am-1:30pm and 2:30-5pm, Th 10am-8pm.) The **post office** is on Main St. (☎947 2010. Open M-F 9:30am-1pm and 2-5:30pm, Sa 9:30am-1pm.)

🔓 **ACCOMMODATIONS. Sive Hostel (IHH) ❶**, 15 East End, Main St., has a welcoming staff, comfortable rooms, and a balcony with amazing views of distant Ballycarbery Castle. The hostel also arranges boat trips to the Skelligs, including transport to the Portmagee pier. (☎947 2717. Laundry €8. Dorms €15; doubles €22 per person. Camping €7 per person.) Those who enjoy a good jog on the beach may find a partner in the avid runner/owner of **O'Shea's B&B ❸**. Keep healthy with their vegetarian breakfast or reward yourself with the full Irish, then kick back in their spacious ensuite rooms with TV and gorgeous views. (☎947 2402. Singles €40; doubles €66-70.) **Mannix Point Caravan and Camping Park ❶**, at the west end of town, adjoins a nature reserve and faces the romantic ruins of Ballycarbery Castle across the water. The common area's turf fire and upright piano create a warmly rustic ambience. (☎947 2806. Wash and dry €3 each. Wi-Fi available. Showers €1. Open mid-Mar. to Oct. Sites €7.50 per person.)

🍴 **FOOD AND PUBS. Centra** sells food and necessities. (☎947 2583. Open M-F 7:30am-10:30pm, Sa-Su 7:30am-10pm.) Incredibly fresh seafood dishes are served at **QC's Chargrill Bar & Restaurant ❹**, Main St.; the fish comes from the owners' shop. The trendy but comfortable dining area is constantly busy. (☎947 2244. Bar menu €8-20; entrees €17-24.50. Kitchen open 12:30-2pm and 6-9:30pm.) **Amartine ❷**, Main St., has satisfying sandwiches (€4-8), decadent desserts, and a sumptuous Sunday lunch special for €10. (☎947 3499. Open June-Sept. daily 8am-10pm.) For classic international dishes, try the **Red Rose Restaurant ❺**, Church St. (☎948 1111. Day menu €4-10; dinner €8.50-12.50. Open July-Aug. daily 8:30am-6pm.) When the kerosene stove quits, or the hostel's kitchen is packed, call on **Chin Fong Chinese**, Main St. (☎947 3588. Entrees €7.50-12. Open daily 5pm-midnight.)

Some of the pubs on Main St. still hearken back to the early 20th century, when establishments served as watering holes and "real" business, be they a general store, blacksmith, or leather shop. **Mike Murt's**, Main St. (☎947 2396), a traditional pub with angling and sports memorabilia festooning the walls and windows, comes alive with trad on Wednesday nights. **Fertha Bar** (☎947 2023) features anything from trad to trendy rock bands on Friday and Saturday nights. **The Shebeen** (☎947 2361) has summer trad on Tuesdays, Thursdays, and Saturdays, with set dancing also on Thursdays. **The East End,** Main St. (☎947 2970), hosts live trad on Monday nights during the summer. Youth from around the Ring head to **The Harp Nightclub** on weekends; it's the place to be Saturday night. (☎947 2436. Attached bar follows standard pub hours. Club open F-Sa midnight-3am. 18+. Cover €7-9.)

🎭 **SIGHTS AND FESTIVALS. O'Connell's Church** is the only house of worship in Ireland named for a layperson. Heroes and major milestones in Irish history are both celebrated and mourned at the **Old Barracks Heritage Centre,** one block down Bridge St., next to the post office. (☎947 2777. Open May to mid-Sept. M-F 10am-4:30pm, Sa-Su 11am-4:30pm. €4, students €3.50, seniors €2, families €9.) The exhibits are brimming with information, but the building has a compelling background as well—its architecture has inspired a rumor that confused officials built it as a colonial outpost while a proper barracks was erected somewhere in India.

The countryside past the bridge farther down the road is home to a wealth of ancient sites. On the left past the bridge and a 40min. walk down the next left off of the main road sits the ruins of 15th-century **Ballycarbery Castle,** which was once owned by O'Connell's ancestors. Two hundred meters past the castle turn-off, two of three area **stone forts** have been partially restored and are some of the best-preserved of their kind. Standing atop **Cahergall Fort's** 3m thick walls provides a great view of the surrounding area, while **Leacanabuaile Fort** still contains small stone dwellings. A few minutes' walk beyond the second fort lies **Cuas Crom Beach** and **White Strand Beach,** both popular swimming spots. Turn right after the bridge to reach **Knocknadobar Mountain,** which makes for a nice half-day hike and holds 14 stations of the cross and a holy well at its base. The map and the manager at the Sive Hostel can help plot the way. During the first weekend in August, Cahersiveen hosts a **Festival of Music and the Arts** (www.celticmusicfestival.com), which features street entertainment, workshops, pub sessions, and numerous free concerts.

VALENTIA ISLAND (DAIRBHRE) ☎066

An escape from the tourist trail, Valentia Island hugs the mainland coastline and provides up-close views of the neighboring mountain ranges. Valentia's tranquility was briefly and famously disturbed over a century ago with the arrival of the first transatlantic cable, which connected Valentia to Newfoundland. Important characters from the world over, including Queen Victoria, came to test it. Today, the island's tiny, winding roads are perfect for biking or hiking; in Knightstown, the gregarious locals keep the *craic* flowing. The much bigger island across the water is only a short car ride away; a bridge and a car ferry at its eastern end connect it to the mainland. No public transportation is available on Valentia.

ⵎⵎ TRANSPORTATION AND PRACTICAL INFORMATION. A quick **car ferry** departs during the summer between **Reenard Point,** 5km west of Cahersiveen, off the Ring of Kerry road, and Knightstown. Taxis from Cahersiveen cost about €10. (☎947 6141. Ferries depart Apr.-Sept. every 8min. M-Sa 8:15am-10pm, Su 9am-10pm. Cars €8 return, pedestrians €2, cyclists €3.) Most cars head for the pier, so hitchhiking is fairly easy, though *Let's Go* never recommends it. The bridge connecting Valentia to the mainland is in **Portmagee,** 16km west of Cahersiveen. To get to Portmagee, head south from Cahersiveen or north from Waterville, then west on R565. The **Kerry Community Transport** offers rides between the Island and **Cahersiveen** every Monday, Thursday and Friday in the summer. (☎18905 28528 or 714 7002. Leaves Valentia 9:30am, Cahersiveen 1:30pm. Call ahead. €4.) For an island **taxi,** call the **Kennedy Bus Hire and Taxi Service** (☎947 6183 or 087 264 8646).

ⵎⵎ ACCOMMODATIONS AND FOOD. Valentia has a surprising variety of budget accommodations. The new owners of **The Royal Valentia ❷** in Knightstown dropped "hostel" from its name, but didn't lose its budget prices. The makeover also includes more B&B-style rooms, but simple bunks (quite unlike what Queen Victoria must have slept in during her stay here) are also available. Some rooms have windows overlooking the bay. (☎947 6144; www.royalpiervalentia.com. Laundry €5. Breakfast €7. Dorms €12. B&B singles €35; doubles €60.) On the contrary, the **Portmagee Hostel (IHH) ❶,** on the Skellig Ring road near the GAA grounds outside of Portmagee, is a proud purpose-built hostel. What it lacks in royalty and centrality it makes up for it in its modern facilities and low rates. (☎948 0018; www.portmageehostel.com. Mar.-Aug. dorms €14.50; doubles €44, with bath €48; family rooms €60. Sept.-Feb. €11/14.50/16.50/30.) Farther up the main street and down to the left on Peter St., **Altazamuth House** ❸ has pretty bedrooms and a pleasant sunroom. (☎947 6300. Open Apr.-Oct. Singles €40; doubles €64.) A 30min. walk down the main road from Knightstown lies tiny **Chapeltown,** home to the **Ring Lyne Hostel and B&B** ❶, which puts guests up in basic doubles and triples above a salty pub. (☎947 6103. Kitchen open daily noon-9pm. Dorms €12; ensuite private rooms €15; B&B rooms €30.)

Limited supplies are available at the **store** in Knightstown, a few doors up from the waterfront. (Open M-Sa 9am-7pm, Su 9:30am-2pm.) ▨**Sea Breeze Cafe** ❷, farther up the street away from the water, is a pleasant and cozy cafe with outdoor tables, tasty midday meals, and a steady stream of local patrons. (☎947 6373. Sandwiches €3-8. Tikka wraps €8.50. Open May-Oct. daily noon-6pm.) Enjoy fine dining with a twist at **Fuchsia** ❹, at the top of the main street, where the 11oz. Sirloin Steak Shakespeare (€20) is cooked "As you like it" or "To be or not to be." (☎947 6051. Entrees €14.50-22. Open M and W-Su 6-9pm.) Next door, **Boston's Bar** ❶ serves quality pub dishes and frequent live acts. (☎947 6140. Entrees €7.50-13. July-Aug. W-Su and Sept.-June Sa live music. Kitchen open daily noon-8pm.)

🔵🔼 **SIGHTS AND OUTDOOR ACTIVITIES.** Valentia's views at several points on the island justify the journey. The hike up to **Bray Head,** at the western end of the island—indeed, the most western point in all of Europe, rewards travelers with the perfect vantage point to survey the distant skelligs. Nearly as awe-inspiring is how close to the edge of the dramatic cliffs the sheep dare to go. The only sign of civilization within miles is the remains of a Napoleonic lookout tower, so its just you, the sheep, and the sea, baby. The road from town to the **old slate quarry** runs past the turn-off to the Coombe Bank House and ends with Valentia's best views across Dingle Bay. Arrive at the quarry (a 1hr. hike from Knightstown) just before sunset to witness the panorama in the rich-hued fading light. Slate from this massive dig was used to create the roof of the British Parliament, and the hollowed-out cliffside now houses a sacred grotto filled with icons dating to 1954. Just outside of Knightstown, a right turn off the island's main road leads to **Glanleam Subtropical Gardens,** a public park housed on a private estate whose awesome collection of rare plants and flowers include the 15m Chilean Fire Bush. (☎947 6176. Open Easter-Oct. daily 10am-7pm. €6, students €5, children €2.50.) The proprietors of Glanleam also have palatial **holiday homes,** complete with full kitchen, jacuzzi, sauna, and 2½ baths, available for rent at reasonable weekly rates. (Contact the gardens with inquiries. Sleeps 10-22. €300-900 per wk., depending on the season.)

The Altazamuth House (☎947 6300) arranges **sea angling. Valentia Island Seasports,** down by the pier, teaches one-week dive certification courses from Easter to October, all equipment included. (☎947 6204; www.divevalentia.ie. €450-550 per person.) Back on the Iveragh peninsula, at its western corner, bikers can follow the gorgeous **Skellig Ring,** an offshoot of the Ring of Kerry that branches from Waterville and runs along the coast through Ballinskelligs and Portmagee before rejoining the main road on the Ring at Cahersiveen.

👁 **WATCH YOUR STEP.** It seems that humans aren't the only species with an ancestral stake in the Emerald Isle. In 1992, Swiss geologist Ivan Stossel discovered a track of small footprints on the rocky shore of Valentia Island. After analyzing layers of volcanic ash in the groove-like prints, scientists concluded that they were stamped out 385 million years ago, making them the oldest fossilized footprints in the Northern Hemisphere. They are believed to be those of a **Devonian tetrapod,** a creature that predates the dinosaurs. The prints, located in the northeastern corner of the island, are clearly signposted.

BALLINSKELLIGS (BAILE AN SCEILG) ☎066

Once visitors turn away from the Ring of Kerry's tourism frenzy and onto R566 or R567 and begin smelling the patches of roadside flowers, they never want to turn back. Across the bay from Waterville, *An Gaeltacht* signs indicate the transition into the Irish-speaking region of Ballinskelligs. The area contains access points to the desolate Skellig Rocks and also boasts a few sights of its own, including a monastery and an artists' community and gallery.

TRANSPORTATION AND PRACTICAL INFORMATION. There is no bus service to Ballinskelligs. Those without cars have the option of a €15 **taxi** from Cahersiveen. R566 runs south along the coast and ends at the Ballinskelligs pier. There is one four-way intersection between Cable O'Leary's and the pier; signs point east to the beach and west to the hostel, the Skellig Ring, and the **Kerry Way.** The **post office** on the main road, across from the Ballinskelligs Inn and Cable O'Leary's, sells snacks, ice cream, and basic provisions and has **Internet** access. (☎947 9221. €2 per 30min., €3.50 per hr. Post office open M-F 9am-1:30pm and 2:30-5:30pm, Sa 9am-1pm; shop with Internet open M-Sa 9am-5:30pm.) The closest banks and other amenities are in Waterville (p. 303) and Cahersiveen (p. 297).

ACCOMMODATIONS. There are two places to stay in Ballinskelligs, and they are both on the beach overlooking Ballinskelligs Bay. Four-year-old Skellig Hostel ❶ is clean and has that inviting new hostel smell. Enjoy plenty of space with two fully equipped kitchens, two dining rooms, and a lounge. Turn right at the four-way intersection on the main road and continue straight through the second; it's a 10min. walk from the beach. (☎947 9942 or 397 7834; www.skellighostel.com. Book ahead. Dorms Sept.-Feb. €12, Mar.-Aug. €14.50. Private doubles €16/22, ensuite €18/24.) The yellow **Ballinskelligs Inn ❸,** before the beach on the main road through town, has 15 bedrooms with gorgeous views of the bay and the inn's pristine lawn. (☎947 9104; www.ballinskelligsinn.com. Rooms May-Sept. €45 per person; Oct.-Apr. €35. No singles.) It is legal to camp on the grass above the beach. Turn down to the beach at the crossroads to find a car park and public toilets.

FOOD AND PUBS. There are a few budget dining options in Ballinskelligs proper, but those who want to cook up their own masterpieces should bring groceries. **Cable O'Leary's Pub and Restaurant ❷** is attached to the Ballinskelligs Inn; look for the American, Irish, and EU flags. The pub is named after a local hero who pulled the first transatlantic cable between America and Co. Kerry up to the Ballinskelligs shore. It plays host to live Irish and country music all summer nights except Mondays and Tuesdays and when it reverts to disco on Sundays. The restaurant serves toasties (€5.75) and entrees starting at €8.50. At **Caiffe Cois Tra (The Beach Cafe) ❶,** Barbara Cassidy sells sandwiches (from €3), desserts, snacks, tea, and coffee in a wooden building by the beach. Browse through her collection of old photographs and maps of Co. Kerry. The shop, as the town's tourist information desk, has the phone numbers of every boat that sails to the Skelligs. (☎947 9323; www.kerryimages.com. Open May to mid-Oct. daily 9am-6pm.)

SIGHTS AND OUTDOOR ACTIVITIES. The **Skellig Cruise** departs daily from Ballinskelligs Pier to the **Skellig Rocks** (p. 305) around 11am. (Contact Sean Feehan for reservations and to check sea conditions ☎947 9182 or 417 6612.) A dozen or so other boats sail to the Skelligs from Portmagee. Names and phone numbers are available at Caiffe Cois Tra at the beach. When the tide is out on the beach, walk to the **"castle,"** remains of a tower house built by the MacCarthy family and excavated from 1988-91 by students from University College at Cork. The

DISTANCE: 45km
DURATION: 2-3 days
BEST TIME TO GO: Summer

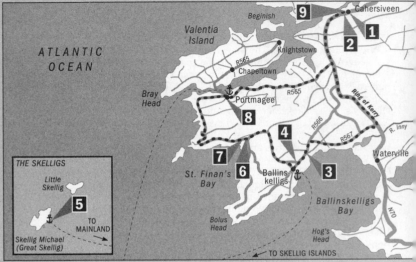

Some of these roads are very narrow for cars, and the distinctive Co. Kerry wildflower smell is more apparent by bike, so grab some wheels and explore this essentially untouristed area adjacent to the famous Ring of Kerry.

1. CASEY CYCLES. Rent a bike at **Casey's Cycles** in Cahersiveen (see p.297).

2. CENTRA. Hit up the store for two days' worth of groceries (see p. 298). Take N70 south, pass the turnoff for Portmagee and continue on to the R566.

3. SIOPA CHILL RIALAIG ART GALLERY. Stop to check out the stellar artwork and have a meal in the upscale cafe (see p. 303).

4. SKELLIG HOSTEL. Drop your stuff off, cook up a storm in the communal kitchen, and spend the night here (see p. 301).

5. THE SKELLIG ROCKS. Daytrip out to visit Skellig Michael's ancient monastic settlement, complete with beehive-shaped dwellings (see p. 305). Stay overnight in Ballinskelligs again, or soldier on.

6. SKELLIG CHOCOLATE COMPANY. Stop on your way as you bike toward Portmagee. Watch the friendly staff cut up mint brittle and coffee fudge, then eat your weight in samples (see p. 303).

7. BEACH. Picnic on the gorgeous no-name beach near the chocolate company (see p. 303). You will need to load up for the steep climb to Coonanaspig; after that you will be coasting all the way to Portmagee.

8. PORTMAGEE HOSTEL. Stay overnight in this brand new hostel if you don't want to cycle all the way back to Cahersiveen (see p. 299).

9. QC'S CHARGRILL. Head back to Cahersiveen, return your bike and reward your athletic self with a square meal of fresh fish (see p. 298).

warm-watered beach is popular with swimmers, many of whom dive off the end of the pier near the castle. Don't miss the ruins of **Ballinskelligs Burial Ground and Priory,** accessible at low tide, which served as a place of worship for the monks of Skellig Michael (p. 305) after 11th-century storms made journeying to the island increasingly hazardous. The remains of the monastery cloister and the hall date back to the 15th century. A **hike** (4-5hr.) to **Bolus Head** leads to a panoramic view of St. Finian's Bay that is worth the trek, but the narrow road makes it easier to walk than to bike. Just before the bay is the **Skellig Chocolate Company,** where you can watch the friendly staff perfect their delicious craft (weekdays 10am-4pm) and get a few free samples of the 60-plus flavors, including gin & tonic or champagne/brandy truffle. (☎066 947 9119; www.skelligschocolate.com. Bags of truffles €7.50; chocolate squares €1. Open M-F 10am-5pm; Apr.-Oct. M-F 10am-5pm and Sa noon-5pm; May-Oct. M-F 10am-5pm, Su noon-5pm.) Bring your goodies to the nearby nameless **beach,** which has tables for pleasant picnicking.

▧Siopa Chill Rialaig Art Gallery, Dun Geagan, 3km before Ballinskelligs on R566, is well worth a stop but nearly impossible to reach without a car or bike. This beautiful, deceptively large gallery and workshop exhibits work by artists who complete residencies at *Cill Rialaig*, a restored pre-famine village at Bolus Head. The free accommodations and studio space draw internationally famed artists to this community; in exchange they often donate some of their work to the gallery. Almost all pieces are for sale, but the original works carry a hefty price tag. (☎947 8277; cillrialaig@esatclear.ie. Ask about the occasional workshops and classes open to the public. Open daily Sept.-June 11am-5pm; July-Aug. daily 10am-7pm.) **▧John Casey's Kitchen** is attached to the gallery. Formerly a chef at London's Savoy and Boston's Ritz Carlton, John Casey serves simple entrees (€9-12), sandwiches (€4.50-7), and desserts made to order in this naturally lit cafe. Stop in for a coffee and homemade apple tart a la mode (€4) on a visit to the gallery. (☎087 993 2246. Open June-Aug. daily 11am-5pm.)

WATERVILLE (AN COIREAN) ☎066

Built between the Atlantic and Lough Currane as a telecommunications portal, Waterville and its scenic shores were flooded every summer by its English founders. Nowadays, Waterville's human traffic piles out of tour buses for a seaside lunch and a shopping excursion in its giant crafts market before rambling on to Sneem. Tourists also clamor around the bronze statue of a certain top-hat-wearing, mustache-sporting, cane-wielding English comedic actor on Main St. for a quick Kodak moment. The real Charlie Chaplin frequented the oceanfront town, which erected the monument in his honor. Those who decide to stay longer than the tour bus allows understand why "the tramp" was so fond of it; its spectacularly close waterfront—most establishments have unimpeded views of the shelf of smooth rocks and sand and the vast expanse of ocean beyond—is irresistible to swimmers, walkers, and sunbathers alike.

◨⁊ TRANSPORTATION AND PRACTICAL INFORMATION. The Ring of Kerry **bus** stops in front of the Bay View Hotel, Main St. (June to mid-Sept. 1 per day), with service to **Caherdaniel** (20min., €3.20); **Killarney** (2hr., €12.20); and **Sneem** (50min., €6.50). Eastbound **Bus Éireann** goes to **Cahersiveen** in the morning once per day en route to **Killarney.** The friendly **tourist office** is above the beach past the Butler Arms Hotel in a low, modern building. (☎947 4646. Open daily 9:30am-5:15pm.) A Bank of Ireland **ATM** is inside Centra (☎947 4257). A small **pharmacy** lies in the town center. (☎947 4141. Open M-Sa 9:30am-6pm, Su 9am-1pm for newspaper and candy only.) **Internet** access is available at Peter's Cafe. (☎947 4608; €3 per hr.; open Apr.-Oct. daily 8am-10pm) and at the **post office,** just across from the tourist office (☎947 4100; €1 per 10min.; open M-F 9am-5:30pm, Sa 9am-2pm).

📵 **ACCOMMODATIONS.** Waterville's closest hostel is a ways away (8 mi. off the Ring of Kerry Rd.; 20min. car ride), but its situation along the Kerry Way means that most of its visitors are looking for a good hike anyway. The remoteness of the **Brú na Dromoda (Dromid Hostel) ❶,** located in Mastergeehy on the Inny River, matters even less as the hostel is part of an enormous community complex that suits any wandering walker, climber, or fisherman's needs. Most hostelers would be happy with its clean bunks, standard kitchen and TV lounge, but the adjacent sports hall (including basketball court), food store, and bar are all the more reason to bust out those hiking boots. From Waterville, head north on N70 out of town; take a right just before the church. (☎947 4782; www.dromid.ie. Free wash and dry. Open May-Oct. Internet access €1 per 10min. Dorms €17-19; family rooms €22-27.) Forward-thinking, long-term-minded budget travelers benefit from per-room (as opposed to per person) rates at **The Huntsman ❸.** Each deluxe apartment has stunning views of the beach below and its own sauna, jacuzzi, and fireplace for you and three buddies; just flip a coin to see who gets the pull-out. To reserve an apartment, call well in advance. (☎947 4124; www.rci.com. Quads €150 per night, €700 per wk.) B&Bs line the main road; one option is **O'Dwyer's ❸,** above the pub of the same name, which provides big, well-furnished rooms with clear views of the beach. (☎947 4248. Rooms €30-35 per person.) Additionally, the **Bay View Hotel ❸** has quiet, private rooms at low rates and two bright, spacious on-site bars. (☎947 4122; www.bayviewhotelwterville.com. Weekend singles €40; doubles €70. Midweek 3-day special €105/198.)

📵📷 **FOOD AND PUBS. Centra** (☎947 4257; open daily May-Sept. 7am-11pm; Oct.-Apr. 7am-10pm), which has a Bank of Ireland ATM inside, and neighboring **Curran's** (☎947 4253; open daily June-Sept. 7am-11pm; Oct.-May 7am-10pm) sell groceries. 📷**The Chédéan ❷,** across from the Butler Arms Hotel, has small-town ambience, some of the best scones in Ireland, and a super-friendly hostess. Peruse the small selection of secondhand books (€2) over a scrumptious home-baked treat. (☎947 4966. Food €2.50-12. Open late Apr. to Oct. daily 10am-6pm.) Across from the tourist office and next to the post office, **Beach Cove Cafe ❶** offers standard burgers and sandwiches at a takeaway counter. Nab a table outside for commanding views of the water. (☎947 4733. Pizza, burgers, and sandwiches €3-7. Open mid-Mar. to Sept. daily 10am-11pm.) **An Corean ❶** is perhaps the quietest of the trio of cafes, but its wholesome fresh food make it a popular choice for those who have high standards and enjoy low prices. (☎947 4711. Lunch €3-10; dinner €11-19. Open daily 9:30am-9pm. MC/V.) Gaelic football legend Mick O'Dwyer lends his name to **O'Dwyer's: The Villa Restaurant & Pub ❷,** at the corner of Main St. and the Ring of Kerry Rd. Enjoy a pint with a young local crowd before jamming to the live music or DJ out back on warm weekend summer nights. (☎947 4248. F and Su live trad; Sa DJ. Sandwiches €3-6; entrees €10-20. Kitchen open daily noon-8:30pm. MC/V.) **The Lobster Bar and Restaurant ❷,** a few doors down, serves dinner and drinks in a spacious and airy room with ocean views. It also showcases live music most nights during the summer. (☎947 4629. Wi-Fi hot spot. W-F trad, Sa-Su alternating trad and live DJ. Entrees €10-20. Kitchen open daily noon-9:30pm.) **The Lodge,** located in the hotel of the same name on the eastern end of Main St., opens its gigantic nightclub for dancing fools and love machines on several summer nights. (☎947 4436. Cover €5. Th teen night. Open June-Sept. W-Th and Sa-Su.) **The Fishermen's Bar** sports big, roomy booths and a loyal set of locals. (☎947 4144. Occasional live music on summer weekends. Kitchen open daily noon-8:30pm.)

◨ ⚠ SIGHTS AND OUTDOOR ACTIVITIES. Lough Currane lies about 3km inland from town; follow the signposts on the main road from Sneem. Locals claim that a submerged castle can be seen in times of low water, but visitors seem to have better luck with the ruins of a monastery on Church Island. The lake is a popular fishing spot; day licenses are available at **O'Sullivan's Tackle Shop,** on the main road near the hostel. The shop also outfits fishermen with bait, rods, boots, and nets. (☎ 947 4433. One-day fishing license €34, €17 goes toward salmon conservation. Open May to late Sept. daily 9am-6pm; otherwise call for an appointment.) For more information about lake and sea angling **boats for hire** and **salmon and sea trout fishing** opportunities, contact John Murphy (☎ 947 5257 or 086 399 1074).

THE SKELLIG ROCKS   ☎ 066

About 13km off the shore of the Iveragh Peninsula, the stunning ◨**Skellig Rocks** rise abruptly from the sea. More than just masses of natural rubble, these islands awe visitors who, as George Bernard Shaw put it, often find them "not of this world, but a place you dream of." While the multitudes rush around the Ring of Kerry, those who detour to the Skelligs are rewarded with an immeasurably more intimate encounter with nature. As **Little Skellig** comes into view, the jagged rock pinnacles appear snow-capped; another look reveals that they are actually covered with a field of crooning **gannets,** the largest such community in Europe.

Boats dock at the larger **Skellig Michael,** where daytrippers have two hours to climb the vertigo-inducing 630 stone steps past kittiwakes, petrels, razorbills, manx shearwaters, fulmars, and puffins to reach an ancient **monastic settlement.** Sixth-century Christian monks carved out an austere but largely self-sustaining niche along one craggy face of the 218m high rock to escape any trace of sin-ridden civilization. Their stone beehive-shaped dwellings and oratories remain amazingly intact and are explained in detail by guides from the Office of Public Works, though the structures' dark interiors and the graveyard's eerie stone crosses speak volumes of the monks' severe—and self-imposed—spiritual journey. The faithful survived Viking raids and harsh winter storms for more than six centuries before abandoning the island for unknown reasons, leaving the world one of its best examples of early Christian architecture. There is no restroom or shelter on the rock, and the Ministry of Tourism does not recommend the trip for young children, the elderly, or those who suffer from serious medical conditions.

On the 1hr. **ferry voyage** (usually €40), rocks seem to materialize silently out of the distant mist. If you have a tendency for seasickness, beware of choppy waves, even in good weather. Most boats depart around 10am from Portmagee, the closest to the Skelligs, and return by 3pm, but some pick up passengers from Reenard Point and Valentia Island. The Sive Hostel and the campsite in **Cahersiveen** (p. 297) arrange trips that include a ride to the dock for no extra cost. Departing from **Ballinskelligs** is Sean Feehan (☎ 947 9182) and from **Caherdaniel** is John O'Shea (☎ 087 689 8431). Some operators departing from **Portmagee** are Michael O'Sullivan (☎ 947 4255) and Joe Roddy (☎ 087 120 9924), who can collect passengers from Waterville, Dermot/Mary Walsh's Boat (☎ 947 6120 or 086 833 9549), and McCrohan Boats (☎ 947 6412 or 087 239 9741). Seanie Murphy picks up passengers in **Reenard** and **Valentia Island** as well as in Portmagee (☎ 947 6214 or 087 236 2344). To arrive at a different town than the one from which you departed, make arrangements directly with the captain. Ferries run from April to October, depending on weather; call ahead for reservations and to confirm departures on the day of the trip.

The grass-roofed **Skellig Experience Visitors Centre** is just over the Portmagee Bridge on Valentia Island. A 15min. video and large-scale models show visitors what it took to live a monastic life in the middle of the ocean; an extra (steep) charge buys a sailboat ride from the Centre to the Skelligs themselves, although the boats do not dock. (☎947 6306. Open daily June-Aug. 10am-7pm; Apr.-May and Sept.-Nov. 10am-6pm; €5, students and seniors €4; with cruise €27/24.50.)

CAHERDANIEL (CATHAIR DONAL) ☎066

There's little to attract the average tourist to the village of Caherdaniel; a small lane with two pubs, a market, and a restaurant is the only evidence of habitation. But there are other chances for fun: Derrynane National Park and its flagship Derrynane House, the ancestral home of patriot Daniel O'Connell, is a 10min. drive out of town. Along the coast, stretches of sparkling white dunes and crystal blue water fill with beachgoers at the first hint of sunlight.

🖅🖬 TRANSPORTATION AND PRACTICAL INFORMATION. The Ring of Kerry **bus** stops in Caherdaniel at the junction of the Ring of Kerry Rd. and Main St. on the way to **Killarney** (1½hr., June-Sept. 1 per day, €14.50) and **Sneem** (30min., June-Sept. 1 per day, €4.40). The **tourist office**, 1.5km east of town at the Wave Crest Camping Park (☎947 5188; open daily mid-Mar. to June and Sept. to mid-Oct. 9am-8pm; July-Aug. 9am-9:30pm), is the only place in town with **Internet** access.

🖬🖸 ACCOMMODATIONS AND FOOD. A relaxing sitting room with fireplace and TV and bedroom-like dorms at **The Travelers Rest Hostel ❶**, across from the gas station and a 3min. walk from the center of the village on the Caherdaniel road, say "home" more than "hostel". (☎947 5175. Dorms €16; private rooms €19.) Right next to the Blind Piper Pub & Restaurant, **Kerry Way B&B ❸** has two bright and spacious rooms with baths open to guests. (☎947 5277. Singles €45; doubles €60.) Campers perch contentedly over the beach 1.5km east of town on the Ring of Kerry Rd. at **Wave Crest Camping Park ❶**. The shop and self-service laundry are handy for campers and passersby. (☎947 5188. Showers €1. Internet access €2 per 15min. Laundry €6 per load. Shop open June-Aug. M-Th 8am-8:30pm, F-Su 8am-9:30pm. Site open mid-Mar. to Oct. €6.50 per person including tent. €20 per couple with car.)

Freddy's Bar and Grocery, on the main corner, stocks food and drink. (☎947 5400. Grocery open in summer daily 8:30am-9pm; in winter 8:30am-7pm. Bar open late.) **O'Carroll's Cove Beach Bar and Restaurant ❸** is Ireland's charming take on a more Bahamas-like institution. When live music isn't playing, the juke box is. If the sun's not out, the family-run family-fun bar ensures that there's always plenty of *craic* about. (☎947 5151. Entrees €11-24. Kitchen open June-Aug. daily noon-9pm.) The **Courthouse Cafe ❷**, on the road to the Derrynane sights, serves satisfying sandwiches by day and Irish favorites for takeaway by night. (☎947 5834. Lunch €6-8. Takeaway dinner €11-19. Cafe open 11am-5pm, takeaway 6-10pm.) The **Blind Piper Pub ❹**, across from the cafe, is a popular local hangout—outdoor tables by the stream are perfect for enjoying a meal. Music drowns out the brook from June to August, when trad or blues is featured on Thursday nights. (☎947 5126. Sandwiches €3-8. Dinner menu €11-25. Kitchen open daily July-Aug. noon-9pm; Sept.-June noon-8pm.) **Keating's Bar** (☎947 5115), over the Mass Path in Derrynane, is the spot to soak up some real Caherdaniel flavor.

🖬 SIGHTS. A trip to Caherdaniel is incomplete without a visit to **Derrynane National Park,** a well-signposted 2.5km drive from the center of the village. The highlighted attraction, **Derrynane House,** was once the residence of Daniel "The Liberator" O'Connell (p. 53). Displayed inside the house are the dueling pistol that O'Connell used to kill challenger John d'Esterre and the black glove he wore to church for years afterward to mourn his victim. A 30min. film (last showing 1½hr. before closing) presents an engrossing image of O'Connell. (☎947 5113. Open May-

Sept. M-Sa 9am-6pm, Su 11am-7pm; Apr. and Oct. Tu-Su 1-5pm; Nov.-Mar. Sa-Su 1-5pm. Last admission 45min. before closing. €3, students and children €1.30, senior €2.10, families €7.40.) A few trails lead through the extensive dunes and gardens down to the beach, which is about a 45min. walk from Caherdaniel. One of the best is the 15min. walk to **Abbey Island** (only a true island during very high tides), which extends into the water to the southwest. There, the **Abbey of St. Finian** shows the wear of 1300 years, enchanting explorers with its graveyard.

Ten kilometers off N70 and several kilometers outside of Caherdaniel on the Sneem road, after a long drive through the countryside, lies the pre-Christian **Staigue Fort.** A remarkably well-preserved ruin and the largest of its kind in Ireland, the empty fort sits serenely on a rise in the middle of a sheep-flecked valley. Stepping through its low T-shaped entrance feels eerily like stepping back in time. (☎947 5288. Fort always open. Free.) For a closer look at the watery side of Caherdaniel at blistering speed, contact **Activity Ireland,** run by the owners of the Kerry Way B&B. They rent the rather pricey but adrenaline-inducing Zapcats. (☎189 022 8483. €80 per hr.) **Derrynane Sea Sports** also rents everything for your windsurfing, canoeing, sailing, snorkeling, water skiing, body and surfboarding needs. (☎087 908 1208. Open June-Sept. daily 10am-dusk. Rentals for 30min. and 1hr.) For land exploration on a friendly beast, try **Eagle Rock Equestrian Centre.** (☎947 5145. Beach treks €25 per hr.) Fishing trips and jaunts to the Skelligs are arranged through **Bealtra Boats.** (☎947 5129. Skelligs trip €40 per person).

SNEEM (AN TSNAIDHM)   ☎064

The hordes tend to make Sneem their first or last stop along the Ring, and the town is well-prepared to receive them. Trad wafts out of the large number of shops on the South Sq. amid clutters of postcard stands. The **Sneem Sculpture Park** includes an unusual variety of works, like a collection of buildings called "the Way The Fairies Went," all of which can be navigated using *Sneem: The Knot in the Ring*, a handy brochure available at the tourist office. Most sculptures have an international connection, like the bronze monument to Charles de Gaulle (who visited for two weeks in 1969) or the beloved white marble panda donated by the People's Republic of China in 1986, whose cuteness matches the town's own charm. Indeed, most people have an inexplicable fondness for the oddly named place, reflected in the popular "I [heart] Sneem" bumper stickers. The town's charismatic nature hits its peak during the **Sneem Family Festival,** featuring a wide range of fun activities for the whole family in late July (☎086 356 1150; www.sneemfestival.com). When the festival's not in full swing, colorful displays still await inside **Rosemary's Art** studio, on the North Sq. Look for the tile-adorned building. (☎45595. Call or just ring the doorbell; Rosemary's is open when she's working inside.)

There are no longer any hostels or campsites in Sneem, but it has several good B&B options. ◙**The Bank House ❸,** North Sq., is all bright and cheery, from its gregarious owners to its facade and flower boxes. Rumor has it that a certain famous Irish actress has stayed here; check the owner's book collection for clues. (☎45226. Open Mar.-Oct. Singles €45; doubles €64-70.) A short walk down the road next to the tourist office lies **Old Convent House ❸,** a stately B&B with comfortable rooms and a lovely proprietress. Enjoy your breakfast out on the stone patio so that you can take in the perfectly manicured grounds with their spectacular mountain view. (☎45181; conventhouse@oceanfree.net. Singles €50; doubles €70.) Just across North Sq. from The Bank House, **Arch House ❸** offers beautiful rooms decorated with prints by local artists. (☎45127. Singles €40; doubles €60.)

Chippers are a dime a dozen, but great chippers are harder to find. The boastful "Best Fish and Chips in Ireland" sign outside **The Hungry Knight ❶,** on the North Sq., makes the search a bit easier. (☎45237. Meals €4-9. Open M-Th and Su noon-10pm,

F-Sa noon-1am.) North of the bridge, **The Village Kitchen ❷** serves seafood and *panini* in a roomy cafe. (☎45281. Sandwiches €3-6; entrees €8-13. Open daily July-Aug. 9:30am-8pm; Sept.-June 9am-6pm.) Ditch hiking boots for fancier footwear before entering **Sacre Coeur ❹,** just past the North Sq., which has served seafood and steak to adoring customers since 1968. (☎45186. Entrees €9-21. Open M-Sa 6-10pm, Su 12:30-2:30pm and 6-10pm.) Massive pub meals and seafood dinners await at **The Blue Bull ❷,** in the South Sq. Proof of the old pub's pride is in its pictures, which line the walls alongside the excerpt mentioning Sneem from the famous Irish play where the place gets its name. Its great reputation comes from its live music. (☎45382. Entrees €11-25. Tu, Th, Sa during summer live music. Kitchen open daily noon-9pm. AmEx/MC/V.) Back in the North Sq., enjoy trad from the comfort of the beautiful back deck at **O'Shea's ❶** during summer weekends. The pub's gourmet sandwich menu is also a delight. (☎45515. Sandwiches €7; entrees €10. Kitchen open daily noon-9pm.) Not many can leave Sneem without having a pint and snapping their picture in front of **Dan Murphy's Bar** and its famous stone.

The Ring of Kerry **bus** goes to Killarney (1hr., June-Sept. 1 per day, €13), and Kenmare (€16). The **tourist office** is in the Joli Coeur Craft Shop between the bridge and South Sq. (☎45270. Open daily June to late Sept. 10:30am-6pm; Mar.-May and Oct.-Nov. 11am-5pm.) **Internet** access is found at **Sneem Resource Center,** Sportsfield Rd., to the right of the Hungry Knight, for €6 per hr. (☎45545. Open M-Th 10am-2pm, F 10am-5pm.) The **post office** is a few doors down. (☎45110. Open M-F 9am-1pm and 2-5:30pm, Sa 10am-1pm.) There is an **ATM** in **Christian's Food-store.** (☎45116. Open M-Sa 8:30am-10pm, Su 9am-8pm.)

KENMARE (NEIDIN) ☎064

Beautiful Kenmare sits at the apex of the Beara and Iveragh peninsulas. Its handy location provides the perfect base for exploring the Ring of Beara and the Ring of Kerry, as the reams of tourists will attest, but its abundance of sights, pubs, and award-winning restaurants are reason enough to make an extended stop here.

▐ TRANSPORTATION

Buses: Depart across from SuperValu on Main St. **Bus Éireann** goes to **Castletownbere** via **Ardgroom** and **Eyeries** (40min., June-Aug. M-Sa 9:30am and 4:10pm, €7-8); **Cork** (4hr., June-Sept. daily 2:30pm, €13.50) via **Glengarriff** (45min.) and **Skibbereen** (2hr.); **Killarney** (1hr.; M-Sa 5 per day 8:40am-6pm, Su 12:45pm, 2:45, 6pm; €7.60), connections to **Tralee** and **Cork; Sneem** (35min., June-Aug. M-Sa 8:50am and 4pm, €6.50), connections available to the **Ring of Kerry** bus in summer as it returns to Killarney (€18.50). Significantly fewer routes and times Oct.-May; check with the tourist office or call the Killarney bus station (☎30011).

Taxis: Finnegan's Tours (☎41491 or 087 248 0800; www.kenmarecoachandcab.com). Also offers bus tours around the Rings of Beara and Kerry (€20 per person) and to Glengarriff and Garinish Island (€25 per person) during summer.

Bike Rental: Finnegan's (☎41083), Henry St. near Shelbourne St. €15 per day, €85 per wk. Bikes available Apr.-Sept. M-Sa 10am-8pm. If closed, enquire at the toy shop on Henry St.

✴ ▐ ORIENTATION AND PRACTICAL INFORMATION

Kenmare's three major streets form a triangle; **Shelbourne Street** runs from east to west off the Glengarriff/Castletownbere road, while the livelier **Main Street** and **Henry Street** meet at the **square,** which contains a small park and is fronted by the tourist office. From here, Main St. becomes N71 to **Killarney;** N70 to **Sneem** and the **Ring of Kerry** branches off Main St. on the way out of town.

Tourist Office: the square (☎41233). Friendly staff offers advice about the Heritage Trail and houses the free **Heritage Centre** (see **Sights,** p. 310). Open June and Sept. M-Sa 9am-6pm, Su 10am-6pm; July-Aug. M-Sa 9am-7pm, Su 10am-6pm; Apr.-May and Oct. M-Sa 9am-6pm.

Bank: AIB, 9 Main St. (☎41010), on the corner of Henry St., and **Bank of Ireland,** the square (☎41255). Both have **ATMs.** Banks open M 10am-5pm, Tu-F 10am-4pm.

Laundry: O'Shea's, Kenmare Business Park (☎41394). Take the Killarney road out of town; it's the 1st left after the road to Sneem. Wash €4, dry €1 per 10min. Open M-F 8:30am-6pm, Sa 9:30am-6pm.

Emergency: ☎999; no coins required. **Police** *(Garda):* Shelbourne St. (☎41177).

Pharmacy: Sheahan's, Main St. (☎41354). Open M-Sa 9am-6pm. **Brosnan's,** Henry St. (☎41318). Open M-F 9am-6:30pm, Sa 9am-6pm, Su 12:30-1:30pm.

Internet Access: Live Wire (☎42714), on Rock St., halfway up Main St., has computers and Wi-Fi. €2 per 30min. Open June-Aug. M-F 10am-8pm, Sa 1pm-9pm; Sept.-May M-F 10am-6pm. The **library** (☎41416), Shelbourne St., near its intersection with Main St., offers free Internet access in 50min. increments. Call ahead to reserve a time. Open Tu-W and F-Sa 10am-1:30pm and 2:30-5pm, Th 10am-1:30pm and 2:30-8pm.

Post Office: Henry St. (☎41490), at the corner of Shelbourne St. Open June-Sept. M-F 9am-5:30pm, Sa 9am-1pm; Oct.-May M-F 9am-1pm and 2-5:30pm, Sa 9am-1pm. Internet access for €1 per 15min. Computers available Apr.-Aug. M-F 8am-8pm, Sa 9am-6pm; Oct.-Mar. M-F 8am-5:30pm, Sa 9am-1pm.

ACCOMMODATIONS

Kenmare Lodge Hostel, 27 Main St. (☎40662; www.kenmare.eu/lodgehostel), toward the intersection with Shelbourne St. Immaculate hostel with bright dorms, private rooms, and a quiet central courtyard. TV lounge with free DVD rental. Laundry wash €4, dry €1 per 10min. Dorms €15; private rooms €35 per person. ❶

Hawthorn House, Shelbourne St. (☎41035; www.hawthornhousekenmare.com). Delightful Noel and Mary O'Brien make guests feel at home in their huge ensuite rooms and luxurious living room. Open year-round. Book ahead July-Aug. Doubles €70-90. ❸

Fáilte Hostel (IHH), at the corner of Henry and Shelbourne St. (☎42333; www.neidin.net). Spacious kitchen, cozy TV room, and convenient location draw backpackers and daytrippers. Just don't stay out too late; curfew Sa 1:30am. Open Apr.-Oct. Dorms €15; doubles €38-46; triples €51; quads €64. ❶

Rose Cottage, the Square (☎41330), next door to Keal Na Gower House. Elegant stone house, part of a former convent, is set off from the road behind a lovely green garden and offers quiet, comfortable rooms. €32-38 per person. ❸

Ring of Kerry Caravan and Camping Park, Sneem Rd. (☎41648; www.kenmare.eu/camping), 5km west of town. Amenities include a kitchen, TV room, and small shop. Laundry €7 per person, €4 per caravan. Showers €0.50. Open Apr.-Sept. 1 person with tent €8; 2-person tent with car €18. ❶

FOOD

Food is plentiful but pricey in Kenmare. Try the smaller cafes for snacks and check the pubs for cheap lunches. **SuperValu** is on Main St. and has a **Bank of Ireland ATM.** (☎41307. Open M-F 8am-9pm, Sa 8am-8pm, Su 9am-6pm.) For the label-conscious consumer, **The Kenmare Food Company** has an extensive array of local artisan and organic products. Its chilled wine cellar also offers free tastings during the day. (☎79800; www.thekenmarefoodcompany.com. Open daily 8am-9pm.) Takeaway is always a cheaper option. There are several on Main St., including the late-night **Wharton's Traditional Fish & Chips ❶**, which serves fried fish, burgers, and chicken. (☎42622. Dishes €2.50-8. Open M-F and Su noon-midnight, Sa noon-4am.) **Jer's ❶**, a few doors down, serves similar fare at similar prices. (☎42045. Dishes €2-6. Open M-Th and Su noon-midnight, F noon-1:30am, Sa noon-4am.) **The Truffle Pig ❶**, a small store in the square, is worth sniffing out. It offers full gourmet meals for takeaway such as the meaty cassoulet in addition to its fine foods selection, allowing the hosteler to eat like a king at a peddler's price. (☎42953. Entrees €3-6. Open M-Sa 9:30am-6pm.)

> **The Purple Heather Bistro,** Henry St. (☎41016). Sample goat cheese, toasted almonds, and seasonal fruit (€8.20) in a cozy red leather booth. Open M-Sa 10:45am-6pm. In the evening, those in search of fine food (entrees €17-29) move upstairs to the owners' newer and more expensive **Packie's** restaurant. Open M-Sa 6-10pm. MC/V. ❸
>
> **Jam,** Henry St. (☎41591). Delicious bakery and deli delights. Try the chocolate rum cake (€3.65) or construct an original toasted sandwich masterpiece (€3.50). Lunch specials €7.50. Open M-Sa 8am-5pm. MC/V. ❶
>
> **Cafe Mocha,** Main St. (☎42133), across from the park. Artsy spot with over a dozen original works satisfies the sweet tooth in hot (baked goods €2-4) or cold (ice cream €1.60) fashion. Open M-F 9am-5:30pm, Sa 11:30am-5:30pm, Su 10am-5pm. ❶
>
> **The Coachman's,** Henry St. (☎41311). Trad music and trad dishes with modern over-tones. M-Th trad sessions. Entrees €11-17. Kitchen open daily noon-9:30pm. MC/V. ❸
>
> **Mulcahy's,** 36 Henry St. (☎42383). Spend an incredible night of pure indulgence here. Wonderful presentation, delightful service, and delicious dishes make dining here an experience that even the most massive Guinness binge won't let you forget. Vegetarian-friendly. Entrees €17-28. Open daily 6pm-10pm. ❸

▼ PUBS

Kenmare's pubs attract a hefty contingent of tourists, making live music easy to come by during summer. The locals still hold their own at most watering holes.

> **The Bold Thady Quill** (☎41368), in the Landsdowne Arms Hotel, at the top of Main St. Wise visitors follow the locals here. Trad F-Su.
>
> **Atlantic Bar,** the Square (☎41094). Relaxed local joint makes sports fanatics feel at home with sports paraphernalia and dart board as primary decor. Su live trad. Breakfast daily 9:30-11:30am, lunch 12:30-2:30pm, dinner 5-9pm.
>
> **Crowley's,** Henry St. (☎41472). Raucous trad sessions pack this intimate pub practically every night. Open daily from 4pm.
>
> **The Square Pint,** Main St. (☎42357). Get down on the dance fl. at the rear of the bar between pints. F-Sa €5 cover for disco. Open until 2:30am.
>
> **Foley's,** Henry St. (☎42162; www.foleyskenmare.com). Huge pub serves heaping Irish faves and trad music to laid-back folk every night. Daily specials €11. Kitchen open daily noon-9:30pm.

◎ SIGHTS

Perhaps the best way to take advantage of Kenmare's prime location is to take to the sea; an exploration through Kenmare Bay allows for simultaneous perusals of the Kerry and Beara peninsulas. The skipper of **Seafari Cruises** is a comedian/singer/entertainer/environmentalist extraordinaire and his crew doubles as his band. Raymond leads his "happy sailors on a happy cruise" through Kenmare

River to its seal colonies, where animals and humans alike are soothed by the sun and the sounds of traditional Irish music. (☎83171 for reservations; www.seafari-ireland.com. July-Aug. 2-3 per day. €20, 18+ students €17.50, ages 12-18 €15, under 12 €12.50, families €60-65. Tea/coffee, cookies and "medicine" included.) The cruises depart from the pier. Take Henry St. out of town and follow the Glengarriff road; turn right just before the bridge. For more fun on the sea, **StarSailing and Adventure Centre,** off R571, a 5min. drive from Kenmare, organizes a host of activities including canoeing, fishing, kayaking, and more. (☎41222; www.staroutdoors.ie.) Back on land, the area in and around town is full of historical sights, most of which are part of Kenmare's **Heritage Trail.** Highlights include the largest **stone circle** in Southwest Ireland, only a short 3min. walk from the tourist office, and **Cromwell's Bridge,** named either after the infamous man himself or for *croimeal*, the Gaelic word for "moustache," which the bridge's shape resembles. A free map of the trail with detailed information about each site is available at the tourist office. Kenmare is also an ideal place for hiking enthusiasts—it's right along the **Kerry Way.** The most direct route to the trail from the tourist office is down the road to the left; passing over a small stone bridge; follow the road up the hill as it dwindles to a path and then runs into the main road. Brown signs announce the beginning of the rail. The new **Heritage Centre,** housed in the tourist office (p. 309), has a model of the town and the stone circle, and small exhibits on topics ranging from the founding of Kenmare to the town's long-standing lacemaking industry. (Same hours as the tourist office. Free.) Above the tourist office, **The Kenmare Lace and Design Centre** has demonstrations of the Kenmare lacemaking technique, invented in 1862 by the local nuns. (☎42636. Open Mar.-Sept. M-Sa 10:30am-1pm and 2:15-5:30pm. Free.) For fishing gear, permits, and info about local spots to cast your line, head to **John O'Hare Fishing Tackle** on Main St. (☎41499. The price for a fly-fishing day permit varies depending on location and species, but generally can be purchased for €10-20. Open daily June-Aug. 9:30am-6pm; Sept.-May 9:30am-1pm and 2-6:30pm.)

Nine miles south on the Glengariff Rd. awaits the nostalgia-inducing **Molly Gallivan's Cottage and Traditional Farm.** Visitors watch a 10min. video detailing the eerie history of the grounds, then take a self-guided 15-20min. walk through them to get a taste of what life must have been like for this famous *poitín*-brewing widow. Unfortunately, they don't get a taste of "Molly's Mountain Dew," the whiskey which she sold here from her *Sibheen* (illegal pub). The homebaking in the **tearooms** is a nice consolation, as is the well-stocked **craft shop.** Other on-site highlights include a Neolithic Stone Row dating back to 3000 BC and a crumbling famine ruin. (☎40714; www.mollygallivans.com. Donations requested. Open Apr.-Oct. daily 10am-6pm.) Along the same route lies **The Lorge Chocolatier** where the French Benoit concocts his award-winning chocolates for your pleasure. (☎087 991 7172. Open daily 10am-6pm.)

The performing arts abound during **Fleadh Cheoil Chiarrai,** a festival of traditional Irish music and dance held annually at the end of June. The festival was founded in Kenmare in the 1950s and moves to a different town in County Kerry every year. For up-to-date information about this year's date and location, contact Joanne ☎087 686 4096. In November, tale-spinners converge in Kenmare for the annual **storytelling weekend.** (Call ☎087 688 6951 or visit www.kenmare.com for details.)

DINGLE (AN DAINGEAN) ☎066

Replete with top-notch accommodations and restaurants (and the vacationers who fill them to the brim), an enviable music scene, and easy access to the most isolated roadways of its namesake peninsula, bayside Dingle draws the well-heeled and the backpack-burdened.

◧ TRANSPORTATION

Buses: Buses stop by the harbor, on the Ring road behind Garvey's SuperValu. Info available from the Tralee bus station (☎712 3566). **Bus Éireann** runs to: **Ballydavid** (Tu 9am and 12:30pm, F 9am and 12:45pm; €3.70, return €6); **Ballyferriter** via **Dunquin** (M and Th 8:50am and 12:45pm; €3.70, return €6); **Tralee** (1¼hr.; M-Sa 6 per day, Su 4 per day; €9, students €7.20).

Taxis: Diarmuid Begley (☎08725 04767), **Foleys** (☎086 381 6277), and **Moran's** (☎800 605 705 or 087 275 3333).

Bike Rental: Foxy John's, Main St. (☎915 1316). Open M-Sa 9am-8pm, Su 11am-8pm. **Paddy's Bike Shop,** Dykegate St. (☎915 2311). Panniers €1 per day. Open Mar.-Oct. 9am-7pm. The going rate in Dingle is €10 per day, €50 per week.

◪ ◧ ORIENTATION AND PRACTICAL INFORMATION

N86 cuts southwest from Tralee into Dingle Town. From town, R559, labeled clearly as Slead Head Dr., heads west to Ventry, Dunquin, and Slea Head. A narrow road runs north through **Conor Pass** to Stradbally and Castlegregory. Downtown, **Strand Street** flanks the harbor along the marina, while **Main Street** runs roughly parallel to it uphill. Approaching the town center, Strand Street splits into **Green Street** and **the Holyground,** which becomes **Dykegate Street.** In the eastern part of town, a roundabout feeds into **The Mall** and the **Tralee road** (N86). Green St., Dykegate St., and The Mall connect Main Street to the waterside and Strand St.

Tourist Office: Strand St. (☎915 1188.) Open mid-June to mid-Sept. M-Sa 9am-7pm, Su 10am-5pm; mid-Sept. to mid-June M-Tu and Th-Sa 9:30am-5pm.

Banks: AIB, Main St. (☎915 1400). Open M 10am-5pm, Tu and Th-F 10am-4pm, W 10:30am-4pm. **Bank of Ireland,** Main St. (☎915 1100). Open M 10am-5pm, Tu-F 10am-4pm. Both have 24hr. **ATMs.**

Laundry: Níolann an Daingin, Green St. (☎915 1837), behind the bakery. Wash and dry from €10 per load. Open M-Sa 9am-1pm and 2-5:30pm.

Emergency: ☎999; no coins required. **Police** (*Garda):* The Holy Ground (☎915 1522).

Pharmacy: O'Keeffe's Pharmacy Ltd., The Holyground (☎915 1310), next to the Super-Valu. Open M-W and F-Sa 9:30am-6pm, Th 9:30am-1pm. Every 2nd Th 2:30-5pm, every 2nd Su 10:30am-12:30pm.

Internet: The **library** (☎915 1499). 50min. free, twice weekly. Call ahead. Open M-W and F-Sa 10am-5pm, Th 10am-8pm. **The Old Forge Internet Cafe,** The Holyground (☎915 0523). New computers, flatscreen TV, comfortable couches, and cappuccinos (€2.20). €1.50 per 15min., €2.50 per 30min., €3.50 per 45min., €4 per hr. Open M-Sa from 9:30am, Su from 11am.

Post Office: Main St. (☎915 1661). Open M-F 9am-1pm and 2-5:30pm, Sa 9am-1pm.

◪ ACCOMMODATIONS

Most of Dingle's hostels are great, but only a few are close to town. Accommodations in town and along Dykegate, Main, and Strand St., are plentiful but fill up quickly, so be sure to call ahead.

▨ **Ballintaggart Hostel (IHH)** (☎915 1454; www.dingleaccommodation.com), on N86. 25min. walk east of town on Tralee Rd. Stone mansion witnessed the strangling of Mrs. Earl of Cork after a poisoning attempt went awry. Her ghost supposedly haunts the bed-

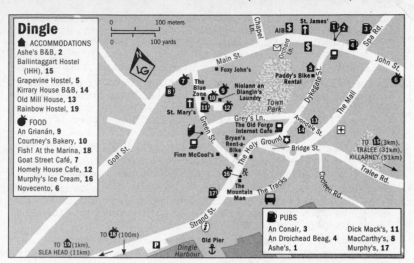

Dingle

🏠 ACCOMMODATIONS
Ashe's B&B, **2**
Ballintaggart Hostel
  (IHH), **15**
Grapevine Hostel, **5**
Kirrary House B&B, **14**
Old Mill House, **13**
Rainbow Hostel, **19**

🍴 FOOD
An Grianán, **9**
Courtney's Bakery, **10**
Fish! At the Marina, **18**
Goat Street Café, **7**
Homely House Cafe, **12**
Murphy's Ice Cream, **16**
Novecento, **6**

🍺 PUBS
An Conair, **3**   Dick Mack's, **11**
An Droichead Beag, **4** MacCarthy's, **8**
Ashe's, **1**   Murphy's, **17**

chambers and elegant, fire-heated common rooms. Self-service laundry €8. 8- to 12-bed dorms €13.50; 4-to-6-bed dorms €17-19; doubles €55-70; family rooms €60-75. **Camping** €8 per single tent; double tent €14, €15 per van. Open May-Oct. ❶

Grapevine Hostel, Dykegate St. (☎915 1434; www.grapevinedingle.com), off Main St. In the middle of town and just a brief stagger from Dingle's finest pubs. Head past a cushy-chaired common room to bunk rooms packed with young travelers. 8-bed dorms €16; 4-bed dorms €18; doubles €44. ❶

Rainbow Hostel (☎915 1044). Take Strand St. west out of town and continue straight through the roundabout for 1km. Tidy, social kitchen. Well-groomed campgrounds. Free lifts to and from town in the Rainbow-Mobile. Bike rental €10 per day, plus €10 deposit. Internet €1 per 10min. Laundry €8. 6- to 12-bed dorms €16; private rooms €20 per person. **Camping** €8 per person. ❶

Ashe's B&B, Main St. (☎915 0989). Peer onto Main St., gaze upon the old graveyard, or drink at the pub downstairs. 4 cream-colored rooms with antique bureaus, all with showers and TVs. Singles €40-60; doubles €60-90. ❸

Old Mill House, 3 Avondale St. (☎915 1120; www.old-mill-house.com). Quietly settled amidst the bustle of Dingle. The O'Neil family serves a hearty breakfast with a side of hospitality. Singles €40-55; doubles €75-90. ❸

Kirrary House B&B, Avondale St. at Dykegate St. (☎915 1606; archeo@eircom.net or collinskirrary@eircom.net). Mrs. Collins pampers guests in pleasant rooms. Book archaeological tours with Sciúird Tours, operated by Mr. Collins (see **Sights,** p. 315), or lounge in the garden with tea and cake. **Bike rental** €8 per day. Doubles €80. ❹

🍴 FOOD

Dingle is home to hot dog stands, gourmet seafood restaurants, and everything in between. Almost all of the nicer restaurants have a two- or three-course early-bird special for €25-35. **SuperValu,** The Holyground, stocks a SuperSelection of groceries and juicy tabloids. (☎915 1397. Open June-Aug. M-Sa 8am-10pm, Su 8am-8pm; Sept.-Apr. M-Sa 8am-9pm, Su 8am-7pm.) **An Grianán,** Green St., in the courtyard side street between Main St. and the Homely House Cafe, sells whole foods and organic vegetables. (☎915 1910. Open M-Sa 9am-6pm.)

Homely House Cafe, Dick Mack's Yard, Green St. (☎915 2431; www.homely-house.com), near the launderette. Perpetually busy 2nd fl. with breezy outdoor seating in the courtyard below. Burritos, bagels, salads, snacks, and home-baked desserts divided into "Just a little hungry," "Pretty darn hungry," and "HUNGRY!!!" sizes. Entrees €4.50-10.50. Open year-round M-Sa 11am-5pm; July-Aug. also open W-Sa 7-10pm. ❷

Courtney's Bakery, Dick Mack's Yard, Green St. (☎915 1583). Breads, cakes, scones, and pastries in this tiny family-run bakery are baked on-site daily. Hit the only early breakfast in town with sausage rolls (€0.70 each) or pick up any of the pastries (€1-4) that taste even better than they look. Open July to mid-Aug. M-Sa 7am-6pm; mid-Aug. to June M-F 7am-6pm. ❶

The Blue Zone, Green St. (☎915 0303). Pizza, wine, and jazz. Not one of them is a weak link here. Upstairs, above the music shop, resides a cove for the coolest cats in Dingle. Pizza €9.50-16. Jazz performances start around 9:30pm. Open daily 6pm-1am. ❷

Goat Street Café, Goat St. (☎915 2770 or 08605 26321). Serves interesting salads (from €10.50), sandwiches (from €5.50), soups, and specials (from €10) like cajun chicken tagliatelle. Homemade desserts €4.80. Open year-round M-Sa 10am-5pm; June-Aug. also F-Su 6-9:30pm. ❷

Novocento, John St. (☎915 2584). Stop in for the 3-course early-bird special (available until 7pm; €25), or spend a few extra Euro on the best pizza in Dingle. Open Mar.-Dec. M-Tu and Th-Su 6-11pm. ❹

Fish! At the Marina, Dingle Marina, Strand St. (☎915 1873). Artful dishes with fresh seafood and plenty of outdoor seating, from where you can watch the boats pass. Entrees €12.50-17.50. Daily special from €12.50. Open daily 10am-6pm; kitchen open noon-4:30pm. ❸

Murphy's Ice Cream, Strand St. (☎915 2644; www.murphysicecream.ie). American brothers Kieran and Sean scoop award-winning homemade ice cream (from €3.20) in innovative flavors, including brown bread. Cappuccino €2.70. Open daily June-Sept. 11am-6:30pm and 7:30-10pm; May and Oct.-Nov. 11am-6pm. ❶

 PUBS

Dingle has a pub for every drinking temperament and much *craic* to spare. Every night brings multiple quality trad sessions, all audible from the streets.

Dick Mack's, Green St., opposite the church. Shoeboxes and whiskey bottles line the walls of this former bar-and-boot store, but if your shoes are broken, you can now only drink your sorrows away. It's all about authentic local *craic* and spirited sing-a-longs; don't expect to blend into the walls here.

Ashe's, Lower Main St. (☎915 0989). Both young and old gather in this plush, intimate pub for a friendly evening of drinking and heart-to-heart in the cozy back lounge. Non-traditional pub food, like salads (€8.50-11.50) served daily noon-4pm and 6-9pm.

An Droichead Beag (The Small Bridge), Lower Main St. (☎915 1723; www.thesmall-bridge.com). Largest and most popular pub in town unleashes 363 sessions of trad each year; M-Th and Su 9:30pm, F-Sa 10pm, and the odd afternoon as well. Many nooks nurture conversation. Snooker table for pub-scale rivalries; huge TV and multiple bars for Su matches. F-Sa disco starts at 9:30pm.

An Conair, Spa Rd. (☎915 2011), off Main St. Hosts anything from modern to truly authentic music. Subdued local crowd enjoys exceptional trad, lusty ballads, and a hidden beer garden to boot. July-Sept. W set dancing; F trad; Sa rock and blues from 9:30pm, Su from 7pm.

MacCarthy's, Main St. (☎915 1205; www.maccarthyspub.com), next to Goat Street Café. Lounge area in back hosts a mixed crowd and spontaneous trad sessions. June-Aug. W and Su trad, Th singer-songwriter.

Murphy's, Strand St. (☎915 1450). Hard to miss with its bright red facade, this classic restaurant and pub by the marina booms with ballads and trad. Listen or chat in cozy corners. May-Oct. live music nightly; Nov.-Mar. Sa only. Kitchen open daily until 9pm.

👁 ⃢ SIGHTS AND OUTDOOR ACTIVITIES

When **Fungi the Dolphin** was first spotted in 1983, the townspeople worried about his effect on the bay's fish population. To say he is now welcome is an understatement, as he single-flipperedly lures droves of tourists and brings plenty of cash to his exploiters. **Dolphin Trips** depart the pier daily 11am-6pm in the summer; call ahead Sept.-June (☎915 2626. 1hr. trips €16, children 2-12 €8. Free if Fungi gets the jitters and doesn't show.) Watching the antics from the shore east of town is a cheaper alternative. Walk two minutes down the Tralee road, turn right at the Skellig Hotel, and follow the strand away from town for about 10min. The small beach on the other side of a stone tower is often crowded with Fungi-fanatics. Anti-dolphinites can be coaxed along by the promise of great views on the walk. At **Dingle Ocean World,** Strand St., all ages ooh and ahh at piranhas, the "Finding Nemo" tank, and the touch tanks with skates and rays. (☎915 2111; www.dingle-oceanworld.com. Open daily July-Aug. 9am-8:30pm; May-June and Sept. daily 10am-6pm; Oct.-Apr. 10am-4:30pm; last admission 30min. before closing. €11, students and seniors €8.50, children €6.50.)

Aquatic explorers **rent wetsuits** from **Brosnan's Wetsuit Hire,** Cooleen Rd., just east of town off the Tralee road behind Brosnan's B&B, opposite the Esso station. The company also runs **swim trips.** (☎915 1967; brosnanswetsuithire@yahoo.co.uk. Wetsuit rental €25 per day. Swim trips 8-10am, weather permitting. €25. Group discounts available.) **Finn McCool's,** Green St., rents **surfboards** and **wetsuits** and has handy info on the peninsula's fabulous beaches. (☎915 0833. Wetsuit €10 per day; surf boards €15; both €20. Open M-Sa 10am-6pm, Su 11am-5pm.) **Dingle Marine Eco-Tours** offers two trips that head in opposite directions along the peninsula, granting insights into bay life and views of archaeological sites. (☎086 285 8802. 2½hr. tours €30, children €15.) To check out the **Blasket Islands** (p. 317), board the *Peig Sayers,* named for one of the island's most famous residents, at the Dingle pier. Tickets are available at **Dingle Marine and Leisure,** at the marina. (☎915 1344 or 087 672 6100; dinglemarina@eircom.net. Departs 11am, 1, 3, 5:30pm. €35 return.) Dingle Marina also organizes **deep-sea angling** trips which leave daily in summer. (8hr. day €90; ½-day €45. Includes equipment and skippered boat.) Adventurers of all levels can take an up-close look under the waves at the Dingle Marina **Dive Centre.** Beginners get right down to business and see some of the area's eerie shipwrecks. (☎915 2789; www.divingdingle.ie. Dives start at €99.)

The Mountain Man camping store sells outdoors gear and *The Easy Guide to the Dingle Peninsula* (€6), which includes walks, cycling tours, information on this area's history, and a map. **Sciúird Archaeology Tours** leads a whirlwind bus tour of the area's ancient spots. (☎915 1606; archeo@eircom.net. 2½hr., daily 10:30am and 2pm, €20. Book ahead.) There are several ways to see the area with **Slea Head Tours,** minibus trips highlighting the peninsula's scenery and historic sights (2hr., €20). **Moran's Tours** (☎915 1155 or 086 275 3333) depart the pier daily at 10am and 2pm. **O'Connor's Tours** (☎087 248 0008) depart daily at 11am and 2pm. **Dingle Horse Riding** gives the chance to explore the peninsula's mountain trails and beaches on horseback. (☎915 2199; www.dinglehorseriding.com. 2hr. ride €52; ½-day beach ride 10am-2pm €97; full-day Slea Head ride 10am-4pm €140.) A **Folk Concert Series** featuring local and international musicians runs from May to September in tiny St. James Church, on Main St. About half of the 2-3hr. performance is traditional Irish music, while the other half is acoustic folk and may feature musicians from *gaeltacht* regions of Ireland, Portugal, Africa, the U.S., and other corners of the world. In July and August, tickets sell out fast; Murphy's Ice Cream sells tickets, as do the Celtic & Prehistoric Museum, the Dingle Record Shop (on Green St.), and The Music House (on Record Ln.). Or, stop by the gate of St. James to view the line-up. (Contact Steve Coulter ☎087 982 9728; stevecoulter@eircom.net. Performances M, W, F 7:30pm. €10, €12 at the door.) The **Dingle Regatta** hauls in salty dogs in early September. In early August, flirt with Lady Luck at the **Dingle Races.**

VENTRY, SLEA HEAD, AND DUNQUIN

Glorious Slea Head presents a coastline alternating between jagged cliffs and green hills, set above a hemline of frothy waves and interrupted only by rough stone walls and the occasional sheep. Hollywood satisfied its craving for classic Irish beauty by filming *Ryan's Daughter* and *Far and Away* here, successfully exploiting the dramatic scenery. The most rewarding way to see Slea Head and Dunquin in a day or less is to bike along the flat Slea Head Dr. (R559).

VENTRY (CEANN TRÁ)   ☎066

Less than 6km past Dingle Town toward Slea Head on R559, the village of Ventry contains little more than a sandy beach and the remnants of lackluster **Rahinnane Castle.** The ▓**Celtic and Prehistoric Museum,** 3km farther down the road, is a must-see. Nowhere else in the region can visitors find such an extensive private collection of Stone, Bronze, Copper, and Celtic Age artifacts packed ceiling to floor, not to mention prehistoric items such as a fully intact skeleton of a baby Psittocosaurus dinosaur. The 40,000-year-old, fully restored skull and tusks of "Millie," recovered off the coast of Holland in 1999, represent the largest complete skull of a **woolly mammoth** in the world. Conversant in half a dozen languages and a virtuoso hammer dulcimer player, proprietor Harris Moore sells everything from fossilized dinosaur droppings to tickets for the local Folk Concert Series. (☎915 9191. Open Mar.-Nov. daily 10am-5:30pm; Dec.-Feb. call ahead. €4, family discounts available.) For a dusty cabin-esque stay near the old castle, **Ballybeag Hostel's ❷** secluded yet convenient location makes it an ideal place to recharge before exploring the western end of the peninsula. To reach the hostel traveling east, turn right onto the Ballyferriter road just after the beach and look for the sign on the right side of the road, or hop on one of seven free daily shuttles from Dingle Town. Ballybeag was built by an Italian tourist who never ended her vacation to Ventry. (☎915 9876; www.iol.ie/~balybeag. **Bike rental** €10 per day. Wheelchair-accessible. Laundry €4. Dorms €17; doubles €48.)

SLEA HEAD (CEANN SLÉIBHE)   ☎066

Slea Head Dr. continues past several Iron Age and early Christian rocks and ruins. Clustered on hillsides overlooking the cliffs, **Dunbeg Fort,** built in 500 BC, and the **Fahan** oratories—beehive-shaped stone huts built by early monks in 2000 BC—are visible from the road and can be explored. (€3, students €2.) Slea Head looks out onto the resplendent **Blasket Islands** (p. 317). Try to pick out the **Sleeping Giant's** profile from among the scattered group. For the best views, locals advise hiking to the top of **Mount Eagle,** which is an easy jaunt from the Ballybeag Hostel (see **Ventry,** p. 316). A number of roadside trails lead to fantastic vantage points, though some can be quite precarious. If rough seas prevent a visit to the Blaskets—or even if they don't—check out the outstanding exhibits at the ▓**Great Blasket Centre,** just outside of Dunquin on the road to Ballyferriter. Thoughtfully designed, the museum evokes the lost way of island life through displays of modern art, island artifacts, photography, and short biographies of better-known islanders. The short movie on the history of the Great Blasket community is worth watching for the dramatic footage of the islands alone. If you grow tired of the representative art, a glassed-in viewing point at the end of the long corridor provides a grand perspective of the real thing. There is also a **cafe ❷** (entrees €7-10; open July-Aug. 10am-5pm) that serves sandwiches and a light lunch. (☎915 6444. Open July-Aug. daily 10am-7pm; Easter-June and Sept.-Oct. daily 10am-6pm. Last admission 45min. before closing. €3.70, students €1.30, seniors and groups €2.60 per person.)

DUNQUIN (DÚN CHAOIN)   ☎066

North of Slea Head, the scattered settlement of Dunquin consists of stone houses, a pub, the guttural lilt of spoken Irish, and no grocery store—stock up in Dingle or in Ballyferriter. At the delightful ▧**Gleann Dearg B&B ❸**, tear your eyes away from the Great Blasket long enough to appreciate the homey rooms and garden conservatory dining room. Homemade orange juice comes with the delicious made-to-order breakfast, and a three-course dinner is available upon request (€25). The four-person family suite is exceptional, and the sitting room has a fireplace and an excellent collection of literature from the Blaskets and books about the Dingle Peninsula. The owner helps organize ferry service to the Great Blasket Island. (☎915 6188. Open Mar.-Nov. Singles €50; doubles €75.) Along the road to Ballyferriter, across from the turnoff to the Blasket Centre, and right on the **Dingle Way,** the **An Óige Hostel (HI) ❶** offers ocean views from the bunks, limited supplies from the mini-general store, and a book exchange. The hostel is popular with bikers, although some object to the daytime lockout. (☎915 6121; www.ire-landyha.org. Sheets €2. Continental breakfast €4.50. Reception 9-10am and 5-10pm. Lockout 10am-5pm. June-Oct. 8- to 10-bed dorms €16; 4- to 6-bed €18, ensuite €19; ensuite doubles €37. Nov. and Feb.-May €1 discount. Closed Dec.-Jan. An Óige members €2 discount.) **Kruger's ❷,** at the turn-off for Dunquin pier, was founded by a local legend who was once a bodyguard for president Eamon de Valera. It is also purportedly the westernmost pub in Europe, featuring year-round music sessions. People of all ages gather for snooker, pints, and the warm fire. (☎915 6127. Upstairs B&B rooms €35-40 per person.)

BLASKET ISLANDS (NA BLASCAODAÍ)   ☎066

Whether bathed in sunlight or shrouded in mist, the Blasket Islands possess an unassuming yet striking beauty; one that may explain the prolific literary masterpieces that have emerged from writers who have called these islands home. The Blaskets comprise six islands: Beginish, Great Blasket, Inishnabro, Inishtooskert, Inishvickillane, and Tearaght. ▧**Great Blasket Island** once supported a community of fishermen, poets, and storytellers, peaking at 176 inhabitants during WWII. However, the subsequent collapse of its fish export market resulted in a tide of emigration, and the village's future became bleak; as one sage resident lamented, "After us, there will be no more." The islands were evacuated in 1953, after their population dropped below a sustainable level. Mainlanders attempted to preserve the dying tradition by sponsoring the autobiographies of Blasket storytellers. The resulting **memoirs** bemoaned the decline of the *gaeltacht* and shared the oral story-telling tradition of the islands. They include Maurice O'Sullivan's *Twenty Years A-Growing*, Thomas O'Crohan's *The Islander*, and Peig Sayers' *Peig*. Seals and fishing boats continue to pass through the Blaskets occasionally, but the unique way of life that once thrived there has faded to an inky echo of the past.

A day on Great Blasket is best spent in uninterrupted rumination. Wander along the white strand, follow grass paths across all six of the island's kilometers, explore silent stone skeletons of houses clustered in the village, and observe the puffins and seals that populate the shores. The isolated Blaskets have no public litter system; **carry out everything you bring here** and honor the maxim "leave no trace."

Two small ferry companies make the 20min. trip to the Great Blasket from Dunquin pier. (Between both companies, there are departures every 30min. late Apr.-early Oct. 10am-5pm. Dependent on weather, so call ahead. Large groups book in advance. €30 return, children €15.) Tickets can be purchased by phone, at the Dingle Marina Booking Office, or at the ticket shacks at Dunquin pier. **Blasket Islands Dun Chaoin Ferry Co.** (☎915 4864 or 087 231 6131; www.blasketislands.ie) and **Blasket Island Ferries** (☎915 6422 or 915 1344; www.blasketisland.com) will help you navigate the islands. Blasket Island Ferries offers a 2½hr. guided boat tour around all the islands for €40. Another boat, the *Peig Sayers*, connects the **Dingle Marina** to Great Blasket Island. (☎915 1344 or 087 672 6100. 35min.; 11am, 1, 3, 5:30pm; €35, children €17, groups over 8 €30 per person.)

Recently, the Irish government has been trying to purchase the islands, especially the Great Blasket, and transform them into a national heritage site, which would provide funding for island tours, preservation of the village ruins, and potential accommodations like the hostel that once operated there. However, private owners of the land have resisted for years offers from the government and have shown no willingness to negotiate.

BALLYFERRITER (BAILE AN FHEIRTÉARAIGH) ☎066

Ballyferriter is western Dingle's closest approximation to a town center. The surrounding settlement is an unpolluted *gaeltacht*. The **Chorca Dhuibhne Museum,** in the center of town, contains photos and text relating to the area's archaeology and history. (☎915 6333. Open May-Sept. daily 10am-5:30pm; Oct.-Apr. by appointment. €2.50, students €1.50.) The small exhibition is a good starting point for visiting nearby ancient sights. Close to Ballyferriter are the remains of the dry-stone circular wall enclosures, *clocháns* (bee-hive huts), and an oratory, as well as a remarkable standing stone, all of which can be found at **Reask Monastic Enclosure** *(Mainistir Riaisc)*. To get there, take the main road east out of Ballyferriter toward the Gallarus Oratory; turn right at the tiny sign for *Mainistir Riaisc*. Continuing east on the main road, follow signs to **Gallarus Oratory,** a mortarless yet watertight masterpiece of 8th-century stonework that was used for worship. Turn left at the signs for the **Visitors Centre,** which shows a 15min. video of Dingle's ancient landmarks. Pass through the Visitors Centre to go straight to the oratory. (☎915 5333. Open daily 9am-8pm. Oratory free. Visitors Centre €3, students €2.50, children free.) The town of **Murreagh** and the **Kilmalkédar Church** *(Cill Mhaoilchéadair)* lie farther east along the main road. The church is a remarkably intact 12th-century specimen with a blend of Romanesque and Irish architecture. Turn right at the Siopa in Murreagh; continue past a small stone church on the right to the graveyard and Kilmalkedar Church on the left. Among the graves overlooking Smerwick Harbour, look for the **ogham stone** (see **Christians and Vikings,** p. 50) and a mysterious **sundial.** Local legend holds that even hapless sinners can ensure entrance to heaven by passing through the rear window of the old church three times consecutively. (The efficacy of this method is likely to be compromised by cutting through the side window—so don't.) The Iron Age **Dún An Óir** ("Fort of Gold") sits northwest of Ballyferriter along the Dingle Way. It was here that the English massacred over 700 Spanish, Italian, and Irish soldiers engaged in a rebellion against Queen Elizabeth in 1580.

Crowds gather in the pubs along Ballyferriter's lone street for dinner, pints, and occasional trad. Visitors longing to gaze at the surf should consider staying elsewhere; the hostel in Dunquin (p. 317) and most of the B&Bs along the Dunquin road have better views than are available from Ballyferriter proper. **An Cat Dubh ❶,** which shares its name with a popular U2 song, provides basic rooms 5min. outside town, on the Dunquin road behind the eponymous shop. (☎915

6286. Rooms €12. **Camping** €6 per person.) There are several Ballyferriter B&Bs: next door to the hostel, quiet **An Spéice ❸** provides gentle comfort. (☎915 6254. All rooms with bath. Singles €45; doubles €35 per person.) For a more raucous time, try the **B&B ❸** at the **Tigh an tSaorsaigh** pub. **Tigh Uí Chathain ❸** is a standard spot for locals to fill up at lunch or dinner. (☎915 6359. Entrees €13.50-22.50. Open daily noon-2:30pm and 6-8:30pm.) **Caife na Cille ❷** is the only true cafe in town, offering delicious wraps (€7) for lunch as well as a dinner menu. (No phone. Entrees €9-10. Open daily 10:30am-8pm.) **Tigh Uí Mhurchú's** (Murphy's) cushioned stools are the perfect place to watch the matches or hear music several times a week. (☎915 6224. Trad Tu and Th in summer. Lunch 12:30-3pm; dinner 6-9pm.) Stop in for pints or a filling meal (entrees €12-20) at **Tigh an tSaorsaigh,** and consider staying the night at the connected **B&B ❸**. (☎915 6344. Open daily 11am-late. Doubles €60-65.) You'll find plenty of space and anything from soup (€4.50) to large burgers (€12) in **Bar an Bhuailtín,** Main St., the shiny new pub attached to the hotel development Ótan Ceann Sibéal. (☎915 6433; www.ceannsibealhotel.com. Kitchen open 12:30-9pm.)

NORTHERN DINGLE

Hikers and beach junkies get their fix on the peninsula's northern shore, far from the tourist bonanzas to the south and the west. Jaw-dropping views from the mountains motivate casual ramblers to make the daytrip from Dingle Town, while the promise of solitude draws some backpackers off the Dingle Way. The seaside villages, though not destinations in themselves, are all pleasant places to find a meal, a pint, or a good night's rest. On Fridays, **Bus Éireann** runs a bus from Tralee to Castlegregory and on to Cloghane. Hitchhiking over the Conor Pass is common during the tourist season, although *Let's Go* never recommends hitchhiking.

From Dingle Town, a winding cliff road runs north through the **Conor Pass** (elevation 457m), the highest mountain pass in Ireland. Buses won't fit on the narrow road, but cars squeeze through, while bikers and walkers huff and puff past valley views on five kilometers of continuous incline. Be wary of inclement weather; low visibility and strong winds can make the trip hazardous. The road crests at **Brandon Ridge,** where dazzling views reward climbers and a car park encourages a brief stop to enjoy the panorama. On clear days, visitors can gaze at lakes hundreds of meters below at the **Magharee Islands** (or **Seven Hogs**) to the north, and even distant **Valentia Island** (p. 299) off the peninsula's southern coast. As the road twists down toward Brandon Bay, a small waterfall, a road-side pull-off, and a picnic table are a 5min. walk from the base of **Pedlars Lake,** named in honor of a traveling tradesman who lost his wares (and his life) to a gang of brigands. These days, a peddler is more likely to encounter geologists than bandits while roaming the glacier-sliced lakes and boulder-pocked landscape.

CLOGHANE AND BRANDON   ☎066

Beyond Pedlars Lake, the road heads downhill to the sea. Signs point out the westward fork to **Cloghane** (Claw-hane; *An Clochán*) and its even smaller northern neighbor, **Brandon** *(Bréanainn).* Both are good starting points for hiking up the 953m **Mt. Brandon** or tackling the seldom trod but magnificent northern region that culminates in **Brandon Point.** To conquer Mt. Brandon, go through Brandon, staying to the left at the fork to Murphy's Pub, and drive up the narrow rode to a car park. Prepare to meet soggy and often disappearing trails, but don't lose heart—the view is worth it. Pick up maps of the area *(Discovery Maps,* €11) and a €0.50 packet with historical information and directions to the Pilgrimage Trail from the friendly staff at the **Information Centre** on the main road in Cloghane. (☎713 8277. Open June to mid-Sept. M-Th 9am-6pm, F-Su 9:30am-4:30pm.) Every July 25, the devout head up the "Saint's Road" on Mt. Brandon, which was misnamed in honor of alleged trailblazer St. Brendan. The rest of the year, the **Pilgrim's Route,** which forks off the Dingle Way west of Ventry and rejoins in Cloghane, attracts hikers who prefer ancient Christian sites and inland ridges to coastal rambles. The 4-6hr. hike passes glassy lakes, a 2000-year-old hill fort, and spectacular views from the summit. A Bronze Age standing stone in the shape of the mountain sits in a nearby valley, in line with the summit. Avoid hiking in foggy conditions and bad weather, and always tell someone where you are going.

Whether you've just conquered the mountain, are preparing for the trek, or prefer to savor a good perch by the sea, ▨**Mount Brandon Lodge ❶** leaves little (or nothing) to be desired. Stretch those weary legs in the glassed-in sitting room and watch the tide recede or curl up on the massive couch and watch a video from the lodge's small but excellent collection. (☎713 8299; www.mountbrandonhostel.com. Wheelchair-accessible. Laundry €6. 3- to 6-bed dorms €18. Singles €20-25; doubles €50. Family rooms available.) The nearest grocery store is in Castlegregory, but a small **food store** attached to the hostel sells basic provisions. (Open June-Sept. M-Sa 9am-8pm, Su 9am-5pm; Oct.-May M-F 9am-7pm, Sa 9am-5pm.) The shop also has a computer with **Internet** access. (€1 per 10min.) Next door, the lively **Tigh Tomsi ❷** pub serves hot meals, which you can enjoy inside with the locals or outside in the convivial beer garden. (☎713 8301. Sandwiches from €3.50, daily specials €10-18. Summer Su live music. Open M-Sa noon-1am, Su noon-11pm.) At ▨**Murphy's Pub,** on Brandon Pier, savor the perfect pint of Guinness and unsurpassed views of Brandon Bay and the majestic hills of Northern Dingle. (☎713 8189. June-Aug. F-Su trad.)

CASTLEGREGORY (CAISLEÁN AN GHRIARE)   ☎066

Castlegregory, situated 2km north of the main road, is home to more than its fair share of excitement and has the only grocery store in Northern Dingle. Residents and visitors take advantage of the winds along the narrow **Magharees Peninsula,** stretching into the sea north of the village, for windsurfing. Swimmers, surfers, snorkelers, and canoeists also find good conditions (and equipment rentals) at Magharees. A good surfing location is just a 10min. walk from the main beach; ask at Waterworld for directions. The conditions pleased competitors in the 2000 **Windsurfing World Championships** so much that the event has chosen Castlegregory as its permanent October venue; contact Jamie Knox for more information. Two companies rent wetsuits, surf boards, boogie boards, canoes, windsurfing and snorkeling equipment; both also give surfing and windsurfing lessons. **Jamie Knox,** past the beach on the right, stays open from Easter to November 10. (☎713 9411; www.jamieknox.com. Equipment rental and tuition are cost-effective in the long run. Windsurfing equipment €25 per hr., €180 for 6 days.) **Waterworld** has trailer shacks on the beach from May to September. (Contact Kevin ☎087 670 9499. Wetsuits €6.50 per hr., €11 per 2hr.; surfing and windsurfing lessons €35 per 1½hr.) Gallop on horseback through the surf with **O'Connor's Trekking** (☎06671 39216), or lower your handicap at **Castlegregory Golf and Fishing Club.** (☎713 9444. €35 per 18 holes; club rental €8.) The **Maharees Regatta** (*curragh* racing) hits the waves in early July. A week or two later, the **Castlegregory Carnival** rouses the town with parades and dances; the winner of the carnival queen competition becomes a contestant to represent Co. Kerry in the Rose of Tralee event.

A **bus** connecting Castlegregory to **Tralee** departs from the tourist office (F 10:30am, €5). The **tourist office** is next to Spar Market. (☎713 9422. Open mid-June to Aug. M-F 9:30am-8:30pm, Sa 9:30am-5pm, Su 9:30am-1pm; Sept. to mid-June M-F 9:30am-5pm.) The office has one computer with **Internet** access. (€3 per 30min., minimum €2.) There is a **post office** on Tailor's Row. (☎713 9131. Open M-F 9am-1pm and 2-5:30pm, Sa 9am-1pm.)

Feel like royalty at the spacious and luxurious **Castle House B&B ❸**, 45m down the Maharees road from the village. Stroll down their private beach before choosing from the extensive breakfast menu. (☎713 9183. All rooms with bath and TV. Singles €45-50; doubles €75.) For a more bare-bones experience, try **Fitzgerald's Euro-Hostel ❶**, above the pub at the junction between the main road and the route to Maharees—not to be confused with the town's two pubs called Fitzgerald's. (☎713 9133. Towels €2. Dorms €15; doubles €54.) Pitch a tent by the water at **Sandy Bay Caravan Park ❶**. There's also a barbecue **restaurant** and a shop stocked with basic necessities. Beware: the bay area tends to have high winds so bring proper stakes and weights. (☎713 9338. Restaurant open mid-June to Aug. daily noon-midnight. Shop open mid-June to Aug. daily 8:30am-9:30pm. Laundry €8. €14 per small tent; €17 per large tent.) The **Spar Market** has an **ATM** inside the store. (☎713 9433. Open June-Aug. M-Sa 8:30am-9:30pm, Su 8:30am-9pm; Sept.-May M-Sa 8:30am-8pm, Su 8:30am-7pm.) **Phil's Cafe ❶**, across from Spar, serves delicious entrees, pancakes, sandwiches and breakfasts in an upstairs cafe. (☎087 773 9123. Open Mar.-Oct. 8am-5:30pm; may stay open in winter. Sandwiches from €2. Breakfast from €4. Loaded pancakes €8.50.) **Ned Natterjack's ❷**, named for the area's rare and vocal Natterjack toad, features a wide range of music and a lively beer garden. (☎713 9491. Full pub menu served noon-9pm. Entrees €11-27. July-Aug. music nightly, Sept. and Easter-June W and Sa-Su. Closed Oct.-Easter.) **Barry's Takeaway ❶**, just before the Spar, is a great spot for burgers (from €2.60), fish (from €3.20), and pizza (from €5.80). (☎713 9878. Open June to early-Sept. M-Th noon-11:30pm, F-Su noon-2am; Sept.-May F-Sa 5pm-2am, Su 5-11:30pm.)

TRALEE (TRÁ LÍ)   ☎066

As the economic and residential capital (pop. 22,000) of Co. Kerry, Tralee's gruff exterior may come as a bit of a shock to those arriving from smaller towns on the peninsula. Still, large storefronts line the city's main streets, and quality pubs serve bar food and trad. Ireland's second-largest museum makes the history of Kerry come to life, and a stroll through the city's famed gardens is a true pleasure. The town gets mobbed in the third week of August during the annual **Rose of Tralee** festival, a competition that keeps Irish eyes glued to their TVs.

▐▀ TRANSPORTATION

Flights: Kerry Airport, in **Farranfore** (☎976 4966), off N22 halfway between Tralee and Killarney. (See **Killarney,** p. 285.)

Trains: Oakpark Rd. (☎712 3522; www.irishrail.ie). Ticket office open daily before departures. Trains to: **Cork** (2½hr.; M-Sa 5 per day, Su 3 per day; €23); **Dublin** (4hr.; M-Sa 6 per day, Su 3 per day; €31); **Galway** (5-6hr., 3 per day, €59); **Killarney** (40min., 4 per day, €8.70); **Rosslare Harbour** (5½hr., M-Sa 1 per day, €56.50); **Waterford** (4hr., M-Sa 1 per day, €47).

Buses: Oakpark Rd. at corner of JJ Sheehy (☎712 3566). Open mid-June to Aug. M-Sa 8:30am-6pm, Su 8:30am-1pm and 1:30-4:15pm; Sept. to mid-June M-Sa 8:30am-5:15pm. Buses to: **Bantry** (2½hr., June-Sept. 2 per day, €19.50); **Cork** (2½hr., 4 per day 8:50am-5:50pm, €14.40); **Dingle** (1¼hr.; M-Sa 4-6 per day, Su 2-5 per day; €9, return €14.40); **Galway** via **Limerick** (M-Sa 8 per day 6:15am-6pm, Su 7 per day 8am-6pm; €17.10); **Killarney** (40min.; June-Sept. M-Sa 13-14 per day 6:15am-6:50pm, Su

10 per day 8:50am-6:50pm; €6); **Limerick** (2¼hr.; M-Sa 9 per day 6:15am-7pm, Su 8 per day 8am-5pm; €13.50); **Skibbereen** (3hr., June-Sept. 12:50pm; €16). A **summer scenic service** travels the **Ring of Kerry** with multiple stops and return service to Tralee. Departs 7:50am and 12:50pm. Student discounts available on all routes.

Taxis: Along the Mall at Denny St.

Bike Rental: O'Halloran Cycles, 83 Boherbee (☎712 2820). €12 per day, €50 per wk. Open M-Sa 9:30am-1pm and 2-6pm.

Car Rental: Several garages in town rent cars. Try **Duggan's Garage** (☎712 1124), **McGelligott's** (☎712 3011), or **Kerry Motorworks** (☎712 1555). Car rental is also available at nearby Kerry Airport.

✦▐ ORIENTATION AND PRACTICAL INFORMATION

Tralee's streets are hopelessly knotted; travelers should arm themselves with free maps from the tourist office. The main avenue—called **the Mall, Castle Street,** and **Boherbee**—has shops, pubs, and restaurants along its roughly east-to-west path. **The Square** is pedestrian-only and lies just south of the Mall; **The Marketplace** is just north. Both have a maze of small alleys with hidden shops and cafes. **Edward Street** connects the main thoroughfare to the bus and train stations. Wide **Denny Street** runs south to the museum, tourist office, and park. Parking is cheaper and safer in some garages than on the street.

Tourist Office: Ashe Memorial Hall basement, at the end of Denny St. (☎712 1288; www.corkkerry.ie.). From the station, head into town on Edward St., turn right on Castle St., then left onto Denny St. Friendly staff provides free maps and can suggest accommodations. Open July-Aug. M-Sa 9am-7pm, Su 10am-6pm; Sept.-May M-Sa 9am-6pm.

Banks: AIB, Denny St. (☎712 1100), at Castle St. **Bank of Ireland** (☎712 1177), a few doors down Castle St. Both open M 10am-5pm, W 10:30am-4pm, Tu and Th-F 10am-4pm. Both have 24hr. **ATMs** throughout town.

Counseling and Support: Samaritans, 44 Moyderwell St. (☎712 2566), 24hr. hotline ☎850 60 9090.

Laundry: Rusk Dry Cleaners, 36 Bridge St. (☎712 5941). Wash and dry €12. Open M-Sa 9am-6pm.

Emergency: ☎999; no coins required.

Police *(Garda):* High St. (☎712 2022).

Pharmacy: Kelly's, the Mall (☎712 1302). Open M-Sa 9am-6pm. Su rotating hours.

Hospital: Bon Secours, Strand St. (☎712 1966). **Tralee County General Hospital** (☎712 6222), off the Killarney Rd.

Internet: Library, Moyderwell St. (☎712 1200). Free 50min. sessions start on the hr.; sign up 15min. in advance. Open M, W, F-Sa 10am-5pm; Tu and Th 10am-8pm. **Talk-Net,** 30 Castle St. (☎718 5637), has extended hours. Open daily 10am-10pm. €2 per hr. **Internet and International Call Centre,** 40 Bridge St. (☎719 1441), has computers, phone booths, and Western Union services. Open June-Sept. M-Sa 10am-10pm, Su 1-9pm; Oct.-May M-Sa 10am-8pm, Su 2-8pm. €2 per hr.

Post Office: Edward St. (☎712 1013), between Castle St. and the train/bus station.

▐▌ ACCOMMODATIONS AND CAMPING

Tralee has an odd mix of accommodations. Most B&Bs lie outside the town center on Oakpark Rd. to Listowel and Limerick, though several pubs have lower-quality rooms above the action. Nestled among the luxury hotels on Denny St. is a beauti-

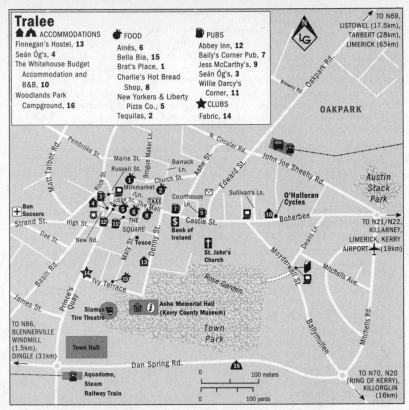

Tralee

🏠🏠🏠 **ACCOMMODATIONS**
Finnegan's Hostel, 13
Seán Óg's, 4
The Whitehouse Budget
  Accommodation and
  B&B, 10
Woodlands Park
  Campground, 16

🍎 **FOOD**
Ainés, 6
Bella Bia, 15
Brat's Place, 1
Charlie's Hot Bread
  Shop, 8
New Yorkers & Liberty
  Pizza Co., 5
Tequilas, 2

🍺 **PUBS**
Abbey Inn, 12
Baily's Corner Pub, 7
Jess McCarthy's, 9
Seán Óg's, 3
Willie Darcy's
  Corner, 11
⭐ **CLUBS**
Fabric, 14

TO N69,
LISTOWEL (17.5km),
TARBERT (28km),
LIMERICK (65km)

OAKPARK

TO N21/N22,
KILLARNEY,
LIMERICK, KERRY
AIRPORT (19km)

TO N86,
BLENNERVILLE
WINDMILL
(1.5km),
DINGLE (31km)

TO N70, N20
(RING OF KERRY),
KILLORGLIN
(16km)

Pembroke St.
Matt Talbot Rd.
Maine St.
Russell St.
Rock St.
Brogue Maker Ln.
Church St.
Barrack Ln.
Ashe St.
N. Circular Rd.
Edward St.
John Joe Sheehy Rd.
Brewery Rd.
Oakpark Rd.
Milkmarket
Bon Secours
Strand St.
High St.
Bridge St.
The Mall
TAXI
THE SQUARE
Mary St.
New Rd.
Dae St.
Basin Rd.
James St.
Prince's Quay
Tesco
Denny St.
Courthouse Ln.
Castle St.
Bank of Ireland
St. John's Church
Sullivan's Ln.
O'Halloran Cycles
Boherbee
Deans Ln.
Moydarvell St.
Mitchells Ave.
Mitchells Rd.
Ballymullen
Austin Stack Park
Ivy Terrace
Siamsa Tíre Theatre
Aquadome, Steam Railway Train
Town Hall
Rose Garden
Ashe Memorial Hall
(Kerry County Museum)
Town Park
Dan Spring Rd.

0   100 meters
0   100 yards

ful and convenient hostel, while south of town there is a fantastic camping park. Ask the tourist office about town houses scattered on the fringes.

Finnegan's Hostel, Denny St. (☎712 7610; www.finneganshstel.com). Set in the middle of town in an old, aesthetically pleasing home with rooms named after great Irish authors. Rose gardens across the street are visible from the windows. Light breakfast included. Dorms €17; singles €30; doubles €40. ❷

The Whitehouse Budget Accommodation and B&B, Boherbee (☎086 866 1868; www.whitehousetralee.com). Good location and comfortable rooms make up for dark, desolate corridors and meager breakfast. Spacious pub downstairs with pool tables, big-screen TV, trad, and Sa DJ. Wheelchair-accessible. Free continental breakfast. Dorms €20; singles €30; doubles €50-60. ❷

Seán Óg's, 41 Bridge St. (☎712 8822). B&B entrance in the back on New Rd. Centrally located B&B has 14 rooms above a pub. An easy crawl to bed after several pints. Doubles €80; triples €105. ❹

Woodlands Park Campground, Dan Spring Rd. (☎712 1235; www.kingdomcamping.com), 1km past the Aquadome; turn at the sign and go straight over the small stone bridge. Clean with beautiful landscape. Game room, kitchen facilities, and shop. Open Mar.-Sept. Showers €1. Laundry wash €4.50, dry €4.50. €8 per person without car, 2-person tent with car €17. Caravans from €18. ❶

FOOD

True gourmet-seekers may be disappointed with the culinary landscape of Tralee, but pub grub and fast food are readily available, and the massive **Tesco** south of the Square on Mary St. is a boon for budding chefs and snackers alike. (☎712 1110. Open M-Sa 8am-10pm, Su 10am-8pm.) **Seancara,** between the Square and Tesco on the pedestrian walkway, sells whole food and organic produce. (☎712 2644. Open M-W and Sa 9am-6pm, Th-F 9am-8pm, Su 1-6pm.) Organic deli **Manna,** 1 New Rd., next to the back entrance of Sean Og's, sells fresh hummus, pesto, and a huge selection of olives. (☎711 8501. Open M-Sa 9:30am-1pm and 2-6:30pm.)

Brat's Place, 18 Milk Market Ln., across the Mall from the eastern side of the Square. Superb vegetarian and vegan dishes made with organic ingredients; the hostess brings warm, spiced breads to those lucky enough to find a table. Soups and desserts €3.50. Entrees €7-10. Open M-Sa 12:30-3pm, or when the food runs out. ❷

Tequilas, Barrack Ln. (☎712 4820), off the Mall; entrance directly across from Denny St. Candlelight, orange walls, and a saddle and stirrups hanging overhead set the tone for delightfully fresh Tex-Mex meals and pasta dishes (nacho plate €6) Starters €3.50-11; entrees €11.50-25. Open daily 5-10pm. ❸

Aínés, the Square (☎718 5388). Friendly cafe and wine bar is a popular place for casual breakfast or lunch. Glass of wine €4-7. Sandwiches €6.50, house specials €8.50. Open M-Sa 8:30am-7pm, Su noon-6pm. ❷

Bella Bia, Ivy Terr. (☎714 4896). A taste of Italy, the early-bird special (5-7pm) offers 3 courses for only €13.50; add a glass of wine for €3. 12 in. pizza €9-14; entrees €10-19. Open daily 5pm-late. ❸

Charlie's Hot Bread Shop, 12 The Mall (☎712 5288). Charlie's is the choice for delicious sweets and pastries starting at €1. Also offers cheap simple sandwiches (€3-4). Open daily 8am-5:30pm. ❶

New Yorkers & Liberty Pizza Co., 4-5 Bridge St. (☎718 0044). Anyone will enjoy the fresh pizza, and New York Yankees fans will appreciate the Derek Jeter posters. Open late for the post-clubbing crowd. 9 in. pizza €7-9. Fried chicken €4.20-6.50. Open July-Aug. M-W noon-3am, Th-Su noon-4am; Sept.-June M-W noon-1am, Th-Su noon-4am. ❷

PUBS AND CLUBS

Seán Óg's, 41 Bridge St. (☎712 8822). Pub's witty subtitle, "drinking consultants" appropriately introduces the town's best *craic*. Hand-crafted fireplace keeps pubbers and snugglers warm on long winter nights. M-Th and Su trad. B&B beds upstairs facilitate long nights at the bar.

Baily's Corner Pub, Ashe St. and lower Castle St. (☎712 6230). Mementos of Kerry's rugby legacy adorn the walls. Players join an older crowd at the bar. Munch on sandwiches or hot food (€4.50-9) while watching matches. M-Th and occasionally Su trad.

Jess McCarthy's, 26 Lower Castle St. (☎712 3170). Sisters Teresa and Phyl keep their lovely family-run pub classy and pour the best pint in Tralee. A place for conversation with true locals instead of trad with tourists. Open daily 10:30am-11:30pm.

Willie Darcy's Corner, the Square (☎712 4343). Just over 3 years old and pure class. All ages meet here over candlelit tables. Genial conversation takes the place of music. Soups and sandwiches served 12:30-2:30pm.

Abbey Inn, Bridge St. (☎712 3390; www.theabbeyinn.ie), across from Seán Óg's. Edgy young crowd comes for the late bar and to hear live rock most weekends. U2 played the Abbey in 1978—they grabbed mops and started scrubbing when a local cop threatened to arrest them for drinking after their show. Th live music; DJ other nights. Kitchen open 9am-9pm. Open M-Sa until 2:30am, Su until 1am.

👁 🌺 SIGHTS AND FESTIVALS

Tralee is home to Ireland's second-largest museum, ⬛Kerry County Museum, in Ashe Memorial Hall on Denny St. A perennial favorite for awards, the museum marshals all the resources of display technology to narrate the county's history. The second floor houses an excellent gallery loaded with dioramas, artifacts, and pictures from each era of Kerry's history; a small video room displays images of Kerry's landscape to slightly creepy orchestral music. The latest exhibit details the exciting life of spymaster William Melville, the original "M" whom Ian Fleming used as inspiration for his James Bond novels. Downstairs, "Geraldine Tralee" leads visitors through a superb recreation of medieval Tralee. Walk through a surprisingly realistic marketplace, Abbey, and public house to the shouts and clamor of the bustling town. The museum also hosts a special exhibition each year with contributions from museums around the world, exploring topics from the wilds of Antarctica to the French Revolution. (☎712 7777; www.kerrymuseum.ie. Open Jan.-Mar. Tu-F 10am-4:30pm; Apr.-May Tu-Sa 9:30am-5:30pm; June-Aug. daily 9:30am-5:30pm; Sept.-Dec. Tu-Sa 9:30am-5pm. €8, students €6.50, children €5, families €22.) Across from the museum, another of Ireland's "second-largests"—the **Town Park**—blooms in summer with the **Rose of Tralee.** Nearby, the tall steeple and the stained glass at **St. John's Church,** Castle St., is hard to miss, though beige carpeting dampens the echo and the Gothic mood.

One kilometer down the Dingle road is the **Blennerville Windmill and Visitors Centre,** the largest operating windmill in the British Isles. The small museum recalls Blennerville during the Famine, when it was Kerry's main port of emigration. A 7min. audio-visual presentation covers the region's history and the windmill's restoration. Ask about the growing database which visitors can search to discover when their ancestors migrated on the infamous "coffin ships" that carried Ireland's sons and daughters to distant shores. Check with the Centre for the database. (☎712 1064. Open Apr.-Oct. daily 10am-6pm. €5.50, students €4.10, children €3, families €14.) The building on the Princes Quay traffic circle looks like a combination of a Gothic castle and space-age solarium, but it's actually Tralee's €6 million **Aquadome,** complete with whirlpools, a steam room, sauna, sun shower, and gym. Waterslides and aquagolf (an 18-hole minigolf course) can entertain kids with even the shortest of attention spans. (☎712 8899; www.discoverkerry.com/aquadome. Open July-Aug. daily 10am-10pm; Sept.-June M-F 10am-10pm, Sa-Su 11am-8pm. €12, children €10. Aquagolf €4.50/3.50.) **Tralee & Dingle Railway,** restored to its days of wine and roses, runs the 3km between the Ballyard Station (near the Aquadome) and the Blennerville complex. (☎712 1064. Trains leave from the Aquadome on the hr. and from the windmill every 30min. July-Aug. 10:30am-5:30pm. Call ahead. Closed 2 days per month for cleaning. €5, students €4, children €3, families €15.)

The **Siamsa Tíre Theatre,** next to the museum and accessible through the park or from Princes Quay, is Ireland's national folk theater. Its summer programs depict traditional Irish life through mime, music, and dance. Various touring productions come through town from October to April. (☎712 3055; www.siamsatire.com. Performances July-Aug. M-Sa; May-June and Sept. M-Th and Sa. May-Sept. shows start 8:30pm; Oct.-Apr. 8pm. Box office open M-Sa 9am-6pm and before showtime.)

Lovely lasses of Irish descent flood the town during the third weekend in August for the annual **Rose of Tralee Festival.** The festival began in earnest in 1959 when local businessmen borrowed a theme from a 19th-century merchant's love song *(The Rose of Tralee)* to relaunch the town's carnival queen festival. Today, regional representatives come from Australia, Dubai, Luxembourg, the US, UK, and most counties in Ireland. A maelstrom of entertainment surrounds the main event (the street parades, concerts and discos draw the biggest crowds), culminating in a "personality" contest to earn the coveted title "Rose of Tralee." Rose-hopefuls or spectators can call the Rose Office in Ashe Memorial Hall for more info. (☎ 712 1322; www.roseoftralee.ie.) As if the live music on every street corner and a five-day party weren't enough, the festival is followed by another six-days of revelry for the **Tralee Races,** held at the Ballybeggan course adjacent to town.

TARBERT (TAIRBEART)   ☎ 068

A peaceful seaside spot on N69, Tarbert's principal draw is the car-and-passenger ferry that runs between the Tarbert pier (about 2km from town) and Killimer in Co. Clare. The 1hr. **John F. Leslie Woodland Walk** begins near the restored Tarbert Bridewell (pick up a free pamphlet on the walk at the gift shop and cafe), and passes by Tarbert House and the pier. The **Tarbert Bridewell** is a restored jail and courthouse built in 1831 to hold prisoners charged with petty crimes. The walk-through exhibition shows prison cells, a courthouse scene, and the keepers' apartments with wax figures. (☎ 36500. Open daily 10am-6pm. €5, students €3.50.) **Tarbert House** has been home to the family of Signeur Leslie of Tarbert since 1690. The recently restored exterior rivals the period pieces and priceless art inside. (☎ 36198. Call ahead for a tour.) The **Ferry House Hostel ❶,** at the intersection of the town's two roads, occupies a 200-year-old building. The friendly owners spent a year traveling and taking notes on the world's hostels before opening their own. Cushy bedding and a cozy common room are nice touches. (☎ 36555. Hostel open year-round. Reception May-Sept. 8am-7pm. Dorms €15.; singles €20; doubles €36-40.) **Enright's ❷,** Main St., serves decent lunches and dinners; the three-course lunch for €13 is well worth it. (☎ 36214. Open daily noon-3pm and 6pm-late.) Small **Coolahan's** is the most notable of Tarbert's pubs, with regulars speaking English and Irish at the bar. Drop down to **The Anchor,** half a block up the hill from the hostel, for a light seafood chowder and live music on Saturday nights.

   Bus Éireann stops in front of the hostel en route between Limerick and Tralee; and in summer, en route to the Cliffs of Moher. Find out the bus schedule before you arrive (try www.buseireann.ie or any major tourist office); schedules are hard to find in town. **Shannon Ferry Ltd.** helps travelers make the 3.6km Shannon crossing between Tarbert and Killimer. (☎ 065 905 3124; www.shannonferries.com. 20min. Departs every hr. on the ½hr. from Tarbert and on the hr. from Killimer Apr.-Sept. M-Sa 7am-9:30pm, Su 9am-9:30pm; Oct.-Mar. M-Sa 7am-7:30pm, Su 10am-7:30pm. €5 per pedestrian, €6 per cyclist, and €15 per car. Pay on board.) The **tourist office** is in the restored jail and courthouse. Walk down the street from the hostel and cross the bridge to the right onto the road toward the ferry. (Open Apr.-Oct. daily 10am-6pm. Tours €5, students €3.50, children €2.50, families €10.50.) The **Day Today** convenience store just down from the hostel on the left has an **ATM.** (☎ 36215. Open daily 7:30am-10pm.) There is also an ATM inside **Martin's Spar,** farther down Main St. (☎ 36931. Open daily 8am-9pm.) The **AIB Bank,** Main St. has a **bureau de change.** (Open M-W and F 10am-12:30pm and 1:30-3pm, Th 10am-12:30pm and 1:30-5pm.) The **Internet Cafe** is on Main St. (☎ 36939. Open M-Th 9:30am-5pm, F 9:30am-1pm. €1 per 15min.)

LIMERICK (LUIMNEACH)   ☎ 061

Although Limerick has long endured a negative reputation as violent, poor, and over-industrialized, the rumors are overblown—Limerick is a city on the rise. With new shops and a brand-new quayside opera house in the works, it's slowly shedding its "Stab City" stigma. Here you will not only find poetic inspiration, but also excellent music, free art museums, and a well-preserved 12th-century cathedral.

A LIMERICK FOR LIMERICK.
There once was a place called Stab City,
That McCourt made to sound fairly gritty.
But with parks and the quay
And pubs on the way
It was, it turns out, very pretty!
-Annie Levenson, RW 2008

▐█ TRANSPORTATION

Trains: ☎315 555. Help desk open M-F 9am-5:30pm, Sa 9am-5pm. Trains to: **Cork** (2½hr.; M-Sa 9 per day 7:55am-10pm, Su 7 per day 8:55am-7:55pm; €22.50); **Dublin** (2½hr.; M-Sa 14 per day 5:35am-7:55pm, Su 12 per day 8:35am-7:55pm; €43); **Ennis** (40min.; M-Sa 12 per day 8:36am-7:30pm, Su 6 per day 10:50am-8:55pm; €8.20); **Tralee** (4hr.; M-Sa 6 per day 7:55am-5:55pm, Su 5 per day 8:55am-7:55pm; €25) via **Killarney** (3½hr.).

Buses: Colbert Station (☎313 333), off Parnell St. Open M-Sa 9am-5:30pm, Su 9am-6pm. **Bus Éireann** sends buses to: **Cork** (2hr., 14 per day, €15); **Derry** (8½hr.; M-Sa 3 per day 8:25am-2:25pm, Su 10:25am and 12:25pm; €32.50); **Donegal** (6hr., 4 per day, €24.50); **Dublin** (3½hr., every hr. 7:30am-7:30pm, €12.50); **Ennis** (45min., every hr. 11:25am-8:25pm, €8.80); **Galway** (2½hr., every hr. 7:25am-8:25pm, €15); **Kilkenny** (1½hr., 3 per day, €16.50); **Killarney** (2½hr., every 2hr. 8:35am-8:35pm, €15.40) via **Adare** (20min., €4.30); **Rosslare Harbour** (4½hr.; M-Sa 4 per day 8:25am-4:15pm, Su 8:25am and 4:15pm; €21) via **Waterford** (3hr., €16.50) and **Wexford** (4hr., €19); **Tralee** (2hr., every hr. 8:35am-7:35pm, €15). **Local buses** run to the suburbs from the city center (M-Sa every 30min. 7:30am-11pm, Su every hr. 10:30am-11:30pm; €1.35. Unlimited day pass €3); #14 runs the university. Most leave from Henry St. or William St.

Taxis: Top Cabs (☎417 417), **Well Cabs** (☎412 727). Most city destinations under €5; to airport about €20.

Bike Rental: Cycleworld, 25 Roches St. (☎415 200). €15 per day (9am-5pm), 24hr. €20. €80 per week. Open M-Sa 9am-5pm.

✈▐ ORIENTATION AND PRACTICAL INFORMATION

Limerick's streets form a grid, bounded by the **Shannon River** to the west and the **Abbey River** to the north. The city's most active area lies in the blocks around **O'Connell Street,** which becomes **Patrick Street, Rutland Street** to the north, and **the Crescent** to the south. Follow O'Connell St. north past Hunt Museum and cross the Abbey River to reach **King's Island,** where St. Mary's Cathedral and King John's Castle loom over the landscape. The city itself is easily navigable on foot, but the number of one-way streets makes it a nightmare for drivers.

Tourist Office: Arthurs Quay (☎317 522; www.shannonregiontourism.ie), in the space-age glass building. From the station, follow Davis St. as it becomes Glentworth; turn right on O'Connell St., then left at Arthurs Quay Mall. Free walking tour **maps** (city maps €1.50) and info on the region. Open June-Sept. M-Sa 9am-6pm, Su 9:30am-1pm and 2-5:30pm. Oct.-May M-F 9:30am-5:30pm, Sa 9:30am-1:30pm.

Budget Travel Office: USIT (☎415 064), O'Connell St. at Glentworth St., issues ISICs. Open M and F 9:30am-5:30pm, Sa 10am-1pm. **Budget Travel,** 2 Sarsfield St. (☎317 404). Open M-Sa 9am-6pm.

Banks: AIB, 106-108 O'Connell St. (☎414 388). Open W 10:30am. 2 branches of **Bank of Ireland,** 94 and 125 O'Connell St. (☎316 822 or 415 055), are among the many banks in the center of town. All 3 have 24hr. **ATMs** and are open M 10am-5pm, Tu-F 10am-4pm.

Luggage Storage: Bus & Railway Station (☎217 331), located in the Fastrack office. €2.50 per item per 24hr. Open M-F 8am-6pm and 6:30-8:45pm, Sa 8am-6pm, Su 9:30am-6pm.

Laundry: Speediwash, 11 Gerard St. (☎319 380). Full service from €10. Open M-F 9am-6pm, Sa 9am-4:30pm. **Mannion Dry Cleaners,** 4 Mallow St. (☎312 712). Full service €12. Open M-F 8am-5pm, Sa 9am-2pm.

Emergency: ☎999; no coins required. **Police** *(Garda)*: Henry St. (☎212 400).

Pharmacy: O'Sullivan's Pharmacy (☎413 808), at the corner of Sarsfield and Liddy St., around the corner from the tourist office. Open daily 9am-10pm. **Charlotte Quay Pharmacy,** Charlotte Quay (☎400 722). Open daily 9am-9:30pm.

Hospital: St. John's, St. John's Sq. (☎415 822). **Regional,** Dooradoyle Rd. (☎301 111), follow O'Connell St. south past the Crescent.

Internet: Limerick Library, Michael St. (☎407 510), in the old Granary. Access is free but only available if no members have signed up for the hourly time slots. Open M-Tu 10am-5:30pm, W-F 10am-8pm, Sa 10am-1pm. **Smile Internet,** 6 Mallow St. (☎634 047), in the basement. €1 per hr. Open daily 10am-10pm.

Post Office: Lower Cecil St. (☎212 058), off O'Connell St. Open M-Sa 9am-5:30pm, Tu 9:30am-5:30pm.

ACCOMMODATIONS

It's a shame that Limerick doesn't have a hostel—with a vibrant student-fed night-life, plenty of beautiful spaces, and big-city museums, it's well-suited to backpackers. Limerick suffered from a series of hostel closures in 2002, and another smaller wave in 2005. Lured by government funding, many of those still operating fill their rooms with long-term residents (mostly Eastern European refugees), and permanent "no vacancies" signs hang on their doors. Others house university students for the majority of the year. Smaller private affordable places are beginning to pop up in the city center, including a row of mid-market B&Bs on southern O'Connell St. and some more rural options lining the Ennis road (over Sarsfield bridge). Be sure to call ahead to book a room, as even in the past year several of the newer accommodations have closed.

Courtbrack Accommodation Hostel, Courtbrack Ave., South Circular Rd. (☎302 500; www.mic.ul.ie), 20min. walk from downtown on Dock Rd. Great kitchen, but it's not the place to meet people—most are long-term working residents. Continental breakfast included. Free Wi-Fi. Laundry €5. Singles €30; doubles €50. MC/V. ❷

Glen Eagles, Vereker Gardens (☎455 521). Take the Sarsfield Bridge; it's just up Ennis Rd. on the left. Located on a quiet cul-de-sac just a 5min. walk from the city center. Lovely owner has a soft spot for cash-strapped backpackers. Singles €40-45; doubles €60-70. MC/V. ❸

Mt. Gerard B&B, O'Connell Ave. (☎314 981). Follow O'Connell St. away from the city center until it becomes O'Connell Ave. Quiet house near bright lights and bustle. Singles €40-55; doubles €65-70. Cash only. ❸

Railway Hotel, Parnell St. (☎413 653; www.railwayhotel.ie), opposite the train station. 30 rooms with TV, tea, and coffee. Most have bathrooms. Full Irish breakfast 7:30-10am. June-Aug. singles €50; doubles €90; Sept.-May €46/80. MC/V. ❹

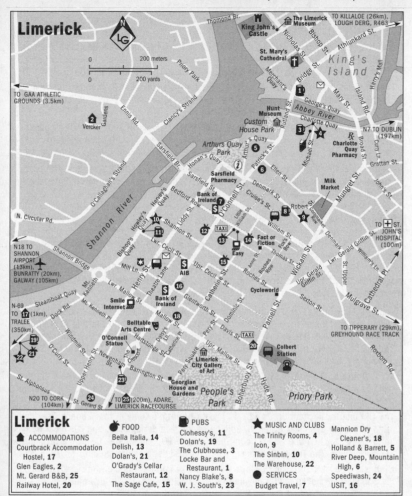

Limerick

ACCOMMODATIONS
Courtbrack Accommodation Hostel, **17**
Glen Eagles, **2**
Mt. Gerard B&B, **25**
Railway Hotel, **20**

FOOD
Bella Italia, **14**
Delish, **13**
Dolan's, **21**
O'Grady's Cellar Restaurant, **12**
The Sage Cafe, **15**

PUBS
Clohessy's, **11**
Dolan's, **19**
The Clubhouse, **3**
Locke Bar and Restaurant, **1**
Nancy Blake's, **8**
W. J. South's, **23**

MUSIC AND CLUBS
The Trinity Rooms, **4**
Icon, **9**
The Sinbin, **10**
The Warehouse, **22**
SERVICES
Budget Travel, **7**

Mannion Dry Cleaner's, **18**
Holland & Barrett, **5**
River Deep, Mountain High, **6**
Speediwash, **24**
USIT, **16**

FOOD

Inexpensive, top-notch cafes in Limerick's center provide refreshing alternatives to pub grub. While O'Connell St. is crowded with fast-food chains, Thomas St. and Catherine St. are full of good cheap eats. To forage for groceries, go to **Tesco** in Arthurs Quay Mall; in the late afternoon, reduced items abound. (☎412 399. Open M-Sa 8am-10pm, Su 10am-8pm.) **Holland & Barrett**, also in the Mall, has a limited selection of natural foods and vegetarian basics. (☎310 466. Open M-W and Sa 9am-6pm, Th 9am-7pm, F 9am-8pm, Su 1:30-5:30pm.) Every Saturday, farmers crowd Limerick's **Milk Market**, off Ellen St., from 8am to 2:30pm.

O'Grady's Cellar Restaurant, 118 O'Connell St. (☎418 286). Above-average service and pub-grub prices are yours in O'Grady's cellar. Candlesticks covered in wax drippings add an air of the unusual to favorites like lasagna (€9.25) and carvery lunches (€10). Open daily 9am-10:30pm. MC/V. ❷

Dolan's, 4 Dock Rd. (☎314 483; www.dolanspub.com). Limerick's best choice for an evening pre-pub meal. Traditional pub grub with a few curveballs, like risotto (€14). Kitchen open M and F-Sa 7:30am-10pm, Tu-Th 9am-10pm, Su 10am-10pm. MC/V. ❸

Delish, 52 Thomas St. (☎214 755.) Makes for great people-watching on a nice day. Tasty open-face brown bread sandwiches (€7-8) and breakfast served all day. Free Wi-Fi. Open M-Sa 8:30am-5pm. MC/V. ❷

The Sage Cafe, 67-68 Catherine St. (☎409 458). Simple interior belies the complex meals, like lamb's liver (€11.25) or goat cheese galettes (€8). Delicious desserts (€5) will stop a diet before it starts. Sandwiches €5-6. Open M-Sa 9am-5:30pm. MC/V. ❸

Bella Italia, Thomas St. (☎418 872) by Catherine St. Cozy little Italian joint with pizza, pasta, and...baked potatoes? It's still Ireland, linguine or not. Potatoes €8. Entrees €9-11, dinner €13-15. Open M-Sa 10am-10pm. AE/MC/V. ❸

PUBS

A variety of musical options cater to Limerick's diverse pub crowd and immense student population. Young *craic*-seekers head toward Denmark St. and Cornmarket Row. Trad-seekers can certainly get their nightly fix, but excellent rock is more plentiful. Unless otherwise noted, all of the following close at standard pub hours: M-Th 11:30pm, F-Sa 12:30am, Su 11pm.

Dolan's, 4 Dock Rd. (☎314 483; www.dolanspub.com). Worth a Shannon-side walk from the city center to join rambunctious locals for nightly trad starting at 9:30pm. Famous Irish musicians show up regularly. F-Sa late bar until 2am. Open M and F-Sa from 7:30am, Tu-Th from 9am. Live rock bands and comedians frequent **The Warehouse** nightclub, in the same building (see **Clubs,** p. 331).

W. J. South's, 4 Quinlan St. (☎318 850). Beautiful pub, renovated 5 years ago for *Angela's Ashes.* Marble floors, sleek counters, and chandeliers. Famed as the watering hole where Frank McCourt quaffed his first pint. MC/V.

The Clubhouse, Michael St. (☎411 177), at Charlotte's Quay in the Granary. Beer garden with palm trees and waterfall. College bands jam during term, and DJs most weekend nights. Kitchen open daily noon-8pm (pizza €10; sandwiches €8.50-11.50). Most F-Sa live music. **The Trinity Rooms** nightclub (p. 331) shares the building. MC/V.

Clohessy's (☎468 100), on Howley's Quay. Classy and cavernous, with sleek hardwood floors, intimate nooks, and a covered patio for rainy evenings. W live music. F-Sa late bar until 2am. Attached **Sinbin Nightclub** (see **Clubs,** p. 331) keeps people dancing through the night. MC/V.

Locke Bar and Restaurant, 3 Georges Quay (☎413 733). Join the classy crowd on the quay-side patio, or head inside to watch sports with owner Richard Costello, a former member of Ireland's national rugby team. Tu and Su trad, Th jazz or country. Pricey food available at the in-pub bistro (entrees €13-23), served until 10pm. MC/V.

Nancy Blake's, Denmark St. (☎416 443). Sawdust covers the floor, where the same family has been running the place for more than 50yr. Spacious beer garden outside. M, W, Sa Trad. Th-Sa late bar until 2am. MC/V.

CLUBS

Limerick's students keep dozens of nightclubs jumping seismically from 11:30pm to 2am. Things slow down over the summer, but there's still plenty of *craic* to go around. Cover charges can be steep (€8-12); keep an eye out for "Ladies' Night" and other promotions.

The Warehouse (☎314 483), behind Dolan's on Dock Rd. Draws big-name bands and rising stars, with something for all ages. Shows more frequent during the winter when the college kids are around. Check www.dolanspub.com for the lineup. Gay night 2 Sa per month. Cover €8-15, higher for well-known acts. Open only for shows.

The Trinity Rooms (☎411 177), inside the Granary on Michael St. Get low to hip-hop, funk, and soul both indoors and under the stars. Open daily until 2am. Cover M-W and Su €5, Th €7, F €10, Sa €12.

Icon, Cornmarket Row (☎310 766), Denmark St. Current hot spot for trendier 20-some-things. Th ladies night. Cover Th €7, F-Sa €12, Su €9. Open daily 11pm-2am.

The Sinbin (☎468 100), inside Clohessy's on Howley's Quay. Mid-20s crowd dances the night away to an eclectic mix of musical styles. Cover W-Th about €8, F-Sa €10-15. Open W-Sa and some Su.

👁 SIGHTS

▓THE HUNT MUSEUM. Located in the old Custom House, Ireland's second largest collection of art and artifacts reaches as far back as the Stone Age. Pieces including Leonardo da Vinci's four "Rearing Horse" sculptures, a gold crucifix given by Mary Queen of Scots to her executioner, and a silver coin reputed to be one of the infamous 30 paid to Judas by the Sanhedrin are presented in an informative fashion. Be sure to check out the room of religious artifacts. Check at the desk for tour times. The **cafe,** which serves sandwiches and tea, also houses a rotating collection of contemporary art. *(Custom House, Rutland St. extension of O'Connell St. ☎312 833; www.huntmuseum.com. Wheelchair-accessible. Open M-Sa 10am-5pm, Su 2-5pm. Cafe closed Su. €7.50, students and seniors €6, children €3.75, families €17.)*

KING JOHN'S CASTLE. Though King John never visited his castle, built in the 13th century, his legacy lives on in a wax likeness. Skip the cheesy audio-visual presentation detailing the siege of 1642 and explore the battlements, which afford a great view of the River Shannon and the city. The underground archaeological excavations which expose the 800-year-old foundations of several houses unearthed below the city are of particular interest. *(Nicholas St. ☎360 788; www.shannonheritage.com. Walk across the Abbey River and take the 1st left after St. Mary's Cathedral. Open daily Apr.-Oct. 9:30am-5pm; May-Sept. 9:30am-5:30pm; Nov.-Feb. 10:30am-4:30pm. Last admission 1hr. before closing. €8.50, students and seniors €6.25, families €20.45.)*

ST. MARY'S CATHEDRAL. St. Mary's, near King John's Castle, was built in 1168 on the site of a Viking meeting place. In the rear of the cathedral, panels marking important events of the last 850 years give away the church's age. Be sure to check out the elaborately carved *misericordia,* Latin for "acts of mercy," which were used by choir members for relief during long services when sitting was prohibited. *(Near King John's Castle. ☎310 293. Open M-Sa 9:30am-4:45pm. Requested donation €2, includes a self-guided tour pamphlet.)*

 A TIP FOR THE MASSES. To dodge the €2 entrance fee at St. Mary's Cathedral—and to get a better idea of its function—stop by any morning at 9am or on Sunday at 11:15am or 7pm for mass.

LIMERICK CITY GALLERY OF ART. The permanent collection, crammed on the walls from floor to ceiling, primarily comprises work of 18th- to 20th-century Irish artists, but the real draw is the avant-garde "ev+a" exhibition, a yearly display of contemporary Irish art. *(Located on Pery Sq. at the main entrance of the People's Park. ☎310 633; www.limerickcity.ie/lcga. Open M-W and F 10am-6pm, Th 10am-7pm, Sa 10am-5pm, Su 2-5pm. Free.)*

THE LIMERICK MUSEUM. For a small museum, it packs a punch—40,000 objects are crammed into its two rooms. Check out everything from hurling medals to lace undies to an underwater diving suit. *(☎417 826; www.limerickcity.ie. Open Tu-Sa 10am-1pm and 2:15-5pm. Free.)*

THE GEORGIAN HOUSE AND GARDENS. Considered one of the best examples of Georgian architecture in Limerick, the house was funded by a tontine, a system in which the last surviving shareholder gains the property. Placards by each room feature limericks thanking big investors. *(2 Perry Sq. ☎314 130; www.georgianlimerick.com. Open M-F 9am-4pm. Other times by appointment. €6, students €4.)*

WALKING TOURS. In the morning, historical tours cover the northern, sight-filled Irishtown and King's Island region. Popular afternoon tours cover the locations described in Frank McCourt's *Angela's Ashes*, and are most enjoyable after recently reading the book. Tour guide Mick O'Donnell recounts anecdotes from the memoir as well as some of his own experiences growing up in Limerick during the same era. *(☎087 622 1906. King's Island tour daily 11am; Angela's Ashes tour daily 2:30pm. Both depart from the tourist office, approx. 2hr. €10.)*

🎵 ENTERTAINMENT

Pick up the *Limerick Events Guide* at the tourist office for info on what's going on in the city (free). **Belltable Arts Centre,** 69 O'Connell St., stages big-name productions year-round as well as smaller music, dance, and poetry performances. Note: the action slows a bit in the summer. The small Georgian building also houses abstract and experimental pieces in its gallery. (☎319 866; www.belltable.ie. Open M-F 9:30am-5:30pm; box office also open prior to performances. Tickets €15-18. Films Tu 8:30pm, €5-6. Gallery free.) **Theatre Royal,** Upper Cecil St. (☎414 224), hosts the town's largest concerts. **University Concert Hall,** on the Limerick University campus, showcases opera and classical music. (☎331 549. Tickets €9-40.) From Irish coffee to hillwalking, Limerick has a festival for you. Shannon's regional tourism authority publishes a yearly pamphlet of Limerick Festivals and events, complete with dates and details, available at the Limerick tourist office. Check www.limerickcityfestivals.com to see what's on before you arrive. The entire city becomes charged with excitement and celebrates the coming of spring during **Riverfest,** held the last weekend in April. Sixty bands hold free performances in 20 venues across the city. For the grand finale, quay-side crowds tilt their heads toward the fireworks erupting over the River Shannon.

🔳 DAYTRIP FROM LIMERICK

BUNRATTY CASTLE AND FOLK PARK

Buses running between Limerick and Shannon airport stop outside the Fitzpatrick Hotel in Bunratty, 13km northwest of Limerick along the Ennis road. 30min.; M-Sa every hr., Su every 2hr. 9:30am-9:30 pm; €5.35 return. Departs from Dunnes on Henry St. and the bus station. Avoid the fanny-packed crowds by arriving early and heading straight for the castle. A 24hr. ATM is across from the hotel in the Village Mills shopping complex.

Bunratty Castle would be great if there were no one else there. The 600-year-old castle is done up splendidly, with tapestries, ornately carved beds, and superbly restored furniture. Unfortunately, swarms of tourists and a poorly designed traffic flow make it a nightmare during the summer months. The **folk park** originated in the 1960s, when builders at Shannon Airport couldn't bear to destroy a quaint cottage in the path of a new runway. Instead, they moved the cottage, now called the **Shannon Farmhouse**, to Bunratty. Since then, reconstructions of turn-of-the-century homes and shops from all over Ireland have been added. Traditional chores of 1900 Ireland are demonstrated on a rotating basis; feel your mouth water as you watch the baking in **Golden Vale Farmhouse**. (Open daily 9am-6pm; last admission to castle 4:30pm. €14, students €9.50, families €32.50.) The weary head back to the main road for oysters (€9) or a sandwich (€3.25-10) on the balcony at **Durty Nelly's** ❸. Music fills the air nightly—trad or "whatever you want to sing" from 9:30pm. The original proprietress earned her nickname in 1620 by serving beer with benefits to Bunratty's soldiers. (☎364 861; www.durtynellys.ie. Entrees €15-20. Open M-Sa 10:30am, Su noon. Kitchen open noon-9:45pm. MC/V.)

ADARE (ATH DARE)   ☎061

Well-preserved medieval architecture and meticulous rows of tiny thatched cottages make Adare the self-proclaimed "prettiest town in Ireland." Yet, you don't need a VIP pass to slip behind the golf course clubhouse for sweeping views of nearly all of Adare's historical sights. Take the path from hole six to reach the ▨**Franciscan Friary,** nicknamed the Poor Abbey because of its monks' commitment to austerity. Its coastal location adds an element of the absurd to the gorgeous, well-preserved stone structure. Next to the golf course is the partially restored **Desmond Castle**, built in the 13th century to protect the fordable river Maigue. Guided tours leave from the **Heritage Center** and point out features like spiral staircases that give an advantage to right-handed sword fighters. (☎396 666; www.adareheritagecenter.com. Tours every hr. June-Sept. €6, students €5.) During the crusades, monks at **Trinitarian Abbey** on Main St. raised funds to liberate Christian captives of the Muslims. The highlight of the **Augustinian Friary,** just before the bridge on the Limerick Rd., is the musty, covered cloister walk surrounding the small garden. Climb passageways for glimpses out of arrow slits. During the school term, the friary is closed from 9am to 3pm, when St. Nicholas' School is in session. Services still take place in the cavernous church. Due to heightened security—and a shiny new security gate—in order to visit the ivy-covered **Adare Manor,** visitors must approach by car and claim lunch reservations. It's worth sweet-talking the guards to see the former estate of the Earls of Desmond, complete with formal, sculpted gardens overlooking the river (☎396 566).

Adare is an easy daytrip from Limerick, but given Limerick's lack of budget accommodations, you might as well stay in this lovely, quiet town. Station Rd., to the right of the heritage center, is lined with B&Bs. A 7min. walk up N21 to Tralee leads to **Ardmore House B&B** ❸, tucked behind a tall hedge. The smooth pine floors are a moonwalker's heaven. (☎396 167. Singles €45; doubles €60. Cash only.) As the last B&B on the Station Rd. strand, set slightly back from the street, **Riversdale** ❸ enjoys a bit more quiet and privacy than its neighbors. (☎396 751. Singles €35; doubles €65. Cash only.) To reach grassy **Adare Camping and Caravan Park** ❶, 4km from town, bear left onto N21 at the uptown fork, turn left at Ivy Cottage toward Ballingeary (R519), and follow the signs. (☎395 376. Open mid-Mar. to Sept. Showers €0.50. Laundry €8. Hot tub €5. Electricity €3.50. €20 per tent with 2 adults; €20 per caravan plus €4 for each additional adult, €2 per child. MC/V.) Sixteen kilometers out of town on N69, nature trails wind through **Curraghchase Forest Park.** Extensive grounds include an arboretum and the former home of 18th-century poet Aubrey DeVere. The more intrepid camp in summer (May-Sept.) at **Curraghchase Caravan Park** ❶. (☎396 349. Showers, kitchen, groceries. Electricity €3. Laundry €8. €16 per tent; €19 per caravan. Cash only.)

Groceries are sold at **Centra** on Main St. (☎396 211. Open M-F 7am-9pm, Sa-Su 8am-8pm.) **The Blue Door ❸,** a 200-year-old thatch-roofed, rose-fronted cottage, is a pricey but beautiful spot for lunch. (☎396 481. Lunches €12-16; dinners €20-25. Open M-F 11am-3pm and 6-10pm, Sa noon-3pm and 6-10pm, Su noon-4pm and 6-9:30pm. AmEx/MC/V.) The menu at **The Arches Restaurant's ❷** has clip-art photos of their plates to help you decide. (☎396 246. Lunches €3-9.50; dinners €16-24. Open M-Sa noon-3pm and 5-9pm, Su noon-3pm and 5-8:30pm. MC/V.) Whatever sort of pub you're seeking, Adare has a Collins for you. **Pat Collins Bar,** next to the post office on Main St., opens early and serves cheap grub (sandwiches €4-9) in a relaxed atmosphere. (☎396 143. MC/V.) Around the corner, **Sean Collins Bar** serves a young crowd and rollicks with trad on Sunday evenings. Cheap burgers (€3.10) and pizza (€12.50) are available for those who work up an appetite on the dance floor. (☎396 400. Th DJ. Cash only.) Farther down the Tralee Rd., **Bill Chawke's** (☎396 160) hosts trad on Thursdays at 9:30pm. Flatscreen TVs make this a good spot to check out hurling or rugby. (Kitchen open 10:30am-6pm. Cash only.)

Buses arrive in Adare from Limerick (25min., every 1-2hr. 8:35am-9:35pm, €6 return), Tralee (1¾hr., every 1-2hr. 8am-7pm, €13.50); and Killarney (1¾hr., 9am and every 2hr. 10am-6pm, €13.50). From the bus stop, head down Main St. to the **Heritage Centre** complex (p. 333), home of the **tourist office** and a computer database that traces family crests. (☎396 255; www.shannontourism.ie. Open daily 9am-6pm.) The center leads tours to Desmond Castle, hosts a small multimedia exhibit on the town's history and several craft and souvenir shops, and serves carrot cake (€3) at the **Dovecot Restaurant.** (Open daily 9am-6pm. Restaurant open daily 10am-5pm. ☎396 666. Exhibit €5, students €3.50. Castle tours June-Sept. every hr., €6, students €5. Combined castle and exhibit ticket €10/8.) To top off the center's long list of services, performers put on evenings of traditional Irish entertainment on summer Tuesdays. (☎381 269. July to mid-Aug. 9pm; €10.) **AIB,** on Main St. across from the knitting and antique shop, has a 24hr. **ATM.** (☎396 544. Open M-Tu and Th-F 10am-4pm, Sa 10:30am-4pm.) The **police** (Garda) is on Main St. (☎396 216). The **library** by the tourist office provides free **Internet** access by appointment. (☎396 822. Open Tu and F 10am-5:30pm and 6:30-8:30pm, W-Th 10am-5:30pm, Sa 10am-1pm and 2-5:30pm.) Down the street is **Adare Pharmacy.** (☎396 147. Open M-Sa 9am-6:30pm.) The **post office** is on Main St. (☎396 120. Open M-F 9am-1pm and 2-5:30pm, Sa 9am-1pm.)

WESTERN IRELAND

Ask any publican—he will probably agree that the West is the "most Irish" part of the island. Yeats (perhaps perched on a barstool) once said, "For me, Ireland is Connacht." For less privileged Irish in more recent centuries, Connacht meant poor soil and emigration. When Cromwell uprooted the native Irish landowners in Leinster and Munster and resettled them west of the Shannon, the popular phrase for their plight became "To Hell or Connacht." The Potato Famine (p. 53) that plagued the entire island was most devastating in the West—entire villages emigrated or died. Today, every western county has less than half its 1841 population. Though wretched for farming, the land from Connemara north to Ballina is a boon for hikers, cyclists, and hitchhikers who enjoy the isolation of boggy, rocky, or strikingly mountainous landscapes. Western Ireland's gorgeous desolation and enclaves of traditional culture are now its biggest attractions.

Galway is a different story: the city has long been a successful port and has begun to harbor young ramblers and music lovers of every kind. Farther south, the Cliffs of Moher, the mesmerizing moonscape of the Burren, and the influential trad music scene attract travelers to Co. Clare. The Shannon River, the longest in all of Britain and Ireland at 214km, pools into holiday-haven Lough Derg and runs south through the city of Limerick, sketching the eastern boundary of the rugged, rocky west. To the north, the farmland of the upper Shannon spills into Co. Sligo's mountains, lakes, and ancient monuments.

WESTERN IRELAND HIGHLIGHTS

ROCK OUT at the **King's Head Bar** in Galway (p. 370).

SPRITZ yourself with wildflower scent at the **Burren Perfumery** (p. 352).

SEARCH for the upside-down rainbow near **Inishmore's worm hole** (p. 378).

COUNTY CLARE

Wedged between the tourist metropolises of Galway and Kerry, Co. Clare is largely free of the traveling hordes. Its historical capital, Ennis, refuses to disappear into urban anonymity. Those tourists who do venture into the county flock to the area's premier attraction, the 213m Cliffs of Moher. Elsewhere, Co. Clare unfurls other geologic wonders: fine sands glisten on the beaches of Kilkee, and 260 sq. km of exposed limestone form Ireland's most peculiarly alluring landscape, the Burren. On the coast, charismatic seaside villages line the strands, while farming communities dot the stark and empty inland.

ENNIS (INIS)   ☎ 065

Growing quickly, the charming capital of Clare cloaks palpitating nightlife under the familiarity of a small town. Narrow, overlapping pedestrian streets run past ancient buildings and chimney stacks—reminders of the town's medieval roots. The River Fergus snakes around much of Ennis, lassoing a large area just north of today's town center—this is the "island" from which Ennis takes its name. Most people come to Ennis

WESTERN IRELAND

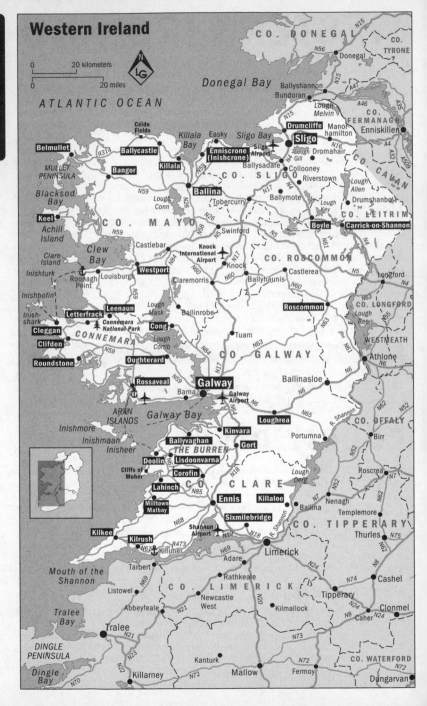

Western Ireland

Scale:
0 — 20 kilometers
0 — 20 miles

ATLANTIC OCEAN

CO. DONEGAL

CO. TYRONE

N15

N56 Donegal

Donegal Bay

Ballyshannon
Bundoran

A47

A46 CO. FERMANAGH

A35

Lough Melvin

N15 Manor-hamilton

Enniskillen

A4 A32

Céide Fields

Killala Bay

Easky

Sligo Bay

Drumcliffe

Sligo

Sligo Airport

Lough Gill

Dromahair

N16

A509

Belmullet

Ballycastle

R314

Killala

Enniscrone (Inishcrone)

N59

Ballysadare

Colooney

Riverstown

CO. CAVAN

MULLET PENINSULA

Bangor

CO. SLIGO

N17

Lough Allen

Drumshanbo

CO. LEITRIM

Blacksod Bay

Lough Conn

N26

Ballina

Tobercurry

Ballymote

Lough Key

N4

Keel

Achill Island

N59

CO. MAYO

N58

N5 Swinford

N5

Boyle

Carrick-on-Shannon

Clare Island

Clew Bay

Castlebar

N84

Knock International Airport

N17

Knock

CO. ROSCOMMON

N61

N4

Longford

Inishturk

Roonagh Point

Louisburgh

Westport

N60

N60

Ballyhaunis

Castlerea

N5

CO. LONGFORD

Inishbofin

Lough Mask

Leenaun

Claremorris

N60

Roscommon

N63

Lough Ree

N55

Inish-shark

Letterfrack

Connemara National Park

Cong

Ballinrobe

N63

WESTMEATH

Inish-bofin

Cleggan

CONNEMARA

Lough Corrib

Tuam

N63

CO. GALWAY

N61

Athlone

N6

N6

Clifden

Roundstone

N59

Oughterard

N84

N17

Rossaveal

Galway

Barna

Galway Airport

N64

N6

Ballinasloe

N6

ARAN ISLANDS

Galway Bay

N65

R. Shannon

CO. OFFALY

Inishmore

Inishmaan

Inisheer

Kinvara

Loughrea

Portumna

Birr

N52

Ballyvaghan

THE BURREN

Gort

N62

N52

Doolin

Lisdoonvarna

N18

Lough Derg

Roscrea

N7

Cliffs of Moher

Corofin

CO. CLARE

N52

N62

Lahinch

N85

Ennis

Killaloe

N7

Nenagh

Templemore

Milltown Malbay

Ballina

CO. TIPPERARY

Thurles

N75

Kilkee

N68

Sixmilebridge

Shannon Airport

N19

N18

R. Shannon

Kilrush

N67

Killimer

R473

N69

Adare

Limerick

N62

Tarbert

Rathkeale

N74

Cashel

Mouth of the Shannon

N69

Listowel

Newcastle West

N20

Kilmallock

Tipperary

N24

N8

Clonmel

N24

Abbeyfeale

N21

CO. LIMERICK

Caher

N24

Tralee Bay

DINGLE PENINSULA

Tralee

N21

N23

Kanturk

N72

Mallow

Fermoy

CO. WATERFORD

N72

Dingle Bay

N70

Killarney

N22

N72

N73

Dungarvan

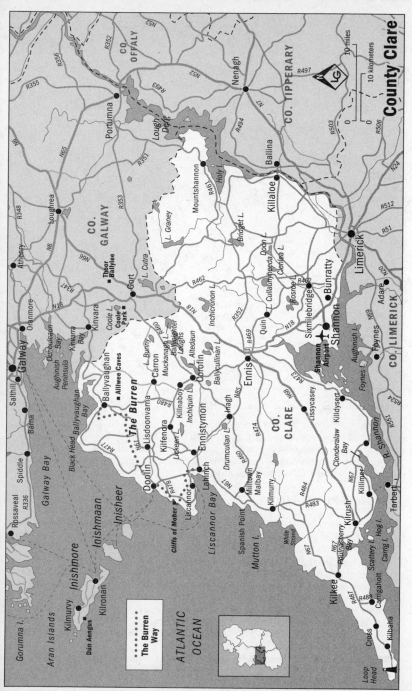

County Clare

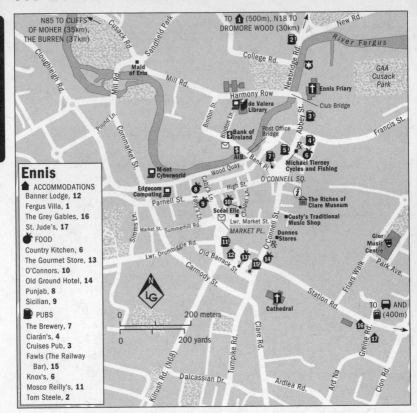

Ennis

🛏 ACCOMMODATIONS
Banner Lodge, **12**
Fergus Villa, **1**
The Grey Gables, **16**
St. Jude's, **17**

🍎 FOOD
Country Kitchen, **6**
The Gourmet Store, **13**
O'Connors, **10**
Old Ground Hotel, **14**
Punjab, **8**
Sicilian, **9**

🍺 PUBS
The Brewery, **7**
Ciarán's, **4**
Cruises Pub, **3**
Fawls (The Railway Bar), **15**
Knox's, **6**
Mosco Reilly's, **11**
Tom Steele, **2**

for its spectacular music, and there's not a whole lot to do there during the day. The town is best experienced on a Saturday, when the pubs and clubs are buzzing and a produce market assembles in Market Square. While Ennis enjoys its visitors, it is at heart a local town, serving as the commercial center of Co. Clare and home to residents who commute to Galway or Limerick.

🚏 TRANSPORTATION

Trains: The station (☎ 684 0444) is a 10min. walk from the town center on Station Rd. Open M-Sa 6:15am-5:30pm, Su 15min. before departures. Trains depart for **Dublin** (M-Sa 7 per day 6:45am-6:45pm, Su 5 per day 7:50am-3:45pm; €43) via **Limerick** (€8.20).

Buses: The bus station (☎ 682 4177) is beside the train station. Open M-Sa 7am-5:15pm. Buses depart to: **Cork** (3hr., every hr. 8:20am-9:20pm, €14); 7:20am-6:20pm to **Dublin** (4hr., every hr. 8:20am-9:20pm, €16.50); 8:20am-9:20pm **Galway** (1hr., every hr. 8:20am-9:20pm, €11); 7:20am-9:20pm **Limerick** (40min., every hr. 8:20am-9:20pm, €8.20). **Shannon Airport** (40min., 22-24 per day 6:55am-11:05pm, €6). Buses head less regularly to **Doolin** (1¼hr.; M-Sa 10:25am, 2:25, 6:25pm; €10) via the **Cliffs of Moher** (50min.) and **Lisdoonvarna** (1hr.); and **Kilkee** (1hr.; M-Sa 4 per day, Su 3 per day; €11.60).

Bike Rental: Michael Tierney Cycles and Fishing, 17 Abbey St. (☎ 682 9433). Dispenses info on bike routes and fishing expeditions. Bikes €20 per day, €80 per wk. Open M-Sa 9:30am-6pm.

✦ 🛈 ORIENTATION AND PRACTICAL INFORMATION

Most of Ennis' winding roads and paths curve back to the town center. **O'Connell Square** marks the center of town; to reach it from the bus and train stations, head left down **Station Road**. At the cathedral, turn right on **O'Connell Street** and go to the end of the street. A soaring statue of Daniel O'Connell stares down from atop a column in the square. From O'Connell Sq., **Abbey Street** and **Bank Place** lead across the river and into the suburbs. **High Street**, which becomes **Parnell Street**, runs almost perpendicular to O'Connell St. through the center of town. **Market Street**, running between O'Connell and High St., leads to **Market Place.**

Tourist Office: Arthur's Row (☎ 682 8366), off O'Connell Sq. **Exchanges currency.** Open Jan. to mid-Mar. M-F 9:30am-1pm and 2-5:30pm; mid-Mar. to mid-June and Sept.-Dec. M-Sa 9:30am-1pm and 2-5:30pm; mid-June to Aug. M-F 9:30am-5:30pm, Sa-Su 9:30am-1pm and 2-5:30pm.

Banks: Bank of Ireland, Bank Pl. (☎ 682 8615). **AIB,** Bank Pl. (☎ 682 8777). Both have 24hr. **ATMs** and are open M-F 10am-5pm, W open 10:30am.

Laundry: Rainbow Laundry, Francis St. (☎ 684 2510). Wash and dry €10. Open M-Th and Sa 8:30am-6pm, F 8:30am-7pm.

Emergency: ☎ 999; no coins required. **Police** *(Garda):* ☎ 684 8100.

Luggage Storage: At the bus/train station, €2 per item. Open daily 6:30am-6:30pm.

Pharmacy: O'Connell Chemist, Abbey St. (☎ 682 0373). Open M-Sa 9am-6pm. **Michael McLoughlin,** O'Connell St. (☎ 682 9511), in Dunnes Shopping Centre. Open M-W and Sa 9am-6pm, Th-F noon-9pm.

Internet: De Valera Library, Abbey St. (☎ 684 6353), over the bridge. Library is 2 blocks from the bridge on the left. Open M and W-Th 10am-5:30pm, Tu and F 10am-8pm, Sa 10am-2pm. **M-Net Cyberland,** Mill Rd. (☎ 684 8100). €1 per hr. Open M-Sa 9am-11pm, Su 10am-11pm. **Edgecom Computing,** River Ln. (☎ 684 8642). €2 per hr. Open M-F 11am-9pm, Sa noon-9pm, Su noon-8pm.

Post Office: Bank Pl. (☎ 682 1713). Open M-F 9am-5:30pm, Sa 9:30am-1pm.

🛏 ACCOMMODATIONS

Banner Lodge, Old Barrack St. and Market Pl. (☎ 682 4224). All rooms with bath, TV, and tea- and coffee-making facilities; most with telephone and windows overlooking the town. Irish breakfast included. Singles €50, with breakfast €55; doubles €70/75. Cash only. ❸

St. Jude's, Greine Rd. (☎ 684 2383), just off Station Rd. Very friendly owner only too happy to give advice on goings-on in town. Doubles €60. Cash only. ❸

Fergus Villa, Gort Rd. (☎ 682 4981), 3min. north of the town center across from the hospital. Clean B&B run by an energetic family of athletes and musicians. All rooms with TV and hair dryer. Doubles €65-70. Cash only. ❸

The Grey Gables, Station Rd. (☎ 682 4487), a short walk from the bus station toward town. Quiet, spacious house with spiral staircases. All rooms with bath. Irish breakfast included. Doubles €70. MC/V. ❸

🍴 FOOD

Enormous **Dunnes,** on O'Connell St., offers enough inexpensive food and beverages to feed all of Clare. (☎ 684 0700. Always open.) A small farmers market assembles in Market Sq. on Fridays (see **Sights and Festivals**, p. 341).

O'Connors, 10 Merchant's Sq. (☎ 682 3660). With low lighting, mermaids floating on the walls, and colorful tablecloths, O'Connors is the best of fun and fancy. Lunch €6-10. Open M-Sa noon-3pm and 5:30-10pm. MC/V for purchases over €20. ❷

The Gourmet Store, 1 Barrack St. (☎684 3314; www.ennisgourmetstore.com). French chef cooks up creative salad combinations best enjoyed at the outdoor tables in front. Sandwiches €5, salads €12-15. Flexible hours; generally open M-W 9:30am-7:30pm, Th-Sa 9:30am-9pm, Su noon-6pm. MC/V. ❷

Country Kitchen, Friary Bow (☎682 9203). Small cafe draws a crowd with home-baked goodies. Sandwiches €3.50-3.70. Open M-Sa 9:30am-6pm. Cash only. ❶

Punjab, Parnell St. (☎684 4656). Excellent Balti and tandoori meals at good prices, especially as leftovers will suffice for the next day's lunch. Big vegetarian section with prices around €9. Entrees €11-16. Takeaway prices about €1 less. Open M and W 5-11pm, Th-Su 5-11:30pm. AmEx/MC/V. ❸

Sicilian (☎684 3873), on the corner of Cabey's Ln. and Parnell St. Bright and cheerful behind the Venetian blinds. A great value, with portions big enough to feed 2. Pasta €10-13; calamari €14. Open daily 5-11pm. MC/V. ❷

The Old Grand Hotel, O'Connell St. (☎682 8127). Musty books and portraits fill this grand pub. Creative dishes, like feta, tomato, eggplant quiche (€9.50) or salmon in yogurt (€10), take the idea of pub grub up a notch. Kitchen open 12:30-9pm. MC/V. ❸

◪ PUBS

With over 60 pubs, Ennis has no shortage of nightlife options. Many host trad sessions that help uphold Co. Clare's reputation for musical excellence. The night traditionally begins with slower tunes, but as time passes it livens up with footstomping impromptu solos. Musical pubs line the streets—just stop and listen. For music listings, grab *The Clare Champion* (€1.35) in just about any shop. To pick up strings for your fiddle or for information on lessons, head to **Custy's Traditional Music Shop,** Cook's Ln. (☎682 1727. Open M-Sa 9am-6pm.)

▨ **Cruises Pub,** Abbey St. (☎684 1800), next to the Friary. High-class restaurant fills the back, while quality Mediterranean grub sneaks through into the lively front pub until session time (9:30pm). Built in 1658, it is one of the oldest buildings in Co. Clare; much of the original interior remains intact. Open M-F 2pm-late, Sa-Su noon-late. MC/V.

Ciarán's (☎684 0180), off O'Connell St., opposite the Queen's Hotel. Traditional music in a contemporary space. Locals turn out in droves for nightly trad sessions. Music nightly from 9:30-10pm. Open from 1pm. Cash only.

Knox's, Abbey St. (☎682 2871). Modern, multi-level pub serves bar food (€9-12) in its comfortably sized downstairs and more expensive fare (€16.50-22.50) in the restaurant upstairs. The young and restless party well into the night at the W-Sa late bar. W live music, Th-Sa DJ. Su band or DJ. Kitchen open from noon. Late bar Th-Sa and July-Aug. W until 2am, Su until 1am. Restaurant MC/V.

Fawls (The Railway Bar), O'Connell St. Only pub left in town with a "snug"—a front room that sits 4 or 5 people. In the old days, when females ventured to houses of drink, they were separated from the males in this cozy area, receiving their beverages through a small hole in the wall that connected to the bar.

Mosco Reilly's, 6 Upper Market St. (☎682 8747). Dark wood, a dart board, and plenty of hurling posters make it clear that this is a sports pub to the core. On weekends, have a seat on a barrel for live music. Open daily from noon. Cash only.

◉ ❋ SIGHTS AND FESTIVALS

A **walking tour** of Ennis spices up a portrait of the town as it was with local lore and political history. Jane O'Brien garners special praise for her gentle yet commanding presence and spirited stories. (☎087 648 3714; www.enniswalkingtours.com.

1½hr. tours leave from the courtyard in Arthur's Row, in front of the tourist office May-Oct. M and W-Su at 11am and 7pm or by appointment. €8.)

The Riches of Clare Museum, attached to the tourist office, traces the history of Co. Clare from the Bronze Age to its present state through concise explanations and audio-visual exhibits. Along with stone axes galore, the museum has an on-site well and a Proclamation of Independence from the early 20th century. Upstairs, learn about Irish emigration through a series of artsy photos. Ennis won an Eircom-sponsored contest designating them an *Information Age Town* and gave Ireland the chance to see what would happen to a little town pumped full of technology; this first-rate museum is one of the results. (☎682 3382; www.clarelibrary.ie. Open Oct.-May Tu-Sa 9:30am-5pm; June-Sept. M-Sa 9:30am-5pm, Su 9:30am-1pm. Last admission 1hr. before closing. Free.) Two blocks along Abbey St., away from O'Connell Sq., rest the ruins of the 13th-century **Ennis Friary,** second only to the Clare hurling team in the local esteem it commands. During the Reformation, the Friary was seized and turned into a jail and a ritzy apartment complex. Be sure to check out the carvings that were discovered when restorers stripped off the plaster that hid them. (☎682 9100. Open daily Apr.-Sept. 10am-6pm; Oct. 10am-5pm. 20-25min. Guided tours upon request. €1.60, students €1.) Across from the Friary, a block of sandstone is inscribed with part of Yeats's "Easter 1916" (see **Easter Rising,** p. 55).

Perched nobly on his monument in the square, **Daniel O'Connell** watches over today's town. A 10min. walk from the town center on Harmony Row, which becomes Mill Rd., leads to the **Maid of Erin,** a life-size statue commemorating one of the three **Manchester Martyrs,** nationalists hanged in Manchester in 1867 (also see **Kilrush,** p. 344). The maid stands with her left hand on a Celtic cross; an Irish wolfhound at her side looks up for guidance. Saturday is **Market Day** in Market Sq., where all conceivable wares are sold beneath a statue of crafty Daedalus. A smaller **farmers' market** operates on Friday from 8am to 2pm. A 30min. walk and sculpture trail winds along the trout-filled **River Fergus;** directions are posted in the parking lot between the river and Abbey St. Ennis's beloved **hurling** team stages matches most weekends. Check the *Clare Champion* on Thursdays or ask local fanatics for game times and buy tickets at **Cusack Park.** (☎682 0172. Tickets €8-20.) Several kilometers north of town off the N18 lies **Dromore Wood,** a beautiful nature reserve centered around a lake. A pamphlet detailing a variety of hikes is available at the Dromore Wood Visitors Centre. (☎683 7166. Centre open mid-June to Sept. M-F 10am-6pm. Grounds open daily year-round during daylight hours. Free.)

While most locals enjoy the free music at pubs, tourists head to the new, state-of-the-art **Glor Music Centre** earlier in the evening. The venue also serves as a regional arts center and has expanded its repertoire to incorporate a diverse mixture of contemporary film, theater, and music, along with performances of traditional music and dance. Pick up a schedule of performances in the tourist office. (☎684 3103; www.glor.ie. Box office open M-Sa 10am-5pm. More performances Sept.-Apr.; call or check online for schedule. Tickets €12-39; student discounts usually available.) The last weekend in May, Ennis takes its musical inclinations for the full ride during the **Fleadh Nua Music and Culture Festival,** when sessions and other festivities spill onto the streets (☎684 0173; www.fleadhnua.com).

THE SHANNON VALLEY AND LOUGH DERG

Northeast of Limerick, the River Shannon widens into the lake region of Lough Derg. Affluent middle-aged tourists powerboat between the small towns of Killaloe, Ballina, Mountshannon, and Portumna; younger, vehicle-challenged travelers are rarer here than in regions to the south and west. Lough Derg's summer water-sport culture provides a good workout but little in the way of archaeological interest. Travelers lured into sleepy Sixmilebridge on their way to and from the airport enjoy a fabulous hostel and a breadth of scenic trails.

SIXMILEBRIDGE   ☎061

Halfway between Shannon and Limerick, quiet Sixmilebridge *(Droichead Abhann Ó gCearnaigh)* has a spectacular hostel and makes a perfect stop en route to the airport. The beauty of the Shannon Valley demands exploration. Hostel co-owner Michael is a great source of information on scenic walks. The most rewarding walks lead to the breathtaking views of Shannon from atop **Gallows** and **Woodcock Hills,** about 5km outside town. From the hostel, take a left when you get to town. Fishermen might pass the time trying to hook dinner at **Castle Lake,** 3km north of town.

The wonderful ▓**Jamaica Inn ❶** is really Sixmilebridge's main attraction. Large, soft beds, a lovely outdoor patio, and knowledgeable staff make it worth a stopover even if you're not on the way to the airport. Head downhill from the bus stop at the center of town and cross the bridge, which, at a distance of exactly six old-Irish miles from Limerick, gave the town its name. Take the first left and follow the signs—it's a short walk from town past the Duck Inn near the old mill pond. The serene central courtyard is a wonderful lounging spot for rare sunny afternoons. (☎369 220; www.jamaicainn.ie. Free Wi-Fi. Laundry €8-10. Dorms May-Sept. €19, Oct.-Apr; €18. Singles €38/35; doubles €58/54. MC/V; 4% surcharge applies.) The inn also serves breakfast in its **restaurant ❶.** (Full Irish breakfast €8.50. Open daily 8:30am-noon.) Pick up groceries at **Centra,** Main St., which also has a small deli and **ATM.** (☎369 176. Open M-Sa 7:30am-9pm, Su 8am-8pm.) Sixmilebridge doesn't have many restaurants, but luckily a few are real gems. A French couple runs cozy ▓**Dine & Wine ❶,** Main St., which serves croque monsieur (€5) and goat cheese sandwiches (€5) with glasses of wine (€4) to class it up. (☎713 900. Open Tu-F noon-9pm, Sa noon-7pm. MC/V.) Up the hill, **Spice Lagoon ❸** has curried dishes for when pub grub gets to be too much. (☎713 688. Entrees €9-13. Open daily 5-11:30pm. MC/V.) Head to the top of the hill to find **Bill McGregors,** an old-school pub with dark wood and a cast of local characters. (☎369 099. F-Su live music. Cash only.) Locals end the night at the **Old House,** where the *craic* continues long after closing time. (☎086 834 7465. Open from noon. Live music Su. Cash only.) The town's six pubs quench the thirst worked up by a long day of hiking. Hurling enthusiasts will enjoy the themed decor at **Casey's.** The second weekend in January is the **winter weekend,** when live music packs Sixmilebridge's pubs.

Buses depart from Sixmilebridge for **Limerick** (€4.30; M-F 8:20, 10:45am, 4:55pm, Sa 8:20am and 10:45am) and **Shannon.** (M-F 7:20am, 1:30, 2:55pm; Sa 7:20am and 1:30pm. Arrive early; buses are known to leave ahead of schedule.) There is a **currency exchange** at the **Credit Union** on Main St. (☎369 322. Open M-W 2-6pm, Th-F 2-8pm.) The green-and-white **pharmacy** is on the first corner when entering town. (☎369 601. Open M-F 9:15am-1:30pm and 2:30-6:15pm, Sa 9:30am-1:30pm.) The **post office** is up the hill on Main St. (☎369 171. Open M-F 9am-1pm and 2-5:30pm, Sa 9am-1pm.) On the first street on the right heading up Main St. is the gorgeous **Kilfinaghty Public Library,** housed in an 18th-century stone church recently refurbished with the financial support of poet laureate Seamus Heaney. (☎369 678. Free **Internet** access for up to 1hr. Open Tu and Th 10am-1pm, 2-5:30pm and 6-8pm, W and F 10am-1pm and 2-5:30pm, Sa 10am-2pm.)

KILLALOE AND BALLINA   ☎061

A wide stone bridge connects spectacular sister towns Killaloe (Kill-a-LOO; *Cill Dalua*) and Ballina (Ball-leen-AH; *Beal an Átha*) across the River Shannon as it becomes the base of Lough Derg, 22.5km northeast of Limerick City. Residents celebrate the rich history of King BrianBorú's old residence, though visitors are more interested in the area's immense beauty and tranquility, broken only by the occasional purr of powerboats. From the center of the old stone bridge that connects the towns, the horizon is dotted by colorful rowboats, downy ducks, and lush hills as far as the eye can see. Picnic tables by the water make it easy for all to take in the lake breezes and beautiful views.

⊡ ⁊ TRANSPORTATION AND PRACTICAL INFORMATION. Transportation to either town enables easy access to both. Local **buses** run between **Killaloe** and **Limerick** (45min., M-Sa 4 per day, €8.20), depositing riders 140m outside town. Rent bikes in Limerick at **Cycleworld**, 25 Roches St. (Bikes €80 per week. Open M-Sa 9am-5pm.) The **tourist office**, in the former Lock House on the Killaloe side of the medieval bridge, has info on walks in the area, including the popular Lough Derg Way and Clare Way. They also offer the brochure *Walks in the Killaloe District* (€0.30), which features waymarked trails ranging from 3½ to 15 miles. (☎376 866. Open May-Sept. daily 10am-6pm.) The tourist office also houses the **BrianBorú Heritage Centre,** which celebrates the fact that Ireland's last high king sat in a highchair here. A 15min. movie and a small exhibit does an excellent job reconciling an ancient story with the context of the modern town and river. (☎376 866. €3.20, students and seniors €2.25, children €1.65, families €7.75. Open daily 10am-5:30pm.) An **AIB** with an **ATM** sits on Main St. (☎376 115. Open M 10am-5pm, Tu and Th-F 10am-4pm, W 10:30am-4pm.) **Grogan's Pharmacy** is on Main St., in Ballina. (☎376 118. Open M-F 9:30am-6:30pm, Sa 9:30am-6pm.) The **library,** in the same building as the tourist office, has free **Internet** access. (☎376 062. Open M-Tu and Th 10am-1:30pm and 2:30-5:30pm, W and F 10am-5:30pm and 6:30-8pm, Sa 10am-2pm.) The **launderette** is to the left after crossing the bridge into Ballina. (Open M-Tu and Th-Sa 9am-6pm, W 1-6pm. 7kg wash and dry €16.) Farther up the hill is the **police** *(Garda)* station. (☎620 540. Open 24hr.) The **post office** is up the hill on Main St. (☎376 111. Open M-F 9am-12:30pm and 1:30-5:30pm, Sa 9am-12:30pm.)

⊓ ACCOMMODATIONS. Killaloe is a manageable daytrip from Limerick, but several nice B&Bs near town make it a pleasant stopover. The stone **Derg House B&B ❸** has a huge kitchen, where the owners bake goods for the nearby **Coffee Pot.** Not only does it smell amazing upstairs, but the large rooms also have a grand view of the lake. (☎375 599; www.derghouseclare.com. All rooms with bath. Singles €40; doubles €70.) Looking out on the river, **Kincora House ❸,** Church St., across from Crotty's Pub, has chandeliers and dark wood. The owners don't take themselves too seriously, though—fishing poles stand right next to the family crest. (☎376 149. Singles €40; doubles €70, all with bath. Cash only.)

⊡ ⊠ FOOD AND PUBS. Purchase groceries at **SuperValu,** up the hill on Abbey St. (☎620 230. Open M-Sa 8:30am-10pm, Su 9am-8pm.) On the **Killaloe** side of the river, the buzzing **Coffee Pot & Deli ❷** whips up sandwiches (€6.50-7), vegetarian lasagna (€9), and homemade breakfasts. (☎375 599. Breakfast 8am-3pm. Open M-Sa 8am-5pm, Su 9am-4pm. MC/V.) **Crotty's Courtyard Bar ❸** serves hearty grub on a patio decorated with flower pots and soap ads. (☎376 965. Pub grub €11-15. Open daily 5-9:30pm. MC/V.) Crossing over into **Ballina** yields several fancier restaurants and hotels. Up from the bridge, **Molly's ❸** serves quality pub grub overlooking the lake. Take your pizza (€10-11) or prawns (€9) to the roof for breezes and *craic.* (☎376 002. Entrees €10-19. Kitchen open M-Sa noon-10pm, Su noon-9pm. F-Su live music during summer. AmEx/MC/V.) On Friday, Saturday, and Sunday nights, people of all ages and a common fashion sense flock to Molly's basement to boogie at the only **nightclub** in town. (Open daily 11pm-2am. Cover €10.)

◙ 兦 **SIGHTS AND OUTDOOR ACTIVITIES.** At the base of the town on Royal Parade lies **St. Flannan's Cathedral,** built around 1200 and still used today. Inside, the **ogham stone** is inscribed in both Scandinavian runes and ogham script with a prayer for the conversion of the Viking Thorgrim to Christianity. The great acoustics also make it a great place for karaoke. (Requested donation €2.) Across the street is **St. Flannan's well** and a **Sheela-na-Gig,** an ancient sexual carving. These former church grounds are now the AIB garden; ask inside the bank to have a look. Market Sq., at the top of Main St., may have once held the **Kincora palace** of legendary Irish High King Brian Ború, granddaddy of the O'Brien clan, who ruled here in 1002, but no trace exists today. **St. Lua's Oratory** was built on Friars' Island in the 9th century. When the Shannon hydroelectric scheme required total submersion of the island, the oratory was moved to its present location at the top of Church St. During the first weekend in July, the **Féile Brian Ború** celebrates Killaloe's most famous resident with four days of music, watersports, parades, and even a quiz bowl. (Contact John Grimes for more information, ☎086 258 7819.)

Quite the people-magnet, the **Lough** has drawn the masses to Killaloe and Ballina for centuries. One option for today's visitor is a relaxing, 1hr. cruise with historical narration on the *Spirit of Killaloe,* operated daily at 2:30pm and other times by arrangement. For tickets (€10, children €6), call skipper James (☎086 814 0559), or go to **Whelan's,** just outside the tourist office. (☎376 159; www.killaloe.ie/thespiritofkillaloe. Open daily 9am-9pm.) Down on the Killaloe side of the bridge, Whelan's also rents **motorboats** for fishing or cruising; boats hold four and include life jackets. (☎086 391 9472. 1st hr. €25. Call for fishing rod availability. Open daily 8am-8pm, depending on weather.) A boat and a bit of navigational prowess grant access to the **Holy Island** (a.k.a. **Iniscealtra**), which has a **round tour** and the remains of five **churches** dating back to the 6th century. For a tour with a local historian, try the **Holy Island Boat Trip,** which departs from Mountshannon Harbour. (☎921 615. €9, children €5. Call for times; trips based on demand.)

CLARE COAST

The Cliffs of Moher form the most famous part of the Clare coastline, with limestone walls soaring 213m over the Atlantic. The spectacular scenery is not limited to this single tourist spot, however; the majority of the western coastline of Clare is composed of similarly thrilling cliffs, and scenic walks and drives delight travelers who trek past the typical tour-bus route, discovering their own favorite ledges, islands, and coves as they go. In several places, the cliffs have lost the battle with the Atlantic, and sandy beaches at Lahinch and Kilkee lie low within the rocky landscape. The southern border of Clare looks across the River Shannon at Kerry from small maritime towns.

KILRUSH (CILL ROIS) ☎065

Despite its small size, Kilrush is home to the coast's principal marina and an active square of shops and pubs. The first permanent settlement here appeared in the 12th century, when monks from nearby Scattery Island built a church in a mainland meadow. Centuries later, famine-stricken tenants banded together to withhold rent from their absentee landlords; "Boycott" was the name of the first deprived debt collector. Today, music, boating, and dolphin-sightings bring steady numbers of travelers to town.

◘ 冈 **TRANSPORTATION AND PRACTICAL INFORMATION. Bus Éireann** (☎682 4177) stops in Market Sq. on the Cork-Galway route. In the summer, service between **Kilkee** and **Ennis** (with connection to **Limerick**) also stops in Market Sq. There is no ticket office in town; buy a ticket on the bus and inquire at the local tourist office or the transportation center in Ennis for times and prices. **Bike rental** is available at **Gleesons**, Henry St. (☎905 1127. €20 per day, €60 per wk. ID required.) The **tourist office** is on Frances St.; stop in for extensive information on the activities in town, its accommodations and bus schedules, and free maps. (☎905 1577. Open May-Sept. M-Sa 9:30am-1pm and 2-5:30pm.) **AIB**, Frances St., has a 24hr. **ATM**. (☎905 1012. Open M 10am-5pm, Tu-F 10am-4pm.) There are also 24hr. ATMs in Market Sq. and on Toler St. **Anthony Malone's Pharmacy**, on the right side of Frances St., has everything for a quick fix. (☎905 2552. Open M-Sa 9am-6pm, Su 11am-1pm.) One hour of **Internet** access is complimentary at **Kilrush Library** on O'Gorman St. (☎905 1504. Open M-Tu and Th 10am-1:30pm and 2:30-5:30pm, W and F 10am-1:30pm and 2:30-8pm, Sa 10am-2pm.) The **post office** is on Frances St. (☎905 1077. Open M and W-F 9am-5:30pm, Tu 9:30am-5:30pm, Sa 9am-1pm.)

⌂ ACCOMMODATIONS. Katie O'Connor's Holiday Hostel (IHH) ❶, on Frances St. next to the AIB, provides clean quarters in rooms that date back to 1797. Hostelers enjoy a central location and a warm welcome from the owners, Mary and Joe. (☎905 1133. Check in at the store next to the sign for the hostel. Self-serve kitchen open 24hr. Dorms €15.) Irish, American, and Canadian flags fly over **The Grove ❸** on Frances St. Inside this guesthouse are spacious rooms with tables and desks for finishing up those long-neglected postcards. Out back, guests volley on the tennis courts. (☎905 1451; www.groveguesthouse.net. Singles €42; doubles €65.)

▯▥ FOOD AND PUBS. A gargantuan **SuperValu** sells groceries at the marina end of Frances St. (☎905 1885. Open M-Sa 8:30am-10pm.) The pleasant aroma wafting down Frances St. comes from **Cosidines Bakery ❶**. (☎905 1095. Soda loaf €2. Open M-Sa 8am-5pm.) For a quick lunch, the **Quayside ❶** restaurant and coffee shop offers soups, salads, and sandwiches from behind baskets of homemade scones. (☎905 1927. Toasted sandwiches €3-4. Salads from €7.50. Open M-Sa 9:30am-5:45pm.) Henry Street offers a variety of options to please the palate. For greasy burgers (€4.50) hop into the new **Taster's Diner ❶**, Henry St. (☎908 0099; www.tasters.ie. Open M-Sa 9:30am-10pm.) The food at **Kelly's Steak and Seafood House ❸**, Henry St., is a notch above typical pub grub. (☎905 1811. Sandwiches for lunch €10.25, dinner entrees €13.50-19.50 Open daily noon-9pm.)

Of Kilrush's 15 or so pubs, at least one is sure to have music on any given night. ▧**Crotty's Pub**, Market Sq., is where concertina player Mrs. Crotty helped re-popularize trad in the 1950s; the pub hosts inspirational tributes to the legendary lady in a set of small, character-filled rooms. (☎905 2470; www.crottyskilrush.com. Trad Tu-Th and Sa after 9pm.) **Charlie Martin's**, next to the hostel on Frances St., hosts trad sessions every Saturday and Sunday.

◩▦ SIGHTS AND OUTDOOR ACTIVITIES. Kilrush's real attractions lie offshore, and most visitors head straight for the marina. The Shannon Estuary is home to Ireland's only known resident population of **bottlenose dolphins.** Climb aboard the *M.V. Dolphin Discovery* for a 98% chance of cruising alongside the playful swimmers. (☎905 1327; www.discoverdolphins.ie. 2-2½hr. May-Sept. 3 per day; sailings based on weather and demand, so call ahead. €20, under 16 €10.) The eco-cruise passes by **Scattery Island,** the site of a 6th-century monastic settlement. The island's resident population took off for the mainland back in the 70s, leaving behind the rubble of monastic ruins, churchyards, and a 36.5m circular tower. The **Scattery Island Centre** gives insight on the island's natural and cultural history and includes a dolphin and marine wildlife display. (☎087 836 2491. Free.) **Scattery Island Ferries** sail often during the summer, departing from the marina, and irregularly during other seasons (May-Sept. 2-4 per day; return €14, under 16 €7). Transportation can be arranged with Gerald Griffins (☎905 1327) or at the marina. More active aquatic exploration starts at the **Kilrush Creek Adventure Centre,** in the gray building across the small bridge from the marina. Instructors lead 1hr. sessions of sailing, kayaking, canoeing, archery (€20-30), and multi-activity sessions (€30-50). Five-day camps, which teach the ins and outs of adventure, start at €200. (☎905 2855; www.kilrush-creekadventure.com. Call ahead for schedules.) In the center of town, a monument facing town hall remembers the Manchester Martyrs of 1867 (see **Ennis,** p. 335).

The **Éigse Mrs. Crotty Festival** ("Rise up, Mrs. Crotty!") celebrates the glory of the concertina with lessons, lectures, and non-stop trad in the pubs and on the streets for a weekend in mid-August. (Contact Rebecca Brew of Crotty's Pub at ☎905 2470 for more info, or check out www.eigsemrscrotty.com.)

KILKEE (CILL CHAOI) ☎065

From the first weekend in June until early September, Kilkee is an Irish holiday town. Families fill the pastel summer homes, teens working resort jobs party until early morning, and beach bums fill the swimming holes along the shore. But the crescent-shaped town overlooking a half-circle of soft sand has a quieter side that emerges when the holiday-makers leave, the population drops back down to 2400, and the countryside is again green and still.

■ ■ **TRANSPORTATION AND PRACTICAL INFORMATION. Bus Éireann** (☎682 4177 in Ennis) leaves from the corner of Grattin St. and Erin St. Leaving the tourist office, take an immediate right and walk to the very end of the street. Buses head to **Galway** with a stop at the **Cliffs of Moher** (4hr.; summer 2 per day; €14.40, students €11.70) and to **Limerick** (2hr.; 2-4 per day; €13.50, students €11.20) via **Ennis** (1hr.). William's, a **pharmacy** (☎056 141; open M-Sa 9am-6pm, Su 11:30am-1pm), and a hardware store that happens to **rent bikes,** are located on Circular Rd., just left of the roundabout at the end of O'Curry St. (☎056 041. Bikes €15 per day; deposit €20. ID required. Open M-F 8:30am-5:30pm, Sa 9am-6pm.) The **tourist office** is next to the Stella Maris Hotel in the central square. (☎905 6112. Open June to mid-Sept. daily 9:30am-1pm and 2-5:30pm.) There is a 24hr. **ATM** at the **Bank of Ireland,** O'Curry St. (☎905 6053. Open M 10am-12:30pm and 1:30-5pm, Tu-F 10am-12:30pm and 1:30-4pm.) **Internet** access, limited to 1hr. per day, is free at the pink **Kilkee Library,** on O'Connell St. (Open M and W 1:30-5:30pm and 6-8pm, Tu and Th-F 10am-1:30pm and 2-5:30pm.) The **post office** is on O'Connell St. (☎905 6001. Open M-F 9am-12:30pm and 1:30-5:30pm, Sa 9am-12:30pm.)

■ **ACCOMMODATIONS.** Visitors to Kilkee often rent a cottage, stay in one of the town's many resort hotels, or base themselves at the hostel in nearby Kilrush (Ireland's Central Reservation Unit ☎8006 6866 8668). There are also a number of B&Bs in town, which start at €35 per person. The Kilkee tourist office has contact information for all board-approved accommodations; the helpful Kilrush tourist office has more information about accommodations in the area. **Duggerna B&B ❸,** a 10min. walk out of town up the left coastal road with the beach on the right, has spectacular cliff views and comfortable rooms. (☎905 6152. Open May-Sept. Singles €40-50; doubles €60-70.) **Halpin's Hotel ❹** is behind the Strand restaurant and bar; the entrance is on Erin St. around the corner from the tourist office. Halpin's has fantastic views, posh rooms, and the Vittles Restaurant. (☎905 6032. Summer rates from €75 for singles, €120 for doubles. Call ahead.)

FOOD AND PUBS. Along the beach in the summer, vendors sell a Kilkee delicacy, **winkles and dillisk.** Winkles are sea snails and dillisk is sea grass, both collected from the tide pools that form during low tide. Both are sold for about €2 a bag. Pub food and hotel-dining options are widely available. **Gala,** on the corner of O'Curry St. and O'Connell St., sells groceries. (☎905 6466. Open June-Sept. M-Sa 9am-11pm, Su 9am-10pm; Oct.-May M-Sa 9am-10pm, Su 9am-9pm.) **The Pantry ❸,** O'Curry St., is a culinary oasis in a desert of bland pub fare. It stocks a large selection of wines and gourmet food to please the palate. (☎905 6576. *Panini* and baps €10; salads €11-12. Open June-Sept. daily 9am-6pm.) The ▒**Country Cooking Shop ❶,** in the alley behind its parent Pantry, bags the same quality baked goods, fish fillets, sandwiches, and salads for considerably cheaper takeaway and also makes desserts. (Fresh scones €0.80 each; fish fillet and sauce €6. Open daily 8:30am-6:30pm.) At night, grab some tasty lo mein (€8.50) from **Gold Sea ❷,** several doors up from The Pantry on O'Curry St., and picnic beneath the stars. (☎908 3847. Open M-Sa 5pm-midnight.) The **Old Bistro ❸,** O'Curry St., is a great find, rebuilt several years ago by a handy Limerick chef and his wife. The restaurant draws weekend crowds with a delicious sea-inspired menu, so call ahead. (☎905 6898. Entrees €16-27. Open for dinner at 6pm; early bird special until 7:30pm.)

After a day spent frolicking or sunbathing at the beach, fritter away even more time by drinking through the dense strip of pubs along O'Curry St. **Naughton's** is a pub that fills up quickly—get there early for a seat or join the jumble of locals and vacationers flooding the floor. **The Myles Creek Pub** features a different live band each summer night. (☎905 6771. Music starts around 10:30pm. Breakfast, lunch, and dinner menus available during summer 9am-9pm, during winter 9am-6pm.) The **Central Bar** has plenty of seating, pool tables, and dark wood to go with the dark pints. It's also a good bet for weekday music beginning in late June. (☎905 6103. M-Th trad, folk, and country bands at 10:30pm.) The **Strand Bar** is a great place to end the crawl. A stone's throw from the beach, the Strand has live music and dancing most nights; the Strand Restaurant has early bird specials from 5:30-7:30pm on weekdays. (☎905 6017. Entrees €17-29.)

SIGHTS AND OUTDOOR ACTIVITIES. The spectacular ▒**West End Cliff Walk** begins at the end of the road left of the seacoast and gently ascends the top

ON THE MENU

IRISH ESCARGOT

While visitors to Ireland may be accustomed to beaches lined with concession stands, in Kilkee, local vendors have replaced hot dogs and ice cream with a regional specialty known as winkles and dillisk. Winkles are small sea snails, and dillisk is a green seaweed found in Kilkee's cliff-sheltered inner bay.

At low tide, Kilkee's shore is pitted with hundreds of tiny, self-contained pools. Local entrepreneurs (and many children) scour the pools for the snails. About 1-2cm across, with a color almost perfectly matching the rocks, the snails are hard to spot, which helps prevent over-harvesting. The seaweed is more obvious and abundant, lending both ample supply to cooking pots and a pungent odor to the beach.

The collected snails are taken to barbecues lining the beach and tossed onto large open pans. After a few minutes, diced seaweed is thrown in the mix and the pan is heavily salted. The mixture is thrown into a separate basket to be cooled and then scooped into white paper bags. The bags go for €2 and include a small "pin," a thin wooden stick used to extract the meat from the shells.

The taste is acquired, the texture takes some getting used to, and it may be a good idea to have a Guinness on hand to wash down the salty aftertaste.

of the cliffs. The curving lines of seacliff and jutting rock formations collapsing into the sea create a different effect than do the cliffs of Moher, but they are equally dramatic and far less touristed. The cliff walk intersects with the similarly scenic **Loop Head Drive** after passing the Diamond rocks, where bits of *Ryan's Daughter* were filmed. The drive passes unusual islands that rise straight out of the water and sport flat, grassy plateaus. A short way into the trip, the road forks two ways. To the right, the photogenic drive runs through small villages, ruined farmhouses, hippie enclaves, and stretches of pasture to the **Loop Head Lighthouse** at the tip of Co. Clare. On the way, it passes through **Carrigaholt,** a village 12km south of Kilkee on the Shannon Estuary. The Loop Head Drive can be biked (48km), though the return trip has some steep climbs. To the left, the road leads back to Kilkee.

If the tide is out, scramble out onto the rock formations in front of the car park of the cliff walk—the three **Pollock Holes** should be exposed. The progressively deep, protected swimming holes offer a change from the main beach. Dry off over a relaxed game of **pitch and putt;** the nine-hole course starts on the other side of the car park at the West End Cliff Walk. (☎906 6152. Open daily during summer 9am-9pm. €7.) Kilkee is famous for its **diving.** For a view of underwater cliffs and boulders, jump in at the **Kilkee Diving Centre,** a 5min. walk down the shore road from town. (☎905 6707; www.diveireland.com. Open Apr.-Oct. daily 9am-6pm; call for Nov.-Mar. hours. 2hr. single beginner lesson €70; discounts for groups. Equipment provided. Check at least a day ahead for weather conditions.)

LAHINCH (LEACHT UI CHONCHUIR) ☎065

In the 1880s, small, lively Lahinch became a summer haven for the well-to-do. The knit sweater-clad moneyed still come to Lahinch for its championship-level golfing and 800m beach, but surfers and teens in wetsuits and board shorts create an interesting mix of cultures. Main St.'s elegant hotels cater to the preppy golfers, while the beach promenade is the surfer's hangout.

■ ? **TRANSPORTATION AND PRACTICAL INFORMATION. Buses** stop near the golf course one to four times per day during the summer, coming from **Cork, Doolin, Dublin, Galway** via **Ennis,** and **Limerick.** Also in the summer, buses run to and from the **Cliffs of Moher** (4-6 per day, €2.50). Individuals run **taxi** services: Paddy Daniels (☎087 674 0226), John O'Shea (☎086 855 5407), Carol's Cabs (☎086 170 9000), or Creedon Cabs (☎087 333 0200). The nearest **bike rental** establishment is **Griffin's,** in Ennistymon. (☎707 1009. €10 per day, €50 per wk. ID deposit. Opens 9am. Bikes can be returned any time to the bar next door.) The Lahinch Fáilte **tourist office,** at the bottom of Main St., offers local info and free area maps and keeps tabs on changing bus schedules, including service to the Cliffs of Moher. (☎708 2082; www.lahinchfailte.com. Open daily during summer 9am-9pm; winter 9am-6pm.) The office also has a **currency exchange** and a 24hr. **ATM.** There is a second ATM inside the **Centra** at the top of Main St. (☎708 1636. Open June-Aug. daily 9:30am-10pm; Sept.-May 9am-8pm.) **Medicare,** on the corner of Main St. across from the tourist office, is the only **pharmacy** in town. (☎708 1999. Open Sept.-May M-Sa 9:30am-1:30pm and 2-6pm; June-Aug. Su 11am-5pm.) **Mrs. O'Brien's Kitchen and Bar,** Main St., has **Internet** access available until late. (☎708 1020; www.mrsobrienskitchen.com. €6 per hr. Open M-Th and Su 9am-11pm, F-Sa 9am-midnight.) Free **Internet** access is available at the **Ennistymon Library,** The Square. (☎707 1245. Open M-Tu and Th 10am-1:30pm and 2:30-5:30pm, W and F 10am-5:30pm and 6:30-8:30pm, Sa 10am-2pm. 1hr. session per day; no pre-booking for non-members. ID required.) The **post office** on Main St. also changes money and has a **Western Union.** (☎708 1001. Open M-F 9am-1pm and 2-5:30pm, Sa 9am-1pm.)

⚑ ⚑ ACCOMMODATIONS AND CAMPING. Book accommodations in advance, especially on summer weekends and during the Willie Clancy music festival in nearby Milltown Malby in early July. The hostel, and a number of local pubs, hire summer staff. B&Bs abound in Lahinch; the weary will find rest on almost any road off Main St. **St. Mildred's B&B ❸,** next to the hostel on Church St., is not only the oldest B&B in Lahinch—it's also the oldest house. Despite its age, the hospitable owners keep it in top condition. The sitting room and most of the bedrooms have sweeping beach views. (☎708 1489. Singles €40; ensuite doubles €56.) The **Lahinch Hostel (IHH) ❷,** Church St., at the end of Main St. away from the tourist office, has dorms that are remarkably free of surfers' sand tracks. (☎708 1040. Laundry €5. 4-, 6-, and 8-bed dorms €17; doubles €70.) Walk 10min. up N67 in the Milltown Malbay direction, past the campground sign, to **Cois Farraige B&B ❸.** This serene house has spotless rooms with light wood paneling and views of the sea and the family's horses. Ask for the spacious upstairs room. (☎708 1580. June-Sept. singles €40; doubles €68; low season €35/60. Student discounts available.) **Lahinch Caravan & Camping Park ❶,** also on N67, makes space for campers amid a well-entrenched set of caravans. (☎708 1424. Open Easter-Sept. Reception daily July-Aug. 9am-9pm; Sept.-June 9am-5pm. Laundry €5. Tents €7 per person.)

◻◼ FOOD AND PUBS. Lahinch's dining options are less than tantalizing, making the shelved food of the **Centra,** Main St., all the more appealing. (☎708 1636. Open daily June-Sept. 8am-10pm; Oct.-May 8am-8pm.) **The Spinnaker Restaurant and Bar ❷,** next to Lahinch Fáilte, serves up traditional fare and hosts dancing most nights. (☎708 1893. Meals €7-17. Live music weeknights; DJ Sa. No cover.) Most Main St. pubs have live music every summer night except Monday and Tuesday. **Danny Mac's ❷,** Main St., is a family-friendly pub extension of Mrs. O'Brien's Kitchen (☎708 1020. Entrees €12-19. Open daily 12:30-9pm.) **Flanagan's,** Main St., is a popular pub that hooks people of all ages with its eclectic mix of nightly live music—everything from reggae to jazz, acoustic, trad, and pop gets a turn within these cozy confines. (☎708 1161.) On weekends, sharply dressed clubbers pack into the modern space of **Coast,** inside the Clare Mont Hotel at the top of Main St. During the week cool cats sip their cocktails in the front bar next to a backlit fish tank. (F-Sa cover €10.)

⚏ OUTDOOR ACTIVITIES. Visitors to **Lahinch Seaworld & Leisure Centre,** at the far end of the promenade, watch as baby lobsters take their first unsure steps, beginning a miraculous cycle of life, death, and butter sauce. The center's aquarium houses crustaceans, giant crawfish, and the sounds and smells of the sea; the pool complex has a jacuzzi, a sauna, and a steam room. (☎708 1900. Pool open daily 10am-10pm; Aquarium open daily 10am-8pm. Aquarium or pool €8, students €6; combined admission €13/11.) Willie O'Callaghan of **O'Callaghan Angling** runs day-long sea angling trips, cruises to the Aran Islands and Cliffs of Moher from Liscannor pier (3km up the coast from Lahinch), and sunset cruises under the cliffs. (☎682 1374 or 086 152 7755; www.ocallaghanangling.com. Apr.-Oct. evening cruises €25; angling trips 9am-6pm €90 (includes lunch at Inisheer); Aran Islands and cliffs cruise €20.) Lahinch is world-renowned for its **golfing.** A trip to the links at the **Lahinch Golf Course,** a short way down the road toward Ennistymon, starts at €60 for the **Castle course** and €130 for the **Championship Course.** Reservations should be made two to three months in advance, although walk-ons are possible. (☎708 1003.) John McCarthy, of **Lahinch Surf School,** which is housed in the white shack at the far end of the promenade, seeks out the breakers year-round. (☎960 9667; www.lahinchsurfschool.com. 2hr. surfboard rental €9; bodyboard €5.50; wetsuit €9. 2hr. lesson with equipment €35, under 16 €22, weekend surf camp

€80. 1 wk. course: 5 lessons €140, 7 lessons €160.) **Surf Report** is a good source of info. (☎081 836 5180). Beachside **arcades** are packed with youngsters.

DOOLIN (DUBH LINN)   ☎065

Something of a national shrine to Irish traditional music, the little village of Doolin draws thousands of visitors every year to its three pubs for nights of *craic* that go straight from tapping toes to Guinness-soaked heads. With four excellent hostels, bikes for rent, and a campsite by the pier, Doolin is the base of choice for trips to the Cliffs of Moher or the Aran Islands (20min. ferry ride to Inisheer). Walk 15min. up Fisher St. to see crashing waves or a few minutes out of town for rolling hills crisscrossed with stone walls. Most of Doolin's 200-odd permanent residents either farm the land or run the town's B&Bs, campsite, hostels, and pubs.

◧ TRANSPORTATION. Buses stop across from the Doolin Hostel and the Rainbow Hostel. Advance tickets can be purchased at the Doolin Hostel, and schedules of current service are available at all four hostels. Buses run to **Limerick** (M-Sa 8am, Su 10:40am; €13, students €10.70), and to **Galway** (M-Sa 8:40am, Su 1:45pm; €12, students €10). There is an express bus to **Dublin** (M-Sa 8am; €17.10, students €14). The Limerick Route also services **Lahinch** (€4), **Liscannor, Lisdoonvarna, Ennistymon** (€5, students €4.70), and **Ennis.** The Galway Route services **Ballyvaughan.** Connections are available to **Clifden, Cork, Dingle, Dongeal, Killarney,** and **Sligo.** There is additional local service in summer. Bus service to the **Cliffs of Moher** departs regularly in the summer, though the times change slightly every year (15min., €2.30). **Ferries** to the **Aran Islands** leave from the town's pier, about 2km from the town center along the main road; if you're headed to Inishmore, take a ferry from Rossaveal are easier (see **Aran Islands,** p. 377). A **tourist office** is located inside the Hotel Doolin between the upper and lower villages on the main road. **Rent bikes** at the **Doolin Bike Store** on the main road, next to the Aille River Hostel (☎707 4260; open daily 9am-8pm; €10 per day) or at the **Rainbow Hostel,** Upper Village (☎707 4415; €10 per day, €8 for hostel guests). Jimmy Garrahy runs a **taxi service** (☎086 813 9090).

◧▨ ORIENTATION AND PRACTICAL INFORMATION. Doolin can be divided into two villages separated by about 1km, though many locals ignore such distinctions. **Fisher Street** runs up from the pier to the **Lower Village** (a.k.a. the Old Village), and traverses a stretch of farms and B&Bs to the **Upper Village,** an area called **Roadford. Toomullen** (also an area name) lies just beyond Roadford. Virtually all of Doolin's human and commercial life resides on the main road from the pier to Toomullen. The 14km paved segment of the **Burren Way** links Doolin to the **Cliffs of Moher.** Pedestrians find the route an exhausting but manageable half-day trip; the steep climb along the road from Doolin to the Cliffs lets cyclists coast the whole way back, saving energy for a night of foot-stomping fun at the pubs. Hiking or biking also saves the parking cost at the cliffs.

A traveling **bank** comes to Lower Village weekly on Thursdays. The nearest **ATM** is in Ennistymon, 7km southeast of town. **Internet** access is available at the **Doolin Internet Cafe,** tucked inside the Doolin Activity Lodge between the Aille River and Doolin Hostel. (☎707 4888; www.doolinlodge.com. €3 per 30min., €5 per hr. Open daily 8am-10pm.) The nearest **post office** is in Ennistymon. Stamps are sold at the Doolin Deli.

◧▨ ACCOMMODATIONS AND CAMPING. Tourists pack Doolin in the summer, so book early; the high season continues through September, with spillover from Lisdoonvarna's six-week matchmaking festival. Locals know where the money is: almost every house on the main road is a B&B. Friendly, laid-back ▨**Aille River Hostel (HIH) ❶,** Main St., is halfway between the villages. Out front, the Aille River gurgles around an island overflowing with wildflowers. Musicians often stop by the hostel to warm up before gigs. (☎707 4260; www.east-clear.ie/ailleriver. Free Internet access. Washer and detergent free, dryer €2. Kitchen open 24hr. Dorms €15; **Camping** €7.50.) 🏠**Doolin Cottage** ❷ is next to the Aille. A friendly proprietress keeps the rooms spotless and bright. Vegetarians savor fresh fruit, natural yogurt, and honey for breakfast, but the full fry is also available. (☎707 4762. Open Mar.-Oct. Rooms with bath Mar.-June and Oct. €28 per person; July-Aug. €30.) **Rainbow Hostel (IHH)** ❶, Toomullin, Upper Village, is steps from legendary pubs McGann's and McDermott's. The newly refurbished wooden interior has comfy pastel rooms. Owners offer free guided Burren walking tours and a slide show of flora and fauna to interested guests. (☎707 4415; www.rainbowhostel.com. Laundry €5.50. Bike rental €8 per day for guests; €10 for non-guests. Dorms €15; doubles €30.) Next door, equally cheery colors decorate the comfortable rooms with coffee, tea, and TV at Shannons' **Rainbow's End B&B** ❸. (☎707 4415. Singles €50; doubles €70.) **Doolin Hostel (IHH)** ❶, Fisher St., Lower Village, is the oldest hostel in town. The hostel includes a small shop, bureau de change, and a bus ticket booth by its entrance. (☎707 4006; www.doolinhostel.com. Open Feb.-Nov. Laundry €4. Kitchen lockout 10pm-7:30am. Reception 7:30am-9pm. Dorms €16; private rooms €22 per person.) **Nagle's Doolin Camping and Caravan Park** ❶, by the Doolin pier, provides a well-kept grassy site for tents and caravans, a self-serve kitchen (bring your own utensils), showers, and laundry facilities. (☎707 4458; www.doolincamping.com. Open Apr.-Sept. Shop with groceries open July-Aug. daily 9am-9pm. Showers €1. Laundry: wash €4, dry €4. 2-person tent €14; 1-person with no car €7.50. 2-person caravan with electricity €17; July-Aug. €18.)

🍴🏠 **FOOD AND PUBS. The Doolin Deli** ❶, Lower Village, is a small convenience store with cheap baked goods. It packages sandwiches (€2.50-3), bakes fresh scones (€1.20) and soda bread (€2.35), and stocks basic groceries. (☎707 4633. Takeaway only. Open June to mid-Sept. M-Sa 9am-9pm; mid-Sept. to May M-Sa 9am-6pm.) **The Doolin Cafe** ❸, Upper Village, serves high-quality dishes in a chill atmosphere. (☎707 4795. Lunches €6-13, dinner entrees €15-24. Open M and W-Su 11am-5pm and 6-11pm.) **Bruach na hAille** ❸, Upper Village, has creative, home-grown dishes (entrees €14-21). The lunchtime *panini* (served with salad) are tasty, if somewhat overpriced at €9. Arrive before 7pm to score main courses at reduced prices. (☎707 4120. Open Apr.-Oct. daily 6-10pm; mid-July to Aug. also noon-3pm.) **The Lodestone** ❶, Lower Village, the thatched cottage just before the bridge, is a small cafe run by Magnetic Music, County Clare's first recording company. Stop by for espresso drinks (€2-4) and desserts or to pick up a schedule of concerts by Ireland's top trad musicians. (☎707 4988; www.magnetic-music.com. Open mid-July to mid-Aug. daily 9am-9pm; otherwise 9:30am-8:30pm. Concerts at 10pm; ticket prices vary but are usually €15 and up, slightly less when purchased in advance).

Local foot-traffic (along with many of the best-known traditional musicians in the country) heads to 🏠**McDermott's**, Upper Village, nightly around 9:30pm. Serious sessions prove that Doolin's trad is more than a tourist trap. (☎707 4328; www.mcdermottspubdoolin.com. Kitchen open until 9:30pm. Live trad nightly early spring to late autumn and on winter weekends.) **O'Connor's**, Lower Village, is the busiest and most touristed pub in town. O'Connor's serves good pub grub until 9:30pm, when music and Guinness take over. Instrument-toting visitors are welcome to join the trad sessions. (☎707 4168; www.oconnorspubdoolin.com. M and F-Su trad. Entrees €9-18.) **McGann's**, Upper Village, has music nightly at 9:30pm and attracts fair weather pubgoers with its outdoor seating. (☎707 4133. Kitchen open daily Mar.-Dec. 11am-9:30pm; Jan.-Feb. 6-9:30pm.)

▶ DAYTRIP FROM DOOLIN: THE CLIFFS OF MOHER. The ■Cliffs of Moher, members of an elite group of Ireland's super-touristed attractions, draw more gawkers on a clear July day than many counties do all year. Although cliffs compose much of Clare's coast, this stretch is popular with tourists because the cliffs are at their highest: 213m of sheer rock face battered by strong winds and Atlantic waves. Touristy they may be (attracting 1 million visitors per year), but with good reason—the views are breathtaking, and unquestionably among Ireland's most dramatic. To the north, the **Twelve Bens of Connemara** form dark and mysterious silhouettes against the skyline; to the west lie the misty Aran Islands; to the south more cliffs jut from the sea along the route to Loop Head, while the Kerry Mountains peak across the River Shannon. The view straight down is exhilarating—gulls whirl far below the edge, and farther down still the overmatched waves explode against unrelenting limestone. Look for the visible layers on the cliff walls—they are composed of shale and sandstone deposited as sediment over 350 million years. **O'Brien's Tower** is a viewing point just up from the car park. Don't fall for its illusion of medieval grandeur—it was built in 1835 as a tourist trap by Cornelius O'Brien, an early tour-promoter. (Tower open, weather permitting, daily Mar.-Oct. 9:30am-5:30pm. €1.) Most tour groups cluster around the tower, safely experiencing the exhilaration of the drop through telephoto lenses and binoculars. The more adventurous, though less intelligent, climb over the stone walls and head left, trekking along a clifftop path (officially closed) for more spectacular views and the possibility of a 213m fall. **Warning:** Winds can be extremely strong at the top of the cliffs, and a few tourists get blown off every year; *Let's Go* strongly discourages straying from the established paths, which are clearly marked and designed to prevent impromptu cliff-diving competitions. The new **Atlantic Edge** exhibit in the Visitors Centre offers a high-tech interactive educational experience, teaching tourists of all ages about the past, present, and future of the cliffs. The center also contains shops and a cafe, though the food options in Doolin are superior and less crowded. (☎708 6141. Open July-Aug. daily 9am-7:30pm, Sept.-June daily 9:30am-5:30pm. €4; students €3.50. Parking fees start at €5.)

Cliffs of Moher Cruises operates a cruise on the *Jack B* from the Doolin and Liscannor piers. The fantastic cruise sails directly under the cliffs; come in April or May to see the puffins. (☎065 708 6060 or 087 204 9583; www.mohercruises.com. 1¾hr.; Apr.-Oct. departs Liscannor 9am, Doolin noon, 3:30, 4:30pm; changes may occur due to weather. Ticket office at Doolin Pier. €20; students €18.) The cliffs are 9km south of Doolin on R478. Bus Éireann sends two to three buses per day on the summer-only Galway-Cork route, sometimes stopping at the cliffs for 30min. The local Doolin-Limerick bus provides an additional three buses per day. In winter, a bus originating in Galway departs Doolin at noon and deposits riders at the Cliffs for 1hr. before retracing its route. Buses depart regularly for **Limerick** via **Ennis** (with connections available), making local stops at Doolin and Lahinch; service increases significantly in early June through mid-September. The well-signposted 32km Burren Way weaves through limestone and wildflowers from Doolin and Liscannor. *Let's Go* never recommends hitchhiking and hitchers reportedly have some difficulty finding rides.

THE BURREN

Mediterranean, alpine, and Arctic wildflowers peek brightly from cracks in kilometer-long rock surfaces, while 28 of Ireland's 33 species of butterfly flutter by. Biologists are baffled by the huge variety of flora and fauna that coexist in the area; their best guess points vaguely to the end of the Ice Age. Disappearing lakes and proud prehistoric tombs—including the 5500-year-old Poulnabrone Dolmen, one of Ireland's most photographed sights—contribute to the mythical aura evoked by the unique landscape. The best way to see the Burren is to **walk** or **cycle**, but be warned that the dramatic terrain makes for exhausting climbs and thrilling descents. Check your brakes before setting out. Burren **bus** service is awful; check with the Ennis transportation center or the Bus Éireann website for bus service info before traveling. Bus Éireann (☎065 682 4177) connects **Galway** to towns in and near the Burren a few times daily in summer but infrequently in winter. Other buses run from Burren towns to **Ennis. Full-day bus tours** from Galway are another popular way to see the area (see p. 359). Hitching in these parts requires patience and, as always, entails risk; *Let's Go* doesn't recommend it.

BALLYVAUGHAN (BAILE UÍ BHEACHÁIN)   ☎065

Along the jagged edge of Galway Bay, about 14km northeast of Lisdoonvarna on N67, the Burren is suddenly interrupted by the little oasis of Ballyvaughan, with its thatched-roof homes and quiet activity. The town center is minutes from caves and castles, making it a frequent stopover for spelunkers and amateur archaeologists and a popular starting point for trips into the Burren. In the evening, walk down to the pier for a view across the bay to Galway City. Just past the turn-off for Aillwee caves on N67 is the turn-off for **Newtown Castle,** where the restored 16th-century home of the O'Loghlens, Princes of the Burren, awaits (free). Beside Newtown Castle, the **Burren College of Art** (☎707 7200; www.burrencollege.ie), offers summer courses, artist residences, and an MFA program. Several week-long workshops, which give participants the opportunity to paint the Burren landscape or learn about the area's botany, are offered in the summer. The college also houses the **Food of the Arts Cafe.** (Open M-F 9am-5pm.) On the way to Ballyvaughan, find solitude interrupted only by the chirping birds at **Corcomroe Abbey,** in Bell Harbor. Founded as a monastery by the Cistercian Order in 1194, the structure actually dates back to 1182. The magnificent walls and arches house centuries-old graves, while the cemetery outside still accepts customers. Prehistoric bears once inhabited the multimillion-year-old **Aillwee Cave** (EYEL-wee), 3km south of Ballyvaughan and 1km into the mountain (take N67 South to the turn-off for R480 and the Aillwee Cave). Anyone scared of the dark should avoid the 40min. tour, which may be too easy for experienced spelunkers. (☎707 7036; www.aillwee.com. Open daily 10am-5:30pm. €12, children €5.) Those itching to do some serious **spelunking** should contact the **Speleological Union of Ireland** (SUI; www.cavingireland.org) or the **Burren Outdoor Education Centre** (☎707 8066).

B&Bs abound in the streets around town. **O'Brien's B&B ❸,** above the pub/restaurant on Main St., has pleasing rooms and a constellation of fireplaces. (☎707 7003. Doubles from €65.) Popular **Oceanville ❸,** next to Monk's Pub on the pier, has gorgeous views and rooms for families and couples. (☎707 7051. Open Mar.-Oct. From €30 per person.) About 3km from the city center on N67, friendly owners welcome guests to **Burren Dale B&B ❸** with comfortable rooms and stories of Jacko McGann, the proprietor's grandfather and discoverer of the famed Aillwee Caves. (☎707 7137. Singles €35, with bath €38; doubles €60.)

Spar sells foodstuffs. (☎77181. Open daily July-Aug. 9am-9pm; Sept.-June 9am-8pm.) There is a lively **farmers' market** in St. John's Hall (across from Spar) on summer Saturdays, from 10am-2pm. **The Soda Parlour ❶,** Main St., serves crepes, pancakes, sundaes, and drinks. (☎708 3999. Savory crepes €7. Open Tu-Su 10am-5pm.) Sunny **Tea Junction Cafe ❷** has sandwiches and vegetarian entrees, but it's tempting to go straight for their rhubarb crumble. (☎707 7289. Vegetarian chili €6.40. Open daily June-Sept. 9am-6pm; Oct.-May 9am-5pm.) Visitors flock to the outdoor tables by **Monk's Pub and Restaurant ❷** on the pier, with a view across the bay to Galway city. Tourists crowd around the huge stone fireplace for trad,

An interview with Willie Daly, the Lisdoonvarna matchmaker.

LG: How did the September matchmaking begin?

WD: It started just before the turn of the century, and it started because Lisdoonvarna was a small market town. There was a doctor who lived there named Dr. Foster who found out there were sulphur and iron waters in the town, and he developed a health spa. The matchmaking started almost accidentally. The people who would come to the spa would be the more wealthy farmers. And they'd start matchmaking their children in conversation over breakfast, saying "now I have a John who is 28..." In the 30s and 40s the festival became popular, and they started having big bands and dances.

LG: What does it take to be a successful matchmaker these days?

WD: Being a successful matchmaker is getting people together...there has to be an element of magic there, and today there has to be an element of love there, quickly. Irish men want a partner, someone to share their home, their life, to share their world with. There's a huge number of men in Ireland. In the past, most of the properties—restaurants, hotels, pubs, farms—would be left to a son; this would be done so that the family name would continue. And in hindsight, it's not good,

while locals gravitate toward the bar. (☎707 7059. Famous seafood chowder €6. Music usually Th and Sa.) Back in town, **Green's** is a small, card-playing locals' pub, frequented by an older crowd. (☎707 7147. Open M-Sa 6pm-midnight.)

Buses come to Ballyvaughan from **Galway, Doolin,** and **the Cliffs of Moher** (M-Sa 3-4 per day, Su 2 per day). The **tourist office,** located behind Spar on Main St., is second to the boutique and souvenir shop in the same room, but it gives information on accommodations. (☎707 7077; www.ballyvaughanireland.com. Open daily June-Sept. 9am-9pm; Oct.-May 9am-6:30pm.) The **post office** is at the Emo Station in the square. (☎707 7001. Open M-F 9:30am-1pm and 2-5:30pm, Sa 9:30am-1pm.) **Bike rental** and **laundry** services are found at **Connoles,** up the road toward N67. (☎707 7061; www.burrenbike.com. Bikes €13 per day, €50 per week. ID required. Laundry from €8.50. Open Apr.-Oct. daily 8am-9pm; Nov.-Mar. M-F 9am-5pm. The **Rising Tide Cafe** next door has **Internet** access. (☎707 7900. €2 per initial 15min.; €1.25 per 15min. thereafter. Open M-Sa 10am-5pm.)

LISDOONVARNA (LIOS DÚIN BHEARNA)☎065

A sign in town proclaims "some matches are made in Heaven...but the best ones are made in Lisdoonvarna." For everyone the Irish, "Lisdoon" is synonymous with the **Matchmaking Festival,** a *craic*-and-snogging fest which has drawn the likes of Jackson Browne and Van Morrison to its all-day music events. More than 10,000 singles descend upon Lisdoonvarna for the festival's six weekends (the first is in early September), and the small town's several luxury resorts host nearly continuous dancing and live music. The festival ends with competitions for two much-sought-after titles: Queen of the Burren and Mr. Lisdoonvarna.

Local celebrity and professional matchmaker Willie Daly from Ennistymon presides over the event. No one talks about how successful the festival is at making matches that last longer than a six-pint hangover, but as one Lisdoon local puts it, "Everything works if you want it to." For more info on the festival, contact the **Hydro Hotel** (☎707 4005; www.whiteshotelsireland.com), or consult the website (www.matchmakerireland.com). The festival weekends are riotous, but during the off-season, the spa-and resort-town can be extremely quiet. In the 1700s, Lisdoon saw carriage upon carriage of therapy-seekers rolling in to try the curative wonders of sulfur and copper; in 1867, the town built a pump room to provide visitors with sulfur baths. Beginning in the summer of 2006, the recently-renovated **Spa Wells Health Center** (at the bottom of the hill, past the Hydro Hotel) has offered a variety of hydrotherapy pools in addition to traditional massages and sulphur baths (☎707 4023). Shane Connolly runs **Burren Walking Tours,** which emphasize a number of options. Some walks highlight botany or visit historical and archaeological sites; others trek through the wilderness and up mountains. (☎77168; http://homepage.eircom.net/ ~burrenhillwalks. Available year-round; depart twice daily in summer. Dawn and sunset walks can be arranged. €15 per person.)

Several B&Bs supplement Lisdoonvarna's luxury hotels. Dermot, of ▨**Dooley's Caherleigh House ❷**, Main St., next to the Hydro Hotel, pampers guests with tea and cookies, crackling fires, and superb breakfasts. (☎707 4543. All rooms with bath. €30-35 per person.) Cathleen O'Connor's **Roncalli B&B ❸** offers pleasant rooms flooded in light, tea and coffee, and a good breakfast. The B&B is a 7min. walk from town; pass the Esso Station across from the town square and continue straight on the Doolin Rd., past the Emo filling station. (☎707 4115. Open Apr.-Oct. €34 per person.) The newest and most comfortable of the three Sleepzone hostels, ▨**Sleepzone Burren ❶**, past the smokehouse on the Doolin Rd., has turned the shell of a former hotel into a friendly hostel with excellent kitchen, dining room, TV room, and bar facilities. (☎707 4036. Free Wi-Fi. All rooms with bath. Dorms €15-22; singles €30-45; prices vary by season and day of the week.) The **Roadside Tavern and Restaurant ❷**, just past the Esso station on the Doolin Rd., serves drinks, desserts, and a good selection of salty entrees (€10-15), which are either traditional Irish dishes or smoked fish. The hot smoked salmon with vegetables and mustard cream sauce (€15) comes with enough potato to feed a small family. The pub itself is dimly lit and decorated with shellacked postcards from around the world. (☎74084. Kitchen open daily noon-9pm. Th-Sa trad Mar.-Sept.) In addition to a tempting array of cheese, crafts, and smoked fish, **The Smokehouse** next door offers a 6min. video about its smoking process (factory tours are no longer available due to health and safety requirements) and free samples of organic smoked salmon. For larger groups, a 50min. lecture can be arranged. (☎74432; www.burrensmokehouse.ie. Open daily 9am-5pm. Lectures €3, students €2.)

A current bus schedule is posted in the town square; buses run regular service to the Cliffs of Moher, Ennis (via Ennistymon), Lahinch, Doolin, and Ballyvaughan. There are also buses to Galway, Sligo,

because there are too many men, and all the women have gone to Dublin, London, and New York. Irish men—the thing that they have that's so very rare in the world—they have a marvelous sense of humor, and a great aptitude for music, singing, dancing, and drinking, and a very relaxed lifestyle. It's this relaxed lifestyle that gives them so much time to make a woman feel cherished and loved. When a man from the West of Ireland finds a woman, he really adores her. He might look a bit rugged, and a bit rough, but he'll have a heart full of love, and his mind won't be confused, like so many people in towns and cities.

LG: What advice do you give your clients?

WD: To someone from another country, I would say that some of the finest men in the world live in Ireland, and especially in the West of Ireland. They're so close to nature themselves; they are unspoiled, and that's important. A lot of women find themselves secure and okay in life, but not in love—I think in one life you owe it to yourself to try to find love, and to find happiness. If you die without that, you have lived life a little bit in vain.

Willie and his daughter, Marie, can be found in the Matchmaker Bar on Th-Sa nights during the festival. They can also be contacted at: ☎707 1385 *or williedaly@tinet.ie.*

Clifden, Dublin, Glengariff, Bunratty and the Shannon Airport, Cork, Tralee, Limerick, Killarney, Liscannor, Waterford, and Donegal. During the summer, local services run as frequently as seven times per day. Peter Mooney's **taxi** service (☎707 4663, mobile 087 206 9019) is a welcome relief from the Burren's inconsistent public transportation system. The tiny Lisdoonvarna **library** is across from the Roadside Tavern and has one computer with free **Internet** access. (☎707 4029. Open Tu and Th 1-4pm and 5-8pm, Sa 10am-1pm). An **ATM**, a **bike rental store,** and a superb public library with Internet access are available in **Ennistymon.** There is a **post office** on Main St. (☎707 4110. Open M-F 9am-1pm and 2-5:30pm, Sa 9am-1pm).

KILFENORA (CILL FHIONNÚRACH)   ☎065

The village of Kilfenora lies 7km southeast of Lisdoonvarna on R476. Its **Burren Centre** and several grocers make it an ideal departure point for trekkers and bicyclists heading into the limestone wonderland—that is, if they already have a bike; the nearest bike rental is in Ennistymon. Visitors shouldn't miss the **Kilfenora Cathedral** with the **high crosses** preserved inside. The town also has an excellent but woefully overlooked trad scene. The **Burren Centre** shows a 12min. video about The Burren and has a walk-through exhibition detailing the region's history and its unique natural and man-made features. The tea room provides a great smoked salmon sandwich (€5). Maps and books are available for sale (the *Ramblers Guide* maps, €3.50-4, show the landscape and sites in each area), and the helpful staff gives directions. (☎708 8030. Open daily Mar.-May 10am-5pm, June-Aug. 9:30am-6pm, Sept.-Oct. 10am-5pm. €5.75, students €4, children €3.50.) Church of Ireland services (1st and 3rd Su of the month at 11am) are still held in the nave of the **Kilfenora Cathedral,** next to the Burren Centre. Kilfenora received official diocesan status in 1152, although a monastery operated on the site of the cathedral for at least 500 years before. Perhaps in conjunction with the town's efforts to obtain official church recognition, Kilfenoran artists produced at least seven (an unusually high number for one area) carved limestone **high crosses** in the 12th century. Walk around the Cathedral to the glass-covered remains of the old abbey to view the aviary carvings on the **Doorty Cross.** The **North Cross** is in the same room; the **West Cross** sits 200m west of the church.

In the yellow house across from the Burren Centre, **Mary Murphy ❷** greets guests with tea and coffee. Rooms are basic but include bath and a sizzling fry. (☎708 8040. Open Feb.-Oct. Singles €35; doubles €60.) **Vaughan's ❶** hosts trad sessions on weekends and set dancing in the adjacent thatched cottage on Thursday and Sunday nights. (☎708 8004. Sandwiches €3-4.50. Seafood chowder €6.50. Kitchen open 10am-9pm.) Kitty Linnane and her *céilí* band of 1954 put Kilfenora on the musical map. Kitty's son Gerard runs **Linnane's,** affectionately called "Kitty's Corner," across from the Burren Centre. Linnane's still hosts trad sessions in a familial environment and has won various awards for food and music. (☎708 8157. Sessions W, and Sa-Su in summer; kitchen open daily noon-8pm.)

CARRAN (AN CARN)   ☎065

Get the Burren without the tourists in Carran. A pub, a hostel, and a sometimes 800m wide by 4.5m deep puddle in the midst of a limestone landscape is the sum total of the town. The lake's dimensions make it Europe's largest disappearing lake. The well-labeled **Burren Way** hiking trail intersects Carran, making it a great launchpad into this unique region. Six kilometers northwest of Carran stands the **Poulnabrone Portal Dolmen,** one of Ireland's most popular and photogenic rock groups. The dolmen is the most impressive of the over 90 neolithic stone burial sites discovered in the Burren and arguably the best-preserved dolmen in Ireland. About 5000 years ago, over 25 people were put to rest with their pots and jewels under the five-ton capstone, only to be dug up by intrepid archaeologists in 1989. To get there, take R480 South of Ballyvaughan. **The Burren Perfumery** turns plant extracts into perfumes, soaps, gels, and salts. Visitors can peer into the distillation room at baskets of strong-smelling plant materials and drying soap cakes or watch the staff wrap and bottle the perfumery's products in the gift shop. Through photographs and a short video, the perfumery introduces the extraordinary diversity of plant life in the Burren. Owner Sadie Chowen has recently started an all-organic tearoom and developed the gardens with educational signs about each plant. To reach the perfumery, take a left out of Clare's Rock Hostel driveway, and a right just after Cassidy's pub; follow the signs from there. (☎ 708 9102; www.burrenperfumery.com. Man of Aran perfume €36. Open daily Nov.-May 9am-5pm, June-Sept. 9am-7pm.) A single magnificent hostel overlooking the giant lough houses half the town's population: ■ **Clare's Rock Hostel ❶**, on the main road, has comfortable dorms with bath, tasteful decor, and bikes (€10) for rent. (☎ 708 9129; www.claresrock.com. Laundry €7. Reception 5-9pm. Open May-Sept.; call for winter openings. Dorms €14; doubles €38.) Across the way, **Cassidy's**, or **Croide Na Barne ❷**, offers gorgeous views over the *turlough* valley, a crackling fire, casual sessions, a pool table, and goat burgers. (☎ 708 9109. www.cassidyspub.com. Quarter-pound burger of organically reared goat meat €8.50; sandwiches from €2.70. Open Apr.-Dec. M-Sa noon-9pm, Su noon-6pm.) The village lies a a few kilometers east of R4 (780), off a small road connecting Bellharbor to Killnaboy; to get there, **drive** (8min.) or **hike** (1½hr.) south from Bellharbor. Alternately, travel due east from the town of Boston. An exhausting **bike ride** from Kilfenora is also possible.

KINVARA (CINN MHARA)   ☎091

Across the bay from the tourist hordes of Galway, this small harbor town of floating swans and passing hookers (the boat type) gets surprisingly lively on weekends. **Dunguaire Castle**, 5min. from town on the Galway Rd., is actually a tower house—a popular type of dwelling for 16th-century country gentlemen. The narrow, winding staircase leads past rooms decorated in the style of each era of occupation to expansive lookouts over sea and countryside. (☎ 637 108. Open daily May-Sept. 9:30am-4:30pm. €5, students €3.10.) Tour groups regularly convene in the castle for the nightly medieval-style feast. The first weekend in May, Kinvarans go crazy at the **Cuckoo Fleadh.** Traditional musicians from around the country bring live music to all 11 of the town's pubs. (See www.kinvara.com for more information.) The second weekend of August is the **Cruinniú na mBád** ("the gathering of the boats") during which the town recreates the arrival of hooker sailboats from Connemara into Kinvara Bay and comes together for live music. **Galway Hooker Trips** (☎ 087 231 1779) gathers boats all year; set sail with skipper Mehall on the *An Traonach*. Alongside Kinvara, **Doorus Peninsula** stretches out into Galway Bay. For hikers, bikers, or families with cars, Doorus is a worthwhile trip; Tracht beach is just steps away from the Doorus House Youth Hostel.

At **Fallon's B&B ❸**, in the center of town on Main St., lovely Maura Fallon and family offer rooms ranging from spacious singles to doubles and family rooms. (☎ 638 988 or 637 483. www.kinvara.com/fallons. All rooms with bath, TV, and tea. Singles €50; doubles €75; quads €110.) Located on the harbor, **Cois Cuain B&B ❸** is a quaint B&B with bright rooms best suited to pairs. (☎ 637 119. Open Apr.-Nov. Doubles with bath €70.) The more upscale **Merriman Hotel ❺**, across from Fallon's, has 32 rooms, each with a bath, TV, and phone. Two rooms accommodate disabled travelers, and the hotel has its own restaurant, **The Quilty Room ❹** (3-course meal €35), and a cheaper bar, **M'Asal Beag Dubh,** to boot. (☎ 638 222; www.merrimanhotel.com. B&B July-Aug. singles €85, doubles €130; Apr.-June and Sept.-Oct. €75/110; Nov.-Mar.; €70/100.) The **Doorus House Youth Hostel ❷**, on the Doorus Peninsula, 6km from Kinvara and several hundred meters from Tracht Beach, offers a spacious and peaceful vacation spot for beach-goers and a relaxed base for tourists. Manager Brent Bishon provides room and board to short-term hostel employees. (☎637 512; www.kinvara.com/doorushouse. €16; under 17 €14).

Londis grocery store is on the main road. (☎637 250. Open daily 8am-10pm.) **Murphy Store,** in a 200-year-old building on the Quay, offers coffee beverages and delicious cakes in a shop filled with locally made crafts and jewelry. (☎637 760; www.murphystore.com. Open M-Sa 10am-6pm, Su noon-6pm.) **Pizza Cafe ❷,** on the quay, offers free Internet access to patrons and serves assorted sandwiches (€5.50-7.50), salads (€6.50-12), pizza (€9.50-12.50), and breakfast. (☎638 129. Open daily 10am-4pm and 5-9pm.) Inside **Keogh's ❶,** a restaurant/bar, a sage sign requests: "If you're drinking to forget, please pay in advance." (☎637 145. Breakfast €5-6.50, sandwiches €7-10, entrees €16-23.) Kinvara's pub scene is the most active thing in town—all are located within seconds of each other on Main St., making it possible to literally crawl from one to the next. A twenty something crowd flocks to **The Ould Plaid Shawl,** named after the Frances Fahy poem (Fahy was born in this building in 1854). Tuesday nights are devoted to dart competitions (€2 to enter), but patrons can take advantage of the jukebox and pool table anytime. (Th trad. Open M-W 5-11:30pm, Th-Sa 5pm-12:30am, Su 5-11pm.) Locals head to **Green's** for spontaneous trad sessions. Reportedly the place to be for music on Monday nights, tiny Green's has been passed down through generations of daughters and remains one of the few Irish bars owned and run by females. (☎637 110. Open M-W 11am-midnight, Th-Sa 11am-1am, Su 11am-11:30pm.)

Buses connect Kinvara to Galway City (€6, students €4.70) and nearby Doolin (€8.80/7) three times per day on weekdays, with additional service in the summer. The bus stop is in the small square by Keogh's. There are two **ATMs** in town: at the Londis Supermarket on Main St. (☎637 250; open daily 8am-10pm) and inside MacMahon's at the Esso Gas Station at the top of Main St. (Open daily 8am-11pm.) There are no laundry facilities in town. **Postscripts,** Main St. sells **area maps** and guides (Ramblers Guide, €3.50), and has three computers with **Internet** access. (☎637 657. Open daily 9am-7pm. €2.50 per 15min.) The **post office,** off Main St., changes currency. (☎637 101; open M-F 9:30am-1pm and 2-5:30pm, Sa 9am-1pm.)

COOLE PARK AND THOOR BALLYLEE ☎091

Two of Yeats's favorite retreats lie about 31km south of Galway near **Gort,** where N18 meets N66. **Coole Park** is now a museum and a national park. **Thoor Ballylee,** Yeats's beloved home, has been restored so it appears as it did when Yeats lived there. The sites are best accessed by car, but biking is another option. Be warned: high winds can make biking the 14km from Kinvara a painful struggle.

The 400-hectare **Coole Park** nature reserve was once the estate of Lady Augusta Gregory, the playwright and folklorist who, along with Yeats, co-founded the Abbey Theater in Dublin (see **The Revival,** p. 69). Although the house was ruined in the 1922 Civil War (p. 56), the yew walk and garden have survived. In the garden area, a great copper beech known as the **"autograph tree"** bears the initials of several historical figures, including George Bernard Shaw, Sean O'Casey, Douglas Hyde (the first president of Ireland), and Yeats himself. Entrance to the park is free. The **Coole Park Visitors Centre** houses a walk-through exhibit based on the memoirs of Lady Augusta's granddaughter. The exhibition displays the Coole Park Estate and the members of the Irish Literary Revival who were frequent guests with stage-sets, video footage, and audio recordings from the book. A 30min. video "Lady Gregory of Coole: A Literary History" is also available. The best guide to Coole Park is *The 7 Woods Trail and Family Trail* (€1.50), which outlines the two main trailways in the park and is available at the Visitors Centre. (☎631 804; www.coolepark.ie. Open daily June-Aug. 10am-6pm; Apr.-May, and Sept. daily 10am-5pm. Last admission 1hr. before closing for the audio program, 15min. for the center. €3, students €1.30.) One kilometer from the garden, **Coole Lake** is where Yeats watched "nine-and-fifty swans...all suddenly mount/And scatter wheeling in great broken rings/Upon their clamorous wings." All three species of swan found in Ireland—**Whooper, Bewick's,** and **mute swans**—still gather here in winter; in summer, they are replaced by cows lumbering down to the beach. Five kilometers north of Coole Park, an 800m-long stretch of road runs from the Galway road to **Thoor Ballylee,** a tower built in the 16th century. In 1916, Yeats bought it for £35 and renovated it with his wife. He and his family lived here off and on from 1922 to 1928. While he was cloistered here writing his "Meditations in Time of Civil War," Republican forces blew up the bridge next to the tower. According to Yeats, they "forbade us to leave the house, but were otherwise polite, even saying at last 'Good-night, thank you.'" The **Visitors Centre** offers a tour of the furnished Tower House and a 17min. film on Yeats's life at Thoor Ballylee. The gift shop has an extensive book selection. (☎631 436. Open June-Sept. M-Sa 9:30am-5pm. €6, students €5.50.)

The Kilartan Gregory Museum greets visitors in a stone house on the road from Kinvara at the turnoff to N18. The building was once the school where Lady Augusta Gregory started one of the first branches of the Gaelic League (see p. 54). It now houses a charming reproduction of a traditional Irish schoolroom, complete with actual posters and books from the turn of the century. (☎632 346 or 631 069. Open June-Aug. daily 10am-5pm; Sept. and May Su 1-5pm. Oct.-Apr. by appointment only. €2.60,families €7.) For a delicious meal in a bright cafe and art space, visit **The Gallery Café ❸,** Market Sq. Gort, in the lime green building across from the town car park. At €4.40, the gallery salad, served with thick slices of homemade herb bread, is a steal. (☎091 630 630. Pizza €8.50-10.50; Vegetarian and meat plates €5-11. Open daily 11am-11p m.)

COUNTY GALWAY

Ireland's third-largest county, Galway is also its most diverse. The potent *craic* of Galway City draws more musicians and travelers than any other city outside Dublin. Thirty kilometers offshore lie the eminent stackled limestone walls of the Aran Islands. The rugged mountain landscape of the county's coastline offers daytripping hikers the opportunity to commune with grazing cattle and provides shade for the beaches that stretch between ridges. Connemara is a largely Irish-speaking region with a harsh rocky interior and hardy locals to match. Clifden, its largest city, has abandoned the native tongue in favor of the international language of tourism. Nearby, Inishbofin and Inishturk provide big doses of island isolation.

GALWAY CITY (GAILLIMH) ☎091

Co. Galway's reputation as Ireland's cultural powerhouse has lured flocks of young Celtophiles to Galway City (pop. 70,000). Mix in over 13,000 students from two major universities, a large transient population of twentysomething Europeans, and tent-loads of international backpackers, and you have the force behind the fastest-growing city in Europe. Street performers show off homegrown tricks while locals and tourists lounge in outdoor cafes. Blue-jeaned hipsters dish out flyers, keys to the night's hottest live music. Follow them into Galway's mesmerizing

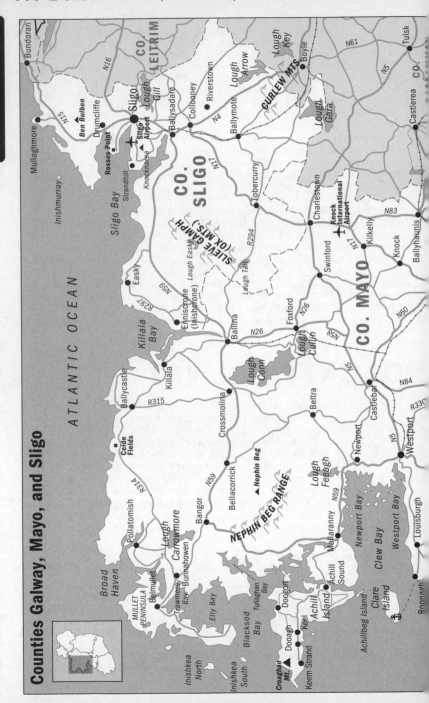

Counties Galway, Mayo, and Sligo

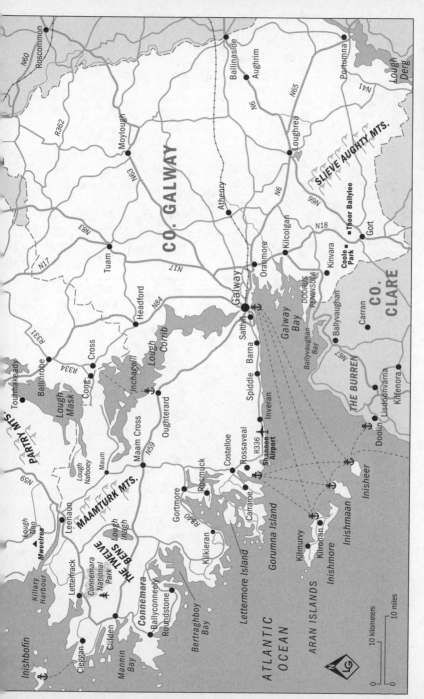

Galway

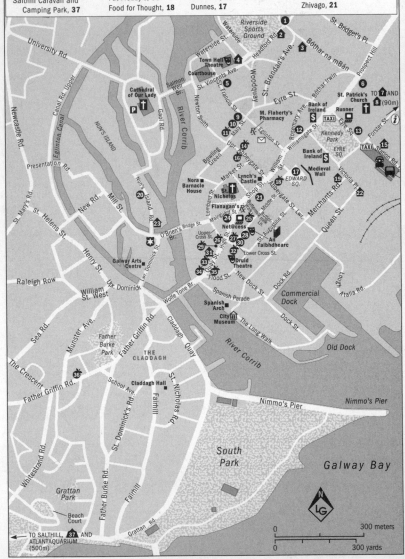

▲▲⛺ ACCOMMODATIONS
Ashford Manor, **7**
Barnacle's Quay St.
    House, **31**
Claddagh Hostel, **22**
The Galway Hostel, **15**
Kinlay House (IHH), **19**
Lynfield House, **8**
Salmon Weir Hostel, **4**
Salthill Caravan and
    Camping Park, **37**

San Antonio, **2**
Sleepzone, **3**
St. Martin's, **23**

🍎 FOOD
Anton's, **36**
Ard Bia Cafe, **26**
Charcoal Grill, **32**
Couch Potatas, **14**
Da Tang, **27**
Fat Freddy's, **35**
Food for Thought, **18**

The Home Plate, **11**
Java's, **16**
McDonagh's, **34**
Pierre's, **29**
Trattoria Magnetti, **33**
Vina Mara, **25**

● SERVICES
The Bubbles Launderette, **9**
Budget rent-a-car, **13**
Charlie Byrne's Bookshop, **28**
Dunnes, **17**

Evergreen Health Food, **24**
Galway Advertiser, **12**
Galway People's
    Resource Ctr., **20**
Murray's Europcar, **1**
Neatsurf, **5**
Prospect Hill Launderette, **6**
River Deep, Mountain
    High, **30**
USIT, **10**
Zhivago, **21**

web of nightlife or simply keep an ear open for the pervasive nightly trad. In the summer, a series of festivals revs up the city's already frenetic energy. Despite all this, Galway manages to stay welcoming, friendly, and easy to navigate—Dublin's cool little sister is more like an extended town than a city.

✈ INTERCITY TRANSPORTATION

Flights: Carnmore Airport (☎755 569), 6km from the city center. **Aer Arann** (www.aerarann.com) jets to **Dublin** (M-F 9am, 1:15, 6:30, 10:30pm; Sa 1:15, 6:30, and 9pm; Su 1:15, 6:30, 10:30pm). **Bus Éireann** shuttles from the main bus station daily at 1, 4:15, 5pm.

Trains: Eyre Sq. (☎561 444). Open M-Sa 9am-6pm. Trains to **Dublin** (3hr., 4-6 per day, €30) via **Portarlington** (€23.50); transfer at Portarlington for all other lines.

Buses: Eyre Sq. (☎562 000). Open M-Sa 8am-6:30pm, Su 8am-7pm. **Bus Éireann** heads to: **Belfast** (7½hr., 3 per day, €30) via **Dublin** (4hr., €13.50; the **Cliffs of Moher** (late May to mid-Sept. daily 8:35, 10:25am, 1:55pm; €14) via **Ballyvaughan** (€10); **Cork** (4½hr., 12 per day, €17); **Donegal** (4hr., 4 per day 11:55am-4pm, €18.50); **Limerick** (2¼hr., 14 per day 7am-8pm, €14). Private coach companies specialize in buses to **Dublin:**

Citylink (☎564 163; www.citylink.ie) departs from the tourist office on Eyre Sq. (17 per day, last bus 6pm; €17 return). Also runs to Shannon Airport (5 per day, €23 return).

Michael Nee Coaches (☎095 34682) drives from Forster St. through **Clifden** to **Cleggan** and meets the **Inishbofin** ferry (M-Su 2-3 per day; €11, €14 return).

Nestor (☎797 144; www.nestorlink.ie) leaves from the tourist office bus park (7 per day 1:45am-6:30pm, €12).

Ferries: Several companies ferry passengers to the **Aran Islands.** Generally the booths all over town offer cheaper fares than the tourist office's ferry desk; the lowest rates hover around €25 round-trip, students €20. It can be difficult to get info about the Doolin-based **O'Brien Shipping/Doolin Ferries** in Galway, but the other companies, like **Aran Direct, Island Ferries,** and **Queen of Aran II** have ticket booths all over town. For more info, see **Aran Islands,** p. 378.

Car Rental: Budget Rent-a-Car, 12 Eyre Sq. (☎566 376). Economy class starting at €50 per day, €250 per wk. 23+. Open M-F 8am-6pm, Sa-Su 9am-6pm. **Murray's Europcar,** Headford Rd. (☎562 222; www.europcar.ie), by the gas station. 22+. Open M-F 9am-5:30pm, Sa 9am-1pm.

▦ ORIENTATION

Buses and trains stop near **Eyre Square,** a central block of lawn, monuments, and lounging tourists; the train and bus stations are up the hill on its southeastern side. Northeast of the square, a string of small, cheap B&Bs lines **Prospect Hill.** To the southeast, **Forster Street** leads to the **tourist office** before turning into **College Avenue,** where larger and fancier B&Bs cluster. The town's commercial zone spreads out in the other direction. Northwest of the square, **Woodquay** is an area of quiet(er) commercial and residential activity. The northwest corner of the square is the gateway to the pedestrian center, filled with hordes of shoppers and coffee-sippers by day and throngs of partiers and pint-chuggers by night. **Shop Street** becomes **High Street** and then **Quay Street,** all pedestrian-only thoroughfares that feel like a single stretch of street-carnival fun. The few pubs along the **docks** in the southeast of the city are largely fishermen hangouts that close up and clear out early in the night. When weather permits, guitar players and paramours lie on the lawn by the river along the **Long Walk.**

Fewer tourists venture over the bridges into the bohemian **left bank** of the Corrib, where great music and some of Galway's best (and largely untapped) pubs await. Just south of the left bank is the **Claddagh,** Galway's original fishing village. Beyond the quays, Grattan Rd. stretches west past many quiet, reasonably priced B&Bs on the way to **Salthill,** a tacky beachfront resort with row-houses and sky-rocketing property values. To the north of the west bank are the university areas of **Newcastle** and **Shantallow,** quiet suburbs of students and families. Galway's Regional Technical College is 2km east of the city center in suburban **Renmore,** which dozes peacefully by its bird sanctuary.

⌨ LOCAL TRANSPORTATION

With its many pedestrian-only and one-way streets, Galway lends itself best to walking. Other forms of transport are mostly of use to those staying outside of the city center or planning excursions away from the city.

Buses: City buses (☎562 000) leave from the top of Eyre Sq. every 20-30min. €1.35, exact fare required. Service M-Sa 7am-11pm, Su 11am-11pm. #1 goes to **Salthill;** #2 to **Knocknacarra** (west) or **Renmore** (east); #3 to **Ballybrit;** #4 to **Newcastle;** #5 to **Rahoon.** Commuter tickets €14 per wk., €47 per month; students €13/40.

Taxis: The biggest companies are **Big O Taxis,** 21 Upper Dominick St. (☎585 858), and **Cara Cabs,** Eyre Sq. (☎563 939). 24hr. taxis can usually be found around Eyre Sq. and near the tourist office.

Bike Rental: Mountain Trail, Middle St. (☎569 888). €10-12.50 per day, €60 per wk. €40 deposit. ID required. Panniers and helmets included. Open M-F 9:30am-1:30pm and 2:30-10pm, Sa 9:30am-10pm.

Parking: Expensive and hard to find in Galway. The cheapest lot, at €4 per day, is by the Cathedral. Open M-Sa 8:30am-6:30pm, free after 6:30pm.

🛈 PRACTICAL INFORMATION

TOURIST AND FINANCIAL SERVICES

Tourist Office: Forster St. (☎537 719). A block south of Eyre Sq. Big, busy office where little is free; ask for free *Galway Tourist Guide* to avoid paying for info. **Exchanges currency.** Books accommodations upstairs for €4 fee. Open June-Sept. and Oct.-May M-Sa 9am-5:45pm. A **kiosk** in Eyre Sq. is open M-F 9am-6pm, Sa-Su 9am-5pm.

Travel Agency: USIT, Mary St. (☎565 177; www.usitnow.ie). Provides flight bookings. Special rates for students. Open M-F 9:30am-5:30pm, Sa 10am-2pm.

Banks: Located throughout the city. **Bank of Ireland,** 19 Eyre Sq. (☎563 181). Open M 10am-5pm, Tu and Th-F 10am-4pm, W 10:30am-4pm. **AIB,** Lynch's Castle, Shop St. (☎567 041). Open M-Tu and F 10am-4pm, W 10:30am-4pm, Th 10am-5pm. Both have 24hr. **ATMs.**

Work Opportunities: See **Long-Term Stays,** p. 366.

LOCAL SERVICES

Bookstores: ▧**Charlie Byrne's Bookshop,** Middle St. (☎561 766). Massive stock of secondhand and discounted books, neatly organized by subject. Open M-Th and Sa 9am-6pm, F 9am-8pm. July also Th 9am-8pm, Su noon-6pm.

Luggage Storage: At the bus/train station. €2.50 per item. Open M-F 8am-6:15pm, Sa 10am-6:15pm.

Library: St. Augustine St. (☎561 666). Open M 2-5pm, Tu-Th 11am-8pm, F 11am-5pm, Sa 11am-1pm and 2-5pm. Internet access available for members only.

Gay and Lesbian Information: Galway Gay Helpline (☎566 134). Line open Tu and Th 8am-10pm; other times recorded message gives info on meetings and events. The

Gay Community News is available at Charlie Byrne's Bookshop (see above), and in Strano's and Zulu's (see **Pubs**, p. 368).

Laundry: The Bubbles Launderette, 18 Mary St. (☎563 434). Basic wash and dry €8. Open M-Sa 9am-6pm. **Prospect Hill Launderette,** Prospect Hill (☎568 343). Self-service wash and dry €6, students €5. Open May-Sept. M-F 8:30am-8:30pm, Sa 8:30am-6pm. Oct.-Apr. M-F 8:30am-6pm, Sa 8:30am-5pm; last wash 1¼hr. before close.

EMERGENCY AND COMMUNICATIONS

Emergency: ☎999; no coins required. **Police** *(Garda):* Mill St. (☎538 000).

Counseling and Support: Samaritans, 14 Nun's Island Rd. (☎561 222 or 85060 9090). Lines open 24hr. **Rape Crisis Centre,** 7 Claddagh Quay (☎589 495 or 850 355 355). Lines open M and W-F 10am-1pm and 3-5:30pm, Tu 10am-noon and 3-5:30pm, Sa 11am-1pm. **Cura,** crisis pregnancy center. Newton Smith Rd. (☎562 558 or 850 622 626). Phone lines open M-F 9:30am-9pm, Sa 9:30am-5pm.

Pharmacies: Pharmacies abound; all keep similar hours. **Flanagan's,** Shop St. (☎562 924). **Matt O'Flaherty's,** Eglinton Shop St. (☎566 670). Open M-Sa 9am-6pm.

Hospital: University College Hospital, Newcastle Rd. (☎524 222).

Internet: Internet cafes abound; some good options are:

Net@ccess, Olde Malt Arcade (☎535 470), off High St. near the King's Head. €3 per hr., €5 per 2hr. Open M-F 10am-10pm, Sa 10am-8pm, Su noon-6pm.

Runner Internet Cafe, 4 Eyre Sq. (☎539 966). Open daily 9am-midnight. Noon-10pm €4 per hr., 9am-noon and 10pm-midnight €2 per hr.

Post Office: 3 Eglinton St. (☎534 720). Open daily 9am-5:30pm.

▮ ACCOMMODATIONS

In the last few years, the number of accommodations in Galway has tripled; it now approaches 1000. Despite that, it's tough to find a hostel bed on summer weekends; call two to three weeks ahead to secure a spot. For festival weeks, especially Race Week, your best bet is to call a few months ahead. Hostels are spread throughout the city, and almost all are well run. Most B&Bs can be found in Salthill or clustered on College St., an extension of Forster St. beyond the tourist office. There are also a few closer to the city center.

HOSTELS AND CAMPING

Barnacle's Quay Street House (IHH), 10 Quay St. (☎568 644; www.barnacles.ie). Spacious rooms in the eye of the Quay St. storm. Perfect for post-pub crawl returns, but that same convenience can make front rooms noisy; ask for back rooms. No alcohol allowed on premises. Excellent security. All rooms with bath. Free Internet access and Wi-Fi. Light breakfast included. Laundry €7. May-Oct. daily and Mar.-Apr. F-Sa 12-bed dorms €17; 8-bed €19.50; 6-bed €22; 4-bed €24; doubles €60. Mar.-Apr. M-Th and Su and Nov.-Feb. F-Sa €15.50/18/19.50/22/54. Nov.-Feb. M-Th and Su €12/15.50/16.50/18.50/51. MC/V. ❷

Sleepzone, Bóthar na mBán (☎566 999; www.sleepzone.ie), northwest of Eyre Sq. A bit institutional, but new and fully loaded: huge kitchen, common room with TV, pool table, luggage room, calm terrace, and car park. Free Internet access and Wi-Fi. Wheelchair-accessible. Free continental breakfast. Coin laundry €7. No alcohol. July-Aug. M-Th and Su, Apr.-June, and Sept.-Oct. F-Sa 8- to 10-bed dorms €20; 6-bed €22; 4-bed €25. Singles €50; doubles €68; triples €84. Apr.-June and Sept.-Oct. M-Th and Su and Nov.-Feb. F-Sa €16/18/20/35/52/66. Nov.-Feb. M-Th and Su €13/15/16/30/44/54. MC/V. ❷

Kinlay House (IHH), Merchants Rd. (☎565 244; www.kinlaygalway.ie), half a block off Eyre Sq. Huge, conveniently located hostel with older showers, but helpful staff and great atmosphere. Currency exchange. Wheelchair-accessible. Breakfast included. Internet €1 per 15min. Laundry €7. Nov.-Feb. M-Th and Su 8-bed dorms €15.50; 4-bed €20, with bath €22. Nov.-Feb. F-Sa and Mar.-Oct. M-Th and Su €17.50/22/24; Mar.-Oct. F-Sa €19.50/24/26. Singles €35-50; doubles €50-58. MC/V. ❷

The Galway Hostel, Eyre Sq. (☎566 959; www.galwaycityhostel.com), right across from the station. Cartoons and wall paintings decorate the walls of the tight dorms and kitchen area. Close to the train station and with small common space. Internet access €1 per 15min. Light breakfast included. 24hr. reception. Large dorms Nov.-Feb. M-Th and Su €15; 4-bed €18, with bath €20; doubles €44; F-Sa €17/20/22/52. Mar.-Oct. €18.50/22/24/54. MC/V. ❷

Salmon Weir Hostel, 3 St. Vincent's Ave. (☎561 133; www.salmonweirhostel.com). True backpacker's hostel: cramped but friendly, with laid-back vibe. Staff and guests commune out back. Free tea and coffee. Laundry €5. Internet €3 per hr. Curfew 3am. 12-bed dorms €13; 6-bed €16; 4-bed €17. Doubles €40. Cash only. ❶

Claddagh Hostel, Queen St. (☎533 555). With only 44 beds and a free-bed-on-your-birthday-rule, this hostel has a fun feel. Free light breakfast. Kitchen, TV room closed 11:30pm-8am. Free Internet access and Wi-Fi. 10 bed dorms M-Th and Su €15, F-Sa €20-25; doubles €60. Cash only. ❷

Salthill Caravan and Camping Park (☎523 972; www.salthillcaravanpark.com). Bayside location, about 1km west of Salthill. 1hr. shore-side walk from Galway. Showers €1. Open Apr.-Oct. €8 per person, with car €10 per person. Cash only. ❶

BED AND BREAKFASTS

▨ **St. Martin's,** 2 Nun's Island Rd. (☎568 286), on the west bank of the river at the end of O'Brien's Bridge. Gorgeous back garden spills into the river. Located near Galway's best pubs and just across the river from the main commercial district. Flat-screen TVs in some rooms and great views of the water falling over the River Corrib in others. All rooms with bath. Singles €35; doubles €70. Cash only. ❸

San Antonio, 5 Headford Rd. (☎564 934), a few blocks north of Eyre Sq. Three cute little kiddies complete the homey feel. Backpacker-friendly. Rooms €23-30, with breakfast €30-37; ask about multiple-night discounts. Cash only. ❷

Lynfield House, 9 College Rd. (☎589 444). Sunny rooms behind the house have a bit more privacy. All rooms ensuite with coffee and teapots and cable TV. Rooms €35 per person. MC/V. ❸

Ashford Manor, 7 College Rd. (☎563 941; www.ashfordmanor.ie), by Lynfield House. Classy B&B with wine bar. Cable TV, direct-dial phone, hair dryer in each room. Plenty of parking. Big breakfast selection. Singles €45-50; doubles €100-110. MC/V. ❺

LONG-TERM STAYS

Galway has a large population of youthful transients who visit, fall in love, find jobs, stay a while, and move on. Most share apartments in and around the city, where low-end rents run €60-90 per week. Rent is lower and apartments easier to find during the summer, when the students clear out. Those staying for less than a month are best off at one of the hostels that have cheap weekly rates. If you're hoping to find an apartment during term-time (Sept.-May), it's best to start looking by the beginning of August. Try the *Galway Advertiser* (€2); apartment hunters line up outside its office at the top of Eyre Sq. at around 1pm on Wednesdays; when the classified section is released at 2pm, they race to the nearest phone box in Eyre Sq. All the information is posted by 3:30pm the same day online at www.galwayadvertiser.ie. Announcement boards in hostels and at the University also fill up with signs from roommate-seekers. An ideal time to start looking for housing or jobs is just before the university lets out, in the latter half of May.

Jobs are also relatively attainable in Galway, with most **short-term work** found in the service industry—ask around at local pubs and restaurants. Citizens of EU countries get priority for jobs; Americans sometimes find it difficult to land a position. A permit (p. 11) is required to work legally. The Thursday morning *Galway Advertiser* has a long list of job vacancies. Galway also has two centers which aid one's introduction to productive society. **FAS,** in Island House to the left of the cathedral, posts employment opportunities. (☎534 400; www.fas.ie. Open M-F 9am-5pm.) **Galway People's Resource Centre,** 19 Nun's Island Rd., intends to guide clients through all aspects of the job search. (☎564 822. Open M-F 9am-5pm.) To try to secure something before arrival, see **Beyond Tourism,** p. 79, for a list of other job-placement services in and around Ireland.

◘ FOOD

The east bank has the greatest concentration of restaurants, the sidestreets leading off Shop and High St. have the best values, and riverside Quay St. is home to the fancier restaurants. Find groceries at **Dunnes,** Edward Sq. (☎530 024. Open M-W and Sa 9am-8pm, Th-F 9am-9pm, Su 11am-7pm.) **Evergreen Health Food,** 1 Mainguard St., has all the healthy stuff. (☎564 215. Open M-W and Sa 9am-6:30pm, Th-F 9am-8pm. July-Aug. also Su 1-5pm.) On Saturdays, an ▨**open market** sets up both with cheap pastries, ethnic foods, and fresh fruit, as well as jewelry and artwork, in front of St. Nicholas Church on Market St. (See **Sights,** p. 371.)

▨ **The Home Plate,** Mary St. (☎561 475). Enjoy huge helpings on tiny wooden tables. Quaint and vegetarian-friendly, with curry dishes and sandwiches big enough to share (but good enough to hoard). All-day breakfast (€8) will tide you over until dinner. Sandwiches €6-7; pasta €8-10. Dessert and tea €5. 10% student discount. Open M-Th noon-8pm, F-Sa noon-9pm, Su noon-7pm. Cash only. ❷

▨ **Anton's** (☎582 067). Just over the bridge near the Spanish Arch and a 3min. walk up Father Griffin Rd. Exhibits by local artists decorate the simple walls of this hidden treasure. Gourmet-caliber sandwiches, like the chorizo and cheddar (€5.50). Open M-F 8am-6pm. Cash only. ❶

Food for Thought, Lower Abbeygate St. (☎565 854). Real student hangout with student-friendly prices. Plenty of vegetarian-friendly options, like the cashew nut roast or moussaka (both €6.50). Baked potato €2.50. Open M-F 7:30am-6pm, Sa 8am-6pm, Su 11:30am-4pm. Cash only. ❶

Java's, 17 Upper Abbeygate St. (☎532 890). Hip, dimly lit cafe. Artsy students flock here at all hours. International options—from tapas (€5.75) to New York-style bagels (€3.30) cater to a different crowd. As reliable as Irish rain—only closes early Christmas Eve. Open M-W and Su 10am-3am, Th 10am-4am, F-Sa 8am-4am. MC/V. ❶

Ard Bia Cafe, 2 Quay St. (☎539 897). Comfy coffee shop overlooking the madness of Quay St. Attachment to fancy restaurant leads to above-average options like blueberry pancakes (€7.50) and rosemary burger (€11) at reasonable prices. Free Wi-Fi. Open M-Sa 10am-5pm, Su noon-5pm. MC/V. ❸

Charcoal Grill, Lower Cross St. (☎532 732). Serves Turkish food and has come to have a bit of a cult following among the young and Guinness-swilling. Huge kebabs €6.40; burgers under €2. Open M-Th and Su noon-3am, F-Sa noon-4am. Cash only. ❶

Trattoria Magnetti, 12 Quay St. (☎563 910; www.magnettifoods.com). Great people-watching from the covered patio of this homey Italian cafe. Cheapest pasta around during lunch €7.50-9. Dinner entrees €13-15. Open daily noon-11pm. MC/V. ❸

McDonagh's, 22 Quay St. (☎565 001). Fish 'n' chips madness. Wait in line, salivate, devour, and try not to feel guilty. Takeaway fish fillet and chips €8.25. Open M-Sa noon-11pm, Su 5-11pm. MC/V over €10. ❷

Fat Freddy's, Quay St. (☎567 279). Low lighting, candlesticks, and...a cartoon cat on the wall. Perfect for the romantic with a sense of humor, or the regular old pizza lover. Gourmet vegetarian pizza (€13.50-16) is delish. Open daily noon-11pm. MC/V. ❸

Da Tang, 4 Middle St. (☎561 443). Some of the best food in town. Pickled mustard mixed with shredded pork in broth (€10, dinner €12.50). Calm, elegant atmosphere. Takeaway available. Open M-Th 12:30-3pm and 6-10:30pm, F noon-3pm and 6-11:30pm, Sa noon-11pm, Su 5:30-10:30pm. MC/V. ❷

Couch Potatas, Upper Abbeygate St. (☎561 664). What could be more Irish than a menu containing nothing but potato-inspired dishes? Spuds adorn the walls, and dishes have silly names like Lord of the Dance (€9). It's goofy, but who can blame them? Takeaway €1 less. Open M-W noon-9:30pm, Th-Su noon-10pm. Cash only. ❷

Pierre's, 8 Quay St. (☎566 066; www.pierresrestaurant.com). Charming French bistro for the severely in love or the complacently alone. An oasis of quiet amid the din of Quay St. Save room for dessert—try the raspberry mousse floating in a chocolate cup. 2-course meal M-F and Su €20. Open M-Sa 6-10:30pm, Su 6-10pm. AmEx/MC/V. ❹

Vina Mara, 19 Middle St. (☎561 610). With multiple awards adorning its foyer, this wine bar and restaurant caters to all appetites. Seafood, meat, and vegan dishes. Lunch still maintains the fancy-food feel: try the Thai fish cakes (€9) or duck liver (€11). Entrees €27-36. Open M-Sa noon-2:30pm and 6pm-late. MC/V. ❹

PUBS

With approximately 650 pubs and 70,000 people, Galway maintains a low person-to-pub ratio. Indeed, the city's intricate constellation of pubs is its primary attraction. Music is alive and well every night, whether it's the latest alternative rock, live hip hop, or some of the best trad in the country. Very broadly speaking, Quay St. and Eyre Sq. pubs cater to tourists, while locals stick to the more trad-oriented Dominick St. scene; *Let's Go's* **Galway Pub Crawl** (see p. 369) sweeps through both scenes. Look for flyers for specific dates or check *Galway First* (free), the Monday edition of the *Galway Advertiser*, available at its office at the top of Eyre Sq.

TIP **STUDENT ADVANTAGE.** Galway is one of the youngest cities in Ireland, and as a result, being a student has its advantages. Having your student ID on hand in restaurants and pubs can often earn you a 10% discount.

DOMINICK STREET

■ **Roisín Dubh ("The Black Rose"),** Dominick St. (☎586 540). Intimate, bookshelved front hides one of Galway's best live music venues. Largely rock and acoustic, but folk and blues put in appearances. Marvel at the musicians pictured on the walls—they've all played here. Cover €5-23 most nights for music in the back room, Th usually free. DJs after midnight play indie and alternative. Late bar nightly. Cash only.

■ **The Crane,** 2 Sea Rd. (☎587 419), a bit beyond the Blue Note. Friendly, musical pub well known as the place to hear trad and spontaneous unaccompanied singing in Galway. Enter through the side door and hop up to the 2nd fl. loft. Authentic, laid-back music. Trad every night and Su 1-4pm. Sometimes cover upstairs, but there's always something free. Open M-Th from 3pm, F-Su 1pm. Cash only.

The Blue Note, 3 William St. West (☎589 116). Twentysomethings dance to the hottest chart-toppers, as well as reggae and soul. Galway's best bet for turntable music with top-notch guest DJs. Open from 4pm. Cash only.

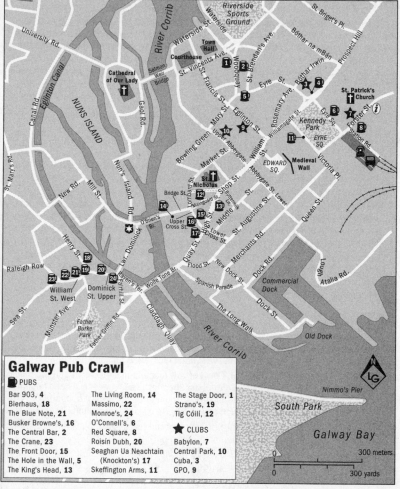

Galway Pub Crawl

🍺 PUBS

Bar 903, **4**	The Living Room, **14**	The Stage Door, **1**
Bierhaus, **18**	Massimo, **22**	Strano's, **19**
The Blue Note, **21**	Monroe's, **24**	Tig Cóilí, **12**
Busker Browne's, **16**	O'Connell's, **6**	
The Central Bar, **2**	Red Square, **8**	⭐ CLUBS
The Crane, **23**	Roisín Dubh, **20**	Babylon, **7**
The Front Door, **15**	Seaghan Ua Neachtain	Central Park, **10**
The Hole in the Wall, **5**	(Knockton's) **17**	Cuba, **3**
The King's Head, **13**	Skeffington Arms, **11**	GPO, **9**

Monroe's, Dominick St. (☎583 397). Middle-aged local crowd fills the pub for "just beer, no bullshit." Nightly music, trad and rock, from 9:30pm. Tu Irish dancing. Open at 9:30am for breakfast. Locals swear that **Vinnie's** chipper, next door, serves the best late-night grease fix in the city. MC/V.

Bierhaus, 2 Henry St. (☎587 766). Around the corner from Roisín Dubh's. Beer connoisseurs fill this unpretentious pub to enjoy 70 top-quality brews from around the world. Th-Su DJs play hip hop and techno. Open from 4pm. Cash only.

Massimo, William St. West (☎582 239). Modern, sleek bar with comfy couches and a young professional crowd. Booths with art above them make for good conversation. F-Sa DJs play funk, soul, reggae. W-Sa late bar until 2am. MC/V.

THE QUAY

Seaghan Ua Neachtain (Knockton's), 17 Cross St. (☎ 568 820). Unchanged for 100yr., it's got plenty of nooks and crannies for conversation. Afternoon pint-sippers eye pedestrians from street-corner tables on Quay St.'s most active patio. W-Su music—everything from jazz and blues to trad. Cash only.

Tig Cóilí, Mainguard St. (☎ 561 294). Place to be for trad on this side of the river. When good weather rolls around, grab a seat outside to watch the street performers who make this particular corner their stage. Sessions M-Sa 6 and 9pm, Su 2 and 7pm. Cash only.

The Living Room, 5-7 Bridge St. (☎ 563 804). Red lights illuminate a towering wall of vodka bottles. Th-Su DJs play a mix of R&B and hits. Impressively un-pub-like menu, with options like bell pepper with tofu and lentils (€10). Th-Su late bar until 2am. Kitchen open 10:30am-6pm. MC/V.

The Front Door, 3 High St. (☎ 563 757). Beams of light criss-cross the dark interior of this traditional pub. More rooms open as it gets busier, filling 3 maze-like stories. Th-Su DJs play a mix of 80s-90s and chart-toppers. Th-Su late bar until 2am. MC/V.

The King's Head, 15 High St. (☎ 566 630). Like visitors to the city itself, pubbers come into King's Head expecting to spend just the night, but soon fall in love and end up living there instead. There's certainly enough room, with 3 fl. and a huge stage devoted to nightly rock cover bands. F-Su late bar until 2am. MC/V.

Busker Browne's, Upper Cross St. (☎ 563 377), in an old nunnery. Upscale bar packs a professional crowd onto wall-to-wall couches. 3rd fl. Chandeliered ▨ **Hall of the Tribes,** easily the most spectacular lounge in Galway, usually manages to stay low-key even when insanity ensues downstairs. Su mornings excellent live jazz downstairs.

EYRE SQUARE

The Hole in the Wall, Eyre Sq. (☎ 564 677). Large pub fills up fast with a beat-seeking college crowd year-round. Nightly DJs spin a mix of chart-toppers and Irish music. During the day, betters are glued to the TV for horseracing and hurling. Cash only.

Bar 903, Prospect Hill (☎ 565 991). Conveniently located under the club and live music venue Cuba (see **Clubs,** p. 371). Colorful bar liberates itself on weekends and becomes an independent rogue club. Music nightly: M wonderful 17-piece jazz band (€7, students €5), W salsa, Su stand-up comedy (€12.50). Nightly late bar until 2am. MC/V.

The Central Bar, Woodquay (☎ 564 596). One of the few all-local pubs left in Galway. No food or music, but plenty of characters. Cash only.

O'Connell's, 8 Eyre Sq. (☎ 563 634). Local barflies swear it has the best Guinness in town. Tu and Sa trad in the beer garden when weather permits. Open M-Sa from 10:30am, Su from 1pm. Cash only.

Skeffington Arms, Eyre Sq. (☎ 563 173). "The Skeff" is a splendid, multi-storied hotel pub with 6 bars and a carved wooden interior. Suspended walkways overlook the rear. A well-touristed, multi-generational pub crawl unto itself. W-Sa DJs. MC/V.

Red Square, 11 Forster St. (☎ 569 633). Monolithic pub with enough space and taps to intoxicate Stalin's army. Rockin' student bar that quiets down during summer. Frequent live rock; DJs on weekends. F-Sa late bar in summer, daily during school year. MC/V.

▨ CLUBS

Between midnight and 12:30am, many pubs drain out, and the tireless go dancing. In the past year, more pubs have started late bar hours and remain open until 2am. Unfortunately, most of Galway's few clubs lag slightly behind its pubs in the fun factor. The place to be rotates at disco-ball speed. A good way to find out what's hot is simply to follow the herd after last call. Most of Galway's clubs require covers, but inquire about free passes, which are often handed out at adjoining or associated pubs and restaurants or from your friendly hostel staff.

 BLOW YOUR COVER. You shouldn't ever have to pay full cover price for a club in Galway. Ask at your hostel for a free or reduced pass, or prowl the streets for workers handing out flyers or stamping hands.

Cuba, on Prospect Hill (☎565 991), right past Eyre Sq. By far the best club. Upstairs provides a little more room, a little less flash, and wonderful live music perfect for busting killer moves. 2 fl., with a band on the 2nd fl. Cover €5-10; get stamped by staff in the street to get in free before midnight. Open nightly 11pm-2am.

Central Park (CP'S), 36 Upper Abbeygate St. (☎565 976). Open nightly 11pm-2am.

GPO, 7 Eglinton St. (☎563 073). Hopping during the term, but less so over the summer. Most evenings feature some form of house, techno, hip hop, or Top 40. Frequent theme nights; W 80s night is the club's most popular. Cover €6-10; pick up a pass dispensed at bars and hostels. Open nightly 11pm-2am.

GBLT NIGHTLIFE

Strano's, 1 William St. Greek nudes sit proudly atop the bar. F-Su DJs, Th and Su drag queens hit the stage. No cover. Open from 5pm. Cash only.

The Stage Door, Woodquay (☎087 224 7763). Traditional pub with good *craic*. Mix of live music—everything from trad to pop—and DJs. Open from 10:30am. Cash only.

Babylon, Foster St. (☎561 528). Galway's only gay nightclub plays a mix of chart-toppers and club standards. Cover €8. Open F-Su 11pm-2am. Cash only.

TOURS

Half- or full-day group tours may be the best way to see the sights of Galway and its environs all at once. Many are cheaper than bus tickets, though hour-long tours in and around the city are generally unnecessary as Galway is compact and walkable, but they might be a good option on a rainy day. These hop-on, hop-off **buses** (most €10, students €8) line up outside the tourist office. The name is somewhat misleading; if you hop-off, you'll wait 1½hr. for the next bus. Several lines depart from the tourist office, bus station, and Merchant's Rd. (by Kinlay House) once per day for both Connemara and the Burren (€20-25, students €15-20): **Bus Éireann** (☎562 000), **Healy Tours** (☎770 066), **Lally Tours** (☎562 905), and **O'Neachtain Tours** (☎553 188). The **Corrib Princess** (☎592 447) sails from Galway's Woodquay and tours Lough Corrib (1½hr., Apr.-Oct. daily 2:30 and 4:30pm, €9). History buffs may enjoy getting the inside story on the medieval city and its turbulent past on a **walking tour.** (☎087 678 3559 or 585 372. 2hr. tours depart from the tourist office May-Oct. M-Sa; call for times. €12, students €10. Reservations required.)

SIGHTS

EYRE SQUARE. If you're traveling by bus or train, the general mayhem of Eyre Sq. will undoubtedly be the first sight you encounter. Visitors and locals gather on this centrally located and recently redesigned square for picnics, sunbathing, and downtime. Mortified city officials are scrambling to get the project completed. Although the park was rededicated officially as **John F. Kennedy Park,** it remains Eyre Sq. in the hearts, minds, and signage of Galwegians. On the south side of the square is **Eyre Square Shopping Centre,** a large indoor mall that

DISTANCE: 5km

DURATION: 5-6hr.

WHEN TO GO: Start in the morning.

GALWAY WALKING TOUR

1. ANTON'S CAFE. Fuel up on the wonderful tea, coffee, and sandwiches in this unpretentious cafe on the less-touristed side of the river. (See p. 367.)

2. CLADDAGH. Though the last thatched cottage was torn down in 1931 for sanitary reasons, a few rudimentary boats are still on display along the Claddagh Quay, an ancient fishing village and the birthplace of the famous rings. (See p. 373.)

3. SPANISH ARCH. Cross **Wolfe Tone Bridge** and take a right. The 1584 Spanish Arch doesn't defend the city like the old days, but its base makes for a good spot to sunbathe and relax on the grassy quayside strip.

4. CHURCH OF ST. NICHOLAS. Wander through the stone-paved pedestrian walkway that starts as **Quay** and becomes **High** and **Shop St.** You may catch a street performance as you make your way to the church. The southern exit goes to **Church Lane,** filled each Sunday with vendors selling everything from horse-shoe wine racks to fried breads. (See p. 373.)

5. NORA BARNACLE HOUSE. Pass by the blue split door to take a look at the tiny two-room home where Nora Barnacle lived with six other family members, or pop in to see the museum dedicated to Nora and her husband, James Joyce. (See p. 373.)

6. MEDIEVAL WALL. Pass **Lynch's Castle** and enter Eyre Sq. Shopping Centre. A passage inside leads to the last existing remnant of the city's original medieval wall. (See p. 371.)

7. EYRE SQUARE. If there is no construction work, sit down for a picnic in the heart of Galway, officially rededicated as John F. Kennedy park. (See p. 371.)

8. CATHEDRAL OF OUR LADY ASSUMED INTO HEAVEN. Crossing the **Salmon Weir Bridge** brings you to the Cathedral, erected in the 60s at the site of the old jail. Atop the Galway limestone structure sits an impressive green copper dome. Check out the mosaics inside. (See p. 373.)

incorporates a section of Galway's 13th-century **medieval town wall** into its architecture.

CLADDAGH. Until the 1930s, this area was a thatch-roofed fishing village. Although stone bungalows replaced the cottages, bits of the small-town feel cling to this predominantly residential area. The famous **Claddagh rings,** traditionally used as wedding bands, are today's mass-produced reminders. The rings depict the thumb and forefingers of two hands holding a crown-topped heart. The heart should be turned outward until marriage; once the heart is turned inward, the wearer's heart is (theoretically) unavailable. *(Across the river, south of Dominick St.)*

GALWAY CITY MUSEUM. Brand-new museum with three floors of excellent exhibits about Galway. Don't miss the exhibit of the Claddagh on the top floor, as well as the view of their village's site. An unusual exhibit features objects that ordinary Galwegians feel symbolize their city. *(Spanish Parade. ☎ 532 460; www.galwaycitymuseum.ie. Open June-Sept. daily 10am-5pm; Oct.-May Tu-Sa 10am-5pm. Free.)*

CATHEDRAL OF OUR LADY ASSUMED INTO HEAVEN AND ST. NICHOLAS. The enormous Catholic Cathedral doesn't look it, but it's only 50 years old. Brilliant mosaics and green Connemara marble glisten inside. The enormous mosaic of the crucifixion caused controversy when it was made: the image follows scientific evidence that Christ's stigmata would have gone through his joints rather than the Catholic doctrine that describes them going through the flesh of his appendages. The dome is visible from almost anywhere in Galway. *(Beside the Salmon Weir Bridge at the intersection of Gaol and University Rd. ☎ 563 577. Open M-F 9am-6pm. Organ practice most weekdays 3:30-5:30pm. Open for mass M-F and Su at 9, 11am, 6pm.)*

CHURCH OF ST. NICHOLAS. A stone marks the spot where Columbus supposedly stopped to pray before sailing. Note the three-faced clock on the exterior; local folklore claims that the residents on the fourth side neglected to pay their church taxes. Artists set up craft exhibitions inside; don't miss the **farmers' market** outside on Saturdays. A plaque behind the church on Market St. marks the spot where a mayor (see **Lynch Mob**) hanged his murderer son. *(Market St., behind the castle. Wheelchair-accessible. Open May-Sept. daily 9am-5:45pm. Suggested donation.)*

NORA BARNACLE HOUSE. The tiny childhood home of James Joyce's life-long companion has hardly changed since its famous-by-association inhabitant left. Original love letters and the table where Joyce composed a few lines attract followers

LOCAL LEGEND

LYNCH MOB

Head behind St. Nicholas's Church on Market St. to the Lynch Memorial Window, the locus of one of Galway's favorite tall tales.

The Lynch family was once one of Galway's 14 ruling families and arguably the most dedicated to the city. According to legend, in the 15th century, Mayor Lynch had a rambunctious son named Walter. When a hot-blooded Spaniard made a pass on Walt's girl, he murdered him in a lover's rage. Daddy Lynch was horrified: what would this mean for Galway's international reputation? Could he let his son go unpunished, or would we have to bring his son to justice?

Mayor Lynch ensured that his son was tried and sentenced to death. On the appointed day, however, the hangman refused to carry out the punishment. Walter's father was so keen to preserve Galway's reputation for law and order that he decided to take matters into his own hands. When no one else would do the deed, he hanged his son from a window. A stone skull-and-crossbones marks the spot where Galway's mayor put city before son. And you thought your relationship with your father was strained?! Incidentally, the event led to the coining of the terms "lynching" and "lynch mob."

Church of St. Nicholas located on Market St., behind the castle. Wheelchair-accessible. Open May-Sept. 9am-5:45pm; suggested donation.

RACING DAYS

Horses gallop and pubbers hop during the last week of July at the annual Galway Races. Primarily a local event, the races are a great opportunity to see the Irish at their best. On Thursday, women don feathered hats, gloves, and long dresses for Ladies' Day. The winning lady doesn't have to run around a track with a small man on her back to earn top honors; she does, however, have to dress the finest.

At the actual races, listen to the whispers around you and try to pick out a "banker"—a horse that's so sure to win it's like money in the bank—and place your bet. Check the local papers for the latest on top horses and pick up a racecard at the tracks, or check online, for a complete lineup. Alternatively, go for the horse from your home country, or choose the jockey with the prettiest silk uniform, and surprise your friends when the underdog lands you a windfall profit. Be mindful at the races: bet wisely and keep a lookout for pickpockets who practice moneymaking methods that leave less to chance than gambling.

☎ 753 870; www.galwayraces.com and www.hri.ie. The racecourse is 6km outside the city on the Tuam Rd. Tickets are available at the gates or the box office. €20-30, children €2, student discount with ID.

of the literary great to Nora's humble abode, but it's probably best left to the fanatics. *(8 Bowling Green; the house with the maroon split-door. www.norabarnacle.com. Open mid-May to mid-Sept. M-Sa 10am-1pm and 2-5:30pm. Last admission 5pm. Mid-Sept. to mid-May by appointment only. Tours on request. €2.50, students €2.)*

NATIONAL AQUARIUM OF IRELAND. With mannequin fishermen overseeing the tanks and an "Octopus Garden," the museum doesn't take itself too seriously. A cartoon salmon on the wall narrates the trip through the exhibits. *(On the promenade, Salt Hill. ☎ 585 100; www.nationalaquarium.ie. Open Apr.-Sept. daily 9am-6pm; Oct.-Mar. W-F 9am-5pm, Sa-Su 9am-6pm. €9, students and seniors €6.50, children €5.50.)*

⚠ OUTDOOR ACTIVITIES

From the Claddagh, the waterfront road leads west to **Salthill.** The coast there alternates between pebbles and sand; watch for the ocean to turn sunset-red. A mini amusement park, complete with casinos and swimming pool, join the unappealing facades of new hotels and condominiums that dominate the esplanade. (**Swimming pool** ☎ 521 455; www.leisureland.ie. Call for lane times. €7, students and children €5. Gym open M-F 7am-10:30pm, Sa-Su 9am-8pm. €10 per day. **Summer carnival** open May-Sept. daily noon-10:30pm. Most rides €2-3.) A 20min. drive on N84 brings you to **Rusheen Riding Centre,** Headford Rd., where the foot-weary can gallop on horseback over the countryside. (☎ 521 285; www.galwayhorseriding.com. Call for reservations.) The nearest **golf course** is **Galway Bay Golf and Country Club,** which is surrounded by the ocean on three sides. (14km east of Galway on N18. ☎ 790 711; www.galwaybaygolfresort.com.) There is also a **GAA Stadium,** Pearse Stadium, Dr. Manix Rd., in Salthill, which plays host to hurling and football matches. (☎ 583 173. Tickets to matches from €10.) Greyhound races take place Thursday through Saturday starting at 7pm at the stadium on College Rd. (☎ 562 273; www.igb.ie. €10, students €5.)

♫ ENTERTAINMENT

ARTS, THEATER, AND FILM
The free *Galway Advertiser* provides listings of events and is available at the Galway Advertiser office at the top of Eyre Sq. **Zhivago,** Shop St., sells

tickets to big concerts and events throughout Ireland. (Ticket hotline ☎509 960. Open M-Sa 9am-9pm, Su 10am-6:30pm. Booking fee €2.25.)

SIAMSA NA GAILLIMHE. At Claddagh Hall, actors, dancers, musicians, and singers stun audiences with their showcase of traditional Irish performances. *(Nimmos Pier, off Claddagh Quay. ☎755 479. Performances July-Aug. M-F 8:45pm. Tickets €10-18.)*

TOWN HALL THEATRE. Galway's premier theater company presents everything from Irish-themed plays and Irish films to international hit musicals. It also hosts the summer **Film Fleadh** and **Arts Festival.** *(Courthouse Sq. ☎569 777. Programs daily in summer; most performances 8pm. Box office open M-Sa 10am-7:30pm. Tickets €15-25; student discounts often available.)*

AN TAIBHDHEARC. An Taibhdhearc (an TIVE-yark), Galways's oldest theater, was founded in 1928 by a group of academics from Galway University and has launched quite a few Irish actors into the spotlight. Poetry readings and musicals alternate with full-blown, mostly Irish-language theatrical dramas. *(Middle St. ☎563 600. Box office open M-F 1-6pm. Tickets €8-15; student discounts often available.)*

DRUID THEATRE. Renowned performances of contemporary Irish plays, all in English. *(Chapel Ln., between Quay and Flood St. ☎568 660; www.druidtheatre.com. Performances nightly 8pm, fewer during summer. Tickets €15-20, students €12-15.)*

FESTIVALS AND EVENTS

Festivals rotate through Galway all year. During the summer, festivals line up back-to-back; it's almost impossible to come to Galway during the warmer months without running into some good *craic*. Reservations are essential during these weeks, especially Race week. It's best to call a few weeks ahead of time. Check www.irelandwest.ie for a full list of festivals.

GALWAY RACES. The gates go up at the end of July, continuing a festival that dates back to the 1760s. The attending masses celebrate horses, money, and stout, but not necessarily in that order. The grandstand bar at the 23,000-seat **Ballybrit track** measures over 65m, making it the **longest bar in Europe.** The major social event is Ladies' Day, when those with the best hats and dresses are officially recognized. Even if you don't go to the races themselves, be prepared for mobbed pubs each night. Book hotels in advance. *(☎753 870; www.galwayraces.com. Tickets €20-30 at the gate or in advance. Student discounts available.)*

GALWAY ARTS FESTIVAL. For two crazed weeks in mid-July, the largest arts festival in Ireland reels in famous trad musicians, rock groups, theater troupes, and filmmakers. Unofficial performers flock to the streets, which are cleared only for parades. *(General information ☎509 700; www.galwayartsfestival.com. Box Office, Victoria Pl. ☎569 777. Open M-Sa 10am-7:30pm. Tickets €7-20.)*

GALWAY POETRY AND LITERATURE FESTIVAL. Also known as the *Cúirt*, this festival gathers the very highest of the nation's brows in the last week of April. Past guests have included Seamus Heaney and J.M. Coetzee. Performances take place all over the city, but the main events are held in Town Hall. *(☎565 886; www.galwayartscentre.ie/cuirt.htm.)*

GALWAY FILM FLEADH. Ireland's biggest film festival is a jumble of films, lectures, and workshops. The Fleadh happens in early July, right before the Arts Festival, and features independent Irish and international filmmakers. *(☎751 655; www.galwayfilmfleadh.com. Tickets €6-8, discounts for students. 5-ticket deals €25-33.)*

WESTERN IRELAND

GALWAY SESSIONS. In mid-July, Galway kicks the trad into overdrive, as pubs open up for three to four sessions per day. Most are free, though better-known acts run €10-18. (☎587 419; www.galwaysessions.com.)

GALWAY INTERNATIONAL OYSTER FESTIVAL. Galway's last big festival of the year takes place in late September. Street theater, parades, and free concerts mark this 53-year-old Galway tradition, which culminates in the **Guinness World Oyster Opening Championship.** (☎522 066; www.galwayoysterfest.com.)

NEAR GALWAY: LOUGHREA AND TUROE STONE ☎091

Loughrea's main sight is **St. Brendan's Cathedral,** a Catholic church constructed at the end of the 19th century during a revival of Celtic craftworks. Irish craftsmen made the 33 stained-glass windows, the magnificent arched dark wood ceiling, the carvings on the pews, and the paintings. Visitors can wander alone or listen to a 30min. audio tour. (☎841 212. Tour from the Presbytery beside the Cathedral M-F 10-11am, 11:30am-1pm, 2-5:30pm. Admission free; tour €2.) The Lough contains **crannogs,** artificial islands which pre-date the town.

Six kilometers from Main St. on N6 is the **Dartfield Horse Museum and Park,** a beautiful 140-hectare expanse including nature trails, stables, and a museum formed from the original farm of Galway horseman Willie Leahy. Equine enthusiasts will enjoy the wagons, antique horse-drawn machines, and the live horses in the stables and surrounding fields. Children can enjoy 5min. pony rides in the courtyard for an extra €2. (☎843 968; www.dartfieldhorsemuseum.com. Open daily 9:30am-6pm; last admission 5pm. €6.80, students and children €10. Trail €25 per hr.; cross-country €35 per hr.) Seven kilometers north of town rests the towering **Turoe Stone,** an intricately carved standing monument dating back to about 300 BC. The stone was moved from a fort several kilometers away and is decorated in the La Tène or Iron Age Celtic style. It may be Ireland's most significant Iron Age relic. Unfortunately, the Turoe Pet Farm has eclipsed the archaeological relic with cheap children's entertainment.

A few B&Bs line the main drag, including **Olde Mill Weir B&B ❸,** just across from O'Dea's Hotel, which represents a comfortable option with four large rooms and gracious hospitality. (☎841 737. Open Jan.-Oct. Singles €40; doubles €60.) The best place to stay is **Cabanas B&B ❸,** Old Galway Rd., a supremely luxurious home with well-groomed gardens and thoughtful hosts. (☎841 159. Singles €42; doubles €70.) Coming from Galway, take an immediate right after the Loughrea roundabout and then a left at the end of the road; the house is on the right—or just call the house and they will give instructions. When Chelsea Clinton visited Loughrea to ride at the equestrian center, she stayed at the elegant **O'Dea's Hotel ❹.** (☎41611 or 41759. Breakfast included. Singles from €65; doubles €100. Call ahead July-Aug.) The attached **restaurant ❺** is the most expensive affair in town, but try the pub across the hall for cheaper fare. (☎41611 or 41759. Entrees €12-28. Dinner served 6-9:30pm.) Main St. is full of other dining options, such as **La Serenata ❷,** Main St., which serves gourmet pizza and pasta dishes for €8-12. (☎871 196. Open daily 11am-11pm.) The **Londis** on Main St. sells groceries for a Lough-side picnic. (☎841 372. Open M-Th and Sa 8:30am-8pm, F 8:30am-9pm, Su 9am-6pm. Off-license open until 11pm.) For lunch, popular ▨**The Weaver's Restaurant ❷,** Main St., is a prime cafe for top-notch pastries and sandwiches. A great carvery offers roast stuffed turkey with bread sauce and cranberries (€7.50), or the delicious *panini* (€7) with melted brie, tomato and red pepper chili. (☎841 783. Sandwiches €3.50-5.50; entrees €6-9.50. Open M-Sa 9am-5:30pm; carvery lunch 12:30-3pm.) **Hope's Bakery ❷,** Main St., has special deals on baked goods (4 scones for €1.50), ample seating space, and an inviting ambience. (☎841 590. *Panini* and wraps €5.50-7.50. Open M-Sa 9am-6pm.) In the evenings, locals lounge in **Kinsella's**

Pub, Main St. (☎ 841 072), an amicable bar with trad on Friday and Saturday nights. For live pop and country and a younger crowd, head to **The Lantern** on Main St. (☎ 841 316. F-Su DJ. Kitchen open daily until 9pm; cover €9-10.)

Buses run between Loughrea and Galway (35min.; 15-17 per day M-Sa 8am-11:50pm, Su 8am-9pm; €7.20, students €6.30) and Athlone (50min., 15-16 per day 7am-9pm, €9.80/8). The Galway bus picks up in front of the AIB on Main St., the Athlone bus in front of Supermacs. For **tourist info,** try **D. Sweeney's** travel office on Westbridge past Dolphin St.; the office provides free brochures to help navigate the area. (☎ 841 552. Open M-F 10am-5:30pm, Sa 10am-4pm.) There are two **banks** in town, both with 24hr. **ATMs.** The **AIB** is on the corner of Main St. and Church St. and has a **bureau de change.** (☎ 841 777. Open M-W and F 10am-4pm, Th 10am-5pm.) The **Bank of Ireland** is also on Main St. (☎ 841 011. Open M 10am-5pm, Tu and Th-F 10am-4pm, W 10:30am-4pm.) **Killian's Pharmacy** is at 55 Main St. (☎ 841 589. Open M-Sa 9:30am-6pm.) Cheap **Internet** access is at **One-Stop Computer Shop,** on Main St. near O'Dea's. (☎ 870 974 or 087 622 9829. €1.50 per 30min.; €2.50 per hr., less with use of own laptop. Open M-Sa 9:30am-6pm.) For laundry, try **ACE Dry Cleaner and Laundry Service** on Main St. (☎ 887 0416. €6 wash and dry. Open M-F 8:30am-6:30pm, Sa 9am-6pm.) A **post office** is beside the bus stop. (☎ 841 111; open Sa 9:30am-1pm and 2-5:30pm.)

ARAN ISLANDS ☎ 099

On the westernmost edge of Co. Galway, isolated from the mainland by 16km of swelling Atlantic, lie the spectacular Aran Islands *(Oileáin Árann)*. The green-and-gray fields of Inishmore, Inishmaan, and Inisheer are hatched with a maze of limestone walls, the result of centuries of farmers piling the stones to clear fields for cultivation. Little is known of the earliest islanders, whose cliff-top forts guard the secrets of their own construction and purpose. Early Christians came seeking seclusion, and explorers can still clamber through the ruins of their churches and monasteries. Irish remains the first language of the islanders, and despite the hundreds of tourists who pour off the ferries each summer day, the islands maintain an untamed character that makes them a highlight of the western coast.

▐ TRANSPORTATION

Four ferry companies service the Aran Islands. **Island Ferries** and **Aran Direct** depart from **Rossaveal** (35min. to Inishmore); **Doolin Ferries** departs from **Doolin** (40min. to Inisheer). Direct connections from Galway are infrequent, but if the ferry leaves from Rossaveal, the company making the trip will provide a shuttle bus from Galway to Rossaveal for an additional fee. The Island Ferries serving Inishmore are reliable and leave daily; the service from Doolin tends to depend more upon weather and tide. If one company cancels for weather (which rarely happens), check with the others, as some are more venturesome. **Purchase all tickets before setting sail.** Aran Direct now offers the only reliable ferry between the islands once a day June-Aug. Otherwise, visitors must return to Rossaveal and embark separately to the other islands.

Island Ferries (☎ 091 561 767 or 568 903, after-hours 572 273; Rossaveal Office ☎ 572 050; www.aranislandferries.com), has main offices in the Galway tourist office and on Forster St., close to Eyre Sq. There are also offices on Merchant's Rd. in Galway and near the Rossaveal pier. 1 ferry sails to **Inishmore** (Apr.-Oct. departs Rossaveal daily at 10:30am, 1, 6:30pm; departs Inishmore daily at 8:30am, noon, 4, 5, 7:30pm Nov.-Mar. departs Rossaveal daily at 10:30am, 6pm; departs Inishmore daily at 8:30am, 5pm), a 2nd goes to **Inishmaan and Inisheer** (Apr.-Oct. departs Rossaveal daily 10:30am and 6:30pm; departs the islands daily approximately 8:15am and 4:30pm; Nov.-Mar. departs Rossaveal 10:30am, 6pm; island departure times the same). Oct.-May call to confirm sailing times, return €25, students €20. July and Aug. Island Ferries runs direct service from **Galway Docks** to **Inishmore** (1½hr.; 9:30am; return €35, students €20).

Aran Direct (☎353 091 566535 or 506786 or 564769; www.arandirect.com), has main offices on Forster St. near the tourist office, at Victoria Place in Galway's Eyre Sq., and at the Rossaveal Harbour. Ferry to Inishmore (Apr.-Oct. and Nov.-Mar. F-Sa departs Rossaveal 10:30am, 1, 6:30pm; departs Inishmore 8am, 12, 5pm; Nov.-Mar. departs Rossaveal 10:30am, 6:30pm, departs Inishmore 8am, 5pm). Ferries to Inishmaan and Inisheer depart Rossaveal daily 10:30am, 6:30pm; depart Inishmaan 9:25am, 4:55pm; depart Inisheer 9:15am, 4:45pm. Aran Direct offers ferries between the islands June-Aug. €6, students €5. Inisheer to Inismaan (11:30am); Inishmaan to Inishmore (11:40am); Inishmore to Inishmaan (2pm); Inishmaan to Inisheer (2:30pm).

Doolin Ferries (☎065 707 4455, after-hours 06570 71710. www.doolinferries.com). 5 ferries per day June-Aug. Apr.-May and Sept.-Oct. Doolin to Inisheer 10am, 1, and 5:15pm, 10am and 1pm go on to Inishmore; Inisheer to Doolin 12:30 and 4:45pm; Inishmore to Doolin 11:30am and 4pm; June-Aug. Doolin to Inisheer 10, 11:30am, 1, 3:30, and 5:15pm; Doolin to Inishmore 9:30am and 1pm; Inisheer to Doolin 9:15am, 12:30, 3, and 4:45pm; Inishmore to Doolin, 11:30am and 4pm. €35 return, €30 students, €20 one-way.

INISHMORE (INIS MÓR)

The archaeological sites of Inishmore (pop. 900), the largest of the Aran Islands, are among the most impressive in Ireland. Of the forts, churches, and holy wells, the most spectacular is the Dún Aengus ring fort, which teeters on the edge of a cliff. Crowds disembark at Kilronan Pier and head to major sights. Minivans and "pony traps" traverse the island, encouraging weary pedestrians to climb aboard and pay up, though bikes are the most scenic and inexpensive way to explore. Exactly 437 types of wildflowers rise from the rocky terrain, and over 4350km of stone walls divide the land. The island is also an excellent locale for birdwatching.

▐ TRANSPORTATION

Ferries: Arrive in Kilronan from **Galway** (via **Rossaveal**) and **Doolin.** See p. 377.

Minibus: At the pier. Confirm route before you board. For rainy days, be forewarned that some tours spend as much as 2hr. outdoors. 2-3hr. €10 and up per person.

Pony Traps: Ponies and their carts also hover by the gangplanks, offering bumpy rides around the island. Prices and times are highly variable and subject to negotiation. Usually around €10 per person per hr. (slightly less for longer rides).

Bike Rental: Aran Bicycle Hire (☎61132). €10 per day. Deposit or ID required. Additional €3 to keep the bike until the following day at noon. Open daily June-Aug. 9am-7pm; Sept.-Aug. 9am-5pm. **Burke Bike Hire** (☎61402), next to the tourist office. €10 per day. Deposit €20. Open daily Mar.-May 9am-5pm; June-Sept. 9am-7pm. Bike theft is common after dark—either lock it up or don't leave it (both bike hires provide locks).

▐ ORIENTATION AND PRACTICAL INFORMATION

Most people hang out in **Kilronan** *(Cill Rónáin)*, the island's main village. Houses and a few restaurants also huddle below Dún Aengus. Kilronan is the only place on the

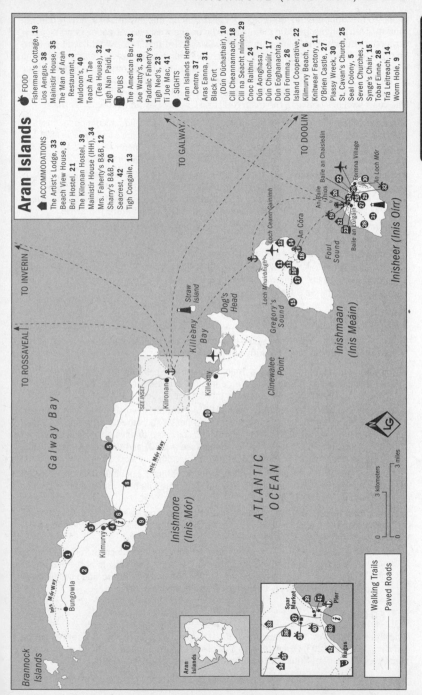

Aran Islands

▲ ACCOMMODATIONS
The Artist's Lodge, 33
Beach View House, 8
Brú Hostel, 21
The Kilronan Hostel, 39
Mainistir House (IHH), 34
Mrs. Faherty's B&B, 12
Sharry's B&B, 20
Seacrest, 42
Tigh Congaile, 13

✦ FOOD
Fisherman's Cottage, 19
Lios Aengus, 38
Mainistir House, 35
The Man of Aran
  Restaurant, 3
Muldoon's, 40
Teach An Tae
  (Tea House), 32
Tigh Nan Paidí, 4

⌂ PUBS
The American Bar, 43
Joe Watty's, 36
Padraic Faherty's, 16
Tigh Ned's, 23
Tí Joe Mac, 41

● SIGHTS
Aran Islands Heritage
  Centre, 37
Aras Eanna, 31
Black Fort
  (Dún Dúchathair), 10
Cill Cheannannach, 18
Cill na Seacht niníon, 29
Cnoc Raithní, 24
Dún Aonghasa, 7
Dún Chonchúir, 17
Dún Eoghanachta, 2
Dún Formna, 26
Island Cooperative, 22
Kilmurvy Beach, 6
Knitwear Factory, 11
O'Brien Castle, 27
Plassy Wreck, 30
St. Cavan's Church, 25
Seal Colony, 5
Seven Churches, 1
Synge's Chair, 15
Tobar Einne, 28
Trá Leitreach, 14
Worm Hole, 9

island to buy supplies, so stock up. The **airstrip** is on Inishmore's east end, while Kilmurvey, Dún Aengus, and the major sights lie on the west end. Anyone spending a few days on the Arans should invest in the *Inis Mór Way* map (€2), available at the tourist office, or the *Robinson Map* (€8), which meticulously documents every rock on all three islands. A free map from one of the bike rentals or ferry companies might suffice for basic exploration. The lack of street names can be confusing for tourists. The **main road** starts at the pier, curves around the American Bar, and heads uphill to the west. The **coast road** lies between the main road and Galway Bay and is relatively flat.

Tourist Office: Kilronan (☎61263). Changes currency, helps find accommodations, and has limited **luggage storage** (€1) during the day. Also sells the *Inis Mór Way* (€2) and provides useful information about navigating the island. Open daily June-Aug. 10am-7pm, Apr.-May and Sept.-Oct. 10am-5pm, Nov.-Mar. 11am-5pm.

Banks: Bank of Ireland, up the hill after the post office. Open Sept.-June W 10am-12:30pm and 1:30-2:30pm; July-Aug. W-Th 10am-12:30pm and 1:30-3:30pm. The only **ATM** in town is located inside **Spar Market,** up the main road from the **American Bar** (see p. 381), but it is frequently out-of-order. **Get cash before you arrive.**

Internet: The Cooperative Office inside the **Heritage Center.** €2.50 per 15min., €4 per 30min. Open M-Th 9am-5pm, F 9am-4pm.

Work Opportunities: The American Bar (☎61130) hires for short-term work in the summer. 1-month min. Min. wage plus tips. Some hostels take on additional summer staff.

Post Office: (☎61101), up the hill from the pier, past the Spar Market. Open M-F 9am-1pm and 2-5pm, Sa 9am-1pm.

ACCOMMODATIONS

Many minibuses make stops at far-away hostels and B&Bs; call ahead or ask at the tourist office (on the pier) for more information.

▨ **The Kilronan Hostel** (☎61255), a 1min. walk from the pier, next to Tí Joe Mac's pub. 4-bed dorms are acceptable, but the free Internet access, continental breakfast, and TV room with a large DVD collection make this a fun stay. Dorms with bath €20. ❶

Mainistir House (IHH), Main Rd. (☎61169), 3km from town past the American Bar. Once a haven for musicians and writers, this hostel still attracts expats to its sitting room, where windows overlook the sea. Dorms converted to private rooms in 2005, but 26 hostel beds remain. Joel prepares dinner (see p. 380) and tasty breakfast biscuits. Light breakfast included. Dorms €18; singles €35; doubles €50. ❶

Seacrest (☎61292), before St. Brendan's House. A bright, spacious B&B near the pier with some of the nicest rooms on the island. All rooms with bath. Book in advance. Singles €40; doubles €70. ❸

Beach View House (☎61141), 5.6km west of Kilronan, on Main Rd. near Kilmurvey. All rooms have warm quilts and views of the sandy beach and rocky fields. Open May-Sept. Singles €40; doubles €60. ❸

The Artist's Lodge (☎61457), take the turn-off to the coast road across from Joe Watty's pub on the main road, continue straight down the path. The lodge is at the end on the right. Inviting, with 3 large 4-bed dorms. Sip free tea and peruse the video collection by a crackling fire. Dorms €17. **Camping** €8 across the street. ❶

FOOD

The **Spar Market,** up the main road, has the only **ATM** in town and serves filling sandwiches. (☎61203. Open July-Aug. M-Sa 9am-8pm, Su 9am-7pm; Mar.-June and Sept.-Oct. M-Sa 9am-8pm, Su 10am-5pm; Nov.-Feb. M-Sa 9am-7pm, Su 10am-5pm.)

▓ **Mainistir House** (see **Accommodations,** above). Dinner here is by far the best deal on the island. Fill up on a largely vegetarian buffet. 8-person tables are arranged to encourage conversation with fellow travelers and locals in search of epicurean bliss. BYOB. Dinner €16, including dessert. Call ahead. ❸

Lois Aengus (☎61030). This cheery cafe next to Spar serves sandwiches (€6), salads (€8), breakfast, and desserts. Open June-Aug. 9am-6pm; Sept.-May 9:30am-5pm. ❸

Tigh Nan Paidi, in a thatched building at the turnoff to Dún Aengus. Specializes in home-made bread with home-smoked fish. Sample the whiskey-cured Aran smoked salmon with salad (€10.50) or sit at the peat fire with a slice of carrot cake (€3.20). Large wooden tables and big crowds promote mingling. Open daily 11am-5pm. ❷

Muldoon's (☎61228), look for the white awning across from the American Bar, by the pier. Serves fish and chips, cheap burgers, and sandwiches. Eat inside or outside on sturdy picnic benches adorned with fresh flowers. Fish and chips €11. Onion rings €2.15. Open daily July-Aug. 10am-9pm; May-June and Sept.-Oct. 11am-7pm. ❷

The Man of Aran Restaurant (☎61301), just past Kilmurvey Beach to the right, with the red trim. Organic lunches in a setting immortalized by the 1934 film. Toasties €5.40; salads €5. Lunch 12:30-3:30pm; dinner by reservation June-Aug. ❷

PUBS

Tí Joe Mac (☎61248), overlooking the pier beside Kilronan Hostel. A popular place to begin the evening. Locals and hostelers savor pints on the terrace and music in the back room. Frequent sessions during the summer; W in winter.

Joe Watty's (☎61155), west of the harbor on the main road. A louder nighttime watering hole, popular with tourists. Weekends usually bring bands and trad.

The American Bar (☎61130), across from the Aran Sweater Market. A traditional Irish pub, despite the name. The 2 sides of the bar attract different clientele—young islanders and tourists stick to the left by the pool table, while older locals chew the fat on the right. Bar food served noon-8pm in summer. Tu and F-Su trad.

👁 🚩 SIGHTS AND ENTERTAINMENT

Inishmore, with its labyrinthine stone walls, rewards wandering visitors who take the day to cycle or walk around its hilly contours. The **Inis Mór Way** is a mostly paved route that makes a great—if tiring—bike ride, circling past a majority of the island's sights. The graveled portion of the path leading from Dún Árran to Kilmurvy offers exhilarating views and bumpy riding. The tourist office's maps of the Inis Mór Way (€2) purportedly correspond to yellow arrows on the trails, but the markings are frustratingly infrequent and can vanish in fog; it's best to invest in a Robinson map for serious exploring, or follow the crowds and hope for the best.

If time is scarce, hightail it to the island's deservedly most famous monument, ▓**Dún Aengus,** 6km west of the pier at Kilronan. One of the best-preserved prehistoric forts in Europe, Dún Aengus opens its ancient concentric stone circles onto the seacliffs' 91m drop, leaving the modern visitor awed and thoroughly humbled. Many visitors are fooled by the occasional appearance of an island on the horizon—a vision so realistic that it appeared on maps until the 20th century. **Be very careful:** strong winds have been known to blow tourists off the cliffs. For those traveling by bike, the best route to the fort follows the **coast road,** and the downward slope of the main road makes an enjoyable ride back to Kilronan. The **Visitors Centre** below guards the stone path leading up to the fort. (☎61008. Open May-Oct. 10am-6pm, Nov.-Apr. 10am-4pm. €2.10, students €1.10.)

The road to *Gort na gCapall*, toward the cliffs, leads to a small freshwater stream. If the wind and light are just right, droplets of water suspended in the air form an upside-down rainbow. Just beyond the stream is a view of the **Worm Hole**, named for a sea serpent once believed to dwell in this saltwater lake. The bases of the surrounding cliffs have been hollowed out by waves and look like pirate caves. For a closer look at the caves, follow the outer cliffs to the left of Dún Aengus for about 2km, climb down into the tidal pool, and walk back beneath the cliffs to the Worm Hole. It's best to keep a bit of distance from the hole, as the flow of water can be unpredictable. The walk is thrilling at high tide but more accessible at low tide. The sound of waves crashing under the rock is worth the 20min. trek.

The road leading to the fort from Kilronan splits near Dún Árann. Either way leads to Dún Aengus; a left up the big hill takes you to Dún Árann, then down through a windy, graveled path to **Kilmurvy,** where it rejoins the flatter, paved coastal route. Inishmore's best beach is at Kilmurvy, with a sandy stretch and frigid water. One kilometer past the beach, a left turn leads to **Dún Eoghanachta,** a huge circular fort with 5m walls. To the right past Eoghanachta are the misleadingly named **Seven Churches**—there were never more than two; the other buildings were likely monks' residences. Most of the structures were built in the 7th and 8th centuries. A few hundred meters down the beach, a collection of large flat rocks plays home to a colony of **seals** and a sizable herd of **trumpeter swans.**

Uphill from the pier in Kilronan, the new, expertly designed ◪**Aran Islands Heritage Centre** provides a fascinating introduction to the islands' monuments, geography, history, and peoples. The center also screens *Man of Aran* several times per day. (☎61355; www.visitaranislands.com. Open June-Aug. 10am-5pm, Apr.-May and Sept.-Oct. 11am-4pm. Exhibit or film only €3.50, students €3. Combined admission €5.50/5.) **Black Fort** *(Dún Dúchathair)*, 1km south of Kilronan across eerie terrain, is larger than Dún Aengus, a millennium older, and greatly underappreciated. Since most tour buses stick to the western end of the island, the Black Fort also offers more elbow room and spectacular views of surf crashing against the cliffsides. Finish off the day on Inishmore with ◪**Ragus,** performed at the Halla Rónáin (down the street from the Aran Fisherman Restaurant)—a 1hr., stunningly energetic display of traditional Irish music, song, and dance that receives rave reviews and costs almost twice as much in Dublin. Tickets are available at the door. (☎61515. Shows June-Sept. at 2:45 and 9pm. €17, students €14.) On summer nights, the hall hosts *ceílís* Friday and discos Saturday at midnight.

INISHMAAN (INIS MEÁIN)

Seagulls circle the cliffs and goats chew their cud, but there's little human activity in the limestone fields of Inishmaan (pop. 200). Largely unaffected by the rapid and dramatic development that has recently swept the other two islands, Inishmaan remains unspoiled by tourism and overlooked by travelers. The island's sites, beaches, and walks make it well worth a daytrip, while travelers looking for a more isolated experience on the islands should stay longer.

The *Inishmaan Way* brochure (€2), available at the craft shop in the Inishmaan Co-op and at the Inishmore Tourist Office describes an 8km walking route that passes all of the island's sights. The ferry deposits passengers at An Córa, half-way up the eastern coast. The single road leading up from the pier cuts west across the island; most of the island's sights and shops are on or near the main road. **Eaglais Naomh Muire gan Smál,** the modern-looking church on the left, 2km down the main road, provides a peaceful escape from the elements on stormy days. A little farther down, a sign indicates the thatched cottage where John Synge wrote much of his Aran-inspired work. (☎73036. Open June-Sept. 12:30-2:30pm and 3:30-4:30pm. €3.) **Dún Chonchúir** (Connor Fort), a stone ring fort which dates to the early centuries AD, sits just beyond Synge's cottage. The fort has several stone walls and structural foundations and is worth the short ascent; a view across the island and surrounding ocean rewards those who climb to the top of the inner fort. At the western end of the road, indicated by a small sign, sits **Synge's Chair,** a large stone seat and semi-circular wall on the seacliff edge, which together provide a view to the Atlantic. An even more dramatic landscape awaits a bit farther down the rocky path; clamber over the rocks along the seacliffs on the southwestern part of the island to reach it.

To the left of the pier, the 8th-century **Cill Cheannannach** church left its rubble on the shore; islanders were buried here under stone slabs until the mid-20th century. There are several beaches north of the pier at An Córa: **Trá Leitreach** lies just ahead (watch for a strong undertow at high tide); the long, sandy beach at **Ceann Gainimh** is easily accessible by following the road to the island's airstrip (a right off the main road) to the northern tip of the island, and it is also possible to swim farther west, at Port na Cora. Entering the **Knitwear Factory,** near the center of the island, is uncannily like stepping into a Madison Ave. boutique. The company sells sweaters internationally to upscale clothiers, but visitors get them right off the sheep's back at better prices; expect to pay anywhere from €30 to €300 for an Aran sweater. The shop is up the stone steps by the flag; in winter months, ask someone in the factory to open the shop. The same building also houses a new modern restaurant and hotel. (☎73009; www.inismeain.com. Shop open July-Aug. M-F 10am-5pm, Sa 11am-4pm, Su noon-3pm. Factory open M-F 10am-5pm.)

For **tourist information,** as well as a variety of local crafts, try the **Inishmaan Co-op,** located by the school and post office; walking west along the main road, turn right just before the church. (☎73010. Open M-F 9am-5pm.) The **post office** (☎73891) is next door. **Caomhán ó Fatharta** sells a small selection of **groceries** and newspapers in a white building just before the church on the main road. (☎73136. Open M-Sa 10am-6pm, Su 10am-2pm.) The **An Dún Shop** (☎73047) sells food at the entrance to Dún Chonchúir. **Bikes** are available on the main road, just past Tigh Conaile B&B and Restaurant. (☎73053 or 73097. €10 per day.)

Angela Faherty runs a **B&B ❸** (from the pier, follow the signs, then look for the yellow house on the left side of the road) and serves dinner at 7pm. (☎73012. Dinner €12. Open mid-Mar. to Nov. Singles €35; doubles €60. Dinner reservations required for non-guests.) **Tigh Congaile ❸,** on the right-hand side of the first steep hill from the pier, is a modern and spacious B&B. (☎73085. Singles €36-40; doubles €65. Call ahead Nov.-Mar.) Its **restaurant ❸** concentrates on perfecting seafood. (Lunch €6-10, dinner from €16. Open daily June-Sept. 11am-5pm and 7pm-late.) The **An Dún Restaurant,** which also serves as a B&B, is open for dinner and serves a light tea or lunch to visitors upon request. **Padraic Faherty's** (☎73003) thatched pub is the center of life on the island. The cozy pub serves a small selection of good grub and has trad on summer weekends.

INISHEER (INIS OÍRR)

The Arans have been described as "quietness without loneliness," but Inishmaan can get pretty lonely, and Inishmore isn't always quiet. Inisheer (pop. 260), the smallest Aran, is the perfect compromise. On clear days, when the island settles into an otherworldly peacefulness, visitors wonder if these few square kilometers hold the key to the pleasures of a simpler life. The sights of the island can be explored alone by foot, by bike, or by any of the pony traps waiting for you at the pier. The first sight on the island is in town, at **Cnoc Raithní,** a bronze-age tumulus (stone burial mound) from 2000 BC. Walking along **An Trá** shore leads to the romantic overgrown graveyard of **St. Cavan's Church** *(Teampall Chaomhain)*. On June 14, islanders hold mass in the church's ruins in memory of their saint; a

festival has recently been added. Cavan's nearby grave is said to have great healing powers. Below the church, a sandy beach stretches back to the edge of town. Farther east along the water, a grassy track leads to majestic **An Loch Mór,** a six-hectare inland lake brimming with wildfowl. The stone ring fort **Dún Formna** is above the lake. Continuing past the lake and back onto the seashore is the eerie **Plassy Wreck,** a ship that sank offshore—the islanders saved all the crew—and washed up on Inisheer in 1960. The wreck has since been taken over by buttercups, crows' nests, and graffiti. A trip down the coast from the shipwreck leads to the **lighthouse,** a perfect place to see the spectacular Cliffs of Moher from a perspective most tourists never witness. The walk back to the island's center leads through **Formna Village** and on out to **Cill na Seacht nIníon,** a small monastery with a stone fort. Remains of both the 14th-century **O'Brien Castle,** razed by Cromwell in 1652, and a tall 18th century tower sit atop a nearby knoll. On the west side of the island, **Tobar Einne,** St. Enda's Holy Well, is believed to have curative powers and is still a place of pilgrimage for the islanders. ⚑**Áras Eanna** is a double-winged building sitting atop one of the island's highest points. The center houses an art gallery, a theater, and a craft workshop where local craftsmen weave baskets of every conceivable size, shape, and pattern, and bodrain players practice their traditional drums. The gallery exhibits the largely island-inspired work of artists who have completed a residency at the center. Its cafe serves up delectable scones for €1. One night a week, the center's theater becomes Aran's **cinema,** while other nights see the occasional concert and theatrical production. The center also hosts talks, lectures and week-long summer schools on topics like Celtic spirituality. Contact Director Aonghus Dwane about internship opportunities. (☎75150 or 087 623 2841; www.araseanna.ie.) Open June-Aug. 11am-5pm; call ahead in winter. Films €5, concerts €7-10. Gallery free.)

Brú Hostel (IHH) ❶, visible from the pier, has pleasant four- and six- bed dorms and great views. Upstairs has skylights, but lower rooms have bigger windows. Call ahead in July and August. (☎75024. Continental breakfast €4.50; Irish breakfast €6.50. Laundry €5. Dorms €13; private family rooms €18 per person. Kitchen lock-out 12:30-8am and 1:30-2:30pm.) **Líos Einne ❸,** to the right of the pier across from Fisherman's cottage (☎75025), provides large, spotless rooms close to all the town's activity (Singles €35; doubles €60). **Sharry's B&B ❸,** behind Brú Hostel, has views and high ceilings. (☎75024. Open summer only. Singles €30, ensuite €35.) Campers who don't mind cold ocean winds stay at **Ionad Campála Campground ❶,** near the beach. (☎75008. Open July-Aug. though campers pitch tents for free in the low season. Showers €2. 2-person tent €8, 4-person tent €10.)

Tigh Ruairí, an unmarked pub and shop in a white building behind the Ostan Hotel, is the best bet for groceries. (☎75002. Shop open July-Aug. daily 9am-8pm; Sept.-June M-Sa 10am-6pm, Su 10:30am-2pm.) **Fisherman's Cottage ❸,** east of the pier past the hostel, serves organic, mostly island-grown meals. They've also been known to offer "Food for Healing" courses in April, May, and September. (☎75053. Soup and bread €3.50, entrees €16-21. Open daily 11am-4pm and 7-9:30pm.) **Teach An Tae ❶** ("the tea house"), just beyond Tigh Ruairí, serves fair-trade coffee, homemade scones (€1.60), and other baked goods. (☎75092. Open daily 9am-6pm.) **Cafe na Trá ❷** ("Cafe on the Beach") is a snacks-and-chipper joint just off the sand. The decor is summery with Mediterranean hues, and the fish is fresh and tasty. (Cod and chips €8. Open daily mid-June to Aug. 10:30am-6:30pm.) **Tigh Ned's** pub, next to the hostel, caters to a young crowd. (☎75004. Pub food served noon-5pm.) The pub at **Ostan Hotel** (☎75020), up from the pier, is as crowded as Inisheer gets.

Rothaí Inis Oírr, directly in front of the pier, rents **bikes** and gives free **maps** of the island. (☎75033. €10 per day, €50 per week. Open daily 9am-6pm.) Looking up and to the left from the pier, the building on the point is the **Inisheer Cooperative,** where a wealth of local information and the town library can be found. (☎75008; www.inisoirr.ie. Open M-F 9am-5pm) Free **Internet** access is available at the library. (Open Tu, Th, Sa 2:30-5pm.) The **post office** is farther up from the pier, to the left of the pier, in a turquoise house. (☎75001. Open M-F 9am-1pm and 2-5:30pm, Sa 9am-1pm.)

LOUGH CORRIB

Three hundred and sixty-five islands, one for every day of the year, dot Lough Corrib. The lough, Ireland's largest, has enough elbow room for all of them. The eastern shores of Lough Corrib and Lough Mask stretch easily into fertile farmland. The west slips into bog, quartzite scree, and the famously rough Connemara country. The island of Inchagoill, in the middle of the lough, has the second-oldest existing Christian monuments in Europe. Lough Corrib is one of Europe's best spots for salmon and trout angling, the principal activity on shore and boat.

OUGHTERARD (UACHTAR ÁRD)   ☎091

With a small population strung along the N59 between Galway and Clifden, Oughterard (OOK-ter-rard) watches most touring vehicles blink briefly in its direction before heading to bigger and better-known attractions. But this little town draws Galway natives to its quiet shores for weekend respites, and the city-weary traveler might do well to follow their lead. Hikers use Oughterard as a base for hikes into the Maumturk Mountains, while the less energetic prefer to angle in Lough Corrib's salmon-rich waters. Aughnanure Castle, a few kilometers from town, is worth a visit even for those just passing through.

▢⚡ TRANSPORTATION AND PRACTICAL INFORMATION. From late June to early September, **Bus Éireann** stops on Main St. and runs to **Galway.** (30min.; M-F 8 per day 7:55am-8pm, Sa 7 per day 9am-8pm, Su 3 per day noon-9:41pm; €6, student €4.70.) During the winter, the Galway-Clifden Bus stops in Oughterard. (Both directions, M-Sa 3-4 times per day, Su 1 per day.) *Let's Go* does not recommend hitchhiking, but those who do report easy going in summer between Galway and anywhere west. An independent **tourist office,** Main St., provides a free town map and information about the area and offers **Internet** access for €1 per 15min. (☎552 808. Open July-Aug. daily 9:30am-5:30pm; Sept.-June M-F 9:30am-5:30pm, Sa 9:30-1:30pm.) **Internet** access is also available at the **Oughterard Library** (☎552 488. Open Tu and Th-F 2-4pm and 7-9pm, W and Sa 11am-1pm) and at **Archers Pizza,** Camp St. (☎552 034. Free. Open daily noon-11:30pm). The **Bank of Ireland** on Main St. has a 24hr. **ATM.** (☎552 123. Open M 10am-12:30pm and 1:30-5pm, Tu-F 10am-12:30pm and 1:30-4pm.) **Flaherty's Pharmacy** (☎557 602. Open M-Sa 9:30am-1pm and 2-6pm), the **post office** (☎552 201. Open M-F 9am-1pm and 2-5:30pm, Sa 9am-1pm), and the **Police** *(Garda)* station (☎552 202) are all on Main St.

▟ ACCOMMODATIONS. The only hostel in Oughterard is **Cranrawer House (IHH) ❶,** 10min. down Station Rd. off Main St. Call ahead; the owner, an experienced fisherman with knowledge of the local fishing scene, has been considering closing. (☎552 388. Laundry €8. Common room lockout midnight-8am. Simple breakfast included. Open Feb.-Nov. 8- to 12-bed dorms €17; private ensuite rooms €16.) The large lawn of the 200-year-old Georgian **Corrib View Farmhouse ❸,** about 5km down the Aughnanure Castle road off N59, descends to the lake, where angling can be arranged. Guests can also use the tennis court. (☎552 345. €40 per person.) B&Bs are easy to find on Camp St. and the Glann road. **Abhainn Ruibe ❸,** on Camp St., is the yellow house on the right. (☎552 144. Singles €45; doubles €35 per person.)

🗓🖼 **FOOD AND PUBS. Keogh's Grocery,** a.k.a. **Spar,** sells food and fishing tackle from its location at the Square at Main St. (☎552 222. Open daily 8am-10pm.) 🖼**The Yew Tree ❷,** Main St., serves as both a bakery and top-notch cafe, serving up gourmet sandwiches (€5.50-8), specialty salads served with foccacia bread and homemade dressing (€6.50-7.50), and tantalizing baked goods (cinnamon buns €2 each). Stop by on Saturdays for local honey, eggs, jams, and organic produce. (☎866 986. Upstairs cafe open Tu-F and Su noon-5pm, Sa 10am-5pm. Evening specials Th-Sa 5-9pm. Downstairs breakfast counter M-Sa 9am-5pm. Wine and coffee bar Th-Su 5-11pm. Market Sa 9am-4pm.) **Breathnach's Bar ❷,** in the Square, serves three solid meals a day in a pleasant, relaxed setting. (☎552 815. Open daily 10:30am-midnight; kitchen open until 9:30pm.) Great pub grub and brilliant *craic* flow from **The Boat Inn ❷,** across from Spar, and spill out onto the sidewalk. (☎552 196. Sandwiches €7.50-11, entrees €11-22. Live music Sa-Su; in summer, every night except Wednesday. Kitchen open 11:30am-10pm.) **Faherty's,** Camp St., is another option for food and drink (☎552194; the sign outside signals live music nights). Across the street at **Keogh's Bar,** fill up on pub grub or just grab a pint. (☎552 222. Th disco; in summer Sa-Su live rock or trad.)

🗓🖼 **SIGHTS AND OUTDOOR ACTIVITIES.** Three and a half kilometers south of town, a turnoff from N59 leads to Oughterard's top attraction, 16th-century **Aughnanure Castle.** Here the Drimneen River curves around the impressively preserved fortified tower that was once home to the O'Flaherty clan but now houses a family of bats. The optional 40min. tour (available upon request; no extra charge) explores highlights such as the secret chamber and the murder hole—a hole that intruders would fall into before being submerged in scalding oil. Be careful—the O'Flahertys were not a tall family, and they intentionally built their spiral staircases to trip up ascending attackers. Near the entrance is the area's only yew tree, a tree that used to grow in abundance and was revered for its magical qualities. (☎552 214. Open May-Sept. daily 9:30am-6pm; Sept.-Oct. Sa-Su 9:30am-6pm; call on weekdays. €3, students €1.30.) The caverns of **Glengowla Mines,** 3km west of town off N59, are Ireland's only silver and lead mines. When mining was abandoned in 1865, Glengowla became Ireland's first show mine. (☎552 021; www.glengowlamines.com. Open daily Mar.-Nov. 10am-6pm. Call for low season hours.) Glann Rd. covers the 13km from Oughterard to a lookout point for viewing the infamous **Hill of Doon,** where the pre-Celtic Glann people annually sacrificed a virgin to the panther goddess Taryn. The 77km **Western Way Walk** begins (or ends) in Oughterard at Glann Rd. and threads through mountains and loughs, affording gorgeous views of the **Twelve Bens, Maumturks,** Clew Bay, and Killary Harbour before finishing in Westport.

Local sports enthusiasts occasionally swarm the **Gaelic football pitch,** near the intersection of Pier Rd. and Main St., where they spend €3-7 to cheer on the local boys in the winter and spring. The last Sunday of August brings an elaborate **Agriculture Fair** to the Gaelic pitch with Connemara pony shows, activities for kids, and a craft show in the Community Centre. Contact the tourist office for information about local competitions and events (☎552 808; oughterardoffice@eircom.net).

Angling on Lough Corrib is the most popular activity in Oughterard and is arranged for visitors almost entirely through the town's accommodations. **Corrib Wave House** (☎552 147), **Camillaun** (☎552 678), **Lakelands** (☎552 121) and **Nomaim Lodge** (☎552 138) hire boats and lead angling expeditions (you don't have to be a guest to participate). Only salmon-fishing requires a license, which can be obtained through the **Western Regional Fisheries Board** in Galway (☎563 118;wrfb@iol.ie). Surprisingly, golfing is usually less expensive than fishing.

Following the hatch of the mayfly in March, a number of angling competitions tangle Lough Corrib with lines between the last two Sundays of the month. Competitors from all over Ireland assemble in June for the Curragh Racing Championships. The family-oriented Oughterard Pony Show comes to town in July.

🔁 **DAYTRIP FROM OUGHTERARD: INCHAGOILL.** Reputed to mean "the Island of the Stranger," **Inchagoill** (INCH-a-gill) has been uninhabited since the 1950s; three families farmed the island when it, along with Ashford Castle, belonged to the Guinness family. Aside from a few ancient monastic ruins and some toppled gravestones, there's little to see on the 52-hectare island. Still, at the right time of day, Inchagoill's eerie beauty and solitude make it as captivating as any of its more touristed island cousins, and the views over the lough and castle are spectacular. Two churches lie just down the right-hand path from the pier. **St. Patrick's Church,** built in the 5th century, has crumbled almost beyond recognition. The famous **Stone of Lugna,** which supposedly marks the gravesite of St. Patrick's nephew and navigator, is 1m tall and stands among the other stones surrounding the church. Its inscription means "stone of Luguaedon, the son of Menueh." (Good thing we cleared that up.) This is the earliest known example of the Irish language written in Roman script, and the second-oldest known inscribed Christian monument in Europe (the oldest are the catacombs of Rome). The second Church, the **Church of the Saint,** where 10 sculpted human heads decorate the arched doorway, dates back to the 12th century. *(The Corrib Queen ☎091 552 808 sails daily from Lisloughrea Quay on Cong's Quay Rd., see p. 398, Ashford Castle, and Quay Rd. in Oughterard; it offers a brief but enlightening tour of the island. 1½hr. May-Oct. 11am, 2:45, and 5pm. €15 return, €22 return including stop at Ashford Castle in Cong with €5 entrance fee to castle grounds included; longer trip 11am Oughterard sailing only. Those interested in extensive exploration should take a morning ferry out and return in the afternoon or camp on the island; no facilities are provided.)*

CONNEMARA (CONAMARA)

Connemara, a thinly populated region of northwest Co. Galway, extends a lacy net of inlets and islands into the Atlantic Ocean. Rough inland mountains, desolate stretches of bog, rocky offshore islands, and a dramatic coastline are among Ireland's most arresting and peculiar scenery. Driving west from Galway City, the relatively tame and developed coastal strip stretching to Rossaveal suddenly gives way to the fishing villages of Roundstone and Kilkieran, with beautiful beaches, frisky wildlife, and constantly changing weather. Farther west, Clifden, Connemara's largest town, offers the most tourist services in the region. Ancient bogs spread between the coast and the rock-studded green slopes of the two major mountain ranges, the **Twelve Bens** and the **Maumturks.** Northeast of the Maumturks is **Joyce Country,** named for a long-settled Connemara clan. Ireland's largest *gaeltacht* also stretches along the Connemara coastline, and Irish-language radio *(Radio na Gaeltachta)* broadcasts from Costelloe. **Connemara National Park** gives a useful introduction to the region's bogs and wildlife.

Cycling is a particularly rewarding way to absorb the region. The 96km routes from Galway to Clifden (via Cong) and Galway to Letterfrack are popular despite challenging dips and curves toward their ends. The seaside route through Inverin and Roundstone to Galway is another option. In general, the dozens of loops and backroads in north Connemara make for worthwhile riding. **Hiking** through the boglands and along the coastal routes is also popular—the **Western Way** footpath offers dazzling views as it winds 50km from Oughterard to Leenane through the Maumturks. A word of caution for those traveling outdoors: **beware the midges.** These mayflies are out in full force during summer. **Buses** serve the main road from Galway to Westport, stopping in Clifden, Oughterard, Cong, and Leenane. N59 from Galway to Clifden is the main thoroughfare; R336, R340, and R341 make more elaborate coastal loops. **Hitchers** report that locals are likely to stop; *Let's Go* does not recommend hitchhiking. If all else fails, Connemara through the windows of a tour bus (see **Galway,** p. 371) is better than no Connemara at all.

> **BOTTLE YOUR SAFETY.** In Connemara, as in other areas of Ireland, ask if the water is drinkable before you imbibe, and be sure to stock up on plenty of bottled water.

ROUNDSTONE (CLOCH NA RÓN)   ☎095

Roundstone is a one-street fishing village that, like many of its neighbors along Coast Rd., would do well in a quaint little Irish town contest. In the distance beyond the bay, a few prominent Bens rise into the clouds. The 2hr. hike up **Errisbeg Mountain,** which overlooks Roundstone's main street, culminates in a view of the entire region. To access the mountain, turn up the street by O'Dowd's and go through the small wooden gate at the road's end. There is no marked path; climbers follow the boggy sheep trails up. The 25min. walk to the mountain is itself also very pleasant. Four kilometers along the coast beyond Roundstone, the white-sand beaches between Dog's Bay and Gorteen Bay fan out to a knobby island.

The town is home to the famed **Roundstone Musical Instruments,** the only full-time *bodhrán* (bough-RAWN) maker in the world (see **Traditional Music,** p. 71). Instruments built here are played across the globe by famous Irish musicians, including

the Chieftains. The owners have taken advantage of this fame by opening a veritable trad megastore with an attached Irish kitsch warehouse, a recently added cafe, and a craft and fashion boutique. A glass partition permits visitors to watch *bodhrán*-makers in the workshop on weekdays. (☎35875; www.bodhran.com. Open May-Nov. daily 9am-7pm; Nov.-Apr. M-Sa 9am-6pm.) Roundstone's annual **arts weeks,** beginning the last weekend of June, are its primary cultural event. Visitors flock to the small village to hear original musical performances by well-known bands and up-and-comers, late-night flute and *uillean* pipe performances, and poetry readings in the local pubs and Community Centre. (☎35977; wwww.roundstoneartsweek.com. Bigger-name bands €7-20; many events free.)

The attentive proprietress of ◪**Wit's End B&B ❸,** located in the town's center, across the street from the water, maintains cozy and immaculately coordinated rooms. (☎35951. Open June-Oct. €40 per person.) Travelers more interested in thrift than in comfort seek out the **Gorteen Bay Caravan and Camping Park ❶,** 3km west of Roundstone on the R341 and just steps away from the beach. (☎35882 or 35787. Open late Apr.-late Sept. Kitchen facilities. Laundry €10. Electricity €4. Hot showers €1.50. €12 per person.) **O'Dowd's Roundstone Cafe ❶** (☎35809), attached to the restaurant next door, has cheap coffee and an upstairs with a view. (Sandwiches €2.50-4.50. Open July-Aug. daily 9am-9pm, Sept.-June daily 9am-6pm.) The cafe has a monopoly on the town's **Internet** access. (€1.25 per 15min.) Next to the cafe, **O'Dowd's Seafood Bar and Restaurant ❸** offers fresh seafood from fried haddock (€13.50) to buttered lobster (€42.50). Music-lovers head to **Shamrock Bar** for live trad, jazz, and folk music on summer Saturdays and some Wednesdays. (☎35760; www.barshamrock.com. Open daily noon-11:30pm; kitchen open 12:30-9pm.) At night, lively **King's Bar** serves up frequent music and all the necessary beverages. (☎35841. Live music weekends late June-Aug.)

The town's only **ATM** is inside **Michael Ferron's Grocery** on Main St. (☎35838. Open late June-Aug. Sa 8am-8pm, Su 9am-8pm; Sept.-May M-Sa 8am-7pm, Su 9am-2pm.) The **post office** is also inside Ferron's. (M-F 9am-1pm and 2-5pm, Sa 9am-1pm.) For more information on Roundstone, call or visit the town's **Information Centre,** hidden away in the Community Centre (walk around the building and enter through the basement entrance by the water). Richard de Stacpoole, who founded the annual arts festival in 1997, runs the center; if he is out of the office, visitors can call him or check his website. (☎35044; www.roundstone-connemara.net.)

CLIFDEN (AN CLOCHÁN)   ☎095

Clifden proper, resting between a small cliff and a pair of modest peaks, is an energetic town fun both for exploring by foot or for just relaxing outside in the Square. In the low season (Sept.-May), the town is relatively quiet. High season begins in late June and brings with it a load of tourists looking for a good launching point into the Connemara wilderness. Saturday nights bring a lively pub scene, and the summer Irish Nights in Town Hall are campy fun. Off the Galway Rd., the old train station has been refurbished into a trendy spot with apartments and shops.

▐ TRANSPORTATION

Buses: Bus Éireann (☎091 56200) leaves from the library on Market St. to: **Galway** via **Oughterard** (1½hr.; late June-Aug. M-Sa 6 per day 8:15am-7:15pm, Su 2 per day, Sept.-May daily 1-3 per day; €10, students €8) and **Westport** via **Leenane** (1½hr., late June-Aug. M-Sa 1 per day; €11.10, students €9). **Michael Nee** (☎34682) runs a private bus from the courthouse (opposite Gannon's Sports) to **Cleggan** (mid-June to Aug. 3 per day, Sept.-May 3 per week; €6) and **Galway** (2hr.; 2 per day; €11, €14 return).

Taxis: C&P Hackney Service (☎21444). **Slevin's** (☎22241 or 087 130 7705). **C&A Cabs** (☎21309 or 086 331 0270). **Joyce's** (☎21076) is in the Clifden Town Hostel.

Bike Rental: Mannion's, Bridge St. (☎21160, after hours 21155). June-Aug. €15 per day, €70 per week; Sept.-May €10 per day. Deposit €20. Open daily 9:30am-6pm.

Boat Rental: John Ryan, Sky Rd. (☎21069). Fishing trips and excursions from €50 per day. Open year-round.

⚡ ℹ ORIENTATION AND PRACTICAL INFORMATION

Local traffic comes in on N59 from Galway (1½hr. to the southeast), which curves at the Esso Station and heads northeast to Letterfrack, Connemara National Park, Westport, and all points north. The town's center is a rounded one-way triangle formed by **Market Street** (where Bus Éireann stops), **Main Street** and **Bridge Street**. **Market Square** sits at the intersection of Main and Market St. **Church Hill** runs uphill from the Main St. side of Market Square. **Sky Road** and **Clifden Beach** are straight out from the Square past the SuperValu and Bank of Ireland. Though *Let's Go* never recommends hitchhiking, hitchers allegedly find rides at the Esso station on N59. If parking a car, remember to pay at the pay station and display the ticket in your car. Additional parking is available in a garage beneath the Supervalu.

Tourist Office: Galway Rd. (☎21163). Extensive info on Connemara, including a free map, transportation schedules, and lists of restaurants and activities in the area. Open July-Aug. M-Sa 10am-6pm, Mar.-June and Sept.-Oct. M-Sa 10am-5pm.

Banks: AIB, the Square (☎21129). **Bank of Ireland,** Sea View (☎21111). Both have 24hr. **ATMs;** both open M 10am-12:30pm and 1:30-5pm, Tu-F 10am-12:30pm and 1:30-4pm.

Laundry: The Shamrock Washeteria, the Square (☎21348). €8 per load; €6 wash only. **Hillview Launderette** (☎21836). Church Hill. €9.50 per load; €6 wash or dry only. Both open M-Sa 9:30am-6pm.

Emergency: ☎999; no coins required. **Police** *(Garda):* ☎22500. Galway Rd.

Pharmacy: Clifden Pharmacy, Main St. (☎21821), just off the Square. Open M-F 9:30am-6:30pm, Sa 9:30am-6pm.

Hospital: ☎21301 or 21302. On the right entering Clifden from Galway.

Internet: Two Dog Cafe, Church Hill (☎22186; www.twodogcafe.ie). Cafe on the 1st fl. (wraps €6-7); Internet access, phone calls, and beverages on the 2nd. Internet €2 per 15min.; €5 per hr. Open M-Sa 10am-6pm; Nov.-May closed M. The **Public Library,** Market St., has free Internet access with a visitor's fee of €3.50. Book sessions in advance during the summer. Open M and W 2:30-6pm and 6:30-8pm; Tu, Th, Sa 10:30am-1pm and 2:30-6pm; F 10:30am-1pm, 2:30-6pm, 6:30-8:30pm.

Post Office: Main St. (☎21156). Open M-F 9:30am-5:30pm, Sa 9:30am-1pm.

⚑ ACCOMMODATIONS AND CAMPING

B&Bs are as plentiful as the wildflowers, especially in the center of town and along Westport, Beach, and Sky roads. The going rate is €35 and up per person.

White Heather House, the Square (☎21655). Great location, with panoramic views from most ensuite rooms. Included Irish breakfast served 8-9:30am. €35 per person. ❸

Clifden Town Hostel (IHH), Market St. (☎21076; www.clifdentownhostel.com). Good facilities, spotless rooms, helpful owners, a quiet atmosphere, and proximity to the pubs endear guests to this hostel. The white plaster in the front hallway covers a several-hundred-year-old stone wall. Open year-round, but call ahead Nov.-Feb. Dorms €15 per person; doubles €36; triples €52; quads €65. ❶

Foyle's Hotel, the Square (☎21801; www.foyleshotel.com). A plain reception area gives way to pretty rooms, all with bath and breakfast. July-Aug. singles €75; doubles €100. Sept.-Dec. and Apr.-May singles and doubles start from €40 per person. Inquire about special weekend and midweek offers. ❹

Ben View House, Bridge St. (☎21256; www.benviewhouse.com). The owner of this antique-laden house loves travelers of all sorts. The price is right for narrow halls and some tiny rooms. €30-50 per person. ❸

Shanaheever Campsite, Westport Rd. (☎22150), 2km outside Clifden and 400m down a bumpy road after the turn-off. The tranquility of this spot compensates for its distance from town. Game room. Free hot showers. Laundry €8. Electricity €4; caravan awning €2. Open May-Sept. only. €9 per person for tent or trailer. ❶

FOOD

Clifden has a surprising number of fine dining options; other offerings include pub snacks, cafe fare, and Chinese takeaway. Most restaurants in town have an early bird special until 6:30 or 7pm. **SuperValu,** Market St., sells groceries. (☎21182. Open June-Aug. M-Sa 9am-9pm, Su 10am-6pm; Sept.-May M-Th and Sa 9am-7pm, F 9am-8pm, Su 10am-6pm.) The **Clifden Fruit & Veg Market,** behind the Esso station, has a wide selection of produce. (☎21531. In summer open daily 9:30am-6:30pm.)

Cullen's Bistro & Coffee Shop, Market St. (☎21983). Family-run establishment prepares hearty meals (Irish stew €16) and tasty desserts (rhubarb crumble €5). Open daily Apr.-Nov. 11:30am-10pm. ❸

Upstairs/Downstairs Coffee and Sandwich Bar, Main St. (☎22809) has salads (€6.50-8) and frappes (€3.50). Open M-F 9am-6pm; Sa-Su 10am-6pm.

Walsh's, Market St. (☎21283). A busy deli and bakery with a large seating area, Walsh's serves soups, baps, fresh pastries, and other morsels, all for €2-5. Open July-Sept. M-F 8:30am-9pm, Sa-Su 9:30am-6pm. Oct.-May M-Sa 8:30am-6pm. ❶

Off the Square, Main St. (☎22281). Chefs Rory and Joe Flaherty prove that Irish cuisine can have flare and flavor. At €20, the 4-course Early Bird Special (5-6:30pm) is an enjoyable dining experience. Open daily for breakfast, lunch, and dinner 9am-10pm. ❸

Mitchell's, Market St. (☎21867). The fresh fish (from €20) is pricey, but it melts in your mouth. Atmosphere not as lively as elsewhere in town. Call ahead to avoid crowds. Open mid-Mar. to early Oct. daily noon-10pm. ❸

E.J. King's, the Square (☎21330). Popular pub serves tasty food. Fish and chips €9. Breakfast served until noon (full Irish, €8). The restaurant upstairs serves upscale fare at higher prices 6-10pm. ❷

Jasmine Garden, Market St. (☎21174). Standard Chinese selections with plenty of vegetarian options. Takeaway available. Entrees €12-16. Open M-F 5:30-11:30pm, Sa-Su 5:30pm-midnight. ❷

✂ PUBS

Mullarkey's, Church St. (☎21801). Pool table, poetry readings, Th open mic nights and good impromptu music (but no food). Revelers sit on the floor when the chairs and pool table fill up. As the sign out front proclaims: "The *Craic* Begins at 6pm!"

Mannion's Bar and Lounge, Market St. (☎21780). A magnet for middle-aged tourists, this bar offers the best pint in town. Music starts at 10pm; summer daily, Sa in winter.

E.J. King's, the Square (☎21330). The largest and most popular pub in Clifden. Nightly live music in summer at 10:30pm. Opens at 10:30am; kitchen open 10:30am-9pm.

Tom King's Bar & Snug, the Square (☎21900). A quiet pub with an older crowd of local men. A relief from the louder E.J. King's next door. Open daily from 10:30am.

The D'Arcy Bar, Main St. (☎21084). Visit this gritty hole in the wall if you want to see old locals pay homage to their town's founder by drinking heavily. Live music on weekends. Open daily until late.

◎ ⚑ SIGHTS AND OUTDOOR ACTIVITIES

The 16km **Sky Road** is a lovely route for hiking, biking, or scenic driving. Starting just past the square, it loops around the peninsula to the west of town, paving the way to beautiful views of green hills and dizzying coastline cliffs. Bicycling is mostly enjoyable, though are a few strenuous climbs lead to the highest vistas. The whole loop takes four to five hours to hike. About 1km down Sky Rd., a sign points to the **John D'Arcy monument.** The small, house-like structure commemorating Clifden's founder isn't much to look at, but the summits above the site yield a bird's eye view of Clifden, the surrounding hills, and the water. Two kilometers down Sky Rd. stands what's left of **Clifden Castle.** Turn left at the stone entrance and follow the dirt road to the castle. Farther out, a peek at the bay reveals the site where US pilots John Alcock and Arthur Brown landed after they made the first nonstop transatlantic flight in 1919, on a bog near Ballyconneely.

One way to get acquainted with Connemara is to hike south to the **Alcock and Brown monument,** a model of a plane's wing erected in 1994. From Clifden, follow signs to Ballyconneely; when the road forks, turn right over the small stone bridge. A sign points you left to the landing site (there's nothing but bog there) and right to the monument. The hilled monument overlooks Clifden and Mannin bays. Those with wheels (of any kind) or the energy to hike should travel down the Galway road for about 9km to **Ballynahinch Castle** (turn right at the small sign, the castle is about 2km after the turn-off). The former home of the O'Flaherty chieftains, Grace O'Malley, and world-class cricketer Maharajah Ranjitsinji, the castle has been converted into a luxury hotel and restaurant. Daytime visitors are welcome to order lunch (€6-13) or dinner (€18-32; reservations required) or to stroll by the river and lake on the 180 hectares of the estate. The hotel has a river stocked with salmon and displays the day's catch each evening. (☎31006; www.ballynahinch-castle.com. Simple lunch 12:30-3pm. Dinner 6:30-9pm.) After visiting the castle, get back to Clifden on **Bog Road,** which invades a 12km stretch of bogland.

Open up to the magic of the bog by joining one of the inspiring tours led by Michael Gibbons, the archaeologist/raconteur of the **Connemara Walking Centre,** Market St. The tours explore the archaeology, folklore, geology, and history of the region and investigate bogs, mountains, and the Inishbofin and Omey islands. (☎21379 or 22278; www.walkingireland.com. Open Mar.-Oct. M-Sa 9am-9pm. Call ahead. Boat tours daily Easter-Oct.; call for info. Tours start at €15 per person.) For some adventure with a relaxed yet rugged guide, call Steve Gannon (☎087 234 9543) of Atlantic Hotel and The Old Monastery Hostel fame.

A family-style **Irish Night** takes place in **Clifden Town Hall,** at the base of the square on Seaview Rd., every Tuesday and Thursday night from late June through August; come from 9 to 11pm for performances by local artists (€5). In late September, during the annual **Clifden Arts Week** (☎21295; www.clifdenarts.com), dozens of free concerts, poetry readings, and storytelling sessions summon large hordes of tourists. Nobel Laureate Seamus Heaney has been known to turn up. On the third Thursday of August, the Connemara Pony Breeders Society hosts the country's prestigious **Connemara Pony Show** (☎21005; www.cpbs.ie) at the center's showgrounds, which are also the backyard of the Brookside Hostel. Over 4000 spectators watch Connemara ponies compete for top awards.

INISHBOFIN ISLAND

☎ 095

Inishbofin (*Inish Bó Finne*), the "island of the white cow," has gently sloping hills (flat enough for pleasant cycling) scattered with rocks, sandy beaches, and an excellent hostel. Due to recent emigration, a pervasive feeling of abandonment adds to the island's charm. During the peak summer months, however, returning islanders and small ferry-loads of visitors give the island a pleasant and not-over-touristed buzz of activity. Eleven kilometers from the western tip of Connemara, the 200 rough-and-tumble islanders keep time according to the ferry, the tides, and the sun, and visitors easily adapt to their low-key system. There's not much to do on the island except scramble up the craggy hills, sunbathe on the sand, explore the rocky ruins, and enjoy a pint and a warm welcome at one of the island's two pubs. It's a rough life, but somebody has to live it.

■ 7 TRANSPORTATION AND PRACTICAL INFORMATION. Ferries leave for Inishbofin from **Cleggan,** a tiny village with stunning beaches, 16km northwest of Clifden. Malachy King operates the **Inishbofin Ferry Island Discovery.** (☎ 44878; low season ☎ 45819 or 45894. 40min.; May-Sept. 3 per day; €15 return, students €13, children €8, under 4 free. Purchase tickets at the office near the Cleggan pier or on the boat.) There is a car park at Cleggan pier (€3 per day). **King's Bicycle Hire** (☎ 45833) rents bikes at the house directly across from the island's hostel on the east side for €15 per day to make sure people see the whole island before the return ferry. The **Community Resource Centre** (☎ 45861), to the left of the pier on the main road, provides information, detailed maps (€2.50), and **Internet** access. (Open M-F 9am-6pm. €1 per 10min.) The **post office** is inside Cloonan's Store, in front of the Community Centre. (☎ 45801. Open M-Sa 11am-1pm and 3-5pm, Su noon-3pm.) Summer **work opportunities** may be available at local places; get contact info from the center.

⌂ ACCOMMODATIONS. Kieran Day's excellent **Inishbofin Island Hostel (IHH) ❶** is a 15min. walk from the ferry landing. Take a right at the pier, bear left at the bottom of the hill, and ascend; the hostel is in the peach-colored building. Visitors enjoy a relaxed atmosphere, several pleasant common areas, and beautiful views. (☎ 45855. Sheets €2. Laundry €7. Dorms €15; singles €40. **Camping** €7 per person.) **The Galley B&B** offers attractive accommodations and home-cooked breakfasts served in the island's only cafe. (☎ 45894. €35 per person.) The people at the **Emerald Cottage ❷**, a 10min. walk west of the pier, greet guests with baked goodies and a veritable museum of religious statuettes. (☎ 45865. €35 per person.) **Horseshoe Bay B&B ❷**, on the east end of the island, is still famed for a visit from Nicholas Cage (or a convincing lookalike) several years back. (☎ 45812. Singles €35-40; doubles €65.) Mary Day-Louvel of the **Lapwing House B&B ❷**, up the road behind the Community Centre, feeds guests through the winter. (☎ 45996. Reservations required in winter. €40 per person; discounts for families with children.)

⊡ ☒ FOOD AND PUBS. Cloonan's Store, the shack in front of the community center, sells basic picnic items and serves as the local post office. For a longer stay at the island's hostel, bring groceries. (☎ 45905. Open M-Sa 10:30am-6pm, June-Sept. Open Su noon-5:30pm.) **The Galley Cafe ❶** in East End Village offers baked goods and simple snacks in a pleasant setting. (☎ 45894. Open Apr.-Sept. 12:30-5pm.) **The Dolphin Restaurant ❹**, next to the Island Hostel, gets rave reviews for its highbrow cuisine of fresh seafood. (☎ 45992. Open daily 12:30-3pm and 5-9pm.) In summer months, the island's nightlife is vibrant and welcoming. An all-age group gathers at one of the island's two pubs most nights. Near the pier, **Day's Pub** (☎ 45829) serves up pool playing, drinking, and occasional evenings of music while its new big brother hotel provides a cushy lounge and flatscreen TV. Smaller, more sedate **Murray's Pub** (☎45804), in the Doonmore Restaurant and Hotel 15min. west of the pier, fills with local farmers around 2pm for good gab and grub.

◙ **SIGHTS.** Days on Inishbofin are best spent meandering through the rocks and wildflowers of the island's four peninsulas. Most good spots are accessible by paths; try not to trespass on the many private plots. Each peninsula warrants about two hours of exploration. East of the hostel lie the barely existent ruins of 7th-century **Colman's Abbey.** The endangered corncrake has decided to nest in the graveyard, so the grass is uncut and visitors can no longer enter. Farther out, a conservation area encompasses beaches and East End Village (a small collection of houses). Spectacular views reward those who scramble up nearby **Knock Hill.** A short distance off the mainland, **Bishop's Rock** is visible at low tide. On the other side of the island, to the west of the pier, is the **Cromwellian Fort and Castle,** which was used to hold prisoners before they were transported to the West Indies.

The ragged northeast peninsula is great for **bird watchers:** gulls, cornets, shags, and peregrine falcons fish among the cliffs and coves. Inishbofin provides a perfect habitat for the corncrake, a bird near extinction everywhere except in Seamus Heaney's poems. Modern farming and development on the island have reduced the ground-nesting bird's population to mere hundreds where it used to thrive in the tens of thousands. Fish swim in the clear water off two massive blowholes, and small land masses called **The Stags** tower offshore. The tidal causeway that connects The Stags to the mainland during low tide is extremely dangerous—stick to the shore proper. **Trá Gheal** ("Silvery Beach") stretches along the northwest peninsula, but swimming there is dangerous. Off to the west is Inishark, an island inhabited by sheep and seals. The seals are most visible during their date-and-mate season in September and October. Archaeologist Michael Gibbons, of the **Connemara Walking Centre** in Clifden (p. 392), offers tours focusing on Inishbofin's history and ecology. Leo Hallissey's fantastic five-day **Connemara Summer School** (☎43443; lfrack@eircom.net) brings artists, scientists, and interested amateurs to study the island's archaeology and ecology. (Tuition €150 for 5 days not including accommodations or food; book at least a month in advance.)

INISHTURK ISLAND (INIS TOIRC)   ☎098

Inishturk (pop. 90), a small, rounded peak rising 182m out of the ocean between Inishbofin and Clare Island, has more spectacular walks and views than either of its more populated neighbors. Lobstering and sheep-raising are the principle sources of income on the island, and in season a fresh lobster dinner can be enjoyed at most of the island B&Bs. Consult locals for directions to the ◙**Sea Cliffs,** a 30min. hike that will not disappoint. You'd never guess it now, but before the Famine, the island teemed with a population of nearly 800. These days, Inishturk appears virtually undiscovered. Those attempting an expedition to Inishturk should bring adequate supplies and a good book. There are no budget restaurants on the island, but the three B&Bs serve enormous home-cooked meals. **Concannon's B&B ❷** is a colorful house just off the pier with vibrant rooms and a flower garden. (☎45610. €35 per person, with dinner €55.) Guests at Mary Heanues' **Ocean View ❷,** up the road from Concannon's, heartily applaud their fantastic meals and rooms. (☎45520. €35 per person, with dinner €55.) **Teach Abhainn ❸** lies far from the pier but close to the island's most striking scenery. (☎45510. €40 per person. 4-course dinner €25, main course only €15.) A 15min. walk up from the pier, the **Community Centre** (☎45655) serves as the town **pub** and hosts trad sessions on Saturday nights from May to September. (Open June-Aug. 1pm-12:30am; Sept.-May 8pm-12:30am.) The island hosts three festivals: **traditional music** during the third week in June, a **regatta** during the third week in July, and a **pilgrimage festival** on August 15th, on which islanders and tourists travel to nearby, deserted Caher Island to visit original 7th-century stations (carvings) of the cross. For **tourist information**, call the informative staff of the **Inishturk Development Office** (☎45778 or ☎45862). From mid-May to mid-September, John Heanue's Atlantic Queen departs **Roonagh Quay** daily at 11am; the return trip departs Inishturk at 5:30pm. (☎45541 or ☎08620 29670. €25 return; buy tickets on the boat.) For transport to and from Roonagh Quay, check with **Port Cabs** (☎087 220 2123).

LETTERFRACK (LEITIR FRAIC)   ☎095

Perched at the crossroads of N59 and the Rinvyle road, Letterfrack compensates for its lack of size with its bevy of exciting sights and attractions. Three pubs and a legendary hostel line the town's center while Kylemore Abbey and Connemara National Park are nearby daytrips. The road from Letterfrack to Leenane passes **Kylemore Abbey,** a looming castle in the shadow of a rocky outcropping. After the castle's completion in 1871 by British Industrialist Mitchell Henry, the extravagant (and nearly bankrupt) Duke of Manchester sold it to Benedictine nuns in 1920. The sisters have lived there ever since, and they run a small girls' boarding school; 5th- and 6th-year boarders live on the second floor of the Abbey, which is closed to visitors. The small neo-Gothic **church,** a 10min. lakeside stroll from the abbey, has an arrestingly beautiful interior. Above the castle a ledge, reached by clambering up a rocky path, affords an exquisite view of the lake. Shuttle buses to the restored 2.4 hectare **Victorian Walled Garden** depart every 10min. A plot of local and tropical plants is a lovely complement to the looming mountains. Since the fees for the garden and abbey have been combined, Kylemore is best visited on a day with good weather and unlimited time for walking. (☎41146. €12, students €17, children free. Open Apr.-Sept., 9am-6pm. Last shuttle to gardens 4:45pm).

Visitors prepared for some fishy business should head to Derryinver's **Ocean's Alive,** otherwise known as the Ocean and Country Museum, a 3km drive north of Letterfrack on the Rinvyle road opposite the direction to the hostel. The museum exhibits shells, seal skulls, fish, pictures of local birds, models of curragh boats, and other relics of a barely extant fishing culture. The museum's own *Queen of Connemara* cruises thrice daily for a 1hr. **seal- and deserted island-viewing expedition** in Ballynakill Harbour. **Angling trips** (2½hr.) depart Derryinver pier at 10am and 6pm and provide all necessary equipment for you to catch a lunker. (☎43473. Open Mar.-Sept. 10am-6pm, Feb. and Oct.-Nov. 10am-5pm. Museum €6.50; students €5. Tours €17. Fishing trip €50.) Leo Hallissey of the Connemara Environmental Education and Cultural Centre has organized **Bog Week** (late May) and **Sea Week** (October) for 22 years. Based in Letterfrack, both include community and cultural events, sporting competitions, musical workshops, and sessions in the local pubs. A Connemara walk-about takes place at the end of Bog Week, and Sea Week offers themed lectures. (☎43443; lfrack@eircom.net.)

A brown signpost will signal you to turn at the intersection across from Veldon's for the ◨**Old Monastery Hostel ❶,** a truly unique accommodation that becomes far more than just a place to sleep. The sheer quantity of intriguing decorations, ranging from vintage instruments to skulls of various animals, keeps boarders entertained and slightly spooked. A peat fire burns in the lounge and bathroom, and framed photos of jazz greats hang in the basement cafe. A new patio bar trumps anything the bars down the street can offer. Owner Steve Gannon serves fresh scones and porridge for breakfast and takes guests on island explorations (€25). Ask Steve about **work opportunities.** (☎41132. Bike rental €10 per day. Free Internet access. Breakfast included. 6- and 8-bed dorms €15; 4-bed €18; doubles €40; **Camping** €10.) Fine pub grub, gourmet groceries, and friendly locals are found at **Veldon's ❷**, which fills at 10:30am and empties late, sometimes after a trad session. (☎41046. Store open M-Sa 9:30am-7pm, Su 10am-7pm.) The hardware store next to Veldon's has a Bank of Ireland **ATM** inside (open M-F 8:30am-6pm, Sa 10am-6pm). The **College Cafe and Pizzeria ❶**, across from Veldon's in the Connemara West Centre, serves breakfast until noon, pizza, and vegetarian snacks (pita of falafel with garlic and natural yogurt dressing €6) to several hundred woodworking students in the winter and to tourists in the summer. (☎41926. Open M-F 9am-10pm, Sa-Su 10am-10pm.)

The **Galway-Clifden bus** (mid-June to Aug. M-Sa 11 per week, Sept. to mid-June M-Sa 4 per week) and the summertime **Clifden-Westport bus** (M and Th 2 per day, Tu-W and F-Sa 1 per day) stop at Letterfrack. **Michael Nee's** private coaches provide two shuttles per day during the summer. Although *Let's Go* never recommends hitchhiking, hitchers report short waits on N59.

CONNEMARA NATIONAL PARK   ☎095

Connemara National Park occupies 2100 hectares of mountainous countryside and is home to a number of curious attractions, including hare runs and roseroot. The park's not-quite-solid terrain comprises bogs thinly covered by a carpet of grass and flowers. To combat erosion, the Park directors have constructed several trails that yield pleasant hikes of varying lengths and difficulty. The **Suffraunboy Nature Trail**, which features alpine views, and **Ellis Wood Trail**, which winds through an ancient forest, are both easy 20min. hikes. The pathway up ▉**Diamond Hill** offers a relatively difficult 2hr. hike that rewards climbers with glorious views of surrounding mountains, lakes, and valleys.

Guides lead free walks through the bogs (June M, W, F 10:30am, July-Aug. daily 10:30am), offer a free children's program (July-Aug. T-Th 11am-1pm), and present a lecture on Connemara ponies (July-Aug. M, W, F 2-4pm). The **Visitors Centre** and its adjoining museum team up with anthropomorphic peat and moss creatures to teach visitors the differences between hollows, hummocks, and tussocks. A 17min. slide show explains the park's ecology, elevating the battle against opportunistic rhododendrons to epic scope. (Every 30min.) The center's wealth of knowledge is limited, though, so head to Clifden's tourist office for better maps and instruction. The Centre has a cafe and picnic area for your gastronomic and aesthetic pleasure. (☎41054. Open Apr., May, Sept., early Oct. 10am-5:30pm, June-Aug. 9:30am-6:30pm. Free.)

More experienced hikers tend to head for the **Twelve Bens** (or Pins, depending on whom you talk to), a rugged range that stretches to heights of 730m. There are no proper trails, and the range is not recommended for novice hikers, but high-quality guides such as Tom Phelan's *Connemara Walking Guide* (€11.50) and Kevin Corcoran's *West of Ireland Walks* (€10), available at the Clifden tourist office, meticulously plot 18 short hikes through the Twelve Bens and the Maumturks. A number of smaller hiking routes are clearly marked by brown signs off N59 on the way to Leenane. For a scenic detour and an inspiring climb, take R344 along Lough Inagh and hike the **Mamean Trail** to **St. Patrick's Oratory**, from which he supposedly banished the snakes of Ireland. Hikers often base themselves at the **Ben Lettery Hostel (An Óige/HI) ❶**, overlooking postcard-quality scenery in Ballinafad, where the staff give good hiking tips. The turnoff from N59 is 13km east of Clifden. (☎51136. Dorms €16; students €14; sheets €2.) A hike from this remote but friendly hostel through the park to the Letterfrack hostel (p. 395) can be made in a day. **Cycling** the 64km loop through Clifden, Letterfrack, and Inagh valley is a great way to see the area, but it's only appropriate for strong bikers.

LEENANE (AN LÍONÁN)   ☎095

Farther east along N59, **Killary Harbour**, Ireland's only **fjord**, slices through coastal mountains and continues inland to the wilderness outpost of Leenane (pop. 47). Wrapped in the skirts of the **Devilsmother Mountains,** this once-populous region was reduced to a barren hinterland during the Famine. Today, the crumbled remnants of farms cover surrounding hills. The obscure movie *The Field* was filmed here in 1989. Those who rank among the movie's most enthusiastic fans note that Aasleagh Falls served as the backdrop for the murder scene. At the **Leenane Sheep and Wool Centre,** on the Clifden-Westport Rd., spinning and weaving demonstrations will answer all your wool-related queries. The center keeps a variety of different sheep, including one with four horns, and has a cafe and gift shop. (☎42323. Open daily Apr.-Oct. 10am-6pm. Call ahead for group reservations Nov.-Mar. €4, students €2, families €8.)

For a dose of excitement, head to **Killary Adventure Company,** 3km outside Leenane. It's Ireland's leading adventure company, offering everything from rock climbing to water skiing to helicopter rides. Archery, clay-pigeon shooting, kayaking, gorge walking, laser wargames, and bungee jumping are other exciting options that fill the void between historical sights. They also offer accommodations with a full breakfast. (☎43411; www.killary.com. Activities start from €20 per hr.; €45 per 3hr. session. 10% discount for groups of 10 or more. Rooms June-Aug. €35; Jan.-May and Sept.-Dec. €32.)

Across from the Killary Adventure Company and down a steep road sits the recently opened **Sleepzone Connemara ❶.** This complex offers 91 beds in modern rooms with continental breakfast, free Internet access and Wi-Fi, and access to a tennis court, kitchen, and bar. Shuttles (€7) to the Galway Sleepzone are available. (☎42949; www.sleepzone.ie. Prices vary by season, room size, and day of the week. Jan.-Feb. and Nov.-Dec. weekday dorms €13, weekend singles €35; Apr.-June and Sept.-Oct. €16/35; Mar. and July-Aug. €18/50). **Killary Harbour Hostel (An Óige/HI) ❶** perches on the fjord's edge 14km west of Leenane; the turnoff from N59 is marked. Aside from its unbeatable waterfront location, this hostel's claim to fame is that esteemed philosopher Ludwig Wittgenstein lived here in 1947. The building's hall windows and front door are no match for harsh harbor winds; pack warm clothes. (☎43417. Sheets €2. Bedroom lockout 10am-5pm. Curfew 11:30pm. Open June-Sept. daily, Mar.-May weekends only. Dorms €18.) If the hostel *craic* has become a bit much, cloister yourself in **The Convent B&B ❺,** on the northern side of town along N59. The dining room features stunning stained-glass windows from its previous life as a chapel. (☎42240. Open Easter-Nov. Doubles from €120.) There are few places to eat in Leenane, but **The Village Grill ❷** is a homey spot to grab a tasty sandwich. (☎087 670 9654; Open daily 10am until whenever they feel like dinnertime is over.)

COUNTY MAYO

Boggy plains and isolated settlements define the dramatic countryside of Co. Mayo. Its inland loughs, curved coastline, and sea cliffs provide a wealth of memorable scenery, including multitudes of majestic islands and small harbor towns. Westport is lively and popular, though more heavily touristed than other parts of the county. These days, Ballina is as famous for its nightlife as it is for its salmon fishing. The county's more remote, coastal destinations are particularly worth visiting. Achill Island, Enniscrone, and the Mullet Peninsula have beautiful beaches; Achill and Clare Islands and the Mullet offer opportunities for walking, hiking, and exploring the county's natural life and historical relics. There are superb hostels on the Mullet and Achill, and a decent campsite in Enniscrone, though budget options are quickly disappearing from Ballina, Westport, and Enniscrone.

SOUTHERN MAYO

Southern Mayo is not often-overlooked, nor is it offensively touristy. Cong can draw crowds, but generally the area seems like a destination between destinations, a place for backpackers to recharge (Westport) and explore (Achill Island) before trekking on. The area itself is rural and quiet, except for the brief moments of summer tourism, and public transport tends to be difficult year-round.

CONG (CUNGA)   ☎09495

Just over the border from County Galway is little emerald-green Cong (pop. 300). A ruined abbey serves as the gateway to the bubbling streams and shady footpaths that criss-cross the gorgeous forests surrounding the town. Nearby, magnificent Ashford Castle towers over the choppy waters of Lough Corrib. Were it not for two events in the mid-20th century, Cong might have slumbered into obscurity. In 1939, Ashford Castle was turned into a luxury hotel, luring the world's rich and famous to Cong. Then, in 1951, John Wayne and Maureen O'Hara made Cong the backdrop for *The Quiet Man*. Thousands of fans come each year to see the location of every scene, which provides locals with both bemusement and profit. However, Cong's unique natural beauty alone makes a visit worthwhile, and the walks, archaeological and historical sites, caves, and legends associated with them can easily fill a day of exploration. The village is technically an island; the River Cong flows underground from nearby Lough Mask, rises in Cong and encircles the village and flows into Lough Corrib, the largest lake in the Republic, with some of the best salmon and trout fishing in Europe.

🖪 🛂 **TRANSPORTATION AND PRACTICAL INFORMATION.** Buses leave for **Galway** from Ryans Hotel (M-F 7:20am and 1pm, Sa 8:40am and 1pm, €9, students €7) and from Ashford Gates (Tu and Th 10:25am), and to **Westport** from Ashford Gates (M-Sa 12:46pm and Tu 2:40pm €8/6.40). During the summer (late June-Aug.), additional service runs from outside Spar to **Leenane** (M-Sa 11:05am and 5:25pm) and **Clifden** (M-Sa 5:25pm; €9.80/7.70). There is additional service to **Galway** from nearby Ballinrobe; in the low season, taking a taxi to Ballinrobe for a bus may be the best option. *Let's Go* does not recommend hitchhiking. Because of infrequent transportation, some hitchhikers find rides at the nearby bus stop at Ballinrobe. **Taxis** and **bikes** are available through **Holian's bus and taxi service** (☎46485 or ☎087 238 6820. Open daily 7am-9pm. €10 per day. ID deposit.) The Cong Hostel **rents bikes** and **boats** on Lough Corrib. (☎46089. Bikes €12 per day; rowboats €40 per day, with motor €45 per day. Office open daily 8:30am-8:30pm.) There is an **ATM** inside the Gala Superstore, at the corner of Main St. and Circular Rd. (☎46485. Open M-Sa 7am-10pm, Su 8am-10pm.) Pick up meds at **Daly's Pharmacy,** Abbey St., by the tourist office. (☎46119. Open M-F 10am-6pm, Sa 10am-1pm.) Across from the tourist office are pay phones and public toilets. **Internet** access is available a few doors down from the tourist office at the **Hungry Monk Cafe.** (☎46866. Open Mar.-early Nov. M-Sa 10am-6pm. €1.50 per 15min., €5 per hr.) The **post office** is on Main St. (☎46001. Open M-F 9am-1pm and 2-5:30pm, Sa 9am-1pm.) The town's **tourist office**, on Abbey St., points visitors toward Cong's wonders, listed in *The Cong Heritage Trail* (€2.65). *Cong: Walks, Sights, Stories* (€4) describes good hiking and biking routes. (☎46542. Open daily Mar.-Nov. 10am-6pm. May be closed 1-2pm in winter). **Inquire about drinking the town's water;** in June 2005, the Health Service Executive issued an advisory after one person in the area tested positively for *E. coli* O157:H7 and several people experienced symptoms of gastroenteritis.

▟ ▞ ACCOMMODATIONS AND CAMPING. The Collinses run an impressive operation at the ▨ **Cong Hostel (IHH)** ❶, a large and immaculate compound on Quay Rd., 1.5km down the Galway road near the entrance to Ashford Castle. The playground, picnic area with barbecue, game room, and TV room (which shows *The Quiet Man* every evening at 8:30pm), and the new fairy tale-themed mini golf course next door keep guests entertained. The tremendous camping area sprouts its own little village every summer. (☎46089. Continental breakfast €5. Sheets €1. 14-bed dorms €13, 4-bed €18; doubles with bath €40. **Camping** with facilities singles €10; doubles €15. Showers €1.) Across the road from the hostel, ▨**Michaeleen's Manor B&B** ❸ (also run by the Collins family) offers comfortable, modern rooms with bath and DVD/VCR/TV, two elegant sitting rooms, a sauna, an outdoor hot tub, and a tennis court. The B&B's theme is *The Quiet Man*, with photographs and posters from the movie and rooms named after characters in it. (☎46089. Wheelchair-accessible. Singles €50; doubles €70.) The family also leases four-person **cottages** in town; inquire at the Cong Hostel. The **Courtyard Hostel (IHH)** ❶, on Cross St. in the small village of **Cross**, 5km east of Cong, offers a rustic farmyard setting, a wild field for camping, and great prices; those who like modern accommodations and comfort should skip it. (☎46203. Dorms €12; **camping** €6.) Signs for B&Bs fill every intersection, making them all too easy to find. **Inisfree House** ❸, on the road out of town to Maum, is a pleasant departure from the camera-happy tourist group in town. (☎46082; Singles €35; doubles €60.) For more scenic roosts, check along the main road between Cong and Cross. The star of this stretch is **Ballywarren Country House** ❺. The elegantly decorated rooms all have large baths, telephones, and complimentary sherry and chocolates. (☎46989; www.ballywarrenhouse.com. Award-winning candlelit French dinners €45. Rooms from €130. AmEx/MC/V.) Camping is free on **Inchagoill Island,** though it costs a bit to get there, and there are no facilities on the island (p. 387).

▐ FOOD. Get your basic items at **O'Connor's Spar Supermarket,** Main St. (☎46008. Open July-Aug. M-Sa 8am-9pm, Su 8am-8pm. Sept.-June M-Sa 8am-8pm, Su 9am-7pm.) At **Danagher's Hotel and Restaurant** ❷, on Abbey St., central location draws the locals for pints and billiards. (☎46028 or 46495. Kitchen open M-Sa 10am-9:30pm, Su noon-9:30pm. Sandwiches €4, entrees €10-21. Sa rock, Su DJ, Th trad session.) "Delicious" is the only word to describe the sandwiches (€7.50-8.50) and homemade desserts (€5) at the **Hungry Monk Cafe** ❷. Try the *panini* (€8) with apple, bacon, brie, and tomato chutney. (☎46866. Open M-Sa 10am-6pm.) **The Quiet Man Coffee Shop** ❶, Main St., mixes cinematic obsession with simple meals. A cheerful street-front counter gives way to a dining room, and both are freckled with film memorabilia. (☎46034. Sandwiches €4-6. Open daily mid-Mar. to Nov. 10am-6pm.) **Fresh Out** ❶, inside the Gala Superstore, sells cheaper lunch fare than the Hungry Monk and stays open for dinner. (☎46485. Sandwiches from €3.50, salads from €6, entrees €7.50-16.50. Open M-Su 9am-8:30pm.)

▐ ▐ PUBS AND CLUBS. Lydon's, Circular Rd. (☎46053), past the Gala Superstore, is the place to attend trad sessions from June to August. (Th, Sa, and some Su live music, mostly trad. The nearest nightclub is at **The Valkenburg,** a hotel in Ballinrobe; a bus (€10 return) picks groups up outside Danagher's Friday through Saturday at 1am and makes return trips until 4am. (☎41099. Cover €10.) Taxis take earlier clubbers to Ballinrobe for around €6-8.

◪ SIGHTS. Lord and Lady Ardilaun, former heirs to the Guinness fortune, were more interested in the scenery of Mayo than in the brewing of beer; accordingly, they spurned Dublin for ▨**Ashford Castle,** where they lived from 1852 to 1939. The original structure dates to 1228. Much of *The Quiet Man* was shot on its grounds, though the castle itself was used as cast housing, not scenery. Now the most luxurious castle/hotel in Europe, the palatial estate has played host to guests like Ronald Reagan, King George V, and, most notably, *Beverly Hills 90210* star Jason Priestley. A 1hr. introductory lesson at ■**Ireland's School of Falconry** (on the castle grounds) isn't for the squeamish, but partnering with the remarkable bird in a mock-hunt is an unforgettable experience. (Introductory lessons €60; www.falconry.ie) The castle **grounds** provide ample opportunity for exploration, from the manicured walkways of the gardens (look for the walled garden, on the way to the school of falconry), to beautiful **Lough Corrib. A swimming beach** sits 2km down the road by the lake. Most days, a guard sits at the estate's entrance from 9am to 5pm collecting a fee from non-guests (€5); entry is free when the guard isn't there, and visitors who tell the guard they are "inquiring about a room" can often get in free.

The sculpted head of its last abbot keeps watch over the ruins of the 12th-century **Royal Abbey of Cong,** near Danagher's Hotel. Founded in the 7th century, the Abbey burned down and was rebuilt five centuries later. (Always open. Free.) Ruairi ("Rory") O'Connor, the last High King of a united Ireland, retired to the abbey for the final 15 years of his life, after multiple losses to Norman troops. At the other end of the abbey grounds, a footbridge spans the **River Cong.** To the left is the **Monk's Fishing House,** a 15th-century stone structure from which monks caught their daily meals. The bridge from the fishing house leads to the lush **Cong Woods,** where nature-lovers can explore the seemingly endless paths and trailways. Follow the nature trail signs to run into the **Pigeon Hole,** the best bet for amateur spelunkers; the steep 61-step descent is worth making. *Cong: Walks, Sights and Stories* (available in the tourist office) outlines two cave walks that take more intrepid explorers to **Giant's Grave, Kelly's Cave** and **Captain Webb's.** The caves are pitch black, narrow, and often wet and slippery; spelunkers, however, should enjoy exploring the dark depths. To spelunk safely, wear waterproof clothing, bring a source of light and extra batteries, and tell a friend when you'll be back.

The Quiet Man Heritage Cottage, down the street from the tourist office, Cong's thatch-roofed imitation of Hollywood's studio replica of a Cong thatch-roofed cottage, provides a dose of fun for postmodernists and *Quiet Man* enthusiasts. Upstairs, there is a succinct timeline of the pre-John Wayne Cong and a 6min. video on the film, and an aerial photograph of Cong. In season, 1hr. tours depart at noon; tour-takers have the opportunity to re-enact scenes from the movie. (☎46089. Open daily 10am-5pm. €4, students €3.20.)

WESTPORT (CATHAIR NA MART) ☎098

If Castlebar is the official capital of County Mayo, Westport is its social and commercial center. Though some visitors find the town over-touristed, many enjoy the busy buzz that permeates the town's brightly colored pubs, cafes, and shops. Small, arched bridges dot the shimmering Carrowberg River, which spills out into Westport Harbor. Visitors may follow the river to the Quay, where they can sit outside and drink in both the rich sunset and a pint. For some pure, unadulterated *craic*, hustle back to Bridge St. Book accommodations in advance to avoid being left out in the cold; tourists eagerly flock to Westport year-round. If you find yourself tired of the constant crowd, take a daytrip to the peaceful Clare Island (p. 404) or Croagh Patrick (p. 403).

▐ TRANSPORTATION

Trains: Trains arrive at the **Altamont St. Station** (☎25253 or 25329), a 5min. walk up the North Mall. Open M-Sa 6:30am-6:30pm, Su 7:30-8:30am and 2-6pm. Train service to **Dublin** via **Athlone** (3½hr. M-Sa 7:10am, 1, 6pm; Su 8am, 2:30, 5:55pm. Day return €42; student €30.50; call for extended stay returns.

Buses: For bus schedules, contact the **Bus Éireann** Travel Centre in Ballina (☎096 71800) or the Tourist Office (☎27511). Student discounts on all tickets. Buses leave from Mill St. and head to: **Achill** (2hr., 1-3 per day, €11); **Ballina** (1hr., 2-6 per day, €10); **Castlebar** (20min.; M-Sa 11-15 per day, Su 6 per day; €4); **Galway** (2hr.; M-Sa 7-8 per day, Su 4 per day; €12.50); **Louisburgh** (40min.; M-Sa 2-3 per day, €5).

Taxis: Taxis are usually individuals with mobile phones and cars. Try **Vinny Moran** (☎ 087 258 8384), **McGuire's** (☎086 813 3933) or **Sid's taxi** (☎087 834 6148).

⚔🛈 ORIENTATION AND PRACTICAL INFORMATION

Bridge Street and **James Street** are the town's parallel main drags. At one end the streets are linked by **The Mall** and the **Carrowbeg River** (the North Mall and the South Mall run along either side of the River). **Shop Street** connects **the Octagon**, at the end of James St., to the **Town Clock**, at the end of Bridge St. **High Street** and **Mill Street** lead out from the Town Clock, the latter into **Altamont Street,** where the Railway Station lies beyond a long stretch of B&Bs. Westport House is on **Westport Quay**, a 30min. walk west of town along **Quay Road.** The original site of the town before it expanded down the river, the Quay is now a miniature Westport with its own set of restaurants and pubs. The N59 passes through Clifden, Galway, and Sligo in addition to Westport. *Let's Go* never recommends hitchhiking, though hitchers report finding rides easily.

Tourist Office: James St. (☎25711). Free town maps and information on ferries to Clare Island. Open M-Sa 9am-5:45pm.

Banks: Bank of Ireland, North Mall (☎25522), and **AIB,** Shop St. (☎25466), both have 24hr. **ATMs** and are open M 10am-5pm, Tu and Th-F 10am-4pm, W 10:30am-4pm.

Work Opportunities: Several of the accommodations in town hire travelers for short-term work, usually for min. 2-3mo. Most offer free housing and a stipend in exchange for reception, cleaning, or pub duties; some prefer prior experience. Inquire at **Old Mill Holiday Hostel** (contact Aoife Carr, ☎27045; oldmillhostel@eircom.net), or **Dunning's Pub and B&B** (contact Mary, ☎25161; info@dunningspub.com).

Laundry: Gill's Dry Cleaner & Launderette, James St. (☎25819). €1 per lb.; min. €6.

Emergency: ☎999; no coins required. **Police** *(Garda):* Fair Green (☎25555).

Pharmacy: O'Donnell's, Bridge St. (☎27347). Open M-F 9am-6:30pm, Sa 9am-6pm, every 4th Sa 12:30-2pm.

Internet: Dunning's Cyberpub, the Octagon (☎25161). Guinness and email kill 2 birds with one stone. Internet €1.40 per 10min., €8 per hr. Guinness €3.50. Open M-Th 10am-11:30pm, F-Sa 10am-12:30pm, Su 10am-11pm. **Gavin's Video and Internet Cafe,** Bridge St. (☎26461). Not much of a cafe (no food or drink), but cheaper than Dunning's. €1 per 15min. Cheaper if you bring your own laptop. Open M-F 10am-10pm, Sa-Su noon-10pm.

Post Office: North Mall (☎25475). Open M-F 9am-5:30pm, Sa 9am-1pm.

🏠 ACCOMMODATIONS

Westport has one hostel and a number of similar B&Bs on Altamount Rd. off the North Mall and along the road to the Quay.

Altamont House, Altamont St. (☎25226). Award-winning Irish breakfasts and hospitality have kept travelers coming back for 42 years. Cheerful owner Mary acts as your mother away from home. Rooms €35, with bath €40. ❸

Old Mill Holiday Hostel (IHH), James St. (☎27045), next to the tourist office. Conveniently located dorms in a renovated mill and brewery. Laundry €6. Kitchen/common room lockout 11pm-8am. Complimentary toast, coffee, and tea at 8am. Dorms €20. ❶

Dunning's Pub and B&B, the Octagon (☎25161). Though it's not the cheapest or most comfortable option in Westport, Dunning's is centrally located and its attached pub and cyber cafe will keep you entertained. Non-smoking rooms available. All rooms with TV and bath; €45. ❸

FOOD

The enormous **SuperValu,** located on Shop St., sells groceries. (☎27000. M-Sa 8:30am-9pm, Su 10am-6pm.) The **country market,** by the town hall at the Octagon, sells farm-fresh vegetables, eggs, baked goods, rugs, and crafts. Come early for a good selection. (Open Th 9am-1pm.) Restaurants, which primarily center around Bridge St. and the Octagon, cater to tourists and are generally crowded and expensive; book ahead after 6:30pm on weekends.

McCormack's, Bridge St. (☎25619), above the Andrew Stone Gallery. An upstairs hideaway with creative dishes and local art adorning the walls. Ravenous locals and tourists feast on open-face sandwiches, salads, and daily specials. Several vegetarian options available. Sandwiches €3.50-6. Open M-Tu and Th-Sa 10am-5pm. ❷

Sol Rio, Bridge St. (☎28944). Italian restaurant popular among local families both young and old. Reasonably priced lunches (€5-10) are delicious. Appetizers, available as main courses upon request, represent the most delectable of vegetarian options, but pizzas, at around €12, are well made and relatively inexpensive. Entrees €10.50-24. Open M and W-Su noon-3pm and 6-10pm. ❸

Gavin's Cafe, Bridge St. (☎087 932 8463). Cheap sandwiches (€3.50-5.50) and pastries (€1.50) served in a nice room. Open M-Sa 9am-6pm; takeaway after 5:30pm. ❶

The Asgard, Quay Harbour (☎25319; www.asgardwestport.com). Formerly The Lemon Peel at the Octogon, the new restaurant joins the bubbling array of Quay eateries and offers an elegant menu with items such as roast half duck (€19; entrees €10-22). Open daily noon-9:30pm; dinner menu 6-9:30pm. ❹

J.W.'s Bar, The Octogon (☎25027). Connected to the Wyatt Hotel, this pub has a delectable selection of open-face sandwiches and fresh seafood (€8-21). Although Bridge St. offers more lively pubs for nightly activity, J.W.'s will pour a good pint over dinner. Open daily noon-10pm. ❸

🍺🍸 PUBS AND CLUBS

Westport's pub scene tends to be overrun by tourists seeking great local *craic;* luckily for them, it's not hard to find.

🍺 **Matt Molloy's,** Bridge St. (☎26655). Owned by the flutist of the Chieftains. Knowing that Molloy's is one of the best-known pubs of the west, tourists flock to the landmark in droves. Officially, trad sessions occur daily at 9:30pm. In reality, any time of day is often deemed appropriate. Go early to get a seat.

Henehan's Bar, Bridge St. (☎25561). A run-down exterior hides a vibrant pub. Beer garden in back is ripe for people-watching. Twenty-somethings jostle eighty-somethings for space at the bar. Music F-Su.

The Porter House, Bridge St. (☎28014). Nightly trad graces this warm establishment and its stout-sipping middle-aged patrons. Open M-Th 1-11:30pm, F-Sa noon-12:30am, Su noon-11pm.

Cosy Joe's, Bridge St. (☎28004). After renovations added elevated booths and a projection-screen TV, cozy has given way to hip. A young crowd keeps the pub's 3 floors and 2 bars full. DJ Th-Sa. Open M-W and Su 10:30am-11:30pm, Th-Sa 10:30am-1am.

McHale's, up Quay Rd. from the Octagon (☎25121). Its excellent sessions are often overlooked by tourists, but not by friendly locals. Slightly older crowd. Trad W and F-Sa; country Su. Open M-W and Su noon-11:30pm, Th-Sa noon-12:30am.

Hoban's, the Octagon (☎27249). A cozy local favorite. Mature crowd. Trad Tu and F-Sa. Open M-Sa 12:30-11:30pm, Su 12:30-11pm.

The Jester, Bridge St. (☎29255). Trendy coffee house by day, enclave for the young and hip by night. Catch the big hurling match on the massive projection screen with crowds of locals. Open M-Th and Su 12:30-11:30pm, F-Sa 12:30pm-late.

Oscar's, Mill St. (☎29200), in the Westport Inn. Upscale bar becomes Westport's primary hopping nightclub on weekends. 18+. Cover €10. Open F-Su midnight-2:30am.

Castlecourt Hotel, Castlebar St. (☎55088). Young clubbers avoid the sedate hotel bar and head to the weekend **Nite Club.** 18+. Cover €12. Open F-Su midnight-2:30am.

SIGHTS AND OUTDOOR ACTIVITIES

Currently owned by descendants of pirate queen Grace O'Malley, Westport House has certainly changed since its oldest part was built by the British nobleman Lord Altamont in 1731. The small log flume, swan boats, train ride, and zoo entertain younger children, but the overcrowded and faded house struggles to hold the attention of older visitors and is hardly worth the price, especially since most rooms are closed off. The grounds are pretty, but they now require an entrance fee. (☎25430 or 27766; www.westporthouse.ie. 30min. walk from town—from the Octagon, ascend the hill and bear right, then follow the signs to the Quay. Open July-Aug. daily 11:30am-5pm; June M-Sa 11am-5pm only house and zoo open, Su 11am-5pm garden, house, rides, and zoo; Apr.-May Su 2-5pm (house and rides only); Sept. daily 2-5pm (house only). Full admission €24, house and gardens €11.50; students €18/9; children €12/6.50.) More interesting is the **Clew Bay Heritage Centre,** located at the end of the Quay. A veritable garage sale of history, this charming but crammed center brims with scraps from the past, including a pair of James Connolly's gloves, a sash belonging to John MacBride, and a stunning original photograph of the not-so-stunning Maud Gonne. The Centre also provides a **genealogical service.** (☎26852. Open Apr.-May and Oct. M-F 10am-2pm; June M-F 10am-5pm; July and Aug. M-F 10am-5pm and Sa-Su 2:30-5pm. €3, students and seniors €2.) The manager of the Heritage Centre also leads historical walks from the Town Clock in July and August. (1½hr.; Tu and Th 8pm; €5.20, children free.) Closer to the center of town is the more basic (and skippable) **Westport Heritage Centre,** housed in the tourist office (see **Orientation and Practical Information,** p. 401). The Centre details the history of the town's development and has an interactive scale model of Westport. (€3.50; students €2.)

Behind the tourist office is **Westport Leisure Park,** which houses a gym, large pool, jacuzzi, and sauna. (☎29160; westportleisure.com. Open M-F 8am-10pm, Sa-Su 10am-8pm. Pool and spa facilities €7.80; students €6.) For an alternative form of relaxation, catch a flick next door at the **Westport Cineplex** (☎24242. €8.50, M-Th students €6). Just outside town, **Carrowholly Stables & Trekking Centre** leads trots to the banks of Clew Bay. (☎27057; www.carrowholly-stables.com. €26 per hr.) In late August, celebrate the Westport Arts Festival (☎66502), a week of free concerts, poetry readings, and plays; or enjoy all things equine at the Westport Horse and Pony Fair Competitions (☎25616) in late September.

DAYTRIP FROM WESTPORT: CROAGH PATRICK

The path up Croagh Patrick begins in the town of Murrisk, several km west of Westport on R335 toward Louisburgh. From Westport, get on N59 South toward Leenane, then turn right on R335 at the small sign for Louisburgh, just after the stone bridge, or follow the coast road to the quay; take a right toward Louisburgh when it intersects with the R335. Buses to Louisburgh and Killadoon stop in Murrisk. (July-Aug. M-F 2-3 per day; Sept.-June M-Sa 1-2 per day.) Call the County Mayo bus information center in Ballina (☎096 71800) or the Croagh Patrick Information Center for departure times. A cab for 2 is cheaper (€8-10) and more convenient. Ballintubber Abbey (☎094 30709) is about 9.6km south of Castlebar on N84, and 35km from Croagh Patrick. The Croagh Patrick Information Centre (☎64114) is at the foot of the mountain on the Pilgrim's Path off R395 and has shower and locker facilities, a car park, bike lock-up, and public toilets.

Conical **Croagh Patrick** rises 765m over Clew Bay. It is a popular hiking destination due to its clear, though moderately difficult, trails and its religious and historical significance (3-4hr. round-trip). The summit has been revered as a holy site for thousands of years. It was considered most sacred to Lug, the Sun God and one-time ruler of the Túatha de Danann. After arriving here in AD 441, St. Patrick fasted for 40 days and 40 nights, argued with angels, and prayed for the conversion of Ireland's people to Christianity. Another tale holds that the Celtic chief Crom Dubh resided at Croagh Patrick until he was thrown by St. Paddy himself into a hollow at the mountain's base (see **Dun Briste,** p. 409, for an alternate account of Crom Dubh's death). Faithful Christians have climbed the mountain in honor of St. Patrick for nearly 1500 years. The barefoot pilgrimage to the summit originally ended on St. Patrick's feast day, March 17th, but the death of 30 pilgrims in AD 1113 during a horrendous thunderstorm prompted the pilgrims to move the holy trek to Lughnasa—**Lug's holy night** on the last Sunday in July—when the weather is slightly more forgiving. Others climb the mountain for the sheer exhilaration of reaching the summit and the incredible views it affords. Pilgrims set out for Croagh Patrick along the Tóchar Phádraig, a path from **Ballintubber Abbey.** Climbers park their cars or bikes in Murrisk and take a path that starts behind the privately run **Croagh Patrick Information Centre** which offers tours, showers, luggage storage (€6 per day; no overnight storage), food, a gift shop, and directions to the summit. *(☎64114; croaghpatrick@ireland.com. Open M-F 10am-5pm, Sa 10am-5:30pm, Su 10am-6pm.)* The 15th-century **Murrisk Abbey** and the **National Famine Monument** lie across the road from the Information Centre. At the Abbey, look for the chapel's east window, which once illuminated the altar of the small Augustian friary dedicated to St. Patrick. Just outside the car park entrance, the stone monument, a narrow ship with skeletons woven through its three cross-like masts, makes a dramatic impact in serene Murrisk Millenium Park.

CLARE ISLAND ☎098

Although only a 15-20min. ferry ride away, Clare Island seems to occupy an entirely different world from that of heavily touristed Westport. The main activities on the island are biking over the hilly roads that connect the island's few historical sites and hiking its two mountains. On a clear day, the views from the island are breathtaking. It is refreshingly free of crowded Westport's tourist traps. A tiny but lovely beach by the harbor provides an ideal location for a picnic. Many of the island's sites and its approximately 165 residents are connected to 16th-century pirate and clan chieftain Grace O'Malley, known locally as *Granuaile*, who ruled the land and the seas from her small **Tower House castle,** which sits above the harbor. The three-story structure is open and free for visitors. *Granuaile* died in 1603 and was supposedly laid to rest under the ruins of the **Clare Island Abbey.**

A free leaflet detailing five walks and hikes around the island is available at the **Bay View Hotel** and at the ferry ticket counters in Westport and Roonagh pier. The road from the harbor forks almost immediately; the left goes to the **Clare Island Abbey** (1km behind O'Malley's Foodstore). The O'Malley family crest depicts 15th-century hunting and fighting scenes and bears the inscription *terra maria pote O'MAILLE,* or "on land and on sea, the O'Malleys are powerful." Ask at O'Malleys if the man who keeps the key to the Abbey is available. At the end of the road, the cliffs of **Knockmore Mountain** rise 472m from the sea on the western coast, where the ruins of a Napoleonic **signal tower** still crumble.

A 2hr. walk along the road to the right of the Abbey runs along the east side of the island to the **lighthouse.** Ten minutes before the lighthouse is the **Ballytougheny**

Loom Shop and Demonstration Centre. The family of weavers spins and dyes its own wool. Sometimes they even let visitors try a hand at the spinning wheel. Longer workshops are offered to those who want a thorough introduction to the trade. (☎25800; bethmoran@eircom.net Open Apr.-Oct. M-Sa 11am-5pm, Su noon-4pm; Nov.-Mar. call ahead.) **Andrew O'Leary** (see **Clare Island**, p. 404), gives **minibus tours** of the island. (Inquire at bike shop. 1¼hr.; €40 flat rate.) After a few hours of trekking, relax on the harbor's pristine sandy beach and contemplate the novelty of becoming the island's 166th inhabitant—not counting sheep, of course.

At the harbor, a sign directs visitors to the **Clare Island Information Centre,** located on the second floor of the island's Community Centre, which has **public toilets** and laundry facilities. The Information Centre shows a 20min. video about the island and has a computer with **Internet** access. (☎29838. Open Tu-Sa 11:30am-3:30pm. €1.50 per 15min.) The €4 map of the island is probably unnecessary as similar maps are posted on billboards near the harbor. The island's **Development Office,** which hosts a tourism committee, can answer any questions about the island (☎25087 or 26525. Open M-F 9am-5pm).

Just past the beach, the hospitable **Sea Breeze B&B ❸** offers comfortable rooms with a view. (☎26746. Singles €40; doubles €70.) Those who want to see Clare's natural charm can stake their tents at the **Clare Island Camp Site ❶,** a grassy plot overlooking the beach. (☎26525. Showers and toilet facilities across the road at the Community Centre. €4.20 per person.) To the right along the coast from the harbor, the **Bay View Hotel ❸** has Clare's only pub and dining establishment. On windy days, the pub is a welcoming respite, and the homemade vegetable soup with brown bread (€4.50) is thick and delicious. (☎26307. Open daily 11:30am-late; kitchen open noon-5pm and 7-9pm. Entrees €6-27. Singles €45; doubles €80.)

O'Malley's Store, 2km along the west road from the harbor, stocks basic provisions and has a **post office.** (☎26987. Open M-Sa 10am-6pm, Su noon-4pm. Post office open M-F 9am-5:30pm, Sa 9am-1:30pm.) To get on and off the island, take either **O'Malley's Ferry** (☎25045; www.omalleyferries.com. July-Aug. 9 per day, May-June and Sept. 3 per day, Oct.-Apr. 2 per day; €15 return; students €12; children €7.50. Bikes free.) or the **Clare Island Ferry** (☎28288 or 086 851 5003; www.clareislandferry.com; 15min.; July-Aug. 5 per day, May-June and Sept. 4 per day, Oct.-Apr. call ahead; €15 return; students €13). Both leave from **Roonagh Pier,** 6km beyond Louisburgh and 29km from Westport. O'Malley's runs a **bus** from the SuperValu in Westport to Roonagh pier (M, W, F departs Westport at 10am, departs Roonagh at 6:30 pm; €10 return). Clare Island Ferry runs a bus from the tourist office in July and August (€10 return; call for schedule details). Once island-side, visit **O'Leary's Bike Hire,** near the harbor. (Hours vary; €10 per day.)

ACHILL ISLAND (ACAILL OILÉAN)

Thirteen kilometers of coastline, spectacular sea cliffs, and a rich archaeological history dating back to the Neolithic period make visiting Ireland's biggest little isle an unforgettable experience. It offers several certified environmentally-minded Blue Flag beaches, great hiking, driving, and cycling, although in good weather you can walk just about anywhere on the island. **The Atlantic Drive** circles Achill's southern peninsula, offering a spectacular first glimpse. Do not leave the Island without making the precarious drive to the end of the road at breathtaking ▨**Keem Strand** just past Dooagh. The 610m cliffs on the northwest face of Croaughan Mountain are thought to be the highest in Europe. Impressionist Paul Henry was inspired by the natural beauty of Achill Island, and especially by that of Keem Bay. In late July and early August, Achill hosts the **Scoil Acla** (☎43414; www.scoilacla.com), a festival of traditional writing, music, and dance during which local musicians and writers return to the island to give concerts and offer lessons and evening workshops for every level. The finale takes place on the last Saturday before the bank holiday (the first Monday in Aug.); this is the busiest weekend of the year on Achill with a celebration of banjos, flutes, and pipes. Registration for the week is €60-70, but some performances in local pubs are free.

Achill's tourist office is beside the Esso station in Cashel, on the main road from Achill Sound to Keel. (☎47353; www.achilltourism.com or www.visitachill.com. Open July-Aug. M-F 10am-6pm, Sa 11am-3pm. Sept.-June M-F 10am-4pm.) The office has information about Achill's many summer sessions, fishing competitions, and lectures; inquire about the **Yawl races**—weekly competitions among the island's 15 traditional sailboats. They can also inform you about the primary walking trails around the island and Mayo county. In July and August, a second tourist office sets up shop in Achill Sound. **Buses** run M-Sa mornings from **Dooagh** and **Keel** to **Westport** (approx. 2hr.); their routes vary, inquire at the tourist office for a schedule. On Sundays, a 4pm bus runs from **Dooagh** and **Keel** to **Westport** and **Galway**. If the buses are too infrequent, call for a **taxi** (☎087 243 7686), "no matter how short the trip." *Let's Go* never recommends hitchhiking, though it is relatively common during July and August.

ACHILL SOUND (GOB A CHOIRE)   ☎098

Development has shifted away from Achill Sound and toward the center of the island, leaving behind a somewhat gloomy village with little to hold visitors' attention other than a quirky religious establishment. Come for the 24hr. **ATM** (near SuperValu) and stay for the internationally famous stigmatic and faith healer Christina Gallagher who holds services at **Our Lady's House of Prayer.** The OLHOP is about 20m up the hill from the town's main church and is open for prayer daily 9:30am to 7pm, as is the gift shop (☎445691), which shows a 25min. documentary about Ms. Gallagher and her healing powers. The healer draws thousands to the town each year, but local opinions remain polarized—some profess faith, others only skepticism. About 9km south of Achill Sound (turn left at the first intersection), two ruined buildings stand in close proximity to each other. The ancient **Church of Kildownet** was founded by St. Dympna after she fled to Achill to escape her father's incestuous intentions. Nearby, a crumbling 16th-century tower house with memories of better days calls itself the remains of **Kildownet Castle,** reputedly built by Grace O'Malley, Ireland's favorite medieval pirate lass. Across the road is the creepy, deteriorating **Kildownet Cemetery.**

The **post office** has a **bureau de change.** (☎45141. Open M-F 9:30am-12:30pm and 1:30-5pm.) Find medicine and band-aids at the **Achill pharmacy.** (☎45248. Open M-Sa 9:30am-1pm and 2-6pm.) **SuperValu** sells groceries. (☎45211. Open M-Sa 9am-7pm.) Just before the bridge to Achill Sound, **Alice's Harbour Bar** flaunts a stonework homage to the deserted village, a boat-shaped bar, and a disco that spins Top 40 hits on Saturdays and many Fridays. (☎45138. Lunch menu €3-12; dinner €9-17. Kitchen open noon-8pm. Disco cover for non-residents €8.)

KEEL (AN CAOL)   ☎098

Keel is an old-fashioned resort town at the bottom of a wide valley. The sandy, cliff-flanked **Trawmore Strand** sweeps eastward for 5km, bordered on one side by the 466m cliffs of Minaun. Stimulated by a government tax scheme, hundreds of vacation homes have sprung up over the past three years. To the relief of locals who prefer their hills green, the pro-development plan has now ended. North of Keel, on the road that loops back toward Dugort, sits **Slievemore Deserted Village,** which (being deserted) is now populated only by the stone houses the Booley cattle ranchers used until the late 1930s. Resist the temptation to crawl up and around the existing structures: not only are many of them dangerously unstable, but doing so also incurs the wrath of the archaeologists who wander the site between June and September searching for ancient artifacts when the **Archaeological Summer School** hits town (see **Dooagh,** p. 407). Along the same road as the abandoned village is **Giant's Grave,** a megalithic multi-chambered tomb.

O'Malley's Island Sports, Costcutter Express, and the **post office** share a building in the town's tiny center. O'Malley's and Costcutter sell basic groceries, fishing tackle, ammunition, and offer bikes for rent. (☎43125. Bikes €12 per day, €60 per week. Open M-F 9am-7pm, Sa 9:30am-7pm, Su 10am-2pm.) Gorgeous vistas abound at the **Richview Hostel ❶,** at the far end of Keel on the way to Dooagh, which offers a taste of the town's laid-back, friendly, and slightly hectic lifestyle. (☎43462. Dorms €12; private rooms €16.) All of the spacious rooms of elegant **Roskeel House ❸** let you gaze out onto Keel Strand and the Minaun cliffs. (☎43537. Breakfast included. Singles €55, doubles €45 per person.) A less expensive B&B option is the popular **Achill Isle House ❷,** also on Keel's main drag. Be sure to book in advance for summer weekends. (☎43355. Singles €30; doubles €40.) On the beach, **Keel Sandybanks Caravan and Camping Park ❶** provides a sandy spot in strikingly beautiful surroundings to escape the B&Bs. (☎43211. Laundry €6. Electricity €2. July-Aug. €15 per tent; late May-June and Sept. €12.) Keel has numerous chippers and other restaurants. The relaxed **Beehive Handcrafts and Coffee Shop ❶** is a popular place to spend a sunny afternoon. The apple rhubarb pie is a slice of heaven. (☎43134. Open daily 11am-5pm.) **Calvey's ❸** offers upscale cuisine with fresh ingredients from Achill Island. (☎43158. Entrees €15-25. Open daily 12:30-4:30pm and 5:30-9:30pm.) **Graceland Chinese Restaurant and Takeaway ❷** serves seafood, meat, fried rice, and noodle dishes in a pleasant dining room. (☎43824. Entrees €8-14. Open Tu-Su 5:30-11:30pm.) The few pubs that have survived in this small town are quite popular, especially **Annexe Inn.** (☎43268. Trad on weekends.) The **Shark's Head Bar** in the **Achill Head Hotel** (☎43108) serves pints daily until 12:30am. On Friday and Saturday nights, people head to the **nightclub** out back (cover €10, open until 2am).

DOOAGH (DUMHACH) ☎098

Corrymore House, 3km up the road from Keel in Dooagh (DOO-ah), was one of several Co. Mayo estates owned by Captain Boycott, whose mid-19th-century tenants went on an extended rent strike that gave new meaning to his surname. In the center of town stands the monument recognizing **Don Allum,** the first man to row both ways across the Atlantic Ocean. Across the street at **The Pub,** Main St. (☎43109), you can grab a pint and see a picture of Allum's 1987 landing on Achill Island (the completion of his journey in an open, 6m plywood boat). A grueling bike ride over the cliffs to the west of Dooagh leads to ◪**Keem Strand,** the most beautiful spot on the island. Wedged between the sea and green walls of weed and rock, the bay was a prime fishing hole for Basking sharks, the plankton-eating second-largest fish in the world (up to 12m long), until the 1970s. Hikers who make it up the quick (30min.) but difficult climb to the sea cliffs at the rear of Keem Bay are rewarded with an impressive view of Croaughan Mt. and Achill Head tapering into the Atlantic Ocean and more ruins related to the Deserted Booley Village.

A seam of purple amethyst crystals runs under the Atlantic and bejewels **Croaghaun Mountain,** rising over Keem Bay. Most of the accessible crystals have been plundered, but local old-timer **Frank McNamara** still digs out the deeper veins with a pick and shovel and sells the haul at his home in Dooagh, which is marked by a small arrow-shaped "amethyst" sign and an enormous crystal rock near the front door. Stop in to see the extraordinary collection of purple amethyst, black smoky quartz, and jasper on display together with his still-functioning 120-year-old gramophone. Necklaces and earrings are available for purchase (☎43581). Dooagh is also home to the **Achill Folklife Centre**, which houses the Achill Archaeological Field School, offers rotating exhibitions (€2-3) and offers free lectures on archaeological research on summer evenings. (☎43564; www.achill-fieldschool.com. Archaeology courses start at €295 and include accommodations and transportation. Open June-Sept. M-Sa 9:30am-5:30pm.)

NORTHERN MAYO

Northern Mayo's Mullet Peninsula is one of the most remote and sublime destinations outside of Donegal and Northern Ireland. Ballina, the region's second claim to fame, is a magnetic commercial and social center that draws crowds from the farthest reaches of this expansive rural region.

BELMULLET (BÉAL AN MHUIRTHEAD) AND THE MULLET PENINSULA ☎097

On the isthmus between Broad Haven and Blacksod Bays, at the beginning of the Mullet Peninsula, Belmullet withstands cold winds and the constant threat of rain, providing a sheltered base for the intrepid traveler. Few tourists make it to the Mullet, and travelers who do journey here seek cultural immersion and solitude. The beaches are nearly empty, as is the soggy moorland covering the peninsula's western half. Thirty-nine different species of fish lure fishermen. For those set on authenticity and rustic relaxation, the Mullet is unbeatable. But be warned, this *gaeltacht* region provides no English translations on its Gaelic-only roadsigns.

☐ 𝌆 TRANSPORTATION AND PRACTICAL INFORMATION. An infrequent **bus** (€9.55) departs from **Ballina** and turns back at Belmullet, stopping outside McDonnell's Pub. (July-Aug. M-Sa 2 per day; Sept.-June 1 per day.) **McNulty Coaches** (☎81085; www.mcnultycoaches.com) runs local buses to **Belmullet** and **Castlebar** (1½hr.; M-F 8:30am, Sa 10am) and to **Galway** via **Ballina** (3hr., F and Su 6pm) and has coaches available for rent. **Lavelle's Taxis** (☎087 639 1278) will also take you to the peninsula. The **Erris Tourist Information Centre** is on American St., just past the Square. (☎81500. Open June-Aug. M-Sa 9:30am-5:30pm, Sept.-June 9:30am-4pm.) **Bank of Ireland** has a 24hr. **ATM.** (☎81311. Open M 10am-12:30pm and 1:30-5pm, Tu-F 10am-12:30pm and 1:30-4pm.) **The Computer Shop** in the Square has **Internet** access. (☎88878. €3 per 30min. Open M-Sa 10am-6pm.) The **post office** is at the end of Main St. (☎81032. Open M-Tu and Th-Sa 9am-1pm and 2-5:30pm, W 9am-1pm.) The friendly owner of the **Fishing Supply Store,** American St. (☎82093), across from the Tourist Information Centre, is the best source of information for angling and summer fishing competitions.

𝌆 ACCOMMODATIONS. The Mullet itself lacks budget accommodations, though the tourist office can direct you to a few scattered B&Bs. Fortunately, the village of **Pollatomish** (Poll a tSomais), 22.5km northeast on the coast road, has a hostel. ▨**Kilcommon Lodge Hostel ①** offers a true outdoors experience with whiskey pot lamps and good company over a fire fueled by bog logs. By bus, request a stop at the lodge on McGrath's coaches. Ask the owners or fellow travelers about the best hiking routes in the area. Steep mountains and a gorgeous bay provide the perfect setting for exploration and relaxation. (☎84621; www.kilcommonlodge.net. Breakfast €6; dinner €14. Dorms €12; private rooms €15.) The owners occasionally welcome young travelers into their home in exchange for help; call for more information. For a bed in Belmullet, try **Western Strands Hotel ❸**, Main St. (☎81096. Buffet and to-order breakfast included. Singles €40; shared rooms €30 per person. Discounts for children.) Church St., off the Square's roundabout, and route 314 into Belmullet have several other B&Bs.

◧▣ FOOD AND PUBS. The **Centra**, located in the Square, sells groceries. (Open M-Sa 9am-7:30pm.) **The Bay Bistro ❷**, in the Square, serves breakfast and lunch (☎82917. Open M-Sa 9:30am-4:30pm; hot food service ends at 2:30pm.) For dinner, try the pub at the **Western Strands Hotel** (open 7pm-late). Belmullet's pubs are in flux, but that certainly does not mean that the town has become dull. Impromptu good cheer abounds at **McDonnell's**, Barrack St. (☎81194). **O'D's**, Main St. (☎81372) is the lively spot for Mullet-goers in their twenties. **Lenehan's**, Main St.(☎81098) is a quieter pub for local flavor.

◩▨ SIGHTS AND OUTDOOR ACTIVITIES. Belmullet features great angling, and Bangor Erris and Glenamoy have the best lake and river fishing. Three companies charter boats for angling and island tours; contact Mattie Geraghty (☎85741), Michael Lavelle (☎85669), or Sean Lavelle (☎086 836 5983). Nearby **Cross Lake** is a popular spot for **fly fishing;** for details, contact George Geraghty (☎81492) or the **Fishing Supply Store** on American St. (☎82093). On a sunny day, these fishermen might also be willing to drop you off at one of the Inishkea islands. Anthony Irwin's **Dulra Nature Tours** offers fishing excursions, ecology courses, island tours, and birdwatching trips (☎85976 or 087 255 3623; www.dulranaturetours.com). The **Ionad Deirbhle Heritage Centre,** at the end of the peninsula in Aughleam, examines all aspects of local history. Its guides also provide info on hikes and boat rides in the area. (☎85728. Open M-Sa 10am-6pm, Su noon-4pm. €4.) To ride through Mullet on horseback, call Georgina of **Dubhailean Riding School** at ☎085 165 7304.

BALLYCASTLE, KILLALA, AND THE CEIDE FIELDS ☎096

Along R314 north of Ballina lies a series of sights and small towns. Though it's small and slightly decrepit, Ballycastle (Baile an Chaisil) provides a place to stop for lunch, provisions, or fuel. Ballycastle's main attraction is the **Ballinglen Arts Foundation,** which acts as a gallery and runs a local artists' colony. In return, each artist leaves behind a work for the foundation's archive. Each piece is a response to the artist's experience in the natural and social environment of Northern Mayo. Follow the brown signs labeled "Tir Saile" to enjoy this sculpture trail. During the summer, the foundation exhibits the works of its artists at the Ballinglen Centre, on Main St., across from Polke's. (☎43189. Open July-Aug. daily noon-6pm, or call for an appointment.) **Bus Éireann** runs from Ballycastle (pickup in front of Polke's Grocery Store and Pub) to **Ballina** via **Killala** (M-Th 8am and 4:55pm, F 8am and 5:20pm; €6.40). A mobile bank comes to town on Thursdays from 1:30-2:30pm (stops at Polke's and the top of Main St.); there is no ATM.

A 10min. walk up the hill from town on R314 leads to the **Keadyville B&B ❸**, where spacious accommodations and a glass-walled dining room encourage afternoons of lounging. (☎43288. Singles €28; doubles €40.) **Polke's**, on Main St., stocks groceries and has a small pub in back (☎43106. Open daily 8:45am-midnight). Pleasant **Mary's Bakery and Cottage Kitchen ❷** serves homemade baked goods, sandwiches (€3.50), and brown bread in an antique-laden nook at the bottom of the hill. (☎43361. Open M-F 10am-5pm, Sa 10am-3pm.)

The **Ballycastle Resource Centre,** housed in the Dun Briste Art & Crafte Shop has **Internet** access for €2.50 per hr. and sells beautiful photographs of Dun Briste. (☎43946. Open June-Aug. M-F 10am-5pm, Sa-Su noon-4pm; Oct.-May closed weekends.) The stunning ▨**Dun Briste** ("broken fort") sea stack, which separated from

WESTERN IRELAND

the mainland in 1393, sits off stoic **Downpatrick Head.** Legend has it that St. Patrick personally struck the land with his staff to exile and kill a pagan chief named Crom Dubh who refused to convert. On garland Sunday (the last Sunday in July), the town celebrates Mass on Downpatrick Head (call the Resource Centre for more information). Downpatrick Head and Dun Briste can also be reached via the **Coast Road** to Killala. The Coast Rd., though narrow and windy with blind curves, has spectacular views of Dun Briste and the ocean. Eight kilometers west of Ballycastle on R314, the ▧**Ceide Fields** (KAYJ-uh) excavation site allows visitors to view the oldest and most elaborate excavated Stone Age farmland in the world. A glass, steel, and peat ziggurat is built to resemble the rock formation visible off the coast and a peat-preserved 5000-year-old pine tree stands in the building's center (500 years younger than the settlement itself). The center displays, through exhibits, tours, and an audio-visual presentation, the dynamic relationship between Northern Mayo's first settlers and their environment. (☎43325. Open June-Sept. daily 10am-6pm; Mar.-May and Oct.-Nov. 10am-5pm. Tours every hr. Film every 30min. €3.70; students €1.30.) If the peat bogs you down, the center's observation deck offers a spectacular view of the 350-million-year-old **Ceide Cliffs.** Bus Eireann runs a day tour from Westport to the Ceide Fields that includes pickup in Ballina; call the tourist office in Ballina (☎71800) for details.

Thirteen kilometers south of Ballycastle, along the Ballina road, is **Killala** (Cill Alaidh), a charming seaport bustling with new residential growth and best known as the site of the French Invasion of 1798 (see **Rebellion and Union,** p. 53). At the peak of international revolutionary fervor, 1067 French soldiers landed at Killala to join the United Irishmen under Wolfe Tone in a revolt against the English (see **Bantry,** p. 273). Instead of a well-armed band of revolutionaries, the French found a ragtag bunch of impoverished, Irish-speaking, and poorly-equipped peasants. Undeterred, the combined forces pressed on, winning a significant victory at Castlebar before being soundly defeated by British forces at Ballnamuck. The **Killala Tourist Office,** in the Community Center on Ballina Rd., has local information, maps, and public restrooms. (☎32166. Open M-F 9:30am-6pm.)

BALLINA (BÉAL AN ÁTHA) ☎096

Ballina (bah-lin-AH), the largest town in Mayo (pop. 11,000) is a fisherman's mecca. Armies dressed in olive-green waders invade the town each year during salmon season (Feb.-Sept.) and venture waist-deep in the River Moy to wait for a bite. On Saturday nights, everyone within a 50km radius descends on the town seeking city-style *craic.* These weekly influxes of visitors shake up the humble hub, leaving it slightly hipper for the wear. Most pubs forgo trad for rock and blues, disco nights, jazz, and folk music; on summer nights, there is almost always live music in several venues around town. Ballina's main claim to fame is that former Irish President Mary Robinson (see **The Republic Today,** p. 57) grew up here.

▐ TRANSPORTATION

Trains: Station Rd. (☎20230), near the bus station. Open M-Sa 6:45am-6pm, Su 10am-6pm. To: **Dublin** via **Athlone** (M-Su 3 per day; M-Th and Sa €30, F and Su €42, students €21.50). From the station, go left, bear right at the fork in the road, and walk 4 blocks to the town center; several signs point the way there.

Buses: Kevin Barry St. (☎71800). Open M-Sa 9:30am-5:45pm. To: **Athlone** (11am, €19.10); **Dublin** via **Mullingar** (4hr.; 6-7 per day, 8am-9pm; €17.50); **Galway** via **Westport** (2hr.; M-Th and Sa 8 per day 7:15am-6:30pm, F 9 per day 7:15am-6:45pm,

Su 5 per day 8:35am-5pm; €14.40); **Sligo** (1½hr.; M-Th 4 per day 7:15am-4:15pm, F 5 per day 7:15am-8:45pm, Sa 3 per day 10am-4:15pm; €12.30).

Local Buses: To **Enniscrone** (first stop on the Sligo bus, 15min.; €3.70), **Ballycastle** via **Killala** (30min.; M-Th 7:25am and 4:15pm; F 7:25, 10am, 4:15pm; €6.40). To **Belmullet** (1½hr.; M-Th and Sa 6:10pm, F 6 and 9:45pm, Su 1pm, July-Aug. additional service M-Sa 1pm; €12.50)

Taxis: Call **John Murphy** (☎087 678 9103 or 087 232 3438). There is a **taxi stand** on Pearse St., in front of the AIB bank.

Bike Rental: Michael Hopkins, Lower Pearse St. (☎21609). €10 per day. Deposit €50. Open M-Sa 9:30am-6pm.

▣▤ ORIENTATION AND PRACTICAL INFORMATION

The cathedral is on the east bank of the **River Moy.** The **Upper Bridge** (closer to the cathedral) crosses to the west bank and the commercial center; the bridge connects to **Tolan Street,** which turns into **Tone Street.** This intersects **Pearse Street** and **O'Rahilly Street,** which run parallel to the river, forming Ballina's center.

Tourist Office: Cathedral Rd. (☎70848), on the river past St. Muredach's Cathedral. Open May-Sept. M-Sa 10am-1pm and 2-5:30pm. **Fishing Permits and Licenses** (€6-35) are available at the **Northwest Regional Fisheries Board** (☎22788), around the corner across from the bridge. Open daily 9:30-11:30am.

Banks: AIB, Pearse St. (☎01055. Open M 10am-5pm, Tu and Th-F 10am-4pm, W 10:30am-4pm), and **Ulster Bank,** Pearse St. (☎21077. Open M 10am-5pm and Tu-F 10am-4pm) have 24hr. **ATMs.**

Laundry: Gerry's Launderette, Garden St. (☎22793). Laundry €8. Open M-Sa 9am-1:30pm and 2:30-6pm.

Pharmacy: Ward's, Pearse St. (☎21110). Open M-Sa 9am-6pm.

Emergency: ☎999; no coins required. **Police** (Garda): Walsh St. off Pearse St., across from the AIB bank and taxi stand. (☎21422; open 24hr.)

Internet: Chat'rnet, Tolan St. (☎094 903 8474). €1 per 15min. Open "early 'til late."

Post Office: ☎21309. At corner of Bury St. and O'Rahilly St. Open M and W-F 9am-5:30pm, Tu 9:30am-5:30pm, Sa 9am-1pm.

▐ ACCOMMODATIONS

There are no hostels in Ballina, but B&Bs line the main roads into town.

Suncroft B&B, 3 Cathedral Close (☎21573; suncroftbb@eircom.net), behind tourist office and cathedral. Walk through car park and turn right. Far enough from town center to be quiet and close enough to be convenient. Bright rooms and a helpful owner. Singles €35; doubles €65. ❸

Greenhill B&B, Cathedral Close (☎22767), 2 doors down from Breda Walsh's Suncroft. Spacious rooms look out onto rose gardens in the back, and the cathedral and River Moy in front. Singles €35-40; doubles €60. Discounts for longer stays. ❸

Belleek Camping and Caravan Park, Killala Rd. (☎71533), 3km from town center toward Killala on R314, behind the Belleek Woods. Laundry €4. Open Mar.-Oct. Tents €8 per person; car or camper €14. ❶

Elm Grove House, Station Rd. (☎70330; pomahoney@eircom.net). Less elaborate than other B&Bs in town; offers cheaper rates and convenience to the train and bus stations as well as the center of town. Singles €32.50; doubles €45. ❷

FOOD

Tesco's, on Market Rd., stocks groceries (☎21056. Open M-W and Sa 8:30am-7pm, Th-F 8:30am-9pm). There are several fruit and vegetable markets, butchers, and fresh fish stores on **Tone, Market,** and **O'Rahilly Streets.** Greasy takeaway and diner fare is cheap and plentiful. For much less grease and a bit of extra cost, the pubs at many of the town's restaurants offer similar menus with lower prices.

Cafolla's (☎21029), up the road from the upper bridge. 1 of the town's 2 Irish diners. Diverse menu serves everything from omelettes (€6-7) to burgers (€3.60) to tongue-tingling milkshakes. Takeaway counter and restaurant open daily 10am-midnight. ❷

Chungs at Tullio's, Pearse St. (☎70888). Serves affordable Chinese and European dishes. Over 90 Chinese standards for €7-8.50 each. Open daily 12:30-11pm. ❷

Dillon's, Dillon Terr. (☎72230), down Pearse St. when it curves into Dillon Terr. and through a stone archway on the left. The most elegant dinner option in Ballina. Wideranging menu with appetizing fish options served at bar and restaurant (entrees €12-25). Outdoor seating available. Trad W nights. DJ F-Su. Pub serves food M-F 3-9pm, Sa-Su 12:30-9pm; restaurant M-Sa 6-10pm, Su 1-10pm. ❸

The Bard, Garden St. (☎21894 or 21324). A variety of heavy chicken and steak dishes. Upstairs serves food daily 6-10pm. Pub serves lunch (€9) and dessert specials. Entrees €10-23. Live music Th-Su; DJ F and Sa. Open M-Sa 11am-10pm, Su noon-9pm. ❸

Padraic's Restaurant, Tone St. (☎22383). A friendly greasy spoon with all-day full Irish breakfast (€9) and diner meals (€8-20). Open M-Sa 8am-8pm. ❷

The Stuffed Sandwich Company, Tone St. (☎72268). Busy lunchtime sandwich bar with a long menu. Hot and cold sandwiches €5-7. Open M-Sa 9am-6pm. ❶

PUBS AND CLUBS

The Loft, Pearse St. (☎21881). A subdued lounge and heavy atmosphere give rise to existential discussion with an older crowd. 3 floors and ample couch space facilitate lounging or rocking. Also serves as a B&B. Poker W 9pm; late bar F-Su.

Gaughan's, O'Rahilly St. (☎70096). Pulling the best pint in town since 1936. No trad—just lively chat over the black brew. Classy meals and snacks served noon-4pm.

Murphy Bros., Clare St. (☎22702), across the river, 3 blocks past the tourist office. A sophisticated and spacious pub for good 'ole boys to meet for dinner and a pint. Its conspicuous size attracts tour buses. Lunch noon-3pm, dinner 6:30-9pm.

Quattro, Pearse St. (☎22750). Ballina's trendy new spot trades traditional pub grub for more cosmopolitan fare. Sucessfully creates a chic bar/restaurant decorated with neon lights and modern art. Live music or DJ on weekends. Food 3-8:30pm. Open late.

The Broken Jug, O'Rahilly St. (☎72379). Large establishment with good service. Though more family friendly than some of Ballina's smaller pubs, it still manages to create an energetic atmosphere. Kitchen open noon-9pm. Open daily until midnight.

SIGHTS AND HIKING

Walking through the idyllic, bird-filled **Belleek Woods,** surrounding **Belleek Castle,** (☎22400) visitors often find it difficult to resist thoughts of mystical Narnia or Sherwood. Cross the lower bridge (just north of the tourist office), take the second right, and follow Nally St. (which becomes Castle Rd.) for 2km to the signposted turn-off for Belleek Woods. Farther down the road, a large map of the woods indicates the castle and additional sites of interest. To dull the pain of returning to modernity, stop in at the castle for a drink or a meal. At the back of the railway station is the **Dolmen of the Four Maols** (the "Table of the Giants"). The Dolmen, which dates from 2000 BC, is said to be the burial site of four Maols who murdered Ceallach, a 7th-century bishop. Turn left as you leave the rail station; signs for the Dolmen point up a small road; the walk takes about five minutes.

The lonely **Ox Mountains,** east of Ballina, are a haven for mountain bikers, with many dirt and asphalt trails criss-crossing the slopes. The 71km **Ox Mountain drive** traces the perimeter of the mountains and is well signposted from Tubbercurry (38km south of Sligo on N17). The **Western Way** begins in the Ox Mountains and winds past Ballina through Newport and Westport to Connemara. The Way then meets the **Sligo Way,** which continues toward Sligo. Tourist offices sell complete guides to both trails. **Coolcronan Equestrian Centre** hires out horses for woodland and riverside treks and offers riding instruction (☎58110). The annual 10-day ◪**Ballina Street Festival** (☎79814; www.ballinastreetfestival.ie) has been swinging through mid-July since 1964. Much of Co. Mayo turns out for the festival's **Heritage Day,** when the streets are closed and life reverts to the year 1910—greased-pig contests, straw-covered streets and all.

ENNISCRONE (INISHCRONE) ☎096

Gorgeous Enniscrone Strand stretches along the eastern shore of Killala Bay, 13km northeast of Ballina on Quay Rd. (R297). Rare sunny days see droves of Irish weekenders vying for real estate on the beach. Across from the beach, the family-run ◪**Kilcullen's Bath House** offers steam baths in personal cedar-wood cabinets and hot or cool seaweed baths in large tubs filled with sea water pumped from Killala Bay. The iodine-tinted water and dark green kelp of the seaweed bath coupled with the the gently rising steam relaxes even the tensest travelers. (☎36238. Seaweed and steam bath €20. 30min. massage by appointment €25. Open May-Sept. daily 10am-9pm; Oct.-Apr. M-F noon-8pm, Sa-Su 10am-8pm.)

Enniscrone itself is a lively resort town. There are more than 20 B&Bs in Enniscrone, but during the summer they can fill up quickly. Call the local **tourist office** (☎36746) to inquire about private cottages, which are often a better deal. The big draw of **Point View House B&B ❸,** Main St., may be its location, but kind Mrs. O'Dowd's tendency to appear with teapot in hand is another plus. (☎36312. All rooms with bath; €35.) **South Lodge ❷,** Pier Rd., offers simple rooms in an attractively restored 100-year-old home. Ask about the history of the house, the castle, and the burial sites in the hills just behind it. For a family of three, the upstairs bedrooms are the best deal in town. (☎36638. Singles €40; large multi-person room €50.) The **Atlantic Caravan Park ❶,** near the end of Main St. at the edge of town, has room for tents. (☎36132. Showers €2. Laundry €8. €15 per tent; €20 per caravan.) For victuals, head to **Tracey's ❶,** Main St. (☎087 682 3745). Run by Tracey herself, this cafe specializes in all-day breakfast and simple treats. (Open June-Aug. daily 9:30am-7pm; Sept.-May M-F 9:30am-5pm and Sa-Su 9:30am-7pm.) **The Pilot's Bar,** Main St., is situated in the middle of town offers another way to relax that doesn't involve seaweed. (Open daily until midnight.)

COUNTY SLIGO

County Sligo is best known as the birthplace and poetic inspiration of William Butler Yeats. The peaks of Knocknarea and "bare Ben Bulben" dominate the carved landscape, which hides the country's oldest megalithic tombs in its hills. In addition to the literary charms of Sligo Town, Sligo's Strandhill Beach attracts wet-suited surfers with its top-notch waves.

SLIGO TOWN (SLIGEACH)   ☎07191

Present-day Sligo Town feels like a cross between a city and a town, with the advantages and disadvantages of both. What the city lacks in cleanliness, it makes up for in sheer energy with cars and pedestrians flooding its narrow streets and cobbled walkways. On summer evenings, the shallow Garavogue River provides a home to both ducks and floating garbage. On weekends, Sligo Town's thriving nightlife is as diverse as any in Ireland, ranging from traditional bars that relish their silence to musical pubs that showcase nightly trad sessions to trendy clubs. The cultural life and cuisine are unimpressive, but a fleet of high-quality accommodations, services, and supplies make Sligo Town a good base for daytripping.

▛ TRANSPORTATION

Flights: Sligo Airport, Strandhill Rd. (☎68280; www.sligoairport.com). Open M-F 8am-5:30pm, Sa-Su 10am-5pm. To **Dublin** (45min., 2 per day, from €25. Book in advance).

Trains: McDiarmada Station, Lord Edward St. (☎69888). Open M-Sa 7am-6:30pm, Su 20min. before departures. To: **Dublin** via **Carrick-on-Shannon** and **Mullingar** (3hr., 3-4 per day, €26 day return).

Buses: McDiarmada Station, Lord Edward St. (☎60066; www.buseireann.ie). Open M-F 9am-5:30pm, Sa 9:30am-5pm. To: **Belfast** (4hr.; 2-3 per day; €24, students €18); **Derry/Londonderry** (3hr., 3-7 per day, €15.40/13); **Donegal** (1hr., 3-7 per day, €11/9); **Dublin** (3-4hr., 4-6 per day, €16/13); **Galway** (2½hr., 4-6 per day, €12.50/10.20); **Westport** (2½hr., 2-3 per day, €14.40/12).

Local Transportation: Buses to **Strandhill** depart from Lord Edward St., across from McDiarmada Station (20min.; M-F 7 per day 7:50am-6pm, Sa 5 per day 10:20am-6pm; €5 return). Buses to **Rosses Point** depart from McDiarmada Station and from Markievicz Rd. at the Bus Éireann sign (20min.; M-F 7 per day 8am-6pm, Sa 5 per day 11am-6pm; €5 return). Book online for occasional discounts.

Taxis: Ace Cabs (☎44444); **City Cabs** (☎45577); **McCormack Cabs** (☎55566); **Sligo Cabs** (☎55015). There is 1 **taxi stand** on Quay St., by Town Hall.

Bicycles: Bike rental is no longer available in Sligo. Most stores will sell bikes and buy them back again; however, this option probably isn't worthwhile unless you want the bike for more than a week.

◀✴ 🔢 ORIENTATION AND PRACTICAL INFORMATION

Trains and buses pull into **McDiarmada Station** on **Lord Edward Street**. To reach the main drag from the station, turn left onto Lord Edward St. and continue straight onto **Wine Street,** then turn right onto **O'Connell Street** at the post office. Take a left off O'Connell St. onto **Grattan Street;** more pubs, shops, and restaurants beckon from **Grattan, Market,** and **Castle Streets.** To get to the river, continue down Wine St. and turn right after the **Yeats Building** onto **Rockwood Parade,** a waterside pedestrian walkway. From here, the bridge leads to **Bridge Street,** where a right turn on **the Mall** leads to the **Model Arts Centre and Niland Gallery.** Rules of thumb are: O'Connell St. and Wine St. for shopping, Rockwood Pde. for breakfast and lunch, Grattan and Market Streets for pubs, and Pearse St. for quiet B&Bs. Quayside Mall off Wine St. has dozens of stores and a few cafes.

Tourist Office: Northwest Regional Office, Temple St. at The Lungy (☎61201). From the station, turn left on Lord Edward St., follow the signs onto Adelaide St., and around the corner to Temple St. Changes currency. Open July-Aug. M-F 9am-6pm, Sa 10am-4pm, Su 10am-2pm; Sept.-May M-F 9am-6pm; June M-F 9am-6pm, Sa 10am-3pm.

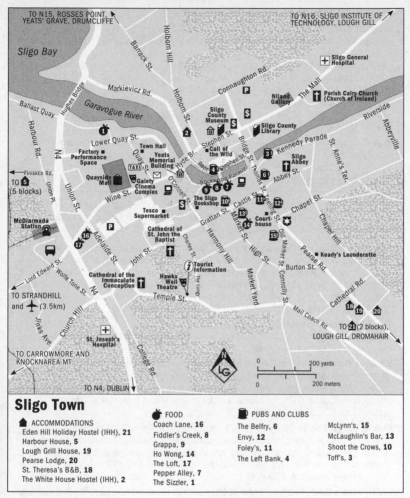

Sligo Town

ACCOMMODATIONS
Eden Hill Holiday Hostel (IHH), **21**
Harbour House, **5**
Lough Grill House, **19**
Pearse Lodge, **20**
St. Theresa's B&B, **18**
The White House Hostel (IHH), **2**

FOOD
Coach Lane, **16**
Fiddler's Creek, **8**
Grappa, **9**
Ho Wong, **14**
The Loft, **17**
Pepper Alley, **7**
The Sizzler, **1**

PUBS AND CLUBS
The Belfry, **6**
Envy, **12**
Foley's, **11**
The Left Bank, **4**

McLynn's, **15**
McLaughlin's Bar, **13**
Shoot the Crows, **10**
Toff's, **3**

Banks: AIB, the Mall (☎42157). 24hr. **ATM.** Open M 10am-5pm, Tu and Th-F 10am-4pm, W 10:30am-4pm. **Permanent TSB,** 16 O'Connell St. 24hr. **ATM.** Open M-Tu and Th-F 10am-5pm, W 10:30am-5pm.

Luggage Storage: At the bus station. Open M-F 7am-7pm, Sa-Su 10:30am-7pm. €2.50 per bag per day; additional €2.50 overnight.

Laundry: Keady's Launderette, Pearse Rd. (☎69791). Full-service. €2.75 per kilo; minimum €8. Open M-Sa 9am-6pm.

Emergency: ☎999; no coins required. **Police** *(Garda):* Pearse Rd. (☎42031).

Crisis Line: Samaritans, 3 the Mall (24 hr. ☎42011). **Rape Crisis Centre,** 42 Castle St. (☎800 750 780; M-F 10:30am-midnight). **Rape Crisis 24hr. Helpline** (☎800 778 888).

Pharmacy: Tohers, O'Connell St. (☎42896). Open M-F 9am-8pm, Sa 9am-7pm, Su noon-6pm.

Hospital: Sligo General Hospital, The Mall (☎71111).

Internet Access: Free at **Reference and Local Studies Library** (14 computers) on Bridge St. and **Stephen Street Branch Library** (6 computers); sign-up available (☎11675; www.sligolibrary.ie). Bridge St. branch open M-F 9:30am-12:45pm and 2-4:45 pm. Stephen St. Branch open T-W and F-Sa 9:30am-5pm, Th 9:30am-8pm. **Café Online,** Stephen St. (☎44892). €3.50 per hr.; students €3 per hr.; Su €2.50 per hr; Open daily 10am-11pm. **Cygo Sligo Internet Cafe,** 19 O'Connell St. (☎40082). €3.50 per hr.; Su and evenings after 7pm €2.50 per hr. Open M-F 10am-10pm, Sa 10am-7pm, Su noon-7pm. **Wi-Fi** available at **Four Star Pizza,** Rockwood Pde. (☎47711); €3 per hr. Open daily noon-midnight.

Post Office: Wine St. (☎59266). Open M and W-F 9am-5:30pm, Tu 9:30am-5:30pm, Sa 9am-1pm.

ACCOMMODATIONS

There are plenty of high-quality and low-cost hostels in Sligo, but they often fill quickly, particularly in mid-August. A collection of small B&Bs and one exceptional hostel lies just a brief 10min. walk down Pearse Rd. (N4).

Eden Hill Holiday Hostel (IHH) (☎43204; http://homepage.eircom.net/~edenhill), off Pearse Rd., 10min. from the town center and 20min. from the bus station. From town, turn right at the Marymount sign before the Esso station and right again after a block. Renovated to complement its Victorian charm with modern comforts, this spotless hostel offers mountain views and a respite from the commotion of town. Yeats often visited his cousin here. Dorms €14; private rooms €18. Parking available. ❶

The White House Hostel (IHH), Markievicz Rd. (☎45160). Take 1st left off Wine St. after Hyde Bridge; reception in the brown house. Convenient location with a water view. Key deposit €3. Dorms €14. ❶

Harbour House, Finisklin Rd. (☎71547; harbourhouse@eircom.net), a 10min. walk from the bus station away from town at the intersection of Finisklin and Ballast Quay Roads. Plain stone front and industrial surroundings hide a luxurious hostel with many TVs and free Wi-Fi. All rooms with bath. Limited kitchen hours. Dorms €18; private rooms €25-30. MC/V. ❷

Pearse Lodge, Pearse Rd. (☎61090; pearselodge@eircom.net). Stay here for the many plants, colors, and delicious breakfast options: french toast and bananas, bagels with cream cheese, and the omnipresent full Irish breakfast are but a few of the choices. Pricey rooms with twin and double bed, tea and coffee, and TV. Singles €45; doubles €65. Parking available. MC/V. ❸

St. Theresa's B&B, Pearse Rd. (☎62230; sainttheresas@eircom.net). Cozy home with shared rooms and TV keeps the rate lower than surrounding B&Bs. Provides hearty breakfast. Parking available. Dorms €32. ❸

Lough Gill House, Pearse Rd. (☎50045). Ivy-laced exterior leads to small but tastefully decorated rooms. A basket of toiletries, digestives, and tissues for the Irish cold is a thoughtful addition to every room. Singles €45; shared rooms €35 per person. ❸

FOOD

Tesco Supermarket, 14 O'Connell St., has a large produce section. (Open M 10am-Sa 10pm; Su 10am-8pm.) **Origin Farmers Market,** held within the Institute of Technology parking lot on the N16, has booths of fresh eggs and fish, organic produce, and fair trade crafts. (Open Feb.-Dec. Sa mornings.) Grab *Discover Sligo's Good Food,* free at many hostels and bookstores, for new restaurant listings.

🦪 **Grappa,** Rockwood Pde. (☎47734). Trade in the usual grilled sandwich for a flavorful *panini* or wrap (€7.50) or enjoy a simple breakfast for under €5. Vegetarian and gluten-free options available. Tapas bar with a menu mostly under €10. Coffeehouse open M-Sa 8:30am-6pm. Tapas bar open Th-Sa 6-9pm. ❷

Fiddler's Creek, Rockwood Pde. (☎41866). New, clean, and large. Pub and restaurant is a welcome relief from the claustrophobia of other local eateries. Sit at the long bar and enjoy the flatscreen TVs or grab a table and have an American burger with pineapple and homemade thousand island sauce (€13.50). Open daily noon-11:30pm. Kitchen closes at 10pm. ❸

Coach Lane, 1 Lord Edward St. (☎62417; www.coachlane.com). Amazing food blends local sensibilities with international flair. A meal might start with a goat cheese purse (€7), followed by monkfish sautéed in Chardonnay (€24), tiramisu (€6), and a hefty bill. Open daily 3-9:45pm. ❹

The Loft, 17-19 Lord Edward St. (☎46770), across from the bus station. A pleasant 2nd-fl. restaurant offers a diverse and appetizing range of pasta and meat entrees (€14-25) and starters such as the tiger prawns in filo pastry (€8.25). Attached to the Gateway Bar. Open daily 6-10:30pm, Su lunch 12:30-4pm. ❸

Pepper Alley, Rockwood Pde. (☎70720). A spacious, well-decorated deli/cafe popular for its prices and central location. Huge selection of basic sandwiches (€3-5) and baked goods. Stick with pastries in the morning instead of the disappointing Irish breakfast (€5). Open M-Sa 8am-5:30pm, Su 10am-4pm. ❶

The Sizzler, Quay St. (☎47682). Conveniently located next to a parking lot, this new Indian restaurant plates all of the country's classics for €11-17 but also strays into traditional Irish territory that should be left to the pubs. Open daily 5:30-11:30pm; lunch buffet noon-2:30pm. ❷

🍺 PUBS

There is something for everyone in the many pubs, night clubs and restaurant/bars filling Sligo Town's main streets. Events and venues are listed in *The Sligo Champion* (€1.50). Many pubs check IDs and post signs restricting clientele to 18+.

🦪 **Shoot the Crows,** Grattan St. Owner Ronin holds court at a pub that is delightfully gothic. Dark fairies and goblins dangle from the ceiling as weird skulls and crazy murals look on in amusement. Welcoming atmosphere banishes any potential anxiety. Trad Tu and Jazz W; frequent impromptu sessions. Open daily 3pm-late.

🦪 **Foley's,** 18/19 Castle St. (☎42381). The Foley family has transformed a decrepit street corner building into the friendliest pub in Sligo. Small and welcoming to all. Chat with the bartender and he'll have you sign the visitors book. Trad Sa. Open M-Sa 9:30am-11:30pm, Su 11am-11pm.

McLaughlin's Bar, 9 Market St. (☎44209). Small and pleasantly gritty. On weekends, the small room bounces with a jovial crowd, but less crowded weekdays allow patrons to admire the impressive collections of keychains, coasters, and other trinkets that decorate the venue. Open M-Th 5-11:30pm, F-Sa 5pm-12:30am, Su 5-11pm.

The Left Bank, 15/16 Rear Stephen St. (☎40100), across the river from the cafes of Rockwood Pde. Spacious, modern club with a 20-something evening crowd. Outdoor patio overlooking the river is one of the best spots in town. Dress to impress on weekends. Have lunch on the river for under €10. DJ F-Sa. Jazz Su. Nightclub 1st Sa of the month. Open M-W 11:30am-12:30am, Th-Sa 11:30am-2am, Su 12:30-11:30pm; food service ends around 5pm.

McLynn's, Old Market St. (☎60743). 3 generations in the making, with a 4th up and coming. Excellent spot for weekend trad with fiddling owner Donal leading the music

Th-Su. Reputed to be Lord of the Dance Michael Flatley's favorite pub. Open M-Th and Su 5:30-11:30pm, F-Sa 5:30-12:30pm.

The Belfry, Thomas St. (☎61250), off the bridge. Modern-medieval decor, with a big bell and bigger chandelier. 2 floors, 2 bars, 30 Irish whiskeys. Toff's nightclub, the Imperial Bar and Lounge, and the Embassy Restaurant are attached. Open M-Th and Su noon-11:30pm, F-Sa noon-12:30am.

Envy, Teeling St. (☎44721; www.envy.ie). Modern, pulsating club for the young "schoolies." Navigate its dark bar rooms, shake it on the dance floor, or retreat to the bathrooms to watch videos on flat-screen TVs. Cover €10. 18+. Bar open 10am-11:30pm; club W-Su 11pm-2:30am.

Toff's, Kennedy Parade (☎61250), on the river behind the Belfry. Geared toward the older crowd, the large, crowded dance floor reveals that locals *can* drink better than they can dance. Th-Su disco. Cover €10-15; €2 discount with card from the Belfry (see p. 418). 18+. Open Th-Su 11pm-2:30am.

◉ SIGHTS

Gray-stoned **Sligo Abbey,** a well-preserved former Dominican friary, is just down Abbey St. Built in the 13th century, the Abbey has well-preserved cloisters and ornate pillars. Most of the walls and many of the ceilings are intact, and visitors are free to duck in and out of the little rooms. Tours are unnecessary, but ask the front desk for the laminated guide sheet, which points out the abbey's more interesting features, including the love-knot carved on one pillar and the lofty reader's desk. (☎46406. Open Apr.-Dec. daily 10am-6pm; Jan.-Mar. call for weekend openings. Tours available on request. Last admission 45min. before closing. €2, students/children €1.) At night, the lit statues and golden clock tower windows visible from the Temple St. entrance to **Sligo Cathedral of the Immaculate Conception** make an impressive sight. Just beyond the Cathedral on John St., the **Cathedral of St. John the Baptist** looks like a medieval fortress in comparison. Built in 1730, the Cathedral of St. John has a tablet dedicated to Susan Mary, Yeats's mother. The **courthouse,** on Teeling St., was built in 1878 on the site of its predecessor.

▓**The Model Arts and Niland Gallery,** on the Mall, holds an impressive collection of Irish contemporary art in a sleek space. White walls suspend one of the country's finest collections of Irish art, including a number of works by Jack Yeats, W.B.'s brother. The gallery also hosts exhibitions of recent works and is home to an experimental black-box theater and cafe with free wireless internet. (☎41405; www.modelart.ie. Arthouse films weekly Sept.-May. Open Tu-Sa 10am-5:30pm; June-Oct. also Su 11am-4pm. Admission and gallery talks free; purchase tickets for performances at reception.) The **Sligo County Museum,** next to the library on Stephen St., preserves small reminders of Yeats, including pictures of his funeral. The collection includes first editions by the man himself, a few illustrated broadside collaborations between Papa Yeats and Baby Yeats, cartoons by Jack Yeats, and Countess Markievicz's prison apron. (Open June-Sept. Tu-Sa 10:30am-12:30pm and 2:30-4:50pm; Oct.-May Tu-Sa 10:30am-12:30pm. Free.) The smaller **Sligo Art Gallery,** in the **Yeats Memorial Building** on Hyde Bridge, has innovative exhibits of contemporary art and an annual exhibition in October of works by artists in Northwest Ireland. (☎45847. Open M-Sa 10am-5:30pm; closed bank holidays.) Also in the Yeats Memorial Building is a small, hastily assembled exhibit by the **Yeats Society.** Photos, snippets of writing, and a history of Yeats complement a brief film matching images of nearby countryside with his poetic descriptions. (☎42693. Open M-F 10am-5pm. Free.)

OUTDOOR ACTIVITIES

For a break from Yeats-worship, head to **Sligo Riding Centre** to horseback-ride through Carrowmore and up Mount Knocknarea, only 3km from Sligo Town. (☎61353. Reservations required. Open daily 8am-10pm. €25, children €20.) Relax at the **Regional Sports Centre** (☎60539), near Doorly Park.

Small brown quill-and-inkwell signs mark the **Yeats trail,** a route that hits most of the must-sees. **Discover Sligo Bus & Coach Hire** (☎47488; www.discoversligo.com) books half and full-day tours for groups of 12 or more. Ask at the tourist office for contact information of individuals who offer tours. Call for info on sunset cruises on the **Rose of Innisfree Boat,** which floats around Lough Gill to the tune of Yeats's poetry. (☎64266 or 087 259 8869; www.roseofinnisfree.com. Departs from **Parke's Castle** (see **Lough Gill,** p. 420) 5 per day Easter-Oct. €15, students €12.)

ENTERTAINMENT

A monthly *Calendar of Events,* free from the tourist office, lists festivals and other events in the northwestern Republic. The popular **Hawk's Well Theatre,** on Temple St. next to the tourist office, stages modern and traditional dramas, ballets, and musicals. (☎61526 or 61518; www.hawkswell.com. Box office open M-F 10am-6pm, Sa 2-6pm; 7:30pm on performance nights. Tickets €8-20, students/children €5-12.) The **Blue Raincoat Theatre Company** is a traveling troupe that puts on theatrical productions, workshops, and community art events. Their 85-seat black box theater, the **Factory Performance Space,** Lower Quay St., through the alleyway just before the road curves, hosts visiting musical, comedic, and theatrical performances as well as workshops. (☎70431; www.blueraincoat.com.) For Hollywood films, try the 12 screens of **Gaiety Cinema Complex,** on Wine St. (☎74002; www.gaietysligo.com. €8, matinees €6, children €6/4.50.)

During the first two weeks of August, the renowned **Yeats International Summer School** (see p. 85) opens some of its poetry readings, lectures, and concerts to the public. International luminaries like Seamus Heaney are regular guests. (☎42693; www.yeats-sligo.com. Applications available on website. Office open M-F 9:30am-5:30pm.)

DAYTRIPS FROM SLIGO

STRANDHILL PENINSULA

The turnoff to Carrowmore is on R292, which loops around the peninsula, about 2km west of Sligo. From town, follow the signs west from John St. Bus Éireann departs from Lord Edward St., across from McDiarmada Station, bound for Strandhill and Carrowmore (M-F 7 per day, Sa 6 per day, Su 2 per day; €3.40). Ace cabs (☎44444) services the peninsula, as do most of the taxi services in Sligo; a taxi to Carrowmore typically costs €8-9. Be sure to visit the Carrowmore Interpretive Centre ☎61534. Open daily Easter-Oct. 10am-6pm; last admission 5pm. Tours available. €2.10, students/children €1.10.

Best known for its 3km stretch of dunes, windy **Strandhill** stretches beneath Knocknarea Mountain at the southern edge of Sligo Bay. The surfing here is excellent for the wetsuited, but swimming is dangerous. Hang ten with an all-inclusive lesson from **Perfect Day Surf School.** (☎68464. Call owner Tom to arrange a lesson ☎087 202 9399. 2hr. lesson €30.) Those who prefer their seaweed heated can indulge in a **Celtic Seaweed Bath,** the ideal cure for all your aches and pains. (☎68686. Open daily 10am-9pm. 50min. bath and steam €20; for 2 €30. Aromatherapy, Swedish and Scalp Massage €32 for 20min., €52 for 50min.) At low tide, a causeway connects the beach to **Coney Island**. Nestled against Knocknarea Mountain, Strandhill Golf Course provides 18 picturesque holes. (☎68188. €40 weekdays, €50 weekends greens fee.) **Strandhill Hostel ❶**, on the shore road, warms surfers with its evening turf fires. (☎68313. Dorms €15; singles €18.)

An assortment of ancient graves gives visitors a history lesson at **Carrowmore**, 4km southwest of Sligo. The site had over 100 tombs and stone circles before modern folks cleared many away, but it's still the largest megalithic cemetery in Ireland. About 35 of the over 60 remaining tombs, some dating from 5400 BC, are open to the public. The **Interpretive Center** guides do their best based on the scant information available, but the self-guided tour is sufficient. (Open daily 10am-6pm. Tours roughly every hr. €2.10, students €1.10.)

█**Knocknarea** ("hill of the moon") perches 328m above the southwestern shore of Sligo Bay. The easy 20-40min. climb to the summit rewards hikers with a stunning 360° view of misty bays, heathered hills, and the mighty Ben Bulben Mountain. Queen Mebdh (or Maeve), the villain of the Táin bo Cuailnge, is reputedly interred in the 9x48m stone cairn on the summit; she stands upright, facing her Ulster enemies. The forested park on Knocknarea's eastern slopes has trails; there are several ways up, but on rainy days it's best to stick with the graveled paths, as the others can get slippery.

LOUGH GILL

The forested 38km road around Lough Gill, southeast of Sligo, runs past woody nature trails, Yeatsian haunts, a castle, and several small towns. It's flat enough for a wonderful bike trip from Sligo, but start early. Take Pearse Rd. and turn left at the signs for Lough Gill. Along the way visit Parke's Castle (☎64149). Open daily Mar.-Oct. 10am-6pm; last admission 5:15pm. 25min. tours on the hour. €3, students/children €2, families €8.

Beautiful Lough Gill, dotted with some 80 tiny islands, is bordered by gnarled mountains on one side and by farmlands and thickly wooded hills on the other. The striking outline of Ben Bulben completes the scene. Legend has it that the bell from Sligo Abbey has sunk into the depths of the lough; only the chosen (or delusional) can hear it ring from beneath the waves.

The first stop on the round-lough route is **Holywell**, a flower-strewn shrine resting near a well and waterfall; Catholics held secret masses here during Penal times. The main road reaches **Dooney Rock**, on the south shore near Cottage Island. Here, Yeats's "Fiddler of Dooney" made "folk dance like a wave of the sea." A forested nature trail around the rock and through the woods leads to views of **Innisfree**, an idyllic island that the young Yeats wistfully wrote about from London: "I shall have some peace there, for peace comes dropping slow/Dropping from the veils of the morning to where the cricket sings."

The next town past the Inisfree turnoff is the blossoming town of **Dromahair**, which shelters the **Creevelea Friary**, founded in 1508 as the Friary of Killanummery. Oliver Cromwell expelled the monks and confiscated their home in 1650. Since 1721, it has been used as a burial site. Dromahair is the farthest point on the route; from here, turn left onto R286 to head to Parke's Castle and back to Sligo Town.

Parke's Castle, a recently renovated 17th-century manor-cum-fortress, was built by English Captain Robert Parke in 1609 to protect himself from dispossessed Irish landowners. The remains of a moat and an earlier interior foundation of the O'Rourke family are still visible. The house now hosts an exhibit on traditional Irish dwellings and shows a film in English, French, and German about area sites. The 30min. tour gives an explanation of the castle's history and its careful restoration by local craftspeople, using only hand-held tools and materials available in the time of the original construction. Three kilometers from town, a left turn leads to **Hazelwood,** the park where Aengus wandered "among long dappled grass" in "The Song of Wandering Aengus." Its sculpture trail makes for a perfect picnic spot.

Lake Districts

DRUMCLIFFE AND BEN BULBEN: YEATS, YEATS, YEATS

Buses from Sligo to Derry/Londonderry stop at Drumcliffe. (10min. Summer M-Sa 9 per day 8:40am-6:45pm, Su 5 per day; winter M-Sa 5 per day. €5.50.) Returns sometimes require flagging down the bus at the Drumcliffe post office, since it's a request-only stop. Let's Go never recommends hitch-hiking, though it is reportedly painless. Glencar Lake is signposted 1.6km north of Drumcliffe on N15. Drumcliffe Church Visitors Centre has turned commercial: sandwiches and Guinness magnets predominate, but a free pamphlet is available. Cemetery grounds free. Lissadell House (call Angela Leonard at ☎ 087 629 6927; for more info visit www.lissadellhouse.com) is open daily May to mid-Sept. 11am-6pm; last tour 45min. before closing. €6, children €3. Grounds free.

Yeats composed the epitaph that was to be placed on his gravestone a year before his 1939 death in France: "Under bare Ben Bulben's head/In Drumcliffe church-yard Yeats is laid... /By his command these words are cut: /Cast a cold eye/On life, on death/Horseman pass by!" Yeats's wife, Georgia, didn't carry out his dying wish to be buried in France, disinterred a year later, and then buried next to Ben Bulben until nine years after his death. (Fun fact: When the two married, he was a venerable 52 years, while she was an innocent 15.) **Drumcliffe's Churchyard** is 6.5km north-west of Sligo off the N15; **Yeats' grave** is to the left of the church door. The 11th-century **ancient cross** and **round tower** across N15 are remnants of the 6th-century Christian site. One side of the cross depicts the crucifixion while the other features Adam and Eve, Cain slaying Abel, Daniel and the Lion, and Christ in glory. A few kilometers northeast of Drumcliffe, **Glencar Lake** and its majestic **waterfall**, mentioned in Yeats's "The Stolen Child," offer another excursion.

Farther north of Drumcliffe, **Ben Bulben** (often written Benbulben) **Mountain** protrudes from the landscape like the keel of a floundered boat. St. Columcille (see p. 59) founded a monastery on the peak in AD 547, and it remained a major religious center until the 16th century. The steep 527m climb is inevitably windy, and the summit can be extremely gusty, but intermediate hikers will have little trouble with the jaunt. Weather permitting, the edge of the cliff offers an unrivaled picnic site. Standing next to the 500m drop at the mountain's edge can be a humbling and beautiful experience that doubly serves as boasting fodder. From N15, follow the signs to Ben Bulben Farm. A dirt road breaks off to mark the beginning of the journey. Farmers own the land around the base of the mountain, and many object to people passing through; the helpful staff at **Call of the Wild** in Sligo Town (see **Practical Information,** p. 414) can direct you to the most acceptable access points.

Eva Gore-Booth and her sister Constance Markievicz entertained Yeats and his friends 6.5km northwest of Drumcliffe at **Lissadell House.** Countess Constance was the first woman elected to the Dáil and was second-in-command for the Easter Rising. Excessive tour bus traffic and a lack of unique features makes this remote stop of little interest. To reach the house from Drumcliffe Rd., take the first left after the Yeats Tavern Hostel and follow the signs.

INISHMURRAY ISLAND

A few individuals run boat services to Inishmurray (1hr.; €30-40 return). Because ground-swells can prevent a safe landing, most will not confirm departure until the day of the trip. Try Joe McGowan (☎ 087 667 4522) or Keith Clarke (☎ 087 254 0190). Rodney Lomax (☎ 66124) and Danny Boyle (☎ 66366) also run boat service to the island.

Across the water from Mullaghmore Head, ◪**Inishmurray Island** appears relatively flat and uninteresting, but those lucky enough to reach it know that a day on Inishmurray is one of the most worthwhile excursions in the area. The island is home to one of the earliest Christian monastic sites in Europe: a stone cashel stands in the middle of the island, enclosing a beehive hut, graves, several churches, and cursing stones. Stone houses that formerly belonged to Inishmurray residents (the last of whom left in 1948) run the length of the small island and are overgrown with grasses and purple flowers. Currently, the island's only inhabitants are a rich variety of birds and plant life. Be sure to bring rain gear, lunch, a camera, an empty bladder, and shoes with traction; there is a slippery clamber over the rocks once you land, and no facilities of any kind on the island.

Much has been written about the island's archaeology, history and folklore; inquire at the **Liber Bookshop** for specific titles. Joe McGowan, a local historian and author, maintains a website with pictures of the island and information about its history and folklore (www.sligoheritage.com).

COUNTIES ROSCOMMON AND LEITRIM

Rivers and lakes meander through untouristed Roscommon and Leitrim, which span a diamond-shaped area between Sligo and Center O'Ireland. Carrick-on-Shannon teems with pubs but remains relaxed, while Boyle is an excellent festival hostess with a soaring abbey. Motor vehicle abound in this region. Due to traffic that is predominantly fly-by and non-local, Roscommon and Leitrim don't always make for easy hitching. **Parke's Castle, Dromahair,** and **Crevelea Abbey** are over the border in Co. Leitrim but are covered in Sligo (p. 414).

CARRICK-ON-SHANNON ☎07196

Nestled on the grassy banks of the River Shannon, Carrick-on-Shannon (Cara Droma Rúisc) maintains a pleasant and low-key tempo. When tourists crowd their own city, Dubliners escape to this posh town to patronize its many shoe stores and hair salons. Despite its lack of sights or inexpensive activities, Carrick-on-Shannon has Gaelic football matches and rollicking nightlife that make the town a worthwhile stop on the way to or from better known destinations. The streets are unmarked, but the clock tower is all you need to orient yourself: Main St., Bridge St., and St. Georges Terr. converge at Market Yard Centre; Bridge St. continues down to the bridge that leads over the Shannon and into Co. Roscommon.

⊏🞂 TRANSPORTATION AND PRACTICAL INFORMATION. Carrick-on-Shannon **Train Station** (☎20036; booking Office open M-Sa 8am-4:15pm, Su 8:30am-noon and 2-9pm) is a 15min. walk southwest of town across the river. **Trains** go to: **Dublin** (2¼hr., 3-4 per day, €22), and **Sligo** (50min., 3-4 per day, €14). **Buses** (☎60066) stop in front of the Landmark Hotel on By-Pass Rd. (about 50m east of Coffey's Pastry Case) to: **Sligo** (M-Sa 6 per day, Su 5 per day) from the river side of By-Pass Rd., and **Dublin** (M-Sa 6 per day, Su 5 per day) from the hotel side of By-Pass Rd. Business cards for **taxis** line most phone-booths and the bulletin boards of local pubs and restaurants. The tourist office on the marina will help orient you in this signless town. (☎20170. Open Tu-Sa 9:30am-5:30pm; may be open July-Aug. M and Su 9:30am-5:30pm.) **AIB** on Main St. (open M 10am-5pm, Tu and Th-F 10am-4pm, W 10:30am-4pm) has a 24hr. **ATM,** as does the **National Irish Bank** on St. George's Terr. (open M 10am-12:30pm and 1:30-5pm, Tu-F 10am-12:30pm and 1:30-4pm), and the **Bank of Ireland** on Main St. (open M 10am-12:30pm and 1:30-5pm, Tu-F 10am-12:30pm and 1:30-4pm). Also on Bridge St. are **Cox's pharmacy** (☎20158; open M-Sa 9:30am-6pm) and **Gartlan's Cyber Cafe**, which has **Internet** access. (☎21735; open M-F 9:30am-6pm, Sa 9:30am-5pm; €1.50 per 15min., €6 per hr.) Free **Internet** access is available at the **Carrick-on-Shannon Library** on Park Ln., off Main St. (☎20789. Open M and W 11am-2pm and 3-8pm, Tu and Th-F 11am-2pm and 3-6pm, Sa 11am-2pm and 3-5pm.) Call to book a 1hr. slot in advance. The **post office** is on St. George's Terr. (☎20051. Open M and W-F 9am-5:30pm, Tu 9:30am-5:30pm, Sa 9am-1pm.)

⌐ ACCOMMODATIONS. Lough Key Campground ❶, just past the entrance to serene Lough Key Forest Park, provides a place to pitch a tent or park a caravan. It also boasts clean facilities, including laundry and hot showers. (☎62212. Showers €2. €10 per small tent; €20 per large tent or vehicle.) **An Oiche Hostel ❷** ("the night"), Bridge St., shares a small entrance and check-in desk with the local veterinary clinic just before the bridge to Co. Roscommon. The hostel is very tidy, with a kitchen and pleasant dining room. (☎21848. Dorms €20.) **The Four Seasons B&B ❸**, on Main St. in the center of town, has large single and double rooms, all with coffee and tea, TV, and private bath. For an additional €5, the owners offer a full Irish breakfast. (☎21333. €40 per person.) Other B&Bs line Dublin Rd., Station Rd., and the manicured lawns of St. Mary's Close.

◖◪ FOOD AND PUBS. Carrick-on-Shannon offers pubs, pastries, and decent sandwiches in abundance, but cheap dinners are hard to come by. **Campbell's Londis Supermarket**, Bridge St., stocks basic provisions. (☎21547. Open M-Sa 8am-9pm, Su 9am-8pm.) For a tasty sandwich, head to **Crumb's Sandwich Bar ❶**, Bridge St. (☎71846; open M-Sa 10am-6pm, Su noon-4pm), or to **Wheat's Sandwich Shop & Bakery ❶**, in the Market Yard Centre, by the clock tower (☎50525; open M-Sa 9am-6pm, Su 10-5pm; closed Su in winter). Try the breakfast *panini* (€4.75) filled with hot sausage, ham, egg, tomato, and tangy relish, with coffee (€1.50). **Coffey's Pastry Case ❶**, Bridge St., also has sandwiches (€3.75), but the real treat is relaxing in the second-floor seating area, enjoying a river view, and savoring a scone or pastry (€1.40) with a dollop of rich cream. (☎20929. Open M-Sa 8:30am-7:30pm, Su 9:30am-7:30pm.) Popular **Chung's Chinese Restaurant ❷**, Main St., tops Carrick-on-Shannon's surprisingly large Chinese food market with heaping portions of decent fare. Get takeaway, or spend a few extra euro to select from a slightly larger menu. (☎21888. Takeaway €9; sit-down €23. Open M-Th and Su 6-11pm, F-Sa 6pm-midnight.) **The Anchorage**, Bridge St. (☎20416), is a popular pub with a traditional feel and mixed crowd. Across the town bridge, the grassy beer garden at **Ging's** invites tourists to sit and watch the passing boats. (☎21054. Open M-Th 3pm-midnight, F-Sa noon-12:30am, Su noon-midnight.) **The Havana Bar**, Bridge St., offers a late bar with live music on Friday nights and a hipper atmosphere than the other local pubs. (☎23333. Open M-Th and Su until 11:30pm, F until 2am, Sa until 12:30am.) Carrick-on-Shannon's nearest nightclub, **Passion**, pulls in partiers from the whole county. It doesn't heat up until midnight, and Saturdays are the most fun. Minibuses (€3) depart from The Anchorage on weekends, and taxis are often available. (Open F-Su. 21+. Cover €5-10.)

◧ ⚑ SIGHTS AND OUTDOOR ACTIVITIES. At the intersection of Main St. and Bridge St., tiny **Costello Memorial Chapel** is, at 5x3.6x9m, reputedly the second-smallest church in the world. Sadly, the Church's interior is indefinitely closed to the public. **St. Mary's Church** (Catholic) sits prominently on the corner of Main St. and Church Ln. Farther up Church Ln., beautiful **St. George's Church** (Church of Ireland) has reopened as a heritage center and fully functioning church. With 41 well-stocked lakes nearby, **fishing** is a popular activity in the area. Licenses are not required; supplies are available for purchase in town. **Moon River Boat Tours** (☎21777; www.moonriver.net) offers daytime boat tours in a classy vessel (€12;

tours leave at 2, 3:15, and 4:30pm); on Saturday nights, the cruiser becomes a floating bar. (Board at Moon River Quay 11:30pm; call-back 1:45am. Buy tickets on board.) When Leitrim battles another county in Gaelic football at the **Pairc Sean MacDiarmada**, it's a must-see event. Ask at the tourist office or any local bar if there's a match on. (Tickets €10-30, students €10-15; pay at the field.) Pick up the *Leitrim Observer* (€1.50) at any news agent for other local listings.

Seven kilometers northwest of Carrick-on-Shannon on the road to Boyle, large signs lead to the 3.5 sq. km and multiple islands of **Lough Key Forest Park** (☎ 73122; www.loughkey.ie.) The park was once the center of **Rockingham Estate**, which burned down in 1957. A new activity center combines cheesy entertainment for children and a base from which to explore the beautiful scenery. The Lough Key Experience (€7.50, students €6.50; €10 deposit for headset) is a walking audio tour of the grounds. **Lough Key Boat Tour** (☎ 67037) offers 1hr. guided tours of Lough Key and its islands. (€10; children €5. Information available from tourist offices in Carrick-on-Shannon and Boyle. Park always open and free.) Nearby is **Lough Key Campground** (see **Accommodations**, p. 424).

BOYLE (MAINISTIR NA BÚILLE)   ☎07196

Settled on a river and squeezed between two lakes, hilly Boyle was once used by clans and troops as a strategic base. The modern explorer would do well to follow their example—Boyle contains numerous historical sights and has convenient access to nearby mountains, lakes, and parks. The Gothic arches of magnificent **Boyle Abbey,** built by Cistercian monks in the 12th century, curve over green lawns at the bottom of Main St. Its high arches and intricate Celtic carvings make it a worthwhile visit. (☎ 62604. Open Apr.-Oct. daily 10am-6pm. Last admission, 5:15pm. Tours every hr. €2, students €1; due to renovations, admissions are free until the work is completed.) In the early 1990s, the Roscommon Council voted to raze **King House**, Main St., to make room for a car park. Luckily for local historians, artists, and visitors, the town decided to restore the building instead upon discovering its sturdy structural base. Built by Sir Henry King circa 1730, the Georgian mansion served as a family home for 40 years and an army barracks for 140 more. Until 1922, it housed the Connacht Rangers, men and boys from the Connacht region who were recruited by the British Army and sent off to battle around the globe, including the 1915 Battle of Gallipoli in WWII. Today, King House contains four floors of historical exhibitions on the Irish kings, the Connacht soldiers, and the productive crafts. The exhibitions are interactive and entertaining (one involves fastening a woolen brat around your shoulders with a heavy metal brooch). It also contains the **Boyle Civic Art Collection** of contemporary Irish sculpture and paintings. (☎ 63242. Open Apr.-Sept. daily 10am-6pm. Free.) The Saturday morning **Origin Farmers Market** (10am-2pm) also takes place at King House. Late July brings the **Boyle Arts Festival** and with it a series of recitals, workshops, and exhibitions. (☎ 63085; www.boylearts.com. Tickets up to €20; full festival ticket €80.) On the road out of town toward Sligo, take a right to stretch your legs at the metal statue of the Gaelic Chieftain, built to commemorate the 1599 Battle of the Curlews. Climbing the horse for a photo shoot is not explicitly prohibited.

The nearest budget accommodation is the hostel in Carrick-on-Shannon (p. 423). However, more comfortable beds abound in Boyle's B&Bs. If you want the Abbey in your backyard, stay at the 170-year-old **Abbey House ❸**, Abbeytown Rd., which will house you in an elegant, antique-laden room. The spacious sitting areas have views of a babbling brook, while some of the rooms look out onto Boyle Abbey. Self-catering family cottages for four are also available. Book a week in advance during the summer. (☎62385; abbeyhouseboyle@eircom.net. All rooms ensuite. €35-40 per person; cottage prices vary.) Cheery **Cesh Corran ❸**, across from the Abbey, is a little rough around the edges with some slightly shabby decor, but the substantial, succulent breakfast and friendly owner will leave you with no regrets. (☎62265; www.marycooney.com. Singles €35; shared rooms €35 per person.) **Londis Supermarket**, Bridge St., stocks groceries. (☎62012. Open M-F 8am-8pm, Sa 8am-7pm, Su 8am-2pm.) **Stone House Cafe ❶**, on Bridge St., is a stone gatehouse turned intimate cafe on the banks of the river. (Vegetarian options available. Sandwiches from €3.25. Open M-Tu and Th-F 9am-6pm, W 9am-3pm, Sa 10am-5pm.) **King House Restaurant ❷**, within the gates of King House, offers tasty, convenient breakfasts and lunches. (☎64805. Food €6-10. Open M-Sa 9am-6pm, Su 9am-5pm.) Any of the pubs along St. Patrick St. or Main St. will provide heavy pub fare for dinner. For perfect pints and rousing trad most nights, everyone heads to **Kate Lavin's**, (☎62855) on Saint Patrick St.

Trains (☎62027), located a few blocks south of the town center, run to **Dublin** (3hr., 3-4 per day, €22.50) and **Sligo** (30min., 3-4 per day, €9). **Buses** stop outside the Royal Hotel on Bridge St. and go to **Dublin** (3½hr., 3-4 per day, €14) and **Sligo** (30min., 3-4 per day, €8). The **tourist office**, inside the gates of King House on Main St., has information on local sites and services, as well as a bus and train schedule. (☎62145. Open May-Sept. M-Sa 10am-1pm and 2-5:30pm.) **National Irish Bank,** at the intersection of Bridge St. and St. Patrick St., has a 24hr. **ATM.** (☎62058. Open M 10am-12:30pm and 1:30-5pm, Tu-F 10am-12:30pm and 1:30-4pm.) **Ryan's Pharmacy** is at the intersection of Saint Patrick St. and Main St. (☎62003. Open M-Sa 9am-6pm). **Internet** access is available at the **library,** in King House. (☎62800. Library membership with unlimited internet use €4; 10min. free. Open Tu and Th 1-8pm, W and F-Sa 10am-1pm and 2-5pm.) The **post office** is on Shop St., just over the bridge and past the bright yellow Royal Hotel (☎62029. Open M and W-F 9am-5:30pm, Tu 9:30am-5:30pm, Sa 9am-1pm and 2-5:30pm.)

NORTHWEST IRELAND

Northwest Ireland consists entirely of Co. Donegal. Among Ireland's counties, Donegal (DUN-ee-gahl) is second to Cork in size and second to none in glorious wilderness. Although its name means "fort of the foreigner," this county is the least touristed, least Anglicized, and most remote of the "scenic" provinces. Its landscape contrasts sharply with that of Southern Ireland, replacing lush, smooth hillsides with craggy, jagged coastlines and rugged mountains. Vast wooded areas engulf many of Donegal's mountain chains, making for some of Ireland's best hiking. Its coastline alternates between beach and sheer rock face, including the towering Slieve League, where the brave traverse Europe's tallest sea cliffs.

NORTHWEST IRELAND HIGHLIGHTS

CHAT with the King of Tory Island and view his artwork (p. 455).

LISTEN IN on Irish-speakers in the pubs of the Northwest gaeltacht (p. 447).

SIFT for amethysts on the raised beaches of **Malin Head** (p. 474).

WATCH weavers and glass-blowers at work in the Donegal Craft Village (p. 433).

COUNTY DONEGAL

Between performing time-honored traditions like fishing and the weaving of Donegal's famous tweeds, locals keep their days busy while retaining a laid-back attitude. Their profound friendliness is on full display in their unbeatable pubs, where the purest traditional music can be found almost any night of the week. Donegal's *gaeltacht* region is the largest sanctuary of the living Irish language in Ireland; it is a legacy of the county's historic resistance to cultural and political Anglicization and a testament to its relative distance from the Irish tourism machine. The Earagail Arts Festival in Co. Donegal distinguishes itself from other Irish arts festivals in its scope and remarkable selection of artists, musicians, and performers.

Although byways are largely devoid of drivers, hitchers report short waits on major roads, particularly those north of Donegal Town. *Let's Go* does not recommend hitchhiking. Many mobile-phoned cab drivers also cater to each region of the county. Donegal has public transportation, but only for those willing to wait. There is **no train service** in the county, and **buses** tend to hit smaller towns only once or twice per day, often in the early morning or late at night. Only a few towns besides Letterkenny, Donegal Town, and Dungloe **rent bikes.** When hopping on a bus, ask if any discount applies. Tourist offices and bus depots have schedules for **Bus Éireann** (Dublin ☎01 836 6111, Letterkenny 07491 21309, Sligo 07191 60066, Strabane 07491 31008; www.buseireann.ie). **Private buses** replace

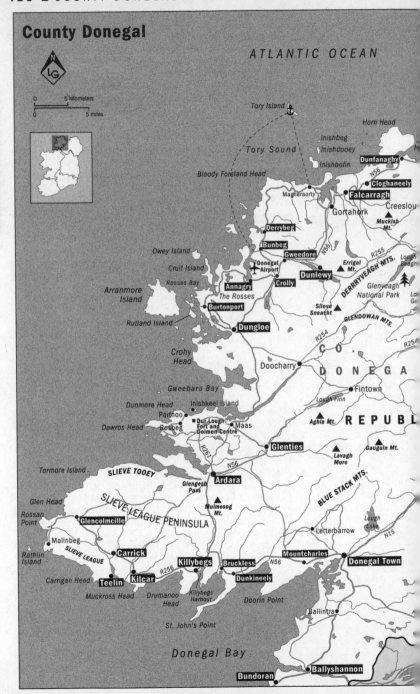

County Donegal

ATLANTIC OCEAN

Tory Island

Horn Head

0   5 kilometers
0   5 miles

Inishbeg
Inishdooey
Inishbofin

Dunfanaghy

Tory Sound

Cloghaneely
N56

Bloody Foreland Head

Magheraorty

Falcarragh

Creeslou

Gortahork

Muckish
Mt.

Derrybeg

Owey Island

Bunbeg

Gweedore
N56

Cruit Island

Donegal
Airport

Crolly

Dunlewy

Errigal
Mt.
R255

Lough
Beagh

Rosses Bay

Annagry

DERRYVEAGH MTS.

Arranmore
Island

The Rosses

Glenveagh
National Park

Lo
Ga

Burtonport

Slieve
Sneacht

GLENDOWAN MTS.

Rutland Island

Dungloe

R254

C O .

R254

Crohy
Head

Doocharry

D O N E G A

Gweebara Bay

Fintown

Dunmore Head

Inishkeel Island

Lough Finn

Portnoo

Dur Lough
Fort and
Dolmen Centre

Maas

REPUBL

Dawros Head

Rosbeg

Aghla Mt.

Glenties

Gauguin Mt.

Tormore Island

SLIEVE TOOEY

N56

Ardara

Lavagh
More

Glengesh
Pass

Muimosog
Mt.

Glen Head

SLIEVE LEAGUE PENINSULA

BLUE STACK MTS.

Rossan
Point

Glencolmcille

Lough
Eske

Malinbeg

SLIEVE LEAGUE

Carrick

Letterbarrow

N15

Rathlin
Island

Killybegs

R256

Bruckless

Mountcharles

N56

Donegal Town

Carrigan Head

Teelin

Kilcar

Dunkineely

Muckross Head

Drumanoo
Head

Killybegs
Harbour

Doorin Point

Ballintra

St. John's Point

Donegal Bay

Bundoran

Ballyshannon

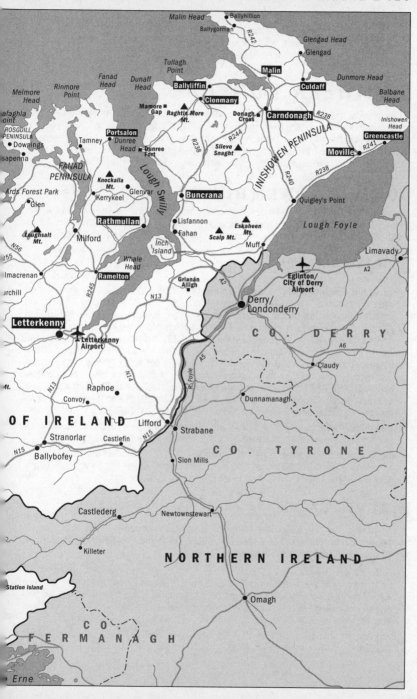

Bus Éireann for most of the major routes in Donegal. Their prices are reasonable and drivers will often make specially requested stops, but the buses don't always run on time. **Feda O'Donnell,** which carries bikes for free, runs along the Donegal coast, connecting the northwest with Galway and Sligo.

SOUTHERN DONEGAL

Without local train service and with buses running infrequently between Donegal town and most other Irish cities, many visitors travel by way of Sligo. Some take a direct bus (1hr.) to Donegal Town, while others stop to relax in the surfing town of Bundoran before continuing northward. The friendly region offers enough sandy beaches and *craic* to sustain visitors before they continue northward.

DONEGAL TOWN (DÚN NA NGALL) ☎07497

A gateway for those headed to destinations in the north and northwest, this sometimes sleepy town ignites on weekends with live music in most pubs, but it reaches fever pitch when festivals arrive. It can swell with tourists in July and August.

▐ TRANSPORTATION

Buses: Bus Éireann (☎21101; www.buseireann.ie. Under 12 ½-price and under 4 free; adult prices listed): **Derry/Londonderry** (M-Sa 7 per day, Su 3 per day; €12.50) via **Letterkenny** (€6.35); **Dublin** (3½hr.; M-Sa 6 per day, Su 7 per day; €17); **Enniskillen** (1hr.; M-Sa 6 per day, Su 5 per day; €9.70); **Galway** (4hr.; M-Sa 4 per day, Su 3 per day; €17); **Sligo** (M-Sa 6 per day, Su 4 per day; €12); **Killybegs** (30min.; July-Aug. M, Tu, Th, Sa 8 per day, W 7 per day, F 9 per day; €6.30) and **Kilcar, Carrick,** and **Glencolumbkille** (1-1½hr.; M, W, F 4 per day, Tu, Th, Sa 5 per day; €7). Bus Éireann stops outside the Abbey Hotel on the Diamond; timetables posted in the lobby. **Feda O'Donnell** (☎07495 48114) leaves for **Galway** from the tourist office (M-Sa 9:45am and 5:15pm; also F 12:45pm; Su 9:45am, 4:15, 8:15pm; €16) and also goes to **Dunfanaghy** via **Letterkenny** (both €8), **Sligo** (€7), **Crolly,** and **Gweedore.**

Taxis: McCallister (☎087 277 1777) and **Michael Gallagher** (☎08741 76600). Or catch one of the many that wait around for customers in the Diamond.

Bike Rental: The Bike Shop, Waterloo Pl. (☎22515), at the bottom of the hill, 1st left off Killybegs Rd. from the Diamond. Bikes €10 per day, €60 per wk. Open M-Sa 10am-6pm during the summer and intermittently otherwise (call ahead).

◀▐ ORIENTATION AND PRACTICAL INFORMATION

The center of town is called **the Diamond,** a triangle bordered by Donegal's main shopping streets. Three roads extend from the Diamond: the **Killybegs Road, Main Street,** and **Quay Street** (the **Ballyshannon Road**).

Tourist Office: Quay St. (☎21148; www.donegaltown.ie). Facing away from the Abbey Hotel, turn right; the tourist office is outside the Diamond on the Ballyshannon/Sligo Rd., next to the quay. Brochures galore on Co. Donegal, a free town map, and accommodation bookings throughout the Republic (€4 fee plus a 10% deposit). Open June-Aug. M-F 9am-6pm, Sa 10am-6pm, Su 11am-3pm; Sept.-May M-F 9am-5pm.

Banks: In the Diamond are **AIB** (☎21016), **Bank of Ireland** (☎21079), and **Ulster Bank** (☎21064). All have 24hr. **ATMs.** All open M 10am-5pm, Tu-F 10am-4pm.

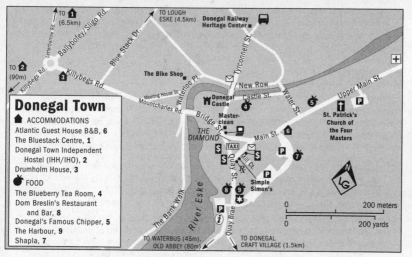

Donegal Town

🏠 ACCOMMODATIONS
Atlantic Guest House B&B, **6**
The Bluestack Centre, **1**
Donegal Town Independent
  Hostel (IHH/IHO), **2**
Drumholm House, **3**

🍴 FOOD
The Blueberry Tea Room, **4**
Dom Breslin's Restaurant
  and Bar, **8**
Donegal's Famous Chipper, **5**
The Harbour, **9**
Shapla, **7**

Laundry: Masterclean, Castle St. (☎22155), Beside the Blueberry Tea Room. Wash and dry 5-10 lb. €10, 11-15 lb. €15, 16-20 lb. €17.65. Open M-Sa 9am-6:30pm.

Emergency: ☎999; no coins required. **Police** ☎21021.

Pharmacy: Begley's Pharmacy, the Diamond (☎21232). Open M-Sa 9:15am-6:10pm.

Hospital: Donegal Hospital, Upper Main St. (☎21019), 4 blocks on the left coming from the Diamond.

Internet Access: The **Blueberry Tea Room** has a cyber-cafe on its 2nd fl. €2 per 30min. Open M-Sa 9am-7:30pm.

Post Office: Tyrconnell St. (☎21007), past Donegal Castle and over the bridge. Open M-F 9am-5:30pm, Tu open 9:30am (first Tu of month 9am), Sa 9am-1pm. 24hr. stamp machine and letter/package drop outside.

▌ ACCOMMODATIONS

Though many budget beds have disappeared in recent years, Donegal Town still boasts one of the most welcoming hostels in the country, and a wealth of B&Bs thrill travelers hooked on the full fry; see the tourist office fir B&B info.

Donegal Town Independent Hostel (IHH/IHO), Killybegs Rd. (☎22805), a 10min. walk from town. With the help of her daughters and their spaniel Scooby, Linda puts her guests at ease. Colorful murals and a common room with a small travel library. Popular with savvy travelers, so call ahead. Dorms €16; doubles €36, with bath €40. **Camping** €9 per person. ❶

The Bluestack Centre, Drimarone Rd. (☎35564), Letterbarrow. Out of town take the Letterbarrow Rd.; after 3.5 mi. there is a T-junction. Take a right and then an immediate left. Clean rooms and modern facilities in the middle of nowhere. Laundry wash €5, wash & dry €13. Reception open 9am-10pm. 10- and 12-bed dorms €16 (YHI €14 members), family room €50, sleeps 4. 2 wheelchair-accessible beds €16 each. ❶

Drumholm House, (☎23126 or 087 648 5734), a 5min. walk from town off the Killybegs Rd. before the roundabout. Plush red carpeting leading up the stairs, nicely furnished rooms, and a breakfast menu make this B&B a cut above the rest. Singles €35; doubles with bath €70. ❸

Atlantic Guest House B&B, Main St. (☎21187). Convenience is the name of the game here: central location, a range of rooms with TVs and phones, and a guest car park. Attractive carpets and reasonable prices round out the value. Singles €40 without bath; doubles €50-60, with bath €70-80. Ask about low-season deals. MC/V. ❸

🍴 FOOD

A good selection of cafes and takeaways occupies the Diamond and nearby streets. For groceries, head to **SuperValu,** a few minutes from the Diamond down Ballyshannon Rd.; inside the shopping center. (☎22977. Open M-Sa 8:30am-9pm, Su 10am-7pm.) **Simple Simon's,** the Diamond, sells fresh baked goods, takeaway meals (€2-4), and homeopathic remedies. (☎22687. Open M-Sa 9:30am-6pm.)

▧ **The Blueberry Tea Room,** Castle St. (☎22933), on the corner of the Diamond toward the Killybegs Rd. Eatery buzzes with patrons packing in for the all-day breakfasts (€6), homemade desserts, and delicious daily specials (around €10.50). Cybercafe upstairs. Sandwiches €3.20; moules frites €9. Open M-Sa 8:30am-7:30pm. ❷

▧ **The Harbour,** Quay St. (☎21702), just up from the car park on the right. Excellent restaurant has quickly become a local favorite for its extensive menu of delicious and well-prepared meals, ranging from pizza (from €9) to Mexican, Indian, and traditional fare. Entrees €11-21. Open M-Sa 4-10pm, Su 3-10pm. AmEx/MC/V. ❸

Dom Breslin's Restaurant and Bar, Quay St. (☎22719), next to the tourist office. Takes the mariner theme to new levels—customers can eat below in the Galley, in the Captain's Office, or at the Crow's Nest above. Steak and seafood specialties €15-20. Trad during the week and July-Aug. F-Sa rock/pop; Sept.-June F-Sa. Bar closes M-Th and Su 11:30pm, F 12:30am, Sa 2:30am. Open during summer daily noon-10pm; low season M-F and Su 5-9:30pm, Sa 5-10pm. AmEx/MC/V. ❸

Shapla, just off Main St. (☎25645), across from the parking lot. Brand-new Indian restaurant serves flavorful dishes from several regions in an elegant setting. Budget-friendly early-bird deal (daily 5-7pm) offers an appetizer, main course, and a side order for €16. Takeaway available. Entrees €12-22. Open for lunch M-Sa noon-2:30pm; for dinner M-Th 5-11:30pm, F-Sa 5pm-midnight, Su 12:30-11pm. MC/V. ❸

Donegal's Famous Chipper, Main St. (☎21428). Name says it all. Renowned throughout the area for its thick, golden chips and fresh fish. Fish 'n' chips €5.50-6.50. Open M-Tu and Th-Su 5-11pm; F 5-11:30pm. ❶

🍸🍷 PUBS AND CLUBS

Donegal's pubs are well equipped to deal with a town's worth of thirsty visitors. To help make the most of these watering holes, *Let's Go* presents the **Donegal Town Pub Crawl.** Whether you're looking to catch a trad session, cut a rug on the dance floor, or enjoy a quiet pint, there's something to suit your nightlife needs.

The Reel Inn, Bridge St. (☎086 251 2004; thereelinn@eircom.net). Formerly Dunnion's Bar, the owners of the now-defunct Scotsman Bar have established the center of Donegal Town's trad circuit (nightly sessions year-round). Open M-Th 10:30am-11:30pm, F-Sa 10:30am-12:30am, Su noon-11pm.

The Coach House, Upper Main St. (☎22855). Spontaneous sing-alongs are standard at this equine-themed locale. Downstairs **Cellar Bar** opens nightly in July and Aug. at 9:15pm for trad, ballads, and the blues (Cellar Bar open low season F-Sa). Cover €2. Open M-Th 11am-11:30pm, F-Sa 11am-12:30am, Su noon-11pm.

The Reveller, the Diamond (☎21201). Caters to a younger crowd that likes loud music and late drinks. Th-Su rock; music videos on flat screens and pop through speakers during the week. Open M-Th 10:30am-11:30pm, F-Sa 10:30am-12:30am, Su noon-11pm.

The Olde Castle Bar and Restaurant, Castle St. (☎21062). Stone walls and corbel windows mirror the medieval feel of its neighbor across the street. Low-key spot for Guinness. Kitchen open noon-9:30pm. Open M-Th until 11:30pm, F-Su until 12:30am.

Charlie's Star Bar, Main St. (☎21158). Well-lit and spacious. Sip Guinness around the huge horseshoe-

Donegal Town Pub Crawl

PUBS
Charlie's Star Bar, **6**
The Coach House, **1**
O'Donnell's, **4**
The Olde Castle Bar and Restaurant, **2**
The Reel Inn, **3**
The Reveller, **5**

shaped bar. Folks gather for GAA games and ballads. Open M-Th 1pm-11:30pm, F-Sa 11am-12:30am, Su 11am-11:30pm. **Linda's Krusty Kitchen** (☎22610), in back, serves sandwiches and soup at the bar for reasonable prices. All-day breakfast (€5-8) and burgers (€9); sandwiches from €3. Open daily 8am-7pm.

O'Donnell's, the Diamond (☎21049). Biggest bar in town packs in well-mannered locals for Sa live music. Kitchen open M-F noon-4pm. Bar open daily 10:30am-11:30pm.

👁 SIGHTS AND FESTIVALS

█ DONEGAL CRAFT VILLAGE. Six craftsmen set up shop around a pleasant courtyard on the outskirts of town and open their studios to the public in Donegal's craft village. The innovative works of a handweaver, a jeweler, a painter, a glassmaker, and two sculptors (one wood, one stone) make great gift alternatives to the legions of mass-produced leprechauns sold elsewhere. *(About 2km south of town on the Ballyshannon Rd. ☎22225. Open during summer daily 10am-5pm; spring and autumn M-Sa, winter Tu-Sa.)* The coffee shop in the village, **Aroma,** is also an award-winning artist for its unusually good espresso (single €1.85, double 2.35). Coffee and cake available 9:30am-5:30pm; lunch specials noon-4pm.

DONEGAL CASTLE. Originally the seat of several chieftains, Donegal was torn apart by the Irish-English conflict during the 17th century. This history is reflected in the castle's architecture: the old tower was constructed under the rule of Red Hugh O'Donnell in 1474, while the newer Manor House was added in 1623 by the English soldier Basil Brooke, who was given the castle in return for his service in the Nine Years War. The ruins have been refurbished and now house exhibits on the history of the castle. *(Castle St. ☎22405. Open mid-Mar. to Oct. daily 10am-6pm; Nov.-Mar. F-Su 9:30am-4:30pm. Last admission 45min. before closing. Guided tours on the hr. €3.70, students and children €1.30, seniors €2.60, families €8.70.)*

OLD ABBEY AND ST. PATRICK'S CHURCH. The stones and doorways of Donegal Castle's grand manor were taken from this ruined 15th-century Franciscan Friary. After the abbey was destroyed in a 1601 explosion, four dispossessed monks went on to write the *Annals of the Four Masters,* the first narrative history of Ireland and the source of many famous myths. An **obelisk** built on the Diamond in 1937 pays homage to these holy men, as does **St. Patrick's Church of the Four Masters,** a

Romanesque church about one kilometer up Main St. *(Old Abbey is a short walk from the tourist office along the south side of town. St. Patrick's open M-F 9am-5pm. Free.)*

WATERBUS. For a different perspective on the area, the Waterbus shuttle provides aquatic tours of Donegal Bay. The tour is at once scenic and morbid, as it encompasses many sights associated with the Famine-era "coffin ship" industry. Among the tour's highlights are a colony of seals, a shoreside castle, and an oyster farm. *(☎ 23666. Ferry leaves from the quay next to the tourist office. Departures depend on tides; call ahead. Wheelchair-accessible. €10, seniors and children €5, under 4 free. Ticket office in the Quay St. parking lot open during the summer daily 9am-5pm.)*

OTHER ACTIVITIES. Railroad buffs can chug over to **Donegal Railway Heritage Center,** where models, exhibits, and a 15min. video tell the story of the railroads that disappeared from Donegal on December 31, 1959. *(☎ 22655; www.countydonegalrailway.com. Open M-F 10am-5pm; July-Aug. also Sa-Su 2-5pm. €3.50, children €2, families €10.)* **Donegal Guided Town and Country Walks** exercise the mind and the legs, educating walkers about the town's history while rambling through the surrounding countryside. Experienced guides are also available year-round to plan excursions to the Slieve League, Bluestacks, Errigal, and Derryveagh Mountains. Call ahead as there is no regular schedule. *(☎ 35967; info@northwestwalkingguides.com.)*

FESTIVALS. One weekend in early or mid-July, the **Donegal Summer Festival** fills the town with craft and antiques fairs, air-sea rescue displays, clay-pigeon shoots, the Bonny Baby show, and plenty of live bands and trad sessions. Call ahead for a room that week—the town doubles in population that weekend. *(Contact the tourist office ☎ 21148 for information and specific dates.)* For two weeks in July, the **Earagail Arts Festival** celebrates the arts throughout northern County Donegal, but does sometimes come as far south as nearby Ballybofey. Twenty towns and over 40 venues host 100 events, from music, dance, and theater to special children's performances. *(Info ☎ 07491 20777; www.donegalculture.com. Ticket hotline ☎ 07491 29186. Ticket prices for individual events vary.)* Closer to town, the new **Bluestacks Bay Festival** celebrates visual art, music, theater, and poetry in the southern portion of the county. *(Call ☎ 07491 21965 for more info, including dates).*

BUNDORAN (BUN DOBHRÁIN)   ☎ 07198

At the mouth of the Dobhran River, Bundoran is the first stop in Donegal for visitors from Sligo or Leitrim. Beautiful beaches, fishing, and some of the best surf in Ireland make this a popular destination for Irish tourists, but tacky seaside amusements and a swelling summertime population may not suit every taste. By day, tourists stroll the 2km shore road. At night, youngsters party in the town's many pubs, saloons, and nightclubs. Bundoran's beach-town bustle, set to the rhythm of crashing waves, makes it a pleasant stop en route to Donegal.

⯅🄵 TRANSPORTATION AND PRACTICAL INFORMATION. Catch **Bus Éireann** (☎ 21101) at the Main St. depot (just past Goodwin's Hire and Sell on the left as you walk from the center of town) for **Donegal** (25min.; M-Sa 7 per day, Su 5 per day; €6.50 adult, €4.10 child), **Dublin** (3hr. 10min.; M-Sa 6 per day, Su 4 per day; €17.50/ 12, leaves from Ballyshannon only), and **Galway** via **Sligo** (3½hr., 5 per day, €18.50/ 12.40). **Ulsterbus** runs to **Enniskillen** (high season M-Sa 7 per day, Su 3 per day; low season M-Sa 3 per day, Su 1 per day; £7); they stop on Astoria Lane, which is the turn-off from Main St. for the Great Northern Hotel, 5min. off the Ballyshannon side of the bridge. **Feda O'Donnell** (☎ 07495 48356) serves **Galway** (3hr.; M-Sa 10:05am and 5:35pm, F also 1:05pm; Su 10:05am, 4:35, 8:35pm; €16) and **Let-**

terkenny (1hr. 10min.; M-Sa 11:40am and 6:40pm, F also 4:05 and 8:25pm; Su 5:40 and 10:40pm; €8); on Feda's buses, under 4 ride free and under 12 pay half-price. Buses stop at the Holywood Hotel (across from the tourist office) en route to Galway and at the tourist office en route to Donegal. **Goodwin's Hire and Sell** rents **bikes** from Main St., at the outskirts of the town center on the road to Sligo, opposite the Bus Éireann stop. (☎41526. Bikes €12 per day, €50 per wk. Open M-Sa 8am-6pm.)

Most stores and accommodations are located on or just off Main St., which runs east to west (the beach being to the north). The most notable landmark on Main St. is the bridge, which is more of a stone wall overlooking the beach than an actual bridge; at the end toward Ballyshannon lies the tourist office, and at the end toward Sligo lies the post office. Any directions you get from the locals will probably be in terms of the bridge and Ballyshannon (east) and Sligo (west). **Donegal Adventure Centre** (p. 424) also **rents surf equipment.** The **tourist office,** over the bridge on Main St., provides brochures covering Donegal's attractions. (☎41350. Open June-Sept. M-Sa 10am-5pm, Su 10am-3pm; Oct.-May F-Sa 10am-5pm. Accommodations booking available for a 10% deposit plus a €4 service fee.) **Bank of Ireland,** on Main St. across from the Grand Central Hotel, has a 24hr. **ATM.** (Open M 10am-4pm, Tu-F 10am-3pm; closed 12:30-1:30pm for lunch.) Short-term **work opportunities** are possible at La Sabbia restaurant, attached to the Homefield Hostel (see **Accommodations,** p. 435). Direct inquires should be made to the owner/chef at the hostel (☎41977) or at the restaurant (☎42253). For **Internet** access, head to the **library;** turn off Main St. at the Railway Bar. (☎29665. €2 per 55min. starting on the ½hr.; students, retirees, and unemployed €1; free if it's for study purposes. Open Tu and F 10:30am-5:30pm, W-Th 10:30am-8pm, Sa 10:30am-4pm.) Free Wi-Fi is available to those with laptops at the **Bridge Bar** and **Central Bar.** (see **Food and Pubs,** p. 436.) The **police** station is up Church St. on the right. (☎984 1203. Open daily 10am-1pm and 7-8pm; after hours, turn the handle on the door to contact the Ballyshannon police who are open later, or just call them at ☎985 8530.) **Cara Pharmacy,** located on the right side of Main St. if you're coming from the bridge toward Ballyshannon, serves your prescription needs. (Open M-Sa 9am-6pm and Su noon-1pm.) The **post office,** Main St., is on the opposite end of the bridge from the tourist office. (☎41224. Open M-F 9am-12:30pm and 1:30-5:30pm, Sa 9am-1pm.)

ⓕ ACCOMMODATIONS. Bundoran has no shortage of B&Bs, but the cheaper and quieter ones are farther down Main St., away from the bridge. There are two hostels in town, but they fill quickly in summer, so call ahead. **Homefield Hostel (IHH) ❷,** Bayview Ave., is off Main St.; head left up the hill between the Church of Ireland and Bay View Guest House. One wing of the huge building, the former summer residence of Viscount Enniskillen, connects to an Italian restaurant, while the other cradles a high-ceilinged parlor. (☎41977; www.homefieldbackpackers.com. Continental breakfast included. Dorms €20; private rooms €25 per person.) Or take advantage of their surf-and-stay deal with **Bundoran Surf Co.** for €50 per day (accommodations and gear rental included). A few steps from the hostel, **Donegal Adventure Centre ❷** caters to youth groups but also welcomes backpackers into its rooms and facilities. Among its smorgasbord of outdoor adventures, the Centre offers **surfing** lessons, a small skateboarding park, and various daring rope-and-climb activities. (☎42418. Surfboard €15 per hr.; wetsuit €8 per hr.; both €20 per hr. 3hr. surf lesson €30. Mar.-Oct. 3-day activity weekend over bank holidays €150. Free laundry. Continental breakfast included. Curfew 3am. Dorms €20; ensuite private rooms €25. Cottages available for groups, 3 beds for 2 days €150. MC/V.) Above a hairdresser just up Church St. from Main St., the **No. 1 B&B ❷,** 1 Church St., provides cheap rooms in the "four walls and a bed" style, but all the usual B&B amenities are still there. (☎984 1247. Singles €25; doubles €50.)

◪◩ **FOOD AND PUBS.** The best restaurant in town is ▨**La Sabbia ❸**, an Italian bistro connected to the Homefield Hostel. Enjoy delicious food in a cozy yet cosmopolitan atmosphere. Like most other locales in Bundoran, La Sabbia welcomes applicants for summer employment; inquire within. By day during the summer, La Sabbia becomes **Cafe Mojo.** (☎42253. Gourmet pizza €10. Pasta €11-12. Open June-Aug. M-Tu and Th-F 6:30-10pm, Sa-Su 6-10pm; Sept.-May Th-Su 6:30-10pm, but call ahead.) Main St. is lined with cafes and cafeteria-style restaurants serving cheap meals, but **McGarrigle's Restaurant ❷** is the best deal. (☎42060. All-day breakfast €6.50. Lunch specials €10; dinner entrees mostly €11-19. Open daily 10am-9:30pm.) Their full menu is available next door at **Sean Rua (Oyster Lounge)**, the bar owned by the same folks. (F-Su music year-round and nightly music during the summer, mostly trad. Open M-Th 10:30am-11:30pm, F-Sa 10:30am-12:30am, Su 10:30am-11pm; kitchen open only during McGarrigle's hours. AmEx/MC/V.)

Madden's Bridge Bar, Main St., over the bridge in a blue building, is a cross between a local pub and a surfer bar. (☎41586. Free Wi-Fi in 2nd fl. lounge. Tu, Th, Su trad. Burgers €10.50-12.50; entrees €14-20. Kitchen open until 7pm. Bar open Easter-Sept. 8am-9pm, otherwise 8am-6pm.) **Railway Bar,** farther up the hill on Main St. in the Ballyshannon direction, pours fine pints to the local wisemen, including the mayor. (☎41196. Pool and jukebox. Open daily 10:30am-12:30am.) Behind the unadorned face of **Brennan's,** Main St., a pair of elderly sisters (part of the family that has owned the bar for 107 years) welcomes a diverse crowd.(☎41810. Open M-Sa 10:30am-11:30pm, Su 12:30-11pm. **The Astoria Wharf** hosts the best weeknight out in Bundoran. Thursday's late bar plays host to YB Sober's "Blasty" and serves pizza from midnight. Take the turn off Main St. for the Great Northern Hotel and it's on the left. (☎42916.)

◧◪ **SIGHTS AND OUTDOOR ACTIVITIES.** A stroll past the Great Northern Hotel affords an impressive view of the mighty Atlantic waves. Curious sights include the **Faery Bridges, Wishing Chair,** and **Puffing Hole,** where water spouts through a bed of rocks. The **Aughross Cliffs** ("Headlands of the Steeds") were once a pasture for warhorses. At the western end of town, down the hill from Thalassa House, a bathing pool is built onto the smooth rock face. In the center of town is the small **Bundoran Beach,** which pales in comparison to the golden sand of its neighbor, **Tullan Strand,** signposted off Main St. toward Ballyshannon. The beaches in this area are better for **surfing** than for swimming. Several accessible breaks are adjacent to town, including a reef break called the Peak at Bundoran Beach and a shore break on the Tullan Strand. **Fitzgerald's Surfworld,** Main St., reports conditions (in person, by phone, or on their website) and serves as local surf oracle; they sell boards and gear, too. (☎41223; www.surfworldireland.com. Open daily 10am-6pm daily.) Rentals and lessons are available from the **Donegal Adventure Centre** (see **Accommodations,** p. 435). **Bundoran's Water World** provides a heated environment for summertime splashing, with a pool and two large water slides. (☎41172; www.waterworldbundoran.com. Open June-Aug. daily; Apr.-May and Sept. Sa-Su. €10, local students €7, seniors €6, under 8 €7.50, under 3 €4.) Parents can retreat to the adjacent **Bundoran Seaweed Baths** for a Seaweed Bath Steam (€20 per hr.), a seat on the psychoacoustic chair (€5 per 10min., €9 for 20min.) to relax on vacation. (☎41173. Open June-Aug. daily 11am-7pm; Easter-May and Sept.-Oct. W-Su 11am-7pm; Nov. Sa-Su 11am-7pm.) The **Homefield Hostel's Donegal Equestrian Holidays** encourages galloping across dunes and beaches. (☎41977; www.donegalquestrianholidays.com. Open Apr.-Oct. Lessons €25 per hr., children €15.) The annual **Bundoran Music Festival,** held over October's bank-holiday weekend in October attracts big names in trad and even the occasional hypnotist.

BALLYSHANNON ☎07198

Though it is rather congested with traffic by day, Ballyshannon *(Béal Átha Seanaidh)* sits unassumingly by the River Erne, offering a quieter alternative to Bundoran's touristed streets and crashing surf. The Falls of Assaroe *(Ess Ruaid)*, west of the bridge, were one of Ireland's oldest pagan holy sites, but now they serve as a shrine for those who worship the fishing rod.

🖃🔁 TRANSPORTATION AND PRACTICAL INFORMATION. All **buses** leave the depot beside the bridge; carriers include **Bus Éireann** (☎07491 31008), **Ulsterbus** (9066 6630), and **Feda O'Donnell** (☎07495 48356). Bus Éireann leaves for **Donegal Town** (20min.; M-Sa 7 per day, Su 5 per day; €5.50, children €3.40) and **Galway** via **Sligo** (3½hr., 5 daily, €18.50/12.40). Ulsterbus runs to **Enniskillen** (high season M-Sa 7 per day, Su 3 per day; low season M-Sa 3 per day, Su 1 per day; £7). And Feda O'Donnell serves **Galway** (3hr.; M-Sa 10am and 5:30pm, F also 1pm; Su 10am, 4:30, 8:30pm; €16) and **Letterkenny** (1hr. 10min.; M-Sa 11:45am and 6:45pm, F also 4:10 and 8:30pm; Su 5:45 and 10:45pm; €8); on Feda's buses, under 4 ride free and under 12 pay half-price. Allingham's Bridge connects the town's two halves. The town lies north of the river, where **Main Street** splits halfway up a hill. This hill, named *Mullach na Sidh* ("hill of the fairies"), is believed to be the burial site of legendary High King Hugh, who supposedly drowned in the Assaroe falls. Visit the **tourist office** on the bridge, next to the bus station, for info or to store luggage for €2 per day. (☎22888. Open M-F 9:15am-1pm and 2-5pm; July-Aug. also Sa-Su noon-4pm.) For quick cash, hit the 24hr. **ATMs** at **AIB**, Castle St. (☎51169), or the **Bank of Ireland** on Main St. (☎54153. Both open M 10am-5pm, Tu and Th-F 10am-4pm, W 10:30am-4pm; all located near where Main St. splits.) **Internet** access is available at **The Engine Room**, in the rear of a small shopping center, across from the Cineplex and at the end of Tirconnail St. (☎52960. Open M-F 9am-5:30pm, Sa 10am-5pm; €1 per 15min) and at **ACL Computers (Ballyshannon Business Center)** in the Saimer shopping center on the left side of Main St. as you face the hill (☎985 2222. €2 per 30min., min. €2. Open M-F 9:30am-6pm, Sa 10am-5pm; closed for lunch 1-2pm.) **Kelly's Pharmacy** is on Main St. next to **Fin McCool's** (☎51183. Open M-Sa 9am-6pm), and **Dorrian's Pharmacy** (☎985 1444; open M-Sa 9am-6pm) is right at the wedge formed where Main and Castle St. meet. The **post office** is in the triangle where Market St. splits from Main St., on the right side if you face uphill. (☎51111. Open M-F 9am-1pm and 2-5:30pm, Sa 9am-1pm.)

🏠🖿 ACCOMMODATIONS AND PUBS. Ten minutes down Belleek Rd., **Assaroe Lake Side Caravan & Camping Park ❶** has a beautiful location and brand-new facilities, including sports fields, a playground, and an on-site restaurant, **Mungo's Kitchen ❷**, with sandwiches from €4. (☎52822. Entrees €10-17. Restaurant open M-F 9am-4pm, F-Su 9am-9pm; hours may change at owner's whim. Showers €1.50. Electricity €4. Laundry €5. 2-person tent €15; 4- to 6-person tent €20; motor homes €20-24; family tents €24; motorcyclists with tent €15; hikers with tent €14; mountain goat with tent: price negotiable). **Shannon's Corner B&B ❸**, at the top of Main St. at Bishop St. (across from Thatch pub), has sunny rooms and affordable meals. (☎51180. Entrees €11. Restaurant open M-Sa 8am-5pm. Book ahead; inquire about discounts for long-term stays. Singles €35; ensuite doubles €70; discounts available during low season.) **Mace Supermarket** sells groceries. (☎58144; open M-Tu 8:30am-7pm, W and Sa 8:30am-7:30pm, Th-F 8:30am-8pm, Su 9:30am-2pm); if Mace is closed, try **Spar**, which is open later (☎51574; open M-Sa 8am-10pm, Su 11am-6:30pm); they're at the end of the street past the Engine Room. **The**

Rowan Tree, on the left side as you climb uphill on Castle St., stocks health food, herbal remedies, and organic vegetables. (☎52438. Open M-Sa 10am-6pm.) **The Market House ❷** serves good pub grub at the bar or in the a la carte restaurant upstairs. Occasionally, it plays host to live music on the weekends. (☎52297. Lunch €7-11; dinner €13-20. Kitchen open daily 11am-9pm. Bar open M-Th 11am-11:30pm, F-Sa 11am-12:30am, Su 11am-11pm.) **Dicey Reilly,** on Market St. behind Finn's, boasts a wide selection of Irish whiskeys, and has a handsome beer garden for whiling away sunny days. (☎51371. Th night during summer bluegrass and country; most Sa rock and pop. Open M-Th and Su noon-11:30pm, F-Sa noon-12:30am.) **Finn McCool's,** on Main St., is the most popular pub in town and reputedly hosts the best trad sessions in Donegal. Get there early; although the pub takes its name from an Irish giant (see **Finn McCool,** p. p. 61), Guinness glasses take up as much space as drinkers. (☎52677. Impromptu trad sessions happen whenever the players show up, typically Th-Sa. Open M-Th and Su 11:30am-11:30pm, F-Sa 11:30am-12:30am.) With its thatched roof, red-and-white facade, and white lace window curtains, **Thatch Pub,** just left off the top of Main St. on Bishop St. toward Rossnowlagh, is about as authentic as it gets. (F-Sa trad during summer starting around 10pm. Open M-Th and Su 8-11:30pm, F-Sa 8pm-12:30am.)

🅖 🎭 **SIGHTS AND FESTIVALS.** From the left fork of Main St., a left turn past the Imperial Hotel leads to **St. Anne's Church,** where William Allingham is buried with all his kin. Along with his celebrated verses, the Ballyshannon poet is known for inspiring Yeats to study the mythic traditions of Co. Sligo. Around June, a fish ladder in the river near the power station allows tourists to marvel at salmon and trout struggling upstream to spawn. The 12th-century Cistercian **Abbey of Assaroe** sits by the river. From town, take the left fork of Main St. past Thatch Pub and take the second left. The Cistercians put a canal in the river, harnessing its hydraulic power for a still-operational water mill. A tiny path outside leads to the **Abbey Well,** blessed by St. Patrick. Pilgrims bless themselves with its water every August 15. To the right of the bridge and 100m down the riverbank, a tiny cave harbors a **mass rock** from Penal days and two hollow stones that once held holy water (see **More British Problems,** p. 52). Things heat up on the bank holiday weekend in August, when the annual **Ballyshannon Music Festival** (☎51088; www.ballyshannonfolkfestival.com) brings raucous Irish folk music to town. Now in its 30th year, the festival is the oldest-running trad festival in Ireland. For rock 'n' roll fans, the **Rory Gallgher International Tribute Festival** celebrates the native guitarist with live music and countless cover bands during a week in July, beginning with the July bank holiday. (Contact Barry ☎086 877 2325; www.barryfest@hotmail.com.)

SLIEVE LEAGUE PENINSULA

West of Donegal Town, the Slieve League Peninsula's rocky cliffs jut into the Atlantic. This sparsely populated area harbors coastal hamlets, remote beaches, and some of Ireland's most dramatic scenery. R263 traces the coast, linking each charming village to the next. Backpackers and cyclists who navigate the hilly terrain are advised to work their way first westward then northward toward Glencolmcille. Stunning coastal vistas, inland paths, and windswept fields of heather await behind every bend and twist in the road. Ardara and Glenties make pleasant stops along the inland route and fine points of departure for a deeper trek into northern Donegal. Though easiest to explore by car, the peninsula offers spectacular cycling. Despite recent improvements in service, buses to area hostels remain infrequent. Hitchers report finding rides in and around Slieve, especially from Donegal. *Let's Go* never recommends hitchhiking.

SOUTHEASTERN SLIEVE LEAGUE ☎ 07497

A handful of tiny villages pepper the coast road between Donegal Town and Slieve League. For those cyclists willing to endure such demanding grades, the route offers rewarding coastal views. About 20km outside of Donegal Town, 16km past the small village of **Mountcharles,** is the tiny **Dunkineely,** surrounded by megalithic tombs, holy wells, and small streams, which are all accessible by round-trip walks of less than 6km. Off the main road in **Bruckless** (about 2km beyond Dunkineely), a turn-off leads to **St. John's Point,** which has views across to the Sligo coast.

KILLYBEGS

A bit further on, the busy fishing port of **Killybegs** is the last outlet for **ATMs** and other major services before continuing on toward the Slieve League. A small **tourist office** is located at the bottom of the hill on Kelly's Quay (signposted from the beginning of town). If you have your own laptop, take advantage of the free Wi-Fi available in **Hughie's Bar** on Main St. (Internet access €2 per 15min. on house computer. Open daily 9am-2am.) For groceries, a **Spar** is just uphill from the tourist office. (Open M-Sa 9am-6:30pm, Su 11:45am-12:45pm.) A **pharmacy** further down Main St. doles out all the essentials. (☎31009. Open M-Sa 9:30am-6pm).

Up the hill behind the Hotel Tara, **The Ritz ❷** ambiguously boasts "budget accommodation," which takes the form of colorful two- to six-person rooms with TVs, bathrooms, and free continental breakfast. A kitchen, laundry facilities, and a large common room with leather couches add a hostel-like touch. (☎31309 or 41852; www.theritz-killybegs.com. Internet access available. Wash €2, dry €1. 3- to 6-bed rooms €20 per person; singles €30; doubles €50.) A few kilometers west of town, signs mark the turn-off for the new **Clock Tower ❸,** resting on an estate dating back to the Plantation of Ulster. Behind the imposing stone facade, a huge modern bar and bistro serves some of the best grub in the area. (☎41922. Meals €12-15. Kitchen open daily June-Aug. 11am-9pm; Sept.-May 5-9pm.)

KILCAR (CILL CHARTHAIGH) ☎ 07497

A breathtaking 13km ride down R263 from Killybegs leads to the village of Kilcar, the gateway to Donegal's *gaeltacht* and commercial base for many Donegal weavers. The main street, which is the scenic coast road running east to Killybegs and north to Carrick, passes Kilcar's main attraction: its accommodations.

☐ ☐ TRANSPORTATION AND PRACTICAL INFORMATION. The **Bus Éireann** (☎21101) route from **Donegal Town** to **Glencolmcille** stops in Kilcar (July-Sept. M-Sa 10:35am, 3:20, 7:20pm; Su 3:20pm; Oct.-June M-Sa 1 daily). The bus from **Donegal Town** to **Dungloe** stops in nearby Killybegs (M-Sa 11 per day). The nearest **banks and pharmacies** are in Killybegs, but **Internet** access is available at the newly renovated **Áislann Cill Chartha** for €5 per hr. (p. 440).

☐ ☐ ACCOMMODATIONS AND CAMPING. Less than 1km from Kilcar toward Killybegs, **☐Dún Ulún House ❷** offers top-notch accommodations for two. It boasts the best campsites anywhere, each having its own semi-sheltered space with a fantastic view. Family-style cottages are also available. (☎38137. Kitchen and shower facilities free. Doubles €45, with bath €60; no singles available. **Camping ❶** €5 per person.) On the scenic road from Killybegs to Kilcar, which becomes Main St. 3km from Kilcar, **☐Inishduff House B&B ❸** sits next to Blue Haven restaurant. Ethna goes beyond the call of duty for breakfast, offering smoked salmon, scrambled eggs, fresh fruit, yogurt, and kippers alongside the good ol' fried heart-attack-on-a-plate; new guests are welcomed by tea and home-baked goodies. Book ahead online during the summer. (☎38542; www.inishduffhouse.com. Internet access available. All rooms with TV and bath. Singles €45; doubles €85.) Located 4km out on the steep Carrick coast road from Kilcar and only 5min. from the beach, **Derryla-han Hostel (IHH)** ❶, a 200-year-old former church, doubles as a hostel and a working farm with great views across Teelin Bay. Call for pickup from Kilcar or Carrick (if arriving by bus, get off at the Rock stop in Kilcar). The best time to visit is in early April during lambing season; book ahead in July and August. (☎38079. Laundry wash €4, dry €4. Dorms €14; singles €16, with bath €18. **Camping** €6, with free separate showers and kitchen. MC/V.)

◪◩ **FOOD AND PUBS. Spar Market,** at the bottom of Main St., sells groceries and fishing tackle. (Open M-Sa 9am-9:50pm, Su 9am-9pm.) A few doors down, **Jack Ban's** ❶, has cheap takeaway grub. (☎38433. Burgers €2.30-3.50; fish 'n' chips €7. Open M-Th 6-11:30pm, F-Sa 6pm-3am, Su 6pm-midnight.) Three kilometers down the road to Killybegs, the **restaurant** ❶ at the Blue Haven Hotel serves food and offers a commanding view of the sea. (Sandwiches €3-6; entrees €8.50-14.50. Kitchen open until 5pm. Open daily 12:30-9:30pm.) Just past the Blue Haven heading toward Killybegs, **Kitty Kelly's** ❷ serves delicious locally caught seafood specialties in a 200-year-old farmhouse. (☎31925; www.kittykellys.com. Entrees €16-22.) Down the street, **John-Joe's** hosts some of Kilcar's liveliest trad often graced by a harp player, a rare instrument these days. (☎38015. Open M-Th and Su 10am-11:30pm, F-Sa 10am-12:30am.) Behind a red facade and a thatch roof, **Piper's Rest Pub,** Main St., is your standard bar, equipped with a beer garden. (☎38205. Open M-F 11:30am-3pm and 7:30pm-12:30am, Sa 11:30am-1am, Su 11:30am-11:30pm.)

◪▨ **SIGHTS AND FESTIVALS. Studio Donegal** sells handwoven tweeds fresh off the loom. Visitors are invited to watch yarn being spun, cloth being woven, and jackets being sewn, all by hand. Viewing is free, but walking away with a new wardrobe will cost a pretty penny. (☎38194. Open M 10am-5:30pm, Tu-F 9am-5:30pm; June-Sept. also Sa 9am-5:30pm.) Next door, **Áislann Cill Chartha** (ASH-lahn khill KHAR-ha) is a multi-tasking community center with a range of services, including genealogical information. The center also offers **Internet** access later than most cafes. (€5 per hr.; min. €1.50. Open M-F 9:30am-10pm, Sa 2-6pm.) The staff at the center can direct you to the surrounding prehistoric and natural wonders, including megalithic tombs, old graveyards, and the Spanish church. Kilcar's **International Sea Angling Festival** casts off during the first weekend in August. (Contact Cara Boyle ☎38341.) It's followed by the **Kilcar Street Festival,** a week of sport, art, and general tomfoolery. (☎38492; kilcarstreetfestival@gmail.com.) The merriment continues into the second week of August with the **Kilcar Fleadh,** a week-long trad festival. (☎38015; johnjoes@hotmailcom.)

CARRICK AND TEELIN   ☎07497

From Kilcar, the coast road passes the villages of **Carrick** *(An Charraig)* and **Teelin** *(Teileann)*, which are about 4km apart. Coming from the east, turn left in the village of Carrick at the Slieve League Bar to continue on to Teelin and the **Slieve League Cliffs.** For most of the year, these tiny towns are but brief stopovers for travelers on their way to the Slieve League (p. 441) or the peninsula's larger villages. However, during the Fall Bank Holiday weekend in late October, the village scene is transformed by the annual **Carrick Fleadh,** when it fills to the brim with people seeking barrels of trad and foaming refreshment. **Fishing** is the other main attraction in the area. The *Nuala Star* in Teelin offers trips of varying length for dolphin- or bird-watching and **diving. Angling trips** (not available in Aug.) are €220 for a half-day and €450 for a full day; up to 10 people can fit on the boat. (☎39365 or 08762 84688; www.nualastarteelin.com. Rod and tackle rental €10 per day. Book ahead.) Dropping lines is especially rewarding around **Teelin Bay,** particularly in an area called **Salmon Leap** on the Glen River. Salmon fishing requires a permit (€20 per day, €50 per wk.), available at **Teelin Bay B&B ❸** across from the river. In addition to permits, Kathleen and Patrick offer comfortable rooms and delicious breakfasts. (☎39043. Rooms €30 per person.) **Glen River** is best for trout; tackle can be bought at the **Spar** in Kilcar. For food that won't try to get away, head 5km up the Ardara road to **Bialann Na Sean Scoile** (BEE-lin nah SHAN skol) ❷ for home-cooked meals and mashed potatoes stacked as high as the Slieve League. (☎39477. Entrees €9-18; dinner specials €10. Open daily Apr.-Sept. 10am-9pm; Oct.-Mar. 11am-7pm.) Or, buy groceries at **Spar** (marked as an ordinary grocery store) in Carrick (☎39120. Open daily 9am-9pm.) Turn left off Carrick's Main St. and head up the Teelin road to reach **The Rusty.** Formerly known as the Rusty Mackerel and **Cúl A' Dúin** (Irish for "behind the fort"), this pub has been owned by international trad megastars and native sons *Altan.* (☎39101. Tu acoustic music; F-Su trad during the summer. Open daily 11am-12:30am.)

THE SLIEVE LEAGUE WAY

◪**Slieve League Mountain** boasts the "highest sea cliffs in Europe." The face of its sheer, 61m drop is spectacular—on a clear day, a hike to the cliffs yields a view of both the infinite expanse of the Atlantic and the compact hamlets that line the peninsula. To reach the mountain from the east, turn left halfway down Carrick's Main St. at the Slieve League Bar and follow the signs for Teelin. Continue on to well-signposted **Bunglass** (1½hr. walk from Carrick), where there are two car parks, the second being at the head of the cliff path. En route to Bunglass, stop for tea and information at **Ti Linn;** the owner is the local Slieve League wise man. From there, the trail heads north and then west along the coast. Written in whitewashed stones to the left of the carpark, the message *Tir Éire* identified Ireland as a neutral state to Nazi aircrafts. A large tower was used by the British to scope out French invaders during the Napoleonic Wars, while the smaller one served as a WWII lookout. One hour along the path from the car park, the mountaintop narrows to 0.5m and becomes the infamous **One Man's Pass.** On one side of this pass, the cliffs drop 548m to the ocean below. No worries, though—the rocky floor on the other side is only 305m down. There are no railings here, and those prone to vertigo generally opt to lower their centers of gravity by slithering across the 30m platform. Never attempt the pass in poor weather; the cliffs at Bunglass are a safer option. The path continues along the cliffs all the way to **Rossarell Point,** 10km southeast of Glencolmcille. While many humans refuse to peer over the edge, herds of sheep calmly graze on the steep inclines. The entire hike from the Teelin car park to Rossarrell Point takes about 4-6hr., depending on the walker's fitness and weather conditions. Other, shorter routes involving loop-like treks can also be plotted. (Carry *Ordnance Survey #10* and ask locals about the day's prospects.)

One possible hiking route starts at the Derrylahan Hostel in **Kilcar** and takes backpackers on a 6hr. trek over the Slieve League Way to the Malinbeg Hostel in **Malinbeg.** Following a short jaunt across the Silver Strand (see **Glencolmcille,** p. 443), backpackers can continue northeast to the Dooey Hostel in **Glencolmcille.**

GLENCOLMCILLE ☎07497

Wedged between two sea cliffs at the northwestern tip of the Slieve League peninsula, **Glencolmcille** (glen-kaul-um-KEEL; *Gleann Cholm Cille*) is actually a parish—a collection of several tiny *gaeltacht* villages regarded as a single entity. Dark and rugged hills in the west give way to the green valley of "The Glen," as it is affectionately known. Named after St. Columcille, who founded a monastery here in the 6th century (see **St. Columcille,** p. 59), the surrounding scenery is rife with ancient remains, including the Stone Age *turas* that the saint inscribed with a cross. The **Feast of Columcille,** celebrated on June 9, still brings barefooted penitents out in droves to follow the ancient pilgrimage that begins at midnight.

⊞ ? TRANSPORTATION AND PRACTICAL INFORMATION. Bus   Éireann (☎21101; www.buseireann.ie) leaves from the village corner to **Donegal Town,** stopping in **Killybegs** and **Kilcar** (July-Sept. M-Sa 4 per day, Su 2 per day; Oct.-June M-Sa 1 per day); also for **Dublin** (7 per day) via **Dungloe, Glenties,** and **Ardara** (M-F 3 per day, Sa-Su 2 per day). **Bikes** can be rented from Sean at **Biddy's** (€10 per day, long-term rates available. Open M-F 11am-11:30pm, Sa 11am-12:30am, Su noon-11pm). The former **tourist office** in the Woolen Mill Factory Shop on Cashel St. is now closed, and a new one is slated to open by summer 2008, probably on Cashel St. The nearest **banks** and **pharmacies** are in Killybegs and Ardara. The Folk Village has a **bureau de change** (but only converts between £ and €). The **post office,** east of the village center, offers **AIB** banking services. (☎30001. Open M-F 9am-12:30pm and 1:30-5:30pm, Sa 9am-1pm.) The **laundromat** is just off Main St.; turn at the Walking Centre. (☎086 874 0138. Open M-Sa 10am-5:30pm.) **Taxi-Hackney Service** (☎087 293 9466) is wheelchair-accessible.

▛ ACCOMMODATIONS. A trip to Donegal wouldn't be complete without a visit to ▨**Dooey Hostel (IHO) ❶,** the original Irish independent hostel. Turn left at the end of the village and follow the signs uphill for a few kilometers. Owners Mary and her son Leo could not be friendlier, funnier, or more helpful. Built right into the hillside with sweeping views of the sea, the hostel looks like a bunker from the outside. The flower-strewn rock face that forms the hostel's corridor ushers visitors into a cavernous wonderland of rooms with private kitchenette and bath. The view from the hostel is so good that the new Walking Centre took its scenic brochure photograph out the window. (☎30130. Dorms €14; singles €14.50. **Camping** €7.50 per tent.) B&Bs surround the Folk Village (see **Sights,** p. 443). The **Glencolmcille Hill Walkers Centre** (☎30302; www.ionadsuil.ie) has double and twin rooms with self-catering kitchen and Internet access available for €22.50. Seven kilometers southwest of Cashel lies Malinbeg and the welcoming arms of **Malinbeg Hostel ❶.** This modern hostel aims to please with amenities like a microwave, laundry (€3.50), and top-notch bathrooms. The amazing views of Rathlin Island's lighthouse and the hostel's proximity to Silver Strand doesn't hurt either. It is a 7km hike from Glencolmcille, but a community bus (☎38913) serves Malinbeg and the owners pick people up when it is not running; call ahead for schedules. The hostel also runs a shop with basic **groceries** and a post office across the street. (☎30006 or 30965; www.malinbeghostel.com. Store open daily 9am-7pm and upon request. Dorms €14-16; singles €16-20. Family rooms available.)

⊡ ▨ FOOD AND PUBS. Byrne and Sons Food Store, Cashel St., supplies groceries, newspapers, and petrol. (☎30018. Open M-F 9am-9pm, Sa 10am-9pm, Su 9:15am-1:15pm and 6-9pm.) **An Chistin ❸** (AHN KhEESHT-ahn; "the Kitchen"), at Foras Cultúir Uladh (see **Sights,** p. 443), is the best restaurant in the area, serving delicious meals ranging from beef and Guinness pie to fresh seafood. (☎30213. Lunches €8.50-9.50; 3-course Su lunch €17; entrees €11.50-18.50. Open Easter-Oct. daily noon-8pm.) The **teashop ❶** in the Folk Village offers delicious sandwiches (€3.50), even better homemade scones (€1.10), and Guinness cake for €2.70. (Open Easter-Sept. M-Sa 10am-6pm, Su noon-6pm.) The town's three pubs share a welcoming, unpretentious atmosphere and a steady lineup of trad sessions. The most famous among them is unassuming 120-year-old **Biddy's,** at the mouth of Carrick Rd. Irish speakers with a bent toward lively conversation add color to the spartan decor. (☎30016. Mid-May to Aug. trad most nights; occasionally other months. Open M-Th 11am-11:30pm, F-Sa 11am-12:30am, Su noon-11pm.) **Roarty's,** the next pub down Cashel St., welcomes guests with trad a few times per week and has a separate bar for quieter chats. (☎30273. Open daily during summer 10am-midnight; otherwise 1pm-11:30pm. **Self-catering accommodations** available for €100 per wk.) Last on the road is **Glen Head Tavern,** the largest of the pint-peddling trio. Nearly the whole village fits into its recently remodeled lounge. Billiards and summer weekend trad sessions enhance the appeal. (☎30008. Open M-Th 10:30am-11pm, F-Sa 10:30am-12:30pm, Su 10:30am-11pm.)

◙ SIGHTS. Glencolmcille's craft movement began in the 1950s under the direction of the omnipresent **Father James McDyer,** who was also responsible for introducing electricity, founding the Folk Village, and building the local football field. Today, the town is renowned for its handmade products—particularly its sweaters, which are on sale at numerous "jumper shops" on the roads surrounding the town. Close to town is **Foras Cultúir Uladh** (FOR-us KULT-er UH-lah; "the Ulster Cultural Institute"), which runs the **Oideas Gael Institute** for the preservation of the Irish language and its culture. Foras offers regular courses of varied lengths on such pursuits as hiking, painting, pottery, local archaeology, traditional music, and Irish language. It also has trad recordings and books on Ireland, as well as concerts, performances, and changing exhibitions on local history. (☎30248; www.Oideas-Gael.com. Weekend course €100, week-long courses €190-220. Other activities €60-170. Open June-Aug. daily 9am-6pm; Sept.-May M-F 9am-5pm, sometimes longer hours depending on course schedules.)

A bit past the village center is Father McDyer's **Folk Village Museum and Heritage Centre,** the town's attraction for non-hiking, non-Irish speakers. Guided tours describe the furniture, tools, and customs of life in three thatch-roof stone cottages dating back to the 18th, 19th, and 20th centuries. There is also an 1850s schoolhouse and an exhibit about Father McDyer's efforts in the area and Glencolmcille's history and archaeology. (€3.50, students and seniors €3, children €2.) A famous **fiddling festival** beginning in the first weekend of August is followed by the **Glencolmcille Folk Festival,** a lively celebration on the first fortnight of the month. (Contact Gerry Gillespie ☎30111.)

Fine beaches and cliffs make for excellent hiking in all directions. Hikers can start their journeys at the newly opened **Glencolmcille Hill Walkers Centre,** on Main St. before the Folk Village. While the Centre has overnight accommodations (€22.50 per person), it also has a day rate (€8) which allows use of showers, changing room, and lockers. Internet access and walking guides are also available upon request. (☎30302; www.ionadsuil.ie. Always open; the phone number diverts to the owner's cell phone after hours. MC/V.) An 8km walk southwest from Cashel leads to **Malinbeg.** This coastal area was once notorious for smuggling *poitín* through tunnels (see **Whiskey Business,** p. 67), some of which may still be in use. Close by Malinbeg, the **Silver Strand** rewards hikers with stunning views of the gorgeous beach and surrounding rocky cliffs. The strand starts a long-distance trek along the Slieve League coastline (see **Slieve League Way,** p. 441). An hour's walk north of town through land dotted with prehistoric ruins (including St. Columcille's stations of the cross, his well, and his church), **Glen Head** is easily identified by the Martello tower at its peak. The Folk Village sells a map and description of *St. Columcille Station* (€1.20) for those wishing to explore the 5km route followed by pilgrims every July 9. A third 3hr. walk from town begins at the Protestant church and climbs over a hill to the ruins of the ghostly "Famine villages" of **Port** and **Glenloch** in the valley on the other side. Port has been empty since its last hunger-stricken inhabitants emigrated. The only current resident, according to local rumor, is an eccentric artist who lives by the isolated bay without electricity or water. The impressive **phallic rock** sticking out of the sea is what it appears to be: the only part of the Devil still visible after St. Columcille banished him to the ocean. Visit the tourist office or any local hostel for maps of major sights.

ARDARA (ARD AN RÁTHA) ☎07495

As the historic center of the Donegal weaving industry, the heritage town of Ardara (ar-DRAH) now tends to attract credit card-toting tweed fiends, though one of the few remaining hostels in the area allows budget travelers to hold their own amid the big spenders. The town is one of the cheapest sources of locally knit and woven articles, although better deals can often be found at small "craft centers" in surrounding villages. During the first weekend of June's Weavers' Fair, weavers from all over Donegal congregate in Ardara to flaunt their weft. Visitors uninterested in merchandise escape to the spectacular scenery along Maghera Caves Rd., leading past a waterfall to stunning sand dunes and cave-riddled beaches.

🖭🔁 TRANSPORTATION AND PRACTICAL INFORMATION. Bus Éireann (☎912 1309) stops in Ardara at the Heritage Center on its way from **Donegal Town** to **Glenties** (10min.; M and F 6 per day, Tu and Th 3 per day, W 4 per day, Sa 1:50 and 10:25pm, Su 10:25pm) and **Dungloe** (40min.; M-Sa 1:50 and 10:25pm, F 8:40pm, Su 10:25pm), to **Killybegs** (25min; M-Sa noon, M-F 9:48am and 4:15pm, M, W, F 11:33am, Su 8am and 3:15pm) and **Donegal Town** (35min.; M-Sa 8:10am and noon; M, W, F also 11:33am, Su 8am and 3:15pm), and **Dublin** (5-6hr. depending on transfers; M-Sa 3 per day, Su 8:10am and 3:30pm). Also departing from the hotel, **Feda O'Donnell's** (☎48114) service between **Donegal** and **Galway** stops in Ardara twice weekly (M 8:50am and Su 3:30pm) with further stops throughout the *gaeltacht*. **Don Byrne's,** past the tourist information point on Killybegs Rd., provides maps and new **rental bikes** (€15 per day, €60 per wk.), as well as **rental fishing rods and tackle** for €10 per day. (☎41658; donbyrne@indigo.ie. Open June-Aug. M-Sa 9:30am-6pm; Sept.-May M-F 5:30-8pm, Sa 9:30am-6pm.) A **tourist information point** is in **Triona Designs,** at the edge of town down Killybegs Rd. The staff displays a 280-year-old loom in action. (☎41422. Open daily 9am-6:30pm, except Dec. 25). Triona also has one of few wheelchair-accessible restrooms in town. Another tourist information point is in the Nesbitt Arms Hotel on the Diamond. (Always open.) **Ulster Bank,** the Diamond, has a 24hr. **ATM.** (☎41121. Open M-F 10am-12:30pm and 1:30-4pm, M until 5pm.) **Sheila's Coffee and Cream ❶,** in the Heritage Center, has one computer with **Internet** access for €5 per hr. (☎37905. Breakfast €6; *panini* €7-8.) The **Ardara Pharmacy** is on Front St. (☎41120. Open M-Sa 9am-1pm and 2-6pm.) The **post office** is on Main St. (☎41101. Open M-F 9am-1pm and 2-5:30pm, Sa 9am-1pm.)

🏠 ACCOMMODATIONS. ▨The Green Gate (An Geata Glas) ❹, 2km outside town, has been showered with superlatives by travel gurus the world over. From the dramatic driveway entrance to the selection of twenty homemade jams at breakfast, this B&B is a unique experience. From the Diamond, take the Donegal road (the only small road at the Diamond), ascend the hill to the north, and follow the discreet white arrows, or call for pickup. (☎41546; www.thegreengate.eu. Book ahead. Irish breakfast included. Singles €45; doubles €90.) Standing its ground in the face of a number of hostel closings in the region, **Ardara Hostel (IHO) ❶** caters to the budget-conscious and offers a prime location, fluffy blankets, and a stone-floored common room and kitchen. The hostel is at the top of the hill at the Diamond. Across the street, the hostel's owners also run the **Drumbarron B&B ❸,** which has ensuite rooms and homemade bread and scones in the morning. (☎41200. Hostel rooms €15. B&B suites €30.) **Rossmore House ❸,** on the Donegal Rd., at the foot of the hill leading to Green Gate, is a simple B&B with an art studio next door, which features the work of the owner's artist son and his friends. On Donegal Rd., take the fork signposted for the Woodhill; just past the blue shack, Rossmore is the 3rd house on the right. (☎41126; dl31@familyhomes.ie. Singles €35; doubles €60.) Campers pitch their tents amid the sand dunes at **Tramore Caravan and Camping Park ❶**, about 9km northwest of town. Go north on R261 and follow the signs for Rosbeg. (☎45274 or 51491; www.campbellireland.com. Laundry and showers available. Electricity €2. 2-person tent €14; family tent €18.)

⬛⬛ FOOD AND PUBS. A **Spar** market sits on Main St. (☎41107. Open M-Sa 7am-10pm, Su 8am-10pm.) **Charlie's West End Cafe ❶**, halfway up Main St., lacks the trendy atmosphere its name suggests, but the service is quick and the quality food is cheap. (☎41656. All-day Irish breakfast €6.80; pizza from €4.80. Open M-Sa 9:30am-9:45pm, Su 5-9:45pm.) Attached to the Nesbitt Arms Hotel on Main St., **Weaver's Bar and Bistro ❷**, the Diamond, serves locally renowned pub grub with a wide variety of options to satisfy any appetite. (☎41103. Food €4-14. Bar open daily 8pm-12:30am; kitchen open 9am-9:30pm.) The attached restaurant serves slightly snazzier fare. With lots of little rooms and old-time relics resting on fireplace perches, enjoying a pint at **⬛Nancy's Bar,** Front St., before the Diamond, feels like having a drink in someone's house. Channel surf at your leisure in the small sitting room or relax in the cozy conservatory. Weekend trad livens up the tranquil vibe and a wooden menu of seafood specials is highlighted by fresh oysters (€9.50 per ½-dozen) and the "Louis Armstrong" (€11.50)—smoked salmon on wheat bread smothered in melted cheese. (☎41187. Kitchen open noon-9pm, but only between St. Patrick's Day and Halloween. Bar open year-round noon-midnight.) Local musician Peter Oliver returned to the pub business with his purchase of the **Corner House.** (☎41736. Open M-Sa 10:30am-midnight, Su 10:30am-10:30pm.) He and his family host nights of excellent trad (July-Aug. nightly, Sept.-June F-Sa), welcoming all willing musicians from the pleasantly relaxed crowd.

◪ SIGHTS. Beautiful walks abound in the area surrounding Ardara. From town, head south toward Glencolmcille and turn right toward **Loughros Point** (LOW-krus) at the "Castle View" horse-riding sign. At the next sign, either turn right for a view of Ardara Bay, or continue straight for views of the sea at the Point (1hr. walk). If you'd rather let a horse do the walking, head to **Castle View Ranch ❸**, a horse-crazy B&B offering independent and guided **horse rides,** located four well-posted kilometers from Ardara off Loughros Point Rd. To get to the road, look for signs along the Killybegs Rd. just outside of town. (☎41212. €30 per hr., €120 per day. B&B doubles €60.) Two kilometers from town on Killybegs Rd., a sign points toward the coastal **Maghera Caves,** which housed weapons during the Irish War for Independence. After the turn-off for the caves, follow the signs several kilometers west on beautiful small roads. The six caves vary in size and depth, but all require a flashlight. Low tide opens up the Dark Cave, once the refuge of *poitín*-makers. Along the way is a gushing waterfall and a stunning beach leading to the caves. (Parking for beach and caves €3; collected daily 9am-6pm. Restrooms and showers available; €0.50.) The road past the caves continues across the Glengesh Pass to Glencolmcille; follow the 10km marked trail to the pass, starting before the waterfall.

Ardara has three sweater shops with superior selections and reasonable prices. The **John Molloy Factory Shop,** 1km from town on Killybegs Rd., offers a wide variety of wares. (☎41133. Open M-Th 9:30am-5:30pm, F 9:30am-4pm; call ahead for weekend hours.) **Kennedy,** Front St., near the top of the hill, sells garments with more contemporary designs. (☎41106. Open M-F 9am-6pm; Apr.-Oct. Sa 9am-6pm; June-Aug. Su noon-6pm.) The town's other manufacturers are **Bonner's** (☎41303; open M-F 9am-6pm, closed 1-2pm for lunch), Front St., and **Triona Design** (☎41422; open daily 9am-6:30pm), at the entrance of town on the Killybegs Rd. Triona offers a quick, free guided tour of its antique machines and inexpensive international shipping. The attached **coffee shop ❶** is open during the same hours as the store.

GLENTIES (NA GLEANNTA) ☎07495

Glenties, repeatedly named "Ireland's Tidiest Town" in the mid-1990s, may ward off party animals with its spic-and-span image, but it has several welcome conveniences and tame, pleasant hikes for visitors passing through northwest Donegal. Hikes are signposted from the crossroads next to the St. Connell Museum. One of the most satisfying routes leads to **Inniskeel Island** (see **Sights in Ardara**, p. 445), 12km past Glenties toward Dungloe; signs point from the car park to lovely, swimmable **Narin Beach.** The island, where the ruins of **St. Connell's** 6th-century church lie, is accessible only when the tide is out; check the *Irish Independent* for tidal information. Another series of trails leads into the foothills south of town. At the far end of Main St. toward Aradara, **St. Connell's Museum and Heritage Center** preserves local culture with a jumble of Glenties-related photographs, artifacts, and exhibitions, including a description of the town's run at the Tidy Town crown and a collection of books associated with Glenties. South of Glenties on N56, an uphill turn-off points to "Meenachallow" and an "organic farm." Three kilometers up the road (turn right at the wooden shed) is Thomas Becht's **Donegal Organic Farm,** a hillside melange of forestry plantations, hydroelectric power plants, and vegetable gardens. In addition to peddling veggies, the farm has tree-sponsorship programs, ECO-Working camps for adolescents, and longer-term opportunities for individuals with serious interests in sustainable agriculture or forestry. Holiday self-catering apartments are also available. (☎51286; www.esatclear.ie/~tbecht. Open M-Sa 9:30am-8pm.) A **nature trail** at the farm guides visitors through the forest and connects to the longer trail bound for **Lough Anney,** Glenties's reservoir. Farther uphill is a waterfall and Special Area for Conservation (SAC) that makes a nice picnic spot. The entire walk is 12km round-trip. A shorter option is the 4km walk along the **Owenrea River** leading to **Mullantayboyne.** From town, head down Main St. toward Glencolmcille and turn right at the sign. The river lies on the right side of the road. *Ordnance Survey #11* provides the best map for walking the area.

September 12th's **Harvest Fair** was once an annual celebration of local agriculture, industry, and beer; the former two have since fallen by the wayside to make more room for the latter. On the first weekend in October, **Fiddler's Weekend** draws musicians from across the globe. (For more info, visit www.glenties.ie.)

Campbell's Holiday Hostel (IHH) ❶, around the bend at the far end of Main St. toward Ardara, behind the St. Connell Museum, provides spare, clean rooms. The common space has a fireplace, satellite TV, and two fully equipped kitchens. (☎51491; www.campbellireland.com. Wheelchair-accessible. Wi-Fi available. Sheets €2. Laundry €5. Open Mar.-Oct. Dorms €15; private rooms €20 per person.) B&Bs are bountiful around Glenties, and the most convenient and best-priced cluster on the far side of town, at the western end of Main St. **Brennan's B&B ❸,** Main St., has antique fireplaces, family rooms, and a menu that offers continental breakfast, omelettes, smoked mackerel, and full Irish fry. (☎51235. Rooms €27.50 per person, with breakfast €35.) On Main St. is a tiny whole foods shop called **Good Earth.** (☎51794. Open M-Sa 10am-6pm.) For normal groceries, **Spar,** Main St., has the goods. (☎51131. Open daily 8am-10pm.) The restaurant at the **Highlands Hotel ❷,** Main St., has a set daily sit-down menu. The 2002 Traditional Irish Music Pub of the Year hosts some of the best Saturday sessions. (☎51111. Sandwiches €2.60; entrees €12-22. Kitchen open 8am-9pm.) **Café Mauds ❷,** next to the post office on Main St., has daily specials, sandwiches, ice cream, and coffee. It also has a touch-screen information stand. (☎51845. Open M-Sa 8am-4pm.)

Like everything else in town, the pubs are on Main St. **Keeney's Pub** has a lakeside beer garden and bathrooms as clean as Glenties's streets. (☎51920. F-Sa live music. Open M-Th 4pm-1am, F-Su 11:30am-1am.) **Paddy's Bar,** at the end of Main St. headed toward Ardara, draws young locals with weekend rock and pop performances. The big-screen broadcasts Sunday matches as the fireplace keeps pubbers warm. (☎51158. Open M-F 5-11:30pm, Sa 5pm-1am, Su 5pm-midnight.)

Bus Éireann stops in front of the post office on its way to **Donegal Town** via **Ardara** (☎912 1309. M-F 8, 11:50am, 4pm, Sa 8am and 11:50am, Su 8am and 3:15pm) and in the other direction toward **Dungloe** (M-Sa 2pm, F also 5:35, 8:50, 10:20pm; M-Th and Sa 8:35pm; Su 10:35pm). **Feda O'Donnell's** (☎48114) serves the Glenties during the college term only: to **Dugnloe** and **Annagry** (daily 9:30pm; F also 7:45pm) and to **Ardara** and **Killybegs** (M 8:40am and 3:15pm). In town, **Bank of Ireland**, Main St., has one of the area's few **ATMs.** (☎51124. Open M-F 10am-12:30pm and 1:30-4pm.) Inquire about **work opportunities** at the Donegal Organic Farm (p. 446). **Glenties Medical Hall,** is on Main St.(☎51289. Open M-Sa 9:30am-6pm.) A **police** station is on Main St. across from the Highlands Hotel. The **post office** is on Main St., inside **The Paper Stop.** (☎51101. Post office open M-F 9am-1pm and 2-5:30pm, Sa 9am-1pm.)

THE NORTHWEST GAELTACHT

The four parishes in Co. Donegal's northwest corner make up the largest *gaeltacht* in the Republic. Though the Rosses, Gweedore, Gartan, and Cloghaneely all maintain distinct identities, they are united by their staunchly traditional Irish culture, which has flourished unperturbed by the *gaeltacht's* geographic isolation. Peddled as cultural showpieces in other parts of the country, Donegal's distinct dialect of Irish and the county's famous style of fiddling remain living aspects of the daily routine for the area's inhabitants.

THE ROSSES

Extending northward from Dungloe, the Rosses are part of a linguistic buffer zone. Locals here regularly speak both the English and Irish language in everyday conversation. While N56 follows the spectacular midwest coast from Glenties to Dungloe, expansive, sandy beaches lie isolated by the eerie stillness of the Derryveagh Mountains. A stay among the Rosses' bogs is an excellent primer for journeys deeper into the *gaeltacht*, the northernmost outpost for information and supplies.

DUNGLOE (AN CLOCHÁN LIATH)   ☎07495

As the capital of the Rosses, Dungloe (dun-LO) is the last bastion of tourist information for visitors continuing northwest. Though it is a rather uneventful stop, its proximity to the beaches of Crohy Head offers an easy outlet for hiking and cycling. The **Crohy Head** *(Ceann na Cruaiche)* peninsula, 10km southwest of Dungloe, is surrounded by a slew of oddly shaped rock formations and sandy beaches. To reach Crohy Head from Dungloe, turn onto Quay Rd. (toward Maghery) halfway down Main St. and follow the bumpy road along the sea for 6km, about 2km past Maghery. Party animals flock to Dungloe during the last week of July, when the population swells to 80,000 for the 10-day **Mary from Dungloe Festival.** The highlight of the festival is the coronation of the new "Mary from Dungloe," although most attendees argue that local favorite Daniel O'Donnell's three concerts really make the festival. Tickets for the singer go on sale in January and sell out almost immediately. For festival information and ticket bookings, call the **Festival Booking Office** in the Lower Main St. car park. (☎21254; www.maryfromdungloe.info. Open M-Sa 10am-6pm.) Traditional music greats tune their fiddles for the **Peader O'Donnell Weekend Festival** in October. For sea-angling and boat tours, visitors should contact Neil and Ann Gallagher at **West Donegal Sea-Angling Charters** (☎48403 or 087 83 32969; www.donegalseaangling.com). For information on inland fisheries or inland boat hire in the Rosses, contact the **Rosses Anglers Association.** (☎21163. Day permit €10; boat fee €15.) Or, march up to **C. Bonner and Sons** on Main St. to chat with Charlie Bonner, the man in charge of area fishing. (☎21163. Open June-Sept. daily 9am-9pm, Oct.-Nov. daily 9am-6pm. Rod and tackle rental €5-8 per day.) International and local **surfers** have discovered the waves just west of Dungloe. Hanging ten is easy with ex-world champ and member of the Irish surf team **Kevin Tobin.** (☎22468 or 08688 68693; www.dooeysurf-school.com. Lessons €25 per 2hr., €75 per wk.) **NaRossa Surf School** (☎08762 96912; www.narossasurf.com) also surfs Dooey Beach and offers pickup.

Dungloe Camping and Caravan Park ❶, Carnmore Rd., off Main St. across from the Bank of Ireland, has backyard-style sights with little natural splendor. (☎21201. Electricity €3. Laundry €6. Open Apr.-Sept. Car or caravan and 2 people €17; tent, car and 2 people €17; tent and 2 hikers or cyclists €12; extra adults €3, children €1.) The **Atlantic House B&B ❷,** conveniently located on Main St., is a cozy little place in which all rooms have bath and TV. (☎21061. Singles €40; doubles €60.) The **Rockeries B&B ❷,** on Cranmore Rd. after the bend off Main St., is a spacious house offering the cheapest B&B rooms in town. (☎22082; www.rockeries.com. All rooms with bath. Singles €35; doubles €60. MC/V.) A 5-10min. walk out of town toward Burtonport, **Sea View ❸** has standard ensuite rooms and advertises its best asset in its name. (☎21353. Singles €45; doubles €64.)

Wandering cooks stock up at **Cope Supermarket,** Main St. (☎21022. Open daily 8:30am-10pm.) **SuperValu** is 1km down Carnmore Rd. and also has a **pharmacy.** (☎21006. Open M-W and Sa 8:30am-8pm, Th-F 8:30am-9pm, Su 9am-7pm.) **Doherty's ❷,** at the midpoint of Main St., provides a variety of cheap dishes in a huge cafeteria/takeaway. (☎21654. All-day breakfast €6; Pizza €5.60-8.50. Open July-Sept. daily 9am-midnight; Oct.-June M-Th 9am-8pm, F-Sa 8am-11pm.) The **Butterrock Restaurant ❶** serves up satisfying meals of Irish, Mexican, and Indian origin. (☎61738. Full Irish breakfast €6; dinners €7.50-9. Open daily 9am-8pm.) **China Town ❷,** at the top of Main St., has cheap, no-frills Chinese grub and a €16 all-you-can-eat buffet for big appetites. (☎21662. Entrees €5.50-8. Open daily 4-11pm.)

Beedy's, Main St., rocks with local bands on weekends. It has a beer garden perfect for sunny days and a pool table for rainy ones. (☎21219. Open daily 2-11pm.) For a quiet pint, **Patrick Johnny Sally's,** up Main St. toward Glenties, is a serene, refined pub with a dark wood interior and an impressive view from the backyard deck. (☎21479. Open M-Sa 10:30am-11:30pm, Su noon-11pm.) Idle youngsters congregate across the street at the **Atlantic Bar** to shoot pool and watch live rock bands on weekends. (☎22166. Open daily July-Aug. 10:30am-12:30am; Sept.-June 10:30am-11:30pm.) For trad, **Ostan na Rossan Hotel** rips it up on Wednesdays. (☎22444. Open M-Th 11am-11:30pm, F-Sa 11am-12:30am, Su 11am-11pm.)

Dungloe is a stop for Bus Éireann (☎071 916 0066) en route to Donegal Town (July-Aug. 3 per day) and to Glencolmcille (M-Sa 3 per day, Su 2 per day). Private bus lines also serve **Dungloe: Doherty's** (☎07495 21105) to **Larne** via **Letterkenny** and **Derry/Londonderry** (Sept.-June M, W, F-Sa; July-Aug. once per day); **Feda O'Donnell** (☎48114) leaves from Greene's Garage to **Galway** (Su 2:40pm, M 8:10pm) via **Glenties, Ardara, Killybegs, Donegal Town,** and **Sligo; Swilly** (☎074 912 2863) to **Derry/Londonderry** via **Burtonport, Annagry, Crolly, Bloody Foreland, Falcarragh,** and **Letterkenny** (M-F 3 per day). **Jack Glackin** (☎086 607 6121) and **Peter Paul Ward** (☎42295 or 06883 42071) provide 24hr. taxi service. Larger parties use **Frank Gallagher's Minibuses** (☎086 821 5936).

The Dungloe **tourist office**, located in the **Ionad Centre** (looks like a chapel and has gravestones out front) just off Main St. across from Patrick John Sally's, is the only such office in northern Donegal. (☎21297. Open M-F 10am-5:30pm; June-Sept. also Sa 11am-3pm.) Main St. has a **Bank of Ireland** with a 24hr. **ATM** (☎21077; open M-F 10am-12:30pm and 1:30-4pm, W open 10:30am), and the flashing green clock-in-a-cross of **O'Donnell's Pharmacy** (☎21386. Open M-Sa 9am-6pm). The **library**, housed in the same building as the tourist office, offers **Internet** access for residents and a computer room upstairs for non-residents. (☎22500. €2 per 30min. Open Tu and Th 10:30am-8pm, W and F 10:30am-5:30pm, Sa 10:30am-4pm.) The **post office** is on Quay Rd., off Main St. toward Crohy Head. (☎21067. Open M-F 9am-1pm and 2-5:30pm, Sa 9am-1pm.)

BURTONPORT AND ENVIRONS (AILT AN CHÓRRAIN) ☎07495

About 8km north of Dungloe, the fishing village of Burtonport is little more than a collection of pubs clustered around a pier. The village makes a good base for **fishing** and **boat trips** to the area's many uninhabited islands. More salmon are landed here than anywhere else in the British Isles. Spirited **sea angling** competitions occur during July and August—call the Dungloe tourist office for details. For a week in July, the **Burtonport Festival** primes locals for the subsequent **Mary from Dungloe Festival** with trad, dance, sport, and an intense karaoke competition. The ferry to Arranmore Island docks in Burtonport, and **Swilly Buses** (☎21380) has one or two stops in Burtonport on its daily Derry-Letterkenny-Dungloe route. The **post office** is on the edge of town, about 300m from the pier. (☎42001. Open M-F 9am-1pm and 2-5:30pm, Sa 9am-1pm.) At the gas station at the edge of town is a **Spar** for your basic grocery shopping needs. A giant lobster clinging to the wall marks Burtonport's most popular pub and the James Joyce Award-winning **Lobster Pot ❸**, on Main St., beside the harbor. Don't go swimming after facing the towering Titanic Seafood Platter (€52.50 for 2 or more); you're sure to sink. Smoked haddock chowder (€6) will satiate sardine-sized appetites. (☎42012. Sandwiches from €8.50; entrees €9-20. Kitchen open daily noon-10pm. AmEx/MC/V.) The yellow and blue **Skippers ❸**, on the left approaching the harbor, serves fresh seafood and some of the best cheap food in the area. (☎42234. Burgers €9; entrees €16-24. Kitchen open 11am-9pm; pub open 11am-midnight.) All of Burtonport's pubs are near the harbor and most are maritime-themed.

ARRANMORE ISLAND (ÁRAINN MHÓR) ☎07495

Arranmore has a full-time population of about 900, but it can swell to over 1500 during the peak of the summer season with visitors seeking a respite from the mainland and young people immersed in Irish-language courses. Despite its small size, the island's late-night *craic* is not to be underestimated.

Walkers who wish to see past the populated part of the area follow the **Arranmore Way** (*Siúlóid Árainn Mhóir*), a well-marked footpath that traces the circumference of the island. Choose from three routes of varying length. The longest of the three trails (about 6hr.) is marked in red and goes to the lighthouse at the far tip of the island, high above cliffs and crashing water. The trail passes The Old Mill, the Old Coastguard Station, the inner-island lakes, a mass rock, an **ancient fort**, and a **WWII lookout hut**. The second walk (about 4hr.) passes the town's main sights, including the craft shop and the Bridge, and affords amazing views of the islands and the Donegal coastline. The third hiking option, only 8km (about 2hr.), sticks mainly to the southeastern part of the island, leading to easily accessible views perfect for the faint of heart or fatigued of foot. All three trails are detailed on the map of the island (€3), usually available at Teac Phil Bán's (p. 439), or for free on the tourist informational sign at the crossroads between the pier street and the street with Early's Bar. Green Island, visible off the southwestern tip, harbors a **bird sanctuary.** Those seeking summertime edification should contact the **Foghlaim Irish Language and Culture Centre,** which offers Irish-language courses on the island. A typical day in this one-week summer program consists of classes in conversational and practical Gaelic, workshops on various aspects of Irish culture, guided historical walks around the island, poetry readings, and set dancing. (☎21593; www.foghlaim.com. Week-long course €175.)

Groceries on the island can be pricey, so stock up on the mainland. A string of pubs and houses stretches along the shore left of the ferryport. Down the street from the ferry lies the **Arranmore Hostel ❶,** a clean, modern building in an excellent seaside location visible from the quay. Call ahead, especially on summer weekends; ask for the popular sea-view dorm. Despite what the brochure says, Internet access is not available; get your online fix before you hop on the ferry. (☎20015 or 20737; www.arainmhor.com/hostel. Wheelchair-accessible. Towel and top sheet €1.30. July-Aug. dorms €14, Sept.-June €12.50. Private rooms €15.50; family rooms €50.) B&Bs on the island are common enough but can fill up during the high season; those in operation vary frequently. Always call ahead, or get contact info at www.arainmhor.com. **Ferryboat B&B ❹,** right off the pier, is easy to find, but spacious ensuite rooms and convenience come at a price. Downstairs, a **restaurant ❷** fills patrons up with satisfying grub. (☎20532. Most meals under €10. Singles €40; doubles €80.) **O'Donnell's B&B ❷** is a pleasant, lemon-colored house with a nice sea view. Young children are often hanging about. Make a left off the ferry, and then another left at the B&B sign about 2km down the road; it's the yellow house on the left. (☎20725. Some rooms with bath. Singles €35; doubles €70.)

Arranmore's famously raucous nightlife has been tamed somewhat by an increased police presence on the island during summer weekends. Nonetheless, pubs keep serving well past the 1am "closing" time. **Early's Bar,** on the right 45m up the hill from the landing, is where local lad Daniel O'Donnell got his start singing. The artist gives an annual concert on the island each August as a token of thanks. The bar also dishes out made-from-scratch stonebaked **pizzas** (from €8.50) that are worth the wait. (☎20515. Summer weekend trad. Open summer M-Th and Su 12:30pm-11:30pm, F-Sa 12:30pm-12:30am; low season open 5pm.) **Teach Phil Bán's** is to the left on the road from the ferry dock. At high tide the ocean slurps against the foundations and crowds slurp beverages at TPB's musty interior bar on rainy days. At the attached **grocery store,** visitors can try a bag of *dulce* (like "pulse"), a local seaweed delicacy, for €3, and buy books on Arranmore genealogy for €10. (Bar ☎20908, store ☎20508. Store open M-Sa 9am-6pm, Su 11:45am-1:30pm. July-Aug. weekend trad sessions. Bar open daily noon-midnight or 1am.)

The **ferry office,** up the road from the pier in Bonner's Restaurant and Amusement Centre, sends boats to Burtonport. (☎20532; www.arainnmhor.com/ferry. Open daily 8:30am-8:30pm. 25min.; June M-Sa 7 per day, Su 6 per day; July-Aug. M-Sa 8 per day, Su 7 per day; Apr.-May and Sept. 4-6 per day; Oct.-Mar. 4-5 per day. €15, students €10, under 14 €7, seniors free; car and driver €30, car and family €45.) The new fast ferry run by **Arranmore Charters** runs every hour or so and takes only about 5min. (M-Sa 7 per day, Su 4 per day, F night extra 2; pedestrians only.) By day, **O'Donnell's** (☎087 260 6833 or 20570) provides taxis and runs tours around the island. **Siob Teo,** a new **minibus service,** carts people all over the island (☎087 135 8028). Former operator of the Taisce Árainn Teo welcome center, **Seamus Bonner** now serves as an unofficial one-man tourist info center (ask around with the locals about finding or contacting him, or go to www.arainmhor.com). Maps of the island (€3) can be purchased at Teach Phil Bán's and most off-shore stores and B&Bs. The **post office** is across from Teach Phil Bán's. (☎20501. Open M-F 9am-1pm and 2-5:30pm, Sa 9am-1pm.)

RANAFAST ☎ 07495

In the heart of the Donegal *gaeltacht*, the village of **Annagry**, 9km past Burtonport on R259, marks the beginning of the **Ranafast** area, famous for its storytelling tradition. Quiet Annagry is upended each summer by flocks of young people piling in to attend Irish-language camps. **Swilly Buses** (☎ 074 912 873) runs to **Annagry** (1 per day) and **Crolly** (3 per day) on its Derry-Letterkenny-Falcarragh-Dungloe route.

Campers rest easy at the family-friendly **Sleepy Hollow's Campsite ❶**, a 2min. walk past Tabbairne Leo. There are no headless horsemen, only a charming wooded campsite with luxurious amenities like laundry (€8 per bag), Internet access (€3 per hr.), and a full Irish breakfast for €6. (☎ 48272; http://homepage.eircom.net/~sleepyhollow. Showers available. Tent or caravan: €9 per adult, €4 per child.) Travelers seeking a luxury B&B find a worthwhile splurge in **Danny Minnie's ❹**. All rooms come complete with bath, gorgeous antique furniture, and inviting beds decorated with country-style pillows and dolls. (☎ 48201. Rooms €50-60 per person.) Downstairs, enjoy a superb candlelit meal in the hotel's elegant **restaurant ❺**, which specializes in local seafood (entrees €25-39). In addition to their storytelling and fine dining, the outskirts of Annagry hold some well-respected trad institutions. About 450m south of the village, in a big beige building on top of a hill to the left of the road, is hotel **Caisleain Oir** ("CASH-lin ore"), which has a pub and restaurant. (☎ 48113. *Panini* €9; entrees €11-24.) Five kilometers west of town is the famous **Tabbairne Leo.** Leo is the father of **Enya** and the members of **Clannad**, and he's created a tourist mecca around his famous family. Though his children's silver, gold, and platinum records decorate the walls, Leo centers the proceedings on himself, serenading bus loads with his well-rehearsed lounge act of ballads and stories. (☎ 48143. Kitchen open daily 1-8:30pm. Bar open M-Th and Su noon-12:15am, F-Sa noon-12:45am.) For a less solipsistic (and more impressive) musical experience, head to **Teác Tessie,** across the street, where a rotating cast of locals and musical pilgrims gathers for spontaneous trad on weekends and whenever the spirit strikes them. (☎ 48124. Kitchen open noon-5pm; bar open until 12:30am.) For groceries, head to **Vivo/Cope** on Main St. as you head into town from Dungloe (☎ 48003. Open M-Sa 9am-10pm and Su 9am-6pm).

GWEEDORE (GAOTH DUBHAIR)

The coastal parish of Gweedore gives way to untouched wilderness as it moves inland toward barren mountain peaks and tiny towns nestled in valleys. It is a patchwork of natural wonders, from the sanguine hues of the Bloody Foreland to the legendary Poison Glen on tranquil Dunlewy Lake, the towering Errigal Mountain, and the forests and bogs of Glenveagh National Park. Gweedore fulfills another role as the weekend amusement center for the *gaeltacht* youth who flood Derrybeg's discos. Tory Island, off Gweedore's northern coast, is a world apart from Ireland, with its own elected king and freedom from Irish taxes.

DUNLEWY AND ERRIGAL MOUNTAIN ☎ 07495

Two kilometers north of the small town of **Crolly,** N56 and the coastal road diverge. N56 turns inland and reaches R251 after about 8km. This road leads east through the village of **Dunlewy** *(Dún Lúiche)*, past the conical **Errigal Mountain,** and on to **Glenveagh National Park.** Dunlewy, which straddles the border of the Gweedore and Cloghaneely parishes, makes a great base for exploring the pristine heaths of the **Derryveagh Mountains.** An interlocking web of trails for hikers of varying abilities extends over the region. These are often hard to follow even with a map; hikers should grab the *Ordnance Survey #1* and *6*, and always inform someone of their plans before setting off. The town itself has its own set of scenic trails, including the ascent to Errigal, a ramble through the Poison Glen, and the numerous paths in Glenveagh National Park (see **Gartan**, p. 452).

A few minutes up the road toward the mountain is a turnoff to Dunlewy Lake and the **Poison Glen**. According to legend, the mighty cyclops Balor was stabbed in the eye with a burning rod at the foot of Errigal Mountain, and the putrid blood that oozed from the fatal wound ran into the glen. Along the paved road lies an unmarked car park that signals the beginning of the trail up **Errigal Mountain** (Ireland's 2nd-highest peak, 751m). In parts, the mountain is too soft or slippery for safe walking. Stick to the grass as much as possible. Expect the challenging scramble to take three hours round-trip. On a clear day, the view from the narrow ridge leading to the tip sweeps over several counties and even more lakes.

Back in Dunlewy proper, follow the signs off the main road for the **Ionad Cois Locha Dunlewy,** or Dunlewy Lakeside Centre. The busy center has 30min. boat tours on Dunlewy Lake, paddle-boat rentals, weaving demonstrations, a craft shop, a playground, a resident red deer, info on the surrounding area, a fire-warmed cafe with snacks, and full meals for €8-10. (☎31699. Open St. Patrick's Day through Oct. M-Sa 10:30am-6pm, Su 11am-6pm. Boat trip or weaving cottage tour €5.75, students and seniors €5, children €4, families €15. Combined ticket €9.50/9/7/24. Playground €3.75, children, students and seniors €3.50, families €13.) The center also provides interested ramblers with descriptions of excellent walks in Dunlewy. Two routes go through the Errigal Mountains: the tourist route (8km, ascending 523m; 2-2½hr.) and the more rugged northwest ridge route (8km, 566m; 2-2½hr.); both lead to the summit.

There is one hostel in Dunlewy; the **Errigal Youth Hostel ❶,** which has recently re-opened its doors. It's the large, modern house two buildings past the gas station, driving out of Dunlewy toward Letterkenney. There are also a few B&Bs along the road that leads to Lake Dunlewy (follow the signs for Poison Glen). Closest to the main road is **Bia Agus Leaba B&B ❸** (whose name means simply "food and bed"), which offers simple rooms, most with a great view of Poison Glen and the abandoned church. From the road leading out of Dunlewy toward Letterkenny, take the turn-off for Poison Glen. Bia Agus Leaba is on the right a few houses down. (☎31835. Singles €37, with bath €40; doubles €64/70.) Hungry chefs should stock up in advance, as the only grocery store within walking distance is the Top service station next to the Errigal Hostel.

Bus Éireann runs a M-F summer-only bus between Bundoran and Letterkenny which stops in Dunlewy, 11:30am toward Letterkenny and 3:05pm toward Bundoran (10:55am and 4:35pm, respectively, for the Glenveagh Park stop). Local buses only come as close as Crolly, 13km west of Dunlewy. **Feda O'Donnell** (☎48114) provides a daily coach service to and from **Galway** and **Donegal Town** (M-Th and Sa-Su 2 per day, F 4 per day); **John McGinley Coaches** (☎35201) go from **Crolly** to **Dublin** (M 3 per day, Tu-Th 2 per day plus 1 Mar.-Sept., F 3 per day plus 1 Mar.-Sept., Sa 2 per day, Su 4 per day); **Gallagher's Bus Service** (☎48356) goes by on its way to **Belfast** via **Letterkenny** and **Derry**. Getting from Crolly to Dunlewy requires a **taxi** ride; try **Charlie Mac** (☎26037) or **Popeye's** (☎32633).

GARTAN   ☎07491

On the eastern side of the Derryveagh Mountains, **Gartan Parish** is the most rural of the *gaeltacht* parishes. As a result, it has few towns and even fewer accommodations. Nevertheless, Gartan is home to some of the *gaeltacht's* greatest attractions. Most travelers base themselves in Dunlewy or daytrip from Letterkenny via **Bus Éireann's** "Glenveagh-Dunlewy" Tour. (☎21309. €22, children €15, students €18. Departs June 25-Aug. 24 M-F 10am and 1:45pm.)

Twelve kilometers from Dunlewy, **Glenveagh National Park** consists of 9500 hectares of forest glens, bogs, and mountains. One of the largest herds of red deer in Europe roams the park; deer-watching is best at dusk and in winter, when the deer come to forage in the valley. Badgers, endangered golden eagles, sandpipers, and other species complete the all-star wildlife cast. Despite Glenveagh's popularity, it's easy to lose the crowd along the park's wide-open spaces. Park rangers lead **guided nature walks** and more strenuous **hill walks.** There are five mountains in and around the park: Dooish is closest to the Visitors Centre, Moylenanav is between two portons of the park, Slieve Snacght is across R254 from Moylenanav, Crocknafarragh is a bit further in its own sections of park, and the great Errigal is just outside of Dunlewy. The **Visitors Centre** has information about these as well as self-guided routes. Head there to watch a 25min. video about the park's wildlife or to enjoy a meal (€8-12) at its cafeteria-style **restaurant ❶.** The *Park Guide* (€6) and *Ordnance Survey #6* (€7) are available at the visitors center on R251 east of Dunlewy. (☎37090; www.heritageireland.ie. Open Feb.-Nov. daily 10am-6pm, Dec.-Jan. daily 10am-5pm; car park gates close at 8pm. Park always open. Call ahead for info or to schedule a walk.) Summertime tourists can take the minibus from the park's entrance to **Glenveagh Castle,** 3.5km away. Although it was built in 1870, the castle looks like a medieval keep with its thick walls, battle-ready ramparts, turrets, and round tower. In 1922 the castle was occupied by the IRA, and its builder, John Adair, infamously evicted 244 tenants from the estate when he purchased it, banishing them either to Australia or to workhouses. (Minibus from park entrance runs every 10-15min.; last departure 1½hr. before closing. €2, students, seniors and children €1. Castle open for guided tours only daily 10am-6pm; last tour 45min. before closing. €3, seniors €2, students and children €1.50.) The surrounding **gardens** were designed by a later owner, American Henry McIlhenny, who left the estate to the government upon his death. Pines and rhododendrons create a buffer against the harsh weather, allowing exotic flowers to flourish inside. Free **tours** of the grounds depart from the castle courtyard. (June-Aug. Su 2pm; call ahead to request a tour July-Aug.) The castle's **tea room** is open daily 10:30am-5:30pm. Three kilometers up the incline behind the castle, **View Point** provides a great panorama of the park.

The delicately manicured 20-acre plot on the northern shore of Gartan Lough, 17km east of Dunlewy, is another Irish Heritage Site, bequeathed to the state in 1981 by the English painter Derek Hill. The site houses two radically different art spaces. The **Glebe Gallery,** formerly Hill's own gallery, displays rotating exhibits of contemporary and 20th century art in a space with wood floors, track lighting, and other modern trappings. **◪Glebe House,** Hill's former residence, contains over 300 paintings and an assortment of craft objects, preserved as they were when Hill lived there. The artist's background in stage design and his innate appreciation of color has created an ornate and eclectic interior, cluttered with porcelain, glasswork, William Morris-designed wallpaper and curtains, his own paintings of Donegal, and countless items covering every available surface. The artist's most impressive purchases include a Picasso plate and some atypical creations of Jack Yeats and Auguste Renoir. Works by the Tory Island "primitive" painters, whom Hill mentored and promoted, are on display in the kitchen. Look for paintings by the current King of Tory Island, Patsy Dan Rodgers (see **Holding Court with the King,** p. 444). The gallery and house are on R251, 7km southeast of Glenveagh National Park's Visitors Centre. (☎37071. Open July-Aug. daily 11am-6:30pm. Easter week and late-May to late-Sept. M-Th and Sa-Su 11am-6:30pm. 45min. tours leave about every 30min. 11:30am-5:30pm. €2.90, students and children €1.30, seniors €2.10, families €7.40. Gallery is self-guided and free, same opening hours as the House.)

St. Columcille (AD 521-97; p. 59), famed for bringing Christianity from Ireland to Scotland, once resided near the shores of Gartan Lough. The countryside around the lough is punctuated with Columcillian ruins. The **St. Columcille Heritage Centre,** across Gartan Lough from Glebe House, is devoted to sharing his legacy and has permanent exhibits about his life and the development of Christianity in Donegal. A 20min. movie details the Columcille-related sights in the area and throughout Ireland. (☎37306 or 37021. Open Easter Week and 1st Su in May through last Su in Sept. M-Sa 10:30am-6pm, Su 1-6pm. €3, students and seniors €2, children €1.) It also functions as an unofficial tourist office; handouts give detailed directions to other saintly sights, including **Columcille's Birthplace, Abbey,** and **Bed of Loneliness.** The latter, a giant stone slab on the southeastern corner of the lake, was where the saint meditated the night before he began his exile in Scotland. Since then, prospective emigrants have lain on the stone overnight to ward off future loneliness.

When it's in full swing with youth groups and other aspiring outdoorsmen, the staff of **Gartan Outdoor Education Center ❷,** which is located just down the road from the St. Columcille Heritage Centre, is happy to put up guests in its spacious dorms and B&B rooms (with meals included), if they have room. (☎37032. Booking required. Rates may vary depending on situation; call ahead. Reception open M-F 9am-1pm and 2-5pm; after hours use the main entrance.)

BUNBEG AND DERRYBEG   ☎07495

Where N56 moves inland to Dungloe, R257 continues along the coast to Bunbeg *(An Bun Beag).* With little traffic, this scenic stretch of road is perfect for cyclists. Though *Let's Go* never recommends hitchhiking, hitchers tend to stay on N56, where cars are more common. **Bunbeg Harbour** is the smallest enclosed harbor in Ireland and was a main exit and entry point during the height of British occupation. Other period relics, such as military barracks, grain stones, and lookout towers line the harbor. A kilometer from bite-size Bunbeg along R257 is the larger **Derrybeg** *(Doirí Beaga),* which stretches its pubs, B&Bs, and services along the main road. However, the two towns have grown into each other, and even the locals are sometimes unclear when explaining where Bunbeg ends and Derrybeg begins. Bunbeg's harbor is one of two docking places for **Donegal Coastal Cruises** (a.k.a. **Turasmara;** Magheroarty office ☎07491 35061, Derrybeg office ☎31320) and the ferry service for **Tory Island,** which departs from R257 at the edge of town once a day at 9am (see **Transportation,** p. 455). Boats also sail from Bunbeg to **Gola Island,** which has deserted beaches and beautiful views. Halfway between Bunbeg and its harbor, a single stone pillar marks a rough path leading to the banks of the **Clady River,** an excellent spot for salmon fishing. In Derrybeg, across from Sean Og's, **Teach Tomáis** (☎31054) is the oldest shop in the parish, dealing Irish books and crafts as well as a decent selection of English-language classics. (Open M-Sa 10am-6pm. If the shop is locked, knock at the door to its right, the home of the owner.)

North of Derrybeg on R257, the **Bloody Foreland,** a short length of rough scarlet rock, juts into the sea. At sunset on clear evenings, the sea reflects the deep red hue of the rocks and sea, composing one of Ireland's most famous views. An old legend holds that the sea is colored with the blood of sailors who perished in the wrecks of Spanish Armada galleons. Farther west, the headland at **Meenlaragh** (2km west of **Magheroarty**) stretches for kilometers of unspoiled beaches. A **holy well** remains full of fresh water despite tidal rushes twice per day.

The left turn immediately after the AIB leads to **An Teach Bán B&B ❸,** run by amiable owners Linda and Paul. A new conservatory with beautiful bay views draws guests out of their comfy rooms, and the breakfasts are top notch. (☎32359; pmcgill@iol.ie. Singles €28-36; doubles €60-64.) Comfort and convenience abound at **Bunbeg House ❸,** on the waterfront, with tranquil rooms and a bar serving meals for €5-15. Coming from town, make a right at the edge of town, down toward the ferry. (☎31305; www.bunbeghouse.com. Kitchen open July-Aug. daily 6-9pm; tea room serves breakfast and tea all day. Singles €35-40;

doubles €70.) Back in Derrybeg, the ivy-clad **Teach Campbell** ❸ has books for visitors to peruse in the lounge and big rooms equipped with TV and phone. (☎31545. All rooms with bath. Singles €40-45; doubles €70.) Guests at **Teach Hudi Beag** ❸ have only 10m to walk to find the best trad in the area; in fact, they can probably hear it from their rooms. (☎31016; www.tradcentre.com/hiudaibeag, hiudaibeag@gmail.com. All rooms with bath. Singles €40; doubles €60.)

At the northern end of town, **Gallagher's Food Store** at the Statoil gas station is the largest grocery store. (Open M-F 8am-8pm, Sa 8am-7pm, Su 8am-2pm.) Just a bit farther down the road, **Spar** sells groceries and has a post office and a cafe, **Molloy's Cafeteria.** (☎31165. Full breakfast €5.75; sandwiches €3-3.50. Cafe open M-Sa 9am-4:30pm. Spar open M-Sa 9am-7:30pm, Su 9am-1:30pm.) Derrybeg's most popular diner and late-night takeway hub is **Pepper's Diner** ❶, which serves a wide selection of the three basic food groups—pizza (from €6.20), ice cream (€1-2), and eight different deep-fried dishes consisting wholly of french fries. (☎31110. All-day breakfast €6. Open daily 8am-10pm; takeaway available F-Sa until 4am.) The irresistible 🖾**Hudi Beag's** pub, a two-story white building at the western (port side) entrance to town, stokes the flames of Derrybeg's musical tradition with its legendary Monday night jam sessions (10pm-1am) drawing 10-25 musicians each time. (☎31016. Occasional F trad; Sa and summer Su rock/pop/oldies. Open M-Th 2-11:30pm, F 2pm-12:30am, Sa noon-12:30am, Su noon-11pm.) Vaulted ceilings and old paintings lend a refined air to the raucous *craic* at **Seán Óg's**, with live music most nights and a Friday night disco. Non-music fans snack on pub grub while fans remain glued to the TVs, which show every game that's playing. (☎32999; www.seanogs.com. Live music Th, Sa-Su. W trad during the summer. Open M-Th 11am-midnight, F-Sa 11am-1am, Su noon-11:30pm.) After pub hours, Bunbeg cuts a rug at the **Millennium Niteclub,** located behind the Sea View Hotel. (Open year-round F-Sa 12:30pm-2:30am; July-Aug. also Su 12:30pm-2:30am. Cover €10.)

To reach Derrybeg by **bus,** try John McGinley (☎07495 35201 or ☎01451), whose Annagry-Dublin route stops at the Bunbeg crossroads (M 3 per day, Tu-Th 2 per day plus 1 Mar.-Sept., F 3 per day plus 1 Mar.-Sept., Sa 2 per day, Su 4 per day). Derrybeg's streets have several banks, but only the **AIB** has both a **bureau de change** and an **ATM. Gweedore Pharmacy** (☎31254) is housed in a white building across the street and a few yards up from Hudi Beag's pub. The Bunbeg **post office** (☎31165) is located across from Hudi Beag's in a small shop; there's also one in Derrybeg, inside Spar. (Open M-F 9am-1pm and 2-5:30pm, Sa 9am-1pm.)

TORY ISLAND (OILEÁN THORAIGH)   ☎07491

The barren landscape of Tory Island, only 13km offshore, is visible from the Bloody Foreland. Named for its many *tors* (hills), the island provides minimal footing for its weather-beaten cottages and eccentric local characters. The independent islanders refer to the mainland as "the country" and still elect a **Rí na nóileán** (king of the island) to a life term that usually entails his becoming the island's PR man. The current Rí, Patsy Dan, relishes his role, maintaining a unique monarchical style with an earring, a cap which never leaves his head, a motorcycle, and accordionist and painter gigs on the side. The island gained mythical status as the home of the demonic Formorians, the original Tory Island pirates who regularly invaded the mainland. This prompted people to equate the word "Tory" with pirate or rascal, a slang term that became associated with British politics. ("Whig," incidentally, originally referred to a Scottish horse thief.) As recently as the last century, Tory Island lived up to its swashbuckling mystique and thrived on an illegal *poitín* trade (see **Whiskey Business,** p. 67). All six layers of the island's turf were burned to produce the alcohol; as a result, today's Tory appears rockier and grassier than the mainland. Residents gradually have been forced to depend

THE LOCAL STORY

HOLDING COURT WITH THE KING

Visitors to the island can look forward to a personal greeting from Patsy Dan O' Ruaidhrí, King of Tory Island, as he meets the ferry whenever possible.

On becoming King: I was given the honor 12 years ago. We had *ceilís* and enjoyed ourselves thoroughly. It was decided by the community to give it to me.

On the relationship between the island and the mainland: It was 10 years ago when we started to get funding from Ireland and from the EU. But before that, trying to get the Irish government to help with development was harder than trying to get a cat through a stocking, and you can understand how hard it is to get a cat through a stocking. The government is a bit more flexible now.

On the future: I'm putting a cry out for young teenagers to get jobs on the island. There's no sense building an island without the young people. If we kept them, eventually the population will go back up again.

On Gaelic: I'm very fond of the language myself and very, very proud, as are the other islanders. This is why I have a slip now and again in my English. I also sing Latin hymns in my church, so in one way or another, I'm struggling with three languages.

On the beginnings of primitive painting on Tory Island: The primitive school of Tory began when an English man named Derek Hill

on mainland supplies as local farming has almost entirely disappeared. Only one tree survives on the island, and livestock herds are almost non-existent. The eastern end of the island breaks into a series of jagged sea cliffs, covered in summer by a swarm of sea birds. Come to the island on the feast of St. John to see the annual bonfire night—a great opportunity to witness traditional entertainment.

Most of Tory's sights are decrepit at best, but a little informed imagination can do wonders. The *Oileán Toraigh/Tory Island* guide book offers stimulating, comprehensive, and bilingual information on the island. At €5, it's an expensive surrogate for the basic information leaflet (pick up a copy at *Siopa Thorai*). A right turn off the pier, **Gailearai Dixon** (Dixon Gallery) showcases the work of the Tory Primitives, a group of local artists promoted by Derek Hill of Glebe House fame (p. 453). Typically painted using donkey-hair brushes, the artwork usually depicts the colorful natural scenery of the island. Today, Rí Patsy Dan himself is the poster child of the primitive style, and much of his eye-catching work can be seen here. (☎35011 or 08706 99240. Call on Anton Meenan—whose work is also featured in the gallery—up the road at cottage #6 if the facility is shut; when you get to the three pairs of attached cottages on the left up the road, his is the last one. If no one answers there, try his studio out back.) The island's historical sights include a crumbling tower marking the **ruins** of the monastery that St. Columcille founded in the 6th century, the **Tau Cross** by the pier, and a **torpedo** that washed ashore during WWII and was erected in the road, dividing east and west Tory.

Legend has it that a stone on one of Tory's hills has the power to fulfill wishes. Dreamers who throw three pebbles onto the stone on the tip of the island's east end (20min. from the pier) on an unapproachable perch will be granted a wish. In addition to the **wishing stone,** the island features a **cursing stone,** which was buried in a secret location by elders to prevent its misuse. The cursing stone has been credited with the 1884 shipwreck of the aptly named *HMS Wasp*, which carried British tax collectors. Six of the victims of the wreck rest in the graveyard near the pier. The bell from the HMS Wasp is kept in the Dixon Gallery. Bird buffs enjoy the free and informal **Tory Mor** (bird sanctuary) near the wishing stone, home to Donegal's largest colony of puffins, along with guillemots, kittiwakes, and seagulls. The islanders still pay no taxes.

Tory tourists have a few options for accommodations, the cheapest being the newly reopened **Teach Bhillie ❷.** Turn left off the ferry and walk 200m along the shore, past the tower; it's the cream-colored house with red trim. The ensuite rooms and modern self-catering kitchen have plenty of sun and great sea views. (☎65145. Call ahead. Continental breakfast included. Singles €25; doubles €50.) **Óstan Thóraig ❹**, in a red-trimmed building in front of the pier, has airy, sweet-smelling hotel rooms with baths and TV. The knowledgeable staff compensates for Tory's lack of a tourist office. (☎35920; www.toryhotel.com. Breakfast included. Singles €55-60; doubles €110-120, prices rise during summer. Ages 5-12 ½-price, under 5 free. Inquire for midweek specials.) The menu at the hotel's **restaurant ❷** changes daily but the prices remain high. (Entrees €18-24; specials €9.50 and €13. Open daily 6:30-9:30pm.) The cheaper **bar ❷** has daytime and evening menus. (Sandwiches €3.50; entrees €7.50-12.50. Kitchen open daily noon-4pm and 6-9pm.) Lighter bites are offered at **Caife an Chreagain ❶**, signposted up to the left from the pier. (☎35856. Toasties €4-4.50. Burgers from €4. Open Easter-Sept. daily 10:30am-10:30pm.) Islanders congregate at **Club Thoraighe (aka Club Soisialta)**, beyond the cafe, a great place to see Irish dance and hear Tory Island trad, which has a slightly stronger rhythmic emphasis than mainland music. (☎65121 or 35502. Open daily 8:30pm-late.) Patsy Dan himself lives across the street in the long cream-colored house. If groceries are what you need, the only game in town is **Siopa Thorai**. (☎65828. Open June-Aug. daily 11am-6pm; Sept.-May M-Sa 11am-2pm and 4-6pm, Su 11:45am-2pm). The store is located before the gallery, right on the main road from the pier.

Donegal Coastal Cruises (a.k.a. **Turasmara;** ☎07495 31320 or 07495 31340; p. 454) runs boats from **Bunbeg** (1½hr.; daily 9am) and, more frequently, from **Magheroarty** (2km east of Meenlaragh) beyond Bloody Foreland on R257 (45min.; Apr.-June and Sept. daily 11:30am and 5pm; July-Aug. 11:30am, 1:30, and 5pm). Call ahead to check departure times and arrive at least 15min. early—unlike most things in Donegal, the ferry is punctual, and the tides may force an early departure. Daytrippers can return on a 4pm ferry or wait until 6pm for a ride to Bunbeg; those who stay the night can catch the 10:30am ferry in the morning. (Bunbeg dock ☎074 953 1991, Meenlaragh ☎913 5061. Return €24, July-Aug. €20, students and seniors €15, under 15 €10, under 5 free.) On the island, **bikes** can be rented from Patrick Rodgers, next to Teach Bhillie's. (€12 per day, deposit of €25 sometimes required. Open June-Aug. daily 9am-9pm; Sept.-May call ahead.) At the hotel, **Dive Tory** arranges accommodations and transportation for diving, sea angling, and bird-watching trips around the island. (☎35920 or 35282. Open from St. Patrick's Day

came here in 1956. He had a great love for Tory and came every summer after that for 30 years. He rented a wee hut here at the top of the hill, and he used to come and paint there.

One day, Derek Hill was painting on the point, and not knowing the name of the islander who was standing there watching him, he turned around to him and said, "What do you think of my artwork?" Now, Derek Hill was expecting him to say, "You're a powerful artist!" But the islander said, "To be honest with you, I think I could do better myself." That man was James Dixon, who became the most powerful primitive painter between Ireland and the British Isles. Imagine!

Derek Hill asked him: "Is there any possibility that if I send you art materials by post I will be able to encourage you to paint?" James said, "of course," and Derek Hill was thrilled. He said, "I'll send you brushes, and colors, and art paper." Well, James said, "Whatever you do, don't bother sending me brushes." It wasn't because he was unmannerly, you see, he was just a very unique islander. He said, "I have a donkey in the field, I will cut its tail twice a year, and I will make my own brushes." They kept in touch, and Dixon, painting with his donkey's tail, became one of the most powerful primitive painters. *The Tory primitive painters have toured all over the world. James Dixon's work can be found in Glebe House, (see p. 453).*

through Halloween. Call ahead for prices. All-inclusive deals with hotel accommodations available, such as B&B, round-trip ferry, dinner, and dive combo €115.)

CLOGHANEELY

East of Gweedore lies the parish of Cloghaneely. Thanks to its *gaeltacht* schools, white-sand beaches, and excellent weather, it's inundated with visitors from the North and English-speaking teens studying Irish in the summer. A bastion of Gaelic culture, Cloghaneely harbors a strong community of artists and poets, lending its pubs and cafes a decidedly bohemian air rarely found in the Irish countryside. The great 20th-century Ulster poet Cathal Ó Searcaigh and other visiting poets and artists make muses of the area's mellow vibe and natural beauty. Whether they frequent Horn Head or the Ards Forest Park, it's no wonder that many visitors feel inspired to stay on longer than expected. The **Samhain International Poetry Festival** in July and classes at the Poets' House also attract visitors.

FALCARRAGH (AN FÁL CARRACH) ☎ 07491

Between the boundless beaches stretching along the coast northeast of the Bloody Foreland rests one of the busiest Irish-speaking villages in the *gaeltacht*. Falcarragh, like many of the settlements in this region, offers little to do in the town during the day, but crowds gathered for writing conferences and summertime Irish language programs create a mellow evening pub scene. At the very least, Falcarragh is worth a few days of beach-bumming and pub-hopping. The towering sand dunes at **Ballyness,** 5km outside of town, are Falcarragh's primary attraction; to reach them, follow the signs for "Trá" (beach) at the south end of town.

🖪🖪 **TRANSPORTATION AND PRACTICAL INFORMATION.** Several private **bus** companies stop in Falcarragh: **Feda O'Donnell** (☎ 07495 48114) traces the West Coast, running from Crolly through Donegal Town to **Sligo** and **Galway** (M-Th and Sa 2 per day, F and Su 3 per day); **McGinley** (☎ 07495 35201 or 01451 3809) passes through on a Donegal-Dublin trek (M 3 per day, Tu-Th 2 per day plus 1 Mar.-Sept., F 4 per day plus 1 Mar.-Sept., Sa 2 per day, Su 4 per day); **Gallagher's Bus** hits Falcarragh en route from **Dungloe** to **Belfast** via **Letterkenny** and **Derry/Londonderry.** Hitching is common in this area, although *Let's Go* doesn't recommend it. For travel over shorter distances, call **Joe's Taxi** (☎ 65017). Off the main road to the south, ferries sail from **Magheroarty Port** to **Tory Island** (June and Sept. daily 11:30am and 5pm; July-Aug. 11:30am, 1:30, and 5pm; €20-24 return; see full info in the Tory Island section) and **Inishbofin Island** (10min.; call **Carmel Olivia** at ☎ 07491 35635 or ☎ 08762 79789). A brand-new **An tSean Bheairic** ("visitors center") runs a craft center and cafe, and offers local art on display, an audio-visual presentation, and reading materials about region. (☎ 80888; www.falcarraghvisitorscentre.com. W trad sessions 8-10pm. Wheelchair-accessible. Open M-F 10am-5pm, Sa noon-5pm.) The **Bank of Ireland,** Main St., has an **ATM** and a **bureau de change.** (☎ 35484. Open M-F 10am-12:30pm and 1:30-4pm.) Inquire about **work opportunities** at **Maggie Dan's,** which is always keen to hire musicians, traditional or otherwise, for accommodation and a small salary per gig. (Contact Milo at ☎ 80600.) **Falcarragh Pharmacy** is on Main St. (☎ 35778. Open M-F 9:30am-6pm, Sa 10am-6pm.) Falcarragh's **post office** is also on Main St. (☎ 35110. Open M-Sa 9:30am-6pm.) For **Internet** access, there are two options, both on Main St.: bookstore **Focal ar Focal** ("word for word") charges €1 per 15min. and offers local art for sale (☎ 80685; open M-Sa 10am-6pm), and **Joe's Taxi,** across from the gas station, which is slightly cheaper at €3 per hr. (☎ 65017. Open M-Sa noon-9pm, Su 2-9pm.)

⬛⬜ ACCOMMODATIONS AND FOOD. The **Shamrock Lodge Hostel (IHH) ❷**, above the pub on Main St., has basic bunks that house poets and artists during the International Poetry Festival. (☎35859. Call ahead. 4-bed dorms €16 per person; singles €40; twins €64. Closed from mid-Dec. to mid-Jan.) Off Main St., on the way to the beach (follow the signs for "Trá"), **Cuan na Mara** ("bay of the sea") ❸, has four comfortable rooms with views of Ballyness Bay out the back. The place is well signposted from Main St. leaving town southbound. (Singles €30, with bath €32, add €5 during summer; doubles €60/64.)

Turn off Main St. at Corner Bar to find **Centra,** which sells groceries and alcohol. (☎35229; open M-Th 7:30am-8pm, F-Sa 7:30am-9pm, Su 8:30am-7pm), as does **Spar,** on Main St. (☎80711. Open daily 8:30am-8pm.) Most days, **outdoor vendors** line Main St. selling just about everything, including fresh fruit, vegetables, and locally caught seafood. The simply decorated, simply delicious **Fulacht Fiadh Cafe ❶**, Main St., satisfies bohemians with tight purses. If your purse-strings are a bit looser, you can purchase the local art hanging on the walls. (☎80683. Breakfast €3.50-4.50; *panini* €5. Open M-Sa 9:30am-5pm.) **Damian's ❶**, at the top of Main St., serves delicious chipper fare. (☎65613. Lunch specials €8; entrees €8-11. Open M-Sa 10am-7pm, Su 1-6pm.) **Shamrock Lodge** (*Lóistín na Seamróige*), in the center of town, has cartoon paintings of Celtic warriors and their female paramours/accomplices on its facade and above its spacious beer garden. Inside, the front room is a traditional pub with a *céilí* room for trad; in back, the swinging doors of the "Mexican" saloon inspire dramatic entrances. (☎35859. Sa trad, Su rock and country. Open M-Sa noon-9pm, Su 2-9pm.) On Ballyconnell Rd., just off Main St. next to Bank of Ireland, the **Loft Bar's** black and white country cottage-style exterior conceals an interior consisting almost entirely of nooks and crannies filled with locals. (☎35992. Occasional weekend music in summer. Open M-Th 10:30am-11:30pm, F-Sa 10:30am-12:30pm, Su noon-11pm.)

Just down the road from town, 1.6km south of Falcarragh on N56, the village of **Gortahork** (*Gort a'Choirce*) argues for quality over quantity with excellent food, pints, and bohemian flair. There are few bed & breakfasts in the area; one is the **An Stoirin B&B,** whose name means "high place" despite its low-lying site. (☎35912. All rooms with bath. Singles €30; doubles €60.) With leather couches and local artwork, ⬛**Maggie Dan's ❷** is as much a cultural center as a tearoom and a tasty pizzeria. Owner Milo hosts musical events all summer, including Monday piano bar and Friday jazz. The upstairs theater hosts regular poetry and dramatic recitals. The helpful staff advises on accommodations and tours. (☎65630; www.maggiedans.ie. 10 in. pizza €5. Open daily 6-11pm.)

◩⬛ SIGHTS AND OUTDOOR ACTIVITIES. Festivals and concerts revolve around **Maggie Dan's** in Gortahork. At Maggie Dan's, a **Jazz and Blues Festival** draws crooners and swingers during Easter week, starting Easter Sunday. The mid-July **Gaelic Festival** celebrates the best of Gaelic culture with performances, readings, and music in Irish and English. Just when revelers think the fun is over, the **Falcarragh Festival** fills the streets with music, dance, and games for 3-4 days. The **Women's Festival** kicks off the second week in August with talks from intriguing international females, such as Bernadette Devlin, the Republican protester and youngest woman elected to the House of Commons. In October or November, €5000 goes to the winner of the **Samhain International Poetry Festival,** hosted by Cathal Ó Searcaigh. The festival emphasizes Irish language and culture. (Event info available through Maggie Dan's or at www.samhainpoetry.com.)

INISHBOFIN ISLAND ☎07491

Inishbofin Island is just a 10min. motorboat ride from Magheroarty Beach, but it seems like it's in a world of its own. (Contact **Carmel Olivia** for a ride at ☎07491 35635 or 08762 79789. Book ahead; prices and schedule are seasonal and by request.) One day every year a sand bar connecting the island to the mainland appears, though it should not be considered an alternate route of transportation. Introduced to electricity in 2002 and tap water in 2003, the village houses a summertime population of about 35 people, along with two tractors, three jeeps, and four dogs, all huddled on one side of the 5km island. The largest population on the island is an assortment of frisky rabbits that bound constantly from the grass and across the rocky beach. The stone arch on the coast is fabled to break if tread upon by a pair of lovers.

DUNFANAGHY (DÚN FIONNACHAIDH) ☎07491

Eleven kilometers north of Falcarragh, Dunfanaghy is a pleasant beach town with a distinctly anglicized character and unique natural features that serves as a summer refuge for Northern Irish tourists seeking to avoid Marching Season. The **Dunfanaghy Workhouse Heritage Centre,** a few hundred meters southwest of town, is a former poorhouse transformed since Famine days. Siphoning her voice through wax figures, "Wee Hannah" narrates her life of hardship, but the bucky lass made it through the Great Hunger in Northwest Donegal and lived past the age of 90. A new exhibit and film also explore the ecology of the area, explaining the formation of New Lake and the surrounding sand dunes. (☎36540. Open mid-June to mid-Sept. M-Sa 10am-5pm; call ahead during other months, especially if you are in a group. €4.50, students and ages 13-16 €3, under 13 €2, seniors €3.50.) The natural attractions within a seven-kilometer radius of Dunfanaghy and Falcarragh are easily accessible by foot, bicycle, or car. Hitching is common, though never recommended by *Let's Go*. The helpful *Walking Donegal: Dunfanaghy* (€3) is available throughout the region and is stocked en masse by the author/proprietor at Corcreggan Hostel. **Horn Head,** signposted on the way into Dunfanaghy, invites long rambles around its pristine beaches, megalithic tombs, and gorse-covered hills. Tireless hikers who make the 14km trek (3½hr., 4½hr. in spring) to the northern tip of Horn Head from Dunfanaghy reach some of the most dramatic sea cliffs in Ireland. The lazy can drive all but the last 3km.

Ards Forest Park, a few kilometers past Dunfanaghy on N56, features a number of nature trails (3-12km) throughout the park's 480 hectares, as well as gorgeous beaches and expansive sand bars for exploration and relaxation. Maps are available at the entrance and in the parking lot. (Open Mar.-Sept. daily 10am-7:30pm; Oct.-Feb. daily 10am-4:30pm. Parking €5.) About 7km south of town on N56, **New Lake**—so called because it was formed in 1912 after a massive storm blocked an estuary—features a world-famous ecosystem and playful otters. Stone walls, relics of where the lake flooded local farmland, can still be seen in the water. The sand dunes surrounding the area have shifted over time, reinventing the landscape and creating a sand bar that connects the mainland to Horn Head, which is thought to have been an island in the past. Beach bums enjoy the spectacular **Tramore Strand,** a 25min. walk through dunes from the Horn Head Bridge.

Turning your back to the sea anywhere in Dunfanaghy brings the expanse of **Muckish Mountain** into view. There are two ways to ascend the mountain. The first, more difficult route takes four hours and covers 12km. It's best to bring along *Ordnance Survey #2* (€9) and a compass. To reach the path, drive from Dunfanaghy toward Creeslough, turn right when the graveyard is on the left, and continue for 4.8km to where the grassy track crosses the road. Park here and walk uphill on the road to the two foundations. The path begins to the right of the upper foundation, across a narrow steam. Once you reach the quarry, the path to the summit is to the right. **Do not climb the mountain in low visibility, as there are some huge drops.** The easier route to the summit takes only two hours. Drive to Muckish Gap (marked by a small roadside shrine), follow the path northeast for 800m, then turn northwest to reach the summit. **Dunfanaghy Stables** (☎00980 or 08682 80552), behind Arnold's Hotel in Dunfanaghy town, leads rides over the dry lakebed and through Ards Forest Park. (1hr. rides along the beach €25, children €20. Longer rides through the forests and mountains available; call for prices.)

One kilometer south of Dunfanaghy toward Falcarragh, the ◾**The Carriage Hostel (IHH, IHO)** ❶ has been built over the course of a decade by the owner, a seasoned traveler who found himself trapped by bad weather while sailing around Ireland. He has converted an old train into comfortable four-bed dorms and private doubles with mahogany floors and equipped the 200-year-old former kiln house with bunks and loft doubles. Most buses will stop at the door. (☎00814; www.the-carriage-hostel-corcreggan.com, book online at www.hostelworld.com. Internet access €3 per hr. Laundry €3 with line dry. Railway bunk singles €17; doubles €42. **Camping** €8 per person.) If you can tolerate the smell of the farm next door, the **Rossman House B&B** ❹ has several large rooms. (☎36273; rossman@eircome.net. Singles €50; doubles €68.) **Ramsay's Store**, next to the parking lot in the town center, stocks groceries. It also has all-day breakfast (€4) and other cafeteria-style meals in the back (lunch specials €7; *panini* €4). The Ramsays sell the local publication "Old Time Jokes & Stories from Falcarragh" for €5. (☎36120. Store open daily 7:30am-9:30pm, occasionally until 10:30pm.) While wine and beer are sold in the back corner of the store, serious boozers head next door to the owners' **Boatshed Bar.** (Open M-Th and Su 5pm-midnight, F-Sa 5pm-1:30am.) In the main square, **Muck n' Muffins** ❶ sells pottery, pastry (muffins €2), and light meals (€8) with lovely bay views. At night, a **wine bar** takes over. (☎36780. Sandwiches from €3. Open for pottery and food M-Sa 9:30am-6pm, Su 10:30am-6pm. Wine bar and food daily 6:30-10pm.) Many of the town's mainstays closed in 2004, but **Patsy's Bar** (☎36198) weathered the storm by reducing the staff to one (the owner).

Transportation to Dunfanaghy is as sparse as it is in the rest of the region. Buses serving the area include **Feda O'Donnell's** (☎48114) route from **Donegal** to **Galway** and **Sligo** (M-Th and Su 2 per day, F and Su 3 per day), **Patrick Gallagher's** (☎07495 31107) route to **Derry/Londonderry** and **Belfast** (1-2 per day), and **McGinley's** (☎35201) service between **Donegal** and **Dublin** (Mar.-Sept. M 4 per day, Tu-Th 3 per day, F 5 per day, Sa 2 per day, Su 4 per day; Oct.-Feb. M 3 per day, Tu-Th 2 per day, F 4 per day, Sa 2 per day, Su 4 per day). While there is no ATM in town, there is an **AIB** branch. (Open M-F 10am-12:30pm and 1:30-4pm, M open until 5pm). Non-locals should secure funds in Falcarragh. For those seeking **work opportunities, The Carriage Hostel** at Corcreggan Mill frequently looks for administrative and gardening help, in exchange it offers accommodations, food, and €40 per week. (☎00814.) The **post office** is on Main St. (Open M-F 9am-1pm and 2-5:30pm, Sa 9am-1pm.)

FANAD PENINSULA

The green fields and sandy beaches of the Fanad Peninsula jut into the Atlantic between Lough Swilly and Mulroy Bay. Most visitors stick to the eastern coastal villages of Ramelton, Rathmullan, and Portsalon, which have colorful old houses and sweeping views across Lough Swilly. These villages may lack the nightlife and cultural offerings of their (relatively) more cosmopolitan southern neighbors, but wanderers who revel in wide-open spaces know what a treasure the Fanad can be. Backpackers enjoy several gentle hikes, either along the northeastern coast or into the Knockalla Mountains. The Fanad Peninsula presents a challenge for those without a car—buses are infrequent and road conditions are not ideal for cyclists. Only one Swilly bus per day runs as far Portsalon; without a car, plan on spending the night. Even with a car, the Fanad Peninsula is infamous for being difficult to navigate, even with good directions and maps.

RAMELTON (RÁTH MEALTAIN) AND RATHMULLAN (RÁTH MAOLÁIN)   ☎07491

At the base of the Fanad Peninsula, 10km north of Letterkenny, lies the town of Ramelton (ra-MEL-ton). Settlements in town began as early as 7000 BC. Surviving buildings from the 17th century onward form a trail of sites which led Ireland to declare Ramelton a national heritage town. These buildings are listed in *The Ramelton Story*, a free pamphlet, and in more detail in the *Ramelton Heritage Town Walk* (€5), both available at the Ancestry Centre. The oldest such building is the **Miller's cottage** from the 17th century on Back Ln. Frances Makemie, founder of the American Presbyterian Church, established the **Old Meeting House**, which still stands at the corner of Back Ln. and Meeting House Ln. Though it no longer stands, the **O'Donnell Castle** once stood on the site now occupied by the **Ramelton Donegal Ancestry Centre** (on the Quay), which helps people trace their roots in County Donegal. A preliminary report is €76, and the price from there depends on the number of sources found. The Centre also has information on Ramelton's history and heritage. (☎51266; www.donegalancestry.com. Open M-Th 9am-5pm, F 9am-4pm.) Just outside of town on the road to Letterkenny, **KS Computers** offers **Internet** access. (☎51940. €3 per hr. on their machines, or €1.50 per hr. on your laptop with their wireless connection. Open M-F 9:30am-6pm, Sa 10:30am-6pm.) Two kilometers toward Letterkenny, follow the signs for the **Lough View B&B ❸**. While the lake view advertised in the name is a bit lacking, guests won't even notice as they're overwhelmed by Jim and Ann's wonderful hospitality. (☎51550. All rooms with bath. Singles €35; doubles €64. Book ahead June-Aug.)

The town of Rathmullan sits 8km north of Ramelton along the main coastal road. It owes its dubious yet prominent place in the history books to Earls Hugh O'Neill and Red Hugh O'Donnell, who surrendered the last stronghold of Gaelic power when they fled from Ireland after suffering numerous defeats to British invaders. They set sail from Rathmullan for Spain to gather military support from the Catholic King Phillip II (see **Feudalism,** p. 51), marking a watershed moment in Irish history that precipitated drastic changes in Irish culture, philosophy, and allegiances. In more recent Anglo-Irish struggles, Wolfe Tone, the champion of Irish independence, was arrested here in 1798 (see **Rebellion,** p. 53). These historical figures are remembered at the **Rathmullan Heritage Centre** (a.k.a. the **"Flight of the Earls" Heritage Centre**), housed in the wind-battered Martello Tower in the town center. (☎58131 or 58178. Open June-Sept. daily 10am-1pm and 2-5pm, Su noon-5pm; Oct.-May F-Su only with the same hours. €5, students and seniors €3, children €2, families €10.) Around the corner toward Ramelton, the picturesque remains of **Rathmullan Priory**, a 14th-century Carmelite monastery, lie shrouded in ivy. For **fishing,** hop aboard the *Enterprise 1* for full- and half-day excursions. (Contact Angela Crerand at ☎58131 before 6pm or 08724 80132 all day. Full-day €400, ½ day €250; boat fits up to 12 people. Bird-watching and sightseeing trips also available.) **Golden Sands Equestrian Centre,** 1.5km up the Portsalon road, offers riders of all levels the opportunity to explore the terrain on horseback. (☎58124. 1hr. ride €20, children €13. Call 3-4 days ahead during summer.)

Mace Supermarket, on the coastal road into town, sells groceries. (☎58148. Open daily 8am-10pm.) Herbivores will be glad to find that **An Stad ❶** serves only vegetarian food, and does it well, under massively high ceilings. (☎58798. Soups, sandwiches, salads all €5-8.50. Open around Christmas, Easter, and mid-June to late-Aug.

M-Th 10am-7pm, F-Su 10am-1pm.) Up a small but well signposted alleyway off Main St. and hidden from the stark coastal scene below, the ivy-covered 🏠**Knoll B&B** ❸ is the picture of extreme elegance, even in dollhouse shades of baby blue and pink. (☎58241. Call ahead. All rooms with bath. Singles €45; doubles €70.) The simply named **Bed and Breakfast** ❸, just outside of town on the Ramelton Rd., has singles for €45 and doubles for €60. (☎58480.) Next door to the Heritage Centre, the **Beachcomber Bar** ❷ offers beach access and prize-winning pub grub—try the sausages (€8). One wall is consumed by a gigantic window displaying a view of the ocean, and a sandy beer garden opens out back in the summer. (☎58080. F-Su live music. Meals €8-11. Open M-Th noon-11:30pm, F-Sa noon-12:30am, Su noon-11pm. Kitchen open July-Sept. daily noon-9pm, Oct.-June F-Su noon-9pm.) Straight up Pier Rd. from the ferry, **Salt 'N' Batter** ❶ should be jailed for battering fresh fish and serving dangerously addictive chips. (☎58800. Catch of the day with chips €6.70. Open M-Th and Su noon-midnight, F-Sa noon-1am.) **Lough Swilly Bus Co.** leaves from the town grocery store to **Derry/Londonderry** via **Letterkenny** (M-F 3 per day, Tu-W and F 5 per day; Sa 2 per day). **Lough Swilly Ferry** departs for **Buncrana** regularly. (☎07493 81901. 30min.; 9 per day 9:40am-8:10pm; €3, cars €15.) **John McGinley Coaches** (☎35201) runs to Milford and Dublin once per day. **Tourist information**, though limited, is happily dispensed at the Heritage Centre. The **post office** (☎58131) is on Main St. (Open M-F 9am-1pm and 2-5:30pm, Sa 9:30am-12:30pm.) The small, home-run **Swilly House Laundry Service** is located a few signposted turn-offs from the Portsalon Rd. (☎58317. Wash and dry €13-18. Open M, W, F 10am-4pm, Sa 11am-3pm.)

NORTHERN AND WESTERN FANAD ☎07491

North of Rathmullan, the road narrows, winding and dipping at the whim of the increasingly wild landscape. These remote roads discourage pedestrians, as towns are few and far between, as bikers who breeze down the enormous hill to Portsalon won't want to go back up. Hitching is nearly impossible here and *Let's Go* never recommends it. The "towns" in this region are generally little more than a group of holiday cottages centered around a post office, but this is also where the peninsula's only budget accommodations lie. North of Rathmullan, the main road becomes disconcertingly steep and breathtakingly scenic. Just before Portsalon, the road crests a hill where the northern tip of the peninsula and sandy **Stocker Strand**—rated the second-best beach in the world by a British writer—suddenly appear. Next to the strand and 5km south of Portsalon, the enormous **Knockalla Holiday Centre** ❶ buzzes in the summer with an army of campers and caravans. Untrimmed hedgerows have provided such a degree of privacy that drivers have to keep their eyes peeled to catch it as they navigate a twisting by-road. (☎59108. Electricity €2. Showers €1 per 6min. Open Easter to mid-Sept. 2-man tent €14; family tent €20.) **Portsalon** (port-SAL-un) was a resort town until its hotel burned down several years ago. Although the best scenery lies just north of town, Portsalon can still make for an entertaining stopover. **Swell Blue Water Sports**, behind Pier Restaurant, leads angling trips and offers great prices for all sorts of fun activities. (☎087 997 4255. Glider sailboard, kayaks, or dinghies €10-15 per hr. Wetsuits €10 per hr., €20 per day, children €15. Showers €2 per 10min. Ask about their new diving school. Open daily 9am-10pm during the summer.) **Pier Restaurant** ❹, on the waterfront, has fine food; the adjoining **fast-food counter** ❶ has better prices. (☎59135. Entrees €12-23; chips €3, burgers €2.60, battered cod €5. Open July-Aug. M-F 10am-9pm, Sa-Su 10am-10pm; Sept.-June Th 6-9pm and F-Su 10am-10pm.) Next door, **The Stores** purveys pints and non-perishables from behind the bar and has a spacious lounge with views across the lough. (☎59107. Open M-Th 10:30am-11:30pm, F-Sa 10:30am-12:30am, Su 10:30am-11pm.) Portsalon has had a recent explosion of building activity, mostly in the way of golfers' holiday homes; **Portsalon Golf Club** is where they gather en masse to play. (☎59459. Greens fee M-F €40, Sa-Su and bank holidays €50.)

Although its famed Ballyhadeen Gardens and Seven Arches have been recently closed to the public, there are still great natural sights not far from Portsalon. Eight kilometers from town lies **Fanad Head,** where the **Great Arch of Doaghbeg** keeps the **Fanad Lighthouse** company. The arch, a 24m rock mass, detached from seaside cliffs, is visible from above, though not from the main road. Cyclists are advised to approach from the west, on the smoother road. From Fanad Head, the route down the western side of the peninsula winds along the inlets of **Mulroy Bay.** Mrs. Borland's ◪**Avalon Farmhouse ❷,** Main St., in tiny **Tamney** (also known as Tawney), has homemade bread, jam, and marmalade. It is also accessible by a road that cuts across the peninsula from Portsalon. (☎59031. Open Easter-Sept. Singles €45; doubles €60, with bath €64.)

LETTERKENNY (LEITIR CEANAINN)   ☎074

Letterkenny is the commercial center of Donegal and the region's primary transportation hub. Though its heavy traffic may be a civil engineer's nightmare, the town is a cosmopolitan breeze through otherwise rustic Donegal, and a large student population supports a lively nightlife scene. Things can get a bit rough Friday and Saturday night after 1am, so try not to go out alone; if you have to fly solo, grab a cab on the way home.

▐ TRANSPORTATION

Buses: The **Bus Depot** is on the eastern side of the roundabout at the junction of Port (Derry) Rd. and Pearse Rd., in front of the Tesco shopping center.

Bus Éireann (☎912 1309). Glenveagh and Dunlewy tour to: **Dungloe, Glenveagh National Park,** and **Gweedore** (June 25 to Aug. 24, M-F 10am and 1:45pm; €22, children €15, students €18; return bus to castle in Glenveagh extra €3/1.5/1.5, castle tour €2/1/2). Regular service to: **Derry/Londonderry** (35min.; M-Th and Sa 7 per day, F 3 per day, Su 3 per day; €7.50, children €4.90); **Dublin** (4hr., 9 daily, €17.50/12); **Galway** (4½hr.; M-Sa 4 per day, Su 3 per day; €18.50/12.40); **Donegal Town** (1hr.; M-Sa 6 per day, Su 4 per day; €8.40/5.35); **Sligo** (2hr.; M-Sa 4 per day, Su 3 per day; €13/8.80).

Doherty's Travel (☎952 1105). To: **Dungloe** and **Burtonport** (M-Sa 3:30pm), from Dunnes Stores.

Feda O'Donnell Coaches (☎954 8114). Leaves from Boyce's Car Park to **Galway** (M-Th and Sa 2 per day, F and Su 3 per day) and **Crolly** (2 daily plus 2 more F and Su) via **Donegal Town** (€6.50).

Lough Swilly Buses (☎22863). To: **Derry/Londonderry** (M-F 9 per day, Sa 4 per day); **Fanad Peninsula** (M-F 3 per day plus 2 Tu-W and F; Sa 2 per day); **Inishowen Peninsula** (M, W, F 6 per day; Tu, Th, Sa 5 per day) via **Buncrana** and **Cardonagh.**

McGeehan's (☎954 6150). To **Glencolmcille** (M-Sa 1 per day) and **Killybegs** (M-Sa 2 per day).

McGinley Coaches (☎913 5201). To Dublin (Mar.-Sept. M, Tu-Th 3 per day, F 5 per day, Sa 2 per day, Su 4 per day; Oct.-Feb. M 3 per day, Th-Th 2 per day, F 4 per day, Sa 2 per day, Su 4 per day).

Taxis: Letterkenny Cabs (☎912 7000) offers 24hr. service and wheelchair-accessible cabs. **Swilly Cabs** (☎912 1666 or 800 272 000) are also at your service. There's a busy taxi stand at Market Sq., in the center of town.

▐ PRACTICAL INFORMATION

Tourist Offices: Bord Fáilte (☎912 1160; www.irelandnorthwest.ie), off the 2nd rotary at the intersection of Port (Derry) Rd. and Blaney Rd. toward Derry/Londonderry; 1km

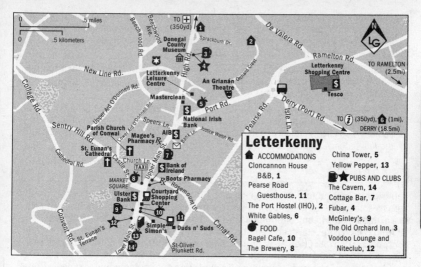

Letterkenny

⌂ ACCOMMODATIONS
Cloncannon House
  B&B, **1**
Pearse Road
  Guesthouse, **11**
The Port Hostel (IHO), **2**
White Gables, **6**

● FOOD
Bagel Cafe, **10**
The Brewery, **8**

China Tower, **5**
Yellow Pepper, **13**

◆★ PUBS AND CLUBS
The Cavern, **14**
Cottage Bar, **7**
Fubar, **4**
McGinley's, **9**
The Old Orchard Inn, **3**
Voodoo Lounge and
  Niteclub, **12**

from town. Accommodations bookings (€4 plus a 10% deposit), info on Co. Donegal, and a **bureau de change**. Open June M-F 9:15am-5:30pm, Sa 10am-4pm; July-Aug. M-F 9:15am-5:30pm, Sa 10am-4pm, Su 11am-2pm; Sept.-May M-F 9am-5pm.

Banks: AIB, 61 Upper Main St. (☎912 2877). **Bank of Ireland,** Lower Main St. (☎912 2122). **Ulster Bank,** Main St. (☎912 4016). All open M 10am-5pm, Tu-F 10am-4pm. All have 24hr. ATMs.

Laundry: Duds n' Suds, Pearse Rd. (☎912 8303). €9 per 10lb. load, €12.50 per 11-15lb. Open M-Sa 8am-7pm. **Masterclean,** High Rd. (☎912 6880), has a more central location. €11.25 per 10lb. load, €14.75 per 11-15lb. Open M-Sa 8:30am-6:30pm.

Hospital: Letterkenny General, north off High Rd. (☎912 5888), past the roundabout.

Pharmacy: Boots, Main St. (☎25499), across from Ulster Bank. Open M-W and Sa 9am-6pm, Th-F 9am-8pm, Su noon-6pm.

Internet Access: Cyberworld, Main St. (☎912 0440), in the basement of the Four Lanterns takeaway. €2 per hr. (min. €1), wireless access 3c per min. Open M-F 10am-9:30pm, Sa 10am-7pm. **Central Library,** corner of Main St. and St. Oliver Plunkett Rd. (☎24950). €2 per hr., students and unemployed €1 per hr. Photo ID required. Open M, W, F 10:30am-5:30pm, Tu and Th 10:30am-8pm, Sa 10:30am-1pm.

Central Library: Corner of Main St. and St. Oliver Plunkett Rd. (☎24950). Open M, W, F 10:30am-5:30pm, Tu and Th 10:30am-8pm, Sa 10:30am-1pm. Internet access.

Post Office: Midpoint of Main St. (☎912 2287). Open M and W-F 9am-5:30pm, Tu 9:30am-5:30pm (except open at 9am first Tu of each month), Sa 9am-1pm.

▲ ACCOMMODATIONS

Most accommodations in Letterkenny are on the outskirts of town.

The Port Hostel (IHO), Orchard Crest (☎912 5315; porthostel@eircom.net), past Cove-hill House B&B. Book way ahead Sa, since the 70 beds fill with bachelor and bachelorette partygoers. Free Wi-Fi on your laptop if you're lucky. Dorms M-F and Su €16, Sa €20; private rooms €20/25 per person. Go to www.porthostel.ie to book ahead for lower, Internet-only prices (not always available). ●

Cloncannon House B&B, High Rd. (☎23114). On the right coming from town, past the Orchard and before the hospital roundabout. Ordinary exterior with yellow walls and flowers gives way to a well-decorated, modern interior and an intriguing spiral plant. All rooms with bath. Singes €35; doubles €60. ❷

Pearse Road Guesthouse (☎912 3002). 7min. walk down Pearse Rd. from the bus depot; look for a large white house. Cool green rooms with bath sweep guests away from the traffic outside. Singles €40; doubles €70. ❸

White Gables, Dromore Rd. (☎912 2583). From the large roundabout (N13-N14) with the circular statue just outside town, take the road to Lifford. Call for pickup. Thoroughly pastoral with cheery rooms. Terrace and conservatory both overlook flocks of sheep and the lough. Singles €35; doubles €60, with bath €65. ❷

◪ FOOD

Letterkenny is a culinary heaven, especially for vegetarians. Relatively cheap meals with fresh ingredients abound and even the grocery options are unusually extensive. **Tesco,** in the Letterkenny Shopping Centre behind the bus station, has it all, including an **ATM.** (Open 24hr.) **Costcutter,** on the lower level of Courtyard, is well-stocked and central. (☎912 5738. Open M-W and Sa 8am-6pm, Th-F 8am-8pm, Su and bank holidays 1-6pm.) Around the corner, **Simple Simon Living Food,** St. Oliver Plunkett Rd., has an admirable selection of organic and vegetarian foods, including a range of fine Irish and imported cheeses. It also has a cafe. (☎912 2382. Daily specials €8 made from locally grown organic vegetables. Open M-W and Sa 9am-6pm, Th-F 9am-7pm.)

The Brewery, Market Sq. (☎912 7330), takes its name seriously and sports barrel tables. Barristers and other young professionals dodge their spouses and wee ones to enjoy the town's best pub food (€10-12) daily 3-10pm. À la carte dinner (€15-25) upstairs daily 5:30-11pm. Carvery lunch M-F noon-3pm (€8-8.50). ❹

China Tower (☎912 9610), up Main St. past the Theatre. From noon until 4pm, lunch specials deliver 3 steaming courses (€6). Light dinner specials (€6.50) delight the 5-11pm crowd with an appetizer and small entree. Night-owls appreciate the restaurant's adherence to the Shanghai time zone. Vegetarian-friendly. Takeaway available. Open M-Tu, and Th 5pm-2am, W and F-Su 5pm-3:30am. ❷

Yellow Pepper, 36 Lower Main St. (☎912 4133). Savory, sophisticated dishes in an interior with an astounding number of mirrors. Lunch specials (€8.50-9.50) change daily but guarantee at least one vegetarian option. Evening à la carte €11.50-22. Open M-Sa noon-10pm, Su 1-10pm. ❷

Bagel Cafe, Main St. (☎26777), next to the Courtyard. Bagel aficionados will find 20 types of specialty bagel sandwiches, featuring names from places the world over: Italy ("The Italian Job"), Bombay, Hawaii, NYC (all €5.25). Open M-Sa 8:30am-5:30pm. ❶

◪◪ PUBS AND CLUBS

McGinley's, 25 Main St. (☎912 1106). Popular student bar upstairs, whose walls are actually taken from an old chapel. American bartender blasts hip-hop from the top bar M nights. Tu quiz night, W trad at 10:30pm, F-Sa rock and blues. Open M-Th and Su 10am-11:30am, F-Sa 10:30am-12:30am.

Voodoo Lounge and Niteclub, 21 Lower Main St. (☎917 7911; www.voodoolk.com), next to McGinley's. Nightlife complex with 3 action-packed bars. Smokers enjoy the large beer garden with outdoor bar. Niteclub cover F-Sa €15-18. Bar open M and W noon-11:30pm, Tu, Th, and F-Su noon-2:30am. Club open M and W 11:30pm-1:30am, Tu, Th and F-Su 11:30pm-2:30am.

The Old Orchard Inn, High Rd. (☎912 1615). Bar, restaurant, nightclub, live music venue, and 3 floors of handsome logwood furniture. Good Ol' Orchard has weathered the seasonal changes of Letterkenny's newer nightlife outcroppings. Downstairs, **Fubar** hosts rock on M, as well as trad and live bands W-F. W and Sa disco until 2am, during summer also Th and Su. Kitchen open daily 12:30-10pm. Sa cover €10. Open M-W 10:30am-11:30pm, Th-Su 10:30am-12:30am.

The Cavern, 46 Lower Main St. (☎912 6733; www.thecavern.ie), past the library. Self-proclaimed #1 nightspot in Letterkenny kicks off the weekend with Th hip hop/R&B and keeps the good times rolling with DJs F-Su at 10pm. MTV and sports on 8 plasma screens, coffee in the afternoon, and W karaoke provide an all-day buzz. Free BBQ every F. Placid upstairs bar portrays an equally placid Irish town in stained-glass windows. Open daily noon-1am.

Cottage Bar, 42 Main St. (☎912 1338). A kettle on the hearth, artifacts of bygone days on the walls, and animated conversation around the bar make for a charming escape. Trad whenever the local band sees fit to show, usually scattered F and Sa. Open M-Th and Su 10:30am-11:30pm, F-Sa 10:30am-1am.

👁 🏔 SIGHTS AND OUTDOOR ACTIVITIES

St. Eunan's Cathedral, perched high above town on Church Ln., strikes an imposing figure when lit at night. (Church Ln. is on the right up Main St. away from the bus station.) Called a "resurrection of the fallen shrines of Donegal," the cathedral's construction took 11 years—all years of economic hardship and depression. The story of St. Columcille (p. 59) is beautifully carved in the arch at the junction of the nave and transept. (☎912 1021. Open daily 8am-5pm, except during Su masses 8-11:15am and 12:30pm. Free.) Across the way, the Church of Ireland's smaller **Parish Church of Conwal** shelters a number of tombstones, some dating back to 1600. (Su services 8 and 10:30am.)

In the old town Workhouse, the **Donegal County Museum,** High Rd., gives Donegal history the once-over, beginning in the Neolithic period and racing forward to the Ulster Plantation, the Famine, and WWII. (☎912 4613. Open M-F 10am-12:30pm and 1-4:30pm, Sa 1-4pm. Free.) Entering its eighth year, the **An Grianán Theatre** serves as the primary venue for July's **Earagail Festival** (p. 434), Co. Donegal's musical, dramatic, and literary extravaganza. (☎912 0777; www.donegalculture.com.) During the rest of the year, it puts on an eclectic program of music, dance, theatre, comedy, and visual art. (☎912 0777; www.angrianan.com. Tickets €15-30. Open M-F 9:30am-6pm. Cafe open M-Sa 9:30am-4pm; serves light food for €6.50-8.)

Ancient history buffs head to **Grianán Ailigh** (p. 471) to view the former seat of the ancient Celtic kings. Anglers hook salmon in a number of nearby lakes. Call **Top Tackle** for more details. (On Port Rd. just past the Theatre leaving town. ☎67545. Open M-Sa 9:30am-5:30pm.) Golfers of all ages perfect their short game at the 18-hole **Letterkenny Pitch & Putt** (☎912 5688 or 912 6000). To hit the long ball try **Letterkenny Golf Club.** (On the Ramelton Road, follow the signs; it's one mile out of town. ☎912 1150. Greens fee €25.) **Ashtree Riding Stables** has treks and lessons for all levels of experience. (From Milford, take Carraigart Rd.; after 4mi., turn on Glen Rd. and the stables are on your left. ☎915 3312.) If horses don't meet your need for speed, rev it up at **Letterkenny Indoor/Outdoor Karting Centre,** signposted three miles out of town on the Ramelton Rd. (☎912 9077. Open M-Sa 11am-10pm. €15 per 14min., €20 per 18min.; children €10 per 15min.) Off-road fun abounds at **Letterkenny ATV Co. Ltd.** (☎912 4604). After strenuous touring, relax in the sauna, swimming pool, and whirlpool at **Letterkenny Leisure Centre** (☎912 5251), on High Rd. The overworked can catch a flick at **Letterkenny Cinema,** next to the Radisson Hotel on Lakeview Ln. (☎912 5050. Open M-Th 1:30-9:30pm, F-Su 1:30-11:30pm. Before 6pm €5, after 6pm €8; students, seniors, and under 12 €6.)

INISHOWEN PENINSULA

The oft-neglected Inishowen Peninsula rewards those who venture off the beaten track with some of Ireland's most stunning and unspoiled landscapes. The peninsula presents a rich collage of scenery dotted with tiny villages and grazing sheep. Most visitors are Irish, swarming up from Derry/Londonderry on summer weekends and buzzing around beaches and golf courses. Signs of development are clear in numerous construction sites for luxury apartments and cottages, but for now the peninsula retains its quiet dignity and unbroken vistas. Moving farther north offers increasingly less touristed and more beautiful sights up until Malin Head, undeniably the crown jewel of Inishowen. Here, a rugged coastline, postcard-worthy beaches, and the call of the corncrake testify to the area's natural splendor.

TRANSPORTATION

The nearest Northern Irish commercial center to Inishowen is Derry/Londonderry. **Swilly Buses** (Derry ☎ 028712 62017, Buncrana 07493 61340) runs buses from **Derry/Londonderry** to points on the Inishowen: **Buncrana** (35min.; M-F 10 per day, Sa 8 per day; Su 4 per day; £3/€6); **Carndonagh** (55min.; M, W, F 3 per day, Tu, Th, Sa 2 per day; £5/€8.50); **Malin** (1hr., extra 30min. to Malin Head; M, W, F 1pm, Sa 11am; £6/€9.60); **Moville** and **Greencastle** (50min.; M-Sa 3 per day; £4/€6.50). **Northwest Busways** (Moville office ☎ 07493 82619) runs through **Ballyliffin, Buncrana, Carndon-**

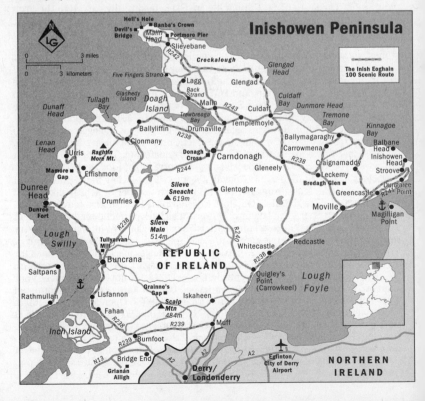

agh, **Clonmany, Culdaff, Fahan,** and **Letterkenny** (M-F 4 per day, Sa 2 per day; €7); Shrove to **Derry/Londonderry** via **Moville** (1hr., M-Sa 4 per day); Derry to Culdaff (M-F 3 per day, Sa 2 per day; €3); **Moville** to **Letterkenny** (express M-F 4 per day, Sa 2 per day; €7); and **Carndonagh** to **Derry/Londonderry** (M-F 4 per day, Sa 3 per day; €5.50). The **Lough Swilly Ferry** joins the Fanad and Inishowen peninsulas at Rathmullan and Buncrana. (☎ 074 938 1901. 10min., Apr.-Sept. every 20min. M-Sa 7:20am-9:50pm, Su 9am-9:50pm; Oct.-Mar. every 20min. 9am-7pm, plus ferries at 7:20, 8, 8:30am, 7:50pm. Cars ₤7/€10, pedestrians ₤2/€3, children and seniors ₤0.70/€1.) **Drivers** follow the signposted **Inis Eoghain 100** road around the peninsula for 160km; hitchers report an easy time finding rides on this road, although *Let's Go* never recommends hitchhiking. **Bikers** enjoy stretches of smooth, if sometimes hilly, roads; cycling can be difficult near the **Gap of Mamore,** due to ferocious northwesterly winds and hilly terrain. The Inishowen Tourism Society map, available at the Carndonagh tourist office, and the *Ordnance Survey #3* help explorers navigate the peninsula; the former is more schematic and easier to read, while the latter provides more detailed topographical information useful for pedestrians.

BUNCRANA (BUN CRANNCHA)   ☎07493

Slieve Snaght looms over Buncrana at Inishowen's southeastern edge. While not terribly exciting, the peninsula's biggest town offers hostel and B&B beds to northbound explorers.

TRANSPORTATION AND PRACTICAL INFORMATION. The **Swilly Buses** (☎61340) at the bus depot in Buncrana travel to: **Carndonagh** (M-F 2 per day) and **Derry/Londonderry** (M-F 10 per day, Sa 8 per day, Su 4 per day). There are three important roads in Buncrana: **Main Street, St. Orans Road, and Cockhill Road.** Most of the shops and pubs are on Main St., but it's one-way toward Letterkenny in the south for most of its length. Just west of Main St. and parallel, Cockhill Rd. is the best bet for northward driving, in particular to the Tullyarvan Mill. St. Orans Rd. splits off Main St. and serves as the road to both the tourist office and the cities of Letterkenny and Derry.The **tourist office,** St. Oran's Dr., a 7min. walk down Main St., dispenses peninsular info and a book of well-marked hikes. Accommodations bookings are made for €4 plus a 10% deposit. (☎62600; www.irelandnorthwest.ie. Open M-F 10am-1pm and 2-5pm, Sa 9am-2pm.) **AIB,** Lower Main St. (☎61087; open M 10am-5pm, Tu-F 10am-12:30pm and 1:30-4pm, W 10:30am-12:30pm and 1:30-4pm), and **Bank of Ireland,** Main St. (☎61795; open M 10am-12:30pm and 1:30-5pm, Tu and Th-F 10am-12:30pm and 1:30-4pm, W 10:30am-12:30pm and 1:30-4pm), have 24hr. **ATMs.** Do your **laundry** at **ValuClean** on Lower Main St. (☎62570. Laundry €6.60 for up to 2.6kg wash and dry. Open M-F 9am-6pm, Sa 9am-5:30pm.) **E. Tierney Chemist's,** 42 Lower Main St. at the corner with St. Oran's Dr., is the local pharmacy. (☎62412. Open M-F 9:30am-6:30pm, Sa 9:30am-6pm.) The **library** has **Internet** access; go down the alleyway on Lower Main St. opposite Bank of Ireland—it is attached to the church. (☎61941. Surfing free; email €2 per hr., students and children €1. Open Tu and F 10:30am-5:30pm, W-Th 10:30am-8pm, Sa 10:30am-4pm.) Or, try the **Inishowen Partnership,** St. Oran's Dr., across the parking lot from the library. (☎61376. €1 per 30min. Open M-F 9am-5pm. The computers will occasionally be unavailable for periods of time, as classes are taught in the room.) The **post office,** Main St., is in **C. & A. McGinley's,** the local newsagent. (☎61010. Open M-F 9am-1:15pm and 2:15-5:30pm, Sa 9am-1pm.)

ACCOMMODATIONS. The cheapest bed in town is the large, newly established hostel at **Tullyarvan Mill ❶,** off of Westbrook Rd. (☎61613. Laundry available. Dorms €15; private doubles €40; family room €60.) To get there, take Cockhill

Rd. north (toward Cardonagh) out of town and make a right onto Westbrook Rd. just after Swan Park. Then, take the signposted right turn for the Mill. Though many B&Bs have closed in Buncrana, others have sprung up to fill in the gaps and beds are generally easy to come by, except during July's music festival. Surrounded by a lovely garden and situated on the River Crana, **Westbrook House B&B ❸**, a 5-10min. walk from the town center before Tullyarvan Mill, offers style and serenity in a spacious Georgian home. Fish right outside the door or arrange an outing; if you prefer to be landlocked, appreciate the huge anchor sitting in the backyard parking lot. (☎63501; mgwest@eircom.net. All rooms with baths. Singles €45; doubles €90.) Golfers will love the short walk to the greens from the **Oak Villa B&B ❸**, on St. Oran's Dr. across from the hotel. After tee-time, enjoy tea-time in the conservatory sitting room. (☎61315. Singles €45; doubles €60-70.) For sheer convenience, **Town Clock Guest House ❸**, above but unaffiliated with the restaurant, ensures that bedtime is never far away with clean and spacious rooms right in the center of town. (☎62146. All rooms with bath. Singles €25; doubles €50.)

🍴🛏 FOOD AND PUBS. Super-cheap German supermarket **Aldi** has recently opened its doors on New Line Rd., which parallel to and east of Main St., away from St. Oran's Rd. (Open M-W 9am-8pm, Th-F 9am-9pm, Sa 9am-7pm, Su 11am-7pm.) **Super Valu,** also at the north end of Main St., sells groceries, and is home to a pharmacy. (☎61719. Open M-Sa 6:30am-11pm, Su 6:30am-9pm.) **Food for Thought,** 12 Lower Main St., sells dried fruit, nuts, herbal remedies, spices, and all manner of ethnic foodstuffs. (☎63550 or 087 281 4870. Open M-Sa 10am-5:30pm.) **O'Flaitbeartai's** (o-FLAH-her-tees) **❷**, Main St., combines old-time elegance with modern fittings to provide something for everyone: noontime feedings, sporting events on the big screen, and the town's best trad keep the bar buzzing. (☎61305. Entrees €6. W trad. Lunch served daily 11am-3pm. Bar open M-Th and Su 10:30am-12:30am, F-Sa 10:30am-1:30am.) The black-clad waitresses at **Town Clock Restaurant ❷**, 6 Main St., serve homestyle favorites from fried breakfasts (€6.50) to toasties and burgers. (☎63279. Most entrees €7-8. Open M-Sa 8:15am-8pm, Su 9:30am-8pm.) Housed in an old Railway Station, **The Drift Inn,** next to the tourist office on Railway Rd., is probably the best pub in town; pints are purveyed from behind a bar plastered with sea-shells, and spontaneous late-night sessions often postpone the closing time. (☎61999. Music scheduled Th-Sa. Open daily noon to at least 11pm.) At the attached **restaurant ❷**, even the cheapest item, a €6.50 plate of mussels, is excellent. (☎22844. Entrees €9-14.50. Kitchen open M-Th and Su 5-9pm, F-Sa 5-10pm. Closed for renovation as of press time, but set to re-open.) **An Tuath Nua,** Upper Main St., has a loyal contingent of young and old who fill its sleek, modern interior for sports and live cover bands Saturdays at 10pm. (☎61564. Open M-Th 11am-11:30pm, F-Sa 11am-12:30am, Su noon-11pm.)

◧⚠ SIGHTS AND OUTDOOR ACTIVITIES. Buncrana's primary attractions stretch along the river north of town. Behind a youth activity center, peaceful **Swan Park** is overlooked by two castles: stately **Buncrana Castle,** where Wolfe Tone was imprisoned after the failed French "invasion" of 1798 (see **Rebellion,** p. 53), and the 1430 **O'Doherty Keep,** a castle that resembles a derelict mansion. Both are closed to the public, but visitors can walk the grounds around the Keep. To reach the park, walk up Main St. toward the shorefront and follow Castle Ave. from the roundabout next to An Tuath Nua and the Cinema. The park is beyond the one-way Castle Bridge, which arcs 100m to the right. A **coastal walk** begins at Castle Bridge, passes the Keep, turns left at the castle, and ascends the hill. **Ned's Point Fort,** also along the coast, built in 1812, seems jarringly modern. The path passes **Porthaw Bay** and terminates in sandy **Sragill Strand. Friar Hegarty's Rock,** beyond the beach, witnessed the friar's murder during Penal times.

Outside the northern edge of the park on Dunree Rd. (a continuation of Main St.) is the community-owned and operated **Tullyarvan Mill**. This renovated corn mill presents a mixture of exhibits on textile history, tracing Buncrana's transition from hand-weaving in 1739 to Fruit-of-the-Looming in 1999. The mill also hosts music and art exhibits, houses a **craft shop** and **coffee shop**, as well as a **hostel**. (☎61613. Open M-Sa 10am-5pm.) **Inishowen Genealogy Centre**, which recently moved south of town onto Inch Island, draws on a multitude of documents from Derry and Co. Donegal. (☎63998. Call ahead. Open daily 9am-6pm or by appointment; www.inishowen.net.) Putters head to **Buncrana Golf Club**, at the turn-off of St. Oran's Rd. right at the tourist office, for a relaxing nine-hole game. (☎20749. Open daily 9am-dusk. Greens fee €13 for men, €8 for women.)

🞂 DAYTRIP FROM BUNCRANA: GRIANÁN AILIGH. At the bottom of the peninsula, 16km south of Buncrana and 5km west of Derry, the stone ringfort Grianán Ailigh (GREEN-in ALL-ya) crowns the hilltop where both locals and visitors have taken advantage of the 360° degree views of the surrounding countryside, stretching from Derry/Londonderry to Loughs Swilly and Foyle. Given its far-reaching vistas, Grianán Hill is a great place to start or finish a tour of Inishowen. The site has been a cultural center for at least 4000 years: first as a druidic temple at the grave site of Aedh, son of The Dagda, divine king of the *Túatha De Dannan;* then as a seat of power for the Uí Néill clan, who ruled Ulster; and finally as a mass rock for secret Catholic worship during Penal times. Much of the present stone structure is a 19th-century reconstruction by an amateur archaeologist from Derry, but the bottom section of the circular wall remains unchanged from the original. Beyond the ringfort, a cross marks a **healing well,** holy since pre-Christian times and supposedly used by St. Patrick to bless Eoghan, after whom the peninsula is named.

Grianán Ailigh is west of the junction of R238 and N16; the 300-year-old **Burt Woods** grow alongside. From Buncrana, follow the Inis Eoghian 100 south to Bridgend, and follow the signs to Burt Woods; the ringfort is 2km to the southeast. To reach the fort from Letterkenny, follow N13 past the turn-off for R265 and R237, and follow the signs. (Open mid-June to Sept. 9am-9pm.) Three kilometers down N13 from Bridgend is the Catholic **Burt Circular Chapel,** a replica of the ancient fort. To reach the fort from the chapel, take the 3km road to the top of the hill. **Swilly Buses** (☎07495 22373) pass by on Derry-Buncrana and Derry-Letterkenny routes.

WESTERN INISHOWEN

From Buncrana, the Inis Eoghain 100 runs through Dunree Head and the Mamore Gap, while R238 cuts through the interior directly to Clonmany and Ballyliffin. Spectacular beaches, raw mountain landscapes, and complete isolation await the traveler who dares to venture this deep into the peninsula.

DUNREE HEAD AND THE MAMORE GAP ☎07493

Fort Dunree and the Mamore Gap were the last areas of the Republic occupied by the British, who handed over the fort keys to the Irish army in 1938. **Dunree Head** juts into Lough Swilly 10km northwest of Buncrana. Peaks rise against the ocean, buffered by the occasional bend of sandy, smooth beach. At the tip of the head, **Fort Dunree** hides in the jagged sea cliffs. Today, the fort holds a military museum and is a superb vantage point for admiring the sea-carved landscapes of the Inishowen and Fanad peninsulas. One of the six **Guns of Dunree,** built during the 1798 Rebellion to defend Lough Swilly against Napoleonic invaders, is among the museum's displayed weaponry. The exhibits detail the mechanics of the massive guns and life in the fort. The fort's location over the lough is a boon for birdwatchers. (Open June-Sept. M-Sa 10:30am-6pm, Su 1-6pm; Oct.-May M-F 10:30am-

4:30pm, Sa-Su 1-4:30pm. Fort and walks €6; students, ages 8-17, and seniors €4; under 8 free; parking €3.50.) The fort's **cafeteria ❶** serves sandwiches (€2) and other cheap baked goods. (Open June-Sept. M-F 10:30am-5:30pm, Sa-Su 1-6pm; Oct.-May M-F 10:30am-4:30pm, Sa-Su 1-4:30pm.)

Farther north along the Inis Eoghain 100 toward Clonmany, a sign points left up a hill to the edge of the **Mamore Gap.** Thirty meters above sea level, the pass slices between Mamore Hill and Urris. The sharply inclined road and fierce winds can prove difficult for hikers and cyclists, but the brave regularly tackle the 30min. climb uphill; most bikers are forced to walk. Driving is easier, although the hairpin turns over the sea are sometimes quite frightening. There is a **pilgrimage well** on the side of the road, in the middle of the gap. Queen Medb of Connacht, Cúchulainn's diva archenemy, is supposedly buried here—and at Knocknarea, Co. Sligo, and a few other places.

The road descends from the gap onto wave-scoured northern beaches. The Inis Eoghain 100 proceeds to **Urris, Lenan Head,** and inviting **Lenan Strand.** Once known for its prodigious *poitín* production (see **Whiskey Business,** p. 67), Urris was the last area in Inishowen to relinquish spoken Irish. The flatbed farms and traditional cottages along the road reveal the endurance of Famine-era style farming. Heading north, the road passes over **Dunaff Head,** and ends at Lenan Strand.

CLONMANY, BALLYLIFFIN, AND DOAGH ISLAND ☎07493

North of the Gap, the two tiny villages of **Clonmany** *(Cluain Maine)* and **Ballyliffin** *(Baile Lifin)* are separated by 2km. Catering mostly to golfers and older travelers, the area is relatively expensive and budget-seekers should consider heading north for the night. Those with a car and the resources to stay will find plenty of B&Bs in Ballyliffin and an abundance of pubs in Clonmany.

Ballyliffin's highlights are its 5km of golden sand on **Pollen Strand** and the world-famous **Ballyliffin Golf Club,** whose two championship 18-hole courses were described by Nick Faldo as "the most natural links I've ever played." Pass the Strand Hotel coming from Clonmany where you'll find the club is signposted half a mile out of town. (☎76119; www.balyliffingolfclub.com. Greens fee Nov.-Mar. €50-65, Apr.-Oct. €75-90.) Grassy dunes now connect the village with misleadingly named **Doagh Island,** where **Carricksbrahy Castle,** a former seat of the MacFaul and O'Donnell clans, is a wave-battered ruin at the end of a 4km beach walk. Area signs point to Doagh Island and the ▨**Doagh Famine Village,** a private museum run by Pat Doherty, who grew up in one of the thatch-roofed houses on display. Pat provides an engaging presentation packed with local wisdom and a contemporary perspective on poverty around the world. Tea and biscuits cap off the thought-provoking tour. (☎78078 or 08684 64749. Wheelchair-accessible. Open Easter-Sept. daily 10am-5:30pm; special Christmas event as well. Admission includes tea and guided tour. Tours every 45min. 10:15am-4:45pm. €6, children €4.) During the first full weekend in August, all the pubs in the square are saturated with trad for the **Clonmany Festival,** now celebrating its 40th year. (Contact Hugo Boyce ☎76477 or 086 342 7373; www.clonmany.com. €5, under 12 free.)

Golfers fill the B&Bs in the area during the summer months. Between Ballyliffin and Clonmany, **McEleney's B&B ❸** ushers guests up a grand central staircase to spacious ensuite rooms. (☎76541. Singles €50; doubles €70.) Travelers enjoy a comfortable stay in the lovely rooms of **Castlelawn House ❸,** behind Strand Hotel in Ballyliffin; coming from Clonmany, turn left just before the hotel. (☎76600 or 087 616 6147. All rooms with bath and TV. Singles July-Aug. €65, Sept.-June €40; doubles €75/50. July-Aug. multiple-night stays can lower the rate to singles €35; doubles €40.) **Centra,** across from the church at the end of Main St. in Clonmany, is the only spot for groceries (☎76105. Open daily 8am-8pm.) There is also a **post office** inside Centra. (Open M-F 9am-1pm and 2-5:30pm, Sa 9am-1pm.) Though no independent restaurants exist in Ballyliffin, some of the hotels have decent meal deals on certain nights. **Strand Hotel ❸** feeds the hungry on Monday and Wednesday nights with a five-course dinner for two (€17 per person; other nights €23). Entrees run €12.50-21 a la carte. (☎76107. Open daily 12:15-10pm.) Weekend country music and occasional trad fill the air in and around **McFeeley's**, Main St. (☎76122. Open M-Th 6pm-midnight, F-Su 6pm-2am.) Bright green **Briney's Bar,** next to the gas station just past McFeeley's, features weekend live music, and summer barbecues. (☎76415. Open M-Th and Su 6pm-11:30pm, F-Sa 6pm-12:30am.)

NORTHERN INISHOWEN

From the southeastern coast, R240 cuts straight up the middle of the peninsula to commercial Carndonagh. North of Carndonagh, R238 veers east to ancient relics of Culdaff. Going north on R242 leads to Malin Head, the northernmost tip of the peninsula. The northern half of Inishowen is the most budget-friendly, containing empty beaches, rugged scenery, and the region's only hostels.

CARNDONAGH (CARN DOMHNACH)   ☎07493

South of Trawbreaga Bay, Carndonagh (known locally as Carn) is Inishowen's main market town—the peninsula's farmers swarm here on alternate Mondays. Commercial Carn has but one sight to offer: the old Church of Ireland, located 10min. down Bridge St. Outside its walls, **Donagh Cross,** a 7th-century Celtic cross, is the sole remnant of the monastery founded by St. Patrick. Two shorter pillars flank the cross: one depicts David playing his harp, and the other displays Christ's crucifixion. The **church's bell** supposedly came from the Spanish Armada ship *Trinidad de Valencera,* which went down in **Kinnagoe Bay** off the Donegal coast.

When a Carn family went to Oregon in search of gold only to return empty-handed, they were known to locals as the "Oregons" forevermore; with the exception of a few modern fixtures the structure of **Oregon House B&B ❷,** down Chapel St. from the church, has changed little since 1911. It's the big white house behind the gate, at the wedge of the road fork across from the graveyard. (☎74113. Singles €25; doubles €50.) The interior of **An Caislean B&B ❸,** just a bit farther down Chapel St. on the left, has enough scenic paintings to make you think you're in Oregon. (☎74537. All rooms with bath. Singles €40; doubles €70.) **Costcutters,** in Cardonagh Shopping Centre on Bridge St., stocks an array of food. (☎74124. Open M-F 8am-8pm, Sa 9am-9pm, Su 10am-7pm.) **Coffee House ❶,** inside the Arch Inn, the Diamond, sells coffee and sandwiches on ciabatta, all under €5. (☎73029. Open M-Sa 10:30am-6pm.) **The Quiet Lady,** Malin St., gets noisy at night when she plays hits and encourages locals to let loose. She also serves filling meals. (☎74777. Roasted meat and vegetables €6.50. F DJ. Kitchen open July-Aug. daily 10:30am-9pm; Sept.-June M-Th 10:30am-4pm, F-Su 10:30am-9pm.)

Carn Cabs, the Diamond (☎74580), provides taxis for late-night jaunts. **McCallion's Cycle Hire,** 5km from town on the Ballyliffin Rd. and signposted on the right, collects and delivers bikes anywhere on the peninsula. (☎74084. €10 per day, €50 per wk. Open M-Sa 10am-6pm.) Although not Bord Fáilte-approved, **Inishowen Tourism,** Chapel St., off the Diamond, provides limited info. (☎74933 or 74934; www.visitinishowen.com. Open M-F 9am-5pm.) On the Diamond is a **Bank of Ireland** branch with a **bureau de change;** it has 24hr. **ATMs** both here and by the post office at the shopping center. (Bank open M 10am-12:30pm and 1:30-5pm, Tu-F 10am-12:30pm and 1:30-4pm.) **AIB,** also on the Diamond, has a 24hr. **ATM** on-site. (☎74388. Open M 10am-12:30pm and 1:30-5pm, Tu-F 10am-12:30pm and 1:30-4pm.) On the way out of town, on a signposted alley off the Moville road, **The Book Shop** sells both locally published and used books, and has an Irish history section. (☎74389. Open M-Tu and Th-Su 2-6pm.) **ValuClean,** Bridge St., does up to 2.6kg of magic for €6.60; €11.50 gets you 5kg of clean clothes. (☎74150. Open M-Sa 9am-6pm.) **McNeill's**, the Diamond, is one of several **pharmacies**. (☎74120. Open M-Sa 10am-6pm.) **Internet** access is available at the **library**, Malin St., across from and past The Quiet Lady in the Public Services Centre. (€2 per hr.; students, seniors, and unemployed €1. Open M and W 10:30am-8pm, Tu and Th-F 10:30am-5:30pm, Sa 10:30am-12:30pm and 1:30-4pm.) The **post office** is on Bridge St. (☎74101. Open Tu and Th 10:30am-8pm, W and F 10:30am-5:30pm, Sa 10:30am-4pm.)

CULDAFF (CÚIL DABHCHA) ☎07493

The area around Culdaff on the eastern side of the peninsula holds a variety of ancient monuments. The "Bronze Age triangle" above Bocan Parochial House, 1km from Culdaff toward Moville, includes the **Bocan Stone Circle, Temple of Deen**, and **Kindroyhead** with evidence of a prehistoric field and fort system. A 4m **high cross** stands next to **Cloncha Church,** signposted 3km from Culdaff toward Moville. The village hosts the **Charles Macklin Festival** (☎79104), during the second weekend of October, with occasional performances of the 17th-century playwright's dramas, poetry competitions, and a slew of trad sessions. **Culdaff Strand,** a short walk east, is the most intimate of Inishowen's beaches and is best seen at daybreak or dusk. Those who want to spend the night will find all they need at the recently renovated █McGrory's ❹, a family-run hotel with exposed stone walls and rustic wood furniture. The **restaurant** ❸ and bar food keep guests well-fed, while famous trad nights and live music in **Mac's Backroom Bar** draw music-lovers from all over the peninsula. If you have your own laptop, grab Wi-Fi **Internet** access for €1 per 2hr. (☎79104; www.mcgrorys.ie. July-Aug. singles M-Th and Su €75, F-Sa €80; doubles €120/130. Sept.-June singles €60/70; doubles €100/120. Call for special deals. Tu and F trad, Sa live bands. Bar open M-Th 11am-11:30pm, F-Sa 11am-12:30am, Su noon-11pm. Kitchen open daily 12:30-8:30pm; entrees €12-14. Open daily 6:30-9:30pm and Su for lunch 12:30-4pm; entrees €13-22.) Also on Main St., the **Village House B&B** ❸ is decked out with leather couches, a beautiful fireplace, and prints on the walls. (☎79972. All rooms with bath. Singles €40-45; doubles €68.)

MALIN HEAD (CIONN MÁLAINN) ☎07493

Inishowen's best asset is Malin Head. Aside from its latitude, the stretch is remarkable for its rocky, wave-tattered coast and sky-high sand dunes. Inis Eoghain 100 continues east from Cardonagh to Malin Head, passing through the tiny, tidy town of **Malin** on its way. Seven kilometers from Culdaff, R242 hits the Inis Eoghain 100 and winds toward Lagg, where the five standing rocks of **Five Fingers Strand** jut into the ocean—follow the signs from the 100. Swift cross-currents and icy waters make swimming treacherous. High above the beach, the **Knockamany Bens** provide fantastic views of the whole peninsula.

Malin Head includes **Banba's Crown,** a tooth of dark rock rising from the ocean spray, noteworthy as the peninsula's northernmost tip. On a clear day, the Head offers views as far as Scotland. Vigilant walkers may catch glimpses of whales off the shore or hear the distinctive call of the **corncrake,** a near-extinct bird indigenous to the area. Written in white-washed stones on a nearby lower cliff, and legible from far above, "S. S. ÉIRE" (*Saor Stát Éire*; "Irish Free State") identified Ireland as neutral territory to Nazi bombers. Tourists have removed many of the stones, but "ÉIRE" is still intact. A path to the left of the car park leads to **Hell's Hole,** a 75m chasm that roars with the incoming tide. Farther down the coast is the naturally formed **Devil's Bridge.** The █raised beaches around Malin Head, the result of glaciers that plowed through the region millions of years ago, are covered with semi-precious stones; walkers sifting through the sands may find jasper, quartz, small opals, and amethysts beneath the more prosaic stones. The **Atlantic Circle** is a 7km circuit of the Inis Eoghain 100 that tours the peninsula's tip.

To reach ▨**Sandrock Holiday Hostel (IHO/IHH)** ❶, Port Ronan Pier, take the left fork off the Inis Eoghain 100, before the Crossroads Inn (also a bus stop). As they warm themselves by the wood stove, visitors may spy passing seals and dolphins through the bay windows. Not a nature fan? Then take advantage of the free Wi-Fi. (☎70289; www.sandrockhostel.com. Bike rental €9 per day. Sheets €1.50. Laundry wash €4, dry €2. 10-bed dorms €12.) Seven kilometers past Malin on the way into Malin Head, ▨**Druim Doo B&B** ❷ has a wonderful wooden ensuite loft and a standard downstairs room, managed with a ready sense of humor by a friendly English couple. (☎70287; www.druimdoo.com. Loft €26; downstairs €27.) On the Inis Eoghain 100, past the phone booth across from the post office, **Malin Head Hostel (HH)** ❶ rewards the brave souls who venture north with an open fire, reflexology (€40), and aromatherapy (€50). Use of the kitchen is encouraged: Mary keeps steaks of wild salmon in the freezer and her homegrown organic vegetables are cheap and delicious. What's more, down at the Malin Fishermen's Cooperative crab claws are free and oysters cost almost nothing. (☎70309. Bike rental €10 per day. Laundry wash €3.50, dry €2.50. 5-bed dorms €13; singles €24; doubles €35.) Newly opened **Cuan na Ron B&B** ❸, next door to Sandrock, has large rooms with decorations which rival the sea views. If the view doesn't do it for you, then maybe the wooden loveseat swing will. (☎70531 or 086 343 3497; mclaughlin_sorcha@yahoo.ie. Singles €30; doubles €60.)

Life in Malin Head centers around the pubs, which all sell groceries and stay open until 1am. Country-rock, fishing tackle, and a Guinness pint poured to perfection—complete with a shamrock settling into the creamy head—await adventurers at family-run **Farren's**, Ireland's northernmost pub. From Sandrock, take your third left, and look for the sign. (☎70128. Open sometime in the afternoon until sometime at night, at the owner's whim.) Just up the road, your first right turn brings you to the aptly named **Seaview Tavern and Restaurant** (☎70117), which fills patrons up with food, beer, and gasoline. The bar, commonly called "Vera Dock's," pours pints beneath shelves of corn flakes and motor oil. (Open M-Th 10am-11:30pm, F-Sa 10am-12:30am, Su noon-11pm.) The **restaurant** ❷ serves local seafood and takeaway, while next door a **grocery store** sells foodstuffs and pumps gas. (Breakfast from €5.50; dinner from €8.50. Kitchen open July-Aug. M-F 12:30-9pm, Sa-Sa 10am-9pm. Store open M-Sa 8am-9pm, Su 9am-9pm.) Inside the store is a **post office**. (Open M-F 9am-1pm and 2-5:30pm, Sa 9am-1pm.)

EASTERN INISHOWEN

Though overshadowed by its northern neighbor Malin Head, **Inishowen Head** draws hundreds of beachcombers to the natural beauty of **Stroove Strand**. On the northernmost beaches, which look over Lough Foyle, smaller crowds go the extra distance to make the most of the stubborn Irish sun. A delightful "shore walk" runs about 10km between the small thumb of Inishowen Head through Greencastle and Moville. Any local can direct shore-explorers to **Port a Doris**, a secluded little cove accessible only at low tide and littered with semi-precious Shroove pebbles.

MOVILLE (BUN AN PHOBAIL)   ☎07493

Tiny Moville straddles the intersection of R239 (from Derry) and R238 (from Culdaff). During the summer, both Moville and its even smaller neighbor, Greencastle, are swamped with Derryites searching for the beach and a game of golf. For a good night's rest, try to snag a room at Mrs. McGuinness's **Dunroman B&B** ❸, off the Derry road across from the football field, where breakfast is served in a conservatory overlooking the River Foyle. (☎82234. Free laundry and Internet access. Singles €35; doubles €60, with bath €70.) The only hostel before Malin Head is the **Moville Holiday Hostel ❷**, just outside town on the Malin Rd. (look for the sign at the edge of town, and take the turn-off at the end of the low stone wall). The old and the new mix freely here, as the original stone-wall interior foundation contrasts the glass blocks in the hallway walls. (☎82378 or 086 851 9795. Free laundry. Key deposit €5. Dorms €20; private rooms €45.) **Barron's Cafe and B&B ❷**, is a one-two punch for the budget traveler. The smallish rooms are reasonably priced and well equipped with baths and TV, while the downstairs cafe doles out hearty portions. (☎82472. All-day breakfast €5.75. Burgers €2-4. Specials €6-14. All rooms but one with bath. Open daily 9:30am-8pm. Singles €30; doubles €50.) The cheapest eats in town are at **The Cosy Cottage ❶**, on Main. St., where burgers (€3-5) and various main dishes (€5-7) can be eaten in the cluttered interior, or outside on picnic benches. (☎85740. Open M-Sa 8am-9:30pm, Su 9:30am-9:30pm.) Everyone keeps time to the music at the **Town Clock Pub**, in the car park on Main St. The high, vaulted ceilings, wood fittings, and old portraits lend a touch of class to proceedings as DJs play chart-toppers until 2am on Friday and Saturday nights. (☎85815. Sandwiches €3.60. Entrees €10.50-22. Kitchen open M-Th and Su 11am-9:30pm, F-Sa 11am-10:30pm. Bar open M-Th and Su 11am-11:30pm, F-Sa 11am-2:30am.) At the well-worn but newly renamed **Bar-A-Cuda** (formerly Eggman's), Main St. (☎82183), old folks huddle around guppy-size tables in the front while a younger crowd of pool and darts sharks hunt their prey in the back. Just off Main St. on Malin Rd., **Rosato's** hosts a lively crowd into the wee hours on Fridays and Saturdays with its stone fireplace and acoustic and folk music. (☎82247. 11 in. margherita pizza €7.50. Kitchen open daily 5-9pm; July-Aug. also daily noon-3pm. Bar open M-Th 5-11:30pm, F-Su 12:30pm-12:30am; July-Aug. open daily 12:30pm.)

Though there's no tourist office, the **library,** in the back corner of the car park next to Susie's Bar, has free info on the peninsula. (☎82110. Open Tu 2-4:30pm and 5-8pm, W-F 10:30am-12:30pm and 1:30-5:30pm, Sa 10:30am-2pm.) A sign in the car park also displays practical and historical info. In Moville, an **AIB** with a 24hr. **ATM** is located on Main St. (☎82050. Open M 10am-12:30pm and 1:30-5pm, Tu-F 10am-12:30pm and 1:30-4pm.) **Ulster Bank,** Main St., also has a 24hr. **ATM.** (Open M 10am-12:30pm and 1:30-5pm, Tu-F 10am-12:30pm and 1:30-4pm.) **Bank of Ireland,** Main St., does as well. (☎82067. Open M-F 10am-12:30pm and 1:30-4pm.) **Foyle's,** on Main St., is a local **pharmacy.** (☎82929. Open M-Sa 9:30am-6pm.) **Internet** access is free at the **library** with a membership (free in Donegal), or check email. (☎918 5110. Email €2 per hr., students €1 per hr. Open Tu 2-4:30pm and 5-8pm, W-Th 10:30am-12:30pm and 1:30-5:30pm, Sa 10:30-2pm.) The **post office** is at the intersection of Malin Rd. and Main St. (☎82016. Open M-F 9am-1pm and 2-5:30pm, Sa 9am-1pm.) **Ulsterbus** runs from Moville to Derry/Londonderry (9 per day, 9:50am-5pm). **McLaughlin's taxi** (☎81500) and **Murphy's** (☎08627 78200) are just a call away.

GREENCASTLE ☎07493

Greencastle, between Moville and Inishowen Head along R239, is a quiet sea-front village resting beneath the ruins of the Red Earl of Ulster's ivy-clad **castle.** Farther north, its blue flag **Stroove Strand** pulls visitors to the end of the peninsula. The **Cairn Visitor Centre** recounts regional history from the time of Celts and Vikings to the recent past. During the summer, it also hosts weekly evening entertainment featuring traditional Irish songs, stories, and dance (tickets €10). To get there coming from Moville, turn left after the Ferryboat Bar, and then left at the T-junction. (☎81104. Open June-Sept. daily 11am-6pm and by appointment. Entertainment July to mid-Sept. W 8pm. Book ahead.) Relics of life on the sea are in the spotlight at the **Greencastle Maritime Museum** on the shorefront. Housed in an old Coast Guard station, the museum's impressive collection includes a traditional Fanad *curragh*, a small Armada room, ship models, photographs, and a 19th-century rocket cart for rescuing passengers of wrecked ships. The new **planetarium** has daily laser light shows. (☎81363. Open Easter-Sept. M-Sa 10am-5:30pm, Su noon-5:30pm; rest of the year M-F 10am-5pm. Last admission 5pm. 40min. planetarium shows run a few times per day; on weekends, a laser light show is held if enough people show up. Call ahead for show times. Museum or planetarium €5; children, seniors, and students €3; families €15. Combined ticket €10/6/30.)

The name of the **Hilltop Lodge B&B ❸** does no justice to its commanding view of Lough Foyle and across to County Derry (two of four bedrooms have the view, and the other two have scenic paintings to compensate). The owners of this beautiful B&B are happy to give rides to and from the pubs in town if you don't feel like a tipsy hill climb yourself. The lodge is a 600m uphill climb, which is reached by a well-signposted left turn off of Stroove Rd., 1km from town. (☎81778. Laundry available. All rooms with bath. Singles €45; doubles €80.) To satisfy fresh fish cravings, head to **Wild Atlantic Salmon,** next to the Maritime Museum, where a whole salmon is about €25-30 per kg. (☎81065. Open M-F 9:30am-6pm, Sa 10:30am-5pm.) Those who prefer their fish battered and greasy head to **Seamy's Fish and Chips ❶,** which dishes out cheap meals from a ship-shaped counter. (☎81379. All takeaway meals under €4. Open M-Th noon-11pm, F-Su 2pm-midnight.) Next door, the faux-brick interior of **Ferryport Bar** makes a second home for most of the youth in Greencastle. (☎81296. Summer Th and Su country, occasional trad on other nights. Open daily 11am until somewhere between midnight and 2am.) **The Drunken Duck,** 3km north of Greencastle toward Stroove Strand, is a friendly pub named for a local woman whose beer leaked into her poultry troughs. Enjoy a pint on the patio with sweeping views of the lough. To get there, take a left uphill after the Ferryport Bar, and take a right at the T-junction. (☎81362. Lunch €8-12; dinner €15-22. Kitchen open M-W 5-11:30pm, Th 5-9pm, F-Su 1-9:30pm. Bar open M-Th 5-11:30pm, F-Sa 1pm-12:30am, Su 1-11pm.)

Across from Seamy's is the **post office** (☎81001. Open M-F 9am-1pm and 2-5:30pm, Sa 9am-1pm). **Lough Foyle Ferry Co.** has frequent service from the town's dock to Magilligan, on Northern Ireland's Antrim Coast. (☎81901; www.loughfoyleferry.com. 10min., Apr.-Sept. every 20min. M-Sa 7:20am-9:50pm, Su 9am-9:50pm; Oct-Mar. every 20min. 9am-7pm, also 7:20, 8, 8:30am, 7:50pm. Cars £7/€10, pedestrians £2/€3, children and seniors £0.70/€1.)

NORTHERN IRELAND

The calm tenor of everyday life in Northern Ireland has long been overshadowed by media headlines about riots and bombs. While acts of violence and extremist groups are currently less visible than many might expect, observable divisions in civil society continue. Protestants and Catholics usually live in separate neighborhoods, attending separate schools, and patronizing different stores and pubs, even playing different sports. The split is sometimes hard for an outsider to discern, especially in rural vacation spots. On the other hand, it would be nearly impossible for a visitor to leave Northern Ireland without seeing curbs in cities and villages painted with the colors of their residents' identity (orange or red, white, and blue for Unionists and green for Nationalists). The 1998 Good Friday Agreement, an attempt to lead Northern Ireland out of the Troubles, has been a mixed success. The Assembly, in Stormont in Belfast, has been suspended on a number of occasions and the lack of progress on various issues, such as the disarmament of paramilitary groups, frustrated peace efforts for many years, although the 2005 announcement from by IRA that they intend to disarm fully has restored a measure of hope to the process. The May 2007 power-sharing agreement has installed a government with the top two executive positions being filled by members of both sides of the conflict, which promises to make their country as peaceful as it is beautiful. And Northern Ireland is certainly beautiful.

Fishing villages dot the strands of the Ards Peninsula, leading to the rounded peaks of the Mournes and the National Park retreats of Newcastle. To the west lie the easily accessible Sperrin Mountains and the tidy-walled farms of the Fermanagh Lake District. Industrial Enniskillen rests just north, though travelers would do well to continue onward to Derry/Londonderry, a city rich in political and historical significance. Nearby lies Northern Ireland's main natural attraction, the Giant's Causeway. This volcanic staircase extends out into the Atlantic while hillside forts and castles loom on the cliffs above. En route to the pubs and clubs of Belfast you'll pass by the waterfalls and valleys of the glorious Glens of Antrim.

NORTHERN IRELAND HIGHLIGHTS

CHECK OUT a ballet at Belfast's historical **Grand Opera House** (p. 510).

CYCLE among puffins at the Kebble Bird Sanctuary on Rathlin Island (p. 561).

GET TIPSY at the **Bushmills Distillery,** the oldest licensed whiskey producer in the world (p. 568).

LIFE AND TIMES

MONEY

Legal tender in Northern Ireland is the pound sterling. Northern Ireland has its own bank notes, which are identical in value to English and Scottish notes of the same denominations but not accepted outside Northern Ireland. Both English and Scottish notes, however, are accepted in the North.

Euro are generally not accepted in the North, with the exception of some border towns which will calculate the exchange rate and will usually add an additional surcharge. Most banks are closed on Saturdays, Sundays, and all public holidays. On bank holidays (see **Appendix,** p. 594), occurring several times per year in both countries, most businesses shut down. Usual weekday bank hours in Northern Ireland are M-F 9:30am to 4:30pm. For more comprehensive information, see **Essentials,** p. 8.

SAFETY AND SECURITY

Although sectarian violence is much less common than in the height of the Troubles, some neighborhoods and towns still experience unrest during sensitive political times. It's best to remain alert and cautious while traveling in Northern Ireland, especially during Marching Season, which reaches its height July 4-12. August 12th, when the Apprentice Boys march in Derry/Londonderry, is also a testy period. In Marching Season, be prepared for transport delays, and for many shops and services to be closed. Despite these concerns, Northern Ireland has one of the lowest tourist-related crime rates in the world.

 Northern Ireland is reached by using the UK **country code 44;** from the Republic dial **048.** The **phone code** for every town in the North is **028.** Remember that when calling from abroad, omit the first digit of each code if it is a zero. See **Telephone,** p. 35, for more details.

HISTORY AND POLITICS

Since the partition of 1920, the people of Northern Ireland have remained steadfast in their determination to retain their individual cultural and political identities, even at the cost of lasting peace. Many continue to defend the lines that define their differences, whether ideological divisions across the chambers of Parliament or actual streets marking the end of one culture and the beginning of the next. Generally speaking, the 950,000 Protestants are **Unionists,** who want the six counties of Northern Ireland to remain in the UK; the 650,000 Catholics tend to identify with the Republic of Ireland, not Britain, and many are **Nationalists,** who wish the six counties to be part of the Republic. The more extreme, and generally working-class, members of either side are known as **Loyalists** and **Republicans,** respectively; these groups traditionally have tended to prefer defending their turf with rocks and gas bombs. In 1998, the world felt a stirring of optimism with the signing of the Good Friday Agreement and subsequent opening of the Assembly in Belfast, but continued tensions over disarmament and political victories by hardliners have kept peace out of reach. For more information about Ireland before the break between the North and the Republic in 1920, see **Life and Times,** p. 49.

A DIVIDED ISLAND: IT STARTS

Ireland's struggle with English occupiers began in earnest when King Henry II arrived in AD 1171, heralding the involvement of England in Irish affairs. In the following centuries, the English took control of Ireland, and King Henry VIII declared himself King of Ireland in 1542. The Irish rose up on various occasions, often supported by their Catholic brethren and fellow English-haters, the French and Spanish. This encouraged King James I to begin a series of plantations in six of the nine counties of **Ulster.** English law was enforced throughout Ireland starting in 1603 and, although various parts of Ireland had been settled previously, the Scottish settlers were "planted" in the Ards Peninsula area of Ulster in large numbers from

Northern Ireland

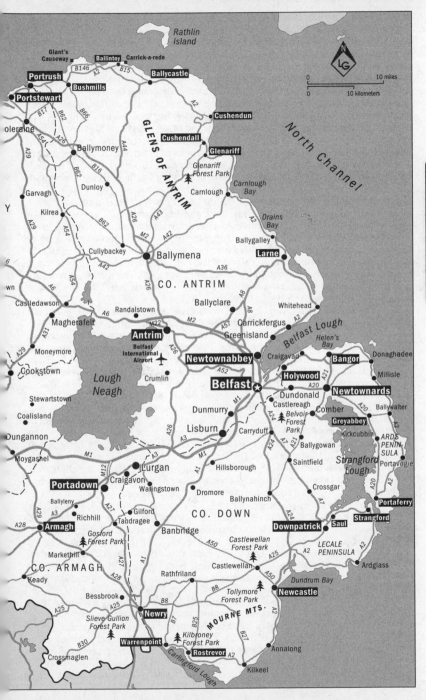

NORTHERN IRELAND

1606 onwards. In 1641, 59% of Ireland's land was owned by Catholics, who formed the majority of the native Irish, but by 1688 this proportion was down to 22%, and reduced to 7% by 1714. Two of the main events currently commemorated by Protestants in Northern Ireland took place during this period: in 1688 the gates of Derry were shut against the troops of Catholic James II (commemorated each August by the **Apprentice Boys of Derry**), and in 1690 William III defeated James II at the **Battle of the Boyne** (commemorated in July by the **Orange Order**).

Over the following two centuries, many merchants and working-class immigrants from Scotland settled in northeast Ulster. Institutionalized religious discrimination limited Catholic land ownership and other rights, but Northern Ireland was an attractive destination for Scottish Protestants who profited from the cheap land options. The British brought the smokestacks of progress to Counties Antrim and Down, while the rest of the island remained agrarian. By the end of the 19th century, Belfast was an industrial center with thriving textile mills and ship-building factories, most of which refused to hire Catholic workers.

As in present-day Northern Ireland, the division between Protestants and Catholics was not simple, but the hate ran deep; as King George III observed, "If you want to baste an Irishman, you can easily get an Irishman to turn the spit." Ironically, **Theobald Wolfe Tone,** a Protestant Presbyterian, is considered the Father of Republicanism. He founded the **United Irishmen,** predecessor of the modern IRA, in Belfast in 1791; the **Orange Order** (referring the color of the uniforms of Protestant William III's army) was formed in County Armagh in 1795. The following year, the first march commemorating the Battle of the Boyne occurred. In 1798 Wolfe Tone instigated an uprising, which was defeated handily at sea.

In the late 19th century, Republicanism continued to develop in pockets in the south, resulting in the formation of **Sinn Féin** under Arthur Griffith in 1905 (see **Parnell and Irish Nationalism,** p. 54). The picture looked very different in the Northeast. During its 300-year existence, the Ulster Plantation had created a working- and middle-class population that identified with the British Empire and did not support Irish Home Rule. The Orange Order's constituency and radicalism continued to grow despite legislative disapproval—it quietly gained momentum, culminating in explosive opposition to the first **Home Rule Bill** in 1886.

In 1912, when Home Rule seemed to be a possibility, **Edward Carson** held a mass meeting, and approximately 447,000 Unionists signed the **Ulster Covenant of Resistance to Home Rule.** As Home Rule grew to appear even more likely, the **Ulster Volunteer Force** formed in 1913 and armed itself by smuggling guns in through Larne. This act prompted the formation of the **Irish Citizen Army** and the **Irish National Volunteers,** who in turn armed themselves by sneaking their own guns in through Howth. As Ireland—the area that would become Northern Ireland in particular—raced toward armed conflict, **WWI** began.

The **36th (Ulster) Division,** originally formed for members of the UVF but later joined by Catholics, fought bravely and is renowned for its role at the Battle of Somme. While WWI continued, the **Irish Republican Brotherhood** organized the **Easter Rising** in 1916 (p. 55). The extreme response of the English converted many to the Republican cause. Out of the remnants of the rebels, **Michael Collins** formed the **Irish Republican Army (IRA)** which became the military wing of the Sinn Féin party. In 1920, a series of meetings between Irish leaders and the British Government led to the **Government of Ireland Act.** This allowed for the creation of two self-governing units, one consisting of the 28 counties of the south, and the other of six counties of northeast Ireland, soon to be Northern Ireland.

The newly constituted statelet of Northern Ireland, governed from **Stormont,** a suburb of Belfast, included only six of the nine counties of Ulster, leaving predominately Catholic **Donegal, Monaghan,** and **Cavan** to the Republic. This arrangement suited the one million Protestants in this area, but it threatened the half-million Catholic Nationalists living within the new Ulster. Protestant groups controlled politics, and the Catholic minority boycotted elections in protest of their "imprisonment within the North." The IRA continued sporadic campaigns in the North through the 1920s and 1930s with little result. In the Republic, the IRA was gradually suppressed.

During **WWII,** the Republic stayed neutral but Northern Ireland welcomed Allied troops, ships, and airforce bases. The need to build and repair warships revived the ship-building industry in Belfast and allowed Catholics to enter the industrial workforce for the first time. Toward the end of the war, Germans firebombed Belfast, making it one of the UK's most damaged cities. In 1949 the Republic was officially established and the **Ireland Act** recognized Northern Ireland's right to self-determination (they would not be booted out of the UK without majority consent).

Over the following two decades, a grateful British Parliament poured money into Northern Ireland. The standard of living remained higher than in the Republic, but discrimination and unemployment persisted for the working class, especially for Catholics. The government at Stormont neglected to institute social reform, and parliamentary districts were obviously drawn to favor middle class Protestants and to disenfranchise Catholics. Religious rifts reinforced cultural divides between and even within neighborhoods. After an unsuccessful attempt at school desegregation, Stormont granted subsidies to Catholic schools. As the Republic gained footing, violence (barring the occasional border skirmish) receded on the island. Between 1956 and 1962, the IRA waged a campaign of attacks on the border, but this ended for lack of support in 1962 and *The New York Times* bid the IRA a formal, eulogistic farewell. **Captain Terence O'Neill,** who became the third Stormont Prime Minister in 1963, tried to enlarge the economy and soften discrimination, meeting in 1965 with the Republic's Prime Minister, Sean Lemass. O'Neill summed up the liberal Unionist view of the time, saying, "If you treat Roman Catholics with due kindness and consideration, they will live like Protestants."

THE TROUBLES

The economy grew, but bigotry festered along with the nationalist community's resentment at their forced unemployment and lack of political representation. In 1966, for fear of this resentment, Protestant Unionists founded the Ulster Volunteer Force (**UVF**—named after the UVF of 1912) and issued a statement: "Known IRA men will be executed mercilessly and without hesitation." The UVF was declared illegal the year it was formed. Both the UVF and the IRA actively bombed each other and civilians throughout 1966. The American civil rights movement inspired the 1967 founding of the **Northern Ireland Civil Rights Association (NICRA),** a religiously mixed organization aiming to end discrimination throughout Northern Ireland. NICRA leaders tried to focus on individual rights, freedom of speech and housing, but Protestants began to fear it as a cover for the IRA. While the first NICRA march was raucous, it was nonviolent. The second, however, held in Derry/ Londonderry in 1968, was a bloody mess disrupted by Unionists and then by the **Royal Ulster Constabulary's** water cannons. The Troubles had begun.

TROUBLED LANGUAGE. Language in both the Republic and the North has become very politicized. Some terms include:

Derry/Londonderry: Because the renaming of Derry by the British during the establishment of Ulster plantations is associated with the taking of land and resources from the native Irish, calling the "maiden city" Derry demonstrates a more Catholic bent, while calling it Londonderry is generally associated with the Protestants. Though both sides say Derry most often, it is a contested term.

Ulster: Originally the province consisted of nine counties. Referring to Northern Ireland as Ulster is typically a Protestant expression of pride.

Catholic **John Hume** and Protestant **Ivan Cooper** formed a new civil rights committee in Derry/Londonderry but were overshadowed by Bernadette Devlin's radical, student-led **People's Democracy (PD)**. The PD encouraged, and NICRA opposed, a four-day march from Belfast to Derry/Londonderry starting on New Year's Day, 1969. On the fourth and final day of the march, seven miles from its destination, the marchers were ambushed by a mob of 200 at Burntollet Bridge. As the march entered Derry/Londonderry it was again attacked at Irish Street, a mainly Protestant area of the city. The march was finally broken up by RUC in the center of the city, sparking widespread rioting. The disorder became so serious that police could no longer enter parts of some cities, particularly Derry/Londonderry, where the slogan **"Free Derry"** became famous.

Civil rights concessions were granted in the hope of appeasing both sides, but mainly served to irritate Unionists. On August 12, 1969, Catholics based in Free Derry threw rocks at the annual Apprentice Boys parade along the city walls. The RUC attacked the Bogside residents, who set up barricades, and a two-day siege ensued. Free Derry retained its independence, but the violence showed that the RUC, even with their use of tear gas, could not maintain order alone. The British Army arrived and responded militarily as if the siege was orchestrated by the IRA, which it was not. "IRA—I ran away" graffiti appeared on Catholic walls after the siege, reproaching the IRA for not protecting their community.

Between 1970 and 1972, leaders alternated concessions and crackdowns to little effect. Rejuvenated by disgust at the British reaction and embarrassed by their failure to participate in the siege, the IRA split in two, with the "official" faction giving way to the new **Provisional IRA** or **Provos** (the IRA that exists today), which took over with less ideology and more guns. British troops became the main target. In 1970, John Hume founded the **Social Democratic and Labor Party (SDLP)**, with the intention of bringing about social change through the support of both Catholics and Protestants; by 1973, it had become the moderate political voice of Northern Irish Catholics. British policies of **internment** (imprisonment without trial, exclusively targeting Nationalists), which lasted from 1971 to 1975, outraged Catholics and led the SDLP to withdraw from government. The pattern was clear: any concessions to the Catholic community might provoke Protestant violence, while compromises that seemed to favor the Unionists risked an IRA response.

On January 30, 1972, British troops fired into a crowd in Derry/Londonderry that was peacefully protesting internment; these actions, called **Bloody Sunday,** and the ensuing reluctance of the British government to investigate, increased Catholic outrage. Fourteen Catholics, none of whom were IRA members, were killed. The soldiers claimed they had not fired the first shot, while Catholics said the soldiers targeted unarmed, fleeing marchers. Only in 1999 did official reexamination of the event begin; the inquiry is ongoing and will likely take several more years.

On February 2, 1972, the British embassy in Dublin was burned down. Soon thereafter, the IRA bombed a British army barracks. After further bombings in 1973, Stormont was dissolved and replaced by the **Sunningdale Executive,** which split power between Catholics and Protestants, and developed ties with the Republic of Ireland. As this power sharing began to take shape, a Loyalist general strike was started to protest the links with the Republic of Ireland. The strike lasted 14 days and brought the end of the executive. A policy of direct British rule from Westminster began, initially for four months.

Legislation in 1976 and 1978 removed special status for prisoners charged with paramilitary, terrorist, or political offences. In 1978, prisoners in the **Maze Prison** began a campaign to have their political prisoner status restored. They employed blanket protests (refusing to wear prison uniforms), dirty protests (smearing excrement on their cell walls), and intensified when Republican prisoners went on **hunger strike** in 1981. Republican leader **Bobby Sands** was elected to Parliament

the walls of belfast

Much of Belfast has changed dramatically since the 1994 cease-fires and the 1998 peace agreement. Signs of the conflict, which engulfed Northern Ireland for 30 years, have nearly vanished from the city center, where cozy cafes, swanky new bars, and bustling shoppers have replaced the army jeeps, battle-scarred buildings, and grim desolation downtown Belfast was once known for. The peace process has been good for business, but take the time to venture just beyond the commercial center, and you'll find that in many neighborhoods at the front lines of the conflict, the peace dividend never arrived.

"Bustling shoppers have replaced...the desolation Belfast was once known for."

Belfast remains a divided city, and the numerous walls (innocently referred to as "peace lines") built along the city's internal frontiers are by far the most visible indication of persistent sectarian divisions. The city is a patchwork of single-identity communities; the 2001 census revealed that two-thirds of the city's population live in areas that are either more than 90% Catholic or 90% Protestant. A peace line marks the dividing line of interface—the area where a majority Catholic/Nationalist community runs up against a majority Protestant/Unionist community. Residential segregation has actually increased since the peace process began and in some areas construction on the walls continues— new ones built and old ones lengthened and heightened, divisions solidified and rigidified amidst the decade-long peace process.

The walls were constructed over the course of the Troubles to separate warring communities, prevent attacks, and sometimes create a buffer zone. Many of the peace-lines in place today stand on ground that has been brutally contested for decades. Tensions run high in areas of such close contact, and attacks on the other community are easily launched from the safety of one's own. Long before the modern Troubles began, there was a history of interface communities building barricades during times of conflict. Riots broke out in Belfast periodically in the first half of the century—during the 1920s with the Anglo-Irish War and subsequent Irish Civil War, and throughout the Depression in the 1930s. In areas affected by the violence, local residents erected barri-

"The walls...are the most visible indication of persistent sectarian divisions."

cades to guard their streets from marauding mobs and, in some cases, the security forces.

When parts of Belfast descended into chaos in the late 1960s and early 70s, many communities constructed barricades to protect themselves from the violence sweeping the city. In the early years much of this was concentrated in the borderland between Catholic/Nationalist Falls and Protestant/Unionist Shankill. British troops arrived in August of 1969, and within a month they assembled the first official peace-line between the two areas to try to prevent some of the rioting. The army's wall ran along the same line as some community barricades, replacing and institutionalizing them with a permanent structure. Originally intended to be a temporary response, what began as a simple fence became

those within, they identify and guard against those beyond. Some look much like the war wounds they are—looming expanses of corrugated metal sprayed with graffiti epithets and crowned with thick coils of barbed wire. Others demonstrate the NIO's recent creative efforts to make the walls less of an eyesore—red and yellow brick with discreet security cameras and tasteful wrought-iron accessories.

"The peace-line solution became an acceptable solution to...conflict."

fortified, elongated, and elevated to the 1.5 mi. brick wall standing today.

The peace-line solution became an increasingly acceptable (and sought after) solution to intercommunal conflict at interface areas. Walls, fences, and official roadblocks were constructed throughout Belfast—with community activists from across the divide sometimes working together to lobby for their construction. By the year 2000, the Northern Ireland Office (NIO) Civil Representative's Office reported a total of 27 separate walls or fences across the city.

Mysteriously, none of these walls appear on most Belfast maps. Standing next to one, it's hard to imagine how such a dominant and obstructive fixture on the urban landscape could be disregarded. The walls forcefully demarcate not only space but identity. As they fortify and contain

Designed to blend more readily into the environment, these new additions achieve a different sense of permanence. This worries some community members who live in interface areas. In recent debates over whether to build new walls and expand others in flashpoint areas, some have argued that once you begin building walls, they're

"These new additions achieve a different sense of permanence."

very hard to take down. Once you go to the effort to make them pretty, the chances they will ever be removed become even more remote.

Brenna Powell has worked at the Stanford Center on Conflict and Negotiation on projects in partnership with grassroots organizations in Northern Ireland.

486

from a Catholic district in Tyrone and Fermanagh while leading the strike. He died at age 26 after 66 days of fasting and became a symbol of resistance; his face appears on murals throughout Northern Ireland. Nine more protesters followed him to their deaths. During the protest, Margaret Thatcher, then Prime Minister of the United Kingdom, said, "We are not prepared to consider special category status for certain groups of people serving sentences for crime. Crime is crime is crime, it is not political." The remaining prisoners officially ended the hunger strike on October 3, seven months and two days after it began. The strikes galvanized Nationalists, and support for **Sinn Féin** surged in the early 80s.

With the increase in support for Sinn Féin and violence continuing, British Prime Minister Margaret Thatcher and Taoiseach Garret FitzGerald had a series of meetings. The **Anglo-Irish Agreement** was signed in 1985, with the first part stating: "the two Governments affirm that any change in the status of Northern Ireland would only come about with the consent of a majority of the people of Northern Ireland." However, the Agreement only granted the Republic a "consultative role," with no legal authority in the governance of Northern Ireland. It improved relations between London and Dublin but infuriated extremists on both sides: Republicans were outraged by the principle of the "consent of the majority of people" in a state they believed to be invalid, while Unionists were enraged by the involvement of the Republic. A protest organized by Unionism used the slogan "Ulster says NO," which was seen around Northern Ireland for many years.

Protestant paramilitaries went on to attack "their own" RUC, while the IRA, buttressed by an estimated 30 tons of arms from Libya, continued its bombing campaigns in England. In 1991 and 1992, the Brooke Initiative led to the first multi-party talks in Northern Ireland in over a decade. The **Downing Street Declaration** was issued at the end of 1993 by Prime Minister John Major and Taoiseach Albert Reynolds, and the interest and cooperation of the Clinton administration served as a foundation for the peace process.

1994 CEASEFIRE

On August 31, 1994, the IRA announced a "complete cessation of military activities." Then on October 13, 1994, the **Combined Loyalist Military Command,** speaking on behalf of all Loyalist paramilitary organizations, offered "to the loved ones of all innocent victims…abject and true remorse" as they announced their ceasefire. Unionist leaders bickered over the meaning of the IRA's statement; in their opinion, it did not go far enough—only disarmament could signify a commitment to peace. Nonetheless, **Gerry Adams,** Sinn Féin's leader, defended the statement. The peace held for over a year.

In February 1995, John Major and Irish Prime Minister John Bruton issued the **joint framework** proposal. The document suggested the possibility of a new Northern Ireland Assembly that would include the "harmonizing powers" of the Irish and British governments and maintain the right of the people of Northern Ireland to choose their own destiny. Subsequently, the British government began talks with both Loyalists and Sinn Féin. Disarmament was the largest problem in the 1995 talks—both Republican and Loyalist groups refused to put down their guns.

The IRA ended its ceasefire on February 9, 1996, with the massive bombing of an office building in London's Docklands. Despite this setback, the stalled peace talks, chaired by US Senator **George Mitchell,** were slated for June 10. Ian Paisley, leader of the extreme **Democratic Unionist Party (DUP),** objected to Mitchell's appointment, calling it a "dastardly deed," but did not boycott the talks, which proceeded sluggishly. Sinn Féin initially refused to participate because it did not agree to the **Mitchell Principles,** which included the total disarmament of all paramilitary organizations. Sinn Féin's popularity had been growing in Northern Ireland, but its credibility was seriously jeopardized on June 15, 1996, when a blast in a Manchester shopping district injured more than 200 people.

As the peace process moved forward, the Orangemen's July and August marches grew more contentious. Parades through Catholic neighborhoods incited violence by marchers and residents. A **Parades Commission** was formed to mediate Unionist claims that their freedom of speech was being curtailed and Catholic arguments that parades were forms of harassment and intimidation. A march in 1996 saw another burst of violence after the Parades Commission banned an Orange Order march through Catholic **Garvaghy Road** in Portadown, Co. Armagh. Unionists responded by chucking petrol bombs, bricks, and bottles at police, who responded with plastic bullets. After four days of violence, police allowed the marchers to go through, but this time Catholics responded with a hail of debris. The nightlife in Belfast and Derry/Londonderry at this time consisted mostly of those rioting.

In May of 1997, the Labour party swept the British elections and **Tony Blair,** riding high on hopes of peace, became Prime Minister. Sinn Féin made its most impressive showing yet: **Gerry Adams** and **Martin McGuinness** (who has recently admitted to being second-in-command of the IRA during Bloody Sunday) won seats in Parliament but refused to swear allegiance to the Queen and were barred from taking their places. The government ended its ban on talks with Sinn Féin. However, hopes for a renewed ceasefire were dashed when the car of a prominent Republican was bombed; in retaliation, the IRA shot two members of the RUC.

GOOD FRIDAY AGREEMENT

The 1997 Marching Season gave Mo Mowlam, the British government's Northern Ireland Secretary, a rough introduction to her new job. The Orange Order started their festivities a week early in Portadown. More than 80 people were hurt in the ensuing rioting and looting, and Mowlam came under scrutiny for allowing the parade without considering the consequences. On July 10, the Orange Order called off and re-routed a number of controversial parades, offering hope for peace. For the most part, the marches went peacefully—police fired a smattering of plastic bullets at rioters in Derry/Londonderry and Belfast, but there were no casualties. On July 19, the IRA announced an "unequivocal" ceasefire to start the next day.

In September 1997, Sinn Féin joined the peace talks without being required to disarm. Members of the **Ulster Unionist Party (UUP),** the voice of moderate Protestants, joined shortly thereafter and were disparaged by Paisley and the DUP for sitting with terrorists. UUP leader **David Trimble** assured Protestants that he would not negotiate directly with Sinn Féin.

The peace process, despite its noble aspirations, did not enjoy universal support. In January 1998, another dozen lives were lost. After two Protestants were killed by Catholic extremists in early February, Unionist leaders charged Sinn Féin with breaking its pledge to support only peaceful actions toward political change, and tried to oust party leaders from the talks. Representatives from Britain, Ireland, and the US continued to push for progress, holding the group to a strict April deadline. Mowlam expressed her commitment by visiting Republican and Loyalist prisoners in Maze Prison to encourage their participation in the peace process.

After a long week of negotiations, during which Blair had physically blocked the doorway to prevent Trimble from walking out, the delegates approved a draft of the **1998 Northern Ireland Peace Agreement** on Friday, April 10—the **Good Friday Agreement.** The pact emphasized that change in Northern Ireland could come about only with the consent of a majority of the people of Northern Ireland, and that the "birthright" of the people is to choose whether to identify personally as Irish or British.

On Friday, May 22, in the first island-wide vote since 1918, residents of Northern Ireland and the Republic voted the agreement into law through a referendum. A resounding majority (71% of Northern Ireland and 94% of the Republic) voted "yes" to divide governing responsibilities of Northern Ireland into three strands. The new main body, a 108-member **Northern Ireland Assembly**, assigns committee posts and chairs proportionately to the parties' representation. Voices of moderation on both sides, David Trimble of the UUP and Seamus Mallon of the SDLP, were elected First Minister and Deputy First Minister. The second strand of the new government, a **North-South Ministerial Council**, serves as the cross-border authority. At least 12 possible areas of focus are still under consideration, including social welfare issues such as education, transportation, urban planning, tourism, and EU programs. The final strand, the **British-Irish Council**, approaches similar issues, but operates on a broader scale, concerning itself with all British Isles.

While many felt that a lasting peace was finally in reach, a few controversial issues remained unresolved. Among other things, calls were made for disbanding the largely Protestant RUC, decommissioning paramilitary weapons, and reducing troop numbers. Blair declared that the RUC would continue to exist, but appointed Chris Patten, former governor of Hong Kong, to head a commission reviewing the RUC's recruiting, hiring, training practices, culture, and symbols.

Just when everything was starting to resolve itself, around rolled Marching Season again. At the end of May 1998, a march by the **Junior Orange Order** provoked violence on Portadown's **Garvaghy Road,** an area still smarting from the unrest in 1996. In light of this disturbance, the Parades Commission hesitated to grant the Orange Day marching permits. On June 15, the Parades Commission re-routed the Tour of the North, banning it from entering the Cliftonville Rd. and Antrim Rd. areas in Belfast. Aside from two short showdowns with the RUC, the parade proceeded without conflict. But the day after the assembly elections, Nationalists and policemen at a parade in West Belfast started the familiar dance of destruction. Early July saw a wave of violence that included hundreds of bombings and assaults.

Other parades passed peacefully, but a stand-off began over the fate of the July 4 **Drumcree parade,** which was forbidden from marching down war-torn Garvaghy Road. Angered by the decision but encouraged by a history of British indecision, thousands of people participated in a week-long standoff with the RUC. Riots erupted in Portadown and elsewhere, and Protestant marchers were angered by what they saw as disloyalty by their own police force. Neither the Orangemen nor the Parade Commission would budge, and the country looked with anxiety toward July 12, Marching Season. On the night of July 11, a Catholic home in Ballymoney was firebombed in a sectarian neighborhood, and three young boys were killed. Marches still took place the following day. Due to the universal condemnation of the deaths of the **Quinn boys,** the **Drumcree Standoff** gradually lost numbers, and the Church of Ireland publicly called for its end. Though some tried to distance the boys' deaths from the events at Drumcree, the deaths led to a reassessment of the Orange Order and a new sobriety about the peace process. Then, on August 15, a bombing in the religiously mixed town of **Omagh** left 29 dead and 382 injured, and a splinter group calling themselves the **Real IRA** claimed responsibility for the attack. The terrorists' motive for one of the worst atrocities of the Troubles was to undermine the Good Friday Agreement.

In October 1998, Nationalist John Hume and Unionist David Trimble received the Nobel Peace Prize for their work in the peace process. The coming year, however, was full of disappointments. The formation of the **Northern Ireland Assembly,** a fundamental premise from Good Friday, ended in failure. Two major provisions of the Agreement highlighted serious rifts between Nationalist and Unionist politicians: the gradual de-arming of all paramilitary groups, and the early release of political prisoners. Disagreement over the **Northern Ireland (Sentences) Bill** fanned the flames and split the UK Parliament for the first time during the talks. The bill required the release of all political prisoners, including those convicted of murder,

NORTHERN IRELAND

by May 2000. Dissenters feared that the bill did not sufficiently link the release of prisoners to their organizations' full disarmament, which was the greatest concern for most Unionists: the military wings of political parties, most notably Sinn Fein, were expected to disarm themselves in time for the June elections. Many saw the lack of a time frame for decommissioning as a fatal flaw of the Agreement.

CURRENT EVENTS

In December 1999 a power-sharing government was formed under the leadership of Trimble and Mallon, but the IRA's hidden weapon caches remained a central point of tension and threatened the collapse of the new assembly. In late January 2000, Trimble gave the IRA an ultimatum to put its weapons "beyond use," and predicted political responsibility being returned to Westminster in London. The IRA's unwillingness to comply hobbled the February peace talks, and the comparatively amateurish **Continuity IRA** bombed a rural hotel in Irvinestown. Every Northern Irish political group, including Sinn Féin, condemned the attack. Though the blast injured no one, it was an unwelcome reminder of the past in the midst of a stalled peace process. Britain suspended the power-sharing experiment just 11 weeks after its implementation and reintroduced direct British rule.

On midnight of May 29, 2000, Britain restored the power-sharing scheme after the IRA promised to begin disarmament. In June, they allowed two ambassadors to inspect their secret weapon caches. The inspectors confirmed that the weapons were unused. In 2002, the IRA broke new ground when they destroyed a small payload of their weapons, marking the first time they had ever voluntarily destroyed any of their resources. In 2000 the last political prisoners in Maze Prison walked free under the Good Friday provisions. Supporters gave them heroes' welcomes, but other civilians and relatives of the deceased found the early release of convicted murderers, some carrying life sentences, appalling. Many of the released men expressed remorse and stated that their war was over, but others refused to apologize. A major stride forward was made in July 28, 2005, when the IRA formally ordered all units to dump their arms, and announced that it will pursue its political goals exclusively through peaceful means.

Both sides are making efforts to repair the past—in 2001, the RUC was reformed into the **Police Service of Northern Ireland,** which some Catholics still regard as suspect. The May 2003 elections were suspended, ostensibly because of the IRA's slow disarmament, but many believe that Britain didn't want Trimble voted out of office. When the elections were held in November, Ian Paisley's Democratic Unionists and Sinn Féin outpolled more moderate parties. The **Bloody Sunday Inquiry** finished in 2006 with testimony from British military and IRA figures. As of May 2007, the Assembly has been re-opened, and Paisley and Martin McGuinness (of Sinn Féin) occupy the First and Deputy First Minister posts, the top two executive positions. While they often fail to communicate, there is widespread hope that the joint government will lead to a lasting era of peace.

LITERARY VOICES

The literature of Northern Ireland deals largely with the divided Catholic and Protestant cultures. Many Northern writers attempt to create works of relevance to members of both communities. Poet **Louis MacNeice** (1907-63) infused his lyric poems with a Modernist concern for struggle and social upheaval, but he took no part in the sectarian politics. **Derek Mahon** tries to focus on the common elements that people of all cultures share. Contemporary poet **Frank Ormsby** addresses larger social concerns through the lens of the everyday, and has collected and edited the works of many other Northern Irish poets. Born in rural Co. Derry, **Seamus Heaney** ("famous Seamus") won the Nobel Prize in 1995 and is the most prominent living Irish poet. His subject matter ranges from bogs to skunks to archaeological remains, and his fourth book, *North* (1975), deals directly with the Troubles. His recent translation of

Beowulf (2000) has given Grendel and his mother a popularity they haven't seen in centuries. Heaney's contemporary **Paul Muldoon** occupies himself more with self-skepticism and an ear for weird rhyme than with politics.

BELFAST (BÉAL FEIRTE)

Belfast still struggles with the stigma of its violent past, it has rebuilt itself from the destruction of the Troubles and now surprises most visitors with its neighborly, urbane feel. The island's second-largest city, Belfast (pop. 330,000) is the focus of Northern Ireland's cultural, commercial, and political activity. Queen's University, once considered the top medical school in the world, bears testament to the city's rich academic history—luminaries such as Nobel Laureate Seamus Heaney and Lord Kelvin (of chemistry fame) once roamed the halls of Queen's, and Samuel Beckett taught the young men of Campbell College. Native son C.S. Lewis spent his youth here but kicked off his literary career in London. The Belfast pub scene ranks among the best in the world, combining the historical appeal of old-fashioned watering holes with more modern bars and clubs. The lively student population enjoys a vibrant nightlife, rollicking trad at the city's many pubs, and a cultural backdrop rich with history and highlighted by murals.

Belfast was founded as the capital of the 17th-century "Ulster Scots" Presbyterian settlement and was William of Orange's base during his battles against Catholic King James II (see **More British Problems,** p. 52). In the 19th century, Belfast

Belfast Environs

TO LARNE (4mi)

0   4 miles

0   4 kilometers

Ballynure

Whitehead

Ballyclare

Woodburn

Antrim

Six Mile Water

Carrickfergus

Dunadry   Templepatrick

Greenisland

Lough Neagh

TO ISLE OF MAN

Newtown-abbey

Belfast Lough

Bangor

Belfast International Airport

Nutts Corner

Holywood

Ulster Folk and Transport Musem

Belfast City Airport

Belfast

Newtownards

Dunmurry

Comber

Strangford Lough

Lisburn

Carryduff

R. Lagan

TO ARMAGH (20mi)

TO OXFORD ISLAND (6mi), CRAIGAVON (10mi)

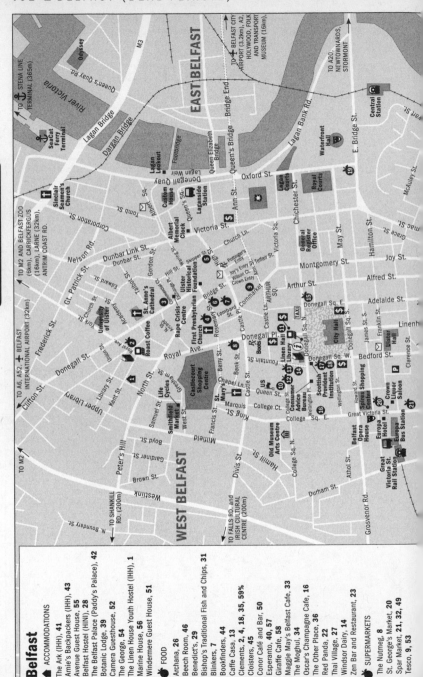

Belfast

▲ ACCOMMODATIONS

The Ark (IHH), **41**
Arnie's Backpackers (IHH), **43**
Avenue Guest House, **55**
Belfast Hostel (HINI), **28**
The Belfast Palace (Paddy's Palace), **42**
Botanic Lodge, **39**
Camera Guesthouse, **52**
The George, **54**
The Linen House Youth Hostel (IHH), **1**
Marine House, **56**
Windermere Guest House, **51**

● FOOD

Archana, **26**
Beech Room, **46**
Benedict's, **29**
Bishop's Traditional Fish and Chips, **31**
Blinkers, **7**
Bookfinders, **44**
Caffe Casa, **13**
Clements, **2, 4, 18, 35, 59%**
Cloisters, **45**
Conor Café and Bar, **50**
Esperanto, **40, 57**
Giraffe Cafe, **58**
Maggie May's Belfast Cafe, **33**
The Moghul, **34**
Oscar's Champagne Cafe, **16**
The Other Place, **36**
Red Panda, **22**
Thai Village, **27**
Windsor Dairy, **14**
Zen Bar and Restaurant, **23**

🛒 SUPERMARKETS

The Nutmeg, **8**
St. George's Market, **20**
Spar Market, **21, 32, 49**
Tesco, **9, 53**

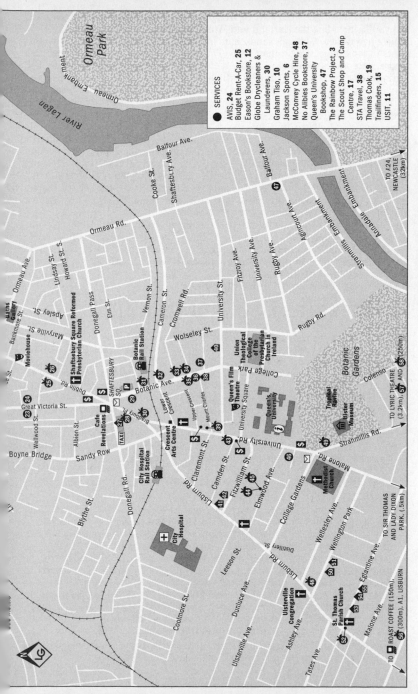

● SERVICES

AVIS, **24**
Budget Rent-A-Car, **25**
Eason's Bookstore, **12**
Globe Drycleaners &
Launderers, **30**
Graham Tiso, **10**
Jackson Sports, **6**
McConvey Cycle Hire, **48**
No Alibies Bookstore, **37**
Queen's University
Bookshop, **47**
The Rainbow Project, **3**
The Scout Shop and Camp
Centre, **17**
STA Travel, **38**
Thomas Cook, **19**
Trailfinders, **15**
USIT, **11**

became the most industrial part of Ireland with its world-famous factories and shipyards, including the Harland and Wolff, birthplace of the *Titanic*. By 1900, Belfast had gathered enough slums, smoke, Victorian architecture, and social theorists to look more British than Irish. The ship-building industry drew Scottish laborers across the channel for jobs, securing the region's allegiance to the UK. During the Troubles (p. 483), armed British soldiers patrolled streets, frequent military checkpoints slowed traffic, and stores advertised "Bomb Damage Sales."

Though sectarian relations remain tense, particularly in the historically divided West Belfast, the Troubles are over and today's city offers a number of distinctive neighborhoods. Belfast City Centre, with its stately City Hall, hums with hurried shoppers, briefcase-toters, and mohawked teens during the day. The industrial docks now hold The Odyssey, a giant entertainment complex and science center that serves as the focal point of the recent riverfront revival. South of Shaftesbury Square, students idle nights away in cafes and keep the streets alive moving between pubs and clubs. In West Belfast, Catholics and Protestants live on opposite sides of the peace line and paint their stories on the walls, while East Belfast remains industrial and predominantly Protestant.

From the first week of July to July 12, a period known as "Marching Season," the "Orangemen"—Protestants celebrating William's victory over James II—parade through Northern Ireland's streets wearing orange sashes and bowler hats. These marches usually meet with Nationalist protests. Tensions inevitably run high with occasional spurts of violence, and much of the city preemptively shuts down for the two weeks surrounding the Marching Season.

■ INTERCITY TRANSPORTATION

Flights: Belfast International Airport (☎9442 2448; www.belfastairport.com) in Aldergrove. **Aer Lingus** (☎0845 084 4444); **British Airways** (☎0845 850 9850); **British European** (Flybe; ☎0870 567 6676); **BMI** (☎0870 607 0555); **Continental** (☎0845 607 6760); and **Easyjet** (☎0870 600 0000; www.easyjet.com) operate from here. **Translink Bus 300** has 24hr. service from the airport to Europa bus station in the city center (M-F every 10min. 7:20am-6:15pm, every 15-40min. otherwise; Sa every 20min. 7:20am-6:40pm, at least once per hr. otherwise; Su every 30min. 8:45am-6:15pm, at least once per hr. otherwise; call ☎9066 6630 or visit www.translink.co.uk for full timetables). £6, round-trip £9 if you return within 1 month. **Taxis** (☎9448 4353) get you there for £25-30. **Belfast City Airport** (☎9093 9093; www.belfastcityairport.com), at the harbor, holds **British European**. To get from City Airport to Europa bus station (near the city center), take **Translink Bus 600** (M-F every 20min. 9:45am-10:05pm, at least every 30min. otherwise; Sa every 20min. 8:05am-6:05pm, at least every 30min. otherwise 6am-9:50pm; Su at least every 45min. 7:30am-9:50pm).

Trains: For train and bus info, contact **Translink**. (☎9066 6630; www.translink.co.uk. Inquiries daily 7am-8pm.) Trains run from City Airport **(Sydenham Halt)** to **Central Station** (M-F 37 per day, Sa 28 per day, Su 14 per day; £1.40). All trains arrive at Belfast's Central Station on E. Bridge St. Some also stop at **Botanic Station**, Botanic Ave. at the northern end of the University, or at **Great Victoria Station**, next to Europa Hotel. To: **Bangor** (22-35min.; M-F 51 per day, Sa 32 per day, Su 14 per day; £4); **Derry/Londonderry** (2hr.; M-F 10 per day, Sa 9 per day, Su 5 per day; £10); **Dublin** (2hr.; M-Sa 8 per day, Su 5 per day; £24); **Larne** (M-F 30 per day, Sa 18 per day, Su 9 per day; £5). To get to Donegall Sq. from Central Station, turn left and walk down E. Bridge St. Turn right on Oxford St., then left on May St., which runs into Donegall Sq. The **Metro** bus service is free with rail tickets (see **Local Transportation**, p. 496).

Buses: Belfast has 2 main stations. Buses traveling to the south and west operate out of **Europa Bus Terminal**, off Great Victoria St., behind the Europa Hotel (☎9066 6630;

ticket office open M-Sa 7:30am-6:30pm, Su 12:30-5:30pm). To: **Cork** (10hr., M-Sa 9:10am, £22.40); **Derry/Londonderry** (1¾hr.; M-F 34 per day, Sa 20 per day, Su 11 per day; £9); **Donegal** (4hr.; M-Sa 10 per day, Su 4 per day; £12.70); **Dublin** (3hr.; M-Sa 17 per day, Su at 11pm, leaving from Glengall St. rather than Europa; £9.65); **Galway** (6¾hr.; M-Sa 3:45pm, Su 3:50pm; £20.30). Buses heading to the west and north operate out of **Laganside Bus Centre,** off Donegall Quay (☎9066 6630; ticket office open M-F 8:30am-5pm). To reach the city center from the station, turn left from the terminal onto Queen's Sq. and walk past the clock tower. Queen's Sq. becomes High St. and runs into Donegall Pl.; a left to City Hall and Donegall Sq. Centrelink buses connect both stations with city center (see **Local Transportation,** p. 496).

Ferries: To reach the city center from **Belfast SeaCat terminal** (☎0870 552 3523; www.seacat.co.uk) off Donegall Quay late at night or early in the morning, a **taxi** is the best bet, as the docks are rather isolated. If on foot, take a left when exiting the terminal onto Donegall Quay. Turn right onto Albert Sq. about 2 blocks down at Customs House (a large Victorian stone building). After 2 more short blocks, turn left on Victoria St. (note: not Great Victoria St.). Turn right again at the clock tower onto High St., which runs into Donegall Pl. Here, a left leads to the City Hall and Donegall Sq. (at the end of the street), where a **Metro** bus stops (see **Local Transportation,** p. 496). **Norfolk Ferries** (www.norfolkline-ferries.co.uk) operates out of the SeaCat terminal and runs to **Liverpool, England** (8hr., starting at £59 with car and £20 without). Book online to avoid a £10 booking fee.) **P&O Irish Ferries** in **Larne** (☎0870 242 4777) run to **Cairnryan, Scotland** and to many other locations in Ireland, England, and France. **Stena Line** (☎0870 570 7070; www.stenaline.com), up the Lagan River, has the quickest service to Scotland, docking in **Stranraer** (1¾hr.; fares seasonal, book online). For information on ferries and hovercrafts to Belfast from **England** and **Scotland,** see **By Boat,** p. 27.

Car Rental: Budget, 96-102 Great Victoria St. (☎0870 156 5656). Economy £51 per day, £185 per week. Ages 23-75. Open M-F 9am-5pm, Sa 9am-noon. **AVIS** (☎9024 0404; www.avis.co.uk) is across Great Victoria St. Other Budget offices at **Belfast International Airport Office** (☎9442 3332; open daily 7am-11pm) and **Belfast City Airport Office.** (☎9045 1111; www.belfastcityairport.com. Open M-Sa 7:30am-9:30pm, Su 9am-9:30pm). At **Belfast International Airport** also look for **Dan Dooley** (☎9445 2522, or use the courtesy phone at the end of the hall past other rental car kiosks) for affordable rates; **Hertz** (☎9442 2533; open M-F 7:30am-10:30pm); **Europcar** (☎9442 3444; www.europcar.ie); another **AVIS** office (☎9422 2333; M-F and Su 7:30am-11:30pm, Sa 7:30am-9:30pm); and **National and Alamo** (☎9032 5522). **Belfast City Airport** has offices of **National and Alamo** (☎9073 9400) and **Hertz** (☎9073 2451), among others. Some bookings can be made at **www.easycar.com.**

■ ORIENTATION

Buses arrive at the Europa Bus Station on **Great Victoria Street** near several landmarks: the Europa Hotel, Crown Liquor Saloon, and Opera House. To the northeast is **City Hall** in **Donegall Square.** A busy shopping district extends north for four blocks between City Hall and the enormous Castlecourt Shopping Centre. Donegall Pl. turns into **Royal Avenue** and runs from Donegall Sq. through the shopping area. In the eastern part of the shopping district is **Cornmarket,** where pubs in their narrow **entries** (small alleyways) and centuries-old buildings offer an escape from the busy streets. **Laganside Bus Centre,** with service to Northeast Ireland, faces the River Lagan on Queen's Sq., northeast of Cornmarket. South of Europa Bus Station, Great Victoria St. meets **Dublin Road** at **Shaftesbury Square.** The stretch of Great Victoria St. between the bus station and Shaftesbury Sq. is known as the **Golden Mile** because of its highbrow establishments and Victorian architecture. **Botanic Avenue** and **Bradbury Place** (which becomes **University Road**) extend south from Shaftesbury Sq. into **Queen's University's** turf, the location of many cafes, pubs, and budget accommodations. In this area, the busiest neighborhoods center around **Malone Avenue** and **Stranmillis and Lisburn Roads.** The city center, Golden Mile, and the university are all quite safe. Though locals advise caution in the East and West, central Belfast is safer than most European cities for tourists.

Westlink Motorway divides working-class **West Belfast,** historically more politically volatile than the city center, from the rest of Belfast. A sharp division remains between sectarian neighborhoods: the Protestant district stretches along **Shankill Road,** just north of the Catholic neighborhood, which is centered around **Falls Road.** The **peace line** separates them. **River Lagan** splits industrial **East Belfast** from Belfast proper. The shipyards and docks extend north on both sides of the river as it grows into **Belfast Lough.** During the week, the area north of City Hall is essentially deserted after 6pm. Though muggings are infrequent in Belfast, it's wise to use taxis after dark, particularly near clubs and pubs in the northeast. West Belfast's murals are best seen by day. Ask the tourist office or local hostels for more information on where and when to exercise the most caution.

The M1 and M2/M5 motorways join north of Belfast's city center. A1 branches off from M1 around **Lisburn** and heads south to **Newry,** where it becomes N1 and continues through **Drogheda** to **Dublin.** M2 merges into A6 and heads northwest to **Derry/Londonderry.** **Larne** is connected to Belfast by A8, off M2. A2 heads west toward **Belfast City Airport, Bangor,** and the **Ards Peninsula.**

THE RAPE OF THE FALLS. The area stretching from Divis Tower to Cavendish Sq. is known as the **Lower Falls.** This area was sealed off by the British Army for 35 hours in July 1970, in an episode known as the **Rape of the Falls.** Acting on a tip that arms were hidden in some of the houses, soldiers searched homes at random while residents were forbidden to leave the area, even for milk or bread. Before this event there were only about 50 Republicans in the area; afterward, over 2000 people had turned to the IRA. Many regard this raid as the biggest tactical mistake ever made by the British Army in Northern Ireland.

▛ LOCAL TRANSPORTATION

All transport cards and tickets are available at the kiosks in Donegall Sq. W. (M-F 8am-6pm, Sa 8:30am-5:30pm) and around the city.

Metro bus service (☎9066 6630; www.translink.co.uk) centers at Donegall Sq. with 12 routes covering the major areas of Belfast, including Europa Bus Terminal, Castlecourt Shopping Centre, Central Train Station, and Laganside Bus Station. Supplemented by Ulsterbus's "blue buses" to the suburbs. Day passes £3. Travel within the city center £1 (£1.30 beyond), under 16 £0.50. 5-journey £5.25-7.25/3.40-4.50, depending on which zones of the city will be visited. 10-day journey £9-13/5.25-7.25. Student discount card for full-time students £7 per year. Grab a timetable at any station.

Nightlink Buses shuttle the tipsy from Donegall Sq. W. to various towns outside of Belfast. (Sa 1 and 2am. £3.50, payable on board or at the Donegall Sq. W. kiosk.)

Taxis: 24hr. metered cabs abound: **Value Cabs** (☎9080 9080); **City Cab** (☎9024 2000); **Fon a Cab** (☎9033 3333).

Bike Rental: McConvey Cycles, 183 Ormeau Rd. (☎9033 0322; www.mcconvey.com). M and F-Su £20; otherwise £10 per day, £40 per wk. Locks supplied. Panniers £15 per week. £50 deposit. Open M-W and F-Sa 9am-6pm, Th 9am-8pm. **Life Cycles,** 36-37 Smithfield Market (☎9043 9959; www.lifecycles.co.uk) rents bikes (£9 per day) and offers **bicycle city tours** (see **Tours,** p. 507).

☑ PRACTICAL INFORMATION

TOURIST AND FINANCIAL SERVICES

Tourist Office: Belfast Welcome Centre, 47 Donegall Pl. (☎9024 6609; www.goto-belfast.com). Offers comprehensive free booklet on Belfast and info on surrounding areas. Books reservations in Northern Ireland (£2) and the Republic (£3). Open June-Sept. M-Sa 9am-7pm, Su noon-5pm; Oct.-May M-Sa 9am-5pm. **Irish Tourist Board (Bord Fáilte),** 53 Castle St. (☎9032 7888). Dishes out info, books accommodations in the Republic, and answers Irish passport inquiries. Open June-Aug. M-F 9am-5pm, Sa 9am-12:30pm; Sept.-May M-F 9am-5pm.

Travel Agency: USIT, College St., 13b The Fountain Centre (☎9032 7111), near Royal Ave. Sells ISICs, European Youth Cards, and every kind of bus or rail pass imaginable. Books ferries and planes and compiles round-the-world itineraries. Open M-F 9:30am-5pm, Sa 9:30am-12:30pm. Additional office at Queen's University **Student Union** (☎9024 1830). Open M-F 10am-5pm. **STA,** 92-94 Botanic Ave. (☎9024 1469; www.statravel.co.uk). Open M-W and F 9:30am-5:30pm, Th 10am-5:30pm, Sa 10am-5pm. **Trailfinders** (☎9032 8260), 1 block up Fountain St. from City Hall. Open M-F 9am-7pm, Sa 9am-6pm, Su 10am-6pm.

Hostelling International Northern Ireland (HINI): 22 Donegall Rd. (☎9032 4733; www.hini.org.uk). Books HINI hostels for free, international hostels for £3. Sells HI membership cards to residents of Northern Ireland (£10, under 18 £6).

Embassies: For an extensive list of embassies and consulates, see **Essentials,** p. 8.

Banks: Find 24hr. **ATMs** at: **Bank of Ireland,** 54 Donegall Pl. (☎9023 4334); **First Trust,** 92 Ann St. (☎9032 5599); **Northern Bank,** 14 Donegall Sq. W. (☎9024 5277); **Ulster Bank,** Donegall Sq. E. (☎9027 6000). Most banks open M-F 9am-4:30pm.

Currency Exchange: Thomas Cook, 10 Donegall Sq. W. (☎9088 3800). No commission on traveler's checks. Open M-W and Sa 8am-7pm, Th 8am-9pm, F 8am-8pm, Su 1-5pm. **Belfast International Airport office** (☎9448 4848; www.belfastairport.com). Open May-Oct. M-Th 5:30am-8:30pm, F-Sa 5:30am-11pm; Nov.-Apr. daily 6am-8pm.

Work Opportunities: The Ark (see **Accommodations,** p. 499) regularly hires travelers to work at the hostel; workers often live in the hostel's long-term housing. **The Belfast Palace** (see **Accommodations,** p. 520) also hires travelers for 2-3 months at a time. Flexible payment and accommodation arrangements available. **The Linen House Hostel** (see **Accommodations,** p. 499) often has openings and posts temporary work throughout the city and island. Those with catering experience may contact Sharon at **Azzura** (see **Food,** p. 500), for stints of at least 2 months. For a formally arranged temporary position, inquire at **Industrial Temps,** 87/91 Great Victoria St. (☎9032 2511); **Adecco,** 38 Queen St. (☎9024 4660); or at one of the city's top agencies, such as **Lynn Recruitment,** 48-50 Bedford St. (☎9023 4324; www.lynnrecruitment.co.uk). **Reed Accountancy,** 1 Donegall Sq. W. (☎9033 0604; fiona-imison@reed.co.uk), appeals specifically to backpackers looking to finance the next leg of their travels. Finally, you should always check the bulletin board or with the staff of hostels.

LOCAL SERVICES

Libraries: Belfast Central Library, 122 Royal Ave. (☎9050 9150). Open M and Th 9am-8pm, Tu-W and F 9am-5:30pm, Sa 9am-1pm. Internet £1.50 per 30min. for non-members. **Linen Hall Library,** 17 Donegall Sq. N. (☎9032 1707; www.linenhall.com), via 52 Fountain St., around the corner. Extensive genealogy, used books, and info on the Troubles. Many activities, especially for children, in May-Aug. Free Irish language courses Sept.-May. Open M-F 9:30am-5:30pm, Sa 9:30am-1pm. (See **Sights,** p. 507.)

Irish Cultural Centre/Cultúrlann: 216 Falls Rd. (☎9023 9303; www.culturlann.ie). Celebrates the Irish language, including music and theater performances with English translation. Open M-W 9am-9pm, Th-Su 9am-10pm, later on performance nights.

Women's Resources: Women's Resource and Development Agency, Mount Charles Ave. (☎9023 0212), works to advance women's equality, especially in the workplace.

GLBT Information: Rainbow Project N.I., 8 Commercial Ct. (☎9031 9030; www.rainbow-project.com), gives mental and emotional support to gay and bisexual men including counseling and drop-in HIV center. Ask about volunteer opportunities. In the same entrance alley as the Duke of York; look for the black door (small sign says Rainbow Project) and ring the bell. Open M-F 10am-5:30pm. **Lesbian Line** (☎9023 8668), open Th 7:30-10pm. **Cara Friends Homosexual Hotline** (☎9032 2023) has resources and information. Open M-W 7:30am-10pm.

Disability Services: Disability Action (☎9029 7880). Open M-Th 9am-5pm, F 9am-1pm.

Laundry: Globe Drycleaners & Launderers, 37-39 Botanic Ave. (☎9024 3956). Less than a block from Shaftesbury Sq. along Botanic Ave. Do-it-yourself laundry £2.20 per load, from £6.75 per bag if you send it out. Dry cleaning service available next or second day; tailoring next week. Open M-F 8am-9pm, Sa 8am-6pm, Su noon-6pm; last wash 70min. before closing.

EMERGENCY AND COMMUNICATIONS

Emergency: ☎999; no coins required. **Police:** 6-18 Donegall Pass and 65 Knock Rd. (☎9065 0222).

Counseling and Support: Samaritans (☎9066 4422). 24hr. hotline lends a sympathetic ear to any topic. **Rape Crisis Centre,** 29 Donegall St. (☎9032 9002, toll-free 0800 77 8888). Open M-F 10am-6pm. If looking for the Centre and embarrassed to mention it by name, ask for "Macfarlane & Smith Estate Agents"—the Centre is next door to this firm. Look for the blue door with graffiti and call for rooms 4, 5, or 6. Phone calls are answered only during business hours, but after-hours calls are diverted to someone who can take them if they are emergencies. **Contact Youth,** 139 Raven Hill Rd. (☎9045 7848, toll-free ☎0808 808 8000). Line open M-F 4-9pm. Open M-F 9:30am-5pm. Offers one-on-one counseling appointments for youths aged 11-25.

Pharmacy: Boot's, 35-47 Donegall Pl. (☎9024 2332). Open M-W and F-Sa 8:30am-6pm, Th 8:30am-9pm, Su 1-6pm. Also on Great Victoria St. and Castle Pl.

Hospitals: Belfast City Hospital, 91 Lisburn Rd. (☎9032 9241). From Shaftesbury Sq., follow Bradbury Pl. and take a right at the fork. **Royal Victoria Hospital,** 12 Grosvenor Rd. (☎9024 0503). From Donegall Sq., take Howard St. west to Grosvenor Rd.

Internet Access: Belfast Central Library (see **Local Services,** p. 497). Wheelchair-accessible. **Revelations Internet Cafe,** 27 Shaftesbury Sq. (☎9032 0337). £4 per hr., students and hostelers £3 per hr. Open M-F 10am-10pm, Sa 10am-6pm, Su 11am-7pm. (Also check out the local art on the walls.) **Belfast Welcome Centre,** 47 Donegall Pl., is the most central. £1.25 per 15min., students £1 per hr. Open M-Sa 9:30am-7pm, Su noon-5pm. **Roast Coffee,** 407 Lisburn Rd. Near the south of the city in B&B territory. £1 per 15min., £5 for 100min. and free coffee. Open M-F 8am-11pm, Sa-Su 9am-11pm. 2nd location at 95-101 Royal Ave. (☎9027 8779), north of City Hall. **Linen Hall Library,** enter via 52 Fountain St. (☎9032 1707; www.linenhall.com). £1.50 per 30min. Open M-F 9:30am-5:30pm, Sa 9:30am-1pm.

Post Office: Central Post Office, 25 Castle Pl. (☎0845 722 3344). Open M-Sa 9am-5:30pm. **Postal Code:** BT1 1BB. Branch offices: **Botanic Garden,** 95 University Rd. (☎0845 722 3344), across from the university. **Postal Code:** BT7 1NG; 1-5 **Botanic Ave.** (☎0845 722 3344). **Postal Code:** BT7 1JG. Both open M-F 8:45am-5:30pm, Sa 10am-12:30pm.

⌐ ACCOMMODATIONS

Despite fluctuating tourism and rising rents, Belfast boasts a solid lineup of hostels. Almost all are near Queen's University; close to pubs and restaurants and a short walk or bus to the city center. This area is by far the best place to stay. If hindered by baggage, catch **Citybus** #69, 70, 71, 83, 84, or 86 from Donegall Sq. to areas in the south. Walking to the area takes 10-20min. from bus or train stations. Reservations are necessary during the summer, when hostels and B&Bs often fill to capacity.

HOSTELS AND UNIVERSITY HOUSING

Arnie's Backpackers (IHH), 63 Fitzwilliam St. (☎9024 2867). Look for a cutout sign of a sky-gazing backpacker. Arnie, the hostel's jovial owner, may greet you with a cup of tea. Relaxed, friendly, in the comfort of a Victorian townhouse. Bunked beds in bright, clean rooms. Library of travel info includes bus and train timetables. Kitchen often has a little stack of free, donated food. If you're looking to find work, check out the bulletin board in the entryway. 8-bed dorms £9; 4-bed £11. ●

The Belfast Palace (Paddy's Palace), 68 Lisburn Rd. (☎9033 3367; www.paddyspalace.com), use the entrance at 70 Fitzwilliam St. Sociable new hostel offers free Internet access (daily 8am-10:30pm), satellite TV, videos in the lounge, and free breakfast with tea and coffee. Kitchen and laundry facilities. Car park. Book ahead in summer. Reception M-Th and Su 8am-8pm, F-Sa 8am-10pm. Dorms from £9.50-16.50. ●

The Ark (IHH), 44 University St. (☎9032 9626). 10min. walk from Europa bus station. Spacious dorms and a busy, stocked kitchen with free tea and coffee. Staff provides info on finding work. Books tours of Belfast (£8) and Giant's Causeway (£16). Internet access £1 per 20min. Weekend luggage storage. Laundry £5. Curfew 2am. Book ahead on bank holidays and in the summer. Co-ed 4- to 6-bed dorms £11; doubles £36; long-term housing from £60 per wk. ●

Belfast Hostel (HINI), 22 Donegall Rd. (☎9031 5435; www.hini.org.uk), off Shaftesbury Sq. Modern rooms and the Causeway Cafe. Groups in the large common room can get loud. Books tours of Belfast and Giant's Causeway. Cafe open daily 8-11am. Full breakfast £4. Wheelchair-accessible. Car park. Internet access 5p per min. on house computers, and £3 per hr. or £10 per 4hr. for Wi-Fi. 24hr. reception. Laundry £3. M-Th and Su 4- to 6-bed dorms £8.50, F-Sa £9.50; ensuite upgrade £1. Triples £42/45. MC/V. ●

The Linen House Hostel (IHH), 18-20 Kent St. (☎9058 6444; www.belfasthostel.com), bordering West Belfast. Converted 19th-century linen factory now packs 130 bunks into bare rooms. Books tours: Black Cab (£24), Giant's Causeway (£20). 24hr. secure parking £4 per day. Posts employment opportunities. Internet £1 per 30min. Luggage storage £0.50. Towels £0.50. Laundry £4. 18- to 20-bed all-female dorms £7.30, co-ed £6.50; 10- to 12-bed dorms £9; 6- to 8-bed dorms £10; 4-bed dorms 12; M-Th and Su doubles £15, F-Sa £18; M-Th and Su singles £20, F-Sa £25. ●

BED AND BREAKFASTS

B&Bs cluster south of Queen's University between Malone and Lisburn Rd. Calling ahead is generally a good idea, though most owners will refer travelers to other accommodations. Options during Marching Season are often very limited, as B&B proprietors are not averse to taking a week's holiday starting around July 12.

Windermere Guest House, 60 Wellington Park (☎9066 2693; www.windermereguesthouse.co.uk). Relatively cheap for a B&B. Leather couches provide comfy seating in the living room. Singles £28, with bath £40; doubles £52/55. Cash only. ●

Camera Guesthouse, 44 Wellington Park (☎9066 0026; malonedrumm@hotmail.com). Quiet, pristine Victorian house is tough to beat. Breakfasts offer wide selection of organic foods and herbal teas that cater to specific dietary concerns. Singles £34, with bath £48; doubles £56/62. MC/V 3% commission; AmEx. ❸

Avenue Guest House, 23 Eglantine Ave. (☎9066 5904; www.avenueguesthouse.com). Four large, airy rooms equipped with TV and Wi-Fi. Comfortable living room has free DVDs and books. £25 per person. ❸

Botanic Lodge, 87 Botanic Ave. (☎9032 7682), corner of Mt. Charles Ave. Larger B&B right in the heart of the Queen's University area, surrounded by restaurants and close to the city center. All rooms with sinks and TV. Singles £30; doubles £45, with bath £50. MC/V 5% surcharge. ❸

Marine House, 30 Eglantine Ave. (☎9066 2828). An airy mansion with high ceilings and wonderful housekeeping, all rooms renovated in 2003. Esteemed 3-star guest house. All rooms with TV, baths, and phones. Singles £45; doubles £60; triples £65. ❹

The George, 9 Eglantine Ave. (☎9068 3212). Fresh fruit at breakfast and saloon-style leather couches in common room entice guests to stay on. All rooms with bath. Singles £30, with bath £40; doubles £50. ❸

🍴 FOOD

Dublin Rd., Botanic Ave., and the Golden Mile, all around Shaftesbury Sq., have the highest concentration of restaurants. Bakeries and cafes dot the shopping areas; nearly all close by 5:30pm, except on Thursdays when most of city center stays open until 8 or 9pm. For dinner in the city center, head to a pub for cheap eats or to a bar for more upscale fare (see **Pubs,** p. 502). The huge **Tesco Supermarket,** 2 Royal Ave., in an old bank building, has better prices than most of the city's convenience stores. (☎9032 3270. Open M-W and Sa 8am-7pm, Th 8am-9pm, F 8am-8pm, Su 1-5pm.) The second location, on Lisburn Rd., is more convenient for those staying near Queen's University, just 11 blocks down on the right from the Church at the corner of Eglatine Ave. (☎9066 3531. Open M-F 8:30am-9pm, Sa 8:30am-8pm, Su 1-6pm.) **Spar Market,** at the top of Botanic Ave. and elsewhere throughout the city, is open 24hr.; order food through a service window at night. Buy high-quality fruits and vegetables at **St. George's Market,** E. Bridge St., in the warehouse between May and Oxford St. (Open F 8am-2pm, Sa 6am-noon.) **The Nutmeg,** 9A Lombard St. (☎9024 9984), supplies health and whole foods. (Open M-Sa 9:30am-5:30pm. MC/V.)

QUEEN'S UNIVERSITY AREA

The Other Place, 79 Botanic Ave. (☎9020 7200). Bustling eatery serves fried break-fasts (until 5pm, from £3; M-F 8-11am special 99p fry), hearty specials, and ethnic entrees. Try the "bang bang chicken," with spicy soy, sweet chili, and crunchy peanut sauce. M steak (£7), Tu and Th tapas (£5-10), W wraps (£5). Open M-Su 8am-10pm. ❷

Bookfinders, 47 University Rd. (☎9032 8269). One block from the University, on the corner of Camden St. and University Rd. Cluttered bookshelves and mismatched dishes on the frequently changing chalkboard are all part of the charm. Occasional poetry readings. Art gallery upstairs features student work. Soup and bread £2.50; sandwiches £2.20. Open M-Sa 10am-5:30pm. ❶

The Moghul, 62A Botanic Ave. (☎9032 6677). Enter around the corner on Cromwell Rd. Overlooks the street from windows. Outstanding Indian Thali lunch M-Th noon-2pm (£3). F noon-2pm buffet (£6). Takeaway available. Open for dinner M-Th 5-11pm, F-Sa 5pm-midnight, Su 5-11pm. ❷

Conor Café & Bar, 11A Stranmillis Rd. (☎9066 3266), across the street from the Ulster Museum. Former studio of artist William Conor (1881-1968) has been converted into a cafe with outdoor seating and a giant portrait. Appetizers £5-6, entrees £9-12.50. Breakfast (£3.50-5.50) served M-F 9am-noon, Sa-Su 9am-3pm. Open daily 9am-5pm.

Maggie May's Belfast Cafe, 50 Botanic Ave. (☎9032 2662). Grab a newspaper from the burlap sacks during the railing and relax in a booth with a thick cappuccino served with a chocolate flake. Lots of vegetarian options. Breakfast served all day. Filled soda bread £3. Dinners around £5. Open M-Sa 7:45am-11:15pm, Su 10am-11:15pm. ❷

Esperanto, 158 Lisburn Rd. (☎9059 0888). 2nd location at 30 University Rd., on the left from Shaftesbury Sq., between Upper Crescent and Mount Charles. Kebab specialists for the budget-conscious. Most meals £3-4. Open daily 4:30pm-1am. ❶

Queen's University Student Union, 1 Elmwood Ave. (☎9032 4803). Two eateries: **Beech Room,** on the 2nd fl., serves cafeteria-style food during the academic year. Open M-F 8:30am-2pm. Closed mid-May to Sept.; **Cloisters,** on the 1st fl., has your usual coffee and espresso selections as well as hot food (until 2:30pm), smoothies (£2.25-2.60), and *panini* (£4). Open daily 8:30am-3:30pm. ❶

THE GOLDEN MILE AND DUBLIN ROAD

Dublin Rd. and the latter portion of the Golden Mile, especially Bradbury Pl., are the places to go for late-night cravings. The area also has the highest density of takeaways in Belfast, as well as a number of quality Asian restaurants.

Benedict's, 7-21 Bradbury Pl. (☎9059 1999; www.benedictshotel.co.uk). Swanky hotel restaurant provides an upscale break from sandwiches and pizza. "Beat the Clock" meal deal offers fine meals daily 5-7:30pm for £7.50-10. Curried chicken, seafood, and vegetarian options. Lunches £7.50-12. Dinners £12-16. Open M-Sa noon-2:30pm and 5:30-10:30pm, Su noon-3:30pm and 5:30-9pm. ❸

Archana, 53 Dublin Rd. (☎9032 3713; www.archana.info). Cozy curry house; dishes made with chicken, lamb, or vegetables. Features Handi dishes, complete with personal candlelit stove. Downstairs Thali lunch £2.50, dinner £7-9; upstairs from £5/8. Takeaway available. Lunch M-Sa 11am-2pm; dinner M-Sa 5-11pm, Su 5-10pm. MC/V. ❸

Red Panda, 60 Great Victoria St. (☎9080 8700), a few doors down from Crown Liquor Saloon toward Shaftesbury Sq. Upscale Chinese restaurant serves a wide variety of meat, fish, and vegetable dishes. Start with the War Tip dumplings stuffed with pork and cabbage (£4.50). Full bar in back. Entrees £8-14. Takeaway available. Open M-F noon-3pm and 5-11:30pm, Sa 4-11:30pm, Su 1:30-10:30pm. AmEx/MC/V. ❸

Zen Bar and Restaurant, 55-59 Adelaide St. (☎9023 2244). Modern take on traditional Japanese decor. Along-the-wall waterfall with Buddhist musings and the imprint of a lotus flower greets visitors. Maki rolls £2-6. Entrees £12-16, or set multicourse meals £24-26. Open M-F noon-3pm and 5-11pm, Sa 6-11pm, Su 1:30-10pm. Closing times may vary with the crowd. MC/V. ❹

Thai Village, 50 Dublin Rd. (☎9024 9269). One of the few, the proud, the only Thai restaurants in Northern Ireland. Tofu dishes and other veggie options available. 2-course lunch £7. Entrees £7-10. Open M-Sa noon-2pm and 5:30-11pm, Su 5:30-10pm. ❸

Bishop's Traditional Fish and Chips, 30-34 Bradbury Pl. (☎9043 9070). Keeps the Th-Sa post-pub crowd satisfied with late hours and a seating area. Fish 'n' chip meals £4.15-6, burgers £3.75-4.55. If you don't want fried food, salt, or vinegar, you can opt for ice cream instead. Other locations throughout the city. Open M-W 11:30am-midnight, Th-Sa 11:30am-2am, Su 11:30am-11pm. ❶

NORTH OF DONEGALL SQUARE

There are a few lunch spots in the shopping district north of City Hall, but a budget meal here requires ducking into a historic pub. Late at night, the hungry are better off strolling the Golden Mile, south of Donegall Sq.

Windsor Dairy, 4 College St. (☎9032 7157). Family-run bakery doles out piles of pastries (under £1), pies, and satisfying daily specials (£2-3). Come early before hungry locals gobble up the best batches. Open M-Sa 7:30am-10:30pm. ❶

Blinkers, 1-5 Bridge St. (☎9024 3330). Inexpensive diner offers burgers (£1.80-3.65) and other greasy eats. Open M-W and F-Sa 9:30am-7pm, Th 11am-8pm. ❶

Clements, 37-39 Rosemary St. (☎9032 2293). More locations at 4 Donegall Sq. W., 66-68 Botanic Ave., 131-133 Royal Ave., and 139 Stranmillis Rd. Modern, comfortable chain of coffee houses sells a standard array of soups, bagels, *panini,* and desserts (£1-4). Open M-W and F 8am-5:30pm, Th 8am-7:30pm, Sa 9am-5:30pm, Su noon-5pm. Botanic and Stranmillis locations open daily until midnight. ❶

Caffe Casa, 12-14 College St. (☎9031 9900). One of many swanky cafes; in good weather, tables spill onto the sidewalk. Sandwiches £4, *panini* and toasties £5. Sumptuous desserts £2.75. Entrees £4.50. Open M-Sa 8am-5pm. MC/V. ❷

Oscar's Champagne Cafe, 11 Chichester St. (☎9043 9400). Voguish take on a Tuscan countryside cafe. Upscale, yet fairly priced menu. Wild boar focaccia £5.45; steak bocata £6.25. Wine, beer, and champagne available. Open M-Sa 8am-5pm. ❸

▓ PUBS

Pubs in Belfast are the place to experience the city's *craic* and meet its colorful characters. Pubs were prime targets for sectarian violence at the height of the Troubles, so most pubs in Belfast are new or restored, though many retain their historic charm. Those in the city center and university area are now relatively safe. *Bushmills Irish Pub Guide,* by Sybil Taylor, relates the history of Belfast pubs (£7; available at local bookstores). Without further ado, *Let's Go* presents the **Belfast Pub Crawl** from north of the city to its southern end (p. 490). The city center closes early and can feel deserted late at night, so start your night early downtown, move to Cornmarket's historic spots, then party near the university. The city's pubbing/clubbing schedule builds in intensity from Thursday night, culminating in blow-out Saturdays during the university term. Off-term months (June-Aug.) are somewhat toned down. The night starts around 9pm; most bars must stop serving alcohol at 1am, though many remain open after that. Many bars and clubs are 21+ and most enforce a "smart casual" dress code, meaning slightly dressy, although presentable does the job. While pubs are more casual, they do not allow football jerseys, baseball caps, or politically charged, visible tattoos due to potential sectarian problems. Sports bars at game time present exceptions to the rule. For a full list of entertainment options at each pub or club grab a free copy of *The Big List* or *Fate,* available in tourist centers, hostels, and certain restaurants and pubs. To savor some history with a pint, take one of the very popular **historical pub tours** of Belfast (see **Tours,** p. 507).

NORTH BELFAST

Given that the city center clears out after 6pm, pubs in this area should be the starting point. After dark, take a cab to the pubs nearer to Donegall Sq.

▓ **The Duke of York,** 7-11 Commercial Ct. (☎9024 1062). Old boxing venue turned Communist printing press, rebuilt after being bombed by IRA in the 60s; now home to the city's largest selection of Irish whiskeys. Students make the long journey from Queen's for good *craic* with a mixed crowd. Kitchen serves sandwiches and toasties daily until 2:30pm. Th trad at 10pm, F acoustic guitar, Sa disco with £5 cover. 18+. Open M 11:30am-11pm, Tu-F 11:30am-1am, Su 11:30am-2am.

▓ **The John Hewitt,** 51 Lower Donegall St. (☎9023 3768; www.thejohnhewitt.com), around the corner from the Duke. Named after the late Ulster poet and run by the Unemployment Resource Centre. Promotes young and unemployed local artists. Half

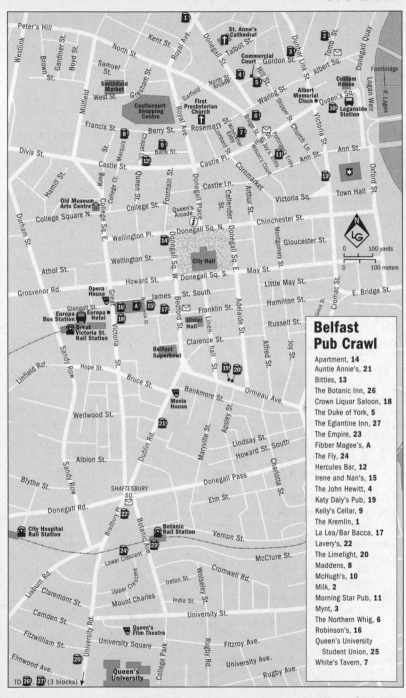

Belfast Pub Crawl

Apartment, **14**

Auntie Annie's, **21**

Bittles, **13**

The Botanic Inn, **26**

Crown Liquor Saloon, **18**

The Duke of York, **5**

The Eglantine Inn, **27**

The Empire, **23**

Fibber Magee's, **A**

The Fly, **24**

Hercules Bar, **12**

Irene and Nan's, **15**

The John Hewitt, **4**

Katy Daly's Pub, **19**

Kelly's Cellar, **9**

The Kremlin, **1**

La Lea/Bar Bacca, **17**

Lavery's, **22**

The Limelight, **20**

Maddens, **8**

McHugh's, **10**

Milk, **2**

Morning Star Pub, **11**

Mynt, **3**

The Northern Whig, **6**

Robinson's, **16**

Queen's University
  Student Union, **25**

White's Tavern, **7**

the profits go to the Centre, so drink up. M singer-songwriter open mic, Tu-W and Sa trad, Th live bands, F jazz; music starts around 9:30pm. W features "The Half Stoned Cowboys." 1st F of each month brings in Hooker ("rock music for grown ups"); other F nights get The Panama Jazz Band, which plays New Orleans-style jazz. Su nights at 9pm, the fiddles and the banjos come out for The Bluegrass Session. 18+. Open M-F 11:30am-1am, Sa noon-1am, Su 6pm-1am.

The Northern Whig, 2 Bridge St. (☎9050 9888; www.thenorthernwhig.com). Expertly blends old-fashioned grandeur with modern swank in a spacious lounge. Full list of well-mixed cocktails (£3.75) headlines the drink menu. Arranges for reasonably priced overnight stays in town. Upscale bar menu serves entrees for £7-14. Sa DJ from 9pm, Su afternoon acoustic music. Kitchen open M-Th and Su until 9pm, F-Sa until 10pm. 21+. Open M-W and Su noon-11:30pm, Th-Sa midnight-1:30am.

McHugh's, 29-31 Queen's Sq. (☎9050 9999; www.mchughsbar.com), across from the Custom House, sells local Belfast Ale. Sleek wrought-iron banisters, a colorful collection of contemporary art, and a chess set featuring caricatures of political figures add to the allure of this historic pub, open since 1711. Restaurant open M-Sa 5-10pm, Su noon-9pm. Th-F and Su live music. Sa DJ Radio K gets the party started for a £5 cover. Open M and Su noon-midnight, Tu-Sa noon-1am.

White's Tavern, 2-4 Winecellar Entry (☎9024 3080), between Rosemary and High St. Tucked away in an entry used for storing wine during Belfast's early days as a port city, this cozy pub has aged well. Still stakes a convincing claim as Belfast's oldest tavern (although this is a popular distinction), serving since 1630. F DJ, Th-Sa live trad. Open M-W 11:30am-11pm, Th-Sa 11:30am-1:30am.

CORNMARKET AND VICINITY

Here stand Northern Ireland's oldest and most inviting pubs. Expect local crowds in most and authentic *craic* in all.

Bittles, 70 Upper Church Ln. (☎9033 3006). Tiny, literary-themed pub draws mixed crowd. Check out the comical portraits of Irish writers—can you name the 6 on the big painting at the back of the room? Pub grub (£2-4.50) served noon-2:30pm. Open M-Th 11am-11pm, F-Sa 11am-1am.

Morning Star Pub, 17-19 Pottinger's Entry (Bar ☎9032 3976, restaurant ☎9023 5986), between Ann and High St. Victorian decor and wooden snugs make this place unique. Old men keep tabs on the horseracing, while a hungry lunchtime crowd enjoys the daily buffet 11:30am-4pm. £4.50, children £2. Kitchen open M-Sa 11:30am-9pm, Su noon-5pm. Open M-Sa 11:30am-11:30pm, Su noon-6pm.

NORTH OF DONEGALL SQUARE

Pubs north of Donegall Sq. offer some of the most authentic music, but the area gets rather deserted at night; pub-crawlers should practice caution in these parts.

Hercules Bar, 61-63 Castle St. (☎9032 4587). Attracts best local musicians and avidly promotes local culture and ethos. F Irish folk night, Sa trad 10pm-1am; Su band Scarlet plays 60s, 70s, and 80s music 4:30-6:30pm. Open M-W 11:30am-11pm, Th 11:30am-midnight, F-Sa 11:30am-1am, Su noon-7:30pm. MC/V.

Maddens, 74 Berry St. (☎9024 4114; www.maddensbar.com). Though its "buzz in" door policy is a relic of the Troubles, this bar is as welcoming as any. Musical instruments adorn the walls. Trad sessions M 9:30pm-12:30am, Tu 9:30-11pm, F 10pm-1am, Sa 10pm-1am (F and Sa upstairs), and live bands Sa—blues, contemporary, and more. W quiz night. 18+. Open M-Tu noon-midnight, W noon-11pm, F-Sa noon-1am.

Kelly's Cellar, 30 Bank St. (☎9024 6058). Self-proclaimed bastion of Irish language and culture with downstairs decor unchanged since 1720. Trad Tu-Sa 7pm- or 9:30pm-closing. F blues night in the upstairs restaurant. Restaurant open M-Sa noon-5pm. Bar open M-Th 11am-11:30pm or midnight, F-Sa 11am-1am, Su 11am-midnight.

CITY CENTER AND SOUTH

Closer to the University area, there are younger crowds and louder music.

■ **Katy Daly's Pub,** 17 Ormeau Ave. (☎9032 5942; www.the-limelight.co.uk). Go straight behind City Hall toward Queen's and make a left on Ormeau Ave. High-ceilinged, wood-paneled, antique pub is a true stalwart of the Belfast music scene, and a young, relaxed crowd keeps coming back for good music. M nights get mocked, grossed out, and roiled up over alternative quiz show, **"Not for the Easily Offended."** Tu adjacent club **Lime-light** and next door bar join up to form the 3-room disco **Shag,** 3 DJs and several drink specials for £3 cover. Th singer-songwriter nights. Sa Limelight again partners up to form the White Album inspired 2-room disco **"Helter Skelter,"** playing only 60s tunes until 2am. Lunch served M-F noon-2:30pm. Bar open M-Sa until 1am, Su until midnight.

Apartment, 2 Donegall Sq. W. (☎9050 9777). Prime real estate and spacious, modern interior make this cafe/bar/bistro the preferred dwelling of Belfast's hip and beautiful. Sip on one of 80 pre-clubbing cocktails (£3.50-5.25) in the swanky upstairs lounge. Arrive before 9:30pm on weekends to beat the crowds. Jeans and sneakers. DJs spin an eclectic mix Th-Su 9pm-1:30am or 2am (last call midnight or 1am). 21+ after 6pm. Happy hour discount daily 5-8pm. Open M-Sa 8am-1am, Su noon-midnight.

Irene and Nan's, 12 Brunswick St. (☎9023 9123; www.ireneandnans.com). Sleek, trendy lounge featuring kitschy 70s decor and a smartly dressed, casual-but-cool crowd. Collection of clocks behind the bar reminds revelers that it's 5 o'clock somewhere— "Workers' Party" Happy hour Th-F 5-7pm (specials like buy 1 get 1 free). F-Sa DJs from 10pm. 21+. Open M-Sa noon-1am, Su 5-10pm.

THE GOLDEN MILE AND THE DUBLIN ROAD

Auntie Annie's, 44 Dublin Rd. (☎9050 1660). Eclectic music and a casual vibe have won this bar a faithful following among all ages (mostly 20s-40s). M-Th and Su live rock music. Tu-W singer/songwriter 10:30pm-1am. Pubby, relaxed downstairs open M-Sa noon-1am, Su 6pm-midnight. 18+. Dance as DJs spin indie rock. F-Sa cover £3-5. Kitchen open M-F 5-7pm, Sa noon-4pm. Open M-Sa noon-1am, Su 6pm-midnight.

Crown Liquor Saloon, 46 Great Victoria St. (☎9027 9901; www.crownbar.com). National Trust-owned pub. Its windows blown in by a bomb attack on the Europa Hotel, but pubbers would never know it: the stained glass and stunning Victorian snugs have been restored. Open M-Sa 11:30am-midnight, Su 12:30-10pm.

Robinson's, 38-42 Great Victoria St. (☎9024 7447). Five venues offer something for everyone. Front saloon provides relaxed pub atmosphere, while the renowned **Fibber Magee's** in the back, with its old-school Irish decor, hosts incredible trad sessions nightly at 10:30pm. In the basement, **BT1** is a quirky nightclub with unisex bathrooms and curtained booths. On the top 2 floors are the more upscale **Lounge** and the "industrial chic" **Roxy Night Club** (dance, retro). F-Sa DJs. Cover F £5, Sa £8. Open M-Sa 11:30am-1am, Su noon-midnight.

Lavery's, 12 Bradbury Pl. (☎9087 1106; www.lavs.co.uk). 3 floors, each dimmer and less polished than the last. Horseshoe-shaped 1st fl. bar. Young crowd dances upstairs in the **Middle Bar** to Top-40 hits, which hosts M reggae nights and W singer-songwriter nights. Sa £1-3 cover. On the 3rd fl., get your billiards fix in the pool room. Outdoor beer garden. 18+. Sa £5-10 cover. Open daily until 1am; upstairs until 2am.

QUEEN'S UNIVERSITY AREA

Close the books and rally the troops—this is where the children come to play.

■ **The Botanic Inn,** 23 Malone Rd. (☎9050 9740). Standing in as the unofficial student union, the hugely popular "Bot" is packed nightly from wall to wall. M singer-songwriter night, Tu quiz night, W "Pinch of Snuff" trad session, and various rock gigs Th-F. Upstairs disco features a DJ W-Sa (£5 cover), Su the DJ moves downstairs (no cover). 20+. Kitchen serves pub grub daily noon-8pm. Su noon-5pm Carvery adds roasts to the menu. Open M-Sa 11:30am-1am, Su noon-midnight.

The Empire, 40-42 Botanic Ave. (☎9032 8110). Big storefront with stairs going both up and down. 120-year-old building was once a church, but its 2 stories were entirely revamped to resemble Victorian music halls. F "Glamarama," a glam rock extravaganza. Sept.-June Tu comedy (£5), Tu and Th-Su live bands. 18+. Cover F-Sa £3-5.

The Eglantine Inn, 32 Malone Rd. (☎9038 1994). Across the road from The Bot, the slightly more upscale "Eg" offers a more refined look. Team up with friends or challenge yourself to go solo on "The Ladder"—a small wooden ladder, whose 6 planks hold a shot each. Daily DJ in the downstairs bar; shake it upstairs with DJ W-Sa (£3 cover during the school year only). Open M and Su 11:30am-midnight, Tu-Sa 11:30am-1am.

■ CLUBS

For information on the city's nightlife, find *The Big List*, a monthly newsletter available at the tourist office, hostels, and certain restaurants and pubs. Ask the staff at the Queen's University Student Union about the hottest night spots.

The Fly, 5-6 Lower Crescent (☎9050 9750). Popular with the yuppie crowd. 1st fl. bar for the pints, 2nd for mingling and dancing, 3rd for more drinks as well as special events (3rd fl. open only Th-Sa). Slick, fly-themed interior will leave you bug-eyed—if the shots don't do the trick. Promotions, theme nights, and Happy hour most nights 5-9pm. Get your Latin groove on Tu with salsa night (lessons, too!). Open M-Th 7pm-1:30am, F-Sa 5pm-2am. Cover £2 before 11pm, £3 after.

La Lea, 43 Franklin St. (☎9023 0200; www.lalea.com), off Bedford St., directly next to Bar Bacca. Features local celebrity DJ Pete Snodden. 21+. Open F-Sa 9pm-3am. Next door, **Bar Bacca** (www.barbacca.com) offers a bit of tranquility with its dim Moroccan decor and small open fires in the wall cubbies. 21+. Open M-Sa 4pm-1am.

Milk, 10-14 Tomb St. (☎9027 8876; www.clubmilk.com). A left at the Albert Sq. Clock onto Tomb Street. Popular club indulges its young, party-crazy crowd with blaring pop music and a fluorescent bar. F funk 'n' disco, Sa "Ritual," and Su "Service" themes. Open W-Su 9pm-3am. Cover £3-10, but look out for free-pass fliers in the town center.

The Limelight, 17 Ormeau Ave. (☎9032 5942; www.the-limelight.co.uk), next door to Katy Daly's Pub. Dark, smoky venue showcases everything from rock to hiphop. Pulls double duty as a nightclub when there is no live performance. Open daily 10pm-2am.

Queen's University Student Union (☎9032 4803). Main bar is the **Speakeasy** (☎9024 1117) on the 2nd fl., a dimly lit and spacious hangout for students. Open June-Sept. M-Th and Su until 11pm, F until 2am; Oct.-May M-Sa noon-2am, Su 7pm-midnight; F-Sa nights, take advantage of £1.60 drinks all night. One Sa per month, the **Shine** (www.shine.net) nightclub event features a guest DJ until 3am. During the school year, check out **Bunatee Bar** in the basement, open M-F 11am-5pm for pizzas and sand-wiches, and 9pm-2am with various promotions and special theme nights. In the base-ment and open only during the school year, **Bar Sub** caters to the gamers: drinks, billiards, and gambling machines abound. Open M-F noon-7pm.

▼ GLBT NIGHTLIFE

Gay and lesbian nightlife is clustered in Northern Belfast.

Mynt, 2-16 Dunbar St. (☎9023 4520; www.myntbelfast.com). Latest offspring of the Parliament and Kube, this spacious club remains a bastion of the Belfast gay scene.

Casual cafebar in front leads to 2 floors of clubbing. Last Sa of each month, famed DJ group **Federation** heats the party up. Two less frequent party nights are thrown by polysexual shindig group **Yello:** Once every 3 months, the **HedKandi** party glams it up and every 2 months, **DTPM** draws a crowd. Open M-Tu noon-1am, W-F and Su noon-3am, and a crazy late Sa noon-6am. F separate gay and lesbian parties for £5 cover. Sa karaoke downstairs and DJ upstairs. Cover: W £3, F and Su £5, Sa £6-10.

The Kremlin, 96 Donegall St. (☎9031 6061; www.kremlin-belfast.com). Look for the statue of Lenin. Beautiful, gelled boys and girls sip and flirt in the downstairs Tsar Bar until they spill onto the dance floor (a.k.a. The Red Square) around 10:30pm. Free Internet upstairs. Although doors close at 1am, the party only heats up inside. Tight security. Cover varies, but free Su. Open Tu 9pm-2:30am, Th-Su 9pm-3am.

TOURS

BLACK CAB TOURS. The one thing every visitor must do is tour West Belfast. Black Cab tours provide commentary on the murals and sights on both sides of the Peace Line. Most drivers have been personally affected by the Troubles, but they make pains to avoid bias. Many hostels book tours with their favored **black cab** operators, usually for £8. **The Original Belfast Black Taxi Tours** give impassioned yet even-handed commentary, and one of the five Protestant and five Catholic drivers will answer any question. (☎0800 032 2003 or ☎077 5165 5359 for Laurence, one of the owners. 1½hr. tour from £8 per person.) Michael Johnston of **Black Taxi Tours** has made a name for himself with his witty, objective presentations. (☎0800 052 3914; www.belfasttours.com. £8 per person for groups of 3 or more.) Walter of **Backpackers Black Taxi Tours** (☎077 2106 7752) is the original of the bunch. Now in his 11th year, he still covers all the bases with his insight and wry humor.

BAILEYS HISTORICAL PUB TOURS OF BELFAST. A departure from recreational pubbing, this tour is a primer in Pint Studies. It guides visitors through seven or more of Belfast's oldest and best pubs with a little sightseeing and city history thrown in. (☎9268 3665; www.belfastpubtours.com. 2hr. tour departs from Crown Dining Rooms, above the Crown Liquor Saloon, May-Oct. Th 7pm, Sa 4pm. £6, £5 for groups of 10 or more; excludes drinks, though a tumbler of Bailey's Irish Cream comes with the tour.)

BIKE TOURS. In addition to bike rental, **Life Cycles** (see **Bike Rental,** p. 496) and **Irish Cycle Tours,** 27 Belvoir View Pk. (☎667 128 733; www.irishcycletours.com), offer tours of Belfast for £15 per day.

BUS TOURS. Mini-Coach (☎9031 5333) conducts tours of Belfast (1hr.; departs M-F noon; £8, children £4) and the Giant's Causeway (M-Sa 9:40am-7pm, Su 9am-5:45pm; £15/10). Tours depart from the Belfast International Youth Hostel. Tickets available at Belfast Welcome Centre.

SIGHTS

DONEGALL SQUARE

Donegall Sq. marks the northern boundary of the Golden Mile and the southern end of the pedestrian-only Cornmarket district. City hall, once a favorite target for IRA bombers, dominates Belfast's old city center.

BELFAST CITY HALL. The most dramatic and impressive piece of architecture in Belfast is also its administrative and geographic center. Towering over the grassy square that serves as the locus of downtown Belfast, its green copper dome (173 ft. high) is visible from nearly any point in the city. Inside, a grand staircase ascends to the second floor, where portraits of the city's Lord Mayors line the halls, moving down the wall each year as the latest portrait is hung. Stained glass and huge paintings depicting all aspects of Belfast industry highlight the impressive rotunda, while glass and marble shimmer in three elaborate reception rooms. The City Council's oak-paneled chambers, used only once per month, are deceptively austere, considering the Council's reputation for rowdy meetings (fists have been known to fly). Directly in front of the main entrance, an enormous marble Queen Victoria stares down visitors with her trademark formidable grimace, while bronze figures representing Shipbuilding and Spinning kneel at her feet. A more sympathetic figure of womanhood stands on East grounds, commemorating the fate of the *Titanic* and her passengers. The interior is accessible only by guided tour. (*☎ 9027 0456. 1hr. tours M-F 11am, 2, 3pm, Sa 2 and 3pm. Tour times may vary; no tours on Bank and Public Holidays. Tours may be cancelled for a period of time starting July 2007, when the Hall begins renovations. Free. Gift shop open 9:30am-4pm.)*

OTHER SIGHTS. One of Belfast's oldest establishments is the **Linen Hall Library** with the red hand of Ulster atop its street entrance. The devoted librarians have compiled a famous collection of over a quarter million items documenting the social and political history of Northern Ireland since 1966. *(Enter via 52 Fountain St. ☎ 9032 1707; www.linenhall.com. Free tours available, but call ahead. Open M-F 9:30am-5:30pm, Sa 9:30am-1pm.)* Nearby, the Victorian **Scottish Provident Institution,** built in 1902, displays a facade featuring panels dedicated to the four main professions of Belfast's industrial history—shipbuilding, ropemaking, spinning, and printing. *(Across the street from City Hall, on the corner of Donegall Sq. N. and East Bedford St.)*

CORNMARKET AND ST. ANNE'S CATHEDRAL

Just north of the city center, a bustling shopping district engulfs eight blocks around Castle St. and Royal Ave. Castle St. was named for the old city castle, whose place has been usurped by the Castle Court Shopping Centre. Although the Cornmarket area is dominated by modern buildings, relics of old Belfast linger in the tiny alleys, or **entries,** that connect the major streets.

ST. ANNE'S CATHEDRAL. Belfast's newspapers set up shop around St. Anne's, the **Belfast Cathedral.** This Church of Ireland cathedral was begun in 1899, but to keep from disturbing regular worship, it was built around a smaller church already on the site. Upon completion of the new exterior, builders extracted the earlier church brick by brick. Each of the cathedral's 10 interior pillars names one of Belfast's professional fields: Science, Industry, Healing, Agriculture, Music, Theology, Shipbuilding, Freemasonry, Art, and Womanhood. Note the marble maze when you enter: the black path leads to a dead end, while the white one leads to salvation. In a small enclave called the **Chapel of Unity,** visitors pray for understanding amongst Christians of all denominations. *(Donegall St., a few blocks from the city center. Open M-Sa 10am-4pm, Su before and after services at 10, 11am, 3:30pm.)*

OTHER SIGHTS. By European standards, most of Belfast's buildings are young, but the city's oldest public building, **The Old Stock Exchange,** on the corner of North and Waring St., is no spring chicken. Tireless Charles Lanyon designed a new facade for the building in 1845 when the original was deemed insufficient. Just one block west on Rosemary St. sits the **First Presbyterian Church of Belfast,** the city's oldest church, founded in 1644. *(☎ 9032 5365. Su service 10:30am.)*

THE DOCKS AND EAST BELFAST

Although the docks were once the beating heart of Belfast, commercial development made the area more suitable for industrial machinery than for people. However, the **Odyssey,** reminding visitors to the east bank of the city's shipbuilding glory days, promises to reclaim the hordes. **Harland & Wolff,** the most famous of the shipyards, proudly claims the *Titanic* as its magnum opus. Today, the twin cranes **Samson** and **Goliath,** towering over the Harland & Wolff shipyard, are the most striking part of the docks' skyline.

ODYSSEY. The posterchild of Belfast's riverfront revival, this attraction packs five distinct sights into one entertainment center. *(2 Queen's Quay. ☎9045 1055; www.theodyssey.co.uk.)* The **Odyssey Arena,** with 10,000 seats, is the largest indoor arena in Ireland. When the Belfast Giants ice hockey team isn't on the ice, big-name performers such as Destiny's Child heat up the stage. *(Performance box office ☎9073 9074; www.odysseyarena.com. Hockey ☎9059 1111; www.belfastgiants.com.)* The **W5 Discovery Centrem** (short for "whowhatwherewhenwhy?") is a playground for curious minds and hyperactive schoolchildren. Design your own racecar and rollercoaster, waltz up the musical stairs, or operate a replica of the Harland & Wolff cranes in a model of Port Belfast. *(☎9046 7700; www.w5online.co.uk. Workshops run throughout the summer. Wheelchair-accessible. Open M-Sa 10am-6pm; closes at 5pm when school is in session, Su noon-6pm; last admission 1hr. before closing. £6.50, children £4.50. Family discounts available.)* The **Sherbidan IMAX Cinema** plays both 2D and 3D films on its enormous 62 by 82 ft. screen, while **Warner Village Cinemas** shows Hollywood blockbusters on its own 14 screens. *(IMAX ☎9046 7014; www.belfastimax.com. £5; M-Th students £4.50, children £4. Multiplex ☎9073 9234. £6/4/3.80. M-F before 5pm £4.50.)* The **Pavilion** contains shops, bars, and restaurants—including that tourist mecca, the **Hard Rock Cafe.** *(Hard Rock Cafe ☎9076 6990. Open M-Sa noon-1am, Su noon-midnight.)*

LAGAN LOOKOUT AND LAGAN WEIR. The £14 million weir was built to reduce pollution and eliminate the Lagan's drastic tides, which once exposed stinking mud flats during its ebb. The refurbished lookout has a near 360° view, a room of displays on the history of Belfast and the purpose of the weir, and a short video highlighting the city's major sights. The statue outside the Lookout is a giant fish covered in panels depicting Belfast's past. Both structures are part of a huge development project that includes the **Laganside Trail** along the far side of the river and **Waterfront Hall,** Belfast's newest concert hall, which hosts a variety of performances. *(Donegall Quay, across from the Laganside bus station. ☎9031 5444. Lookout open Apr.-Sept. M-F 11am-5pm, Sa noon-5pm, Su 2-5pm; Oct.-Mar. Tu-F 11am-3:30pm, Sa 1-4:30pm, Su 2-4:30pm. £1.50, students and seniors £1, children £0.75, families £4.)*

SINCLAIR SEAMEN'S CHURCH. Designed to accommodate the hordes of sinning sailors landing in Belfast port, this quirky church does things its own way—the minister delivers his sermons from a pulpit carved in the shape of a ship's prow, collections are taken in miniature lifeboats, and the choir uses an organ from a Guinness barge with port and starboard lights. The exterior was designed by the prolific Charles Lanyon. *(Corporation St., down from the SeaCat terminal. ☎9071 5997. Open W 2-5pm; Su service at 11:30am and 7pm.)*

OTHER SIGHTS. Belfast has its own leaning tower of Pisa and Big Ben rolled into one impressive timepiece: the **Albert Memorial Clock Tower,** which keeps watch over Queen's Sq. Named for Victoria's prince consort and designed in 1865 by W. J. Barre, the tower slouches precariously at the entrance to the docks. On New Year's Eve, the locals run to the clock at the first stroke of midnight and try to reach it by the last toll, smashing their glasses around it to ring in the New Year. The stately **Custom House,** Lanyon's 1857 masterpiece, stands between Queen Sq. and Albert Sq., approaching the river from the clock tower. Designed in an E-shape, it rests on an elaborate pediment of Lady Britannia, salty Neptune, and Mercury, the god of trade.

THE GOLDEN MILE

"The Golden Mile" refers to a strip along Great Victoria St. where historic buildings surround more modern shops and restaurants. Because it drew a number of powerful Englishmen to its sparkling establishments and was funded largely by the British-based government, the Golden Mile was once a target for IRA bombers. Today, it occupies safer territory within the city center.

GRAND OPERA HOUSE. As the city's pride and joy, the opera house was cyclically bombed by the IRA, restored to its original splendor at enormous cost, and then bombed again. Visitors today enjoy the calm in high fashion, while tours offer a look behind the ornate facade and include a complimentary coffee and danish at their cafe, Luciano's. *(See Theatre, p. 515. ☎9024 1919; www.goh.co.uk. Office open M-F 8:30am-9pm. Tours begin across the street at the office W-Sa 11am. Times may vary, so call ahead. £3, seniors/students/children £2.)*

THE CROWN LIQUOR SALOON. The Crown had its windows blown in from an IRA blast across the street at the **Europa Hotel**. The National Trust restored this popular pub as a showcase of carved wood, gilded ceilings, and stained glass. Victorian snugs with hinged doors accommodate groups of two to 10 comfortably. Once upon a time, hitting the buzzer in the booth would order another round, but now pubbers must stagger to the bar. (See **Pubs,** p. 502.)

EUROPA HOTEL. Having suffered 31 attacks, the Europa long held the dubious distinction of being "Europe's most bombed hotel." In March of 1993, Europa installed shatterproof windows; luckily, they haven't yet been tested and likely won't be anytime soon. Staff working at reception recall the last chilling attack, for which no warning was received—if approached sensitively, they may even produce photographs of the aftermath, which miraculously caused no injuries. Also check out their two bars, which remain open until 10 or 11pm every night.

ORMEAU BATHS GALLERY. Once the site of Victorian swimming baths, this spacious gallery is now Belfast's premier contemporary visual art space. Four exhibits run simultaneously. *(www.ormeaubaths.co.uk. Open Tu-Sa 10am-5:30pm. Wheelchair-accessible entrance around the corner at Aspret St. Free.)*

QUEEN'S UNIVERSITY AREA

Though the student population dwindles in the summer, its leafy stomping grounds are worth a wander any time of the year. The walk from the city center only takes 15-20min., but Metro bus #8 goes there as well.

QUEEN'S UNIVERSITY BELFAST. Charles Lanyon designed the beautiful Tudor Gothic brick campus in 1849, modeling it after Magdalen College, Oxford. The **Visitors Centre,** in the Lanyon Room to the left of the main entrance, offers Queen's-related exhibits and merchandise, as well as a free pamphlet detailing a walking tour of the grounds. Upstairs, the **Naughton Gallery** displays rotating exhibits of contemporary art. *(University Rd. Visitors Centre ☎9033 5252; www.qub.ac.uk/vcentre. Wheelchair-accessible. May-Sept. open M-Sa 10am-4pm with tour Sa noon; Oct.-Mar. open M-F 10am-4pm, tours by request. Gallery open M-Sa 11am-4pm. Free.)*

BOTANIC GARDENS. Join birds, bees, and Belfast's student population as you relax in the peaceful gardens behind the university. The rare spurt of sunshine brings droves of people to the park. Inside the gardens lie two 19th-century greenhouses: the humid **Tropical Ravine,** and the more temperate Lanyon-designed **Palm House,** which shelters an impressive array of flowers. *(☎9032 4902. Open daily 8am-dusk. Tropical House and Palm House open Apr.-Sept. M-F 10am-noon and 1-5pm, Sa-Su 1-5pm; Oct.-Mar. M-F 10am-noon and 1-4pm, Sa-Su 1-4pm. Free.)*

ULSTER MUSEUM. Don't try and enter from Stranmillis Rd.—you can't. Enter the Gardens at the intersection of University Rd. and the Malone-Stranmillis fork and walk up the path to the right of the statue of Lord Kelvin. This eclectic museum has exhibits that run the gamut from Irish and modern art to local history, dinosaur bones, and 18th-century fashion. The most popular are the blackened, shriveled Mummy of Takabuti and the treasure salvaged from the *Girone*, a Spanish Armada ship that sank off the Causeway Coast in 1588. Unfortunately, the museum is closed for renovations until Spring 2009. *(In the Botanic Gardens, off Stranmillis Rd. ☎ 9038 3000. Open year-round M-F 10am-5pm, Sa 1-5pm, Su 2-5pm. Free, except for certain exhibits.)*

SOUTH BELFAST

Riverside trails, ancient ruins, and idyllic parks in south Belfast make it hard to believe that it's only a few minutes from the city center. The area can be reached by bus #8 from Donegall Sq. E., though it's still a bit of a hike from the drop-off. The **Belfast City Council Parks Section** can provide further information; they offer a map at most parks, the Welcome Centre, and Belfast Castle.

SIR THOMAS AND LADY DIXON PARK. The most stunning of the parks, visitors find it sitting pretty on Upper Malone Rd. 20,000 rose bushes of every variety imaginable bloom here each year. The gardens were founded in 1836 and include stud China roses, imported between 1792 and 1824. *(Open M-Sa 7:30am-dusk, Su 9am-dusk.)*

GIANT'S RING. Four miles north along the tow path near Shaw's Bridge lies an earthen ring surrounding a dolmen, which is remarkable as it's older than dirt (birthdate 2500 BC or thereabouts). Little is known about the 600 ft. circle, but experts speculate that it was built for the same reasons as England's Stonehenge. In other words, no one really knows. *(Always open. Free.)*

NORTH BELFAST

The sights of North Belfast cluster in and around **Cave Hill Forest Park.** A sunny and unhurried day is best for visiting, as walking is the primary mode of transportation after taking Antrim Rd. or Metro bus #1 to the park.

BELFAST ZOO. Set in the hills alongside Cave Hill Forest Park, the zoo's best attribute is its natural setting—catching sight of a lumbering elephant against the backdrop of Belfast lough can be a surreal experience. The recommended route highlights the standard lineup of tigers, giraffes, camels, zebras, and the acrobatic spider monkey. *(4 mi. north of the city on Antrim Rd. Take Metro bus #1. ☎ 9077 6277. Open daily Apr.-Sept. 10am-7pm; Oct.-Mar. 10am-4pm. Last admission 1hr. prior to closing. Apr.-Sept. £7.80, children £4.10; Oct.-Mar. £6.30/3.20. Seniors, under 4, and disabled free.)*

BELFAST CASTLE. Constructed in 1870 by the Third Marquis of Donegall, the castle sits atop **Cave Hill,** long the seat of Ulster rulers, and offers the best panoramas of the Belfast port—on a clear day views extend as far as Scotland and the Isle of Man. The ancient King Matudan had his McArt's Fort here, where the more modern United Irishmen plotted rebellion in 1795, though these days it sees more weddings than skirmishes. Marked trails lead north from the fort to five **caves** in the area, which historians postulate are ancient mines; yet, only the lowest is accessible to tourists. For those on foot, the small path to the right of the gate makes for a far shorter and prettier walk than the road. *(☎ 9077 6925; www.belfastcastle.co.uk. Open M-Sa 9am-10pm, Su 9am-5:30pm. Free.)*

WEST BELFAST AND THE MURALS

West Belfast has historically been at the heart of political tensions in the North. The Troubles reached their peak in the 1970s; the particularly violent year of 1972 saw 1000 bomb explosions and over 400 murders. While there have not been any large-scale outbreaks of violence in recent years, tensions remain high. The Catholic area (centered on **Falls Road**) and the Protestant neighborhood (centered on the **Shankill**) are separated by the **peace line,** a grim, gray wall with a number of

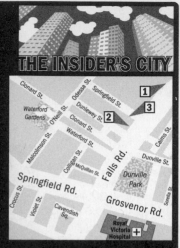

THE CATHOLIC MURALS

The murals of West Belfast are a powerful testament to the volatile past and fierce loyalties of the divided neighborhoods. Many of the most famous Catholic murals are on Falls Rd., an area that saw some of the worst of the Troubles.

1 Mural illustrating protestors during the **Hunger Strikes of 1981,** in which they fasted for the right to be considered political prisoners.

2 Portrayal of **Bobby Sands,** the first hunger-striker to die, is located on the side of the Sinn Féin Office, Sevastopol St. Sands was elected as a member of the British Parliament under a "political prisoner" ticket during this time and is remembered as the North's most famous martyr.

3 Formerly operating as Northern Ireland's National RUC Headquarters, the most bombed of any police station in England, the Republic, or the North. Its fortified, barbed wire facade is on Springfield St.

gates that close at nightfall. Along the wall, abandoned buildings and barricaded homes testify to a tumultuous history and an uneasy future. One bit of the peace line, near **Lanark Way,** connecting the Falls and Springfield roads, contains peace paintings and signatures—left mostly by tourists—promoting hope for a brighter future. The Falls and Shankill exude both the raw sentiment that drives the Northern Irish conflict and the casual calm with which those closest to the Troubles approach daily life. West Belfast is not a tourist site in the traditional sense, though the walls and houses along the area's streets display political **murals** which speak to Belfast's religious and political divide. These murals are the city's most striking and popular attraction.

Those traveling to these sectarian neighborhoods often take **black taxis,** community shuttles that whisk residents to the city center, transporting passengers along their set routes. Some black taxis and **black cabs** can also be booked for tours of the Falls or Shankill (p. 507). *Let's Go* offers two **neighborhood maps** (see **Catholic and Protestant Murals**) of the Catholic and Protestant artistic representations of the past, allowing individuals to explore the murals for themselves.

It is best to visit the Falls and Shankill during the day, when the neighborhoods are full of locals and, more importantly, the murals visible. Do not visit the area during Marching Season (the weeks around July 12) when the parades are underscored by mutual antagonism that can lead to violence (see **History and Politics,** p. 479). Because the area around the peace line remains politically charged, travelers are advised not to wander from one neighborhood over to the other, but to return to the city center between visits to Shankill and the Falls.

New murals in the Falls and Shankill are constantly produced, so the descriptions below and the neighborhood maps describe only a fraction of what is there. For a guide to the murals' iconography, consult our glossary of common mural symbols (see **The Mural Symbols of West Belfast,** p. 514). Before taking a camera, ask hostel or B&B owners about the current political climate. Taking pictures is generally poorly advised during Marching Season. However, photography is acceptable on black cab tours, as drivers have agreements with the communities. But **do not take photographs of military installations,** as film may be confiscated.

THE FALLS. This Catholic and Republican neighborhood is larger than Shankill, following Castle St. west from the city center. As Castle St. continues across A12/Westlink, it becomes **Divis Street.** A high-rise apartment building marks **Divis Tower,** an ill-fated housing development built by optimistic social planners in the 1960s. The project soon became an IRA stronghold and saw some of the worst of Belfast's Troubles in the 1970s. The British Army still occupies the top floors. Continuing west, Divis St. turns into **Falls Road.** The **Sinn Féin** office is easily spotted: one side of it is covered with an enormous portrait of Bobby Sands (see **The Troubles,** p. 483) and an advertisement for the Sinn Féin newspaper, *An Phoblacht*. Continuing down Falls Rd. reveals a number of murals, most of which are on side streets. In the past both the Falls and the Shankill contained many representations of paramilitaries (the IRA in the Falls, UVF and UDA in the Shankill) with armed men in balaclavas; this and commemorative murals were the main subjects in the past, but both communities have focused on historical and cultural representations for the newest murals, even replacing many older works. The newest Falls murals recall the ancient Celtic heritage of myths and legends, and depict The Great Hunger, the phrase Northern Catholics use to refer to the Famine. Earlier militant murals certainly still exist including a few that depict the Republican armed struggle.

Falls Rd. soon splits into **Andersonstown Road** and **Glen Road,** one of the few urban areas with a predominately Irish-speaking population. On the left are the Celtic crosses of **Milltown Cemetery,** the resting place of many fallen Republicans. Inside the entrance, a memorial to Republican casualties is bordered by a low, green fence on the right; the grave of Bobby Sands lies here. Nearby, **Bombay Street** was the first street to be burned down during the Troubles. Another mile along Andersonstown Rd. lies a housing project that was formerly a wealthy Catholic neighborhood—and more murals. The Springfield Rd. Police Service of Northern Ireland station, previously named the RUC station, was the **most attacked police station in Ireland and the UK.** It was recently demolished, perhaps as a sacrifice to the peace process. Its defenses were formidable, and the **Andersonstown Barracks,** at the corner of Glen and Andersonstown Rd., are still heavily fortified.

SHANKILL. The Shankill Rd. begins at the Westlink and turns into Woodvale Rd. as it crosses Cambrai St. The Woodvale Rd. intersects the **Crumlin Road** at the Ardoyne roundabout and can be taken back into the city center. The **Shankill Memorial Garden** honors 10 people who died in a bomb attack on Fizzel's Fish Shop in October 1993; the garden is on the Shankill Rd., facing Berlin St. On the Shankill Rd., farther toward the city center, is a mural of James Buchanan, the 15th President of the United States (1857-1861), who was a descendant of Ulster Scots (known in the US as the "Scots-Irish"). Other cultural murals depict

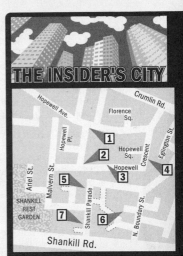

THE PROTESTANT MURALS

The Protestant murals, in the Shankill area of West Belfast, tend to be overtly militant. Most are found near Hopewell St. and Hopewell Cr., to the north of Shankill Rd., or down Shankill Parade, and are accessed by traveling south from Crumlin Rd.

1 Mural commemorating the **Red Hand Commando,** a militant Loyalist group.

2 Painting of a **Loyalist martyr,** killed in prison in 1997.

3 Depiction of the **Grim Reaper,** with gun and British flag.

4 A collage of Loyalist militant groups including the **UVF, UDU,** and **UDA.**

5 Mural of the **Battle of the Boyne,** commemorating William of Orange's 1690 victory over James II.

6 The **Marksman's** gun seems to follow you as you pass by.

7 Portrait of the infamous **Top Gun,** a man responsible for the deaths of many high-ranking Republicans.

the 50th Jubilee of the coronation of Queen Elizabeth in 1952 and the death of the Queen Mother in 2002. These are at the beginning of the Shankill near the Rex Bar. Historical murals include a memorial to the UVF who fought at the Battle of the Somme in 1916 during WWI (see **A Divided Island**, p. 479), also near the Rex Bar. In the **Shankill Estate**, some murals represent Cromwell suppressing the 1741 Rebellion against the Protestant plantation owners. The densely decorated **Orange Hall** sits on the left at Brookmount St. McClean's Wallpaper; on the right was where Fizzel's Fish Shop stood before being demolished. Through the estate, Crumlin Rd. heads back to the city center, passing an army base, the courthouse, and the jail.

SANDY ROW AND NEWTOWNARDS ROAD. This area's Protestant population is growing steadily, partly due to the redevelopment of the Sandy Row area, and also because many working-class residents are leaving the Shankill. This stretch is a turn off Donegall Rd. at Shaftesbury Sq. An orange arch topped with King William once marked its start. Nearby murals show the Red Hand of Ulster, a bulldog, and William crossing the Boyne. East Belfast is a secure and growing Protestant enclave, but as in other areas use caution when traveling in this area around Marching Season. A number of murals line Newtownards Rd. One mural depicts the economic importance of the shipyard to the city's industrial history. On the Ballymacart road, which runs parallel to Newtownards Rd., is a mural of local son C.S. Lewis's *The Lion, the Witch, and the Wardrobe*.

THE MURAL SYMBOLS OF WEST BELFAST.
PROTESTANT MURALS. Blue, White, and Red: The colors of the British flag; often painted on curbs and signposts to demarcate Unionist murals and neighborhoods. **The Red Hand:** The crest of Ulster Province, the central symbol of the Ulster flag, which includes a red cross on a white background, used by Unionists to emphasize the separation of Ulster from the Republic. Symbolizes the hand of the first Norse King, which he supposedly cut off and threw on a Northern beach to establish his primacy. (The crest also appears on Catholic murals which depict the 4 ancient provinces—evidence of the overlap in heritage.) **King Billy/ William of Orange:** Sometimes depicted on a white horse, crossing the Boyne to defeat the Catholic King James II at the 1690 Battle of the Boyne. Ironically, his campaign was funded by the Pope, who opposed James' creation of the Church of England. The Orange Order was later founded in his honor. The **Apprentice Boys:** A group of young men who shut the gates of Derry to keep out the troops of James II, beginning the great siege of 1689. They have become Protestant folk heroes, inspiring a sect of the Orange order in their name. The slogan "No Surrender," also from the siege, has been appropriated by radical Unionists, most notably Rev. Ian Paisley. **Lundy:** The Derry leader who advocated surrender during the siege; now a term for anyone who wants to give in to Catholic demands. **Scottish Flag:** Blue with a white cross; recalls the Scottish-Presbyterian roots of many Protestants whose ancestors were part of the Ulster Plantation (see **Cromwell**, p. 52). **CATHOLIC MURALS. Orange and Green:** Colors of the Irish Republic's flag; often painted on curbs, mailboxes, and signposts in Republican neighborhoods. **The Irish Volunteers:** Republican tie to the earlier (nonsectarian) Nationalists. **Saoirse:** Irish for "Freedom"; the most common term found on murals. **Éireann go bráth:** (erin-go-BRAH) "Ireland forever"; a popular IRA slogan. **Tiocfaidh ár lá:** (CHOCK-ee-ar-LA) "Our day will come." **Slan Abhaile:** (Slawn ah-WAH-lya) "Safe home"; directed at the primarily Protestant RUC police force. **Phoenix:** Symbolizes united Ireland rising from the ashes of British persecution. **Lug:** Celtic god, seen as the protector of the "native Irish" (Catholics). **Green Ribbon:** IRA symbol for "free our POWs." **Bulldog:** Britain. **Bowler Hats:** A symbol for Orangemen.

🎵 ARTS AND ENTERTAINMENT

Belfast's many cultural events and performances are covered in the monthly *Arts Council Artslink*, free at the tourist office, while the bi-monthly *Arts Listings* covers arts and entertainment throughout Northern Ireland. Listings appear daily in the *Belfast Telegraph* (which also has a Friday Arts supplement) and in Thursday's issue of the *Irish News*. For summer events, check *What About?*, *The Big List*, and *Fate*, which all have concert listings. The **Crescent Arts Centre,** 2 University Rd., supplies some general arts info, but mostly broadcasts specific news about its own exhibits and concerts, which take place September through May. The Centre also hosts three seasonal terms of eight-week courses in yoga, writing, traditional music, dance, theater, and drawing. (☎9024 2338. Classes £40-48, children £24-32. Open M-Sa 10am-10pm.) **Fenderesky Gallery,** 2 University Rd., inside the Crescent Arts building, hosts contemporary shows and sells the work of local artists. (☎9023 5245. Open Tu-Sa 11:30am-5pm.) The **Old Museum Arts Centre,** 7 College Sq. N., is Belfast's largest venue for contemporary artwork. (☎9023 5053; www.oldmuseumartscentre.org. Open M-Sa 9:30am-5:30pm.) A small gallery hosts rotating exhibits, but its focus is on performance art. Pick up a booklet detailing upcoming workshops and a variety of dance, theater, and music performances. (Tickets ☎9023 3332. Most tickets £6-9, students and seniors £3.) July and August are slow months for arts; around July 12, the whole city shuts down for Marching Season.

THEATER

The Grand Opera House, 4 Great Victoria St., presents a mix of opera, ballet, musicals, and drama. (☎9024 0411; www.goh.co.uk.) Tickets for most shows can be purchased either by phone until 9pm or in person at the box office. (☎9024 1919, 24hr. info line ☎9024 9129. Tickets £9-27. Open M-F 8:30am-9pm.) The Lyric Theatre, 55 Ridgeway St., which counts Liam Neeson amongst its esteemed alums, presents a mix of classical and contemporary plays with an emphasis on Irish productions. (☎9038 1081; www.lyrictheatre.co.uk. Box office open M-Sa 10am-7pm. Tickets M-W £14, concessions £11; Th-Sa £17.) The Group Theatre, Bedford St., produces comedies and farces in the Ulster Hall from September to May. (☎9032 9685. Box office open M-F noon-3pm. Tickets £4-8.)

MUSIC

Ulster Hall, Bedford St. (☎9032 3900), brings Belfast everything from classical to pop. Unfortunately, it is currently under renovation and not hosting performances. Check the website at www.ulsterhall.co.uk for updates. The **Grand Opera House** (see **Sights,** p. 510) resounds with classical choral arrangements but more commonly stages musicals and ballet performances. **Waterfront Hall,** 2 Lanyon Pl., is one of Belfast's newest concert centers, hosting a variety of performances throughout the year. Its concourse features visual arts exhibitions. (☎9033 4400; www.waterfront.co.uk. Student discounts usually available.) The **Ulster Orchestra** plays concerts at Waterfront Hall and Ulster Hall. (☎9066 8798; www.ulster-orchestra.org.uk. Tickets £8-24.)

FILM

There are two major movie theaters in Belfast, besides the new one at the Odyssey (see **Sights,** p. 509). Hollywood films are shown at **Moviehouse,** 14 Dublin Rd. (24hr. info ☎0870 155 5176. £5, students £3.75, seniors and children £3.50; all seats before 5:30pm £3.50, all Tu shows £2.50.) **Queen's Film Theatre,** in a back alley off Botanic Ave., draws a more artsy crowd with a full lineup of foreign films and cult classics. (☎9024 4857, box office ☎9097 1097. Book online at www.queensfilmtheatre.com. £5, students and seniors £4. "Meal and movie" discounts for certain restaurants.)

FESTIVALS

QUEEN'S UNIVERSITY BELFAST FESTIVAL. Belfast reigns supreme in the art world for three weeks between October and November during the university's annual festival. Over 300 performances of opera, ballet, film, and comedy invade venues across the city, drawing internationally acclaimed groups. Tickets for the most popular events sell out months ahead of time, but there's always something to see without planning ahead. *(Box office ☎ 9066 5577; www.belfastfestival.com. For advance schedules, write to: The Belfast Festival at Queen's, 25 College Gardens, Belfast BT9 6BS. Tickets sold by mail and phone from mid-Sept. through the festival's end. Prices £2.50-33.50; for additional info on area festivals, see* **Holidays and Festivals,** *p. 75.)*

WEST BELFAST ARTS FESTIVAL (FÉILE AN PHOBAIL). This week-long series of events, held the second week of August, is the high point of the year for Falls residents. The Nationalist festivities celebrate traditional Irish culture, bringing in both big-name trad groups and rockers who owe something to Irish music. *(473 Falls Rd. ☎ 9028 4028; www.feilebelfast.com.)*

THE BELFAST FILM FESTIVAL. Celebrating its seventh year in Spring 2007, this film festival presents a full schedule of film screenings from cult to classic, with a particular emphasis on Irish filmmakers and film as a political medium. Recent themes have included *Reconciliation and Divided Societies*, *Irish Women Filmmakers*, and most recently, *Societies in Transition: Policing for the People. (☎ 9032 5913; www.belfastfilmfestival.org.)*

◪ SPORTS AND OUTDOOR ACTIVITIES

The state-of-the-art **Belfast Superbowl** has 20 glow-in-the-dark bowling lanes. (4 Clarence St. ☎ 9033 1466. £3.30 per round; students £2.70 (ISIC not accepted); children before 7pm £2.70, after 7pm £3.30. Open M-Sa 10am-11:30pm, Su noon-11:30pm.) **Lagan Valley LeisurePlex,** 12 Lisburn Leisure Park, Lisburn, is one of the biggest family-fun facilities in all of Ireland and comes complete with a huge galleon, master-blasters, and thrilling water rides. (☎ 9267 2121. 8 mi. from Belfast along M1.) Dominating the skyline just north of Belfast, **Cave Hill** offers adventure sports of a different kind. The **Cave Hill walk** starts from the parking lot of the **Belfast Zoo** (p. 485), trails the Ulster Way for a short distance, and then branches off on its own on a straight shot toward **McArt's Fort** (1100 ft.) at the summit. During the three-hour climb, hikers pass **caves** that were carved into the hill many years ago by Neolithic wanderers searching for shelter. Hikers will also be granted panoramic views of Belfast and its port. (For more info call ☎ 9032 1221.) On the nine-mile **Lagan Valley Towpath Walk,** travelers temporarily join with the Ulster Way for part of their journey along the canal towpaths to **Sir Thomas and Lady Dixon Park** (☎ 9023 1221).

Rather sit and watch than walk and run? Take a cab to the **Odyssey Arena** to catch the **Coors Belfast Giants** battle it out on the ice with county competitors (☎ 9059 1111; www.belfastgiants.com). **Football** (soccer) fanatics catch a game at the **Windsor Park** pitch, located on Donegall Ave. (☎ 9024 4198.) **Gaelic Footballers** run to Anderson-stown, West Belfast, to enjoy Sunday afternoon matches. (Contact the Gaelic Athletic Association at ☎ 9038 3815; www.gaa.ie.) Belfast is crazy about **horse racing;** see the action down at the Maze in Lisburn. (☎ 9262 1256; www.downroyal.com.) Located just 10 mi. from Belfast, the racecourse has a dozen events throughout the year, including the **Mirror May Day** fixture and the **Ulster Harp Derby** in June. **Ulster Rugby,** recent winners of the European Cup, play at **Ravenhill Stadium** (☎ 9049 3222).

🔽 DAYTRIPS FROM BELFAST

ULSTER FOLK AND TRANSPORT MUSEUM

The Museum stretches across 170 acres in the town of Holywood. Take the Bangor road (A2) 7 mi. east of Belfast. Buses and trains stop here on the way to Bangor. ☎ 9042 8428; www.uftm.org.uk. Open July-Sept. M-Sa 10am-6pm, Su 11am-6pm; Mar.-June M-F 10am-5pm, Sa 10am-6pm, Su 11am-6pm; Oct.-Feb. M-F 10am-4pm, Sa 10am-5pm (Nov.-Jan. the Rural Area closes Sa at 4pm), Su 11am-5pm. Folk Museum £5.50, students, seniors, and ages 5-18 £3.50, families £15.50 for 2 adults and 3 children and £11 for 1 adult and 3 children, disabled free. Transport Museum has the same prices, except disabled. Combined admission £7, ages 5-18 £4, 2 adults with 3 children £19, 1 adult with 3 children £13, seniors and students £4. Group discounts and season passes available.

Established by an Act of Parliament in 1958, the ▨**Folk Museum** aims to preserve the way of life of Ulster's farmers, weavers, and craftspeople. The Museum contains over 30 buildings from the past three centuries divided into a town and rural area, the latter containing cottages from all nine Ulster counties, including the usually overlooked Monaghan, Cavan, and Donegal in the Republic. All but two of the buildings are transplanted originals. They have been artfully integrated into a landscape befitting their rural origins; the size of the property and the natural surroundings provide full immersion in the lost-in-time wonderland, creating a remarkable air of authenticity. Unobtrusive attendants in period costume stand nearby to answer questions. In Ballydugan Weaver's House, John the Weaver, a fourth-generation practitioner of his craft, operates the only working linen loom in Ireland. A fully functional printer's press still runs on Main St. Along with a cornmill and a sawmill from Fermanagh, the town is currently in the process of recreating a silent film house from Co. Down. The museum hosts special events, including trad sessions, dance performances and workshops, storytelling festivals, and textile exhibitions. Go on a sunny day and leave time to wander.

 GULL WINGS. In 1978, John Z. de Lorean, then the Vice President of General Motors, raised the hopes of Belfast by deciding to construct a new **car factory** just outside the city. With a pair of cowboy boots and a heap of great salesmanship, de Lorean gathered $200 million from investors and earned the status of savior among Northern Ireland's unemployed population. There was reason, however, to mistrust the hype. In 1982, the factory shut down after producing just 10,000 cars, due to consistently high and unrealistic sales projections. Fast-talking de Lorean was arrested the same year on drug charges. His dream car—with its "gull wings" and sleek design—lives on in popular memory as Marty McFly's time-traveling vehicle in the *Back to the Future* film series.

The **Transport Museum** is across from the Folk Museum. Inside the aircraft hangar-sized main building, horse-drawn coaches, bicycles, cars, and locomotives tell the history of vehicles in motion. The presentation begins with 25 old railway engines, including the largest locomotive built in Ireland. The motorcycle exhibition follows the evolution of the vehicle from the bicycle to Harley-mania, while the car exhibition showcases an array of bizarre cars, including a model of de Lorean's ill-fated vehicle. In a second building, the "Flight Experience" focuses on airborne travel with a life-sized airplane cabin and hands-on displays explaining the physics involved. The ship section is highlighted by a *Titanic* exhibit including original blueprints, china, photographs, and letters from passengers on board.

COUNTIES DOWN AND ARMAGH

Locals flock to this sleepy, scenic area to take advantage of the seaside—the coast of Down and the Ards Peninsula are covered with fishing villages, holiday resorts, and 17th-century ruins. The Mourne Mountains, south of Belfast and a lough away from the Irish Republic, rise above the town of Newcastle, the largest seaside resort in County Down. An inland county surrounded by rivers and lakes, Armagh is an ancient ecclesiastical city set on the rolling hills of Northern Ireland's Drumlin Belt. The best time to visit County Armagh is during apple blossom season in May, when the countryside, known as the "Orchard of Ireland," is a veritable sea of pink. At the southern end of the Ards, Downpatrick celebrates the legacy of the beloved St. Patrick, while stunning mansions like Castle Ward and Mount Stewart Estates add a shimmer of grandeur and historical significance to the region.

BANGOR (BEANNCHOR)

Bangor found a place on early medieval maps of Ireland with its famous abbey. By Victorian times, the town had again become eminent, this time as the seaside resort for Belfast residents seeking the leisure and health benefits of fresh air. Today, the hilly town is one of the top destinations on the Ards Peninsula. While Bangor caters to families and older vacationers during the week, its nightlife draws Belfast partygoers on the weekends. Such traffic does not affect the serene air about the town, however, and its location makes it an inevitable (and enjoyable) stop on the way down the Ards Peninsula.

⌐ TRANSPORTATION

Trains: Abbey St. (☎9127 1143; www.translink.co.uk), the south end of town. Trains run to: **Belfast** (40min.; M-F at least every ½hr. 6am-11pm, Sa every ½hr. 6am-10:30pm, Su every hr. 9am-10pm; £4); **Newry** (1½hr.; M-F 12 per day, Sa 7per day, Su 5 per day; £10); **Portadown** (1¼hr.; M-F every ½hr.-1hr. 6am-10:30pm, Sa every ½hr. 8:30am-9pm then every hr. until midnight, Su every hr. 9am-10pm; £9.40). Tickets for bus and rail available at **Bangor Station.** (Ticket office open M-F 7am-6pm, Sa 7am-5pm.)

Buses: Abbey St. (☎9127 1143), joined to the train station. To: **Belfast's** Laganside Bus Station (45min.; M-F at least every ½hr. 6:40am-9pm, Sa every ½hr. 7:15am-9pm, Su 8 per day; £3). All **Ards Peninsula** towns accessed via **Newtownards** (30min.; M-F every ½hr. 7:15am-10:20pm, Sa every ½hr. 7:40am-10:40pm; £2) Station (☎9181 2391). There is a Bangor-area **local bus** system (£1 single ride, £1.70 all-day pass).

Taxis: Atlastaxi (☎9145 6789; £3 per min.) and **LA Cabs** (☎9127 0848).

◄◼ 🛈 ORIENTATION AND PRACTICAL INFORMATION

The road from Belfast runs north-south through town, changing names several times along the way—**Abbey Street** becomes **Main Street** at the roundabout, then **Bridge Street,** then **Quay Street,** and finally **Seacliff Road.** A left turn at the marina leads to B&B-lined **Queens Parade.** The train and bus stations are where Abbey St. becomes Main St. From there, Main St. intersects three important roads: **Castle Park Avenue** becomes restaurant-filled **Dufferin Avenue** as it crosses Main St.; **Hamilton Road** becomes **Central Avenue** and leads to Crawfordsburn and its park; and **High Street,** lined with pubs and restaurants, divides Bridge St. and Quay St. **Free public parking** is available on Dufferin Ave. and on Quay St., across from the tourist office.

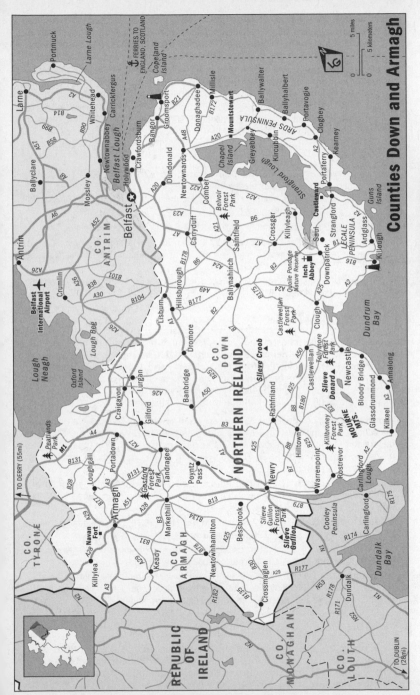

Counties Down and Armagh

NORTHERN IRELAND

Tourist Office: Tower House, 34 Quay St. (☎9127 0069; www.northdown.gov.uk, and www.bangorgoesglobal.com). Books all accommodations (£2 plus 10% deposit) and has a **bureau de change.** Open July-Aug. M-F 9am-6pm, Sa 10am-5pm, Su 1-5pm; Sept.-June M-Tu and Th-F 9am-5pm, W 10am-5pm, Sa 10am-4pm; June also Sa until 5pm.

Banks: First Trust, 85 Main St. (☎084 5600 5925). Open M-Tu and Th-F 9:30am-4:30pm, W 10am-4:30pm. **Northern Bank,** 77 Main St. (☎9127 1211). Open M 10am-5pm, Tu and Th-F 10am-3:30pm, W 9:30am-3:30pm, Sa 9:30am-12:30pm. **Ulster Bank,** 75 Main St. (☎9127 0924). Open M-F 9:30am-4:30pm, W opens at 10am. **Bank of Ireland,** 82a Main St. (☎9145 3800). Open M-F 9:30am-4:30pm; W opens at 10am. All 4 have 24hr. **ATMs.**

Pharmacy: Boots Pharmacy, 79-83 Main St. (☎9127 1134). Open M-Sa 9am-5:30pm, July-Aug. also Su 1-5pm.

Work Opportunities: The Marine Court Hotel, 18-20 Quay St. (☎9145 1100; www.marinecourthotel.net). Travelers work in its restaurant for min. 2 months. Experience preferred. Min. wage. Most positions available early summer and Christmas.

Emergency: ☎999; no coins required. **Police:** Castle Park Ave. (☎9145 4444).

Hospital: Bangor Hospital, Hamilton Rd. (☎9147 5120), treats minor injuries.

Internet Access: Bangor Library (☎9127 0591), in the Flagship Shopping Centre, lower level (between Bridge and High St.). £1.50 per 30min., members free. Open M-Sa 9am-5:30pm, Th-F open until 9pm.

Post Office: 143 Main St. (☎9146 3000), on the corner of Dufferin Ave. Open M-Sa 9am-5:30pm. **Postal Code:** BT20.

ACCOMMODATIONS

Although Bangor lacks a hostel and a campground, it teems with B&Bs; check the tourist office window for details. Rooms with private bath are less common and more expensive. B&Bs cluster along coastal Seacliff Rd. and inland Princetown Rd., Dufferin Ave.'s extension. Choosing among them can be a challenge, as all are cozy, homey, and on the small side. Those on Seacliff Rd. have spectacular sea views to recommend them. Book ahead during the summer.

Cairn Bay Lodge, 278 Seacliff Rd. (☎9146 7636; www.cairnbaylodge.com). Turn-of-the-century B&B includes large rooms with sitting areas and elegant guest lounges decorated to Victorian perfection. Owners also run a health and beauty salon on premises. All rooms with bath, TV, DVD player, and fridge. Free laundry and Internet access. Singles £45; doubles £70-80. ❸

No. 108 Superior B&B, 108 Seacliff Rd. (☎9146 1077; www.bandb-bangor.co.uk). Set back on a large, terraced lawn, it's worth the walk from town. Singles £25-30, with bath £37; doubles £38/48. ❷

The Dolly Rocks Guest House, 72 Seacliff Rd. (☎9147 2644). Two snug rooms and a lovely visitors lounge. Singles £20; doubles £40. ❷

Anglers Rest B&B, 24 Seacliff Rd. (☎9127 4970). Friendly owner invites guests into rooms with big TVs. Rooms £22-25 per person. ❷

Hebron House, 68 Princetown Rd. (☎9146 3126; www.hebron-house.com). 5 AA stars and 3 ensuite rooms, including a luxurious ground floor room with a whirlpool for the romantic (or just weary) traveler. Free Wi-Fi. Singles £45; doubles £70. ❸

FOOD

Like any resort town, Bangor has no shortage of places to eat. Every third store on Main St. doles out baked goods and sandwiches, while most pubs in town also serve food. Pubs and clubs cluster along High St. and the waterfront. Inside the **Flagship Shopping Centre,** wedged between Bridge St. and High St., is the **Co-**

op (☎9147 4714; open M-W 9am-6pm, Th-F 9am-9pm, Sa 9am-8pm, Su 1-5pm), which sells groceries and has a nearby food court.

Ava Bar and Restaurant, 132 Main St. (☎9146 5490; www.theava.co.uk), across from the bus and train station. Snug pub decorated with mahogany and velvet. Serves pub grub (£5-7) and more serious restaurant fare (2-course lunch £7.50; entrees £8.50-16.50). Next door, the colorful floors and muraled walls of the bistro/cafe provide a funky atmosphere for enjoying *panini* (£5) and entrees. Bar open M-F 11:30am-11:30pm, Sa 11:30am-midnight, Su 12:30-10pm. Lunch M-Sa noon-2:30pm, Su 12:30-2:30pm; dinner M-Th 5-8:45pm, F-Sa 5-9:30pm, Su 5-7:30pm. ❸

Taj Tandoori, 61-63 High St., 2nd fl. (☎ 9146 1644). Encyclopedic menu of Indian cuisine and other Southeast Asian specialities. 3-course lunch special (M-Sa noon-1:45pm; £6) is hard to beat. Takeaway available. Entrees £5.50-8.50. Open M-Th 5-11:30pm, F-Sa 5pm-midnight, Su 5-11pm. ❷

Cafe Brazilia, 13 Bridge St. (☎9127 2763). Whitewashed halls and colorful paintings whisk diners away to an Irish designer's vision of Brazil. But the name of this cafe is specifically meant to evoke the Brailiza coffee bean, 1 of 4 types offered by the coffee connoisseur owner. Wide selection of sandwiches (£4-5.50) and omelettes (£5.50). Brazilian brunch £5. Open M-Sa 8:30am-4:30pm. ❷

Spice, 7-9 Market St. (☎9147 7666), off Main St., across from the Monary's shopping center. Gourmet grocer specializes in cheeses, spices, and Mediterranean specialities and has some of the best sandwiches in town (£2.50-3.50). Grab something to go or snag one of the few seats. Kitchen open until 4pm. Open daily 9am-5pm. ❷

Piccola Pizzeria, 3 High St. (☎9145 3098). Turkish management serves burgers and the town's best takeaway pizza and kebabs from £3.50. Avoid Sa 1:30am when scavengers satisfy their late-night appetites. Open M-Sa 4:30pm-late. ❷

🅿 PUBS

Fealty's, 35 High St. (☎9146 0088; www.fealtys.com). Popular hangout known for spreading turf on its floor for rugby season's most important games. Past guests include a horse (for the Euro Football 2000) and a donkey (Easter). Come for the local characters and one of the best Guinness pints in the North. F trad 9:30pm, F-Sa live music. Open M-Sa 11:30am-1am, Su 12:30pm-midnight.

Jenny Watts, 41 High St. (☎9127 0401). Draws an older crowd, except for Su jazz (1-3pm). Low-ceilinged underpass feels like the cave where the pub's namesake, an 18th-century rogue, allegedly hid from the authorities. F-Sa 10pm-1am DJs spin at the club upstairs. Tu trad, W acoustic, Th live band, Su night soul. Bar open M 11:30am-11pm, Tu and Th-Sa 11:30am-1am, W 11:30am-midnight, Su 12:30pm-midnight.

Mocha, 18-20 Quay St. (☎9145 1100), in a little alley off Quay. From Main St. toward Seacliff Ave., take a right after the green courthouse. Difficult to find, but many Belfast natives make the trek. 21+. Cover F after 10pm £3, Sa before 10pm £3, Sa after 10pm £4. Open W and F-Sa 8pm-late.

Coyle's Bar and Restaurant, 44 High St. (☎9127 0362). Advertising "Real Music and Hard Liquor," award-winning bar offers Su 12:30-8pm "Picture Yourself" performance, featuring guitar playing and poetry reading. Pub grub (£6.50-7.50) served M-Th noon-3pm and 5-9pm, F-Sa noon-9pm, Su 12:30-8pm. Bar open M-Sa 11:30am-1am, Su noon-midnight.

👁 🎵 SIGHTS AND ENTERTAINMENT

North Down Museum, adjacent to Bangor Castle (Town Hall) on Castle Park, dispenses visitor information and houses a nostalgic collection of photographs and artifacts from Bangor's past. (☎9127 1200; www.northdown.gov.uk/heritage. Open Tu-Sa 10am-4:30pm, Su 2-4:30pm; July-Aug. and bank holidays also M 10am-

4:30pm. Free.) The rest of the Hamilton Estate, named for the wealthy Hamilton family who once owned all the land around Bangor, consists of 129 acres of shady trails and grassy fields that now compose the public **Castle Park.** Nearby, 37-acre **Ward Park,** up Castle St. or Hamilton Rd. from Main St., entices visitors with tennis courts, bowling greens, a cricket pitch, a pitch-and-putt, and a string of lakes harboring a wildlife sanctuary. Contact the **Bangor Castle Leisure Centre** to reserve plots. (☎9127 0271 and 9145 8773. Tennis courts £3.30-4.30 per hr.; rackets £1.80. Bowling £5; children, students, and seniors £2.75. Pitch-and-putt £3/2.00/1.75. Sports facilities open daily Easter to Sept. Centre open M-F 7:30am-10pm, Sa 7:45am-6pm, Su 2-6pm.) The Centre provides a swimming pool (£2.00/1.55/1.10), a gym and spa (£5.00/3.80/4), and squash courts (£5.40 peak times, £4 off-peak). Like any good port town, Bangor has its share of aquatic options. **Fishing** trips and sightseeing tours depart from the North Pier on the Purple Heather across from the tourist office. (☎077 960 0607 or 070 5060 8036; www.bangorboat.com. Fishing trips July-Aug. 9:30am-noon and 7:20-9:40pm. £10, children £7. Sea cruises July-Aug. afternoons; weekends in spring and fall, £3/2. Birdwatching in June, £8/5.) The **North Down Coastal Path** forays 16 miles along the bay's edge from Holywood through Bangor and Groomsport to Orlock Point. Along the way lie abandoned WWII lookouts, Helen's Bay (a popular bathing spot), Crawfordsburn Country Park, Greypoint Fort (an old fort with a massive gun), and a giant redwood. The region is renowned for its colonies of **black guillemots,** more widely known as the Bangor penguins. In addition, seals play and fish among the rocks at Ballymacormick Point and Orlock Point, both of which are National Trust areas. If you want a break from all the tree-hugging, enjoy the great indoors at **Bangor Multiplex,** 1 Valentine Rd., off Castle Park Rd., just past the turn for Town Hall. (☎9145 4007. Ticket window open daily 11:30am-9:20pm.)

The path also passes through the picturesque village of **Crawfordsburn,** three miles from Bangor and home to Ireland's oldest hotel. The creatively named **Old Inn,** Main St., dates from 1614 and maintains many of its original wood decorations, including a stately desk with intricate carvings. The Inn has been visited by celebrities ranging from Peter the Great of Russia to C.S. Lewis and serves meals in its wood-panelled **Parlour Bar ❷.** (☎9185 3255. Sandwiches £3-5; entrees £9.50-12. Set 2-course meal with wine £40 per couple. Kitchen open M-F noon-7pm, Sa-Su noon-9pm. Bar open M-Sa 11:30am-11pm, Su 11:30am-10pm.) The **Crawfordsburn Country Park,** off B20 (A2) at Helen's Bay, offers coastal paths, forests, and a waterfall. To walk there, turn onto the easily missed footpath behind the inn, just before the Texaco station. (Open Apr. to Sept. or mid-Oct. daily 9am-8pm; Oct.-Mar. 9am-5pm. For pedestrians, the park is always open.) Inside the park, a **Visitors Centre** provides info on trails and natural history and has a **cafe ❶.** (☎9185 3621; www.ehsni.gov.uk. Open daily 9am-5pm.) The Bangor **bus** and **train** both run through Crawfordsburn (£1.70).

Bangor claims to be the **festival** capital of Northern Ireland. The hills are alive with the sound of music in April for the **Bangor International Choral Festival,** and all the world's a stage earlier in the month during the town's popular weeklong **Drama Festival.** The **Ultimate Bank Holiday Weekend** sweeps through town in late August—the foam machines, trapeze artists, and DJs galore are all free, but cost concerns have prompted speculations regarding future cancellations. For more information, contact the Bangor tourist office, or see the pamphlet **Let's Go,** which is published by the tourist office. In late September, crowds gather for five days of **Aspects,** one of Ireland's premier literary festivals, which drew the likes of Seamus Heaney in its heyday. Contact the Arts Deptartment of the Borough Council for details (☎9127 1200).

ARDS PENINSULA

The Ards Peninsula is bounded on the west by tranquil Strangford Lough and on the east by the rough Irish Sea. The shore of the lough from Newtownards to Portaferry is crowded with historic houses, decaying ruins, and spectacular lake views. Several wildlife preserves maintain the fauna and fragile ecosystems of the lough—the area supports 80% of all the species found along Ireland's coast. On the Irish Sea side, minnow-sized fishing villages dot the shore.

Ulsterbus leaves Laganside Station in **Belfast** to cruise the length of the peninsula, stopping in almost every town. **Trains** roll no farther than Bangor. From the south, a **ferry** crosses frequently between Strangford and Portaferry (p. 527). **Biking** is another excellent and fairly painless way to see the Ards Peninsula.

NEWTOWNARDS

At the head of the Strangford Lough lies Newtownards, Ards borough's capital city. This relatively quiet town falls in the shadows of the iconic Scrabo Tower, provides a wealth of information on its southern neighbors, and serves as a convenient base for further exploration of the Ards Penninsula.

▐▀ TRANSPORTATION

Buses: 33 Regent St. (☎9181 23910; www.translink.co.uk), next to the tourist office. To **Belfast** (35min.; M-F every 10-30min. 6:15am-9:35pm, Sa at least 1 every hr. 7am-9pm, Su at least every 1½hr. 8am-9pm; £2.30), to **Bangor** (M-F every 15-30min. 6:45am-6pm and every hr. until 10pm, Sa every ½hr. 8:15am-6pm and every hr. until 10pm, Su every 2hr. 9:30am-9:30pm; £2), and **Ards Peninsula** towns, including **Portaferry** (50min.; M-F 15 per day, Sa 10 per day, Su 5 per day; £4.50). A bus to **Comber, Downpatrick, Killyleagh,** and **Newcastle** runs July-Aug. M-F at 10:10am, noon, and 2:55pm (returns from Newcastle at 12:15; 2:30, 4:45pm); £7.70 round-trip. All buses stop at Gibsons Ln. between Regent St. and Mill St. The station can hold baggage.

Taxis: Call **Ards Cabs,** 5 Gibsons Ln. (☎9181 1617); **A&G,** Lower Mary St. (☎9181 0360); or the wheelchair-accessible **Rosevale Taxis,** Unit 11 North St. (☎9181 1440 or 9182 1111). Taxis also operate from the bus station at Regent St.

◢▌ ▐ ORIENTATION AND PRACTICAL INFORMATION

Conway Square is home to the town hall and a small pedestrian area. Running north to south on either side of the square are **Church Street,** which becomes **Regent Street** and then **Frances Street** as it progresses southeast to Donaghadee, and **Mill Street,** which becomes **High Street.** Between the two main streets toward the tourist office is **Gibsons Lane,** where all buses stop and leave.

Tourist Office: 31 Regent St. (☎9182 6846; www.ards-council.gov.uk). Books accommodations for a £2 fee and 10% deposit. Stays open year-round and has ample information on all destinations in Northern Ireland. The office is also home to the **Ards Crafts** store, which sells the work of local artisans. Open July-Aug. M-Th 9am-5:15pm and F-Sa 9am-5:30pm; Sept.-June M-Sa 9am-5pm.

Banks: Bank of Ireland, 12 Conway Sq. (☎9181 4200). Open M-Tu and Th-F 9:30am-4:30pm, W 10am-4:30pm. **Northern Bank,** 35 High St. (☎9181 2220). Open M 10am-5pm, Tu-W and F 10am-3:30pm, Th 9:30am-3:30pm, Sa 9:30am-12:30pm.

Ulster Bank, 22 Frances St. (☎9182 7840). Open M-Tu and Th-F 9:30am-4:30pm, W 10am-4:30pm. All have 24hr. **ATMs.**

Pharmacy: Boots, 12-14 Regent St. (☎9181 3359). Open M-Sa 9am-6pm.

Work Opportunities: Contact **Grafton Recruitment,** 13 High St. (☎9182 6353).

Emergency: ☎999; no coins required. **Police:** John St. (☎9181 8080).

Hospital: Ards Community Hospital, Church St. (☎9181 2661), treats minor injuries. Open daily 9am-5pm. Emergencies and under 4 go to **Ulster Hospital,** Upper Newtownards Rd. in **Dondonald** (☎9048 4511).

Internet Access: The **Newtownards Library,** on Regent St. in Queen's Hall, a few doors from the tourist office toward Conway Sq., provides Internet access at £1.50 per 30min. (☎9181 4732. Open M-W 10am-8pm, Th 10am-5pm, F 9:30am-5pm, Sa 10am-4pm.)

Post Office: 8 Frances St. (☎084 5722 3344). Open M-F 9am-5:30pm (Tu 9:30am), Sa 9:30am-12:30pm. Also has a **bureau de change.** There is another office in the **Asda** supermarket at **Ards Shopping Center** (☎9182 0203). Open M-F 9am-5:30pm, Sa 9am-1pm. **Postal Code:** BT23.

ACCOMMODATIONS

Despite its centrality and accessibility to the rest of the Ards, Newtownards itself does not have a developed accommodations market. There is only one hotel in town, but a 5-10min. taxi or car ride outside the city yields a variety of B&Bs.

Strangford Arms Hotel, 92 Church St. (☎9181 4141; www.strangfordhotel.co.uk). A legitimate reason to indulge, as the town's only hotel just happens to be a 3-star oasis in a land of B&Bs. Singles £79; doubles £99. AmEx/MC/V. ❹

Woodview B&B, 8 Ballywalter Rd. (☎4278 8242; www.kingdomsofdown/woodview), in Greyabbey. Follow signs for Ballywalter; after passing the abbey, the easily missed driveway is on the left where the church wall ends. Peaceful B&B surrounded by farmland. Kind Mrs. Carson welcomes visitors to her home with a cup of tea and biscuits with homemade jam. Singles £25; doubles £44. Discount for stays of 3+ nights. ❷

Rockhaven B&B, 79 Mountain Rd. (☎9182 3987; www.kingdomsofdown.com/rockhaven). Secluded modern home with interesting world art and 2 comfortable rooms just a short drive toward Crawfordsburn (A2). Pass the Leisure Centre and the subsequent traffic light; then make a right on Mountain Rd. Rockhaven is ½ mi. on the right. Parking available. Free Wi-Fi and laundry. Singles £35; doubles £60. ❸

FOOD AND PUBS

Tesco (☎9181 5290; open M-F 8:30am-9pm, Sa 8:30am-8pm, Su 1-6pm) and **Asda** (☎9181 5577; open M-Sa 8am-10pm, Su 1-6pm) lie at the edge of town in the **Ards Shopping Centre** off Church St. after the Strangford Arms Hotel. Bakeries and fruit stands line Regent St. between Frances St. and the tourist office and Conway Sq.

Cafe Mocha, 23 High St. (☎9181 2616). Tranquil and delicious haven amid town square's bustle. Breakfasts £3-5; sandwiches £2.50-3.65; lunches £3.50-6.50. Open M-Th 8am-4:30pm, F-Sa 8am-10pm, Su 9am-3pm. ❶

Regency Restaurant, 5A Regent St. (☎9181 4347). Family-oriented bakery/restaurant features grill options from £6-8.50 and sandwiches (£2) for takeaway. Try the "Ulster Fry" breakfast special—sausage, bacon, eggs, and bread (8:30-10:45am £2, after 10:45am £5). Open M-F 7:30am-5pm, Sa 7:30am-6:30pm. ❶

The Blue Room, 12 Frances St. (☎9182 1217). Foccacia, bagels, croissants, and wraps with a variety of fillings round out the sandwich roster. All-day breakfast features 4 sizes of fried dishes, including the "Bellybuster" (£5.50). Lunches around £5. Open M-Sa 8:30am-4:30pm. ❷

👁 🔺 SIGHTS AND OUTDOOR ACTIVITIES

Newtownards is the closest hub to the **Scrabo Tower and Country Park,** 203A Scrabo Rd., one of Northern Ireland's favorite postcard subjects. To take your own pictures, head north out of Newtownards taking Blair Maine Rd. from the Newtownards Shopping Centre roundabout, then make a right at Scrabo Rd. and the second left on that road. The bus to Comber also stops at the tower upon request (one-way £1, all-day ticket £1.70). The 200 ft. tower was erected in 1857 as a memorial to Charles William Steward, Third Marquee of Londonderry (1778-1854), in commemoration of the struggles his tenants faced during the Great Famine. Though Charles Lanyon's elaborate plan for the tower was never realized due to lack of funding, it is one of Northern Ireland's most recognizable landmarks. Visitors enjoy exhibits on the tower's history and the park, as well as an audio-visual presentation. Those who brave the steep spiral staircase leading to the top are rewarded with a fantastic 360° view. The adjoining park's quarries supplied the stone for **Greyabbey,** down the road (p. 527), and the Albert Memorial Clock in Belfast. Ramblers and birdwatchers are welcome in **Killyneater Wood,** home to many tree-lined walks. (☎9181 1491; www.ehsni.gov.uk. Open Easter-Sept. daily 10:30am-6pm. Free.)

Six miles from Newtownards (12 mi. from Belfast), the Wildfowl and Wetlands Trust maintains **Castle Espie,** 78 Ballydrain Rd., a wetlands preserve that protects endangered birds and has the largest population of ducks, geese, and swans in Ireland. From Newtownards, take C2 toward Comber, then A22 toward Killyleagh. Take the first left at Ballydrain Rd. An emphasis on conservation and environmental education govern the site's woodland walks, children's activities, sustainable garden, and art gallery. Activity is especially high in fall and winter when migrating flocks from the Arctic seek refuge in Northern Ireland's comparatively temperate climate. The Visitors Centre has free maps and wildlife information. (☎9187 4146; www.wwt.org.uk. Open Mar.-June and Sept.-Oct. M-F 10:30am-5pm, Sa-Su 11am-5:30pm; Nov.-Feb. M-F 11am-4pm, Sa-Su 11am-5:30pm; July-Aug. M-F 10:30am-5:30pm and Sa-Su 11am-5:30pm. £5, Gift Aid £5.50; students, seniors, and unemployed £3.77/4.15, children £2.49/2.75, under 4 free.) At **The Ark Open Farm,** 296 Bangor Rd., about one mile from Newtownards, right off A21, visitors are encouraged to return to their agrarian roots. Milk a cow named Kathy, feed red deer, pet a llama, or ride a pony. The working farm specializes in caring for over 80 rare species of domestic animals, including White Bud cows, which are believed to have been brought to Britain by the Romans. (☎9182 0445; www.thearkopenfarm.com. Open Apr.-Oct. M-Sa 10am-6pm, Su 2-6pm; Nov.-Mar. M-Sa 10am-5pm, Su 2-5pm. £4, ages 3-18, seniors, and students £3.20, under 3 free.) Fishermen look to the **Movilla Trout Fishery** to practice a little catch and release. Fly fishers cast their lines on Movilla Lake, four miles down Donaghadee Rd. (B172) from Newtownards, on Movilla Rd.; make a right after Movilla H.S., and after two miles the fishery will be signposted. (☎9181 3334. 1 fish £16, 2 fish £19; catch and release £12. Open daily 9am-dusk.) Note that a rod license is necessary and can be purchased at **Country Sports,** across from the bus station at 48 Regent St. (☎9181 3403.) For indoor sports, head to the **Ards Leisure Centre** on William St. From Regent St., heading away from town hall, make a right on William St. and walk a quarter of a mile to the compound. Go for a swim, play some badminton or ping pong (£1.65/1.10), or opt for one of their fitness classes (£4-6); afterward, grab a bit at the **cafe ❶.** (☎9181 2837; www.leisureards.org.uk. Pool £1.60; children, students, and seniors £1.10. Open M-F 9:30am-8:30pm, Sa 9:30am-4:30pm, Su 1-4:30pm.) After your workout, take a trip to **Movieland,** Blair Mayne Rd. South, to negate all that exercise with an enormous bucket of popcorn. The movie theater is in the same parking lot as the shopping center; take Mill St. out of town to reach it. (☎9182 0000. Matinees £3.90, children £3.30; evening shows £4.90, students and children £3.90.)

DV Diving, 138 Mount Steward Rd., leads dives in Belfast and Strangford loughs and around the peninsula. Leave Newtownards on Portaferry Rd. (E4) and pass Ards Sailing Club after 3½ miles, then make a left onto Mount Steward Rd.; it is 2 mi. down on the left. Certified instructors provide equipment and offer diving qualification courses. (Bangor office ☎9146 4671; dive center 9186 1686; www.dvdiving.co.uk. £20 per dive; £40 full-equipment hire. 1½hr. introductory lessons £25. 5- to 7-day courses with equipment £225-295.) Land and lough lovers alike delight in the double-whammy bike and kayak rental offered at **Mike the Bike,** 53 Francis St. (☎9181 1311. Bikes £12 per day; kayaks £15 per day. Open daily 9:30am-5:30pm) For an aeronautical thrill, look into **flight lessons** or **helicopter hire** from the **Ards Airport.** Ards Tourist Information organizes occasional tours from Easter through September, ranging from historical guided walking tours of Newtownards to a folklore-themed jaunt. Contact the Tourist Board for schedules.

Festivals are common throughout the peninsula. In August, **The Creative Peninsula** showcases artists and craftsmen's work at the **Ards Arts Gallery** in the Newtownards Town Hall. (☎9182 3131; arts@ards-council.gov.uk. Open M-Th 10am-5pm, F-Sa 10am-4pm. Contact either the gallery or the tourist office for additional info.) For four days around mid-October, the **Ards International Guitar Festival** fills local cafes, bars, and halls with six-string sounds ranging from folk to blues to flamenco. Late September presents the Ards-wide **Festival of the Peninsula,** when musicians, dramatists, dancers, storytellers, and other performers come from Donegal, Scotland, and all over Ireland to entertain visitors (contact the tourist office for more info).

South of Newtownards, gnat-sized fishing villages buzz along the eastern shoreline. **Donaghadee, Millisle, Ballywalter, Ballyhalbert, Portavogie, Cloughey,** and **Kearney** make good stops on an afternoon's drive, but none merits a special visit. **Donaghadee** has a lifeboat and a functioning lighthouse. **Portavogie** is famous for its prawns, and **Millisle** is home to the **Ballycopeland Windmill.** A2 runs the length of the shore. Hitching is reportedly easy, although *Let's Go* doesn't recommend it.

MOUNT STEWART

Fifteen miles southeast of Belfast on A20 sits ▨**Mount Stewart House and Gardens.** To reach Mount Stewart from Belfast, take the Portaferry bus from Laganside Station (1hr.; M-F 16 per day, Sa 14 per day, Su 4 per day). From Newtownards, take the Portaferry Rd. (C4); the estate is two miles before Greyabbey. Held by many Marquess of Londonderry, the Mount Stewart House was brought to its current splendor as an upper-crust Shangri-La in the 1920s by Lady Edith, Marchioness of Londonderry. Both house and garden are now National Trust property, although Lady Edith's daughter Lady Mairi Stewart still resides in the house. The stately 18th-century Mount Stewart House is packed with eccentricities, and its halls have been graced with summer visits by the likes of Winston Churchill, George Bernard Shaw, and European royalty. Among the treasures are George Stubbs's life-size painting of the Stewart family horse and race champion, Hambletonian—one of the Royal Academy of Painting's top 10 British paintings. The BBC's "Antiques Roadshow" came to the house in July 2003 to investigate its other fascinating artifacts, including a galleon-shaped chandelier hanging in Lady Edith's sitting room—before the gardens were built, it appeared to float on the waters of Belfast Lough when viewed from across the room. (☎4278 8387. Gardens open daily Mar. 10am-4pm; Apr.-Oct. 10am-6pm; May-Sept. 10am-8pm. House and gardens open Mar.-Sept. daily noon-6pm, Oct.-Feb. Sa-Su noon-6pm. 40-45min. tours every 15-30min.; 1st tour at noon, last tour at 5pm. Gardens alone £4.54, Gift Aid £5; children £2.72/3.)

Mount Stewart's **gardens,** spanning 94 acres, are more of an attraction than the house itself and they are currently nominated as a UNESCO World Heritage Site. Lady Edith took advantage of Ireland's temperate climate to create a weird and wonderful landscape of flowers, shrubs, and trees from as far as Africa and Australia. Her **Dodo Terrace** contains a menagerie of animal statues representing the members of her upper-crust circle of friends dubbed "the Ark Club." Each member adopted an animalian alter-ego and Lady Edith, the group's matriarch, was named "Circe the Sorcerer" after the character in Homer's *Odyssey* who turned Ulysses's men into swine. Other elite critters include Winston "the Warlock" Churchill and Nelson "the Devil" Chamberlain. The ◲**Shamrock Garden,** whose name belies its shape, contains a Red Hand of Ulster made of begonias and a topiary Irish Harp planted, appropriately enough, over a cluster of the Emerald Isle's shamrocks. The Lake Walk leads to **Tír na nÓg** ("the land of the ever young"), the beautiful family burial ground above the lake. The gardens also host the wildly popular **Summer Garden Jazz Series** on the last Sunday of each month from April to September, as well as murder mystery evenings and car engine shows. Check the website for details. (☎4278 8387; www.nationaltrust.org.uk. Open May-Sept. daily 10am-8pm; Mar. Sa-Su 10-4pm; Apr. and Oct. daily 10am-6pm.) Based on the Tor of the Winds in Athens, the **Temple of the Winds,** used by Mount Stewartians for "frivolity and jollity," sits atop a hill with a superb view of Strangford Lough. To reach the temple from the house, turn left on the main road and go about one quarter of a mile. (Temple open Apr.-Oct. Su and bank holidays 2-5pm; you can walk around any time.)

GREYABBEY

A few miles down from Mount Stewart through the tiny town of **Greyabbey** lies its famous ruined Cistercian abbey. Founded in AD 1193 by Affreca, wife of Norman conqueror John de Courcey, who also built Inchabbey near Downpatrick, the abbey was the first fully Gothic building in Ireland. The abbey is located a few blocks from the town's crossroads at the bend in the road on Church St.; it is well signposted. The beautiful ruins have an adjoining cemetery and a medieval ◪**Physic Garden,** where healing plants were cultivated to cure such common monastic ailments as flatulence, melancholy, and lunacy. Visitors can touch and taste the plants, and often take some home as well. A medieval vegetable garden grows elephant garlic, kale, and white carrots, which seasoned monks' meals before their orange counterparts came into existence in 1500. (Bus #10 from Belfast's Oxford St. Bus Station to Portaferry goes via Greyabbey. ☎9054 4278. Open Apr.-Oct. M-Sa 9am-6pm, Su 1-6pm; Oct.-Mar. for groups by appointment. Free.) Abandon the ascetic life and have a pint or generous meal in the yellow **Wildflower Inn ❷,** 1-3 Main St. (☎4278 8260. Entrees £8-9; M-F and Su 5-7pm, Sa noon-7pm 2 for £10. 4-course Su lunch 12:30-8pm £10. Kitchen open M-Th 12:30am-3pm and 5-8:30pm, F noon-3pm and 5-9pm, Sa noon-9pm, Su noon-8pm.) Across the street, **Pebbles Coffee Shop ❶,** 12 Main St., has coffee, baked goods, sandwiches, and an adjoining craft shop. (☎4278 8031. Meals around £6. Open Tu-F 10am-5pm, Sa 9am-5pm, Su 2-5pm. MC/V.)

PORTAFERRY (PORT AN PHEIRE)

Portaferry lies on the southern tip of the Ards Peninsula and peers at Strangford town across the waters of Strangford Lough. Tourists stop in this seaside town to relax, explore the southern Ards, and enjoy Northern Ireland's largest aquarium.

◪ **TRANSPORTATION.** To reach Strangford Lough from the bus stop, follow **Ferry Street** or **Castle Street** downhill for about 100 yd. **Ulsterbuses** from Belfast drop off visitors at **The Square** in the center of town. (1½hr.; M-F 15 per day, Sa 10 per day, Su 5 per day; £5.) **Ferries** leave Portaferry's waterfront at 15 and 45min. past the hr. for a 10min. chug to Strangford, returning on the hr. and ½hr. (☎4488

1637. M-F 7:45am-10:45pm, Sa 8:15am-11:15pm, Su 9:45am-10:45pm. £1.10, children 50p, seniors free; return £2/1/8.50. Car and driver £5.30.)

■: ■ **ORIENTATION AND PRACTICAL INFORMATION.** To reach the **tourist office** from the bus stop, take **Castle Street** downhill toward the lough. The tourist office is on the corner of Castle St. and **the Strand,** the shoreline's official name, in front of **Portaferry Castle.** Beyond the usual brochures, accommodations bookings (£2 plus 10% deposit), and a **bureau de change,** it also has a 12min. video on the medieval "tower houses" of Co. Down, precursors of the grand estates. (☎4272 9882. Open July-Aug. M-Sa 10am-5:30pm, Su 1-6pm; Easter-June and Sept. M-Sa 10am-5pm, Su 2-6pm.) Get **Internet** access at the **library,** 45 High St., at the end of the block on the right. (☎4272 8194. £1.50 per 30min. Open M and W 2-8pm, F 10am-1pm and 2-5pm, Sa 10am-1pm.) **Portaferry Pharmacy,** 39 High St. (☎4272 8226), is on the north side of town. (Open M and F 9am-6pm; Tu, Th, and Sa 9am-5:30pm; W 9am-5:45pm; closed 1-2pm.) Near the bus station is **Northern Bank** and its 24hr. **ATM,** 1 The Square (☎4272 8208; open M 10am-5pm, Tu-W and F 10am-3:30pm, Th 9:30am-3:30pm; closed daily 12:30-1:30pm), and the **post office,** 28 The Square (☎4272 8201; open M-W and F 9am-1pm and 2-5:30pm, Th 9am-1pm, Sa 9am-12:30pm). **Postal Code:** BT22.

☗ ACCOMMODATIONS. A peaceful stay awaits residents of the **Portaferry Barholm Youth Hostel ❶,** 11 the Strand, across from the ferry dock. Offering both hotel- and hostel-style accommodations, Barholm is a cut above standard hostels and is ideally located right on Strangford Lough, with a conservatory dining room and excellent views. (☎4272 9598. Weekend reservations are necessary. Wheelchair-accessible. Weekend tearoom open daily noon-5pm; sandwiches £2.20. For groups: breakfast, lunch, and 3-course dinner £16 per day. Laundry £3. Dorms £13; singles £15; ensuite doubles from £35.) The digs at **Fiddler's Green B&B ❸,** located above the pub on Church St., are unbeatable. Hardwood floors, private baths, and airy rooms with matching bedsheets and curtains add that extra touch of class. Call ahead as it fills up on weekends. (☎4272 8393, bookings 078 1603 0058; www.fiddlersgreenportaferry.com. Free Wi-Fi. Singles £22-35.)

❒ ☒ FOOD AND PUBS. Numerous fresh fruit and veggie **markets** and convenience stores are scattered around High St. and The Square. For opening hours, you can't beat **Spar,** 16 The Square. (☎4272 8957. Open daily 6:30am-9pm.) Every Saturday from Easter through September, Market House in The Square welcomes a **country market** (9:30am-noon). For a quick and greasy bite, **Ferry Grill ❶,** 3 High St. across from Spar, stays open late on weekends and serves burgers and fries or fish 'n' chips. (☎4272 8568. Food under £3. Open M-Th noon-2pm and 4:30-8pm, F noon-9:30pm, Sa noon-2pm and 4:30-9:30pm, Su 4:30-9pm.) **White Satin ❷,** 2-8 Castle St., before Exploris and Portaferry Castle, serves Chinese food. Try the two-course weekend lunch deal (F-Su noon-5pm; £6.50). Entrees include a wide selection of duck and squid dishes. (☎4272 9000. Most entrees £7-9. Open M-Th 5-11pm, F-Su noon-11pm.) **Deli-licious ❶,** 1a Castle St. (☎4272 9911), has a warm interior despite the copious amounts of ice cream (from £3). It rounds out the menu with its hot breakfasts for £3 and lunches for £3-5. (Open daily 9am-3pm; July-Aug. until 5pm; during Gala Week 8am-8pm.) At night, everyone stumbles to ☒**Fiddler's Green,** 10-14 Church St., where publican Frank and his sons lead rowdy sing-alongs on weekends. As the wall proclaims: "There are no strangers here. Just friends who have not yet met." (☎4272 8393. F-Su live folk, trad, rock, or pop. Open daily 11:30pm-1:30am.) Across the street, locals gather for booze and billiards at **The Milestone,** 1-3 Church St. (☎4272 9629. £5 deposit for billiards. Open daily 11:30am-12:30am.) **M.E. Dumigan's,** 9-11 Ferry St., is up from the waterfront. This pub is so small, you'll have no choice but to rub shoulders with the local crowd. (Open M-Sa 11:30am-11pm, Su 12:30-10pm.)

◙ **SIGHTS.** Portaferry's pride and joy is ◙**Exploris,** Northern Ireland's only public aquarium and one of the UK's best. Near the pier, beneath the crumbling **Portaferry Castle,** Exploris holds first-rate exhibits on local marine ecology. The journey begins in the shallow waters of Strangford Lough, proceeds through the Narrows, and ends in the depths of the Irish Sea, where one of Europe's largest tanks houses sharks and other large fish. Touch-tanks and interactive displays keep kids educated and engaged. The aquarium is renowned for its **seal sanctuary,** which focuses its efforts on the rehabilitation of injured or orphaned seals along the coastline. Very young injured seals are kept in pens where they are carefully monitored. As they heal they are free to play in the open-air sanctuary before being released back into the wild. October through December is the best time for seal sightings; check out Ballyquinton Point and Cloughy Rocks or ask at the aquarium for the best spots. (☎4272 8062; www.exploris.org.uk. Open Apr.-Aug. M-F 10am-6pm, Sa 11am-6pm, Su noon-6pm; Sept. Mar. until 5pm. ₤7; children, students and seniors ₤4; families ₤20; under 4 free.) July brings the massive **Gala Week** of boat races, crowds, performers, drink, and general revelry (www.portaferrygala.com). A lineup of events is available from the tourist office; alternatively, contact Caroline Mageean at ☎077 4216 7917.

LECALE PENINSULA

Dubbed "The Island of Lecale" by some, this region spans the west coast of Strangford Lough from the village of Strangford to Downpatrick, then continues inland to Ballynahinch in the north and Dundrum in the west. It was once bounded entirely by bodies of water, including the Irish Sea, Strangford Lough, and a series of streams and ponds, until these waterways were re-routed for mills and hydrocentered agricultural pursuits. Industrialization bypassed Catholic Lecale, concentrating on the wealthier Protestant-populated areas of County Down, which left the area culturally isolated. Today, animals are raised on its rolling green hills, as the rocky farmland can't support heavy cultivation. Beautiful parks, lavish estates, and St. Patrick-related sights draw visitors from afar.

STRANGFORD (BAILE LOCH CUAN)

This tiny harbor village lies just across the Lough from Portaferry, northeast of Downpatrick on A25 and north of Ardglass on A2. Strangford has limited (namely, one) accommodation; its tourist appeal lies in its proximity to the **Castle Ward House and Estate** (p. 530). **Buses** to Downpatrick leave from the center of town, called the Square. (25min.; M-F 10 per day, Sa 5 per day; ₤2.20.) **Ferries** leave for Portaferry every 30min. (M-F 7:30am-10:30pm, Sa 8am-11pm, Su 9:30am-10:30pm; ₤1.10, cars ₤5.30.) The **Castleward Caravan Park ❶** stands on the Castle Ward National Trust property; headed out of town, take a right off the road to Downpatrick. (☎4488 1680. Open daily mid-Mar. to Sept. Warden's cottage closed daily 1-2pm and 5-6pm. Free showers. Small tent ₤6, family tent ₤8, large igloo-style tent ₤10; caravans ₤12. Fee collected by the warden.) At the cozy old **Cuan Bar and Restaurant ❹,** the Square, enjoy a warm welcome and quality pub grub. (☎4488 1222. Fresh seafood chowder ₤8.95; most meals ₤8-13.50. Last F of every month live music. Bar open daily 11:30am-11:30pm. Open M-Sa noon-9pm, Su noon-8pm.) The Cuan does triple duty as the **Cuan Guest House ❹.** Its hardwood floors, big cushy beds, and tidy bathrooms recommend it, as does its lack of competition. (Free Wi-Fi. All rooms with bath and TV. June-Aug. singles ₤52.50; doubles ₤85; Sept.-Apr. ₤47.50/75.) Back in town, a small 16th-century tower house optimistically called **Strangford Castle** stands to the right of the ferry dock as you disembark. Wander into its dark, spooky interior and find a humbling view from the 3rd fl. (Gate key available from Eimon Seed, 39 Castle St., across from the tower house's gate; open daily 10am-6pm.) If you turn off the main road at the Mace convenience store and drive toward Kilclief, a short drive brings you to the **Kilclief Castle,** one of the oldest castle towers in Ireland. Built in the 15th century for the Bishop of Down, it has four well-preserved (albeit fairly empty) floors. The steep spiral staircase's tiny steps are a fun climb but may not be for the faint of heart or the careless of foot. (☎9181 1491. Open July-Aug. Tu-Sa 10am-6pm, Su 2-6pm; closes for 30min. lunch daily at varying times. Contact the Enivornmental Heritage Service for more information: ☎028 9054 6754.)

CASTLE WARD HOUSE AND ESTATE

To get to ▨**Castle Ward House and Estate** by car or bus (request to be dropped off) from Strangford, take A25 toward Downpatrick. The entrance is about two miles up the road on the right. Pedestrians seeking a leisurely and pleasant stroll along a shady and cool path should take the **Loughside Walk** (see **Strangford,** p. 529). This 18th-century estate, once owned by Lady Anne and Lord Bangor and now the property of the National Trust, lies atop a hill with a spectacular view of the lough. The house, built in 1768, is marked by its conflicting architecture. It is split lengthwise down the middle—one wing is classical, which satisfied Lord Bangor, and the other is Gothic, which suited Lady Anne. Thick double doors, one in each design, leave no room for crossover. The divide even went as deep as the dessert table, with jelly molds available in both styles. Having literally etched their differences into the walls, the couple eventually split, but they left the house intact and spared its curious artifacts, including a **"living cartoon"** of stuffed squirrels duking it out in a series of 3D tableaux. The front room features a sculpture shortcut—real objects, such as a violin and a hat, were dipped in plaster and mounted on the walls. The 800-acre estate features a stable, Victorian laundry room, and kitchen, and on its grounds are a rectangular lake, a restored mill, two tower houses, and a "Victorian Pastimes Centre" for children. Earnings from the secondhand bookshop in the stableyard help maintain the grounds. (☎4488 1204; www.ntni.org.uk. Grounds open daily Oct.-Apr. 10am-4pm; May-Sept. 10am-8pm. House and Wildlife Centre open May-June and Sept. Sa-Su 1-5pm, July-Aug. daily 1-5pm. Bookstore open 2-5pm when the center is open. House tours either hourly 1-5pm or 1:30, 3, and 4:30pm; call ahead to see which schedule is running. Grounds and Wildlife Centre £4.08, Gift Aid £4.50, children £1.81/2, family £9.53/10.50. House tours £2, children £1, families £5.50.)

The **Strangford Lough Wildlife Centre** is located on the estate and provides information on both the natural environment of the lough and on microscopes, whose development owed much to the groundbreaking work of Lady Anne. On foot, follow A25 past the causeway and take an immediate sharp right, which leads to the entrance to the Castle Ward Caravan Park (p. 529). Follow the driveway to the right fork and go through the brown gate on the right. This leads to the Loughside Walk, a 30min. stroll along the coastline to the Centre. Step lively, or risk stepping on one of the many birds scuttling along the path. (☎4488 1411. Same hours as estate.) During the first three weeks of June, the **Castle Ward Opera** sings to a tuxedoed crowd. (☎9066 1090. Tickets £40-45.) From March through September, **Jazz in the Garden** sounds every second Sunday of the month. Occasional piano recitals culminate in a **music festival** the first weekend in August as trad, rock, and country regales the public.

DOWNPATRICK (DÚN PÁDRAIG)

The final resting place of Saints Columcille, Brigid, and Paddy himself, Downpatrick is the county's administrative center and capital. Though nights can be slow, shoppers, schoolchildren, and heavy traffic from nearby villages pack the town by day. The surrounding countryside, peppered with St. Patrick-related sites, is best seen in a daytrip by car or bike.

TRANSPORTATION

Buses: 83 Market St. (☎4461 2384). To: **Belfast** (1hr.; M-F every 5-35min. 6:30am-6:45pm and 9:05pm, Sa every 5-35min. 7:30am-6:10pm and 9:05pm, Su every 2hr. 9am-7pm; £4.50, children £2.25), **Newcastle** (35min.; M-F every 30-60min. 7:30am-6:25pm and 9:45pm, Sa 13 per day, Su 4 per day; £3, children £1.50), and **Strangford** (25min.; M-F 11 per day, Sa 6 per day; £2.70, children £1.35).
Taxis: Downpatrick Taxis, 96 Market St. (☎4461 4515).

ORIENTATION AND PRACTICAL INFORMATION

Market Street is the town's main throughfare. Continuing left from the station, the first right is **St. Patrick's Avenue.** Farther on, Market St. meets **Irish Street** on the right and **English Street** on the left. Market St. becomes **Church Street** and continues straight. **Scotch Street** lies between Church and Irish St.

Tourist Office: 53a Market St. (☎4461 2233; www.downdc.gov.uk), in the **St. Patrick Heritage Centre,** books accommodations for a £2 fee and 10% deposit and provides useful info about the area and county. Also distributes a free map of town and the surrounding areas. Open July-Aug. M-F 9am-6pm, Sa 9:30am-6pm, Su 2-6pm; Sept.-June M-F 9am-5pm, Sa 9:30am-5pm.

Banks: Northern Bank, 58-60 Market St. (☎4461 4011). Open M 9:30am-5pm, Tu-F 10am-3:30pm, Sa 9:30am-12:30pm. **Bank of Ireland,** 80-82 Market St. (☎4461 2911). Open M-Tu and Th-F 9:30am-4:30pm, W 10am-4:30pm. **First Trust,** 15 Market St. All 3 have 24hr. **ATMs.**

Laundry: Crawford's Dry Cleaners, 16 St. Patrick's Ave. (☎4461 2284). £5 per load. Open M-Sa 9am-5:30pm.

Emergency: ☎999; no coins required. **Police:** Irish St. (☎4461 5011).

Pharmacy: Foy's Chemist, 16 Irish St. (☎4461 2032). Open M-F 9am-1pm and 2-5:30pm. **Deeny,** 30a St. Patrick's Ave. (☎4461 3807). Open M-Sa 9am-5:30pm.

Hospital: Downe Hospital, Pound Ln. (☎4461 3311), off Irish St.

Internet Access: Downpatrick Library, 79 Market St. (☎4461 2895), next to the bus stop. Internet access free with membership. Open M-Tu and Th 9:30am-8pm, W and F 9:30am-5pm, Sa 10am-5pm. **e-Learn Shop,** 102 Market St. (☎4461 1500), across from the bus stop. £1 per hr. Open M and W 9am-9pm, Tu and Th-F 9am-5pm, Sa 10am-1pm. The **St. Patrick Centre** has a **Cybercafe,** £1.50 per 30min.

Post Office: 65 Market St. (☎4461 2061), inside The Grove next to the St. Patrick Centre. Open M-Tu 8:30am-5:30pm, W-F 9am-5:30pm, Sa 9am-1pm. **Postal Code:** BT30.

ACCOMMODATIONS

Downpatrick's B&Bs are pricey and often on the outskirts of town; visitors usually stay in Portaferry, Newcastle, or the caravan parks near Strangford.

Dunleath House, 33 St. Patrick's Dr. (☎4461 3221 or 077 9186 8792; www.dunleathhouse.com). Luxurious rooms with satellite TV and bath; all have private doors leading to 1 of 2 patios. Hospitable proprietress stays current on town events. Breakfast included. Singles £32; doubles £60. ❸

Hillside B&B, 18 Cathedral View Ring (☎4461 3134), off Stream St. Sheltered home has three comfortable rooms (one with bath). Since its move to this new location, its name has become a misnomer. Rooms £20 per person. ❷

Ardmore House, 1 Ardmore Ave. (☎4461 3028; www.kingdomofdown.com/ardmore), about a 5min. walk from the town center. Friendly proprietress welcomes travelers in a quiet residential neighborhood just outside of town. Free Internet access and laundry. Singles £25; doubles £40. ❷

Denvir's Hotel, 14-16 English St. (☎4461 2012; www.denvirshotel.co.uk), a left onto English St. from Market St. One of the oldest coaching inns in Ireland. Homey 6-room tavern, with private baths and TV, has slept the likes of Jonathan Swift and Daniel Day Lewis. Breakfast included. Singles £37.50; doubles £60. MC/V. ❸

◖ FOOD

Downpatrick's eateries surpass those of many nearby towns in both quality and quantity. The cheapest groceries are at **Lidl**, Market St., across the street from the library. (Open M-Sa 8am-9pm, Su 1-6pm.) Try the deli in **Hanlon's Fruit and Veg**, 26 Market St. for unsurpassable takeaway sandwiches (☎4461 2129; sandwiches £1.70-2.10; open M-Sa 8am-6pm), or the supermarkets around the bus station. Finding a square meal after the local workday proves more difficult. At night, restaurants hike up their prices significantly, but some pubs quiet rumblings at lower cost.

Daily Grind Coffee Shop, 21a St. Patrick's Ave. (☎4461 5949), just off Market St. An upbeat upstairs orange-and-blue cafe serving tasty sandwiches (£2.50-2.75) and mega salads (£5-6); try the Ultimate Club Sandwich (£4.25), a triple-decker take on the BLT. Takeaway available. Open M-Sa 10am-3:30pm. ❶

Denvir's Restaurant and Pub, 14 English St. (☎4461 2012). Good cooking in a historical setting. Pub dates from 1642. United Irishmen fighting for Home Rule in 1798 met here as a literary society (see **Rebellion and Union,** p. 53). Rumored to have served revolutionary Thomas Russell his last meal before he was hanged outside of the Down County *Gaol*. Th and Sa live music. Lunch noon-2:30pm £6-10; dinner 5:30-9pm £9-13. Kitchen open daily noon-9pm. Pub open daily noon-12:45am. ❸

Roubles, 36 Market St. (☎4461 3131). Inexpensive lunches (£4-5) and an all-day breakfast (£3-5) refuel travelers. Vegetarian options available. Open M-Sa 9am-5pm. ❷

Oakley Fayre, 52 Market St. (☎4461 2500). Join Downpatrick's old ladies for tea and scones or their robust grandchildren for full meals in a diner-esque seating area. Sandwiches £3-4; lunches £5. Open M-Sa 9am-5:15pm. ❷

🎇 PUBS

Mullans Pub, 48 Church St. (☎4461 2227). Worth the short walk from the town center for good *craic* and walls with pictures of famous rockers. Odd collection of Americana. F live rock band, Sa blues (10pm-1am). 21+. Open daily noon-11pm.

Hogan's, 78 Market St. (☎4461 2017; www.hogans-bar.com). Most modern hangout in town offers a relaxed lounge, a restaurant, and **Indigo,** where Downpatrick's partiers get down. Kitchen open M-Th noon-4:30pm, F-Su noon-8pm. Often 18+, but Sa downstairs 21+ while the club is on upstairs. Club open Sa 9:30pm-2am. Cover £5. Open M-W 11:30am-11:30pm, Th-F 11:30am-1am, Sa 11:30am-2am, Su 11:30am-12:30am.

👁 🎿 SIGHTS AND OUTDOOR ACTIVITIES

The state-of-the-art 🏴**Saint Patrick Centre**, 53a Market St., teaches visitors that there's more to St. Paddy than green Guinness. An incredible interactive journey narrated by the saint starts with his capture and enslavement by Irish pirates and continues to his later teachings and enduring legacy. The Centre's key display is a 20min. IMAX field trip to all the sites in Ireland associated with St. Patrick (see **St. Patrick,** p. 59), displayed on five huge screens to provide sweeping panoramic views of the Irish landscape. The center contains a rooftop garden, craft shop, and art gallery, as well as the local **tourist office.** (☎4461 9000; www.saintpatrickcentre.com. Open June-Aug. M-Sa 9:30am-6pm, Su 10am-6pm; Apr.-May and Sept. M-Sa 9:30am-5:30pm, Su 1-5:30pm; Oct.-Mar. M-Sa 10am-5pm, until 7pm on St. Patrick's Day). Last admission 1½hr. before closing. IMAX and exhibit £5, students and seniors £3.30, children £2.50. IMAX without exhibit £2.15. Garden and art gallery free.)

Past the car park to the right of the St. Patrick Center is the **Downpatrick Railway Museum,** featuring restored trains, a replica of a turn-of-the-century Belfast and County Down railway station, and behind-the-scenes tours of train restorations. On weekends from July to September, trains run around the site from 2-5pm and take trips to Inch Abbey, a restored cornmill, and Viking King Magnus's grave. (☎4461 5779; www.downrail.co.uk. Tours June-Sept. M-Sa 11am-2pm. £5; children and seniors £4; families(2 adults, 3 children) £17.50; under 3 free.)

At the southwest corner of Strangford Lough and a five-mile drive from Downpatrick along A22 toward Killyleagh, **Delamont Country Park** has nature trails, woodlands, and the **Strangford Stone,** the tallest megalith in Ireland. Formerly the estate of a wealthy 18th-century Scottish family, the site was first settled between 1100 and 600 BC, in the so-called "Fairy Forts." The Strangford Stone was quarried in the Mourne Mountains and erected in 1999 for the millennium. The Visitors Centre has info on the history of the estate and the stone. (☎4482 8333. Park open daily 9am-dusk. Pedestrians free; parking £3.50.) The area also has a **caravan park ❶.** (£5.65 per site; £5 per adult, £2.50 per child. Gates closed 11pm-7am.)

The **Down County Museum and Historical Gaol,** at the end of English St., is housed in the jail where Thomas Russell, early father and martyr of Irish republicanism, was hanged. The museum features artifacts from County Down dating back to the Stone Age and a wax gang of 19th-century prisoners in the preserved cells of the *gaol.* The former Governor's Residence now contains historical galleries and activities. (☎4461 5218; www.downcoutymuseum.com. Open M-F 10am-5pm, Sa-Su 1-5pm. Free.) Beside the museum is the Church of Ireland **Down Cathedral** (☎4461 4922). A Celtic monastery until the 12th century, the cathedral went Benedictine under the Norman conqueror John de Courcey and was demolished in the 1316 invasion by Edward Bruce of Scotland. Rebuilt in 1818, the present cathedral incorporates stone carvings from its medieval predecessor and houses the only private pew boxes still used in Ireland. The entrance proclaims 1500 years of Christian heritage, beginning with St. Patrick's settlement in nearby Saul (p. 534). In the cemetery, a slab of granite commemorates the **grave of St. Patrick,** though most believe the saint rests in peace beneath the church itself, joined by the remains of **St. Brigid** and **St. Columcille** (p. 59). Choral Evensong showcases the church's world class organ every 3rd Sunday of the month at 3:30pm. (Open M-Sa 10am-4:30pm, Su 2pm-5pm. Free.)

The top of the **Mound of Down,** behind the Down County Museum, affords a view of the surrounding hills. By car, head down English St. away from the museum and turn left on Mt. Crescent; from the car park walk back toward the Cathedral and take the gravel path on the right through the green gate. This Bronze Age hill fort was once known as Dunlethglaise, or "fort on the green hill," and was a seat of power for the local kings of Ulster. Later, during the Iron Age, an early Christian town flourished on the mound until Anglo-Norman invaders defeated the Irish chief MacDunleavy. Today, visitors are hard-pressed to find signs of the fort or the city, but the green hill remains a lovely spot for a ramble. (☎9054 3034. Open daily dawn-dusk.) In town, on Saturday mornings (9am-noon) from February to October, **Gaelic football** or **soccer matches** are played at Dunleath Park, next to the **Down Leisure Center** (☎4461 3426), past the bus stop on Market St.

FESTIVALS

In Downpatrick, festivals commemorate the obvious (St. Patrick's Day) and more obscure holidays. The days leading up to March 17 mark the **St. Patrick's Festival and Cross-Community Parade.** Children's entertainment, guided historical walks, music, theater, and storytelling vary with the annual theme, but green Guinness is a constant. (☎4461 2233; www.st-patricksdayfestival.com.) On the last weekend in March, **The Magnus Barelegs Viking Festival** ransacks Downpatrick and County Down and celebrates their Viking aggressor with reenacted battles, fierce longship races, and other Norse pastimes. Taking its cue from the Castleward Opera season, Downpatrick lifts the red velvet curtain for the **Fringe Opera Festival** in June (www.operafringe.com; tickets up to £10). Information on all festivals is available from the tourist office (☎4461 2233; events@downdc.gov.uk).

 DAYTRIPS FROM DOWNPATRICK

SAUL AND THE STRUELL WELLS. Although County Down reveres anything touched by St. Patrick's hands, **Saul** may be the most beloved sight of all. After he was converted to Christianity by the saint, local chieftain Dichu gave Patrick the barn *(sabhal)* that later became the first parish church in Ireland (see **Saint Patrick,** p. 59). Replicas of an early Christian church and round tower commemorate Big Paddy's arrival from Scotland at the peaceful **St. Patrick's Memorial Church.** A little over one mile farther down Saul Rd., **St. Patrick's Shrine** stands on the summit of Slieve Patrick. The monument consists of a huge granite statue of St. Patrick, bronze panels depicting scenes from his life, and an open-air temple. The statue was made from the wedding rings, donated as tributes to the saint, of the sculptors and many townspeople. Indecisive about Pat's preferred footwear, the sculptors gave the saint a boot and a sandal, one on each foot, to cover their historical bases. Even nonbelievers appreciate the 360° view of the lough, the mountains, and, on a clear day, the Isle of Man. At the **Struell Wells,** southeast of Downpatrick on the Ardglass road (B1), healing waters run through underground channels beneath ruins vaguely associated with St. Patrick, until they reach the 200-year-old bathhouses at the base of the hill. Belief in their curative powers originated long before Christianity spread to the area. Water pours into the women's bathhouse, but travelers might do better to wait for a shower. *(Follow the signs on the Saul road for ½ mi. past Downpatrick and a golf course to reach Saul Church on the site where St. Patrick is believed to have landed in the 5th century. Bus to Raholp stops here upon request. Church ☎4461 4922. Open daily until 5pm. Su services 10am. Other sites always open to the public. Free.)*

INCH ABBEY AND THE QUOILE PONDAGE NATURE RESERVE. The Cistercian **Inch Abbey,** the earliest standing Gothic ruin in Ireland, was built in 1180 by the Norman conqueror John de Courcey to make amends for his destruction of the Eneragh monastery a few years earlier. The Abbey, off-limits to Irishmen until it closed in 1541, is near the marshes of the River Quoile. Though only low foundation walls remain, the Abbey's enchanting grounds make an excellent picnic site. Enjoy hiking and birdwatching around a manmade pond at nearby **Quoile Pondage Nature Reserve.** The pond was created in 1957 when a tidal barrier was erected to prevent the flooding of Downpatrick. The barrier has since attracted an assortment of vegetation, fish, and insects. The **Quoile Countryside Centre** provides information about the area. *(Abbey is 1 mi. from Downpatrick on Belfast Rd. (A7). Bus to Belfast stops at Abbey Lodge Hotel on request; the abbey is ½ mi. walk down the road. Nature Reserve is 1 mi. from Downpatrick off Strangford Rd. ☎4461 5520. Open Apr.-Aug. daily 11am-5pm; Sept.-Mar. Sa-Su 1-5pm.)*

NEWCASTLE (AN CAISLEÁN NUA)

Newcastle has all the trappings of a tacky seaside town—its allure lies in the fresh air of the Mourne Mountains rising majestically to the south. On weekends, packs of kids prowl the streets in search of fun, while July and August bring the rest of the family to the sun-flooded beach. Weekend ramblers and hardcore mountaineers flock to the miles of trails that wind through forested parks, along the dunes of the coast, and up the mountains. Newcastle is often used by travelers as an inexpensive base for exploring the Mourne Mountains and nearby parks.

TRANSPORTATION

Buses: Ulsterbus, 5-7 Railway St. (☎4372 2296), end of Main St. away from the mountains. To: **Belfast** (1½hr.; M-F 19 per day, Sa 15 per day, Su 8 per day; £6.30, children £3.15); **Downpatrick** (30min.; M-F 24 per day, Sa 12 per day, Su 5 per day; £3/1.50); **Dublin** (3hr., £11.70/5.85) via **Newry** (50min.; M-F 7 per day, Sa 6 per day, Su 10am and 7pm; £5/2.50). The summertime **Rural Rover** service provides personalized pickups upon request (☎4372 7200) in the Mourne area. It runs between Newcastle (departs 10am and 2:25pm) and Belfast (departs noon and 4pm); total ride 1½hr. £6.30, children £3.15.

Taxis: Donard Cabs (☎4372 4100 or 4372 2823) and **Shimna Taxis** (☎4372 6030).

Bike Rental: Wiki Wiki Wheels, 10b Donard St. (☎4372 3973). From the bus station, turn right onto Railway St. £8 per day, children £6 per day; £35/28 per wk. ID deposit. Open Jan.-Mar. M-W, F, Su 9:30am-5:30pm; Apr.-Dec. M-Sa 9am-6pm, Su 2-6pm.

ORIENTATION AND PRACTICAL INFORMATION

Newcastle's main road runs parallel to the waterfront; initially called **Main Street** (where it intersects with **Railway Street**), its name changes to **Central Promenade** and then to **South Promenade** as it approaches the Mournes. **Railway Street** runs down to the water at the end of Main, and **Downs Road** runs parallel to Main St. for several blocks, closer to the water, starting at Railway St.

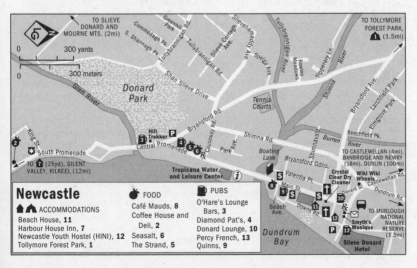

Newcastle

ACCOMMODATIONS
Beach House, 11
Harbour House Inn, 7
Newcastle Youth Hostel (HINI), 12
Tollymore Forest Park, 1

FOOD
Café Mauds, 8
Coffee House and Deli, 2
Seasalt, 6
The Strand, 5

PUBS
O'Hare's Lounge Bars, 3
Diamond Pat's, 4
Donard Lounge, 10
Percy French, 13
Quinns, 9

NORTHERN IRELAND

Tourist Office: 10-14 Central Promenade (☎4372 2222), 10min. from the bus station. Free map and visitor's guide. Late arrivals can use the 24hr. touchscreen computer in front for basic info on accommodations, services, events, and places to visit. Open July-Aug. M-Sa 9:30am-7pm, Su 1-7pm; Sept.-June M-Sa 10am-5pm, Su 2-6pm. Books accommodations (£2 plus 10% deposit) and changes money (to £ only).

Banks: First Trust Bank, 28-32 Main St. (☎084 5600 5925) and **Ulster Bank,** 115-117 Main St. (☎4372 3226) are open M-Tu and Th-F 9:30am-4:30pm, W 10am-4:30pm. **Northern Bank,** 60 Main St. (☎084 5602 6544 or 9004 5490) is open M 9:30am-5pm, Tu-F 10am-3:30pm. All three have 24hr. **ATMs.**

Laundry: Crystal Clear Dry Cleaner, in a small shopping center at 14 Main St. (☎4372 3863). 10 lb. load £5. Open M-Sa 8am-5:30pm.

Emergency: ☎999; no coins needed. **Police:** S. Promenade (☎4372 3583).

Pharmacy: Gordon's, 14 Railway St. (☎4372 2724). Open M-F 9am-6pm, Sa 9:30am-5pm. **Thornton's (MediCare),** 49 Central Promenade (☎4372 3248). Open M-Sa 9am-6pm. Pharmacies have rotating Su noon-1pm opening hour in case of emergency.

Internet Access: Newcastle Library, 141-143 Main St. (☎4372 2710). £1.50 per 30min. Open M, W, F 10am-5pm, Tu 1-8pm, Th 2-8pm, and Sa 10am-1pm and 2-5pm.

Post Office: 6 Railway St. (☎4372 2651), inside the Hallmark Card Shop. Open M-Tu and Th-F 9am-5:30pm, W and Sa 9am-12:30pm. **Postal Code:** BT33.

🏠 🏕 ACCOMMODATIONS AND CAMPING

Of the area's **campsites,** Tollymore Forest Park is probably the most scenic. Since the land is privately owned, camping in the Mournes themselves is illegal; to gain permission from landowners contact the Countryside Access and Activities Network. (☎9030 3930.)

Newcastle Youth Hostel (HINI), 30 Downs Rd. (☎4372 2133; leave a message for reservations). Central seaside location less than 1min. from the bus station. Well-furnished kitchen and basic single-sex dorms. Lockers £0.50 per day. Laundry £2. Check-in 5-11pm. Dorms June-Aug. £13, Sept.-Apr. £12, under 18 £10, members £9, HI £1 discount. MC/V; under £30 £1 surcharge, over £30 3.5%. ❶

Beach House, 22 Downs Rd. (☎4372 2345; beachhouse22@tiscali.co.uk). Splash of luxury by the sea and a few treasures harbored by a proprietress with an eye for antiques, such as the intricately carved acorns on the staircase. Most rooms have terrace access. Singles £50; doubles £80. ❹

Harbour House Inn, 4-8 South Promenade (☎4372 3445). Just outside of town along the seafront. Offers hotel-style rooms with bath, a bar decorated with sailing paraphernalia, a restaurant serving local seafood specialities, and a lounge with great views. Singles £40; doubles £60; under 14 £15, under 2 free. ❸

Tollymore Forest Park, 176 Tullybrannigan Rd. (☎4372 2428), a 2 mi. walk along A2 or 10min. on the "Rural Rover," which leaves the Newcastle Ulsterbus station daily at 9:10am and 12:25pm (£6.30). Excellent **camping** facilities include clean, piping-hot showers, a cafe with tasty doughnuts, and 140 acres of well-marked walks and gardens. Electricity £1.50. Single tent or caravan July-Aug. £13 per night; May-June and Sept. £9. The **Castlewellan Forest Park's** campsite charges the same rates (☎4377 8664); see **Outdoor Activities,** p. 537. ❶

🍴 FOOD

The density of fast-food joints, candy stores, and ice cream parlors on the waterfront leaves greasemongers satisfied and sweet tooths in a sugar coma. More nutritious meals can also be found at reasonable prices, and two- or three-course set meals are often good values. **Tesco,** 21 Castlewellen Rd., is a 10min. walk out of town on Railway St. or toward Castlewellan on A50. (☎4372 5753. Open M-F 8:30am-10pm, Sa 8am-10pm, Su 9am-6pm.) Produce vendors gather on Main St. near the bus station.

🍴 **Seasalt,** 51 Central Promenade (☎4372 5027; www.seasaltnewcastle.co.uk). Modern, sleek interior. Create your dream *panini* with gourmet fillings (£4.40-5) or go epicurean with daily specials that generally span at least two continents (£5-10). Accommodates special dietary needs. Hours are inconsistent, but roughly daily 9am-10pm. ❷

Café Mauds, 106 Main St. (☎4372 6184). On busy weekends, the glass facade of this cafe reveals a full cross-section of the Mourne milieu: hungry hikers devouring *panini* (£5) and crepes (£4-5), old ladies nibbling on pastries, and children dribbling ice cream (small cone 90p; sundae £3). Plop down on a squishy couch or relax on the small terrace overlooking the water. Open M-F 9am-10pm, Sa-Su 9am-11pm. ❷

The Strand, 53-55 Central Promenade (☎4372 3472; www.thestrand.net). Family restaurant with filling dinners (£6-10), including tea and pastry. Snacks and ice cream in the front room takeaway. Open daily July-Aug. 8:30am-11pm, May-June and Sept. 8:30am-8:30pm, Oct.-Apr. 8:30am-6pm. ❸

The Coffee House and Deli, 67a South Promenade (☎4372 3576). Small eatery on the outskirts is worth the walk. Customize your breakfast with a la carte items (60p-£1.50 each), or go for the lunches (£5). Open July-Aug. M-Tu and Sa-Su 8:30am-6:30pm, W-F 8:30am-10pm; Sept.-June M-Tu and Sa-Su 8:30am-6:30pm, W-F 8:30am-8pm. ❶

🎵 🍺 PUBS AND CLUBS

With a few exceptions, the pubs of Newcastle cater to the older set, although on karaoke nights young'uns crowd in for the spotlight.

Quinns, 62 Main St. (☎4372 6400). Packed with artifacts from its days as a pub/grocer in the 1920s. Snag a cozy, dark green snug for a more private chat. M jazz, W local radio DJ, Su drinking games (think boat races). Cover W £3, F-Sa £1. Kitchen open daily noon-5pm. Open M-Sa 11:30am-1am, Su noon-12:30am.

Percy French (☎4372 3175) right outside the Slieve Donard Hotel, where Railway St. meets the sea. Adorned with the flowery lyrics of the popular late 19th-century Irish bard, attracts an older crowd who sip their pints and G&Ts amid the classy surroundings. 18+. Entrees £10-13. Kitchen open daily noon-3pm and 6-9:45pm. Open M-Sa 11:30am-midnight, Su 11:30am-11pm.

Donard Lounge, Main St. (☎4372 2614), by the Donard Hotel. Th karaoke popular with twentysomethings; mixed crowd swills pints all week watching football. Th-Su nights live bands play blues, rock, trad, and folk. 18+. Open daily 11am-1am.

O'Hare's Lounge Bars, 121 Central Promenade (☎4372 2487; www.ohareslounge-bars.com). Entertainment behemoth packs in 4 bars, 3 beer gardens, a club (**Coast**), a lounge, and a restaurant. Club open F (18+) and Sa (21+) 10pm-2am, and sometimes Th or Su as well (call ahead or check the website). Cover £5 after 11pm. **Front Bar** has pool and M karaoke. Open M-Sa 11am-2am, Su 11am-midnight.

🎯 🏔 SIGHTS AND OUTDOOR ACTIVITIES

While Newcastle is not blessed with much of a festival lineup, the unique **Herrings Gutters Festival** is the most interesting highlight of the town's calendar, taking place over four days in early August. Besides the gutting itself, the festival brings free music, barbecues, karaoke, games, dress-up competitions, and more to the streets and pubs of Newcastle. Pick up a list of events from either the tourist

NORTHERN IRELAND

office or the Harbour House Inn. After 9:30pm, all children vacate the festival, and the liberated parents take the boozing up a notch. All times and events, according to the official schedule, are subject to Murphy's Law.

Hikers find paradise in the majestic Mournes (see **Hiking: The Mourne Mountains**, p. 539), while equestrians choose between the beach and forest for riding. Three parks managed by the Department of Agriculture are just a hop, skip, and a jump from Newcastle. **Tollymore Forest Park** lies just two miles west of town in Bryansford. A beautiful entrance lined with gigantic, gnarled trees leads toward ancient stone bridges, a fort, and well-marked trails through woods and over rushing waters. The **Shimna River** runs from east to west and cuts the park in half. From the four main trails, ranging in length from one to eight miles, hikers encounter diverse wildlife including deer, foxes, badgers, and otters. The threemile "Rivers Trail" encompasses most of the park and is highly recommended, as is the 3½ mi. hike to the Curraghard viewpoint overlooking the Irish sea, accessible via the eight-mile "Long Haul Trail." The park also maintains an arboretum featuring a strawberry tree and the only three tree species native to Ireland that are not also native to Great Britain. While hikers are welcome, mountain bikers must stick to paved areas. (☎4372 2428. Open daily 10am-dusk. Cars £4, pedestrians free.) The park is equipped with a campground (see **Accommodations**, p. 536), ranger station with trail info, Visitors Centre, cafe, and impressive outdoor arboretum. If you're not up for the rambling walk to Tollymore, take one of Ulsterbus's "Rural Rover" shuttles from the Newcastle bus station (10min., 10am and 2:25pm, £6.30). Excursions into the Tollymore forest can be arranged through **Tollymore Mountain Center** (☎4372 2158), a left off the exit onto Newry Rd. The center has a climbing wall and offers deals on hiking and canoeing.

Castlewellan Forest Park spreads over the hills north and east of the Mournes. From the Newcastle bus station take Castlewellan Rd. into town, turn left on Main St. at the roundabout, and continue for 420 yd. The entrance is at the top of the main street in Castlewellan, and the campground is opposite the library. (☎4377 8664. Open daily 10am-sunset. £4 per car, pedestrians free. Call M-F 9am-5pm for info. **Camping:** electricity £1.50; tents and caravans July-Aug. £13, May-June and Sept. £9.) The park contains accessible attractions: a Scottish **baronial castle** (now closed to the public but still visible from across the park), an impressive **Sculpture Trail** (2½ mi. of sculpted natural materials), the North's **National Arboretum**, and the recently added Peace Maze, which is purportedly the "largest hedge maze in the world," encompassing 17 mi. of paths. The park's lake overflows with trout; fishing permits are available at the **ranger station**, the first building on the right near the lake, from April to mid-October. Buses run from Newcastle to Castlewellan (10min.; M-F 30 per day, Sa 19 per day, Su 7 per day; £1.60).

Less than one mile past the opposite end of town is the **Murlough National Nature Reserve**, on the Dundrum Rd. (A24) toward Belfast. Home to sand dunes and woodlands, Murlough boasts marvelous swimming (for the polar bear crowd), and seal-watching during the summer/fall molting season. In July, over 150 seals stretch out on the sand. Plenty of critters are visible throughout the year, including badgers, foxes, skylarks, meadow pipits, and the endangered marsh fritillary (a checkered insect). To get there, take the Downpatrick or Belfast bus from Newcastle and get off at Murlough. (☎4375 1467. Beach and walks open dawn-dusk. May-Sept. £2.70 per car, pedestrians free; Jan.-Apr. and Oct.-Dec. free. Car park open 8am-9pm all year.)

Mount Pleasant Equestrian Centre, a cozy, family-run riding center on 15 Bannonstown Rd. in Castlewellan, leads forest or beach rides for all experience levels. Following the Castlewellan Road, the Centre is sign-posted from town, about a one-mile drive from the main road. (☎4377 8651. Bookings required. £15 per hr., children £14 per hr.; helmet included. 6+. Open daily 10am-4:30pm.) More experienced riders head to the **Mourne Trail Riding Centre,** two miles toward Castlewellan at 96 Castlewellan Rd., for 2hr. rides in Tollymore Forest Park. (☎4372 4351. £15 per hr.; helmet included. 10+. Daily rides approx. 11am, 2:30pm, and during the summer also 6pm. Call for other ride times. Book ahead.)

🏔 HIKING: THE MOURNE MOUNTAINS

Before heading for the hills from Newcastle, stop at the **Mourne Countryside Centre** and **Mourne Heritage Trust,** 87 Central Promenade. Friendly and knowledgeable staff leads hikes and offers a broad selection of guides to the mountains. Those planning short excursions can purchase *Mourne Mountain Walks* (£6), which describes 10 one-day hikes, while those planning to camp in the Mournes overnight should buy the *Mourne Country Outdoor Pursuits Map* (£7), a detailed topographical map. (☎4372 4059; www.mournelive.com. Open M-F 9am-5pm.) If the Centre is closed, get maps at the Newcastle tourist office (p. 536). Seasoned hikers looking for company can join the **Mourne Rambling Group,** which sends gangs into the Mournes each Sunday. (Call the secretary, Dora McCavern ☎9049 2114, for meeting locations. Walks generally 4½-5hr., at varying levels of difficulty.) Another such group is the **Down Danderers** (contact Collette Walsh, ☎9756 1167). Shuttle buses run between Silent Valley and Ben Crom Reservoirs. (☎4372 2296. June and Sept. Sa-Su 1pm; July-Aug. 3 per day; £2.15.) In late June, join in the **Mourne International Walking Festival** for planned group walks along designated trails of varying lengths and difficulties. (☎4176 9965; www.mournewalking.com.)

The **Mourne Wall,** built between 1904 and 1923, was a landlord's idea of a barrier, though at an unimpressive 1m tall, one wonders why the mountains wouldn't suffice. It encircles 12 of the mountains just below their peaks. Following the length of the 22 mi. wall takes a strenuous 8hr.; many people choose to break it up with a night under the stars. The Mournes' highest peak, **Slieve Donard** (850m), towers above Newcastle. The trail up is wide, well maintained, and paved in many places with flagstones and cobblestones (5hr. return). **Donard Park,** on the corner of Central Promenade and Bryansford Rd., provides the most direct access to the Mournes from Newcastle. (Always open. Free.) It provides convenient access to Slieve Donard and **Slieve Commedagh** (767m), both three miles from town. Follow the dirt path behind the car park as it crosses two bridges. It eventually joins the Glen River Path for about 1½ mi. to reach the Mourne Wall. At the wall, turn left for Slieve Donard or right for Slieve Commedagh. Those seeking a more remote trek might try **Slieve Bernagh** (739m) or **Slieve Binnian** (747m), most easily accessed from **Hare's Gap** (430m) and **Silent Valley,** respectively. The two craggy peaks, both with tremendous views, can be combined into a 12 mi. half-day hike. Hare's Gap is accessible through a car park. From Newcastle, pass Tollymore Park, and make a right on Trassey Rd. at a sign marked "Meelmore Amenity Area." The car park is closest to the track and a 1min. walk up the **Trassey Track** to Hare's Gap. The ascent crosses the **Ulster Way,** a walking trail that runs east to west. Most of the land in and around the Mournes is privately owned, so trekkers should treat the environs with respect.

Camping in forest areas is strictly prohibited due to the risk of forest fires and because the land is privately owned; stick to designated "wilderness" areas. Camping is allowed along the Mourne Wall, and other common spots include the **Annalong Valley, Lough Shannagh, Trassey River, Hare's Gap,** and the shore of **Blue Lough** at the foot of Slievelamagan, though it is best to contact the Countryside Access and Activities Network (☎9030 3930) before pitching a tent in the Mournes. Remember to bring warm clothing; the mountains get cold and windy at night, and weather conditions may change suddenly. A local volunteer **Mountain Rescue** team (☎999) is available in case of emergency.

NEWRY

In the 5th century, St. Patrick is said to have planted a yew tree at the head of the Clanrye River. From this sacred seedling bloomed the city of Newry, which takes its name from the Irish *Iúr Chinn Trá* ("yew tree at the head of the strand.") Still conscious of its ancient origins, today's Newry proudly proclaims its city status, bestowed by the Queen during her Golden Jubilee Celebration in 2002. A retail and business center between Counties Antrim and Down, Newry entices customers across the border from the Republic to visit its shopping centers and independent stores, and its strategic location between the Mournes and the Ring of Gullion make it a convenient transportation hub.

E TRANSPORTATION. One mile out on Camlough Rd. to the northeast of town is the **train station** (☎3026 9271), from which shuttle buses make the trip into town regularly (runs during all train times; free). To: **Dublin** (80min.; M-Sa 7 per day, Su 4 per day; £16, children £8) and **Belfast** (55min.; M-F 11 per day, Sa 10 per day, Su 5 per day; £8/4). **Buses** run from the Ulsterbus depot on the Mall to: **Belfast** (1½hr.; M-F at least every ½-hr. 6am-9:15pm, Sa 13 per day, Su 9 per day; £7/3.50); **Downpatrick** (1hr.; M-Sa 6 per day, Su 11:20am and 8:30pm; £7/3.50); **Dublin** (2½hr.; daily every hr. 6:55am-9:55pm, and additional buses at least every 2hr. all night; £9.65/4.83). **ABC** (☎3025 2511) and **ACE** (☎3026 2666) run 24hr. **taxis.**

🖪🛈 ORIENTATION AND PRACTICAL INFORMATION. Newry has two main streets that run parallel to each other and the **Newry Canal,** which flows between them. From its northern end at **Kildare Street, Hill Street** runs southward into town and changes to **John Mitchell Place,** while farther west, **Merchant's Quay,** home to shopping and **free parking** havens **Buttercrane Shopping Centre** and **Old Creamery Retail Park,** runs along the canal and shopping area to become **Buttercrane Quay.** Connecting the two streets is **Mill Street,** which becomes **Francis Street** as it crosses the canal onto the Merchant's Quay side. The **Mall** runs along the canal, parallel to Hill St. The **tourist office,** on Abbey Way inside Bagenal's Castle, books accommodations (£2 plus a 10% deposit) and provides information about Newry and its surroundings. Take Mill St. away from the canal and make your second right after Hill St. (☎3026 8877; www.seenewryandmourne.com. Open Apr.-June M-F 9am-1pm and 2-5pm, Tu-F 9am-5pm, Sa 10am-4pm; July-Sept. M 9am-5pm, Tu-F 9am-6pm, Sa 10am-4pm; Oct.-Mar. M 9am-1pm and 2-5pm, Tu-F 9am-5pm.) **Camping equipment** as well as hunting and tack can be purchased at **Smyths Sports and Saddlery,** 5-9 Kildare St. (☎3025 2332; www.smythsports.co.uk. Open M-Sa 9am-5:30pm.) **First Trust Bank,** 42-44 Hill St. (☎3026 6221), **Northern Bank,** 58 Hill St. (☎084 5602 6545 or 9004 5500; open M 9:30am-5pm, Tu-F 10am-3:30pm), and **Ulster Bank** have 24hr. **ATMs;** Ulster Bank has one for £ and one for €. For free Wi-Fi, head to **Ground Espresso Cafe,** 2a Monaghan St. From Francis St., walk along Merchant's Quay with the river on the right; the cafe is on the corner at the next street bridge. (☎3083 3868. Open M-Sa 8am-10pm, Su 11am-10pm). The **library,** 79 Hill St., has **Internet** access. (☎3026 4683. £1.50 per 30min., free for members. Open M and F 9:30am-6pm, Tu and Th 9:30am-8pm, W and Sa 9:30am-5pm.) The **post office,** in the SuperValu on Hill St., has a **bureau de change.** (Open M and W-Sa 8:30am-5:30pm, Tu 9:30am-5:30pm.) **Postal Code:** BT34 1JD.

🛏 ACCOMMODATIONS. A few fancy hotels confirm that Newry is the mover and shaker it claims to be. For cheaper price tags and a bit more character, seek out B&Bs just outside of town along the Belfast road. 🖪**Belmont Hall ❹,** 18 Downshire Rd., invites visitors into enormous rooms with massive oak beds, high ceilings, fluffy comforters, big windows, private baths, free Internet access, and coffee-making facilities. A large apartment through the greenhouse sleeps six to 10 in a dark-oak interior with velvet couches and a fireplace. (☎3026 2163; www.bellmonthall.co.uk. Singles £35-45; doubles £70; apartment £120-150 with breakfast.) **Marymount B&B ❸**, 15 Windsor Ave., up a steep hill and a 7min. walk from town off the Belfast road, is a pleasant white bungalow that offers three airy, wood-floored rooms with large windows and TV; two of these have doors to the porch. (☎3026 1099. Free Internet access. Singles £30; doubles £54.) **Ashdene House B&B**, 28 Windsor Ave., is much more welcoming than the imposing black and gold iron gate that precedes it would suggest. (☎3026 7530. Singles £30-35; doubles £60.)

🍴🍽 **FOOD AND PUBS. Supervalu,** 41-51 Hill St., sells groceries. (☎3026 1410. Open M-W 8am-8pm, Th-F 8am-9pm, Sa 8am-6pm, Su 9am-6pm.) **Spar,** 92 Hill St., sells groceries and serves sandwiches and hot snacks from its deli. (☎3025 1083. Open daily 8am-9:30pm.) Also on Hill St., **The Shelbourne Bakery ❷** serves fresh baked goods (under £1) and sandwiches to go (from £2.25), as well as larger meals in its sit-down restaurant (specials £7), while a poster of Clint Eastwood watches over and keeps the peace. (☎3026 2002. Open daily 8am-6pm.) Overlooking the canal, classy **Cobbles ❸**, 13-15 The Mall, serves international entrees such as Mexican steak and Lebanese chicken at reasonable prices. (☎3083 3333. Lunch daily noon-5pm; £5-7. Entrees £8-10. Open daily 10am-midnight.)

Pubs also serve decent meals. Canal Court Hotel's swanky **Granary Bar,** on Merchant's Quay, offers a popular carvery meal (£8) of assorted meats and side dishes. (Kitchen open daily noon-3pm. Bar menu available M-Sa 3:30-7:30pm.) Wash down the feast with pints and a side of 80s-90s music at the enormous, elegant bar. Party on weekends at the upstairs disco **The Miller Suite.** (☎3025 1234; www.canalcourthotel.com. Su karaoke. Bar 18+. Club 23+. Club cover £10. Bar open M-Th 11:30am-11:30pm, F 11:30am-12:30am, Su noon-1pm. Club open Sa 10pm-2am, last entrance 1:15am, last call 1:30am.) Yuppies hand over their bills to the **Bank Bar** and its corresponding **Vault Club,** 2 Trevor Hill, housed in an old Northern Bank building kitty-cornered from the tourist office before the Belfast road. A swank bar on the ground floor is eclipsed by an enormous club area with more sound and light equipment than a U2 concert. A projector above the dance floor lets those gettin' jiggy check their moves on the big screen and acts as a surveillance camera for catching potential dancemove burglars. (☎3083 5501; www.thebanknewry.com. Kitchen open daily noon-9pm. Bistro lunch menu £5-7; dinner £6-15. F night "Vogue" plays music from 80s-present, Sa "Decks in the City" plays pop and dance. 20+. Cover F £6, Sa £8. Bar open daily 9am-1am. Club open daily 10pm-2am.) A younger crowd gets down at **O'Dowds,** 17-19 Francis St. The bar spills into refurbished **Club Velvet.** (☎6936 6926. Cover F £5, Sa £7. Bar open daily 11:30am-1am. Club open F-Sa 11pm-1:30am.)

🔲🎿 **SIGHTS AND OUTDOOR ACTIVITIES.** The tourist office equips enthusiastic visitors with a free guide to the Newry Town Trail, which highlights most of the city's historic sites, including **St. Patrick's Church,** the first Reformation church in Ireland, begun in 1578. Jonathan Swift is said to have preached in the church during his trips to Newry. **Newry Canal Way** is a marked trail from Portadown to Newry with ancient monuments and birdwatching along the way. Also in Banegal's Castle with the tourist office, the **Newry and Mourne Museum** has exhibits detailing the town's history and a restored 18th-century room with period furniture. Its newest display explores Newry's role in WWII. (☎3031 3170; museum@newryandmourne.gov.uk. Open M-Sa 10am-4:30pm, Su 1-4:30pm. Free.) Newry's **shopping** is nationally renowned with **Quays Shopping Centre** on Bridge St. and **Buttercrane Shopping Centre** on Buttercrane Quay. Boutiques line the area between Hill and Merchant's Quay. The town hosts unique festivals. The year kicks off in January with the annual **pantomime** held at Town Hall, a satirical rendering of some traditional yarn or fairy tale. (Call Town Hall ☎3026 6232 or Charlie Smith ☎3082 1643. Tickets £6.) March introduces Newry to 10 plays on 10 consecutive nights as theater troupes from all over the Republic and the North compete to advance to the **Newry Drama Festival.** (Contact Miss Eileen Mooney ☎3026 6407. Admission to each play £7, children £6.) **Newry Musical Feis** (FEESH) sees Irish and contemporary dancers, choirs, and classical musicians compete for two creative weeks in February and March. (Contact Mary Goss ☎3026 2849; a.m.goss@bt.internet.com. Individual sessions £1 each.) **Newry Agricultural Show** gets the summer started in late June when dog and livestock shows, vintage cars, pig races, and homemade crafts deck the lawn of Derrymore House, a landed estate 2½ mi. from town. (Show office ☎3026 2059.)

WARRENPOINT (AN POINTE)

Down the coast from Newcastle, on the north side of Carlingford Lough, lies the harbor town of Warrenpoint. It first gained fame as a resort town in the 1800s, when just a half-decent beach satisfied tourists. Today, a fortuitous Gulf Stream keeps Warrenpoint several degrees warmer than its neighbors. Much of its tourist appeal lies in its proximity to Rostrevor, which overflows with visitors for the annual Fiddler's Green Festival. The end of the pier provides an unparalleled view of the Mourne and Cooley Mountains rising up in the Republic. While visitors might be tempted to spend most of their time in the town staring out toward the lough and nearby mountains, they would do well to make the two-mile trek down A2 toward Newry to see Narrow Water Castle; bus drivers stop on request. The 16th-century structure, built for defense and toll collection, is one of the best-preserved tower houses in Ireland. In the 19th century, it became a dog kennel. (Tower usually open July-Aug. Tu and F-Sa 10am-1pm; W-Th 2-8pm. Hours may vary; call the tourist office. Free.)

A tragic event in recent years resonates with locals who recall the **IRA bombing** of a British army truck on August 27, 1979. Michael Hudson, a 29-year-old onlooker from the opposite shore, was mistaken for the bomber and shot by the survivors. Across the shore in the Republic, a commemorative stone memorializes the slain man. Since 1990, mid-August has been dominated by the **Maiden of the Mournes Festival,** for which lasses from Ireland, Europe, and the US gather to strut their stuff in a no-holds-barred beauty pageant. Bookies accept bets a week before, but the **Junior Miss Maiden of the Mournes** competition, involving seven- to eight-year-olds, leads to much less betting. (Contact Brendan Bradley ☎4177 2346.) On the last weekend in May, the town gets soulful for **Blues on the Bay,** which brings local and national acts to the waterfront and local pubs. (☎4175 2256; www.bluesonthebay.com. Most shows are free, some ticketed at £10-40.) Warrenpoint also serves as a base for the **Mourne International Walking Festival** in late June (☎4176 9965; www.mournewalking.com.)

Accommodations in Warrenpoint are expensive; the budget-conscious should set up camp in Rostrevor's Kilbroney Park. The sleek, modern **Whistledown and Finn's ❹,** 6 Seaview, on the waterfront, next to a playground at the end of Church St., offers a restaurant, a bar, and hotel-quality rooms with comfy canopy beds. (☎4175 4174. Breakfast included. Singles £40; doubles £70.) The **Ryan B&B ❸,** 1.5mi. from town at 19 Milltown St., is a less pricey option. Leaving town, take Duke St., which becomes Upper Dromore Rd.; then take the signposted right turn at the intersection. (☎4177 2506; dryanbb@hotmail.com. All rooms with bath. Singles £30/€45, doubles £50/€75.) Most of Warrenpoint's eateries offer takeaway, so take your food to the pier. **Diamonds Restaurant ❶,** 9a The Square, is famous for having the best food at the best price. It is usually packed with locals and their wee ones devouring burgers, seafood, pasta, and all-day breakfast. (☎4175 2053. Entrees £5-10.50. Open M-Th 9:30am-9pm, F-Su 9:30am-10pm. MC/V.) **Genoa Café ❶,** 5 The Square, has served fish and chips to Warrenpoint since 1910. Practice made perfect and won them several local chipper competitions. Don't pass up the smooth vanilla ice cream for just 80p. (☎4175 3688. Open daily noon-11pm.) **Vecchia Roma ❸,** 1 Marine Parade at the docks, serves Italian fare under a trellis. (☎4175 2082. Pizza £5-8; other entrees £8-15. Open M-Th 5-10pm, F-Sa 5-11pm, Su 12:30-2:30pm and 5-9:30pm.)

Though quite a few locals go into Newry, enough seek *craic* in town to maintain a decent nightlife. **Jack Ryan's,** 18 The Square, serves eats (most dishes £2-5), hosts live music Sunday at 9pm in its spacious lounge, and games it up with Wednesday quiz night and Thursday pub bingo. The brand-new **Attic** nightclub upstairs hosts a disco on Saturdays. (☎4175 2001. Kitchen open M-F 12:30-2:30pm, Sa-Su 12:30-8pm. Bar open M-Sa 11:30am-1am, Su 12:30pm-midnight. Cover £5.) At **The Square Peg,** 14 the Square, twenty- and thirtysomethings pour into the spacious back bar and fill up the cozy green booths after 11:30pm. (☎4175 3429; www.thepeg.org. Strong music lineup with Th open mic, F disco, Sa live rock, and Su live band. Cover £3-4 for some bands. Pool 50p. Open M-Sa 11:30am-1am, Su 12:30pm-12:30am.)

The bus drop-off is in **The Square;** facing the water, the street bordering the Square and parallel to the lough coast becomes **Church Street** on the left and **Charlotte Street** on the right. B&Bs cluster around **The Promenade,** which becomes **Seaview** and eventually merges with Rostrevor Rd. The **tourist office,** two blocks right from the bus stop when facing away from the water, offers a town map and armloads of free glossy regional guides. They also book accommodations for free. (☎4175 2256. Open M-F 9am-1pm and 2-5pm.) **Ulster Bank,** 2 Charlotte St. (☎4175 2323; open M-Tu and Th-F 9:30am-4:30pm, W 10am-4:30pm), **Northern Bank,** 1 Queen St. (☎084 5602 6558 or 9004 5550; open M 9:30am-5pm, Tu-F 10am-3:30pm), and **First Trust,** 1 The Square, at the corner of Church St. (☎084 5600 5925; open M-Tu and Th-F 9:30am-4:30pm, W 10am-4:30pm) have 24hr. **ATMs.** The **library,** located underneath a health clinic on Summerhill, has **Internet** access (£1.50 per 30min.), which is free for members (membership is easy to obtain with any photo ID). From the tourist office, leave to the right and take the first two rights, and the library is on your left on the block behind the office. (☎4175 3375. Open M and F 10am-5pm, Tu and Th 10am-8pm, and W 2-6pm.) **Rent bikes** at **Stewart's Cycles,** 14 Havelock Pl., beside the Surgery Clinic on Marine Parade. (☎4177 3565. Also does repairs. £10 per day, £50 per wk. Open M-Sa 10am-6pm.) The **police station** is located on Charlotte St. (☎4175 2222). In an **emergency** dial ☎999. **Walsh's Pharmacy** is at 25 Church St. (☎4175 3661. Open M-Sa 9am-6pm.) **Taxis** are run by A.V. Taxis (☎4177 3966). The **post office** is at 9 Church St. (☎4175 2225. Open M-F 8:30am-5:30pm, Sa 9am-12:30pm.) **Postal Code:** BT34 3HN.

(BURNING) WASHINGTON MONUMENT. About midway between Warrenpoint and Rostrevor stands a dull, massive gray spike. The unadorned monument stands in honor of General Robert Ross, commemorating his victory over American forces at Bladensburg, Maryland, in 1814 and subsequent entry into the capital, where he reputedly burned down every public building, including the White House. President James Madison fled amid the pandemonium, leaving Ross to literally finish his breakfast for him, so the story goes. The general's hometown has honored him with the pointed monument, whose ironic resemblance to the Washington Monument may or may not be intentional.

ROSTREVOR (CAISLEAN RUAIRI)

The tiny village of Rostrevor, which lies three miles from Warrenpoint along A2, has a "downtown" of one sharply sloped block (the #39 **bus** from Newry to Kilkee frequently makes the journey). At its bottom, a short bridge ends at **Fairy Glen,** a small park with a bike path that runs along a peaceful stream. Next to Fairy Glen, ramblers can wander into the rolling hills of the much larger **Kilbroney Park** or drive 100 yd. farther down to the car park. For those seeking a longer stay, the park offers 52 well-appointed **campsites.** In addition to a cafe and some wonderful climbing trees, Kilbroney holds the town's crown jewel: **Rostrevor Forest,** one of the few remaining virgin Irish Oak forests in Ireland. A mildly exerting walk up the main gravel path from the car park and a jaunt down the small left arching path unveils a sweeping view of Carlingford Lough below, the Cooley Mountains beyond, and a huge, anomalous hunk of sandstone called the Cloughmore Stone. Locals swear that the suspicious stone was thrown by the Irish hero Finn McCool (see **Finn McCool,** p. 61) during a fight with a Scottish giant. The giant allegedly responded by tearing a handful of earth out of the ground and hurling it at Finn, who coolly ducked out of the way. The hunk of earth landed in the sea and became the Isle of Man, while the divot filled with water to form Lough Neagh, the UK's largest lake. In an ironic twist of fate, that ancient act of ire has inspired couples to carve their monumental expressions of love onto the rock's side. (Open daily July-Aug. 9am-10pm, Sept.-June 9am-5pm. Parking and admission free. **Camping:** Easter-Oct. £7.40 per tent; £13.50 per caravan.) Aside from its idyllic parks, Rostrevor is known for its annual **Fiddler's Green Festival.** During the last week of July, fans and performers gather to enjoy traditional Irish music, poetry readings, storytelling, and dancing in the streets. (Call tourist information ☎4173 8236; www.fiddlersgreen.co.uk. Tickets ☎4173 9819 or bought locally from Hanna's Newsagent in Rostrevor or Carlin Records in Newry.) As a young girl, President of Ireland and Rostrevor native Mary McAleese tipped half-pints at her father's **Corner House Bar,** 1 Bridge St., the big, shamrock-green storefront at the top of the town's steep main drag. (☎4173 8236. Tu and F trad 10pm. Open daily 11:30am-1:30am.) **The Glenside Inn,** 33-35 Bridge St., at the bottom of the Main St. hill, draws scores to its excellent trad sessions on Sunday evenings, especially during the Fiddler's Green Festival, when it fills with the drunk, the dancing, and those who can't find the exit. (☎4173 9485. Open daily 11:30am-1am.)

ARMAGH (ARD MACHA)

Armagh challenges Downpatrick's claim to the title "City of St. Patrick." In the 5th century, St. Patrick ostensibly based his saintly mission on the hill *Druim Saileach,* strategically close to the nearby Navan Fort, an ancient stronghold for pagan kings. Today, the Church of Ireland's St. Patrick's Cathedral rests where the original church was built in AD 445. On a facing hilltop, St. Patrick's Catholic Cathedral also overlooks town, tracing Ireland's historic divisions into the skyline. In the 19th century, Archbishop Robinson filled Armagh with Georgian architecture, seen today in the observatory, the district council office, and the Robinson Library, which was formerly his palace. Only the streets of Dublin can match such architecture; unsurprisingly, Robinson also had a hand in that city's construction. Under the watch of the two ancient and sacred behemoths, modern Armagh goes about its daily business quietly, enjoys a lively pub scene by night, and turns into a sea of orange on Saturdays when ardent fans cheer on their beloved Gaelic football team.

▐ TRANSPORTATION

Buses: Ulsterbus station (☎3752 2266), Lonsdale Rd. To: **Belfast** (1½hr.; M-F 12 per day, Sa 7 per day, Su 11 per day; £7, children 5-15 £3.50, under 5 free), **Monaghan** (45min.; M-F 11 per day, Sa 5 per day, Su 3 per day; £4.50/€5, children 5-15 £2.30/€2.50), and **Dublin** via **Monaghan** (2¾hr.; M-F 6 per day, Sa 5 per day, Su 2 per day; £11.40, children 5-15 £5.70) or via **Newry** (2-3hr. depending on connection; M-Sa 6 per day, Su 2 per day; £14.15/7.08). **Local buses** to areas like **Markethill** and **Newry** stop along the Mall West. Check the station on College St., the tourist office, or www.trankslink.co.uk for schedules.

Taxis: Eurocabs (☎3751 1900) is the largest 24hr. cab company in Armagh.

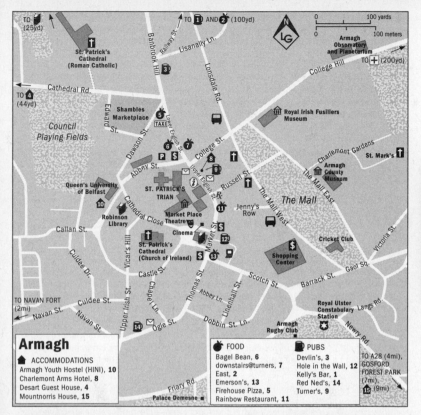

Armagh

▲ ACCOMMODATIONS
Armagh Youth Hostel (HINI), **10**
Charlemont Arms Hotel, **8**
Desart Guest House, **4**
Mountnorris House, **15**

🍴 FOOD
Bagel Bean, **6**
downstairs@turners, **7**
East, **2**
Emerson's, **13**
Firehouse Pizza, **5**
Rainbow Restaurant, **11**

🍺 PUBS
Devlin's, **3**
Hole in the Wall, **12**
Kelly's Bar, **1**
Red Ned's, **14**
Turner's, **9**

TO A28 (4mi),
GOSFORD
FOREST PARK
(7mi),
15 (9mi)

NORTHERN IRELAND

✦ 🛈 ORIENTATION AND PRACTICAL INFORMATION

English Street, Thomas Street, and **Scotch Street** compose Armagh's city center, wrapping around **St. Patrick's Trian.** Just to the east lies the Mall, a former race course that became a grassy park after betting was deemed detrimental to the city's collective morality. Wedged in between Market St. and The Mall is the **Armagh Shopping Center.** To the west, the two cathedrals sit on neighboring hills: the Catholic Cathedral rears its neo-Gothic spires, while a tower represents the Church of Ireland. North of Shambles marketplace is a primarily **Nationalist area;** the city's **Protestant neighborhood** lies south and east of Scotch St. While the city center is generally safe, the area on the Mall West has been the site of the occasional weekend brawl.

Tourist Office: Old Bank Building, 40 English St. (☎3752 1800; www.visitarmagh.com). Booking service 10% deposit plus £2 fee. *Armagh Miniguide* covers the city's sights and attractions. Pious pedestrians can grab a free copy of the *Armagh Pilgrim's Trail,* a walking tour of holy sites. The office also offers a **bureau de change.** Open July-Aug. M-Sa 9am-5pm, Su 1-5pm; Sept.-June M-Sa 9am-5pm, Su 2-5pm.

Banks: First Trust, English St. (☎3752 2025; open M-Tu and Th-F 9:30am-4:30pm, W 10am-4:30pm); **Ulster Bank,** 7 Upper English St. (☎3752 2053); **Northern Bank,** 78 Scotch St. (☎3752 2004). All have 24hr. **ATMs.**

Emergency: ☎999; no coins required. **Police:** Newry Rd. (☎3752 3311).

Pharmacy: J.W. Gray (☎3752 2092), at the corner of Russell and English St. Open M-Sa 9am-6pm. Rotating Su schedule for prescriptions.

Hospital: Armagh Community Clinic, Tower Hill (☎3752 2967), off College Hill.

Internet Access: Armagh City Library, Market St. (☎3752 4072), has **Internet** access for £1.50 per hr. Open M, W, F 9:30am-5:30pm, Tu and Th 9:30am-8pm, Sa 9:30am-5pm. While the Armagh Robinson Library on Abbey St. is public, it does not have Internet access. **Armagh Computer World,** 43 Scotch St. (☎3751 0002), is located inside the Wise Buy and up the stairs; another entrance located around the corner at a direct staircase. Open M-Sa 9am-5:30pm. £1.50 per 30min. Printing 10p per pg.

Post Office: 31 Upper English St. (☎084 5722 3344), through a convenience store. *Poste Restante* mail cools its heels across the street at 46 Upper English St. (☎3752 2079). Avoid lines at 5 Ogle St. office, but only for sending mail. Open M-F 9am-5:30pm, Sa 9am-12:30pm, except Ogle St. W 9am-12:30pm. **Postal Code:** BT6 17AA.

🔓 ACCOMMODATIONS

Travelers not toting tents find refuge at Armagh's in-town hostel and B&Bs outside the city; the more rugged, outdoorsy types camp near **Gosford Forest Park** (p. 550).

Armagh Youth Hostel (HINI), 39 Abbey St. (☎3751 1800), next to Queen's University campus. Huge and squeaky clean, if a little sterile, with superb kitchen, TV room, and lounge. Excellent security. Wheelchair-accessible. Wash and dry £1.50 each. Reception 8-11am and 5-11pm. Check-in 5-9pm. Dorms £12.50; singles £14. 4-bed dorm June-Aug. £15, Sept.-May £14; 2-bed dorm £16/15. Under 18 £2 discount. ❷

Desart Guest House, 99 Cathedral Rd. (☎3752 2387), a 7min. walk from the city center and a right onto Desart Ln. Formidable mansion so long as the embalmed birds in the hall don't give you Norman Bates nightmares. A bastion of character among legions of "quaint" B&Bs. £25 per person, children free. ❸

Mountnorris House, 41 Main St., Markethill (☎3750 7543), about 9 mi. from Armagh near Gosford Forest. Situated in a calm 1-street village with a post office, a pub, and more cows than people. Floral-patterned rooms and huge baths. If no one answers when you knock, call the phone number on the door. Singles £27; doubles £44. ❸

Charlemont Arms Hotel, 57-65 Upper English St. (☎3752 2028; www.charlemontarmshotel.com), across from tourist office. Slightly stodgy family-run hotel with 30 large rooms with TV, tea/coffee facilities, and bath. Attached bar **Turner's** and restaurant **downstairs@turners** (see **Food,** p. 546) ensure guests don't go to bed hungry (or sober). Includes full Irish breakfast. Singles £50; doubles £80; twin £85. ❺

🍴 FOOD

Finding affordable grub in Armagh is a challenge. The best bet is to get groceries at **Sainsbury's** in the Mall Shopping Centre, Mall West (☎3751 1050; open M-W and Sa 8:30am-8pm, Th-F 8:30am-9pm), or at **Emerson's,** Scotch St. (☎3752 2846; open M-F 8am-8pm, Th-F 8am-9:30pm, Sa 8am-6pm). Some pubs also serve cheap meals.

Bagel Bean, 60 Lower English St. (☎3751 5251). Tiny storefront has big poster of New York City skyline. Creative daily specials, like the "chicken tikka" bagel sandwich; in all, dozens of daily melts and lunch options, all around £2.50-3. Smoothies and milkshakes £2. Open M-Sa 7:30am-5pm, Su 9am-1pm. ❶

Firehouse Pizza, 70 Upper English St. (☎3751 8800). Small Philly-born pizzeria produces the famous cheesesteaks of its hometown. Along with Bagel Bean, one of 2 good, cheap meals in town: pizzas £3.25-7.50 (8-16 in.), burgers £2-3.50. Late hours F-Sa draw the post-pub crowd. Open M, W-Th, Su 5-11pm, F-Sa 5pm-3am. ❶

Rainbow Restaurant, 13 Lower English St. (☎3752 5391). Cafeteria-style lunches and all-day breakfast make this a popular student hangout. Full bar and air conditioning. Sa dinner with bistro menu starts at 10pm. Lunch from £4. Open M-F 9am-5:30pm, Sa 9am-9pm, Su 6:30-9:30pm. ❷

downstairs@turners (☎3752 2719), under Turner's bar, attached to Charlemont Arms Hotel. Even the subterranean location can't hide Armagh's best, most popular Asian fusion style restaurant. Manager recommends the fish (salmon £14); entrees £9-17. Meal deal Th-Sa before 7:30pm offers either 2 courses and a bottle of wine for 2 people or 3 courses for £17 per person. Call ahead for dinner F-Sa. Lunch Tu-Su noon-3pm; dinner Th-Sa 6-9:30pm. MC/V, and AmEx if you ask politely. ❸

East, 143-147 Railway St. (☎3752 8288), above Kelly's Bar; formerly known as **Zen.** 3-course lunch special (M-F noon-1:45pm; £5) and early bird dinner (M-Th 5-7pm; £8.50 for 2 courses) are a blessing for the budget-conscious. Book ahead for Sa dinner. Open M-Th noon-1:45pm and 5-11:30pm, F noon-1:45pm and 5pm-12:30am, Sa 5pm-12:30am, Su 5-11:30pm. AmEx/MC/V. ❸

🔋 PUBS

As in almost any part of Northern Ireland, Armagh's nightlife is segregated along sectarian lines. Visitors should orient themselves with the help of locals (such as hostel workers) before going out on the town. The majority of action occurs on weekends, and pubs can be quiet during the working week.

Red Ned's, 27 Ogle St. (☎3752 2249), follow English St. to Market St. and Thomas St. Formerly named "O'Neill's" after its founder Edward O'Neill, the 3-generation-old pseudonym still recalls his hair color. Business is a family affair; everyone is next-of-kin every other W for trad (winter only, starts 9 or 10pm) and Gaelic football matches. Horse races, football, and rugby on several TVs. Varied promotional nights. 18+. Open M-Sa 11:30am-11:30pm (after 11:30 customers can often stay until 1am but the doors are closed), Su noon-midnight.

Kelly's Bar, 147 Railway St. (☎3752 2103), also known as **Platform 1.** Cluttered bar attracts Armagh's 18-30 crowd. Aspiring crooners grab the mic for karaoke Th and Su, dancers cut a rug F-Sa to live bands or discos, and pool sharks troll the table looking for chum. Pool £0.50. Open M-Sa 11:30am-1am, Su noon-12:30am.

Devlin's, 23 Lower English St. (☎3752 3865). A mixed crowd of all ages comes to watch the horse races from the comfortable lounge-style seating. Tons of football jerseys on the walls. Open M-F and Su 11:30am-11:30pm, Sa 11:30am-1am.

Hole in the Wall, 9 Market St. (☎3752 3515). Locals gather for billiards and arcade games over pints. Beer garden for smokers. Open M-Sa 11:30am-11:30pm.

Turner's, 56-57 Upper English St. (☎3752 2028), attached to Charlemont Arms Hotel. Mixed crowd enjoys pints in this well-worn hotel bar. Early-bird menu from downstairs 6:30-7:30pm. Rustle up pub grub daily noon-3pm or 5:30-8:30pm. 18+. Trad Sa 10pm-12:30am. Open M-Th and Su 11:30am-11pm, F-Sa 11:30am-1am.

👁 SIGHTS

THE ROMAN CATHOLIC CATHEDRAL OF ST. PATRICK. To the north on Cathedral Rd. sits the 1873 Roman Catholic **Cathedral of St. Patrick.** The imposing twin spires and exquisite mosaic interior contrast with the shiny granite sanctuary. (☎3752 2802; www.armagharchdiocese.org. Open daily until dusk. Free.)

NORTHERN IRELAND

THE CHURCH OF IRELAND CATHEDRAL OF ST. PATRICK. South of the city is the Protestant cathedral. Authorities claim that the 13th-century church rests upon the site where St. Patrick founded his stone church in AD 445. Though it has been restored numerous times, the cathedral contains ancient relics and is the final resting place of great 10th-century Irish King Brian Ború. (☎3752 3142; www.stpatrickscathedralarmagh.org. Open Apr.-Oct. daily 10am-5pm; Nov.-Mar. daily 10am-4pm. Tours June-Aug. M-Sa 11:30am and 2:30pm by arrangement with Dean. Suggested donation £2.)

ST. PATRICK'S TRIAN. In the center of town, ⊠St. Patrick's Trian shares a building with the tourist office. Most exhibits emphasize St. Patrick's role in Armagh, although his link to the town is historically dubious. The **Armagh Story** is a walk-through display and audio-visual presentation where plaster Vikings, priests, and pagan warriors relate the lengthy history of the town. **Patrick's Testament** introduces the curious to the patron saint's writings, most pertinently to the *Book of Armagh*, also known as *The Confessions of St. Patrick*. A smaller display pays homage to Jonathan Swift's **Land of Lilliput.** Following the adventures described in the first part of *Gulliver's Travels*, the exhibit culminates with a gigantic Gulliver narrating his own tale. (☎3752 1801; www.visit-armagh.com. Open M-Sa 10am-5pm, Su 2-5pm. £4.50, students and seniors £3.50, children £2.75, families £11.)

ARMAGH OBSERVATORY. Up College Hill, north of the Mall, is the **Armagh Observatory,** founded and designed in 1790 by Archbishop Robinson, architect of Armagh's and Dublin's Georgian buildings. The star-struck observe a modern weather station and an 1885 refractory telescope. Ireland's largest public telescope is free to families and small groups during nights from October to April. (☎3752 2928. By appointment only, although the grounds are open M-F 9:30am-4:30pm.) More celestial wonders await in the nearby **Planetarium,** which displays a few centimeters of Mars. From the Observatory, visitors can wander into the outdoor **Astropark,** which scales the entire solar system down to human level. Walk up the "Hill of Infinity," where every 10 m represents a distance 10 times farther on the cosmic level. (☎3752 3689; www.armaghplanet.com. Call ahead for tours and prices.)

PALACE DEMESNE. Palace Demesne (dah-MAIN) sprawls south of the town center. The palace, chapel, and stables were another of the Archbishop of Armagh's efforts to rebuild the city. The County Council now occupies the main building, relegating the public to the **Palace Stables Heritage Centre,** where a multimedia show presents "A Day in the Life" of the closed palace; in the 3-D world, Georgian characters enact traditional tasks. A **Franciscan Friary** occupies a peaceful plot near the entrance to the grounds. (☎3752 9629; www.visit-armagh.com. Open June-Aug. M-Sa 10am-5pm, Su noon-5pm; Apr.-May, and Sept. Sa 10am-5pm, Su noon-5pm. £4.75, children £3, seniors £3.75, families £14; group discounts available.)

OTHER SIGHTS. Visitors can peek at a first edition of **Gulliver's Travels**—covered with Swift's own scrawled comments—and a facsimile of the "Book of Armagh" at the **Armagh Public Library (Robinson Library);** tours available for £2. (43 Abbey St. ☎3752 3142; www.armaghrobinsonlibrary.org. Wheelchair-accessible. Open M-F 10am-1pm and 2-4pm; other times available by appointment. Access to rare books by appointment.) **Cardinal Thomas O'Fiaich Memorial Library and Archive** contains materials pertaining to Irish diaspora, history, language, and sport based on the Cardinal's collection. (15 Moy Rd. ☎3752 2981; www.ofiaich.ie. Open M-F 9:30am-5pm. Following the Moy Rd., follow the signs for the Cathedral; the library is next door.) Computerized genealogical resources focusing on Co. Armagh unite families with their ancestors at the **Armagh Ancestry.** (38A English St. ☎3752 1802; ancestry@acdc.btinternet.com. Call ahead. Search fees based on extent of request; initial consultation £15.) Bargain-hunters fill the walled **Shambles Marketplace.** Regular car-boot sales dredge up old records, Jackie Collins bestsellers, and other "antiques." A farmers market makes an irregular appearance. (At the *foot of the hill where Cathedral Rd., Dawson St., and English St. meet. ☎3752 8192. Open Tu, F, and alternating Sa 9am to mid-afternoon.)* The **Armagh County Museum,** on the east side of the Mall, displays a seemingly random assortment of 18th-century objects—old wedding dresses, photographs, stuffed birds, folk crafts, a giant earthworm preserved in a jar, and militia uniforms. *(☎3752 3070. Wheelchair-accessible. Open M-F 10am-5pm, Sa 10am-1pm and 2-5pm. Free.)* A bit farther down the Mall East at the corner of College Hill, the **Royal Irish Fusiliers Museum** charts the history of the famous regiment—originally nicknamed the "Eagle-Takers" after becoming the first unit to capture one of Napoleon's Imperial Eagle Standards in 1811—with a collection of uniforms, weaponry, and artifacts. *(☎3752 2911. Open M-F 10am-12:30pm and 1:30-4pm. Individuals free; groups £1 per person.)*

ENTERTAINMENT

Armagh's cultural offerings center around the white-tiled **Market Place Theatre and Arts Centre,** Market Sq., which offers a varied program of dance, music, theater, and visual arts. The theater also organizes the **Tara Music and Arts Festival** in August. (☎3752 1821; www.marketplacearmagh.com. Open M-Sa 9am-4:30pm, performance nights 9am-8pm.) Around the first week of June, Armagh holds the annual **Comhaltas Ceoltori Traditional Music Festival** (for info call Liz Watson ☎3752 5353). In mid-June, the Ulster **Road Bowls Finals** (see **Sports and Recreation,** p. 73) are held on 10 designated roads throughout the county, while August ushers in the All-Ireland Finals. (for info call Sammy Gillespie ☎3752 5622). May's **Apple Blossom Festival** brings craft shows to town. (For info call tourist information ☎3752 1800). On March 17, **St. Patrick's Day** inspires revelers to celebrate Big Paddy. **Céilí** dancing at St. Patrick's Parochial Hall on Cathedral Rd. demonstrates the Irish version of a hoe-down. (Th 9-10pm. Contact Brendan Kirk or Seamus McDonagh ☎3752 6088.) **Set dancing** also welcomes visitors on Monday nights at the **Pearse Og Social Club** on Dalton Rd. (Contact Pat Prunty ☎3755 18414.)

OUTDOOR ACTIVITIES

The area surrounding Armagh contains tons of outdoors activities. **Angling** is popular; one-day permits are available from GI Stores (☎3752 2335), including the one on Dobbin St. **Loughgall County Park** promises a 37-acre fishery with daily and yearly permits available. (☎3889 2900; www.visitarmagh.com. Daily permits £3.20, children £2.15; annual £27/16. Open M-F 9am-10pm, Sa 7am-10pm, Su 7:30am-10pm. Parking £2 per car.) For more horsepower, head to **Moy Riding School,** 131 Derryclaw Ln., where an equine escort awaits. The school presents **show jumping** on Friday nights. Take A29 toward Dungannon, pass through Carlemark, and take the next right for Portadown. Take the first left, and then another left at the T intersection; the school is about two miles on the right, opposite the Agory. (☎8778 4440. £8 per hr.) **Gosford Karting** satisfies the fast and furious. Take A28 toward Dinnahorra; the track will be about ten miles on your left. (☎3755 1248; www.gosfordkarting.co.uk. 15/30min. practice sessions £10/20; grand prix tournaments £20-30 depending on group size.)

DAYTRIPS FROM ARMAGH

NAVAN FORT. On the outskirts of Armagh, the mysterious Navan Fort, also called *Emain Macha* (AHM-win ma ka), was the seat of the Kings of Ulster for 800 years. Today, all that remains is an unusually large mound of earth. Surveying the surrounding land from its high vantage point, visitors can easily see the strategic power it would have granted its occupants, once the symbolic center of religious, political, and cultural ceremony in the province. In 94 BC, a huge wooden structure 40 yd. in diameter was constructed where the mound now stands; it was filled with stones, burnt to the ground in a religious rite, and covered with soil. Fairy Queen Macha is said to have founded the fort, although it is also associated with St. Patrick, who probably chose *Ard Macha* as a Christian center because of its proximity to this pagan stronghold. Adding to the site's mysterious allure is the belief that druids used the fort as a halfway structure between man and the sacred cosmos; the giant post in the center may have been an *axis mundi*, which marks the center of the world and links the underworld, surface, and sky. Walk to the fort from the nearby Navan Centre, recently reopened after a fire and a lack of funding nearly shut it down. The Centre explores the "Vanished World" of lost myths, the "Real World" of regional archaeology, and the "Other World" of legends surrounding the ancient Ulster kings. A cafe and gift shop are also available. *(Killylea Rd. A28, 2 mi. west of Armagh; there is plenty of signage. www.visitarmagh.com. While the Centre is only open for tours M-Sa 10am-5pm, Su 2-5pm, the Fort itself is always freely available to anyone who walks up to it. Tour £4.75; includes both guided and self-guided portions.)*

LOUGH NEAGH AND OXFORD ISLAND. Birdwatching and various aquatic activities are the principle amusements in the towns around Lough Neagh, a lake some believe was created supernaturally (p. 543). The lough's **Kinnego Marina** offers boat trips aboard the *Master Mc'Gra.* (☎ 3832 7573. Trips Apr.-Oct. Sa-Su £4, children/seniors £2.) Some say that a Scottish giant once scooped a prime heap of Ulster earth out of the ground to hurl at Irish Giant Finn McCool (p. 61), who nimbly sidestepped the massive projectile. The heap of earth landed in the Irish sea, creating the Isle of Man, while the massive divot filled with water to form Lough Neagh, the UK's largest lake. The **Lough Neagh Discovery Centre,** on the **Oxford Island National Nature Reserve** in **Craigavon,** has acres of wooded parkland ready for exploration. Audiovisual displays inside the center detail the lake's ecosystem and wildlife. For children, educational programs are available as well. And recently, the Reserve hired two resident artists, now living in the Reserve's **Art Space;** inquire at the Discovery Centre about visiting. There are also cycle paths throughout the Reserve. *(Route A3 runs northeast from Armagh to loughside Craigavon and Lurgan. Follow the signs for the marina and the Discovery Center; once you turn off of A3, the Discovery Centre is all the way at the end. ☎ 3832 2205; www.oxfordisland.com. Open Sept.-Easter M-F 9am-5pm, Sa 10am-5pm, Su 10am-5pm; Easter-June M-F 9am-5pm, Sa 10am-5pm, Su 10am-6pm; July-Aug. M-F 9am-6pm, Sa-Su 10am-6pm. Last admission 1hr. before closing. Free, audio-visual displays £1.60.)* **Kinnego Caravan Park,** on the Kinnego Marina in Lurgan, hosts hundreds of species of wild campers. *(☎ 3832 7573. Electricity £2. £10 per tent, £13 per caravan.)*

GOSFORD FOREST PARK. The Gosford Forest Park, seven miles southeast of Armagh, offers a respite from the city streets with 590 acres of woodland and open fields. Four well-marked walking trails ranging from one to four miles take in the park's sights, as does one new four-mile bike trail. The short and gentle **Castle Trail** (1¼ mi.) meanders to a handsome walled garden, the battlements of Gosford Castle, and the chair in which Jonathan Swift is rumored to have written some of his verses. The park also harbors a number of rare breeds of farm animals, along with campers who make use of the wooded **campsites.** Ten miles north of Armagh on the A29 (the Moy road) lies **The Agory,** 144 Derryclaw road, Moy. Built in 1824, this small estate house remains just as it was left, complete with a still-functional cabinet barrel organ built by James Bishop, which is considered one of the most significant of its kind. Original gas fixtures, central stove heating, and a Victorian laundry room illustrate the hardships of 19th-century life. *(Agory: ☎ 8778 4753; www.nationaltrust.org. Wheelchair-accessible. Open Mar.-May and Sept. to mid-Oct. Sa-Su 1-6pm; June-Aug. daily 1-6pm. £2.50 per car, grounds and house £6.50, children £2.20, families £11. Park: Take A28 for about 7 mi. or take the #40 bus to Markethill. Or from M1, take junction*

13 and follow the signs for about 3 mi. ☎3755 1277 or 3755 2169. Open daily 8am-sunset. Pedestrians £1.50, children £0.50; or admission and parking, £4 per car. Youth site £2.50 per tent; May-June and Sept. £9.50 per site; July-Aug. tent or caravan £11.50, electricity £1 extra.)

ANTRIM AND DERRY

The A2 coastal road connects the scenic attractions of Counties Antrim and Derry, providing a fantastic and easily accessible journey for visitors. North of Belfast, industrial Larne gives way to lovely seaside villages. The breathtaking scenery of the nine Glens of Antrim sweeps visitors north toward the Giant's Causeway, which spills its geological honeycomb into the ocean off the northern coast. This mid-section of the coast road is a cyclist's paradise. Seaside novelties replace natural wonders with the carnival lights of Portrush and Portstewart, and the road finally terminates at Derry/Londonderry, the North's second-largest city.

LARNE (LATHARNA)

Although it claims royal roots—Prince Lathar lent his name to the original settlement of Latharna—today's Larne is a working man's town whose interest to travelers is limited to its ferries to and from Scotland, Britain, and France. **P&O Ferries** (☎087 0242 4777; www.poirishsea.com) operates boats from **Larne** to **Cairnryan, Scotland** (1¾hr.; M-Sa 7 or 8 per day, Su 5 per day; July-Aug. from £59 with car, Sept.-June from £49; pedestrians £20, extra passengers £12, children £5) and **Troon, Scotland** (2hr., Apr.-Sept. 7:15am and 5:30pm, same prices). Ferries leave up to 15 minutes early due to tides, so call ahead; best fares are available online well in advance. **Stena Line** (☎087 0520 4204) sends ferries to **Fleetwood, England** (8hr.; 2 per day, exact times depend on the tide and often vary greatly, so call at least a day ahead; car and driver £68-118, additional adults £20, children 4-15 £10, under 4 free). The **train station** is adjacent to a roundabout, down the street from the tourist office on Narrow Gauge Rd. (☎9066 6630; www.translink.co.uk. Open M-F and Su 6:50am-5pm, Sa 8:30am-5:20pm.) Trains chug into Central Station in **Belfast** to **Larne Town** and **Larne Harbour**, 15min. from town. (50min.; M-F 20 per day, Sa 17 per day, Su 6 per day; £5), and run from Larne to **Belfast** (same price as Belfast to Larne), **Coleraine** (£10), and **Derry** (£10). Various special deals are available seasonally; for example, on Sundays in summer unlimited travel is £5 per day. The **bus station** is south of town, on the other side of the A8 overpass. (☎2827 2345. Open M-F 9am-5:15pm.) **Buses** depart from Station Rd. for Laganside Station in **Belfast** (1½hr., express 50min.; M-F at least every hr. 7am-4pm, Sa 6 per day, Su 1pm and 4pm; £4, return £7.20, discount for same-day return) and stops along the coast. **T. T. Cabs** (☎077 9630 7117) is a local **taxi** service.

Larne is not a town where people linger. If you're coming from central or heading south by car, the **Ford Farm Hostel ❶**, 8 Low Rd. on Islandmagee, is an ideal choice. Islandmagee is a misnomer; it's a peninsula you turn onto from A2 north of Larne. Once on the peninsula, take the first left and the hostel will be signposted. (☎9335 3204. Free laundry. 2-bed dorms £10, with linens £12.) Instead of crashing at the harbor near the ferry, head to the B&Bs lining **Glenarm** and **Curran Road**, which spring from Main St. as it nears the terminal. **Inverbann ❷**, 7 Glenarm Rd., offers satellite TV and two more ensuite rooms. (☎2827 2524. Singles £30; doubles £50.) **Curran Caravan Park ❶**, 131 Curran Rd., between the harbor and town, is a congested campground. (☎2827 5505. Tents £12.) Less industrial sites are also available 2½ miles north of town in the **Carnfunnock Country Park ❶**. (☎2827 0541. Open Mar.-Nov. Tents M-Th £7-14, F-Sa £7.50-15; July and Aug. £7.50-15/8-16. Caravans £12.50-15/13-16.) Or opt for the **Curran Court Hotel ❷**, 84

THE BIG SPLURGE

COASTEERING ANTRIM

You're walking along a rocky, treacherous coastline, and you come to a wide, turbulent river in your way. You know how the song goes: "can't go over it, can't go under it." While the reasonable rambler would try to find a safer passage, the coasteerer finishes the verse properly: "can't go around it, gotta go through it!"

Coasteering, a sport popular in coastal regions such as the Antrim Coast and the southern coast of England, consists of traversing a rocky coastline by any means necessary. This can include, but is certainly not limited to: walking anywhere, climbing up rocks and scrambling along cliffs, jumping and diving into various pools of water or even the sea, and swimming right through rapids. It's an adventure sport not for the faint of heart.

Although it sounds dangerous, and probably is quite dangerous no matter how you swing it, coasteering can be responsibly done with a professional guide and proper equipment. In the Glens of Antrim area, contact the Ardclinis Outdoor Adventure Centre, which runs coasteering trips for groups of six or more from April through October. Rates are generally £45 per person, which includes equipment and a guide.

Ardclinis Outdoor Adventure Centre (028 2177 1370; www.ardclinis.com.). Office located in back of 11 High St., Cushendall, Co. Antrim.

Curran Rd. (☎2827 5505. Entrees £11.50-17.50. Dinner served M-Sa 5:30-7pm, Su 5-8:30pm. Singles £30, with bath £45; doubles £50/60.) The giant **Co-op Superstore** is on Station Rd. next to the bus station. (☎2826 0737. Open M-W 8am-9pm, Th-F 8am-10pm, Sa 8am-8pm, Su 1-6pm.) For fresh fruit, vegetables, fish, or knock-off designer gear, hit the **farmer's market** in the Market Yard across the street from the bus station (W 8am-noon). Larne's main street is lined with cheap sandwich shops. Popular with the younger crowd, **Caffe Spice ❶**, 7 Dunluce St., serves *panini* and wraps (£4-5) with ingredients like roasted peppers and brie. (☎2826 9633. Open M-Th 10am-5pm, F-Sa 10am-10pm.) **Chekker's Wine Bar ❷**, 33 Lower Cross St., serves a broad selection of bistro food as well as basic burgers and fish and chips in a leisurely atmosphere. A £2 breakfast special (daily 9am-noon) is a blessing for the ferry-bound. (☎2827 5305. Lunches £5-6; entrees £6-10. Kitchen open daily noon-9pm.) Larne's nightlife heats up at **The Kiln,** half a mile out of town on Glenarm Rd. The restaurant serves up various meal deals (M-W 5-9pm 2-for-1 entrees; most entrees £12-15) during dinner. (F DJ, Sa-Su live band, Th students' night. Kitchen open noon-9pm. Bar open M-W noon-11pm, Th-Sa noon-1am, Su noon-midnight.) During the entire month of June, the **Larne Alive Festival** brings art, dance, crafts, and music to the town (contact the tourist office for specific events ☎2826 0088).

To reach the town center from the harbor, take the first right outside the ferry port. As the road curves left, it becomes **Curran Road** and then **Main Street.** The rest of the town is a maze of side streets, so make sure to grab a free map from the tourist office. It's best to take a cab in the evening, as the route passes through a fairly rough neighborhood. The **tourist office,** Narrow Gauge Rd., books accommodations for £2 plus a 10% commission, offers a free town map and points visitors up the coastline. (☎2826 0088; www.larne.gov.uk. Open Easter-Sept. M-Sa 9am-5pm; Oct.-Easter M-F 9am-5pm.) **Northern Bank,** 19 Main St. (☎2827 6311; open M 9:30am-5pm, Tu-F 10am-3:30pm, Sa 9:30am-12:30pm) and **Bank of Ireland,** 51 Main St. (open M-F 9:30am-4:30pm; open W 10am), have 24hr. **ATMs. The library,** 36 Pound St., at the top of High St., has **Internet** access. (☎2827 7047. £1.50 per 30min., members free. Open M and Th 10am-8pm, Tu-W and F 10am-5:30pm, Sa 10am-5pm.) **Boots Pharmacy,** 38 Main St., has your meds. (☎2827 4701. Open M-Sa 9am-5:30pm.) The **post office** is at 98 Main St. inside the Booknote Newsagency. (☎2826 0489. Open M-F 9am-5:30pm, Sa 9am-12:30pm). A 24hr. **ATM** is also outside the store. A second post office is located inside the Co-op. **Postal Code:** BT40.

GLENS OF ANTRIM

During the Ice Age, glaciers plowed through the coastline northeast of Antrim, leaving nine deep scars in the mountains. Over the years, water collected in these valleys, nourishing trees, ferns, and other flora not usually found in Ireland. The A2 coastal road connects the mouths of these glens and provides entry to roads inland. Still relatively unspoiled and much less touristed than the northern coast, the nine glens are rich in their own lore and distinct character. While the road offers stunning coastal vistas, the mountains and waterfalls are best explored on daytrips inland from the coastal villages of Glenarm, Waterfoot, and Cushendall.

Most visitors travel the glens by car, but two **Ulsterbus** routes serve the area year-round (Belfast ☎9032 0011; Larne ☎2827 2345). Bus #150 runs between **Ballymena** and **Cushendun** (M-F 5 per day, Sa 4 per day; £4.50) with intermediate stops at **Waterfoot** and **Cushendall** (M-F 4 per day, Sa 3 per day; £5.50). The **Antrim Coaster** (#252) runs year-round, stopping at every town on the road from **Belfast** to **Coleraine** (M-F and Su 2 per day, one of which runs only Belfast to Larne; £4 to Larne and £9 to Belfast). **Cycling** the glens is fabulous. The **Ardclinis Activity Centre** in Cushendall **rents bikes** (p. 554). The coastal road from Ballygally to Cushendun is both scenic and relatively flat. Once the road passes Cushendun, however, it becomes hilly enough to make even motorists groan. Crossroads are reportedly the best places to find a lift, though *Let's Go* never recommends hitchhiking.

GLENARIFF

Known as the "Queen of the Glens," Glenariff is crowned by the peak of Lurigethan. Access the glen through the village of **Waterfoot,** nine miles up the coast from Glenarm. Thackeray dubbed this area "Switzerland in miniature" because of the steep, rugged landscape. Keeping watch over Waterfoot is **Red Castle,** atop **red arch,** a lookout from which Irishmen scouted for marauding Englishmen. It now marks the beginning of the Cushendall natural conservation area. A43 toward Ballymena, past Waterfoot, leads to the large **Glenariff Forest Park,** where the natural delights of the glen lie in wait. The **bus** (M-Sa 3-5 per day) between Cushendun and Ballymena (#150) stops at the official park entrance. (☎2175 8769 or 2177 1796. Car park open daily 10am-8pm; park always open. £4 per car, £1.50 per pedestrian, children 50p.) Inside the park, marked trails range in length from ½ mi. to 5 mi. The awesome three-mile ◪**Waterfall Trail,** marked by blue triangles, follows the cascading, fern-lined Glenariff River from the park entrance to the Manor Lodge. The entrance to the **Moyle Way,** a 17 mi. hike from Glenariff to Ballycastle, is directly across from the park entrance. All the walks begin and end at the car park and the **Glenariff Cafe ❷.** This bay-windowed restaurant has fresh snacks (sandwiches £4-6), high tea (£10), full meals (£6-11), and a lovely view. The attached shop has **free maps** of the park's trails. (☎2175 8769. Open daily 10am-5pm.) An **exhibition** space displays local flora and fauna, as well as information on rocks, mining, farming, and biodiversity.

Those who wish to commune with beautiful Glenariff for longer than an afternoon lodge in and around Waterfoot. **Dieskirt Farm B&B ❷,** 104 Glen Rd., is on a working farm a few hundred yards from the waterfalls. Make the hike to find reasonably priced luxury, a lovable donkey, and summer work for inexperienced farm hands. As a bonus, the B&B lies at the waterfall end of the glorious waterfall trail, and guests enjoy free access to the park. (☎2177 1308 or 078 0134 6792; book online at www.dieskirtfarm.co.uk. Singles £35; doubles £46. **Camping** free, with shower and breakfast £5. MC/V.) To find **Lurig View B&B ❷,** 38 Glen Rd., hang a left onto Glen Rd. before Waterfoot and go about 2½ mi. The country house provides colorful beds, ensuite rooms, and tasty breakfasts. (☎2177 1618. Singles £32; doubles £50. MC/V.) Pitch a tent at **Glenariff Forest Park Camping ❶,** 98 Glenariff Rd., across the street from the park entrance. There's no office; just pay when the ranger visits in the morning or the evening. Guests enjoy free park access as a bonus. (☎ 2175 8232. Electricity £1.50. Tents £11.) Before trekking into the wilderness, buy provisions at **Kearney's Costcutter,** 21 Main St. (☎ 2177 1213. Open daily July-Aug. 9am-10pm, Sept.-June 9am-9pm.) There is just one eatery in Waterfoot, the Chinese restaurant **Rainbow Kitchen** ❶, 32 Main St. Try the £3.80 mixed appetizer dish called the "special snack." (☎ 2177 1700. Open daily 4:30pm-midnight). The blue and yellow **The Saffron Bar,** 4-6 Main St., is a mellow pub where locals gather to watch, talk about, and get ready for hurling. **Cellar Bar,** downstairs, has live music ranging from various live acts Friday and Saturday to Sunday "Barryoke" (disco plus karaoke) and occasional trad sessions. (☎ 2177 2906. Saffron open daily 11:30am-1am. Cellar open F-Sa 9pm-1am.) The nautically themed **Mariners' Bar,** 7 Main St., hosts a variety of live music on Saturday nights, with trad sessions during the summer. (☎ 2177 1330. F quiz night. Open daily 11:30am-1am.)

CUSHENDALL (BUN ABHANN DALLA)

Cushendall is nicknamed the capital of the Glens, thanks to its natural wonders. The four streets in the town center house a variety of goods, services, and pubs unavailable anywhere else in the region. The town's proximity to Glenaan, Glenariff, Glenballyeomon, Glencorp, and Glendun reinforce its importance as a commercial center. Unfortunately, the closing of its hostel means that budget travelers are diverted to the camping barn outside of town.

■⁊ **TRANSPORTATION AND PRACTICAL INFORMATION. Ulsterbus** (☎ 9033 3000) stops at the Mill St. tourist office where current bus times are posted. Bus #162 has limited service from **Belfast** (£6.50) via **Larne** and **Cushendall** (£7), then north to **Cushendun** (M-F 3 per day, the first of which doesn't go up to Cushendun). Bus #252 (a.k.a. the **Antrim Coaster**) goes coastal from **Belfast** to **Coleraine,** stopping in Cushendall and most everywhere else. (M-F and Su 1 per day between Belfast and Coleraine £9, 1 per day between Belfast and Larne £4.) Bus #150, from **Belfast** via **Ballymena,** stops in **Glenariff** (a.k.a. Waterfoot; M-F 5 per day, Sa 3 per day; £4.50). **Ardclinis Activity Centre,** in back of the house at 11 High St., **rents bikes** and provides advice and equipment for hill-walking, canoeing, cycling, rafting, and other outdoor pursuits. They also lead "coasteering" trips which involve jumping, climbing, swimming, and negotiating the coastline by any means necessary. (☎ 2177 1340; www.ardclinis.com. Mountain bikes £10 per day; deposit £50. Wetsuits £5 per day. Coasteering from £180 for trips of around 10 people.)

The busiest section of Cushendall is its crossroads. From the center of town, **Mill Street** turns into **Chapel Road** and heads northwest toward Ballycastle; **Shore Road** extends south toward Glenarm and Larne. On the north side of town, **High Street** leads uphill from **Bridge Road,** a section of the **Coast Road** (an extension of the A2) that continues toward the sea at Waterfoot. The **tourist office** hands out info at 25 Mill St., near the bus stop at the northern (Cushendun) end of town. (☎ 2177 1180. Open mid-June to mid-Sept. M-F 10am-5pm, Sa 10am-1pm; Oct.-May Tu-Su 10am-1pm.) The **library** across from the tourist office offers **Internet** access for £1.50 per 30min. (☎ 2177 1297. Open Tu 2-8pm, Th and Sa 10am-1pm and 2-5pm). **Cushendall Development Office,** behind the tourist office, has Internet access and info on many local events. (☎ 2177 1378. £2 per ½hr., £3.50 per hr.; students and seniors £1.50/2.50. Open M-Th 9am-1pm and 2-5pm, F 9am-1pm and 2-3pm, although Fridays often don't recover from the lunch break.) **O'Neill's,** 25 Mill St., sells fishing and hiking gear. (☎ 2177 2009. July-Aug. M-Sa 9:30am-6pm, Su 12:30-4pm; Sept.-June M-Sa 9:30am-6pm, Tu close at 1pm).

Northern Bank, 5 Shore Rd., has a 24hr. ATM. (☎2177 1243. Open M 9:30am-12:30pm and 1:30-5pm, Tu-F 10am-12:30pm and 1:30-3:30pm.) **Numark Pharmacist** is on 8 Mill St. (☎2177 1523. Open M-Sa 9am-6pm.) The **post office** is inside the Spar Market, on Coast Rd. (☎2177 1201. Open M and W-F 9am-1pm and 2-5pm, Tu and Sa 9am-12:30pm.) **Postal Code:** BT44.

ACCOMMODATIONS. Ballyeamon Camping Barn

❶, six miles south of town on B14 at 127 Ballyeamon Rd., is Cushendall's last bastion of budget travel. The barn has views of Glenariff Forest Park, and owner Liz is a professional storyteller happy to regale visitors with her repertoire of ghost stories and fairy tales. It's far from town but near the Moyle Way and well worth the trip. The Cushendall-Cargan bus will stop across the field. (☎2175 8451 or 2175 8699; www.taleteam.demon.co.uk. Internet access £1 per 30min. Dorms £10. Call for pickup.) A bevy of B&Bs surround Cushendall, but the majority are located just south of town. Overlooking the sea and surrounded by grazing cows, **Glendale ❷**, 46 Coast Rd., has huge rooms and colorful company. Tea, coffee, candy, and biscuits are in each room. (☎2177 1495. Internet access available. Singles £25; doubles £40. MC/V.) **Mountain View ❷**, 1 Kilnadore Rd., a few minutes walk out of town toward Glenariff and a right onto Kilnadore just after the police station, has four smallish but comfortable rooms with bath. (☎2177 1246. Singles £25; doubles £40.) The **Central B&B ❷**, right in the middle of town at 7 Bridge St., is your most convenient choice. (☎2177 1730. All rooms with bath. Singles £25; doubles £50.) The town's caravan parks aren't particularly suited to tents, but campers in need can find a bit of earth. Strong winds can make camping rugged at **Cushendall Caravan Park ❶**, 62 Coast Rd. (☎2177 1699. Free showers. Laundry £1.50. 2-person tent £8.30; family tent £12.40; caravans £16.55 with electricity.)

FOOD AND PUBS. Spar, 2 Coast Rd., past

Bridge Rd., sells groceries. (☎2177 1763. Open daily 7am-10pm.) **Arthur's ❶**, 6 Shore Rd., is a family-run cafe that serves simple, fresh sandwiches and full breakfasts from £2.75. (☎2177 1627. *Panini* £3.85-4.45. Open daily 9am-5pm.) Renowned throughout the Glens for its big portions of delicious fish and meat dishes (£5.30-8), **Harry's Restaurant ❸**, 10-12 Mill St., serves upscale pub grub (£4-8) by day and big dinners (entrees £8-13) by night. (☎2177 2022. Kitchen open daily noon-9:30pm; dinner served 6-9:30pm.) One of the Isle's best pubs for Irish music, **Joe McCollam's (Johnny Joe's)**, 23 Mill St., packs in

NO WORK, ALL PLAY

AN UPHILL BATTLE

For 10 days during the second week of August, folks from all over Northern Ireland gather in the small coastal town of Cushendall for a lovely, idyllic nature festival called the Heart of the Glens Festival.

But for a competitive few, the Heart of the Glens becomes a heart-racing adventure in the Lurig Challenge Run, one of the premier events. The spectacular Lurigethan Hill, or Lurig for short, looms 1153 ft. over Cushendall, shaped like a giant wave about to break upon the town. During the race, men and women start in the center of town and scramble up the 4 mi. north face of that wave, whose upper portion is nearly vertical, climbing almost 1200 vertical ft. The current records for men and women are 26min. and 34min., respectively. Starting in July, passers-by can see would-be champions training on Lurig's face. The winners of the 2006 race were Neil Carty (27:26) and Shileen O'Kane (34:32).

For information on this and other area trail races, visit the Northern Ireland Mountain Running Association's website and calendar at www.nimra.org.uk

Think you have what it takes? Contact the Cushendall development office at ☎028 2177 1378; the office is located behind 25 Mill St., Cushendall, Co. Antrim.

crowds for ballads, fiddle-playing, and slurred limerick recitals. (☎2177 1876. Weekend live music. Opens between 3 and 7pm; last call at midnight, drinkers get booted out at 1:30am.) **An Camán** ("hurling bat"), 5 Bridge St. at the foot of the bridge, is marked on one side of the building by a giant mural of a hurler (but don't be confused by the much larger mural next to the library). Needless to say, they like their hurling, and the game room in the back draws the town's younger crowd. (☎2177 1293. W and F-Su Live music or disco. Open daily 11:30am-1:30am.)

◪ **SIGHTS.** The sandstone **Curfew Tower** in the center of town, on the corner of Mill St. and High St., was built in 1817 by the eccentric and slightly paranoid Francis Turley. This Cushendall landlord made a fortune in China. When he returned to Ireland he built a tower based on a Chinese design. He added openings for pouring boiling oil onto nonexistent attackers in a mad attempt to protect his riches. The bell on the tower was co-opted by the British forces during the Irish Revolution (see **History and Politics**, p. 479) and sounded at the designated curfew, at which time Catholics were confined indoors under watch from on high—hence the tower's name. Today, the structure is privately owned and closed to the public. The extensive remnants of **Layde Church,** a medieval friary, lie along Layde Rd. When it was established in 1306, the church was valued at 20 shillings for tax purposes. Its ruins are noteworthy for their extensive burial sites, which have raised the ground by about a meter, evident in the low portals and windows. The graveyard includes **Cross Na Nagan,** an unusual pagan holestone used for marriage ceremonies and later Christianized into a Celtic cross. Sloping down toward the cliffside, the site also offers spectacular seaviews of Scotland and the pretty **seaside walks** that begin at its car park. (Always open. Free.) **Tieveragh Hill,** ½ mi. up High St., is known locally as Faery Hill, inspired by the otherworldly "little people" who supposedly reside in the area. Although it would make a fine patch of farmland, locals have honored the "wee folk" and let the hedgerows grow. The summit of similarly supernatural **Lurigethan Hill,** more commonly "Lurig Mountain," flattens out 1153 ft. over town. During the **Heart of the Glens** festival, locals have clocked records of 26min. (men) and 38min. (women) racing up the hill for the Lurig Run. The less eager amble up in about 45min. The festival is a 10-day affair that starts the 2nd week of August and ends in a giant block party. During the 2nd week of June, ramblers put on their hiking boots for the new **Glens Walking Festival,** when the *Walk the Glens* groups lead a series of free Glens treks. **Oisín's Grave** (OH-shans) is a few miles away on the lower slopes of **Tievebulliagh Mountain.** Actually a neolithic burial cairn dating from around 4000 BC, it is linked by tradition with the Ulster warrior-bard Oisín, who was supposedly buried here around AD 300. The A2 leads north from Cushendall toward Ballymoney and the lower slopes of Tievebulliagh, where a sign points to the grave. The steep walk up the southern slope of **Glenaan** rewards travelers with views of the lush valley. The **Walk the Glens** group leads occasional (usually monthly) walks around the area for a nominal fee. (Contact the development office for more info ☎2177 1378.)

CUSHENDUN (COIS ABHAINN DUINE)

In 1954, the National Trust bought the minuscule seaside village of Cushendun, five miles north of Cushendall on A2, to preserve its unusual whitewashed, black-shuttered buildings. Along with its distinctive Cornish architecture, the town also harbors some natural structures of note—murky **caves** carved into the red seacliffs can be explored along the beach. The less intrepid will enjoy a relaxing meander around the **historic monuments** in town and in nearby **Glendun,** a preserved village and another fine example of Cornish architecture. The **Maud Cottages** lining the main street were built by Lord Cushendun for his wife in 1925; tourist information signs in town remind visitors not to mistake them for almshouses. During the 2nd week of July, usually sleepy Cushendun swarms with sports fans for the annual **Sports Week.**

In the fields northwest of town (toward Ballycastle), various games are played all week; the highlight is the big hurling match that takes place on the last day.

Buses pause on the coast road at Cushendun's **Mace grocery shop**, which also features a **post office** and an **ATM**, on their way to **Waterfoot** via **Cushendall**. (#162; M-F 10 per day, Sa 5 per day, Su 3 per day. Mace open daily 7am-8pm.) Guests at 🏠**Drumkeerin, 201a** Torr Rd., signposted west of town off the A2, may choose between the immaculate **B&B ❸** and the **camping barn ❶**. The barn has unisex dormitory rooms with foam mattresses and a common room with TV and table tennis. Each B&B room boasts a gorgeous view of Cushendun and the coast. Mary was named Landlady of the Year for the whole of the UK in 2002; it's no wonder—she makes her own bread and jams, and offers eggs from her hens. Joe leads hill walks and historical tours. (☎2176 1554; www.drumkeeringuesthouse.com. Camping barn £12. B&B singles with bath £35; doubles £55.) **Cushendun Caravan Site ❶**, 14 Glendun Rd., 50 yd. from the end of the beach, is usually pretty packed and will soon open a game room with TV and a DVD player. (☎2176 1254. No kitchen. Laundry £1. Open Easter-Sept. 2-person tent £8.30, family-size tent £12.40, caravan with electricity £16.55.) The town's most popular attraction is also its only real pub: **Mary McBride's**, 2 Main St., used to be in the *Guinness Book of World Records* as the smallest bar in Europe. The original wee bar has been expanded to create a lounge for viewing GAA matches (see **Sports and Recreation**, p. 73). Cushendun's characters leave the bar only when musicians start a session in the lounge. (☎2176 1511. Summer Sa-Su music, usually trad or country. Bar food £6.50-7.50. Kitchen open daily 12:30-8:30pm. Bar open daily noon-1am.) **Cushendun Tea Rooms ❷**, across the street, serves typical cafe fare while patrons relax on a green lawn. (☎2176 1506. Burgers and sandwiches £2.50; entrees £5-9. Open Apr.-Sept. daily 10am-6pm.)

CAUSEWAY COAST

Past Cushendun, the northern coast shifts from gentle to dramatic, paving the way for Northern Ireland's postcard superstars. Sea-battered cliffs and castle ruins tower 600 ft. above white, wave-lapped beaches before yielding to the geological splendor of the Giant's Causeway (p. 567). Lying between stretches of scenery, the Causeway is a hopscotch of 40,000 black-and-red hexagonal stone columns, formed by volcanic eruptions 65 million years ago. The site today swarms with visitors, although few take time to explore the rest of the stunning and easily accessible coastline.

The A2 is suitable for **cycling** and is the major thoroughfare for the main towns along the Causeway. **Ulsterbus** #172 (Coleraine Bus and Rail Center ☎7032 5400, timetable info 9066 6630; www.translink.co.uk) runs between Ballycastle and Coleraine (and to Portrush once daily) along the coast (1 hr.; M-F 7 per day, Sa 1 per day, Su 3 per day; £5) and makes frequent connections to Portstewart. The #140 "Triangle" service connects Portrush, Portstewart, and Coleraine (M-Sa every 10-30min. 7am-10:30pm, Su every hr. 7am-10:30pm; £2). The #252 "Antrim Coaster" runs up the coast from Belfast to Portstewart via about every town imaginable (£4 to Larne, £9 to Belfast). Ulsterbus also runs package **tours** that leave from Belfast, Portrush, and Portstewart (£10-30). The orange, open-topped **Bushmills Bus** traces the coast between Coleraine, 5 mi. south of Portrush, and the **Causeway**. (Coleraine bus station ☎7032 5400. July-Aug. 5 per day.) Hitching along A2 or the inland roads is difficult due to the low number of passing cars and is never recommended by *Let's Go*.

CUSHENDUN TO BALLYCASTLE

The coastline between Cushendun and Ballycastle is one of the most famous stretches in Ireland. Although motorists and other travelers seeking a speedy trip between the two towns opt for the wide A2, this road seems tame compared with its coastal counterpart, the scenic 🏠**Torr Road**. And by scenic we mean occasionally terrifying. This narrow coastal road affords incomparable views and sheer

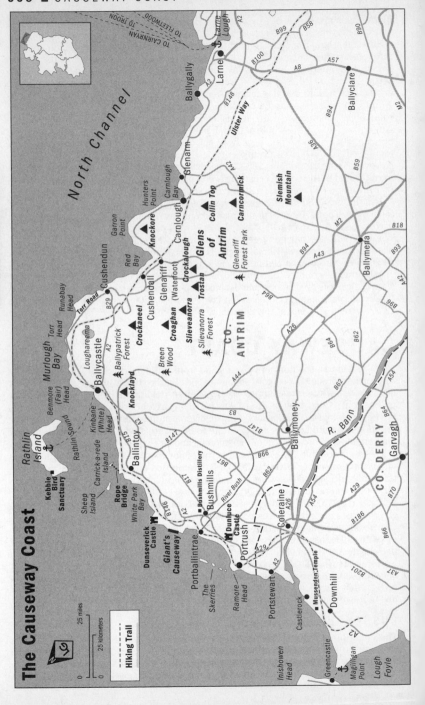

The Causeway Coast

Hiking Trail

0 25 miles

0 25 kilometers

NORTHERN IRELAND

North Channel

TO CAIRNRYAN
TO TROON
TO FLEETWOOD

A2
B99
B58
B90
Larne
Larne Lough
B100
Ballygally
B148
Uister Way
A8
A57
B58

A2
Glenarm
Carnlough Bay
Hunters Point
Garron Point
AA2
Glenariff Forest Park
B94
A43
A36
B59
B94
Ballymena
B18
B93

Rathlin Island
Kebble Bird Sanctuary
Rathlin Sound
Sheep Island
Carrick-a-rede Island
White Park Bay
Rope Bridge

Benmore (Fair) Head
Torr Head
Kinbane (White) Head
Murlough Bay
Loughareema
Torr Road
Red Bay
Runabay Head
Cushendun
Cushendall
B29
Glenariff (Waterfoot)
Crockalough
Trostan
Slievanorra Forest
Slievanorra
Breen Wood
Croaghan
Crockaneel
Ballypatrick Forest
Knocklayd
Knockore
Collin Top
Carncormick
Carnlough
Slemish Mountain
Glens of Antrim

CO. ANTRIM

Ballycastle
Ballintoy
B15
B17
B147
Bushmills Distillery
Bushmills
River Bush
B62
B66
B17
Ballymoney
B147
B99
A26
A44
A26
B64
B62
B62

Dunseverick Castle
Giant's Causeway
Dunluce Castle
Portballintrae
Portrush
Coleraine
A26
A29
A54
A54
R. Bann
Garvagh
CO. DERRY
A29
B70
B64
B186
A37
B201

The Skerries
Ramore Head
Portstewart
Castlerock
Mussenden Temple
Downhill
A2

Inishowen Head
Greencastle
Magilligan Point
Lough Foyle

cliffs but also demands tricky maneuvers around steep corners and tight squeezes with oncoming traffic. The most famous vista is **Torr Head**, the site of many ancient forts and the closest point on the Isle to the Scottish coast, 12 miles away. Past Torr Head is **Murlough Bay**, protected by the National Trust, where a stunning landscape hides the remains of the medieval church **Drumnakill**, once a pagan holy site. A small gravel car park above the bay leads to the north and east vistas. The east vista is accessible by car and thus more crowded than the pedestrian-only north vista. The road then bumps on to **Fair Head**, 7 miles north of Cushendun and 3 miles east of Ballycastle. This rocky, heather-covered headland winds past several lakes, including **Lough na Cranagh;** in its middle sits a *crannog*, an island built by Bronze Age Celts as a fortified dwelling for elite chieftains. **Bikes** should be left at the hostel: the area is steep and rainy, and it's only a 1½hr. hike from Ballycastle.

The more direct A2, the official bus route, does have its advantages—the road passes its own set of attractions and is more manageable for cyclists, with only one long climb and an even longer descent from a soft, boggy plain. Sparse traffic makes hitching impossible. A few miles northeast of Cushendun, a high hollow contains a vanishing lake called **Loughareema** (or **Faery Lough**), which during the summer can appear and disappear into the bog in less than a day. When it's full, the lake teems with fish. When it empties, the fish take refuge in caverns beneath the porous limestone. Locals claim that the lough is still haunted by the ghosts of Colonel McNeill and his horses after the coachmen misjudged the shifting water levels and drowned. Farther along, part of the plain was drained and planted with evergreens. The result is the secluded **Ballypatrick Forest**, with a scenic drive and pleasant, pine-scented walks. Before Ballycastle town, and roughly 1 mile into the woods, **Ballycastle Forest** contains the eminently climbable 1695 ft. **Knocklayde Mountain.**

BALLYCASTLE (BAILE AN CHAISIL)

The Causeway Coast leaves the sleepy Glens behind at Ballycastle, a friendly seaside town shelter for Causeway-bound tourists. More accommodating than many of its neighbors, Ballycastle is a nice base for budget travelers exploring the coast and the unspoiled Rathlin Island, which is just a ferry ride away.

▐ TRANSPORTATION. Buses stop at the Marine Hotel at the end of Quay Rd. **Ulsterbus** runs: #131 to **Ballymena** (3hr.; M-Sa 4 per day, Sa 2 per day; £5.50); #171 to **Coleraine** via **Ballymoney** (1hr.; M-F 6 per day, Sa 3 per day; £5) and #162A to **Waterfoot** via **Cushendun** (50min., M-F 1 per day). The #252 Antrim Coaster runs from the **Glens of Antrim** and **Larne** to **Belfast** (4hr.; M-F and Su 1 per day to Belfast £9, 1 per day to Larne £4). **Castle** (☎2076 8884) and **Grab-a-Cab** (☎2076 9034) run **taxis** in Ballycastle.

▐ ORIENTATION AND PRACTICAL INFORMATION. The town's main street runs perpendicular to the waterfront, starting at the ocean as **Quay Road**, becoming **Ann Street**, and then **Castle Street** as it passes the **Diamond**, which is the geometrically distinctive town square. Most restaurants and shops cluster along Ann St. and Castle St. As Quay Rd. meets the water, it takes a sharp left onto **North Street**, which houses more stores, pubs, and restaurants. East of Quay Rd. are tennis courts, the tourist office, and the town strand on **Mary Road**. B&Bs line **Quay Road** on the way into town. The **tourist office**, Sheskburn House, 7 Mary St. (☎2076 2024; ballycastle@hotmail.com), has brochures on Northern Ireland and the Antrim coast and a free guide detailing the Ballycastle Heritage Trail. The books *Rathlin Island as I Knew It* (£6) and *Bird of Rathlin* (£5) are sold here. The office books accommodations for £2 plus a 10% deposit and holds baggage for £1. (fcampbell@moyle-council.org. Open year-round M-F 9:30am-7pm; July-Aug. also Sa 10am-6pm, Su 2-6pm.) **First Trust Bank**, Ann St. (☎2076 3326; open M-F 9:30am-4:30pm, W 10am-4:30pm) and **Northern Bank**, 24-26 Ann St. (☎2076 2238; open M

9:30am-12:30pm and 1:30-5pm, Tu-F 10am-12:30pm and 1:30-3:30pm), have 24hr. **ATMs.** In an **emergency,** dial ☎999; no coins required. **McMullan's NuMark,** 63 Castle St., is a local **pharmacy.** (☎2076 3135. Open M-Sa 9am-6pm, alternating Su noon-1pm.) The **police** are on Coleraine Rd. (☎2076 2312 or 2766 2222.) The **library** (☎2076 2566), on the corner of Castle St. and Leyland St., has **Internet** access. (£1.50 per 30min. Open M and F 10am-1pm and 2-5:30pm, Tu and Th 10am-1pm and 2-8pm, Sa 10am-1pm and 2-5pm.) The **post office** is at 3 Ann St., with an additional location in the Super Shop on Quay St. (☎2076 2519. Open M-Tu and Th-F 9am-1pm and 2-5:30pm, W 9am-1pm, Sa 9am-12:30pm.) **Postal Code:** BT54.

Г₁ ACCOMMODATIONS. Most of Ballycastle's housing clusters around the harbor at the northern end of town. Plan ahead for the 🏴Ould Lammas Fair, held the last Monday and Tuesday in August—B&Bs fill almost a year in advance, and hostels fill weeks before the fair. **Ballycastle Backpackers (IHO) ❶,** North St., is next to Marine Hotel. The view of sunrise on the strand compensates for an occasionally absent management. (☎2076 3612 or 077 7323 7890. Dorms £10.) Although **Fragrens B&B ❷,** 34 Quay Rd., is one of Ballycastle's oldest houses, renovations have brought a modern sheen to the immaculate hotel-quality rooms with TV and bath. Fresh fruit at breakfast is a welcome change from the typical artery-clogging fare. (☎2076 2168; http://members.aol.com/JGreene710. All rooms with bath. Singles £35; doubles £45. MC/V.) Another option is the **Ammiroy House B&B ❷,** 24 Quay Rd. (☎2076 2621. Laundry and Internet access available. Singles £22.50; doubles £45, under 11 £10.) The recently renovated **Marine Hotel ❺,** 1-3 North St., has beautiful views, spacious rooms, and an on-site bar and restaurant. (☎2076 2222; www.marinehotel.net. Breakfast, pool, and gym included. Singles £60-65; doubles £70-95; family rooms £140. MC/V.)

❑🍴 FOOD AND PUBS. The **SuperValu,** 54 Castle St., is a 10min. walk from the hostels. (☎2076 2268. Open M-Sa 8am-10pm, Su 9am-10pm.) Right in the center of town at the Diamond, the **Co-op** is the most convenient grocer in town. (☎2076 8166. Open M-Sa 8am-10pm, Su 8am-6pm.) Splurging on a proper meal may be necessary in one of Ballycastle's many top-notch restaurants. **Flash-in-the-Pan ❶,** 74 Castle St., has won fish-frying awards for its tasty fish supper, which will fill you up for £5.40. (☎2076 2251. Open M-Th and Su 11am-11pm, F-Sa 11am-midnight.) **Wysner's ❹,** 16 Ann St., caters to a sophisticated palate, using local ingredients to make Mediterranean-, Asian-, and Mexican-influenced dishes. (☎2076 2372. Lunch £6-8. Dinner special £11-16. Open daily June-Aug. 12:15-2:30pm and 6-9pm; Sept.-May 8am-8pm. MC/V.) The young staff at **Thyme and Co. ❸,** 5 Quay Rd., serves fresh gourmet sandwiches (£2-3.20) and keeps Ballycastle awake with good espresso drinks. The weekend four-course menu (£13) is tasty and popular, so book ahead. Daytime takeaway is less expensive. (☎2076 8563. Open M-Sa 9am-6pm, F-Sa 7pm-10 pm, Su 11am-5pm.) The intimate **Cellar ❸,** the Diamond, has evening meals (think crab claw starters) and lunch dishes served in a classy cellar hung with plants. Try the steak, chicken, or beef burgers with chips for £7. (☎2076 3037. Lunches £5-10; entrees £9-20. Open daily noon-10pm. MC/V.) Grab a takeaway pie from **Pizza Haven ❷,** North St., and take it to the nearby beach or back to the hostel. (☎2076 9999. 10 in. £4.50, 12 in. £6. Open M-Sa 4-11:30pm, Su 4-11pm.)

Ballycastle has a bustling weekend pub scene and has plenty of trad sessions in the summer months. Every two weeks during the summer, **Harbour Bar,** 6 North St. next to the hotel, rocks the 'Castle with the **Fat Dad Sessions,** complete with BBQ, beer, and live music. (☎2076 2387. For upcoming sessions, visit www.myspace.com/thefatdadsessions. Bar open M-Th and Su 2pm-midnight, F-Sa 2pm-1am.) Behind its shiny black facade, **Central Bar,** 12 Ann St., hosts musical fun ranging from impromptu piano sing-alongs to Wednesday trad, Thursday karaoke, and live bands Friday and Saturday. Also on Saturdays, the upstairs disco pumps tunes for dancing fools. (☎2076 3877. Sa disco cover £3-5. Kitchen open daily noon-5pm. Open daily noon-1:30am.) **O'Connor's Bar,** 7-9 Ann St., draws a lively, mixed crowd. The beer garden in the back beckons pint-swillers on sunny afternoons. (☎2076 2123. Th trad, F-Sa live bands, Su karaoke. Open M-Th 11:30am-11pm, F-Sa 11:30am-2am, Su 11:30am-10pm.) **The Diamond Bar,** 6 the Diamond (☎2076 2142), recently expanded to make room for its popular weekend trad sessions. **House of McDonnell,** 71 Castle St., opens at the owner's whim (usually in the afternoon or evening) but guarantees Friday trad sessions and Saturday folk music throughout the year and Wednesday and Sunday sessions during the summer. (☎2076 2975.)

🅶 🕱 **SIGHTS AND FESTIVALS.** With its bizarre octagonal spire, the **Holy Trinity Church of Ireland** (a.k.a. **Boyd Church**) is an easy landmark to spot. Built by 18th-century landlord Hugh Boyd—also responsible for Quay Rd., Ann St. (named for his wife), and local industrialization the improvements fell into ruin when industrial profiteering lost its groove. Half a mile out of town on the Cushendall Rd., the 15th-century **Bonamargy Friary** sits in the middle of a golf course, complementing its graveyard and climbable priory with a par-3 hole. A small stone cross with a hole in it marks the grave of the 17th-century recluse and prevaricator Julia McQuillan, better known to locals as 'The Black Nun." It is said that her headless figure still haunts the grounds. (Always open. Free.)

Moyle Outdoor Angling & Leisure, 23 Ann St., hosts fishing and sightseeing tours. (Contact Dan McCauley at ☎2076 9521. 1-day license £11, 8-day £23.50.) For **boat hire,** charter the *Lady Linda* for a fishing excursion. (☎2076 9665 or 077 1216 7502. £30 per person; £160 per day for the entire boat, which fits 7.) For deep-sea fishing, contact **Ballycastle Charters.** (Call Christopher McCaughlan ☎2076 2074 or 077 5134 5791. Open M-Sa 11am-7pm. £15 per person, children £10. Rod rental included.) For pony rides, fishing, boating, and kids' outdoor activities, head to **Watertop Farm,** located halfway to Cushendun along A2. (☎028 2076 2576; watertopfarm@aol.com. Open July-Aug. daily 11am-5:30pm. £2, children £1, seniors £1.50; call ahead for activities prices.) The 🕱**Ould Lammas Fair,** Northern Ireland's oldest and most famous fair, has been held in Ballycastle for 414 years. Originally a weeklong fiesta, the festival is now crammed into two frenzied days, the last Monday and Tuesday of August. Following the traditions of the ancient Celtic harvest festival, the fair jams Ballycastle's streets with vendors of cows, sheep, crafts, and baked goods, while trad musicians pack pubs. (Contact the tourist office for info, or the Environmental Health Agency ☎2076 2225.)

Hikers begin the 🕱**Moyle Way** here, a 17mi. trail that stretches all the way down to Glenariff. Pick up the guide book (50p) at the tourist office before setting out, and consider carrying *Ordnance Survey #5* and *#9;* to get to the trail, follow the blue and yellow signs from town. In the other direction, the 🕱**Causeway Coast Way** is a 31 mi. trail with several great sights, culminating of course in a trip to Giant's Causeway. Pick up the guidebook (50p) at the tourist office and consider carrying along *Ordnance Surveys #4* and *#5.* A free leaflet with six different **cycling routes** in the **Ballymoney** area is also available at the tourist office (routes range from 4.5 to 18 mi.).

RATHLIN ISLAND (REACHLAINN)

Off the coast of Ballycastle, bumpy, boomerang-shaped Rathlin Island ("Fort of the Sea") is home to only about 70 human inhabitants, but in the summer it becomes the nesting ground for 20,000 loveable puffins, swarms of seabirds, the odd golden eagle, and four daily ferryloads of tourists. Although its windy surface supports few trees, the island does harbor a paradise of orchids, purple heather, and seabirds. The contrast between the white chalk and black basalt cliffs encircling the island led the novelist Charles Kingsley to compare Rathlin to a "drowned magpie." During 20 years of Famine, the island's population dwindled from 1200 to 500, and by 1993 there were just over 100 islanders left; most of Rathlin's emigrants sailed for America and settled in Maine. Even though electricity only arrived in Rathlin in 1992, the island holds a unique place in the history of technology. In 1898, Italian scientist Guglielmo Marconi sent the first wireless telegraph message from here to Ballycastle. The island is rich in history, from its days as a hideout for Robert the Bruce in 1306 to its more recent adventure care of Sir Richard Branson, whose round-the-world hot air balloon trip ended with an explosion that sent the balloon out to sea, just offshore of the island. Branson was rescued and later returned to donate £25,000 to the renovation of the Manor House.

A leaflet from the Ballycastle **tourist office,** on Mary St. by the shore, has a decent map and a description of the island's walks and sights. For a more complete presentation of its storied history and intriguing myths, visit the island's **Boat House Heritage Centre** (a.k.a. the Rathlin Island Visitors Centre), a right turn from the ferry. The Centre also offers books, maps, and birdwatching advice. (☎2076 2225; www.moyle-council.org. Open May-Aug. daily 10am-4pm, Sept.-Apr. by appointment. Free.) The most rewarding route heads 4½ mi. out from the harbor to the West Light Viewpoint and the ⬛**Kebble Bird Sanctuary.** The walk back is easier and **Raghery Tours** runs shuttles between the two points. (☎2076 3949. 20min., every 45min., £3). The magnificent Kebble Bird Sanctuary is operated by the RSPB (Royal Society for the Protection of Birds) and comprises unique cliffs formed by pounding seas that caused caves to collapse, leaving detached sea stacks that are ideal breeding grounds for kittiwakes, guillemots, razorbills, and other seabirds, who vie for their preferred spots. Meanwhile, the famous and adorable puffins potter about like wind-up toys on the grassy slopes at the bottom of the cliffs. The breeding season lasts from May to July, with June being the peak month for birdwatching. A warden is generally on duty to provide binoculars, answer questions, and point out the different species. (☎2076 3948. Viewpoint open most days Apr.-Aug., but visitors should contact warden Liam McFaul during low-season months to ensure access.) Another walk leads 2½ mi. southeast of the harbor to the classic black-and-white lighthouse at **Rue Point,** past cows, sheep, goats, and the ruins of farm buildings from the island's past populations. From the crumbled remains of **Smuggler's House,** whose wall cavities once hid contraband during the days when pirates and smugglers fueled Rathlin's economy, visitors can access **Ushet Point,** where **seals** bask on the rocks and frolic in the sea during the summer. Finally, a shorter 1½ mi. hike to the northeast corner of the island offers a glimpse of the **East Lighthouse,** the site of Marconi's historic transmission. On the cliffs below is **Bruce's Cave** where the Scottish King plotted his revenge. Visitors less inclined to animal-watching can enjoy a walking tour of the island's more unusual botanic specimens. (Call Paul ☎077 4556 6924. £3 per person.)

Kinramer Camping Barn (ACB) ❶, a four-mile hike from the harbor (west from the ferry), has clusters of bunks and pull-out beds isolated by plywood partitions. (☎2076 3948. Dorms £6 with your own sleeping bag; **camping** £3.) **Soerneog View Hostel ❶** is a simple, functional option closer to the bustle of the ferry landing. To get there, take a right from the dock and turn left at the side road before the pub. At the top of the road, turn right; the hostel is a quarter of a mile down on the left. Call ahead for pickup or to reserve one of six beds. (☎2076 3954. Bike rental £7 per day. Laundry wash £3, dry £2. Dorms from £10.) A fancier option is the **Manor House ❸,** located directly in front of the ferry terminal, a late Georgian gentleman's abode with private rooms. (☎2076 3964; www.rathlinmanorhouse.co.uk, info@rathlinmanorhouse.co.uk. Dinner £10-24; served during summer 6-8pm. Singles £30, with bath £35; doubles £60/65.) Most people buy groceries on the mainland, although **Morgan's,** located east of the ferry, carries the basics. (☎2176 1355. Open daily 7am-8pm; hours may vary.) **McCuaig's and Bruce's Kitchen ❷** pulls double duty as the island's only bar and restaurant apart from the hotel. (☎2076 3974. Sandwiches £2.20; toasties, burgers £2-4; limited entrees £4-6. Kitchen open daily 10:30am-6pm; bar open until late.)

For three days in early August, the **Jigs & Rigs** festival brings DJs, bands, and swarms of rockers to the island. (Visit www.the-session.com for more info.)

Caledonian MacBrayne runs a **ferry** service from Ballycastle. In summer, the ferry runs four times per day from the pier at Ballycastle on Bayview Rd., up the hill from Quay Rd. and by the harbor. The small MacBrayne office at the Ballycastle pier opens before departures to sell tickets; buying at the central office ensures a timely return. (☎2076 9299. 45min.; departs Ballycastle Apr.-Sept. M-F 10am, noon, 4:30, 6:30pm; Oct.-Mar. 10:30am and 4 or 4:30pm. Departs Rathlin Apr.-Sept. 8:30, 11am, 3:30, 5:30pm; Oct.-Mar. 9am and 3pm; £10, ages 5-16 £5, under 5 and seniors free, families £26.50; bikes £2.60.) The **Aquasports** company also runs a **fast ferry.** (☎079 6230 9670; www.aquasports.biz, alanwilson@aquasports.biz.)

BALLINTOY, SHEEP AND CARRICK-A-REDE ISLANDS, AND ROPE BRIDGE

Five miles west of Ballycastle on the B15, the modest village of **Ballintoy** *(Baile an Tuaighe)* consists of a church, a harbor, a hostel, two pubs, and a fisherman's bridge that is one of the most frequented tourist destinations in all of Northern Ireland. The **Causeway Rambler** bus connects Bushmills to Carrick-a-Rede bridge with a stop in Ballintoy. (☎7032 5400 or 9066 6630; www.translink.co.uk.) Two diminutive islands, Sheep and Carrick-a-rede, put Ballintoy on the map. Visible from the village but inaccessible to visitors, **Sheep Island** is home to puffins, razor bills, kittiwakes, and the largest cormorant colony in Ireland. Indeed, it was originally named Puffin Island until farmers started grazing their sheep on its grassy top, although its capacity was fairly limited—an old saying warned that it would "fatten ten sheep, feed eleven, and kill twelve." Smaller but better-known, **Carrick-a-rede Island** lies off-shore east of Ballintoy. Meaning "rock in the road," Carrick-a-rede presents a barrier to migrating salmon returning to their home rivers. For 350 years fishermen cast their gigantic nets in the salmon's path, stringing a **rope bridge** between the mainland and the island from April to September to retrieve their haul. Due to depleted salmon populations, fishing has stopped now, but the bridge is faithfully rebuilt by engineers each summer as a folly for tourists. Crossing the shaky, 48 in. wide, 67 ft. long bridge over the dizzying 80 ft. drop to rocks and sea can be a harrowing experience, but it's much safer than it used to be—the bridge is engineered to support six tons of weight, and wardens on site during opening hours monitor traffic and close the bridge in windy weather. During particularly busy summer days, timed tickets may be distributed, so go in the morning to avoid crowds. A sign about ½ mi. east of Ballintoy, on the Coast road, marks the turn-off for the bridge. The car park is a quarter of a mile farther, and the bridge is less than one mile beyond that.

The walk to the bridge runs along the limestone **Larrybane sea cliffs,** nesting place of the unusual black-and-white razor bill, the quirky brown- and white-bellied guillemot, and the mundane gull. The National Trust's leaflet, available from the wardens, has a map of the area's geological notables. A fishing hut teeters on the eastern side of the island. The **tearoom** by the car park sells snacks, posts information, and gives local advice. (☎2076 2178 or 2073 1582. Sandwiches £2.75-3. Bridge open July-Aug. daily 10am-7pm. Last ticket sold at 6:15pm. Footbridge £3, Gift Aid £3.30, children £1.64/1.80, families £7.64/8.40; National Trust members free.)

Quiet Ballintoy provides beds and grub for Carrick-a-rede's daredevils. A wooden statue of an intrepid backpacker points up the driveway to the aptly named **Sheep Island View Hostel (IHH) ❶**, 42A Main St., which welcomes the adrenaline-drained with bunked rooms and a top-notch kitchen. Sheep graze on the grass outside and eye the island longingly, while frequent summertime barbecues illuminate the outside courtyard. Call for pickup from anywhere between Ballycastle and Portrush. (☎2076 9391; www.sheepislandview.com. Wheelchair-accessible. Group catering available; call ahead. Laundry wash £1, dry £1. Dorms £12, under 12 £9. Private rooms available, same per-person prices. MC/V.) In town, **Fullerton Arms ❸**, 22 Main St., was once the site of an illegal drinking *shabeen* shut down by the puritanical Dr. Fullerton when he purchased Ballintoy in the 18th century. It's a less prudish affair today—a pub takes his name and offers quality grub and three-star **B&B** ❸ rooms with satellite TV. (☎2076 9613; www.fulertonarms.co.uk. Internet access and laundry available. F-Sa live music. Pub food £7-11. Kitchen open daily 9am-9pm. Open daily 11:30am-1am. All rooms with bath. B&B singles £38.50; doubles £60. MC/V.) Across the street, **Carrick-a-rede Pub** is cheaper and less ostentatious with both its food and music. (☎2076 2241. July-Aug. trad at least once per week. Food £3-7.50. Kitchen open daily noon-9pm.) Halfway to Ballycastle (2.5 mi. from Ballintoy) is **Glenmore,** 94 White Park Rd., which has both a **B&B** ❸ and a small **caravan park** ❶. The owners emphasize that they allow only quiet, respectful guests, but if you're lucky their children will raise the roof with their homemade trad sessions. They also have a fishing lake. (☎2076 3584. Catch and release £10. Laundry £5. Internet access £2 per day. Tents and caravans with electricity £12. B&B singles £37; doubles £54.) Just over two miles west along the coast road from Ballintoy is the **Whitepark Bay Youth Hostel (HINI)** ❶. Its out-of-the-way setting, overlooking one of the most famous—and least swimmable—beaches on the Antrim Coast, is either a blessing or a bane, depending on whether or not you have a car. Clean rooms, dependable facilities, and a number of walks leading from the doorstep make it worth the trip. Portrush-Ballycastle bus (#172) or the Antrim Coaster (#252) will stop 200 yd. from the hostel, but there are no shops or pubs for 2½ miles. (☎2073 1745; www.hini.org.uk. Open daily Mar.-Nov., closed daily 11am-2pm. Reception 8am-10:30pm. Check-in 2-10pm. Laundry wash £3, dry £1. Dorms July-Aug. £15, Sept.-June £15, HINI £1 discount. Discounts for guests under 18. MC/V.)

PORTRUSH (PORT RUIS)

Portrush's name should be taken quite literally: in the fall, when the universities reopen, students flood the city center; in July, when their summer holidays begin, they give way to an even more rapid influx of tourists. The streets boil over on summer days with families flocking to amusements and carnival rides. In the evenings, teens swamp the town's discos. The tacky seaside kitsch is redeemed by sandy beaches and some of the best surf in the North. Portrush is also the town most conveniently located near the region's major attractions.

🖹🛂 TRANSPORTATION AND PRACTICAL INFORMATION. Trains run from Eglinton St. (☎7082 2395) in the center of town (open July-Aug. M-F 11am-8pm; Sept.-June M-F 8am-4pm) to: **Coleraine** (10min.; M-F 6:40am and 4:15pm, Sa 5pm, Su 3:30pm), where connections can be made for **Belfast** (1½hr.; M-F 11 per day, Sa 10 per day, Su 5 per day; £8.20) and **Derry/Londonderry** (1hr.; M-Sa 9 per day, Su 5 per day; £8). Most causeway-bound **buses** stop at Dunluce Ave. **Ulsterbus** #140 ("Triangle Service") runs to **Coleraine** via **Portstewart** (30min., daily every 10min. 7am-10:30pm, £2). #402, "The Causeway Rambler," runs to **Bushmills** (20min., 7 per day); **Giant's Causeway** (25min.); **Ballintoy** (40min.); and **Ballycastle** (1hr.). #252, the "Antrim Coaster," reaches Belfast after stopping at every sight along the Antrim coast, from **Bushmills** and **Ballycastle** to **Larne** (M-F and Su 1 per day to Larne £4, 1 per day to Belfast £9). For night owls, **Radio Taxis** (☎7035 3709) provides eight-seater cabs. **Andy Brown** (☎7082 2223) is another convenient option.

The **tourist office,** located in the Dunluce Centre off Sandhill Dr. south of the city center, has a **bureau de change** and books accommodations for £2 plus a 10% commission. (☎7082 3333. Open July-Aug. daily 9am-7pm; Apr.-June and Sept. M-F 9am-5pm, Sa-Su noon-5pm; Mar. and Oct. Sa-Su noon-5pm.) Or, try **First Trust,** 25 Eglinton St. (☎7082 2726. Open M-Tu and Th-F 9:30am-4:30pm, W 10am-4:30pm.) Surf the **Internet** at the public **library** opposite MacCool's on Causeway St. (☎7082 3751; open M and Th-F 10am-1pm and 2pm-5:30pm, Tu 10am-1pm and 2-8pm, Sa 10am-1pm and 2-5pm; £1.50 per 30min.) or at **Ground Espresso Bar,** 52 Main St. (£1 per 20min.; see

Food, p. 565). The **post office** is on Eglinton St. (☎7082 3700. Open M-Tu and Th-F 9am-12:30pm and 1:30-5:30pm, Sa 9am-12:30pm.) **Postal Code:** BT56.

▮▯ ACCOMMODATIONS AND FOOD. Portrush's sole hostel has closed, and the flow of constant seaside weekenders make booking any B&Bs along the coast tough. If the recommended B&Bs are full, a stroll down **Kerr, Mark, Eglinton,** and **Main Streets** in town could prove fruitful. For more remote lodgings, **Landsdowne Crescent** and **Ramore Avenue,** north of the city center, are at the peninsula's end. The luxurious **Clarmont Guest House ❸,** 10 Landsdowne Crescent, has decadent seaview rooms with TV and jacuzzi baths. (☎7082 2397; www.clarmont.com. Rooms £15-40 per person. MC/V.) **Harbour Heights ❸,** 17 Kerr St., has elegant blue rooms and tasty breakfasts. (☎7082 2765; www.harbour-heights.co.uk. Singles £30; doubles £50. Ages 10-15 £15, ages 5-10 £10, under 5 free.) The friendly, family-run **Ashlea House ❷,** 52 Mark St., has eight comfortable rooms. (☎7082 3094; ashleahouse@hotmail.com. Wheelchair-accessible. Rooms £18-20 per person, with bath £20-22.50.) After a long day of beach-combing, 'ave a rest at **Avarest House B&B,** 64 Mark St. (☎7082 3121. All rooms with bath. Internet access £1 per hr., free if you connect your own laptop. Laundry £5 per load. Singles £40-50; doubles £55-70.) Although its owners prohibit nightclubowls from staying, more sedate tourists enjoy the private parking lot at the **Beulah House B&B ❸,** 16 Causeway St. (☎7082 2413. All rooms with bath. Singles £40; doubles £56-80.) Campers can set up tents at the family-oriented **Carrick Dhu Caravan Park ❶,** 12 Ballyreagh Rd., less than one mile west of Portrush on A2. (☎7082 3712. Showers 20p. Laundry £1 per wash and 50p per dry. Open Easter-Sept. daily, Oct.-Easter weekends only. Tents £14; caravans with electricity £15.)

Greasy chippers and pricey eateries dominate Portrush's culinary offerings, while groceries are available at **Costcutter,** 106 Lower Main St. (☎7082 5447. Open daily 7am-10pm.) At **◪D'Arcy's ❹,** 92-94 Main St., adventurous specials like the crocodile starter (£5.50) and ostrich (£13.25) add a touch of flair to the menu. (☎7082 2063. Lunch £6-8. Early evening menu £5-7. Dinner £11-14. Open M-Th and Su noon-9:30pm, F-Sa noon-10pm. Book ahead. MC/V.) For a good, cheap meal, the **Silver Sands Restaurant ❶,** 27-29 Eglinton St. is your best bet. (☎7082 4113. Breakfast £3.60-5; entrees £4-10. Open daily 8:30am-11pm.) Find solace in the fishy arms of **Spinnaker ❸,** 25 Main St., where the spoils of the sea are broiled, grilled, sauteed, and smothered in butter. (☎7082 2348. Specials £6-10. Open M-Sa 12:15-9:30pm, Su 12:15-9pm.) Don't be put off by the garish facade of **Don Giovanni's ❸,** 9-13 Causeway St., where tasty Italian dishes are served on red-and-white checkered tablecloths. (☎7082 5516. Entrees £11-13.50. Open daily 5:30-11pm, may close earlier on slow nights.) Beneath **Ramore** (see **Pubs and Clubs,** p. 566), the modern **Coast ❷** serves pizza (from £4.50) in a sleek interior. (☎7082 3311. Open M-F 5-10pm, Sa-Su 3-10pm.) If you're looking for a caffeine buzz, head over to **Ground Espresso Bar ❶,** 52 Main St.,

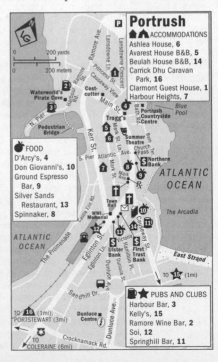

🅟 Portrush

🏠🅰 ACCOMMODATIONS
Ashlea House, 6
Avarest House B&B, 5
Beulah House B&B, 14
Carrick Dhu Caravan Park, 16
Clarmont Guest House, 1
Harbour Heights, 7

🍴 FOOD
D'Arcy's, 4
Don Giovanni's, 10
Ground Espresso Bar, 9
Silver Sands Restaurant, 13
Spinnaker, 8

🍺⭐ PUBS AND CLUBS
Harbour Bar, 3
Kelly's, 15
Ramore Wine Bar, 2
Soi, 12
Springhill Bar, 11

which advertises itself as "the gates to coffee heaven." Don't pass up their gelato. (☎ 7082 5979. Gelato from £1. Open daily July-Aug. 9am-10pm, Sept.-June 9am-5pm.)

◪ ▩ **PUBS AND CLUBS.** Portrush plays host to the premiere club scene in the North. Weekend partiers come from as far as Belfast and Derry/Londonderry to black out at the town's multi-venue nightlife complexes. Although bar crowds remain mixed, the (very) young set seems to prevail on disco nights. Those who are overwhelmed by choice can find solace in the simplicity of **Springhill Bar,** 15-17 Causeway St., across from the library, which features the best trad on Wednesday and Thursday nights, live bands Friday and Saturday, and free food occasionally showered on unassuming college students. The upstairs lounge has pool and darts and hosts a 60s-80s themed disco Friday and Saturday nights. Summertime brings all-you-can-eat barbecues Wednesday nights at 8:30pm for £1. (☎ 7082 3361. Open M-Sa 11am-1am, Su noon-midnight.) The laid-back **Harbour Bar,** 5 Harbour Rd., tries its best to remain a sailor pub with bands rocking on weekends (☎ 7082 2430; F-Sa live music; cover Sa £5), while **Ramore Wine Bar,** the newest and classiest conglomerate, sits pretty atop North Pier off Harbour Rd., and boasts three restaurants, a pub, a wine bar, and a lounge. (☎ 7082 4313. Open M-Sa 12:15-2:15pm and 5-10pm; F closes 10:30pm, Su 12:30-3pm and 5-9pm.) The significantly less classy **Soi** packs quite a crowd onto its dance floor, while the older folk sway to the live music at **Shunter's** and relative innocents gyrate to hard techno at **Trak's Nightclub** by way of **Station Bar.** (☎ 7082 2112. M student night. Shunter's open summer Tu-Sa, winter Th-Sa. £5 cover grants access to all venues. Open M and Th-Sa.) Finally, **Kelly's,** outside town on the Bushmills road, is the North's top clubbing venue; it regularly draws big-name DJs. Something like the palatial bachelor pad of a debaucherous playboy, the wonderland of club kitsch features 10 themed bars and three clubs, including the main disco **Lush!** (open W and Sa), as well as discos **Wild** (name says it all) and **Synk** (house and dance music). This behemoth has a niche for every type of teenager. (☎ 7082 2027. Covers vary £3-10 depending on the event, but a student discount is sometimes available.) If the appeal draws you to Kelly's all the way from afar, a shuttle is available (☎ 077 4770 0820), including one that runs from Derry (☎ 077 7926 7049).

◨ ▣ **SIGHTS AND OUTDOOR ACTIVITIES.** Portrush's best-advertised attraction, **Dunluce Centre,** in Dunluce Arcade, is perfect for kids. It hosts an interactive computer Treasure Hunt, **4D Turbo Tours Hydraulic Movie Room,** and **Finn McCool's Playground,** the largest soft-play area in Ireland. (☎ 7082 4444. Open July-Aug. daily 10:30am-6:30pm; Sept.-Mar. Sa-Su noon-5pm; last weekend in Apr. noon-6pm; May-June M-F noon-5pm, Sa-Su noon-6:30pm. Playground and treasure hunt £3.50 each; Turbo Tours £4; complete access £8.50.) Escape the special effects at **Portrush Countryside Centre,** 8 Bath Rd., next to East Strand. The displays, which cater to children, include a tidal pool with sea urchins and starfish. A new "Time and Tide" exhibit, which targets a wider age range shows how natural coastal processes interact with human activities. It is set to open soon. (☎ 7082 3600; www.ehsni.com. Open Easter-Sept. daily 10am-5pm. Free.)

Beyond all the amusement-park revelry, sandy **East Strand Beach** stretches 1½ miles from town toward the **Giant's Causeway** (p. 567). The best **surfing** on the North Antrim coast is found at **Portballintree Beach,** where the waves soar almost as high as the nearby castle. Outfit a surfing excursion at **Trogg's,** 88 Main St. (☎ 7082 5476. Boards £10. Wetsuits £7. Open daily July-Aug. 10am-9pm; Sept.-June 10am-6pm.) **Carl Russell** teaches the timid to conquer the surf and hang ten like a pro. (☎ 7082 5476 or 4825 7717; surflessons@troggs.com. £25.) Before hitting the amazing Antrim waves, make sure to check the **surf report** (☎ 0906 133 7770). After a hard day of surfing, retire to **Waterworld's Pirate's Cove,** on the North Pier, where you can enjoy two water slides, a water playground, and a swimming area. (☎ 7082 2001. Open July-Aug. M-Sa 10am-10pm, Su noon-10pm; June M-Th 10am-5pm, F-Sa 10am-10pm, Su noon-10pm; Sept. F 6-10pm, Sa 10am-10pm, Su noon-10pm. Last tickets sold 1hr.

NORTHERN IRELAND

before closing. 45min. sessions £4, children £3, family tickets from £12.) Afterward, in the same building, **Pirate Bowl bowling lanes** is a fun way to dry off. (☎7082 2334. Open July-Aug. M-Sa 10am-8pm, Su noon-8pm; June M-F 10am-3pm, Sa 10am-6pm, Su noon-6pm; Sept. Sa 10am-6pm, Su noon-6pm. £4.50, under 8 £2.50.)

Portrush's **Summer Theatre** stage, St. Patrick's Hall, Causeway St., is a venue for several Northern Irish theater companies. (☎7082 2500; www.audf.org.uk/portrush.html. Box office open W-Sa 11am-noon and 6-8pm. Shows W-Sa 8pm. Tickets £6, seniors £5, children £3.) For festive family fun, May's **Portrush Raft Race** (☎6981 4605; www.portrushlifeboats.com) incorporates street theater, music, and homemade raft-racing. Also in May, motorcycle racers rev their engines on the famous "Triangle" course between Portrush, Portstewart, and Coleraine during the **Junction One North West 200 Race Week Festival,** Ireland's biggest international sporting event. (Contact Coleraine Tourist Information Centre ☎7034 4723.)

▶ DAYTRIPS FROM PORTRUSH

DUNLUCE CASTLE. Perched dramatically on top of a craggy sea cliff, the remarkably intact ruins of this 16th-century fortress seem to merge seamlessly with their rocky foundation. Indeed, the castle is built so close to the cliff's edge that the kitchen once fell into the sea during a grand banquet, resulting in the arrest of the host and the relocation of the lady of the house (who despised the sound of the sea) to an inland residence. Built as the seat of the MacDonnell family, the castle was considered unbreachable by any army, and it can only be accessed across a small bridge, which was originally a narrow, rocky pass. The east wall has cannons from the *Girona,* a Spanish Armada vessel that sunk nearby. Beneath the castle, a covert **sea cave** offered a quick escape route toward Rathlin Island or Scotland; climbing down can be slippery, but adventurers are rewarded with a different perspective of the castle's cliffside location. While a small fee is required to get up close and personal with the castle, the most spectacular views are afforded by stopping along the A2 coming from Bushmills. From mid-June until mid-September, a free "living history" exhibit shows the castle ruins being used as they would have been before they were, well, ruined. *(The castle is located along A2, between Bushmills and Portrush; served by Causeway Rambler bus. ☎7032 5400 or 9066 6630; www.translink.co.uk; daily 10:15am-5pm. Open daily Oct.-Mar. 10am-5pm, last admission 4:30pm; Apr.-Sept. 10am-6pm, last admission 5:30pm. £2, under 16 and seniors £1, under 4 free.)*

THE GIANT'S CAUSEWAY. Geologists believe that the unique rock formations found at ■**Giant's Causeway** were created some 60 million years ago by lava outpourings that left curiously shaped cracks in their wake. Although locals have different ideas (see **Finn McCool,** p. 61), everyone agrees that the Causeway is an awesome sight to behold. Comprising over 40,000 symmetrical hexagonal basalt columns, it resembles a descending staircase leading from the cliffs to the ocean's floor. Several other formations stand within the Causeway: **the Giant's Organ, the Wishing Chair, the Granny, the Camel,** and **the Giant's Boot.** Advertised as the 8th natural wonder of the world, the Giant's Causeway is Northern Ireland's most famous natural sight, so don't be surprised if 2000 others pick the same day to visit. Visit early in the morning or after the center closes to avoid crowds.

Once travelers reach the Visitors Centre, they have two trail options: the more popular low road, which directly swoops down to the Causeway (20min.), or the more rewarding high road, which takes visitors 4½ mi. up a sea cliff to the romantic Iron Age ruins of Dunseverick Castle. Bus #172 and the #252 "Antrim Coaster" stop in front of the castle, from which it's 4½ mi. farther to Ballintoy. The trail is well-marked and easy to follow, but you can also consult the free map available at the Visitors Centre. The center also offers a 12min. film about the legend of Finn McCool and posits on the geological explanation for the formations. *(The Causeway is always open and free to pedestrians. Ulsterbus #172 to Portrush, the #252 Antrim Coaster, the "Causeway Rambler," and the Bushmills Bus drop visitors at Giant's Causeway Visitors Centre, in the shop next to the car park. The Causeway Coaster minibus runs to the columns. ☎9066 6630; www.translink.co.uk. 2min.; every 15min.; £1, round-trip £2, children 50p/£1. Centre info ☎2073 1855; www.northantrim.com. Open daily July-Aug. 10am-6pm, Sept.-June 10am-5pm. Movie 10am-5pm every 15min.; £1, child £0.50. Parking £5. To avoid the fee, park at nearby Heritage Railway Centre's free car park, a 2min. walk away, or behind the Causeway Hotel.)*

BUSHMILLS DISTILLERY. Ardently Protestant Bushmills has been home to the Old Bushmills Distillery, creator of Bushmills Irish Whiskey, since 1608, when a nod from King James I established it as the oldest licensed whiskey producer in the world. Travelers have been stopping at the distillery since ancient days, when it lay on the route to Tara from castles Dunluce and Dunseverick. In those days, the whiskey's strength was determined by gunpowder's ability to ignite when doused with the fiery liquid. When the plant is operating, the tour shows the various stages involved in the production of Irish whiskey, which is distilled three times rather than the paltry two involved in making Scotch. During the three weeks in July when production stops for maintenance, the far less interesting experience is redeemed only by the free sample at its end. Serious whiskey fans should work their way to the front as the tour winds down to get a chance at eight different whiskeys when the guide makes his cryptic request for "help." Note: request for volunteers had been discontinued as of press time, but there are rumors that it may return.

The sleepy town of Bushmills caters to visitors who decide they can't move on (or move at all, for that matter) after visiting the distillery. The brand-new **Mill Rest Youth Hostel (HI) ❶**, 49 Main St. just up the road from the Diamond, away from the distillery, is a blended whiskey of a hostel—the spacious common room and spotless, lofted rooms are of single malt quality, but the lack of character reminds you that you're still drinking the cheaper stuff. Check back in 12 years to see if it's aged well. (☎2073 1222; www.hini.org.uk. Reception closed daily 11am-5pm. Coin-operated **Internet** access 5p per min. Laundry £4. Dorms July-Aug. £15, Sept.-June £14; singles £35/33; doubles £41/41. HINI £1 discount per night.) Down the street, the **Hip Chip ❶**, 82 Main St., will line your stomach for whiskey-drinking with a £4.85 fish supper. *(☎2073 1717. Open M-Th 11:30am-11pm, F-Sa 11:30am-11:30pm, Su 1-11pm. The distillery and Bushmills are at the intersection of A2 and B17, 3 mi. east of Portrush and 2 mi. west of the Causeway; served by the Causeway Rambler bus ☎7032 5400 or 9066 6630; www.translink.co.uk; daily 10:15am-5pm; and the Bushmills open-top bus #9, which connects Coleraine to the Giant's Causeway, 5 per day. The Giant's Causeway and Bushmills's Railway connect the two. ☎2073 2594; www.giantscausewayrailway.org. Runs Mar.-Dec. irregularly; June-Sept. daily 11:15am-4:30pm, every 15min. and 30min. after the hr. £5, children £3.50. Distillery ☎2073 1521; www.whiskeytours.ie. Open Apr.-Oct. M-Sa 9:30am-5:30pm, Su noon-5:30pm, last tour 4pm; Nov.-Mar. daily 10am-4:30pm, tours M-F 10:30, 11:30am, 1:30, 2:30, 3:30pm; Sa-Su 1:30, 2:30, 3:30pm. £5, students and seniors £4.)*

PORTSTEWART (PORT STÍOBHAIRD)

The twin ports of Portstewart and Portrush enjoy a friendly sibling rivalry. Although it's no more populous than Portrush, Portstewart feels far more expansive; its more affluent crowd lends the town a more refined ice-cream-parlor aesthetic. Recent overcrowding in 'Rush has pushed some of its famous nightlife over the border—'Stewart's visitors can now couple their beachy fun with a dose of clubbing.

◫ ◪ **TRANSPORTATION AND PRACTICAL INFORMATION. Buses** stop in the middle of **the Promenade.** Ulsterbus #140 ("The Triangle") connects **Portstewart, Portrush,** and **Coleraine** (M-Sa every 10-30min. 7am-10:30pm, Su every hr. 7am-10:30pm; £2). **Cromore Cabs** (☎7083 4550) is a local taxi service. Portstewart's **tourist office,** located in the red-brick library/town hall complex, sits on the crescent at the southern end of the Promenade before the Diamond. (Open July-Aug. M-Sa 10am-1pm and

2-4:30pm.) **Ulster Bank,** 52 the Promenade, has a 24hr. **ATM.** (☎7083 2094. Open M-F 9:30am-12:30pm and 1:30-4:30pm; W opens at 10am.) **McElhone's Pharmacy,** 22A the Promenade, has prescriptions and other essentials. (☎7083 2014. Open M-Sa 9am-5:30pm.) The **library** provides **Internet** access for £1.50 per 30min. (☎7083 2286. Open M, W, F 10am-1pm and 2-5:30pm, Tu and Th 10am-1pm and 2-8pm, Sa 10am-1pm and 2-5pm.) The **post office,** 90 the Promenade, is inside the Spick and Span cleaners. (☎7083 2001. Open M-F 9am-5:30pm, Sa 9am-12:30pm.) **Postal Code:** BT55.

ſſ ſ⁀ ACCOMMODATIONS AND CAMPING. Most beds in the area lie near the Victoria Terr., on the left heading out of town on the Portrush road. When visitors arrive at **Rick's Causeway Coast Independent Hostel (IHH/IHO) ❶,** 4 Victoria Terr., they are greeted with a hot cup of tea or coffee and invited into its high-ceilinged rooms. (☎7083 3789; rick@causewaycoasthostel.fsnet.co.uk. Barbecue available. Laundry £4, free with stays of more than two nights. Dorms £10; private rooms £13 per person, with bath £16. Singles often not available in summer.) Just next door, the **Chez-Nous B&B ❷,** 1 Victoria Terr., has bright, sunny rooms, and a host with a matching disposition. (☎7083 2608; www.chez-bousbb.co.uk. Wheelchair-accessible. Free laundry and Wi-Fi. Rooms £19.50 per person, with bath £24.50.) The **Craigmore House B&B ❷,** 26 the Promenade, has a more central location. (☎7083 2120. Dinner available for £10. Rooms £22 per person, some with bath.) Next to Anchor Bar and Skipper's Wine Bar, the **Anchorage Inn ❹** makes the late-night stumble back to luxury rooms short and indulges hangovers with a noon check-out time. (☎7083 4401. All rooms with bath. Singles Jan.-Mar. and Oct.-Dec. M-Th £40, F-Sa £50; Apr.-Sept. £45/55. Doubles Jan.-Mar. and Oct.-Dec. £70/75, Apr.-Sept. £75/85.) Campers are welcome to pitch their tents on a limited number of sites at **Juniper Hill Caravan Park ❶,** 70 Ballyreagh Rd., on A2 toward Portrush. (☎7083 2023. Laundry £1 per wash, 50p per dry. Check-in 2-8pm; gates closed 7pm-midnight. Apr.-Oct. sites £14, with electricity £15.)

ſ⁀ ſ⃟ FOOD AND PUBS. Restaurants line the waterfront along the **Promenade** leading toward the **Diamond.** While the town has no grocer, there is a **Costcutter** in the Texaco gas station just outside of town at 171 Coleraine Rd. (☎7083 2722. Open daily 7am-11pm.) **ſ⃟Morelli's ❶,** 53-56 the Promenade, serves burgers (£3.75) and omelettes (£5.75), but the five generations of ice-cream expertise whipped into their waffle cone sundae (£2.50-3.50) is a treat too good to miss. (☎7083 2150. Open daily June-Aug. 9am-11pm; Sept.-June 9am-5pm.) Farther along the Promenade, **Bon Apetit Cafe ❶,** 67a the Promenade, has coffee beans at various stages of the roasting process in its tables. (☎7083 3808. Breakfast £4-5; *panini* £4.75; hot meals from 11am £5-6. Open daily 9am-10:30pm.) The **Seaview Seafood Restaurant ❷,** 12 the Diamond, at the top of the Promenade, serves quality Indian cuisine with a seafood flare. (☎7083 6999. Entrees £7-12.50. Open daily 3pm-midnight.) Catch fish and chips (£4.25) at **The Harbour ❶,** 31 the Promenade. (☎7083 3030. Open daily noon-midnight.)

As Portrush's slightly less scandalous twin sister, Portstewart boasts its own multi-venue entertainment spots—O'Hara's and The Anchor—both at the southern end of the Promenade, uphill from the shore. Each consists of a few bars and a music venue or club. **The Anchor,** 87 the Promenade, purveys pints and spares pretension. Downstairs, the party rages with Tuesday karaoke, Wednesday quiz night, and Thursday trad. **Club Aura** houses a live music venue and a disco Tuesday and Thursday nights (cover £2), as does **Skipper's Wine Bar** next door. Both serve food, but Skipper's is a bit more expensive. (☎7083 2003. M and Th-Su live music. Anchor Bar kitchen open M-Th and Su noon-9pm, Sa noon-7pm. Anchor Bar open M-Sa 11:30am-12:50am, Su 11:30am-11pm. Club Aura open Th-Su 10pm-1:30am; cover F-Sa £5.) Across the street at 78 the Promenade, **Shenanigans** gastropub courts a mature see-and-be-seen crowd, serving sophisticated eats to accompany the thumping dance beat. Upstairs, partygoers enjoy the latin rhythms of the **Havana Disco.** (☎7083 6000; www.shenaniganscomplex.com. Bar: M quiz, Tu trad, W karaoke, Th and Sa live band, F and Su DJ. Restaurant open daily noon-9:30pm; entrees £7-10. Bar open M-Sa noon-1am and Su noon-midnight. Disco open F-Sa 10pm-1:30am.)

◘ ⚠ SIGHTS AND OUTDOOR ACTIVITIES. Beachcombers have a full day in store on the six-and-a-half-mile coastal path that leads east from Portstewart Strand, on the west side of town, toward Portrush. The path passes sea cliffs, blow holes, an ancient hermit's house, and plenty of other odd sights that a free map from the tourist office helps to identify. The sandy beach of the **Portstewart Strand,** less than one mile west of town, is owned and preserved by the National Trust. (Site open year-round. Visitors facilities open Mar.-Sept. daily 10am-6pm; Oct. Sa-Su 10am-5pm. £4 per car, free after 6pm.) The **Port-na-happle rock pool,** between the town and the beach, is ideal for bathing. A small but dedicated group of surfers calls these waters home. Surfers, whether beginner or expert, should check the surf report, tide charts, and other useful info. (☎0906 133 7770. Updated daily 8am.) **Ocean Warriors,** 80 the Promenade on the Strand, rents wetsuits (£7 per day, children £5 per day), body-boards (£5), and surfboards (£10); they have a sister store in Portrush as well. (☎7083 6500. Open July-Aug. daily 10am-6pm, Sept.-June F-Su 10am-6pm.) According to locals, the best waves hit the shore from September to March and reach heights of five to six feet. **Fishing** is possible aboard the *M.F.V. Boy Matthew.* (☎7083 4734. Sails June-Sept. daily 2 and 6pm.) **Scuba** lovers indulge with **Portstewart Sub Aqua** (☎015 0476 5169 or 015 0430 1409). **Aquaholics,** 14 Portmore Rd., across from Wanderin' Heights B&B, leads dives, including night dives upon request. (☎7083 2584, after 6pm 079 6816 4748; www.aquaholics.org. Open daily 9am-5:30pm. Introductory "try" dive £60 with equipment; diving course £460. Experienced divers £25 without equipment.) **Flowerfield Arts Centre,** 185 Coleraine Rd., displays traveling art exhibits, runs a variety of workshops, and holds lectures on subjects from local history to the royal family. (☎7083 3959. Open M-F 9am-1pm and 2-5pm.) For the last week in July, Portstewart hosts bands, karaoke, fishing, and fireworks during the **Red Sails Festival.** (Contact Sean Graham ☎7083 3005.)

DOWNHILL

The land between Castlerock and Downhill once belonged to the Earl Bishop Frederick Hervey, Earl of Bristol and Derry, who will long be remembered as one of the wackiest members of British aristocracy ever to experiment with the Irish landscape. His construction of **Downhill Castle** in the late 18th century set this shrine to human privilege against the barren backdrop of a raw cliff face. Alas, it suffered a disastrous fire and was abandoned after WWII. The residence was later bought by an American, who gutted it and sold the windows, chandeliers, furnishings, and even the roof, leaving behind only the stone shell of a former palace.

On the cliffs in front of the castle, **Mussenden Temple** is a piece of sheer architectural folly barely clinging to its precarious perch close to the cliff's edge. Typifying the Victorian love of juxtaposing romantic natural landscape with manmade structures, this circular library was based on the Temples of Vesta in Italy and was named after the niece with whom it was speculated Earl Bishop Fred had an affair. Behind the castle sit the remains of another of Hervey's architectural frivolities—the **mausoleum** he built for his brother. Ignoring warnings that the windy clifftop would not support the structure he had planned, Hervey erected a monument twice the height of the one that survives today. Pedestrians wishing only to walk around and not enter the Temple can do so for free; the grounds are always open. Park at Downhill Forest to avoid the fee. (☎7084 8728; www.nationaltrust.org.uk. Temple and castle open Apr. to mid-June and Sept. weekends and bank holidays, June-Aug. daily 11am-7:30pm. £1.98, Gift Aid £2.20, children £1.58/1.75, families £5.54/6.15; free for National Trust members.) On the road from Downhill to Castlerock, **Hezlett House** is a 17th-century thatched cottage and Victorian mini-museum. (☎7084 8728. Open Apr. to mid-June and Sept. weekends and bank holidays, June-Aug. daily 11am-

7:30pm. £2.73 or Gift Aid £3, children £1.81/2, families £7.27/8.) **Downhill Forest,** on the same road, has waterfalls, streams, wildfowl, and paths through the lush forest for hikers and bikers. (Open dawn-dusk. Free.) **Downhill Beach,** one of the most beautiful on the Northern coast, lies below the forest in front of the hostel.

Leaving Downhill may be difficult, especially once you experience the gentle embrace of ⬛**Downhill Hostel ❶,** 12 Mussenden Rd. The hostel, a late Victorian house with high ceilings, has a beach out front and cliffs out back with a view of Mussenden Temple. High bunks, hand-sewn quilts, and a luxurious shower provide more reasons to stick around. The hostel houses a working pottery studio; guests are invited to paint and decorate their own. (☎7084 9077; www.downhillhostel.com. Call ahead; pottery may not always be available. Pottery painting £6-25. Wetsuit rental £10, boogie board rental £10 per day. Internet access £1 per 15min. Laundry with machine dry £4. Dorms £11; private doubles M-F £30, Sa-Su £35; private quad £50.) The closest food sources are the grocery stores two miles away in **Castlerock** and **Artaclave.** While Downhill lacks a pub of its own, guests are regularly sent to the **Village Tavern,** 24 St. Paul's Rd., in Artaclave. (☎7084 8106. Lunch served 12:30-3pm; dishes £4-6. Dinner served 5-9pm; entrees £7-10. Bar open M-Sa noon-11pm, Su noon-10pm.)

Getting to Downhill is easy. **Bus** #134 from Coleraine to **Limavady** often passes nearby (M-F 9 per day, Sa 6 per day; £4.50); ask the driver to stop at the hostel, which is a 2min. walk straight ahead. The **train** (☎9066 6630; www.translink.co.uk) stops at Castlerock on its way between Belfast and Derry/Londonderry (both directions M-Sa 9 per day, Su 5 per day). From Co. Donegal, the ferry from Greencastle on the Inishowen Peninsula sails straight to Magilligan, 10 miles away. (☎7493 81901; info@loughfoyleferry.com. 15min.; April-Sept. every 20min. M-Sa 7:20am-9:50pm, Su 9am-9:50pm; Oct.-Mar. daily every 20min. 9am-7pm, plus ferries at 7:20, 8, 8:30am, 7:50pm. Cars £7/€10, pedestrians £2/€3, children and seniors 70p/€1.) Pedestrians can catch one of **Tony's Taxis** (☎7084 8147 or 079 7626 8076) from Magilligan and anywhere in and around Downhill.

DERRY/LONDONDERRY (DOIRE CHOLM CILLE)

Derry became a major commercial port under the Ulster Plantation of the 17th century (see **Cromwell,** p. 52), a feudal system established to create an outpost of London's authority. Originally christened *Diore,* meaning "oak grove," the city's name was anglicized to Derry and finally to Londonderry. The city's label remains a source of contention, as the minority Protestant population uses the official title while many Republican Northerners and informal Protestants refer to the city as Derry. In an effort to remain impartial, the BBC reported on "Derry-stroke-Londonderry" at the height of the troubles. The past three centuries of Derry's history have given rise to the iconography used by both sides of the conflict. The city's troubled history spans from the siege of Derry in 1689, when the now-legendary Apprentice Boys closed the city gates on the advancing armies of the Catholic King James II (see **More British Problems,** p. 52), to the civil rights turmoil of the 1960s, when protests against anti-Catholic discrimination exploded into violence. In 1972, the Troubles reached their pinnacle on Bloody Sunday, a public massacre in which British soldiers fired into a crowd of peaceful protesters. None of the soldiers were ever convicted, and Nationalists are still seeking redress from the British government (see **1994 Ceasefire,** p. 487). Hearings into the Bloody Sunday Massacre were recently held in Derry's Guildhall, and the report (2006) can be seen at the Bloody Sunday Centre.

Although tourism is relatively new to Derry, visitors are rewarded with an intriguing juxtaposition of the 400-year-old history of the city walls and the more recent memory of the Troubles painted on the walls of the conflict-ridden neighborhoods. The walkable city has a manageable but cosmopolitan vibe, and citi-

NORTHERN IRELAND

zenry and government alike pride themselves on the leaps that Derry has made in its clean and cohesive appearance, as well as the emotional and practical compromises made by both sides of the political and religious divide. Perhaps due to the town's reputation, natives are quick to stand up for their beautiful and intimate city, and with good reason. It is hard to beat the city's hopping pub scene, with free live music and merry locals keeping the *craic* flowing late into the night.

◥ INTERCITY TRANSPORTATION

Flights: Eglinton/Derry Airport, Eglinton (☎7181 0784). 4 mi. from Derry. Flights to **Dublin, Glasgow, London-Stansted,** and **Manchester.** The **AIRporter** runs buses from Quayside Shopping Centre to Belfast International and Belfast City airports. (☎7126 9996; www.airporter.co.uk. M-F 13 per day 6am-6pm; Sa-Su 6 per day. £15, under 16 £7.50, seniors free; families £35, couples £25, groups of 3 or more £12 per person.)

Trains: Duke St., Waterside (☎7134 2228), on the east bank. A free **Rail-Link bus** connects the bus station to the train station. Call the rail or bus station to find the corresponding bus; the Rail-Link runs during all connecting times. Trains from Derry go east to: **Belfast** via **Castlerock, Coleraine, Ballymoney, Ballymena,** and **Lisburn** (2hr.; M-Sa 9 per day, Su 4 per day; £9.80, children £5). Connections may be made from Coleraine to **Portrush** (Derry to Portrush £8, children £4). Bus and train combo passes £14 per day, families £17.50 per day.

Buses: Most stop at the Ulsterbus depot (☎0128 9066 6630) on Foyle St., between the walled city and the river. Open 7am-10pm. **Ulsterbus** (☎7126 2261) serves all destinations in the North and a few in the Republic. (ROI routes are in €, since they are operated by Bus Éireann. Both companies offer ½-fare for children on all routes.) #212 and #273 to **Belfast** (1½-3hr.; at least 1 every 30min. M-F 5:30am-5pm, Sa 8am-1pm; at least every hr. M-F 5am-8pm, Sa 7am-8pm; Su 10 per day; £8.70); #234 to **Coleraine** (during university term only M-F 7 per day, Su 2 per day; £6.30); #275 to **Donegal** (1½hr., 5 daily, €8.40); #274 to **Dublin** (£13.40) via **Omagh** (9 daily, £6.30); #296 to **Galway** via **Longford** and **Athlone** (7hr.; M-Sa 4 per day, Su 3 per day; €18.50); #273 and 274 to **Omagh** (M-F 12 per day, Sa 11 per day, Su 5 per day; £6.30). **Swilly Buses** (☎7126 2017) head to the **Fanad Peninsula,** the **Inishowen Peninsula, Letterkenny,** and other parts of northwest Donegal. Buses to: **Buncrana** (35min.; M-F 10 per day, Sa 8 per day, Su 4 per day; £4); **Letterkenny** (1hr.; M-F 11 per day, Sa 5 per day; £6); **Malin Head** (1½hr.; M, W, F 1pm, Sa 11am; £7.40). **Northwest Busways** (Republic ☎0778 2619), depart from Patrick St. opposite the Multiplex Cinema to: **Buncrana** and **Inishowen** (M-Sa 5 per day, £2.50); **Carndonagh** (M-F 4 per day, Sa 3 per day; £3.20); **Malin** (town, not all the way to the head; M-Sa 5:10pm, £4.20). **Patrick Gallagher Coaches** (Republic ☎07495 31107), which stops at Water St. next to the library, has a once daily route servicing **Belfast** (1½hr.) via **Dungiven** (30min.; M-Sa 10am, Su 7:15pm) and **Letterkenny, Falcarragh, Gortahork, Bunbeg, Crolly,** and **Annagry** (M-Sa 7pm).

◢ ORIENTATION

Derry straddles the **River Foyle** just east of Co. Donegal's border. The **city center** and the **university area** both lie on the Foyle's western banks. The old city, within the medieval walls, is Derry's downtown, even though its hilltop setting literally makes it "up-town." At the center lies the **Diamond,** from which four main streets radiate: **Shipquay Street** to the northeast (downhill), **Butcher Street** to the northwest, **Bishop Street** to the southwest (uphill), and **Ferryquay** to the southeast. Outside the city walls, Butcher St. intersects **Waterloo Street,** which holds the pedestrian shopping district. **Magee University** is to the north off **Strand Road,** the northern extension of Waterloo St. The famous Catholic **Bogside** neighborhood that became Free Derry in the 1970s (see **The Troubles,** p. 483) is west of the city walls. On the south side of the river is the tiny Protestant enclave of the **Fountain.** The residential areas of the Foyle's western bank are almost entirely Catholic, while most of Derry's Protestant population lives on the eastern bank, in the hous-

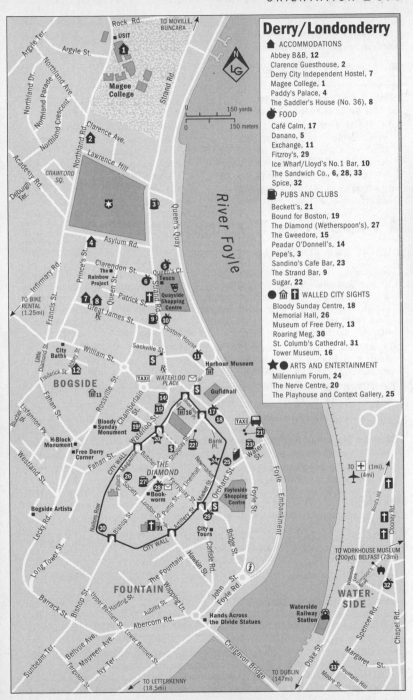

Derry/Londonderry

🏠 **ACCOMMODATIONS**

Abbey B&B, **12**
Clarence Guesthouse, **2**
Derry City Independent Hostel, **7**
Magee College, **1**
Paddy's Palace, **4**
The Saddler's House (No. 36), **8**

🍎 **FOOD**

Café Calm, **17**
Danano, **5**
Exchange, **11**
Fitzroy's, **29**
Ice Wharf/Lloyd's No.1 Bar, **10**
The Sandwich Co., **6, 28, 33**
Spice, **32**

🍺 **PUBS AND CLUBS**

Beckett's, **21**
Bound for Boston, **19**
The Diamond (Wetherspoon's), **27**
The Gweedore, **15**
Peadar O'Donnell's, **14**
Pepe's, **3**
Sandino's Cafe Bar, **23**
The Strand Bar, **9**
Sugar, **22**

● 🏛 🛡 **WALLED CITY SIGHTS**

Bloody Sunday Centre, **18**
Memorial Hall, **26**
Museum of Free Derry, **13**
Roaring Meg, **30**
St. Columb's Cathedral, **31**
Tower Museum, **16**

★● **ARTS AND ENTERTAINMENT**

Millennium Forum, **24**
The Nerve Centre, **20**
The Playhouse and Context Gallery, **25**

ing estates commonly referred to as **Waterside.** The train station is on the east side of the river and can be reached from the city center by way of the double-decker **Craigavon Bridge,** or via a free shuttle at the bus station.

▐ LOCAL TRANSPORTATION

Taxis: Derry Taxi Association (☎ 7126 0247). For up to 7-8 people; also gives 1hr. tours of city center or Portrush and Donegal for around £20. **Delta Cabs** (☎ 7127 9999).

Car Rental: Enterprise, 70 Clooney Rd. Campsie (☎ 7186 1699 or 0800 800 227; www.enterprise.com), rents cars at the most competitive rates. Pickup and drop-off in a number of towns around the North. (From £18.42 per day.) **Europcar,** City of Derry Airport (☎ 7181 2773; www.europcar.ie). 24+ in theory, but negotiable in practice. Cars from €42.29 per day. Airport pickup. Open M-F 8:30am-5:30pm, Sa 8:30am-1pm.

Bike Rental: An Mointean Rent-A-Bike, 245 Lone Moor Rd. (☎ 7128 7128), a 20min. walk from the city center. £10 per day, £40 per wk. ID deposit.

▐ PRACTICAL INFORMATION

TOURIST AND FINANCIAL SERVICES

Tourist Office: 44 Foyle St. (☎ 7126 7284; www.derryvisitor.com), inside the Derry Visitor and Convention Bureau. Be sure to ask for the free and useful *Derry Visitor's Guide* and *Derry Visitor's Map.* 24hr. computerized info kiosk. Books accommodations (£2 plus 10% deposit) and **exchanges currency.** Runs guided walking tours of the city. **Bord Fáilte** (☎ 7136 9501) keeps a desk here, too. Both desks open Mar.-June and Oct. M-F 9am-5pm, Sa 10am-5pm; July-Sept. and Nov.-Feb. M-F 9am-5pm.

Banks: Bank of Ireland, Shipquay St. (☎ 7126 4992). Open M-Tu and Th-F 9:30am-4:30pm, W 10am-4:30pm. **Northern Bank,** Guildhall Sq. (☎ 7126 5333). Open M-W and F 9:30am-3:30pm, Th 9:30am-5pm, Sa 9:30am-12:30pm. All have 24hr. **ATMs.**

Work Opportunities: Derry Independent Hostel accepts temporary help and offers housing and a small salary. Contact Steve and Kylie ☎ 7137 7989.

LOCAL SERVICES

Disability Resources: Disability Action, 58 Strand Rd. (☎ 7136 0811). Serves the mentally and physically disabled. Open M-Th 9am-5pm, F 9am-2pm.

GBLT Resources: Rainbow Project, 12a Queen St. (☎ 7128 3030). Drop-in counseling and other support services for GBLT individuals. Free condoms.

EMERGENCY AND COMMUNICATIONS

Emergency: ☎ 999; no coins required. **Police:** Strand Rd. (☎ 7136 7337).

Pharmacy: Gordon's Chemist, 3a-b Strand Rd. (☎ 7126 4502). Open M-Sa 9am-5:30pm, F 9am-8pm. **O'Hara's Pharmacy,** 43 Great James St. (☎ 7126 2695). Open M-Sa 9:15am-6:15pm, Su 9:30am-5:30pm.

Hospital: Altnagelvin Hospital, Glenshane Rd. (☎ 7134 5171). Cross the bridge to the Waterside and follow the signs.

Internet Access: Central Library, 35 Foyle St. (☎ 7127 2300). £3 per hr. Open M and Th 8:30am-8pm, Tu-W 8:30am-5:30pm, Sa 9:15am-5pm. Snack bar open M-F noon-4pm. Same rates at **Waterside Library,** 23 Glendermot Rd. (☎ 7134 2963). Open M and W 9:15am-7:30pm, Tu and Th 9:15am-5:30pm, Sa 9:15am-1pm.

Post Office: 3 Custom House St. (☎ 7136 2563). Open M-F 9am-5:30pm, Sa 9am-12:30pm. Another is at the Diamond, inside the city walls. **Postal Code:** BT48. Unless addressed to 3 Custom House St., *Poste Restante* letters will go to the **Postal Sorting Office** (☎ 7136 2577), on the corner of Great James and Little James St.

⬛ ACCOMMODATIONS

▓ **Derry City Independent Hostel,** 44 Great James St. (☎ 7137 7989 or 7128 0280). With so much imagination and expense invested in the decor of the 2 buildings, it's little wonder so many hostelers flock to fill Steve and Kylie's 70 beds year after year. Steve greets the crowds with a rundown of Derry's offerings and inspires a laid-back, sociable vibe. With free breakfast, free Internet access, and all-you-can-eat barbecues for £2.50, who could resist the offer to stay a 5th night for free? Dorms £10; doubles £28. ❶

The Saddler's House, 36 Great James St. (☎ 7126 9691; www.thesaddlershouse.com). Knowledgeable owners welcome guests into their lovely Victorian home. Same family runs the more upscale **Merchant's House,** Queen St., an award-winning, restored Georgian townhouse with a gorgeous lounge, elegantly decorated rooms, and fluffy beds. Free Internet access. Ask for the decadent "blue room" (#4 Merchant's House). Singles £25-35; doubles £45-50. ❸

Paddy's Palace, 1 Woodlie Terr. (☎ 7130 9051; www.paddyspalace.com). Though a bit rough around the edges from the regular busloads of tour groups that come by, this relatively new hostel offers a cheap and friendly bed near the city center. Meet new friends at the billiards table in the lounge. Free Internet access. Cereal breakfast included. Laundry £5. 6-bed dorms £12, Aug. £15. ❶

Abbey B&B, 4 Abbey St. (☎ 7127 9000 or 077 2527 7864; www.abbeyaccommodation.com). Close to the city center and in the heart of the Bogside neighborhood near the murals. Greets visitors with coffee and spacious peach rooms. Free Internet access. Singles £30; doubles £48. Discounts for families. MC/V. ❷

Clarence Guesthouse, 15 Northland Rd. (☎ 7126 5342; guesthouseireland.co.uk, clarencehouse@zoom.co.uk). Well-equipped guesthouse has quality rooms stocked with phones, hair dryers, TV, irons, and bottled water. 3-courses for £20. All rooms with bath. Singles from £35; doubles from £65. Discounts for longer stays. MC/V. ❷

Magee College (☎ 7137 5283 or 7137 5870; www.ulster.ac.uk/accommodation.bunk.com), on the corner of Rock and Northland Rd. The Housing Office is on the ground floor of Woodburn House, a red brick building just past the main building. Rooms with desk and sink. Wheelchair-accessible. Wash/dry £1.60 each. Bookings by phone required. Reception M-Th 9am-5pm, F 9am-4pm. Available mid-June to Sept. £48.50 per person per wk., with bath £55.50. ❷

◖ FOOD

Groceries are available at **Tesco,** in the Quayside Shopping Centre, along Strand Rd. (☎ 7137 4400. Open M-Th 9am-9pm, F 8:30am-9pm, Sa 8:30am-8pm, Su 1-6pm.) **Iceland,** in the Foyleside Shopping Centre, is another option. (☎ 7137 7650. Open M-Tu 9am-6pm, W-F 9am-9pm, Sa 9am-7pm, Su 1-6pm.)

Danano, 2-4 Lower Clarendon St. (☎ 7126 9034). Watch chefs shove tasty pizzas and confused lobsters into the only wood-burning oven in Northern Ireland at this modern Italian eatery. Adjoining takeaway offers pizzas (£6.40-8.40), pastas, and salads for slightly less; call ahead if you're in a hurry. M-Tu 2 pizzas for price of 1 at the takeaway window next door. Open daily 5-11pm. ❸

Exchange, Queens Quay (☎ 7127 3990), down Great James St. toward the River Foyle, right at the Derry City Hotel. Trendy eatery with private booths. Lunch specials £6-7. Dinner £10-15. Open for lunch M-Sa noon-2:30pm; dinner M-Sa 5:30-10pm, Su 4-9pm. ❹

Ice Wharf/Lloyd's No. 1 Bar, 22-24 Strand Rd., across from The Strand nightclub. Part of the Wetherspoon's pub chain. 2 meals for £6 all day, a £6 "curry club" Th 5-10pm, and a £6 carvery roast Su noon-3pm. Breakfast £2.10 before noon. Open M-W and Su 10am-midnight, Th-Sa 10am-1am. ❷

Spice, 162 Spencer Rd. (☎ 7134 4875), on the east bank. Cross Craigavon Bridge and continue as it turns into Spencer. Seabass with tomato and coriander salsa £16. Appetizers £3-6.50; entrees £11-15. Separate vegetarian and vegan menu has £4 appetizers and £10 entrees. Open M noon-2:30pm and 5:30-10pm, Tu-F 12:30-2:30pm and 5:30-10pm, Sa 5-10:30pm, Su 5-9pm. ❸

The Sandwich Co., The Diamond (☎7137 2500), 61 Strand Rd., (☎7126 6771), and 33 Spencer Rd., Waterside (☎7131 3171). Trio of eateries lets customers design their own from a selection of breads and fillings. Eat at the Strand location to avoid downtown lunch-break queues. Sandwiches £2.60-4. Open M-F 8am-5pm, Sa 9am-5pm. ❶

Fitzroy's, 2-4 Bridge St. (☎7126 6211), next to Bishop's Gate. Modern cafe culture and filling meals, from simple chicken breast to mango lamb. Lunch options £5-6.50; dinners £8-13. Open M-Sa 11am-10pm, Su noon-8pm. ❷

Café Calm, 4 Shipquay Pl. (☎078 8996 3858). Enjoy a cappuccino and filled bagel (£3.30) while surfing the Web (Internet access £1 per 15min.) or people-watching at this contemporary cafe. Try the Sa evening tapas menu for a taste of Spain. Open M-W 8:30am-6pm, Th-Sa 8:30am-10pm. Open during summer Su 10am-3pm. ❶

🗹 🄟 PUBS AND CLUBS

Most pubs line Waterloo St. and the Strand, although new ones are popping up within the city walls. Trad and rock are available almost any night of the week, generally starting around 11pm, and pubs stay lively until the 1am closing time.

🄟 **Peadar O'Donnell's,** 53 Waterloo St. (☎7137 2318). Named for the Donegal socialist who organized the Irish Transport and General Workers Union and took an active role in the 1921 Irish Civil War. Celtic and Orangeman paraphernalia hang beside chalkboards of drink specials. Nightlife hub for tourists and locals. Live music 11pm. W and Sa trad 7-9pm, sometimes Su 10pm. Open M-Sa 11:30am-1am (last call at 1am; doors close at 2am), Su 12:30pm-midnight.

The Gweedore, 59-61 Waterloo St. (☎7126 3513). Back door has connected to Peadar's since Famine times. Peadar's little brother handles overflow and caters to a slightly younger crowd with rock, bluegrass, and funk bands nightly. Tu-Su live music. Open M-Th 4:30pm-1am, F-Su 4:30pm-2am.

Sandino's Cafe Bar, 1 Water St., next to the bus station (☎7130 9297; www.sandinos.com). Named after Nicaraguan guerrilla leader Augusto Sandino, this left-wing watering hole is plastered with pictures of Che and Fidel. Venue for poetry readings, local up-and-coming bands, and international music artists. In you're not up for pint-slugging or poetry-slamming, locals say this is also the best cup of coffee in town. F live bands. Tu and Sa DJs. Su afternoon trad. Open M-Sa 11:30am-1am, Su 1pm-midnight. Upstairs venue opens at 10pm.

Bound for Boston, 27-31 Waterloo St. (☎7127 1315). Young crowd relaxes in spray-painted booths with TV by day and rocks out to alternative bands by night. Upstairs, pool sharks and their prey watch sports at **Club Q.** Tu and Th-Sa live music. Su karaoke. 3-level terraced beer garden. Open M-Sa 1pm-1am, Su 12:15pm-1am.

The Strand Bar, 31-35 Strand Rd. (☎7126 0494). 4 floors of decadently decorated space pull in young partiers, especially on F when DJs spin dance faves from Top 40 to electronica. Downstairs has live music or Tu and Th-Sa DJs. Top fl. is the scandalous **Buddha.** W karaoke. Su R&B. Open daily noon-1am. Nightclub open Th-Sa 10pm-1:30am. Cover £5.

Sugar, 33 Shipquay St., next to Downey's. Biggest party available in Derry on W. Big-name DJs drop in on weekends. F 70s and 80s, Sa R&B. Cover £5 every night. W 18+, F 23+, Sa-Su 21+.

The Diamond (Wetherspoon's), The Diamond (☎7127 2880). 2-for-1 meals, cheap curry specials (Th 5-11:30pm; £5), and even cheaper drinks make this a good place to start the night before moving onto pubs with more character. Frequent promotions stretch a few quid a long way. Th 10pm karaoke. Breakfast £2.10 before noon. Kitchen open until 10pm. Open M-Th and Su 10am-midnight, F-Sa 10am-1am.

Beckett's, 1-4 Leslie House, Foyle St. (☎7136 0066). Sam Beckett may have been a writer, but the patrons of this bar are mostly there to watch the numerous sports games on TV. Th salsa. F-Sa live music. Open M-W 12:30pm-midnight, Th-Su 12:30pm-1am.

Pepe's, 64 Strand Rd. (☎7137 4002). Center of Derry's GLBT nightlife, features live music on some weekends and a smoke machine on overdrive every night of the lung-clogging week. Open M-Sa 7pm-2am, Su 8pm-1am.

⚅ TOURS

▨ **FREE DERRY TOURS.** General tours cover the city walls, the Fountain area, and the Bogside, introducing visitors to the city's conflicts by candid nationalist locals. Political tours and other special-interest tours can be arranged. *(Contact Ruiari ☎7136 6931 or 077 9328 5972; www.freederry.net.. Departs daily at 10am and 2pm from The Museum of Free Derry on Rossville St.; other tours by arrangement. Book ahead. From £4.)*

THE DERRY VISITOR AND CONVENTION BUREAU GUIDED TOURS. Most walks circle the top of the city walls, descending to visit various sights. The Derry Visitor and Convention Bureau Guided Walking Tours leave from the tourist office and take visitors around the city walls, including a brief tour of St. Columb's Cathedral. Other tours follow narratives ranging from the 1689 Siege to Emigration. *(☎7126 7284; www.derryvisitor.com. July-Aug. M-F 11:15am and 3:15pm; Sept.-June M-F 2:30pm. 1½hr. tours. £6/€9; students and seniors £5/€7; under 16 £4/€6.)*

CITY TOURS. Acclaimed City Tours urges the curious to lace their walking shoes and pound the pavement for about 2hr. It is possible to arrange tours through the Sperrins or literary tours throughout Northern Ireland. *(11 Carlisle Rd. ☎7127 1996; www.irishtourguides.com. Depart daily at 10am, noon, 2pm. Book ahead. From £4.)*

CITYSIGHTSEEING BUS TOURS. Survey sights from the top of an open-air touring bus, hopping on and off at your leisure. Buses depart from the Tourist Information Centre and from Guildhall. *(☎078 0895 7330 or 078 1218 8607. 1hr. tour Mar.-Oct. daily 10am-4pm on the hr. £8, students and seniors £7, children £5.)*

FOYLE CRUISES. Sailing trips along the Foyle reveal the city's beauty from the water. Daytime ships float over to Culmore Bay, while 4hr. night cruises sail to Greencastle in Co. Donegal and include live music. *(☎7136 2857. Boats leave from the Harbour Museum Apr.-Sept. daily at 2pm. 1¼hr. £7, seniors and children £5, families £20. Evening rides leave at 8pm. 4hr. £12, with barbecue £20; students and seniors 15/10.)*

⚆ SIGHTS

Derry was once the main emigration point in Ireland—massive numbers of Ulster Catholics and Scottish Presbyterians fled the area's religious discrimination. In fact, Derry was the only point of emigration to Australia, a journey of 26 seasickening weeks. Around the time of the Famine, many Catholics gave up on emigration and settled in the peatbog area outside the city walls, now called the **Bogside** neighborhood. The creation of the Republic made Derry a border city, and a Catholic majority made it a headache for Unionist leaders; it became the site of blatant civil rights violations, including gerrymandering and religious discrimination. The civil rights marches that sparked the Troubles originated here in 1968. The following places and events became powerful touchstones for Catholics in Derry and for Nationalists everywhere: **Free Derry,** the western, Catholic part of the city, seized by the IRA in retaliation for the constant siege the neighborhood experienced at the hands of the British, and an effective "no-go" area for the army from 1969 to 1972; **Bloody Sunday,** January 30, 1972, when British troops fired on peaceful demonstrators and killed 14 (see **The Troubles,** p. 483); and **Operation Motorman,** the July 1972 military effort to penetrate Free Derry and arrest IRA leaders. Although the

NORTHERN IRELAND

cityscape was once razed by years of bombings, Derry has since been rebuilt and looks sparklingly new. No violent incidents have erupted for the past five years, even during Marching Season and other contentious sectarian events.

■ **THE CITY WALLS.** Derry's city walls, 18 ft. high and 20 ft. thick, were erected between 1614 and 1619. The mile-long periphery has never been breached, hence the Protestant nickname "the Maiden City." However, such resilience did not save the city from danger; during the **Siege of 1689,** 600 mortar bombs sent from the nearby hills by fleeing English King James II and his brigade of Catholic Frenchmen went over what they could not go through, decimating the 30,000 Protestants crowded inside. Seven **cannons**—donated by Queen Elizabeth I and the London Guilds who "acquired" the city during the Ulster Plantation—are perched along the northeast wall between Magazine and Shipquay Gates. A plaque marks the water level in the days when the Foyle ran along the walls (it now flows 300 ft. away). The 1½ mi. walk around the city walls leads past most of Derry's best-known sights, including the raised portion of the stone wall past New Gate that shields **St. Columb's Cathedral,** the symbolic focus of the city's Protestant defenders. The same area also affords a perfect view of the red-, white-, and blue-painted Unionist **Fountain** neighborhood. Stuck in the center of the southwest wall, **Bishop's Gate** received an ornate face-lift in 1789, commemorating the victory of Protestant William of Orange 100 years earlier. The southwest corner supports **Roaring Meg,** a massive cannon donated by London fishmongers in 1642 and used in the 1689 siege. This corner affords a sprawling view of the **Bogside** neighborhood and a look at some of the murals, which are best accessed from **Butcher's Gate.** Just south of Butcher's Gate, the **Memorial Hall** is the traditional clubhouse of the Apprentice Boys, famous for closing the city gates in 1689.

THE MUSEUM OF FREE DERRY. Covering the Catholic civil rights struggle in Northern Ireland up until Bloody Sunday, the museum tells an eye-opening story, which includes civil rights marches, the Battle of the Bogside, internment, Free Derry, and of course Bloody Sunday. They also serve as the replacement for the old Bloody Sunday Centre. The Free Derry tours depart from here (see **Tours,** p. 577). The museum is located across Rossville St. from the Bloody Sunday monument. *(55 Glenfada Pk. ☎ 7136 0880; www.museumoffreederry.org. Open M-F 9:30am-4:30pm; Mar.-Sept. M-F 9:30am-4:30pm, Sa 1-4pm; June-Sept. M-F 9:30am-4:30pm, Sa-Su 1-4pm. £3/ €4.50, students, seniors, and children £1.50/€2.25.)*

ST. COLUMB'S CATHEDRAL. Named after St. Columcille (p. 59), whose monastery was the foundation on which Derry was built, the cathedral was constructed between 1628 and 1633 and was the first Protestant cathedral in Britain or Ireland (all older ones were confiscated Catholic cathedrals). The original wooden steeple burnt down after being struck by lightning, while the second (a leaden and rounded replacement) was smelted into bullets and cannonballs during the Great Siege of 1689. The same fate did not befall the cathedral itself, as it was designed to double as a fort with 6-inch- thick walls and a walkway for musketeers to shoot from the spire. The porch still holds the mortar shell that delivered the terms of surrender directly to the courtyard. The roughly hewn stone interior holds an exquisite Killybegs altar carpet, an extravagant bishop's chair dating from 1630, and 214 hand-carved Derry-oak pews, of which no two are the same. A small museum in the **chapter house** at the back of the church displays the original locks, along with keys of the four main city gates and other relics. The tombstones lying flat on the ground in the **graveyard** outside were leveled during the siege to protect the graves from Jacobite cannonballs. The small **Mound of Martyrs,** in the back left corner toward the walls, contains the 5000 dead previously buried in the cellars of the nearby houses, transplanted here during the city's redesigning efforts. *(London St., off Bishop St. in the southwest corner of the city. ☎ 7126 7313; www.stcolumbscathedral.org. Open Easter.-Oct. M-Sa 9am-5pm; Nov.-Mar. M-Sa 9am-4pm. Tours 30-60min. £2. Services M-F 10:30am, Su 8, 11am, and 4pm.)*

GUILDHALL. This Neo-Gothic building was formerly home to the City Council. First built in 1887, the original structure was wrecked by fire in 1908. As the seat of the Old Londonderry Corporation, notorious for its discriminatory housing and job policies toward Catholics, it incurred the wrath of the IRA and was destroyed again in 1972 by bombs. When one of the IRA bombers was later elected to City Council, he opened his first speech: "Last time I was here, I brought the house down." Among the many rarities is the mayor's chain of office, which was officially presented to the city by William of Orange. The hall also sponsors various concerts, plays, and exhibitions throughout the year. Until recently, the hall was home to the public hearings of the Bloody Sunday Inquiry. The hearings concluded in June 2004, and a verdict was expected in October of the same year but has been delayed indefinitely. The ghost of Sam Mackay, a turn-of-the-century superintendent and the sole Guildhall tenant, is rumored to haunt the place and has been seen pacing the viewing gallery. *(Shipquay Pl. at Shipquay Gate. ☎ 7137 7335. Open M-F 8:30am-5pm. Guided tours July-Aug. Free.)*

TOWER MUSEUM. Derry's top museum has had two great exhibits. The **Story of Derry** gives a non-partisan history of the city from St. Columb until the present. The **Armada in Ireland** tells the story of the Spanish Armada's journey around the Irish Coast, offering interactive exhibits on underwater archaeology and investigating the recovery of artifacts from *La Trinidad Valencera*, which was shipwrecked off the coast of Donegal in 1588. Various temporary exhibits keep the selection fresh. *(Union Hall Pl., inside Magazine Gate. ☎ 7137 2411. Open July-Aug. M-Sa 10am-5pm, Su 11am-3pm; Sept.-June Tu-Sa 10am-5pm. Last entrance 4:30pm. £4; children, students, seniors, and unemployed £2; families £9.)*

APPRENTICE BOYS MEMORIAL HALL. The Apprentice Boys, a fraternal order which remembers the acts of the original 13 Apprentice Boys during the siege of Derry, holds an exhibit on their history and the history of the siege on the second floor of their meeting house. Free tours can be requested on the first floor. *(13 Society St. ☎ 7126 3571. 30-45min. tours. Open July-Sept. M-F 10am-4pm. Free.)*

WORKHOUSE MUSEUM. Located in a recently restored Victorian building on the east side of the River Foyle, this workhouse-turned-showplace now houses displays dealing with poverty, health care, and the history of the Famine in Northern Ireland, which it compares with the famine in Somalia. A horse-drawn hearse once used to transport the dead from the workhouse is one of the few artifacts on display. The museum also houses the Atlantic Memorial exhibition that examines the role of the city in the WWII Battle of the Atlantic. Pass through Simpson's Brae and turn left at Clooney Terrace; then take the first right after the Clooney Methodist Church and a left after Glendermott Rd. The museum is on the right, above the Waterside Library. *(23 Glendermott Rd. ☎ 7131 8328. Open M-Th and Sa 10am-4:30pm. Free.)*

MAGEE COLLEGE. This Neo-Gothic building, outside the city walls, shines among its clumsier neighbors. Originally a member of the Royal University of Ireland in 1879, by 1909 the university was part of Trinity College Dublin. It has been part of the University of Ulster since 1984. *(University of Ulster Campus, a 12min. walk out on Northland Rd. from the city center. ☎ 7137 1371.)*

OTHER SIGHTS. The **Harbour Museum** features paintings and artifacts related to Derry's harbor history. It has also inherited the "Story of Derry" from the Tower Museum. The exhibit follows Derry's history from its days as an oak grove through the Troubles. A short video offers an overview of Derry's economic, political, and cultural heritage. *(Guildhall St., on the banks of the Foyle. ☎ 7137 7331. Open M-F 10am-1pm and 2-5pm. Last admission 4:30pm. Free.)* The **Genealogy Centre** conducts research on ancestry in Counties Derry and Donegal. *(14 Bishop St. ☎ 7126 9792; www.irishroots.net. Open M-F 9am-1pm and 2-5pm.)*

NORTHERN IRELAND

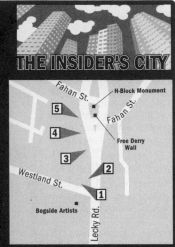

THE BOGSIDE MURALS

The Bogside Artists have created a series of murals, known as the "People's Gallery," that provide a narrative of the Troubles on the way north from the Bogside Artists studio toward William St.

1 Painted in 1997 to commemorate the 25th anniversary of **Bloody Sunday**, this mural depicts all 14 victims against the background of a red circle.

2 Portrait of 14-year-old **Annette McGavigan**, 100th victim of the Troubles and the first child casualty in Derry.

3 A boy carrying a petrol bomb wears a mask to protect against gas used by the Royal Ulster Constabulary during the 1969 Republican riots.

4 A mural of **Bernadette Devlin** pays homage to the women of the Republican movement. Devlin played a leading role in the Battle of the Bogside and recovered from seven gunshot wounds after she and her husband were gunned down outside their home.

RESIDENTIAL NEIGHBORHOODS AND MURALS

Near the city walls, Derry's residential neighborhoods, both Catholic and Protestant, display brilliant murals. Most pay tribute to historical events. The most famous are the 11 Bogside murals created by the Bogside Artists. Known as the "People's Gallery," they tell the story of the Troubles based on the artists' symbolic representation of many of the most moving photographs and film clips taken from the conflict. Meanwhile, those on the Unionist side focus on Ulster-American heritage and portray para military casualties and aims. Several murals are visible from points along the city wall. A sculpture at the west side of Craigavon Bridge looks forward optimistically, with two men reaching out to each other across a divide.

WATERSIDE AND THE FOUNTAIN ESTATE. These two neighborhoods are home to Derry's Protestant population. The Waterside, on the east side of the River Foyle, is nearly split in its percentage of Catholics and Protestants, but the Fountain, right outside the Derry city walls, is almost entirely Protestant. The Fountain can be reached from the walled city by exiting through the left side of Bishop's Gate; it is contained by Bishop, Upper Bennett, Abercorn, and Hawkin St. This small area of 600 residents holds the more interesting Protestant murals, among them a stark whitewashed house with black letters declaring "No Surrender," a slogan carried through from siege days and touted by present-day Protestants. It stands opposed to the Bogside "Free Derry Corner," dating back to the barricaded beginnings of the Troubles when Bogside Derry was successfully closed to military and police patrols. The flat, tiled area across from it is publicly designated for the Orangemen's annual bonfire on July 12; the surrounding lamppost glasses have been warped by the heat. The few Loyalist murals in the Waterside lie along Bonds and Irish St. and portray famous Ulster-descended US Presidents, including George Washington and James Buchanan, beside a likeness of the Queen.

THE BOGSIDE. The Bogside is hard to miss—a huge facade just west of the city walls at the junction of Fahan St. and Rossville Sq. declares "You Are Now Entering Free Derry." Surrounded by the striking Bogside artist pieces, as well as independent nationalist murals, this area is referred to as Free Derry Corner. Free Derry Tours offers tours of the area, led by locals who helped shape its history. Those interested can also stop by Bogside Artists studio to speak with the men who made the murals. Groups can arrange for slide presentations delivered by the artists, followed by a question and answer session. (☎ 7128 4123 or 7135 7781; www.bogsideartists.com. M-Sa 10am-5pm. £4.) For more information on the symbols in the murals and monuments, see p. 514.

🔊 ARTS AND ENTERTAINMENT

The Millennium Forum, Newmarket St., has a 1000-seat theater that hosts big name performances. (Box office ☎ 7126 4455; www.milleniumforum.co.uk. Performances from £9 and (way) up, discounts often available.) **The Nerve Centre,** 7-8 Magazine St., is a much-acclaimed multimedia center, hosting local and international performances on its main stage, independent films in its **cinema,** and music and art lessons in its workshops. (☎ 7126 0562; www.nervecentre.org. Bar and music venue £10-15. Open M-Sa 9am-5pm. Films play at 8pm, and during summer 2pm; £1.50.) For more mainstream films, **Orchard Hall Cinema,** on Orchard St., in **St. Columb's Hall,** and the **Strand Multiplex,** Quayside Centre (☎ 7137 3900), on Strand Rd., screen feature films daily. (Orchard Hall Cinema ☎ 7126 2845. £9, children, students, and seniors £6. Multiplex open M-Th and Su 11:30am-9:15pm, F-Sa 11:30am-11:30pm. £5, children £3.50. Before 1pm all tickets £3.50; M-F before 6pm £4; M-Th £3.80 seniors and students.) **The Playhouse,** 5-7 Artillery St., showcases the work of young playwrights. Until at least January 2009, it has moved into St. Columb's Hall on Orchard St. while their main space is under renovation. Also now in St. Columb's Hall, the adjoining **Context Gallery** displays contemporary art exhibits. (Playhouse ☎ 7126 8027; www.thesource.org.uk. Tickets usually £9, students £6. Gallery: ☎ 7137 3538; www.contextgalleries.blogspot.com. Open Tu-Sa 11am-5:30pm. Free.)

Derry's most boisterous and festive time of year is the week leading up to October 31, when the whole city, including thousands of visitors, dresses up and revels at the **Banks of the Foyle Halloween Carnival** (contact the city council at ☎ 7136 5151 or the tourist office). The event culminates in a fireworks show over the river. During the last week in June, the **Celtronic Festival** (☎ 078 1491 8452; www.celtronic.co.uk) caters to a younger crowd with electronica-Celtic fusion music. Throughout each July and August, the **Walled City Cultural Trail** pamphlet, available free at the tourist office, details tons of arts and activities going on in the city. August once brought the **Maiden City Festival** (☎ 7134 9250), an arts festival run by the Apprentice Boys in memory of the siege of Derry, but recent funding cuts have postponed the festival two years in a row. Contact the tourist office (p. 574) to see if it's back on.

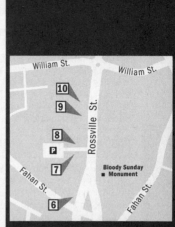

5 **Edward Daly,** a priest, helps rush gunshot wound victim **Jackie Duddy** from the Bloody Sunday crossfire.

6 The soldier beating down a door recalls the invasion of the Bogside no-go area by British troops on July 31, 1972. They knocked down barricades and doors with bulldozers, bringing an end to **Free Derry.**

7 Although this mural depicts a peaceful march in the 1960s, the subsequent clash between protesters and the RUC on March 5, 1968 precipitated the Troubles.

8 A rioter holds a coil mesh window guard up against a British tank during the **1969 Battle of the Bogside.**

9 This mural depicts **Raymond McCartney** during the hunger strike in the Maze Prison. The female figure represents the women who joined the strike.

10 Unveiled by the mayor in 2004, this **peace mural** includes a dove and an oak leaf, both symbols of Derry.

🏃 OUTDOOR ACTIVITIES

Sporting events in Derry are prevalent and exciting. **Gaelic football** and **soccer** are played at **Brandywell** on Lone Moor Rd. (Gaelic football info ☎7126 7142. Games June-Sept. Su afternoon. Tickets £6. Soccer info ☎7128 1337. Games Aug.-May. Tickets from £7.) Brandywell also hosts **greyhound racing** (about £5). **Rugby** can be caught at **Judges Road Pitch.** (☎7186 1101. Sept.-Mar. Sa 2:30pm. Tickets £2-5.) **Brooke Park Leisure Centre,** Rosemount Ave., has tennis and squash courts, a fitness room, and sporting equipment. (☎7126 2637. Open M-F 9am-10:30pm, Sa-Su 11am-6pm. Generally £2-7.) The **City Baths,** on William St., offers public swimming. (☎7126 4459. Open M-F 10am-2pm and 6-9pm, Sa noon-4pm. £2.50, children £2, seniors and under 4 free; Sa £1.50/1. Sessions last 40-105min. depending on crowd.)

🥾 HIKING

The **Sperrin Mountains** span a 40 mi. arc northeast from **Strabane** to **Milltown** to **Downhill.** The new **Sperrin Way,** an ambitious collection of waymarked trails, makes a portion of this land more accessible to outdoors enthusiasts. **Hikers** and **bikers** who embark on the trail can expect rambles through the best-preserved high-elevation blanket bogs and moorlands in Ireland, as well as some fantastic inland stretches of lush countryside. A number of maps and guided walks to the area are available; for travelers expecting an extended stay in the Sperrins, *Ordnance Survey #13* (£5.60) is an invaluable guide to the southern part of the range. *Walking in the Western Sperrins* (£0.50) has concise instructions and miniature maps for five short walks (5-10 mi.) focused on the area around **Gortin,** north of Omagh. *Walk the Sperrins* (£5) provides a selection of 10 hikes (5-13 mi.) with more detailed narrative descriptions of the routes and geological information about the area. Guides are available at the Omagh tourist office (p. 584) and the Sperrins Heritage Centre (p. 582).

Hikers can also take advantage of the **Central Sperrins Way,** newly signposted in August 2001. A product of the fragmentation of the former Ulster Way into several more manageable pieces, the Central Way runs 30 mi. through the mountains between the **Glenelly** and **Owenkillew Rivers** in Co. Tyrone. The route can be picked up at any point, but the car park at **Barnes** (where there is also **free camping**) is a logical starting location. The longest segment of the trail extends northeast from Barnes, following the **Glenelly River** to **Corratary Hill.** The Way then crosses the mountains and circles back to **Scotch Town,** which is connected to Barnes by a well-trodden path. To the west of Barnes and Scotch Town is the Way's shorter loop, which traverses higher elevations and the expansive bogs of **Craignamaddy Hill.** The *Central Sperrins Way* (£0.50) brochure details the route's segments and sights.

The bounty of the Sperrins is not restricted to pedestrians. **Cyclists** can enjoy the **National Cycle Network,** which connects Derry, Strabane, and Omagh via smooth, low-traffic roads. The route is labeled on *Ordnance Survey* maps and is signposted in most areas. Further options for Sperrin-edification abound. Visitors to the Sperrins often base themselves in **Gortin** (p. 586) or **Omagh** (p. 583), the towns closest to the most heavily traveled stretch of the range. Distant **Dungiven,** on the A6 in Co. Derry, provides access to the less-traveled northeastern region.

DUNGIVEN (DUN GEIMHIN)

Dungiven is located on the main road between Derry and Belfast. Perfectly situated at the foot of the Sperrins, the town also sports sights of its own. The ornate 14th-century tomb of Cooey na Gal, a Chieftain of the O'Cahans, is one of the best preserved tombs in Northern Ireland. The town is also home to two of the North's most interesting—and affordable—accommodations. The 🏠**Flax Mill Hostel (IHH) ❶,** just outside of town, is an out-of-the-way treasure not to be missed. Take the first right after passing through Dungiven toward Derry; if coming from Derry, take a left immediately before the sign announcing Dungiven town. The sign for the hostel is on the left about 400 yd. from the main road. Hermann and Marion charm visitors with their pastoral utopia. They mill flour for bread, grow organic vegetables, and make jam, cheese, and muesli. Despite being without electricity (ask Hermann or Marion for the story), the hostel facilities remain top-notch thanks to gas lamps and gas-heated showers and baths. Marion doubles as a weaver, working a manual loom on-site (scarves £25), and the hostel also hosts the **Trad Session Festival,** a weekend of world-renowned trad on the second Saturday in September. (☎ 7774 2655. Call for pickup from town. Festival admission based on suggested donation; book far in advance. Breakfast £2—and well worth it. Dorms £6. **Camping** £4.) If you fancy yourself more of a village king than a countryside baron, shack up in the newly renovated **Dungiven Castle B&B ❸.** The castle grounds comprise 22 acres of parkland and near-wilderness, and all the rooms have inland views. (☎ 7774 2428; www.dungivencastle.com. 1 wheelchair-accessible room. Rooms £35-40 per person.) Before leaving the hostel or castle for a trek into the Sperrins, stock up on food at **Mace,** 108 Main St. (☎ 7774 1670; open daily 7am-11pm), on Main St., or **SuperValu,** at 2 Garvargh Rd., behind the post office building (☎ 7774 1214; open daily 8:30am-9pm). The family-run **Street Cafe ❶,** 87 Main St., doles out breakfasts and gourmet sandwiches. (☎ 7774 0222. Sandwiches £2.50-4.50. Open M-Sa 9am-4:30pm, Su 11am-4pm.) **Skippers Takeaway ❶,** Main St., fills the tank. (☎ 7774 0370. Hamburgers, fish, and sandwiches all under £4. Full breakfast £3.20. Open M-Th 9am-10:30pm, F-Su 9am-11:30pm.)

Though off the beaten path, Dungiven is not beyond reach. An hourly **bus** service to Derry and Belfast runs Monday to Saturday and stops in front of Dungiven Castle. Inside the castle is a small **tourist enclave** with free reading material on the Sperrins and the Roe Valley. The castle's front desk can answer additional questions. **Northern Bank,** Main St. (☎ 084 5602 6524), has a 24hr. **ATM.** (Bank open M 9:30am-12:30pm and 1:30-5pm, Tu-F 10am-12:30pm and 1:30-3:30pm.) Visitors also have the option of **Ulster Bank,** 83 Main St. (☎ 7774 1732. Open M-F 9:30am-12:30pm and 1:30-4:30pm, W open at 10am.) **Numark Pharmacy,** 111 Main St., has all of the essentials. (☎ 7774 1288. Open M-Sa 9am-6:30pm, Su 12:30-1:30pm.) The **library,** Main St., has **Internet** access. (☎ 7774 1475. £1.50 per 30min. Open M 2-5:30pm, Tu 10am-1pm and 2-5:30pm, W 2-7pm, Sa 10am-1pm.) The **post office,** 144 Main St., is inside a convenience store. (Open M-W and F 9am-12:30pm and 1:30-5:30pm, Th and Sa 9am-12:30pm.)

COUNTY TYRONE

As lakes are to Fermanagh, forests are to Co. Tyrone. Moving toward the Sperrin Mountains, which span the border between Tyrone and Derry/Londonderry, well-maintained and protected woodlands precede forest wilds too unruly to contain. Along with its peaceful countryside, the county showcases its rich history of emigration at the sprawling Ulster American Folk Park, an homage to Ulstermen who made their way to America and a must-see for history buffs. Omagh is the county's commercial center and provides bus access to the rest of Ireland; it's also the place to pick up supplies before heading to Gortin Glen Forest Park.

OMAGH (AN OMAIGH)

On August 15, 1998, a bomb ripped through Omagh's busy downtown area, killing 29 people and injuring hundreds more. "The Real IRA," a splinter group of the Provisional IRA, took responsibility for the act. Despite the persistent memory of this tragedy, the town's sloping main street is once again the center of frenzied commercial activity. Tourists rarely stay in Omagh for long, and most simply see the bus station and the river in the rearview mirror as they head to the Ulster American Folk Park (www.folkpark.com), the nearby forests, and the mountains to the North.

E TRANSPORTATION. Ulsterbus runs from a station on Mountjoy Rd. (☎8224 2711. Open M-F 7:30am-5:45pm, Sa 7:30am-12:30pm; Sept.-June also Su 3:30-7:15pm.) Buses go to: **Belfast** (2hr.; M-F 16 per day, Sa 11 per day, Su 5 per day; £9, children £4.50); **Derry/Londonderry** (1hr.; M-F 12 per day, Sa 11 per day, Su 5 per day; £6.30/3.15); **Dublin** (3hr., 18 per day, £13.40/8.10); **Enniskillen** (1hr.; M-F 6 per day, Sa 4 per day, Su 7:25pm; £6.30/3.15). **Taxis** (☎8229 1010) are at the bus depot and have fixed fares to the town center (£3), the hostel (£5), and the Folk Park (£6).

> **GET WITH THE TIMES.** For other taxi service, call Urgent Taxis at ☎8224 8999, or text message ☎82820 with "TAXI OMAGH <where you are> <your name> <where you're going>." Available 24/7; office located at 24 Bridge St., just before the bridge on the left.

⊞⑦ ORIENTATION AND PRACTICAL INFORMATION. Omagh's buildings cluster to the south of the **River Strule.** The town center, across the bridge from the bus depot, is bounded by one street with three names that marches uphill to the town courthouse: **Market, High,** and finally **George Street.** At the top of the hill, High St. splits into pub-lined **John Street.** Warm welcomes and town maps, including the *Historical Walks of Omagh Guide,* are free at the **tourist office** in the basement of the Strule Arts Centre (access from High St., or just before the bridge on Bridge St., on the left; look for signs). *Ordnance Survey #13* of the Sperrin Mountains is also available for £5.20. Accommodation bookings are free for Omagh establishments and a £2 fee for those elsewhere in Ireland. (☎8224 7831. Open M-Sa 10am-6pm.) From High St., the **Foundry Lane** shopping center is a walkway with a wide variety of shops: food, clothing, and more. **Ulster Bank,** 14 High St., has a 24hr. **ATM.** (☎822 51750. Bank open M-Tu and Th-F 9:30am-4:30pm, W 10am-4:30pm.) **Boots** pharmacy is at 43-47 High St. (☎8224 5455. Open M-Th 8:45am-5:45pm, F 9am-9pm, Sa 9am-5:45pm.) For **Internet** access, walk downhill on Market St. and turn right onto the Dublin road; the **library** is at 1 Spillars Pl. Its 40 terminals rarely require waiting. (☎8224 4821. £1.50 per hr. Free for members; use your hostel's address to register for free membership. Open M, W, F 8:30am-5:30pm, Tu and Th 9:15am-8pm, Sa 9:15am-5pm, closed 1-2pm.) If a visit to the Folk Park is in the cards, its **Centre for Migration Studies** (open M-F 10:30am-5pm) has free **Internet** access. Do laundry at **Spick and Span Cleaners,** 36 Main St. (☎8224 7535. £6-7 per load. Open M-Tu and Th-Sa 9am-5:30pm, W 9am-2pm.) The **Travelcare** travel agency at 2 Market St. is just opposite from Scarffes Entry. (☎8824 2055. Open M-F 9am-5:30pm, Tu 9:45am-5:30pm, Sa 9am-5pm.) The **post office** is at 7 High St. (☎8224 2015. Open M-F 9am-5:30pm, Sa 9am-12:30pm.) **Postal Code:** BT78 1AB.

⌐ ACCOMMODATIONS. The **Omagh Hostel ❶,** 9a Waterworks Rd., perches atop a remote hill overlooking the town, sharing its space with cattle and sheep. Clean rooms and a conservatory perfect for sipping tea and watching the sunset guarantee a relaxing stay. The owners, Billy and Marella, are avid organic farmers who may throw in a free night in exchange for help around the garden. They are also involved in the ecotourism movement and even keep a binder about it on the kitchen table for guests to peruse. Campers have access to all hostel facilities. Call for pickup or head north from town on Gortin Rd., B48; turn right and follow the signs that start about 800m out of town. A series of roads, each thinner and less paved than the last will guide you. (☎8224 1973; www.omaghhostel.co.uk. Internet access available. Laundry £3. Open Apr.-Sept. Dorms £8; private rooms from £10. Family rooms available. Camping £6 per tent.) The **Silverbirch Hotel ❹,** 5 Gortin Rd., just north of town, has red rooms with plenty of lighting and mirrors, a restaurant and bar, and three rooms for disabled or elderly guests. (☎6224 2520; www.silverbirchhotel.com. Breakfast included. Book ahead on weekends. Singles £60-70; doubles £85-102. Weekend and mid-week getaway deals available.) The **4 Winds ❸,** just outside town at 25 Comber

Counties Tyrone and Fermanagh

Rd., has two family-size rooms in a newly built house and an owner (a former chef) who serves a hearty Irish breakfast. (☎8224 3554; www.fourwinds.org.uk. Call for pickup. Free Internet access. 4-person rooms £23-25 per person.)

🛒🍴 **FOOD AND PUBS.** Grab groceries at **SuperValu,** next to Northern Bank on Market St. (☎8224 2310; open M-Tu and Sa 8:30am-8pm, W-F 8:30am-9pm), or at **Iceland,** on Kelvin Ave. across the street from the parking lot. (8225 2664. Open M-W and Sa 9am-6pm, Th 9am-7pm, F 9am-8:30pm.) **The Sandwich Co. ❶,** 50 Market St., sells coffee and all types of sandwiches, including bagels, *panini*, and wraps. Walking from High and George St., it's on the left just before the intersection with Dublin Rd. (☎8225 1119. Sandwiches £2.50-3; *panini* £3-4. Open M-F 8am-5:30pm, Sa 8:30am-5:30pm; takeaway only during the last 30min.) Recalling the rich history of Irish emigration, **Grant's** (a.k.a. **Ulysses S. Grant's**) ❸, 29 George St., across from the cathedral, dispatches hunger with heaping portions of American favorites ranging from pastas to steak to seafood. (☎8225 0900. Entrees £6.50-14. Open M-Th 4-10pm, F 4-10:30pm, Sa noon-10:30pm, Su noon-10pm. AmEx/MC/V.) **Dragon Castle ❷,** 2 High St., doles out tried-and-true Chinese takeaway. It's the oldest Chinese restaurant in Omagh, as hypercolor scenes of Shanghai attest. (☎8224 5208. 3-course lunch special £4.50; entrees £4-6. Open Th-F 12:30-2:15pm for lunch; M-Th and Su 5-11:45pm, F-Sa 5pm-midnight for dinner.) With tons of outdoor seating and a big bar with an even bigger mirror above it, **Bar Ten,** the new bar from the owners of now-closed McElroy's, is where the young people of Omagh come to chill. Walking from the Courthouse, take the yellow walkway just after Foundry Lane Shopping; Bar Ten is at the end on the left. (☎8224 4440. Th karaoke, F live band or disco, and Sa disco; no cover. Breakfast served daily 10:30am-noon and dinner noon-6pm; bar open Th-Sa until 1:30am and M-W and Su until midnight.) **Sally O'Brien,** 33-35 John St. (end of the long block on the right coming from town center), began as a tea merchant in the 1880s but has since moved on to stronger brews (Th trad, F-Su live music). On weekend nights, clubbers shake it in the back at colorful **Eden.** (☎8224 2521. Bar 18+, club 20+. Cover £5-6. Bar open M-Th 11am-1am, F-Sa 11am-1:30am, Su noon-midnight; club open F-Sa 11pm-1:30am, Su 11pm-1am.)

◙ **SIGHTS.** The ▣**Ulster American Folk Park,** sprawling seven miles north of Omagh on the Strabane road (A5), bears proud testament to the two million folk who left Ulster in the 18th and 19th centuries. The indoor museum tracks the plight of immigrants who chose to seek a new life in America and has a full-scale tableaux of a Famine cottage and a New York City tenement. The open-air museum is spread around the Mellon (of Mellon Bank and Carnegie-Mellon fame) homestead, the only building in its original location. The buildings in the rest of the park were transplanted from all over Ulster and are "inhabited" by historical actors. Frequent special events include July 4th celebrations on the weekend nearest the 4th, an Appalachian and Bluegrass Festival in September, and occasional farming demonstrations and craft workshops. The Omagh-Strabane bus (M-F 13 per day, Sa 11 per day, Su 5 per day; £1.75) runs directly to the park. (☎8224 3292; www.folkpark.com. Open Apr.-Sept. M-Sa 10:30am-4:30pm, museum closes at 6pm; Su 11am-5pm, museum 6:30pm; Oct.-Mar. M-F 10:30am-3:30pm, museum 5pm. Last admission 1½hr. before closing. £5, students/children/seniors £3, families £11-13.) Next door is the **Centre for Migration Studies,** which includes an extensive collection of books on Irish-American culture and emigration. It also offers **Internet** access. (☎8225 6315; www.qub.ac.uk/cms. £1.50 per 30min. Open M-F 9:30am-4:30pm.)

The **Gortin Glen Forest Park,** seven miles out of town on the Gortin Rd., is the crown jewel of the county's protected woodlands. A number of shaded nature trails and a scenic drive run through the park, while wildlife enclosures harbor wildfowl and deer. (☎8167 0666; www.forestserviceni.gov.uk. Open daily 8am-dusk. Cars £3.) The annual **Omagh Agricultural Show** is held the first Saturday of July on the Gillygoolly road beyond the Derry road. Its barnyard animals, tractor rides, and great carnival food make for great family fun. Archaeology enthusiasts should check out Ireland's answer to Stonehenge on A505 between Omagh and Cookstown. The **An Creagán Visitor Centre** points visitors toward 44 well-preserved Neolithic monuments in the surrounding area, including stone circles and megalithic tombs. The center also has a **restaurant** (entrees £6-12; open M-W 10am-3pm, Th-Su 10am-9pm), craft shop, **bike rental** (£10 per day), and Sa trad around the turf fire. (☎8076 1112; www.an-creagan.com. Open Apr.-Sept. daily 11am-6:30pm; Oct.-Mar. M-F 11am-4:30pm.) Buses from the Omagh bus station run to the Visitor Centre Monday through Friday at 9:15am and 1:30pm. On the first weekend in May, born-again Celts descend on the village of **Creggan** for the **Bealtaine Festival,** an ancient rite of fertility and fun.

GORTIN

North of Omagh, one-street Gortin provides access to the walking trails of the **Central Sperrins Way** and the **Gortin Glen Forest Park** (p. 586). Despite its ideal location right on the edge of the **Sperrin Mountains,** Gortin feels largely undiscovered. Short walks surround the town—the **Gortin Burn Walk,** for instance, offers a two-mile meander along a riverbank toward the forest park. The trailhead is up a gravel road just before the post office. Walking routes and guides can be found at the **Gortin Activity Centre,** 62 Main St. (☎8164 8346 or 8164 8390). **Fishing permits** can be purchased along with sausages at **Treanor Meats,** 56 Main St. (☎8164 8543; permits £10 per day).

The **Gortin Accommodation Suite and Activity Centre ❶,** 62 Main St., is modern and child-friendly, with a number of accommodations ranging from four- to eight-person apartments (£60-120 per night; £300-600 per week) to family rooms (£40-50 per night) to hostel beds (£12.50). Kitchen, laundry, and a lounge with a fireplace can't compete with the playground out back. The apartments have all modern appliances, including microwave and TV. If no one is around when you come, there will be a local contact name, address, and phone number to check in. (☎8164 8346; www.gortin.net. Linens £2.50. Laundry £1 per load; no linen charge.) The renovated schoolhouse on the Omagh road is actually the **Gortin Hostel ❶,** 198 Glenpark Rd., uphill on the Omagh road off Main St., across from the Church of Ireland. The hearthside chairs are as comfortable as the beds in the lofty rooms. (☎8164 8083; if no answer, call the warden who lives next door at ☎8164 8087. Dorms £7.) Pitch a tent in a forest plot at the **Gortin Glen Caravan Park ❶,** two miles south of town on the Omagh road. (Contact the tourist office ☎8224 7831 for bookings. Laundry £2. 2-person tent £4.50 per night, £26 per week.) **McSwiggen's Costcutters,** 14 Main St., sells groceries. (☎8164 8810. Open daily 8am-9pm.) **Glenview ❶,** down the street, fries up takeaway goodies. (☎8164 8705. Open M-Th and Su 5-11:30pm, F-Sa 5pm-1:30am.) Next to the Gortin Activity Centre, **The Pedlar's Rest ❷,** Main St., serves reasonable lunches (£3.50-4.50) and weekend dinners (£6.50-11), as well as a fortifying multiple-course Sunday lunch (£12). Make reservations for weekend lunch 1-2pm, as locals fill the place. (☎8164 7942. Open M-Th 10am-4pm, F-Su 10am-8pm.) **Foot Hills,** 16 Main St., formerly Badoney Tavern, no longer feels at all like its pub ancestor—it's a surprisingly modern and sleek-looking restaurant for such a small town. (☎8164 8157. Entrees £10-14. Open M-F 4:30-6:30pm for tea, 6:30-9pm for dinner; Th-F 12:30-3pm for lunch; Sa-Su 12:30-6pm for tea and Su lunch, 6-9:30pm for dinner.)

The **Ulster Bank,** on the corner of Main St. and B48, has a 24hr. **ATM.** (Open M-F 9:30am-12:30pm and 1:30-4:30pm.) **Badoney Pharmacy,** 36 Main St., relieves maladies. (☎8164 8020. Open M-Sa 9:30am-1pm, also M-W and F 2-6pm.) The **post office** is in the **Day Today** convenience store on Main St. (☎8164 8160. Store open M-Sa 7am-9pm, Su 8am-8pm; post office open M-F 9:30am-5:30pm, Sa 9:30am-12:30pm.)

FERMANAGH LAKE DISTRICT

Rough southern roads make crossing the border into Co. Fermanagh from Sligo a jarring experience. Heading inland, the landscape changes dramatically as hills become more wooded, fields become more orderly, and gentle dips descend into small lake-filled valleys. Along with Upper and Lower Lough Erne, a number of smaller lakes make a matrix of waterways, whose gentle streams creep from Sligo in the west, across Enniskillen, and south into Co. Cavan. Vacationers, mostly from Northern Ireland, crowd into this "Lake District of Northern Ireland" in July and August to enjoy fantastic hikes and bike rides, to explore grand castles and mansions, and to breathe the fresh air.

ENNISKILLEN (INIS CEITHLEANN)

On a gently sloped island between Upper and Lower Lough Erne, industrial Enniskillen is the transportation hub between Northern Ireland and the Republic. The attractive town is packed with shops, pubs, and a number of outstanding restaurants, making it a thoroughly pleasant base for explorations of the Lake District. Enniskillen's residents are renowned for their friendliness, although many still bear the emotional scars of the Remembrance Day 1987 IRA bombing, which killed 11 and injured 61 at a war memorial service. In 2001, the Clinton Centre, named and inaugurated by the former US President and Fermanagh Co. descendant, was finished on the site of the bombing. The ultra-modern edifice, which houses a working peace and reconciliation center, a top-notch hostel, and a restaurant, is a cherished landmark for locals and visitors alike.

⌐ TRANSPORTATION

Buses: Wellington Rd. (☎6632 2633), across from tourist office. Open M-F 8:45am-5:15pm, Sa 8:45am-2:45pm. To: **Belfast** (2½hr.; M-F 8 per day, Sa 9 per day, Su 7 per day; £9); **Derry/Londonderry** via **Omagh** (2-3hr.; M-F 8 per day, Sa 4 per day, Su 5:40pm; £9); **Dublin** (3hr.; M-Sa 7 per day, Su 5 per day; €16); **Galway** (4hr. 20min.; M-Sa 9:25am, 1:30, 5:35pm, Su 3:35, 6:30pm; €19.50); **Sligo** (1hr.; M-Sa 6 per day, Su 3:35pm, 6:30pm; €11.10).

Taxi: County Cabs (☎6632 8888) available daily from 7am-3am. **Speedie Cabs** (☎6632 7327) operates all day except from 3 or 4am until 5am.

Bike Rental: Lakeland Canoe Centre, Castle Island (☎6632 4250). Press the blue button at the dock to summon the free ferry. Bikes £12 per day. Canoes also available; £20 per 2hr.

◼◼ ORIENTATION AND PRACTICAL INFORMATION

Enniskillen's primary streets run laterally across the island: **Queen Elizabeth Road** borders the town to the north, while **Wellington Road** runs along the southern part of town. **Ann, Darling, Church, High, Townhall,** and **East Bridge Streets** are the six segments of the middle street as it heads west to east through the center of town. Because of Enniskillen's proximity to the Republic of Ireland, most places accept the euro as well as the pound sterling.

Tourist Office: Fermanagh Tourist Information Centre, Wellington Rd. (☎6632 3110; www.fermanagh.gov.uk), next to the bus station. Accommodations booking (£2 + 10% deposit; £3 for self-catering accommodations) and a 24hr. touch-screen information system. Open July-Aug. M-F 9am-7pm; Sept.-June M-F 9am-5:30pm; Easter-Sept. also Sa 10am-6pm, Su 11am-5pm; bank holidays 10am-5pm. After hours, all brochures and a map are available next door at the Lakeland Forum Leisure Complex. Open M-F 8am-10:30pm, Sa 10am-6pm, Su 2-6pm.

Banks: Bank of Ireland, 7 Townhall St. (☎6632 2136). Open M-Tu and Th-F 9:30am-4:30pm, W 10am-4:30pm. **Ulster Bank,** 16 Darling St. (☎6632 4034). Open M-F 9:30am-4:30pm, opens W 10am. **Northern Bank,** 24 Townhall St., has 24hr. ATM; bank open M-W and F 10am-3:30pm, Th 9:30am-5pm, Sa 9:30am-12:30pm.

Laundry: Paragon, 12 East Bridge St. (☎6632 5230). Wash/dry from £5. Drop off by 11am for same-day service, except W and Sa. Open M-Sa 9am-1pm and 1:30-5:30pm.

Hospital: Erne Hospital, Cornagrade Rd. (☎6632 4711), north of town across the river.

Emergency: ☎999; no coins required. **Police:** Queen St. (☎6632 2823), at the northernmost tip of the island.

Pharmacy: Gordon's, High St. (☎6632 2393). Open M-F 9am-6pm, Sa 9am-5:30pm. Rotating Su 9am-5pm among the 6 pharmacies in town. Across from Scoffs restaurant on Belmore St. is **Numark.** Open M-Sa 9am-5:30pm. Also on Belmore St., closer to the Clinton Centre, is **Lloyds Pharmacy.**

Internet Access: East End Restaurant (see **Food,** p. 590), in the Clinton Centre, has longer hours than most and is convenient for hostelers. (Open daily 8am-11pm. £2 per 30min.) The **library,** Queen Elizabeth Rd. (☎6632 2886). £1.50 per 30min. or free for members (for membership eligibility, you must live or work in the Enniskillen area). Open M, W, F 9:15am-5:15pm, Tu and Th 8:30am-8pm, Sa 9:15am-1pm and 2-5pm.

Post Office: E. Bridge St. (☎6632 4525), at the back of Dolans Centra, across Water St. from the Town Hall. Open M-F 8am-5:30pm, Sa 9am-2pm. **Postal Code:** BT7 47BW.

ACCOMMODATIONS

Backpackers have a couple of hostel options in Enniskillen, while quality B&Bs are surprisingly scarce and farther from the town center. Campers head 10 mi. north of town on the B82 to reach **Castle Archdale Country Park.** (☎6862 1333. Open Apr.-Oct. £10-15 per tent; £15 per caravan.)

The Bridges (HINI), Belmore St. (☎6634 0110; www.hini.org.uk). 5min. walk from bus depot. State-of-the-art hostel is a blessing for the eco-friendly traveler; the curved facade collects solar rays to reduce energy waste. Internet access £1 per 20min., downstairs in Stopgo Cafe (open M-F 8am-4pm). Reception Sept.-June M-F 8-11am and 5-11pm, Sa-Su 8am-11pm; July-Aug. daily 8am-11pm. 4- to 6-bed dorms £15; singles £20; doubles £32. HI £1 discount. MC/V, £1 surcharge or 3.5% of bill over £30. ❷

Ashwood House B&B, Sligo Rd. (☎6632 3019), 2 mi. on the right as you take the Sligo Rd. (A4) out of town. 3 of the 7 rooms have baths, but there is no difference in price. Singles £30; doubles £45. ❸

Sharvedda B&B, 1 Dublin Rd. (☎6632 2659), a 10min. walk from town, next to Ardhowen Theatre. Guests are housed in converted stables that renovations have made fit for the finest. TV in double rooms only. Singles £30; ensuite doubles £50. ❸

Railway Hotel, 34 Forthill St. (☎6632 2084), a left off Belmore St. out of town. Yellow, blue-trimmed family-run hotel with TV and bathrooms in big rooms. Downstairs restaurant and bar; most entrees £6-10. Restaurant open M-Th 12:20-9pm, F-Sa 12:20-9:45pm, Su 12:20-7:45pm. F-Sa live music. Bar open M-Th and Su until midnight, F-Sa until 1am. Book ahead. Breakfast included. Singles £37.50; doubles £75. ❸

Three Ways Inn, Sligo Road (☎6632 7414), 3-4 mi. on the right as you take the Sligo Rd. (A4) out of town. Small, cheap hotel with simple rooms. Otherwise conventional bar has donation cups for charity and a large portrait of Elvis Presley in the back. Book ahead June-July. Singles £22.50; doubles £35; 6- to 7-person chalet suites £44. ❷

FOOD

Connoisseurs of good food will be impressed by Enniskillen's top-notch restaurants; this is a good place to splurge a bit. The budget-conscious buy groceries at

Dunnes, Forthill St. (☎6632 5132; open M-Tu and Sa 9am-6pm, W-F 9am-9pm, Su 1-6pm) or at **Iceland,** across Wellington Rd. from the bus station. (Open M-W and Sa 8:30am-6pm, Th-F 8:30am-9pm, Su 1-6pm.)

▨ **Oscar's,** Belmore St. (☎6632 7037; www.oscars-restaurant.co.uk). Book-lined shelves, portraits of writers, and walls emblazoned with rules from Enniskillen's Portora Royal School (attended by both Wilde and Samuel Beckett). Mediterranean-influenced dishes, thin-crust pizzas (£6-10), and ample veggie options served by young, earnest staff. Most meals £7-10. Open daily 5-11:30pm. MC/V. ❸

Franco's, Queen Elizabeth St. (☎6632 4424), at Water St. Hopping Italian eatery is a local favorite known for its fresh seafood, pastas, and pizzas (£7.45-9.25). Entrance draped with plants and flowers adds a touch of Tuscany. Entrees £12-22. Open daily noon-11pm. AmEx/MC/V. ❸

Cafe Mauds, 26 Shore Rd. (☎6632 6208), directly across Wellington Rd. from the foot bridge to the Shopping Centre. Serves pizzas, sandwiches (£2-4), salads (£3-5), ice cream, and the best espresso in town. Open M-Sa 10am-8pm, Su 1-8pm. ❶

Scoffs Restaurant, 17 Belmore St. (☎6634 2622). The amazing shank of lamb (£11.50) is nothing to scoff at in this warm, dark-wood eatery. Entrees £9-15. Attached wine bar, **Uno ❶,** has cheaper fare; entrees £6.20-8.20. Uno menu available in Scoffs M-Tu. Open daily 5-11pm. MC/V. ❷

East End Restaurant, Belmore St. (☎6632 2226), in Clinton Centre. Great patio for sunny days and hefty meals. Su lunch with free glass of wine £5. Internet access (p. 589). A la carte dinner £6-12. Open daily 8am-11pm. MC/V. ❷

Forthill Fine Foods, 2 Forthill St. (☎6632 2228), across the street from Dunnes at the roundabout. Butcher shop and deli also sell sandwiches (£2), filled rolls (£2.20), and pies (small £3.50 feeds 3, large £4.50 feeds 4). Open M-Sa 9am-6pm, with prepared food starting at 10:30am. ❶

▧ PUBS

▨ **Blake's of the Hollow,** 6 Church St. (☎6632 2143; blakesofthehollow@utvinternet.com). Ancient red facade reads "William Blake." Gated mahogany snugs, modern pub upstairs, airy beer garden out back, Greco-Roman wine bar in the cellar, and mod 60s club to top the building. F Trad. Club cover Sa £4, F after midnight £2. Club open W-Su 10:30pm-late. Bar open M-Sa 11:30am-1am, Su 11:30pm-1am. Upstairs, find Sa disco (11pm-closing) and live music at the second-floor **Atrium Bar.** Downstairs (enter via Blake's bathroom door or around the back on Wellington Rd.), **Cafe Merlot** ❷ serves classy meals and Enniskillen's only jazz & blues night (Sa 10pm-closing). Entrees £13-15.50. Kitchen open M-Sa noon-3pm and 5:30-9pm, Su 1-4pm and 5:30-8:30pm. Bar open F-Sa until 1:30am, otherwise 11pm.

Pat's Bar, 1-5 Townhall St., (☎6632 7462), directly across from town hall. Enormous bar hosts live music W and F-Su, from trad to rock (with frequent cover bands). Sa band plays downstairs while popular disco pulses upstairs; in total, 3 bars on 2 floors. 18+. Open daily 11am-1am.

The Crowe's Nest, 12 High St. (☎6632 5252; www.thecrowsnest.20m.net). Firearms and whiskey barrels adorn this central pub/grill with a patio out back. Tu live music ranges from country to trad and all sorts of music W and F-Su 10pm. Th karaoke. 18+. Upstairs **Thatch Niteclub** runs the musical gamut and draws its biggest crowds W and Sa. 21+. No cover W and Su; disco F £3, Sa £5. Most meals around £7.50-11. Kitchen open M-Sa 10am-9pm, Su noon-9pm. MC/V.

Charlie's, 1 Church St., (☎6632 5303). Homey, eclectic decorations such as bottles, jars, books, and figures adorn this crowded pub. F 7pm-close £2 pint. Disco on 2nd floor F-Sa 11pm-1:30am (last call 1am). On game day, Charlie's fills up with sports fans; football fanatics for Manchester United meet here. Open daily noon-1am.

👁 ⚠ SIGHTS AND OUTDOOR ACTIVITIES

CASTLES AND MUSEUMS. At the end of Wellington Rd., the jumbled buildings of Enniskillen Castle were home to the fearsome Gaelic Maguire chieftains in the 15th century before becoming Elizabethan barracks; these days they house two separate museums. The castle's heritage center presents a comprehensive look at the natural history of rural Fermanagh. Two museums make up the **Enniskillen Castle Museums:** first, **Inniskillings Museum,** in the castle keep, displays guns, uniforms, and row upon row of military medals. Other exhibits detail the history of the castle and religious sites in the surrounding area. Then the **County Museum** has various displays and events about the art, history, and current events of County Fermanagh. *(☎6632 5000; www.enniskillencastle.co.uk. Both museums open M and Sa-Su 2-5pm, Tu-F 10am-4pm. Admission to both £3, children £2, students and seniors £2.50, families £8.)*

One and a half miles south of Enniskillen on A4, **Castle Coole** rears up in Neoclassical pride. Prolific British architect James Wyatt put his obsession with symmetry to good use when he completed this impressive mansion in 1798, going so far as to place faux-keyholes on the doors to ensure complete balance. The showhouse feel is compounded by the numerous *scagioli* columns (hollow columns encased by fine marble) designed by Italian craftsman Bartoli, and £7 million worth of restoration from the National Trust. Gadget-lovers will appreciate the face of the French clock in the dining room; it turns while the hands remain immobile. Other artifacts of interest include the regal State Bedroom, outfitted with decadent Regency furnishings for King George IV's visit in 1821. The saloon holds a wedgewood piano with plaques embedded in its body, one of only three in the world. The castle grounds contain a number of trails and quiet picnic spots; they lie just 10min. along the Dublin road; the castle itself appears at the end of a 20min. hike up the driveway. *(☎6632 2690; www.nationaltrust.org.uk. Grounds open Oct.-Mar. daily 10am-4pm; Apr.-Sept. daily 10am-8pm. House open July-Aug. daily noon-6pm; June M-W and F-Su noon-6pm; mid-Mar. to May and Sept. Sa-Su noon-6pm. Admission to house by guided tour only. Last tour 5:15pm. £4.20, children £2.10, families £10.50.)*

OTHER SIGHTS. Diagonally across from Castle Coole, the **Ardhowen Theatre** sits by the shore, satisfying dance, drama, music, and comedy enthusiasts. *(☎6632 5440; www.ardhowentheatre.com. Performances generally Th-Sa. Box office open M-Sa 10am-4:30pm, until 7pm performance nights. Tickets £7-15.)* On Church St., **St. Macartin's Cathedral** (Church of Ireland) towers over the surrounding area. *(Open daily 11am-1pm and 2-5pm.)* Nestled between Market St., Queen Elizabeth Rd., and Down St., the **Buttermarket** is the unofficial home of local craftspeople. *(Hours vary by store; most open M-Sa 10am-5pm, a few closed W.)*

OUTDOOR ACTIVITIES. Fermanagh Lakeland Forum, behind the tourist office, has a swimming pool and squash, badminton, and tennis courts. *(☎6632 4121; www.lakelandforum.com. Pool £2.50, children £1.60; badminton, table tennis, bowls, and cricket £8, seniors all games £1.50. Open M-F 8am-10:30pm, Sa 10am-6pm, Su 2-6pm.)* Lakeland Canoe Centre (see **Transportation,** p. 588) rents bikes for £12 per day and canoes for £20 per 2hr. The **Castle Archdale Marina** rents boats and **bikes** (£6 per ½-day, £10 per day), sells fishing rods and bait (£30), and runs pony trekking expeditions.

(☎ 6862 1892. Boats £30 per 2hr.; £50 per ½-day, £75 per full day. Fishing rod and bait £5.) To get to Castle Archdale Country Park, take B206 (the Kesh Road) out of town and follow the signs; within the park, follow the signs for the marina. Also departing from the marina are ferries to **White Island,** which is home to the remains of a 12th-century church, as well as eight unexplained, enigmatic 6th-century stone figures. Ferries leave on the hour except for 1pm (lunch) during opening hours. The whole trip takes about an hour, and all passengers cost £3, regardless of age. *(Call ☎ 6862 1892 for more information. Open Apr.-June and Sept. Sa-Su 11am-5pm; July-Aug. daily 11am-5pm, and all public holidays 11am-5pm.)*

Also in the park and near the marina are the **Castle Archdale Stables,** where you can arrange a pony for trekking. *(£10 per 30min. or £5 for a shorter ride. Open July-Aug. daily 9:30am-6pm, Sa-Su year-round.)* **Castle Archdale Park** features a two-mile trail and a wildflower meadow. To get to the park, take B206 (Kesh Rd.) out of town and follow the signs. *(Open July-Aug. daily 10am-9pm; Sept.-June 10am-5pm.)*

A **GAA Pitch** lies on Factory Rd. Experienced spelunkers check in with **Correlea Activity Centre** in Belcoo *(☎ 6638 6123; www.activityireland.com)* or **Gortatole** in Florence-court *(☎ 6634 8888)* for planned trips into the **Marble Arch Caves.** The Speleological Union of Ireland *(www.cavingireland.org)* has information about sites outside the Lake District. Towering over the city but almost completely obscured by trees is the **Forthill Park,** which is home to **Cole's Monument,** dedicated to a general from the area and erected in 1843. The park is always open and has good southward views. The monument itself only opens daily 1:30 to 3pm; tickets are available at town hall.

▶ DAYTRIPS FROM ENNISKILLEN

FLORENCE COURT AND FOREST PARK. Florence Court, which once housed the Earls of Enniskillen, is a mid-18th-century mansion built by Sir John Cole. Now owned by the National Trust, the home is preserved as a splendid example of Georgian architecture, Rococo plasterwork, and traditional Irish furniture. Much of the original artwork has been restored, and the third Earl left behind his fossil collection. To reach the castle, take the Sligo road (A4) out of Enniskillen, then turn left onto the A32 (Swanlinbar Rd.) and follow the signs. *(☎ 6634 8249. Open June daily 1-6pm except Th; July-Aug. daily noon-6pm; Sept. Sa-Su 1-6pm; special hours apply around Easter and St. Patrick's day, so call ahead. £4.55, children £2, but a price including a suggested donation (Gift Aid) is £5/2.20. Parking costs £3.50 per car, £16.50 per minibus.)*

MARBLE ARCH CAVES. Four miles farther down the road to Belcoo are the Marble Arch Caves, a subterranean labyrinth of hidden rivers and strangely sculpted limestone. A boat trip begins the 1¼hr. tour, which leads to spectacular formations carved over thousands of years. A good imagination and some gentle prodding from guides reveals angels, elephants, bacon, cauliflower, and other real-life objects in rock form. The adjacent **geopark** is free and open to the public. It contains the actual **marble arch** through which water flows. To reach the caves, take the Sligo bus to Belcoo and follow the 3 mi. of signposts. A £12 taxi ride is the only alternative. *(☎ 6634 8855; www.marblearchcaves.net. Open Easter-June and Sept. daily 10am-4:30pm, July-Aug. 10am-5pm. Tours every 15-20min. £8, children £5, students and seniors £5.25, families £18. Book ahead. Tours may be canceled after a heavy rain.)*

CUILCAH MOUNTAIN PARK. Farther down the road from Florence Court and the Marble Caves *(5min. by car)* lies a rugged piece of protected peatland and white sandstone cliffs; it's the next left after the Marble Arch Caves, look for a sign. The caves and the park were jointly recognized by UNESCO in 2001 as the first endorsed European geopark. The **Legnabrocky Trail** from the park's road leads to a stupendous mountain overlook. Check in at the **Visitors Centre** at the Marble Arch Caves for information. *(☎6634 8855; mac@fermanagh.gov.uk. Free and always open.)*

DEVENISH ISLAND. Lough Erne is sprinkled with "holy islands" used for religious rites and pilgrimages, of which the largest is Devenish Island *(Daimh Inis)*, where St. Molaise founded a monastery in the 6th century. Among the island's most popular sights are a well-preserved 81 ft. **round tower** dating from the 12th century, the ruins of **St. Molaise's Church** and St. Mary's 15th-century Augustinian **priory,** and a 15th-century **high cross.** To reach the island, sail with **Devenish Ferries** from Trory Point, 4 mi. from Enniskillen on Irvinestown Rd., or a one-mile walk to the left from the bus stop on the Pettigoe route. More information is available from the Environment & Heritage Servies at ☎9023 5000 (Belfast) or ☎6862 1588 (Irvinestown). *(☎07702 052873. Apr.-Sept. 10am, 1, 3, and 5pm. £3, children and seniors £2.)*

BELLEEK. Belleek lies 25 mi. from Enniskillen on the A46. Buses run six times per day from Enniskillen *(1hr., return €6.30)*. At the northern tip of Lower Lough Erne, tiny Belleek would go unnoticed were it not for its famously delicate china, the legacy of John C. Bloomfield's quest to turn a humble toilet manufacturer into a powerhouse of fine pottery. Tours of the **Belleek Pottery Factory** showcases the craftsmanship that goes into each unique piece. *(☎6865 8501. Open Apr.-June and Sept. M-F 9am-6pm, Sa 10am-6pm, Su 2pm-6pm; July-Aug. M-F 9am-6pm, Sa 10am-6pm, Su 11am-6pm; Oct. M-F 9am-5:30pm, Sa 10am-5:30pm; Nov.-Mar. M-F 9am-5:30pm. 2 tours per hr. Last tour 4:15pm, F 3:15pm. £4/€6, students and seniors £2/€3.)*

NORTHERN IRELAND

APPENDIX

TIME DIFFERENCES

Ireland and Northern Ireland are on **Greenwich Mean Time (GMT),** which is: 1 hour behind most of continental Europe; 5 hours ahead of New York (EST); 6 hours ahead of Chicago, IL (CST); 7 hours ahead of Phoenix, Arizona (MST); 8 hours ahead of Los Angeles, California (PST); 8 hours (Perth), 9½ hours (Adelaide), and 10 hours (Victoria) behind Australia; and 12 hours behind Auckland, New Zealand.

MEASUREMENTS

MEASUREMENT CONVERSIONS	
1 foot (ft.) = 0.30m	1 meter (m) = 3.28 ft.
1 yard (yd.) = 0.914m	1 meter (m) = 1.09 yd.
1 mile (mi.) = 1.609km	1 kilometer (km) = 0.62 mi.
1 acre (ac.) = 0.405ha	1 hectare (ha) = 2.47 ac.
1 square mile (sq. mi.) = 2.59km²	1 square kilometer (km²) = 0.386 sq. mi.

TEMPERATURE AND CLIMATE

°CELSIUS	-5	0	5	10	15	20	25	30	35	40
°FAHRENHEIT	23	32	41	50	59	68	77	86	95	104

To convert from °C to °F, multiply by 1.8 and add 32. °F is roughly 25 more than twice °C. To convert from °F to °C, subtract 32 and multiply by 0.55. For a rough approximation, subtract 25 from °F and cut it in half.

AVERAGE TEMPERATURE AND RAINFALL

Avg. Temp. (low/high), Precipitation	January			April			July			October		
	°C	°F	mm	°C	°F	mm	°C	°F	mm	°C	°F	mm
Dublin	2/7	37/46	63	5/11	41/52	48	12/18	54/66	66	7/12	46/55	73
Cork	3/7	38/46	124	4/11	40/52	66	11/18	53/65	68	7/12	46/65	106
Belfast	4/7	40/45	83	6/10	44/51	51	13/17	56/63	79	8/11	47/52	85
London	2/7	36/45	60	5/12	41/55	43	13/22	56/72	45	7/14	46/58	78

DISTANCE (IN KILOMETERS)

In the Republic, distances are now measured in kilometers. The general speed limit is 95km/hr.; in urban areas it is 45km/hr., and on motorways 110km/hr. Since there are few motorways, expect to average about 65km/hr.

	Athlone	Belfast	Cork	Donegal	Dublin	Galway	Limerick	Derry	Portlaoise	Waterford
Athlone	—	227	182	114	126	93	121	209	74	174
Belfast	227	—	425	181	167	305	323	118	253	333
Cork	219	425	—	402	258	209	105	428	174	126
Donegal	183	181	402	—	222	204	296	402	257	357
Dublin	126	167	258	222	—	218	198	237	84	158

	Athlone	Belfast	Cork	Donegal	Dublin	Galway	Limerick	Derry	Portlaoise	Waterford
Galway	93	305	209	204	218	–	105	272	150	220
Limerick	121	323	105	296	198	105	–	328	114	123
Derry	209	118	428	402	237	272	328	–	282	383
Portlaoise	74	253	174	257	84	150	114	282	–	100
Waterford	174	333	126	357	158	220	123	383	100	–

GLOSSARY

For a brief history of the Irish language, see **The Irish Language,** p. 68. On the left side of the table below is a list of Gaelic/Irish words (or English words marked by a distinct Irish dialect). The glossary on the right side of the table should help sort things out. Spelling conventions do not always match English pronunciations: for example, "bh" sounds like "v," "mh" like "w," "dh" like "g" and "ai" like "ie."

IRISH	PRONUNCIATION	(AMERICAN) ENGLISH
Getting to Know the Locals		
Ba mhaith liom pointa.	ba WHY-lum pee-yunt-ah	I would like a pint.
Ceann eile le d'thoil.	cahn EYE-leh led-TOIL	Another one, please.
Conas tá tú?	CUNN-us taw too	How are you? (informal)
dia dhuit	DE-ah ghwuit	good day, hello (formal)
dia's mhuire	Jee-as MWUR-a	the reply to "good day"
fáilte	FAHL-tchuh	welcome
go raibh maith agat	guh roh moh UG-ut	thank you
mór	more	big, great
oíche mhaith dhuit	EE-ha woh ghwuit	good night
sláinte	SLAWN-che	cheers, to your health
slán leat	slawn lat	goodbye
Tá sé fluich.	tah SHAY fluck	It's raining.
Tá sé tirim!	tah SHAY trim!	It's not raining!
Tóg é go bog é.	TOG-ah BUG-ay	Take it easy.
Tuigim.	tiggum	I understand.
Sleeping and Living		
bedsit	–	one-room apartment, sometimes with kitchen
biro	BEE-roh	ball point pen
caravan	–	RV, trailer
fir	fear	men
first floor	–	first floor up from the ground floor (second floor)
flat	–	apartment
ground floor	–	first floor (are you confused yet?)
half-ten, half-nine, etc.	–	ten-thirty, nine-thirty, etc.
hoover	–	vacuum cleaner
jacks	–	bathrooms
lavatory, lav	–	bathroom
leithreas	LEH-hrass	toilets
lift	–	elevator
loo	–	bathroom
mná	min-AW	women
Oifig an Phoist	UFF-ig un fwisht	Post Office

IRISH	PRONUNCIATION	(AMERICAN) ENGLISH
to queue up, "the Q"	CUE	waiting line
teach	chock	house
torch	—	flashlight
siopa	SHUP-ah	shop
Locations and Landmarks		
An Lár	on lahr	City Center
Baile Átha Cliath	BALL-yah AW-hah CLEE-ah	Dublin
drumlin	—	small hill
Éire	AIR-uh	Ireland; official name of the Republic of Ireland
gaeltacht	GAYL-tokt	a region where Irish is the everyday language
inch, innis	—	island
quay	key	a waterside street
slieve or sliabh	shleev	mountain
sráid	shrawd	street
strand	—	beach
trá	thraw	beach
Getting Around		
bonnet	—	engine
boot	—	trunk (of a car)
coach	—	bus (long distance)
hire	—	rental
left luggage	—	luggage storage
a lift	—	a ride
lorry	—	truck
petrol	—	gasoline
return ticket	—	two-way ticket
roundabout	—	rotary road interchange
self-drive	—	car rental
single ticket	—	one-way ticket
Sightseeing		
Bord Fáilte	Bored FAHL-tchuh	Irish Tourist Board
concession	—	discount on admission for seniors and students
dolmen	—	chamber formed by huge stones
dún	doon	fort
gaol	jail	jail
kil	kill	church; monk's cell
ogham	OHG-um	early Irish, written on stones
rath	rath or rah	earthen fort
Money, Please		
cheap	—	inexpensive (not shoddy)
dear	—	expensive
fiver	—	€5 note
sterling	—	British pound
tenner	—	€10 note
Civic and Cultural		
chemist	—	pharmacist
garda, Garda Síochána	GAR-da SHE-och-ANA	police

IRISH	PRONUNCIATION	(AMERICAN) ENGLISH
OAP	—	Old Age Pensioner, "senior citizen"
RTÉ	—	Radio Telefis Éireann, the Republic's broadcasting authority
RUC	—	Royal Ulster Constabulary, the police force of Northern Ireland
Please, Sir, May I Have Another		
bangers and mash	—	sausage and mashed potatoes
bap	—	a soft round bun
bill	—	check (in restaurants)
biscuit	—	cookie
carvery	—	meal of meat, potatoes, and carrots/vegetables
chips	—	french fries
chipper	—	fish and chips vendor
crisps	—	potato chips
rashers	—	bacon
takeaway	—	takeout, "to go"
Pubs and Music		
bodhrán	BOUR-ohn	traditional drum
brilliant	—	great, awesome
busker	—	street musician
céilí	KAY-lee	Irish dance
concertina	—	small, round-button accordion
craic	krak	good cheer, good pub conversation, a good time
faders	FOD-ers	party poopers who go to bed early
fag	—	a cigarette
feis	fesh	an assembly or Irish festival
fleadh	flah	a musical festival
knackered	—	exhausted
off-license, offy	—	retail liquor store
pissed	—	drunk
poitín	pah-CHEEN	moonshine; sometimes toxic homemade liquor
pub grub	—	bar food
publican	—	barkeep
to slag	—	to tease and ridicule
to snog	—	to kiss
stocious	—	very drunk
to take the piss out of	—	to make fun of in a joking way
trad	—	traditional Irish music
uilleann pipes	ILL-in	"Elbow pipes," a form of bagpipes
táim	thaw im	I am...
súgach	SOO-gakh	tipsy
ar meisce	uhr MEH-shka	drunk
caoch ólta	KWEE-ukh OLE-ta	blind drunk
Sports		
football	—	Gaelic football in the Republic, soccer in the North
GAA	—	Gaelic Athletic Association; organizes Gaelic sports

IRISH	PRONUNCIATION	(AMERICAN) ENGLISH
peil	pell	football
snooker	—	a game similar to pool
Politics in the Republic		
Dáil	DOY-il	House of Representatives in the Republic
dole, on the dole	—	welfare or unemployment benefits
Fianna Fáil	FEE-in-ah foil	"Soldiers of Destiny," political party in Éire
Fine Gael	FINN-eh gayl	"Family of Ireland," political party in Éire
Seanad	SHAN-ud	the Irish Senate
Taoiseach	TEE-shukh	Irish Prime Minister
Oireachtas	OR-ach-tus	both houses of the Irish Parliament
Politics in the North		
Bloody Sunday	—	30 January 1970, when 14 Catholic civilians in Derry were gunned down by the British Army
Bobby Sands	—	elected to British Parliament; the first IRA member to die during the 1980s hunger strikes
Catholic	—	someone of the Roman Catholic faith, usually implies loyalty to the Republic of Ireland
DUP	—	Democratic Unionist Party, right-wing party led by Ian Paisley
INLA	—	Irish National Liberation Army, an IRA splinter group
IRA (Provisional IRA)	—	Irish Republican Army, a Nationalist paramilitary group
Loyalists	—	pro-British Northern Irish (see Unionists)
Nationalists	—	those who want Northern Ireland and the Republic united (see Republicans)
Orangemen	—	a widespread Protestant Unionist secret order
Protestant	—	someone of the Anglican Protestant faith, usually implies allegiance with the British Crown
Provos	—	slang for the Provisional IRA
Real IRA	—	small splinter group of radicals who claimed responsibility for the 1998 Omagh bombing
Republicans	—	Northern Irish who identify with the Republic (see Nationalists)
SDLP	—	Social Democratic and Labor Party, moderate Nationalist Party in the North
Sinn Féin	shin fayn	"Ourselves Alone," Republican party affiliated with the IRA
the Troubles	—	the period of violence in the North that started in 1969
UDA	—	Ulster Defense Association, an Unionist paramilitary group
UFF	—	Ulster Freedom Fighters (synonymous with UDA)
Unionists	—	those who want Northern Ireland to remain part of the UK (see Loyalists)
UUP	—	Ulster Unionist Party, the ruling party in the North
UVF	—	Ulster Volunteer Force, Unionist paramilitary group

INDEX

INDEX

GET CONNECTED & SAVE WITH THE HI CARD

An HI card gives you access to friendly and affordable accommodations at over 4,000 hostels in over 60 countries, including across Britain and Ireland. Members also receive complementary travel insurance, members-only airfare deals, and thousands of discounts on everything from tours and dining to shopping, communications and transportation.

Join millions of HI members worldwide who save money and have more fun every time they travel.

 Hostelling International USA

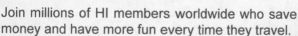

MAP INDEX

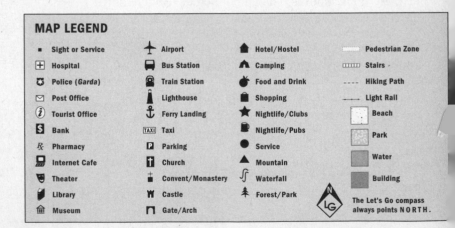

MAP LEGEND

▪ Sight or Service	✈ Airport	🏨 Hotel/Hostel	▬▬ Pedestrian Zone
✛ Hospital	🚌 Bus Station	⛺ Camping	⊞ Stairs
✪ Police (*Garda*)	🚂 Train Station	🍔 Food and Drink	---- Hiking Path
✉ Post Office	🛄 Lighthouse	🛍 Shopping	── Light Rail
ⓘ Tourist Office	⚓ Ferry Landing	★ Nightlife/Clubs	Beach
$ Bank	TAXI Taxi	Nightlife/Pubs	Park
℞ Pharmacy	P Parking	● Service	
💻 Internet Cafe	✝ Church	▲ Mountain	Water
🎭 Theater	⚜ Convent/Monastery	∫ Waterfall	Building
📗 Library	♜ Castle	🌲 Forest/Park	The Let's Go compass
🏛 Museum	⊓ Gate/Arch	LG	always points NORTH.